SEARCHING FOR PEACE
IN ASIA PACIFIC

EUROPEAN
CENTRE
FOR
conflict prevention

A project of the European Centre for Conflict Prevention
(Utrecht, the Netherlands) in cooperation with the
Gaston Z. Ortigas Peace Institute (Manila, Philippines)
and the Center for Security and Peace Studies (Yogyakarta, Indonesia).

Financially supported by the Ministries of Foreign Affairs
of Canada, the Netherlands, and New Zealand, the
Department for International Development of the United Kingdom,
and the Dutch nongovernmental organization Cordaid.

SEARCHING FOR PEACE IN ASIA PACIFIC

An Overview of Conflict Prevention and Peacebuilding Activities

edited by
Annelies Heijmans, Nicola Simmonds,
and Hans van de Veen

LYNNE
RIENNER
PUBLISHERS

BOULDER
LONDON

Published in the United States of America in 2004 by
Lynne Rienner Publishers, Inc.
1800 30th Street, Boulder, Colorado 80301
www.rienner.com

and in the United Kingdom by
Lynne Rienner Publishers, Inc.
3 Henrietta Street, Covent Garden, London WC2E 8LU

Library of Congress Cataloging-in-Publication Data
Searching for peace in Asia Pacific : an overview of conflict prevention
and peacebuilding activities / Annelies Heijmans, Nicola Simmonds, and
Hans van de Veen, editors.
    Published in association with the European Centre for Conflict
Prevention.
    Includes bibliographical references and index.
    ISBN 1-58826-214-6 (hardcover : alk. paper)
    ISBN 1-58826-239-1 (pbk. : alk. paper)
1. Asia—Politics and government—1945–   2. Oceania—Politics and government.
3. Conflict management—Asia. 4. Conflict management—Oceania. 5. Peace-building—
Asia. 6. Peace-building—Oceania. I. Heijmans, Annelies. II. Simmonds, Nicola, 1973–
III. Veen, Hans van de. IV. European Centre for Conflict Prevention.
DS35.2.S43 2004
320.95'09'049—dc22

                                                                2004009267

British Cataloguing in Publication Data
A Cataloguing in Publication record for this book
is available from the British Library.

Printed and bound in the United States of America

         The paper used in this publication meets the requirements
    ∞   of the American National Standard for Permanence of
         Paper for Printed Library Materials Z39.48-1992.

    5 4 3 2 1

Contents

Foreword

Kevin P. Clements

It gives me great pleasure to write the foreword to this important book on conflict in the Asia Pacific region. During the economic boom of the late 1980s the Asia Pacific region was predicted to become one of the major motors of the global economy by the end of the twentieth century. Pundits saw all the "Asian Tigers" continuing to generate high levels of economic growth and playing a major leadership role in the development of a more integrated global economy. It was assumed, further, that this growth would be accompanied by the development of higher levels of possessive individualism, and an expanded civil society, since modern, democratic political systems are considered most congenial to modern market conditions. The Asian financial crisis of 1997 put a question mark over the speed of both of these predictions.

In relation to economic growth, however, there is absolutely no doubt at all that this region will become a leading economic actor in the twenty-first century and develop economic power matching that of Europe and the United States. Taken as a whole, East Asia, Southeast Asia, and the Southwest Pacific region represent a vast reservoir of human, economic, social, political, and material resources. When these are added to the entrepreneurial spirit and energy that exists within the region, the financial crisis of the 1990s will be rapidly forgotten as the region achieves higher and higher levels of prosperity.

The second prediction—that capitalism and the expansion of the market will automatically generate pressures for higher levels of individualism, a more pluralistic civil society, respect for human rights, and popular movements for democracy—is much more problematic. This prognosis overlooks the deep hierarchy of Confucian and other Asian cultures, for example, not to mention the heavy stress placed on collective familial and kinship obligations and responsibilities. It also tends to underestimate the impact of strong authoritarian rule. It overlooks the fact that when confronted by order and chaos, most people will prefer the former to the latter, even if this means strong and sometimes autocratic government. Thus political systems in the Asia Pacific region have, by and large, proved fairly resistant to democratic rule.

Singapore, for example, is a spectacular case of a jump from a simple entrepôt to a major player in the world economy. It moved in this direction under a very authoritarian political system, which placed more stress on economic security rather than political freedom and on order and conformity rather than anarchic diversity. It was a formula that most Singaporeans accepted, and most Malaysians and Chinese seem to have done so as well. Even though there are significant numbers pushing for more liberty and real democracy in all these societies, there is an "Asian authoritarianism" that seems to have delivered high levels of economic growth. This has come at a price. In the absence of openness, transparency, and political accountability, many of the governments in the region have become corrupt and inefficient. They have failed to deliver growth with equity. Because of this, social, health, and educational services, as well as other public goods, have not received as much attention as that lavished on the entrepreneurial private sector. There has been spectacular economic growth without a corresponding increase in democratic participation, political accountability, and inclusion in decisionmaking processes. One of the paradoxes of democracy is that it amplifies social and political divisions. Thus when Asian states take a tentative step in a democratic direction, this is often accompanied by a new consciousness of old fault lines, the emergence of community-based conflict, and a coercive response from the state. Thus the democratic process then generates first authoritarian democracy and then simple authoritarian dictatorial rule. This has often been accompanied by the political repression of dissent, willful or benign neglect of minority interests, and the emergence of radical inequalities between rich and poor. It is in these sorts of conditions that deeper social and political conflict flourishes.

Asia Pacific recently has witnessed renewed instability and the reemergence or continuation of political violence in countries/regions such as Burma, Indonesia, Thailand, Malaysia, the Southern Philippines, Cambodia, the Solomon Islands, Papua New Guinea, and Vanuatu. These events demonstrate some disturbing trends. In a region that was assumed to be relatively stable, there are now instabilities; in a region that was supposed to be relatively democratic, there are signs of a remilitarization of politics and a return to violence; in a region that was supposed to have relatively stable political leadership, such leadership now seems fragile and unstable. In a region that used to be characterized by an ability to mobilize considerable public will (e.g., People's Power in the Philippines), citizens now have difficulty mobilizing for a common purpose. Across the whole region, there is now a dearth of diplomatic and nonviolent approaches to the resolution of deep-seated conflicts. Frustrated political actors are turning to violent rather than nonviolent methods as matter of first recourse. This situation needs to change if the region is to achieve a political role commensurate with its economic power.

This book is an excellent account of the genealogy of many of these internal and interstate conflicts, and explains well their persistence and prospects for management, resolution, or transformation. It highlights the similarities and dissimilarities between these diverse conflicts. It identifies which are sui generis and which have deep commonalities.

There are some important questions that policymakers and nongovernmental organizations have to ask. Are existing global mechanisms—within the UN and regional organizations—apprised of and capable of dealing with the interstate conflicts that have shown remarkable persistence since World War II? What mechanisms need to be developed in addition to those identified in Chapter 3 by Desmond Ball to ensure timelier, more proactive and effective conflict prevention? Would it be useful for something like the Organization for Security and Cooperation's Office of the High Commissioner on National Minorities to be developed within the Association of Southeast Asian Nations (ASEAN) and the Pacific Islands Forum (PIF)? Which countries have the best track record for "altruistic" preventive diplomacy? How can these skills and techniques be used more effectively? How can the role of China in brokering peace negotiations between the United States and North Korea be acknowledged more fully? Also, shouldn't other countries in the region encourage China to utilize its formidable power to generate stable peaceful relations among all states in the region? The question of course is: Are all these diverse states within the region willing to allow China to assume a stabilizing role in collaboration with others? What should be the role of the predominantly European states/societies that border the region: Australia, New Zealand, the United States, Canada, and at a greater distance Latin America? How are they dealing with their ambivalent status as essentially West European societies within an Asian environment? Are they sensitive to Asian national and regional interests and willing to play a support rather than an interfering role in the development of distinctive "Asian" mechanisms for Asia Pacific conflict transformation, and how might these differ from those on offer in Europe?

These questions are addressed here. This book is an invitation to an ongoing dialogue about ways of ensuring that the growing arc of instability that stretches from the Indian Ocean to the Southwest Pacific does not become as volatile as the tectonic fault line that stretches around the Pacific Rim. How do states and peoples within and outside the region ensure that violent conflict in Asia is dealt with early, creatively, and positively? Do the regional organizations that exist—ASEAN, the Asia Pacific Economic Cooperation, the PIF, for example—have the political nerve and courage to utilize the formidable economic wealth that is being created to help individual states generate stable, inclusive, effective, and capable political systems that serve rather than exploit their citizens and that generate human security for all?

Do the members of ASEAN have the courage to move beyond "golf course" diplomacy to develop mechanisms capable of identifying emergent violence early and, more important, capable of working to close the early warning–early response gap so that the needs underlying these conflicts might be addressed and the parties helped to seek resolution? Are they willing to marshal a wide range of economic, political, and social resources and actors in order to give as much attention to peacebuilding as to economic growth? This is the challenge facing the region. It's a challenge that has to be engaged. It is not an optional extra.

The twenty-first century will belong to Asia Pacific if the states, peoples, and regional institutions within the region take seriously the importance of ensuring that political systems serve the interests of all citizens and peoples rather than just the elites; and if national and regional security systems and economic actors focus their efforts on the pursuit and maintenance of human security.

> Human security in its broadest sense embraces far more than the absence of violent conflict. It encompasses human rights, good governance, access to education and health care and ensuring that each individual has opportunities and choices to fulfill his or her own potential. . . . Freedom from want, freedom from fear and the freedom of the future generations to inherit a healthy natural environment—these are the interrelated building blocks of human, and therefore national security.[1]

Achievement of human security for all peoples within the Asian region is not an impossible goal. All it requires is political will and the development of mechanisms that remove the root causes of violence and a desire to utilize economic prosperity in the service of all. Asian states and societies have all the resources to make this possible. All that is needed are national and regional visions of how to realize this goal. This book is an important contribution toward understanding the impediments. It is up to all who live within the region, with the support of others outside, to transcend the impediments and realize the possibilities.

Kevin P. Clements is director of the Australian Centre for Peace and Conflict Studies, University of Queensland.

Note

1. Commission on Human Security, *Human Security Now* (New York: Communications Development, 2003), p. 4.

Acknowledgments

This book is one of the major outcomes of the Searching for Peace in Asia Pacific project of the European Centre for Conflict Prevention (ECCP). Numerous individuals and organizations from the Asia Pacific region, Europe, the United States, and Canada provided their advice, insights, and support in shaping the project, participated in workshops and seminars, gave feedback on draft texts, contributed chapters for the book, and assisted in the compilation of the directory. The book represents the involvement and ideas of many more persons than those whose names are mentioned as authors. We are indebted to all of them.

The project would not have been possible without generous grants from several funding sources. We are grateful to the Ministries of Foreign Affairs of Canada, the Netherlands, and New Zealand, the Department for International Development of the United Kingdom, and the Dutch nongovernmental organization Cordaid for providing financial support.

The Searching for Peace in Asia Pacific project started in January 2000 with preliminary research done by the staff of the ECCP. Soon, the need to produce two volumes, in order to give full justice to the region's diversity and to cover this huge continent in sufficient detail, became clear. The first volume, *Searching for Peace in Central and South Asia,* was published in August 2002. Work on the present volume began in January 2002.

The aim of this book is to provide a concise overview of the conflict prevention and peacebuilding efforts in Asia Pacific. Our own staff conducted the initial research, but we relied heavily on the expertise of several practitioners and scholars. We benefited greatly from the intellectual advice and guidance provided by Peter Cross, Owen Green, Rolando Modina, Maria Lorenza Palm-Dalupan, Jan Nielen, Nico Schulte-Nordholt, Stephanie Powell, Shelina Thawer, Marika Vicziany, Rob Watson, and Lisette van der Wel in the identification of major issues causing conflict in Asia Pacific, and in helping to broaden our contact base in the region.

A preparatory workshop organized by the Gaston Z. Ortigas Peace Institute in June 2002 in Manila helped us in further shaping the Searching for

Peace in Asia Pacific project, particularly in gathering recommendations on regional issues, key conflicts, and causes of conflict in the Southeast Asian and Pacific region. Cooperation was discussed and developed with many participants, and potential authors were identified. We would like to thank the organizers and participants of the Manila workshop for their input: Kamarulzaman Askandar, Volker Böge, Aisake Casimira, Jone Dakuvula, Eda Detros, Miriam Coronel-Ferrer, Ed Garcia, Suwit Laohasiriwong, Ed Legaspi, Emma Leslie, Linh Doan Mai, Gus Miclat, Soth Plai Ngarm, Maria Lorenza Palm-Dalupan, Madelene Sta. Maria, Elga Sarapung, Eliakim Sitorus, Karen Tañada, Erik Torch, Lambang Trijono, Fernand de Varennes, and David Wright-Neville.

Similarly, a meeting focusing on Northeast Asia was held in October 2002, organized by Bradford University. We would like to thank the following persons for their valuable suggestions and comments on how we could best obtain a balanced picture of (potential) conflicts involving China: Mike Bourne, Malcolm Chalmers, Dru Gladney, Owen Green, Glen Hook, Christopher Hughes, Francis Lee, Rex Li, Eirin Mobekk, Neil Renwick, and Michael Yahuda. Based on this consultation, ECCP staff visited Hong Kong–based organizations in November 2002 to further discuss this approach and to meet with potential authors. We are thankful to the following persons for their suggestions and support: Chine Chan, Joseph Cheng, Max Edigar, Basil Fernando, Apo Leung, Jeannie Manipon, Roger Ricafort, and Hazel Wong.

The chapters and surveys are written by practitioners and scholars with long-term expertise on specific conflicts or issues. Many of the authors wrote on conflicts in the areas where they live and work, others wrote on conflicts and issues in which they gained extensive experience from researching them. We greatly appreciate the authors' outstanding efforts in presenting a balanced view of the conflicts in which they are, inevitably, involved. We hope their analyses will help a broad audience to better understand and appreciate local situations. We want to express our sincere gratitude to all the authors for the willingness and flexibility shown in revising and updating their texts in short time frames.

All authors had their draft texts reviewed by a widely composed pool of resource persons. We would like to thank the following people for giving their valuable time to review draft chapters and to provide feedback: Erkin Alptekin, Youdon Aukatsang, Muhammad Najib Azca, David de Beer, Roland Bleiker, Volker Böge, Theo van den Broek, Fr. Angel Calvo, Aisake Casimira, Kevin Clements, Ralph Cossa, Koila Costello-Ollson, Malcolm Chalmers, Joseph Cheng, James Cotton, Harold Crouch, Zha Daojiong, Sinclair Dinnen, Thierry Dodin, Paul Evans, Henny van der Graaf, Awang Hasmadi, Eric Hiariej, Johnson Honimae, Glenn Hook, Xiaoming Huang, Caroline Hughes, Tim Huxley, Otto Syamsuddin Ishak, Michio Ito, Oh Jaeshik, Wang Jian-min, Chen Jie, Vanessa Johanson, Vikki John, Stephanie Joubert, Diah Kusuman-ingrum, Gabriel Lafitte, Htoo Htoo Lay, Samuel Lee, Tse-Kang Leng, Viktor Kasiëpo, Leo Ladjar, Faye Leone, Emma Leslie, Rex Li, Ruth Liloqula, Liem Soei Liong, Marcell Lodo, Colin McKerras, Ichsan Malik, Gus Miclat, Eirin

Mobekk, Tetty Naiborhu, Nguyen Nam Duong, John Olsen, Maria Lorenza Palm-Dalupan, Nancy Lee Peluso, Barbara Pillsbury, Nathan Quimpo, Grace Rebellos, Neil Renwick, Rudy Rodel, Delsey Ronnie, Robert Ross, John Roughan, Faisal Saifuddin, Kabini Sanga, Irene Santiago, Catherine Scott, Nico Schulte Nordholt, Heinz Schurman-Zeggel, Kirsten Schultz, Laura Shipler Chico, John Sidel, Neb Sinthay, Martin Smith, Dionisio Soares, Ashley and Bellay South, Ian Storey, Julia Strauss, Park Sunsong, Takao Takahara, Sandra Tarte, Teresia Teaiwa, Fuad Mardhatillah Tiba, Luigi Tomba, Fernand de Varennes, Marika Vicziany, Jusuf Wanandi, Rob Watson, Erich Weingartner, Robert Winzeler, David Wright-Neville, Harumi Yoshino, Hoang Young-ju, and Lobsang Nyandak Zayul.

Participants at the Manila preparatory meeting expressed the need for a subsequent meeting to share experiences, to strengthen networks, and to draw lessons from peacebuilding efforts in Asia Pacific. The Centre for Security and Peace Studies in Yogyakarta, Indonesia, offered to organize such a meeting, which took place in Bali in May 2003. The participants' backgrounds included journalism, academic research, human rights monitoring and advocacy, interfaith dialogue, humanitarian assistance, mediation, and lobbying. Several of them are contributors to this book.

We would like to thank all the participants at the meetings for their input and openness: Riza Noer Arfani, Kamarulzaman Askandar, Saifuddin Bantasyam, Sara Carley, Brother Richard Carter, Miriam Coronel-Ferrer, Diana Devi, Kristina Sintia Dewi, Nani Farida, Charlotte Gordon, Rufa Guiam-Cagoco, Yayah Khisbiyah, Diah Kusumaningrum, Vanessa Johanson, Suwit Laohasiriwong, Bert Layson, Ichsan Malik, Vivi Elvira Marantika, Jane McGrory, Gus Miclat, Carolina Monteiro, Adriano Nascimento, Soth Plai Ngarm, Hofni Rumbiak, I Wayan Sadra, Elga Sarapung, Adang Setiana, Prak Sokhany, Line Sofiani Sumantri, Arif Surachman, Ema Tagicakibau, Karen Tañada, Ronald Rischard Tapilatu, Mateus Tilman, Lambang Trijono, Jim Wake, Matthew Wale, Ni Komang Widiani, and Rev Akuila Yabaki.

For the compilation of the directory we are indebted to many people. First of all, thanks to Iris Wielders, who made a start and produced a working list and questionnaires to establish the first contacts with organizations. We want to express our gratitude to Jane McGrory and Jan Nielen of Catholic Relief Service/Cordaid for their advice and support in developing the directory for Indonesia in particular. We also acknowledge the *Indonesian Peacebuilding Directory,* published through a Cordaid–CRS–CERIC–Ohio University partnership (www.direktori-perdamaian.org). Renata Arianingtyas was very helpful in translating the questionnaires and responses from Bahasa Indonesia into English. We would further like to thank the National Coordinators of the Southeast Asian Conflict Studies Network for sharing with us profiles of key organizations from their country directories, and the staff of the European Centre for Pacific Concerns for assisting in compiling the Pacific directory. Simon Foster was instrumental in developing the profiles of local organizations in East Timor. Without the invaluable cooperation of these individuals it would not have been possible to provide profiles of organizations in these regions.

The cooperation provided by the Bureau M&O–Environment and Development Productions in Amsterdam was constructive and enjoyable. Several journalists at the bureau provided an invaluable service in editing the chapters and surveys. We thank Bas Jongerius, Jan van der Putten, Niall Martin, and Jim Wake. Karel Meyer of MMS Grafisch Werk developed the maps. Special thanks go to Berto Jongman, who was willing to produce the "Human Rights and Conflict Map for Asia Pacific" illustrating Chapter 1.

Our managerial home was the European Centre for Conflict Prevention. We gratefully acknowledge the support of our colleagues there, particularly the continuous advice and moral support of Monique Mekenkamp, Paul van Tongeren, and Juliette Verhoeven, who know from experience the joys and hardships of managing the production of such a publication. Last, but far from least, a number of interns have been constructive in research, assistance in organizing seminars, compilation of the directory, and support for the project and organization in general: Chikako Minei, Renata Arianingtyas, Xavier Hédiard, Alex Grainger, Annelies Claessens, and Anna Gerrard. In the last phase of the preparation of this book, Pieter Schultz provided very useful support in cross-checking the references and endnotes. Further we express our gratitude to Linda Schouten for her instrumental assistance in the final editing of this publication.

While thankful for all the support we received, we assume full responsibility for this publication.

—The Editors

Introduction

Annelies Heijmans, Nicola Simmonds, and Hans van de Veen

Work on this book began in January 2002, just three months after the September 11 attacks in the United States and the announcement of the "war on terrorism." Afghanistan was the initial target of the global war, followed by Iraq in 2003. The impact of these events on the Asia Pacific region has been enormous. Many governments reasserted their security policies, believing that militaristic responses are the only right means to crush phenomena such as "terrorism." Efforts to establish standards for human rights protection and humanitarian law through long and difficult processes of collaboration between governments and civil society organizations were overruled and fragile peace processes stagnated. Human rights and development goals are being subsumed into governments' goals of maintaining alliances or promoting security agendas.

The Asia Pacific region is a vast area, populated by peoples with largely divergent ethnic backgrounds and religious beliefs. There are huge gaps in socioeconomic development of the Asian Pacific countries, ranging from Japan to Cambodia or the Solomon Islands. Large parts of the region are affected by war and violent conflicts. People have taken up arms because of issues that are rooted in legacies of colonization and the Cold War; others fight against authoritarian rule, economic inequality, or the politics of exclusion or corruption, to assert their identity or sovereignty, for access to resources, and over border and territorial disputes. In some cases conflicts are stimulated by transnational political movements, whether rooted in leftist revolutionary traditions or the more recent radical Islamic movements. On top of these specific causes and dynamics of conflicts lies the global dimension of both the macroeconomic and sociocultural effects of globalization and the impact of the U.S.-led "war on terrorism." Instead of dealing with these deep-seated grievances and causes of violent conflicts, most governments seem more preoccupied with maintaining the status quo, especially their own position.

Many of these conflicts have been analyzed thoroughly and much is known about their causes and the reasons for their escalation and violence. Far less information is available on what has been done and what is currently being undertaken to deescalate these conflicts. Nor is sufficient information available about the people and institutions that have gained expertise in specific conflicts or subregions. This is especially true for local nongovernmental organizations (NGOs) and other civil society groups, and their increasing role in conflict prevention and peacebuilding. Civil society actors as a whole can make an important contribution toward generating strategies and processes for addressing these many conflict arenas—in terms of both causes and ameliorating their effects. The context of conflict greatly matters in shaping what civil society can do to prevent "new" conflicts and resolve existing ones.

Civil society groups represent pluralities and diversity in society rather than concentrations of interests. They are active in many different fields, such as humanitarian assistance, education, health services, development, security services, and the like, but within a framework that shows concern for environment, good governance, human rights, justice, and peace. However, communication and coordination among these different civil society organizations, in order to be more effective, need to be improved. Further, interdisciplinary networks and forums connecting academics, civil servants, and practitioners hardly exist. There is a heart-felt need for facilitating the exchange of information, experiences, and lessons learned among participating organizations, which will stimulate cooperation and synergy. *Searching for Peace in Asia Pacific* is meant to meet these challenges.

As with the previous Searching for Peace projects of the European Centre for Conflict Prevention (ECCP), the goals of the Searching for Peace in Asia Pacific project are threefold. The first is to provide essential information about different actors in conflict prevention and transformation in the Asia Pacific region; this includes information on who is doing what, comprising hundreds of organizations, as well as important publications, resources, contacts, websites, and databases. Second, with the survey chapters we aim to provide insights into various approaches to conflict prevention and peacebuilding in different contexts to help actors become better coordinated and more effective. The third objective is to provide space for the voices of local civil society organizations. A further objective is to act as a bridge between NGOs and networks of different regions, between practitioners, academic institutions, policymakers, media, and the donor community, thus enhancing the capacity for the prevention of violent conflict.

As the "war on terrorism" deepened, the third objective increasingly became seen as the most important. Anxiety over U.S. unilateralism in managing certain conflicts, and the threat of terrorism in particular, became the norm across networks during the two years we worked on the project. This concern was shared by almost all involved in the field, from academics to activists, and was evident in both Asia Pacific and Europe. Members of the European Platform on Conflict Prevention and Transformation made public statements opposing U.S. unilateralism and calling for dialogue, greater protection for human rights, and democratic processes. A commonly stated concern, and one that is central to the Searching for Peace projects, was that local civil society actors are not being adequately considered, and are certainly not being genuinely included in official conflict management processes. There is still a gap between the official and the unofficial approaches to violent conflicts, and multi-track diplomacy is the exception rather than the rule. It was our guiding hope throughout the project to help mitigate this trend and build bridges between official and unofficial actors.

During this period of international protest against the U.S.-led "war on terrorism" and rapid change in the contexts surrounding many conflicts in Asia Pacific, the ECCP entered into a long process of consultation toward defining the content and focus of this book. Many individuals and organizations were involved in shaping the project through their advice, insights, and support. The uniqueness and strength of this book is that the chapters are written and commented upon by practitioners and scholars with long-term expertise on specific conflicts and issues, and many of the authors wrote on conflicts in the areas where they live and work.

Our first steps were to meet with the members of the European Platform on Conflict Prevention and Transformation, for which the ECCP is the secretariat, to learn from their experience and of their concerns in Asia Pacific, and to broaden the ECCP's contacts in that region. After compiling an initial draft outline for the book, based on what was shared by platform members and on initial research, we held a workshop—coorganized by the Gaston Z. Ortigas Peace Institute in Manila—and meetings in the Asia Pacific region with local civil society organizations. This workshop and these meetings determined the final content of the book, and of the broader Searching for Peace project.

One main impact of these meetings was the decision to place more emphasis on exploring the lessons learned by civil society organizations in transforming and preventing violent conflicts. A workshop titled "Lessons Learned from Peacebuilding in Asia-Pacific" was held in Bali in May 2003, organized in cooperation with the Centre for Security and Peace Studies in Yogyakarta. Lessons were shared from particular aspects of peacebuilding like disarmament, the role of the media, security-sector reform, and indigenous and religious approaches. Participants further focused on lessons, gaps, and recommendations for better cooperation and coordination of peacebuilding efforts among various actors at different levels. The seminar was also an opportunity, of course, to network and explore how to support each other better in our efforts to bring peace to this diverse and divided region. Chapter 7 in this book builds upon the workshop's findings.

The structure of *Searching for Peace in Asia Pacific* follows that of previous *Searching for Peace* volumes. It consists of three parts. The chapters in Part 1 provide readers with reflections and analyses of issues that are influencing conflicts and communities everywhere in the Asia Pacific region, like regional security cooperation, globalization, democratization, and the impact of the "war on terrorism." This part starts with an overview of the main violent conflicts in Asia Pacific, their causes, and trends. It further provides insights into the current field of conflict prevention and transformation in the region, and closes with a wide range of lessons learned from the peacebuilding practices of civil society organizations.

Part 2 consists of chapters written mainly by local peacebuilders and researchers about specific violent conflicts that they are working to resolve. This part presents regional surveys, including general chapters that describe the dynamics and political developments in each region. While respecting the many interrelated issues that draw Asia Pacific together as one region, we considered it helpful to group the conflict survey chapters into three subregions: Northeast Asia, Southeast Asia, and the Pacific Islands. The surveys in Part 2 provide a brief background analysis of seventeen of the major (potential) violent conflicts in Asia Pacific. Among these, several conflicts are either actually (sporadically) violent or are in a postsettlement phase with the possibility of new conflicts. The primary focus of each survey is the activities of key local and international actors working to resolve the conflict. The initial selection of conflicts was based on both the list of high- and low-intensity conflicts identified by the *World Conflict and Human Rights Map 2001–2002* (produced by the Research Program on Causes of Human Rights Violations—PIOOM), and the annual *States in Armed Conflict* (published by the Department of Peace and Conflict Research at Uppsala University). This initial selection was discussed and validated with resource persons and experts from the region during several workshops and meetings.

Part 3 of the book contains a directory of some 350 leading organizations in the area of conflict prevention and transformation active in Asia Pacific. A short profile and practical contact information are provided for each organization.

Throughout the Searching for Peace in Asia Pacific project it has been our intention and hope to bring the perspectives of those close to the grassroots to international attention. Thus the analyses of the backgrounds and dynamics of these conflicts, the descriptions of the roles of official and unofficial actors in the conflicts, and the recommendations are written mostly by those whose lives have been directly impacted, and who are involved in the transformation of the conflicts they are writing about in this book. At the same time, we have placed primary importance on providing balanced analyses and descriptions of the conflicts. Sometimes tensions arose between bringing a local perspective to the fore and ensuring political impartiality in an analysis; however, the process of the project has been one of considered discussion and collaboration, and we hope that the reader will find the book both balanced in perspective and of fresh importance.

We do, however, recognize that there are still gaps in information and we therefore see this undertaking as an ongoing process.

Annelies Heijmans is program coordinator for the Asia Pacific Region of the European Centre for Conflict Prevention, based in Utrecht, the Netherlands.

Nicola Simmonds was officer for the Searching for Peace in Asia Pacific project until June 2003. She is currently coordinating for the Pacific region for the 1,000 Women for the Nobel Peace Prize project and is working freelance in New Zealand.

Hans van de Veen is senior journalist and coordinator of an independent network of journalists, Bureau M&O (Environment and Development Productions), based in Amsterdam.

PART I

Reflections

1

Conflict Through Asia and the Pacific: Causes and Trends

Benjamin Reilly and Kennedy Graham

The search for peace in the Asia Pacific region is both a historical drama and a modern challenge. The region has never been without conflict since earliest times. The emergence of the original Chinese and Indian civilizations some five millennia ago was itself born of violence and trauma, to be followed by the long, drawn-out interplay of differing cultures and rival polities through the broad expanse of the region—from the Korean Peninsula across the high Mongolian steppe, the Himalayas and subcontinent, and out across the archipelagos of Sri Lanka, Indonesia, the Philippines, and Japan. Concomitantly, the early inhabitants of the region faced military incursion from outside—in the form of European, Arab, and Turkic invaders from the west. And finally, the "sea peoples" in the east of the region sought over time to escape such human pressures, recording extraordinary feats of navigation across the greatest ocean of all, the Pacific, settling in the subregions of Micronesia, Melanesia, and ultimately Polynesia. The contemporary tapestry of conflict and struggle across this vast and heterogeneous region is in many ways the child of a long, violent past.

The modern era of conflict in the region, however, can be traced to the struggle for the independence of Asia Pacific peoples during the final stages of World War II some sixty years ago. Since at least the 1940s, societies within the region have struggled to achieve independence from centuries of colonial rule by Europe and the United States and indeed from their own kind within Asia. Since independence, many states in the region have faced new conflicts that stem not from external colonizers, but from their own internal cleavages. Indeed, the bloodiest and most persistent conflicts in the region over the past decade have all been internal, intrastate wars that stem, in many cases, from the heterogeneous nature of the postcolonial state.

9

Taking this sweep of history as a starting point, this book aims to capture and assess the search for peace in the Asia Pacific region. It seeks to analyze the causes of conflict in the region, and identify the principal trends at play as regional societies, with support from the international community, aspire to marry freedom with stability, security with justice. In so doing, it also seeks to explore the techniques of conflict prevention and peacebuilding currently being practiced in the region in the face of the postmodern challenges of resurgent ethnic identities, globalization, and terrorism.

This chapter identifies the major conflict areas in the Asia Pacific region, analyzes their causes, and assesses the trends currently apparent in the efforts under way on the part of the international community to contain these conflicts and ensure a sustainable peace in the region.

A Brief Overview

We live in an age of transition in which conflict takes place both between and within nation-states. In the Asia Pacific region, the tension between India and Pakistan over the disputed territory of Kashmir is one of the major potential nuclear flashpoints of the world. The potential interstate conflicts on the Korean Peninsula and in the Taiwan Straits represent two other major threats to international security in the world today. Another potential interstate conflict comes from competing claims over sovereignty of islands in both the Kurils and the South China Sea, both of which have thwarted repeated attempts at resolution. In some areas (Burma's civil war, China's problems with Tibet and Xinjiang, and several Pacific Island conflicts), internal unrest has the potential to drag neighboring states into a conflict situation.

But in the modern age the balance of armed conflict has shifted away from war between states toward those predominantly within states.[1] Such conflicts have beset many Asia Pacific states in recent years. Academic studies have found a higher incidence of ethnic conflict and more independent ethnopolitical groups involved in such struggles in this region than anywhere else on earth.[2] Asia Pacific also had the largest number of "major armed conflicts" of any region in every year between 1989 and 1997.[3] Almost all of these were intrastate conflicts.

Most such internal conflicts are based around communal, linguistic, religious, or other kinds of "identity" issues. Major conflicts of this sort have been present during the last decade in Indonesia, Burma, the Philippines, Papua New Guinea, Fiji, and the Solomon Islands.

In many cases, however, ethnic animosities are also convenient cloaks for mobilizing support around political and economic issues, such as control over resources, changing social relations, increasing group inequalities, and the tensions created when traditional lifestyles and power bases are confronted by the inexorable forces of modernization. The highly intermixed and fragmented ethnic demography of parts of the region, like Southeast Asia, creates distinctive problems, making international disputes out of domestic tensions and complicating territorial prescriptions for conflict management.

Interstate Conflicts

The Korean Peninsula. Tension has been high on the Korean Peninsula ever since the end of World War II and the establishment of rival regimes backed by the United States and the Soviet Union. The invasion of the south by "North Korean forces" in June 1950 led to the first UN-mandated enforcement action (known as the Korean War, 1950–1953), ending in an armistice that to this day has not been consummated with a peace agreement. During this early period the Democratic People's Republic of Korea (North Korea) was not recognized at the United Nations as a legitimate government, but with the end of the Cold War in Europe the two Koreas were admitted to the United Nations as sovereign states in 1991. Cross-border tensions remain rife, however, and the continued presence of a large U.S. military force deployed in the south is an indication of the intractable stalemate that persists. North Korea's announced withdrawal from the Non-Proliferation Treaty (effective April 2003) and its claimed development of a nuclear weapons capability have increased tensions to crisis level. The issue is currently under consideration in the UN Security Council, and talks are under way among the United States, Russia, China, Japan, and the two Koreas.

The South China Sea. The South China Sea, surrounded by China, Vietnam, Brunei, Malaysia, Indonesia, and the Philippines, has long been a source of tension and conflict. Territorial disputes over the Paracel and Spratly islands have caused violent clashes especially between China, Vietnam, and the Philippines; seabed exploration has caused friction between China and Vietnam; and the seaway itself is notorious for pirate activity. All of the Spratly Islands are claimed by China, Taiwan, and Vietnam, while some are claimed by Malaysia and the Philippines. Brunei has a maritime claim in the area, and Indonesia's Exclusive Economic Zone is affected by such claims. Military clashes with significant loss of life occurred in 1974 and 1988, and skirmishes have taken place as recently as 1999. For their part, most nonregional states, including the United States, do not recognize any claim and consider the sovereignty of the islands to be in dispute. U.S. and British commercial enterprises have undertaken oil exploration on behalf of China and Vietnam—a source of further potential friction within the subregion. Above all, the United States is concerned to maintain its "rights of free passage" for its naval ships and military aircraft in international territory. China has itself deliberately kept its claim to the islands and the waters of the South China Sea rather vague. The April 2001 incident involving the U.S. spy plane forced down on Hainan focused U.S. and Chinese attention on the issue, but without permanent resolution. Apart from bilateral talks between China and Vietnam, and China and the United States, no serious effort has been made to seek a peaceful settlement of the South China Sea issue through multilateral means such as the International Court of Justice.

Kuril Islands. The islands between Japan and Russia (known to the Japanese as the Northern Territories and to the Russians as the Southern Kuriles) remain a source of deep friction between these two powerful countries. Occupied by Russia at the end of World War II, the islands have been retained ever since as a route to the Pacific Ocean from the Russian Far East. Historical claims by Japan, together with the islands' rich fishing waters, prompt Japan to seek restoration of its sovereignty over the disputed territories. The dispute has prevented the conclusion of a peace treaty between the two countries that would formally terminate hostilities from World War II, and they failed to fulfill a joint pledge in 1997 to meet a five-year deadline to settle the matter. At a summit in January 2003 the two countries confirmed their determination that, based on agreements already reached, bilateral relations should be fully normalized by solving "the issue of the attribution of the four islands" and concluding a peace treaty at the earliest possible date. The two leaders agreed to accelerate negotiations toward concluding such a treaty.[4]

Taiwan. Taiwan itself stands as a potential flashpoint in the region because of the ideological importance attached to the issue by China and the United States. The replacement of the Republic of China (Taiwan) by the People's Republic of China (PRC; communist mainland China) at the United Nations in 1971 caused a seismic tremor through the international community that has not totally subsided. The strict "one China" policy maintained by Beijing makes it clear that the PRC will not tolerate any international recognition of Taiwan by other states; and China has even employed its Security Council veto or otherwise opposed UN assistance to countries that transgress (Guatemala, Solomon Islands). Tensions continue between Beijing and Taiwan, a strong military capacity is retained by both parties, and the issue continues to be an emotive and volatile one inside the United States.

Intrastate Conflicts

China. While internal conflicts are relatively uncommon in North Asia, they are a growing problem in the three non-Han regions of China: Tibet, Xinjiang, and Inner Mongolia. All of these regions are currently in a state of low-level, simmering conflict born out of the desires for self-determination of the majority populations of these areas (Tibetan, Uighur, and Mongolian). As well as being driven by strong ethnoreligious distinctiveness, Uighur nationalists in particular have also been encouraged by a growing pan-Islamic consciousness and the creation of new Turkic-speaking Central Asian states on China's western border.

Burma. Burma has been afflicted by ethnic conflict throughout its history as a modern state. Currently, a range of such conflicts exist between the (predominantly Burmese) military government and peripheral ethnic groups such as the Shan, Karen, Kachin, Mon, and Arakanese. A further incipient conflict is the political tension between the prodemocracy movement and its imprisoned leader, Aung San Suu Kyi, and the military government of Burma. There is considerable variation in the level and intensity of these various conflicts. In recent years, the Burmese military has concluded cease-fire agreements with promises of regional autonomy with a view to gaining a short-term cessation of ethnic insurgencies from some fifteen different groups. But armed conflict continues with other groups such as the Karen, while the question of the legitimacy of the central government remains unresolved, particularly as international support for the regime has largely evaporated. Only the Association of Southeast Asian Nations (ASEAN) maintains dialogue with the military regime through "constructive engagement."

Indonesia. Southeast Asia's largest state, Indonesia is wracked by a range of violent internal conflicts and self-determination disputes that threaten the very viability of the country itself. The two most persistent conflicts, in Aceh and Papua, at the western and eastern extremities of the country, have a strong self-determination focus. The resource-rich, strongly Islamic province of Aceh, located in the northern part of Sumatra, has been waging an ongoing campaign for independence for decades. Unlike most of Indonesia's separatists, the Free Aceh Movement is well organized and well armed. Serious negotiations over greater autonomy are likely to be the only alternative to ongoing violence. A similar conclusion applies to Papua, at the eastern end of the Indonesian archipelago, which has cultural and historical claims to kinship with neighboring Papua New Guinea (PNG) and to separate nationhood from Indonesia. There have also been violent interethnic clashes in other Indonesian outer provinces such as Maluku, Kalimantan, Sulawesi, and Riau. Further tension between "immigrant" and "migrant" groups has also been a major cause of conflict in various regions: for example, between Islamic migrant groups and local Christians in Maluku; indigenous resistance to immigrants from other Indonesian provinces in Papua; and Dyak attacks on Madurese migrants in Kalimantan.

The Philippines. In the Philippines, a predominantly Christian country, conflict is concentrated in the remote hinterlands and on Mindanao, the southern region where a predominantly Muslim population continues its campaign for a Muslim homeland. Ongoing peace talks between the Philippine government and the Moro National Liberation Front (MNLF) have been brokered by the Organization of the Islamic Conference, with the particular involvement of Indonesia and Malaysia. The 1996 peace agreement resulted in the establishment of an autonomous regional government. The Moro Islamic Liberation Front (MILF), a more militant rebel group, split from the MNLF in 1977 in pursuit of a separate Islamic state. In July 2003 a cease-fire agreement was concluded between the government and the MILF following the latter's renunciation of terrorism the previous month. Abu Sayyaf is the smallest and most radical movement, labeled a "terrorist group" by both Manila and Washington. However, despite the peace agreements, Mindanao continues to suffer from ongoing violence, including conflict between hard-liners and moderates, guerrilla war between rebels and the government, and the kidnapping for ransom.

A recent development is the intervention of U.S. troops as "trainers" for their Philippine counterparts. In addition, a communist rebellion has been waged for over three decades, with a 10,000-strong military wing (the New People's Army) spread over the whole nation, including Mindanao. Although the United States has labeled the Maoist group a terrorist organization, the Philippine government has not done so and continues to push for a resumption of peace negotiations following their breakdown in mid-2001.

Malaysia. Conflicts are of a lower level of intensity in Malaysia, in part due to the effective state apparatus and quasi-authoritarian forms of governance of the central government. As in the other Southeast Asian states, however, center-periphery tensions are present. There are ongoing disputes in the eastern provinces of Sabah and Sarawak, as well as growing threats from some of the northern sultanates for greater autonomy on religious matters and, in some cases, for the establishment of an Islamic state.

East Timor. Since its emergence under UN auspices as an independent state in 2002, East Timor has had to deal with its own internal politics. Conflict has continued since independence, fueled by cross-border raids by Indonesian militias based in West Timor as well as by disgruntled local youths and others, resulting in local riots in December 2002.

Papua New Guinea. The region's most ethnically diverse country, Papua New Guinea suffers from a score of local conflicts—in part the result of having over 800 ethnolinguistic groups within its borders. In recent years, armed conflict has been an especially serious problem in the Southern Highlands, where tribal tensions degenerated into outright armed conflict during the 2002 elections. However, the long-running separatist struggle in the eastern island province of Bougainville appears to have been resolved, in the short term at least, through a successful peace deal brokered by the New Zealand and Australian governments. Papua New Guineans are also intimately connected to the secessionist struggles of their fellow Melanesians in the neighboring Indonesian province of Papua.

Pacific Islands. Internal conflicts currently afflict a number of the island countries of the South Pacific. The most serious of these, in the Solomon Islands, resulted in the overthrow of an elected government in 2000 amid armed conflict between residents of the main island groups of Guadalcanal and Malaita. The Australian government facilitated the Townsville Peace Agreement, which brought a fragile cessation of hostilities. In June 2003 a regional military intervention initiated and led by Australia (Operation Helpem Fren) resulted in the reestablishment of legitimate government there. Elsewhere, low-level conflicts remain in Fiji (where the May 2000 coup led to calls for the separation of the western half of the main island from the traditional power centers in the east), and in the French overseas territory of New Caledonia, where society is split between indigenous Kanaks in the island's north and French settlers in the south). Indeed, the prevalence of such separatist movements is one of the hall-marks of what might be called the "Africanization" of the South Pacific.[5]

Causes of Conflict

What explains the many different kinds of conflict in such a varied range of countries and contexts? While the causes of such events are complex and multi-dimensional, a number of themes, both political and economic, stand out. Some of the most diverse and fragmented societies in the region have had weak and artificial state structures imposed upon them. Weakened systems of gov-ernment invite corruption and organized crime; outlaw groups operate beyond the rule of law, not only in criminal gangs but in professional and political cir-cles that occasionally act beyond judicial reach. Economically, the impact of modernization, with the pervasive effects of globalization and the strains and uncertainties caused by unregulated trading and fragile financial systems, ex-acerbates these weaknesses and tensions.

Weak States, Many Societies

A fundamental problem facing many countries in the region is the weakness of state structures in the face of resurgent religious and ethnic identities. The explosion of internal conflicts reflects, at least in part, the artificiality of some states and the intrinsic salience of ethnicity, and more generally the ongoing strength of traditional society in the face of modern state structures. While the concept of a strong state is highly valued in most of Asia, and some countries (Thailand, Cambodia) have historical claims to "stateness," many states in Southeast Asia and the South Pacific are artificial creations of the twentieth century. The division between peninsular and eastern Malaysia, for example, is a product of British colonialism, as is the territorial manifestation of Burma. Indonesia, a country created by Dutch colonialism's amalgamation of sul-tanates and stateless tribes, has famously been described by Benedict Ander-son as a country "imagined" and hence invented by Javanese nationalists.[6] In PNG and the Solomon Islands the concept of a state is even more artificial. In the South Pacific generally, small stateless traditional societies were aggre-gated for the purposes of international statehood into weak and impoverished modern "states," some of which lack the capacity to fulfill such fundamental state tasks such as tax collection or the delivery of basic services. In addition, in most such cases there is no dominant culture, as in Indonesia, but rather hundreds of languages and thousands of small clans and tribal groups.

The term "Island Asia" is now being used to describe the broad region encompassing maritime Southeast Asia (i.e., Malaysia, Brunei, Indonesia, and the Philippines), East Timor, Papua New Guinea, and the Pacific Islands.[7] Eth-nically this region is, quite simply, the most diverse area of the world. It encapsulates over 1,000 languages and related ethnolinguistic groups, and an astonishing diversity of cultures and societies, including four of the world's great religions. Ethnic heterogeneity, however, does not necessarily lead to conflict; indeed, recent studies have shown that highly fragmented ethnic constellations are less prone to internal conflicts than those in which only two or three groups are present.[8] In addition, as noted earlier, it is often the case that demands for self-determination are as much demands for the redistribution of economic power as they are quests for genuine political self-determination.

The region is also home to small but economically significant populations of an extensive Chinese and Indian diaspora. Such communities control much of the private economy in Indonesia (where the Chinese represent an economically privileged and resented minority) and Fiji (where a coup in May 2000 ousted the country's first ethnic Indian prime minister). These communities tend to suffer periodic victimization in times of political upheaval—such as the 1998 anti-Chinese riots in Jakarta. This presents at least the potential that major external powers will become involved in the region to support ethnic kin abroad.[9]

The historical context of state building in many Asia Pacific countries also creates difficulties in addressing contemporary conflicts. Accordingly there is today some pressure for such countries to move away from a unitary structure toward a more decentralized or even federal model, and to grant "special autonomy" to rebellious outer provinces. But critics argue that granting such concessions only assists those wanting to break away and may serve to fragment rather than unify fragile multiethnic states. Such geopolitical tensions between central government and peripheral regions are prominent in Indonesia (Aceh, West Papua), Malaysia (Sabah, Sarawak), the Philippines (the Cordilleras, Mindanao), Thailand (the Muslim region in the south and the borders with Burma and Laos), and PNG (Bougainville). In each case, the peripheral regions see themselves as being ethnically, religiously, and linguistically separate from the dominant culture of the center.

Crime and Corruption

The Asian region is characterized by several important features that influence money-laundering methods used in the region. These include narcotics production centers, a well-established and growing drug-abuse problem, an international underground banking system, the widespread use of cash, and the existence of highly structured organized-crime groups.[10] Other recent criminal developments in the region include "cybercrime" and the production and export of illicit synthetic drugs. Trafficking in human beings, estimated to be the third-largest source of profit for organized crime, is prevalent within and from Southeast Asia and is a serious problem throughout the entire Asian region. Female trafficking for prostitution, in particular, is rife. A vicious circle is established whereby such crime further weakens state structures and opens the way to organized violence within societies.

By comparison, Pacific states have traditionally been relatively free of organized crime. But their vulnerability to such criminal networks because of their small size and limited investigative and enforcement capabilities makes them an increasingly attractive arena for criminal networks.

Modernization and Globalization

Many countries in the Asia Pacific region are in the throes of enormous social and economic change from tradition to modernity[11]—and this process is in itself conflict-creating. Because economic modernization creates winners and losers, social cleavages have provided a way of mobilizing coalitions of common interest to be part of the winning side—for example, in competition for scarce natural or economic resources. The various peoples' uprisings in China,[12] and the labor protest clashes with the establishment in South Korea, constitute clear evidence of the strains to which society is subjected as a consequence of political modernization. One society, North Korea, has removed itself completely from the forces of modernization through a strict isolationist policy, resulting in international tensions of an entirely different sort.

Trends in Conflict Management, Democratization, and Peacebuilding

How can such internal conflicts in the region be managed or accommodated peacefully? One possible approach is to design political institutions that can effectively defuse, reduce, or reshape conflicts. This is particularly timely because so many of the region's political institutions now have the potential for redesign and reform, due to ongoing democratization and recognition of the weakness of transplanted political systems across the region. One clear need in many cases is the restructuring of internal political systems to accommodate the realities of social diversity. The confluence of increasing democratization and increasing internal conflict has naturally redirected attention to the capacity of the political institutions of countries in the region to respond to and effectively manage conflict. So far, most of these institutions have been found wanting. Three broad areas of institutional design have received particular attention: the territorial structure of the state (questions of federalism, autonomy, confederation); the form of the state's legislative and executive functions (presidential, parliamentary, or "semipresidential"); and a state's rules of political representation (electoral systems, political parties, and local representation).

These political institutions are increasingly central to the debate over state security and survival in the region. The issue of parliamentary versus presidential government, and the balance of forces between the legislature and the executive, was a major source of dispute in Indonesia during the Wahid presidency. Similarly, Indonesia's ongoing process of decentralization to the local government level *(kapupatem)* represents an important experiment in devolution that will inevitably have serious impacts on the state's capacity to manage conflict prevention. Likewise, the provision of "special autonomy" for Aceh and West Papua in Indonesia, for Mindanao in the Philippines, and for Bougainville in Papua New Guinea, is genuinely applied in those regions. Discussions of electoral system reform are also prominent in many countries, including Indonesia, Papua New Guinea, and Fiji. In each case, accommodation of diversity and management of conflict is central to the broader debate about the design of institutions.

Beyond these concerns there are many "extraconstitutional" institutions and policies requiring attention from those seeking solutions to intrastate conflict. These include measures to combat the proliferation of small arms; policies to reintegrate former combatants; the promotion of local peace accords; social and economic "pacts" between contending elites; truth, reconciliation, and justice commissions; the formation of civic "peace committees"; changes to language and education policy; and minority rights instruments, indigenous group bodies, and gender commissions. All of these devices have the potential to address and ameliorate conflicts in the region.[13] But so far only a few have been seriously investigated as options for peacebuilding, and often only after the initial conflict has already occurred. A greater emphasis on these institutional approaches to conflict management will become more important as Asia Pacific states are forced to grapple with these issues into the future. These issues are explored in Chapters 3 and 6.

In contrast to these devices for managing intrastate conflict, the search for lasting solutions to potential interstate conflicts relies more on the familiar tools of diplomacy, coercion, and international engagement. Yet even here, increasing focus has been placed on the importance of internal political arrangements, especially via the so-called democratic peace theory—the empirical fact that democracies are far less likely to go to war with each other than with other regime types—a thesis much cited in speeches by former U.S. president Bill Clinton during his term in office.[14] A paradox, however, exists: while "democracy" is held by the international community to be an intrinsically desirable goal and a necessary condition of a sustainable peace, the process of democratization itself is often seen to unleash forces of opposition and tension within a society that make conflict more likely. While enduring democracies are, in general, less likely than their authoritarian counterparts to experience high levels of internal conflict or to go to war with each other, countries undergoing the wrenching process of democratization are neither safer internally nor less prone to war.[15] Indeed, many indicators of conflict—both inter- and intrastate varieties—tend to *rise* in the initial period of democratization. One of the weaknesses of rapid democratization in multiethnic states is thus the greater probability of the rise of ethnically based self-determination and secessionist movements.[16] This is explored in Chapter 4.

This phenomenon has been evident in a number of the established and emerging Asia Pacific democracies such as Indonesia, the Philippines, and Papua New Guinea, where disaffected groups claiming self-determination and/or independence as a fundamental aim have tended to take up arms to achieve their aims. Thus, within the putatively "democratic" states of the region, minorities have eschewed the ballot box as a route to self-determination, reverting to force instead (the Tamils in Sri Lanka, Kashmiris in India, Jammu peoples of the Chittagong Hill Tracts in Bangladesh, Moros in the Philippines, and Bougainvilleans in PNG). Similarly, some of the internal conflicts and secessionist movements in Indonesia have been prompted not just by the successful (if bloody) separation of East Timor but also by the ongoing democratization of national politics in the country.

West Papua/Nabire, March 2000. Papuans selling calendars
with the Bintang Kejora, the Morning Star, the flag of an independent West Papua.
The money they raise will be used to support the Free Papua Movement.

Across Southeast Asia—a region that only ten years ago was dominated by repressive and authoritarian governments—there is now a clear trend toward democratic governance as a new norm.[17] The primacy of democracy as a form of government is now established in Thailand, the Philippines, and Indonesia—three of the four biggest countries in ASEAN. This has dramatically altered prospects for the management of self-determination and other kinds of internal conflict through democratic compromise and accommodation rather than the repressive responses that typify authoritarian regimes. But this same process of democratization is also sowing the seeds for ongoing internal conflicts and the possible breakup of some countries that were previously held together by force.

Internal conflicts are notoriously difficult to solve through conventional measures. Because of the deep-seated nature of ethnic identities, they are particularly unsuited to "cake cutting," split-the-difference solutions. They also tend to be immune to traditional approaches to international security based on international law and diplomacy, using intergovernmental organizations as the vehicle. Such institutions were designed for the maintenance of international peace and order, not for events that take place within state borders. Consequently, they are often impotent or irrelevant in the face of internal conflicts, which often involve nonnegotiable claims to separate statehood. Similarly, the existing international architecture of world governance, in the shape of the United Nations, is founded on the assumption that states are the basic unit of international order and not, as so many of the Asia Pacific's conflicts suggest, artificial and ephemeral creations of colonialism and circumstance.

Intrastate conflicts also present problems for those attempting to resolve disputes through measures such as preventive diplomacy, early warning, and international intervention. These have so far had little impact on contemporary intrastate conflicts in the Asia Pacific region, most of which are not amenable to international involvement. Nor do they usually attract direct international intervention. Especially in Asia, the concept of a strong state is highly valued, and most countries oppose any attempt at interference in their internal affairs, just as they resist demands for self-determination that involve a redefinition of their existing territorial boundaries. In most cases, lasting solutions to internal conflicts must be based on internal reforms rather than external intervention. External actors can assist, guide, and pressure, but they cannot solve a conflict themselves.

Conclusion: The Effect of Changing International Norms

A new force driving modern conflict and thwarting the efforts at peaceful settlement is the perceived change in international norms regarding secessionism and the creation of new states. It has been noted that the twentieth-century bias against political divorce (secession) was as strong as the nineteenth-century bias against marital divorce.[18] If that is the case, then the twenty-first-century attitude to secession may follow the relaxation of prevailing norms against marital divorce that occurred over the course of the twentieth century. Today, the constraints that the international community puts against the creation of new states, while strong, are also less prohibitive than they were for most of the twentieth century, particularly the Cold War period. Indeed, since the fall of the Berlin Wall, there have been many new states created around the world. Most of these have come from the dissolution of the Soviet empire, but others have come from mutual separation (the Czech Republic and Slovakia), war (Ethiopia and Eritrea), a combination of the two (Yugoslavia), or direct international intervention (East Timor).

Are the self-determination claims currently advanced in the region likely to be recognized or supported by the broader international community? Why do the region's most savage conflicts (such as the Christian-Muslim clashes in Ambon and North Maluku) scarcely make the international news media? For most of the world, the Pacific Islands are even more obscure and their strategic importance is extremely limited. Yet it is a measure of how important international support has become for the prospects of successful secession that activists from two of the region's most persistent conflicts have been assiduously seeking to internationalize their conflicts: Aceh in the Islamic world (within the Middle East) and Papua in the Pacific Islands Forum and the Netherlands (where a legal challenge to the province's incorporation into Indonesia is now under way).[19]

The search for peace in the Asia Pacific promises to be as elusive as that in other complex regions beset with equally intractable problems, such as the Middle East and Central Africa. Success in conflict prevention and peace-building in the region will demand all the innovative conceptual contributions that scholars can make and the dedicated talent of the practitioners in the international organizations and civil society groups, both at headquarters and in the field. The further development of conflict-prevention and peacebuilding techniques, the process of democratization, and ways of accommodating the diverse impacts of globalization, localization, resurgent ethnic identities, and the renewed focus on international terrorism all contribute to this. The following chapters explore these issues in greater detail.

Benjamin Reilly, Ph.D., is currently a senior lecturer in the Asia Pacific School of Economics and Government at the Australian National University, Canberra. He has previously served with the UN Development Programme, New York, and the International Institute for Democracy and Electoral Assistance, Stockholm. He is the author of several books on democracy and conflict management, most recently Democracy in Divided Societies *(Cambridge: Cambridge University Press, 2001).*

Kennedy Graham, Ph.D., is currently senior fellow in the Peace and Governance Division of United Nations University. He served in the New Zealand Foreign Service for sixteen years, subsequently working in New York and Stockholm before joining the United Nations. He was director of the university's Leadership Academy in Amman, Jordan, from 1999 to 2002. He is the author of three books on global governance and international relations, most recently The Planetary Interest *(UCL Press/Rutgers University Press, 1999).*

Notes

1. Peter Wallensteen and Margareta Sollenberg, "Armed Conflict 1989–99," *Journal of Peace Research* 37, no. 5 (2000): 635–649. Of the 110 "major armed conflicts" in the world during that decade, only 7 were traditional interstate conflicts; the remaining 103 took place within existing states, mostly based on identity issues such as language, religion, and ethnicity. A "major armed conflict" is defined as a conflict over government and/or territory that incurs over 1,000 battle-related deaths.

2. Ted Robert Gurr, "Peoples Against States: Ethnopolitical Conflict and the Changing World System," *International Studies Quarterly* 38, no. 3 (1994): 349–353.

3. Margareta Sollenberg, Peter Wallensteen, and Andrés Jato, "Major Armed Conflicts," in Stockholm International Peace Research Institute, *SIPRI Yearbook 1999: Armaments, Disarmament, and International Security* (Oxford: Oxford University Press, 1999).

4. Statement by Prime Minister of Japan, Russian-Japan Summit, 10 January 2003 (Prime Minister's Office) http://www.kantei.go.jp/foreign/koizumispeech/2003/01/10kaiken_e.html.

5. Ben Reilly, "The Africanisation of the South Pacific," *Australian Journal of International Affairs* 54, no. 3 (2000): 261–268.

6. Benedict Anderson, *Imagined Communities: Reflections on the Origin and Spread of Nationalism* (London: Verso, 1983).

7. See, for example, Bruce Vaughn, ed., *The Unraveling of Island Asia? Governmental, Communal, and Regional Instability* (Westport, Conn.: Praeger, 2002).

8. See Paul Collier and Anke Hoeffler, "On the Economic Causes of Civil Wars," *Oxford Economic Papers* 50, no. 4 (1998): 563–573; and Benjamin Reilly, "Democracy, Ethnic Fragmentation, and Internal Conflict: Confused Theories, Faulty Data, and the 'Crucial Case' of Papua New Guinea," *International Security* 25, no. 3 (2000): 162–185.

9. See Zha, Daojiong, "China and the May 1998 Riots of Indonesia: Exploring the Issues," *Pacific Review* 13, no. 4 (2000): 557–575.

10. See Interpol's website for details, www.interpol.int.

11. "Modernization" in this section refers to two things: (1) the historical sweep of modernity—the Cartesian dualism, secularism, and materialism since eighteenth-century European revolutionary thought, translated into twenty-first-century neoliberalism; and (2) the closely related concept of globalization, which is to some extent technology-driven. These forces together threaten traditional societies across the planet—especially in the Muslim world and in indigenous cultures.

12. Uprisings such as the peasant uprising in the rural areas and the spiritual challenge of movements such as Falun Gong in urban areas.

13. For a survey of these "constitutional" and "extraconstitutional" options, see Peter Harris and Ben Reilly, eds., *Democracy and Deep-Rooted Conflict: Options for Negotiators* (Stockholm: International Institute for Democracy and Electoral Assistance, 1999).

14. See Bruce Russett, *Grasping the Democratic Peace* (Princeton: Princeton University Press, 1993).

15. Edward D. Mansfield and Jack Snyder, "Democratization and the Danger of War," *International Security* 20, no. 1 (1995): 5–38.

16. See Renée de Nevers, "Democratization and Ethnic Conflict," in Michael Brown, ed., *Ethnic Conflict and International Security* (Princeton: Princeton University Press, 1993).

17. See Ben Reilly, "Regionalism and the Spread of Democracy in the Asia Pacific," in Bert Edström, ed., *Interdependence in the Asia Pacific* (Stockholm: Swedish Institute for International Affairs and Center for Pacific Asia Studies, 2001).

18. Samuel P. Huntington, foreword to Eric A. Nordlinger, *Conflict Regulation in Divided Societies* (Cambridge: Center for International Affairs, Harvard University, 1972).

19. "West Papua Separatists Prepare to Fight in Court," *Sydney Morning Herald,* August 9, 2001.

2

Empowering People to Build a Just Peace in the Asian Arena

Ed Garcia

Historically beset by violent political upheavals and internal armed conflicts, political leaders in diverse regions of the world have tended to take the path that is traditionally well traveled. The inclination to advance military solutions to address problems of security and the safety of peoples has drawn adherents from across the political divide. Perceived to be both more logical and more politically plausible, it seems to be a preferred option of those in power. It is no wonder then that at the onset of the twenty-first century, we are witnessing an unprecedented and unconventional global war on terror.

For the peace practitioner, however, the challenge of envisioning alternative approaches to the unending task of making and building peace now seems more urgent and compelling than at any other time. Experience has shown us time and again that military means employed to combat insecurity often lead to more war and less security for people. It has moreover clearly demonstrated the dearth of diplomatic means at our disposal and the lack of appropriate approaches in today's peace practice. Thus it is no longer possible to think that protracted violence can be addressed only by one set of actors or by unilateral initiatives. Undoubtedly, today's imperative is to take action at different levels, involving diverse stakeholders and sectors of society at given times and in ways that may complement each other so that efforts on different tracks become collaborative and subsequently more effective.

Unconventional Global War's Impact on Asia
Waged in the shadow of the Twin Towers tragedy in New York and the ensuing global war on terror, the second war on Iraq in 2003 and its aftermath have made increasingly clear what thoughtful conflict practitioners have previously observed: a paradigm shift in our ways of thinking, in the way politics is conceived, economics is conducted, wars are fought, and governments are run. More people demonize the enemy, divide the world into right or wrong, or

readily label the other as terrorist or part of evil empires. The trend to rely on military means is matched by the propensity to wage all-out war, where violence is readily tolerated, the habits of dialogue are crushed by the flourish of rhetoric, and the appeal to reason is drowned out by loyalty to the flag.

The impact of these events on the Asia Pacific region has been both immediate and incalculable. Afghanistan, nestled in West Asia, has been the initial epicenter of what has turned out to be an unconventional global war. The island of Basilan, Mindanao, in the Southern Philippines soon became a second front, while the bomb blast in Bali extended its frontiers. Meanwhile, critical concerns confront countries of South and Southeast Asia, now polarized by events in the Middle East and in the Gulf.

In Asia, where efforts to establish the universality of human rights standards and the relevance of common instruments and mechanisms have taken considerable dedication, the fallout of this war on terror has, so to speak, been terrifying. Standards that have taken time to nurture, institutions that are in process of being built, and situations of violent conflict that require patience and deep understanding to address are today deeply affected.

Work to establish a set of international standards of acceptable behavior in the fields of human rights and humanitarian law required painstaking collaboration between governments and nongovernmental organizations. Efforts to build viable institutions, vested with legitimacy, universally acclaimed, and made available for the redress of grievances in cases where gross violations, war crimes, or crimes against humanity have been committed, now risk being stalled. The Rome Statute of the International Criminal Court, the special international tribunals, and the parallel truth and reconciliation commissions are testaments to the resolve of the international community to build imperfect but nevertheless worthy institutions to respond to acts of inhumanity that have caused untold suffering.

Diplomacy has been short-circuited. Attempts to expand the capacity of international diplomacy and strengthen the rule of law to respond to dissent or political conflict have been undermined. The practice of exhausting diplomatic efforts and employing the creative arsenal of conflict resolution approaches available to the UN and its agencies has been discarded in favor of shortcuts and emergency measures—all in the name of the war on terror. Efforts to help resolve intractable conflicts through negotiated political settlements have become more difficult and the spaces for dialogue have been reduced, polarizing potential dialogue partners and undermining attempts to bridge the divide.

Consider the vast Asia Pacific region—3.3 billion people. Two-thirds of the 800 million people considered by the UN to be the world's poorest live in the great Asian expanse. The majority of those who live in the region are the young, under eighteen years of age. The region is diverse, with the world's most populous nations, such as China, India, and Indonesia, living side by side with some of the least populous countries among the island nations of the Pacific. The per capita income gap differs radically from Japan to Cambodia.

It is home to different religions (Buddhism, Hinduism, Islam, Christianity, and Confucianism, among others) and is the cradle of civilizations. It is, finally, the site of some of the most complex conflicts in the world, and the greatest number of internal armed conflicts and intractable ethnopolitical conflicts on the planet.

If one looks back on Asian history, one is struck by the different forms of struggle people have waged to address diverse situations. In the Asia Pacific, Filipinos fought one of the earliest wars of independence in their quest to end Spanish colonial rule at the turn of the twentieth century. In the 1940s and 1950s, from India to China to Burma to Indonesia, different forms of struggle took place, from the nonviolent struggle led by Mahatma Gandhi to end British rule, known as satyagraha, to efforts to end Dutch domination of the Indonesian archipelago. As recently as the 1960s and 1970s, in what was known as Indochina, the people of Vietnam, Cambodia, and Laos took on France, the United States, and their collaborators in protracted guerrilla wars.

The context of the Cold War provided the backdrop to some of the deadliest conflicts of the past half century. Issues such as dictatorial rule, economic inequality, the politics of exclusion or corruption, the question of identity or ideology, access to resources, and disputes over borders and territories have driven people to take up arms. Some of these issues remain unresolved in diverse conflict areas in Asia Pacific. At the onset of the present century, however, the overarching reality of the global war on terrorism seems to have diverted attention away from those unfinished quests for profound change and the deep differences existing across the region that have been the source of so much internal armed conflict. It is thus more than probable that as governments engage in the war on terror, they will once again fail to address these deep-seated grievances that lie at the root of so much violent conflict.

Imperatives in the Conflict Conjuncture

If we are to prevent further wars in the future and the escalation of current conflicts, there is no option but to address these underlying sources of armed conflicts, in particular those of a protracted nature. In the field of conflict prevention and transformation, it has become apparent that no single path to peace exists nor are there any shortcuts to build a just peace in response to the violent challenges facing the global community. If efforts are to be effective in this difficult period in the aftermath of the war on Iraq, with all its consequences for international relations, the imperative of the hour is to adopt multilateral approaches, seeking broader support for peace efforts, and higher levels of collaboration so as to forge more effective strategies to build durable peace.

From Somalia to Rwanda, from Chechnya to Georgia/Abkhazia, from Indonesia to the Philippines, and from the Middle East to Colombia, to name but a few, the last decade has seen a failure on the part of governments and intergovernmental organizations, as well as nongovernmental organizations, to address armed conflicts in effective ways. Solutions conceived only on the official levels of governments and the parties to the conflict, without taking into account communities and people's organizations (or vice versa), have largely been incomplete efforts, tending crucially to fail the test of sustainability. Unless there is greater understanding of what causes violent conflicts and until more comprehensive responses are designed to meet these situations, then our failures are bound to continue as conflicts recur or intensify.

To better understand how the work to transform situations of violence can prosper, it is essential that there is sound and shared analysis of the situation, that stakeholders are identified, options for action studied, strategies formulated before work is begun, and processes of engagement initiated. In this analysis, there may be a need to incorporate organizations within regional or global contexts, especially in situations where those responsible for state security and the safety of citizens are incapable of delivering on this responsibility or are themselves the cause of this insecurity. Without prior analysis and an understanding of the sociopolitical and economic contexts, it may not be possible to assist in designing or implementing helpful or collaborative processes.

Working Effectively with Others

The rethinking required in the field of conflict prevention and transformation deals with overcoming the often artificial and at times unhelpful boundaries between official and unofficial, governmental and nongovernmental, regional and global, which at times impede rather than facilitate the formulation of sound strategies for addressing conflicts in ways that are appropriate, and more comprehensive. Distinctions obviously exist and they must be recognized, and the primacy of one actor over another at different phases of the conflict certainly can influence the approaches taken to resolve them. However, what needs to be highlighted and recognized is the fact that the contributions of all relevant actors, both official and unofficial, are important, so as to be able to achieve the aims of comprehensive human security in the context of stable peace. There are limits to what politicians and government leaders can achieve, just as there are limitations with respect to the experience and competence of nongovernmental organizations and the representatives of civil society. But a willingness to explore ways of working together, showing respect for appropriate strengths while acknowledging certain constraints, would go a long way toward creating the kind of complementarity needed now more than ever to handle the armed conflicts of our time.

Primacy of People

In the various areas of conflict, it is increasingly clear that there are no lasting ways of building a just peace unless people are placed at the heart of peace processes. Peace endures when there is support from local communities through processes they respect and own. Peace cannot be imposed from the outside, but must be built patiently and intelligently, primarily by those who have lived and suffered through the conflict and with the assistance of others who are sensitive to the primacy of local peoples but sufficiently skilled to navigate through processes that are trustworthy and truly helpful.

Sustainable Peace

The core of work aimed at transforming conflicts is the building of sustainable peace. This undertaking implies that the underlying causes of the conflict are addressed, including their structural sources; or that the flawed policies or weak institutions that create conditions for the breakdown of workable relationships are properly tackled. It is necessary but not sufficient to deal with the manifest violence and the tensions between parties to the conflict that result in the loss of lives and suffering to noncombatants and that themselves must be either reduced or eliminated. If the peace is to be sustained over the long term, an awareness of the sources of the violence is vital and a capability to deal with the underpinnings of such situations equally crucial.

Peace, Power, and Politics

Moreover, it is important to highlight the fact that making or building peace is intimately related to power and politics—the reality of states and the power wielded by those who make decisions in the political and economic spheres. Practitioners in the field of conflict resolution often work to change situations by means of working with and through civil society organizations or representatives. While this may be an important venue to modify attitudes or behavior, it may not be sufficient to influence policies and impact on structures to bring about more peaceful processes. Thus conflict practitioners would be well advised to incorporate approaches that are more sensitive to the role played by politics and initiatives emanating from the state, while the political leadership in those states come to accept the fact that coercive means and the use of force or state power have their limits and that less adversarial approaches to "conflict sensitive politics" may hold more promise for successful conflict resolution.

Civil Society Representatives in Parallel Efforts

Among other things, the twentieth century will be remembered as the period when civil society organizations and social movements flourished more than at any other time in recorded history. People from different walks of life and from diverse political contexts became more aware of the possibilities for relevant and sustained action: in alleviating human suffering, advancing human rights, advocating priorities in development or environmental protection, or working to build peace. Thus nongovernmental organizations or people's groups evolving into social movements flourished in relevant areas of human endeavor.

Social Movements

These organizations and the social movements they have spawned have assumed roles that previously were the unique preserve of the nation-states. More and more organized groups in the voluntary sector are providing emergency humanitarian assistance, health and educational services, support for development efforts in communities, agriculture and livelihood endeavors, and the protection of forests and waters. They are also supporting campaigns to bring about more peaceful relationships within and among nation-states, such as the vast antiwar movement, spanning borders and continents, that sprouted around the issue of the war in Iraq.

On some continents more than in others, there has been a landscape change in this regard. Not only in Europe but also in the Americas, in Africa, in Latin America, and in the Asia Pacific area these nongovernmental or civil society groups and private voluntary organizations are beginning to play a more critical role in defining and advancing policy, in influencing decisions, and in mobilizing people and creating constituencies for profound social change.

Areas of Engagement

In general, organizations dealing with conflict situations tend to make their contributions in at least four major areas of work: emergency relief and assistance; economic and social development, including social justice issues, to provide assistance in the medium or long term; human rights and international humanitarian law; and the nonviolent resolution of conflict and the building of sustainable peace.

Cooperative Efforts

Increasingly, organizations working in one area have become more sensitive to the interrelatedness of various fields of effort. They recognize that work in one area can have significant impact on other fields; for example, work for peace requires collaboration on development efforts to enable communities to survive and thrive. Likewise, peace, to be just and durable, needs to be accompanied by efforts focused on the promotion and protection of human rights and humanitarian law.

Grounded in the reality of local conditions, most of these groups bring knowledge of local conditions and access to committed individuals and relevant groups or country networks that can make a difference. In general, they are relatively independent, flexible, and innovative. Their unique advantage often lies in the fact that they can operate with fewer constraints than most high-profile political or diplomatic leaders.

However, they suffer from other limitations that severely constrain their effectiveness. Thus there is a greater willingness to learn from past mistakes and a growing conviction of the need to be more professional to ensure that the work becomes more effective. There is also a growing realization, that all of the groups and organizations in these fields need one another if they are going to make any real difference in addressing the deep-rooted and intractable conflicts that they are called upon to deal with.

Multi-Track Approaches

Practitioners and organizations engaged in conflict resolution and peacebuilding enhance their efforts by taking "multi-track" approaches that recognize different paths to tackle common problems while availing themselves of valuable

North Sumatra, Indonesia, 1999.
An investigator with Aceh's independent legal aid office talks to witnesses
of a massacre supposedly perpetrated by the Indonesian armed forces.

human and scarce material resources. This type of parallel and unconventional diplomacy—combining so-called Track One and Track Two efforts—seeks to advance peacemaking from a variety of perspectives, taking into account various groups whose particular strengths may differ, while recognizing their respective limitations. These multifaceted endeavors bring together various stakeholders and aim to make a significant impact and effectively work at many levels of society.

In effect, multi-track approaches essentially bring together two related efforts: official diplomacy, where governmental or intergovernmental representatives work to bring about solutions to violent situations; and unofficial citizen efforts, which encompass the efforts of civil society representatives to reduce violence and to address the underlying causes of the violence. There can be other parallel attempts, such as those, sometimes described as "semi-official," taken by parliamentarians or the private or corporate sector, which provide an additional layer of involvement. In reality, however, the combined diplomacy of both official and unofficial endeavors tends to be both creative and constructive in the long run.

Official Tracks

Among official-track efforts, the more significant have been those of intergovernmental diplomacy as carried out by the United Nations and, increasingly, a large number of regional organizations including the European Union, the Organization of American States, the Association of Southeast Asian

Nations, and subregional groupings such as the Economic Community of West African States, the Intergovernmental Authority on Development in East Africa, or their equivalent formations in southern Africa or South Asia.

There is the peacemaking work of governments through official diplomacy, such as the negotiations conducted by Norway in relation to the Sri Lankan conflict or the efforts of the Irish and British governments in Northern Ireland. A variation of this effort is the use of unofficial channels by officials or people close to policymakers, such as the 1993 Norwegian negotiations that eventually led to the Oslo Accord between Israel and the Palestine Liberation Organization, or the work of representatives of the Italian government in collaboration with the Comunità di Sant'Egidio in relation to the Mozambique conflict.

In more recent experiences in Asia, the Organization of the Islamic Conference, and the efforts of both the Indonesian government (with regard to the Moro National Liberation Front in 1996) and the Malaysian government (in relation to the Moro Islamic Liberation Front in 2002–2003) have been notable in the case of the protracted conflict in Mindanao in the Southern Philippines. The role of the Commonwealth Secretariat in Fiji, as well as representatives of both the New Zealand government and the Australian government, has been substantive. More important, the roles of both New Zealand and Australia have also been highlighted in the peace accord reached in Bougainville, Papua New Guinea.

Unofficial Tracks

The diplomacy exercised by citizens or private organizations or at times practiced through respected elders or recognized personages provides an illustration of the usefulness of the unofficial track. In Asia, there have been examples of tribal elders who have used traditional methods to resolve disputes, such as the *Bodong,* or peace pipe ritual, in the Cordilleras in the mountain provinces of Central Luzon in the Philippines, or kinship networks to address communal problems.

The role that women played in weaving consensus in the case of Bougainville, Papua New Guinea, has been documented extensively, showing how women on both sides of the divide took initiatives to advance a delicate process. In the case of other conflicts in the Asia Pacific region, such as those in the Philippines, Fiji, Sri Lanka, and Cambodia, women working side by side with men as peace advocates have played significant roles.

The role of religious leaders engaged in interfaith dialogue or in reconciliation initiatives have been remarkable on numerous occasions in Latin America, in Africa, and in Asia. The examples of the Quakers in Nigeria during the Biafra war and or the Comunità di Sant'Egidio in Mozambique in the 1990s provide illustrations of the impact of unofficial tracks. The Buddhist monks in Cambodia played a significant role through their peace marches to galvanize political will to address the intractable problems that had been caused by the excesses of the Khmer Rouge and their successor regimes.

Not as frequent but equally crucial can be the role of the private or corporate sectors, such as occurred in South Africa or Northern Ireland, where their contributions to the peace process meant a stronger constituency for peace, providing an economic impetus to the work of peacebuilders.

Work by peace advocates in media has proved to be a valuable tool in mobilizing public opinion and influencing policymakers. For example, Search for Common Ground in Indonesia hosts a radio soap opera that broadcasts messages across the archipelago of tolerance and conflict transformation, and its War and Peace Film Festival promoted dialogue across religious and cultural divides at a time when the world had split over how to understand and effectively work against terrorism.

Grassroots community efforts have resulted in "peace zones," "peace corridors," and "territories or municipalities of peace" created by unarmed citizens in Colombia and the Philippines, for example. Other examples of peace and reconciliation efforts include the work of the Community Relations Council in Northern Ireland, the Melanesian Brotherhood in the Solomon Islands, and the private sector in the cases of initiatives to promote reconciliation between North and South Korea, and China and Taiwan. Search for Common Ground has likewise done exemplary work in Kalimantan, Indonesia, employing media to create conditions for better understanding.

Other citizens' initiatives involve peace education in schools or in broader areas such as those undertaken through the UN Educational, Scientific, and Cultural Organization's Culture of Peace campaign and the work with youth and children advocating more peace-related learning and activities. Relevant to this area is the work for peace undertaken by artists and sports personalities who contribute to the making of a more peaceful world through music, dance, theater, and games.

Empowering Citizens to Transform Violent Conflicts

In both North and South, peacebuilders are seeking to maximize their resources wherever possible, seeking "higher levels of communication and cooperation" with people working in government, intergovernmental institutions, or nongovernmental organizations.

Nongovernmental organizations in collaboration with other institutions are helping to create conditions where local peoples can engage in initiatives that can make a difference in the peace processes required in their communities. Obstacles, however, abound. Resources are limited, and their capacity to challenge the prevailing sociopolitical order is more limited still. Citizens, as one reflective observer put it, cannot "mediate with muscle" nor can they enforce solutions to problems. Their strength lies in their capacity to organize and mobilize, their flexibility, and their ability to respond readily to urgent situations without the constraints of bureaucracies or the protocol of intergovernmental institutions. They can create alliances with local peoples who live and suffer through their conflicts, and they can help facilitate ways to resolve obstacles and respond to the needs of people—in brief, to promote human security—through sensitive dialogue.

However, to be effective there is a need for strategic linkages. Effective peacebuilding processes require better collaboration between those who attempt to develop communities and those who aim to transform conflicts—since peace cannot be durable without one or the other, just as the benefits of humanitarian assistance can be short-lived without a longer-term development framework.

The main challenge, however, remains how to explore ways of empowering citizens and societies so that they can bring about the profound social changes in society required not only to put a stop to violence today, but also to address the issues that are left unresolved and that often become the causes of future violent conflicts. In the current conjuncture in Asia, particularly, where fragile peace processes are found in Sri Lanka, Nepal, parts of Indonesia, and the Philippines, among others, it is crucial that citizens are empowered to participate more meaningfully in the peace processes that are currently under way or are being besieged by forces determined to undermine them. Track-one efforts that focus on the formal peace negotiations need to be accompanied closely by efforts on other and parallel tracks so that a social infrastructure of peace, so to speak, is created for the medium and long term. Otherwise, these fragile processes, and even agreements that may reached, will soon either collapse and be unable to withstand serious challenges from more established forces.

Advancing Peace Processes: Key Elements
While taking into consideration the diversity of armed conflicts in the Asia Pacific region and its subregions, it is useful to look at a framework for understanding peace processes and possible paths to peace. As a way of helping to address the causes of conflict and contributing to effective peace processes, three interrelated elements can be discussed:

- Peacemaking and peacebuilding
- Efforts that may be conducive to a durable peace
- Exploration of viable outcomes—especially in a period such as that experienced under the regime of the global war on terrorism, where long-term goals of sustainable peace may be undermined by the more immediate focus on security concerns

The major elements that can, moreover, be considered significant in understanding peace processes include people's participation; third-party facilitation and mediation; phased, partial agreements; preparation and framework of negotiations; and the pursuit of parallel tracks.

People's Participation
In reflecting on peace processes, one begins with the primacy of people and their effective participation. If the combatants on both sides claim to be fighting in the people's name, why limit the efforts to resolve these disputes to official peace conference tables or high-level negotiations among elite leaders? Consulting people, exhorting the sectors to articulate their aspirations, and incorporating the work of trade unions or peasant farmers, the urban poor and

the displaced, the unemployed and the dispossessed, are essential ingredients for meaningful processes. Examples of these efforts abound in a number of Southeast Asian countries. In the Philippines, they include community-based "sanctuaries of peace," the National Peace Conference, the Citizens' Council of Peace, and the Bishops-Ulama Conference. In Cambodia, there have been peace marches, or *dayamietra,* led by Buddhist monks and other peace advocates. In Indonesia and in Thailand, academics and nonviolent activists find common spaces for collaboration. In South Asia, examples range from the vast and rich experience of Gandhian-inspired peace advocacy in both India and Pakistan to the interfaith groups in Sri Lanka.

Third-Party Facilitation and Mediation
Often, the parties to the conflict reach dead ends, becoming unable to advance and condemned to repartition blame or to resort to name-calling or the use of slogans. Third parties, whether local or international, acting as friends of the process, facilitators of dialogue, or if required, as mediators, have frequently played a crucial role in overcoming stalemates and advancing processes that had bogged down. The example of the weaving of consensus in the Papua New Guinea–Bougainville peace process is a case in point.

Phased, Partial Agreements
The perfect, at times, becomes the enemy of the good. Partial agreements, imperfect in content yet approached in phases, thus becomes a possibility—modest, step-by-step efforts, recognizing the fact that solid structures are built block by block, in rigorous and painstaking ways.

Preparation, Framework of Negotiations
To accomplish the task there is a need for careful preparation for negotiations and the creation of conditions for constructive dialogue as well as a framework of talks that enables themes or issues to be identified and tackled seriously, thoroughly, and systematically. Public fanfare and dramatic breakthroughs often do not represent the hard reality that results in helpful outcomes.

Pursuit of Parallel Tracks
A last element is the exploration of parallel tracks. Stable structures stand on several pillars or multiple legs; and similarly, conflict resolution efforts are more likely to succeed when parallel tracks are pursued that complement one another to create synergy and unleash creativity.

Pursuing a Just Peace Requires a Marathon Mentality
Those engaged in the work for peace require a marathon mentality. Not unlike Sisyphus, the advocates trudge through the valley, trekking upward undaunted by repeated falls, undeterred by the obstacles posed by the towering heights. The call of the hour is for people who can commit their lives to advance the work toward a just peace even in the midst of adversity, continuing to strive toward the common task of building a durable peace for future generations.

In Southeast Asia, in the intense conflict areas of the South Asian sub-continent, in the island countries of the Pacific, there are those who labor—but not in vain—for a just peace to be enjoyed by children deserving a better future, refusing to be condemned to a recurring past. The legacies of Gandhi, Aung San Suu Kyi, Xanana Gusmão and Bishop Belo, Maha Ghoshananda in Cambodia, Senator Jose W. Diokno and Lorenzo Tanada in the Philippines, the interfaith dialogue groups in Indonesia and the cross-border relations groups forged by Koreans, the women of Bougainville and Papua New Guinea, the professionals in Fiji, and the interreligious groups in Sri Lanka and Mindanao somehow weave a common thread: peace demands a high price, and requires a focus on the long term. The task is for people to broaden the horizons and their perceptions of the possible, to help sustain the work—though the burden may be heavy and the peace all too distantly removed from our times.

Box 2.1 Addressing Substantive Issues and Pursuing Viable Outcomes

Comparing the content of relatively successful peace efforts that have resulted in some form of meaningful accord, one can identify the following broad areas that may form part of partial or comprehensive agreements:

Human Rights, Humanitarian Law
The promotion and protection of universally accepted human rights standards and the principles of international humanitarian law as found in the Geneva Conventions (Common Article 3, and their two protocols) are basic and indispensable.

Economic Reforms
The issue of poverty and inequality, the access to land and natural resources, the question of livelihood, of basic services, of health and nutrition, of shelter and clothing, of adequate healthcare and social security, have to be addressed.

Political and Constitutional Reforms
The politics of exclusion has created a generation of vulnerable people who are not or do not feel represented, heeded, or heard, who do not feel responsible for or accountable to others for their actions or their inaction. Electoral reform that allows for genuine involvement of villagers or communities may be a starting point for more important political and constitutional reforms to be put in place to respond to the diverse demands of a divided society.

Sociocultural Reforms
The reform in sociocultural norms, attitudes, and behavior, allowing for greater participation of people from the grassroots or from different ethnic or regional areas to respect differences in terms of faith or language, of ethnicity or identity, is of paramount importance.

(continues)

Box 2.1 Cont.

Security-Sector Reform

This area deals with the reform in the military, police, and intelligence services and the establishment of civilian supremacy over the military at all times, ensuring that there is oversight concerning their professional services and compliance with relevant human rights and humanitarian law standards. Viable outcomes can reasonably be expected from processes that deal with relevant issues—those that parties to the conflict and the people in whose name the combatants claim to fight find significant. Five possible outcomes can perhaps be considered.

Respect

Respect for the other is a first important outcome of a negotiated process. At the opposite end of the table, the other side acquires a name and face, allowing for listening to take place, and for the development of an understanding of the motives and/or grievances of the other party. Even so-called enemies will be seen to possess a humanity, making it possible to identify common ground and, in time, to respect the common values of those involved. Restoring the centrality of respect—a quality that is sadly missing in conflict situations and that explains their deterioration—can thus be a critical outcome.

Sustainable Development

"Development" is another name for "peace," and no peaceable situation can be sustained unless the lives of people are improved, the quality of their lives enhanced, and the environment and resources protected and preserved for future generations.

Accountable Governance

Governance that is accountable and political leadership that is responsible are viable outcomes that are both indispensable and required, so that measures taken in the context of accords forged are implemented or executed at the appropriate levels of government and society.

Reconciliation and Political Tolerance

Deep changes in attitude may be required to accompany economic or political reforms. The response of a Palestinian journalist who, when asked what he could say to Americans in the aftermath of terrorist attacks of September 11, 2001, is illustrative: "America, we feel your pain. Isn't it time you felt ours?" The sense of shared grief, of political tolerance and respect for diverse experiences, can somehow help bring about the required reconciliation, which may take time, but which must take place if peace is to be durable.

Human Security

The security that is sought at the end of the day is not merely one that is confined to national borders or guaranteed by the force of arms, but one that is comprehensive, that is commonly enjoyed, and that can be called human security—addressing the shared concerns of communities confronted by common challenges.

Ed Garcia, professor in peace studies/political science, serves as senior policy adviser at International Alert, where he participates in work on Asia, Africa, and Latin America. He taught political science and peace studies at the University of the Philippines and Ateneo de Manila University. He was a member of the Philippine Constitutional Commission, which drafted the 1987 charter. He worked with the International Secretariat of Amnesty International from 1978 to 1980, and was founding convenor of Amnesty International–Philippines in the 1980s. He has authored A Journey of Hope *(Quezon City, Philippines: Claretian, 1994) as well as the* Filipino Quest Triology *(Quezon City, Philippines: Claretian, 1988), and has coedited* Waging Peace in the Philippines: Looking Back, Moving Forward *(Quezon City, Philippines: GZO-PI, 2003).*

Note

The insights of Kevin Clements, former secretary general of International Alert, on multi-track approaches and nongovernmental organizations expressed in two of his 2000 works, *Civil Society and Conflict Prevention* and *Towards Conflict Prevention and a Just Peace* (both London: International Alert, 2000), inform the analysis presented in this chapter and are gratefully acknowledged.

3

Security Cooperation in Asia Pacific: Official and Unofficial Responses

Desmond Ball

At the beginning of the 1990s, there was almost no security coopera-
tion in the Asia Pacific region apart from the bilateral alliance rela-
tionships established during the Cold War. No regionwide mechanism
existed for discussion of security matters, and the prospects for multi-
lateralism looked very bleak.[1] The United States, and indeed most of
the countries in the region, were firmly committed to the maintenance
of the bilateral structures; multilateral endeavors were represented as
being incompatible with fundamental aspects of Asia Pacific strategic
cultures, and even viewed as damaging to the architecture of bilateral
arrangements that had arguably served the region well during the
previous decades. The Asia Pacific region was simply too large and
the diversity too great in terms of the size, strength, culture, interests,
and perception of threat among the constituent states, to support any
meaningful regionwide security architecture. It soon turned out, how-
ever, that these "realities" were not so immutable as to rule out the
establishment of an active, purposeful, and productive regional secu-
rity cooperation process.[2]

By the mid-1990s, mechanisms for regionwide security dialogue had been
firmly established. One of the important preliminary achievements was the
creation of a community of knowledgeable professionals concerned with security issues.[3] The Association of Southeast Asian Nations (ASEAN), through its
Regional Forum (ARF), which is the centerpiece of the regional security dialogue activity, began meeting in 1994. Numerous confidence- and security-
building measures (CSBMs) were soon implemented, of which many were
designed to enhance *transparency* throughout the region. Considerable progress
was made with the development and institutionalization of maritime CSBMs
and other maritime cooperative measures. Cooperation among regional defense
forces burgeoned, involving reciprocal visits of senior officers, joint exercises,
and joint training programs. Concepts and mechanisms for preventive diplomacy

began to receive serious official consideration. In the intervening years there has also been considerable interest in the institutionalization of mechanisms for the prevention of proliferation of weapons of mass destruction (WMD).

This chapter discusses the achievements and the limitations of multilateral security cooperation in the Asia Pacific region, including both its Track-One and Track-Two dimensions, especially with respect to conflict prevention and conflict resolution processes. It defines the terms "Track One" and "Track Two" and discusses the relationship between them, using the ARF and Council for Security Cooperation in Asia Pacific (CSCAP) as exemplary case studies. It briefly outlines the principal security concerns in the region, to which this multilateral diplomacy is a response. Finally, it discusses some of the opportunities and challenges facing multilateral security processes in the region.

The Dynamics of the Regional Security Environment

The burgeoning activity in the 1990s concerning security dialogue and cooperation in the region was a response to concerns that regional security policymakers and analysts had about certain aspects of the emerging regional security environment:

• *The uncertainty pervading the region.* At the end of the Cold War, regional security policymakers and analysts were very perturbed by the extreme uncertainty. The Soviet Union had collapsed and effectively withdrawn from the region. The future commitment of the United States to a strategic presence in East Asia and the Western Pacific was questioned. Plans regarding military capabilities, and the strategic intentions of the major regional powers (China, Japan, and India), were unclear. And there was a very real possibility that the widespread efforts to achieve greater defense self-reliance in response to these developments might provoke regional tensions and generate competitive arms acquisitions programs. Mechanisms for regionwide dialogue, confidence building, transparency, and cooperation were considered to be essential to the management of this uncertainty.

• *The rise of China.* The most important geostrategic concern has been the rise of China and its inevitable impact on regional and international relations. It has had the fastest-growing defense budget in Asia (averaging about 15 percent a year since 1988), with sustained growth in nuclear weapons and missile systems as well as conventional power projection capabilities. In the early 1990s, regional leaders believed it was imperative to engage China in multilateral dialogues, confidence-building arrangements, preventive diplomacy, and other forms of security cooperation.[4]

• *Territorial and sovereignty disputes.* There are numerous issues of simmering and potential conflict in Asia, involving competing sovereignty claims, challenges to government legitimacy, and territorial disputes. The great majority (more than twenty) involve interstate (rather than intrastate) disputes.[5]

• *Arms acquisition (or "defense modernization") programs.* Asia's share of world military expenditure doubled from 1986 to 1996, and its share of world expenditure on arms transfers increased nearly threefold from the mid-1980s (15 percent) to the late 1990s (41 percent). In part, this reflected a decline in defense spending in Europe and the former Soviet Union, but it was also due to unprecedented real increases in Asian defense budgets. A regionally destabilizing arms race was widely feared.[6]

• *Proliferation of weapons of mass destruction.* Since the end of the Cold War, the proliferation of WMD and long-range missile delivery systems has proceeded much more rapidly and extensively in Asia, or at least South Asia and Northeast Asia, than in any other part of the world.

• *Maritime issues.* The security environment of the Asia Pacific region is essentially maritime. Many countries are islands or archipelagos or have long coastlines. The seas and straits are among the busiest in the world. There are more than a dozen interstate disputes over islands, continental-shelf claims, Exclusive Economic Zone (EEZ) boundaries, and other offshore issues. These maritime concerns are evinced in the major weapons acquisition programs (such as naval surface combatants, submarines, antiship missiles, and maritime strike aircraft), and have been reflected in the robust maritime dimension of security cooperation in the region.

• *The new security agenda.* The concept of security has become broader and more complex, encompassing the so-called new security agenda, which involves both economic and environmental security issues as well as transnational crime (e.g., human trafficking, drug trafficking, and money laundering), and, especially since September 11, 2001, terrorism.[7]

Confronting Difficulties on the Road to Multilateralism

Multilateral security processes were severely damaged by the regional economic crisis in 1997–1998, which diverted the attention of policymakers away from security matters. The security processes suffered because of the cuts in regional defense budgets, which hit training and exercise activities—the basis of most defense cooperation—particularly hard. And multilateralism suffered because of the perceived impotency of the major regional institutions.

None of the regional multilateral institutions contributed much to the identification of solutions to the economic crisis or to any comprehension of its strategic and security implications—neither economic institutions such as the Asia Pacific Economic Cooperation, nor important political organizations such as ASEAN, nor security forums such as the ARF, nor so-called second-track organizations such as CSCAP.[8]

Moreover, from the mid-1990s onward, the multilateral security cooperation process suffered from a lack of effective leadership. Japan had been very active in pushing the case for a pan-regional official security dialogue arrangement in 1991–1992, culminating in the establishment of the ARF in 1993,[9] but burdened and distracted by persistent economic malaise, it was unable to continue providing diplomatic leadership. The collapse of the Suharto regime in Indonesia in 1998, caused in large part by the economic calamity, effectively removed Indonesia from the leadership role it had been playing within ASEAN.

The events in East Timor in 1999, including the death and destruction that the Indonesian army and its proxy militia groups inflicted following East Timor's independence referendum in September, and the subsequent peacekeeping intervention of the Australia-led International Force for East Timor (INTERFET), gravely fractured Australian-Indonesian relations. The East Timor crisis undermined both defense cooperation, which had become the closest bilateral defense cooperative arrangement in Southeast Asia and which formed the core of the December 1995 "Australia-Indonesia Agreement on Maintaining Security" (subsequently abrogated in 1999), and a diplomatic partnership that had hitherto produced important regional initiatives. And although most East Asian countries supported the INTERFET operation, there was considerable disquiet in the region about the implications for the sacrosanct principle of nonintervention in the internal affairs of other states.

But the multilateral security process was losing momentum by 1997 in any case. The extraordinary growth in cooperative activities during the previous five years could not have been sustained. Establishing mechanisms for dialogue and institutionalizing a regionwide confidence-building process were fundamentally important achievements of the first five-year period, but they were relatively easy undertakings when compared to more substantive activities such as preventive diplomacy, crisis management, conflict resolution, or arms control.

The terrorist attacks against the U.S. homeland and the subsequent "war on terrorism" have resuscitated regional security cooperation at both Track-One and Track-Two levels, and have strengthened the relationship between them. Numerous forums have been organized to discuss counterterrorism matters, and measures have been implemented at both bilateral and multilateral levels to increase intelligence exchanges and cooperation between law enforcement agencies.

Official and Unofficial Responses

The terms "Track One" and "Track Two" now have generally accepted meanings in the Asia Pacific region, honed by a decade of intensive dialogue—meanings that are not necessarily completely synonymous with usage in other regions. "Track One" is defined as official, government-led multilateral organizations and processes, such as ASEAN, the ARF, the Shanghai Five, and multilateral defense cooperation programs. "Track Two" refers to unofficial activities, involving academics, think-tank researchers, journalists, and former officials, as well as current officials participating in their private capacities.[10] A defining characteristic is the existence of some linkage to Track One, either through the participation of officials and/or institutionalized reporting arrangements, such as have been formed between CSCAP and the ARF.

The essential elements of Track Two diplomacy are seen in particular in the establishment of CSCAP, which has emerged as the premier Track Two institution in the Asia Pacific region.[11] CSCAP was set up in 1992–1993 to provide "a more structured regional process of a non-governmental nature . . . to contribute to the efforts towards regional confidence building and enhancing regional security through dialogues, consultation and cooperation."[12] Three essential themes permeated the discussions that attended its establishment. The first was that the council should be a nongovernmental institution but that it should involve government officials, albeit in their private capacities. Although it was considered essential that the institution be independent from official control in order to take full advantage of the extraordinary vitality and fecundity of nongovernmental organizations (NGOs) engaged in the Track-Two process—as well as to allow relatively free discussion of diplomatically sensitive issues that could not be brought up in official forums—it was also recognized that official involvement was necessary in order to attract government resources and to ensure that the value, relevance, and feasibility of the NGO efforts secured official appreciation. In other words, the prospects for implementation should count as much as the intrinsic worth of any ideas generated in the Track-Two process. It was considered important that the official involvement include senior military personnel as well as defense civilians and foreign affairs officers.

The second theme derived from the experience of NGOs such as the Pacific Asia Free Trade and Development Conference and the Pacific Economic Cooperation Conference in the promotion of Asia Pacific economic cooperation throughout the 1970s and 1980s. These NGOs contributed to the regional economic cooperation process in several important ways. To begin with, they developed and disseminated the ideas and stimulated the discussion that engendered the process. They conducted the technical economic studies and analyses that showed the benefits of liberalization of trade in the region, either through formal free trade arrangements or, more recently, the concept of "open regionalism." They demonstrated to government officials that meaningful and productive dialogue on complex and important policy matters is possible notwithstanding the extraordinary disparity in the sizes and interests of the numerous parties involved. By providing forums for officials to engage in "unofficial" dialogue, the NGOs contributed to greater official interaction and enhanced mutual confidence, as well as providing a sound "building block" for supporting cooperative arrangements at the governmental level itself.

The third theme in the foundation of CSCAP was the acceptance of the need to build on extant arrangements in the region wherever possible rather than construct new structures and processes. In practice, this meant building upon the arrangements and processes developed by the ASEAN Institutes of Strategic and International Studies (ISIS), and particularly ISIS Malaysia, which was the most advanced in the region in terms of both its infrastructure and its cooperative arrangements and practices.

With regard to CSCAP's relationship to Track One, while it has numerous linkages with a variety of Track-One processes, its highest priority has been to serve the ARF. As Jusuf Wanandi (the first CSCAP cochair) argued in June 1994: "The main challenge for CSCAP is whether its work will be relevant to the ARF."[13] And as the planning group of the CSCAP steering committee reported in June 1996, "CSCAP's utility . . . will largely hinge on the relationship between CSCAP and the ASEAN Regional Forum."[14] Indeed, the degree to which CSCAP has been useful to the ARF, together with the latter's recognition of its contribution, provides an important standard for measuring its success.

The terminology has also been extended to include Track-One and Track-Three processes.[15] Track-One initiatives are officially sponsored, the participants include a large proportion (typically a majority) of officials, usually in their official capacities, but nonofficials from Track-Two (and sometimes even Track-Three) entities are also included; the activities generally involve exchanges of views, and are generally exploratory rather than conclusive with regard to policy outcomes. "Track three" is defined as those other organizations and individuals, including academics and many NGOs, that are active in the security domain but that are not directly concerned with influencing official government policies.

The Record of the ARF

The ARF is the centerpiece of the institutionalization of multilateral security dialogue and confidence building in the region. It held its first meeting in July 1994, and its progress, especially since its adoption of a concept paper and appended agenda at its second meeting in Brunei in August 1995, has been quite remarkable.

The concept paper outlined "a gradual evolutionary approach to security cooperation," which is supposed to take place in three stages: promotion of confidence-building measures, development of preventive diplomacy mechanisms, and development of conflict-resolution mechanisms. The paper covers some three dozen proposals for CSBMs, preventive diplomacy, maritime cooperation, and other cooperative measures. These are divided into two lists: the first (Annex A) contains "measures which can be explored and implemented by ARF participants in the immediate future," and the second (Annex B) contains "an indicative list of other proposals which can be explored over the medium and long-term by ARF participants and also considered in the immediate future by the Track Two process."[16]

The terms "immediate future" and "medium and long-term" were not defined, but it was generally reckoned by the ARF senior officials in 1995 that measures in Annex A could be achieved within one to two years, while some of the measures in Annex B could take three to five years and others perhaps a decade or so. In terms of the progression from confidence building to preventive diplomacy and conflict resolution, dialogue and consultations about the latter were to begin immediately, with the expectation that some preventive diplomacy mechanisms would be devised and implemented within about five years, with some conflict resolution mechanisms to follow in about ten years.

According to this schedule, Annex A should have been substantially implemented by now. In fact, there has been considerable progress with most of the sixteen measures contained in it. Many of them were fairly simple, such as the organization of "seminars/workshops on peacekeeping issues," "exchanges between military academies [and] staff college," and "enhanced contacts, including high level visits and recreational activities." Some required novel activity on the part of many of the members, such as the preparation and publication of defense white papers or "equivalent documents," although some of the products have involved little real transparency. An important achievement was the Southeast Asia Nuclear Weapons Free Zone treaty, which entered into force on March 27, 1997. Some of the measures in Annex A are still some years away from implementation, however, such as the development of "a set of guidelines for the peaceful settlement of disputes," or the adoption by all ARF members of the principle of "comprehensive approaches to security."

It is fair to say that a good start has been made with some of the nineteen measures in Annex B. This is especially the case with regard to maritime CSBMs, where there has been considerable progress with the development of maritime information databases, such as the Australian-developed Strategic Maritime Information System; "a multilateral agreement on the avoidance of naval incidents," produced by the CSCAP Working Group on Maritime Cooperation as "Guidelines for Maritime Cooperation" and submitted to the ARF in early 1998; and exploration of "the idea of joint marine scientific research" and other aspects of oceans management, which are currently also being explored by the CSCAP Working Group on Maritime Cooperation. It is quite likely that other measures will be implemented over the next few years, such as the development of a "mechanism to mobilize relief assistance in the event of natural disasters," and exploration of "the possibility of establishing a [regional] peacekeeping center," as well as more maritime cooperation measures.

On the other hand, it is clear that some proposals have stagnated, such as the notion of a regional arms register. Others are unlikely to be implemented during the next decade, such as the "establishment of zones of cooperation in areas such as the South China Sea." More generally, there is unlikely to be much progress with the institutionalization of conflict resolution or arms control during the next decade, and only modest progress on preventive diplomacy is likely.

The concept paper described preventive diplomacy (Stage II of the ARF agenda) as "a natural follow-up to confidence-building measures," and Annex B contains three specific proposals: to "explore and devise ways and means to prevent conflict"; to explore the idea of appointing UN special representatives to undertake "fact-finding missions" and to "offer their good services"; and to explore the idea of establishing a center for regional risk reduction.

Progress with preventive diplomacy has been very slow. The ARF sponsored three seminars in 1995–1997 (the third of which, in Singapore in September 1997, was organized by CSCAP), but these neither reached any consensus about the conceptual basis of preventive diplomacy nor identified any concrete measures.[17] The first moves forward began with the meeting of the ARF Intersessional Group (ISG) on Confidence Building in Bangkok in March 1999, which was arranged to immediately follow a meeting on preventive diplomacy, organized by the CSCAP Working Group on CSBMs and attended by most of the ISG participants. It considered four proposals, which were deemed to lie in "the overlap between CBMs and preventive diplomacy": an enhanced role for the ARF chairman, particularly a "good offices" role; the development of a register of experts and eminent persons among ARF partici- pants; production of an *Annual Security Outlook;* and voluntary background briefings by ARF participants on regional security issues.[18]

Over the ensuing four years, progress has involved the acceptance by the ARF of a paper (drafted by Singapore) on concepts and principles of preven- tive diplomacy; the production of three *Annual Security Outlooks* (in 2000, 2001, and 2002); acceptance of an enhanced role for the ARF chairman to serve as a liaison to external parties, including the United Nations and the Organization for Security and Cooperation in Europe; and a start on compiling a register of experts and eminent persons.

With regard to Stage III of the ARF agenda (i.e., conflict resolution), the concept paper stated: "It is not envisaged that the ARF would establish mech- anisms for conflict resolution in the immediate future. The establishment of such mechanisms is *an eventual goal* that ARF participants should pursue."[19]

In the case of nonproliferation and arms control, the ARF agenda prom- ises little. Even transparency measures concerning arms acquisitions are unac- ceptable to most ARF members, let alone constraints on the acquisition and deployment of weapons systems.

Substantial progress on hard-core security issues such as current and po- tential conflicts (and hence conflict resolution) and defense acquisition pro- grams (and the prospect of an East Asian arms race, and hence the issue of arms control) is effectively ruled out within the ARF process not so much by

ROC soldiers guarding a road junction on Taiwan's frontline Kinmen Island, situated just two miles away from PRC's Xiamen City and home to around 50,000 troops.

formal agreement as by prevailing conventions. In particular, the fundamental norm of noninterference in the internal affairs of other countries proscribes efforts to address intrastate conflicts and national defense programs, while the principle of consensus removes most contentious issues from the agenda.[20] For example, China's insistence that the South China Sea and its relations with Taiwan are internal matters has prevented these flashpoints from being considered in the ARF process.

Other Track One Achievements

The ARF is very much an ASEAN (that is, Southeast Asian) creature in both substantive and procedural terms. Its mechanisms are not well suited for serious dialogue about, let alone resolution of, Northeast Asian security issues, and its purview excludes Central and South Asia. The major powers in Northeast Asia, for instance, cannot be expected to pay much attention to a body in which two-thirds of the members are extraregional and extrasubregional, at least where issues affecting their important security interests are involved. In these other subregions, dialogue arrangements have been made by the parties most directly concerned.

In Northeast Asia, there have been many attempts to institute Track-One dialogue arrangements and CSBMs with respect to the Korean Peninsula, mostly initiated by the United States, but they have proved ephemeral as mechanisms of crisis management (which has been primarily conducted on the basis of bilateral diplomacy between the United States and North Korea). The most important multilateral initiatives have been the Korean Energy Development Organization, which, although ostensibly about economic cooperation, was supposed to moderate North Korea's nuclear weapons program and promote political change on the peninsula, but which has become moribund; and the Four Party Talks, between North and South Korea, the, United States and China, which began in 1996, and which have been mainly (but unsuccessfully) concerned with designing a peace agreement for the peninsula.[21] The Trilateral Coordination and Oversight Group, involving the United States, Japan, and South Korea, was formed in 1999 and involves quarterly meetings of officials to share perspectives and coordinate policies with respect to North Korea.[22]

The most successful subregional Track-One organization has been the Shanghai Cooperation Organization (SCO), which began as the "Shanghai Five" (China, Russia, Tajikistan, Kyrgyzstan, and Kazakhstan) in 1996 and became the SCO (with the accession of Uzbekistan) on June 15, 2001. The original purpose was to provide an informal forum to discuss settlement of border disputes between China and its neighbor from the former Soviet Union, but its scope has expanded to include counterterrorism, defense cooperation, and economic cooperation.[23]

Defense Cooperation

Defense cooperation burgeoned from the late 1980s to the late 1990s, particularly among the ASEAN countries and Australia. In this region, cooperative defense activities such as reciprocal visits by senior defense officers, joint exercises, training programs, and personnel exchanges soon accounted for the great weight of cooperative activities concerning regional security. Australia was at the center of cooperative defense activities in Southeast Asia. Most of the ASEAN countries, and especially Indonesia, Singapore, and Malaysia, became more engaged with Australia with respect to cooperative defense activities than with any other country, including their own ASEAN neighbors.[24]

The rationale for such reciprocal visits by senior officers has been that they provide a mechanism for increasing "openness" and closer personal relationships, and enhancing mutual understanding and trust. Training programs provide a very useful means of imparting much-appreciated staff and technical skills, sharing operational concepts and doctrines, creating networks of personal friendships and professional contacts, reducing the likelihood of misunderstandings and misinterpretations, and building trust. Joint military exercises can be extremely productive in terms of building closer defense relations.

However, in part because of the impact of the Asian economic disaster in 1997–1998 on most regional defense budgets, and in part because of the collapse of Australian-Indonesian defense cooperation that followed the Australian-led intervention in East Timor in 1999, defense cooperation floundered in the late 1990s. After the terrorist attacks on the United States on September 11, 2001, and the subsequent "war on terrorism," defense cooperation was pursued with new energy. Defense agencies have been involved in a range of new initiatives to enhance cooperation to combat terrorism, including more extensive intelligence exchanges and joint counterterrorist training programs. As Admiral Dennis C. Blair, commander in chief of the U.S. Pacific Command, said in Jakarta on November 27, 2001, "The exchange of intelligence among countries in the region is unprecedented."[25] In February 2002, Australia and Indonesia agreed to increase intelligence cooperation and exchanges between Australian agencies and Indonesia's National Intelligence Agency, following the rupture of the intelligence relationship in 1999.[26] Australia has resumed some defense cooperation with the Indonesian armed forces and, in the wake of the Bali bombing on October 12, 2002, is considering resumption of cooperation with the notorious Kopassus special forces with respect to counterterrorism.[27] In March 2003, Australia and the Philippines signed an agreement to expand exchanges of information and intelligence about terrorist activities, to enhance cooperation on defense science and technology, and to increase joint training exercises, with a special emphasis on counterterrorism.[28] Malaysia is setting up a counterterrorism center that will be open to all ten ASEAN countries, and which will provide counterterrorism training and a locus for the transfer of relevant technology and expertise as well as the exchange of information about developments relating to terrorism.[29]

The most significant recent initiative with respect to multilateral defense cooperation was the meeting of defense ministers and senior defense officials in Singapore in June 2002. Referred to as the Shangri-la meeting, it was convened by a Track-Two organization (the International Institute for Strategic Studies, based in London), and functions in a Track-One mode, but it could well generate a defense cooperation process more active and more innovative than the ARF process. The June 2002 meeting, for example, produced an ambitious proposal for regional cooperation with respect to recovery from terrorist attacks.[30] Defense ministers and their senior officials will use the Shangri-la meetings to discuss not only counterterrorism but the whole gamut of current security concerns. A second meeting was held in June 2003.

CSCAP's Achievements

CSCAP's progress since its establishment a decade ago has been remarkable, at least as measured in terms of its own institutionalization. The number of member committees has doubled from the original ten in 1993 to twenty in 2000 (including a European committee, which became a full member in December 1998). The individual memberships of CSCAP's committees have also grown substantially—from a total of 452 members (in thirteen countries) in 1995, when the first *CSCAP Directory* was compiled, to some 750 in 2000. They include most of the leading international scholars of Asia Pacific security affairs, and current and former diplomats, defense officials, and military personnel with great practical experience. The primary mechanism for CSCAP activity consists in its five working groups—on CSBMs; concepts of cooperative and comprehensive security; maritime cooperation; the North Pacific; and transnational crime. Some of these have been extremely productive and of direct assistance to the ARF (such as the Working Group on CSBMs with respect to the ARF's work on preventive diplomacy). The working groups have held about fifty meetings and have produced about twenty volumes of edited papers and eight "CSCAP Memoranda," some of which have been quite influential.[31]

CSCAP is linked to Track-One processes at steering committee, working group, and member/national committee levels. The relationship with the ARF has been considerably strengthened over the past few years. There are now fairly regular communications between the CSCAP cochairs and the ARF senior officials. Working arrangements have been developed to directly support the ISGs, as initiated by the Working Group on CSBMs with the ISG on Confidence Building at the meeting on preventive diplomacy in Bangkok in March 1999, and as more recently evinced in the workshop "Countering the New Terrorism: Options and Strategies for Policymakers," which the working group organized in Vientiane in March 2003 for the ARF's new ISG on Counterterrorism. In May 2002 the CSCAP cochairs produced a report titled *The ARF Into the Twenty-First Century,* to "contribute to the further evolution of the ARF by presenting a set of policy recommendations . . . to energize the ARF."[32] It proposed six "menus" for consideration by the ARF: augmenting the ARF's achievements with regard to CSBMs; the further development of preventive diplomacy practices; further institutionalization of the ARF (e.g., the establishment of an ARF Secretariat); enhancing defense participation; strengthening the ARF's ability to address transnational security issues, such as organized transnational crime, unrestricted population movements, trafficking in women, cybercrimes, and terrorism; and strengthening the linkages between Tracks One and Two. The ARF has been receptive to these proposals. In addition, the CSCAP steering committee has established new arrangements for coordinating policy-related work on cooperative approaches to counterterrorism, and for ensuring its relevance to the ARF.

Prospects and Recommendations

Multilateral security cooperation is now an important part of the security architecture in the Asia Pacific region. Although its prospects initially looked bleak, it has now become institutionalized, at both Track One and Track Two levels, and provides a substantial countervailing force to the exercise of crude power politics in the region. There is great scope for further progress, as exemplified in the "menus" submitted by the CSCAP cochairs to the ARF in May 2002.[33] These include both institutional measures (such as further strengthening of the linkages between tracks one and two) and new policy initiatives (especially in the areas of preventive diplomacy and counterterrorism). However, the ability of multilateral institutions to affect the major regional security dynamics and to address the hard-core security issues (requiring, for example, conflict resolution and arms control arrangements) remains severely circumscribed by the "gospel" of noninterference.

September 11 and the "war on terrorism" have provided opportunities for collective action to refashion the security architecture in the Asia Pacific region—for further coalition building at the strategic level, for exploiting the ground swell of abhorrence regarding international terrorism at the public level, and for promoting regional security cooperation more generally.

The war on terrorism has invigorated the regional security cooperation process; it has also provided a new institutional dimension, drawing law enforcement agencies into the cooperative discourse. In early 2002, Indonesia and Australia began discussions to improve their extradition processes, as well as to examine other forms of legal cooperation.[34] In May 2002, Malaysia, the Philippines, and Indonesia signed a wide-ranging agreement to increase the sharing of information between their law enforcement agencies to "boost the fight against terrorism and cross-border crime" (including money-laundering, drug trafficking, hijacking, trafficking of women and children, and piracy).[35]

It is critically important that these opportunities be exploited to the fullest—to address not only the security issues generated by terrorism itself but also the erstwhile and more fundamental dynamics (such as the geostrategic developments in Northeast Asia, the proliferation of WMD, and the emergence of a regional arms race). These remain profoundly disturbing challenges—but the war on terrorism has distracted attention from as well as exacerbated (rather than alleviated) them.

Track-one processes in the Asia Pacific region are not yet ready to seriously consider the complex, consequential, and potentially intrusive issues of arms control (including nonproliferation of WMD) and conflict resolution. On the other hand, Track-Two organizations should not feel constrained about addressing conflict resolution issues, and their engagement should extend to consideration of possible institutional mechanisms for conflict resolution.

An essential precursory project would involve a study of the most likely characteristics of possible conflicts in the Asia Pacific region—in terms of their scale, intensity, naval and air dimensions, level of technology, and sorts of casualties. The spectrum of the conflict issues in East Asia is much more extensive and the character of possible conflict much more variegated than in any other region. Most of the interstate disputes are about maritime boundaries and offshore territorial claims, such as the competing claims to the Paracel and Spratly islands in the South China Sea. Many others are about land borders, mostly involving disputes over borders established during the European colonial period, but some having much deeper roots. Analysis of these conflict issues, including the types of forces likely to be employed, should inform thinking about conflict resolution.

Finally, Track-One and Track-Two processes should more actively promote "human security" in the region. Since the end of the Cold War, there has been not only a broadening of the concept of security to encompass the "new agenda" issues such as economic and environmental security, but also a more fundamental questioning of objectives of security and whom it should benefit, with a reassertion, in particular, of primacy of the individual as compared to the state (wherever these are inconsonant). The notion of "human security" focuses on the individual as the referent.[36]

Despite the progress described in this chapter toward improved security cooperation, gross violations of human rights, state-sponsored killings, torture, extreme cruelty, injustice, exploitation of fellow human beings (including women and children), and grinding poverty persist in many countries in East Asia, and there is little hope for the future. Neither Track-One nor Track-Two organizations can truly claim to be promoting real security in the region unless and until the human dimension becomes a central feature of their activities. These tracks will have to forge closer relations with Track-Three entities (such as human rights and voluntary aid organizations), which are stronger in this field.

Desmond Ball is a professor in the Strategic and Defense Studies Center, Australian National University, Canberra, which he headed from 1982 to 1991. He is the author or editor of more than forty books on nuclear strategy, Australian defense policy, intelligence matters, and security issues in the Asia Pacific region, including regional weapons acquisition programs, security cultures, and regional security cooperation. He served as cochair of the Council for Security Cooperation in Asia Pacific from 2000 until 2002.

Notes

1. See Desmond Ball, introduction to Desmond Ball, ed., *The Transformation of Security in the Asia/Pacific Region* (London: Frank Cass, 1996), pp. 1–14.

2. Desmond Ball, "A New Era in Confidence Building: The Second Track Process in the Asia-Pacific Region," *Security Dialogue* 25, no. 2 (June 1994): 157–176.

3. Miles Kahler, "Institution-Building in the Pacific," in Andrew Mack and John Ravenhill, eds., *Pacific Cooperation: Building Economic and Security Regimes in the Asia-Pacific Region* (Sydney: Allen and Unwin, 1994), pp. 31–32. See also Sheldon W. Simon, "Evaluating Track II Approaches to Security Diplomacy in the Asia-Pacific: The CSCAP Experience," *Pacific Review* 15, no. 2 (2002): 170–175.

4. Amitav Acharya, "ASEAN and the Conditional Engagement of China," in James Shinn, ed., *Weaving the Net: Conditional Engagement of China* (New York: Council on Foreign Relations Press, 1996), chap. 10.

5. Desmond Ball, "Arms and Affluence: Military Acquisitions in the Asia-Pacific Region," *International Security* 18, no. 3 (Winter 1993–1994): 87–90.

6. Ibid.

7. Alan Dupont, *East Asia Imperiled: Transnational Challenges to Security* (Cambridge: Cambridge University Press, 2001); and Alan Dupont, "Preventive Diplomacy and Transnational Security Issues," in Desmond Ball and Amitav Acharya, eds., *The Next Stage: Preventive Diplomacy and Security Cooperation in the Asia-Pacific Region,* Canberra Papers on Strategy and Defence no. 131 (Canberra: Strategic and Defence Studies Centre, Australian National University, 1999), chap. 7.

8. See Desmond Ball, "Implications of the East Asian Economic Recession for Regional Security Cooperation," Working Paper no. 331 (Canberra: Strategic and Defence Studies Centre, Australian National University, January 1999).

9. See Desmond Ball, *Building Blocks for Regional Security: An Australian Perspective on Confidence and Security Building Measures (CSBMs) in the Asia/Pacific Region,* Canberra Papers on Strategy and Defence no. 83 (Canberra: Strategic and Defence Studies Centre, Australian National University, 1991), pp. 53–54.

10. See the entry for "Track Two" in David Capie and Paul Evans, *The Asia-Pacific Security Lexicon* (Singapore: Institute of Southeast Asian Studies, 2002), pp. 213–216; and Brian L. Job, "Track Two Diplomacy: Ideational Contribution to the Evolving Asia Security Order," in Muthiah Alagappa, *Asian Security Order: Instrumental and Normative Features* (Stanford: Stanford University Press, 2003), chap. 7.

11. For a more comprehensive discussion of CSCAP, see Desmond Ball, *The Council for Security Cooperation in the Asia Pacific (CSCAP): Its Record and its Prospects,* Canberra Papers on Strategy and Defence no. 139 (Canberra: Strategic and Defence Studies Centre, Australian National University, October 2000); Sheldon Simon, "Evaluating Track Two Approaches to Security Diplomacy in the Asia Pacific: The CSCAP Experience," National Bureau of Asian Research Special Report, September 2001; and Sheldon W. Simon, "Evaluating Track Two Approaches to Security Diplomacy in the Asia-Pacific: The CSCAP Experience," *Pacific Review* 15, no. 2 (2002): 167–200. See also the CSCAP website, www.cscap.org.

12. The quote is from the website of the Council for Security Cooperation in Asia Pacific (see www.cscap.org).

13. Jufus Wanandi, "The Future of the ARF and CSCAP in the Regional Security Architecture," in Bunn Nagara and Cheah Siew Ean, eds., *Managing Security and Peace in the Asia-Pacific* (Kuala Lumpur: ISIS Malaysia, 1996), p. 288.

14. Cited in Ball, *The Council for Security Cooperation in the Asia Pacific,* p. 47.

15. See the entries for "Track One-and-a-Half" and "Track Three" in Capie and Evans, *Asia-Pacific Security Lexicon,* pp. 211–212, 217–219.

16. ASEAN Senior Officials, "The ASEAN Regional Forum: A Concept Paper," in Desmond Ball and Pauline Kerr, *Presumptive Engagement: Australia's Asia-Pacific Security Policy in the 1990s* (Sydney: Allen and Unwin, 1996), app. 2, pp. 111–119.

17. Desmond Ball, "Introduction: Towards Better Understanding of Preventive Diplomacy," in Ball and Acharya, *Next Stage,* pp. 2–4.

18. Cochair's summary report of the meetings of the ARF Intersessional Support Group on Confidence-Building Measures held in Honolulu, Hawaii, November 4–6, 1998, and in Bangkok, Thailand, March 3–5, 1999, p. 15.

19. ASEAN Senior Officials, "ASEAN Regional Forum," p. 114 (itals. added).

20. Desmond Ball, "Strategic Culture in the Asia-Pacific Region," *Security Studies* 3, no. 1 (Autumn 1993): 51–54, 59–60.

21. Peter Brookes, "The Four Party Talks: A Perspective," *PacNet Newsletter,* March 20, 1998, available at www.ciaonet.org/pbei/csis/pac98/brp04.html; Hanns W. Maull, "The Role of Multilateralism: Germany's Two + Four Process and Its Relevance to the Korean Peninsula," June 2001, available at www.fes.or.kr/k_unification/u-paper1.htm; and David G. Brown, "Reconsidering Four Party Talks in Korea," *PacNet Newsletter,* January 11, 2002, available at www.csis.org/pacfor/pac0202.htm.

22. See, for example, "Joint Press Statement by the United States, Japan, and the Republic of Korea Trilateral Coordination and Oversight Group (TCOG) Meeting in San Francisco, November 27, 2001," U.S. Department of State, Press Statement, November 27, 2001, available at www.state.gov/r/pa/prs/2001/6401.htm; "Joint Press Statement of Trilateral Coordination and Oversight Group (TCOG), Tokyo, April 9, 2002," U.S. Embassy, Tokyo, April 9, 2002, available at http://tokyo.usembassy.gov/wwwhpr0051.html; and "TCOG: Joint Press Statement," June 16, 2003, available at www.globalsecurity.org/wmd/library/news/rok/2003/rok-030616-korea-net02.htm.

23. Zhang Jiang, "The Shanghai Cooperation Organization and Its Future," *Australia and Security Cooperation in the Asia Pacific,* AUS-CSCAP Newsletter no. 14 (November 2002): 12–15.

24. See Ball and Kerr, *Presumptive Engagement,* pp. 58–72.

25. "Adm. Blair Says Intelligence Sharing Helps Fight Terrorism," U.S. Department of State, International Information Programs, November 27, 2001, available at http://usinfo.state.gov/topical/pol/terror/01112812.htm.

26. Hamish McDonald, "Australia's Bloody East Timor Secret: Spy Intercepts Confirm Government Knew of Jakarta's Hand in Massacres," *Sydney Morning Herald,* March 14, 2002, available at www.smh.com.au/news/0203/14/text/national991.html.

27. "We Must Deal With Kopassus: Hill," *News.Com.Au,* March 31, 2003, available at www.news.com.au/common/story_page/0,4057,5459472^421,00.html. See also Allan Behm, "Cooperation with Kopassus? Take Care!" *Agenda* 10, no. 1 (2003): 13–18; and Alan Dupont, "The Kopassus Dilemma: Should Australia Re-Engage?" *Agenda* 10. no. 1 (2003): 19–26.

28. Raymund Quilop, "Australia and Philippines to Forge New Military Links," *Jane's Defence Weekly,* March 12, 2003, p. 22.

29. "KL to Go Ahead with Anti-Terrorism Centre," *Straits Times Interactive,* April 3, 2003, available at http://straitstimes.asia1.com.sg.

30. Ross Babbage, *Recovering from Terror Attacks: A Proposal for Regional Cooperation,* ASPI Occasional Paper no. 1 (Canberra: Australian Strategic Policy Institute, July 2002).

31. Ball, *Council for Security Cooperation in the Asia Pacific,* chap. 2; Sheldon Simon, "Evaluating Track Two Approaches to Security Diplomacy in the Asia Pacific: The CSCAP Experience," National Bureau of Asian Research, Special Report, September 2001; Simon, "Evaluating Track Two Approaches to Security Diplomacy in the Asia-Pacific: The CSCAP Experience," *Pacific Review;* Sheldon W. Simon, "The ASEAN Regional Forum Views the Council for Security Cooperation in the Asia Pacific: How Track Two Assists Track One," National Bureau of Asian Research, *NBR Analysis* 13, no. 4 (July 2002), available at www.nbr.org/publications/analysis/vol13no4/arf%20views%cscap.html; and the CSCAP website, www.cscap.org.

32. Desmond Ball and Barry Desker, CSCAP cochairs, *The ARF Into the Twenty-First Century,* Kuala Lumpur, May 29, 2002.

33. Ibid.

34. "Bid to Review Australia-Indonesia Treaty," *Canberra Times,* April 11, 2002, p. 8.

35. Reme Ahmad, "Three-Way Pact to Tackle Terrorism," *Straits Times,* May 8, 2002, available at www.straitstimes.asial.com.sg/primenews/story/0,1870,118419,00. html?.

36. See, for example, Ken Booth, "Security and Emancipation," *Review of International Studies* 17, no. 4 (October 1991): 313–326; David Long, "The Harvard School of Liberal International Theory: A Case for Closure," *Millennium: Journal of International Studies* 24, no. 3 (1995): 489–505; Ramesh Thakur, "From National to Human Security," in Stuart Harris and Andrew Mack, eds., *Asia-Pacific Security: The Economics-Politics Nexus* (Sydney: Allen and Unwin, 1997), pp. 53–54; entry for "Human Security" in Capie and Evans, *Asia-Pacific Security Lexicon,* pp. 139–146; International Commission on Intervention and State Sovereignty, *The Responsibility to Protect* (Ottawa: International Development Research Centre, 2001); Pranee Thiparat, ed., *The Quest for Human Security: The Next Phase of ASEAN?* (Bangkok: Institute of Security and International Studies, Chulalongkhorn University, 2001); and David Dickens, ed., *The Human Face of Security: Asia-Pacific Perspectives,* Canberra Papers on Strategy and Defence no. 144 (Canberra: Strategic and Defence Studies Centre, Australian National University, 2002).

4

East Asia and the "War on Terror": Why Human Rights Matter

David Wright-Neville

Wars usually become nightmares that last far longer than expected, and their ultimate consequences can rarely be predicted.
—*Gabriel Kolko*[1]

Since the attacks of September 11, 2001, the United States has been engaged in a worldwide "war on terror." The United States has argued that success in this war to defeat terrorism is so important that it justifies extraordinary measures, even including the suspension of civil liberties. Other nations fighting global terrorism—or purporting to fight terrorism—including many in East Asia, have also compromised on the protection of civil liberties and human rights and democratic principles. In some cases, the "terror" argument has been used as a smokescreen to justify actions against political opponents and to strengthen the positions of privileged elites. But tolerance for violations of human rights and undemocratic practices poses a variety of threats: Where civil society is still fragile, there is the serious risk that trends toward democracy will be reversed and that civil society will be eroded; where autocratic regimes have grudgingly relaxed their grip on power, the war on terror offers an excuse to clamp down on dissent and opposition; and where disaffected ethnic and religious minorities come to feel even more marginalized, the possibility exists that such policies will further alienate significant segments of the population and even contribute to increased risks of terrorism in the future.

Although it has yet to run its course, the U.S.-led "war on terror" will surely mark a pivotal moment in global politics—one that could dramatically redraw the international political landscape. Two years after the tragic events of September 11, 2001, the world had already seen two significant wars, in Afghanistan and Iraq, while a new set of dynamics had altered the course of smaller civil conflicts in places like Sri Lanka, and with similar effects possible in conflict-prone places such as Chechnya and the Southern Philippines.

Yet there are many aspects of this inappropriately named war on terror that have attracted much less attention. Notable in this regard has been the apparent resignation with which many have accepted as a necessary evil the assault on political and civil liberties launched under the pretext of making society "safe" from the terrorists who might lurk among us. While initiatives like the U.S. Patriot Act[2] and the powers of detention and interrogation[3]— especially after the revelations of torture and humiliating treatment of Iraqi prisoners by U.S. military—have generated a lot of disquiet in the world, the level of anxiety about the abuse of human rights in many parts of Asia has been much less evident. Minor exceptions to this phenomenon are Indonesia and the Philippines, where nascent civil society movements have enjoyed enough political space to mount successful rearguard actions against proposals that might jeopardize recent democratic gains. On the whole, however, fear of terrorism throughout East Asia has provided a pretext for a series of counter-terrorism measures that have increased state policing and surveillance powers at the expense of civil liberties and human rights.

It is stating the obvious to point out that both political rights and the ideal of civil society remain highly contestable and inherently fragile concepts in many parts of East Asia. Recalcitrant authoritarian regimes in Burma, China, Laos, and Vietnam sit cheek by jowl with recently democratized societies such as Indonesia and nations with slightly more democratic experience such as the Philippines and Thailand. On the other hand, there are those states whose outward democratic appearance is belied by strong authoritarian instincts, states such as Brunei, Malaysia, and Singapore, where restrictions on franchise and the systematic harassment of opposition voices effectively negate the outward appearance of participatory democracy. Yet it is this diversity of political organization, coupled with both ongoing political and strategic tensions and cultural and religious pluralism, that renders East Asia "an important window for assessing the implications of September 11 for world order."[4]

This chapter focuses on one particular aspect of the war on terror in East Asia, namely its consequences for political and civil rights and the relationship between the state and civil society. It aims to tease out more fully the complex interplay of social and political dynamics unleashed by the war on terror in the region and to argue that the promotion of human and civil rights and the further nurturing of civil society must be a key component to any counterterrorism strategy. Or to put it slightly differently, the curtailment of civil and political rights and the assaults on civil society launched under the pretense of protecting society from terrorist attack risk increasing the alienation and anger upon which terrorism feeds. However, as a first step it is worth briefly examining how individual East Asian states have responded to the events of September 11.

East Asia in the War on Terror

From China to Indonesia and Nepal to the Philippines, most East Asian governments moved quickly to address the possibility that attacks similar to September 11 might be perpetrated on or launched from their own territory. In the majority of cases these responses have reflected a belief that effective counterterrorism requires some restrictions on existing civil and political rights. Clearly, this trend is not peculiar to East Asia and is similarly evident in many other parts of the world, including in the West itself. What makes East Asia somewhat unique, however, is that the reactive urge to limit rights in the name of national security has occurred at a time when these rights are only tenuously grounded and have only been established as result of a long and often difficult transition from authoritarian rule. In many cases this transition is yet to play itself out fully, and we are still a long way from saying with any confidence that civil and political rights are permanent features of the East Asian social landscape. Indeed, there is a risk across East Asia that fears generated by terrorism will bring about a reversal of the democratic trend and interrupt the development of a more vibrant civil society. Of course this dynamic is unevenly spread throughout the region, with some states, such as Indonesia and the Philippines, showing much greater resistance to the dubious claim that combating terrorism requires a curtailment of rights and limits on civil society.[5] Other states, such as China and Malaysia, have responded to the fears generated by the attacks of September 11 to justify the intensified suppression of opposition voices and the imposition of further restrictions on civil society. Despite this variation in responses, East Asia as a whole shares with many other parts of the world a sense of panic and bewilderment about how to respond to the threat of terrorism.

Also like other parts of the world, East Asia has its fair share of political groups eager to use the terrorist bogey to justify a return to the repressive practices of the past, especially in the treatment of ethnic and religious minorities. Even in the cases of Indonesia and the Philippines, the new international obsession with terrorism has been used by their respective militaries to justify fresh military operations, accompanied sometimes by more frequent and serious violations of human rights, in places like Aceh and West Papua in the case of Indonesia,[6] and across the Philippine archipelago in the context of ongoing battles between government forces and communist and Muslim insurgents.[7] Hence, with few exceptions, counterterrorism across East Asia has become a justification for an assault on civil liberties, giving fresh life to those elites who for the past decade have struggled to hold back the rising tide of civil society groups.

From a civil society perspective, the impact on different political and cultural groups resulting from the enhanced authority granted to agents of the East Asian state to monitor, harass, arrest, and in some cases kill is especially worrying. Across the region, counterterrorist operations have been directed mainly against cultural and religious organizations and individuals whose activities are at odds with the prevailing political and cultural status quo. This has been especially evident with respect to Islamic groups, but by no means have they been the only targets. It isn't possible here to provide an extensive list of those groups targeted for special attention. But several specific examples can be used to highlight the point.

In the Philippines, the administration of President Macapagal-Arroyo has been emboldened by U.S. support under the aegis of the war on terror to change the ground rules for peace talks with Marxist insurgents. Especially worrying has been Manila's threat to lobby the United States to designate leftist militants as terrorists and to invite U.S. assistance in quashing the rebellion unless the militants submit to "peace talks" conducted almost exclusively on terms set by the state.[8] The use of the U.S. State Department's designated list of foreign terrorists as a bargaining chip in negotiations between the Philippine government and rebels risks for the sake of political expediency the goodwill and trust needed for future peace talks to reach a successful conclusion. It also threatens to further radicalize sections of the leftist insurgency and harden their opposition to a negotiated peace.

Further south, peace talks between the government and the Moro Islamic Liberation Front (MILF) have stalled as the Macapagal-Arroyo administration's "get tough" approach has elicited similar belligerence from MILF leaders and resulted in fresh outbreaks of violence.[9]

Meanwhile, in China, the government has used post–September 11 atmospherics as an excuse to step up its harassment of dissident labor organizations, Tibetan separatists,[10] the Falun Gong sect (now referred to in official Chinese statements as "a quasi-terrorist sect"),[11] and many other organizations and individuals whose only crime is peaceful opposition to the prevailing political status quo. The focus on the threat of terrorism in the region has also distracted attention from ongoing human rights abuses in other countries such as Myanmar, where the army continues to use rape and torture as instruments in its campaign against Shan and Karen "terrorists," and among other places, in Nepal, where Maoist rebels and government forces are both guilty of gross brutality against ordinary citizens.

However, it is Muslim individuals and groups that have borne the brunt of East Asia's counterterrorism campaign. In China, Uighur separatists in the Xinjiang Uighur Autonomous Region have been targeted for particularly harsh treatment.[12] In Malaysia, the administration of former prime minister Mahathir Mohamad jailed more than seventy alleged Islamist "terrorists" under the Internal Security Act, even though evidence against a considerable number of them was scanty and many of the arrests were motivated by a deliberate strategy to demonize the opposition rather than because of genuine concerns about the terrorist potential of these individuals. Kuala Lumpur has also moved to limit the ability of Muslims to educate their children in religious schools (despite there being no evidence that any Malaysian Islamic schools have links to terrorist organizations) by starving these institutions of state funds. Kuala Lumpur has also mooted a possible strengthening of the already draconian Internal Security Act, which allows for indefinite detention without trial. State

Jakarta, December 2002. Habib Rizieq, leader of the Front Pembela Islam
(FPI, Islamic Defenders Front). The FPI was funded, some say created,
by the police in 1997 and was used by the Jakarta police to crack down on
prodemocracy demonstrators. A few weeks after the Bali terrorist bombing in October 2002 the militant branch of FPI was dissolved. "We need to cleanse the organization from infiltrators," said Rizieq, who is a big fan of Osama bin Laden.

governments controlled by the ruling United Malays National Organization
(UMNO) are also doing their bit, with the government of the state of Kedah
foreshadowing the introduction of video and audio recording devices in
mosques so that police and intelligence agents can more readily identify opposition activists.[13]

Washington's New Democratic Push

An intriguing paradox underlies this authoritarian dynamic unleashed by the
new fear of terrorism. The paradox lies in the apparent tension between, on the
one hand, the assault on civil society launched under the rubric of countering
terrorism and, on the other hand, Washington's post–September 11 rhetorical
commitment to enhancing democracy across the globe, in the Muslim world in
particular.

Although it is true that Washington's immediate reaction to the September
11 attacks was a reflexive military response, by late 2003, with U.S.-led military operations in Afghanistan and Iraq failing to stem the tide of anti-U.S.
sentiment, the George W. Bush administration had begun to advocate greater
political freedom and the nurturing of civil society as a component of its wider
counterterrorist agenda. For instance, in an address in late 2003 to the U.S.
National Endowment for Democracy, President Bush observed:

> Our commitment to democracy is . . . tested in the Middle East, which is my focus today, and must be a focus of American policy for decades to come. In many nations of the Middle East—countries of great strategic importance— democracy has not yet taken root. And the questions arise: Are the peoples of the Middle East somehow beyond the reach of liberty? Are millions of men and women and children condemned by history or culture to live in despotism? Are they alone never to know freedom, and never even to have a choice in the matter? I, for one, do not believe it. I believe every person has the ability and the right to be free.[14]

For anybody interested in furthering human dignity and freedom, the president's observations and his corresponding commitment to a new policy, a "forward strategy for freedom," mark an interesting and outwardly positive development. On the surface this newfound focus on democracy offers hope that Washington might adopt a less obstructionist position when it comes to international scrutiny of the actions of habitual human rights offenders not only across the Middle East (including Israel), but also in other parts of the developing world.

The Bush initiative reflects the belief that criminal violence and terrorism are more likely to thrive under conditions of cultural, political, and social deprivation—a position supported by a large amount of contemporary research.[15] The nexus between terrorism and civil society is also suggested by data included in the U.S. Department of State's *Patterns of Global Terrorism Report* issued in 2004. The report shows that the vast majority of terrorist attacks occurred in states and regions with questionable records on rights and political accountability and/or where restricted notions of citizenship impede the development of civil society.[16]

This view is also supported by more scholarly studies. For example, in a recent study of extremist groups in Egypt, Jeffrey Nedoroscik highlights how sustained repression from the secular state, especially under Gamal Abdul Nasser, played a key role in dividing the Islamic movement into two distinct strands: a moderate mainstream fundamentalism and, on the other hand, a radical fundamentalism committed to violence as the only form of political agency likely to secure an Islamic future.[17] The observation is shared by John Esposito, who notes how suppression by the Nasser regime radicalized elements of the Muslim Brotherhood and led individuals such as Sayyid Qutb to transform the ideology of modernist Islamists like Al-Banna and Mawdudi into a rejectionist call to arms.[18]

While activist and militant Islamic groups have been a part of the political landscape in East Asia for many years, only recently is there evidence that accumulated political frustration brought about by repressive political elites has led some of these groups to follow a similar path. In other words, President Bush's comments suggest that Washington might have begun to accept that terrorism is more than the outcome of a handful of power-crazed maniacs bent on destroying the *American way of life*. Rather, terrorism is a phenomenon incubated under conditions of oppression and deprivation. Seen in this way, the fostering of democratic principles, the nurturing of key civil and political rights, and the promotion of civil society must constitute key elements of any successful long-term policy designed to minimize the risk posed by terrorist violence.

But are there really grounds for optimism? It is worth noting that President George W. Bush grounded his commitment to the promotion of freedom in the tradition of a predecessor, Ronald Reagan. While Reagan's democratic credentials are celebrated by U.S. neoconservatives, his record attracts much more criticism among a wider and more critical U.S. constituency. One suspects that a similar level of skepticism will characterize the responses of the many thousands of victims of U.S. military action launched by the Reagan administration in Grenada and Panama as well as in places like El Salvador and Nicaragua, where U.S.-backed right-wing paramilitaries were responsible for a litany of human rights abuses.[19] Moreover, to the extent that the promotion of democracy has become a leitmotif of U.S. neoconservatives, it has also assumed an almost missionary character. In the hands of the U.S. right, democratization and Americanization are mutually dependent concepts, a point underscored by the inevitable correlation in presidential speeches between democracy and free enterprise. The significance of these parallel themes in Washington's foreign policy after September 11 underscores an observation by Vibeke Schou Pedersen that adversity has again been used "as a resource for renewing the [U.S.] national sense of purpose."[20] While it remains to be seen whether the Bush administration's record on human rights and democracy will prove better than that of its predecessors, the early signs are not good. Not only does the current U.S. administration thumb its nose at the United Nations on issues where it perceives international opinion to be against its own national interests, but in its treatment of alleged terrorists detained at Guantanamo Bay, Washington continues to disregard international criticism that it is in breach of international human rights conventions. Nor is there any convincing evidence that the United States will carry through its rhetorical commitment to democracy in places like Saudi Arabia and Egypt if so doing were to mean the election of Islamist governments in this resource-rich and strategically vital part of the world.

The United States, Democracy, and Human Rights in East Asia

From the perspective of this volume, a more intriguing aspect of Washington's post–September 11 focus on democracy and human rights has been the relative anonymity afforded East Asia. Although in his speech to the U.S. National Endowment for Democracy the president mentioned countries such as Burma, China, and North Korea, there is little evidence that the Bush administration is prepared to exert anything more than a modicum of diplomatic pressure on the respective regimes in these countries.

There are a variety of reasons for this cautious approach. Clearly China is simply too big to be pushed around by the United States on human rights issues. Instead, the president referred to democratization in China as something that would occur naturally as a result of capitalist development, and as such it would eventually bring about an end to the one-party state. At a slightly different level, the post–September 11 U.S. military presence in Central Asia and Washington's fragile counterterrorism partnership with Pakistan means that Washington feels a need to avoid irritating Beijing. Accordingly, it has expressed sympathy with the Chinese government over the latter's struggle with the Turkic insurgency in the Western province of Xinjiang, going so far as to list the East Turkestan Islamic Movement (ETIM) as a proscribed terrorist organization despite the absence of any reliable evidence that the group is linked, as Beijing claims, to Al-Qaida.[21]

Meanwhile, North Korea also has shown unique resiliency in confronting U.S. pressure. There are few signs that the apparent indifference of the regime in Pyongyang to the suffering of its people will translate into a popular uprising against the government. Denied a grassroots movement that it might use to lever the current leadership from power, the United States has little option but to deal through conventional diplomatic means—meaning without any tangible access to ordinary citizens—with a North Korean leadership that is erratic and armed with nuclear weapons. Moreover, Washington clearly feels a need to treat Pyongyang with caution, worried that pushing too hard on either nonproliferation or human rights issues might prompt the North Korean leadership to retaliate by sharing its knowledge of technologies for producing weapons of mass destruction with U.S. enemies, including various terrorist networks.[22]

Washington has also evinced little determination to confront seriously the junta in Rangoon over its ongoing disregard for human rights and its determination to resist moves toward a more democratic and accountable form of government. While it is true that Washington has adopted a harder line with Rangoon than have its traditional Western allies in the region, notably Australia, its behavior suggests that it is unwilling to risk the opprobrium of Burma's partners in the Association of Southeast Asian Nations (ASEAN), most of whom see defending Burma from outside criticism as a litmus test for regional states to stand together on sensitive issues of domestic political sovereignty. While ASEAN gently chastised Rangoon for the mid-2003 arrest of Aung San Suu Kyi, for some ASEAN members, notably Vietnam, Malaysia, and Singapore, defending Burma sets a useful precedent for any future criticisms of their own less-than-free political environments.[23] What makes this tentative approach to human rights in Burma all the more unusual is an emerging body of evidence that links members of Burma's displaced Muslim community, the Rohinga, to extremist organizations in Bangladesh, groups that through their links to like-minded groups in Pakistan are connected to Washington's current nemesis, Osama bin Laden's Al-Qaida network. Indeed, one scholar recently claims to have unearthed evidence that places Rohinga volunteers fighting alongside fellow mujahidin in Kashmir and Chechnya.[24]

Looking at the region more broadly, it is curious that in its trumpeting of a new human rights agenda the White House has paid only scant attention to Southeast Asia as a region. This is unusual because of a convergence of issues including the fact that Southeast Asia is home to almost 300 million Muslims. Southeast Asia is also home to at least one indigenous terrorist group, the Jemaah Islamiyah, which has clear links to Al-Qaida and which, in its bombing attacks in Bali in October 2002 and against the Marriott Hotel in Jakarta in mid-2003, has proven itself a deadly presence. Moreover, the proliferation of insurgencies and public dissatisfaction with often corrupt and unaccountable secular governments has generated a groundswell of support for groups pushing sometimes militant agendas overtly hostile to the United States and its allies.[25]

One possible explanation for this lack of attention on human rights in East Asia is that the United States feels that to push regional countries too hard on the issue risks jeopardizing their willingness to cooperate with Washington in counterterrorist operations. Yet this would not explain why President Bush has singled out Saudi Arabia and Egypt. In the overall scheme of things, counterterrorism cooperation with those two nations is considered to be even more important—and equally problematic—than that with East Asian states. Another possible explanation, then, could be that Washington tends to equate terrorism with Middle Eastern political currents, a perspective that pushes East Asia's Muslim community to a lower level of importance in Washington's thinking.

Why Human Rights Matter in the War on Terror

A more persuasive explanation for the lack of attention to the nexus between terrorism and authoritarianism in East Asia lies in the ambiguity of the terrorist threat in the region. There is something artificial about the war on terror in East Asia. For instance, there is a nagging lack of certainty about the authenticity of officially designated targets, whether they be Islamist critics of the UMNO-led administration in Malaysia, Acehnese separatists in Indonesia, Muslim rebels in Mindanao, or Uighur nationalists in Xinjiang. In the panicked post–September 11 atmosphere, it seems as though a vital distinction between terrorists on the one hand and dissidents, rebels, and cultural nationalists on the other, has been blurred. Sometimes this collapse of distinctions is the result of the urgency with which officials feel they have to move if they are to prevent more atrocities like those in New York and Washington, as well as the bombings in Bali barely twelve months later. However, as suggested above, this confusion results more often from a deliberate strategy by East Asian political elites to solicit Western support for the intimidation and brutalization of their critics.

While curtailing rights and rolling back civil society might temporarily complicate the activities of terrorist networks in the region, in the longer term this strategy carries a significant degree of risk. Indeed, unless it is rescued from the obfuscating tactics of autocratic elites, there is a serious risk that the war on terror will provoke escalating violence in troubled parts of East Asia.[26]

Another problem lies at the level of perception. Among Muslim communities in East Asia as a whole, Washington's war on terror has generated more skepticism, and occasional outright hostility, than support. This reflects deeply rooted cultural and political hostilities among pious and nonpious Muslims alike. This in turn is underpinned by a widely held image of the United States as the main prop to an international system that denies Muslims their cultural, economic, and political rights. At a practical level it is irrelevant that this view might be naively simplistic or that its prevalence often results from deliberate disinformation spread by the political elites in these countries as a way of deflecting critical attention away from themselves. What matters is that *the myth is believed* and that it is for many a reality. Indeed, Richard Bett's observation that "U.S. leaders can say that they are not waging a war against Islam until they are blue in the face, but this will not convince Muslims who already distrust the United States," appears especially prescient in the case of East Asia.[27]

Ignoring the plight of ordinary folk in East Asia in the name of better counterterrorist cooperation with regional governments will do nothing to address in the long term the threat posed by terrorist groups in the region. Indeed, the lessons of the Middle East, North Africa, and elsewhere suggest that the actions of authoritarian governments foment more political violence than they solve.

If history has taught us anything, it is that the dynamics driving an increasing number of modern Muslims toward Islamic politics, and occasionally violence, cannot be reversed by oppression and intimidation. Inherent in this dynamic are decades of accumulated frustrations with the unresponsive and unaccountable governments of the region. Of similar importance is skepticism about the policies and intentions of the United States, which is seen as the source of the cultural and political challenges they confront. As it is currently being waged in East Asia, the war on terror brings these two drivers—authoritarianism and U.S. belligerence—together in a dangerous combination that poses real risks for the long-term stability of much of the region.

But skepticism does not have to metamorphose into visceral hatred, and counterterrorism initiatives in East Asia need to be better calibrated to avoid this possibility. While counterterrorism cooperation with some of these regimes might be a necessary temporary evil, Washington needs to balance such partnerships through an engagement with those Muslims who have come to see Islam and Islamic democracy as an "alternative to the Faustian bargain of serving an authoritarian regime."[28]

This is not just an issue of ethical foreign policy; it's also practical politics. Writing in the *New Republic,* Peter Maass has observed, "Arbitrary arrests and executions, carried out by unloved governments at the bidding of the unloved United States, can lead to those governments being replaced by ones that support terrorists instead."[29] While the coming to power of Islamist governments is not in prospect in any part of East Asia, such groups still have the potential to complicate governance and foment violence. The rise of Islamic politics in East Asia is part and parcel of that region's integration into the wider global cultural and political milieu. It cannot be reversed, nor can it be controlled from outside. Political tensions must be allowed to play themselves out through an open, democratic, and accountable political environment. Accordingly, the

United States will serve its own and the region's interests much more effectively if it works to facilitate this process. Good relations with diverse elements across the Islamic community in East Asia, from Xinjiang to Mindanao, are essential to this end. So too is a more critical eye to the self-serving agendas of corrupt secular authorities.

There is a need to resist the temptation to pigeonhole all Islamic groups as vehemently anti-U.S. and as antidemocratic. Indeed, as John Esposito and John O. Voll have pointed out, "The efforts of Muslims to develop an authentic and viable Islamic democracy . . . reflect concerns prominent in Western efforts to create more effective forms of participatory democracy."[30] U.S. recognition of nonviolent Islamic groups as part of a legitimate opposition and a vibrant civil society with, in many instances, justifiable complaints against authoritarian and corrupt regimes, would deny the extremist fringe one of their most potent symbolic weapons: the image of the United States as the anti-Muslim fulcrum upon which the power of repressive and undemocratic secular governments rests. By establishing a dialogue with these groups, the United States would contribute to the establishment of a discursive public space and help bring nonviolent Islamic groups into a mainstream discourse. By fostering participation and a sense of ownership over the democratic process, such a strategy would also make it harder for the violent Islamic fringe to secure fresh recruits.

Conclusion

In the wake of September 11 and the terror attacks in Bali in October 2002, civil society in many parts of East Asia has suffered a profound setback. So too have the associated goals of further advancing the cause of human rights and achieving the peaceful resolution of the many conflicts that continue to bedevil the region. Even in those areas where individuals have successfully resisted attempts to restrict rights, civil society still faces a stiff challenge from groups determined to use the threat of terrorism to restore their own privileged positions by undoing many of the achievements of recent years.

Even if we were to concede the suspect argument that violence and the curtailment of rights is the answer to the threat posed by terrorism, however, the fact remains: Without the rule of law, without judicial systems free of state and corporate corruption, and without the participation in politics of a wide range of social groups, there is no guarantee it will be the genuine terrorists who are subjected to these "get tough" policies. Unless the media is free, well informed, and critically engaged, there is no check on the abuse of state power. Unless minority peoples and the culturally, economically, and politically disenfranchised are given a voice and some space to exercise their rights, there will be a steady supply of replacements for every suspected terrorist arbitrarily arrested or executed. As Joseph Nye has observed with regard to the unilateralist tendencies of the Bush administration, "Those hard nuggets of hate are unlikely to catalyze broader hatred unless we abandon our values and pursue arrogant and overbearing policies that let the extremists appeal to the minority in the middle."[31] In short, unless counterterrorist strategies in East Asia are true to the principles of a civil society, human rights, and respect for human dignity, the cycle of violence will not be broken.

For those of us who understand that there is no short-term easy solution to the scourge of terrorism, the task is to try and avoid this scenario. Those experts who dismiss as "a reflexive and sanctimonious" dream of the "softies of the world" any counterterrorism agenda that is premised on a respect for human rights and an expansion of civil society ought not forget that the path of peace and dignity is in many respects a harder road to travel.[32] But history tells us that it is the only road to success.

David Wright-Neville, Ph.D., is senior lecturer in the School of Political and Social Inquiry at Monash University in Melbourne, where he is also a member of the multi-disciplinary Global Terrorism Research project. Before returning to academe in 2002 he worked as a senior terrorism analyst in the Australian intelligence community, specializing in terrorist and militant groups in Southeast Asia.

Notes

1. G. Kolko, *Another Century of War?* (New York: New Press, 2002), p. 86.

2. For example, see collected essays in C. Brown, ed., *Lost Liberties: Ashcroft and the Assault on Personal Freedom* (New York: New Press, 2003).

3. See J. Hocking, *Terror Laws: ASIO, Counter-Terrorism, and the Threat to Democracy* (Sydney: University of New South Wales Press, 2003).

4. A. Acharya, "State-Society Relations: Asian and World Order After September 11," in Ken Booth and Tim Dunne, eds., *Worlds in Collision: Terror and the Future of Global Order* (London: Palgrave Macmillan, 2002), p. 194.

5. For an example of this argument, see T. Homer-Dixon, "The Rise of Complex Terrorism," *Foreign Policy* no. 128 (January–February 2002).

6. See International Crisis Group, "Aceh: How Not to Win Hearts and Minds," ICG Indonesia Briefing, Brussels/Jakarta, July 23, 2003.

7. See Amnesty International, *Philippines: Torture Persists—Appearance and Reality Within the Criminal Justice System,* ASA35/001/2003 (London: Amnesty International, 2003).

8. See "Reds Must Sign Peace Accord to Get Off Terror List: Ople," *Philippines Daily Inquirer,* February 1, 2003.

9. "Death Toll Nears 2000 in Mindanao Fighting," *Philippine Daily Inquirer,* February 14, 2003.

10. See J. Pomfret, "China Executes Tibetan Monk for Alleged Bombing," *Washington Post,* January 28, 2003.

11. See A. Demaria, "China: Falun Gong a Global Threat," *CNN.com,* August 6, 2002, available at http://cnn.worldnews.

12. See P. P. Pan, "In China's West, Ethnic Strife Becomes 'Terrorism,'" *Washington Post,* July 15, 2002, p. A12; Amnesty International, "China: Extensive Crackdown on Uighurs to Counter 'Terrorism' Must Stop," Press Release, March 22, 2002, AI Index ASA 17/012/2002.

13. "Anti-Government Sermons to Be Caught on Camera in Mosques," *Malaysiakini.com,* November 5, 2002.

14. George W. Bush, "Remarks by the President at the Twentieth Anniversary of the National Endowment for Democracy," November 6, 2003, available at www.whitehouse.gov/news/releases/2003/11/20031106–2.html.

15. For example, see K. Worcester, S. Avery Bermhanzohn, and M. Ungar, eds., *Violence and Politics: Globalization's Paradox* (New York: Routledge, 2001); and Charles

Tilly, *The Politics of Collective Violence* (Cambridge: Cambridge University Press, 2003).

16. U.S. Department of State, *Patterns of Global Terrorism Report 2001* (Washington, D.C.: U.S. Department of State, May 2004), app. 1, Statistical Review.

17. J. A. Nedoroscik, "Extremist Groups in Egypt," *Terrorism and Political Violence* 14, no. 2 (2002): 47–76.

18. J. L. Esposito, *Islam: The Straight Path,* 3d ed. (New York: Oxford University Press, 1998).

19. See essays in J. D. Martz, ed., *United States Policy in Latin America: A Decade of Crisis and Challenge* (Lincoln: University of Nebraska Press, 1995).

20. V. Schou Pedersen, "In Search of Monsters to Destroy? The Liberal American Security Paradox and a Republican Way Out," *International Relations* 17, no. 2 (2003): 223.

21. For a brief overview of the ETIM and doubts about its links to larger terrorist networks, see U.S. Council on Foreign Relations, "East Turkestan Islamic Movement" Terrorism: Questions and Answers," August 2002, available at www.terrorismanswers.com/groups/etim.html.

22. See R. A. Wampler, ed., "North Korea and Nuclear Weapons: The Declassified U.S. Record," *National Security Archive Electronic Briefing Book* no. 87 (April 25, 2003), available at www.gwu.edu/~nsarchiv/nsaebb/nsaebb87.

23. See L. Jagan, "ASEAN Takes Up Burma: But Only Very Reluctantly," *Bangkok Post,* June 17, 2003, available at http://search.bangkokpost.co.th/bkkpost/2003/june2003/bp20030617/news/17Jun2003_opin55.html. For a fuller treatment of ASEAN's approach to human rights, see M. Maznah, "Towards a Human Rights Regime in Southeast Asia: Charting the Course of State Commitment," *Contemporary Southeast Asia* 24, no. 2 (2002): 230–252.

24. Z. Abuza, *Militant Islam in Southeast Asia: Crucible of Terror* (Boulder: I. B. Taurus, 2003), p. 174.

25. See D. Wright-Neville, "Dangerous Dynamics: Activists, Militants, and Terrorists in Southeast Asia," *Pacific Review* 17, no. 1 (forthcoming 2004).

26. Kolko, *Another Century of War?* p. 90.

27. R. K. Betts, "The Soft Underbelly of American Primacy: Tactical Advantages of Terror," *Political Science Quarterly* 117, no. 1 (2002): 26.

28. G. Kepel, *Jihad: The Trial of Political Islam* (London: I. B. Taurus, 2002), p. 97.

29. P. Maass, "How America's Friends Really Fight Terrorism," *New Republic,* November 11, 2002, p. 19.

30. J. L. Esposito and John O. Voll, *Islam and Democracy* (New York: Oxford University Press, 1996), p. 32.

31. J. S. Nye, *The Paradox of American Power: Why the World's Only Superpower Can't Go It Alone* (Oxford: Oxford University Press, 2002), p. x.

32. See B. Hoffman, "A Nasty Business," *Atlantic Monthly,* January 2002.

5

Globalization, Insecurity, and Overextension

Walden Bello

With the launch of the World Trade Organization (WTO) in 1995, it seemed that a new economic order was taking hold in which, according to its adherents, both prosperity and security would be enhanced by the process of globalization. But the globalization project has run into difficulties and can now be said to be in crisis. These difficulties have roots in economic, environmental, and political realities. Significantly, there is a growing belief among critics of globalization that rather than increasing security, it has actually contributed to increased insecurity. This insecurity has been further aggravated by resentment against the United States, which has paid lip service to "globalization" while pursuing a unilateralist agenda to secure its own interests without sufficient regard for either the opinion of the outside world or the impact of its policies on the international community. There are now indications, however, that the United States may have overextended itself as it has attempted to assert its power.

The offspring of eight years of negotiations, the World Trade Organization was hailed in the establishment press as the gem of global economic governance in the era of globalization. The nearly twenty trade agreements that underpinned the WTO were presented as composing a set of multilateral rules that would eliminate power and coercion from trade relations by subjecting both the powerful and the weak to a common set of rules backed by an effective enforcement apparatus. The WTO was a landmark, declared George Soros, because it was the only supranational body to which the world's most powerful economy, that of the United States, would submit itself.[1] In the WTO, it was claimed, the powerful United States and lowly Rwanda had exactly the same number of votes: one.

Triumphalism was the note sounded during the first ministerial meeting of the WTO in Singapore in November 1996, with the WTO, International Monetary Fund (IMF), and the World Bank issuing their famous declaration saying that the challenge now is to make their policies of global trade, finance, and development "coherent" so as to lay the basis for global prosperity.

The Crisis of the Globalist Project

By the beginning of 2003 the triumphalism was gone. Since then, the organization had seemed to be in gridlock. A new agreement on agriculture is nowhere in sight as the United States and the European Union (EU) continue to defend multibillion-dollar subsidies paid to their farmers. Brussels is on the verge of imposing sanctions on Washington for maintaining tax breaks for exporters that have been found to be in violation of WTO rules, while Washington has threatened to file a case with the WTO against the EU's de facto moratorium against genetically modified foods. Developing countries, among them some that were once hopeful that the WTO would in fact bring more equity to global trade, unanimously agree that most of what they have reaped from WTO membership are costs, not benefits. They are dead set against opening their markets any further, except under coercion and intimidation. Instead of heralding a new round of global trade liberalization, the Cancun ministerial meeting resulted in a stalemate.

These failings, which some would say amount to a crisis for the globalist project, unfolded within a world that seemed to be plunging into even greater instability in the late 1990s. In 1991, President George H. W. Bush spoke about a "New World Order" that would replace the bipolar world of the Cold War, which had now passed from the scene. In the next few years, his successor, Bill Clinton, painted a future of peacefully coexisting societies integrated by free trade and multilateral governance systems.

But wars would not go away, and the Balkan conflicts of the 1990s appeared to be a direct product of the end of the Cold War, since this eliminated the discipline imposed on those who would fight national and ethnic conflicts as a result of the global competition between the two ideological blocs. Equally disturbing was the proliferation of civil wars in Africa, and many wondered if the phenomenon was related to the volatile combination of increased poverty, increased inequality, and economic stagnation that accompanied the imposition of IMF–World Bank structural adjustment programs throughout the continent in the 1980s and 1990s. Despite its visions of an emerging benign order, the Clinton administration resorted to the use of force to resolve conflicts that seemed, as the globalization process progressed, to increase rather than decrease. By the end of Clinton's second term in 2001, his administration, in the words of one analyst, had "made long-range precision air strikes an emblem of American statecraft."[2]

The context for the dramatic change from the triumphalism of the first half of the 1990s to the sense of an unraveling international order in the past few years is the crisis of the globalist project. But first, some notes on globalization and the globalist project.

Globalization is the accelerated integration of capital, production, and markets globally, a process driven by the logic of corporate profitability. Globalization has actually had two phases, the first lasting from the early nineteenth century until the outbreak of World War I in 1914; the second from the early 1980s until today. The intervening period was marked by the dominance of national capitalist economies characterized by a significant degree of state intervention and an international economy with strong constraints on trade and capital flows. These domestic and international constraints on the market, which were produced by the dynamics of class conflict internally and inter-capitalist competition internationally, were portrayed by the advocates of "neoliberalism" as having caused distortions that collectively accounted for the stagnation of the capitalist economies and the global economy in the late 1970s and early 1980s.

As in the first phase of globalization, the second phase was marked by the increasingly dominant influence of this neoliberal ideology, with a particular focus on "liberating the market" via accelerated privatization, deregulation, and trade liberalization. There were, broadly, two versions of neoliberal ideology—a "hard" Thatcher-Reagan version and a "soft" Blair-Soros version (globalization with "safety nets"). But underlying both approaches was the goal of unleashing market forces and removing or eroding constraints imposed on transnational firms by labor, the state, and society.

Three Moments in the Crisis of Globalization

There have been three moments in the deepening crisis of the globalist project. The first was the Asian financial crisis of 1997. This event, which laid low the proud "tigers" of East Asia, revealed that one of the key tenets of the globalization—the liberalization of the capital account to promote freer flows of capital, especially finance or speculative capital—could be profoundly destabilizing. The Asian financial crisis was, in fact, shown to be merely the latest of at least eight major financial crises since the liberalization of global financial flows began in the late 1970s.[3] How profoundly destabilizing capital market liberalization could be was shown when, in just a few weeks' time, 1 million people in Thailand and 21 million in Indonesia were pushed below the poverty line.[4]

The Asian financial crisis was the "Stalingrad" of the IMF, the prime global agent of liberalized capital flows. The IMF had encouraged "structural adjustment" in some 100 developing and transitional economies, but with the Asian crisis, these policies were subject to reevaluation. Criticism articulated as early as the late 1980s by such agencies as the UN Development Programme and UN Conference on Trade and Development was shown to have been prophetic. The structural adjustment programs designed to accelerate deregulation, trade liberalization, and privatization had almost everywhere institutionalized stagnation, worsened poverty, and increased inequality.

As Thomas Kuhn pointed out in his classic work *The Structure of Scientific Revolutions,*[5] a paradigm is really in crisis when its best practitioners desert it, and something akin to what happened during the crisis of the Copernican paradigm in physics occurred in neoclassical economics shortly after the Asian financial crisis, with key intellectuals leaving the fold—among them Jeffrey Sachs, noted earlier for his advocacy of "free market" shock treatment in Eastern Europe in the early 1990s; Joseph Stiglitz, former chief economist of the World Bank; Columbia professor Jagdish Bhagwati, who called for global controls on capital flows; and financier George Soros, who condemned the lack of controls in the global financial system that had enriched him.

The second moment of the crisis of the globalist project was the collapse of the third ministerial meeting of the WTO in Seattle in December 1999. At Seattle, three separate currents of discontent and conflict, which had all been growing stronger for some time, converged:

- Developing countries resented certain aspects of the Uruguay Round agreements, perceived to be inequitable, which that they had felt compelled to sign in 1995.
- Widespread popular opposition to the WTO emerged globally from myriad sectors of global civil society, including farmers, fisherfolk, labor unionists, and environmentalists. All of these sectors perceived the globalization process as threatening, with the result that much of civil society could unite in opposition to the WTO, which symbolized the perceived threat.
- There were unresolved trade conflicts between the EU and the United States, especially in agriculture, which had been simply been papered over by the Uruguay Round agreements.

These three volatile elements combined to create the explosion in Seattle. Inside the Seattle Convention Center, the developing countries were rebelling against what they sensed was an effort by the leading economies of the developed world to impose their will on the rest of the world, while outside, 50,000 people were massing militantly in the streets. Meanwhile, differences between the EU and United States made it impossible for the wealthy nations of the developed world to act in concert to salvage the ministerial. In a moment of lucidity right after the Seattle debacle, British secretary of state Stephen Byers captured the essence of the crisis: "The WTO will not be able to continue in its present form. There has to be fundamental and radical change in order for it to meet the needs and aspirations of all 134 of its members."[6]

The third moment of the crisis was the collapse of the stock market and the end of the Clinton boom. This was not just the bursting of the bubble but a rude reassertion of a recurring problem of capitalism—overproduction manifested especially in substantial overcapacity. Prior to the crash, corporate profits in the United States had not grown since 1997. This was related to overcapacity in the industrial sector, the most glaring example being seen in the troubled telecommunications sector, where only 2.5 percent of installed capacity globally was being utilized. The stagnation of the real economy led to capital being shifted to the financial sector, resulting in the dizzying rise in share values. But since profitability in the financial sector cannot deviate too far from the profitability of the real economy, a collapse of stock values was inevitable, and this occurred in March 2001, leading to prolonged stagnation and the onset of deflation.

There may well be a broader structural reason for the length of the current stagnation or deflation and the inability of the global economy to definitively escape the threat of renewed recession. It is conceivable, as a number of economists have stated, that we are at the tail end of the famous "Kondratieff cycle." This is the central feature of a theory, advanced by the Russian economist Nikolai Kondratieff, that suggests that the progress of global capitalism is marked not only by short-term business cycles but also by long-term "supercycles." Kondratieff cycles are roughly fifty- to sixty-year waves. The upward curve of the Kondratieff cycle is marked by the intensive exploitation of new technologies, followed by a crest as technological exploitation matures, then a downward curve as the old technologies produce diminishing returns while new technologies are still in an experimental stage in terms of profitable exploitation, and finally a trough or prolonged deflationary period.

The trough of the last wave was in the 1930s and 1940s, a period marked by the Great Depression and World War II. The ascent of the current wave began in the 1950s and the crest was reached in the 1980s and 1990s. The profitable exploitation of the postwar advances in the key energy, automobile, petrochemical, and manufacturing industries ended, while that of information technology was still at a relatively early stage. From this perspective, the "New Economy" of the late 1990s was not a transcendence of the business cycle, as many economists believed it to be, but the last glorious phase of the current supercycle prior to a descent into prolonged deflation. In other words, the uniqueness of the current conjuncture lies in the fact that the downward curve of the current short-term cycle coincides with the move into descent of the Kondratieff supercycle. To use the words of another famous economist, Joseph Schumpeter, the global economy appears to be headed for a prolonged period of "creative destruction."

Environmental Crisis and the Globalist Project

The focus above has been on "moments" or conjunctural crystallizations of the crisis of the globalization project. These moments were manifestations of fundamental conflicts or contradictions that were unfolding unevenly over time. A central smoldering contradiction was that between globalization and the environment. It is worth devoting a few words to how the environmental crisis has proven to be a central factor not only undermining the legitimacy of the globalization project, but also exposing inherent weaknesses of capitalism as a mode of economic organization itself.

Both before and after the World Summit on Environment and Development in Rio de Janeiro in 1992, there was a sense that while the world environmental situation was worsening, consciousness of this fact was leading to the creation of the global institutional and legal mechanisms to deal with the problem. The Rio Summit's agreeing on Agenda 21, a global program for environmental improvement that would have counterpart country programs, seemed to mark a major step forward in terms of global cooperation.

The late 1980s and early 1990s were, moreover, a period when a number of multilateral environmental agreements were inked and appeared to be making headway in reversing the global environmental crisis, like the Montreal Protocol putting controls on the production of chlorofluorocarbons to preserve the ozone layer, and the CITES Treaty putting tough controls on trade in endangered species. Also, with the coming to power of Bill Clinton and Al Gore in 1992, an environmentally "correct" administration seemed to be in place. Several moves stalemated this process.

The first was the establishment of the WTO. As Ralph Nader put it, the WTO put corporate "trade über alles," meaning that trade subordinates all our consumer, environmental, health, safety, and workplace standards. In other words, laws protecting natural resources and the environment needed to be changed if they were seen as imposing standards that were perceived as unfair to foreign trading interests. In a series of landmark cases—the tuna-dolphin case between the United States and Mexico, the turtle-shrimp controversy pitting the United States and Asian countries against each other—it seemed that national environmental laws were being subordinated to free trade. The thrust seemed to be to establish a lowest common denominator applicable in all countries, rather than to bring those with low standards up to a higher level.

Second, the aggressive push by corporations to exploit advanced food technology and biotechnology caused great alarm among environmentalists and ordinary citizens around the globe. The EU's ban on hormone-treated beef from the United States—enacted in response to popular demand in Europe—was

EPA Photo/Ardiles Rante

Jakarta, 13 September 2003.
Indonesian Muslim women protest
during an anti-WTO demonstration.

sustained despite the WTO's view that it was illegal. Likewise, genetic modifications in agricultural production, coupled with resistance to eco-labeling on the part of U.S. firms like Monsanto, triggered a consumer backlash in Europe and other parts of the world, with the precautionary principle being invoked as a powerful weapon against the U.S. corporations' criterion of "solid science." Also, the aggressive efforts by U.S. biotech firms to claim patents on life-forms and seeds produced through biotechnology led to strong resistance by farmers' groups, consumer groups, and environmentalists to what was denounced as the inappropriate "privatization" of a domain—where man and nature interact—which had existed for eons with no such interference or regulation.

Third, the steadfast refusal of many within the U.S. industrial sector to acknowledge the fact of global warming at a time when the speed of the melting of the polar ice caps was accelerating was perceived as a brazen attempt to put profits ahead of the common interest. This perception could only be reinforced by the successful corporate effort to stymie a collective global effort to effectively deal with global warming during the Clinton administration, and then finally to kill it when the second Bush administration refused to sign and ratify the already weak Kyoto Protocol on Climate Change.

The aggressive antienvironmental posture dominant among U.S. corporations was one of the factors that led to a great distrust of business even within the United States, with 72 percent of Americans surveyed by *Business Week* in 2000 saying that business "has too much power over their lives," leading the country's prime business weekly to warn: "Corporate America, ignore these trends at your peril."[7]

At the same time, developing countries felt that the United States was using environmental arguments to slow down their development with its position that the greenhouse gas emissions of developing countries needed to also be subject to substantially the same restrictions imposed on the developed countries as a condition for Washington signing the Kyoto Protocol. Indeed, such suspicions were, perhaps, not unfounded, since Bush administration people were targeting China, whose rapid development was seen by some administration officials as a strategic threat to the United States. Environmentalism, if this were indeed the case, was being employed by the United States as a tactic to help it to maintain its geoeconomic and geopolitical edge.

By the early 2000s, then, the global consensus represented by the Rio Summit had unraveled, and it all but collapsed under the massive corporate "greenwashing" campaign—where corporations tried to project images of environmental responsibility while pursuing their own interests with little regard for the environment—that was unleashed at the World Summit on Sustainable Development (also known as Rio Plus Ten) in Johannesburg in September 2002. "Sustainable development," a vision that attempted to reconcile economic growth with ecological stability, fell by the wayside, and Herman Daly's apocalyptic image of an economic system marked by hypergrowth outstripping an ecological system created over the eons seemed closer to realization as corporate interests in the United States, Europe, and Japan worked closely with a "pollution friendly" government in China to make that high-growth nation both the workshop and the wastebasket of the world.

Globalization and Insecurity in the Asia Pacific Region

Globalization and environmental crisis are positively correlated. So too are globalization and insecurity, according to many observers. The relationship between economic globalization, poverty, and insecurity has been articulated cogently by Susan George:

> Between 1990 and the end of 1996 there were ninety-eight major wars—overwhelmingly civil wars, not inter-country ones—and the Peace Research Institute in Oslo has found that these conflicts share the following characteristics. One, they take place chiefly in poor countries where agriculture is still the main contributor to the GDP. Two, the environmental factors most frequently associated with civil conflict are land degradation, low fresh water availability per capita, and high population density, in that order. Three, a particularly strong correlation exists between high external debt and the incidence of civil war. Four, falling export income from primary commodities is closely associated with the outbreak of civil war. Five, a history of vigorous IMF intervention is also positively linked with all forms of political and armed conflict.[8]

This picture holds in general terms for the Asia Pacific region, which is the primary zone of interest here. Globalization and insecurity have evinced a disturbing positive correlation in East Asia, particularly in recent times. While the period of East Asian prosperity from 1975 to 1997 was marked by the near absence of external wars except on the Indochinese Peninsula, in fact the dynamics of economic growth were marked by great internal strife. In Korea, the accelerated exploitation of labor with little in the way of worker rights led to a very unstable social situation that could only be maintained by means of massive state repression, resulting in a major confrontations between management, backed by the state, and labor. As I and Stephanie Rosenfeld wrote in 1990, along with labor repression, "rising income inequality, conspicuous consumption, and the housing crisis jarred the sensibility of a people who had been socialized by the government to the myth of a relatively egalitarian Korea, and the engendered dissatisfactions fueled the flame of labor's rebellion in the late 1980s to an even greater intensity. By then, suspicion of wealth had become so deeply ingrained that one ruling party legislator remarked, 'The mood of the country is like a people's court in a communist country.'"[9]

Despite external peace and high growth rates, the same volatile state of social relations was found in other "development dictatorships" in Taiwan, Indonesia, and the Philippines that were rushing to integrate their societies into the world economy. The onset of formal democratization in the late 1980s throughout most of East Asia did help lower social tensions, even if respect for both human rights and political rights on the part of the military and security forces left much to be desired. But the respite was short. After the "high boom" of Southeast Asia in the second half of the 1990s, social conflicts intensified with the onset of the Asian financial crisis, a disaster directly related to the liberalization of global capital flows. The plunge below the poverty line of so many millions of people heightened economic insecurities and social tensions. The intervention of the IMF, with its budget-cutting measures, then ended up exacerbating the already bad situation, with the resulting social tensions erupting in uncontrolled crime and race riots in Indonesia. In South Korea, renewed class conflict accompanied the IMF-driven government effort to "rationalize" the economy by laying off workers, and confidence in the system was eroded by the realization that the social safety net was completely inadequate in times of economic crisis.

Nevertheless, there was a silver lining to the crisis, at least in Indonesia. There, having staked its own future and legitimacy on the smooth management of the economy, the Suharto dictatorship collapsed when the economy went bust. The resulting weakening of Jakarta's central control emboldened East Timorese to intensify their demands for the end of Jakarta's rule over their country. After a horrifying transition in which Indonesia-backed militias went on a murderous rampage, the UN-supervised transition to independent status took place in 1999–2002. However, here too, the free-market bias prevailed, with the World Bank, brandishing billions of dollars in reconstruction aid, playing a leading role in the economic redevelopment process and pushing Timorese development along neoliberal lines.

One of the most damaging impacts of the Asian financial crisis was the deflation of the prestige of the ASEAN Regional Forum (ARF). In the mid-1990s the ARF, centered on the ASEAN countries, had made a strong bid to become a key player in regional security affairs. The ARF played an important role in pushing to resolve territorial disputes through diplomacy rather than the use of force. ASEAN's neighbors, including China, Japan, Russia, and eventually North Korea, were eager to participate in the yearly meetings that followed the annual ASEAN foreign minister meeting for fear that otherwise, they might be seen as uncooperative. And even though the United States periodically dismissed the ARF as a "talk shop" and warned that it must "supplement our alliances and forward military presence, not supplant them,"[10] it was forced to take the meetings seriously.

Why was Washington so wary of the ARF? Because, as a report of the Congressional Research Service put it:

> A problem would arise if East Asian governments used the ASEAN Regional Forum and other future regional security consultative organizations in attempts to restrain the United States from acting on certain security issues. The impasse between the United States and the NATO and OSCE countries over policy toward Bosnia-Herzegovina points up the potential for disagreements as Cold War–based mutual interests decline. Four areas of US security policy in East Asia would appear to be subject to potential differences between the United States and some East Asian governments: US attempts to restrain Chinese missile and arms sales; US policy toward Taiwan, especially

if Taiwan-China relations should worsen; US efforts to prevent North Korea from developing nuclear weapons; and US policy towards Japan's future regional and military roles. The US Government and friendly East Asian governments might agree on some basic objectives on these issues, but they may disagree on the strategies and tactics to employ. Regional security consultative organizations could be focal points for the airing of such differences.[11]

In other words, there was concern that the ARF could evolve as an increasingly influential check on U.S. unilateralism. The Asian financial crisis, however, pulled the carpet out from under the ARF. Political prestige, the ASEAN countries found, was greatly dependent on the perception of prosperity. So long as the ASEAN countries were exhibiting impressive growth rates, their political influence was not inconsequential. However, their collapse in 1997 greatly diminished respect for them, not least from the Big Three—China, Japan, and the United States. By the time of the ARF meeting in 1999, the ARF had degenerated into an inconsequential assembly, and the ASEAN governments, which were preoccupied with economic crisis, were on the defensive. Their position was not helped by their continuing reluctance to speak out against the continuing violation of human and democratic rights in Burma.

With the ARF diminished, there was one less check on U.S. unilateralism. This could only lead to more regional instability. The restraining influence of an influential ASEAN and ARF was sorely missed after the September 11, 2001 events, when full-fledged unilateralism came to totally dominate U.S. foreign policy. Determined to push its punitive campaign against real or perceived terrorists, the United States took advantage of disarray within ASEAN to reintroduce a military presence in the Philippines. By late January 2002, U.S. special forces were present on Basilan Island in the Southern Philippines, ostensibly to assist Philippine troops tracking down Abu Sayaff, an Islamic fundamentalist group that specialized in kidnapping for ransom. The more strategic objective of the United States, many analysts claimed, was to establish a forward base to strike against militant Islamic movements in the Southern Philippines, Indonesia, and Malaysia.[12]

With the invasion of Afghanistan, followed by the invasion of Iraq, the consequences of this even more single-minded U.S. unilateralism seem to be an increase rather than a decline in Islamic extremism in Indonesia, which had long prided itself on its tradition of Islamic tolerance. The Bali bombing of October 2002 underlined how counterproductive a purely punitive approach toward terrorism was. But Washington has been undeterred in its strategy and continues to fight terrorism by striking militarily at suspected terrorist networks—which are essentially symptoms of a sociopolitical malady—without addressing the root causes of terrorism, which can be traced back to poverty, inequality, and cultural alienation. Indeed, the constant refrain of U.S. officials at multilateral gatherings has been to press the fight against terror, even as evidence has mounted that the war against terror is enhancing the appeal, in many quarters, of the extremists.

The Unilateralist Politics and
Economics of the Bush Administration

The crisis of globalization, neoliberalism, overproduction, the environment, and security provides the context for understanding the economic policies of the George W. Bush administration, notably its unilateralist thrust.

The military dimension of unilateralism was essentially a resurrection of the Project for a New American Century study initiated at the Pentagon in the early 1990s by Paul Wolfowitz, then a senior official at the administration of President George H. W. Bush. The key message of this document was that the United States should build up its military superiority to the point where its hegemony would be permanent and unchallengeable by any rival or any coalition of rivals. But by the time it was put into effect with the return of the Republicans under George W. Bush after September 11, 2001, and formalized in a national security doctrine issued by the White House on September 17, 2001, the strategy had become not so much an effort to address great power rivalries as an effort to contain what it saw as the innumerable threats posed to U.S. security and hegemony by nonstate actors or "terrorists." The proliferation of terrorists was an acknowledgment that instead of reducing risks, globalization might actually be increasing them. For many in the U.S. elite, September 11 represented a stunning refutation of the globalists' belief that globalization would enhance global peace and stability. U.S. conservatives were inclined to argue that the terrorists were motivated to attack the United States out of resentment of U.S. prosperity and political influence in global politics. The liberal interpretation was that poverty, inequality, and stagnation promoted by corporate-driven globalization had served as the breeding ground of terrorism.

While the military dimension of unilateralism has been widely discussed, the economic dimension has not been subjected to the same level of scrutiny. Many continue to see globalization as a U.S.-inspired project pushed by George W. Bush. But is this in fact the case?

The globalist corporate project has been backed by capitalist elites all over the world, because they share a common interest in an expanding global economy, and it reflects their fundamental dependence on one another. But globalization does not mean that the owners of capital will not compete with each other. In fact, in both the United States and Europe, there are important segments within the corporate world—the military-industrial complex in the United States, for example—that are strongly nationalistic in character and dependent on the state for their well-being and even survival. Indeed, since the 1980s there has been a sharp struggle between the more globalist faction of the ruling elite, stressing the common interest of the global capitalist class in a growing world economy, and the more nationalist, hegemonist faction, seeking to ensure the supremacy of U.S. corporate interests.

As Robert Brenner has pointed out, the policies of Bill Clinton and his treasury secretary, Robert Rubin, put prime emphasis on the expansion of the world economy as the basis of the prosperity of the global capitalist class. For instance, in the mid-1990s they pushed a strong dollar policy meant to stimulate the recovery of the Japanese and German economies, so they could serve as markets for U.S. goods and services. The earlier, more nationalist Reagan administration, on the other hand, had employed a weak dollar policy to regain competitiveness for the U.S. economy at the expense of the Japanese and German economies.[13] With the George W. Bush administration, we are back to economic policies, including a weak dollar policy, that are meant to revive the U.S. economy, even if that revival occurs at the expense of other nations and economies, and primarily promotes U.S. corporate interests with little regard for the interests of global capitalist class as a whole, which has continued to suffer the consequences of a global downturn.

Several features of this approach are worth stressing:

- There is significant wariness of any process of globalization that is not managed by the United States, so as to ensure that the process does not diffuse the economic power of the United States. There is concern that the consequences of a truly free market could be that key U.S. corporations actually become victims of globalization and thus compromise U.S. economic interests. The result is that despite the free-market rhetoric, we have a group that is very protectionist when it comes to trade, investment, and the management of government contracts. It seems that the motto in the Bush administration is protectionism for the United States and free trade for everyone else.
- The Bush approach includes great skepticism about multilateralism as a way to achieve global economic governance, since multilateralism may promote the interests of the global capitalist class in general, but could still have negative consequences for particular U.S. corporate interests. The Bush team's growing ambivalence toward the WTO stems from the fact that the United States has lost a number of cases related to trade issues to the detriment of U.S. interests but the benefit of global capitalist interests.
- Within the Bush administration, the view prevails that strategic power is the ultimate modality of power. Economic power is a means to achieve strategic power. This is related to the fact that under Bush, the dominant faction of the ruling elite is the military-industrial establishment that won the Cold War. The conflict between globalists and unilateralists or nationalists along this axis is evident in the approach toward China. The globalist approach put the emphasis on engagement with China, seeing its importance primarily as an investment area and market for U.S. capital. The nationalists, on the other hand, see China mainly as a strategic enemy, and they would prefer to contain it rather than assist its growth.
- From the Bush perspective, management of the environment is a low priority. The administration is happy to let others worry about environmental issues. There is, in fact, a strong corporate lobby that believes

that environmental concerns such as that surrounding genetic modification is a European conspiracy to deprive the United States of its high-tech edge in global competition.

If these features are seen as the premises for action, then the following prominent elements of recent U.S. economic policy make sense:

- *Asserting control over Middle East oil.* While oil was not the only reason that the Bush administration decided to invade Iraq, it undoubtedly was one of its most important considerations. With competition with Europe becoming one of the prime aspects of the transatlantic relationship, this was clearly aimed partly at Europe. But in view of the Bush administration's view of China as a strategic enemy, another reason may have been to ensure that energy-poor China did not end up controlling the region's resources.[14]
- *Aggressive protectionism in trade and investment matters.* The United States has pursued an aggressively protectionist strategy, including, notably, successfully blocking any movement at the WTO negotiations by violating the spirit of the Doha Declaration's provision holding that intellectual property rights—specifically patents on medicines—should not be exercised in such a way as to prevent governments from supporting public health. In response to pressures from the powerful U.S. pharmaceutical lobby, the United States pushed to limit the declaration's applicability to just three diseases. While it seems perfectly willing to see the WTO negotiations unravel, Washington has put most of its efforts into concluding bilateral or multilateral trade deals such as the Free Trade of the Americas (FTAA) before the EU can reach similar agreements. Indeed, the term "free trade agreements" is a misnomer since these are actually preferential trade deals.
- *Incorporating strategic considerations into trade agreements.* In a recent speech, U.S. trade representative Robert Zoellick stated explicitly that "countries that seek free-trade agreements with the United States must pass muster on more than trade and economic criteria in order to be eligible. At a minimum, these countries must cooperate with the United States on its foreign policy and national security goals, as part of 13 criteria that will guide the U.S. selection of potential FTAA partners." New Zealand, perhaps one of the governments most supportive of free trade, has nevertheless not been offered a free trade deal because it has a policy that prevents visits by nuclear ships, which the United States feels is directed at itself.[15]
- *Manipulation of the dollar's value in such a manner that the costs of the economic crisis are borne by rivals among the center economies and the U.S. economy regains a competitive advantage.* A slow depreciation of the dollar vis-à-vis the euro could be interpreted as market-based adjustments, but the 25 percent fall in value cannot but be seen as, at the least,

a policy of benign neglect. While the Bush administration has issued denials that this is a beggar-thy-neighbor policy, the U.S. business press has seen it for what it is: an effort to revive the U.S. economy at the expense of the European Union and other center economies.

- *Aggressive manipulation of multilateral agencies to push the interests of U.S. capital.* While this might not be too easy to achieve in the WTO owing to the weight of the European Union, it can be more readily done at the World Bank and the IMF, where U.S. dominance is more effectively institutionalized. For instance, despite support for the proposal from many European governments, the U.S. Treasury recently torpedoed the IMF management's proposal for a sovereign debt-restructuring mechanism (SDRM) to enable developing countries to restructure their debt while giving them a measure of protection from creditors. Already a very weak mechanism, the SDRM was vetoed by U.S. Treasury in the interest of U.S. banks.[16]
- *Forcing other center economies, as well as developing countries, to bear the burden of adjusting to the environmental crisis.* While some in the Bush administration do not even believe that there is an environmental crisis, others know that the current rate of global greenhouse gas emissions is unsustainable. Their attitude, it would appear, is to let others bear the brunt of adjustment, since that would mean not only exempting environmentally inefficient U.S. industries from the costs of adjustment, but also hobbling other economies with even greater costs than would arise if the United States were to participate in an equitable adjustment process. Such a strategy would give the U.S. economy a strong edge in global competition. If such an analysis is indeed true, then it is raw economic realpolitik, rather than fundamentalist blindness, that lies at the root of Washington's decision not to sign the Kyoto Protocol on Climate Change.

The Economics and Politics of Overextension

Being harnessed very closely to strategic ends, any discussion of the likely outcomes of the Bush administration's economic policies must take into account both the state of the U.S. economy and the global economy and the broader strategic picture. A key condition for the success of what might be called "imperial" management is expanding economies at both the national and the global levels—something that would be precluded by the extended period of deflation and stagnation that may be looming, and that would be more likely to spur intercapitalist rivalries. Moreover, resources include not only economic and political resources but political and ideological resources as well. For without legitimacy, without what Gramsci called "the consensus" of the dominated that a system of rule is just, such a scheme of imperial management cannot be stable.

Faced with a similar problem of securing the long-term stability of its rule, the ancient Romans came up with the solution that created what would become the furthest-reaching case of collective mass loyalty ever achieved and thus prolonged the empire for another 700 years. The Roman solution was not merely or even principally military in character. The Romans realized that an important component of successful imperial domination was consensus among the dominated of the "rightness" of the Roman order. As sociologist Michael Mann notes in his classic work *Sources of Social Power,* the "decisive edge" was not so much military as political. "The Romans," he writes, "gradually stumbled on the invention of extensive territorial citizenship." The extension of Roman citizenship to ruling groups and nonslave peoples throughout the empire was the political breakthrough that produced what "was probably the widest extent of collective commitment yet mobilized."[17] Political citizenship combined with the vision of the empire providing peace and prosperity for all to create that intangible but essential moral element called legitimacy.

Clearly, extension of citizenship plays no role in the U.S. imperial order. In fact, U.S. citizenship is jealously reserved for a very tiny minority of the world's population, and entry into the United States is tightly controlled. Rather than pursuing a policy of integration with respect to have-nots and dependent peoples, the United States asserts its dominance either by force or the threat of force, or by supporting a system of global or regional rules and institutions—the World Trade Organization, the Bretton Woods system, the North Atlantic Treaty Organization—that are, according to many, increasingly manipulated to serve the interests of the imperial center with little concern for world opinion.

Though extension of universal citizenship was never a tool in the U.S. imperial arsenal, during its struggle with communism in the post–World War II period Washington did come up with a political formula to legitimize its global reach. The two elements of this formula were multilateralism as a system of global governance and liberal democracy.

In the immediate aftermath of the Cold War, there were, in fact, widespread expectations of a modern-day version of a Pax Romana. There was hope in liberal circles that the United States would use its sole superpower status to undergird a multilateral order that would institutionalize its hegemony but ensure an Augustan peace globally. That was the path of economic globalization and multilateral governance, but with George W. Bush's pursuit of unilateralism, this path has been abandoned.

As Frances Fitzgerald observed in *Fire in the Lake,* the promise of extending liberal democracy was a very powerful ideal that accompanied U.S. arms transfers during the Cold War.[18] Today, however, Washington- or Westminster-type liberal democracy is in trouble throughout the developing world. Rather than offering a promise of liberal democracy, it provides a façade behind which oligarchs exercise power, as in the Philippines, pre-Musharraf Pakistan, and much of Latin America. In fact, liberal democracy in the United States has become both less democratic and less liberal. Certainly, few in the developing world want to emulate a system that is to such a large extent fueled and corrupted by corporate money.

Recovery of the moral vision needed to create consensus for U.S. hegemony will be extremely difficult. Indeed, the thinking in Washington these days is that the most effective consensus builder is the threat of use of force.

Moreover, despite their talk about imposing democracy in the Arab world, influential neoconservative writers like Robert Kagan and Charles Krauthammer seem more intent on manipulating liberal democratic mechanisms to encourage pluralistic competition and undermine Arab unity. For these neoconservatives, bringing democracy to the Arabs is not the real objective, but it does serve as a convenient rallying cry, even if the words ring hollow.

Ultimately, the Bush administration is not interested in creating a new Pax Romana, but rather a Pax Americana in some regions such as the Arab world, where the threat posed by the potential exercise of power serves to maintain order, and elsewhere, such as in the Philippines, loyalty is purchased with the promise of cash. But without a moral vision to bind the global majority to the imperial center, this mode of imperial management is likely to inspire just one thing: resistance.

The great problem for unilateralism is overextension: in this case a mismatch between the goals of the United States and the resources needed to accomplish these goals. Overextension is relative—it is to a great degree a function of resistance. An overextended power may in fact be in a worse condition, even with a significant increase in its military power, if resistance to its power increases by an even greater degree. Among the key indicators of overextension are the following:

- Washington's continuing inability to create a new political order in Iraq.
- Its failure to consolidate a pro-U.S. regime in Afghanistan outside of Kabul.
- The spread of Islamic fundamentalism throughout the Middle East, South Asia, and Southeast Asia, brought about to a large extent by U.S. policies that have played into the hands of extremists like Osama bin Laden by inflaming Arab and Muslim passions.
- The deepening divisions within the Atlantic Alliance and the assertive independence and leadership of Germany and France on matters of international security and trade.
- The forging of a burgeoning global civil society movement opposing U.S. unilateralism, militarism, and economic hegemony, whose most recent significant expression is the global antiwar movement.
- The electoral victories of anti-neoliberal and in some cases even anti-U.S. governments in Washington's own backyard in Brazil, Venezuela, and Ecuador.
- An increasingly negative impact of militarism on the U.S. economy, with military spending adding hundreds of billions of dollars to the budget deficit, and deficit spending adding to the dependency of the United States on financing from foreign sources. The result is additional stress and strain within an economy that is already in the throes of stagnation.

In conclusion, the globalist project is in crisis. A comeback if either a Democrat or a liberal Republican were to be elected U.S. president should not be ruled out, especially as there are influential globalist voices in the U.S.

business community—among them George Soros—who are voicing opposition to the unilateralist thrust of the Bush administration.[19] In my view, however, this is unlikely, and unilateralism will reign for some time to come.

The world has, in short, entered a historical maelstrom of prolonged economic crisis, the spread of global resistance, the reappearance of the balance of power among center states, and the reemergence of acute interimperialist contradictions. U.S. power should not be underestimated, but neither should it be overestimated. There are signs that the United States is seriously overextended, and that what appear to be manifestations of strength might in fact signal strategic weakness.

Walden Bello is professor of sociology and public administration at the University of the Philippines and executive director of the Bangkok-based Focus on the Global South. He is active in the peace and anti-corporate-globalization movements and is the author of some thirteen books, including Deglobalization *(London: Zed, 2002) and The Future in the Balance (Oakland: Food First, 2001). He is the recipient of the Right Livelihood Award (also known as the Alternative Nobel Prize) for 2003.*

Notes

1. George Soros, *On Globalization* (New York: PublicAffairs, 2002), p. 35.

2. Andrew Bacevich, *American Empire* (Cambridge: Harvard University Press, 2002), p. 154.

3. See UN Conference on Trade and Development, *Trade and Development Report 1998;* and Barry Eichengreen and Donald Mathieson, *Hedge Fund and Financial Markets,* Occasional Paper no. 166 (Washington, D.C.: International Monetary Fund, 1998).

4. Jacques-chai Chomthongdi, "The IMF's Asian Legacy," in *Prague 2000: Why We Need to Decommission the IMF and the World Bank* (Bangkok: Focus on the Global South, 2000), pp. 18, 22.

5. Thomas Kuhn, *The Structure of Scientific Revolution* (Chicago: University of Chicago Press, 1962).

6. Quoted in "Deadline Set for WTO Reforms," *Guardian News Service,* January 10, 2000.

7. The quote comes from a cover story in *Business Week,* Issue 37, September 11, 2000. Available at www.businessweek.com/2000/00_37/b3698002.htm

8. Susan George, "The Corporate Utopian Dream," in Proceedings of the Forum on the Global War System, Hildebrand Hall, Plymouth Congregational Church, Seattle, Washington, November 28, 1999.

9. Walden Bello and Stephanie Rosenfeld, *Dragons in Distress: Asia's Miracle Economies in Crisis* (San Francisco: Food First, 1990), p. 40.

10. U.S. Department of Defense, *United States Security Strategy for the East Asia Pacific Region* (Washington, D.C.: Office of International Security Affairs, February 1995), p. 13.

11. Larry Niksch, *Regional Security Consultative Organizations in East Asia and Their Implications for the United States,* CRS Report for Congress (Washington, D.C.: Congressional Research Service, January 14, 1994), pp. 13–14.

12. See, for instance, *Report of the International Peace Mission to Basilan: Focus on the Global South,* Manila, March 2002.

13. See Robert Brenner, *The Boom and the Bubble* (New York: Verso, 2002), pp. 128–133.

14. David Harvey, speech at the Conference on Trends in Globalization, University of California at Santa Barbara, May 1–4, 2003.

15. "Zoellick Says FTA Candidates Must Support U.S. Foreign Policy," *Inside U.S. Trade,* May 16, 2003. This article summarizes a May 8, 2003, speech by Zoellick.

16. For the sharpening conflicts between the U.S. Treasury Department and IMF officials, see Nicola Bullard, "The Puppet Master Shows His Hand," *Focus on Trade,* April 2002, available at http://focusweb.prg/popups/articleswindow.php?id=41.

17. Michael Mann, *The Sources of Social Power,* vol. 1 (Cambridge: Cambridge University Press, 1986), pp. 254.

18. Frances Fitzgerald, *Fire in the Lake* (New York: Random House, 1973), p. 116:

> The idea that the mission of the United States was to build democracy around the world had become a convention of American politics in the 1950's. Among certain circles, it was more or less assumed that democracy, that is electoral democracy combined with private ownership and civil liberties, was what the United States had to offer the Third World. Democracy provided not only the basis for American opposition to Communism but the practical method to make sure that opposition worked.

19. See George Soros, "America's Role in the World," speech at the Paul H. Nitze School of Advanced International Studies, Washington, D.C., March 7, 2003. Noting that he was in favor of intervention in the Balkans, including a "NATO intervention without UN authorization," Soros denounced the war with Iraq on the grounds that it stemmed from a fundamentalism that was unsound and was wreaking havoc with U.S. relations with the rest of the world. The arguments he mustered are those heard not only in liberal democratic circles in Washington but also in "pragmatic" Republican Party circles and on Wall Street.

6

Transition and Conflict in Asia Pacific: The Role of the International Community in the Democratization Process

Kennedy Graham

The relationship between democracy and conflict is complex and elusive. Conflict is often, though not always, generated by an absence or repression of democracy. Democracy is often, though not always, thwarted by the occurrence of conflict. Democracy is conducive to, though not always, the avoidance of aggression and the peaceful resolution of disputes.

A permanently peaceful society is one where in preventative structures that minimize the causes of conflict and preempt its occurrence are in place, where peacemaking mechanisms exist for rapid activation when conflict occurs, and where enforcement and reconciliation procedures are well enough integrated to strike an optimal balance between the frequently competing demands of stability and justice. The cyclical, self-regenerative nature of this societal process—conflict prevention, peacemaking, and peacebuilding—is evident, which is to say that these sustainable preventative structures depend, in turn, on maintaining that optimal balance between stability and justice.

The perfect "permanently peaceful" society does not exist. But as the world shrinks and societal tensions become more acute, efforts at the international and national levels are under way to develop theoretical and institutional means of assisting the attainment of "sustainable peace" through the democratization of human society, both nationally and globally.

This chapter addresses the role of the international community in the "democratization process" in the Asia Pacific region, in particular the transition toward democracy that certain societies are undergoing and the tensions and conflicts they are experiencing as a result. Fundamental to this analysis is a clear understanding, not yet fully embraced by those institutions engaged in the process, of the nuances of "democracy" that must be sensitively appreciated to meet the aspirations of different cultures throughout the subregion. Until that understanding is genuinely reflected in institutional policies, the trend toward sustainable peace in all societies will continue to be impeded by misunderstanding and, occasionally, prejudice.

The chapter addresses three issues. It analyzes contemporary theoretical aspects of democracy and the role of the international community in the democratization process. It identifies the transition certain societies in the subregion are experiencing. And it stresses the need to understand democracy better in a cultural sense, if democratization is to be less traumatic and more enduring.

Theoretical Framework

The international community can assist countries in the democratization process to move toward a dynamic rather than a static state of democracy.[1] While the process itself is accepted within the international community now after a decade of experience, sensitivities and misunderstandings remain rife, in particular over two areas. First, there is a widespread misapprehension that democracy presupposes independence. Second, the struggle continues over the component elements of "democracy" that make up its very nature. There is a need for greater clarity on these issues, and until this is achieved, conflict will continue.

Democracy and Independence

The attainment of "democracy" does not always result in independence, nor should it. The sovereignty of a society, and its internal nature, are separate things. Much of the conflict in the world, not least in the Asia Pacific region, is due to an erroneous conflation of these two concepts.

The dichotomy between democracy and independence is best illustrated today in modern Europe. The nation-states of that region, among the most enduring and benign democracies on the planet, are "pooling" their national independence in common economic and social and, in due course, security structures. This is being done through a circumspect sharing of sovereignty on the basis of the subsidiarity principle, with attendant increased powers to Scotland and Flanders, Tuscany and Thuringia. Conversely, national "independence" can simply result in an undemocratic, smaller nation-state (contemporary Belarus and Uzbekistan come to mind). The world is tending toward systems of governance wherein the assignment of jurisdiction is increasingly complex, spread across many levels from the global through the regional and national to the municipal. Sovereignty is being spread with increasing insight in a manner that can potentially guarantee democracy, in all its facets, for all peoples. The dynamic twists and turns of most societies today, so often marked by anguish and conflict, will no doubt be recognized by future historians for what they are—manifestations of a painstaking but ineluctable process of discovering the optimal "layering of sovereignty," genuflecting to the democratic imperative, for all peoples around the world.

The key concept facilitating this—clarifying the relationship between democracy and independence—has been "self-determination." This is simply the action of a people to freely decide their own future. "Self-determination" has become one of the major forces guiding the international community over the past half century. The UN Charter in 1945 identified the "self-determination of peoples" as one of its basic principles, and in 1960 the General Assembly "upgraded" that principle to a "right" in its Declaration on Decolonization. The Assembly recognized the "passionate yearning for freedom" felt by all dependent peoples. It was aware of the increasing conflicts resulting from the denial of such freedom, which constituted a "serious threat to world peace." All peoples, said the Assembly, had an "inalienable right" to complete freedom, sovereignty, and the integrity of their national territory. By virtue of their right to self-determination, they could freely determine their political status and pursue their economic, social, and cultural development.[2]

But this did not necessarily mean independence: Self-determination could also be exercised through free association with, or by integration with, an existing independent state.[3] And the Assembly added that any attempt to disrupt a country's national unity was incompatible with UN principles.

Thus the balancing of two competing forces—justice (through the self-determination of peoples) and stability (through the unity of the nation-state)—was struck in the theoretical framework laid down early on by the international community. This dialectic lies at the heart of modern-day conflict, in all its forms, as will be seen below. Sustainable peace is more than stability at any one time; it is the proper fusion of stability and justice, on a self-regenerating basis.

The theory of self-determination begs many questions, however. What constitutes a "people," who decides, how, and upon what? In assisting non-self-governing territories to that end, all UN member states recognized that "the interests of the inhabitants of these territories are paramount." The administering powers accepted, as a "sacred trust," the obligation to promote to the utmost the well-being of such territories.

The Nature of Democracy

In contrast to "self-determination," the term "democracy" is not to be found in the UN Charter, which speaks rather of human rights and fundamental freedoms. Thus the international community recognized democracy as a politically subjective concept, rather than a juridical concept. The Universal Declaration of Human Rights (1948) speaks of a "democratic society" without defining the phrase.[4] The Vienna Declaration (1993) identifies "democracy" as an objective of the international community, also without defining the concept.[5] So while democracy has become established as a global goal, the term has been left so all-encompassing as to invite a continuation of struggle, and often conflict, within and between societies over its meaning and its attainment.

Although "democracy" is not explicitly identified, the Charter identifies respect for "human rights" and "fundamental freedoms" as one of the UN's four purposes. Both the Universal Declaration and its associated political rights covenant assert that "everyone has the right to take part in the government of his country, directly or through freely chosen representatives."[6] The authority to govern is to be based on "the will of the people as expressed in periodic and genuine elections." Those elections are to be held by universal and equal suffrage, and by secret vote or equivalent voting procedures, guaranteeing the free expression of the will of the electors.[7]

The balance between universality and particularity was explicitly captured for the first time in the Vienna Declaration, which accorded special recognition to the societal context of human rights. And successive General Assembly resolutions speak of the sovereign right of each state freely to choose and develop its political, economic, and cultural systems, "whether or not they conform to the preferences of other States." No single political system or electoral method, says the Assembly, is equally suited to all nations and their people.

In the real world, however, striking the correct balance between the "universal" and the "particular" in the democratization process is not a simple task. It is significant that Vienna, in its theoretical formulation, rendered the "particular" subordinate to the "universal." "All human rights," said the declaration, "are universal, indivisible and interdependent and interrelated. The international community must treat human rights globally in a fair and equal manner, on the same footing, and with the same emphasis. While the significance of national and regional particularities and various historical, cultural and religious backgrounds must be borne in mind, it is the duty of States, regardless of their political, economic and cultural systems, to promote and protect all human rights and fundamental freedoms."[8]

The institutional diversity of democracy has been explicitly affirmed by the UN Secretary General. While warning that resistance to the democratization process in some cases seems to "cloak authoritarianism in claims of cultural difference," he stresses the "undeniable fact" that there is no one model of democratization or democracy suitable to all societies. The reality is, he suggests, that individual societies decide if and when to begin democratization, and that, throughout that process, each society decides the nature and pace of democratization. "The starting point from which a society commences democratization will bear greatly upon such decisions."[9]

"Democracy" has always been subject to differing interpretations throughout the world. The modern era has witnessed tension over what might be called the "trialectic of democracy"—a dispute over three competing contexts: the political and the economic, the secular and the theocratic, and the modern and the traditional. Such a debate is subjective, however, since there is discord even over the frame of reference within which it must be pursued. Some embrace one form of "democracy" (liberal, secular, free-market) as the only genuine model of democracy, perceiving other "models" as threats to democracy itself. Others see that form as simply one model of democracy, reflecting one cultural background, and believe that other models can be realized. Yet others simply reject "democracy" as a concept if it is to be defined in purely liberal terms. But this preoccupation with definitions tends to impede a genuine debate over democracy and democratization at the international level.

Whether it comprises a challenge to democracy or a struggle between different versions, the points at issue have shifted markedly over time. The debate, for example, between capitalism ("political democracy" involving freedom of speech and enterprise) and communism ("economic democracy" involving freedom from poverty and inequality) characterized the global rivalry between the major powers from the 1950s through the 1980s. Whatever the theoretical merits of the issue, it was capitalism that ended up prevailing in the real world. It offered a vision of economic opportunity along with its political goals, while the latter failed to guarantee minimum political freedoms with its primary economic goals.

This ideological contest was replaced in the nineties by the debate between Asian and Western values and their implications for democracy. The impressive growth of many Asian economies generated theories that traditional values, based on social hierarchy and deference to authority in both private and public life, would trump modern values of liberalism and capitalism. Excessive freedoms and a lack of discipline within the West, it was held, spawned a social aimlessness and anomie, inviting the breakdown of societal cohesion and a sense of misdirection. The economic crisis of these economies peremptorily ended this debate, but the belief that modernity threatens traditional values and that an alternative to the liberal model of democracy must be found is a view still held by many.

Tension between traditionalism and modernity takes a milder, more poignant form in the democratization process of countries whose societal structures are still largely based on indigenous values, such as those in the South Pacific, some Buddhist societies in Asia, and some Arab and African nations. Such societies tend to prefer leadership through lineage—whether through legitimized monarchies (Jordan, Morocco, Tonga) or family dynasties (India, Sri Lanka, Pakistan, Syria, and perhaps Egypt and Azerbaijan in the future).[10] Such societies, however, embrace traditional values that have tended to minimize the political (though not necessarily the economic or social) status of women, and this is proving problematic to them as Western modernity sweeps around the planet. For its part, the United Nations strikes a balance between a vigorous promotion of women's rights and a certain deference to the stated need for the pace of change to be pursued within the context of national unity and stability.

With the waning of these two ideological contests a third has arisen more recently through an Islamic challenge to Western values. The Shiite theory of sovereignty, based on the philosophical premise that all authority (legislative, executive, judicial) derives from a single common source, the Quran, represented in the Velayat-e Faqih, challenges the separation theory of the West.[11] Comparable Sunni and Wahabi beliefs pertaining to communal and gender relationships also contrast with their Western counterparts. Yet the Islamic picture is inevitably complex—the Muslim world covers an array of political structures—from secular republics (Egypt, Turkey) through constitutional monarchies (Jordan, the Gulf states) to religious theocracies (Saudi Arabia, Iran).[12]

These theoretical contests are more than rhetorical—they reflect the intense struggle for global power that is the hallmark of human affairs. The first such struggle was manifested in a strategic nuclear confrontation that threatened the planet. The second contest was more economic than military in nature, and conducted with a Confucian dignity. The third has translated, in its extreme Taliban and Al-Qaida forms, into a seething opposition to Western values, ignited into violence by the Western military presence on the Arabian Peninsula, and culminating in the specter of global terrorism aimed at the leading Western power. The hot wars of the early twentieth century (1914–1945) were replaced by the Cold War of the late twentieth century (1948–1990) and the "war on terror" in the early twenty-first century (1998–?).

Not only in the Middle East but also in Southeast Asia, this interplay between contestable values forms the permeable membrane dividing liberation movements from terrorist activity in the confused struggle for the self-determination and self-expression of all peoples. Territorial dispute may be the most visible cause and independence the common goal of such conflict, but competition over "democracy" is the underlying issue.

During the past decade the United Nations has become increasingly active in the process of democratization. In 1989 the General Assembly initiated action for "enhancing the effectiveness of the principle of periodic and genuine elections"—the principle enshrined forty years earlier in the Universal Declaration. It asked the Commission on Human Rights to devise appropriate ways of promoting the principle.[13] In the early 1990s it noted the work of the commission and the UN Development Programme (UNDP) in assisting countries, at their request, "including those in transition to democracy." It affirmed that electoral verification by the UN should remain an "exceptional activity" to be undertaken in "well-defined circumstances," primarily in situations "with a clear international dimension." And it noted the Secretary General's criteria for agreeing to requests for electoral verification, and the establishment of an Electoral Assistance Unit.[14] In the mid-1990s it reaffirmed that "electoral assistance and support for the promotion of democratization" should be provided only at the specific request of a member state. But it also recalled the Vienna assertion that assistance in conducting free and fair elections was of particular importance for the strengthening of a "pluralistic civil society." It therefore endorsed further actions in support of democratization, including human rights education, legislative and judicial reform, civil service reform, and "governance."[15] By 2002 it had recognized the need for strengthening democratic processes, electoral institutions, and national capacity building (for fair elections, citizen participation, and civic education). It wished to continue to respond to the "evolving nature" of requests for assistance.[16]

Within that mandate for democratization the UN has become involved in constitutional reform, judicial administration, crime prevention, military demobilization and depoliticization, and capacity building in political participation, civil society, and media freedoms. The mandate does not explicitly acknowledge the relationship between democratization and conflict resolution, but rather rests its justification on the principle of periodic and genuine elections enshrined in declarations dating back to the 1940s. But in his *Agenda for*

Peace and his *Agenda for Development,* the Secretary General has drawn this link clearly enough, with the Assembly's endorsement.

The democratization process takes more forthright action when intervention is considered. The atrocities of the 1990s (Rwanda, Bosnia-Herzegovina, Kosovo), and indeed in the 1970s before that (Cambodia), gave rise to the notion of the "right of humanitarian intervention." This has been reshaped of late into the more politically palatable doctrine of a "responsibility to protect": if a government proves unable or unwilling to protect its own citizens from continuing and gross violations of human rights, then the responsibility to do so falls by default to the international community.[17] The aim of such intervention is to protect human rights, including those pertaining to democracy, and restore those rights to the people. But the doctrine of "protective intervention" has not yet been explicitly endorsed by the United Nations.

Amid these theoretical complexities the international community strives to defend and promote "democracy" without an agreed consensus over what it precisely is. Some progress has been made within the UN in recent years, however, in developing greater clarity toward a consensus on what is a politically charged concept. In February 2003 (and the preceding two years) the General Assembly declared that everyone was entitled to a "democratic and equitable international order." Democracy was not only a political concept but also had economic and social dimensions. It was imperative to ensure that globalization became a positive force "for all the world's people"; intolerance everywhere was aggravated by the inequitable distribution of wealth, marginalization, and social exclusion. Only through broad and sustained efforts, based on "common humanity in all its diversity," could globalization be made fully inclusive and equitable.[18] And in September 2003 the Secretary General stressed the important role civil society was playing in promoting good governance—without space for civil society, he said, the simple casting of votes becomes an "empty exercise."[19]

The Practical Experience: Democratization and Conflict

How does this theoretical framework relate to the democratization process in the East Asia Pacific subregion? How does the democratization process relate to conflict there?

Three stages can be identified for the countries of this subregion: those that have been through the democratization process, those experiencing violent conflict as they undergo the process, and those that may be experiencing tension but where violent conflict has not broken out and may never do so.

Some countries, such as Cambodia and East Timor, have formally been through the democratization process. They have, with UN assistance, been transformed from one-party systems to multiparty systems, with elections organized and verified by the UN. This is not, of course, to say that they have achieved the perfect "permanently peaceful" society.

In Cambodia the UN organized and conducted the elections in 1993 as part of the peace plan, and since then it has provided technical assistance for

Ineke Siegt/Panos Pictures

Queue of people waiting to vote in the referendum on East Timor's future. 78% voted for independence, which became a reality in May 2002.

national elections in 1998 and municipal elections in 2001. It has also provided judicial and human rights training and negotiated an arrangement for the joint prosecution of former combatants accused of genocide. In February 2003 the General Assembly recognized that the "tragic history" of Cambodia required "special measures" to ensure human rights protections. It acknowledged that the efforts of the Cambodian government had provided the basis for the restoration of peace and stability with the aim of achieving national reconciliation throughout the country. It remained concerned, however, over the continued problems pertaining to the rule of law and judicial administration. It encouraged the government to work toward "free and fair elections" in July, bearing in mind the concerns over acts of intimidation, violence, and reports of vote-buying.[20] In fact while Cambodian elections of the past decade have generally been marred by violence and corruption, the 2003 election featured less political disruption and greater opposition access to media than in the past.[21] Cambodia has come a long way in the past ten years, but there remains a long way to go before restorative justice and human rights are fully in place. The same must be said of East Timor, whose act of self-determination and successful UN-organized elections remains marred by continuing tensions and violence. In terms of a "strategic structure" for democracy, however, these two may be regarded as successes to date. The challenge facing East Timor now is to make these structures work toward achieving genuine democracy according to the will of the people.

Currently, the main conflict areas in the subregion are in China (Xinjiang, Tibet), Burma, Indonesia (Aceh, Maluku, East Timor, Irian Jaya/West Papua), Philippines (Mindanao), Papua New Guinea (Bougainville), the Solomon

Islands, and Fiji. The process of democratization through external assistance has attended to only some of these countries. But there are other localities in the subregion that have not broken into conflict because of UN involvement in the democratization process through successful acts of self-determination.

Self-Determination in Asia Pacific

In 1945, only fifty-one states signed the UN Charter, while some eighty-three colonies still existed. Eleven of these—those that had belonged to the defeated powers—became trust territories under the administration of victorious powers, and seventy-two others remained "non-self-governing territories" also under the latter's control. The acknowledged goal in all cases was an act of self-determination. Some other entities, such as East Timor, were added to the list after 1945. To date, all but sixteen territories have exercised their right to self-determination.

Three of the eleven trust territories were in the Pacific (none was in Asia). Each of these (Samoa, Papua New Guinea, and the Pacific Island Trust Territories), as well as several other non-self-governing territories in the subregion (Cook Islands, Tonga), have had unique experiences that have, for the most part, resulted in an avoidance of conflict.

Samoa. The Samoan islands came under foreign supervision in 1889 but were politically divided under a treaty arrangement whereby the United States annexed Eastern Samoa while Western Samoa became a German protectorate. Following World War I the League of Nations gave a mandate for Western Samoa to New Zealand but opposition to this arrangement led to a nationalist movement (1927–1936). Following World War II a Samoan request for independence was rejected, and it continued as a UN Trust Territory. Cabinet government was introduced in 1959, a new constitution adopted in 1961, and full independence achieved by agreement with New Zealand and the UN in 1962. Eastern Samoa, however, remains an "unincorporated territory" of the United States administered by the Department of the Interior. Its indigenous inhabitants are U.S. nationals but not citizens. It elects a governor and has a bicameral legislature, the Senate being chosen by tribal chiefs and the House being directly elected. It also elects a nonvoting delegate to the U.S. Congress.

Papua New Guinea. Papua New Guinea is an amalgam of several colonies. British New Guinea became Papua in 1906 under Australian control. Northeast Guinea was a German colony which Australia administered from 1920 under a League mandate, and Eastern New Guinea also came under Australian control. Administered as a UN Trust Territory from 1945, Papua New Guinea elected to merge into one independent state in 1975. With 3 million inhabitants speaking 700 languages, this was a remarkable achievement, and it is no less remarkable that, with the exception of Bougainville, there has been no significant conflict there.

Cook Islands. The Cook Islands, administered by New Zealand, opted in 1965 for the new arrangement of "free association" with the former administering power. Since then the Cooks have repeatedly declined full independence, preferring the benefits of an associative status with a larger country while enjoying increasing freedom of action including in the area of foreign policy.

Trust Territories. The Pacific Island Trust Territories opted for the same status. Sold by Spain to Germany and subsequently seized by Japan in 1914 before being taken over in 1945 by the United States, the territories achieved self-determination in 1994 by splitting into different entities. Between 1986 and 1994 the Marshall Islands, Micronesia, and Palau chose sovereign status in free association with the United States. The inhabitants of the Northern Marianas became U.S. citizens in 1986 under U.S. law, and the UN Security Council removed it from trusteeship in 1990.

Unresolved Conflicts
There remain, however, many unresolved conflicts in East Asia Pacific. How is the international community handling these, and to what extent is the process of democratization facilitating a transition?

Tibet. In the case of Tibet, the People's Republic of China announced shortly after the 1949 revolution the need to "liberate all Chinese territories" including Tibet, Xinjiang, Hainan, and Taiwan. Over the following two years Chinese forces occupied Tibet. El Salvador requested that China's "aggression against Tibet" be put on the UN agenda but India argued that a peaceful solution that would be advantageous to China, Tibet, and India could be reached by the three parties concerned. Thus Tibet has never been handled by the UN as a peace and security issue.

It has, however, been perceived as an issue of human rights. In 1951 China and Tibetan leaders signed an agreement governing the relationship between them, but an uprising in 1959 was suppressed by China and the Tibetan leader fled to India, where he has resided ever since. After renouncing the agreement he established a government-in-exile and formulated a plan offering to accept regional autonomy in exchange for recognition.[22] But China had itself already established an Autonomous Government of Tibet and thus rejected the plan.

China claims that before its liberation, Tibet was a feudal theocracy with slavery and serfdom, and that its economic system has advanced under the "plan of modernization" ever since. Although the Dalai Lama is feted in the West, he has been denounced by China as corrupt and a stooge of Western interests. During the 2000 Millennium Summit, the UN Secretary-General at China's behest omitted an invitation for him to attend a conference of religious leaders, explaining that the UN was "a house for the member states and their sensitivities matter." For their part the Tibetan exiles claim that China's occupation is a form of colonialism. In October 2002 the Dalai Lama called for reform of the United Nations to make itself more democratic by setting up a chamber of "representatives of humanity." The General Assembly and Human Rights Commissions have regularly condemned China for human rights violations in Tibet, but the issue is not seen at the UN as one of self-determination. A judgment of the democratic nature of Tibet as an autonomous part of China turns on one's understanding of the meaning of "democracy."

September 2003 saw signs of a potential rapprochement when the Dalai Lama met with Chinese academics in Boston, assuring them that Tibetans are not seeking independence today but rather a "meaningful form of self-rule within China." He recalled that he had once been attracted to the ideals of communism but had lost faith following the Great Leap Forward, the Cultural Revolution, and the Tibetan repression. He described a vision of a future in which Tibetans could govern themselves and preserve their unique culture, within China. The meeting itself could perhaps augur future contact for an amicable settlement on the Tibetan issue.

Burma/Myanmar. As with China, the principal issue in Burma/Myanmar concerns an opposition between "order" and "freedom," with the government ranking economic modernization as the top national priority. But unlike in China, whose government seeks to strike a balance, in Myanmar the military has simply taken power, ignored the democratic election results of 1990, and violated the human rights of its citizens. In the 1940s and 1950s, Burma enjoyed a reputation under its founding leader, U Nu, as an internationalist-minded country and a cofounder of the nonaligned movement. The 1962 coup by Ne Win, however, resulted in the abolition of the federal system and introduction of the "Burmese Way to Socialism," with a nationalized economy and single-party state. The new constitution of 1974 transferred power from the military to a People's Assembly and a multiparty system was reintroduced. In reaction to an economic crisis and riots in the late 1980s, however, the military assumed power again through the State Law and Order Restoration Council (SLORC), which declared martial law. The overwhelming electoral victory by the opposition National League for Democracy (NLD) was annulled by the SLORC,[23] which has detained the NLD leader, Aung San Suu Kyi, for extended periods on several occasions since the annulled elections.

Despite the clear violation of democracy in Myanmar, both China and the Association of Southeast Asian Nations (ASEAN), which have the greatest influence on the country, accept the situation as, on balance, in the best interests of the people. China's president visited Myanmar in 2001, declaring support for the regime while urging faster economic progress. ASEAN admitted Myanmar to its membership in 1997 and has developed supportive economic links with it. ASEAN stresses the "centrality of the principle of consent by the parties concerned in paving the way for third party adjudication" and thus has no intention of pressuring the regime to surrender power to the opposition party based on an election result from over a decade ago. For ASEAN as for China, stability and the avoidance of interstate conflict override liberal aspirations in determining the pace of the democratization process.

The UN has a different approach. The General Assembly, in its most recent action, has affirmed that the "will of the people" had been clearly expressed in the 1990 elections and that a "genuine democratic government" there was essential for the realization of all human rights. It expressed concern over the "ongoing systematic violation" of those rights, and urged the government to "restore democracy and implement the 1990 election results," ensuring that contact with the NLD leaders move without delay into "substantive and structured dialogue towards democratization."[24] The Secretary-General has appointed a special envoy to engage in dialogue with the regime and the Assembly has appealed for a constructive response from Myanmar, but progress is slow.

Philippines. The Philippines, predominantly Roman Catholic, has faced an independence movement from Islamic groups in the southern islands, centering on Mindanao. This is a complex situation between the competing groups. The Moro National Liberation Front (MNLF), with mediation from the Organization of the Islamic Conference (principally from Libya and Indonesia), concluded a peace agreement with the government (1976, finalized in 1996). This led to the establishment of an autonomous region in Muslim Mindanao, with an MNLF leader as governor (his predecessor having been jailed for an insurrection in November 2001). The Moro Islamic Liberation Front (MILF), a more militant rebel group, split from the MNLF in 1977 in favor of a separate Islamic state. The stalled peace talks between the MILF and the government of the Republic of the Philippines may resume in Oslo in June 2004, after the general elections of May 10. Another group, Abu Sayyaf, is smaller and more radical still. It is labeled a "terrorist group" by both Manila and Washington.

Essentially, the conflict derives from a belief within the religious minority that their basic human rights have been systematically violated by the "colonial government" in Manila. As with so many cases (Tibet, Bougainville, Aceh) the question turns on whether autonomy or independence is sufficient for their stated interests. In December 2001 the MNLF petitioned the Secretary-General to put the issue of Mindanao independence, along with a draft declaration of independence, before the UN Decolonization Committee, but this has not been done.

Fiji. In the South Pacific the UN has promoted democratization through electoral assistance and observation. In Fiji, following a coup in 2001 and in response to a request from the caretaker government, the UNDP provided technical support to the electoral authorities and the Secretary-General authorized the UN Fiji Electoral Observer Mission to monitor the general elections there and the immediate postelection environment.[25] Prior to that, following an earlier coup in 1987, the British Commonwealth had organized a review commission to redraft the constitution. Fiji's political instability is rooted in the ethnic makeup of the nation. Native Fijians compose only slightly more than half of the population. Indo-Fijian descendants of contract laborers from the Indian subcontinent compose about 44 percent of the population, but they have a disproportionately dominant position in the Fijian economy. Resentment on the part of native Fijians has been a recurring theme throughout the postindependence period. The revised constitution adopted in 1997 provided for a power-sharing arrangement but after elections were held in 2002, the new prime minister formed a government that contravened this principle, excluding in particular the major Indo-Fijian party. In July 2003 the Fiji Supreme Court ruled that the prime minister had breached the constitution.

Bougainville. In Bougainville a separatist movement seeking independence from Papua New Guinea (PNG) developed in the 1980s over mineral exploitation by "postcolonial" interests. Mediation was undertaken by Australia and New Zealand with the approval of the Pacific Forum. The UN endorsed the regional peace monitoring group and an international civilian transition team is now helping to establish genuine autonomy there. This twenty-year conflict has been settled through the democratization process and successful conflict resolution techniques.

West Papua/Irian Jaya. West Papua/Irian Jaya was part of the Dutch East Indies during colonial times. Ethnically Papuan and an integral part of the Papua-New Guinea island, it was retained by the Netherlands after Indonesian independence but subsequently turned over to the UN on the understanding that administrative authority would be transferred to Indonesia pending an act of self-determination. In 1969 Indonesia staged an "act of free choice" by convening eight regional consultative assemblies, all of which voted for annexation with Indonesia. Many Papuans complained of repression and expressed a desire for independence. In 1971 a "provisional revolutionary government of West Papua New Guinea" was established by insurgents. The Free Papua Organization (OPM) has been active ever since and in the 1980s a series of offensives by the Indonesian armed forces resulted in a refugee influx into PNG. In 1998 a cease-fire was signed between Indonesia and the OPM, but the political issue has yet to be resolved.

New Caledonia. New Caledonia was annexed by France in 1854 and is administered as an "overseas territory." An independence movement gained momentum in the late 1970s, followed by a decade of violence during which the South Pacific Forum successfully petitioned the United Nations to reinscribe the territory on its list of non-self-governing territories. The Matignon Accords of 1988 divided the territory into three autonomous regions (one dominated by French settlers and two by the indigenous Kanaks), envisaging a referendum on independence by 1999. In the late 1990s tensions continued over the precise nature of the proposed referendum (a "consensus proposal" or a choice between independence or continued French status). The 1998 Nouméa Accord established "shared sovereignty" with a newly elected national congress. The UN welcomed the accord as aimed at "taking more broadly into account" the Kanak identity in the political and social organization of the territory. In February 2003 the General Assembly invited France and New Caledonia to promote a framework for the peaceful progress of the territory toward an act of self-determination "in which all options are open." This would be based on the principle that "it is for the populations of New Caledonia to choose to control their own destiny."[26]

French Polynesia. French Polynesia is also a French overseas territory, but France has opposed its inscription as a non-self-governing territory at the UN. In the late 1990s nationalist leaders petitioned the South Pacific Forum to have it reinstated on the UN's decolonization agenda.[27] The relationship between democracy and independence in French Polynesia will become an issue for the future.

Understanding Democracy: The Cultural Dimension

As the Secretary-General has observed, "while democracy can and should be assimilated by all cultures and traditions, it is not for the United Nations to offer a model of democratization or democracy or to promote democracy in a specific case. Indeed, to do so could be counter-productive to the process of democratization which, in order to take root and to flourish, must derive from the society itself. Each society must be able to choose the form, pace and character of its democratization process. Imposition of foreign models not only contravenes the Charter principle of non-intervention in internal affairs, it may also generate resentment among both the Government and the public, which may in turn feed internal forces inimical to democratization and the idea of democracy."[28]

The unanswered question that derives from this observation, however, is whether an indigenous kind of democracy can be devised without the institutional features of the liberal model. More than most regions, the Pacific holds the prospect of developing insights into this issue because of its distinctive cultural traditions.

The Pacific Way

Efforts to marry the modern with the traditional in the democratization process have been under way in the Pacific region for some time now. The conventions and declarations of the regional body, the Pacific Islands Forum, reflect this dualism. They defer to universal democratic principles yet also stress "indigenous values" and "Pacific customs and traditions."[29] These values and traditions downplay separateness, competitiveness, and exclusion in society and politics, and stress unity, consensus, and inclusiveness. The interplay between European and Polynesian values within a "liberal" democratic context is evident in several current issues within New Zealand/Aotearoa (see Box 6.1).

Pacific nations, moreover, wish to proceed at their own pace with the process of democratization. For a rare glimpse into how the process might be softly and slowly encouraged in a traditional society with respect and deference to the indigenous lines of authority, the Modern House of Tokelau—on three tiny atolls in the South Pacific—is perhaps as good as it gets (see Box 6.2).

Box 6.1   Bicultural Value Differences Within a Democratic Nation: Two Current Issues in New Zealand–Aotearoa

Two issues under debate in New Zealand–Aotearoa during 2003 give some insight into the political forces at play in a bicultural society that aspires to maintain a sustainable democracy. They highlight the imperative of striking "middle ground" between different value systems within the same society.

The Nation's Foreshore and Seabed
An issue has arisen over title to the nation's foreshore and seabed. For the indigenous Maori people, who have held grievances over loss of land since early British colonial days in the mid–nineteenth century, not only the "ownership" of the land is a sensitive issue but also the nature of that "ownership." The government's proposal of August 2003 to designate the foreshore and seabed as "public domain" rather than claim Crown title is an attempt to strike middle ground between extreme *pakeha* ("white person"—i.e., European) and Maori views. The proposal involves (1) clarifying legislation to ensure that the foreshore and seabed are not subject to private rights of ownership and (2) recognition and protection of Maori customary rights in relation to these areas including recognition of their *mana* (influence plus prestige) over, or ancestral connection with, an area. The proposal deliberately states that nobody "owns" the foreshore and seabed—that is, no one has fee simple title.[30] This issue, however, has become a "defining moment" in the building of a country's nationhood. As Colin James has put it:

> A nation is built on agreed foundations and the shared experiences of many generations. In the 1970s this was easily stated: we were building a European nation with Pacific tack-ons. The law was derived from the common law. The institutions were English. The ethic was Judeo-Christian. Reason and scientific enquiry were the bases of knowledge. . . . But there has always been another foundation and another set of experiences here. That other nation is animist, its knowledge spiritual as much as experiential. The institutions are tribal. The law is derived . . . from relationships. Those relationships are not just with people or even just with other living things, but with everything. "*Pakeha* law is sterile and devoid of connection to spiritual relationships," [Maori lawyer Annette] Sykes said. . . . In Sykes' law, in the Maori-descended nation, ownership is a relationship for a particular purpose. Those in a *whanau* (extended family group), *hapu* (sub-tribe) or *iwi* (tribe) who share the connection share the ownership. The exclusion is of other *whanau, hapu* and *iwi* (including *tau iwi,* non-Maori) and is exclusion from the particular use, not title in the English sense. . . . So this is a defining moment for Maori. But for non-Maori from the one-nation 1970s, it is a long trek.[31]

Pacific Style of Justice
New Zealand's system of "restorative justice" is being adopted in Britain. The system has transformed the way juvenile offenders are treated, bringing criminals and victims face-to-face and assigning responsibility for retribution

(continues)

Box 6.1 Cont.

to families and the community. Based on concepts rooted in ancient Maori and Pacific tradition, it is internationally admired and is being emulated by a number of countries. The aim is to keep young people out of court, reduce recidivism, and give victims a meaningful role in the legal process. A punishment plan, often involving an apology, community work, and financial reparation, is drawn up and must be approved by all parties before ratification by a judge. The offender gets a clean slate after completing the plan. If not, a court case and possible custodial sentence are in store. Neal Cleaver, senior restorative justice manager in the New Zealand government, says, "A lot of people think it's a soft option. But it's actually harder than going to court. Facing your victim across the room is probably the hardest part of all. It's about shaming people—in a positive way—and healing. Europeans usually deal with criminals by outlawing them. Maori and Pacific Islander culture is inclusive. You're born into a structure that you are kept within, no matter how unacceptably you behave."[32]

Box 6.2 Democratization: Slowly and Softly—The Tokelau Experiment

An effort to marry the modern with the traditional in the democratization process is under way with Tokelau. The process of planning and developing Tokelau's future has been cautious and gradual. In recent years it has revolved around the concept of the "Modern House of Tokelau." This is an initiative of the Tokelauans themselves, and it aims to provide a "governance structure that fits Tokelau's cultural context." The project is seen as a critical part of the movement toward Tokelau's act of self-determination. The leadership views it as the framework within which future decisions as to Tokelau's development will be made.

A project approach was selected by New Zealand and Tokelau for the flexibility it allowed in concentrating on the tasks that needed to be done. Overseeing the project is a joint committee, which includes the political leaders of Tokelau and its (New Zealand) administrator. The committee has established a transition team to support the implementation of the project and facilitate the intensive consultation that is necessary to ensure its success. Over half the adult population of Tokelau has been involved in the consultation phase.

The movement involves building and developing Tokelau's future governance structure around the traditional authority of the village council. It is based on the principle that the traditional *taupulega* (village council) should be the foundation of any such structure, while recognizing that it is appropriate to have some functions performed through a national administration. Establishing the balance between these considerations will be a matter to be determined at the local level—with the *taupulega*. This is to be done in various ways: first, by combining traditional decisionmaking processes with modern advice and support, thereby allowing decisionmaking to meet the modern needs of Tokelau; second, by reestablishing the village as the focus of

(continues)

Box 6.2 Cont.

---

social and economic activity; and third, by transferring appropriate functions from national level of management to village management, while consolidating other functions that can be more effectively carried out at the national level.

Experience with the movement has demonstrated the need for different approaches and structures, and a different pace of progress, on each atoll. Of greatest concern is the need for constant communication with the *toeaina* (elders) and the *nuku* (village). Even though there have been many meetings with the *taupulega* and their communities, and many publications and radio contact, there remains a need to gain an understanding with, and regularly inform, the people of Tokelau about the project's goals and its progress.[33]

Experience shows that the pluralistic, competitive, multiparty system can exacerbate ethnic divisions, as has occurred in Fiji and elsewhere outside the region.[34] The two Eminent Persons Groups of the Pacific Forum in the Solomons and Fiji and the Commonwealth Special Envoy to Tonga all find themselves obliged to address this issue. To this day traditionalism still confronts modernity in the democratization process in the Pacific. In American Samoa, for example, the island's representative to the United States once reminded a nonplussed Congress that "only the chiefs tend to speak at village meetings, demonstrating once again the classic difficulty of overlaying Western institutions on non-Western societies."[35]

Yet even the "Pacific Way" is under siege as an indirect result of the modern pressures of terrorism. The urgent need for radical action to safeguard national security felt by the United States at the global level and Australia at the regional level is making inroads on the "softer approach" to life and society in what was once a genuinely tranquil subregion. Reference to traditional values appears to have been downgraded in the Biketawa Declaration of 2000, and is completely absent in the latest Nasonini Declaration of 2002. Both declarations are seen to be facilitating intervention in the subregion. But the regional peacekeeping force that recently entered the Solomon Islands was deployed in direct response to a governmental request to rescue a state that had nearly collapsed. The intervention was endorsed by both the Pacific Forum and the UN, and has not engendered any real opposition. It remains to be seen, however, whether Australia will, as it has indicated, intervene one day without such approval if it perceives its vital interests to be at stake.

The process of globalization, which imposes Western cultural values and economic values upon these societies faster than they wish, often tends to exacerbate a situation where a society is in any case already threatened with conflict. In such cases, no amount of well-intentioned assistance from multilateral or Western donors to promote "good governance" (crime prevention and anticorruption, public administration and law reform) will ameliorate matters until an underlying consensus is reached on the philosophical tenets of democracy. Indeed, these tensions become more acutely felt as the focus moves along the "spectrum of democratization" from the "safe" to the "sensitive" issues—from issues such as effective public administration and law enforcement, toward issues such as media freedoms, judicial independence, and multiparty politics.

In the final analysis, the ultimate goal of "democracy" needs to be better understood. If it is to confer participatory rights on the people, different methods can be devised. If it is to establish sovereignty and legitimize the exercise of supreme powers, different beliefs can prevail. If it is to provide a mechanism for changing leadership, different models can suffice that account for cultural variations in respect for authority and accountability. And all of this can be done while faithfully hewing to universal rights within each society. Only when an appreciation of the different models for democracy is realized will the international community achieve lasting progress in the painstaking process of democratization and its contribution to conflict resolution.

Dr. Kennedy Graham is currently senior fellow in the Peace & Governance Division of the United Nations University. He served in the New Zealand Foreign Service for sixteen years, subsequently working in New York and Stockholm before joining the United Nations. He was director of the UNU's Leadership Academy in Amman, Jordan, from 1999 to 2002. He is the author of three books on global governance and international relations, most recently The Planetary Interest: A New Concept for the Global Age *(UCL Press/Rutgers University Press, 1999).*

Notes

1. "Democratization is a process which leads to a more open, more participatory, less authoritarian society. Democracy is a system of government which embodies, in a variety of institutions and mechanisms, the ideal of political power based on the will of the people." UN Secretary-General Boutros Boutros-Ghali, *Supplement to "An Agenda for Democratization,"* December 1996 [hereafter: *Supplement*]. See also *Support by the UN System of the Efforts of Governments to Promote and Consolidate New or Restored Democracies,* A/50/332, August 1995 and A/51/512, October 1996.

2. *Declaration on the Granting of Independence to Colonial Countries and Peoples,* UNGA Resolution 1514 (XV). This was made binding law in the International Civil and Political Rights Covenant (Article 1.1), concluded in 1966, in force since 1976.

3. UNGA Resolution 1541 (XV).

4. The declaration refers to the "just requirements of morality, public order and the general welfare in a democratic society." This appears in Article 29 on "duties and limitations" of individual rights, and ironically it was (precommunist) China that proposed that this become the declaration's penultimate rather than its second article on the grounds that it was illogical to foresee limitations on rights before identifying them. See A. Eide et al., *The Universal Declaration of Human Rights: A Commentary* (Oslo: Scandinavian University Press, 1992), pp. 449–465.

5. World Conference on Human Rights, *Vienna Declaration and Programme of Action,* June 1993.

6. UDHR, art. 21.1; ICCPR, art. 25.1.

7. UDHR, art. 21.3; ICCPR, art. 25.2.

8. World Conference on Human Rights, *Vienna Declaration and Programme of Action.*

9. *Supplement,* para. 4.

10. Among Western societies, only the United States tends to have dynastic political families.

11. Three views of Velayat-e Faqih compete. The "official" view of the Iranian government is that the "absolute, appointive, velayat-e faqih" is binding on the people as a religious duty, that legitimization of public decisions rests on the supreme jurist; and that democracy is neither desirable nor beneficial. The "reformist" view holds that neither absolute appointive velayat-e faqih nor democracy is entirely acceptable, and an Islamic democracy can be attained through "elective, conditional velayat-e faqih." The "intellectual" view is that Velayat-e Faqih, being an autocratic rule of God through the divine right of jurists, is incompatible with democracy. See Mohsen Kadivar, "Veleyat-e Faqih and Democracy," www.kadivar.com/Htm/English/Papers/Velayat-e%20Faghih.htm

12. Several states observe "Islamic values" (Pakistan, Sudan) yet remain secular republics. Some subnational states have adopted *sharia* law and become theocracies, for example in Malaysia and Nigeria.

13. A/RES/44/146, December 15, 1989.

14. A/RES/46/137, December 17, 1991; and A/RES/47/138, December 18, 1992.

15. A/RES/49/190, December 23, 1994.

16. A/RES/56/159, February 20, 2002.

17. See "The Responsibility to Protect: Report of the International Commission on Intervention and State Sovereignty" (Ottawa: IDRC, 2001).

18. A/RES/57/213, February 25, 2003 (and 56/151 and 55/107 before it).

19. Statement by UN Secretary-General to the Fifth International Conference on New or Restored Democracies (UN Press Release, September 10, 2003). Two months earlier the Assembly had also recognized the "important supporting role" of civil society in conflict prevention (A/RES/57/337, July 3, 2003).

20. A/RES/57/225, February 26, 2003.

21. International observers are reported to have been pleased with the election process. See http://news.bbc.co.uk/2/hi/asia-pacific/3102025.stm.

22. The Five-Point Plan of 1987, subsequently expanded upon in the Strasbourg Proposal.

23. Subsequently renamed the State Peace and Development Council.

24. A/RES/57/231, February 28, 2003.

25. UN Doc. A/56/344, October 19, 2001.

26. A/RES/57/136, February 25, 2003.

27. *Political Handbook of the World 1999,* Arthur S. Bankis and Thomas C. Muller, eds. (CSA Publications, Binghamton University/State University of New York Press, 1999), p. 351.

28. *Supplement,* para. 10.

29. See the Honiara (1992), Aitutaki (1997), and Biketawa (2000) Declarations of the South Pacific Forum.

30. See the New Zealand government website, www.beehive.govt.nz.

31. *New Zealand Herald,* August 26, 2003.

32. See *The Independent,* and *New Zealand Herald,* August 26, 2003.

33. See the Tokelau website, www.tokelau.org.nz.

34. A similar situation is faced in Guyana, in Latin America.

35. *Political Handbook 1999,* p. 1051.

7

Lessons Learned from Peacebuilding Practices in Asia Pacific

Jim Wake

War, we were told by Karl von Clausewitz,[1] is nothing but the continuation of politics by other means. Unfortunately, it often seems easier to engage in warfare than in politics. In some parts of the world, including much of Asia and the Pacific, politics is especially difficult. The legacy of colonialism has forced some peoples together who have little in common, and divided others who belong together. Traditional systems of governance have been replaced by newer ones that may be alien, if not inappropriate, to indigenous cultures and their traditional structures of governance. Civil society is underdeveloped, and military structures, by comparison, are highly developed. Often, when conflict looms, there are no spaces where political discourse can take place. Violence is not so much the continuation of politics by other means, but rather the path of least resistance.

One of the most important elements of peacebuilding in Asia and the Pacific, then, involves the creation of those spaces—both actual and metaphorical— where people can come to know each other, know and understand each other's grievances, engage in dialogue, and discover where their common interests intersect, rather than conflict

When we speak of "lessons learned," "best practices," or as some prefer, merely "better practices," we can mean several things. First, these terms may refer to the type of intervention selected to try to address a conflict or a potential conflict. Clearly, there are many choices available at each level (though not all choices are available to all actors). Some have proven to be more effective than others. At any rate, the particular context in which one operates, and the specific objectives one identifies, will be of crucial importance in informing these choices. Second, best practices and lessons learned may refer to the actual *implementation* practice—how to structure an intervention, what particular strategies work well, what to look out for, what sorts of individuals should be involved, how to get the message out, and so on. Beyond that, there are lessons to be learned from an examination of the ways in which a range of initiatives—multi-track approaches—complement each other (or in some cases, sow confusion and distrust).

Interventions take place at various levels—from the grassroots to the international arena, with a range of methodologies and a range of objectives. Some are direct efforts to resolve or transform conflict or, following a conflict, to achieve reconciliation by reducing the levels of antagonism between communities and healing the emotional wounds suffered during the conflict. Others focus on creating an environment where the risks of violent conflict are reduced by disarmament, demobilization, or security-sector reform. Still others focus on building the institutions of a stable and nonviolent society—democratic institutions, systems of justice, and civil society itself. And some aim to change attitudes through education or the use of the media, or try to provide those working to prevent and transform conflict with the skills, tools, and connections to be more effective in their work. Conflict resolution scholar Kevin Clements, discussing the objectives of those intervening in conflict zones, distinguishes four main categories:

- Those supplying emergency relief and assistance
- Those working on the medium- to long-term economic and social development
- Those concerned with social justice, human rights advocacy, and monitoring
- Those specifically focused on the nonviolent resolution of conflict and long-term peacebuilding[2]

This chapter surveys a wide (but not exhaustive) range of interventions that run the gamut, in terms of focus, methodologies, and objectives. Loosely, they are organized from small-scale grassroots to massive international efforts. They are "exemplary" not in the sense that they are models to be copied exactly, or that they represent any "ideal," but rather in the sense that each case discussed offers important lessons to those confronted with similar issues and challenges. Indeed, these cases are intended to provide a view of both what works and what doesn't, based on both published reports and the first-hand experiences of peacebuilders. Each of the following nine sections represents both a general lesson on the application of a strategy or tactic, as well as more specific lessons relating to that strategy.

Learning from the Experience of Others

What's All the Fighting About? Identifying the Issues

In many civil conflicts, the conflict seems to take on a life of its own and the adversaries lose sight of their objectives. It may well be that what separates the adversaries is far less than what it appears to be, and that "winning" becomes an end in itself, more important even than solving those problems or redressing those grievances that originally sparked the conflict. By implication, it can be extremely useful, early on in a conflict intervention, to identify the underlying issues. In so doing, it will also be evident where there is common ground—shared objectives, common grievances, mutually compatible agendas.

Matthew Wale, who has been deeply involved in conflict resolution work in the Solomon Islands, notes that in the civil conflict that has devastated this country since 1999—and this is true in many other conflict situations as well—the antagonists probably agree on far more than they disagree on. The conflict broke out in 1999, sparked by resentment on the part of the Isatabu, the indigenous residents of Guadalcanal, against immigrants from the neighboring island of Malaita. But that resentment was not rooted in racism or ethnic hatred. Rather, says Wale, it was rooted primarily in a sense of injustice about the ownership and exploitation of land, with a history dating back to colonial times under the British. The British had sidestepped the traditional landownership system, in which land is passed on to succeeding generations through the maternal line, and given to settlers from other islands, including Malaita. However, explains Wale, the settlers went further, and began—outside of the traditional system of land transfer—to make deals for land with some of the Isatabu men. Tensions grew steadily and eventually evolved into an organized campaign to drive the Malaitan settlers from Guadalcanal, involving deadly clashes between rival militias. The Isatabu have the sense that the Malaitans are occupying Isatabu land. But the Malaitans came as settlers, not as conquerors, originally settling on land offered by the British, and now have nowhere to go. "It's a just cause—the exploitation of land and redistribution of the profits," observes Wale. "They are bona fide issues that don't concern one group; they concern everybody. The land issue is a national issue."

Rather than focusing on what were the flashpoints in the conflict—demands that prisoners be released, that free access be granted to areas cut off by roadblocks, or that compensation be given for losses suffered in the conflict—"we decided to look at the underlying issues," Wale explains. Those underlying issues, he says, relate to principles of reciprocity—the notion that if you don't want a certain fate, such as murder or rape, to befall one of your own people, then you will agree that it also should not happen to the other. As such, then, it is an acceptance of certain basic human rights, including land rights. "Once we found those, we saw that they were fundamentally the same—70 percent in common. And this builds confidence. These people both have just cause."[3]

Finding the common ground creates an opportunity for resolution. In this case, that might have been achieved by addressing those common grievances through legal or constitutional channels. Unfortunately, even best practices cannot overcome intransigence: The situation in the Solomons did improve briefly, but violence and lawlessness continued—until the Australia-led intervention in July 2003.

Identifying the *underlying* issues may also reveal that a conflict that is perceived to be "ethnic" or "religious" in nature is nothing of the sort, or that it is far more complex. The conflicts in Mindanao and Maluku, for example, are often viewed as Muslim-Christian conflicts—which they are, in a sense, but not in the sense that they pit the groups against each other on the basis of their religious beliefs.

It may be true, in the conflict in Mindanao, as well as in others in Bougainville, the Solomons, and Kalimantan, that the antagonism is often couched in ethnic and religious rhetoric. But in fact, quite often these conflicts are far more about perceptions of justice and injustice, about power, and about the sharing of resources. And many are about the marginalization of a weaker or less developed group by a dominant group and culture. If mediators, and indeed the parties to the conflict, can come to recognize this, and to distinguish between differences in culture and belief that result in conflict, they will be more inclined to address the real, underlying sources of conflict and to find strategies for resolving the conflict.

Using What You've Got: Drawing upon Moral Agency and Customs

In many of the conflicts that have afflicted Southeast Asia and the Pacific, outside parties have stepped in to act as mediators, relying on what might be described as "classic" conflict resolution approaches—negotiating around a table to achieve cease-fires, to separate adversaries, to seal peace agreements, and to enforce the terms of those agreements. But often—perhaps far more often than the international community recognizes—mechanisms already exist, and have existed for generations, that can be utilized to resolve conflict.

In the Solomon Islands conflict, Australia played a leading role in efforts to end the fighting, and in October 2000 rival militias signed the Townsville Peace Agreement. But the agreement failed to bring real peace or to resolve the fundamental issues around the conflict, violence continued to flare, and the armed elements within the conflicting parties faced off against each other at many locations on Guadalcanal.

In these circumstances, several initiatives were undertaken to try to reduce tensions using the moral authority of religious and traditional leaders. These local efforts, which used "customary" structures and the influence of the religious communities, did have a significant effect.

Matthew Wale explains how it was possible to assert that moral authority. "We've got chiefs, [but] we don't have a highly structured chiefly system. There are people both in the traditional structure and also in the religious community. So it's a fairly convenient mechanism to use. Obviously we have a vested interest—to re-empower the traditional structures and to see how they might re-emerge stronger. And so in that sense, we used religion. We used the church to re-empower the traditional governing structures."[4]

What Wale did, among other things, was to write several pastoral letters, and then, especially in areas where militancy was prevalent, distribute them in the name of the bishop to local churches. The letters were then read from the pulpit on selected Sundays. The message—the sermon of the week—in the reading would be that violence was inappropriate because the traditional system was in place to resolve the disputes. "We were sort of channeling all that grievance back into the traditional system. The traditional system can handle this—it's a tried and tested system. It's what we've got—the only thing we've got—so we should work towards using it."

Wale says that the Solomon Islands government and the militants who were involved in the violence actively attempted to undermine the system, and that for several years a small minority refused to acknowledge the authority of the traditional structures. "But now we see they are all coming back," he says, "because they know of no other system that is robust enough to address their grievances. So I think we are seeing a resurgence of recognition for the traditional structures." But the turmoil has caused serious damage. The traditional structures still do not enjoy the recognition that they previously enjoyed, but Wale believes a recovery is under way and will continue.

Another strategy that proved effective in the Solomons was to engage women, who occupy a position of respect in the island cultures, in a peacemaking role. The woman visited the camps of the militias engaged in the conflict and appealed, as mothers speaking to their sons, to end the violence.

A third significant agent for peace, actually beginning well before the Townsville Peace Agreement, was a religious order known as the Melanesian Brotherhood, a male Anglican religious community with a significant presence in the Solomons. As described in a paper by Brother Richard Carter, "The ethos of the community is to live the religious life but in a Melanesian, indigenous way" that "tries to reflect many of the strengths of Melanesian tradition."[5] The Melanesian Brotherhood is especially notable because it draws members from all communities of the Solomons, and thus could bridge the ethnic divide between the indigenous residents of Guadalcanal and the Malaitan settlers. According to Carter, the brotherhood is highly respected and trusted in Melanesian society, with people ascribing an almost mystical "spiritual power and holiness" to it. And so the brotherhood came to play both a humanitarian and a peacemaking role in the conflict. When Malaitans were driven from their homes, the brotherhood and an affiliated female Christian order offered them refuge in their own headquarters, and the Isatabu militias respected the sanctuary provided by the religious communities. The religious communities were also able to move freely when, at the height of the conflict, the militias were severely restricting movement on Guadalcanal. In this way, they were able to escort people across battle lines, and to provide medicine and vital supplies to villages and homes cut off by the fighting.

In May 2000, writes Carter, the Melanesian Brotherhood took the decision to work actively for peace, rather than simply engaging in humanitarian activities. Members of the brotherhood were sent into conflict zones and placed themselves—unarmed—between the opposing militias, appealing "in the name of Jesus Christ" to end the killing, hatred, and vengeance.[6]

Largely through the moral authority they asserted, they were able to keep the two sides apart, and on several occasions were able to successfully negotiate the release of hostages taken by the militias. Carter believes that the religious communities were able to function as peacemakers because "in a very real sense people feel they belong to the whole of Melanesia," that they had no ulterior motive for their engagement, and that they represented a "Christian expression of indigenous Melanesia culture."[7] He adds that many of the brothers were contemporaries of the militants, had known them personally before the conflict began, or forged friendships in the midst of the conflict.

Militants treated them with a mixture of annoyance, gratitude, and awe, since even though they were getting in the way of their plans and lines of attack, they were nevertheless bringing a sense of providential protection to the front line. Militants were frightened of disobeying the requests or demands the brothers made for fear that they would lose the blessing and thus the protection of God. Melanesians have a deep belief in the world of spirits, devils, and ancestors and were nervous of the consequences of God's anger or curse.

Carter points to several important lessons learned from the experience of the Melanesian Brotherhood and other religious communities in the Solomons:[8]

- The *adat* system had been undermined and so it was necessary to restore its credibility as a system for conflict resolution.[9]
- The brotherhood had credibility because its integrity was unquestioned and it was viewed as an impartial mediator.
- The reconcilers were themselves reconciled—the diversity of the community was not itself a source of conflict.
- The brotherhood was viewed as "belonging" to the people, and living according to and embracing both indigenous and Christian values. Their credibility was enhanced because they had a history of community peacebuilding.
- The peacemakers' credibility was enhanced because they didn't seek publicity, recognition, or personal gain.
- The restoration of the community was viewed as more important than individual rights and wrongs.
- Respect for traditional authority was enhanced by inclusiveness, extending to inclusion of the young and disaffected.
- Peacemaking involved not just words but also symbol and action.
- Conflict reconciliation involved reciprocal action and the conscious choice to renew a relationship.

Empowering People at the Grassroots: Bottom-Up Organizing

How can individuals and organizations make a difference in conflict situations if they are working at the grassroots level? From a grassroots initiative in Ambon, Maluku (Indonesia), come important insights.

In Ambon, Ichsan Malik has, through persistence and patience, succeeded in bringing Christians and Muslims together for an ongoing dialogue aimed at halting communal violence.[10] Without a bottom-up approach, Malik believes, conflict management efforts in situations of sectarian violence are doomed to failure. He also emphasizes the importance of first strengthening the local base, and only addressing the national government when the local base is secured. Malik stresses that the purpose of the bottom-up approach is not to undermine efforts on the part of authorities in government or international organizations to resolve conflict, but to give the people involved in the conflict a sense of empowerment.

Malik serves as the facilitator of BakuBae (Reconciliation), which has been active in Maluku since early 2000, a little more than a year after the sectarian violence erupted on Ambon. Getting the project going took some considerable effort. "I tried to knock on doors of Christian and Muslim militants, and the police and the military for two months," he says. "I asked: Can I do something as a mediator?" But his offers were rejected. People, it seemed, believed that all peace initiatives should originate with the government or with the military. In fact, hard-line Muslim clerics even issued a fatwa prohibiting Muslims from cooperating with Malik's initiatives.

What finally made the difference, he says, was demonstrating that ordinary people supported his position. To do that, he undertook public opinion polling with the help of six Muslims and six Christians who canvassed people in their communities. A first poll showed fairly low levels of support, but a second poll showed a marked increase, and with the benefit of a "mandate" based on the polling results, Malik felt confident enough to begin actual conflict transformation work.

He describes a three-stage approach in a BakuBae's brochure titled *Reweaving Maluku's Future:*

Stop violence. In the first stage, a joint working group is established with representation from local figures. Workshops are held to bring together key figures such as traditional village heads, community defenders, local dignitaries from the conflicting communities, and victims. Gradually, more people are brought into the network as the campaign to end violence progresses, including village leaders, youth leaders, traditional leaders, military and police officers, lawyers, educators, religious leaders, women, nongovernmental organization (NGOs), and small vendors. The campaign includes dialogue, media activities, and also efforts to build solidarity in the international community and the Maluku expatriate communities outside Indonesia.

Social empowerment. "This stage," writes Malik, "could be initiated when all the fundamental social structures of 'Stop violence' drives have been firmly established. The minimal indication is at least if the people are no longer easily provoked into 'warring clashes' again." Malik envisions three primary types of activities: a "popular consultative conference" with representation from all elements of society; economic, educational, and public health services in "neutral zones"; and activities to pave the way for legal action to redress the grievances of victims and reinforce the rule of law. Malik envisions, for example, the establishment of an independent investigation team to address the nature and roots of the conflict, and also the possibility of introducing an unarmed observer mission.

Legal enforcement. Here, an in-depth investigation would take place, and courts would be established to prosecute those accused of crimes. Simultaneously, educational programs would be initiated with the aim of preventing future outbreaks of violence.

Certain themes become apparent from this example and other grassroots initiatives:

- To work at grassroots level and in bottom-up fashion, you must show that you have credibility or a "mandate." That mandate can be the endorsement of a position through public polling, the support of a respected figure or institution, such as the church or a religious leader, or it can be a reputation for effectiveness—a track record that people on the ground will respect.
- Trust and solidarity between conflicting parties come from the process itself. If they are not talking, they have no basis for trust, so *any* sort of process that involves contact and dialogue can be helpful, because greater trust will develop.
- Structure a negotiation so there is some balance of power between the parties. This can, of course, be difficult in some cases, where one party appears to have all the power. But if at all possible, try to find the points of leverage that the weaker party may also be able to bring to the discussion.
- Patience is not just a virtue—it is a necessity. If you intend to engage in grassroots conflict resolution, you must be committed for the long term.
- If you find common ground and a basis for discussion and negotiation, focus on confidence building based on reciprocity. Examples of such measures would include prisoner releases, easing of travel restrictions, humanitarian gestures, and the establishment of zones of peace.

Deadlines Can Be Deadly: Don't Rush the Process

The causes of conflicts may percolate for generations, and the conflicts themselves may drag on for years, but the international community can be notoriously impatient when it comes to negotiating peace and working toward reconciliation. Donors provide support to self-contained, discrete projects, but are less inclined to support more sustained processes that may have more profound but less immediately apparent impact. And negotiators frequently set deadlines for peace negotiations, to pressure the parties to bargain seriously.

Such deadlines may focus people's energies on an important objective, but trust and confidence develop over time, and it is usually not possible to know in advance how long it will take to build sufficient trust to engage in meaningful dialogue and to live up to commitments.

A comparison of the peace processes in Bougainville and the Solomon Islands shows how rushing the process can backfire. Both have been afflicted by ugly civil conflicts, and in both cases outside parties have acted as mediators between the adversaries—New Zealand in a leading role in the case of

Bougainville and Australia in the case of the Solomon Islands—but both the approaches and the outcomes have been quite different. Volker Böge, in his analysis of the peace processes in these two cases, concludes that in the case of the Solomon Islands conflict, Australia's decision to impose a deadline on the peace talks it had organized was counterproductive.[11]

According to Böge, the Australian mediators believed that an agreement could be reached by setting an extremely tight schedule; at the Townsville peace talks in October 2000, they gave the participants three days to reach an agreement and then extended the deadline by a further three days. Although agreement was reached, the "outcome"—an agreement signed by the adversaries—was given priority over the process, and this has had negative consequences for the long-term prospects for reconciliation. Distrust and suspicion still prevail, and violence and instability continue to plague the Solomons. Where the very structures of society are at the root of a conflict, it is, most probably, unrealistic to assume that a stable peace can be reached by imposing such time pressure. By contrast, says Böge, the Bougainville peace process was conceived of as a long-term process, and ample time was provided for the early sessions of the peace talks in New Zealand. "This proved to be very important for overcoming the tense atmosphere which almost naturally prevails when people start talking to each other who have been at war with each other for years," notes Böge. The actual peace agreement provides for a ten- to fifteen-year transitional period, during which Bougainville will enjoy substantial autonomy.

Similar differences in approach characterized the disarmament provisions reached in the two conflicts. In the Townsville Peace Agreement, a thirty-day deadline was set for weapons disposal. Such a deadline could not possibly be met, which undermined the credibility of the process itself. In the Bougainville Agreement, the disarmament/weapons disposal process was conceived of as a staged, long-term process, with the pace of disarmament dependent on local conditions. First, weapons would be stored under the control of local commanders. In the second stage, a "double key" scheme would be put into effect, whereby a local commander would hold one key, and a UN representative would hold the other. The third stage proposed a "final state" for the weapons, without specifying what that would be.

The Media as a Tool for Conflict Prevention

Conflict resolution is not just about stopping the fighting. It is also about education and about changing attitudes. And one of the most effective mechanisms for both education and changing attitudes is the media. Common Ground Indonesia's parent organization, Search for Common Ground, has had considerable success with a range of media projects focused on conflict prevention and conflict resolution, which it carries out in most of the fifteen countries where it works. Since 2001, Common Ground Indonesia has started up a number of media projects, including a radio soap opera called *Menteng Pangkalan* (the name refers to a fictitious, poor, multiethnic neighborhood in

Jakarta) that is broadcast three times a week on about 180 stations across the country.

"The main outcomes that we hope to have from the show," explains Common Ground Indonesia's director, Vanessa Johanson, "are helping people to understand how to communicate across cultures and religions and giving people practical methods or examples of how to deal with conflicts at the local level. We also want to address the negative impacts of stereotypes."[12] Johanson points out that one of the advantages of the soap opera format is that it is extremely flexible, so plots and subplots can be introduced to address a wide range of issues, characters can develop and change in response to new elements in the show, and the show can incorporate events from real life—for example, the national elections held in 2004.

To ensure success, Common Ground carried out extensive research at three different locations in Indonesia before starting on scripts and production. The research focused on the attitudes of the target audience, including their attitudes about ethnic and religious conflict, and about pluralism in Indonesian society. Beyond that, audience media habits were also studied, to make certain that a radio soap opera would draw a sufficiently large audience. Common Ground established a partnership with the psychology department of the University of Indonesia to carry out the research.

After the initial research had been carried out, six pilot episodes were produced and broadcast, and then additional research was carried out to gauge the impact and acceptance of the programs. Says Johanson, "We went back and did more focus groups using the pilots. What did people like? What did they not like? What did they understand? How authentic did they think it was?"

Another advantage of the soap opera format is that it lends itself to all sorts of media tie-ins—discussions and talk shows, call-in programs, singing contests, and so forth—all of which can be used to help to maintain a high level of interest in the program and to further the goals of conflict resolution.

It may be obvious, but is still worth noting, that one of the great advantages of the radio soap opera is simply that it is entertaining. People are not generally inclined to consciously devote much time or effort to conflict resolution as a way to relax from their busy and often difficult lives. But with the soap opera, they are exposed to ideas that can influence their attitudes in ways that reduce the possibility of conflict. And although, with the increased availability of television, radio is less popular than it once was, radio soap operas have been one of the most popular forms of entertainment in Indonesia for decades.

Common Ground Indonesia has also been involved in other media-based projects. One of these was initiated as it became increasingly clear that war was likely in Iraq in early 2003. Common Ground Indonesia organized a film festival with the goal of depicting images of tolerance and intercommunal relations during times of tension and war. "We had a feeling that there was a rising hatred against the West," explains Johanson, "and that there was a perception that this was a Christian war against Muslims, which has a big impact in Indonesia. We were afraid of repercussions between Christians and Muslims, and of violence against Westerners, so we decided to do this sort of reactive thing."

In fact, though one lesson of the film festival was that it required a great amount of work in a short time, the advantage of this sort of project is precisely that it can be put together quite quickly, since the films themselves already exist; in this case, Search for Common Ground had already compiled a collection of suitable films, many of which were used in the festival. Another lesson of the project was that with the exploitation of "portable" media such as film and video, the reach could be extended considerably beyond the audience of the festival. Common Ground Indonesia received dozens of requests to repeat the festival or to make the films available for screenings at other locations, including university campuses. Some of these requests have been granted, including screenings in Indonesia's conflict areas.

Johanson notes that another advantage of the film festival approach was that it offered an alternative to more common public gatherings—meetings, seminars, workshops, and the like—which tend to attract a more homogeneous audience. She is convinced that the film festival format is an effective one. The films addressed a range of issues—the ethnic-based conflict in Kosovo, the India-Pakistan conflict and the conflict in Aceh, and racism in Canadian schools—with screenings followed by discussions. The screenings and discussions aimed not to promote any particular point of view but rather to promote discussion and debate on what the real issues and conflicts were and what alternatives might exist to resolve them without violence. Most films, says Johanson, were documentaries, but she says that she would be inclined to include more feature films in a festival if she were to do it again, because the documentaries tend to be "heavy," and the festival would be enhanced if the films had been more "entertaining." Finding suitable Indonesian films proved to be difficult, which highlights the need, says Johanson, for more locally produced films addressing peace and conflict issues.

Strengthening the Effort by Sharing the Load: Networking

When individuals and small organizations attempt to take action as advocates for peace, it is usually difficult to make their voices heard above those with resources at their disposal. Governments, interest groups, and even well-funded insurgencies are at a distinct advantage. And yet peace advocacy from below can be an effective tool, especially if advocates leverage their influence through networking activities.

One experienced networker is former journalist Gus Miclat, executive director of Initiatives for International Dialogue (IID) in the Philippines. Miclat has been engaged in organizing against the Marcos dictatorship in his own country, but has also played a key role in the launch of the Asia Pacific Coalition for East Timor (APCET) and, through IID, in building "South-South solidarity"—by which he means a movement bringing together people of the southern part of the world who share common experiences to work for peace, justice, freedom, and democracy.

Networking is not easy, warns Miclat. "You have to have the stomach for it. It means being diplomatic, dealing with various types of people, even people that you personally wouldn't want to be with, given the choice, and that you respect these people for what they are and understand where they're coming from."[13]

Networking, of course, is all about organizing, and that means having the right people to tackle the right jobs—such jobs as communications, research, interaction with governments and outside organizations, community organizing, and so forth. Miclat encourages the establishment of a "core group" of individuals who may assume a central leadership role, who will maintain momentum, and who may also act as the "public face" of the coalition.[14] It is also important to establish a secretariat that is, as Miclat puts it "creative, independent and professional in the conduct of its work."

In grassroots organizing and networking activities, money will almost inevitably be a near-constant problem. Miclat approaches the funding problem in much the same way as he approaches networking in general. "What you try to do is to work within coalitions, or to establish coalitions for the particular project or issue that you are dealing with at the moment. And in that way, you distribute the bill, so to speak." Clearly, most grassroots organizations will not have the resources to pay extra staffing costs that result from their involvement in the network, but they are usually capable of offering in-kind contributions that will help to keep operating costs down. It probably doesn't make much sense to go to institutional funders for start-up funding, says Miclat, but once a networking activity is up and running and manages to achieve a track record, funders will not only be open to providing support, but will actually come forward to offer it.

"You are able to bring that project success story to the funders and sell it," says Miclat. But "connections" can also be important. "It is helpful to identify individual friends within funding agencies who resonate with what you are doing. . . . In our case, our organization was funded by an organization that had someone in charge of the Asia-Philippines desk who was working for the solidarity movement for the Philippines during the Marcos era. He also believed in the concept that we were involved in—the concepts of South-South solidarity that we wanted to pursue. That guy lobbied within his organization, and we got the funding. And it even went beyond his organization. He sold the idea to other funders that were in partnership with his foundation."

In a sense, Miclat is almost pursuing parallel network activities. There is a network of activists, and under ideal conditions there is a parallel network of funders prepared to support the activist network. But funders can't be taken for granted—they quickly become partners as well, both out of courtesy to them for their engagement, but also because it is tactically important. "Once you deal with them as partners and involve them in the advocacy work as well," says Miclat, "you sell your advocacy to their own sources of funding. And then they need to keep you around because to *their* sources and *their* community, you are also *their* success story. This is what we're trying to do, so the stakeholdership of the funder in your organization would be developed more in a partnership framework rather than a funding framework." There is one risk that Miclat points out when forging close relationships with funders—the risk that the network will become "fund driven," allowing its own activities to be determined on the basis of the priorities of the funder.

Networkers can sometimes lose sight of their objectives. After all, the goal is not to build a strong network, but to make a difference in the real world. And so it is important to develop strategies for engaging the principle players in a conflict—at all levels. This may include government officials, and it may also include representatives of an insurgency or opposition movement. Indeed, the network can fill an odd function for rebels, who may not be able to communicate directly with the government. In that sense, a network may provide an outlet for the rebel movement and a point of contact with the authorities.

Clearly, the public, and civil society organizations as well, should also be engaged. "We shouldn't avoid them," comments Miclat. "But first those networks need to understand them, before they are able to engage them properly. I would personally back this kind of trend as part of a comprehensive framework of any network or any organization. My analogy would be a rice cake. You cook the rice cake on the top and the bottom. So you develop capacities in networks, among people, and organizations, and at the same time you advocate on the top, with policymakers, etc."

As a former journalist, Miclat is probably more aware of the importance of the media than most organizers. But it's not just about publicity, he stresses. Equally important is more substantive work. Journalists need to be "educated" to understand the issues from the grassroots perspective. Networking activists should "target" journalists as they would target other constituencies in order to win their support (or at least a sympathetic ear). After all, a sympathetic or supportive report carried by the major media reaching an audience of millions becomes the most effective advocacy platform any activist could dream of.

Miclat provides a neat, six-point summary of the requisites for effective networking:

- All members agree on a common issue around which to organize.
- Each member of the network clearly understands its own role within the coalition.
- There is a core group providing leadership and guidance.
- There is reliable secretariat, with a "point person," to manage networking activities.
- There are adequate resources to get the job done.
- There is an understanding of the importance of the media and sufficient skills to use the media to communicate the network's main message to a broader public.[15]

East Timor. Villagers and Falintil guerrillas.

Truth and Reconciliation: Healing the Wounds

East Timor's Commission for Reception, Truth, and Reconciliation (CAVR). During East Timor's years of occupation by Indonesia, human rights were violated on a massive scale, by the Indonesian security forces especially, by militias allied with the Indonesian military, and also by supporters of East Timorese independence. Since the withdrawal of the Indonesian security forces from East Timor, various measures have been undertaken to move toward reconciliation after the many years of trauma. Indonesia itself has brought some members of its security forces to trial, but these trials have been criticized as halfhearted efforts aimed more at appeasing international opinion than truly seeking justice, and most of those found guilty—particularly high-ranking officers—have received light sentences. In East Timor itself, a far more important and meaningful initiative has been the establishment of the CAVR, whose mandate is, among other things, to "inquire into human rights violations committed on all sides, between April 1974 and October 1999, to facilitate community reconciliation with justice for those who committed less serious offenses," and to make proposals to the government for further action on reconciliation and the promotion of human rights.[16]

At the swearing-in of CAVR's commissioners in January 2002, a few months prior to East Timor achieving full independence, Nobel Laureate and Foreign Minister of East Timor José Ramos-Horta spoke of what he hoped the commission could achieve: "As part of our preparation for this new reality, we have chosen to take a long and hard look at the past. We want to learn from the lessons of the past so that we will be able to prevent similar tragedies in the future. At the same time, we wish to open the door of forgiveness and acceptance to those who were caught in the vicious cycle of violence. . . . Victims of past violations will have recognition of their suffering, an important part of their healing process. This will also be an important part of our healing as a nation. It is also important to acknowledge that many of those responsible for lesser crimes were victims as well. As a people we must find a way to end the cycle of violence and rise above those who committed atrocities against us."

Notably, the mandate of the CAVR differs from that of the frequently cited South African Truth and Reconciliation Commission in that it specifically withholds the power to grant amnesty, and also is restricted to "less serious offenses." The United Nations mission in East Timor and the UN Human Rights Commission established a separate "Serious Crimes Unit." This was a sort of "hybrid" tribunal, functioning in a fashion similar to the war crimes tribunals for the former Yugoslavia, Rwanda, and Sierra Leone, but including both East Timorese as well as international judges and prosecutors. One of the reasons for separating out the serious crimes from those under the purview of CAVR was the sheer scale of serious crimes that had been committed, and the sense that it would not be appropriate to extend a blanket grant of amnesty to those who might have been involved in murder, rape, war crimes, crimes against humanity, and acts of genocide. If, during CAVR's work, evidence is uncovered of "serious crimes," then these are supposed to be referred to the Serious Crimes Unit. Furthermore, notes Adriano do Nascimento, of La'o Hamutuk—the East Timor Institute for Reconstruction Monitoring and Analysis—President Xanana Gusmão has initiated a national dialogue in which the political elite can meet to address the issues that continue to divide the nation. Nascimento feels that such a dialogue is essential in parallel with the truth-seeking and reconciliation activities.[17]

The CAVR has also been engaged in activities to reintegrate refugees, many of whom fled to West Timor into East Timorese society. And since the reconciliation process can only be achieved if the public itself is sufficiently well informed to feel that a healing process is really taking place, public information has been an important element in the CAVR's activities.

By mid-2003, the Truth-Seeking Division had conducted thousands of interviews, taken more than 5,000 statements from the victims of human rights violations, and established a system for organizing and archiving these records for possible future reference. It also began holding a series of public hearings on themes related to human rights violations, war crimes, and other political themes.

The CAVR's activities in facilitating community reconciliation have been quite extraordinary. The process, as described by the CAVR, "is a voluntary one, where a perpetrator comes forward and admits his wrong in a statement; this statement is sent to the Office of the Prosecutor General for confirmation that it is appropriate for a community reconciliation process; with this approval a hearing is organized by the CAVR in the community, where perpetrator, victim and community members all speak before a panel of community leaders headed by a Regional Commissioner. The aim is to facilitate communities to effectively reintegrate people who have harmed the community." These "perpetrators" have acknowledged such acts as forced detention, destruction of livestock, threatening behavior, slander, beatings, house burnings, and so forth. The reintegration/reconciliation has been achieved in most cases by specifying a "community reconciliation act." These have included simple apologies and pledges not to repeat the act, requirements to fulfill community service for a specified period of time or to attend church services, and in some cases, ceremonial offerings of money or possessions such as food or livestock. Individuals who fulfill the terms of a community reconciliation agreement are granted immunity from further civil or criminal liability for those acts.

A summary of the primary lessons learned from the truth and reconciliation process in East Timor includes the following:

- The healing process following a conflict is furthered by a genuine effort to learn the truth, and by acknowledging the suffering of victims of the conflict.
- Those who are involved in violations of the rights of others are often themselves victims and need to be acknowledged as such.
- Symbolic compensation of victims can be an important element of reconciliation, especially when victim and perpetrator both accept the terms of the compensation arrangement, and when a perpetrator offers, and a victim accepts, an apology.
- Reconciliation within communities is furthered by establishing a community-based rather than a regionally or nationally based process.
- A national dialogue to address divisive issues at the root of the conflict should complement that locally based process.
- Justice for the perpetrators of serious crimes—crimes against humanity and war crimes—may be pursued in a process separate from that pursued for lesser crimes during reconciliation.

Reforming the Military, Disarming the Adversaries, Destroying the Weapons

Security-sector reform in Indonesia: a work in progress. Throughout Indonesia's history, and especially during the "New Order" regime of President Suharto, Indonesia's security forces occupied a central place in society, often acting more to preserve the regime in its position of power and privilege than to protect the public. The military embraced a doctrine known as *dwi fungsi*—dual functions.[18] In addition to a traditional military function, the second function was in the political sphere.

But the New Order regime came crashing down in 1998, and since then an effort has been under way—albeit haltingly—to reform Indonesia's security forces along with the rest of Indonesia's political culture. Indeed, the two are inextricably linked—true democracy in Indonesia can only take place when the disproportionate political and economic influence of Indonesian security forces has been effectively eliminated, and military abuses of human rights end. But progress on security-sector reforms is closely linked to progress toward greater democratization of Indonesian society.

Indonesia is a large and complex nation experiencing dramatic change, feeling its way toward a more democratic government. It would be unrealistic to expect that reform of the security forces could be achieved quickly or easily, but concrete, positive moves toward reform have been made. Perhaps the most important of these include the following, outlined by Rizal Sukma and Edy Prasetyono, of the Dutch foreign policy think tank Clingendael, which can be considered essential elements of any security sector reform initiative:

- A clear articulation of the function that the military would play in society, including defending the nation's territorial integrity, safeguarding the people and the nation, and participating in international and regional peacekeeping missions.[19]
- The separation of internal police activities from those activities more properly under the purview of the military.
- The ending of the military's involvement in day-to-day politics and administrative functions in the government. Specific measures in Indonesia have included the following:
  - The requirement that military officers resign their military positions before taking up civilian positions.
  - The reduction of the allotted seats in the People's Consultative Assembly from seventy-five to thirty-eight.
  - The agreement to reduce the number of military representatives in local parliaments.
  - The cutting of ties between the military and political parties, including, especially, Golkar, which had been the ruling party under the New Order regime.
  - A commitment to political neutrality in elections.
  - A revision in the doctrines under which the military operated.[20]

Furthermore, the security forces have acknowledged past wrongdoing, and apologized for their past sins.

But as noted, security-sector reform in Indonesia is a work in progress. And Sukma and Prasetyono point to three important deficiencies in the reforms to date, namely (1) the failure to codify the reforms through legislation; (2) the failure to move beyond acknowledgment of past wrongs and to hold individuals, including high-ranking officers and commanders, accountable for their actions; and (3) the failure to effectively address the pervasive involvement of the military in economic activities, which presents great opportunities for corruption and can only be eliminated by providing for adequate funding via normal budgetary mechanisms and instituting proper financial management.

Demobilization: Mindanao's lost opportunity. Ending hostilities is crucial—but often it is not enough. The means to wage war must be removed from the arena as well. Otherwise, combatants who have agreed to a truce can easily return to violence. This is at least one of the lessons that can be drawn from what can only be viewed as a lost opportunity in Mindanao, where the rebels fighting under the banner of the Moro National Liberation Front (MNLF) signed a peace agreement with the government of the Philippines in September 1996. By the end of 2001, however, the peace in Mindanao was in tatters.

What has led to these dashed hopes? A variety of political factors have played a role, but Filipino scholar Miriam Coronel Ferrer believes that one inherent weakness in the 1996 agreement—a failure to provide a mechanism for the demobilization of the great majority of MNLF fighters—has proved crucial in the collapse. Although the agreement provided for the integration of a substantial number of the MNLF fighters into the Philippine armed forces and police, these provisions were not sufficient to cover all the rebels.[21] As a result, a large rebel army continued to exist, with easy access to weapons. Ferrer readily concedes that total disarmament prior to the final implementation of the peace would not have been a realistic option, but she argues that the failure to include an enforceable demobilization and disarmament provision in the 1996 agreement ultimately resulted in an increase in the supply of weapons in Mindanao and contributed substantially to the breakdown of the agreement.

Making the world safe for normal life: weapons reduction in Cambodia. When the UN Transitional Authority in Cambodia (UNTAC) ended its eighteen-month peacekeeping mission in 1993, it left behind not just an uneasy peace, but also a sizable arsenal of mostly small arms and light weapons after decades of war. Those weapons, says Soth Plai Ngarm of the Alliance for Conflict Transformation in Phnom Penh, presented a considerable threat to security.[22] They were held by political factions, who saw them as a trump card to hold in reserve in case of a new outbreak of violence. They were used by groups and individuals to gain control over resources and businesses in Cambodia. They were used by criminals in the commission of crimes. And they were held by private citizens to defend their homes, families, and property.

In 1997, political violence flared up briefly. In response, members of civil society, including local and international NGOs, began considering the issue of weapons and actions that might be taken to respond to the threat posed by the easy availability of weapons. In early 1998 they carried out a feasibility study that concluded: "Weapons and the fear of them are blocking the progress toward development, democracy and a peaceful and healthy society. We recommend that a campaign to reduce the number of weapons and the practice of using weapons to solve problems, start now."[23]

A decision was taken shortly thereafter to begin such a campaign, and in August 1998 the Working Group for Weapons Reduction in Cambodia was established. Since then, it has achieved important successes, including:

- Mobilizing civil society to engage in disarmament activities, and putting the issue of weapons availability on the agenda.
- Undertaking research and disseminating information on weapons issues in Cambodia.
- Providing a platform for grassroots voices and opportunities for individuals and organizations to be involved in peacebuilding work.
- Pushing for weapons collection and disposal programs.

The working group's first major success involved its consultation with the municipality of Phnom Penh, in 1998, which led the following year to a weapons collection and destruction program in the capital: 3,855 weapons were collected, and then publicly destroyed in May 1999. At the instigation of the working group, similar activities followed outside Phnom Penh, with a total of more than 110,000 weapons collected, and nearly 80,000 weapons destroyed, between 1999 and February 2002.

The working group has continued its efforts in public education and information, weapons reduction advocacy, and monitoring and research, and has built up an extensive network both inside Cambodia and internationally. It is now broadening its activities to include peace education and community security. One lesson is to begin peacebuilding activity with a focus and achievable objectives. Building on the success and credibility that comes with success, it is possible to tackle new challenges and to assert greater influence.

A number of lessons emerge from the working group's experience:

- In view of the fact that many people possess arms to protect themselves against crime, Soth Plai Ngarm observes that the collection of weapons can decrease rather than increase security if it is not undertaken in conjunction with programs to develop police and security forces.
- Weapons collection and disarmament programs can be manipulated by those in power as a strategy for disarming and neutralizing political opponents. In the case of the Working Group for Weapons Reduction in Cambodia, the strategy to reduce these risks was to work closely with the government and establish a monitoring protocol.
- Successful weapons collection programs can help to reduce suspicion or, conversely, to increase trust and confidence among opposition groups in society.
- Education to raise public awareness about the negative impacts of weapons on peace and development should be an essential part of a weapons collection program. Furthermore, public education efforts should be undertaken in conjunction with weapons reductions programs to reassure the

public that the government is taking actions to guarantee security through improvements in police protection services and other public security measures.

• Management and control of weapons stockpiles need to be integrated into weapons collection programs, so that these weapons are not removed from weapons storage centers and allowed to replace those that have been collected. Similarly, concerted efforts need to be undertaken to control illegal weapons trafficking, especially in an environment like Cambodia, which has a history of weapons smuggling and porous national borders.

Moving to higher ground: weapons disposal in Bougainville. In Bougainville, the three-stage weapons disposal program described earlier was conceived of as a major, integral part of the peace and reconciliation strategy, rather than as an adjunct that would follow a peace settlement in order to ensure that the adversaries would not revert to violence in the future. That is, agreeing to disarm and giving up weapons was seen as an essential part of a process that would build confidence and encourage reconciliation, and conversely, that process of negotiation and discussion of the root causes of the conflict enabled the disarmament to occur.

Indeed, the peace, reconciliation, and disarmament process in Bougainville was infused with an almost spiritual aspect. As James Tanis, vice president of the Bougainville People's Congress explains, "To the parties to the conflict, disposal of weapons is not a symptom of weakness. It is simply moving on to a higher ground. Therefore all sides see that the disposal of weapons strengthens the process toward the achievement of goals and objectives they stand for."[24]

Tanis also explains, "We believe that weapons have blood [and] weapons taken to war have spirits of the slain. . . . If a weapon that has blood is taken around in public, it will arouse the spirits of those that were killed to cry out for more blood. Therefore to avoid more killings, disposal of weapons is . . . demanded after the war. Even though modern man may brush this aside as superstition, this is one important asset for disarmament on Bougainville."

Another important aspect in the disarmament process was the prominent role played by women. According to Tanis, "The mothers, the wives and sisters of the former enemies often would make the first ice breaking contact. Women's groups are active in making demands for weapons disposal while at the same time organizing peace related meetings. For the reconciliation, the women representing each side perform a symbolic breaking of bows and arrows. This is an important step in the process of disposal of weapons."

It is also notable that once weapons had been collected, they were disposed of in public ceremonies that combined elements of traditional and religious culture with the cultures of politics and diplomacy. Thus politicians, members of the peace monitoring group and the UN observer mission, traditional chiefs, former combatants, and members of the religious community all attended and participated in these ceremonies.

Drastic Measures for Intractable Struggles: UN Intervention in Cambodia
In October 1991, following the signing of the Paris Peace Agreement to end decades of conflict in Cambodia, the UN embarked on what was, at the time, the most ambitious peace mission it had ever undertaken. For the first time, the UN was involved not just in "peacekeeping" and "peacemaking," but also in peacebuilding.[25] Although nominal power was given to Cambodia's Supreme National Council (SNC), all effective power was ceded by the SNC to the UN Transitional Authority in Cambodia. The mandate given to UNTAC included aspects relating to human rights, the organization and conduct of free and fair general elections, military arrangements, civil administration, the maintenance of law and order, the repatriation and resettlement of the Cambodian refugees and displaced persons, and the rehabilitation of essential Cambodian infrastructure during the transitional period. UNTAC was also charged with monitoring the cease-fire and withdrawal of foreign forces.[26]

UNTAC began its operations in March 1992 and continued until September 1993. A decade later, Cambodia enjoys a shaky but imperfect peace, a functioning government in what is, at least in name, a multiparty democracy, and a growing economy. By the time UNTAC completed its mission, it had played a crucial role in building the foundations of civil society in Cambodia, and restoring a sense of legitimacy for the state. Its most important success was almost certainly the organization, management, and monitoring of elections, with the participation of nearly 90 percent of eligible voters. It also contributed significantly to the process of national reconciliation after the years of conflict.

A number of features of the UNTAC intervention have been widely praised, and can serve as positive lessons for future large-scale interventions:

- The establishment of an informal group known as the "Friends of the Secretary General." The Friends comprised the five permanent members of the Security Council plus Australia, Indonesia, and Japan, as well as several other nations. The Friends were able to exert pressure on the parties to the conflict to work to ensure successful implementation of the peace agreement. Because the various nations had a common interest in the success of the process, but unique relations with the parties to the conflict, they were able to exert that pressure to keep the process moving forward.
- Giving an important role to Prince (and later King) Norodom Sihanouk during the transition process. As a widely respected, charismatic figure, the prince helped to unify the country and rally the Cambodian population to support the peace agreement.
- Extending a strong mandate to UNTAC. In an environment where the credibility and the structures of a state had crumbled due to a conflict, this decision had much to do with the ultimate success in stabilizing the situation.

Still, in both its conception and its implementation, the UN's intervention in Cambodia suffered from flaws: (1) there was an excessive time lag, which resulted in lost momentum, between the signing of the Paris Peace Agreement in its implementation under UNTAC; (2) the UN found itself with inadequate resources—financial and human—and infrastructure; (3) during the negotiations, planning for the future was inadequate; (4) UNTAC's authority was at times subverted, because remnants of those administrative structures that had existed prior to the agreement were utilized, especially by politicians and military officers at the provincial level, to sidestep UNTAC; (5) the UNTAC mission was unable to effectively enforce the cease-fire and to effectively deal with cease-fire violations—the Khmer Rouge, in particular, failed to adhere to the demobilization provisions of the agreement, and so the other parties felt less compelled to adhere to these provisions as well.

Multi-Track Approaches: Many Weapons, Many Targets

Even the most straightforward conflict is complex, colored not just by conflicting objectives, but also by conflicting perceptions of the issues; by complicated relationships between the adversaries; by history, emotion, and memories; by the relationships of the adversaries to outside parties; and sometimes by cultural differences and diverging standards of what and who is right and wrong.

It only makes sense, then, that conflict resolution and conflict prevention must also be complex. And it is not surprising that, as Kevin Clements notes, "When one looks at all of the conflicts that have convulsed the world since 1990 . . . none have been finally resolved by military means nor have there been any final political solutions." Interventions from the international community have not brought stability and lasting peace, suggests Clements, because "the levels of analytic and conceptual coherence in our understanding of violent conflict have been inadequate." There are, says Clements, no "magic solutions," but peacemaking efforts will remain inadequate until we have "more integrated and coordinated responses" to conflict.[27] Indeed, he adds, "distinctions between official and unofficial, governmental/non-governmental, regional/global have, more often than not, been impediments towards the development of sound and comprehensive strategies for dealing with these problems" and so, he argues, peacemakers must acknowledge that "violent conflict requires the energy of all actors (official and unofficial) if human security, structural stability and peace are to be achieved." Elsewhere, Clements further asserts that "it is vital to adopt a *multi-disciplinary and multi-leveled analysis to the conflict.*"[28]

So it is only logical to employ multi-actor and multi-track approaches to try, if possible, to prevent conflict from turning violent, to end violence when it erupts, and to reconcile the parties when the fighting has come to an end. In the last decade or so, the term "multi-track" has been adopted in the conflict resolution community to refer to efforts involving both *official* conflict transformation efforts, undertaken by governments, international agencies, and the like, and *unofficial* efforts, undertaken by actors such as civil society organizations, NGOs, individuals, and religious organizations. The beauty of multi-track approaches is that they afford an opportunity for anyone, at any level, to contribute to the peacebuilding process with the means that they have available to them.

Of course, the outcomes of efforts at the grassroots often will not produce visible changes in the course of a conflict. And it is important that those engaged in multi-track conflict resolution efforts know and accept this reality. Rather, they need to understand that *incremental* contributions will have their effect, but that those effects occur over time, and only become visible when enough incremental contributions have been made to produce the beginnings of a structure of peace—changes in attitudes, relations between conflicting parties, greater trust between communities and individuals, alternate ways of resolving disputes, objective sources of information, structures of governance that are responsive and accountable to the needs of the people they purport to serve, agencies to monitor human rights, progress in the area of economic justice, and so on.

The various efforts and lessons described in this chapter are illustrations of the many paths to peace that are possible. They include initiatives that rely on traditional conflict resolution mechanisms—the tried and true approaches developed over generations that are widely known as *adat,* and people-to-people initiatives that rely on dialogue to build (or rebuild) trust between adversaries and communities. Some are more internal—focusing on strengthening the networks of like-minded advocates of peace, for example, and improving their ability to influence public opinion. Some focus on changing attitudes by using the media. Others more directly address issues of governance, justice, and in some detail, security—removing weapons from society, demobilizing armed groups, and reforming the security sector.

As noted at the start of this chapter, this is not an exhaustive catalog of methodologies. In fact, that is precisely the point about multi-track approaches. The possibilities are virtually endless. Ideally, for maximum impact, an intervention is preceded by a good, solid analysis of the situation and the range of choices available, and preferably there is some degree of coordination among the actors, but that is not always possible (in fact, it is probably the exception rather than the rule). And, again citing Clements, every conflict is unique, and therefore, not every strategy applicable in one situation will be applicable in other situations.[29]

Every conflict is unique, but they all share in common their capacity to destroy. In modern conflict, that destructive capacity has become ever more terrible. The armies of the Cold War relied on jet fighters and tanks, but the weapons of today's conflicts include passenger airplanes and pickup trucks. Ten-year-old children armed with machine guns can wreak terror as well. Even the most ill-equipped armies can cause horrible human suffering. Still, peacemakers too have a broad arsenal of weapons at their disposal to wage peace and, to extend the metaphor, a range of targets as well. If enough peacemakers take aim at enough targets with the properly chosen weapons, the sum total of their individual, incremental contributions can be a powerful force with which to successfully confront and overcome violence and injustice.

Box 7.1 Best Practices and Lessons Learned: A Compendium of Useful Strategies

Building Peace
- Identify the underlying issues and look for shared objectives and mutually compatible agendas that can be addressed to bridge the divide and build trust.
- Build peace one block at a time, one person at a time.
- Talk to all the stakeholders at all levels over and over again, and keep them continually informed about what is going on.
- Peace is only possible when there is authentic dialogue, and authentic dialogue is only possible when there is mutual respect. Conversely, respect and trust develop from the process.
- Mediators need to establish their credibility.
- If hard-liners walk away from face-to-face talks, set up parallel discussions to keep the process on track, and keep both sides informed via a trusted go-between.
- If the outcome—an agreement signed by the adversaries—is given a higher priority than the process—genuine acceptance of peaceful coexistence, justice, reconciliation—prospects for long-term peace will be adversely affected.
- Complex conflicts require complex conflict resolution strategies. Each action can make an incremental difference in the overall situation, but multi-track, multi-actor approaches combining a range of strategies at all levels have the best chance of making significant and lasting impact.

Preventing Violence and Maintaining Peace

Addressing Problems in the Security Sector
- Clearly articulate—and codify—the role that the security forces are to play in society.
- Separate military forces from police forces; require that military officers resign their commissions in order to participate in politics.
- Establish mechanisms to hold the security services accountable for their actions.

Disarmament and Demobilization
- Include programs of disarmament, demobilization, and reintegration in any peace settlement.
- Disarmament programs should be undertaken in conjunction with programs to enhance the capabilities and competence of police and security forces, and a long-term peacebuilding strategy.
- Communication and cooperation with civil society—in both urban and rural areas—is essential to ensure full understanding of both weapons reduction programs and related security-sector reforms. Organizations working on these programs should use consultative and participatory processes to ensure that available resources and knowledge are used effectively and to build trust within civil society for the new security sector.

(continues)

Box 7.1 Cont.

Constitutional and Legal Measures
- Introduce checks and balances into the governmental structures, including, especially, an independent judiciary and accountability to the voters on the part of both the executive and legislative branches.

Indigenous and Religious Approaches
- Indigenous mechanisms can be utilized in times of crisis or emergency to restore order when governmental structures have collapsed.
- Outside parties involved in postconflict nation building should educate themselves about traditional governance systems and incorporate them into the governance and justice systems they establish.

Reconciliation
- Reconciliation at all levels—personal, between individuals, and between larger groups—requires a variety of approaches and focuses—cultural, political, economic, and indigenous and religious—and a full range of actors.
- Mechanisms for achieving reconciliation include revitalizing and/or exploiting customary law practices as frameworks for reconciliation; people-to-people approaches; working through neighborhood organizations; involving respected persons and groups; organizing public forums; engaging in trauma-healing processes; and arranging for compensation—often symbolic—from the perpetrators to the victims.
- Reconciliation can take place through official or unofficial channels, at the grassroots level or at the national level.
- Truth and reconciliation commissions have been show to be highly effective in healing the wounds caused by conflict and injustice.

Strengthening Organizations and Maximizing Impact
- Develop networks and coalitions with like-minded partners.
- Don't overlook the necessity to create solid organizational foundations for networks, with a core group to provide leadership and guidance, a reliable secretariat to coordinate activities, and adequate funding.
- Distribute the responsibilities among network members to take advantage of experience, skills, and access.
- Identify individual friends within funding agencies who resonate with what you are doing, and work with funders to develop mutually beneficial partnerships.
- Take a "rice cake approach" to advocacy and organizing: work at the grassroots level to build support, but focus as well on public officials, lawmakers, policymakers, the media, the international community, NGOs, and so on.
- Continually evaluate effectiveness, and document lessons learned to apply in future actions.
- Strategize about how to use peacebuilding as an overarching concept to bring together a broad range of organizations and actors for a common purpose.

(continues)

Box 7.1 Cont.

Communications and Media

For Activists and Peacebuilders
- Learn the appropriate ways to deal with the press—the rules, parameters, and limitations.
- View the media as a "tool" to be used for communication and advocacy to maximize any opportunities for publicity, and anticipate media reactions to your actions.
- "Package" the message so that it is attractive and "marketable" to mainstream media.
- Target the media themselves—including journalists, editors, and owners—as objects of advocacy.

For Journalists and Other Media Professionals
- Develop training programs to enhance the professional skills of journalists and acquaint them with peace journalism practices; provide journalists with information on security management so they can accurately gauge and minimize the risks they face.
- Be aware that both sides will try to manipulate the media.
- The media can contribute both to the escalation of conflict, by sensationalizing violence and spreading hate, or to conflict resolution, by showing the costs of conflict and the possibilities of peace.
- The media can serve as a channel of communication between warring parties who refuse to talk to each other directly.

Resources

Publications

"Armed to the Teeth." By Miriam Coronel Ferrer. *Kasarinlan* 16, no. 2 (2001). Available at www.upd.edu.ph/~twsc/arms_and_militaries/tws_desk_v16n2-ferrer.htm.

The Battle for the Rule of Law in Thailand: The Constitutional Court of Thailand. By James Klein, p. 1. Available at www.kpi.ac.th/download/james%20klein.pdf.

"Best Practice in Networking and Coalition-Building: The Story of APCET." By Gus Miclat. Paper presented at the Workshop on Lessons Learned from Southeast Asian and Pacific Peacebuilding Efforts, Bali, May 5–7, 2003. Available at www.csps-ugm.or.id/bali/paper/gusmiclat.html or www.csps-ugm.or.id/bali/paper/gusmiclat.pdf.

Breaking Spears and Mending Hearts. By Pat Howley. Leichhardt, NSW, Australia: Federation Press, 2002.

Cambodia: The Legacy and Lessons of UNTAC. By Trevor Findlay. SIPRI Research Report no. 9 (abstract). Available at http://editors.sipri.se/pubs/cambodia_pr.html.

Civil Society and Conflict Prevention. By Kevin Clements. Bonn: Center for Development Research, 2000. Available at www.zef.de/download/ethnic_conflict/clements.pdf.

Human Development Report 2002: Deepening Democracy in a Fragmented World. By the UN Development Programme. New York: Oxford University Press, 2002. Available at www.undp.org.in/hdr2002/hdr2002complete.pdf.

"Lessons Learned from a Comparison Between the Cases of Bougainville and Solomon Islands." By Volker Böge. Paper presented at the Searching for Peace in Southeast Asia and the Pacific Workshop, Manila, June 4–6, 2002. Available at www.geocities.com/ccom_pacific_forum/documents/ccom_pacific_forum_boege_bougainville_solomon_islands.htm.

"Lessons Learnt from Indigenous Methods of Peacemaking in Solomon Islands, with Particular Reference to the Role of the Melanesian Brotherhood and the Religious Communities." By Brother Richard Carter. Paper presented at the Workshop on Lessons Learned from Southeast Asian and Pacific Peacebuilding Efforts, Bali, May 5–7, 2003. Available at www.csps-ugm.or.id/bali/paper/brother.html or www.csps-ugm.or.id/bali/paper/brother.pdf.

Security Sector Reform in Indonesia: The Military and the Police. By Rizal Sukma and Edy Prasetyono. Working Paper no. 9. Netherlands: Netherlands Institute of International Relations "Clingendael," Conflict Research Unit, February, 2003, p. 16. Available at www.clingendael.nl/cru/pdf/working_paper_9.PDF.

"Towards Conflict Transformation and a Just Peace." By Kevin Clements. In *Berghof Handbook for Conflict Transformation.* Berline: Berghof Research Center for Constructive Conflict Management, 2001. Available at www.berghof-handbook.net/cf.htm.

"War and Peace in Cambodia." By Michael W. Doyle. Draft working paper. Available (subscribers only) at www.ciaonet.org/wps/dom01.

"Weapon Reduction Experience in Cambodia." By Soth Plai Ngarm. Paper presented at the Workshop on Lessons Learned from Southeast Asian and Pacific Peacebuilding Efforts, Bali, May 5–7, 2003. Available at www.csps-ugm.or.id/bali/paper/ngarm.html or www.csps-ugm.or.id/bali/paper/ngarm.pdf.

In Between: Personal Experiences in the Nine-Year-Long Conflict on Bougainville, and Habuna Momouqu—Violence and the Guadalcanal Uprising in Solomon Islands. By James Tanis and George Gray. Available at www.exkiap.net/articles/miscellaneous/james_tanis.htm.

Organizations

The following organizations served as primary sources for the information presented in this chapter, or are engaged in activities described herein:

Berghof Research Center for Constructive Conflict Management
e-mail: info@berghof-center.org
www.berghof-center.org
The center publishes the excellent *Berghof Handbook for Conflict Transformation,* which is available at www.berghof-handbook.net.

Center for Development Research (ZEF)
e-mail: presse.zef@uni-bonn.de
www.zef.de/download/ethnic_conflict/clements.pdf

Commission for Reception, Truth, and Reconciliation (CAVR)
www.easttimor-reconciliation.org/mandate.htm
Reports on ongoing activities of the CAVR are available at www.easttimor-reconciliation.org/updates.htm.

Common Ground Indonesia
e-mail: commonground@indocg.org

Initiatives for International Dialogue
e-mail: iid@skyinet.net
www.iidnet.or

Institute for Multi-Track Diplomacy
e-mail: imtd@imtd.org
www.imtd.org

La'o Hamutuk (East Timor Institute for Reconstruction and Development Monitoring and Analysis)

e-mail: laohamutuk@easttimor.minihub.org
www.etan.org/lh/default.htm

Search for Common Ground
e-mail: search@sfcg.org
www.sfcg.org
Information on the Indonesian program described in this chapter is available at www.
sfcg.org/locations.cfm?locus=indonesia.

Third World Studies Center
University of the Philippines, Diliman
e-mail: twsc@kssp.upd.edu.ph; www.upd.edu.ph/~twsc

Working Group on Weapons Reduction (WGWR)
e-mail: wgwr@online.com.kh
www.wgwr.org

The following organizations served as secondary sources for the chapter, or are engaged in noteworthy conflict resolution activities in the Asia Pacific region:

Center for Security and Peace Studies, Gadjah Mada University
w-mail: csps-ugm@jmn.net.id
www.csps-ugm.or.id

Citizens' Constitutional Forum
www.ccf.org.fj

The Collaborative for Development Action, Inc.
w-mail: cda@cdainc.com
www.cdainc.com

International Alert
w-mail: general@international-alert.org
www.international-alert.org

Pacific Concerns Resource Centre
w-mail: pcrc@connect.com.fj
www.pcrc.org.fj

Jim Wake is a freelance journalist based in the Netherlands. This chapter has been written with narrative contributions from the region.

Notes

I would like to thank Renata Arianingtyas for her research assistance.

1. Karl von Clausewitz (1780–1831) was a Prussian general, military strategist, and the author of the influential volume *On War,* in which he advanced the doctrine of "total war" expressed in the quotation.

2. Kevin Clements, *Civil Society and Conflict Prevention* (Bonn: Center for Development Research, 2000), p. 6, available at www.zef.de/download/ethnic_conflict/clements.pdf.

3. "Workshop on Lessons Learned from Southeast Asian and Pacific Peace Efforts," small group discussion on negotiating with hardliners, Bali, Indonesia, May 6, 2003.

4. Interview with author during "Workshop on Lessons Learned from Southeast Asian and Pacific Peace Efforts," Bali, Indonesia, May 5, 2003.

5. Brother Richard Carter, "Lessons Learnt from Indigenous Methods of Peacemaking in Solomon Islands, with Particular Reference to the Role of the Melanesian

Brotherhood and the Religious Communities," paper presented at the Workshop on Lessons Learned from Southeast Asian and Pacific Peacebuilding Efforts, Bali, May 5–7, 2003, p. 4, available at www.csps-ugm.or.id/bali/paper/brother.html or www.csps-ugm.or.id/bali/paper/brother.pdf.

6. Carter is here quoting from a letter that was published in Richard Carter, *A Resource Book for the Training and Mission of the Melanesian Brotherhood* (n.p., 2000), pp. 80–81.

7. Unfortunately, despite the successes described in this section, the security situation in the Solomons deteriorated in the first half of 2003, and seven members of the Melanesian Brotherhood were murdered. Several others were taken hostage but subsequently released. An Australia-led international peacekeeping force was deployed in July 2003. As of September 2003, progress has been made toward the restoration of order and the disarmament of armed militias.

8. Carter, "Lessons Learnt," pp. 10–11.

9. *Adat* is a system based on traditional, indigenous custom.

10. "Workshop on Lessons Learned from Southeast Asian and Pacific Peace Efforts," small group discussion on negotiating with hardliners, Bali, Indonesia, May 6, 2003.

11. Volker Böge, "Lessons Learned from a comparison between the cases of Bougainville and Solomon Islands," presented at the "Searching for Peace in Southeast Asia and the Pacific Workshop," Manila, June 4-6, 2002, available online at m_pacific_forum_boege_bougainville_solomon_islands.htm.

12. Interview with the author during "Workshop on Lessons Learned from Southeast Asian and Pacific Peace Efforts," Bali, Indonesia, May 6, 2003.

13. Much of the information presented here on networking is derived from an interview with Gus Miclat on May 6, 2003, during the "Workshop on Lessons Learned from Southeast Asian and Pacific Peace Efforts," Bali, Indonesia.

14. Gus Miclat, "Best Practice in Networking and Coalition-Building: The Story of APCET," paper presented at the Workshop on Lessons Learned from Southeast Asian and Pacific Peacebuilding Efforts, Bali, May 5–7, 2003.

15. Ibid., pp. 1–2.

16. Background information from the official website of the Commission for Reception, Truth, and Reconciliation in East Timor, www.easttimor-reconciliation.org/mandate.htm. Reports on ongoing activities of the CAVR are available at www.easttimor-reconciliation.org/updates.htm.

17. "Workshop on Lessons Learned from Southeast Asian and Pacific Peace Efforts," plenary presentation, Bali, Indonesia, May 6, 2003.

18. Rizal Sukma and Edy Prasetyono, *Security Sector Reform in Indonesia: The Military and the Police,* Working Paper no. 9 (Netherlands: Netherlands Institute of International Relations "Clingendael," Conflict Research Unit, February, 2003), p. 16, available at www.clingendael.nl/cru/pdf/working_paper_9.pdf. Much of the section on security-sector reform in Indonesia is derived from this excellent paper.

19. Sukma and Prasetyono, *Security Sector Reform,* p. 17.

20. Ibid., p. 23.

21. Miriam Coronel Ferrer, "Armed to the Teeth," *Kasarinlan* 16, no. 2 (2001), available at www.upd.edu.ph/~twsc/arms_and_militaries/tws_desk_v16n2-ferrer.htm.

22. Soth Plai Ngarm, "Weapon Reduction Experience in Cambodia," working paper for "Workshop on Lessons Learned from Southeast Asian and Pacific Peace Efforts," Bali, Indonesia, May 5-7, 2003; available as html or pdf file at www.csps-ugm.or.id/bali/papers.html.

23. Much of the information on the Cambodian weapons reduction activities is drawn from Soth Plai Ngarm, "Weapon Reduction Experience in Cambodia," paper presented at the Workshop on Lessons Learned from Southeast Asian and Pacific Peacebuilding Efforts, Bali, May 5–7, 2003. See also www.wgwr.org, the website of the Working Group on Weapons Reduction.

24. James Tanis and George Gray, *In Between: Personal Experiences in the Nine-Year-Long Conflict on Bougainville, and Habuna Momouqu—Violence and the Guadalcanal Uprising in Solomon Islands,* available at www.exkiap.net/articles/miscellaneous/james_tanis.htm.

25. Michael W. Doyle, "War and Peace in Cambodia," draft working paper, available (subscribers only) at www.ciaonet.org/wps/dom01. Doyle, professor of politics and international affairs at Princeton University and senior fellow at the International Peace Academy in New York, is citing a quotation from former UN Secretary-General Boutros Boutros-Ghali.

26. See www.un.org/depts/dpko/missions/untac.htm; and Trevor Findlay, *Cambodia: The Legacy and Lessons of UNTAC,* SIPRI Research Report no. 9 (abstract), available at http://editors.sipri.se/pubs/cambodia_pr.html.

27. Clements, *Civil Society and Conflict Prevention,* p. 1.

28. Kevin Clements, "Towards Conflict Transformation and a Just Peace," in *Berghof Handbook for Conflict Transformation* (Berlin: Berghof Research Center for Constructive Conflict Management, 2001), p. 22 (itals. in orig.), available at www.berghof-handbook.net/cf.htm.

29. Ibid.

PART 2

Surveys of
Conflict Prevention and
Peacebuilding Activities

8

NORTHEAST ASIA

8.1

Regional Introduction: The Changing Regional Security Agenda in Post–September 11 Northeast Asia

James Tang

As Northeast Asia emerged from the Asian financial crisis, strength-
ened by the recognition that it had survived a most difficult economic
downturn and with more promising prospects for closer regional
cooperation at the beginning of the new millennium, it was con-
fronted with the dual challenge of dealing with the post–September 11
world order and a rising China. The world has been transformed
since the terrorist attack against the United States on September 11,
2001. Although Northeast Asia has not been the focus of attention in
the U.S.-led global campaign against terror, the terrorist attacks have
altered both U.S. perceptions of the security role of the region as well
as Northeast Asian calculations of regional security concerns. One
critical question is China's attitude toward security problems in the
region. With an outward-oriented economic strategy, China has also
become more engaged and active in both regional and world affairs
in the last few years. The implications of China's growing importance
in the region has been a matter of debate, but as one Asian commen-
tator put it in the Korean Times, *"That China is rising is not a matter*
of debate."[1] The future of Northeast Asian security has to be seen in
the context of the emergent post–September 11 world order and
China's changing role in the region.[2]

Global insecurity has been brought home vividly by a devastating act of terror against the world's financial center in New York. The elevation of homeland security in U.S. foreign policy and the military action against Afghanistan and Iraq have raised important questions in international relations. The
U.S. military action fundamentally altered the balance of power in Central
Asia and the Middle East and confirmed U.S. military and political dominance. By declaring a war on terror and launching military action against
Afghanistan and Iraq, the Bush administration has also practically redefined
the meaning of war and introduced new military doctrines in U.S. security

strategy (such as the so-called shock and awe strategy), and established the preemptive strike as a key principle in U.S. security policy.[3]

Northeast Asian governments have responded to the U.S. call for support in different ways. While most supported U.S. efforts to combat terrorism, Japan and Korea were the only East Asian countries that joined the "coalition of the willing"—the alliance of thirty states against Iraq. China has remained opposed to military action against Iraq. North Korea, which has been identified as a potential security threat by the Bush administration as part of the Axis of Evil, has made public its nuclear program and thus complicated the global security picture and created uncertainty in the region.

The strategic landscape of Northeast Asia has been dominated for a long time by major power politics in a region divided by diverse political, economic, and social conditions. The key players include not only Asian countries in the region such as China, Japan, and the two Koreas, but also two extraregional powers: the United States and Russia. Although the region saw some of the most violent military conflicts during the Cold War, it has been one of the world's most economically dynamic regions during the past several decades. Since the end of the Cold War era, Northeast Asia has been referred to as the world's most peaceful region.[4] However, potential conflicts across the Taiwan Strait and on the Korean Peninsula are still threatening regional peace. The region is not completely free from the legacy of the Cold War.

Compared to the security environment in Southeast Asia, where the myriad ethnic populations and religiously defined civil conflicts and human security crises have become far more worrying, the threat to regional peace in Northeast Asia comes still largely from interstate conflicts that tend to be military in nature. Moreover, bilateralism has remained the hallmark of the security architecture, despite the establishment of the Association of Southeast Asian Nations (ASEAN) Regional Forum (ARF) in 1994.[5] Although multilateralism took a new turn in the form of the ASEAN "plus" processes involving Southeast Asian countries and China, Japan and South Korea, traditional security problems that have haunted the region for a long time continue to be major problems for Northeast Asia. However, with the Asian financial crisis in 1997–1998 and the September 11 terrorist attacks against the United States, the Northeast Asian states have to confront the twin challenges of economic turmoil and terrorism beyond traditional threats such as territorial disputes. In providing an overview of the security situation in Northeast Asia, this chapter also examines the extent to which the twin challenges of economic problems and terrorism have altered the regional security agenda.

Following the end of the war against Iraq in May 2003, the Northeast Asian states have had to grapple with a number of challenging security issues. Although China has been able to improve its relations with the United States—a key economic partner—it is also uncomfortable with the dominance of the United States in the region and, in particular, U.S. support of Taiwan. China's relations with Japan are also complex. While the two are neighbors with mutual economic interests, regional rivalry and the legacy of Japanese atrocities in China during World War II are still key problems in their bilateral relations. However, the two do share the common security objective of regional stability, especially over the Korean Peninsula, which has remained turbulent politically.

North Korea's nuclear weapons program is a major security threat to the region. While details about the program are not known, many observers also maintain that North Korea's nuclear ambition has been driven by domestic economic woes. Indeed, even in other Northeast Asian states such as China, there is recognition that domestic economic and social issues have become increasingly intertwined with security issues. The new security concept, articulated by President Jiang Zemin in public at the Shanghai Cooperation Organization meeting in 2001, emphasized mutual trust and cooperation and also recognized the importance of nontraditional threats.[6] China's role in mediating the six-way talks over the nuclear issue in North Korea at the end of August 2003 demonstrated its willingness to address a regional security concern actively through a multilateral framework.

However, the debates over human rights standards and ideological differences between states such as China and the West have yet to be resolved. Unlike in Southeast Asia, where a multilateral framework for managing interstate regional conflicts has been highly institutionalized regionally and the importance of nontraditional security problems is more widely recognized, the processes and mechanisms for conflict management in Northeast Asia are still fluid and the role of track-two activities are more tentative.

Historical Legacies

The longer-term impact of September 11 has to be seen within the historical context of the region. Territorial disputes and national rivalry have always remained high on the security agenda in Northeast Asia. The relationship between the two Koreas, and mainland China's relations with Taiwan, are two potential flashpoints that are rooted in historical rivalry.

The situation on the divided Korean Peninsula has remained volatile since the end of the Cold War. While South Korea has undergone dramatic economic and political transformation, the socialist North has become ever more isolated and faces a domestic food shortage. President Kim Dae-jung of South Korea initiated the "Policy of Reconciliation and Cooperation Toward North Korea," widely known as the "Sunshine Policy," after he came into office in 1998. By promoting dialogue with Pyongyang instead of seeking containment of the North Korea regime, the Kim administration sought to move beyond the legacy of the Cold War and secure a long-term settlement of the Korean problem.[7] The first inter-Korean summit, of June 2001, having raised high hopes, turned out to be a disappointment. The emotional reunion of families separated by a divided nation did not result in any concrete developments toward reunification. More important, North Korea has remained "economically challenged, diplomatically isolated, and militarily unpredictable."[8]

Although the Bush administration officially endorsed the Sunshine Policy, the administration has been skeptical of North Korea's intentions. By grouping North Korea together with Iraq and Iran as part of an "axis of evil,"[9] the United States openly identified North Korea as a threat to international security. The September 11 attacks deepened U.S. suspicion of North Korea and generated tensions in U.S.–South Korean relations. Paradoxically, the U.S. response to a nontraditional security threat imposed constraints on the South Korean efforts in breaking away from the Cold War framework by engaging with North Korea. President Roh Moo-hyun has been successful in pursuing a more moderate policy toward North Korea without damaging U.S.–South Korean relations.[10]

North Korea's disclosure of its nuclear arms program in October 2002, however, has created a new security challenge for the region. The Bush administration responded by stopping oil supplies to North Korea. Under an agreement between the two governments signed in 1994, the North Korean government had agreed to freeze its nuclear weapon program in exchange for international aid and oil supplies. The crisis escalated when the North Korean government announced in December 2002 that it would reactivate nuclear facilities at Yongbyon, which had been frozen according to the 1994 agreement. North Korea's confrontational stance against the United States, and its announcement in January 2003 that it was pulling out of the Nuclear Non-Proliferation Treaty, brought the region closer to the brink of a major military conflict than it had been at any other time since the end of the Cold War. By the end of 2003 regional concerns were vividly expressed by a new report that stated, "The Korean nuclear standoff has become a high stakes, no-bluff game, where the threats are potentially greater than that posed by Iraq."[11]

The nuclear crisis in Korea, however, provided an opportunity for a concerted effort in securing peace. China successfully persuaded North Korea to take part in a six-party talk in August 2003. The six countries involved with the talks—both Koreas, China, the United States, Japan, and Russia—failed to find a solution to the problem. The talks lasted for only three days and did not produce concrete results, and the deadlock remained. In January 2004 the Institute of International and Strategic Studies suggested the North Koreans might have had one or two nuclear weapons prior to 1992, and might have obtained plutonium for two to five nuclear weapons from existing spent fuel in storage.[12] On February 5, 2004, North Korea and the United States agreed to enter into another round of six-party talks at the end of the month.

While the threat posed to regional security by North Korea's stance on its right to maintain a nuclear program is serious, China's willingness to mediate and the agreement of all the six countries to come together was a major breakthrough. A peaceful solution to the Korea problem is clearly not easy to find. In fact it was only after much prompting from the Chinese government and international pressure, that North Korea agreed to a second round of the six-party meeting. Nonetheless, the talks, which have set the precedent of a multilateral approach to one of the most critical security problems in the region, may serve as a model for wider acceptance of multilateral discussions on security issues in Northeast Asia.

The anxiety over possible military conflict across the Taiwan Strait is another major legacy of the Cold War. Although the situation has become more stable since the Sino-American rapprochement in the 1970s, tensions over the strait have not been removed. In fact, it is probably the only issue that could lead to a military confrontation between China and the United States. In 1996 a series of military exercises involving the firing of missiles in the waters near Taiwan by the People's Liberation Army became so alarming that the United States sent two aircraft carrier battle groups to the strait. While the danger of war across the strait has receded since then, the situation has remained difficult especially following the electoral victory of Taiwan's proindependence Democratic Progressive Party at the presidential election. As Kurt Campell and Derek Mitchell argue, September 11 may have significantly altered international affairs, but not the tension over the Taiwan Strait. They remarked in 2002 that "cross-strait trends remain highly troublesome despite initiatives that may appear on the surface to facilitate reconciliation over time."[13]

Both sides have remained reluctant to enter into genuine negotiations and are highly suspicious of each other. Recent military, economic, and social trends do not bode well for a long-term solution to the problem. Mainland China's growing economic power and attempts to promote economic ties with Taiwan are seen to have facilitated the mainland's ability to achieve unification on Beijing's terms. The worrying thing is that on the one hand, China is gaining ground in terms of military capabilities and could well be in the position to pose a more credible military threat to Taiwan; and on the other hand, the population in Taiwan seemed to have become less enthusiastic about the idea of reunification. Moreover, with a U.S. president sympathetic to Taiwan's position, President Chen Shuibian had taken steps to assert a more independent political identity. To the dismay of Beijing, the word "Taiwan" now appears on the cover of passports issued by "the Republic of China." Beijing also responded very strongly to Chen's remarks in early August 2003 about a referendum on Taiwan's political status.[14]

However, post–September 11 improvement of Sino-U.S. relations did provide an opportunity for the new Chinese leadership under President Hu Jintao and Premier Wen Jiabao to maintain a stable and cooperative relationship with the United States. The Bush administration also recognized the importance of Sino-U.S. relations to wider U.S. interests including terrorism, nuclear proliferation, and North Korea. During Premier Wen Jaibao's U.S. visit in December 2003, Beijing managed to persuade President Bush to declare his administration's opposition to Chen Shuibian's plan for holding a referendum on Taiwan. Responding to reporters with Wen at his side at the White House, Bush declared: "We oppose any unilateral decision by either China or Taiwan to change the status quo. And the comments and actions made by the leader

Taipei, 2000. Police battling protesters one day after the elections. The KMT—the ruling party since the Republic of China was installed on Taiwan in 1949—had just lost power for the first time. KMT supporters took to the streets to express their anger at the former president (and at the time still acting head of the KMT) Lee Teng-Hui, who was suspected of offering behind-the-scenes support to the victorious opposition party, the DPP.

of Taiwan indicate that he may be willing to make decisions unilaterally to change the status quo, which we oppose."[15] The Bush administration was clearly trying to diffuse the "referendum crisis." In fact the new Chinese leadership had also adopted a less confrontational approach. But the Taiwan question would continue to be a troubling issue in Sino-U.S. relations for a long time to come.

Since the end of the 1990s, the security structure in Northeast Asia remains very much rooted in the Cold War framework. Regional security has been built upon alliance systems that are bilateral in nature. Such bilateral arrangements have been challenged by the growing complexities of the regional security environment, including the changing role of China in the management of regional security and also the domestic political dynamics of Japan and South Korea.

Critics of the alliance system argued that it had undermined regional security. One such critic, Anthony DiFilippo, suggested in his work *The Challenges of the U.S.-Japan Military Arrangement* that the alliance itself is a source of instability in the region.[16] Responding to the new security challenges, Washington has been reluctant to abandon the "hub and spoke" approach of bilateral agreements with its key allies. Instead, the United States has attempted to strengthen the bilateral alliances in face of the new challenges. The joint declaration on security by the United States and Japan in

1996 and the revision of defense guidelines in 1997 are good examples of such an approach. In fact, Japan's commitment to the alliance has been demonstrated with the deployment of the Maritime Self-Defense Force to the Indian Ocean in support of the U.S. military action against Afghanistan in 2002 as well as its offer of aid to Iraq and its decision to deploy Japanese personnel to Iraq for reconstruction purposes in 2003. Yet the future of the U.S.-Japan security alliance, described as the most durable and successful security partnership to have emerged from the Cold War, has been increasingly questioned. This durability will be tested by the strategic change on the Korean Peninsula and by new security priorities in the aftermath of September 11.[17]

Similarly, both Washington and Seoul have attempted to renew their commitments to the bilateral security arrangements. South Korea's participation in the "coalition of the willing" in support of U.S. action in Iraq, and the Roh administration's decision to deploy Korean personnel to aid the reconstruction of postwar Iraq, are significant in this respect. The U.S.–South Korean security alliance is rather fragile given its narrow focus on the North Korean threat. Once the strategic environment on the Korean Peninsula undergoes significant change, the U.S.–South Korean alliance arrangements may not be able to broaden their application to wider security challenges or accommodate domestic political opposition in South Korea. One leading observer suggested that the most critical foreign policy issue that the Roh Moo-hyun presidency will have to contemplate before its departure in 2008 will not be North Korea but the alliance with the United States.[18]

While the bilateral alliance system has been challenged, alternative regional security arrangements have yet to emerge. Multilateral mechanisms have been established, but they are largely regarded as weak, as is the ARF, or insufficiently comprehensive, as are the Shanghai Cooperative Organization institutions. However, track-two activities and organizations such as the Council for Security Cooperation in Asia Pacific (CSCAP) have become more significant.[19] The limited success of CSCAP in providing new ideas and building confidence demonstrates not only that the regional security agenda has been changing, but also that political, economic, and social and technological developments in the region have created new dynamics in both the nature of conflicts and potential conflicts and the way such conflicts are being managed.

Dynamics Reshaping Northeast Asia and Its Conflicts

Economic, social, political, and technological changes have fundamentally transformed the regional security environment since the 1990s. In fact, from the 1970s onward, a number of East Asia countries have become highly successful economically. By the early 1990s, East Asian economies were growing faster than all other regions in the world and have since been able to narrow the gap between the rich and the poor more effectively than have economies in other parts of the world. In fact, the "high performance" Asian economies— Hong Kong, Indonesia, Japan, Malaysia, the Republic of Korea, Singapore, Taiwan, and Thailand—as the World Bank described them, not only maintained high growth but also achieved declining inequality. The economic miracle was possible because East Asian economies have made a number of sound policy choices.[20] By 1997 the East Asia and Pacific region had surpassed Western Europe as the largest regional trading partner of the United States, with an exchange valued at U.S.$529.75 billion, close to 40 percent of the latter's total trade.[21]

The East Asian success story, however, soon turned into a spectacular story of economic collapse when the region was hit by a financial crisis toward the end of 1997 and beginning of 1998. The financial turmoil that followed not only demolished the confidence in the economic dynamism in East Asia, but also revealed how vulnerable the region is to wider global forces. In the words of Alan Greenspan, the highly efficient globalized financial system not only "exposes and punishes underlying economic imprudence swiftly and decisively," but also "facilitated the transmission of financial disturbances far more effectively than ever before."[22]

The economic miracle was shattered following the Asian financial crisis. The turbulence that was created, referred to as a new breed of crisis by the International Monetary Fund,[23] not only brought devastating economic hardship and chaos to the region, but also had far-reaching social and political consequences. With the collapse of the financial and property markets, the majority of East Asian states were hit by the most serious economic downturn in recent history. The economic situation—lower wages, rising unemployment, greater poverty, less equitable distribution of income—created hardship in general. The impact on migrant workers and minorities was particularly severe. The economic downturn therefore led to major social and political problems for many states throughout East Asia.[24] Northeast Asia weathered the financial storm better than Southeast Asia. With the exception of South Korea and Hong Kong, other Northeast Asian governments managed to keep their financial markets stable. In fact, China emerged as the most resilient economy and continued its phenomenal growth despite the general downturn in the region.

As a result of the crisis, Asian leaders developed a much better understanding of the limits of state autonomy and came to accept that their abilities in managing the many economic and social problems within their national boundaries often depend on developments beyond their control. The financial crisis facilitated wider appreciation that transnational problems such as illegal migration across borders (especially of workers), drugs, the smuggling of small arms, terrorism, and the spread of infectious diseases such as SARS would require transnational responses. This reassessment of sovereign power also led to a reassessment of regional security concerns beyond the traditional agenda. Asian governments have become more interested in closer regional cooperation, and new ways of defining the security challenges have emerged.

The building of region institutions is not new to East Asia. The political divide during the Cold War, and economic and social diversities of the region, however, have prevented the rapid development of regionalism. Regional cooperation was more successful in Southeast Asia than in Northeast Asia. In the early years of the Cold War, Western powers sponsored the Southeast Asian Treaty Organization, and ASEAN was established in 1967. In 1989 the Asia Pacific Economic Council (APEC) was established, serving as a forum for addressing mainly economic issues for countries around the Pacific Rim. There were no regional institutions for East Asian countries alone. In fact, efforts to establish an East Asian grouping by Malaysian prime minister Mahatir Bin Mohamed in 1990 failed to gain support partly because of U.S. opposition. For governments in the region, the Asian financial crisis has highlighted that in a globalized world, nonmilitary forces can have major impact on state security and, at the same time, international institutions or the leading Western countries can only offer limited help. The crisis therefore helped strengthen the cooperative process in the region. The bitter experience helped bring Northeast and Southeast Asia closer together through "ASEAN Plus Three" (APT)—the informal summit between heads of government of the ten ASEAN states and Japan, China, and South Korea. The APT grew steadily since its first informal summit meeting in Kuala Lumpur in 1997.

The APT process, as Richard Stubbs has suggested, is the latest manifestation of the evolving development of East Asian regional cooperation. He also identified five regional trends that have nurtured the process:

- There are common threads in East Asia's recent experience, including the economic and social dislocation during World War II, the rise of Asian nationalism in the postwar period, major conflicts in Korea and Vietnam, and Japan's economic expansion, that have brought countries in the region together.
- There are common cultural traits, such as the importance attached to family, community, social harmony, and duty, the acceptance of hierarchy and respect for authority, that are shared among many throughout the region.
- There is a distinctive set of institutions and approaches to economic development characterized by weak societies and interventionist developmental states.
- There is an emerging East Asian capitalism that is rooted in business networks and strong state-business relations, with emphasis on production interests rather than consumer interests and results rather than ideology.
- The crosscutting pattern of the inflow of foreign direct investment has helped to bring the region's economies together.

Stubbs believes that the APT will most likely emerge as the key organization in East Asia.[25]

China's role in the APT process has been critical. It is also worth noting that the Chinese government has been willing to engage with the emerging regionwide nontraditional security agenda. In November 2002, China and ASEAN signed a joint declaration on cooperation in the field of nontraditional security issues. The declaration identified issues such as "trafficking in illegal drugs, people smuggling including trafficking in women and children, sea piracy, terrorism, arms smuggling, money laundering, international economic crime, and cyber crime" as nontraditional security problems that were "affecting regional and international security and are posing new challenges to regional and international peace and stability." China and ASEAN countries maintained that the nontraditional security issues had to be addressed with an integrated approach combining political, economic, diplomatic, legal, scientific, technological, and other means. They declared that regional and international cooperation would have to be strengthened.[26]

In fact, China's growing stature as the lead regional power had brought new dynamics to the region. The willingness displayed by China to be cooperative with its neighbors in addressing common regional problems is consistent with China's foreign policy priorities for securing a peaceful environment for economic growth. In fact earlier concerns among policymakers around the world that a rising China may pose a threat to international security seem to have given way to preoccupation with China competitiveness and the opportunities offered by a rapidly expanding Chinese economy.[27] In the aftermath of September 11, China became an important partner to U.S. efforts to combat global terrorism. Although China did not support U.S. military action against Iraq, it has remained cooperative on the broader global antiterrorism campaign, and has mediated in the six-way talks over North Korea's nuclear program. In September 2003, Secretary of State Colin Powell declared that "US relations with China are the best they have been since President Nixon's first visit." While suggesting that while there were still major differences between the two countries on issues such as human rights and the proliferation of missile technology, Powell highlighted the fact that China and the United States had managed to cooperate closely over the question of North Korea's nuclear program. He suggested that neither government would like to see nuclear weapons developed and deployed by North Korea and a worsening refugee crisis on China's border, and that both would like to avert war on the Korean Peninsula.[28]

There are encouraging signs that major players in the region are more willing to engage in multilateral dialogues to deal with the new security concerns. China even went so far as to assert that in addition to its willingness to engage with ASEAN on nontraditional security challenges, its commitment to the ARF, and active role in the establishment of the Shanghai Cooperative Organizations demonstrated it is serious about a new security concept.[29]

While the attitude toward nontraditional security threats underwent significant changes, and nations appear to have embraced the virtue of multilateral cooperation, East Asian states had been spending more on weapons than had the rest of the world. Between 1993 and 2002, military expenditures edged upward at 3 percent for the world as a whole, but increased by 22 percent in East Asia (see Figure 8.1.1). China and the Koreas have accounted for

Figure 8.1.1 Military Expenditure in East Asia, 1993–2002

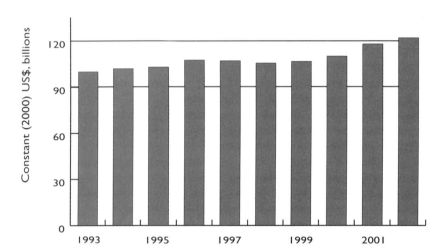

the majority of the region's overall military spending during the past two decades. However, as a result of the financial crisis in 1997, the military expenditure in the region decreased through 2002, when the three major Northeast Asian countries, China, Japan, and South Korea, were again among the top ten military spenders in the world and were accountable for a 6 percent increase in global military expenditure in real terms to U.S.$794 billion.[30]

While the increase in global military expenditure can be attributed to U.S. efforts to combat terrorism, the increases in East Asia have been driven by military reform and the buildup of greater military capacity by major powers such as China. However, China has demonstrated its growing maturity as a regional power in the aftermath of the Asian financial crisis and following September 11. Its domestic need for economic development has also driven it to pursue a stable security environment. There are signs that Northeast Asian countries are more prepared to engage in multilateral dialogues and broaden the definition of security, but the potential for military conflicts remains high on the regional agenda. The first six-way talks on North Korea's nuclear program represented a major step forward in developing a multilateral framework for managing conflicts in Northeast Asia, but have not yet found a solution to the problem. The political divide between China and the West may have been shifted, but differences remain.

On October 4, 2003, in response to a U.S. congressional report on human rights in China, the Chinese Foreign Ministry rejected the findings of the report by saying that it had "distorted the facts and attacked China by using the issues of human rights, religion and the Falungong." Foreign Ministry spokesman Kong Quan stated, "This only shows the report drafter's arrogance and prejudices. We express strong displeasure and resolute opposition over the issue."[31]

China's domestic political development may prove critical in the longer-term development of regional security. While China has enjoyed unprecedented prosperity in recent years, critics have also pointed out "mounting governance deficits." In a *Foreign Affairs* article Minxin Pei of the Carnegie Endowment for International Peace discussed China's governance crisis, with reference to what he called "dot communism," by arguing that the country's political system is not compatible to the requirements of the rule of law, a market economy, and an open society. He challenged those who predicted the further rise of China by asking "whether China, without restructuring its political system, can ever gain the institutional competence required to generate power and prosperity on a sustainable basis."[32] While it is difficult to predict the future, China's long-term political situation may not remain stable if the Chinese leadership is not prepared to address the inherent contradiction between political institutions and economic policy as well as the social transformation taking place.

Outside China, however, social and economic changes have facilitated the growth of a more dynamic civil society. For example, the number of Track-Two meetings on nontraditional security matters involving nongovernmental organizations (NGOs) has increased steadily in the region. The inventory on multilateral meetings in Asia Pacific listed forty-five Track-One events, but ninety Track-Two meetings and twenty-three Track-Three meetings for 2002.[33] Although civic society is much weaker in East Asia compared with Europe or North America, NGOs are becoming more important as partners to governments in the region as the security agenda broadens to incorporate issues such as food security, environmental degradation, and drug and human trafficking.

Prospects

Although no major military conflict has occurred for more than two decades in Northeast Asia, the danger of war and other security threats is real. The security agenda presents a myriad of challenges, from traditional conflicts over the Korean Peninsula and the Taiwan Strait—problems remaining from the days of the Cold War—to newer concerns such as global economic turbulence and other nontraditional security issues such as terrorism, transnational crime, and environmental and public health problems.

The impact of September 11 on Northeast Asian regional security has far-reaching consequences. In the aftermath of the terrorist attacks against the United States, the Bush administration adjusted its security policy in East Asia. Instead of confronting China as a potential strategic competitor, the United States sought China's cooperation in the war on terror. Unlike Southeast Asian states, where Islamic sentiments can be volatile, Northeast Asian states' support of the United States has been unequivocal. But concerns about U.S. unilateralism have also been expressed.

In meeting the new security challenges in the post–September 11 world, Northeast Asian states have recognized the value of regional cooperation and developed a greater acceptance of multilateralism and Track-Two diplomacy.

Prior to the terrorist attacks, Northeast Asian states had been gradually moving toward a greater sense of regionalism as they struggled to recover from the economic devastation brought by the Asian financial crisis. Nontraditional security concerns and transnational threats in the form of terrorism and other crimes, environmental degradation, public health, and illegal migration have also become accepted as major issues on the regional agenda.

The APT process had provided the region with a viable way forward in developing a regionwide institution to address a full range of political, economic, and social issues that are critical to the security of Northeast Asia. A combination of Track-One, Track-Two, and Track-Three activities has also provided a basis for the development of stronger institutions and a more coherent framework in the management of regional conflicts. The difficulties of institutionalizing such a framework, however, cannot be exaggerated. The security landscape is being transformed in complex ways. While Northeast Asian states seem positive about the concept of common security and have been able to identify mutual interests in managing the new security challenges, deep-rooted historical animosity has not been removed and domestic political issues have yet to be fully addressed. The outlook for a more secure Northeast Asia is promising in the longer run, but the process will be tortuous.

James Tang is director of the Institute of China and Global Development, and head and associate professor in the Department of Politics and Public Administration at the University of Hong Kong. Specializing in the field of international relations, his research and teaching interests include Chinese foreign policy, international political economy in Asia Pacific, and political transition in Hong Kong. His current research topics include localization of Chinese foreign policy, Hong Kong's role in the World Trade Organization, and nontraditional security in East Asia.

Notes

1. Frank Ching, "China: Threat or Opportunity?" *Korean Times,* 18 December, 2002. See http://times.hankooki.com/lpage/opinion/200212/kt2002121816322911600.htm.

2. One comprehensive account of China's changing role from a Chinese perspective is Wang Jisi, "China's Changing Role in Asia," The Atlantic Council, January 2004. See www.acus.org/Publications/occasionalpapers/Asia/WangJisi_Jan_04.pdf.

3. The Bush administration's "shock and awe" military strategy in Iraq was conceived by Harlan K. Ullman and James P. Wade in their coauthored book *Shock and Awe: Achieving Rapid Dominance* (Washington, D.C.: National Defense University Press, 1996). On the principle of preemptive strike, see "The National Security Strategy of the United States of America," released by the White House, available at www.whitehouse.gov/nsc/nss.html.

4. Robert Ross, "The U.S.–China Peace: Great Power Politics, Spheres of Influence, and the Peace of East Asia," paper presented at the International Conference on East Asia, Latin America, and the "New" Pax Americana, February 14–15, 2003, Weatherhead Center for International Affairs, Harvard University.

5. See Michael Leifer, ASEAN Regional Forum, *Adelphi Paper* no. 302, International Institute for Security Studies (London: Oxford University Press, 1996). Official documents are available at the ARF website, www.aseansec.org/arf.htm.

6. Chinese Ministry of Foreign Affairs, "Position Paper on the New Security Concept," June 8, 2002. For a scholarly analysis of the development of the concept, see

Michael Yahuda, "Chinese Dilemmas in Thinking About Regional Security Architecture," *Pacific Review,* 16, no. 2 (2003): 189–206. A good background of earlier discussions by Chinese strategists on the security environment is provided in Michael Pillsbury, *China Debates the Future Security Environment* (Washington, D.C.: National Defense University Press, 2000).

7. An outline of Kim's Sunshine Policy can be found in "New Challenges for the Korean Peninsula and Northeast Asia: The Role of the Republic of Korea and the United States," remarks by President Kim Dae Jung at a luncheon given by the Korea Society, the Asia Society, and the Council on Foreign Relations, June 8, 1998.

8. "Korean Security: The Highest Hurdle," *Proliferation Brief* 3, no. 30 (October 20, 2000).

9. State of the Union Address, January 2002, available at www.whitehouse.gov/news/releases/2002/01/20020129-11.html.

10. For an early assessment of implications of Roh's election as president of South Korea on U.S.–South Korean relations, see "Korea: U.S.–Korean Relations—Issues for Congress," Issue Brief for Congress, update, March 17, 2003.

11. North Korea: What are the options?" CNN December 10, 2003. See http://edition.cnn.com/2003/WORLD/asiapcf/east/08/28/nkorea.options/index.html.

12. Kurt M. Campbell and Derek J. Mitchell, "Crisis in the Taiwan Strait?" *Foreign Affairs* 80, no. 4 (July–August 2001): 14–25. See author update, August 2002, available at www.foreignaffairs.org/20020801faupdate10331/kurt-m-campbell-derek-j-mitchell/crisis-in-the-taiwan-strait.html.

13. Press statement by Dr. John Chipman, IISS Director on the IISS report *North Korea's Weapons Programmes: A Net Assessment,* Jan 21, 2004.

14. For Beijing's position, see "Taiwan Referendum Plays with Fire," *Commentary on People's Daily,* updated *(Beijing Times)* July 11, 2003, available at http://fpeng.peopledaily.com.cn/200307/11/eng20030711_119989.shtml.

15. Press release by the White House December 9, 2003, "Remarks by President Bush and Premier Wen Jiabao in Photo Opportunity. The Oval Office." See www.whitehouse.gov/news/releases/2003/12/20031209-2.html. See also *China Daily,* December 10, 2003. See www1.chinadaily.com.cn/en/doc/2003-12/10/content_288832.htm.

16. Anthony DiFilippo, *The Challenges of the U.S.-Japan Military Arrangement: Competing Security Transitions in a Changing International Environment* (New York: M. E. Sharpe, 2002).

17. See Charles M. Perry and Toshi Yoshihara, *The U.S.-Japan Alliance: Preparing for Korean Reconciliation and Beyond* (Cambridge: Institute for Foreign Policy Analysis, 2003).

18. Victor D. Cha, "The Coming Change in the U.S.-Korea Alliance," *National Interest* 2, no. 14 (April 9, 2003). For a more comprehensive analysis, see *Stability and Confidence Building on the Korean Peninsula* (Cambridge: Institute for Foreign Policy Analysis, August 2003), available at www.ifpa.org/pdf/interim-srkorea.pdf.

19. Sheldon W. Simon, "Evaluating Track II Approaches to Security Diplomacy in the Asia-Pacific: The CSCAP Experience," *Pacific Review* 15, no. 2 (May 2002): 167–200.

20. World Bank, *The East Asian Miracle: Economic Growth and Public Policy* (New York: Oxford University Press, 1993).

21. "U.S. Economic Relations with East Asia and the Pacific," Fact Sheet released by the Bureau of East Asian and Pacific Affairs, U.S. Department of State, October 26, 1998.

22. Statement by Alan Greenspan, chairman, Board of Governors of the Federal Reserve System, before the Subcommittee on Foreign Operations of the Committee on Appropriations, U.S. Senate, March 3, 1998.

23. "Recovery from the Asian Crisis and the Role of the IMF," International Monetary Fund Brief, June 2000.

24. For an analysis of the social impact of the crisis, see Jong-Wha Lee and

Changyong Rhee, *Social Impacts of the Asian Crisis: Policy Challenges and Lessons,* Occasional Paper no. 33, prepared for the UN Development Programme, Human Development Report Office, January 1999. See also "The Social Impact of the Asian Financial Crisis," technical report for discussion at the High-Level Tripartite Meeting on Social Responses to the Financial Crisis in East and South-East Asian Countries, Bangkok, April 22–24, 1998.

25. Richard Stubbs, "The ASEAN Plus Three: Emerging East Asian Regionalism?" *Asian Survey* 42, no. 3 (May–June 2002): 440–445.

26. See for example, "the Talk of the town at Davos: China," *International Herald Tribune,* January 24, 2004 at IHT Online http://iht.com/articles/126444.html; "China is the Talk of Davos," Jan. 23, 2004, *Businessweek Online* www.businessweek.com/bwdaily/dnflash/jan2004/nf20040123_3923.htm.

27. The full text of the joint declaration is available at the Chinese Foreign Ministry website, www.fmprc.gov.cn/eng/topics/zgcydyhz/dlczgdm/t26290.htm.

28. Remarks at the Elliott School of International Affairs, Secretary Colin L. Powell, George Washington University, Washington, D.C., September 5, 2003; see the State Department website, www.state.gov/secretary/rm/2003/23836.htm.

29. Chinese Ministry of Foreign Affairs, "Position Paper on the New Security Concept."

30. Based on the latest information from the Stockholm International Peace Research Institute's database, http://databases.sipri.se. See also Kul C. Gautam, UNICEF regional director, East Asia and the Pacific region, "Weapons or Well-Being? East Asia's Most Important Choice for the New Millennium," presentation at the Manila Social Forum, November 9–12, 1999.

31. *Xinhua News* (Beijing), October 4, 2003.

32. Minxin Pei "China's Governance Crisis," *Foreign Affairs* 81, no. 5 (September–October 2002): 96–109.

33. *Dialogue and Research Monitor: Inventory of Multilateral Meetings on Asia Pacific Security Issues and Community Building,* Japan Center for International Exchange, New York, available at http://www.jcie.or.jp/drm/research.html#7.

8.2

Introduction:
Japan—Accepting the Challenges of
Conflict Prevention and Peacebuilding

Nobuhiko Suto

Japan's entry into the field of peacebuilding in conflict zones represents the end of an era. In August 2003 the Japanese Diet (House of Representatives) approved a law that enables the significant deployment of self-defense forces to Iraq. The bill was passed in response to the urgent request from the United States under the title of "peace and reconstruction of Iraq."[1] Behind this dramatic and challenging shift in Japanese military policy from self-defense to international cooperation, however, lies a fundamental transformation of Japan's posture for global peacebuilding in the post–Cold War world system. Although Japan has been known as a major provider of official development assistance (ODA), it has been silent both in actual conflict resolution and in peacebuilding.[2] Now, Japan is recognizing its political responsibility for peacebuilding, particularly in Asia, and trying to mobilize its power, resources, and ideas to be used for peacebuilding in the eastern Asia Pacific region. Simultaneously, the government is recognizing the importance of the concept of "human security" and the power of emerging civil society organizations, and is trying to change the entire posture of its foreign policy and diplomacy.

The purpose of this chapter is to describe recent developments in Japan in the field of conflict prevention and peacebuilding in East Asia (Northeast and Southeast Asia) and the Pacific region. These developments are the result of structural changes in the post–Cold War system. This chapter also addresses the role that Japan is likely to play in the next few years to enhance its efforts to secure peace and stability in this region.

Following World War II, Japan decided—or was forced to decide by the Occupation forces—not to intervene in any international conflicts. Intervention was proscribed even for the purposes of peacemaking, since most of Japan's military aggression in 1930s and 1940s had been conducted under the guise of bringing peace and stability to conflict zones. The combination of

153

legal restrictions, especially as set out in Article 9 of the Japanese constitution,[3] the stance taken by bureaucrats and political leaders regarding international disputes, and a peace culture that developed among the population at an early stage of the postwar era resulted in an enduring "pacifism" and a passive attitude in Japan toward peacebuilding in the world.

Japan has maintained a conservative posture toward peacebuilding and peacekeeping activities, even toward peacekeeping operations carried out under the auspices of the United Nations. Japan's reticence toward peacekeeping is due to several factors, including:

- The nation's "historical trauma"
- The constraints of its constitution, which explicitly prohibits the exertion of military strength beyond Japan's territory as a means of conflict resolution.
- Other related regulations regarding self-defense forces and guidelines such as the ban on the export of arms.

These factors can be seen to have impeded Japan's military involvement even in peacekeeping or peacebuilding roles. In fact, Japan was absent from any kind of military involvement outside its borders, including peacekeeping operations by the UN in the 1960s and 1970s, because of the legacy of military invasions and occupations in Asian countries before and during World War II.[4] These invasions caused huge casualties throughout the entire eastern Asia Pacific region including, ultimately, Japan.

Japan's nonmilitary resources, by contrast, have been used to enhance the peace and security of the region. ODA has been used frequently as a diplomatic tool, replacing a military contribution to the international security system.

The Gulf War: A Turning Point

The invasion of the sovereign state of Kuwait by Iraq in 1990 was a great shock to all who believed that war had become a "dead language" in the post–Cold War world. It also led to enormous pressure being put on Japan by the international community (mainly the United States) to intervene in the ensuing conflict alongside other members of the assembled allied forces.

The Japanese government took this international pressure seriously, and tried to comply with the request by contributing militarily in support of its ally, the United States, in the form of peacekeeping operations. However, such a sudden change of fundamental security policy from self-defense to international cooperation aroused severe public criticism. In consequence, the Japanese government responded only by financing the military operations of the allied forces, instead of actually dispatching its self-defense forces to Kuwait.

Besides facing criticism from the general public, the Japanese government realized that it lacked a fundamental legal framework under its constitution for sending its self-defense forces overseas. It needed laws and regulations regarding the forces, and standard operational procedures such as rules of engagement in using arms.

Yokosuka, 16 December 2002. People wave Japanese navy flags from a pier as the Aegis-equipped destroyer *Kirishima* of Japan's Marine Self-Defence Force leaves Yokosuka Naval Base, suburban Tokyo. The *Kirishima* was being sent out to bolster the U.S. fleet in the Indian Ocean as it turned its attention to the possible war in Iraq.

This unexpected crisis and the request for a military contribution by the United States provoked a series of intense discussions in the Japanese Diet. These debates led to a gradual recognition of the need to review and soften the regulations of the self-defense forces to enlarge their activities. This recognition in turn led to a dramatic transformation of government policy in the field of international peacekeeping activities.

Although Japan failed to answer the request for a military contribution to the Gulf War, contributing instead U.S.$13 billion to cover almost one-fourth of the military expenditures of the operation, there emerged a kind of consensus among the population that Japan should contribute more in the military domain and should dispatch more human resources to solve global problems.

The Gulf War thus prompted a realization in Japan, on the part of both the government and individual citizens, of the need to cooperate in peacebuilding activities. At that time, however, the activities of Japanese civil society organizations were not highly developed and were not responding to global crisis, though some low-level humanitarian efforts were undertaken by a number of citizen action groups.

There were a number of precedents for Japanese participation in peacebuilding activities. In 1980s, the refugee outflows in Cambodia, Laos, and Vietnam had attracted the attention of a some citizen groups. The famines and humanitarian crises in the former Yugoslavia, Somalia, and Rwanda in the early 1990s had also aroused the concern of Japanese civil society in general.

Volunteer organizations such as the Japan Volunteer Center and the Association for Aid and Relief had responded to those humanitarian crises by providing emergency aid to the refugees.[5]

Cambodia had been suffering from the trauma of the Khmer Rouge period and in order to alleviate this situation, the United Nations created a major peacekeeping operation called the UN Transitional Authority in Cambodia (UNTAC). UNTAC was to carry out a comprehensive peacebuilding program, from cease-fire to democratization. The appointment of Yasushi Akashi, special envoy of the UN Secretary-General, attracted great interest in Japan. Japan would play a role in peacekeeping under the auspices of the UN for the first time, and this again had the effect of stimulating debate regarding Japan's contribution to peace and stability in Asia, breaking something of a political taboo that had prevailed since the end of World War II.

Although Japan's contribution to UNTAC was limited, it sent a self-defense engineering battalion for the construction of roads, as well as liaison officers for UNTAC headquarters and a group of civilian police officers to provide security for the impending elections. The dispatch of a battalion of engineers to Cambodia, which was a success, helped to lower the public's psychological resistance to Japanese intervention, and promoted the idea of expanding the role of the self-defense troops in various noncombat functions. In 1996, another self-defense battalion was sent to the Israeli-occupied Golan Heights to participate in the UN mission supervising Israel's disengagement.

Meanwhile, one Japanese volunteer's life was lost in support activities during the election supervision, and a civilian police officer was killed in an ambush by Khmer Rouge in the peacekeeping operations in northern Cambodia. Despite these losses, more and more people were welcoming the idea of Japan making a more direct contribution to peace and stability in Asia.

At this stage, however, the Japanese government, the mass media, and the general public alike tended to regard UN peacekeeping operations as the sole measure for peacebuilding, and they focused almost exclusively on developing Japan's contribution to peacekeeping operations. The psychological, institutional, and legal barriers to sending its self-defense forces abroad had been so overwhelming that Japanese institutions were incapable of recognizing the gravity of the problems inherent in peacebuilding and the need to take a holistic approach to it.

Developing Civil Society Organizations

Traditionally, civil society organizations such as nongovernmental organizations (NGOs) and nonprofit organizations have played a minor role in Japanese society compared with the government and private sectors, which have been dominant especially in the post–World War II era. There are several reasons for this imbalance. One reason is the weakness of religious groups in social activities. During Japan's Age of Civil Wars in the fifteenth and sixteenth centuries, some Buddhist factions were very aggressive in pushing for the incorporation of their religious ideals into secular life. They confronted the warlords, but were ruthlessly oppressed. Religious organizations then survived by keeping out of sensitive political and social problems, and by concentrating instead on secular religious ceremonies such as funerals. This trend continued throughout the Edo Period and remained a kind of social norm even after the Meiji Restoration (1868). Although Christian missions were allowed following the restoration, they remained on the margins of society, and volunteer organizations that in other countries might ordinarily have developed through historical incidents (such as the continuous outbreak of wars in Europe) were not active.

Perhaps the toughest obstacle to the development of NGOs is the Japanese tax system, which discourages donations from private corporations and wealthy individuals. Japanese tax authorities do not generally provide any incentive through tax exemptions or deductions for charitable contributions. And ironically, the Japanese constitution (Article 89) also prohibits the transfer of governmental money to organizations that are not under the control of the government. As a result of these historic and institutional factors, NGOs remained undeveloped.

However, facing a mushrooming of regional conflicts and an outflow of refugees or internally displaced persons (IDPs), and keeping pace with the growing interest in Japan's contribution to peacebuilding, from the 1980s onward many NGOs were formed, mainly in the field of humanitarian assistance to provide food, shelter, medicine, and medical services. Such organizations included the Association of Medical Doctors of Asia and Peace Winds Japan.

As humanitarian tragedies occurred in Rwanda, Bosnia, Kosovo, Afghanistan, and elsewhere, the Japanese government began providing emergency funds for NGOs to tackle human crises. The government eventually created an umbrella organization named the Japan Platform, which also had the support of the business community, to accelerate and reinforce the emergency relief activities of Japanese NGOs. The Ministry of Foreign Affairs also established a new section for overseeing NGOs, via the Economic Cooperation Bureau.

Traditionally, the Japanese government had been cautious about providing funds directly to NGOs. For bureaucrats in the Ministry of Foreign Affairs, such projects were not necessarily legitimate uses of taxpayer money, and even for projects that aimed to provide medical care and education, only hardware such as buildings and equipment were liable to be financed. The government was rarely willing to cover the "soft parts" of the project, such as miscellaneous expenses and NGOs' administration costs.

These rigid guidelines in allocating financial resources did not meet the actual and urgent needs of NGOs operating on the front lines, and as a result severe antagonism built up between the government and NGOs. As a compromise, the Japanese government introduced a system of small, grassroots grants (up to U.S.$50,000 per project) for the quick and flexible transfer of funds to NGOs.

At that point, governmental support and the scope of activities of Japanese NGOs remained at a preliminary stage and in value-free areas, providing, for example, emergency relief, food, and medical and educational support, generally regarded as clear human necessities and thus not subject to political debate. More sensitive fields such as democratization, disarmament, and capacity building, which can involve social and political conflicts of interests among the donors, host-country governments, and recipients, were still not recognized as legitimate fields for NGO activities.

The publication of the *Agenda for Peace* in 1992 by Boutros Boutros-Ghali, then UN Secretary General, made a positive impression on both Japanese scholars and the NGO community, and a few NGOs emerged that specialized in the fields of preventive diplomacy, peacebuilding, and support for democratization. For example, Interband, established in 1992 to meet the growing need for early warning and crisis prevention around the world, gradually expanded its activities into the fields of election monitoring, small arms reduction, postconflict peacebuilding, and disarmament, demobilization, and reintegration of soldiers.[6]

The rise of Track Two diplomacy as a way of breaking through deadlocks in official diplomacy, and the successes of the international campaign to ban land mines and the Ottawa Process gave additional impetus to Japanese NGOs. They recognized that fields that had hitherto been regarded as the exclusive preserves of governments could be addressed by civil society organizations, and they started to develop their capacities in these fields.

Two additional factors contributed to the development of Japanese NGOs. One was the Great Hanshin Earthquake of 1995. Faced with the destruction of their hometown, citizens became acutely aware of the limitations of local and national governments. Many people set up their own organizations to deliver food and water and to take care of victims, and unprecedented numbers of students and citizens from all over the country mobilized to help them.

About the same time, Japan was starting to suffer from rapid demographic aging and other social problems inevitable in mature economies. Meanwhile, local governments had to cut their budgets and scale down their operations. These circumstances prompted the establishment of volunteer and civil society organizations. Finally, in 1998 the Japanese government enacted a law granting legal status to nonprofit organizations.

A Changing Security Environment

Since the late 1990s, the Japanese government has drastically changed its fundamental posture on peacebuilding. Then prime minister Keizo Obuchi signed the Ottawa Treaty, banning land mines, in 1997, after long and tedious lobbying of the Defense Agency, which had been opposing the ban and the destruction of Japan's land mines. The signing of this treaty was welcomed with surprise by the NGO community in Japan. Simultaneously, the Japanese government, which had been widely criticized for its traditional diplomatic posture and its conventional usage of ODA, realized a number of ambitious programs for peacebuilding, conflict resolution, and prevention. These programs were influenced by the emerging concept of "human security."

In December 1998, Prime Minister Obuchi made a speech in Hanoi that called for the establishment of a trust fund for human security in the United Nations. This was realized in March 1999 by the donation of approximately U.S.$4.6 million. That same year, the Japanese government contributed an additional U.S.$5.5 million to the fund to support projects for Kosovar refugees and for the reconstruction of East Timor after independence from Indonesia. The purpose of this fund is to support UN-related projects dedicated to solving contemporary problems in the human security domain, such as refugee/IDP problems, HIV/AIDS, environmental deterioration, regional and ethnic conflicts, land mines, small arms, narcotics, and poverty. According to the Japanese government, the total sum raised was U.S.$170 million in 2001; the fund became the largest trust fund established in the United Nations.

Backed up by the growing interest of the general public in humanitarian assistance, and faced with growing criticism, on the other hand, from the public and politicians that Japan was just funding and not acting, the Japanese government promoted a number of projects and actually participated in various UN peacebuilding projects. The government participated in international election monitoring in Cambodia in 1998 and Indonesia in 1999. At about the same time, the Japanese government recognized the importance of small arms as a key element hindering the stability of conflict areas, and with the moral underpinning of its own policy of never having exported weapons, it became very active in the field of small arms reduction, appointed a special ambassador on the issue, and organized a number of conferences.

Toward a Full Commitment

In the late 1990s the Japanese government started to position peacebuilding activities as an essential part of formal diplomacy in a rapidly changing international political environment. This meant that Japan had to shift its resources drastically from traditional diplomacy to peacebuilding. Policy changes were also required, starting with enormous improvements in diplomatic structure. The Ministry of Foreign Affairs started to mobilize nondiplomatic resources and to establish tools for peacebuilding.

This dramatic change in policy was not easy for Japan, since sooner or later it was bound to confront two sensitive constitutional issues: Article 9, which prohibits any military activities outside Japanese territory; and Article 89, which prohibits direct government funding of NGOs. Changing laws and regulations regarding the self-defense forces, which at present are unable to participate fully in peacekeeping activities even under the clear mandate of the United Nations, could cause additional tension in domestic politics.

What is missing in Japan's shift in diplomatic goals, however, is not just clear legitimacy in utilizing military force for peacemaking purposes, or far-reaching reforms of Japan's traditional development assistance policies and the organizational response mechanisms inside the Ministry of Foreign Affairs. To make multi-track diplomacy successful, Japan also needs to develop a capacity to mobilize a wide range of human resources, including NGOs specializing in relevant fields, and to convince stakeholders in society to actively engage in peacebuilding.

In order to cope with these serious shortcomings, the Japanese government has been carrying out experimental programs and projects to address the issues and to develop necessary human resources. One example was the commitment, noted above, to support the reconstruction and rehabilitation of East Timor after its independence in 2002. In addition to ordinary economic assistance in various rehabilitation projects, Japan sent a self-defense battalion, the so-called Japan Engineering Group, for the reconstruction of roads, while the Ministry of Foreign Affairs proposed a number of projects in the field of post-conflict peacebuilding, including an especially noteworthy project to reintegrate former combatants into society. The reintegration of former soldiers and civilians who had participated in clandestine operations is difficult, but it is regarded as one of the most crucial tasks in war-torn societies such as East Timor. Japan's efforts in disarmament, demobilization, and reintegration, combining disarmament and demobilization with the development of rural society, may achieve a breakthrough in this challenging field.

Japan has also started experimental work in Cambodia and is now undertaking ambitious commitments in Afghanistan. The government started a special program called the Ogata Initiative, led by Sadako Ogata, former head of the UN High Commissioner for Refugees, with a trust fund of U.S.$2.2 million. The initiative comprises a package of economic aid in order to support the stability of regions outside Kabul, with special financial support of U.S.$750,000 dedicated to accelerating the establishment of a new constitution in Afghanistan.

In addition, Japan is promoting slow but steady efforts toward the reconstruction of peace and harmony in conflict areas. Roundtables and other initiatives for peacebuilding are now frequently used, making the most of Japan's neutral position, unique location, and financial support. For the recovery of democracy in Myanmar, Japan used private and public efforts to soften the attitude of the military government, using economic incentives on one hand and political pressure on the other. These efforts led eventually to the release of Aung San Suu Kyi from house arrest, representing an important step toward the general democratization of society. Unfortunately, those continued efforts were drastically undermined by violence that occurred in Depayin on May 30, 2003, and led to the rearrest of Aung San Suu Kyi.[7] The Japanese government responded quickly by applying diplomatic pressure on the Myanmar government, suspending economic assistance and demanding the immediate release from jail of Aung and other National League for Democracy leaders.

With respect to the ongoing conflict in Sri Lanka, the Japanese government has been working for the peace and stability of the region, supporting the efforts by the Norwegian government to facilitate peace negotiations between the Sri Lankan government and the rebels. In order to promote the peace process, the Japanese government appointed a special envoy, Yasushi Akashi, in October 2002 to help to accelerate dialogue between the government and the Liberation Tigers of Tamil Eelam (LTTE), and to continue Japan's efforts to foster reconciliation and rehabilitation.

It is not an easy task to ensure constant progress, and there are always ups and downs in such peace processes. Even when there were growing expectations for the acceleration of peace negotiations, the LTTE's sudden boycott of the Tokyo Peace Conference in June 2003 deeply disappointed all countries concerned. In response, the Japanese government sent a vice minister in July 2003 to Jaffna (the LTTE's stronghold, which has been badly damaged by the conflict), to call for further dialogue with the Sri Lankan government.[8]

In December 2002, when the world was focused on the situation in Iraq and the attitude of the UN weapons inspection team, news of a cease-fire agreement between the Indonesian government and the Aceh Independence Movement Group (GAM) was welcome news for the Japanese government, which had been patiently working to promote dialogue between the two conflicting parties. Both parties had agreed to a preparatory meeting in Tokyo on peace and reconstruction in Aceh.

Unfortunately, the expectation of the world was betrayed again by the military aggression of the Indonesian military forces in May 2003, which swept through villages in Aceh province. This kind of flare-up not only is an expression of antagonism between GAM and the government, but also reflects the political struggle in the Indonesian political arena over future leadership. This incident shows the difficulties and limitations of peace negotiations and additional facilitation activities, and how they are inextricably linked to the internal and structural political problems of the country.

Remaining Questions

Responding to the turbulent climate of the world in the post–Cold War era, the Japanese government, and the Ministry of Foreign Affairs in particular, have drastically changed Japan's fundamental policy of almost half a century, and started to promote ambitious endeavors to cope with the growing demands of the international community. Even conventional ODA has been transformed, and is now being used strategically for the peace and stability of the eastern Asia Pacific region. This approach will likely continue in the next few years.

The Ministry of Foreign Affairs has published the "New ODA Charter," drawn up in response to advances in globalization and political changes after the terrorist attacks in the United States on September 11, 2001. The document proposes that the Japanese government should use ODA more strategically, should establish targets for the elimination of poverty and humanitarian crises, and should work more in partnership with citizens and NGOs.[9]

In addition to these considerable challenges for policymakers, government-oriented peacebuilding initiatives face a number of uncertainties. Due to the immaturity and inexperience of civil society organizations and the short history of genuine mutual cooperation, the partnership between the Japanese government and NGOs is still at an early stage and remains fragile. The government is prone to regard NGOs either as hindrances to official diplomacy or as subcontractors who should follow the instructions of the contractor—that is, the government. In fact, there is growing disharmony between the two entities over objectives and views of the contemporary world.

In the wake of unilateral actions of the United States following the September 11 terrorist attacks, and in particular the military attack against the Iraqi regime without authorization from the UN, and the Japanese government's blind support for the military actions of the Bush administration in Afghanistan and Iraq, the majority of Japanese NGOs working in the field are finding themselves seemingly at odds with the government with respect to their perspectives on international political developments.

Some of the internal tensions are evident in Japanese policies toward North Korea; the attitude of the Japanese government has arguably changed frequently, shifting between a so-called Sunshine Policy of supplying foods and medicine through channels of the Red Cross and NGOs and a stern attitude against North Korea in reflection of Japan's antipathy to the regime's abductions and nuclear weapons program.[10] Resulting friction between the government and NGOs involved in peacebuilding will continue or even be exacerbated if the political uncertainty in the eastern Asia Pacific region worsens and instability increases. The sheer number of unresolved regional issues left over from the Cold War makes such increases in uncertainty and instability inevitable.[11]

Since the government has been slow and reticent to directly confront and resolve the North Korean issues, a number of NGOs and citizens have tried to rescue refugees from North Korea, providing shelters and ways to escape to freedom. Some of these organizations have helped refugees flee into Japanese embassies and consulates in search of sanctuary, where they can then request transfer to third countries.[12] Although these are unique cases involving Japan's unusual relations with North Korea (there are no official or diplomatic relations between the two countries), some of these NGOs are in fact overtly challenging Japanese foreign policy.

Almost certainly, the relationship between the government and civil society organizations will become more complex, interdependent, and delicate. Differences over organizational missions and goals are likely to remain or even widen, depending on whether the government of Japan continues to automatically accede to the demands and embrace the views of a U.S. administration whose policies on international peace, security, and stability are shaped in large part by a group of neoconservative policymakers. Civil society in Japan needs to be more vocal in calling for the government to intensify its peacebuilding efforts, and both the government and NGOs must work harder to achieve a genuine partnership.

Last but not least, we must focus on emerging risks, including in particular the inadequacies of the UN system as revealed by its inability to effectively deal with the war against Iraq; the increased risks of ethnoreligious conflicts in the eastern Asia Pacific region; and the risks of escalating conflict in Indonesia, in the Taiwan Strait, and on the Korean Peninsula. The failure of the United Nations will inevitably weaken Japan's resolve to engage in peacebuilding in the region. What is not yet certain is whether both the government and NGOs will remain important mediators or whether they will become active participants in the process of resolving conflicts, under the auspices of a regional "peacebuilder."

Nobuhiko Suto is chairman of InterBand, professor at Tokai University, and member of the Japanese House of Representatives.

Notes

1. "The Law Concerning the Social Measures on Humanitarian and Reconstruction Assistance in Iraq" was established on June 26, 2003.

2. Japan's economic assistance to least-developed countries started from compensation for war damages and gradually shifted toward development assistance. Until recently, the major focus was the social and industrial infrastructure of the recipient countries, which also benefited Japanese enterprises involved in construction work.

3. Constitution of Japan, Chapter 2, Renunciation of War, Article 9:

> Aspiring sincerely to an international peace based on justice and order, the Japanese people forever renounce war as a sovereign right of the nation and the threat or use of force as means of settling international disputes. In order to accomplish the aim of the preceding paragraph, land, sea, and air forces, as well as other war potential, will never be maintained. The right of belligerency of the state will not be recognized.

Contrary to the negative description of Article 9, the preamble of the constitution mentions the spirit of contribution by Japan to peacebuilding in the world:

> We, the Japanese people, desire peace for all time and are deeply conscious of the high ideals controlling human relationship, and we have determined to preserve our security and existence, trusting in the justice and faith of the peace-loving peoples of the world. We desire to occupy an honored place in an international society striving for the preservation of peace, and the banishment of tyranny and slavery, oppression and intolerance for all time from the earth. We recognize that all peoples of the world have the right to live in the peace, free from fear and want. We believe that no nation is responsible to itself alone, but that laws of political morality are universal; and that obedience to such laws is incumbent upon all nations who would sustain their own sovereignty and justify their sovereign relationship with other nations. We, the Japanese people, pledge our national honor to accomplish these high ideals and purposes with all our resources.

4. Although it occurred in a neighboring country, Japan was not involved militarily in the Korean War. But facing a threat in East Asia, the occupation forces changed their policy of demilitarizing Japan completely, and asked the government to form a kind of armed police, which later developed into the self-defense forces. Japan did not participate in the Vietnam War.

5. With respect to the activities of Japan-based nongovernmental organizations involved in peacebuilding, refer to the *Directory of Organizations for Conflict Prevention in Asia and the Pacific 2002*, p. 61, published by the Japan Center for Conflict Prevention, February 2002, and to Part 3 of this book.

6. Regarding InterBand, refer to the directory mentioned in endnote 5, and www.interband.org.

7. Suu Kyi was campaigning with other NLD leaders and supporters in the Depayin area when they were attacked by a mob and local security forces. See "Preliminary Report of the Ad Hoc Commission on Depayin Massacre," July 4, 2003 (e-mail: eace@loxinfo.co.th).

8. For the results of Tokyo Conference on Reconstruction and Development of Sri Lanka, see www.mofa.go.jp/announce/press/2003/6/0610.html#1.

9. See www.mofa.go.jp/policy/oda/reform/measure0207.html.

10. In the 1970s the North Korean government systematically sent spy ships to the coast of Japan in order to abduct Japanese citizens to be used as language and culture training staff for their clandestine operations inside Japan. Although North Korean government has continuously denied such illegal operations, the fact was revealed and confirmed at a 2002 summit meeting between Prime Minister Jyunichiro Koizumi and Secretary Jyon-Il Kim. Since then, at the request of the families of the victims and backed up by the heated resentment of the general public, the Japanese government declared that there will be neither concessions nor negotiations without the return of all citizens abducted by North Korea.

11. One example concerns the Japanese wives who married North Korean nationals and returned with them to their country in the 1960s. Contrary to their expectations of finding a people's heaven, they led miserable lives under the Kim regime and were not allowed to return home. Because of the deterioration in bilateral diplomatic relations during the Cold War era, communications between relatives were cut off and the Japanese government could obtain no information about them. Recently, some of them escaped the country by crossing the border and hiding in northern China. Although they have Japanese nationality, and there are growing requests from the public that the government should do more to rescue them, the Japanese government cannot fully respond to their request because of the lack of diplomatic relations with North Korea.

12. Japan has accepted the smallest number of refugees of any developed country. That said, few North Koreans want to go to Japan for asylum. Most refugees ask to be sent to South Korea, which has an official program for accepting them and integrating them into Korean society.

8.3

CHINA

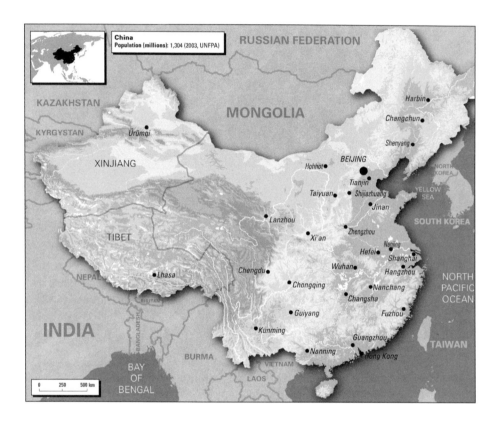

8.3.1

The Potential for
Civil Unrest in China

Yu-shek Cheng and K. L. Ngok

In June 2002, three prominent Chinese scholars issued a stark warning to the Chinese leadership: Civil discontent in China is growing fast and Chinese society is on the verge of a dangerous crisis. If not handled properly, the crisis could spin out of control and the government could lose power.

This chapter examines the sources of discontent in China, its recent history of civil unrest, and the potential for future domestic conflict. It looks at the risks to social and political stability, potential outcomes, and the government's policy responses. We argue that civil unrest in post-Mao China can be primarily attributed to a traditional dualistic society divided between urban and rural sectors, the social inequality resulting from the transition from a planned economy to a market economy, the lack of adequate social security, and rampant political corruption.

China's post-Mao leaders have accorded primacy to economic development, and largely based their own legitimacy on the growth of gross domestic product. Although market-oriented economic reforms in the past twenty-odd years have brought unprecedented economic growth, and improved the living standards of over 1 billion people in China, a development strategy emphasizing growth has nonetheless led to a serious imbalance between economic and social development. That imbalance is apparent in a widening gap between rich and poor, an increasing urban-rural divide, and destabilizing regional disparities. These developments and the grievances of those who have lost ground as a result of the economic reform process have led to the unrest to which the Chinese scholars allude.

Basically, two main types of potential civil unrest exist in China: One derives from the economic demands of peasants and workers; the other originates from dissident sociopolitical groups, such as the Falun Gong, ethnic separatists, and prodemocracy activists. Other factors that may affect China's social and political stability include its further integration into the global economy following its accession to the World Trade Organization, its booming nonstate sector, and the influx of foreign investment.

To head off the crisis that these scholars and others have warned about, the government has pursued a two-track policy. It has attempted to respond to the grievances of workers and peasants by implementing or modifying social and economic policies—offering some tax relief and improving social security, for example. At the same time, it has clamped down on all forms of political dissent, emphatically demonstrating that activities that threaten the political order will not be tolerated.

Market Transition, Social Inequality, and Social Instability

Under Mao, China aspired to be an egalitarian society, though that egalitarianism was distinguished by a sharp divide between rural and urban dwellers. In the villages, Chinese peasants might have been equal, but they were poor. In the cities, urban workers enjoyed free housing, education, health care, and job security. However, the market-oriented reforms initiated by Deng Xiaoping have fundamentally transformed the egalitarian society and created an increasingly unequal China.

Social inequality in China is first reflected by income inequality. Before the economic reforms, income inequality in China was relatively low, but the Gini coefficient, a common indicator of income inequality, has been rising rapidly since (see Table 8.3.1.1), with widening income gaps between rural and urban areas, and between the prosperous coastal region and the interior in China.

A huge gap between the rich and poor has also correspondingly developed. In the top 1 percent—a newly rich class comprising film stars, famous singers, fashion models, writers, athletes, owners of private enterprises, professionals, intellectuals, real estate developers, corrupt officials, and managerial staff in foreign-invested enterprises (FIEs) and financial institutions enjoys an average annual family income of 200,000 yuan (about U.S.$24,160). A well-off middle class has also been growing in China.[1] Meanwhile, in 2000, the average annual per capita urban income in China was 6,300 yuan (about U.S.$750).[2]

Table 8.3.1.1 The Rising Gini Coefficient in China

1980	0.300
1994	0.434
1998	0.456
1999	0.457
2000	0.458

Source: Yang Yiyong and Xin Xiaobo, "The Current Pattern of Income Distribution and Its Development Trend in China," in Ru Xin, Lu Xueyi, and Shan Tianlun, eds., *Zhongguo Shehui Xingshi Fenxi Yu Yuce* [Analysis and Forecast of Social Conditions in China] (Beijing: Social Science Documentation Publishing House, 2002), pp. 144–152.

Note: The Gini coefficient is an indicator of the level of income inequality, with 0 representing absolute equality, and 1 representing absolute inequality.

The economic reforms have created a substantial underclass of about 40 million rural poor and 10 million urban poor, about 4 percent in both sectors. Among them, laid-off workers, retirees, workers in poorly run enterprises, the unemployed, poor peasants, migrant workers, and teachers in poorer areas are worst affected. Although official poverty lines have been set locally since the mid-1990s, many living under the poverty lines have not been offered official relief. An official survey conducted in 1999 revealed that the per capita monthly income was less than 100 yuan (about U.S.$12) for 6 to 10 percent of all urban families. Those in the top 20 percent secured 42.4 percent of the total income of the country, while the bottom 20 percent earned just 2.2 percent of the total income.[3]

Despite the economic reforms, the urban-rural divide has been an enduring problem, and China now has the biggest urban-rural gap in the world, with per capita income among urban residents about four times that of rural residents, compared to the global average ratio of about 1.5.[4] Rural income has been in decline since 1997,[5] and the urban-rural income gap has led to the largest internal migration in the world in peacetime, as 100 million peasants currently move from city to city looking for work in the so-called *mangliu* (blind flow).

Wide disparities exist between the coastal and inland regions, especially regions with substantial ethnic minorities. Some scholars have described China as "a country with four worlds"—the first world comprising the most prosperous urban areas, the second the relatively prosperous coastal provinces, the third the poor interior provinces, and the fourth the poverty-stricken border regions and the rural areas dominated by ethnic minorities. In 1999, the average income in Shanghai (U.S.$15,516) was twelve times that in Guizhou province (U.S.$1,247), an interior province in the "fourth world."[6]

The result is rising tension in Chinese society and, since the mid-1990s, increasing worries concerning potential social instability. In 2001 a report by a Communist Party research organization about mounting public anger over inequality, corruption, and official aloofness in China described a spreading pattern of "collective protests and group incidents" arising from economic, ethnic, and religious conflicts. The report cited growing inequality and corruption as major sources of discontent, and warned that even greater social conflicts are likely as China continues to open its markets to foreign trade and investment.[7] The following year, the three scholars issued the warning cited at the beginning of this chapter, pointing to unemployment, political corruption, the heavy tax burden on peasants, the increasing gap between the rich and poor, and the deterioration of law and order as the primary sources of social discontent.[8]

Labor Unrest: The Biggest Threat to Social Stability

With the transition from a planned economy to a market economy, guaranteed employment for urban workers, and its associated social welfare, has been severely challenged. Market reforms have resulted in massive layoffs, and many workers in state-owned enterprises (SOEs), once considered "masters of the state," have since joined the urban poor. A sense of alienation is widespread among workers. They have resorted to collective action in their struggle to protect their interests. Their chief grievances are layoffs, unemployment, wage arrears, delayed pension payment, and enterprises' failure to pay labor insurance. The usual forms of labor unrest include everyday workplace resistance, petitions, work stoppages and strikes, public protests, outbreaks of violence, independent unionism, and political movements. Incidents of labor unrest have become so widespread that party and government leaders have identified labor problems as the "biggest threat to social stability."[9]

Since the mid-1990s, with the increasing integration of the Chinese economy into the global market system and reform of SOEs, more and more workers have lost their jobs, relegating many without adequate social security into the ranks of the urban poor. Grievances related to the labor contract system and the prevalent corruption in SOEs have further fueled workers' anger. According to the figures from the Ministry of Labor and Social Security, incidents of collective action (usually strikes or slowdowns with a minimum of three people taking part) have increased steadily in recent years (see Table 8.3.1.2).[10]

Such incidents usually occur when workers' livelihood is threatened. For example, in 1997 a wave of worker protests arose mainly because of delayed wage and pension payments in several cities in Sichuan. In March 1997 in Nanchong city, 20,000 workers from the biggest textile factory paralyzed the community by occupying the city government building to protest delayed wage payments.[11] Similar worker protests also occurred in Mianyang and Doujianyan.[12]

Such actions have continued in recent years. Workers' protests in northeast China in 2002 were particularly serious. From early March until May, thousands of displaced workers in Daqing, Heilongjiang province, and in Liaoyang, Liaoning province, engaged in large-scale protests over unpaid benefits and the corruption of cadres. The protests spread to a number of cities, and probably constituted the largest social protest movement since the 1989 prodemocracy movement.[13] These protests were defensive in nature and driven basically by economic interests, but are notable for a number of reasons: the number of the protests, the level of interfactory dialogue among workers, the spontaneous nature of the protests, and political connotations of the workers' demands. Labor unrest in Daqing was very significant, as workers there

Table 8.3.1.2 Workers' Collective Actions in China

	Number of Incidents	Workers Involved
1998	6,767	251,268
2000	8,247	259,445
2001	9,847	287,000

Source: See www.molss.gov.cn/news/2002/6101.htm.

were presented as the model of new China's working class before the economic reforms. Immediately after the protests in Daqing and Liaoyang, similar protests broke out in the mining city of Fushun, Liaoning province, and in Guangyuan.

Labor unrest does not occur only among disgruntled state workers. The emerging new working class, comprising employees in FIEs and private enterprises and recruited mainly from the rural sector, has also become a new source of labor conflict. These workers are denied basic rights. Labor abuses in the private sector often involve arbitrary production quotas, no pay for overtime work, excessive working hours, wages below the legal minimum, and arbitrary fines and punishment of workers. Various types of corporal punishment, humiliation, and even beating are not uncommon.[14] As a labor activist at a government research center observed, "Labor relations in China have gone back to the level of the Industrial Revolution in the nineteenth century in Europe. The conditions of workers in many private and foreign-owned companies are those of primitive capitalism."[15] As this new working class grows, builds solidarity, and gains awareness of its rights and interests, it has been struggling for more legal protection, challenging China's repressive labor regime, and since the mid-1990s it has been increasingly engaged in collective actions.[16] In early 2003 an article in *Outlook,* a popular official magazine, warned that if the legitimate rights and interests of peasant laborers were denied, social disturbances, even large-scale ones, would break out.[17]

The Communist authorities understand the seriousness of labor unrest. Political dissidents, too, understand the implications of labor unrest for their cause. Indeed, one direct result of the unrest has been the reappearance of politically motivated labor organizers and labor lawyers and even the resurgence of a reformist wing in the official All-China Federation of Trade Unions. In order to pacify labor unrest, the central government has adopted a carrot-and-stick policy—frequently arresting the organizers of labor protests, while tending to curry favor with disgruntled workers by making quick concessions. Local governments have been instructed not to exacerbate the situation by using force to disperse protesting workers. So far, this mixture of carrot and stick has been effective in dealing with individual crises. However, offering "carrots" to workers tends to encourage them to pursue additional demands, with the increased chance of further labor unrest. In some extreme cases, local governments may adopt a hands-off policy concerning worker protests and deliberately make them appear serious so as to secure financial assistance from the central government. Realizing the potential convergence of disgruntled workers and political opposition, the Chinese government has adopted various methods to prevent intersector linkages, such as banning news reports, suppressing independent unions, and closing down labor journals.

Peasant Uprisings

Although peasants have benefited considerably from private farming since the early 1980s, unrest among the rural poor remains a threat to the Chinese leadership. The primary reasons for peasant unrest are the heavy tax burden, corrupt and abusive officials, income inequality, and decaying social ethos. Though there have been no large-scale peasant rebellions, the Chinese government has faced frequent protests against the high taxes imposed by local authorities, especially in densely populated and underdeveloped central provinces.

As early as in the mid-1980s, a "rebellious psychology" was spreading among Chinese peasants, who complained of high taxes, low grain prices, appropriation of their land, pollution, cultural and social conflicts, and abusive officials.[18] Beginning in the 1990s, this rebellious psychology was expressed in several waves of peasant unrest—especially in the interior provinces, such as Hunan, Sichuan, Jiangxi, and Anhui—including demonstrations, violent confrontations between individual peasants and cadres, riots, damage to Party/government buildings and property, the blocking of roads and railways, the burning of automobiles, and the killing of cadres and police.[19]

Tax revolts have become common throughout rural China since 1985, especially as the financial burden on peasants has been increasing. In 1994–1995, in order to stop the continuing decline of central government revenues in relation to provincial revenues, a new tax-sharing system was introduced in China. This system increased the central and provincial revenues at the expense of county and township authorities. With insufficient funds from the central government, local authorities were plunged into financial crisis.[20] The financial resources of the township and village authorities are dependent on the fees and taxes collected from peasants, which county and township officials have often increased in an uncontrolled manner.[21] Peasants throughout China have responded by lodging complaints collectively at higher levels.[22] And while the financial burden has been increasing, peasant incomes have been declining, aggravated since 1997 by the fall in domestic grain prices and a sharp decline in employment offered by town and township enterprises.[23] Where rural incomes have stagnated or declined, the conflicts between poor peasants and the local authorities have intensified. The corruption of rural cadres has further fueled peasants' anger, epitomized in the comments of a peasant from Yuandu county, Jiangxi province, where in August 2000 an estimated 20,000 peasants engaged in a week of protests against excessive taxation and fought battles with the armed police sent to suppress them: "We peasants do not have enough to eat while even a junior township official will be able to own at least a car and a house. We are feeling very bad about this, we have been forced to fight."[24]

From time to time, rural revolts in China produce headlines in the international media. In April 2001, armed police confronted 1,400 villagers from Yuntang in Jiangxi province (see Box 8.3.1.1). Two peasants were shot dead and twenty villagers and twenty-three police were wounded.[25] Although most peasant protests have been short-lived spontaneous eruptions, clandestine organizations have been involved in some cases. Most often the organizers have been demobilized soldiers (see Box 8.3.1.2).[26]

Box 8.3.1.1 Yuntang Incident, 2001

Yuntang, like thousands of other communities, was devastated by the 1998 flooding of the Yangtze River. Government officials stole relief money assigned to rebuild ruined rice terraces and then the local authorities attempted to levy a tax on villagers. Yuntang residents refused to pay, organized a mass rally, and erected roadblocks to prevent police and tax collectors from entering the village in February 1999 and again in July 2000. In April 2001 the authorities declared the villagers a "criminal gang" and in the early hours of April 15 dispatched a 600-man force of riot police and armed paramilitaries to the village. When hundreds of villagers tried to block their entry, the police opened fire. Two peasants were shot dead.

Box 8.3.1.2 Zhajiang Incident, 1998–1999

In September 1998 the peasant Peng Rongjun from the Yantian management district in the town of Zhajiang organized a group of peasants to lobby for the reduction of their financial burden. The leaders were all demobilized military personnel. Peng was a farmer who had previously served in the People's Liberation Army, and was a core member of the "representatives' network" for the reduction of peasants' financial burden in Hunan. On September 15 the network collected over 600 signatures and went to the provincial capital to petition. On September 19 the network read documents from the central, provincial, and city governments on the reduction of peasants' financial burden over the loudspeakers in the market. The following day, a violent confrontation occurred between the network and cadres of the Yantian management district. In October the network organized over 3,000 peasants to engage in protest activities, and burned a vehicle belonging to the local government. On January 17, 1999, the Zhajiang government called a meeting, attended by 10,000 people, for the purpose of strengthening law and order. Six members of the network, arrested earlier, were presented at the meeting, bound, and forced to wear signs describing their "crimes." This angered those attending the meeting, and led to violent clashes involving an estimated 6,000 people, with many casualties and damaged vehicles.

In contrast to its attitude toward the prodemocracy activists, the central government has a generally tolerant attitude toward the peasant uprisings, for two reasons. First, the government itself is cognizant of the excessive tax burden,[27] and is therefore willing to tolerate some protests.[28] Beyond that, intimidation and violence would only make the peasantry more militant. And while it firmly puts down major protests by using the regular police and the armed police, the government tries to create the impression among peasants that it supports them in their fight against high taxes by punishing local officials whom it blames for excessive taxation. This, ironically, has emboldened peasants to submit more petitions and organize more protests against local authorities. Without effective reforms in the administrative and financial systems in rural China, peasant protests will not stop.

Aware of the threat that widespread rural unrest can pose to its rule, particularly if it is linked with worker discontent in the cities, the government attempts to placate peasant discontent by criticizing the excessive taxes and corruption in local governments, promoting village elections, and improving social security by setting minimum prices for agricultural commodities and the purchase of surplus grain. It is also introducing a radically reformed tax scheme that limits taxes to 5 percent of rural household income, but the plan is encountering resistance from local governments.

The Falun Gong: A Powerful Organized Opposition

Beyond labor protests and peasant disturbances, the Chinese regime faced a significant challenge in the late 1990s from the Falun Gong, a movement that began a few years earlier and quickly developed into an organization with millions of adherents. The Falun Gong draws on *qigong*—the healing and cultivating of the mind—though it also incorporates elements of traditional Chinese religions. China has a long and pervasive tradition of *qigong,* and since initiation of its open-door policy and economic reforms, and especially since the 1989 crisis, *qigong* has been promoted by the Chinese government. After the Falun Gong was founded in May 1992, the Chinese authorities actually

AFP Photo

Hong Kong, 1 August 1999. Falun Gong followers exercise in a rally outside a building of Xinhua, China's official news agency. More than 150 Falun Gong members staged a peaceful protest against the mainland government's treatment of the sect.

facilitated its spread, giving the sect assistance to publish and distribute its ideology, to lecture around the country and internationally, and to establish teaching centers in most major Chinese cities. Numerous government and Party officials practiced the Falun Gong.

Further, the popularity of the Falun Gong is rooted in China's economic and social discontent and the inequalities that have accompanied reform. The Falun Gong made its earliest gains in the mid-1990s in northeast China, where industry was declining and workers had been laid off without an adequate safety net. With the cost of medical care rising, incomes falling, and no access to publicly funded health care, self-healing without medicine, a power claimed by the Falun Gong, had a powerful attraction.

The Falun Gong remains strongest in the industrial cities in the northeastern and central provinces, which have been hardest hit by the market reforms. The old social security system has been eliminated, but no suitable replacement has been established. The mutual aid provided by members serves as a substitute for social security.

Beyond the sense of insecurity and alienation rooted in economic hardships, the growth of the Falun Gong can also be attributed to the ideological crisis facing the population and Communist Party members. Increasing social inequality, rampant corruption, and the deteriorating sense of security have created a spiritual vacuum in China. More and more people are looking for an alternative creed. Many Falun Gong followers are elders who once followed the Communist revolutionary cause and who have not benefited from the economic reforms (see Box 8.3.1.3).

Obviously, the rapid spread of the Falun Gong presented a major political crisis to the Chinese Communist regime, which has reserved for itself the exclusive right to promulgate an ideology in China, and views any other ideology or religion with deep suspicion.[29] In response to a major demonstration by Falun Gong members in Beijing on April 25, 1999, the government began

---

Box 8.3.1.3 Profile of Falun Gong Practitioners

A survey on Falun Gong practitioners in Beijing conducted in late 1999 revealed that the majority of the followers were marginalized, disadvantaged people, including retirees, jobless workers, and farmers. According to the survey, three-quarters of the respondents were either retired persons (22.4 percent), laid-off workers and unemployed persons (6.5 percent), or rural residents (46.2 percent). Only 25 percent of them were employed. Among the 1,790 leading members, 39.2 percent were employed, 13.9 percent were retired, 3.8 percent were unemployed, and 43.1 percent were rural residents.

Source: Kang Xiaguang, Guanyu "Falun Gong Wenti" de Sikao [Reflections on the Problem of the Falun Gong] (Beijing: Research Center of State Situation, China Academy of Sciences, January 2000).

a crackdown (see Box 8.3.1.4), and in July the Falun Gong was banned. The government accused the Falun Gong of "spreading fallacies, hoodwinking people, inciting and creating disturbances and jeopardizing social stability" and described it as a notorious cult with an evil political will.[30]

In the eyes of Chinese leaders, the Falun Gong is perceived as falling within the tradition of other sectarian resistance movements in Chinese history. It is not surprising, then, that the Chinese government takes a harsh line toward the movement. Repression of the Falun Gong sect has been among the most serious acts of state repression in China since the Tiananmen Square massacre in June 1989. To fight the Falun Gong and other spiritual sects, the Chinese government set up a special task force in 1999, the Anti-Cult Office. But Falun Gong followers have managed to resist, organizing sporadic protests, hijacking satellite signals, interrupting cable broadcasts, and beaming their own messages into the homes of Chinese viewers, much to the dismay of the government.[31] This resistance reflects the impressive dedication of Falun Gong followers.

Prodemocracy Activists

Unlike the labor unrest and peasant insurgencies, which are driven by bread-and-butter issues, prodemocracy activists aiming to end the rule of the Communist Party pose a direct threat to the authoritarian regime in China. Prodemocracy activists in post-Mao China have their roots in the Democracy Wall Movement of late 1978 and early 1979, when activists in Beijing were allowed to record news and ideas on a designated wall in the city. The movement was then suppressed and the wall was torn down, but the movement reemerged with the large-scale student protests in Beijing in 1989.

With the arrest or forced exile of the leading figures in the student movement after the Tiananmen incident, the prodemocracy movement in China was effectively silenced for a long time. But since the advent of the Internet in China

---

Box 8.3.1.4 Falun Gong Protest Incident, 1999

On April 25, 1999, about 10,000 Falun Gong members gathered to protest in Zhongnanhai, the location of the private residences and offices of China's highest leadership. The protest was the largest mass gathering in the capital since the student prodemocracy movement of 1989. It was a silent and orderly demonstration, organized to protest against defamation of the sect by the state media. Such a large-scale demonstration in the Communist regime's headquarters shocked the top leadership in Beijing and led in July to the banning of the Falun Gong. Since then, Falun Gong books and tapes have been collected and destroyed across the country. Its websites have been shut down or blocked. Practice of its beliefs now constitutes a criminal offense. Tens of thousands of Falun Gong practitioners have been arrested, beaten, detained, or sent to psychiatric hospitals, labor camps, and prisons.

in the mid-1990s, dissident e-mail publications and websites have proliferated online and a network of prodemocracy activists has developed. The signing of the international human rights covenants by the Chinese government and the visit of then U.S. president Bill Clinton to China in 1998 further encouraged the Chinese prodemocracy activists. In this context, a new wave of activism emerged in 1998, when the prodemocracy activists in Beijing, Tianjin, and Zhejiang announced the creation of an opposition party—the China Democracy Party (CDP), which they hoped to make the country's first opposition party since 1949. Such organizations of prodemocracy activists are still illegal, so they can only operate underground.

Chinese authorities responded with a severe campaign of repression in late 1998 and 1999. Thirty-nine activists were arrested for involvement in the CDP's formation, including Xu Wenli, the head of the party. Xu was charged with subversion and sentenced to thirteen years in prison.[32] Many other dissidents were subsequently arrested, including some 100 members of the fledgling party. Despite these arrests, the authorities have been unable to completely curb the spread of the movement. Relying on modern communication technology, high-profile prodemocracy activists have established close contacts with each other, and can make use of international networks to exercise their influence and gather external support.

Prodemocracy activists usually time their public statements to coincide with significant political occasions and the anniversaries of major historical events (see Box 8.3.1.5).[33] In the absence of a democratic political culture, with little awareness about individual rights and limited desire for freedom, the development of a prodemocracy movement is a long and difficult process and China's democratic forces are still weak and poorly organized. In theory, the existing social trends in China described above should provide favorable conditions to draw new blood into a prodemocracy movement in China, but in reality this has not occurred. Most activists belong to the generation that participated in the 1989 student movement. Over 60 percent of China Democracy Party members were students in the Tiananmen movement.[34]

Box 8.3.1.5 Dissident Activities Before the Sixteenth National Congress of the Communist Party

On the eve of the Sixteenth National Congress of the Communist Party of China, Zhao Changqing, a dissident in Xian city, Shaanxi province, launched a signature campaign, calling for a reassessment of Beijing's official verdict on the 1989 Tiananmen massacre, the release of purged Party chief Zhao Ziyang, and the termination of the suppression of dissidents. Almost 200 dissidents nationwide signed the open letter. In response, Chinese authorities toughened their political control and suppression. Zhao was arrested in November 2002 and charged with "incitement to subvert state power." Several signatories to the letter were also arrested on the same charge.

Although prodemocracy activists only play a limited role within China, they have established wide international connections and attracted substantial international coverage. Their activities and the harsh crackdown by the Chinese government tend to be important factors affecting China's international image and its relations with other countries, especially the United States. On several occasions, in fact, the Chinese government has permitted well-known activists to go to the United States for medical treatment in the hope that such moves would help to improve the fragile bilateral relationship. As China integrates further into the international community, it will become more susceptible to international pressure.

Conclusion

Civil unrest in China is primarily a result of the social inequality associated with high levels of unemployment and poverty, which has followed the introduction of market-oriented reforms, as well as the public's abhorrence of rampant corruption in government and bureaucracy. Unless effective social security policies are adopted, it is reasonable to predict that as the economic reforms accelerate and China integrates more fully into the global economy, spaces will continue to emerge wherein the disaffected can express their views and civil unrest will continue to increase.

The key question is whether, as some predict, civil unrest will develop into a social revolution, leading to the collapse of the Communist regime.[35] Our basic judgment is that while small-scale civil unrest will continue, major social crises are unlikely in China in the foreseeable future, especially if economic growth continues and the government continues to manage unrest as it has to date.

China's political and social stability is premised on such growth. Economists predict economic growth of around 7 percent per annum in the coming decade and 6 percent per annum in the following decade.[36] But serious structural imbalances exist in the Chinese economy. Slackening economic growth, rampant corruption, and political infighting at the top could undermine those policies that have succeeded in controlling social unrest. While Chinese leaders understand well the present situation and the challenges ahead, they may not have the political will and support to implement the necessary reforms to transform the conflicts.

The Chinese government has developed relatively effective strategies for dealing with the social unrest resulting from the economic reforms, and the leadership is well aware of various threats such as labor unrest associated with those reforms. The Chinese authorities have adopted a variety of countermeasures to deal with different types of civil unrest. They have been relatively tolerant of labor protests and peasant uprisings, but have responded to the prodemocracy movement, the Falun Gong, and other organized opposition groups that challenge the regime politically with a policy of intimidation, exile, imprisonment, administrative detention, and house arrest.

Traditional measures of political control, including the use of state violence, are still sufficient to suppress any potential political challenge. In 1998, in view of the deteriorating sociopolitical situation, the Communist Party set up an office for maintaining social stability to coordinate the efforts of the police, the Ministry of State Security, the People's Armed Police, and those agencies responsible for ideology and propaganda, trade unions, social security, and the ethnic minorities. In recent years, the Chinese authorities have been strengthening the capacity of the People's Armed Police to handle domestic disturbances. China's admittedly belated response to the SARS crisis in 2003 demonstrates that the Communist regime's ability to effect mass mobilization can still be effective in response to social crisis. The regime has also moved ahead with various reforms of the party and the government, and continues to wage a war against rampant official corruption. The Chinese leadership clearly understands that social problems combined with official corruption could trigger more serious civil unrest.

With the suppression of prodemocracy activists and the Falun Gong, the most serious threats to stability are economic. But it is almost impossible for workers and peasants to develop centrally organized protests, particularly in the absence of a strong alliance between the intellectuals and workers. The government is now attempting to redress the grievances of the victims of socioeconomic change. It realizes that, if resources are available to address the financial grievances of workers and peasants, unrest can be contained, and that the benefits of economic development have to accrue to the majority of the people.

The Chinese leadership, especially the new leadership with Hu Jintao as its core, has accorded top priority to the improvement of the livelihood of the socially disadvantaged groups. In particular, it has tried to lighten the tax burden felt by peasants, and is now considering radical reforms of local government.[37] To pacify angry workers, more money has been invested in a national public income–maintenance scheme to guarantee minimum living standards for laid-off workers and the urban poor.

Despite impressive economic growth, China will find it difficult to provide a satisfactory social security system that covers the entire population. Unemployment and poverty will continue to affect a significant segment of the population. The Chinese leadership therefore tolerates protests from the poor peasants and the urban unemployed. It promises long-term improvement in livelihood, and offers subsidies and relief for the short term. These protesters are not allowed to organize themselves or to engage with similar groups in neighboring localities, under threat of arrest. The Chinese leadership adopts a much harsher attitude toward the prodemocracy activists and Falun Gong, because they attempt to establish autonomous organizations outside Party control and therefore are seen as a threat to the regime. Individual critics, especially those with some reputation, are often tolerated and escape persecution as long as they do not organize politically. These different methods of treatments are basically related to the Chinese Communist Party's past experience and perception of threat.

Although we do not anticipate a social revolution, we are cognizant of a dilemma confronting the Chinese Communist regime. It is unlikely that it can totally eliminate social and political instability, but as China becomes more and more integrated into the global economy, and its society is subjected to new pressures, its ability to control civil unrest through political repression or even violence may be increasingly constrained by both domestic and international opinion. At some point, the regime could well be forced to choose between international isolation and tolerance of some level of political freedom.

Yu-shek Cheng is Professor (Chair) of Political Science at the City University of Hong Kong. He is the founding editor of the Hong Kong Journal of Social Sciences *and the* Journal of Comparative Asian Development. *His recent publications include the edited work* China's Challenges in the Twenty-First Century *(Hong Kong: City University of Hong Kong Press, 2003).*

K. L. Ngok, Ph.D., teaches in the Department of Public and Social Administration, City University of Hong Kong. His publications cover labor law and industrial relations, education development, public policy, and administrative reform in China. His recent publications include a special issue of Chinese Law and Government: The 1998 Administrative Reform of the State Council of the People's Republic of China *(New York: M. E. Sharpe, 2003).*

Notes

1. Azizur Rahman Khan and Carl Riskin, *Inequality and Poverty in China in the Age of Globalization* (New York: Oxford University Press, 2001). Also see Kang Xiaoguang, "The Challenge of the Wealth Distribution," in Lu Rongqiang, ed., *Ershiyi Shiji Zhongguo Mianlin de Shier Da Tiaozhan* [Twelve Challenges Facing China in the Twentieth-First Century] (Beijing: World Affairs Press, 2001), pp. 342–385.

2. Yang Yiyong and Xin Xiaobo, "The Current Pattern of Income Distribution and Its Development Trend in China," in Ru Xin, Lu Xueyi, and Shan Tianlun, eds., *Zhongguo Shehui Xingshi Fenxi Yu Yuce* [Analysis and Forecast of Social Conditions in China, 2002] (Beijing: Social Science Documentation Publishing House, 2002), pp. 144–152.

3. Ibid.

4. Zhong Dajun, "The Impacts of Dual-Structure on Chinese Society," in Xin, Xueyi, and Tianlun, *Analysis and Forecast,* pp. 197–213.

5. Yiyong and Xiaobo, "Current Pattern of Income Distribution," pp. 144–152.

6. Zouping Hu Angang and Li Chunpo, "The Regional Disparity in Economic and Social Development in China Between 1978 to 2000," in Xin, Xueyi, and Tianlun, *Analysis and Forecast,* pp. 167–184.

7. Erik Eckholm, "Chinese Warn of Civil Unrest Across Country," *International Herald Tribune,* June 2, 2001.

8. Wang Shaoguang, Hu Angang, and Ding Yuanzhu, "Jingji Fanrong Beihou de Shehui Weiji" [The Social Crisis Behind the Economic Prosperity], *Zhanglue yu Guanli* [Strategy and Management] no. 3 (June 2002): 26–33; Eckholm, "Chinese Warn of Civil Unrest."

9. Ching Kwan Lee, "Pathways of Labor Insurgency," in E. Perry and M. Selden, eds., *Chinese Society: Change, Conflict, and Resistance* (London: Routledge, 2000), pp. 41–61.

10. See www.molss.gov.cn/news/2002/6101.htm.

11. *Far Eastern Economic Review,* June 26, 1997.

12. *Ming Pao,* July 18, 1997; *October Review,* September 20, 1997.

13. *Yazhou Zhoukan,* May 20–26, 2002, p. 21.

14. For the details of labor abuse in FIEs, see Anita Chan, *China's Workers Under Assault: The Exploitation of Labor in a Globalizing Economy* (Armonk, N.Y.: M. E. Sharpe, 2001).

15. Mark O'Neill, "Trouble at the Workplace," *South China Morning Post,* October 3, 2001, electronic edition, available at www.prctaxman.com.cn/trouble_at_the_workplace_scmp_oneil_3_oct_2001.htm.

16. Qiao Jian, "Employees and Labor Under the Situation of Entering WTO," in Xin, Xueyi, and Tianlun, *Analysis and Forecast,* pp. 313–328.

17. *Outlook* (Liaowang), January 27, 2003, p. 4.

18. Thomas P. Bernstein, "Instability in Rural China," in David Shambaugh, ed., *Is China Unstable?* (Armonk, N.Y.: M. E. Sharpe, 2000), pp. 95–111.

19. Ibid.

20. Lu Xueyi, "The Current Situation of Rural China and the Reasons of Its Problems," in Xin, Xueyi, and Tianlun, *Analysis and Forecast,* pp. 159–166.

21. Ibid.

22. Kevin J. O'Brien and Lianjiang Li, "The Politics of Lodging Complaints in Rural China," *China Quarterly* no. 143 (1995): 756–783.

23. Fang Ping, "The Changing Rural China and the Peasantry," in Xin, Xueyi, and Tianlun, *Analysis and Forecast,* pp. 252–259.

24. Carol Divjak, "Rural Protests in China Put Down by Riot Police," September 7, 2000, available at www.wsws.org/articles/2000/sep2000/chin-s07.shtml.

25. John Chan, "Rural Revolts in China Reveal Widespread Disaffection over Tax Burdens," May 2001, available at www.wsws.org/articles/2001/may2001/chin-m25.shtml.

26. The data on the Zhajiang Incident came from Yu Jianrong. In October 2002, Yu gave a public seminar on the political crisis in rural China at the Chinese University of Hong Kong.

27. Li Lianjiang and Kevin J. O'Brien, "Villagers and Popular Resistance in Contemporary China," *Modern China* 22, no. 1 (1996): 28–61.

28. Bernstein, "Instability in Rural China."

29. Beatrice Leung, "China and Falun Gong: Party and Society Relations in the Modern Era," *Journal of Contemporary China* 11, no. 33 (2002): 761–784.

30. He Ping, ed., *Jiepi Falun Defa Xieshuo* [Unmasking and Denouncing the Heretical Ideas of Falun Gong] (Beijing: Xinhua Press, 1999), p. 20.

31. James Tong, "An Organizational Analysis of the Falun Gong: Structure, Communication, Financing," *China Quarterly* no. 171 (2002): 636–660.

32. *Open Magazine,* February 2003, p. 59.

33. *South China Morning Post,* January 3, 2003.

34. Wang Dan, "Working for a Peaceful Transformation: The Road Ahead for the Chinese Democracy Movement," *Harvard Asia Pacific Review* (Winter 1999–2000), available at http://hcs.harvard.edu/~hapr/winter00_millenium/issue.html.

35. Gordon G. Chang, *The Coming Collapse of China* (New York: Random House, 2001).

36. See http://big5.china.com/gate/big5/news.china.com/zh_cn/finance/11009723, and Zhang Zhuoyuan, ed., *Ershiyi Shiji Zhongguo Jingji Wenti Zhuanjiatan* [Experts on China's Economic Issues in the Twenty-First Century] (Zhengzhou: Henan Remin Chubanshe, 1999).

37. *South China Morning Post,* February 11, 2003.

8.3.2

China and Regional Security— External Perceptions and Responses

Rex Li

The emergence of China as a key actor on the international stage is undoubtedly a significant phenomenon in the early twenty-first century. Some view the awakening of the "sleeping giant" with great interest. Others are troubled by the rapid augmentation of Chinese power, fearing that it might bring about unpredictable repercussions in Asia Pacific and the wider world.

This chapter examines the debate among Western scholars and security specialists on the "China threat," focusing on two main schools of thought on what a rising China means and what are the associated security implications beyond its borders. It also analyzes the threat perceptions of the United States and other Asian countries, and concludes with a consideration of the debate on how to respond to the China challenge.

China: Rising Power or Fragile Kingdom?

Since the late 1970s, Chinese leaders have been actively developing China's "comprehensive national strength" in order to be in a position to compete with other great powers politically, economically, and militarily. Between 1992 and 1995 the People's Republic of China (PRC) enjoyed double-digit economic growth each year. Since 1996 it has maintained an average growth in gross domestic product of 8 percent.[1]

From 1978 to 2002 China's exports grew from U.S.$9.8 billion to U.S.$325.6 billion, and its imports grew from U.S.$10.9 billion to U.S.$295.2 billion. Actual foreign direct investment in China increased from less than U.S.$1 billion to more than U.S.$50 billion in less than twenty years.[2] In terms of total trade volume China has become the seventh-largest trading nation in the world.[3] Indeed, the PRC has been actively involved in global economic activities and is fully integrated into the Asia Pacific economy. It is now a member of all the major international and regional economic organizations. Some suggest that China will soon overtake Japan and become the second-largest economy in the world;[4] others predict that it may even replace the United States as "the number one economy in the world."[5]

Apart from its growing economic strength, there has been significant progress in China's military modernization.[6] According to the estimates of the International Institute for Strategic Studies, the PRC increased its defense spending from U.S.$24.3 billion in 1992 to U.S.$47 billion in 2001.[7] It has been purchasing a variety of weapons from Russia, Israel, and other countries to upgrade its air and naval power. Beijing is reported to have spent an average of £650 million on Russian fighter jets and warships each year.[8]

Over the past two decades, substantial improvement has been made in the People's Liberation Army (PLA) navy's surface combatants, destroyers, frigates, and submarine forces. Recent acquisitions from Russia include the well-known Sovremenny-class destroyers. In 2002 China ordered eight Project 636 Kilo-class submarines from Russia.[9] The purchase of Russian aircraft such as Su-27s and Su-30s and the development of indigenous fighters (e.g., Jian-10 fighter-bomber) are further evidence of the PLA's efforts to modernize its air force.

Strategic forces are also a very important part of China's defense modernization. A sustained effort has been made to improve the range and accuracy of its missile force. Ten years ago China had only eight intercontinental ballistic missiles; today it has about twenty. Similarly, the number of China's intermediate-range ballistic missiles increased from 60 in 1992 to 130–150 in 2002. In addition, Beijing now possesses 335 short-range ballistic missiles.[10]

There are many weaknesses in China's military capabilities, of course, but PRC leaders seem determined to press ahead with their defense modernization. They have introduced serious reforms in every aspect of their military forces. If the reforms continue, in the next two decades the PLA may well become a very powerful army with a capability to project force beyond China's borders.

Many believe that the size, population, and resources of China, combined with the enormous economic and military potential, make it almost inevitable that the country will achieve great-power status. Others, however, are somewhat more skeptical about the prospects of a rising China. Indeed, following the collapse of the communist regimes in Eastern Europe and the former Soviet Union, there were speculations that China would follow the Soviet path of disintegration.[11] Some researchers argued that Chinese provinces had gained much autonomy in economic decisionmaking since the 1980s as a result of a greater emphasis on the market economy and economic decentralization. They pointed out that regional authorities had become more assertive in promoting and protecting their interests, and that the central government had found it more difficult to coordinate the national economy. The rise of economic regionalism, according to their analysis, might lead to political and military regionalism and even the breakup of China.[12]

Contrary to these predictions, the Chinese communist regime was able to survive and sustain its reform program in the 1990s. However, the achievement

Hong Kong, 1999. Chinese troops arrive in Hong Kong
at sunrise after the official handover of power from Britain.

of rapid economic growth in China is not without its costs. Critics have
pointed to the numerous problems, such as regional disparities, income
inequalities, widespread corruption, rising unemployment, labor unrest, rural
discontent, environmental degradation, and so on, that could seriously threaten
the economic development of China. More fundamentally, some scholars are
questioning whether the PRC's economic growth can be sustained because of
substantial institutional and structural constraints and weaknesses in its banking and financial system.[13]

Some analysts argue that the accession of China to the World Trade Organization (WTO) will present Chinese leaders with a formidable economic
challenge. This, combined with other social and political problems, could trigger a major systemic crisis in the PRC. In his controversial book *The Coming
Collapse of China,* Gordon Chang predicts that China is "in long term decline"
and "on the verge of collapse."[14] He contends that Beijing's WTO commitments can only hasten the demise of the communist regime. Some scholars
agree with Chang's observations and analyses; others have challenged his bold
prediction, arguing that it lacks a sophisticated methodology or convincing
evidence. Nevertheless, the book has generated yet another round of debate on
the future of China.[15]

The "China Threat" Debate

While the prospects of a fragmented China have not been ruled out by foreign
leaders and analysts, most of them are working on the assumptions that China

will continue to grow both economically and militarily and that it will become a great power in the not-too-distant future.[16] If that is the case, it could alter the regional balance of power fundamentally and pose an immense challenge to the United States and Japan. This in part explains their concerns over the economic and security implications of a rising China.

China as a Potential Threat to Regional Security

The rapid development of the Chinese economy since the late 1970s has led to speculation that the rise of China may constitute a long-term threat to the stability and security of the Asia Pacific region.[17] According to some security specialists, a great power's behavior is determined not so much by its intentions but by its capabilities. As a state's economy vastly expands, it will use its newfound power to extend its spheres of influence and defend its economic interests whenever and wherever these interests are challenged.[18]

International relations scholars have pointed out that the emergence of great powers has invariably caused instability and international conflict.[19] "Big countries are more likely to be difficult to live with," Gideon Rachman notes, "if they have a strong sense of cultural superiority or historical grievances about their treatment by the rest of the world."[20] China is widely known as a dissatisfied and non–status quo power seeking to "right the wrongs" of its humiliating history and alter the existing rules of the international system— rules, in its view, created and dictated by the West.[21] Thus, some analysts predict that an economically and militarily powerful China would pursue a more assertive foreign policy, and that it would be less likely to accommodate the other great powers in the Asia Pacific region.[22] To those proponents of "civilizational realpolitik," like Samuel Huntington, China represents one of the hostile non-Western civilizations that will challenge Western security interests.[23]

The lack of transparency in the PRC's defense spending and its growing military capabilities have added to the fear of Chinese hegemonic intentions. To be sure, Beijing has a track record of utilizing military force to deter potential enemies and achieve diplomatic and security objectives.[24] Its assertive stance in a variety of territorial disputes in the South China Sea and its menacing posture toward Taiwan have led some analysts to conclude that a more open and prosperous China will not necessarily be a pacific China. Critics point to the inconsistency of Chinese official declarations and foreign policy behaviors. The PLA's large-scale military exercises and missile tests in the Taiwan Strait in 1995–1996 were an indication that Chinese leaders were willing to resort to military means to regain lost territories.[25]

In addition, China's determination to fulfill its great power potential and rising nationalistic sentiments among Chinese elites and citizens since the early 1990s have reinforced external perceptions of an emerging "China threat."[26] Despite its economic success and greater openness, the PRC remains, to most Western analysts, a communist regime governed by a group of self-selected leaders. In today's China, criticisms of the political leadership are still prohibited and dissent is harshly suppressed. Such a nondemocratic government is believed to be less inclined to adopt a peaceful approach to conflict resolution and territorial disputes. It is also more susceptible to pressures from the military to follow a more assertive security policy.[27]

Many security specialists are critical of the assumption that economic interdependence would reduce the possibility of military conflict. Both Taiwan and Association of Southeast Asian Nations (ASEAN) member states are important trading partners of China, yet their close economic relationships have not prevented the PRC from acting assertively in the South China Sea and across the Taiwan Strait. Given China's increasing energy needs, these specialist maintain, the country will sooner or later press its claim to the South China Sea area, leading to military confrontation with ASEAN states.

To some analysts, a weak and chaotic China could also pose a threat to regional stability and security. They are worried about the consequences of a possible economic disaster and political upheaval in China. As the PRC is now a trading partner of many nations and has extensive economic links with the wider world, an economic failure in the country would undermine regional and global economic stability. Should the communist regime fail to maintain the political cohesion of China, internal strife or even civil war may ensue, which, some scholars predict, could lead to a massive refugee crisis[28] and great-power competition for control over the fragmented kingdom.[29]

China as a Stabilizing Force in East Asia

Not all analysts agree that a rising China would threaten global and regional security. Some argue that a China that is committed to reform and trade should be welcomed by the international community, for economic change will gradually transform it into a more open and liberal country that will in turn be a stabilizing force in East Asia.[30] As China becomes more prosperous, it is argued, its emerging middle class will demand more political freedom and a greater degree of participation in the decisionmaking process. Indeed, economic decentralization and increasing competition for economic benefits among different groups, organizations, and regions have resulted in the rise of interest-group politics in the PRC. Moreover, rapid technological change combined with growing economic and cultural interactions between China and the external world have made it difficult for the regime to maintain tight social and political control.[31]

Scholars have often referred to the experience of Taiwan, South Korea, and other East Asian countries where economic modernization was followed by political liberalization and democratization.[32] While the pre-Tiananmen democracy movement suffered a serious setback in 1989, the trend toward greater liberalization in China has accelerated as a result of further economic progress. Competitive elections at the local level have been introduced that allow Chinese villagers to choose their local officials.[33] Some observers are of the view that the limited democratic experiment will eventually result in more substantial reforms of institutions at higher levels and, over a longer term, a fundamental change in the political system.[34]

Based on the theory of democratic peace,[35] some analysts argue that a China that is moving toward political liberalization and democratization, albeit at a very slow pace, is less likely to use force to resolve territorial disputes with neighboring countries and to achieve its great-power ambition through military means. More important, a China that is increasingly linked to the world economy and that has an interdependent relationship with its trading partners is less inclined to take aggressive actions that will be detrimental to its own economic interests. Thus, growing economic linkages between the PRC and its neighbors would make military confrontation too costly to contemplate.[36] Chinese leaders, as Michael Yahuda observes, have recognized that economic interdependence plays a vital part in sustaining China's economic growth, maintaining its social stability, and legitimizing the rule of the Chinese Communist Party (CCP).[37]

Indeed, some scholars argue that interdependence in one sphere helps facilitate interdependence in other spheres.[38] They point out that since the end of the Cold War, China has developed cooperative relations with most of its Asian neighbors, promoted regional economic cooperation, participated in bilateral and multilateral security dialogues in Asia, signed the Nuclear Non-proliferation Treaty, and acted on most occasions as a responsible member of international organizations.[39] "China is a revisionist power," says Robert Ross, "but for the foreseeable future it will seek to maintain the status quo."[40] To liberal scholars, a poor and underdeveloped China would present a much greater threat to the outside world, as an economically unstable Chinese regime will be less likely to be a cooperative member of the international community.[41]

China as Perceived by the United States

The country that is most concerned about an ascendant China is arguably the United States. Some scholars argue that the post–Cold War international system is one of unipolarity dominated by the United States, and that no other country is capable of challenging its dominance.[42] Even Chinese security specialists acknowledge that the military capabilities, economic strength, and technological advantages of the United States will allow it to retain its predominant position for years to come.[43] There is every incentive for the United States to preserve "the unipolar moment,"[44] particularly after the success of U.S. military operations in Afghanistan and, more recently, in Iraq. In this sense, China's great-power ambition and active promotion of a multipolar world are perceived as a direct challenge to U.S. interests.

Washington is particularly worried about the PRC's rising military power, especially its nuclear capability, which is considered to be a potential threat to U.S. security. Beijing's alleged arms sales and transfer of missile technology to some "irresponsible and dangerous" countries are also a major concern to the United States, especially after the September 11, 2001, terrorist attacks.[45] The nature of the current Chinese regime has further increased U.S. distrust of China. Indeed, the United States has long been an outspoken critic of the PRC's human rights record.

As the United States has extensive security interests in the Asia Pacific region, it is apprehensive of China's growing assertiveness there. Despite Chinese criticisms, Washington has strengthened its defense cooperation with Japan since the mid-1990s. During his February 2002 visit to Tokyo, President George W. Bush called Japan the "bedrock for peace and prosperity in the Pacific." The United States is also planning to develop and deploy a theater missile defense system in Asia, a move also opposed by China. The most controversial area concerns the close, albeit informal, relations that the United States has with Taiwan. To Washington, Taiwan is a loyal ally and a valuable trading partner, and it is also a successfully democratized regime. The United States feels that it has a moral, if not political, responsibility to protect its security. If Taiwan were to be taken over by China, it would enormously strengthen the PRC's economic and military power, which could pose a threat to U.S. regional interests.

The United States also has a vital interest in ensuring freedom of navigation in the South China Sea. While the United States is not a claimant in South China Sea disputes, it is concerned about the destabilizing effects of a potential conflict between China and U.S. allies such as the Philippines. Washington has thus urged all claimant states to resolve their disputes through peaceful negotiations. The last thing the United States wishes to see is China resorting to the use of force to assert its territorial claims in the area.[46]

During the Clinton era, the term "strategic partnership" was used to describe U.S.-China relations, although there were fundamental differences on a wide variety of issues between the two nations.[47] Indeed, the Bush campaign saw China as a strategic competitor of the United States. Immediately after taking office, President Bush took steps to strengthen U.S. security relations with friends and allies across the Asia Pacific region, especially with Japan, Australia, and Singapore. The consolidation of U.S. defense links with these countries was viewed by Chinese leaders as a strategy of encircling China. Relations between Washington and Beijing deteriorated substantially in April 2001, when a EP-3 spy plane collided with a Chinese fighter jet over the South China Sea, resulting in an unauthorized emergency landing of the U.S. plane on China's Hainan Island.

Following the tragic events of September 11, optimism was expressed in the Western media over the prospects for a significant improvement in U.S.-China relations. While the "war against terrorism" may have provided a new opportunity for the United States and China to work together, it does not appear to have provided a lasting basis for their cooperation.[48] This is because the two countries have different views on the origins of international terrorism, the approaches to fighting it, and the expected outcomes of their antiterrorist cooperation. In fact, the expansion of U.S. antiterrorist networks since September 11 has led to deeper concern in China about the future role of the United States in the global system.[49]

Clearly, Chinese support for the U.S. antiterrorist campaign has not altered its perceptions of the implications of the PRC's military modernization.

A Central Intelligence Agency report of 2002 estimated that China's ballistic missiles will increase severalfold by 2015 and that they would be deployed primarily against the United States.[50] Concerns about China's defense modernization and its growing military capabilities were also expressed in two Pentagon reports published in 2002 and 2003.

In particular, China's continued military intimidation of Taiwan is interpreted as a threat to U.S. interests in the region. Thus, President Bush has approved the sale of a massive arms package to Taipei. The package includes four Kidd-class destroyers, eight diesel-electric patrol submarines, twelve P-3 Orion maritime patrol aircraft, submarine- and surface-launched torpedoes, and other naval systems. Together they would enhance Taiwan's capability to break potential Chinese blockades. President Bush has also stated publicly that the United States would do "whatever it took to help Taiwan defend herself."[51] In the meantime, Washington has developed closer defense ties with the Taiwanese military and allowed senior Taiwanese leaders and officials to visit the United States. A leaked Pentagon report has allegedly suggested that nuclear weapons could be used against China in the event of a conflict across the Taiwan Strait.[52]

This is not to say that an armed conflict between the United States and China is inevitable. After all, the two nations share a common interest in maintaining regional stability and economic prosperity in East Asia. The United States also needs Chinese cooperation in handling a wide range of regional and global issues such as the North Korean nuclear crisis.[53] For example, China may have played an instrumental role in persuading Pyongyang to accept the six-party negotiations on dismantling its nuclear program.[54] Moreover, the China market is too important for the U.S. business community to ignore. For all these reasons, the U.S. government has been trying to engage China over the past decade. However, as the sole superpower in the world, the United States is bound to view a stronger and more assertive China as a tremendous challenge to its global primacy.

China as Perceived by Its Neighbors

Most countries in East Asia have mixed feelings about an increasingly powerful China. On the one hand, they are disturbed by growing Chinese power and its long-term implications. On the other, they tend to believe that China is preordained to become a major power in the region and hope to gain from the China trade. Indeed, most of them have close economic and commercial links with the PRC. The extent to which they see Beijing as a potential threat would depend on their historical and current relations with China. These ambivalent attitudes are analyzed below with reference to the perceptions of Taiwan, India, ASEAN states, Japan, and Russia.[55]

Taiwan

Of all of the PRC's neighbors, Taiwan is doubtlessly the one that feels most threatened by China. After all, Beijing has never renounced the use of force in achieving its goal of reunification with Taiwan. The modernization of

China's air and naval forces since the 1990s is closely related to the preparation for a cross-strait confrontation.[56] "Over the past few years," according to some security analysts, "the training regimen, doctrine, writings, weapons procurement, and rhetoric of the People's Liberation Army have all turned to focus on a Taiwan attack scenario."[57] Indeed, Taiwan is constantly under the threat of over 300 Chinese short-range ballistic missiles. Since the election of the Chen Shui-bian government in 2000, China has stepped up its military buildup to deter Taiwanese independence and potential U.S. intervention in a conflict over Taiwan.[58]

However, military coercion from the PRC is not the only concern for Taiwanese leaders. They are also worried about China's rapid economic growth and its prominent economic role in Asia, which could result in the marginalization of Taiwan's economy. Indeed, Chinese leaders have consistently trying to frustrate Taiwan's aspirations to become a regional economic center.

Meanwhile, China has succeeded in attracting enormous Taiwanese investment and in forcing the Taipei government to ease its trade restrictions on cross-strait trade. Closer economic links and trade interactions between Taiwan and China could make Taipei more dependent on the mainland for its future economic development. In this sense, Taiwan's ability to resist PRC pressure for cross-strait talks could be weakened by its rapidly expanding economic ties with China in the past few years.[59] Nevertheless, President Chen seems determined to reject Beijing's "one-China principle" as the basis for any future negotiations. Following his recent reelection as Taiwanese president, Chen insisted that "Taiwan is one country and the other side in another country" and that "neither side exercises jurisdiction over the other."[60]

India

India, China's South Asian neighbor, also views rising Chinese power with some apprehension. Like China, India has great-power aspirations and perceives Beijing as its potential rival in Asia. While the Chinese believe that India seeks to become a dominant power in South Asia and the Indian Ocean, the Indians regard China's growing nuclear capabilities as a threat to regional security. Prior to New Delhi's nuclear tests in 1998, Indian officials voiced their concern about a "China threat" to India's security. The roots of Indian-Chinese tension can be traced to the events of the 1950s following China's occupation of Tibet and the Dalai Lama's flight to India. This was exacerbated by their boundary disputes and border clash in 1962.[61]

Although the boundary question remains unresolved, there has been much pragmatism on both sides in handling their bilateral relations in other areas. Indeed, Sino-Indian economic and security cooperation has expanded considerably in the past decade. The visit of Prime Minister Atal Bihari Vajpayee to Beijing in June 2003 signifies India's desire to develop a better relationship with China.[62] However, the PRC's close military relations with Pakistan and its alleged transfer of nuclear and missile technology to Islamabad continue to arouse mistrust in India.

ASEAN States

Given China's dominant role in the history of Southeast Asia and its extensive links with communist forces in the region during the Maoist era, ASEAN countries are wary of growing PRC military and economic strength. Nevertheless, they tend to accept the inevitability of a rising China and have benefited from the lucrative Chinese market.[63] At the "ASEAN Plus Three" summit in November 2002 in Phnom Penh, ASEAN leaders and then–Chinese premier Zhu Rongji decided to establish a China-ASEAN free trade area by 2010, which could become the world's third-largest trading bloc.[64]

Very few, if any, ASEAN leaders would expect China to reclaim its historical preeminence by conquering neighboring countries. However, they are not confident that Beijing would not use force to deal with unresolved territorial disputes in future. Of particular anxiety to the ASEAN states are China's territorial claims in the South China Sea. It is true that Chinese leaders have indicated their willingness to shelve the sovereignty issue for the time being, but they have never relinquished their nationalist goal of regaining "lost territories" in due course. Despite a common concern over the PRC's intentions, there is no unanimity among ASEAN members in their perceptions of the "China threat."

The most pessimistic assessment of the security implications of the rise of China can probably be found in Indonesia.[65] Jakarta's perceptions of a threat are rooted in its historical encounters with China and its views of the role of overseas Chinese in the Chinese communist revolution. Beijing's support for the Indonesian Communist Party in the 1950s, coupled with controversies over the legal status and economic position of ethnic Chinese residents in Indonesia, have contributed further to the instability in Sino-Indonesian relations for decades.[66]

Indonesian leaders also see an emerging China as a challenge to Indonesia's regional aspirations. As the de facto leaders of ASEAN, Indonesia initiated in 1990 a series of annual workshops on managing potential conflicts in the South China Sea. But Indonesian officials are frustrated by the lack of tangible outcomes from these workshops. Jakarta's suspicion of China is heightened by Beijing's claim to a gas-rich area close to the Natuna Islands, occupied by Indonesia. However, a greater emphasis has been placed on economic cooperation with the PRC since the end of the Suharto era.[67]

The other country that is most skeptical of Chinese intentions in the South China Sea is the Philippines. For two decades prior to 1995, Sino-Philippine relations were by and large stable. However, the Philippines' threat perceptions have changed following the PRC's occupation of Philippines-claimed Mischief Reef in 1995 and its incursions into the Scarborough Reef since 1997.[68] Although efforts have been made by both countries to establish various confidence-building measures, China's "creeping assertiveness" in the Spratly Islands[69] and its military modernization have led to a growing fear of Chinese expansionism among Filipino politicians and the public alike. This has in part contributed to the enhancement of U.S.-Philippines security relations in the past few years.[70]

To Vietnam, the "China threat" is by no means a recent phenomenon. For over 2,000 years the Vietnamese have lived under the shadow of China. As Vietnam's policy toward China is tightly constrained by geographical reality, it has sought to maintain a delicate balance between accommodating its powerful neighbor and defending Vietnamese national interests. Despite repeated conflict with the PRC over ideology, disputed territorial claims, the treatment of ethnic Chinese, and other issues, Hanoi has been able to achieve a substantial improvement in its relations with China since the late 1980s, largely due to the fact that each is trying to develop a market-oriented economy within a socialist system. Beijing's experience in economic reform is no doubt of immense value to Vietnam.[71]

Nevertheless, the South China Sea dispute remains a "main irritant" in Sino-Vietnamese relations.[72] Indeed, Vietnam fought two naval battles with China in the South China Sea, in 1974[73] and in 1988. China won both battles and succeeded in occupying the Paracels in 1974 and several reefs in the Spratly area in 1988. In 1992 China signed a contract with the U.S. company Crestone Energy Corporation to explore oil in the Vietnam-claimed area of the Spratly Islands. Vietnam's decision to join ASEAN in 1995 must have been driven partly, if not primarily, by its fear of China's readiness to challenge Vietnamese interests in the South China Sea. From Hanoi's perspective, ASEAN membership may help counter further Chinese moves in the Spratlys.

Like Vietnam, Malaysia has territorial disputes with China in the South China Sea. For several decades the Malaysian government resented Beijing's support for Malaysian communist insurgency movements and the Communist Party of Malaya. However, Malaysian leaders are reluctant to say that China would present a threat to their country's security. Former Malaysian prime minister Mahathir Mohammad has rejected the "China threat" theory, arguing that treating China as a potential enemy could result in regional tensions. Clearly, Malaysia does not see the South China Sea dispute as an obstacle to the development of a cordial relationship with the PRC.[74] In fact, Malaysia has argued against exerting pressure on Beijing to make concessions on the South China Sea dispute.[75] Meanwhile, Malaysia is critical of the role of the United States in Southeast Asian economic and political affairs.

This is a reflection of Mahathir's "Look East" policy and a common position between Malaysian and Chinese leaders on a range of regional and international issues.[76] Nevertheless, Kuala Lumpur shares the view of other ASEAN states that a U.S. military presence in Southeast Asia is essential to regional stability. Indeed, Malaysia's defense planners are less sanguine about China's strategic intentions. They have serious misgivings about the PRC's military buildup and its naval modernization in particular. The long-term aim of China, according to the chief of the Malaysian army, appears to be "dominance, though not necessarily aggression."[77]

Brunei, Thailand, Cambodia, Laos, Myanmar, and Singapore do not seem to see China as a threat to regional security, at least not in public. They have all been rather restrained in questioning China's security intentions in the region. Singaporean leaders have argued that China's behavior will likely be constrained by its national goal of economic modernization and increasing trade and commercial links with other Asian countries.[78] Nevertheless, Singapore does have some concern over the PRC's growing military power and regional policy. It is actually a strong advocate of a continued U.S. military presence in Southeast Asia. In recent years Singapore has made a serious effort to modernize its armed forces.[79] Singapore's military modernization may not be intended as a counterbalance to Chinese forces, but it provides the country with a fallback position should engagement fail.[80]

Japan

China and Japan are historical rivals in East Asia. While there is a high level of economic and trade interactions between the two countries, the Japanese are aware that growing Chinese power would present a formidable challenge to Japan's position in the region. China's internal developments and foreign policy are therefore of special interest to Japan.

In the Cold War years, Tokyo's policy toward China was based primarily on the assumption that the PRC could be integrated into the international system through trade and economic interactions. Since the early 1990s, Japanese politicians and analysts have become increasingly worried about China's military modernization, missile technology exports, nuclear testing, and assertive stance on the Taiwan issue and the South China Sea disputes.[81] After all, 70 percent of the oil that Japan needs passes through the waters in the South China Sea area. In any case, Japan has a long-standing territorial dispute with China over the sovereignty of the Diaoyu/Senkaku Islands. Following the Taiwan Strait crisis in 1996, Japanese public opinion on China became rather negative.[82] Beijing's belligerent behavior certainly contributed to the Japanese decision to strengthen the U.S.-Japan security alliance.[83] Indeed, Japanese leaders were forced to accept what Michael Green and Benjamin Self called "reluctant realism" in their China policy.[84]

By the end of the 1990s, the voice of those in the Japanese government, academia, and media who had advocated a tougher approach to China became more prominent.[85] This seemed to mirror a growing suspicion of Japan's security intentions among PRC elites and analysts.[86] While the Koizumi government does not wish to promote the idea of a "China threat," concern about the potential threat to Japanese interests from a militarily powerful China remains strong.

From the Japanese perspective, the relative strength or weakness of China will have profound implications for Japan and pose great challenges to its policymakers. A rich China with a strong military capability could become more aggressive on regional security issues and provoke a further arms buildup in the Asia Pacific region. On the other hand, an economically weak and politically fragmented China could result in mass migration of Chinese people into Japan and other Southeast Asian countries, which would also threaten regional stability and prosperity.[87] This is why Tokyo is keen to engage China economically while strengthening its alliance with the United States.

However, the emergence of China as a great power in the international system is seen by many Japanese as a challenge to Japan as a regional power. According to this view, a close economic relationship between Japan and China does not preclude the possibility of economic rivalry. In fact, the two nations are engaged in a political-strategic rivalry in Asia, where they both aspire to assume the role of regional leader. This is why Japan decided to begin talks over the establishment of a free trade agreement with ASEAN countries in late 2002 soon after China and ASEAN announced their plan to set up a free trade area by 2010. On a global level, Japan and China are also competing for economic and political influence on various issues.[88] Their competition is likely to intensify in the coming years as China grows stronger.

Russia
Russia's relations with the PRC have improved immensely since the collapse of the Soviet Union. Russian leaders certainly do not perceive China as a security threat, at least not for the foreseeable future. The two countries are far more concerned about the predominant position of the United States in the post–Cold War world, and are keen to encourage the development of a multipolar international system. As both countries are actively engaged in a process of economic reform, a peaceful security environment in East Asia, especially along the Sino-Russian borders, would serve their interests. Over the past decade, there has been a fairly high degree of economic and military cooperation between the two nations, and Moscow is currently the PRC's main provider of weapons. On numerous occasions Russian and Chinese leaders have referred to their relationship as a "strategic partnership."

However, there is considerable skepticism among Russian officials and intellectuals about their country's relations with China. The radical Westernizers see the PRC as a potential threat because of its undemocratic political system, while the radical nationalists believe that the Chinese are working closely with the West to encircle Russia. As China's economic and military power increases, Russian analysts argue, it may become an expansionist power.[89] This explains Russia's reluctance to offer Beijing cutting-edge weapons systems.[90] Indeed, some Russian specialists have expressed their concern about the strategic implications of arms sales to the PRC despite short-term benefits.[91]

The most negative perceptions of China are found in the Russian Far East where the local residents are worried about an influx of Chinese immigrants. This "demographic expansion" is seen by some inhabitants in the border areas as a threat to Russian interests.[92] Nevertheless, according to a recent national survey 52 percent of the respondents considered Russian-Chinese relations as friendly.[93]

Responding to the China Challenge
The challenge of a more stalwart and confident China to Asia Pacific security seems formidable, but there is no commonly accepted strategy to deal with a rising China. Those who see a "hegemony on the horizon" have advocated

various strategies of containing or constraining China. By far the most extreme form of containment is recommended by Charles Krauthammer, who argues that the United States must do everything within its power to contain an aggressive and expansionist China, including developing and strengthening U.S. security relations with China's neighboring countries and supporting Chinese dissidents to destabilize the communist regime in Beijing.[94]

A less confrontational strategy is proposed by Denny Roy, who believes that Asian and Western countries should try to "slow the growth of China's military and economic power."[95] Roy has also advanced a strategy of "enmeshment,"[96] which is more or less the same as Gerald Segal's proposal of the "constrainment of China." Segal argues that Chinese behavior cannot be moderated by economic interdependence alone and that the balance-of-power strategy is indispensable. China can be "constrained," Segal maintains, if Asian and Western countries are willing to act together to defend their interests "by means of incentives for good behavior, deterrence of bad behavior, and punishment when deterrence fails."[97]

A somewhat similar strategy is recommended by Gideon Rachman, who argues for a combination of "economic engagement and strategic containment." The West should encourage economic and trade interactions with the PRC, he suggests, but Western countries and China's neighbors must unite in dissuading Beijing from using force to settle disputes in East Asia. They should make it absolutely clear that any Chinese military actions will provoke a strong and concerted response from the outside world that will severely damage China's economic interests. The key to this strategy, according to Rachman, is to sustain and expand the U.S. military presence in the Asia Pacific region.[98]

Other analysts who are less worried about the "China threat" argue that it is important to seek to integrate the PRC into the international society through engagement and dialogue. Proposals of containing or constraining China, they contend, are unrealistic and irresponsible and will only provoke Chinese hostility, heighten regional tension, and undermine international cooperation.[99] Instead, they have proposed various strategies to engage China. The more moderate approaches include "comprehensive engagement"[100] and "constructive engagement"[101] relying primarily on cooperative measures to integrate China into the international community. More assertive approaches such as "conditional engagement"[102] and "coercive engagement"[103] place more emphasis on punitive measures should Beijing fail to follow the rules and regulations of the international institutions and regimes. Still others suggest that the outside world should try to "incorporate" the CCP leaders "by creating vested interests for them in the current international system."[104]

Despite the differences in their strategies, scholars of the "engagement school" believe that engagement offers the best hope that the rise of China will not threaten regional security.[105] In reality, however, the distinction between "containment" and "engagement" is not as clear-cut as it appears to be. One can certainly find elements of both approaches in the response of the U.S. and East Asian governments to the emerging China challenge.

For the moment, the United States and all other East Asian nations have made it clear that they wish to engage China both bilaterally and multilaterally. At the same time, they have accepted certain elements of the balance-of-power strategy. While there may be different views among them on the utility of engagement, few would place their hope entirely on the self-restraint and benevolence of a rising China. Even those countries that do not subscribe to the "China threat theory" have made a conscious attempt to enhance their military capabilities in recent years.[106]

With the possible exception of Russia, all the governments in East Asia appear to welcome a continued U.S. military presence in the region. This does not mean that they have no disagreements with Washington on other issues. But they feel that only U.S. military power can deter Beijing from using force to tackle unresolved territorial disputes. Meanwhile, U.S. and Asian leaders do not wish to antagonize the PRC by treating it as a potential enemy. At the November 2002 ASEAN summit in Phnom Penh, for example, the ten ASEAN member states signed an important accord with China with the objective of avoiding armed conflict over contested areas of the South China Sea.[107] It was a concrete example of the dominant sentiment among them: Through economic interactions and diplomatic efforts, they hope to persuade China to follow a peaceful path in its pursuit of great-power aspirations.

Rex Li is senior lecturer in international relations, Liverpool John Moores University, and an associate editor of Security Dialogue, *International Peace Research Institute, Oslo. In recent years, he has been a visiting lecturer at the Joint Services Command and Staff College, UK Defence Academy. A regular speaker at high-level security conferences and Track Two diplomatic dialogues, he has published widely on Asia Pacific security and China's foreign relations. His recent works have appeared in* Journal of Strategic Studies, World Today, Pacifica Review, Journal of Contemporary China, *and other international publications.*

Notes

I would like to thank the editorial staff of the European Centre for Conflict Prevention and three external referees for their helpful comments on an earlier version of this chapter.

1. Stephen Green, *Reforming China's Economy: A Rough Guide* (London: Royal Institute of International Affairs, 2003), p. 1; *The Military Balance* (London: Brassey's/Oxford University Press for the International Institute of Security Studies [IISS], 1994–2003).

2. Nicholas R. Lardy, *China in the World Economy* (Washington, D.C.: Institute for International Economics, 1994), pp. 30, 63; People's Republic of China (PRC), Ministry of Foreign Trade and Economic Cooperation, "The Information on Import and Export Statistics, 2002, 12," available at http://english.moftec.gov.cn/article/200301/20030100064844_1.xml; PRC, Ministry of Foreign Trade and Economic Cooperation, "Statistics About the Utilization of Foreign Investment in 2002, 1–12, of China," available at http://english.moftec.gov.cn/article/200301/20030100063756_1.xml.

3. Shi Guangsheng, Chinese minister of foreign trade and economic cooperation, "Remarks at the Reception Hosted by EU-China Business Association and Belgium-Chinese Economic and Commercial Council," December 9, 2002, available at http://english.moftec.gov.cn/article/200212/20021200056451_1.xml.

4. Mamdouh G. Salameh, "China, Oil, and the Risk of Regional Conflict," *Survival* 37, no. 4 (Winter 1995–1996): 142.

5. Nicholas D. Kristof, "The Rise of China," *Foreign Affairs* 72, no. 5 (September–October 1993): 59.

6. For a recent assessment of China's military modernization, see David Shambaugh, *Modernizing China's Military: Progress, Problems, and Prospects* (Berkeley: University of California Press, 2002).

7. *Military Balance.*

8. *The Times,* May 3, 2003, p. 22.

9. Ibid.

10. *Military Balance,* 1992–1993 (1992), p. 145, 2002–2003 (2002), p. 145. According to a recent Pentagon report, China has as many as 450 short-range ballistic missiles. See United States Department of Defense, "Report to Congress Pursuant to the FY2000 National Defense Authorization Act: Annual Report on the Military Power of the People's Republic of China," July 2003, p. 48, available at http://www.defenselink.mil/news/Jul2003/n07312002_200307315.html.

11. For a critical consideration of these speculations, see Peter Ferdinand, "Russian and Soviet Shadows over China's Future," *International Affairs* 68, no. 2 (April 1992): 279–292.

12. Gerald Segal, *China Changes Shape: Regionalism and Foreign Policy,* Adelphi Paper no. 287 (London: Brassey's for the IISS, 1994).

13. Callum Henderson, *China on the Brink* (New York: McGraw-Hill, 1999); Carsten A. Holz, "Economic Reforms and State Sector Bankruptcy in China," *China Quarterly* no. 166 (2001): 342–367.

14. Gordon G. Chang, *The Coming Collapse of China* (London: Century/Random House, 2001), p. xvi.

15. See, for example, the "Special Book Review" section in *Issues & Studies* 38, no. 2 (June 2002): 235–263.

16. Given space constraints, the international relations theories that underpin the arguments in the "China threat" debate cannot be examined in detail in this chapter. For a fuller consideration of the scholarly debate, see Denny Roy, "The 'China Threat' Issue: Major Arguments," *Asian Survey* 36, no. 8 (August 1996): 767–770; Avery Goldstein, "Great Expectations: Interpreting China's Arrival," *International Security* 23, no. 3 (Winter 1997–1998): 62–71; Herbert Yee and Ian Storey, "Introduction" in Herbert Yee and Ian Storey, eds., *The China Threat: Perceptions, Myths, and Reality* (London: RoutledgeCurzon, 2002), pp. 6–10; and Rex Li, "Security Challenge of an Ascendant China: Great Power Emergence and International Stability," in Suisheng Zhao, ed., *Chinese Foreign Policy: Pragmatism and Strategic Behavior* (New York: M. E. Sharpe, 2004), chap. 2.

17. Richard Bernstein and Ross H. Munro, *The Coming Conflict with China* (New York: Alfred A. Knopf, 1997).

18. This pattern of great-power emergence has recurred many times in history: Britain, France, Germany, Japan, the former Soviet Union, and the United States all followed similar paths. See Aaron L. Friedberg, "Ripe for Rivalry: Prospects for Peace in a Multipolar Asia," *International Security* 18, no. 3 (Winter 1993–1994): 16; and Roy, "The 'China Threat' Issue," p. 762.

19. According to the power transition theory, a rising power will seek to challenge the status of the leading power in the international hierarchy, which could result in a war between them. See A. F. K. Organski, *World Politics* (New York: Knopf, 1958); and A. F. K. Organski and Jacek Kugler, *The War Ledger* (Chicago: University of Chicago Press, 1980).

20. Gideon Rachman, "Containing China," *Washington Quarterly* 19, no. 1 (Winter 1995): 132. For comparisons of Wilhelmine Germany and today's China, see Kristof, "Rise of China," pp. 71–72; and Arthur Waldron, "Deterring China," *Commentary* 100, no. 4 (October 1995): 18.

21. Barry Buzan and Gerald Segal, "Rethinking East Asian Security," *Survival* 36, no. 2 (Summer 1994): 6; Denny Roy, "Hegemon on the Horizon? China's Threat to East Asian Security," *International Security* 19, no. 1 (Summer 1994): 161; David Shambaugh, "Containment or Engagement of China? Calculating Beijing's Responses," *International Security* 21, no. 2 (Fall 1996): 186–187.

22. Roy, "Hegemon on the Horizon?" pp. 159–160; Denny Roy, "China's Reaction to American Predominance," *Survival* 45, no. 3 (Autumn 2003), p. 74.

23. Samuel P. Huntington, "The Clash of Civilizations?" *Foreign Affairs* 72, no. 3 (Summer 1993): 22–49. See also Huntington's book *The Clash of Civilizations and the Remaking of World Order* (New York: Simon and Schuster, 1996).

24. See Allen S. Whiting, "China's Use of Force, 1950–96, and Taiwan," *International Security* 29, no. 2 (Fall 2001): 103–131.

25. Alastair Iain Johnston, "China's Militarized International Dispute Behavior, 1949–92: A First Cut at the Data," *China Quarterly* no. 153 (1998): 1–30.

26. For a penetrating analysis of the growth of nationalistic sentiment in China since the early 1990s, see Suisheng Zhao, "Chinese Intellectuals' Quest for National Greatness and Nationalistic Writing in the 1990s," *China Quarterly* no. 152 (1997): 725–745.

27. This is especially true in the case of the communist leaders in the post-Deng era. Unlike Mao, Deng, and other leaders of the older generation, they do not have an impressive military record or personal charisma that can command respect and loyalty from the military. According to a recent study, Jiang Zemin was forced to take bellicose actions to intimidate Taiwan in 1995–1996 in order to secure full support from the military in fortifying his position as Deng Xiaoping's successor. See Jianhai Bi, "The Role of the Military in the PRC Taiwan Policymaking: A Case Study of the Taiwan Strait Crisis of 1995–1996," *Journal of Contemporary China* 11, no. 32 (August 2002): 539–572.

28. Akihiko Tanaka, "China: Dominant, Chaotic, or Interdependent?" in Trevor Taylor and Seizaburo Sato, eds., *Future Sources of Global Conflict* (London: Royal Institute of International Affairs, 1995), pp. 56–57.

29. Bryce Harland, "For a Strong China," *Foreign Policy* 94 (Spring 1994): 51.

30. Kenneth Lieberthal, "A New China Strategy," *Foreign Affairs* 74, no. 6 (November–December 1995): 36.

31. George Gilboy and Eric Heginbotham, "China's Coming Transformation," *Foreign Affairs* 80, no. 4 (July–August 2001): 26–39.

32. See, for example, Barber B. Conable Jr. and David M. Lampton, "China: The Coming Power," *Foreign Affairs* 71, no. 5 (Winter 1992–1993): 146; Thomas W. Robinson, "Interdependence in China's Foreign Relations," in Samuel S. Kim, ed., *China and the World: Chinese Foreign Relations in the Post–Cold War Era* (Boulder: Westview, 1989), p. 197; Yoichi Funabashi, Michel Oksenberg, and Heinrich Weiss, *An Emerging China in a World of Interdependence* (New York: Trilateral Commission, 1994), p. 65.

33. Tianjian Shi, "Economic Development and Village Elections in Rural China," *Journal of Contemporary China* 8, no. 22 (November 1999): 425–442.

34. William H. Overholt, "China After Deng," *Foreign Affairs* 75, no. 3 (May–June 1996): 71, 75–76. See also Minxin Pei, "Is China Democratizing?" *Foreign Affairs* 77, no. 1 (January–February 1998): 68–82.

35. According to the democratic peace theory, democracies are restrained by constitutional mechanisms from fighting wars, as an unjustified war will not be supported by the people who have to bear the burdens of armed conflict. Moreover, democracies do not fight democracies, because of their shared democratic ideals and moral values,

greater transparency in communication, and more peaceful approaches to the resolution of conflict. Finally, within the "pacific union" war can be prevented by trade inter-action and economic interdependence among democratic nations. See Georg Sorensen, "Kant and Process of Democratization: Consequences for Neorealist Thought," *Journal of Peace Research* 29, no. 4 (1992): 398–399.

36. Vincent Cable and Peter Ferdinand, "China as an Economic Giant: Threat or Opportunity?" *International Affairs* 70, no. 2 (April 1994): 259.

37. Michael Yahuda, "How Much Has China Learned About Interdependence?" in David S. G. Goodman and Gerald Segal, eds., *China Rising: Nationalism and Inter-dependence* (London: Routledge, 1997), p. 22.

38. Robinson, "Interdependence in China's Foreign Relations," p. 198.

39. Robert S. Ross, "China and the Stability of East Asia," in Robert S. Ross, ed., *East Asia in Transition: Toward a New Regional Order* (New York: M. E. Sharpe, 1995), pp. 115–117; Gary Klintworth, "Greater China and Regional Security," in Gary Klintworth, ed., *Asia-Pacific Security: Less Uncertainty, New Opportunities?* (Melbourne: Longman, 1996), p. 36.

40. Robert S. Ross, "Beijing as a Conservative Power," *Foreign Affairs* 76, no. 2 (March–April 1997): 34.

41. Funabashi, Oksenberg, and Weiss, *Emerging China*, p. 2; Cable and Ferdinand, "China as an Economic Giant," p. 259; Conable and Lampton, "China," p. 149.

42. Charles Krauthammer, "The Unipolar Moment," *Foreign Affairs* 70, no. 1 (1990–1991): 23–33; William C. Wohlforth, "The Stability of a Unipolar World," *International Security* 24, no. 1 (Summer 1999): 5–41.

43. Rex Li, "Unipolar Aspirations in a Multipolar Reality: China's Perceptions of U.S. Ambitions and Capabilities in the Post–Cold War World," *Pacifica Review* 11, no. 2 (June 1999): 141–147.

44. Michael Mastanduno, "Preserving the Unipolar Moment: Realist Theories and the U.S Grand Strategy After the Cold War," *International Security* 21, no. 4 (Spring 1997): 49–88.

45. Aaron L. Friedberg, "11 September and the Future of Sino-American Relations," *Survival* 44, no. 1 (Spring 2002): 37–38.

46. Lee Lai To, "China, the USA, and the South China Sea Conflicts," *Security Dialogue* 34, no. 1 (March 2003): 25–39.

47. Rex Li, "U.S.-China Relations: Accidents Can Happen," *World Today* 56, no. 5 (May 2000): 17–20.

48. Friedberg, "11 September and the Future of Sino-American Relations"; Adam Ward, "China and America: Trouble Ahead?" *Survival* 45, no. 3 (Autumn 2003), pp. 35–56.

49. Chinese leaders and analysts are disturbed by the augmentation of U.S. power in the post–September 11 world. They believe that the "war on terror" has enabled the United States to fortify its defense ties with traditional allies and develop new security relations across Asia. Pakistan's military cooperation with the United States in removing the Taliban regime and the presence of U.S. forces in Central Asia are of particular concern to Beijing. China is worried that it would be encircled by the United States through a series of security networks in Central, South, Southeast, and Northeast Asia. For an analysis of China's assessment of its changing security environment since September 11, see Rex Li, "A Rising Power with Global Aspirations: China," in Mary Buckley and Rick Fawn, eds., *Global Responses to Terrorism: 9/11, Afghanistan, and Beyond* (London: Routledge, 2003), chap. 18.

50. National Intelligence Council, "Foreign Missile Developments and the Ballistic Missile Threat Through 2015," January 2002, available at www.cia.gov/nic/pubs/other_products/unclassifiedballisticmissilefinal.htm.

51. United States Department of Defense, "Report to Congress Pursuant to the FY2000 National Defense Authorization Act: Annual Report on the Military Power of

the People's Republic of China," July 2002, available at http://www.defenselink. mil/news/Jul2002/20020712china.pdf; United States Department of Defense, "Report to Congress Pursuant to the FY2000 National Defense Authorization Act: Annual Report on the Military Power of the People's Republic of China," July 2003, available at http://www.defenselink.mil/news/Jul2003/n07312003_200307315.html.

52. David E. Sanger, "U.S. Would Defend Taiwan, Bush Says," *New York Times,* April 26, 2001, p. A1.

53. BBC News, "U.S. 'Has Nuclear Hit List,'" March 9, 2002, available at http://news.bbc.co.uk/1/hi/world/americas/1864173.stm. Excerpts of the Pentagon's "Nuclear Posture Review" can be found at www.globalsecurity.org/wmd/library/policy/dod/npr.htm.

54. Donald MacIntyre, "Talking About Talks," *Time,* August 11, 2003, available at www.time.com/time/asia/magazine/printout/0,13675,501030811-472921,00.html.

55. Pakistan and South Korea do not appear to consider China as a threat to their security interests. See Perviaz Iqbal Cheema, "The China Threat: a View from Pakistan," in Yee and Storey, *The China Threat,* pp. 302–311; and Victor D. Cha, "Engaging China: the View from Korea," in Alastair Iain Johnston and Robert S. Ross, eds., *Engaging China: The Management of an Emerging Power* (London: Routledge, 1999), pp. 32–56.

56. Rex Li, "War or Peace? Potential Conflict Across the Taiwan Strait," *World Defense Systems* (London: Royal United Services Institute for Defence Studies, August 2002), pp. 157–160.

57. Kurt M. Campbell and Derek J. Mitchell, "Crisis in the Taiwan Strait," *Foreign Affairs* 80, no. 4 (July–August 2001): 17.

58. For a succinct review of China's recent military development programs in relation to the Taiwan issue, see Sheng Lijun, "Peace over the Taiwan Strait?" *Security Dialogue* 33, no. 1 (March 2002): 101–103.

59. Rex Li, "Changing China-Taiwan Relations and Asia-Pacific Regionalism: Economic Cooperation and Security Challenge," in Christopher M. Dent, ed., *Economic and Security Cooperation in the Asia-Pacific Region* (Basingstoke: Palgrave Macmillan, 2004), chap. 11.

60. BBC News, "Interview: Chen Shui-bian," March 30, 2004, available at http://news.bbc.co.uk/go/pr/fr/1/hi/world/asia-pacific/3582853.stm.

61. C. V. Ranganathan, "The China Threat: A View from India," in Yee and Storey, *The China Threat,* pp. 288–301.

62. "China and India: Friendly Giants," *The Economist,* June 28–July 4, 2003, p. 78.

63. Lee Lai To, "China's Relations with ASEAN: Partners in the 21st Century?" *Pacifica Review* 13, no. 1 (February 2001): 66–67.

64. "China and ASEAN Agree to Create World's Biggest FTA," *Digital Chosunilbo* (English edition), November 5, 2002.

65. Rizal Sukma, "Indonesia's Perceptions of China: The Domestic Bases of Persistent Ambiguity," in Yee and Storey, *The China Threat,* pp. 181–204.

66. Michael Leifer, "Indonesia's Encounters with China and the Dilemmas of Engagement," in Johnston and Ross, *Engaging China,* pp. 87–108.

67. Sukma, "Indonesia's Perceptions of China," pp. 191–195.

68. Aileen San Pablo-Baviera, "Perceptions of a China Threat: A Philippine Perspective," in Yee and Storey, *The China Threat,* pp. 252–253, 257–260; Liselotte Odgaard, "The South China Sea: ASEAN's Security Concerns About China," *Security Dialogue* 34, no. 1 (March 2003): 16.

69. Ian James Storey, "Creeping Assertiveness: China, the Philippines, and the South China Sea Dispute," *Contemporary Southeast Asia* 21, no. 1 (April 1999): 95–118.

70. Greg Austin, "Unwanted Entanglement: The Philippines' Spratly Policy as a Case Study in Conflict Enhancement?" *Security Dialogue* 34, no. 1 (March 2003): 41–54.

71. Carlyle A. Thayer, "Vietnamese Perspectives of the 'China Threat'" in Yee and Storey, *The China Threat*, pp. 265–287.

72. Stein Tonnesson, "Sino-Vietnamese Rapprochement and the South China Sea Irritant," *Security Dialogue* 34, no. 1 (March 2003): 55–70.

73. China's naval battle over the Paracels in 1974 was with what was then South Vietnam.

74. Abdul Razak Baginda, "Malaysian Perceptions of China: From Hostility to Cordiality," in Yee and Storey, *The China Threat*, p. 244.

75. In negotiating a code of conduct between China and ASEAN member states, Malaysia maintained that it should have the status of a guideline rather than that of a treaty. See Odgaard, "South China Sea," p. 15.

76. Baginda, "Malaysian Perceptions of China," p. 243.

77. Amitav Acharya, "Containment, Engagement, or Counter-Dominance? Malaysia's Response to the Rise of China," in Johnston and Ross, *Engaging China*, p. 132.

78. Ian Storey, "Singapore and the Rise of China: Perceptions and Policy," in Yee and Storey, *The China Threat*, pp. 216–219.

79. An excellent analysis of Singapore's armed forces and military capability can be found in Tim Huxley, *Defending the Lion City: The Armed Forces of Singapore* (St. Leonards: Allen & Unwin, 2001).

80. Yuen Foong Khong, "Singapore: A Time for Economic and Political Engagement," in Johnston and Ross, *Engaging China*, p. 121.

81. Reinhard Drifte, *Japan's Security Relations with China Since 1989: From Balancing to Bandwagoning?* (London: RoutledgeCurzon, 2003), pp. 43–55.

82. Ibid., pp. 50–51.

83. The renewal of the U.S.-Japan security alliance can be traced to the early 1990s, when the United States suspected that North Korea was developing a nuclear program. In response to the situation, Washington and Tokyo began to review the 1978 "Guidelines for U.S.-Japan Defense Cooperation." This intention was to be stated in a joint declaration during a scheduled visit of then–U.S. president Bill Clinton to Japan in 1995. However, due to the cancellation of the visit the announcement of the declaration had to be postponed until April 1996, a month after the Taiwan Strait crisis. I am indebted to Harumi Yoshino for drawing my attention to these important events.

84. Michael J. Green and Benjamin L. Self, "Japan's Changing China Policy: From Commercial Liberalism to Reluctant Realism," *Survival* 38, no. 2 (Summer 1996): 35–57. See also Michael Jonathan Green, "Managing Chinese Power: The View from Japan," in Johnston and Ross, *Engaging China*, pp. 152–175.

85. Gilbert Rozman, "Japan's Images of China in the 1990s: Are They Ready for China's 'Smile Diplomacy' or Bush's 'Strong Diplomacy'?" *Japanese Journal of Political Science* 2, no. 1 (May 2001): 97–125.

86. See the analysis in Rex Li, "Partners or Rivals? Chinese Perceptions of Japan's Security Strategy in the Asia-Pacific Region," *Journal of Strategic Studies* 22, no. 4 (December 1999): 1–25.

87. Tanaka, "China," pp. 56–57.

88. For a perceptive analysis of Sino-Japanese economic and political-strategic rivalry, see Drifte, *Japan's Security Relations with China*, pp. 147–157.

89. Alexander Lukin, "Russian Perceptions of the China Threat," in Yee and Storey, *The China Threat*, pp. 99–100.

90. S. Bilveer, "East Asia in Russia's Foreign Policy: A New Russo-Chinese Axis?" *Pacific Review* 11, no. 4 (1998): 501.

91. Dmitri Trenin, "Russia and the Emerging Security Environment in Northeast Asia," *Security Dialogue* 29, no. 1 (March 1998): 83.

92. Lukin, "Russian Perceptions," pp. 92–94.

93. Ibid., p. 104.

94. Charles Krauthammer, "Why We Must Contain China," *Time,* July 31, 1995, p. 72.

95. Denny Roy, "Consequences of China's Economic Growth for Asia-Pacific Security," *Security Dialogue* 24, no. 2 (June 1993): 190.

96. Roy, "Hegemon on the Horizon?" pp. 165–168; Roy, "The 'China Threat' Issue," pp. 770–771.

97. Segal, "East Asia and the 'Constrainment' of China," p. 134.

98. Rachman, "Containing China," pp. 129–130.

99. Lieberthal, "New China Strategy," pp. 47, 37–38.

100. Ibid.

101. Audrey Kurth Cronin and Patrick M. Cronin, "The Realistic Engagement of China," *Washington Quarterly* 19, no. 1 (Winter 1996): 145–146.

102. James Shinn, ed., *Weaving the Net: Conditional Engagement with China* (New York: Council on Foreign Relations Press), 1996.

103. Michael J. Mazarr, "The Problems of a Rising Power: Sino-American Relations in the 21st Century," *Korean Journal of Defense Analysis* 7, no. 2 (Winter 1995): 7–39.

104. Fei-Ling Wang, "To Incorporate China: A New Policy for a New Era," *Washington Quarterly* 21, no. 1 (Winter 1998): 77.

105. Shambaugh, "Containment or Engagement of China?" p. 184; Bates Gill, "Limited Engagement," *Foreign Affairs* 78, no. 4 (July–August 1999): 66; Asia Project Policy Report, *Redressing the Balance: American Engagement with Asia* (New York: Council on Foreign Relations, 1996), pp. 18–20.

106. There are of course many other economic and strategic factors that have influenced East Asian states' military modernization. For analyses of these factors, see Desmond Ball, "Arms and Affluence: Military Acquisitions in the Asia-Pacific Region," *International Security* 18, no. 3 (Winter 1993–1994): 78–112; and Richard K. Betts, "Wealth, Power, and Instability: East Asia and the United States After the Cold War," *International Security* 18, no. 3 (Winter 1993–1994): 33–77.

107. "ASEAN, China Sign Landmark Accord," *The Guardian,* November 4, 2002, available at www.guardian.co.uk/worldlatest/story/0,1280,-2143239,00.html.

8.3.3

China's Perception
of External Threats
to Its Security and Stability

Suisheng Zhao

China's perception of external threat has been shaped by many factors. Among the most important are national security objectives, China's position in the international system, and its relations with major powers and Asian neighbors. Since Chinese leaders decided to open up China to the outside world in the late 1970s, economic modernization and political stability has been set as the overarching national goal. At the conclusion of the sixteenth congress of the Chinese Communist Party in October 2002, China's fourth-generation leadership, headed by Hu Jintao, presented a blueprint for its long-term national goal of quadrupling the 2000 gross domestic product by 2020 and transforming China into what is known as a xiaokang *society, wherein the Chinese people would enjoy a much more abundant and comfortable life. To achieve this goal, pragmatic Chinese leaders have tried to create and maintain a stable and favorable international environment and remain alert to any threat, at home and abroad, that could subvert its modernization program.*

Since the end of the Cold War, one potential external threat has been perceived as coming from the structural conflict between China as a rising power and the United States, the only superpower left in the post–Cold War world. While avoiding a confrontational approach, China has tried to promote a multipolar international system in which it could interact with the United States and other major powers on a more or less equal footing. In addition, China has identified many new threats to its national security. As an *Outlook Weekly* article celebrating the sixteenth party congress indicated, "Along with the development of new technology and the acceleration of globalization, the national security issues have become more and more complicated. In addition to traditional military security, many non-traditional security issues, including economic security, financial security, information security, and organized transnational crime, international terrorism, etc. have threatened the international community." Therefore, "Chinese leaders have quickly realized the new challenges to our national security . . . and proposed a new security concept."[1] This new security concept has stressed the development of China's comprehensive national strength, promotion of a multipolar international system, and the maintenance of equal and cooperative relations with major powers and its Asian neighbors. This chapter starts with an examination of China's modernization goal and its perception of threat to this overarching goal, then explores China's perception of international system, and ends with an analysis of China's perception of its relations with Asia Pacific neighbors.

The New Concept of Security
and Threat to Economic Modernization

Concentrating on achieving its overarching goal of economic modernization, Chinese leaders have been particularly concerned with any threat to their country's economic security. This concern has colored China's perception of external threat and national security. As one Western reporter observed, "Economic development in an unstable international setting is unthinkable. Without economic improvement, China would not have the international profile it has now, and thus winning the hosting rights of the 2008 Olympic Games and 2010 Expo would have remained nothing but a dream."[2] Therefore, China has worked hard to identify any threat to its effort to maintain an international environment that is acceptably stable, peaceful, and favorable to the success of its modernization program.

Placing top priority on economic security in its national security strategy is a major departure from its previous perception of national security, which was based on a military security strategy of surviving external attacks. As Wu Baiyi, an analyst at the China Strategic Research Institute, indicated, during the Cold War, China stayed with a zero-sum perception of its security relations with the outside. Restrained by limited political and economic resources, China managed its security by adopting an isolationist policy of "self-reliance." Economic, technological, and environmental elements were hardly recognized in official security documents. Since the end of the Cold War, a new concept of national security has been developed and emphasized: "The integrity of national sovereignty and territory, the intactness of its political institutions, social stability, the capability to resist internal or external revolts, and the safety of its economic prosperity and natural resources."[3] In particular, China has tried to enhance what it has called "comprehensive national strength" *(zhonghe guoli),* composed of international competitiveness, an efficient and flexible diplomacy, and a compatible military capability.

While emphasizing comprehensive national strength, Chinese political leaders have paid special attention to any threat to their country's economic stability and sustained development. Wu Baiyi identified five aspects of the threat:

- The obvious superiority of multinationals and foreign direct investment firms places Chinese counterparts at a disadvantage in capital, technology, and policy treatment. It produces problems such as a shrinking market share by Chinese enterprises and heavy loss of state assets through the process of joint venture.

- A transfer of economic sovereignty is quickening as China embraces international norms and regimes. The shift not only occurs from national to international organizations but, more alarmingly, also moves from the state to localities and firms.

- The increasingly frequent assertions of the "China menace" in recent years have led to rising political concerns. In this context, the maintenance of a security environment conducive to China's reforms and growth will become more difficult.

- With sliding agricultural output, lagging high-tech productivity, and declining state-owned enterprises, China's economic fundaments are now in serious question. This presents immediate as well as long-run challenges to central governance over the macroeconomy.

- The economic fragility can also be seen in interruptive factors like local protectionism, corruption, economic crimes, and the like. In addition to the growing regional disparity, the expanding gap between rich and poor poses a socioeconomic danger to the entire nation. To overcome these threats and achieve economic security, China has tried to maintain a favorable business environment and strong international competitiveness. The accession to the World Trade Organization (WTO) has been an integrate part of this effort.

On the latter point, China's accession to the WTO has greatly enhanced the confidence of the Chinese leadership in its effort to overcome external threats by working with the international community. Since the inception of market-oriented economic reform, China has achieved a phenomenal economic growth, which has depended to a great extent on China's access to international resources and the international marketplace. As a result, a new perception of the world of interdependence has been accepted by many of Chinese political elites. They have recognized that a globalization process is inevitable and indispensable for the country's modernization. Neither violent revolt nor isolated development will be effective in the interdependent world of today. China should and can take advantage of international interdependence to pursue its dream of being an equal to its peers, including Western powers. The nature of its security policy, therefore, should be accommodative, rather than confrontational.

However, Chinese political elites are also very concerned about the threat to China's modernization program as a result of the potential conflict between China and the Western powers, particularly the United States. Because China is the only "communist" country in the post–Cold War world, Chinese leaders have a deeply rooted sense of political insecurity. Working to defend the eternal survival of their political power and principles, Chinese leaders have sought to establish normal state-to-state relationships with various foreign countries. To their dismay, however, the end of the Cold War coincided with the deterioration of China's relations with major Western countries, particularly the United States, and the rising advocacy for the containment of China in the Western media of the 1990s. With a profound concern over the regime's survival after the crackdown on prodemocracy demonstrations in 1989, they worried that the United States had a hidden agenda to prevent China from rising as an equal. As two Chinese scholars accused in an official publication, "A few Western countries do not want China to become powerful too fast and inevitably will plot in many aspects to divide China."[4] The communist regime created a sense of besiegement by citing numerous examples of interference in China's domestic affairs by hostile foreign forces. China's failed bid to host the 2000 Olympic Games was interpreted as an anti-Chinese plot. The debate on China's most-favored-nation trade status in the United States and the international campaign for human rights in China were construed as attempts to "Westernize" China. Frictions with the United States over intellectual property rights were labeled as U.S. attempts at cultural intrusion. A visit by President Lee Teng-hui of Taiwan to the United States was portrayed as a U.S. scheme to tear China apart. And Hong Kong residents' demands for more democracy were described as an international effort to turn Hong Kong into an anti-China base. The regime thus created a sense of crisis among the Chinese people in an attempt to convince them that international "hostile forces" were doing everything they could to prevent China from rising as a competitor. The Chinese people were asked to bear in mind that weakness, disunity, and disorder at home would invite foreign aggression and result in the loss of Chinese identity, as China's century-long humiliation and suffering before 1949 demonstrated.

Immediately after the Tiananmen incident, this perception of threat was seen most in official media and not shared by many Chinese intellectuals. Only a few scholars who supported the official position of suppressing the demonstrations expressed suspicion about Western intentions. This situation began to change after the disintegration of the Soviet Union in August 1991. The postcommunist transformation was not as smooth and positive as expected. Western values and systems did not seem to make that much difference to postcommunist countries. Although Russia adopted a democratic system, Western countries still appeared to weaken Russia's standing in international affairs and refused to provide Russia with sufficient assistance as it struggled internally with reform programs. For those liberal intellectuals who supported the 1989 demonstrations, there was the added realization that if China had gone the way promoted by the West, the nation could well have shared a fate similar to that of Russia. A prominent scholar in Shanghai, Xiao Gongqin, criticized those who called for immediate democratization in China and predicted that "the combination of radical political liberalism and highly mobilized political participation would inevitably bring a tragedy to China."[5] Many Chinese intellectuals took pride in China's incremental economic reform of the 1990s, which had brought about rapid growth and avoided a Russian-style collapse. Vigorous economic development led to China's rising power status, which some Chinese came to believe would inevitably lead to a conflict of interest with Western countries.

This conflict of interest was revealed vividly to many Chinese after Beijing's failure to win its bid to host the 2000 Olympic Games and then in the dispute between China and the United States regarding most-favored-nation trading status and entry into the World Trade Organization. Although the Chinese government was at least partially responsible for the conflicts, many Chinese drew the conclusion that Western countries, especially the United States, were afraid of the emergence of a strong China. This conviction was seemingly supported by a series of speeches by Western leaders and publications by journalists in the debate over whether and how to contain China in the 1990s.

The Confucian-Islamic Challenge

Suspicions were exacerbated by Samuel P. Huntington's 1993 influential article "The Clash of Civilizations," published in *Foreign Affairs,* which was expanded into a widely read book in 1996, *The Clash of Civilizations and Remaking the World Order.* Huntington argued that geopolitical struggles in the post–Cold War world were not ideologically motivated but defined by different civilizations. Huntington was especially worried that, while Western civilization would face challenges from all other civilizations, the Confucian and the Islamic civilizations might join together to form the most serious challenge to Western civilization. A summary of Huntington's book was translated immediately into Chinese and appeared in China's journal *Can kao Xiaoxi* (Reference News), which had more than 1 million readers. More and more Chinese intellectuals were convinced that after the end of the Cold War, countries that used to be united by ideology had come to realize their own national identity, interests, and values. As a result, a confrontation between different nation-states and cultures under the banner of nationalism was going to replace the struggle between communism and capitalism. Wang Xiaodong (using a pen name, Shi Zhong), published an article in the first issue of *Zhanglue yu Guanli* (Strategy and Management) to rebuff Huntington. He argued that there was no desire on the part of the Chinese to Confucianize the rest of the world. The Chinese generally welcomed Western values apart from the instances where their transmission constituted imperialism. Any future conflicts would depend on economic interests. The thesis of a clash of civilizations was little more than a guise for the clash of national interests. If China were to come into conflict with the United States, it would be because of its present economic strength and potential, which made it seem a threat.[6] Guan Shijie, a scholar at Beijing University, argued that the West made use of the human rights campaign and other civilizational and cultural clashes to cover their "closed-minded intentions of suppressing China and the rest of Asia."[7]

After September 11

When President George W. Bush came to office in 2001, he talked of China as a "strategic competitor" and many in his administration saw China as a nascent threat to U.S. interests. Only after the terrorist attacks of September 11, which led the United States to heavily preoccupy itself with the war on terrorism and request China's cooperation in the war against Iraq and nuclear crisis in North Korea, has the U.S.-China relationship dramatically improved. However, some Chinese leaders and strategists have expressed their concern about the changing strategic environment since September 11. They are suspicious of the U.S. military presence and growing U.S. influence in Central Asia. The closer security relationship between the United States and Pakistan, China's traditional ally in South Asia, has also troubled them. These developments have exacerbated their fear of a strategic encirclement of China and a unipolar world dominated by the United States.

After all, the perception of a structural conflict with the United States has not disappeared. As Thomas J. Christensen observed, the improvement in the Sino-U.S. relationship has been "conditioned largely on Washington's problems and distractions elsewhere. That means that Beijing's confidence on that score could prove mercurial if international conditions were to change and Washington's security challenges elsewhere were to seem less severe."[8]

Indeed, even when U.S. secretary of state Colin Powell stated in a September 2003 speech that U.S. relations with China were the best they have been since President Richard Nixon's first visit to China in February 1972,[9] many U.S. politicians blamed China's currency policy for the decline of the manufacturing industry and the broader job market in the United States. High-ranking U.S. officials, including President Bush, Federal Reserve Chairman Alan Greenspan, and Treasury Secretary John Snow, have indicated that China will have to alter its currency policy. Snow made the point personally and repeatedly during a high-profile trip to Asia in September 2003. In this case, while the war on terrorism has brought China and the United States closer, China's concern over its economic security has not been reduced.

China's Position in the Changing International System

China's position in the international system is another very important factor shaping its perception of external threat to its security and stability. Chinese scholars and officials in recent years have often started their analyses of international relations from *liliang duibi* (balance of forces) in the world, a Chinese term similar to the conception of "distribution of power" in Western literature on international relations. The dynamics of international politics are understood as changes in power distribution across the world. As Wang Jisi indicated, "Without a study of *liliang duibi*, policy-makers in Beijing presumably would not be able to adjust foreign policy accordingly."[10]

The implicit emphasis on power relations in the international system has been a new development in the recent decade. For many years in the Mao Zedong era, China's perception of international relations was expressed largely by moralist/communist ideological language. Perceiving international relations through ideological concepts, Chinese leaders believed in the inevitable victory of anti-imperialism, socialist revolution, and national liberation struggles.

Since Mao's death and the inception of Deng's market-oriented economic reform, the importance of ideology has dramatically declined and the power consideration has become crystal clear. A Xinhua (China's official news agency) article states that, in foreign activities, "China does not define its stand according to the ideologies and social systems of other countries, but entirely on the basis of the merits of the matters themselves."[11]

That is, China's stand is defined solely on the basis of enhancing its national interest and international influence. This change is significant. Yan Xuetong, a Berkeley-trained Chinese scholar based in Beijing, published a book titled *Guanyu Zhongguo de Guojia Liyi Fenxi* (Analysis of China's National Interests) in 1996. Yan claims that his book is "designed to clarify the confusing concept of national interest, provide an analysis of China's national interest after the Cold War and propose some strategic suggestions for realizing national interest."[12] This serious scholarly book gained unusual popularity because of Yan's argument that China is facing a competitive international environment, and that it is therefore crucial that China's leaders place emphasis on its economic, political, and security interests. Yan suggests that while China should avoid military conflict with other powers, particularly the United States, it should be assertive in defending China's national interests against any external erosion.

In light of the power consideration, the dynamics of international politics have been perceived, in Beijing, as a change of power distribution across the world that is structured around several great powers or a few poles. Major-General Wang Pufeng, deputy director of the Department of Research on Strategy at the Academy of Military Science of China, explains that "the term *pole* represents the interests of one party which has the capacity to exert influence on international affairs and has certain control over other world forces." According to the major-general, "each country deals with international affairs in accordance with its own interests and exerts its influence."[13]

To act in accordance with its own interests and to exert its influence on international affairs, Beijing has worked hard, since the early 1970s, to find (or shape) an international system that is in its favor or at least not to its disadvantage. A hierarchical structure of three worlds was put forth in Beijing in the 1970s. According to this perception, in cooperation with developing countries (the Third World), a developed Japan and Western Europe (the Second World) could be a force to counter the alleged hegemonism of the two super-powers that constituted the First World.[14] China thus could act as a leader of the Third World. After the United States extended diplomatic recognition to Beijing in 1979, Beijing, while admitting a Washington-Moscow bipolar system, was also very much looking forward to a strategic triangle in which China played a global role by maneuvering between the United States and the Soviet Union. Since the demise of the Cold War strategic triangle temporarily weakened China's immediate strategic leverage in the global balance of power, Beijing's foreign policy makers have tried to resist the emergence of a unipolar world that is perceived not to be in China's favor. To find an alternative, Beijing's foreign policy analysts have suggested that "the world has undergone a transition to multipolarization *(duojihua)* since the end of the Cold War. A relative balance of power has resulted in an effective check on all global powers."[15]

Early in 1990 some Chinese scholars, such as Chen Qimao in Shanghai and Song Yimin in Beijing, began to express the view that, with the end of the Cold War and a bipolar system, the world had entered a new period of transition toward multipolarization.[16] At first, the official view about the change in the international system was very cautious. In an interview in December 1990, Qian Qichen, China's foreign minister at the time, said that the world was in a transition phase. The old order had dissolved but no new one had emerged to take its place.[17] A similar view was expressed in March 1991 by Li Peng, chairman of the National People's Congress (NPC), when he told the NPC that "the old world structure, which lasted for over four decades, disintegrated and a new one has yet to take shape."[18]

After the end of the Gulf War and the breakup of the Soviet Union in 1991, Beijing's view became clear-cut in its assertion that the world was evolving toward a multipolar system. In the 1991 year-end assessment of the international situation, Qian Qichen stated, "Although the world is in the transitional period and a new pattern has not yet taken shape, there is a rough structure in international relations, in which one superpower and several powers depend on and struggle against each other." To make his point clear, Qian indicated that "this is the initial stage of the evolution towards multipolarization."[19] In a press conference on March 23, 1992, Qian said once again, "The breakup of the old world pattern means the end of the post-war bipolar system characterized by the hostility between the two superpowers. A new world . . . is likely to be a multipolar pattern."[20] Multipolarity has since become the official perception of China. In his speech at the Fortune Forum in 2001, Jiang Zemin put forth multipolarization, together with economic globalization and the growth of science and technology, as fundamental world trends.[21]

While pursuing multipolarity, Chinese scholars have been debating about a different configuration of such a world. Xi Shuguang, a policy consultant in the Security Market Research Center of China, presented a new structure of one system (the Western capitalist system) and five "geopolitical plates" (European, African, Middle Eastern and Central Asian, Asia Pacific, and North-South American).[22] Two other types of multipolarization are also perceived. One is a three-polar world, in which the European Community constitutes the European pole, the United States, Canada, and Mexico may form the North American pole, and Japan is working toward an Asia Pacific economic rim, leading to the formation of the Asia Pacific pole. Another is a five-polar structure, which consists of the United States, Germany, Russia, China, and Japan.

The most frequently mentioned configuration in Chinese strategic studies literature has been that of "one superpower and four big powers." Chinese strategists admit that the United States has remained the sole superpower because of its comprehensive national strength, whether in terms of its economy, scientific and technological strength, military might, or foreign influence. The United States, as the sole superpower, has had strong security interests and competed energetically for its dominant position in the world. In this case, China must live with and even accommodate the superpower status of the United States while trying to retain its independent power aspirations and building a united front with other nations to protect its national interests. This view also holds that the United States has failed to enact an effective strategy of controlling the globe unilaterally. The U.S. government not only is subject to strong domestic resistance to foreign military intervention due to the American public's concern with domestic problems but also faces the reality that the traditional control of its allies has become more difficult as some European powers have adopted more independent policies. One major feature of global politics after the Cold War is that a growing number of big powers have become bold enough to say no to the sole superpower. In the words of Qian Qichen, "The development of the world multipolarization tendency has brought to an end of the era in which one or two superpowers tended to dominate the world."[23]

Beijing's perception of multipolarity apparently stands against the speculation of neoconservatives in the Bush administration that a unipolar world characterized by U.S. predominance has emerged from the ashes of the Cold War. Beijing's leaders reacted with great alarm to Bush's "preemptive war" doctrine, its justification for the U.S. attack on Iraq in 2003. They are concerned that this could be a ruse for extending U.S. hegemony throughout the globe. As Alastair Iain Johnston observed, "Statement that multipolarity is an objective trend and a normative good explicitly challenges any continued US hegemony or primacy."[24] Promotion of multipolarity thus became a way to reduce the threat of a unipolar world dominated by the United States.

Talking about multipolarity, however, does not mean that China has launched a major challenge to U.S. power. It is a wish that U.S. power is on the wane. Beijing's analysts have calculated that a unipolar world is not sustainable. According to this view, after the United States became the sole superpower in the world, some Americans believed that "it has obtained a thorough triumph but fails to recognize the wounds it suffered during the Cold war. Being dizzy with success, it is prone to arrogance. As a result, 'an arrogant army will necessarily lose,' and 'sole self-importance' (in international affairs) is the attitude of hegemony, which leads to isolation."[25]

Before the United States launched the war against Iraq in 2003, a Chinese scholar at Beijing University, Zhu Feng, asked how the United States could "deal with the anti-Americanism the second Iraq War would arouse." He predicted that "if the United States marches toward Baghdad, it will provoke anti-American sentiment, and perhaps even incite international terrorist organizations to take action."[26] Unfortunately, his prediction has become the reality at the aftermath of the war. In addition, the U.S. search for global dominance will come at a very high economic cost, which it may not be able to afford itself. Major-General Wang Pufeng took the example of the 1991 Gulf War and suggested that, "although the United States appears to have won the Gulf War, in fact, it demonstrates a weakening capability of controlling the world. In the past, the US financially supported foreign troops in fighting wars. This time, however, it sent its troops to the Gulf, backed financially by other countries. This reflects its weak economy."[27] As a Chinese analyst summarized, "The US dreams of a unipolar hegemony, but it cannot afford it economically."[28]

Beijing's perception of a multipolar system is more a matter of normative truth than an empirical or analytical assessment, which should surprise no one familiar with the history of Chinese analysis of the world situation. To an extent, it may be argued that because a multipolar system may provide more opportunities than a unipolar system for Beijing, and because a multipolar system has become its goal, Beijing has "perceived" it. Indeed, a multipolarizing world may bring about a change of order from superpower contention toward more egalitarian international relations. It may be a world of multiple opportunities for China to assert itself forcefully on multiple chessboards, increasing trade, peddling arms, attracting foreign aid and investment, and exporting construction workers, all designed to enhance China's domestic modernization and to improve its international relations.

Perceptions of Challenges in Relations with Neighboring Countries

While China's national objective of modernization and its position in the international system have been the most important factors shaping its perception of external threat, many others are also significant, particularly its relations with neighboring Asian countries. In spite of China's traditional cultural complacency and the legacy of sinocentrism, which took China as the center of Asia, political leaders in China have always been concerned about their neighboring countries becoming security threats. China has supported Washington's antiterrorist campaign in Asia because it has worried about the possible links between Islamic fundamentalist movements and Muslim separatists in Xinjiang and external terrorist threats that may well lead to domestic instability. Chinese leaders have paid special attention to at least three challenges in relations with periphery countries: border disputes, power rivalries, and the "China threat" in the eyes of weaker neighbors.

Border disputes have always been a threat to China's security and stability. One scholar has divided China's border disputes into three categories: disputes over land boundaries, disputes over so-called lost territories (Hong Kong, Macao, and Taiwan), and disputes over maritime boundaries involving both bilateral and multilateral relations.[29] The border issue is related to sovereignty, which is Beijing's most important concern in its foreign relations. Beijing has been firm in negotiations over all three categories of territorial disputes, particularly on the second category because it believes that people in these territories are ethnically and historically Chinese. Taking back these territories involves not only the vital security interests of China but also the legitimacy of the regime. Beijing recovered Hong Kong in 1997 and Macao in

1999. Taiwan is now the focus of dispute in this category. Since the early 1980s, Beijing has tried to use the same method to recover Taiwan as it did with Hong Kong and Macao—economic inducement and proposing a "one country, two systems" formula. But this peaceful offensive has not resulted in the achievement of its objectives. While Taiwan has become the second-largest supplier (after Japan) to the mainland and China the third-largest market of Taiwanese goods, the political relationship between the two governments remains officially nonexistent and hostile. In frustration and to show its determination, Beijing launched a series of military exercises in the Taiwan Strait in 1995–1996.[30] However, military coercion has not stopped Taiwan's political centrifugal tendency either. President Lee Teng-hui proposed a "special state-to-state relationship" in July 1999 in spite of Beijing's military threat. Chen Shui-ban of the Democratic Progressive Party was even elected as Taiwan's tenth president in the fiercely contested 2000 election. Although Beijing has made it clear that it is willing to fight a war if necessary to recover Taiwan, it still has to concern itself with the reactions of the United States and Asia Pacific countries as well as the resultant rupture of China's economic development.

Progress in the third category of disputes is extremely limited. In the cases of the Tonkin Gulf and the Senkaku/Diaoyutai Islands, no agreement or compromise has been reached with Vietnam and Japan. In the South China Sea, while Beijing has showed certain degree of flexibility by suggesting "shelving the disputes and working for joint development" *(gezhi zhengyi, gongtong kaifa)*, China's maritime neighbors have been very assertive in contesting Beijing's sovereignty claims. As one study indicated, "Although China has offered joined development to other claimants, its concept of joint development seems to involve joint development of the producing oil and gas fields on other claimants' continental shelves—and then only after China's sovereignty has been recognized." In addition, as the same study pointed out, Beijing has continued to "insist on bilateral solutions and its interest and sincerity in participating in a multilateral cooperative solution remains in doubt."[31] China's position has been criticized and even ridiculed by other claimants in the South China Sea. No resolution was found over the two large island groups—the Paracels (or Xisha and Zhongshao), which China has occupied since 1974 and over which it had a military clash with Vietnam in 1988. Vietnam still occupies most of the Spratlys to which China claims sovereignty. The Philippines has stepped up its claims over the Spratlys in recent years. Beijing has not given up its claims of sovereignty over these islands because they are extremely important for China's security and energy supply. Sovereignty over these islands keeps all of China's options open regarding resources, should any be discovered. However, Beijing's sovereignty claim may eventually bring China to the fore with all countries in Southeast Asia.

The second major challenge to China's peripheral security is how to work with other regional powers, namely Japan and India, to secure peace and stability in the Asia Pacific region. For obvious historical and geopolitical reasons,

China's relationship with Japan has always been difficult. Although a Sino-Japan peace treaty was signed in 1978, this formerly friendly relationship has been largely superficial. While China has regarded Japan as a successful model of economic modernization and tried to lure Japanese trade and investments, Japan has been unwilling to build up a potential rival unnecessarily. Disappointed Beijing leaders have thus blamed Japan for its arrogant and unfair trading practice. In particular, they have been extremely alert against any signs of Japan's remilitarization. Beijing has done everything to discourage Japan from aspiring to leadership of the region or taking on a greater global or regional political role. At a seminar on Northeast Asian security held in Shanghai, Chinese strategists asserted that "Northeast Asia is the only region where China has a strategic advantage. One of China's strategic goals should be to delay Japan's advancement toward becoming a major military power."[32] However, China's strategy has not been very effective. When President Jiang visited Japan expecting to dominate the scene, the Japanese refused a formal written apology over the war atrocities even though South Korea received this apology earlier. The Japanese also refused to exclude the Taiwan Strait from its security agreement with the United States. Finally, Japan refused to utter the "three no's" (no support to Taiwan independence, no support to one China, one Taiwan, and no support to Taiwan's bid to join the United Nations) on the Taiwan issue, although earlier President Bill Clinton had made the pledge during his visit to Beijing. No matter what China's stance, Japan has taken a more and more critical position on China's military modernization efforts. As June Teufel Dryer indicated, "China's economic growth was accompanied by increase in the defense budget that averaged 12–13% each year. Given the absence of any external invasion threat and the presence of many domestic problems, this worried the PRC neighbors. Japan began to complain about the lack of transparency in Beijing's defense decision-making."[33] In response, Japan has made China the major target of its national defense strategy. It is hard, in this case, to be optimistic about the future relationship between these two important countries in the Asia Pacific region.

India is another budding rival of China in Asia. Although these two countries befriended each other by working together in the promotion of the national independent movement in the Third World during the 1950s, they became enemies and engaged in a military clash in 1962. Sino-Indian relations began to improve in the late 1980s. China and India signed two agreements, on maintaining peace and tranquillity and on undertaking confidence-building measures in the border area, in 1993 and 1996 respectively. President Jiang Zemin visited India in November 1996. However, Sino-Indian geopolitical rivalry has never ceased regarding three issues. The first is the Pakistan issue. While China has sought to improve relations with India, it has maintained a long-term strategic partnership with Pakistan, which India has waged three wars against in the five decades since its independence. New Delhi believes that China has used the Sino-Pakistan alliance to check the growing influence

China's incorporation of Tibet and India's allowance to the Dalai Lama and his exile government to reside in Dharamsala and to campaign for Tibetan independence, is a big issue between the two countries.

of India in Asia. Tibet is the second issue. Although India has publicly affirmed Beijing's position that Tibet is part of China, it did not welcome China's incorporation of Tibet, which otherwise may serve as a buffer between these two countries. China has been irritated that India has allowed the Dalai Lama and his exile government to reside in Dharamsala and to campaign for Tibetan independence. The third issue is the two segments of the 2,500-mile Sino-India border that are still disputed: the southeastern Himalayas, now administered by India, and the Aksai Chin Plateau, through which a major Chinese highway linking Tibet and Xinjiang runs. Solutions to these troubled issues have to be found in order for China to establish a truly good neighboring relationship with India.

How to deal with the concerns of its weaker neighbors is the third challenge in China's search for peace and security. With rapid economic growth, China has been regarded as the coming superpower of the twenty-first century, a realization that has given rise to speculation about a "China threat." China's weaker neighbors worry that, after China modernizes, Beijing will pursue an expansionist policy in East Asia, seeking to make the region its exclusive sphere of influence, a modern equivalent of the traditional tributary system. Beijing has denied this speculation and offered repeated assurances that "China will never seek hegemony." However, these assurances have not eased the fear of China's weaker neighbors. Although military expansion cannot be considered a serious Chinese objective at least in the foreseeable future— because China lacks the military power and faces immense internal and external challenges to take an expansionist policy in Asia—there has been a perception gap between China and its weaker neighbors. "China, viewing itself in global terms, does not always realize how strong it is when placed in a regional context. The rest of Asia, viewing China in a regional perspective, does not always realize how weak it is on a global scale."[34]

In this case, although China remains relatively weak in many of the measurable indicators of power, China's weaker neighbors see it in terms of its considerable potential and its long historical record of cultural and political domination of the region. China is slow to understand and properly respond to the suspicion and fear of its weaker neighbors. Discussing China's relations with Southeast Asian countries, for example, a Chinese scholar maintained that, "as soon as the mutual trust is established, good neighboring relations and partnerships would be able to complete." He asserted that "the foundation for the mutual trust has been laid. The only problems are to overcome some barriers to the mutual trusts."[35]

However, the nature of the relationship is much more ambivalent. As one Western scholar indicated, "While most of ASEAN's policies towards China are guided by the economic perspectives of a huge Chinese market, explaining ASEAN's constructive engagement strategy towards China, Beijing's ambiguous foreign and security policies are simultaneously a major concern in the region." According to this scholar, "The rapid modernization programs of China's armed forces (including its nuclear arsenal), Beijing's territorial claims in the entire South China Sea and its gunboat policies towards Taiwan have raised widespread concern over irredentist tendencies in China's foreign security agenda."[36] The fear of the perceived China threat is partially responsible for stimulating a rush to arms in many Asia Pacific countries after the end of the Cold War.[37] Many of China's weaker neighbors have determined to enhance their defense self-reliance capacities and military preparedness to better deal with regional contingencies.

Conclusion

China's perception of external threat reflects its effort to defend its national security and modernization program and an attempt to redefine its position in post–Cold War international strategic relations. It also reveals the importance attached to relations with major powers on the part of the Chinese leadership, who look upon China as a rising power pursuing legitimate interests on the world stage. Since the end of the Cold War, the new generation of Chinese leaders have confronted an increasingly complicated world as the more or less predictable and manageable bipolar competition and ideological confrontations are replaced by unpredictable and hardly manageable ethnic, religious, and nationalistic conflicts among states as well as nonstate and transnational actors.

Chinese leaders have perceived the threat and opportunities from a pragmatic perspective. While keeping their overarching goal of modernization in mind, in spite of the concern over the rising debate about a China threat and the containment of China in the West after the end of the Cold War, China's leaders have placed a great priority on sustaining an international environment amicable to its economic development. While working hard to encourage multipolarity, Beijing in fact finds a unipolar reality in the post–Cold War era and has accommodated to it through pragmatic foreign policy adjustment.

As Robert Sutter's research indicates, the Chinese leadership since mid-2001 has carried out what appears to be its "most important adjustment in Chinese foreign policy toward the United States and US interests in world affairs since the end of the Cold War, strongly emphasizing the positive while eschewing pressure, confrontation and conflict. Beijing now only rarely refers to previous staples in its post cold war repertoire regarding US 'hegemonism,' 'power politics,' and alleged US schemes to 'contain' and 'hold back' China. China also rarely refers to its previous commitment to join with other world power centers to wear down the US superpower and create a 'multipolar' world. Strident PRC opposition in recent years to NATO expansion, US missile defense programs, and enhanced US-Japan security cooperation appears to be a thing of the past, and authoritative threats to use force if Taiwan delays reunification have fallen still."[38]

In relations with Asia Pacific neighbors, Chinese leaders have tried very hard to found common ground in order to protect the national interests of their country. In one study, Yan Xuetong divided China's neighbor countries into three categories according to their degrees of agreement with China's terms of strategic balance. The first category of countries shared China's interest in developing a regional multipolarization in which China would be an important strategic power and play a balancing role. These countries included Pakistan, North Korea, Burma, Nepal, Cambodia, Malaysia, Singapore, Russia, and Central Asian states, as they hoped to see China becoming powerful enough to reduce the pressure of the United States intervening in their internal affairs. The second category of countries included Australia, Canada, Indonesia, Thailand, the Philippines, Vietnam, New Zealand, and India, which hoped to maintain the current strategic balance, in which the United States had the strategically advantaged position. These countries didn't want to see China become a balancing power to the United States. But they did not have major conflicts of interest with China. The third category of countries, mainly the United States and Japan, concerned over the rise of China, wanted to establish a multilateral mechanism in China's periphery to prevent China from becoming a security threat to their interests. Yan believed that because China shared common strategic interests with most of the periphery countries, it had enjoyed and could continue to enjoy a favorable security environment in the periphery for the near future.[39]

Suisheng Zhao is associate professor at the Graduate School of International Studies, University of Denver, and executive director of its Center for China-U.S. Cooperation. He is on the board of directors of the U.S. Committee of the Council for Security Cooperation in the Asia Pacific, founder and editor of the Journal of Contemporary China, *and a research associate at the Fairbank Center for East Asian Research, Harvard*

University. His most recent books include Across the Taiwan Strait: Mainland China, Taiwan, and the Crisis of 1995–96 *(1999),* China and Democracy: Reconsidering the Prospects for a Democratic China *(2000), and* Chinese Foreign Policy: Pragmatism and Strategic Behavior *(2003). His most recent book,* Chinese Nationalism and the Construction of a Nation-State, *is forthcoming from Stanford University Press (2004).*

Notes

1. "Shiliuda Tebiebaodao: Yiqizhouguo Shishannian" [The Sixteenth Party Congress Special Report: Walk Through Thirteen Years Together], *Liaowang Zhoukan* [Outlook Weekly], November 4, 2002, p. 31.

2. Jaewoo Choo, "China: National Interest = Foreign Policy," *Asia Times* (online), August 20, 2003, www.atimes.com/atimes/China/eh20ad02.html.

3. Wu Baiyi, "The Chinese Security Concept and its Historical Evolution," *Journal of Contemporary China* 10, no. 27 (May 2001): 279.

4. Yan Xuetong and Li Zhongcheng, "Xia Shiji Chu de Guoji Zhengzhi" [Forecasting International Politics at the Beginning of the Next Century], *Xiandai Guoji Guanxi* [Contemporary International Relations] no. 6 (June 1995): 8.

5. Xiao Gongqin, "Zouxiang Chengshu: Zhongguo Gaige de Fansi yu Zhanwang [Toward Maturity: Reflections and Prospects of China's Reform], in *Xiao Gongqin Ji* [Collected Works of Xiao Gongqin] (Harbin: Heilongjiang Jiaoyu Chuban She, 1995), p. 132.

6. Shi Zhong (Wang Xiaodong), "Weilai de Chongtu" [Future Conflicts], *Zhanlue yu Guanli* [Strategy and Management] no. 1 (1993): 46–50.

7. Guan Shijie, "Cultural Collisions Foster Understanding," *China Daily,* September 2, 1996, p. 4.

8. Thomas J. Christensen, "PRC Security Relations with the United States: Why Things Are Going So Well," *China Leadership Monitor* no. 8 (August 2003): 7.

9. Associated Press, "Powell: U.S., China Ties at Thirty-Year High," September 6, 2003.

10. Wang Jisi, "International Relations Theory and Study of Chinese Foreign Policy: A Chinese Perspective," in Thomas W. Robinson and David Shambaugh, eds., *Chinese Foreign Policy: Theory and Practice* (Oxford: Clarendon Press, 1995), p. 489.

11. *Beijing Review* 35, no. 19 (May 11–17, 1992): 16.

12. Yan Xuetong, *Guanyu Zhongguo de Guojia Liyi Fenxi* [Analysis of China's National Interests] (Tianjin: Tianjin Renmin Chuban She, 1996), p. 1.

13. *Beijing Review* 34, no. 47 (November 25–December 1, 1991): 11.

14. "Chairman Mao's Theory of the Differentiation of the Three Worlds Is a Major Contribution to Marxism-Leninism," *Beijing Review* 20, no. 45 (November 4, 1977): 29–33.

15. Feng Lidong, "An Interview with Yang Chengxu, Director of International Studies Institute," *Banyuetan* [Bimonthly Talk], January 10, 1995, p. 67.

16. See, for example, Chen Qimao, "A Study of the Development of the World System from Bipolarity to Multipolarity," *Guojiwenti Yanjiu* [Studies of International Issues] no. 4 (1990): 1–6; Song Yimin, "The New Problems Associated with the Changing World Situation," *Liaowang Zhoukan* no. 36 (1990): 39–42; Wang Guang, "What New World Order Does the West Want?" *Liaowang Zhoukan* no. 37 (1990): 38–43; and Huang Dingwi and Wang Yulin, "The Rapidly Changing World Situation," *Xiandai Guoji Guanxi* no. 3 (1990): 1–8.

17. *Remin Ribao, Haiwaiban* [People's Daily, overseas edition], December 17, 1990.

18. *Beijing Review* 34, no. 15 (April 15–21, 1991), doc. 20.

19. "Adhering to Independent Foreign Policy," *Beijing Review* 34, no. 52 (December 30, 1991–January 5, 1992): 7, 10.

20. *Beijing Review* 35, no. 14 (April 6–12, 1992): 15.

21. Jiang Zemin, speech at the Fortune Forum, *China Daily,* September 5, 2001.

22. Xi Shuguang, *Shijie Xinjiegou* [The New Structure of the World] (Chendu: Sichuan Remin Chuban She, 1992). Quoted from Min Chen's book review in *Journal of Contemporary China* 2, no. 1 (Winter–Spring 1993): 97.

23. "Qian Qichen on International Situation and China's Diplomacy," *Xinhua,* June 16, 1995.

24. Alastair Iain Johnston, "Is China a Status Quo Power?" *International Security* 27, no. 4 (Spring 2003): 29.

25. Liu Ji, "Making the Right Choices in Twenty-First Century Sino-American Relations," *Journal of Contemporary China* 7, no. 18 (March 1998): 90.

26. Zhu Feng, "The Second Gulf War: Is There Any Suspense?" *Beijing Review* 46, no. 6 (February 6, 2003): 13.

27. *Beijing Review* 34, no. 47 (November 25–December 1, 1991): 11.

28. *Beijing Review* 35, nos. 5–6 (February 3–16, 1992): 15.

29. Harold C. Hinton characterized them into four categories and I regroup them into three. Harold C. Hinton, "China as an Asian Power," in Robinson and Shambaugh, *Chinese Foreign Policy,* pp. 352–357.

30. For a study of this crisis, see Suisheng Zhao, ed., *Across the Taiwan Strait: Mainland China, Taiwan, and the 1995–1996 Crisis* (New York: Routledge, 1999).

31. Mark J. Valencia, Hon M. Van Dyke, and Noel A. Ludwig, *Sharing the Resources of the South China Sea* (Honolulu: University of Hawaii Press, 1997), pp. 77, 99.

32. Ren Xiao, "Tongbeiyia Anquan Xingshi de Xianzhuang yu Weilai" [The Current and Future Security Situation in Northeast Asia], *Guoji Zhanwang* [International Outlook] no. 7 (1996): 11.

33. June Teufel Dryer, "Sino-Japanese Relations," *Journal of Contemporary China* 10, no. 28 (August 2001): 375.

34. Steven I. Levine, "China in Asia: The PRC as a Regional Power," in Harry Harding, ed., *China's Foreign Relations in the 1980s* (New Haven: Yale University Press, 1982), p. 107.

35. Zhang Xizheng, "Zhongguo Tong Dongmeng de Muling Huxin Huoban Guanxi" [The Good Neighboring, Mutual Trust, and Partnership Between China and ASEAN], in Zheng Yushou, ed., *Huolengzhan Shiqi de Zhongguo Waijiao* [Chinese Diplomacy in the Post–Cold War Era] (Hong Kong: Tiandi Tushu, 1999), p. 224.

36. Frank Umback, "ASEAN and Major Powers: Japan and China—A Changing Balance of Power?" in Jorn Dosch and Manfred Mols, eds., *International Relations in the Asia-Pacific: New Patterns of Power, Interest, and Cooperation* (New York: St. Martin's Press, 2000), p. 174.

37. For one illumination of the arms race in the post–Cold War Asia Pacific, see Desmond Ball, "Arms and Affluence: Military Acquisitions in the Asia-Pacific Region," *International Security* 18, no. 3 (Winter 1993–1994): 78–112.

38. Robert Sutter, "Bush Administration Policy Toward Beijing and Taipei," *Journal of Contemporary China* 12, no. 36 (August 2003): 478–479.

39. Yan Xuetong, *Zhongguo de Jueqi: Guoji Huanjing Pinggu* [The Rise of China: An Evaluation of the International Environment] (Tianjin: Tianjin Renmin Chuban She, 1998), pp. 234–236.

8.3.4

Taiwan:
Building Cooperation Across the Taiwan Strait

Chyungly Lee

Two concurrent developments in recent cross-strait relations—the growing political hostility and military confrontation at the state-governmental level, and the rapidly increasing social and economic interdependence among the people on either side of the divide—complicate the process of conflict prevention to increase security across the Taiwan Strait. "One China" controversies, involving both external diplomatic stakes and internal political capital, require immediate but delicate handling. In the meantime, if functional frictions and civil tensions emerging out of the dynamics of the de facto integration taking place across the strait are not to serve as catalysts for greater political hostility, multi-track diplomatic initiatives will be necessary. The proliferation of technical and functional collaborations and their impact on wider policy considerations have come to be viewed as more relevant, in assessing what the costs of war might be, than the potential costs or benefits of military measures, and thus both China and Taiwan refrain from taking irrational measures against each other.

In 1949, the Nationalist Party of the Republic of China (ROC), the Kuomintang (KMT), withdrew from mainland China and settled in the island of Taiwan in the wake of a civil war. The People's Republic of China (PRC), a communist regime, was then established on the mainland.[1] The reunification of China was the primary goal of both regimes in the 1950s. The PRC prepared to invade Taiwan, while Chiang Kai-shek, leader of KMT, also considered the use of force to recover the lost territory. The outbreak of the Korean War brought a U.S. military presence to the region to defend South Korea, including a military presence in the Taiwan Strait to counter the PRC's support of North Korea. The United States declared that its Seventh Fleet would "neutralize" the Taiwan Strait, thereby protecting the KMT government from invasion. Beijing asserted its power by undertaking two significant military actions in 1954–1955, and again in 1958, on Kinmen and Matsu, the two small ROC-held offshore islands close to the PRC coast. During this period of military

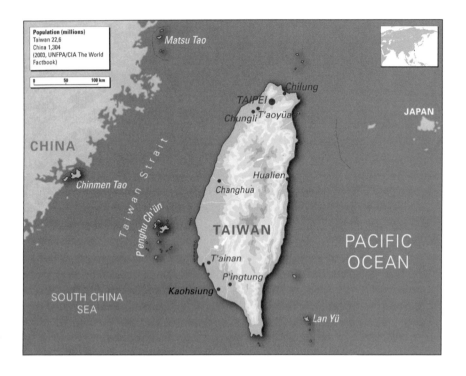

Population (millions)
Taiwan 22.6
China 1,304
(2003, UNFPA/CIA The World Factbook)

confrontation, Taiwan relied on its military alliance with the United States to counter military threats from Beijing.

With diplomatic support from the United States, the ROC retained the "China seat" at the United Nations until 1971. In the Shanghai Communiqué of 1972, signed between the United States and the PRC, the United States acknowledged that "all Chinese on either side of the Taiwan Strait maintain there is but one China and that Taiwan is a part of China." In 1979 the United States normalized its diplomatic relations with the PRC and passed the Taiwan Relations Act to retain an unofficial tie with the ROC.[2] Such developments in U.S.-China-Taiwan triangular relations drastically shrank the international diplomatic space available to the ROC. The ROC was forced to withdraw its memberships from international organizations for which statehood was required. The number of formal allies was reduced to about thirty. Nevertheless, the so-called one-China principle commonly held by both governments in Beijing and Taipei restrained both sides from using force despite the ongoing diplomatic tensions. The KMT regime in Taipei declared that the ROC was the legitimate regime of China, consisting of two separate but equal political entities: Taiwan and China. Beijing introduced the concept of "one country, two systems" in early 1980s. The concept asserted the "one country" as a Beijing-ruled China, with Taiwan being folded under Beijing's wing as a special administrative region with independent political and economic systems.

After Lee Teng-hui took office as president of Taiwan, a pragmatic approach was adopted to proactively expand Taiwan's international diplomatic space. The ROC regime formally acknowledged the Beijing government by redefining ROC-governed territory as extending only to Taiwan and its outlying islands, and no longer claimed jurisdiction over mainland China. Nevertheless, the territorial definition in the constitution of the ROC remains unchanged. Between 1989 and 1995, besides making visits to Taiwan's formal allies, president Lee took several landmark overseas trips to enhance Taiwan's bilateral relations with other friendly countries, including a 1989 visit to Singapore, 1994 visits to Latin America and Africa, and a 1995 visit to the Middle East. In his speech at Cornell University in the United States in June 1995, President Lee repeatedly claimed the existence of "the ROC on Taiwan." This assertion was interpreted by Beijing as a nascent step toward a reversal of Taiwan's reunification policy. Beijing responded with propaganda assaults, suspended all ongoing cross-strait communications, and conducted intensive military exercises along the mainland's southeast coast near Taiwan. Two aircraft carriers, the *Nimitz* and the *Independence,* and their accompanying fleets, were sent by the United States to the waters adjoining the Taiwan Strait to monitor China's intentions. The crisis of military confrontation continued to escalate throughout Taiwan's first direct presidential election campaign in March 1996.[3]

After the PRC's fifteenth national congress in 1997, the PRC urged its allies to reinforce their one-China policy and aggressively pursued its one-China principle in international institutions.[4] By blocking Taiwan's international links, China hoped to persuade Taiwan to resume cross-strait talks under the one-China principle. However, these measures only pushed Taiwan further away and in July 1999, Taiwan's leader, President Lee, overtly rejected the notion of "one China" and redefined cross-strait relations as "state to state," or at the very least, "a special state-to-state relationship." From China's perspective, Taiwan in fact embarked on an intolerable policy of permanent separation. In response, waves of missile were launched in a show of force directed at Taiwan. China modified its Taiwan policy from "peaceful reunification" to "the use of force to prevent independence," or even "the use of force to prevent the facilitation of independence."

Paradoxically, despite the continuing escalation of political hostility, diplomatic tensions, and military confrontation between the two governments across the Taiwan Strait, the extensive economic and social exchanges among people across the strait have hardly been affected. According to an estimate of the ROC's Mainland Affairs Council, the share of cross-strait trade as a percentage of Taiwan's total trade increased from 0.64 percent in 1983 to 15.39 percent in 2002, while the share of China's total foreign trade conducted with Taiwan increased from 0.64 percent to 6.03 percent over the same period. The cumulative amount of Taiwan's investment in the mainland from 1952 to April 2003 accounted for 46.33 percent of Taiwan's total approved outward investment. In contrast, the combination of Taiwan's indirect investment via Hong Kong and direct investment in the mainland from 1979 to April 2003 accounted for more than 50 percent of China's foreign capital inflow. After Taiwan lifted the ban on visiting the mainland in November 1987, the total number of Taiwanese tourist visits to mainland China reached 28.3 million by

Kinmen Island, Taiwan. A soldier from the ROC army keeping lookout,
with the Chinese mainland in the distance.

April 2003, while the number of mainland visits to Taiwan during the same
period was almost 5 million. The number of cross-strait marriages has also
grown rapidly since 1992. By 2003, there were more than 200,000 Chinese
spouses in Taiwan.

Conflict Dynamics

The year 2000 is a turning point in Taiwan's transition to democracy. Right
before the second presidential election in March, China delineated three conditions for the use of force against Taiwan in a white paper on the one-China
principle and the Taiwan issue (February 2000)—among them, if Taiwan were
to indefinitely refuse to enter into negotiations on reunification. This pro-
nouncement, however, did not dissuade voters from supporting the proindependence candidate. Instead, the candidate of the Democratic Progressive
Party (DPP), Chen Shui-bian, won the election.

Chen chose, however, to avoid provocative rhetoric and pledged that Taiwan would only declare independence if the PRC were to use force.[5] With a
reservoir of great mistrust, the PRC adopted a "wait and see" posture toward
Chen. In the wake of DPP's victory, both sides were cautious not to increase
cross-strait tensions. But a political impasse on the one-China issue, with no
sign of compromise between the DPP regime and the communist regime,
remains the major obstacle to a peaceful resolution of cross-strait tensions.

The specifics of the one-China principle have been modified several times
by Beijing as it has attempted to persuade Taiwan to accept the principle as a

precondition for the resumption of cross-strait talks.[6] The syllogism released by Qian Qi-Chen in July 2000 no longer stresses that the Beijing-ruled regime is the central government of China. Instead, it states that Taiwan and mainland China are both parts of China and thus implies equal footing at the negotiating table. This new notion of "one China" was later formally accepted at the sixteenth national congress of the Communist Party in November 2002. On the other side of the Taiwan Strait, the DPP regime in Taiwan accepted that "one China" could be on the agenda for discussion, but insisted that no prior conditions for talks should be set. After he took over the chair of the DPP, President Chen described Taiwan and China as "one country on each side" of the Taiwan Strait and highlighted the "equal sovereignty" doctrine. This statement immediately struck a raw nerve in Beijing and strengthened its resolve to continue its freeze on any formal contacts with the DPP government.

Moreover, China has deployed an increasing number of short-range missiles designed to intimidate—or if necessary, attack—Taiwan. In response, Taiwan is exploring an increase in its military budget and increased arms purchases from the United States. After George W. Bush assumed the presidency in 2001, he showed stronger support for Taiwan than had his predecessor. He suggested that unification could be delayed, but not denied, that the timing of it will be decided by the people of Taiwan and not the leaders in Beijing, and that until that happens, Taiwan will remain a part of China and, though without the status of statehood, will continue as a self-governing entity. The United States rejects forced unification or unilaterally declared independence of Taiwan, and will do whatever it takes to block such moves. Recent enhanced bilateral military ties between the United States and Taiwan through upgrades of arms sales and dialogue between high-ranking defense officials have caused great concern in China. However, the events of September 11, 2001, have resulted in a U.S. swing back to China in order to gain China's support for the war on terror.

The dynamics of social and economic interdependence across the Taiwan Strait have brought about a new dimension of conflict potential—cross-border threats to human security. Although both sides implicitly agree on a "middle line" in the Taiwan Strait as the jurisdictional boundary, the cross-boundary movements and activities between people on both sides have often been beyond control. According to Bureau of Entry and Exit, Ministry of Interior, ROC, the total number of illegal entrants from mainland China captured between 1987 and March 2003 was 44,471. Criminal elements engaged in human trafficking, drug and gun smuggling, and armed robbery at sea often take advantage of the lack of collaboration between the two sides. The high level of crime at sea not only endangers travelers passing through the strait but also results in serious negative social and economic impacts on both sides, and causes concerns about the deteriorating human security environment. In addition to crime at sea, the high frequency of other types of incidents in the Taiwan Strait has raised the alarm that any inappropriate handling of such incidents could potentially increase mistrust and could possibly trigger armed conflict across the strait.[7]

Official Conflict Management

At the global level, after the PRC took the China seat at the United Nations in 1971, the ROC was forced to withdraw its membership from international organizations for which statehood was required. Taiwan's restricted participation in global intergovernmental organizations and institutions has limited the ability of international institutions to initiate cross-strait conflict prevention measures. From China's perspective, cross-strait issues are internal affairs, and thus any external interference, even public debates or discussions, cannot be justified. China's veto power in the UN Security Council and its leverage in other intergovernmental institutions not only impede Taiwan's representation in world organizations, but also ensure that issues relating to Taiwan Strait security will be excluded from the formal agendas of international meetings.

At the regional level, the Association of Southeast Asian Nations (ASEAN) Regional Forum (ARF), the only multilateral security forum in Asia Pacific, has adopted an evolutionary approach to regional security.[8] Since none of the ARF member states, constrained by China's strong opposition, has formal diplomatic ties with Taiwan, whatever preventive diplomacy concepts and measures the forum has adopted, or may adopt in the future, are taken without consideration of the Taiwan Strait tensions.

At the bilateral level, the concept of confidence-building measures has been in use in conflict areas for decades to reduce military tensions and political uncertainties among state adversaries, but the perceptions of state-centered and military-based requirements for these measures have hampered both Beijing and Taipei from taking such initiatives in the past. With the increasing human security concerns associated with the growing social and economic interdependence, developing a management mechanism to establish codes of conducts has become more urgent. In the early 1990s, the Taiwan-based Strait Exchange Foundation (SEF) and the China-based Association of Relations Across the Taiwan Strait (ARATS) were established to negotiate institutional arrangements for people-to-people exchanges as a strategy to help prevent civil disputes. After the 1992 mutual understanding on "one China," with each side being entitled to its respective interpretations, Taipei and Beijing were able to put aside the highly sensitive issue of sovereignty and reunification and initiate more constructive contacts through official proxies. On this basis, Koo Chen-fu, chairman of SEF, and Wang Daohan, chairman of ARATS, met in Singapore in April 1993; several functional meetings followed, yielding several positive results and laying the foundations for the cross-strait dialogue. The agreement upon an ambiguous definition of "one China" indeed allowed some measures of trust building across the Taiwan Strait and temporarily stabilized relations.

However, the previously initiated semiofficial communications on functional collaboration—the foundation for cross-strait conflict prevention—have had an intermittent history, suspended after president Lee's trip to the United States in 1995, resumed in October 1998, and then again suspended after Lee articulated his "special state-to-state" theory. During the first three years of

Chen's presidency, both sides relaxed the tough rhetoric. The DPP regime in Taipei has recognized that people-to-people contacts are the first step toward economic and cultural integration, which could in turn lead to a framework for permanent peace in the future. The DPP regime modified Taiwan's investment policy toward China from "no haste, be patient" to "active opening, effective management" in November 2001. In January 2001, "three small links" were initiated to permit the direct exchange of people and goods between offshore islands and adjacent territory on the mainland. Taiwan began allowing tourists from China to visit in January 2002. As for China, although it has made some concessions on the "equal footing" position regarding negotiations, and no longer insists on bilateral talks to be conducted between a central government and a provincial government, Beijing still maintains that in order for talks to resume, the government in Taiwan must explicitly acknowledge the principle of "one China." Anything can be discussed under the general, mutually accepted rubric of the one-China principle—even that the "one China" does not have to mean the PRC. In other words, Taiwan's acknowledgment of the 1992 mutual understanding of "one China" with different interpretations would be sufficient for Beijing to resume the cross-strait dialogue.

Multi-Track Diplomacy

Encouraging multi-track cross-strait diplomacy is particularly critical to the security of the Taiwan Strait, since the controversies of the one-China issue have frozen the ability of both sides to conceptualize confidence-building measures or conflict-prevention measures at the governmental levels. The most critical part of developing cross-strait conflict-prevention measures is to design an achievable implementation agenda and a format that is politically acceptable to both Beijing and Taipei. Measures that exceed the political will on both sides can easily become sources of contention rather than accommodation. This section summarizes major ongoing nongovernmental efforts that might reduce cross-strait mistrust and help to eliminate those conditions that could lead to conflict.

Track Two

Track Two diplomacy refers here to interactive collaborative reflection and problem solving, as well as reciprocal and noncommittal discussions involving academics, think-tank researchers, and both former officials and current officials participating in their private capacities. More important, it serves to provide an alternative to the more constrained format of official diplomacy.

At the regional level, the Council for Security Cooperation in Asia Pacific (CSCAP) provides one such platform for Track-Two diplomacy. Established in 1993, it currently comprises twenty leading think tanks from countries across the Asia Pacific region. Although CSCAP does not engage in official diplomacy, China has effectively blocked Taiwan's membership by insisting that security issues can only be discussed among delegations of sovereign states. In December 1996 the steering committee of CSCAP—in exchange for China's

consent to join—agreed on a set of conditions for Taiwan's unofficial participation: although think tanks from Taiwan could not be formal members of
CSCAP, and cross-strait issues could not be included on the council's formal
agenda, scholars and security experts from Taiwan could be invited to participate in working-group meetings in their individual capacities. CSCAP is thus,
despite the restrictions, the only multilateral security forum in which delegations from both Taipei and Beijing have a chance to engage and exchange
views on regional security. Through such informal communications, it is
hoped that both sides will be able to gradually build trust and exchange candid
comments on cross-strait issues in an "off the record" capacity. Currently, the
Institute of International Relations at National Chengchi University is coordinating Taiwan's participation, while the China Institute of International Studies, an official think tank linked to the PRC's Ministry of Foreign Affairs, is
representing Beijing in CSCAP.

In terms of the role of the third party, U.S.-based think tanks try to influence
policies on both sides of the Taiwan Strait. The KMT regime in Taiwan did not
welcome the U.S. mediation through Track-Two diplomacy, while Beijing
clearly has preferred cross-strait issues to be addressed only in bilateral discussions between Taipei and Beijing. However, since the suspension of communications between SEF and ARATS in 1995, Track-Two diplomacy has been
envisaged by some as an alternative to the currently stalled semiofficial contacts
between SEF and ARATS. U.S. think tanks have been welcomed by the DPP
government in Taiwan to act as facilitators, but not mediators, of dialogue
between Taipei and Beijing. The "Roundtable on U.S.-China Policy and Cross-
Strait Relations," organized by the U.S.-based National Committee on American
Foreign Policy, was initiated in 1996 to bring together important security experts
and scholars from Washington, Taipei, and Beijing to exchange views on issues
of security in the Taiwan Strait. Nevertheless, Beijing has recently indicated that
it will not talk with Taiwan through this communication channel.

At the bilateral level, intellectual exchanges and informal dialogues have
been undertaken among think tanks and research institutes on both sides. So
far, these cross-strait intellectual interactions have not amounted to actual policy discussions and thus have been less affected by the political impasse. In
Taiwan, institutions actively involved in cross-strait exchanges include the
Institute of International Relations at National Chengchi University, the Foundation on International and Cross-Strait Studies, the Prospect Foundation Taiwan, and the China Reunification Alliance. On the mainland, active institutions include the Institute of Taiwan Studies at the Chinese Academy of Social
Sciences, the Institute of International Relations at Beijing University, the
China Institute of Contemporary International Relations, the Fujian Academy
of Social Science, and the Shanghai Academy of Social Science.

Party-Based Legislative Delegations to the Mainland

Since 2000, party caucuses in Taiwan's lawmaking body, the Legislative Yuan,
have organized several visits to China. The first trip was organized by the People First Party (PFP), a new party established after the second direct presidential

election in August 2000. In early 2001, both PFP and KMT legislators organized group visits to China. The party-based legislative visits reached a peak in June–July 2002. At least five group visits were organized by legislators representing different parties. Retired military officials also joined legislators and were received by high-ranking generals from the People's Liberation Army. Even the DPP party caucus was able to organize a group to visit the mainland in July 2002. Basically, Beijing welcomed such party-based delegations. The groups were well received by ARATS and the Office of Taiwan Affairs in the State Department of the PRC. Some delegations were even able to meet with high-ranking officials in Beijing.

Nevertheless, such missions involve the risk of consuming domestic political capital without the backing of a domestic consensus on Taiwan's identity. Most legislators have been cautious about stating the purpose of the trips, because there have been voices against political figures or retired officials visiting China. A coalition against "selling Taiwan" formed by proindependence activists proposed that before departing, political figures should hold press conferences to explain the purposes of their trips. Thus the goal of improving cross-strait political relations would not be explicitly expressed. Issues of "three direct links" have been the most popular topics of discussion between officials in Beijing and legislators from Taipei. Meetings with officials of the Chinese Ministries of Transportation, Foreign Trade, Postal Affairs, and Civil Aviation held to address technical issues related to the three direct links have been welcomed.

Cooperation to Combat Crime

In the Kinmen Agreement, signed by the Red Cross societies of Taiwan and China on September 12, 1990, both sides agreed on crime-fighting issues and the repatriation of illegal immigrants. The SEF-ARATS joint agreement, effective in 1993, also identified issues related to joint combat of crime and mutual assistance on judicial proceedings. It is hoped that through consultation on these issues, a formal channel for joint crime control can be established. However, the institutionalized approaches to jointly combating crime have been suspended due to the current political impasse. Apart from daily verification of notarized documents, there has been no progress with respect to the exchange of other intelligence related to cross-boundary crimes, which has meant that effective crime fighting has been impossible. Recently, efforts were resumed at the nongovernmental Track-Two level. Academic and research communities from both sides of the Taiwan Strait organized seminars and dialogues in which public security officers were able to participate without causing political controversy. A seminar on cross-strait cooperation for combating crime was held in May 1998 in Taipei. Two Shanghai public security officers and several scholars and experts from mainland China attended the seminar. On June 20, 2001, another cross-strait academic exchange was held in Taipei. Central Police University in Taiwan and the Chinese Police Society in Mainland China co-organized the conference. The nature of engagement shifted from invitations extended to individuals toward more institutional coordination.

Recently, contacts have been upgraded to the level of officials, but still only acting in their private capacities. In July 2001, fifteen mainland Chinese incumbent and retired senior public security officers made a low-profile visit to Taiwan. In December 2001 the Criminal Investigation and Prevention Association, formed in 1992 by retired and current high-ranking police officers and legislators to combat crime committed by Taiwan's citizens abroad, organized a trip to China. It was the first time that senior police officers of the ROC visited the PRC to promote bilateral cooperation in cracking down on crime. The group also functions as a semiofficial channel for the ROC to establish links with external police authorities. On the other side of the Taiwan Strait, the China Police Society is considered to be a front organization of the Department of Public Security and acts as an informal contact point with foreign counterparts from police studies associations, especially that of Taiwan and its police force. Both organizations have some contact through the exchanges and Track-Two activities. In January 2002, criminal investigation authorities on both sides of the Taiwan Strait agreed tentatively to install a hotline to exchange information on crime. However, the idea has not been realized.

De Facto Economic Integration

The Taipei-based Cross-Strait Common Market Foundation, established in March 2001 and led by former premier Vincent Siew, is an initiative to further political integration by pursuing economic integration. This objective is formally supported by President Chen. Beijing has responded positively to the idea so far. The foundation is Taiwan's only representative in the Boao Forum for Asia, a regional version of the World Economic Forum. Although the forum is a nongovernmental and nonprofit organization to promote dialogue, coordination, and cooperation among Asian economies, it facilitates engagement between delegations from Taiwan and China in a multilateral economic forum.

At the bilateral level, the Taiwan-based Chinese National Federation of Industries (CNFI) has played an active role in promoting cross-strait economic dialogue. In June 2000 a high-powered business delegation visited mainland China. At a meeting with then-president Jiang Zemin, Jiang indicated to the CNFI that conflict with Taiwan should be avoided and that the two sides should strive for greater dialogue and economic cooperation. In March 2001, He Shizhong, director of the Economics Bureau in the Taiwan Affairs Office of the Beijing government, was invited by the CNFI to hold talks with business leaders in Taipei. Nevertheless, no meeting was scheduled with governmental officials of the ROC during the visit. In general, SEF restricts itself to activities in the private sectors to promote cross-strait conflict prevention. It fears that the views of the private sectors might deviate too far from official positions and could then inadvertently serve to give Beijing an excuse to be dismissive of SEF. Instead, SEF calls upon Beijing to return to the formal channels of negotiations through ARATS.

Prospects

Domestic politics on both sides of the Taiwan Strait have been and will continue to be a critical factor in shaping cross-strait policies. Reaching internal consensus on Taiwan's identity poses a difficult challenge, but failing to do so will jeopardize Taiwan's internal stability and weaken the bargaining power of the Taiwanese government in relation to China. After Chen became president, a "supraparty task force" on cross-strait relations was established to try to reach internal consensus on issues related to national development and cross-strait relations among all domestic political parties and civil societies. To date, however, differences among political parties remain and the task force is hardly able to function. The third presidential election in 2004 is another opportunity to test Taiwan's identity. The so-called pan-green coalition, including the DPP and the Taiwan Solidarity Union, launched a "renaming Taiwan" campaign in September 2003, and proposed a revision of the current constitution. Cross-strait relations would be more likely to improve and the chance of resuming a functional dialogue would increase if the KMT-PFP coalition, the so-called pan-blue camp, wins the election.

Leadership politics in Beijing is another important factor. The new president, Hu Jintao, has so far indicated that China's policy toward Taiwan will remain unchanged. Nevertheless, China's U.S. policy and other regional policies could very well have an impact on cross-strait tensions. China's new cabinet is alleged to be taking a tougher stand against the United States and it would be less likely for Beijing to accept the United States as a facilitator of cross-strait dialogue if U.S.-Taiwan military ties continue to strengthen.

Moreover, China's recent policies toward the region, especially the initiative of the China-ASEAN free trade agreement, indicate China's intent to use its geoeconomic leverage to influence regional development. As a consequence of this developing trend, Taiwan may have to contend with both diplomatic obstructionism as well as renewed international isolation. Exclusion from the process of regional economic integration would increase Taiwan's economic vulnerability and thus undermine the very foundations that make it possible for Taiwan to participate in the international arena. The cross-strait conflict would then, to some extent, be transformed from a dispute about diplomatic recognition into a conflict with an important economic component.

With rapidly growing economic and social ties, continuing civil disputes and tensions are to be expected, but are insufficient to trigger armed conflict at the state level. However, nontraditional cross-border security issues such as drug trafficking, illegal trading, smuggling, gunrunning, and the like, have emerged as a result of the increasing economic and social interdependence, and these issues have caused tremendous human security concerns for both sides. The current suspension of cross-strait functional communications could, over time, threaten the long-term economic welfare and prosperity of people on both sides of the Taiwan Strait. The increasing awareness that cooperation is necessary in order to cope with these common nontraditional security concerns could create opportunities for cross-strait détente.

Recommendations

Measures of conflict prevention in the context of cross-strait tensions should extend to wider policy considerations beyond military and political means. First, in order to move beyond the current situation, wherein political and military conflict is preeminent, both sides would have to sensitively address the one-China issue. Before direct talks at the governmental level take place, *bilateral dialogue at the Track-Two level* (with or without a third party as a facilitator) should be conducted to encourage a convergence of views on the one-China issue, as well as other critical institutional arrangements for future coexistence. The possibility for flexibility and creativity in Track-Two dialogues provides opportunities for Beijing and Taipei to avoid direct political confrontations; Track-Two dialogues could also facilitate the process of "integration" by including voices from civil society on both sides of the Taiwan Strait. Think tanks from both sides that have conducted regular intellectual exchanges (as discussed above) should put the discussion of the one-China issue on their agendas and try to provide policy inputs on critical issues rather than just reflecting the official line.

Second, an incremental building-block approach effected through the cumulative efforts of social and economic functional cooperation (at both semiofficial and nongovernmental levels) could increase the stake at risk from the use of force to resolve political conflicts. *Functional or sectoral cooperation* means neither political concession nor directly implies any form of *political integration*. The reactions of political extremists on both sides is expected to be less vehement, and thus the cost in terms of domestic political capital would be lower. With the current political impasse, however, communications through governmental proxies are more feasible. Bilateral communications through SEF and ARATS, an established channel, should be resumed. Issues of "three links" involving tremendous social and economic interests are common concerns of both governments and are expected to be the next hot topic on the policy agenda.

Third, increasing economic and social interdependence has created new cross-strait tensions, as there are no appropriate measures to respond to the incidents of nontraditional security that frequently occur in the Taiwan Strait. *A bilateral mechanism for crisis management* that provides a framework for promptly responding to such incidents, particularly those with strong humanitarian concerns, would be helpful in ensuring that political recriminations do not accrue from situations that are not essentially political. Both Beijing and Taipei would have to extend mutual respect to their respective jurisdictions so that transboundary threats, such as the smugglings of arms, people, and trade items, the breakout of epidemic diseases, and other maritime safety issues could all be combated effectively. To a significant degree, successfully dealing with these cross-border issues requires Taiwan's participation in the efforts to effect global governance on these matters. Talking to the government in Taipei on these common concerns, either bilaterally or within international institutions, does not necessarily imply any encouragement of Taiwan's independence, but reflects a pragmatic approach to the crisis management of cross-border human security threats.

Resources

Books

Across the Taiwan Strait: Mainland China, Taiwan, and the 1995–1996 Crisis. Ed. Suisheng Zhao. New York: Routledge, 1999.

China's Dilemma: The Taiwan Issue. By Sheng Lijun. London: I. B. Tauris, 2001.

China and Taiwan: Cross-Strait Relations Under Chen Shui-Bian. By Sheng Lijun. London: Zed Books, July 2002.

Contemporary Taiwan. Ed. David Shambaugh. New York: Oxford University Press, 1998.

Cooperation or Conflict in the Taiwan Strait? By Ralph N. Clough. Lanham, Md.: Rowman and Littlefield, 1999.

The Costs of Conflict: The Impact on China of a Future War. Ed. Andrew Scobell. Carlisle, Penn.: Strategic Studies Institute, 2001.

A Historical Account of the Consensus of 1992. Eds. Su Chi and Cheng An-kuo. Taipei: National Policy Foundation, 2002.

Island China. By Ralph N. Clough. Cambridge: Harvard University Press, 1978.

The Making of Chinese Foreign and Security Policy in the Era of Reform. Ed. David Lampton. Palo Alto, Calif.: Stanford University Press, 2001.

Reaching Across the Taiwan Strait: People-to-People Diplomacy. By Ralph N. Clough. Boulder: Westview, 1993.

The Taiwan-China Connection: Democracy and Development Across the Taiwan Straits. By Tse-Kang Leng. Boulder: Westview, 1996.

Taiwan in World Affairs. Ed. Robert Sutter. Boulder: Westview, 1994.

Taiwan Strait Dilemmas. Ed. Gerrit Gong. Washington, D.C.: Center for Strategic and International Studies, 2000.

Taiwan's Presidential Politics. Ed. Muthiah Alagappa. New York: M. E. Sharpe, 2001.

The United States and Cross-Strait Relations. Ed. Kenneth Klinker. Urbana: University of Illinois at Urbana-Champaign, 2001.

Articles

"Can China Conquer Taiwan?" By Michael O'Hanlon. *International Security* 25, no. 2 (2000): 51–86. Available at www.brookings.edu/dybdocroot/views/articles/ohanlon/2000fall_is.pdf.

"China Eyes Taiwan: Why Is a Breakthrough so Difficult?" By Sheng Lijun. *Journal of Strategic Studies* 21, no. 1 (March 1998): 65–78.

"Chinese Decision-Making Toward Taiwan, 1979–1997." By Michael Swaine. In David Lampton, ed., *The Making of Chinese Foreign and Security in the Era of Reform, 1978–2000.* Stanford, Calif.: Stanford University Press, 2001, chapter 10.

"Chinese Missiles and Taiwan Theater Missile Defense." By Bonnie Glaser. *American Foreign Policy Interests,* December 1999, pp. 20–31.

"Chinese Perceptions of the Cost of Conflict." By David M. Finkelstein. In Andrew Scobell, ed., *The Costs of Conflict: The Impact on China of a Future War.* Carlisle, Penn.: Strategic Studies Institute, 2001, pp. 9–28.

"The Contemporary Security Dilemma: Deterring a Taiwan Conflict." By Thomas J. Christensen. *Washington Quarterly,* August 2002. Available at www.twq.com/02autumn/christensen.pdf.

"Crisis in the Taiwan Strait." By Kurt M. Campbell and Derek J. Mitchell. *Foreign Affairs* 80 no. 4 (July–August 2001): 14–25.

"Cross-Strait Relations: Bilateral Strategies and Tactics." By George W. Tsai. In Martin Edmonds, Chyungly Lee, and Greg Mills, eds., *Preventing Insecurity: Lessons from and for East Asia*. Johannesburg: South African Institute of International Affairs, 2003, pp. 59–78.

"Cross-Strait Trade and Investment: Economic and Security Implications for the Republic of China." By J. D. Kenneth Boutin. *Issues and Studies* 33, no. 12 (December 1997): 70–93.

"Developing Economic CBMs as a Foundation for Security Across the Taiwan Strait: Opportunities After the WTO Accessions." By Chyungly Lee. In Martin Edmonds, Chyungly Lee, and Greg Mills, eds., *Preventing Insecurity: Lessons from and for East Asia*. Johannesburg: South African Institute of International Affairs, 2003, pp. 25–40.

"Dynamics of Taiwan–Mainland China Economic Relations: the Role of Private Firms." By Tse-Kang Leng. *Asian Survey* 12, no. 5 (May 1998): 494–509.

"Economic Interdependence and Political Integration Between Taiwan and Mainland China: A Critical Review." By Tse-Kang Leng. *Chinese Political Science Review* (June 1996): 27–43.

"If Taiwan Chooses Unification, Should the United States Care?" By Nancy Bernkopf Tucker. *Washington Quarterly* 25, no. 3 (2002): 15–27.

"The Impact of the PRC's Domestic Politics on Cross-Strait Relations." By Szu-chien Hsu. *Issues and Studies* 38, no. 1 (March 2002): 130–164.

"The Making of Taiwan Policy in Mainland China: Structure and Process." By George W. Tsai. *Issue and Studies* 33, no. 9 (September 1997): 1–30.

"Maritime Confidence Building Measures Across the Taiwan Strait: Technical Collaboration for Human Security at Sea." By Chyungly Lee. *Cooperative Monitoring Center Occasional Paper* no. 26. Albuquerque: N.M.: Sandia National Laboratories, March 2003.

"Missile Defenses and the Taiwan Scenario." By James Mulvenon. Report no. 44. Washington, D.C.: Henry L. Stimson Center, 2002. Available at www.stimson.org/china/pdf/cmdwp2.pdf.

"Navigating the Taiwan Strait: Deterrence, Escalation Dominance, and U.S.-China Relations." By Robert S. Ross. *International Security* 27, no. 2 (Fall 2002). Available at http://mitpress.mit.edu/journals/pdf/isec_27_02_48_0.pdf.

"The 1995–6 Taiwan Strait Crisis: Coercion, Credibility, and the Use of Force." By Robert S. Ross. *International Security* 25, no. 2 (2000): 87–123.

"The 1996 Taiwan Strait Crisis. Lessons for the United States, China, and Taiwan." By Robert S. Ross. *Security Dialogue* 27, no. 4 (1996): 463–470.

"A Political Analysis of Taiwan's Economic Dependence on Mainland China." By Tse-Kang Leng. *Issues and Studies* 34, no. 8 (August 1998): 132–154.

"The Political Economy of Taiwan's Mainland Policy." By Yun-han Chu. *Journal of Contemporary China* 6, no. 15 (1997): 229–257.

"Securing Cross-Straits Economic Relations: New Challenges and Opportunities." By Tse-Kang Leng. *Journal of Contemporary China* 11, no. 31 (April 2002): 261–279.

"The Security Implications of the New Taiwan." By Bernice Lee. *Adelphi Paper* no. 331. New York: Oxford University Press, 1999, chap. 4, pp. 43–51.

"The Stability of Deterrence in the Taiwan Strait." By Robert S. Ross. *National Interests* no. 65 (Fall 2001): 67–76.

"State, Business, and Economic Interaction Across the Taiwan Straits." By Tse-Kang Leng. *Issues and Studies* 31, no. 11 (November 1995): 40–58.

"Taiwan's Security: Maintaining Deterrence amid Political Accountability." By David Shambaugh. In David Shambaugh, ed., *Contemporary Taiwan*. London: Oxford University Press, 1998, pp. 240–274.

"Taiwan and China Cross-Strait Negotiations: The International Connection." By Jawling Joanne Chang. *International Journal of Business* 7, no. 3 (2002). Available at www.craig.csufresno.edu/ijb/v73-7.pdf.

"Taiwan Domestic Gridlock, Cross-Strait Deadlock." By Willem van Kemenade. *Washington Quarterly* 24, no. 4 (August 2001): 55–70.

"Theorizing on Relations Across the Taiwan Strait: Nine Contending Approaches." By Yu-Shan Wu. *Journal of Contemporary China* 9, no. 25 (November 2000): 407–428.

"An Uncertain Relationship: The United States, Taiwan, and the Taiwan Relations Act." By Steven M. Goldstein and Randall Schriver. *China Quarterly* no. 165 (March 2001): 147–172.

"WTO and the Taiwan Strait." By Karen Sutter. *China Business Review*, January–February 2000, pp. 28–33.

Speeches and Statements

"Always in My Heart." By Lee Teng-hui. The Spencer T. and Ann W. Olin Lecture at Cornell University, Ithaca, June 9, 1995. Available at www.taiwanpresident.org/page17d.htm.

"Bridging the New Century." By Chen Shui-bian. New Year's Eve address, Taipei, December 31, 2000. Available at www.taipei.org/chen/chen891231.htm.

"Continue to Promote the Reunification of the Motherland." By Jiang Zemin. Address, Chinese New Year speech, Beijing, January 30, 1995.

"Diplomatic Rivalry Between the ROC and the PRC, 1972–1992." By Lang Kao. Speech delivered at the ninetieth annual meeting of the American Political Science, New York, September 1–4, 1994.

"Domestic Determinants of Taiwan's Mainland Policy." By Su Chi. Presentation to the Oxford University Conference, May 2002.

"The Impact of WTO Accession on Political and Economic Relations Between the Two Sides of the Taiwan Strait." By Michael Y. M. Kau. Address at the Cross-Strait Forum, organized by the Center for National Policy, Washington, D.C., July 23, 2002. Available at www.cnponline.org/press%20releases/transcripts/michael%20kau%20remarks.pdf .

"Solving the Taiwan Strait Crisis: Can Preventive Diplomacy Work?" By Desmond J. Ball. Presented at the conference "Taiwan Security in the Year 2000: Retrospect and Prospects," Taipei, December 15, 2000. Available at www.dsis.org.tw/peaceforum/symposium/2000-12/121510.pdf.

"White Paper on the One-China Principle and the Taiwan Issue." Taiwan Affairs Office and Information Office of the State Council, PRC, Beijing, January 21, 2000. Available at www.taiwandocuments.org/white.htm.

"Taiwan Stands Up: Toward the Dawn of a Rising Era." By Chen Shui-bian. Inauguration address, Taipei, May 20, 2000. Available at www.taipei.org/chen/chen0520.htm.

"Taiwan–Mainland China Relations From Negative Isolation to Positive Transformation—An Episode of History in the 21st Century." By Paul S. P. Hsu. Presented at the conference "Asian Approaches to International Negotiations: Borders and Territories," Honolulu, September 1998. Available at www.taiwansecurity.org/ts-hsu.htm.

U.S.-Sino Joint Communiqués. Available at www.taiwandocuments.org/communique01.htm, www.taiwandocuments.org/communique02.htm, www.taiwandocuments.org/communique03.htm.

Organizations

Taiwan

Chamber of Taiwan Businessmen in China
11F.-2, No. 10, Linsen S. Rd.
Jhongjheng District, Taipei City 100, Taiwan R.O.C.
tel: +886 2 2358 2353
fax: +886 2 2358 2301

Chinese National Federation of Industries
12th FL., 390, Fu-Hsing S. Road, Section 1, Taiwan R.O.C.
tel: +886 2 2703 3500
fax: +886 2 2705 8317
e-mail: cnfi@cnfi.org.tw
www.cnfi.org.tw/

Cross-Strait Common Market Foundation
7F., No.97, Sec. 2, Dunhua S. Rd., Taipei, Taiwan R.O.C.
tel: +886 2 2702 7411
fax: +886 2 2702 7448
e-mail: webmaster@crossstrait.org
www.crossstrait.org/version1/

Future China Research, Cross-Strait Interflow Prospect Foundation
1F., No. 1, Lane 60, Sec. 3, Tingjhou Rd.
Taipei, Taiwan R.O.C.
tel: +886 2 2364 366
fax: +886 2 2367 6511
e-mail: info@future-china.org.tw
www.future-china.org

Foundation on International and Cross-Strait Studies
14F., No. 88, Sec. 2, Jhongsiao E. Rd.
Taipei, Taiwan R.O.C.
tel: +886 2 2396 8760
fax: +886 2 2391 7350
www.fics.org.tw

Institute of International Relations—National Chengchi University
No. 64 Wan Shou Rd.
Taipei, Taiwan R.O.C.
tel: +886 2 8237 7277
e-mail: iir@nccu.edu.tw
http://iir.nccu.edu.tw

Mainland Affairs Council, Executive Yuan, R.O.C.
15 FL., No. 2-2, Sec. 1, Jinan Rd.
Taipei, Taiwan R.O.C.
tel: +886 2 2397 5589
e-mail: macst@mac.gov.tw
www.mac.gov.tw

National Policy Foundation
16 Hang Chow S. Rd., Sec. 1
Taipei 100, Taiwan R.O.C.
tel: +886 2 2343 3399
fax: +886 2 2343 3357
email: npf@npf.org.tw, npf@npf.org.tw
www.npf.org.tw/english/main-eng.htm

Strait Peaceful Re-unification Association
Room 2405, 24F., No. 333, Sec. 1, Jilong Rd.
Songshan District, Taipei City 105, Taiwan R.O.C.
tel: +886 2 8789 0538
fax: +886 2 2757 7271

e-mail: spra@tpts.seed.met.tw
www.spra.org.tw

Taiwan Straits Exchange Foundation
17F., No.156, Sec. 3, Minsheng E. Rd.
Taipei, Taiwan R.O.C.
tel: +886 2 2718 7373
fax: +886 2 2514 9962/3/4
e-mail: service@sef.org.tw
www.sef.org.tw

China

Association for Relations Across the Taiwan Straits
No. 6-1, GuangAnMen South Street, XuanWu District, Beijing, China P.R.C.
tel: +86 10 8353 6622
fax: +86 10 6357 1505
www.gwytb.gov.cn/

China Reform Forum
No.35, Bao Fang Hu Tong, Dong Cheng District, Beijing, China P.R.C.
tel: +86 10 6512 5829
fax: +86 10 6512 6148
e-mail: article@crf.org.cn
www.crf.org.cn/

Chinese Institute of International Studies
No. 3, Tai Ji Chang Tou Tiao, Beijing, China P.R.C.
www.ciis.org.cn/

Institute of International Relations—Beijing University
Beijing University, Beijing, China P.R.C.
e-mail: webmaster@sis.pku.edu.cn
http://162.105.189.100

Institute of Taiwan Studies—Chinese Academy of Social Sciences
No.15, YiHeYuan, BeiBoShang Village, Beijing, China P.R.C.
tel: +886 10 6258 3509
fax: +886 10 6258 3520
www.cass.net.cn/webnew/index.asp

Chyungly Lee received her Ph.D. from the Department of Government and Politics, University of Maryland, in 1995 and then joined the Institute of International Relations, National Chengchi University. She is an active participant in the Council for Security Cooperation in Asia Pacific (CSCAP) and has been coordinating Taiwan's participation in CSCAP-related activities since May 2000. Her recent international experiences also include visiting scholarships at the Cooperative Monitoring Center, Sandia National Laboratories, United States, in spring 2002, and at the Center for International Relations, University of British Columbia, since fall 2002. Her recent publications and research include topics of Asia Pacific security multilateralism, East Asian regionalism, and nontraditional security issues in Asia Pacific, with particular focus on issues of economic security and human security in the region.

Notes

1. "Republic of China" and "Taiwan" are both used in this chapter. The former emphasizes the official and formal status of the country, while the later tends to be more frequently used in most of the recent literature. Use of "People's Republic of China" and "China" reflect similar distinctions between official and nonofficial references.

2. The Taiwan Relations Act of 1979 and the three U.S.-Sino Joint Communiqués of 1972, 1979, and 1982 have provided the guidelines for U.S. cross-strait policy. Basically, the United States has adopted a "one China" policy to recognize the government of the PRC as the sole legal government of China, but it has also agreed to provide any arms necessary to enable Taiwan to maintain sufficient self-defense capacity.

3. Lee Teng-hui, who received his Ph.D. from Cornell University in 1968, delivered a speech at the Olin Lecture on June 9, 1995, as part of the university's alumni reunion weekend. In the speech, "the Republic of China on Taiwan" was mentioned sixteen times. Later, in July 1995, China fired six DF-15 missiles from Fujian province to an East China Sea impact site ninety miles north of Taipei. On the eve of Taiwan's first presidential election, China launched four DF-15s into two ocean impact zones that would bracket the island. One zone was forty-seven miles west of the southern port of Kaohsiung and the other was just thirty miles east of the northern port of Keelung.

4. For instance, in July 1998, President Bill Clinton proclaimed "three no's" in his visit to China. The United States denies any support for Taiwan's independence and rejects the idea of two Chinas or "one Taiwan, one China." Furthermore, the United States does not agree that Taiwan should be a member of any organization for which statehood is a requirement. This new policy has significantly reduced Taiwan's bargaining space in its diplomatic battle against China.

5. In his inauguration speech, President Chen articulated the principle of "four no's, one not-do"—that is, no declaration of independence, no change of country name, no revision of constitution to reflect state-to-state theory, no referendum on issues of unification and independence, and no abandonment of the unification guideline.

6. In the 1993 "White Paper on the Taiwan Issue and the Unification of China," the "one China" was equated with the PRC, with Taiwan ruled by the central government in Beijing. In the 1995 "Jiang's Eight Points," Beijing insisted on the inseparability of China's sovereignty and territorial integrity. In the 1998 Koo-Wang Meeting, Wang expressed the belief that people of both sides of the Taiwan Strait ought to work on the future China together.

7. From January 1990 to May 2000 there were 237 fishing disputes, including 127 related to collisions, labor disputes, and entangled nets between Taiwanese and Chinese fishing boats; 55 involved Taiwanese fishing boats allegedly inspected and harassed by the mainland coast guard; and 55 involved alleged robberies by pirates.

8. Three stages are suggested in the approach: promotion of confidence-building measures, development of preventive-diplomacy mechanisms, and development of conflict-resolution mechanisms. ARF is currently at the stage of developing preventive-diplomacy mechanisms. Two key principles are reiterated among members of ARF: first, respect for state sovereignty and noninterference in the internal affairs of a state, and second, that preventive diplomacy practices are entirely voluntary and are to be employed only at the request of the parties or with their consent.

8.3.5

Tibet: Still Searching for Solutions

Jane Caple

Since the military annexation of Tibet by China fifty years ago there has been a high level of tension between the Tibetan population and the Chinese government. China maintains that Tibet is experiencing unprecedented economic growth and political stability, but the fundamental issue of the Tibetan right to self-determination remains unresolved. Although diplomatic solutions proposed by the Dalai Lama have won international approval, they have been met with little substantive movement from the Chinese authorities. The role of civil society in conflict resolution in Tibet is insignificant. Activity by nongovernmental organizations (NGOs) is largely confined to localized, small-scale environmental, aid, and development projects. Traditional community-based organizations are generally not recognized as stakeholders in decisionmaking, or are circumscribed in practice by suspicions that they harbor political agendas. The success of far-reaching conflict-resolution strategies will be largely dependent on political reform within China.

The political histories of Tibet and China have been interrelated since Tibet emerged as a nation-state in the seventh century. However, a historical shift in their relationship occurred following the victory of the Chinese Communist Party (CCP) in China's civil war in 1949. For the first time, China established centralized control over Tibet. Its land, resources, economy, culture, religion, politics, and society all came under direct control of the government in Beijing, with huge impact on its inhabitants.

The Chinese authorities have ideological, strategic, and economic interests in Tibet. Although Tibetans only constitute roughly half of 1 percent of China's population, Tibetan areas account for almost one-quarter of China's landmass.[1] Tibet's borders with India and Nepal make the region of strategic importance in China's national security concerns, contributing to its militarization and construction of nuclear bases.

Tibet's inclusion within the People's Republic of China is important to the CCP's legitimacy and hold on power. Tibet is one of the territories viewed as

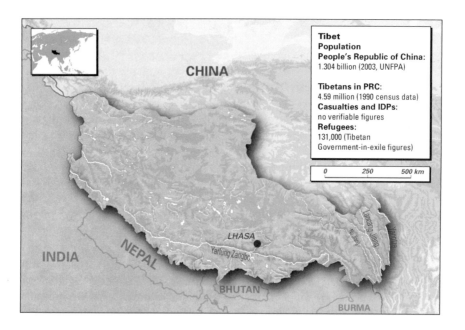

Tibet
Population
People's Republic of China:
1.304 billion (2003, UNFPA)

Tibetans in PRC:
4.59 million (1990 census data)
Casualties and IDPs:
no verifiable figures
Refugees:
131,000 (Tibetan
Government-in-exile figures)

lost to imperialists that the Communist leadership vowed to reclaim upon assuming power. The current leadership's claim to sovereignty over Tibet is derived from the Mongol Yuan dynasty, which controlled much of Central and East Asia (including China and Tibet) in the thirteenth century. China's major rivers rise from the Tibetan plateau and the leadership of the country has always maintained an interest in Tibet's natural resources.

In political opposition, the Tibetan government-in-exile, based in Dharamsala, India, claims to be the legitimate government of the Tibetan people. It holds that Tibetans have never conceded their sovereignty to a foreign power and that China's status is one of occupier and colonizer.[2] The Tibetan government-in-exile was formed by the fourteenth Dalai Lama after he escaped into exile in 1959, followed by 80,000 Tibetans. The Tibetan diaspora continues to grow with roughly 2,000–3,000 Tibetans illegally crossing the border into Nepal each year, most of them moving straight on to India under auspices of the UN High Commissioner for Refugees (UNHCR), although numbers have decreased in the past three years due to more stringent border controls.[3]

Conflict arising from Chinese control over Tibet has been exacerbated by authoritarian implementation of the CCP's ideology and policy. Clashes between traditional Tibet and communist China in every sphere of life have strengthened the collective identity, as well as nationalism, among Tibetans, who seek to retain their cultural integrity and aspire to genuine autonomy. Most Tibetans appear to share a desire for a solution that will end Chinese dominance over Tibet's politics, culture, and economy and the visible Chinese presence in Tibet.

However, China's policies in Tibet are driven by the imperative of protecting national unity through firm control. Prior to 1949, Tibet comprised three areas: U-Tsang (central and western Tibet, administered by the Lhasa government), Amdo, and Kham. Under Chinese administration, central Tibet has been redesignated the Tibet Autonomous Region. Other Tibetan areas are incorporated into neighboring provinces (Qinghai, Sichuan, Gansu, Yunnan). Areas where Tibetans have compact inhabitancy are designated "Tibetan autonomous," although in practice local governments in these areas must implement the directives of higher-level authorities.[4]

The CCP exercises tight political control over local government and population. Over the past decade, its security operations at the grassroots level have become increasingly pervasive. Chinese security officials are active within communities. Intelligence is gathered through networks of informants and surveillance.[5] Local Tibetan security personnel are instrumental in day-to-day control, while the armed police and army have the capability to suppress open opposition (e.g., political demonstrations).

Since the beginning of the 1990s, the Chinese authorities have been pursuing fast-track development policies in Tibet. These policies focus on large-scale infrastructure projects, exploitation of natural resources, and urbanization. Efforts were intensified in 1999 following the launch of China's campaign to develop its western regions. Critics of this development model, including some mainstream Chinese academics (e.g., Hu Angang of Qinghua University),[6] argue that it is environmentally unsustainable. They also argue that it will not alleviate poverty and will increase urban-rural wealth disparities, providing few benefits to the majority of Tibetans who are farmers and herders. Despite China's subsidization of development in Tibetan areas, levels of education and healthcare provision remain among the lowest in China.[7]

Current development policies, notably the construction of a railway to Lhasa, will intensify migratory trends that have fueled ethnic tension and resentment against the state. The threat of assimilation and marginalization through in-migration of nonindigenous peoples (primarily Han Chinese and Hui Muslims) is of overriding concern to Tibetans, irrespective of their political views.

Conflict Dynamics

China's official position is that deep-rooted conflict (i.e., the broad Tibetan desire for self-determination) does not exist and that the majority of Tibetans are satisfied with Chinese rule. The government claims that Tibetans' human rights are protected and views international criticism as interference in China's internal affairs, intended to undermine national unity.

China's military, political, demographic, and economic strengths far outweigh those of Tibetans. The state has been able to quash open resistance and implement its central policies. However, the authorities have been frustrated by their failure to eradicate Tibetan opposition and the vigor and persistence of Tibetan resistance to being drawn away from their language, religion, and customs.

The Tibetan response to Chinese rule has included diplomacy and resistance (including violent and nonviolent protest and noncompliance). Despite the power imbalance, Tibetans have garnered considerable popular support outside China and the Tibet issue has received greater international attention than other conflicts in China (e.g., the Sino-Uyghur conflict). However, China's rising stature politically and economically has dissuaded foreign governments from involving themselves in the conflict beyond calling for dialogue and an improvement of the human rights situation.

In terms of deaths and displacement caused by the conflict, the most acute periods were the 1950s and 1960s. This was a result of China-wide policy-induced famines (notably the Great Leap Forward), armed conflict during the 1950s, and reprisal campaigns following the 1959 Tibetan Uprising, which continued through the Cultural Revolution until 1979. During this period tens of thousands of Tibetans were sent to labor camps. Traditional culture, religion, and society were attacked and nearly all of Tibet's monasteries destroyed.

From the late 1970s to mid-1980s, reforms instituted throughout China resulted in relative liberalization of the economy and society, leading to a religious revival in Tibet. Dialogue was established between the Dalai Lama and Beijing, and three Tibetan government-in-exile fact-finding missions were invited into Tibet.

By the end of the 1980s, a modern political protest dynamic, incorporating Western concepts of democracy and human rights, had emerged, starting with a series of nonviolent proindependence protests in Lhasa. Following three days of mass demonstrations during which at least seventy Tibetans were killed by security forces,[8] martial law was imposed at midnight on March 7, 1989, and kept in place through April 1990.

During the 1990s, control was tightened through increased security measures, harsh punishment of Tibetan political prisoners, regulation of monasteries, and political campaigns. China's position toward the Tibetan government-in-exile also hardened and dialogue broke off in 1993. Beijing intensified efforts to discourage and prevent loyalty to the Dalai Lama through denunciatory propaganda and bans on open worship.

Restrictions on religious freedom and government regulation of monasteries and popular religion have exacerbated the conflict, as they have intensified Tibetan antipathy against China's role in the region. State interference in the selection of reincarnations of senior lamas has caused deep-seated resentment. Notably, the disappearance of the boy recognized in 1995 by the Dalai Lama as the eleventh Panchen Lama, and subsequent enthronement of Beijing's candidate, gave rise to deep anger among Tibetans. A "Patriotic Education Campaign," launched in monasteries, schools, and offices in the mid-1990s, required Tibetans to recognize China's Panchen Lama and denounce the Dalai Lama.

The Tibetan government-in-exile's position for negotiations is based on the "middle path" peace proposal put forward by the Dalai Lama in June 1988.[9] This proposal calls for the establishment of a self-governing democratic entity, including the regions of Kham and Amdo, to operate in association with China. The Chinese government would remain responsible for foreign policy. Tibetans would have genuine autonomous control over domestic affairs.

Although his decision to drop calls for independence was controversial among Tibetans, the Dalai Lama's proposal received international approval, and he was awarded the Nobel Peace Prize in October 1989. However, the compromise he proposed has not yet demonstrably moved forward Sino-Tibetan dialogue. The Chinese leadership remains suspicious that the real aim of the exiles continues to be independence. Over the past fifteen years, the authorities have perceived a growing threat from the internationalization of the Tibet issue, which is personified in the Dalai Lama, who is welcomed by many governments around the world as a religious leader.

Preconditions that China has set for dialogue are unlikely to be met by the Tibetans. They include an acknowledgment that Tibet and Taiwan have always been part of China. At the same time, China is unlikely to accept the territorial claims made by the Tibetan government-in-exile (see endnote 2). The Chinese government have generally given the impression that the only issue on the table is the Dalai Lama's return to Tibet.

Despite this stalemate, contact has now been reestablished between the Tibetan exiles and Beijing. Envoys of the Dalai Lama made two visits to China, in September 2002 and spring 2003, with the stated purpose of building trust and starting a dialogue process. These visits were a significant step for the Tibetan side, but China has not publicly acknowledged them as official.

Official Conflict Management

Official conflict management in Tibet is dominated by the Chinese authorities. They use a combination of incentives, deterrence and repression to deal with tension in Tibet. The emphasis has been on stability at the expense of political reform and improvements in human rights and civil liberties. This approach to the conflict has caused deep resentment and suspicion of Chinese rule and policies among Tibetans.

Policies to protect China's national unity include accelerated economic development in ethnic minority regions. This leads to greater integration of Tibetan areas into the wider Chinese economy, society, and culture, which are dominated by Han Chinese, and to the demographic restructuring of these areas. As centralized control strengthens, minorities become increasingly dependent on subsidized development efforts.

Some opportunities and incentives have been offered to Tibetans in the form of limited economic, social, cultural, and religious latitude. The authorities have also sought to win Tibetans over through ideological education campaigns and propaganda emphasizing the benefits of Chinese rule and policy over life in "old Tibet," as well as attempts to undermine widespread popular reverence for the Dalai Lama. The Chinese authorities appear to be genuinely frustrated when Tibetans continue to take the high risks of opposition, which includes violent suppression of protests and severe treatment of political prisoners.

Where incentive-based measures and political education have not succeeded in eradicating dissent, the following methods of deterrence and repression have been employed:

- Tight regulation and control of religion and other sectors of society
- Development of an increasingly sophisticated domestic security operation, particularly during the 1990s
- Imprisonment and reeducation-through-labor, with particularly harsh
  treatment of political inmates
- Military repression of opposition—for example, the imposition of martial law in 1989

China has also renewed efforts to sway international opinion on the Tibet issue
through increased propaganda. These efforts include publication of English-
language materials, guided media tours, and cultural and academic exchanges,
apparently aimed at influencing opinion about the Tibet issue.[10]

Regional organizations within Asia, such as the Association of Southeast
Asian Nations (ASEAN), have largely deferred to China in treating Tibet as
China's internal problem. The European Parliament, on the other hand, has
stated that China is illegally occupying Tibet and has passed twenty-four resolutions condemning human rights violations there. In July 2000 it passed a
particularly significant resolution, calling on European Union member states
to seriously consider recognizing the Tibetan government-in-exile as the legitimate government of the Tibetan people if no agreement had been signed
between China and the exile government within three years. This is likely to
have been a factor in the recent permission of visits by envoys of the Dalai
Lama. In view of these visits, the European Parliament decided to continue to
observe developments before taking any further steps to implement the resolution, but renewed calls on China to ensure dialogue with the Dalai Lama's
representatives in April 2002.

Some individual states have raised the Tibet issue during bilateral dialogue with China. The United States has been the most vocal, with Congress
passing nine resolutions, ten public laws, and one foreign relations authorization act in relation to Tibet between 1988 and 1995. The United States has also
created the post of "Tibet coordinator," with the main mandate of seeking dialogue between China and the Dalai Lama.

China's seat on the UN Security Council limits the effectiveness of the
UN in addressing the conflict. The attention given to Tibet within the UN has
largely been restricted to human rights issues and avoided the question of
political status. The UN General Assembly has passed three resolutions on
Tibet, in 1959, 1961, and 1965, calling for cessation of practices depriving the
Tibetan people of their fundamental human rights and freedoms, including
(1961 resolution) their right to self-determination. However, at the time these
resolutions were adopted, the UN recognized the Chinese Nationalist (Kuomintang) government, based in Taipei, as the representative of China. Since the

Communist government in Beijing was admitted to the UN in 1971, the scope of the UN discussion about Tibet has changed.

During the past twenty years, the United States and some European countries have sponsored resolutions at the annual UN Commission on Human Rights, calling for UN investigations into human rights abuses in Tibet. However, implementation of these resolutions has been blocked by votes in favor of "no action" motions set forth by China. According to Human Rights Watch, resolutions critical of China's human rights have been sponsored and supported by the United States and Europe because such multilateral initiatives are seen as less damaging to bilateral relations and business interests. Since 1997, Western governments appear to have been ready to take any promise of improvement from China as a pretext for delaying lobbying and avoiding conflict at Geneva.[11]

Multi-Track Diplomacy

Despite far-reaching economic reforms, China remains a one-party state with an authoritarian political structure. Party control is at its tightest in ethnic minority areas, where fears of political instability are heightened by ethnic nationalism and desires for separation from China.

There is a marked lack of organized local civil society groups or NGOs able to participate in debate and decisionmaking in Tibet. As a result, there are no broad or inclusive conflict resolution/transformation frameworks in operation. However, some local officials have sought solutions to conflict that satisfy both the community and higher levels of authority, while other popularly respected community figures, often religious leaders, have played a role in unobtrusively managing and preventing conflict.

Tibet has one of the smallest concentrations of NGOs in the world. The atmosphere in which they work is very difficult. In order to operate with any level of success, they have to handle national and local political interests and sensitivities, and deal with systemic corruption and a system in which the best interests of the local community and environment are often accorded a low priority by officials. China still has a deep distrust of foreign NGO programs in Tibet, perceiving them as part of the West's attempt to intervene in China's internal affairs. There is frequent government interference and all projects are closely monitored.

Opportunities for international NGOs working in Tibet have largely been limited to aid and development or the environment. A few have worked on religious and cultural preservation initiatives. Projects carried out by international, regional, and local groups tend to be small-scale, focusing on improving living conditions, training and educating Tibetans, and preserving Tibetan culture, traditions, and religion at a localized level.

International NGOs working outside China on the Tibet issue have more freedom to pursue explicit conflict transformation goals, but are unable to coordinate with grassroots society within Tibet. Most of the advocacy work that has been carried out by such groups has focused on building awareness of

Lhasa. Chinese troops in front of the Potala Palace.

the conflict and human rights abuses in order to garner international support. These international NGOs have sustained pressure on governments and international agencies to push the Chinese government toward internal reform and negotiations with the Tibetan government-in-exile.

Tibet support groups exist in over fifty countries. Most have the explicit agenda of working toward an independent Tibet and are primarily concerned with campaigning and lobbying to generate international support on specific issues, such as the disappearance of Gedun Choekyi Nyima, the boy recognized by the Dalai Lama as the eleventh Panchen Lama. International human rights advocacy NGOs, such as Amnesty International and Human Rights Watch, have highlighted abuses and launched public campaigns, such as letter writing and petitions.

Specialist Tibet-monitoring organizations also exist, with the aim of ensuring a continued flow of information about what is happening in the region. These include the Tibet Information Network, an independent news and research service, and the Tibetan Center for Human Rights and Democracy, established by Tibetan exiles. Other organizations, such as the Dharamsala-based Tibetan Women's Association and Tibetan Youth Congress, also publish literature on issues such as environmental degradation and women's rights.

Aid and development NGOs have been involved in Tibet in emergency relief and longer-term projects in rural development, education, and vocational skills training. They also work in the field of health care (Western and Tibetan medicine) and entrepreneurship development. Some of these organizations are set up and run by Tibetan exiles (e.g., the Rokpa Trust and the Tibet Foundation) and specialist Tibet development agencies (e.g., the Trace Foundation, the Bridge Fund, and the Tibet Poverty Alleviation Fund). International NGOs Save the Children Fund (UK) and the Red Cross also run emergency aid and development projects in Tibetan areas, as do evangelical Christian organizations such as English Language Institute/China (ELIC), Jensco, and World Concern.

Some organizations focus on cultural and religious development and preservation. Buddhist groups and NGOs have funded religious and cultural projects inside Tibet, such as monastery renovation or training of Tibetan medical practitioners. Tibetan organizations and Tibetan community groups abroad have focused on maintaining traditions while in exile. Tibetan and non-Tibetan groups outside China have organized cultural fairs, art exhibitions, and concerts.

Environmental NGOs have worked in cooperation with the authorities in Tibet, with programs aimed at reforestation and protection of forest, flora, and fauna (e.g., the Rokpa Trust, the Nature Conservancy, and the World Wildlife Fund). International NGOs have also been involved in the development of nature reserves in Tibet, including Qomolangma (Everest).

The activities of NGOs have helped to place Tibet on the international agenda. Their efforts have helped to put pressure on governments, international agencies, and multinational corporate investors to acknowledge that a conflict exists and to contribute to its transformation and resolution.

The public support generated for Tibetans has helped NGOs to attract funding for projects inside Tibet and for exiled Tibetan communities. Although these projects have had positive impact on local communities, NGOs have been unable to engage the Chinese authorities in actively promoting conflict transformation due to the official position that deep-rooted conflict does not exist.

One organization that has been skillful in its use of diplomatic and legal tools is Dui Hua (Chinese for "dialogue"). Dui Hua is a U.S.-based NGO that seeks to facilitate the release of political prisoners through contact and discussions with the Chinese government. Several Tibetan political prisoners were released from prison following Dui Hua involvement. Recently, in February 2004, the nun Phuntsog Nyidrol, who was serving seventeen years in prison, was released. Others who were released include:

- Ngawang Choephel, a Fulbright scholar and musicologist who was serving eighteen years for espionage
- Tagna Jigme Zangpo, imprisoned for a third time in 1983 and serving the longest sentence of Tibetan political prisoners (twenty-eight years) and, at age seventy-seven, the oldest
- Ngawang Sangdrol, a nun from Garu nunnery serving a total twenty-one-year sentence, including multiple extensions for political recalcitrance in prison

The possibilities for civil society in Tibet to engage in conflict resolution activities are even more circumscribed than the work of NGOs. Organized action taken at a civil level is frequently perceived as opposing government policy and treated as a political attempt to undermine party control and therefore a threat to stability.

Environmental groups are the most tolerated sector of organized civil society in China, but even these groups have to operate within strict parameters. During the past decade, environmental NGOs have played a role as intermediaries between the state and local communities in the implementation of ecological protection projects. NGOs in major Chinese cities have called for greater protection of Tibetan wildlife and river sources, but no equivalent Tibetan NGOs exist.

The Chinese authorities maintain a tight rein over dissemination of information and the media remains under Communist Party control. Some societal and political issues are being discussed more openly, but only if the government recognizes them as problems and sees their resolution as crucial to the long-term health of the state and legitimacy of the party. Public discussion of issues such as Tibetan desires for separation from China would qualify as an official acknowledgment that Tibetans are dissatisfied. As a result, their coverage in the media remains framed within official propaganda.

Although lacking the power to resolve the root causes of the conflict, local figures have tried to manage and prevent conflict within their communities. Some local party and government leaders, for instance, have attempted to work within the system to preserve and develop Tibetan culture and traditions while keeping their political superiors satisfied. The following examples are from Tibetan areas outside the Tibet Autonomous Region, which tends to harbor the harshest, most repressive policies:

- When the Patriotic Education Campaign was implemented in monasteries in Qinghai province, starting in 1997, there were several reports of local officials seeking to defuse potential conflict. Finding themselves personally responsible for implementing policies that they knew would cause conflict and with which they did not agree (most Tibetans, including officials, still hold loyalties to the Dalai Lama), some attempted to persuade monks to pay lip service to official ideological demands. Others simply filed reports to higher authorities, telling them the campaign had been successfully implemented, while turning a blind eye to local noncompliance.[12]
- During the 1990s, resentment grew among nomads in Gansu province over gold-mining activities that were generating wealth for county officials but had degraded land and harmed livestock. Some of the younger nomads took direct action in protest, camping out at the mine site and halting production. The authorities sent religious and government leaders respected within the local community to mediate. The dispute was eventually resolved, without recourse to violence, after the announcement of a plan to increase the yearly payment from the mine to the township.

Monks and nuns have played a central role in resistance to Chinese control. They also constitute the majority of Tibet's political prisoners. However, religious leaders have also played an important role in promoting nonviolence and compromise to protect Tibetan interests. Best known was the tenth Panchen Lama, who worked within the system to prevent erasure of Tibetan culture, identity, and religion, and at the same time tried to find ways to promote economic development and relative autonomy.[13] Lesser-known figures have also used their positions of respect and devotion in similar ways to respond to and manage ethnic tensions within local communities.

Individuals outside the established power structure who have influence over local populations remain politically vulnerable. Official hostility toward religion makes the situation particularly sensitive for religious leaders. In recent years, several charismatic religious leaders with great potential to negotiate conflict resolution have been arrested including Tenzin Deleg Rinpoche and Sonam Phuntsog. Their arrests were linked to their religious and social activism and loyalty to the Dalai Lama. The authorities have displayed increasing concern in recent years over the influence of religious leaders and monasteries within local communities, viewing this as a threat to the legitimacy and control of local party and government leaders. One of the charges brought against Tenzin Deleg, who received a commuted death sentence in 2002, was that he illegally usurped the prerogatives of state power by settling local conflicts.

The possibilities and potential for civil society to play a meaningful role in conflict resolution within Tibet will largely depend on the extent and speed of political reform in China over the next decade. Despite the difficulties facing NGOs operating in Tibet, there are a growing number of projects and initiatives. The potential for foreign-funded development and environmental projects to become influential over the situation on the ground is likely to increase as China tries to attract foreign investment for its "Western Development Campaign." However, there is a high risk that such potential will be offset by the speed with which Tibet is being transformed as a result of the policies and interests of the central government.

Prospects

China's interests in Tibet and the opposing positions of the primary parties on the question of Tibet's status constitute a formidable barrier to conflict resolution. There is some room to maneuver over secondary causes of conflict, such as uneven development, but these issues are often firmly embedded in the conflict's ideological and political roots. As a result, progress in conflict transformation is difficult to achieve.

Since the Chinese government is the most important actor in conflict prevention, it is difficult for international organizations and other governments to have a broad impact on the situation in Tibet without China's cooperation. China's relatively strong international position means that it is not as susceptible to foreign pressure as much of the developing world is. Any potential solution to the conflict in Tibet will be influenced by China's geostrategic concerns, such as unresolved border issues and nuclear-potential conflict with India.

Political change and reform in China will strongly influence the potential for a long-lasting solution of mutual benefit to both parties. At present, Tibetans have little to bring to the negotiating table other than China's desire for prestige and international respect. There are signs that this desire has motivated some recent goodwill gestures from China—for example, the release of several high-profile political prisoners and the resumption of contact with exile officials. However, the barriers to effective long-term resolution remain high. Fragmentation of Chinese political interests could allow more room for Tibetans to intervene and negotiate for their own interests. However, while the current stalemate between Chinese and exile political forces ensues, there is little incentive for China to affect any long-lasting changes that would benefit Tibetans. As the far more powerful party to the conflict, China has time to prevaricate.

The effectiveness of conflict prevention initiatives will largely be determined by the rate of development of civil society in China and Tibet. The main gap and weakness in discussions over the future of Tibet is the exclusion from any open debate of Tibetans inside Tibet. For Tibetans, the situation is one of increasing urgency as fast-track development policies are pushed forward. Urbanization and economic development will probably intensify rather than eradicate Tibetan nationalism and resistance. The newly emerging educated Tibetan middle class is likely to be dissatisfied with economic benefits and will become more assertive in its demands for cultural autonomy. An increasing interest in Tibet among the Chinese middle class could also help to build bridges and deepen mutual understanding.

Recommendations

While civil society remains constrained by China's political structure, efforts should focus on local education and development for Tibetans within their communities. These efforts should coincide with initiatives to reach diplomatic solutions. Projects to strengthen Tibetan community life should be encouraged, as well as initiatives aimed at reducing Tibetan dependence on the central government with regard to the construction of schools and health clinics and investments to improve agriculture. Specific measures that are recommended include the following.

- The European Parliament should continue to seek ways to facilitate substantive dialogue between the Chinese government and the Dalai Lama and his representatives, following up on its July 2000 resolution by seeking further mechanisms to hold both parties accountable for moving the process forward.
- Western NGOs should keep Tibet questions visible and the idea of conflict resolution alive. They should research and produce good, balanced information. NGOs working in China should exchange information and analyze their work within the wider context of China and East Asia.

- NGOs should continue to encourage international financial institutions to make funding conditional on progress in addressing social and political problems that constitute violations of human rights and civil liberties, impede poverty alleviation and sustainable development, and restrict accountability of governance. Donors and investors should be made fully aware of the politicization of economic development in Tibetan areas and the conflict that this can cause.
- The authorities have publicly recognized the importance of environmental protection of the Tibetan plateau. This provides some leverage for NGOs to encourage the Chinese authorities, regional organizations (e.g., ASEAN), and international agencies (e.g., the World Bank, the World Food Programme, the UN Development Programme, the International Fund for Agricultural Development, the Asian Development Bank) to explore alternative paths to economic development and wealth creation in Tibetan areas, as advocated by some mainstream Chinese academics.
- Donor agencies and investors such as the World Bank should focus at the micro level on promoting and strengthening the capacities of local communities, particularly in rural areas, where most Tibetans live. They should work hard to educate and involve local communities to ensure that development is creating direct benefits for Tibetans, is meeting local needs, and is being carried out appropriately. Development programs should be environmentally sustainable and do nothing to encourage or facilitate an influx of nonindigenous persons.

Resources

Newsletters
World Tibet News (daily compilation of international press coverage on Tibet, prepared and distributed via e-mail by the Canada Tibet Committee; includes official Chinese press and Tibetan government-in-exile statements)

Reports
Tibet Information Network. The *Hostile Elements* series of reports on political imprisonment in Tibet, 1999, 2001, 2002. By Steven D. Marshall.
———. Reports on development: *China's Great Leap West*, 2000; *Mining Tibet*, 2002; *Delivery and Deficiency*, 2002.
Tibet Information Network and Human Rights Watch/Asia. *Cutting off the Serpent's Head: Tightening Control in Tibet, 1994–1995*. London: Tibet Information Network, 1996.
Tibetan Center for Human Rights and Democracy. Annual reports on human rights and monthly newsletter.
Tibetan government-in-exile. Department of International Relations newsletter *Tibet Bulletin* and reports on human rights, development, and the environment.

Other Publications
China and Its National Minorities: Autonomy or Assimilation? By Thomas Heberer. New York: M. E. Sharpe, 1989.
The Dragon in the Land of Snows: A History of Modern Tibet Since 1947. By Tsering Shakya. London: Pimlico, 1999.
A Poisoned Arrow. Translation of the tenth Panchen Lama's 80,000-character petition. London: Tibet Information Network, 1997.

Resistance and Reform in Tibet. Eds. Robert Barnett and Shirin Akiner. London: Hurst/Bloomington: University of Indiana Press, 1994.

Tibet Outside the TAR. By Susette Cooke and Steven D. Marshall. CD-ROM published by the authors, 1997.

Tibetan Nation: A History of Tibetan Nationalism and Sino-Tibetan Relations. By Warren W. Smith Jr. Boulder: Westview, 1996.

Websites

www.tibet.com, www.tibet.net, www.tibetnews.com (websites of the Tibetan government-in exile)

www.tibetinfo.net (Tibet Information Network)

www.tibetinfor.com (Chinese perspective on Tibet and daily news bulletins)

www.tibetjustice.org (Tibet Justice Center, formerly the International Committee of Lawyers for Tibet; website contains documents on the Tibet issue)

Resource Contacts

Youdon Aukatsang, independent Tibet specialist, e-mail: yennyla@yahoo.com

Robert Barnett, lecturer in modern Tibetan studies, East Asian Institute no. 939, Columbia University, 420 W. 118th, New York, NY 10027, tel: 212 854 1725

Jane Caple, e-mail: jane_caple@yahoo.co.uk

Kate Saunders, independent Tibet specialist, e-mail: ks@insidetibet.net

Organizations

Dui Hua Foundation
850 Powell St.
Suite 404
San Francisco, CA 94108
www.duihua.org

Tibet Foundation
1 St. James's Market
London SW1Y 4SB, UK
tel: +44 20 7930 6001
fax: +44 20 7930 6002
e-mail: enquiries@tibet-foundation.org

Tibetan Government-in-Exile
Department of Information and International Relations
Central Tibetan Administration
Dharamsala 176215 (H.P.) India
e-mail: admin@tibetnews.com

Tibet Information Network (TIN)
188-196 Old St.
London, EC1V 9FR, UK
tel: +44 207 814 9011
fax: +44 207 814 9015
e-mail: tin@tibetinfo.net

Tibetan Center for Human Rights and Democracy
Top Floor, Narthang Building
Gangchen Kyishong
Dharamsala 176 215 (H.P.) India
tel: +91 1892 23363
fax: +91 1892 24957
e-mail: dsala@tchrd.org

Tibetan Women's Association
Central Executive Committee
Bhagsunath Rd.
P.O. Mcleod Ganj, Dharamsala-176219
Kangra (H.P) India
tel: +91 1892 221527/221198
fax: +91 1892 221528
e-mail: twa@del2.vsnl.net.in

Jane Caple has been researching and writing about China and Tibet for the last decade, with a particular focus in recent years on political and socioeconomic issues in contemporary Tibet. She worked for four years at the independent Tibet Information Network in London. Her most recent publication is a comprehensive study of mineral exploitation in Tibetan areas under the administration of the People's Republic of China.

Notes

1. These areas do not just refer to the Tibetan Autonomous Region, but include all Tibetan areas under the administration of the People's Republic of China. China's strategic position in the region is strengthened by its ability to militarize areas like Tibet and Xinjiang, including placement of nuclear weapons. Tibet's strategic position serves as a buffer zone in the region, particularly between China and India. China can place weapons within relatively short range of India's capital and population centers, whereas the lowly populated, but vast expanse of Tibet provides a buffer for China's population centers.

2. It should be noted that the Tibet government-in-exile's territorial claims include the whole of ethnographic Tibet (i.e., including Amdo and Kham—areas outside the control of the original Lhasa government) and include areas that are predominantly inhabited by other nationalities, for example Mongols, Tu, and Salar.

3. UNHCR figures. Although many of these Tibetans are refugees, it should be noted that some only leave temporarily, to go to India on pilgrimage, to educate their children in the Tibetan exile schools in India, or to visit family in exile.

4. According to law, autonomous areas must "place the interests of the state as a whole above anything else and make positive efforts to fulfil the tasks assigned by state organs at higher levels." Article 7 of the Regional National Autonomy Law of the People's Republic of China, 1984, amended 2001.

5. For more information, see Steven D. Marshall, *Hostile Elements* (London: Tibet Information Network, 1999).

6. See, for example, Hu Angang and Wen Jun, *The Problem of Selecting the Correct Path for Tibetan Modernisation* (Beijing: China Tibetology, 2001–2001), pp. 3–26. Hu Angang is a professor of the Development Research Academy for the Twenty-First Century at Qinghua University, Beijing. Since 2000, he has been a commissioner on the Experts Commission on Territory Resources of the Chinese Academy of Sciences. For a discussion of the views of Hu Angang and other Chinese academics, see *Mining Tibet* (London: Tibet Information Network, 2002) and *China's Great Leap West* (London: Tibet Information Network, 2000).

7. See, for example, the UN Development Programme's 2002 *Human Development Report on China,* which places Tibetan areas among the lowest in China according to its Human Development Index (taking into account life expectancy, education, and income).

8. *A Struggle of Blood and Fire* (London: Tibet Information Network, 1999).

9. Put forward at the European Parliament in Strasbourg and sometimes referred to as the "Strasbourg proposal."

10. See *Propaganda and the West,* Tibet Information Network special report (London: Tibet Information Network, 2000).

11. *Western Hypocrisy and Chinese Diplomacy* (New York: Human Rights Watch, 1999).

12. For further details, see *A Sea of Bitterness: Patriotic Education in Qinghai Monasteries* (London: Tibet Information Network, 1999).

13. See *A Poisoned Arrow: The Secret Report of the Tenth Panchen Lama* (London: Tibet Information Network, 1997).

8.3.6

Xinjiang: History, Cultural Survival, and the Future of the Uyghur

Dru C. Gladney

In 2002, both the United States and the United Nations supported China's claim that an organization known as the East Turkistan Islamic Movement (ETIM) should be recognized as an international terrorist organization.[1] It is important to note, however, that China makes little distinction between separatists, terrorists, and civil rights activists—whether they are Uyghur, Tibetans, Taiwanese, or Falun Gong Buddhists. One person's terrorist may be another's freedom fighter. Are the restive Uyghur of Xinjiang terrorists, separatists, or freedom fighters? How can the incidents of recent years be seen in terms of patterns of cooperation and opposition to Chinese rule in the region?

Chinese histories notwithstanding, every Uyghur firmly believes that their ancestors were the indigenous people of the Tarim Basin, which did not become known in Chinese as *Xinjiang* (New Dominion) until the eighteenth century. Nevertheless, the identity of the present people known as Uyghur is a rather recent phenomenon related to great game rivalries, Sino-Soviet geopolitical maneuverings, and Chinese nation building. While a collection of nomadic steppe peoples known as the Uyghur have existed since before the eighth century, this identity was lost from the fifteenth to the twentieth century.

It was not until the fall of the Turkish Khanate (C.E. 552–744) to a people reported by the Chinese historians as *Hui-he* or *Hui-hu* that we find the beginnings of the Uyghur empire. At this time the Uyghur were only a collection of nine nomadic tribes.[2] Gradual sedentarization of the Uyghur, and their defeat of the Turkish Khanate, occurred precisely as trade with the unified Chinese Tang state became especially lucrative. The traditional shamanistic Turkic-speaking Uyghur came increasingly under the influence of Persian Manichaeanism, Buddhism, and eventually Nestorian Christianity. Extensive trade and military alliances along the old Silk Road with the Chinese state developed to the extent that the Uyghur gradually adopted cultural, dress, and even agricultural practices from the Chinese.

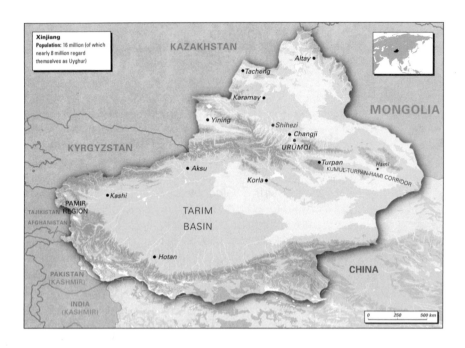

Xinjiang
Population: 16 million (of which nearly 8 million regard themselves as Uyghur)

KAZAKHSTAN

Altay •

•Tacheng

Karamay •

• Yining   •Shihezi
            • Changji
MONGOLIA

KYRGYZSTAN   URÜMQI

            •Turpan   Hami
            KUMUL-TURPAN-HAMI CORRIDOR

    • Aksu
         Korla •

•Kashi

PAMIR
TAJIKISTAN REGION   TARIM
AFGHANISTAN   BASIN

    • Hotan

PAKISTAN   CHINA
(KASHMIR)

INDIA
(KASHMIR)

0   250   500 km

Until major migration of Han Chinese was encouraged in the mid-nineteenth century, the Qing emperors were mainly interested in pacifying the region by setting up military outposts that supported a vassal-state relationship. Colonization was cut short by the Yakub Beg rebellion (1864–1877),[3] the fall of the Qing empire in 1911, and the ensuing warlord era that dismembered the region until its incorporation as part of the People's Republic in 1949. Competition for the loyalties of the peoples of the oases further contributed to divisions among the Uyghur according to political, religious, and military lines. The peoples of the oases, until the challenge of nation-state incorporation, lacked any coherent sense of identity.

Thus the incorporation of Xinjiang for the first time into a nation-state required unprecedented delineation of the so-called nations involved. The reemergence of the label "Uyghur," though arguably inappropriate as it was last used 500 years previously to describe the largely Buddhist population of the Turfan Basin, stuck as the appellation for the settled Turkic-speaking Muslim oasis dwellers. It has never been disputed by the people themselves or the states involved. For Uyghur nationalists today, the direct lineal descent from the Uyghur kingdom in seventh-century Mongolia is accepted as fact, despite overwhelming historical and archaeological evidence to the contrary.[4]

The end of the Qing dynasty and the rise of great game rivalries between China, Russia, and Britain saw the region torn by competing loyalties and marked by two short-lived and drastically different attempts at independence: one in Kashgar in 1933, with proclamations of an "East Turkistan Republic," and another in Yining (Ghulje) in 1944.[5] These rebellions and attempts at self-rule did little to bridge competing differences within the Turkic Muslim people who became officially known as the Uyghur in 1934 under successive Chinese Kuomintang (KMT) warlord administrations.[6] Andrew Forbes describes the great cleavages during the period from 1911 to 1949 that pitted Muslim against Chinese, Muslim against Muslim, Uyghur against Uyghur, Hui against Uyghur, Uyghur against Kazak, warlord against commoner, and Nationalist against Communist.[7] This extraordinary factionalism caused large-scale destruction of lives and resources in the region, which still lives in the minds of the population. Indeed, it is this memory that many argue keeps the region together, a deep-seated fear of widespread social disorder.

Today, despite continued regional differences, there are nearly 8 million people spread throughout the area that regard themselves as Uyghur.[8] Many of them dream of, and some agitate for, an independent "Uyghuristan." The "nationality" policy under the KMT identified five peoples of China, with the Han in the majority. The Uyghur were included at that time under the general rubric of "Hui Muslims," which included all Muslim groups in China. This policy was continued under the Communists, eventually recognizing fifty-six nationalities, the Uyghur, and eight other Muslim groups split out from the general category "Hui" (which was confined to mainly Chinese-speaking Muslims).

A profoundly practical people, Uyghur and regional leaders actually invited the People's Liberation Army (PLA) into the region after the defeat of the Nationalists in 1949. The "peaceful liberation" by the Chinese Communists of Xinjiang in October 1949, and their subsequent establishment of the Xinjiang Uyghur Autonomous Region on October 1, 1955, perpetuated the Nationalist policy of recognizing the Uyghur as a minority nationality under Chinese rule. The ongoing political uncertainties and social unrest, however, led to large migrations of Uyghur and Kazak from Xinjiang to Central Asia between 1953 and 1963, culminating in a Central Asian Uyghur population of approximately 300,000. This migration stopped with the Sino-Soviet split in 1962 and the border was closed in 1963, reopening twenty-five years later.[9]

The separate nationality designation awarded the Uyghur in China continued to mask very considerable regional and linguistic diversity, with the designation also applied to many "non Uyghur" groups. At the same time, contemporary Uyghur separatists look back to the brief periods of independent self-rule, in addition to the earlier glories of the Uyghur kingdoms in Turpan and Karabalghasan, as evidence of their rightful claims to the region. Contemporary Uyghur separatist organizations all share a common vision of a continuous Uyghur claim on the region, disrupted by Chinese and Soviet intervention. The independence of the former Soviet Central Asian republics in 1991 has done much to encourage them, despite the fact that the new, mainly Muslim, Central Asian governments all signed protocols with China in Shanghai in the spring of 1996 that they would not harbor or support separatists' groups. These protocols were reaffirmed in the August 25, 1999, meeting between Boris Yeltsin and Jiang Zemin, committing the "Shanghai Five" nations (China, Russia, Kazakhstan, Kyrgyzstan, Tajikistan) to respecting border security and suppressing terrorism, drug smuggling, and separatism.[10] The policy was enforced on June 15, 1999, when three alleged Uyghur separatists were deported from Kazakhstan to China, with several others in Kyrgyzstan and Kazakhstan awaiting extradition.[11]

In terms of religion, the Uyghur are Sunni Muslims, practicing Islamic traditions similar to their co-religionists in the region. In addition, many of them are Sufi, adhering to branches of Naqshbandiyya Central Asian Sufism. However, Islam was only one of several unifying markers for Uyghur identity, depending on those with whom they were in cooperation at the time. This suggests that Islamic fundamentalist groups such as the Taliban in Afghanistan will have only limited appeal among the Uyghur. For example, to the Hui Muslim Chinese in Xinjiang, numbering over 600,000, the Uyghur distinguish themselves as the legitimate autochthonous minority, since both share a belief in Sunni Islam. In contrast to the formerly nomadic Muslim peoples, such as the Kazak, numbering more than 1 million, the Uyghur might stress their attachment to the land and oasis of origin. Modern Uyghur are marked by their reaction to Chinese influence and incorporation. It is often Islamic traditions that become the focal point for Uyghur efforts to preserve their culture and history. One such popular tradition that has resurfaced in recent years is that of the Mashrap, whereby generally young Uyghur gather to recite poetry and sing songs, dance, and share traditional foods. These evening events have often become foci for Uyghur resistance to Chinese rule. However, Uyghur continue to be divided from within, as evidenced by the attack in May 1996 on

Kashgar/Xinjiang. Muslim family walking past the gleaming concrete statue of Chairman Mao in this northwestern China city.

Chris Stowers/Panos Pictures

the imam of Idgah Mosque in Kashgar by other Uyghur, as well as the assassination of at least six Uyghur officials in September 2003. It is this contested understanding of history that continues to influence much of the current debate over separatist and Chinese claims to the region.

Minority Nationalities Policy

The Uyghur are an official minority nationality of China, identified as the second-largest of ten Muslim peoples in China. The fact that over 99.8 percent of the Uyghur population is located in Xinjiang, whereas other Muslim peoples of China have significant populations in other provinces (e.g., the Hui) and outside the country (e.g., the Kazak), contributes to the important sense of belonging to the land, despite the fact that the early Uyghur kingdom was based in what is now Outer Mongolia and the present region of Xinjiang is under the control of the Chinese state.

Unprecedented sociopolitical integration of Xinjiang into the Chinese nation-state has taken place in the last forty years. While Xinjiang has been under Chinese political domination since the defeat of the Zungar in 1754, until the middle of the twentieth century it was but loosely incorporated into China proper. The extent of the incorporation of the Xinjiang region into China is indicated by Chinese policies encouraging Han migration, communication, education, and occupational shifts since the 1940s. Han migration into Xinjiang increased their local population enormously between 1940 and 1982, with an average annual growth of 8.1 percent. Indeed, many conclude that China's primary program for assimilating its border regions is a policy of integration through immigration.[12] This was certainly the case for Inner Mongolia, where the Mongol population now stands at 14 percent.

The increase of the Han population has been accompanied by the growth and delineation of other Muslim groups. While the Hui population in Xinjiang increased with an average annual growth of 4.4 percent between 1940 and 1982, the Uyghur population has followed a more natural biological growth of 1.7 percent. This dramatic increase in the Hui population has also led to significant tensions between the Hui and Uyghur Muslims in the region, and many Uyghur recall the massacre of the Uyghur residents in Kashgar by the Hui Muslim warlord Ma Zhongying and his Hui soldiers during the early 1930s.[13] These tensions are exacerbated by widespread beliefs held among the exile Uyghur community and international Muslims that the Chinese authorities vastly underreport the Muslim populations of China. Some Uyghur groups claim that there are upwards of 20 million Uyghur in China, and nearly 50 million Muslims, with little evidence to support those figures.[14]

Chinese incorporation of Xinjiang has led to a further development of ethnic socioeconomic niches. The 1982 census revealed vast differences in socioeconomic structure. Differences in occupational structure between the Uzbek and Tatar on the one hand, and the Uyghur and Hui on the other, suggest important class differences, with the primarily urban Uzbek and Tatar groups occupying a much higher socioeconomic niche.

However, among the elderly elite, there continues to be a high standard of traditional expertise in Persian, Arabic, Chagatay, and the Islamic sciences, which is not considered part of Chinese "culture" and education. Although elementary and secondary education is offered in Uyghur, Mandarin has become the language of upward mobility. Many Uyghur have been trained in the thirteen nationalities colleges scattered throughout China. It is these secular intellectuals trained in Chinese schools who are asserting political leadership in Xinjiang, as opposed to traditional religious elites. Many Uyghur in Urumqi point to the establishment of the Uyghur Traditional Medicine Hospital and Madrassah complex in 1987 as a beginning counterbalance to this emphasis on Han education.[15] However, most Uyghur feel that their history and traditional culture continues to be downplayed in the state schools and must be privately reemphasized to their children. It is through the elementary schools that Uyghur children first participate formally in the Chinese nation-state, dominated by Han history and language, and most fully enter into the Chinese world. As such, the predominant educational practice of teaching a centralized, mainly Han, subject content, despite the widespread use of minority languages, continues to drive a wedge between the Uyghur and their traditions, inducting them further into the Han Chinese milieu.

The increased incorporation of Xinjiang into the political sphere of China has not only led to the further migration of Han and Hui into the region, but also opened China to an unprecedented extent for the Uyghur. Uyghur men are heavily involved in long-distance trade throughout China. As Uyghur continue to travel throughout China, they return to Xinjiang with a firmer sense of their own pan-Uyghur identity. International travel has also resumed for the Uyghur. An important development in recent years has been the opening of a rail line between China and Kazakhstan through the Ili corridor to Almaty, and the opening of several official gateways with the surrounding five nations on its borders. With the resumption of normal Sino–Central Asian relations in 1991, trade and personal contacts have expanded enormously.

Conflict Dynamics

After denying the problem for decades and stressing instead China's "national unity," official Chinese reports and the state-run media began in early 2001 to detail terrorist activities in the regions officially known as the Xinjiang Uyghur Autonomous Region.[16] Until then, the term "Eastern Turkistan" was not allowed to be used in the official media. Anyone found using the term could be arrested, even though this is the term that Uyghur and other Turkic-speaking peoples most often use outside China to refer to the region. In the northwestern Uyghur Autonomous Region of Xinjiang, there has been an ongoing series of incidents of terrorism and separatism since the large riot in the Xinjiang town of Yining of February 1997, with multiple crackdowns and arrests that have rounded up thousands of terrorist suspects, large weapons caches, and printed documents allegedly outlining future public acts of violence.[17] Amnesty International has claimed that these roundups have led to hurried public trials and immediate, summary executions of possibly thousands of locals. One estimate suggested that in a country known for its frequent executions, Xinjiang had the highest number, averaging 1.8 per week, most of them Uyghur.[18] In his April 16, 2002, speech to the UN High Commission in Geneva, Enver Can, president of the East Turkistan (Uighuristan) National Congress, based in Munich, claimed that between 1997 and 1999, 210 death sentences were recorded. Since September 11, 2001, claims have been made that arrests and executions have increased, but there is little accurate documentation. The Uyghur service of Radio Free Asia (RFA) announced a January 2002 roundup of 350 suspected Uyghur separatists in Xinjiang.[19]

Troop movements to the area, related to the nationwide campaign against crime known as "Strike Hard," launched in 1998, which included the call to erect a "great wall of steel" against separatists in Xinjiang, were reportedly the largest since the suppression of the Akto insurrection in April 1990 (the first major uprising that initiated a series of unrelated and sporadic protests).[20] Alleged incursions of Taliban fighters through the Wakhan corridor into China, where Xinjiang shares a narrow border with Afghanistan, led to the area receiving increased Chinese security forces and large military exercises, beginning at least one month prior to the September 11, 2001, terrorist attacks in the United States. Under U.S. and Chinese pressure, Pakistan returned one Uyghur activist to China, apprehended among hundreds of Taliban detainees, which follows a pattern of repatriations of suspected Uyghur separatists from Kazakhstan, Kyrgyzstan, and Uzbekistan.[21]

In 1997, bombs exploded on two buses on March 7 (killing two) and in a city park in Beijing on May 13 (killing one), as well as in the northwestern border city of Urumqi, the capital of Xinjiang, on February 25 (killing nine), with over thirty other bombings in 1999 and six in Tibet alone. Most of these are thought to have been related to demands by Muslim and Tibetan separatists. Eight members of the Uyghur Muslim minority were executed on May 29, 1997, for alleged bombings in northwest China, with hundreds arrested on suspicion of taking part in ethnic riots and engaging in separatist activities. Though sporadically reported since the early 1980s, such incidents have been increasingly common since 1997 and are documented in a recent scathing report of Chinese government policy in the region by Amnesty International.[22] A report in the *Wall Street Journal* of the arrest on August 11, 1999, of Rebiya Kadir, a well-known Uyghur businesswoman, during a visit by the U.S. Congressional Research Service delegation to the region, indicates that China's random arrests have not diminished since the report, and that China is unconcerned with Western criticism.[23] Interestingly, however, despite this history of ethnic tensions, unrest, and terrorism in the late 1990s, there has been very little documented activity since that restive period.

Most confirmed incidents have been directed against Han Chinese security forces, recent Han Chinese émigrés to the region, and even Uyghur Muslims perceived to be too closely collaborating with the Chinese government. Most analysts agree that China is not vulnerable to the same ethnic separatism that split the former Soviet Union. But few doubt that should China fall apart, it would divide, like the Soviet Union, along centuries-old ethnic, linguistic, regional, and cultural fault lines.[24] If China did fall apart, Xinjiang would split in a way that, according to Anwar Yusuf, president of the Eastern Turkistan National Freedom Center in Washington, D.C., "would make Kosovo look like a birthday party." It should be noted that due to this fear of widespread civil disorder, Yusuf indicated that the Eastern Turkistan National Freedom Center did not support a free and independent Xinjiang.[25] On June 4, 1999, Yusuf met with President Bill Clinton to press for fuller support for the Uyghur cause.[26]

Estimates differ widely on the number of Uyghur living outside of China in the diaspora. Uyghur in Central Asia are not always well represented in the state censuses, particularly since 1991. Yitzhak Shichor estimates approximately 500,000 living abroad, about 5–6 percent of the total world Uyghur population.[27] Uyghur websites differ dramatically on the official Uyghur population numbers, from up to 25 million Uyghur inside Xinjiang, to up to 10 million in the diaspora.[28]

International campaigns for Uyghur rights and possible independence have become increasingly vocal and well organized, especially on the Internet. Repeated public appeals have been made to Abdulahat Abdurixit, the Uyghur people's government chairman of Xinjiang in Urumqi. International organizations are increasingly including Uyghur indigenous voices from the expatriate Uyghur community. Notably, the 1995 elected chair of the Unrepresented Nations and Peoples Organization, based in The Hague, is an Uyghur: Erkin Alptekin, son of the separatist leader, Isa Yusuf Alptekin.[29] Supporting primarily an audience of mostly expatriate Uyghur, there are at least twenty-five international organizations and websites working for the independence of "Eastern Turkistan," based in Amsterdam, Munich, Istanbul, Melbourne, Washington, D.C., and New York. This growing influence of "cyber separatism" is of increasing concern to Chinese authorities.

Supported largely by Uyghur émigrés who left China prior to the Communist takeover in 1949, these organizations maintain a plethora of websites and activities that take a primarily negative view of Chinese policies in the region. Although not all organizations advocate independence or separatism, the vast majority of them do press for radical change in the region, reporting not only human rights violations, but also environmental degradation, economic imbalances, and alternative histories of the region. In general, these websites can be divided roughly into those that are mainly information-based and others that are politically active advocacy sites.[30]

Although most of these websites have limited funding and circulation, they should not be dismissed as forming only a "virtual" community without any substantial impact on events within Xinjiang. These websites have served as an important source of information not available in the official Chinese media. While cyber-separatism would never be able on its own to unseat a local government, it is clear that it does link like-minded individuals and raise consciousness about issues that were often inaccessible to the general public.

For an isolated region such as Xinjiang, and the widely dispersed Uyghur diaspora, the Internet has dramatically altered the way the world sees the region. The Chinese state must respond to issues within it.

The East Turkistan Islamic Movement was recognized by the United Nations in October 2002 as an international terrorist organization responsible for domestic and international terrorist acts, which China claimed included a bombing of the Chinese consulate in Istanbul and assassinations of Chinese officials in Bishkek and Uighur officials in Kashgar thought to be in collaboration with Chinese officialdom.[31] China and the United States, however, presented little public evidence to positively link ETIM with the specific incidents described.[32] In 2001 the U.S. State Department released a report that documented several separatist and terrorist groups operating inside the region and abroad, militating for an independent Xinjiang.[33]

The list included the United Revolutionary Front of Eastern Turkistan, whose leader, Yusupbek Mukhlisi, claims to have thirty armed units with "20 million" Uyghur primed for an uprising; the Home of East Turkistan Youth, said to be linked to Hamas, with a reported 2,000 members; the Free Turkistan Movement, whose leader, Abdul Kasim, is said to have led the 1990 Baren uprising; the Organization for the Liberation of Uighuristan, whose leader, Ashir Vakhidi, is said to be committed to fighting the Chinese "occupation" of the "Uighur homeland"; and the so-called Wolves of Lop Nor, who have claimed responsibility for various bombings and uprisings. The State Department report claims that all of these groups have tenuous links with Al-Qaida, the Taliban, the Hizb-ut-Tahrir ("Islamic Revival"), and the Tableeghi Jamaat. Many of these groups, but not ETIM, were listed in the Chinese report that came out in early 2002. It came as some surprise, therefore, when at the conclusion of his August 2002 visit to Beijing, Deputy Secretary of State Richard Armitage identified ETIM as the leading Uyghur group to be targeted as an international terrorist group.[34] At the time, very few people, including activists deeply engaged in working for an independent East Turkistan, had ever heard of ETIM. Even the U.S. military did not seem to be aware of the group.[35]

Many Uyghur have complained that they do not see the United States ever siding with China in condemning a Tibetan independence organization as terrorist. The real issue is that there are Uyghur-related activist groups that can be said to support terrorism, but cannot be directly implicated in any specific incident.

The Chinese State Council issued its own report on January 21, 2002, charging that from 1990 to 2001 various Uyghur separatist groups "were responsible for over 200 terrorist incidents in Xinjiang" that resulted in the deaths of 162 people and injuries to 440 others. The report, titled *East Turkestan Terrorist Forces Cannot Get Away With Impunity,* also dismissed allegations that Beijing had used the U.S.-led war on terror as a pretext to crack down on Uyghur. The report condemned numerous Uyghur groups. These organizations and many of the Internet news and information organizations have rarely if ever claimed responsibility for any specific action, though many are sympathetic to isolated incidents regarded as challenges to Chinese rule in the region. Interestingly, there seems to be very little support for radical Islam, and a search for the term *jihad* (holy war) turns up almost no instances, nor any calls for a religious war against the Chinese. Many of the Uyghur nationalists are quite secular in their orientation, and overthrow of Chinese rule is related to issues of sovereignty and human rights, rather than those of religion. By contrast, Uyghur expatriates tend to be quite religious, yet they rarely call for a holy war against the Chinese.[36]

Since September 11, 2001, very few groups have publicly advocated terrorism against the Chinese state, and most have denied any involvement in terrorist activities, though they may express sympathy for such activities.[37] Chinese authorities are clearly concerned that increasing international attention to the treatment of its minority and dissident peoples has put pressure on the region, with the United States and many Western governments continuing to criticize China for not adhering to its commitments. In 2002, China ratified the International Covenant on Economic, Social, and Cultural Rights. Article 1 of the covenant states: "All peoples have the right of self-determination. By virtue of that right they freely determine their political status and freely pursue their economic, social and cultural development." Although China continues to quibble with the definition of "people," it is clear that the agreements are pressuring China to answer criticisms by high-ranking human rights advocates about its treatment of minority peoples. Clearly, with Xinjiang representing the last Muslim region under communism, large trade contracts with Middle Eastern Muslim nations, and five Muslim nations on its western borders, Chinese authorities have more to be concerned about than just international support for human rights.

On December 15, 2003, two days after the capture of Saddam Hussein, China issued a list of four "terrorist" groups and eleven individuals, all of them living abroad, calling for international help to wipe them out. The groups identified were ETIM, the Eastern Turkistan Liberation Organization, the World Uighur Youth Congress, and the East Turkistan Information Center. The last two groups, both based in Germany, have been operating legally for years. It has not been made clear why these groups were singled out, unless it was for the political purpose of strengthening U.S.-China relations. On December 22, 2003, Hasan Mahsum, one of the eleven people labeled as wanted terrorists, dubbed China's most-wanted man by the Ministry of Public Security, was killed in a joint Pakistani-U.S. operation, according to the Chinese state agency Xinhua. The ministry maintained that Mahsum's movement was responsible for a series of robberies and murders in Xinjiang in 1999, which left six people dead. It maintained also that his organization raised funds through drug and weapon smuggling, kidnapping, blackmail, and robbery. Osama bin Laden was said to have also supplied the group with millions of dollars. The *Oxford Analytica* report on the ETIM issue concludes that ETIM and other "scapegoat terrorists" are only a "dubious threat" and have been used as an excuse for increased repression.[38] Interestingly, the Mukhlisi's United

Revolutionary Front was not included, despite its frequent claims of responsibility for violent acts in Xinjiang. Human rights groups accused China of using counterterrorism to punish Uyghur who were exercising peaceful dissent.

Official Conflict Management

Although the 1931 Communist Party constitution recognized the right of self-determination of the minorities in China—including their right to separation and to the formation of an independent state—this commitment was not kept after the Communists came to power in 1949. China's policy toward the Uyghur and other minorities involves official recognition, limited autonomy, and unofficial efforts at control. Maintenance of national unity and social stability is China's main concern in Xinjiang, even more important than economic development. Beijing considers Uyghur activists as "terrorists," comparing them to the armed resistance in Chechnya and Middle Eastern militants. Interference of external actors in China's "internal affairs" is not accepted.

The United Nations maintained a very critical position toward China's Xinjiang policy during the mandate of Mary Robinson as High Commissioner for Human Rights. She said she feared that the Chinese regime was using the "war on terror" as a mere pretext to annihilate its internal opposition and to commit abuses against its own Muslim minority, trying to submit the Uyghur to forced assimilation.

The European Union (EU) has repeatedly expressed its concern about the violation of the cultural rights of the Uyghur people, on the same, somewhat rhetoric level as its concerns about Tibet and human rights in China in general. The EU is engaged in a "dialogue" on human rights with Beijing; sustaining this will be conductive to a gradual improvement. Critics affirm that this dialogue is nothing substantial.

The official U.S. attitude toward China's Xinjiang policy—that the fight against terrorism cannot be a pretext for violation of Uyghur rights—has been watered down considerably after September 11. The labeling by the U.S. government of ETIM as a terrorist group and its silence after Beijing's classification of three other Uyghur groups as terrorist, are clear indications that respect for human rights in Xinjiang has no priority anymore in Washington.

Following the breakup of the Soviet Union, the Chinese government feared that the new independence of the neighboring Central Asian republics might inspire separatist goals in Xinjiang. It also worried that promoting regional economic development could fuel ethnic separatism by resurrecting old alliances. China, however, was reassured by an agreement reached in April 1996 with Russia, Kazakhstan, Kyrgyzstan, and Tajikistan to avoid military conflict on common borders. It is also resting easier after assertions from Muslim states that they would not become involved in China's internal affairs. Thus China's policy of encouraging economic development while keeping a tight lid on political activism seems to have the support of neighboring governments, despite not satisfying the many demands of local and cross-border ethnic groups.

With the decline in trade with most Western nations after the Tiananmen massacre in the early 1990s, the importance of China's Middle Eastern trading partners rose considerably. This may account for the fact that China established diplomatic relations with Saudi Arabia in August 1990. In the face of a long-term friendship with Iraq, China went along with most of the UN resolutions in the war against Iraq. Although it abstained from Resolution 678, on supporting the ground war, China enjoys a fairly solid reputation in the Middle East as an untarnished source of low-grade weaponry and cheap, reliable labor. Recent press accounts have noted an increase in China's exportation of military hardware to the Middle East since the Gulf War.[39] But because China has a significant Muslim population, 20 million, any mishandling of its Muslim problems will alienate trading partners in the Middle East, who are primarily Muslim as well. Already, after the 1997 riot in Yining, which led to the death of at least nine Uyghur Muslims and the arrest of several hundred, Turkey's defense minister condemned China's handling of the issue. China responded by telling Turkey to not interfere in its internal affairs.

Since the breakup of the Soviet Union in 1991, China has also become an important competitor for influence in Central Asia and is expected to serve as a counterweight to Russia. China is already constructing such a link with rails and pipelines. Muslim nations on China's borders, though officially unsupportive of Uyghur separatists, may become increasingly critical of harsh treatment extended to fellow Turkic and Muslim co-religionists in China. However, the April 1996 signing of border agreements between China and the five neighboring Central Asian nations suggests that there is little hope that the Uyghur separatists will receive any official support from their Central Asian sympathizers. The importance of trade is the primary reason. In addition, none of the countries in the region wishes to have border problems with China. At a popular level, however, the Uyghur receive much sympathy from their Central Asian co-religionists, and there is a continuing flow of funds and materials through China's increasingly porous borders.

The Oil Factor

Opportunities in Xinjiang's energy sector attract many migrants from other parts of China. In 1993, with domestic oil consumption rising faster than production, China became a net importer of oil for the first time.[40] As China develops into a modern economy, it should see a rise in demand comparable to that experienced in Japan, which is why it has begun to look elsewhere to meet its energy needs. Li Peng signed a contract in September 1997 for exclusive rights to Kazakhstan's second-largest oil field. This move also indicates declining expectations for China's own energy resources in the Tarim Basin, estimated ten years ago to have contained 482 billion barrels of oil. Today, even the president of China National Petroleum Corporation admits that there are known reserves of only 1.5 billion barrels.

China hopes to make up for its dependence on Kazakhstani oil by increasing trade, and China's two-way trade with Central Asia has increased dramatically since the Chinese government opened Xinjiang to the region following the collapse of the Soviet Union. Xinjiang has already become dependent on Central Asian business, with the five republics accounting for more than half of its international trade in 1993. Most China–Central Asia trade is between Xinjiang and Kazakhstan.

There is a risk that unrest in the Xinjiang Uyghur Autonomous Region could lead to a decline in outside oil investment and revenues, with such interests already operating at a loss. The World Bank currently has investments of over U.S.$780.5 million in fifteen projects in the Xinjiang Region alone, with some of that money allegedly going to the Xinjiang Production and Construction Corps (XPCC), which human rights activist Harry Wu has claimed employs prison *laogai* labor. Already, Treasury Secretary David A. Lipton has declared that the United States will no longer support World Bank projects associated with the XPCC. International companies and organizations may not wish to subject their employees and investors to social and political upheavals. China also recently canceled plans to build an oil pipeline from Kazakhstan to Xinjiang and inland China, citing lack of outside investment and questionable market returns.

Landlocked Central Asia and Xinjiang lack the road, rail, and pipeline infrastructure needed to increase economic cooperation and foreign investment in the region. New links from Central Asia could follow several routes west. All the routes pass through vast, remote, and perhaps politically unstable regions.

China's relations with its neighbors and with internal regions such as Xinjiang and Tibet have become increasingly important not only for the economic reasons discussed above, but also for China's desire to participate in international organizations such as the World Trade Organization and the Asia Pacific Economic Council. Uyghur have begun to work closely with Tibetans internationally to put political pressure on China in international forums. Their meetings are unable to force China to change its policy. Nevertheless, they continue to influence China's ability to cooperate internationally. As a result, China has sought to respond rapidly, and often militarily, to domestic ethnic affairs that might have international implications.

Despite increasing investment and many new jobs in Xinjiang, the Uyghur and other ethnic groups complain that they are not benefiting as much as recent Han immigrants to the region. They insist that the growing number of Han Chinese not only take the jobs and eventually the profits back home with them, but also dilute the indigenous people's traditional way of life and leave them with little voice in their own affairs.

Multi-Track Diplomacy

Civil society, with its nongovernmental organizations (NGOs) and its small and medium-size private enterprises, is on the rise in the rest of China; in Xinjiang, however, it is next to nonexistent.[41] The only well-organized Uyghur force, the religious movement, is under strict government control. Religious leaders who have good connections with moderate Islamic leaders outside China—which is wooing the Arab world because of its oil—could become a driving force behind a peace process, but are unable to fulfill that role at the moment. NGOs identified with Uygur activity of any kind are also strictly controlled.

It seems next to impossible that initiatives coming from outside China to improve the situation in Xinjiang will succeed without some help from inside. And that seems thinkable only if major changes within the Communist Party were to take place, to allow the birth of different currents of opinion. Nevertheless, external NGOs can perhaps accelerate this process by stressing that China has nothing to lose and a lot to win—stability, development—by giving more autonomy to the Uyghur.

The lack of a civil society partly reflects the ongoing role and power of the Bingtuan Production and Construction Corps, a paramilitary force that controls about 40 percent of the economy, runs prisons and businesses, and is one reason why Xinjiang will not fall apart. The corps holds it together—a perpetual subterranean force of coercion. Another dimension of this coercion and lack of a civil society seems to be reflected in the persistence of the *hasha* system, so-called voluntary labor but in fact forced labor for a whole range of community tasks.

The position of women in Xinjiang in general is not very positive, notwithstanding the fact that there have been some interesting experiments with schools for Uyghur girls, founded by moderate religious people. A rich Uyghur businesswoman, Rebiye Kadeer, was hailed by the Han Chinese authorities as a shining example of the emancipation of Uyghur women—until the suspicion arose that she was a "separatist." In 1999 she received an eight-year jail sentence for sending newspaper articles from Xinjiang to relatives abroad.

An irritant to the Chinese government, but one of a few sources of information to Uighurs that addresses issues of human security, is Radio Free Asia. Created by the U.S. Congress in 1994 and incorporated in 1996, RFA currently broadcasts in many languages, including Uyghur. Although the service claims to adhere to the highest standards of journalism and aims to exemplify accuracy, balance, and fairness in its editorial content, local governments have often complained of bias in favor of groups critical to the regimes in power. The Uyghur service has been regularly blocked and criticized by the Chinese government, and has been cited in the past for carrying stories supportive of so-called separatists, especially the case of Rebiya Kadeer, but despite the new cooperation between the United States and China in the war on terrorism, the site has continued its regular broadcasting. Frequent Uyghur listeners to the program have complained that the site—since the increased Sino-U.S. cooperation on terrorism—no longer criticizes China as strongly or frequently for its treatment of Uyghur in Xinjiang.

Outside Xinjiang, there are a number of informational websites generally traceable to academic organizations. There are also many advocacy sites often run by exiled Uyghurs. Other than the United States, which supports the RFA Uyghur service, there is no other government that officially supports dissemination of information related to Uyghur human rights issues. However, many Uyghur organizations in the past have claimed sympathy and tacit support from Turkey, Saudi Arabia, Iran, Australia, Germany, France, the Netherlands, and Canada.

In addition to sites that focus on human rights abuses, there are advocacy sites that openly promote international support for Uyghur- and Xinjiang-related causes. These sites and organizations often take a strong and critical stance against Chinese rule in Xinjiang, giving voice, they say, to a "silent majority" of Uyghur in Xinjiang and abroad who advocate radical political reform, if not outright independence, in the region.[42]

Prospects

To an extent never seen before, the continued incorporation of Xinjiang into China has become inexorable, and perhaps irreversible. The need for the oil and mineral resources of the region means that Chinese influence will only grow. To be sure, the Uyghur are still oriented culturally and historically toward Central Asia in terms of religion, language, and ethnic custom, and interaction has increased in recent years due to the opening of the roads to Pakistan and Almaty. Certainly, pan-Turkism was appealing to some, but not all, Uyghur during the early part of the past century. Historical ties to Central Asia are strong. Turkey's late prime minister Turgut Özal espoused a popular Turkish belief when, on his first state visit to Beijing in 1985, he commented that the Turkish nation originated in what is now China. Yet separatist notions, while perhaps present, are not practicable. But if China should fail at the center, the peripheries will certainly destabilize, with Xinjiang and Tibet having the strongest prospects for separation. The problems facing Xinjiang, however, are much greater than those of Tibet if it were to become independent. Not only is it more integrated into the rest of China, but the Uyghur compose less than half of the population and are primarily located in the south, which has less industry and fewer natural resources, except for oil.

The history of Chinese-Muslim relations in Xinjiang has been one of relative peace and quiet, broken by enormous social and political disruptions. The opposition to Chinese rule in Xinjiang has not reached the level of resistance seen in Chechnya or the Middle East, but similar to the Basque separatists of the Euskadi ta Askatasuna (ETA) in Spain, or the former Irish Republican Army in Ireland and England, it is one that may erupt in limited, violent moments of terrorism and resistance. The admitted problem of Uyghur terrorism and dissent, even in the diaspora, is thus problematic for a government that wants to encourage integration and development in a region where the majority population are not only ethnically different, but also devoutly Muslim. How does a government integrate a strongly religious minority into a Marxist-capitalist system? China's policy of intolerance toward dissent and economic stimulus have not seemed to resolve this issue.

China's Uyghur separatists are small in number, poorly equipped, loosely linked, and vastly outgunned by the People's Liberation Army and People's Police. China's nine other official Muslim minorities do not in general support Uyghur separatism. Local support for separatist activities is ambivalent and ambiguous at best. Memories of mass starvation and widespread destruction during the Sino-Japanese and civil war, including intra-Muslim and Muslim-Chinese bloody conflicts, not to mention the chaotic horrors of the Cultural Revolution, are strong in the region. Many local activists are calling not for complete separatism or real independence, but generally express concerns over environmental degradation, nuclear testing, religious freedom, overtaxation, and recently imposed limits on childbearing. Many ethnic leaders are simply calling for "real" autonomy according to Chinese law for the five autonomous regions, each of which is led by a First Party secretary, each of whom is a Han Chinese controlled by Beijing.

Mosques are full in the region and pilgrimages to Mecca are often allowed for Uyghur and other Muslims. But recently there has been an increase of political control over spiritual leaders, and more restrictions have been put in place against mosque attendance by youth, students, and government officials. Travelers to Kashgar have reported a general resentment against state control of religion. Although Islamic extremism does not yet appear to have wide-spread appeal, especially among urban, educated Uyghur, the government has consistently rounded up any Uyghur suspected of being "too" religious, especially those identified as Sufis or the so-called Wahabbis. These periodic roundups, detentions, and public condemnations of terrorism and separatism have not erased the problem, but have forced it underground, or at least out of the public eye. During the 2001 Asia Pacific Economic Cooperation (APEC) meetings in Beijing, it was widely reported that Uyghur travelers were not allowed to stay in hotels in the city and often were prevented from boarding public buses due to fears of their supposed terrorist links.

Recommendations

Many positive policies, increased domestic and international investment, and extraordinarily heavy repression have not eradicated tension and unrest, which continue to simmer. It is clear that China needs a new approach to resolve tensions in the region. Purely Marxist and Keynesian economic development strategies are not enough. First of all, it is necessary to identify some fundamental, pragmatic reforms that Xinjiang needs, such as more autonomy and tolerance, less political and social discrimination, and freedom of culture and religion.

In a recent *Foreign Affairs* article, Chien-Peng Chung of the Singaporean Institute of Defense and Strategic Studies called for immediate political changes in the region to avoid further deterioration in ethnic relations.[43] To further this discussion, starting from the reforms mentioned above, I suggest some possible new models for Xinjiang's future, peaceful development, something that all Uyghur and Chinese, as well as the other twenty-four ethnic groups in the region, seem to want:

- *The Alaska model.* Award residents of Xinjiang direct dividends for returns on wealth derived from regional natural resources, in accord with

Article 2 of the International Covenant on Economic, Social, and Cultural Rights. By according benefits to all second- or third-generation residents of Xinjiang, China can perhaps obviate interethnic tensions in the region and deflect criticisms that recent nonlocal migrants "lured to the region" by a government interested in integration through immigration are the real beneficiaries of China's increased investment of the region.

- *The Scotland model.* Although it is clear that China would never consider granting full independence to the region (lest it lose its authority over Tibet and Taiwan as well), an approach that grants Xinjiang more control over its own resources and governance, while maintaining central control over national defense and international trade, would not only seem to make sense in the modern era, but also parallel traditional models of Chinese imperial control of the region under the last dynasty.

- *The Hawaii model.* China must find a way to allow its local peoples to legally, democratically, and officially express their concerns about the development process in the region, the future directions of tourism and trade, and the prospects for greater autonomy and sovereignty. There should be state and federal funding available for elected representatives of indigenous peoples that have real input into the legislative process, such as the elected Office of Hawaiian Affairs.

- *The Australia model.* Peoples regarded by themselves and international organizations as aboriginal and indigenous must have the right to address land and environmental rights issues, despite government disagreements about historical migration to the region. As yet, China's extremely beneficial special entitlement laws for the official minority nationalities, including nationwide bilingual education, exemption from many taxes and birth-planning restrictions, and educational advancement opportunities, apply only to those regarded by the state as designated official minorities, and not to those regarded as indigenous to a region or district (Korean migrants to Xinjiang have as many rights as Uyghur). China has no laws pertaining to indigenous rights, and often regards treaties relating to "peoples" as affecting all the peoples of China, including the Han majority, when their original intent was to alleviate suffering of underprivileged indigenes.

International observers and frequent visitors to the region are concerned that if China does not explore other options besides repression, restriction, and investment, millions of Uyghur Muslims might become increasingly marginalized and disenfranchised, encouraging some of the more disgruntled among them to look to the Intifada, the Taliban, or Al-Qaida for inspiration. This would not be in China's or the West's best interest in the region.

China is a sovereign state and, like all modern nations in the era of globalization, faces tremendous challenges from migration, economic imbalance, ethnic unrest, and cyber-separatism. Clearly, the Xinjiang model must be as unique to the region as the region is to China itself. Not unlike Hong Kong and Taiwan, the situation in Xinjiang, and possibly Tibet, calls for dramatic and creative solutions. The future of this vastly important region, which Owen Lattimore once called the "pivot of Asia," depends upon it. Since September 11, 2001, the entire region has once again become pivotal to the rest of the world.[44]

Resources

Reports

Amnesty International. *People's Republic of China: Gross Violations of Human Rights in the Xinjiang Uyghur Autonomous Region.* London, April 21, 1999.

Eastern Turkistan Information Center. *Kasakistan Government Deport Political Refugees to China.* Munich, June 15, 1999. Available at www.uygur.org/enorg/ reports99/990615.html.

―――. *Population of Eastern Turkistan: The Population in Local Records.* Munich, n.d. Available at www.uygur.org/enorg/turkistan/nopus.html.

Eastern Turkestani Union in Europe. *Brief History of the Uyghers.* N.d. Available at www.geocities.com/capitolhill/1730/buh.html.

International Taklamakan Human Rights Association (ITHRA). "How Has the Population Distribution Changed in Eastern Turkestan since 1949?" N.d. Available at www. taklamakan.org/uyghur-l/et_faq_pl.html.

People's Republic of China. Department of Population Statistics of State Statistical Bureau and Economic Department of State Nationalities Affairs Commission. *Zhongguo Minzu Renkou Ziliao (1990 Nian Renkou Pucha Shuju)* [Population of China's Nationality (Data of 1990 Population Census)]. Beijing: China Statistical Publishing House, 1994.

―――. National Population Census Office. *Major Figures of the Fourth National Population Census.* Vol. 4. Beijing: China Statistical Publishing House, 1991.

―――. National Population Census Office. *Population Atlas of China.* Hong Kong: Oxford University Press, 1987.

Articles

"Central Asia and Xinjiang, China: Emerging Energy, Economic, and Ethnic Relations." By James P. Dorian, Brett Wigdortz, and Dru Gladney. *Central Asian Survey* 16, no. 4 (1997): 461–486.

"China Arrests Noted Businesswoman in Crackdown in Muslim Region." By Ian Johnson. *Wall Street Journal,* August 18, 1999.

"China's Ethnic Reawakening." By Dru C. Gladney. *Asia Pacific Issues* no. 18 (1995): 1–8.

"China's 'War on Terror': September 11 and Uighur Separatism." By Chien-Peng Chung. *Foreign Affairs* 81, no. 4 (July–August 2002): 8–12.

"Ethnogenesis and Ethnic Identity in China: Considering the Uygurs and Kazakhs." By Dru C. Gladney. In Victor Mair, ed., *The Bronze Age and Early Iron Age People of Eastern Central Asia,* vol. 2. Washington, D.C.: Institute for the Study of Man, 1998, pp. 812–834.

"The Ethnogenesis of the Uyghur." By Dru C. Gladney. *Central Asian Survey* 9, no. 1 (1990): 1–28.

"Guanyu 1990 Nian Renkou Pucha Zhuyao de Gongbao" [Report Regarding the 1990 Population Census Primary Statistics]. *Renmin Ribao* [People's Daily] (Beijing), November 14, 1991.

"Introduction." By Victor Mair. In Victor Mair, ed., *The Bronze Age and Early Iron Age People of Eastern Central Asia,* vol. 2. Washington, D.C.: Institute for the Study of Man, 1998, pp. 1–40.

"Legal Reform and Minority Rights in China." By Barry Sautman. In Stuart Nagel, ed., *Handbook of Global Legal Policy.* New York: Marcel Dekker, 1999, pp. 49–80.
"Making Muslims in China: Education, Islamicization, and Representation." By Dru C. Gladney. In Gerard A. Postiglione, ed., *China's National Minority Education: Culture, State Schooling, and Development.* New York: Garland Press, 1999, pp. 55–94.
"Muslim and Central Asian Revolts." By Morris Rossabi. In Jonathan D. Spence and John E. Wills Jr., eds., *From Ming to Ch'ing.* New Haven: Yale University Press, 1979, pp. 169–199.
"Press Release." Turkistan News and Information Network, June 8, 1999.
"Russia, China, and Central Asian Leaders Pledge to Fight Terrorism, Drug Smuggling." By Rym Brahimi. CNN News Service, August 25, 1999. Available at www.uygur.org/enorg/wunn99/990825e.html.

Other Publications
Cambridge History of China. Vol. 6, *Alien Regimes and Border States (907–1368).* By Herbert Franke and Denis Twitchett. Cambridge: Cambridge University Press, 1994.
China's Changing Population. By Judith Banister. Stanford, Calif.: Stanford University Press, 1987.
China's Minorities: Integration and Modernization in the Twentieth Century. By Colin Mackerras. Hong Kong: Oxford University Press, 1994.
Ethnic Identity in China. By Dru C. Gladney. Fort Worth, Tex.: Harcourt Brace, 1998.
Exit Voice and Loyalty: Responses to Decline in Firms, Organizations, and States. By Aklbert O. Hirschman. Cambridge: Harvard University Press, 1972.
The Ili Rebellion: The Moslem Challenge to Chinese Authority in Xinjiang, 1944–1949. By Linda Benson. New York: M. E. Sharpe, 1990.
Making Majorities: Constituting the Nation in Japan, Korea, China, Malaysia, Fiji, Turkey, and the United States. By Dru C. Gladney. Stanford, Calif.: Stanford University Press, 1998.
Muslim Chinese: Ethnic Nationalism in the People's Republic of China. 2d ed. By Dru C. Gladney. Cambridge: Harvard University Press, 1996.
National Minority Policy in Southwest China, 1911–1965. By David Deal. Ph.D. diss., University of Washington, 1971.
Oasis Identities: Uyghur Nationalism Along China's Silk Road. By Justin Jon Rudelson. New York: Columbia University Press, 1998.
The Party and the National Question in China. By George Moseley. Cambridge: MIT Press, 1966.
Pivot of Asia: Sinkiang and the Inner Asian Frontiers of China and Russia. By Owen Lattimore. Boston: Little, Brown, 1950.
The Political Forms of Modern Society: Bureaucracy, Democracy, and Totalitarianism. By Claude Lefort. Ed. Roger B. Thompson. Cambridge: Polity Press, 1986.
The Sinkiang Story. By Jack Chen. New York: Macmillan, 1977.
Waiting for Uyghurstan. By Sean R. Roberts. Los Angeles: University of Southern California, Center for Visual Anthropology, 1996. Video documentary.
Warlords and Muslims in Chinese Central Asia. By Andrew Forbes. Cambridge: Cambridge University Press, 1986.
Xinjiang Tongji Nianshu [Xinjiang Statistical Yearbook, 2002]. Ed. Statistics Bureau of Xinjiang Uygur Autonomous Region. Beijing: China Statistics Press, 2002.

Websites
www.ccs.uky.edu/~rakhim/et.html (virtual library of the Australian National University based in Eastern Turkistan)
www.eurasianet.org (Open Society Institute)
www.euronet.nl/users/sota/turkistan.html (Turkistan newsletter)
www.utoledo.edu/~nlight (work on Xinjiang by Nathan Light of the University of Toledo)

www.uyghuramerican.org. (Uyghur organizations and links)
www.uyghurinfo.com (Uyghur Information Agency)
www.vic-info.org (interactive question-and-answer site with a special report: "Uighur Muslim Separatists"; Virtual Information Center, open-source organization funded by USCINCPAC)

Dru C. Gladney is professor of Asian studies and anthropology at the University of Hawaii. Further background material and analysis relevant to the subject of this survey can be found on the author's website, www.hawaii.edu/dru, and in Ethnic Identity in China *(Fort Worth: Harcourt-Brace, 1998),* Making Majorities: Constituting the Nation in Japan, Korea, China, Malaysia, Fiji, Turkey, and the United States *(editor) (Stanford, Calif.: Stanford University Press, 1998),* Muslim Chinese: Ethnic Nationalism in the People's Republic of China, *2d ed. (Cambridge: Harvard University Press, 1996); and* Dislocating China: Muslims, Minorities, and Other Subaltern Subjects *(Chicago: University of Chicago Press, forthcoming).*

Notes

1. Erik Eckholm, "U.S. Labeling of Group in China as Terrorist is Criticized," *New York Times,* September 13, 2002, p. 1.
2. For an excellent historical overview of this period, see Herbert Franke and Denis Twitchett, *Cambridge History of China,* vol. 6, *Alien Regimes and Border States (907–1368)* (Cambridge: Cambridge University Press, 1994).
3. Morris Rossabi, "Muslim and Central Asian Revolts," in Jonathan D. Spence and John E. Wills Jr., eds. *From Ming to Ch'ing* (New Haven: Yale University Press, 1979), pp. 169–199.
4. The best "Uyghur nationalist" retelling of this unbroken descent from Karakhorum is in the document "Brief History of the Uyghers," which originates from the Eastern Turkistani Union in Europe, available at www.geocites.com/capitolhill/1730/buh.html. For a recent review and critique, including historical evidence for the multiethnic background of the contemporary Uyghur, see Dru C. Gladney, "Ethnogenesis and Ethnic Identity in China: Considering the Uygurs and Kazakhs," in Victor Mair, ed., *The Bronze Age and Early Iron Age People of Eastern Central Asia,* vol. 2 (Washington, D.C.: Institute for the Study of Man, 1998), pp. 812–834. For a discussion of the recent archaeological evidence derived from DNA dating of the desiccated corpses of Xinjiang, see Victor Mair, introduction to Mair, *Bronze Age,* pp. 1–40.
5. The best discussion of the politics and importance of Xinjiang during this period is that of an eyewitness and participant, Owen Lattimore, in his book *Pivot of Asia: Sinkiang and the Inner Asian Frontiers of China and Russia* (Boston: Little, Brown, 1950).
6. Linda Benson, *The Ili Rebellion: The Moslem Challenge to Chinese Authority in Xinjiang, 1944–1949* (New York: M. E. Sharpe, 1990).
7. Andrew Forbes, *Warlords and Muslims in Chinese Central Asia* (Cambridge: Cambridge University Press, 1986).
8. Justin Jon Rudelson, *Oasis Identities: Uyghur Nationalism Along China's Silk Road* (New York: Columbia University Press, 1998), p. 8. On Uyghur ethnogenesis, see also Jack Chen, *The Sinkiang Story* (New York: Macmillan, 1977), p. 57; and Dru C. Gladney, "The Ethnogenesis of the Uyghur," *Central Asian Survey* 9, no. 1 (1990): 1–28.
9. The best account of the Uyghur diaspora in Central Asia, their memories of migration, and their longing for a separate Uyghur homeland is contained in a video documentary by Sean R. Roberts, *Waiting for Uyghurstan* (Los Angeles: University of Southern California, Center for Visual Anthropology, 1996).
10. Rym Brahimi, "Russia, China, and Central Asian Leaders Pledge to Fight Terrorism, Drug Smuggling," CNN News Service, August 25, 1999, available at www.uygur.org/enorg/wunn99/990825e.html.

11. Eastern Turkistan Information Center, "Kasakhstan Government Deport Political Refugees to China," Munich, June 15, 1999, available at www.uygur.org/enorg/reports99/990615.html.

12. On China's minority integration program, see Colin Mackerras, *China's Minorities: Integration and Modernization in the Twentieth Century* (Hong Kong: Oxford University Press, 1994).

13. Forbes, *Warlords and Muslims,* pp. 56–90.

14. See the discussion of population numbers in Eastern Turkistan Information Center, "Population of Eastern Turkistan: The Population in Local Records," Munich, n.d., available at www.uygur.org/enorg/turkistan/nopus.html. A useful guide with tables and breakdowns is found in International Taklamakan Human Rights Association (ITHRA), "How Has the Population Distribution Changed in Eastern Turkestan Since 1949," n.d., available at www.taklamakan.org/uyghur-l/et_faq_pl.html, wherein it is reported that the Xinjiang Uyghur population declined from 75 percent in 1949 to 48 percent in 1990. The problem with these statistics is that the first reliable total population count in the region did not take place until 1982, with all earlier estimates highly suspect according to an authoritative study by Judith Banister, *China's Changing Population* (Stanford, Calif.: Stanford University Press, 1987).

15. The late Uyghur historian professor Ibrahim Muti'i, in an unpublished 1989 paper, provides an excellent historical synopsis of the role of the Central Asian Islamic madrassah in traditional Uyghur education.

16. Chinese State Council, *White Paper on Xinjiang Uyghur Autonomous Region,* Beijing, February 2002; "China Also Harmed by Separatist-Minded Eastern Turkestan Terrorists," *People's Daily,* October 10, 2001.

17. Brahimi, "Russia, China, and Central Asian Leaders."

18. Amnesty International, *People's Republic of China: Gross Violations of Human Rights in the Xinjiang Uighur Autonomous Region* (London: Amnesty International, April 21, 1999), p. 24.

19. Radio Free Asia, Uyghur service, "Separatist Leader Vows to Target Chinese Government (RFA)," January 24, 2003, available at www.rfa.org/service/index.html?service=uyg.

20. Charles Hutzler, "Trade Is China's Carrot to Muslim Separatists," *Wall Street Journal,* September 21, 2001.

21. Erik Eckholm and Craig S. Smith, "Fearing Unrest, China Pressures Muslim Group," *New York Times,* October 5, 2001; Pamela Pun, "Separatists Trained in Afghanistan, Says Official," *The Standard,* posted at hk-imail.singtao.com/inews/public/article_v.cfm?articleid=30156&intcatid=2, October 22, 2001.

22. Amnesty International, *People's Republic of China.*

23. Ian Johnson, "China Arrests Noted Businesswoman in Crackdown in Muslim Region," *Wall Street Journal,* August 18, 1999.

24. Dru C. Gladney, "China's Ethnic Reawakening," *Asia Pacific Issues* no. 18 (1995): 1–8.

25. Anwar Yusuf, president of the Eastern Turkistan National Freedom Center, Washington, D.C., personal interview, April 14, 1999.

26. Turkistan News and Information Network, press release, June 8, 1999.

27. See Yitzhak Shichor, "Virtual Transnationalism: Uygur Communities in Europe and the Quest for Eastern Turkestan Independence," unpublished paper, 2002.

28. See, for example, www.uyghur.org, the website supported by Anwar Yusuf, who has suggested that there are up to 25 million Uyghur worldwide.

29. See writings by Isa Yusuf Alptekin's son, Erkin Alptekin, which also present histories of the Uyghur alternative to that of the Chinese state: Erkin Alptekin, *Uygur Türkleri* [The Uyghur Turks] (Istanbul: Boğaziçi Yayinlari, 1978); and Erkin Alptekin, "Xinjiang a Time Bomb Waiting to Explode," *South China Morning Post* (Hong Kong), May 29, 2002. On Alptekin's involvement with the Unrecognized Nations and People's Organization in The Hague, see www.unpo.org/member/intro.htm.

30. There are a growing number of Central Asia–related websites that increasingly contain information on and discussion of events in Xinjiang, even though Xinjiang is often normally not considered a part of Central Asian studies and, due to its rule by China, often falls under Chinese studies or Inner Asian studies. See, for example, Harvard's Forum for Central Asian Studies, www.fas.harvard.edu/~centasia, which is run by John Schoeberlein and maintains the "Central Asian Studies World Wide" website, www.fas.harvard.edu/~casww, and the list-serve "Central Asia-L," www.fas.harvard.edu/~casww/casww_centralasia-l.html, which frequently reports on Xinjiang-related issues. An informational website, titled "For Democracy, Human Rights, Peace, and Freedom for Uzbekistan and Central Asia," with links to Uyghur and East Turkistan sites is www.uzbekistanerk.org/.

31. The East Turkistan Islamic Movement is a shadowy group known to be previously active only in Afghanistan and founded in the mid-1990s by Hassan Mashum. Mahsum had served three years in a labor camp in Xinjiang and recruited other Uighurs, including his number-three leader, Rashid, who was captured with the Taliban and returned to China in spring 2001. See Charles Hutzler, "China-Iraq Policy Is Risky for U.S.," *Asian Wall Street Journal,* September 10, 2001.

32. "China Also Harmed by Separatist-Minded Eastern Turkestan Terrorists," *People's Daily,* October 10, 2001; Erik Eckholm, "U.S. Labeling of Group in China As Terrorist Is Criticized," *New York Times,* September 13, 2002; Charles Hutzler, "U.S. Gesture to China Raises Crackdown Fears," *Wall Street Journal,* September 13, 2002.

33. Dewardic L. McNeal, "China's Relations with Central Asian States and Problems with Terrorism," U.S. Department of State, Congressional Research Service report, 2001. See also Scott Fogden's excellent thesis *Writing Insecurity: The PRC's Push to Modernize China and the Politics of Uighur Identity,* University of Wales, Aberystwyth, 2002.

34. "Conclusion of China Visit" press conference, Deputy Secretary of State Richard L. Armitage, Beijing, August 26, 2002.

35. See "Special Report: Uighur Muslim Separatists," *Virtual Information Center,* September 28, 2001, p. 6, available at www.vic-info.org.

36. For a discussion of the various meanings of "jihad" in Islam, see John L. Esposito, *Unholy War: Terror in the Name of Islam* (Oxford: Oxford University Press, 2002), pp. 26–35. For studies among Uyghur and other Turkic communities in Istanbul, see Dru C. Gladney, "Relational Alterity: Constructing Dungan (Hui), Uyghur, and Kazakh Identities Across China, Central Asia, and Turkey," *History and Anthropology* 9, no. 2 (1996): 445–477; and Ingvar Svanberg, *Kazak Refugees in Turkey: A Study of Cultural Persistence and Social Change* (Stockholm: Almqvist and Wiksell International, 1989).

37. Radio Free Asia, Uyghur service, "Separatist Leader Vows to Target Chinese Government."

38. See "China: China Increases Suppression in Xinjiang," *Oxford Analytica,* December 20, 2002. The report concludes: "Distinguishing between genuine counterterrorism and repression of minority rights is difficult and the Uighur case points to a lack of international guidelines for doing so. In any case, Chinese policies, not foreign-sponsored terrorism, are the cause of Uighur unrest. China's development and control policy in Xinjiang is unlikely to stabilise the region as long as development benefits remain so unevenly distributed."

39. James P. Dorian, Brett Wigdortz, and Dru Gladney, "Central Asia and Xinjiang, China: Emerging Energy, Economic, and Ethnic Relations," *Central Asian Survey* 16, no. 4 (1997): 469.

40. Ibid., p. 480.

41. A useful reference in this regard is Ross Garnaut, Ligang Song, Yang Yao, and Xiaolu Wang, *Private Enterprise in China,* ANU China Center for Economic Research, Peking University, Asia Pacific Press, 2001.

42. These sites include that of the International Taklamakan Human Rights Association, which contains links to several articles and websites concerning East Turkistan, Uyghur, and Uyghuristan, www.taklamakan.org; that of the Uyghur American Association, which contains links to articles and websites concerning issues of human rights and territorial freedom among Uyghur in Xinjiang, as well as a listing of twenty-two other organizations around the world that do not have websites, www.uyghuramerican.org; and that of the East Turkistan National Congress, led by Enver Can in Munich: www.eastturkistan.com. The Uyghur Human Rights Coalition (www.uyghurs.org), directed by Kathy Polias, and located near the Georgetown University campus, tracks human rights issues and has organized several demonstrations and conferences in the Washington, D.C., metro area, especially pushing for the release of Rebiya Kadir. See also the website of the Eastern Turkistan National Freedom Center (www.uyghur.org), whose leader is Anwar Yusuf. One of the earliest Uyghur advocacy organizations established in the United States, in 1996, is the International Taklamakan Human Rights Association (www.taklamakan.org), whose president is Ablajan Layli Namen Barat; the association maintains an active list-serve, UIGHUR-L.

43. Chien-peng Chung, "China's 'War on Terror': September 11 and Uighur Separatism," *Foreign Affairs,* 81, no. 4 (2002): 8–12.

44. Owen Lattimore, *Pivot of Asia: Sinkiang and the Inner Asian Frontiers of China and Russia* (Boston: Little, Brown, 1950).

8.4

Korea:
Perilous Crossing and New Dangers

Francis Daehoon Lee

Despite the general thaw in relations and economic cooperation between the two Koreas since the 1990s—and especially the Korean Summit of 2000 and increasing inter-Korea trade and exchange— occasional military clashes signal the existence of clear tension. Recently a new crisis appeared on the horizon with the designation of North Korea as a member of the "axis of evil" by Washington in 2002. In the meantime, South Korea saw a great surge of nongovernmental peace initiatives, greatly diminishing the militarist-confrontational stance toward the north and actively inviting North Koreans to enter a new space of engagement.

After Japan's defeat in August 1945, Soviet troops entered the north of Korea, while U.S. troops entered the south. In December 1945 the three victorious allies of World War II decided to rule Korea as a trust territory, dividing Korea into north and south along the thirty-eighth parallel, with the Soviet Union and the United States being given the authority to oversee each part respectively. Nationalists and the left led the political process in the north, while the U.S. military forces took power in the south.

In February 1946, local forces of the left, with the support of the Soviet Union, began setting up their own government in the north, and put Kim Il Sung into power. By August 1948, with U.S. backing, the south on its own held the first election and declared the Republic of Korea for the whole country. North Korea followed suit a month later and formed the Democratic People's Republic of Korea. The nation was thus divided. Political instability quickly ensued in South Korea. Rebellions and spontaneous revolts led by the left erupted around the country. By June 1949, all foreign forces had withdrawn from Korea while the two Korean governments became involved in military clashes around the division line, approaching a de facto civil war.

On June 25, 1950, a full-scale war broke out as the North Korean troops invaded the south, declaring unification of the country by force. The UN Security

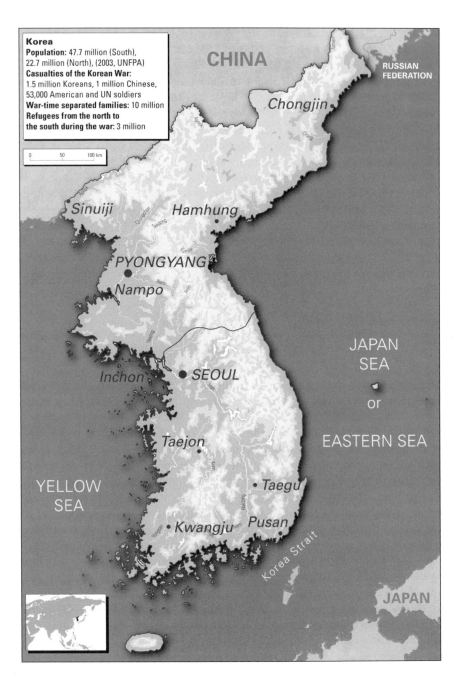

Korea
Population: 47.7 million (South),
22.7 million (North), (2003, UNFPA)
Casualties of the Korean War:
1.5 million Koreans, 1 million Chinese,
53,000 American and UN soldiers
War-time separated families: 10 million
**Refugees from the north to
the south during the war:** 3 million

Council decided to intervene, and the war turned into an international conflict. The U.S.-led United Nations troops fought alongside the South Koreans to push back the North Koreans, while Chinese troops began to fight alongside the North Koreans soon after in 1950. Over the next three years, the country and the international troops were dragged into exhausting back-and-forth war-fare. The Korean War ended in July 1953 with a truce, but the two sides remain technically at war to date. While the U.S. forces remained in the south by a mutual security pact with South Korea, all of the Chinese forces had withdrawn from the north by 1958. So far, no peace treaty has been signed between any parties involved in the war.

After the war, both Koreas maintained a hostile stance and policy toward each other. Secret forces conducted various unlawful operations in each other's territories, some of which developed into major crises. In 1968, in reaction to South Korea's active involvement in the Vietnam War on the side of the United States, North Korea sent a unit of special armed forces into Seoul and created serious tension. North Korea's kidnapping of a U.S. intelligence naval ship in 1968 triggered another crisis. In 1969 a U.S. intelligence plane was shot down near North Korea, and in 1976 a dispute in Panmunjom, a small area for holding talks inside the demilitarized zone (DMZ) separating the two Koreas, led to the deaths of a few U.S. servicemen at the hands of North Koreans.

However, throughout the Cold War period, there was in the Korean Peninsula a relative balance of power between the communist bloc (North Korea, China, and Soviet Russia) and the capitalist bloc (South Korea, the United States, and Japan), which was seen as a guarantor of relative stability of the region. North Korea signed friendship treaties with Beijing and Moscow, receiving military, political, and economic aid from both. Similarly, South Korea received aid from the United States, while hosting a significant number of U.S. forces.

Since the mid-1960s, under the military-backed authoritarian politics led by Park Jung-hee, South Korea was turned from an impoverished country into a rapidly industrializing power. But the people paid a high price for this trans-formation in terms of human rights violations, ideological indoctrination, and the use of politics of terror. A regimented society was created to sustain eco-nomic growth. In 1979, Park Jung-hee was assassinated by his own chief of security in the name of "democracy." Park's prime minister, Choe Gyu Wha, succeeded Park and for several months there was hope of a democratic elec-tion—until Chun Doo-hwan, a pro-Park general, mounted a coup and ousted Choe. However, in response to the military coup, popular uprisings took place, particularly in Kwangju city. In 1980, security forces led by generals Chun Doo-hwan and Roh Tae-woo, killed hundreds of protesters. With growing popular demands for democracy, Chun's government was effectively pressured into accepting the first multiparty election in the country in 1987. In 1992, South Korea saw its first civilian government in three decades.

Until the mid-1970s, North Korea surpassed South Korea in economic growth, but its economy and national power have continuously declined ever since. When Soviet president Mikhail Gorbachev introduced perestroika, and the Soviet Union began to crumble, North Korea's only remaining external support came from Beijing. The country has so far greatly suffered from long-term underdevelopment, the breakdown of the economic system, poor resource supply, and international isolation.

The major conflict today centers on the relationship between North Korea and the United States. After the end of the Cold War at the global level, a new tension has arisen, bringing North Korea's intention of using its nuclear program for direct bargain with the United States, largely pressed by domestic economic problems, into a direct clash of interest with the plans of the United States to place such attempts under stronger control. None of the neighboring countries is happy about this development, which could escalate into a nuclear arms race in the region. The economic instability of North Korea has also produced grave concerns about the predictability of situations in relation to negotiating with North Korea.

Conflict Dynamics

There are three outstanding features in the conflicts in Korea: the military confrontation between the two Koreas, the systemic internal crisis of North Korea, and the continuation of the adversarial relationship between North Korea and the United States. The fact that there is no peace treaty to replace the 1953 armistice[1] and that the overwhelming military power manifested by the Republic of Korea–U.S. alliance and the U.S.-Japan alliance has convinced North Korea that it is under threat, and this situation obstructs the confidence building process.

Since the 1953 armistice, the two Koreas and the United States have been involved in numerous small-scale armed conflicts and conducted large-scale regular military exercises that each side considered a serious threat to security. Both sides have sent special forces and armed agents to the other side. Occasional conflict surrounding armed incursions and espionage operations has tended to result in heightened security measures.

A few other cases involved alleged terrorist attacks. During a visit to Rangoon, Myanmar, in 1983 by a South Korean delegation headed by President Chun Doo-hwan, a bomb killed seventeen high-ranking officials. North Korea has been blamed for the bombing. In 1987, Pyongyang was accused of bombing a South Korean airliner and killing all of the 115 people aboard. While the truth of this case remains unresolved, it contributed to the deepening of North Korea's international isolation at that time. In each case, the incident created great fear in South Korea and reinforced authoritarian politics on each side.

Since 1992, North Korea has attracted international concern over its potential nuclear and missile programs. The initial inspection of the International Atomic Energy Agency (IAEA) failed to produce a convincing report and, in 1993, North Korea announced its intention to secede from the Nuclear Nonproliferation Treaty. The IAEA decided to bring the case to the UN Security Council for sanctions, which North Korea took as a grave threat. All inter-Korean talks were frozen. Mounting hostility and failure of the talks between North Korea and the United States placed the peninsula within a hairsbreadth of war.

With the help of mediation by former U.S. president Jimmy Carter, and pressured by various domestic problems, North Korea agreed to allow international inspection of its nuclear sites in 1994 and to have its nuclear reactors replaced with light-water reactors. In return North Korea was promised fuel oil supplies through the framework agreement signed in Geneva in 1994 by the United States and North Korea.

Tensions rose again when a defunct North Korean submarine ran aground and was found during its incursion into South Korean waters in 1996, and again when small-scale naval battles were fought in 1999 and 2002 between the two Korean navies escorting fishing boats in the Yellow Sea. Both sides refrained from military action, and the crises were resolved without further escalation.

When North Korea test-fired a ballistic missile with a range of 1,800–2,300 kilometers over Japan in 1998, Japan responded by strengthening its naval and ground forces in the region and also by moving toward a controversial missile defense system. After some diplomacy, North Korea unilaterally decided to stop the tests as long as negotiations continued. In 1999, a new site in Kumchangri, North Korea, was suspected of being used for possible nuclear development, but the case was resolved when North Korea accepted a visit by U.S. inspectors, who later refuted the allegation, in return for economic aid from the United States.

The foremost conflict in Korea is currently the military tension between North Korea and the United States. Since 2001, North Korea has been on high alert as a result of Washington's new hard-line and often incoherent approach that sometimes calls for "regime collapse." One reaction to it came in October 2002, when North Korea told a visiting U.S. official that it was entitled to produce weapons of nuclear substance, which Washington regarded as a violation of the 1994 framework agreement. The United States reacted by suspending delivery of fuel oil supplies. North Korea took steps for restarting its nuclear reactor, taking the fuel oil suspension as a significant breach of the framework agreement. New talks for diplomatic resolution of the case started in April 2003 with China's active mediation role. Soon afterward, the first six-nation talk was held over the issue among the United States, Russia, China, Japan, and North and South Korea, marking a step toward a peaceful resolution of the conflict.

International isolation and the failure of the economic system paralyzed the North Korean economy throughout the 1990s. An average of 1.5 million tons of food aid from outside is needed every year. Famine, malnutrition, and economic refugee problems have caused grave concerns in neighboring countries. Key governments have been sensitive to the potential politicization of these problems. For example, China has been sensitive to accusations of returning North Korean refugees that international human rights norms have been violated, and the South Korean government considers it a dilemma whether or not to raise human rights issues against North Korea.

Panmunjom border post/North Korea. A North Korean soldier
being "psyched out" by South Korean soldiers at the Demilitarized Zone.

Official Conflict Management

Under the favorable conditions emerging from international détente since
1970, the two Koreas made an initial approach to each other and signed the
first official agreement of cooperation in 1972. The 1972 joint statement laid
down basic principles of peaceful unification. The spirit of this statement did
not materialize into any specific steps, as both governments soon intensified
their internal control in order to remedy the weakening legitimacy of their
political power.

Until 1984 the two governments continued to exchange declaratory statements on principles of mutual nonaggression, exchanges, cooperation and confidence building, and sending proposals for dialogue and cooperation to each
other, but without hard results. The two sides made competing proposals for a
blueprint of unification as it related to the political legitimacy of each regime.
It was only in 1984 that the first talks on economic cooperation and cultural
exchanges were agreed upon and conducted. The first meeting of families separated by the war took place in 1985. North Korea often cited disputes over
the Republic of Korea–U.S. military exercise and the use of the notorious
National Security Act by the South Korean government in repressing dissidents as the cause of breaking off talks with the south.[2]

The two Koreas began a new round of talks in 1990, three years after the
1987 democratic movement in the south, as peaceful approaches were regaining momentum in Korea. In 1991, the two Koreas signed a breakthrough
agreement, the North-South Reconciliation, Nonaggression, Exchange, and

Cooperation Agreement, opening the way to comprehensive political settlement of the long-held conflict. From then on, the two Koreas were able to sign several other important agreements by 1992, which would serve as a key confidence-building step toward further engagement. These included agreements on the organization of joint committees on military affairs, exchange-cooperation affairs, and communication affairs. The agreements of 1991–1992 included most of the key principles and policy guidelines for political settlement of any disputes arising from inter-Korean affairs. This was the cornerstone of a comprehensive track-one Korean conflict-prevention initiative.

The two sides were also able to reach the first-ever agreement on a nuclear-free Korea in 1992, the Joint Declaration of Denuclearization in Korea, stipulating the peaceful use of nuclear energy and banning any measures related to potential and actual weaponization of nuclear materials. Mutual inspection was also agreed. The so-called North Korean nuclear crisis in 1993–1994, started by North Korea's secession from the Nuclear Nonproliferation Treaty, pushed the region to the brink of war in April 1994, but North Korea and the United States managed to reach an agreement to resolve the issue. However, the 1994 nuclear crisis showed that inter-Korean agreement was not by itself a sufficient guarantee of peace. The Joint Declaration of Denuclearization in Korea is also handicapped because it does not have any authority on the nuclear affairs of foreign troops, notably the U.S. forces in Korea. Officially, the United States removed all nuclear weapons stationed in South Korea, the verification of which, however, remains free of public scrutiny.

The Sunshine Policy toward North Korea, adopted by the Kim Dae-jung government (1998–2003), in concert with the 1994 agreement between the Democratic People's Republic of Korea and the United States, resulted in the first-ever summit of the two Koreas, which was held in Pyongyang in June 2000 (the Korean Summit). The summit increased mutual understanding and reaffirmed basic principles of reconciliation and mutual progress in its June 15 joint declaration. It also opened opportunities for North Korea in international relations: after the summit, North Korea embarked on diplomatic normalization with European Union member states and increased economic cooperation with Western countries. It also speeded up its diplomatic efforts with the United States and Japan.

After the Korean Summit, the two Koreas—elites and public alike—began to develop a new trust in each other's intentions for reconciliation and cooperation, even though internal hard-line resistance remained significant. Especially in South Korea, the newly established policy of building trust greatly changed the public perception of North Korea: Public tolerance toward North Korea is now much greater than before. The outlook toward North Korea also differs widely across the generations. This in turn widens policy options for the government. Continued and consistent dialogues expanded human relationships on both sides and deepened the level of trust. These developments also left a clear mark among neighboring countries in relation to their attitude toward Korea.

Two aspects stand out as new confidence-building measures during this period. Although the payment to North Korea for tourism was relatively low, at U.S.$900 million, during the first six years—considering North Korea's trade volume of U.S.$2 billion in 2000—the magnitude and the importance of this tourism project can be easily seen. At the same time, Kim Dae-jung's administration actively recommended to Bill Clinton's administration an improved relationship with North Korea, as the latter was in the process of reexamining its relationship with Pyongyang, later formalized into the soft-line Perry Process.[3] The roles of the South Korean government and opinion leaders in South Korea were crucial in this process. For Japanese–North Korean relations, Kim's government took the same approach. By October 2000, normalization with North Korea became highly likely for both Japan and the United States.

After its legalization in 1988, trade between South and North Korea increased steadily, reaching U.S.$402.96 million in 2001. Trade has been halted by political tensions, but since 1998 and Kim Dae-jung's policy of separating economics from politics, it is on a stable course, serving as an important confidence-building measure. The two governments have been working toward increasing the number of goods and easing restrictions on trade and joint ventures. Now South Korea allows business trips to and meetings in the North. Construction work on reconnecting railways across the DMZ has been completed and consultations are in progress for various projects such as building dams and industrial complexes in North Korea. Along with the current highly popular Kumgang Mountain Tour and Kaesung Special Administrative Zone, inter-Korea economic cooperation as such is thought to bring in much more economic benefit and trust to each side.

Multi-Track Diplomacy

During the time of the authoritarian regimes in the south, NGOs focused mainly on political democratization and peaceful reunification. While unable to engage with any North Korean partners due to national security legislation, they advocated instead alternative principles and a road map to unification to the Cold War–style official policies: Key points were lessening U.S. influence, opening gates between the two Koreas, and the people's initiatives to unification. Leaders of such initiatives were regarded as dangerous dissidents and were arrested and imprisoned in large numbers. This in turn contributed to the weakening of the political legitimacy of the dictatorial governments, because in the process their usual invocation of *national security* from the "North Korean threat" came to be viewed merely as an attempt to preserve *regime security.*

The state's control over security issues was vital in the legitimization of the authoritarian governments. Civil society groups trying to redefine security issues and the perception of threats were in fact working to ease the state's monopoly control over national security, which in turn prompted delegitimization of the authoritarian rule and consequently a democratization process.

With a political process toward democracy on track since the late 1980s, nongovernmental organizations (NGOs) and religious groups began illegal communication with, and visits to, the north in order to hold direct talks with the North Korean authorities despite severe legal consequences. Such visits were regarded as sensational for demonstrating the possibility of friendly talks and of reaching common understanding across the ideological divide, and they shook the foundation of the public belief in a "mutual enemy." An outlawed visit to North Korea in 1989 by a young student, Lim Soo-Kyong, for example, caused such public sensation and celebration at the same time within the two Korean societies that huge and constructive debates ensued over the legitimacy of hostility in Korea. In general, peaceful unification was widely accepted in civil society in South Korea, but possible withdrawal of the U.S. forces, disarmament issues, and a formula for joint unified government were vigorously debated.

Along with democratization, public pressure to depoliticize the military gained momentum, as did successful campaigns to bring to justice two former presidents who were responsible for coups in 1979 and 1980, and by the mid-1990s politics were conducted free from the Korean military influence. At the same time, NGOs began to raise issues of human rights violations during the compulsory military service, out of which a conscientious objectors' movement was born. The revival of parliamentarian politics and civil society campaigns to depoliticize the military have helped to shape an initial form of civilian control over the military, which is vital in conflict management in Korea.

After 1993, as the world became aware of the serious economic failure in North Korea, new civic groups began to emerge in order to enhance humanitarian aid to the north and raise such concerns in the south. Legal constraints on nongovernmental groups sending aid to North Korea began to ease in the late 1990s. Noted for their initiatives and success in mobilizing public donations and sending food and aid to the north are the South-North Sharing Campaign, Good Friends: International Peace, the Human Rights and Refugees Center, and the Korean Sharing Movement. In addition to food aid, such nongovernmental humanitarian aid focuses on health care, the modernization of hospitals, agricultural infrastructure, and forestation. The total amount reached U.S.$51 million in 2002, in comparison to U.S.$8,375 in governmental humanitarian aid.

With the introduction of Kim Dae-jung's Sunshine Policy in 1998, social and cultural exchanges between the two Koreas expanded rapidly. Civic groups actively supported the human exchange aspect of the new policy and began to organize regular sports events, joint academic meetings, cultural exchange visits, and joint commemoration events, such as sending a delegation to the May Day ceremony in Pyongyang. At the same time, the sheer number of civilians visiting the other side for various civilian purposes rose dramatically. Compared to the single case of a civilian visit to North Korea in 1989, more than 12,000 South Koreans visited the north and 1,000 North Koreans visited the south in 2002. The humanitarian impact of these visits and their effect on boosting mutual understanding are enormous and are slowly but surely affecting each society.

In the meantime, the U.S. issue began to surface as pressure for silence waned with democratization. Various groups representing the victims of offenses arising from the daily activities of the U.S. military bases led this trend, stimulating many civic and religious groups to question the legitimacy of the U.S. forces while North-South relations were thawing. Anti–land mine campaigns also highlighted the long-hidden reality of the unfair treatment of the victims and arrogant stance of the U.S. forces on this matter. Scholars and religious groups in the two Koreas began to hold joint meetings on such agendas. In general, South Korea in the 1990s saw a great surge of NGO peace initiatives in humanitarian, academic, religious, sports, and political fields, greatly diminishing the militarist-confrontational stance toward the North and actively inviting North Koreans to enter a new space of engagement.

As a result of these challenging peace initiatives by civic groups, political taboos weakened and sensitive issues were more freely discussed. Now politicians had to deal with growing public interest in nonconfrontational and Korean-initiated settlement of the Korean affairs. When Kim Dae-jung's engagement policy came in 1998, it also opened a new era for civil society initiatives for peace. Most notable was a huge body called the Korean Council for Reconciliation and Cooperation, a unique organization composed of political parties, governmental bodies, and nongovernmental groups that resolved to work for reconciliation based on wider cooperation. This body also served as a platform for reconciliation among the left- and right-wing forces within South Korea in relation to their views toward North Korea. At the same time, a majority of the nongovernmental groups joined the Council for National Reconciliation and Independent Unification to express their support for the June 15 North-South Joint Declaration, which strengthens the peaceful course of inter-Korean affairs.

As tension grew between Seoul and Washington along with the Bush administration's new approach to North Korea, there was deep disappointment among the Korean public. Some of it was expressed in large-scale anti-American demonstrations in South Korea in 2002–2003. NGOs continue to advocate for a peaceful settlement of the tension between North Korea and the United States, and hope to build a "peace buffer" by further expanding North-South exchange and cooperation. The large-scale demonstrations against the Korean troops being dispatched to Iraq in 2003 also shows the nature of the growing public sentiment concerning U.S. arrogance over Korean affairs. There is a concern over the implications for Korea of the U.S. preemptive strike doctrine applied to Iraq. Another concern is the hierarchical nature of decisionmaking between South Korea and the United States, especially in military affairs. The rapid rise and expansion of the peace movement reflects this change in the public mind, centered on rationalizing relations between the United States and the Republic of Korea beyond the Cold War tradition.

A new NGO initiative was noted in summer 2003: Peace groups in the United States and in South Korea have developed closer cooperation in advocating peaceful resolution of the tension. Along with many advocacy works, they organized a "lobby" tour of a delegation from South Korea, composed of members of the National Assembly (the legislative), scholars, and peace advocates, to the United States to have alternative discussions on North Korean issues with key policymakers, civil society leaders, and parliamentarians. After the visit, an awareness-raising campaign was jointly planned, to introduce a broader perspective of North Korean issues to the wider public in the United States.

NGO initiatives for peaceful settlement of Korean affairs reflect the structural nature of the Korean conflict, the division of the nation into two different systems ruled by militarist "national security regimes" and backed by powerful nations around the world. In short, they reflect a continuing interest in shifting security politics toward normal politics. In South Korea, NGO initiatives for inter-Korean conflict resolution centered on political democratization (de-securitization of the national security state) and independence from the U.S. influence (de-securitization of foreign policies). Political democratization since 1987, resulting from a series of popular revolts against national security regimes since the 1970s, has strengthened such a course and cultivated the ground for Kim Dae-jung's engagement policy since 1998. Now, new focus is being laid on de-securitizing the tension between the Democratic People's Republic of Korea and the United States over nuclear and missile issues. In the long term this will invite civil society groups to work for new international relations in Northeast Asia, including the military alliance between the Republic of Korea and the United States.

Prospects

While South Korea has been undergoing rapid industrialization and political evolution, North Korea has continuously suffered from international isolation since the demise of the socialist bloc, which compounded its domestic difficulties, such as its energy crisis, and foreign currency holdings and food crises.

In view of the mood for appeasement among neighboring countries and given the unfavorable military balance, military action by North Korea seems unlikely. The hard-line policy of the Bush administration may become the biggest obstacle on this course, but the renewed six-party talks of 2003 give some hope for a diplomatic solution. Amid growing skepticism of the need for U.S. forces in the south, the U.S. military presence in Korea will continue, with its capability highly strengthened. The current U.S. defense policy entails equipping the military with state-of-the-art ammunition and restructuring it in a way that allows rapid deployment and mobility.[4]

Recommendations

Despite some new hard-line developments in the region, there are lessons to be learned from the past. The peaceful approach to Korean conflicts worked toward tilting the policy balance in favor of restraint and moderation. The peaceful approach itself was a key confidence-building measure. Equality was a major condition for peace negotiations: After the Korean Summit, which was carried out by mutual recognition on an equal footing, optimism grew and reconciliation was in the air. The best way of coordinating different interests in the region is to have all bilateral negotiations (the United States and North Korea), special bilateral negotiations (North and South Korea) and multilateral negotiations (the United States, North and South Korea, China, Japan, and Russia) proceed in parallel.

Economic support for North Korea is vital in terms of maintaining the regional stability and security that are crucial for stable negotiations. All sides should drop hostile attitudes, including pursuit of regime change.

Conflicts and tensions in and around Korea can best be resolved if all parties concerned start by agreeing to some key principles as proposed by peace researchers and activists in Korea: clear denouncement of a military approach to the crises, an expression of commitment to peaceful resolution, uninterrupted initiatives for peace and reconciliation by the two Koreas, a multilateral approach toward regional cooperative security arrangements, and the coexistence and coprosperity of different political systems in the region.

In order to resolve military tension, North Korea demanded a binding nonaggression pact or treaty with the United States. President George W. Bush has several times said that the United States has no intention of attacking North Korea. But for North Korea this "expression" is not enough. On the U.S. side, and basic to the six-party talks, the key issues are the nuclear program and the long-range missile program. Energy supply and humanitarian aid to North Korea are vital in building trust and stability in the country, which in return should take steps to improve the economic situation as well as its human rights situation. Such security and economic deals can best be achieved as a package agreement involving the two Koreas, the United States, and other key partners like Japan and the European Union. The United States wants a multilateral guarantee, so that if North Korea reneges on agreements, all the parties concerned will be affected.

To maintain stability in the region, the following initiatives should continue uninterrupted by any politically motivated developments: humanitarian aid and energy supply to North Korea, and cultural exchange and cooperation of nongovernmental groups in the two Koreas. Economic cooperation should continue and expand in order to bind North Korea more closely to the international community.

Steps to reach a peace treaty between the two Koreas will greatly ease military tension in the region. To this end, South Korea should be allowed to operate its military affairs independently of the command of U.S. forces in Korea. A peace regime in Korea should be developed in parallel with the development of a regional, multilateral cooperative security arrangement involving China, Russia, and Japan in addition to the two Koreas and the United States. The alliance between the Republic of Korea and the United States should be modified to allow a more neutral U.S. stance.

Resources

Newsletters and Periodicals

Foreign Policy in Focus (ASIA & PACIFIC RIM in Focus). English-language periodical published by the Washington, D.C.–based Institute for Policy Studies and the Interhemispheric Resource Center.

Korea Now. English-language biweekly published by the Korean Information Service, Republic of Korea.

Korea Peace Letter. English-language e-mail newsletter produced by a network of peace groups in South Korea.

Korea Times. South Korean English-language daily

The People's Korea. English-language web daily produced by the Korean Central News Agency (www.korea-np.co.jp/pk), representing the official views of the Democratic People's Republic of Korea.

Worker's Daily. Korean-language official daily of the Democratic People's Republic of Korea.

YonhapNews. Daily news from the United Press in South Korea (www.yonhapnews. co.kr).

Reports

A Comprehensive Approach to North Korea. By Richard L. Armitage, National Defense University, Strategic Forum. March 1999.

A Comprehensive Solution to the Korean Peninsula Problems (Korea Peace Report). Report by South Korean peace researchers. Seoul, October 2002.

Review of United States Policy Toward North Korea: Findings and Recommendations. Unclassified report by William J. Perry, U.S.–North Korea policy coordinator and special adviser to the president and the secretary of state. Washington, D.C., October 12, 1999

Turning Point in Korea: New Dangers and New Opportunities for the United States. Report of the Task Force on U.S. Korea Policy, chaired by Selig S. Harrison of the Center for International Policy. February 2003. Available at www.ciponline.org/asia/taskforce.pdf.

Other Publications

Korea Briefing 1997–1999: Challenges and Change at the Turn of the Century. Ed. Kongdan Katy. New York: M. E. Sharpe, 2000.

Korean Endgame: A Strategy for Reunification and U.S. Disengagement. By Selig S. Harrison. Princeton: Princeton University Press, 2002.

Peace and Security in Northeast Asia: The Nuclear Issue and the Korean Peninsula. Eds. Young Whan Kihl and Peter Hayes. New York: M. E. Sharpe, 1997.

The Politics of Democratization in Korea: The Role of Civil Society. By Sunhyuk Kim. Pittsburgh: University of Pittsburgh Press, 2000.

The Two Koreas: A Contemporary History. By Don Oberdorfer. London: Little, Brown, 1998.

Websites

http://ifes.kyungnam.ac.kr/ifes/ifes/eng/default.asp (Institute for Far Eastern Studies)

www.fpif.org/indices/regions/asia.html (Foreign Policy in Focus)

www.kcna.co.jp (Korea Central News Agency, Democratic People's Republic of Korea)

www.kimsoft.com/korea.htm (Kim Soft Korea Web Weekly)

www.kois.go.kr (KoreaNet, official homepage of the Republic of Korea)

www.peacekorea.org/eng/index_eng.html (Civil Network for a Peaceful Korea)

www.sejong.org (Sejong Institute)

Resource Contacts

Park Gunyoung, professor at Catholic University, author of *Korea Peace Report* (2002),
  e-mail: think@catholic.ac.kr
Lee Hyunsook, Women Making Peace, e-mail: wmp@peacewomen.or.kr
Oh Jaeshik, former president of World Vision Korea, e-mail: oh_jaeshik@wvi.org
Lee Samuel, director of the UNESCO Asia-Pacific Center of Education for International Understanding, e-mail: samlee@unesco.or.kr
Park Sunsong, inter-Korean affairs specialist, professor at Donguk University, e-mail:
  sunsong@dongguk.edu
Jung Wookshik, inter-Korea and Korea-U.S. specialist, e-mail: civil@peacekorea.org.

Organizations

Civil Network for Peaceful Korea (CNPK)
5F Kyungkimhoigwan
53-8 Manli-Dong
1 GaJung-Gu,
Seoul, Korea
tel: +82 2 393 3509
e-mail: civil@peacekorea.org
www.peacekorea.org
CNPK monitors national and international reporting of Korean relations and makes issue of military policies. It holds frequent public forums on Korean relations and advocates peace options through public media.

Korean Council for Reconciliation and Cooperation (KCRC)
4F Donggu International Bldg.
Youido-Dong, Youngdeungpo Gu, Seoul, 150-010 Korea
tel: +82 2 761 1213
fax: +82 2 761 6590
e-mail: kcrc@kcrc.or.kr
www.kcrc.or.kr
The KCRC promotes national reconciliation and peaceful reunification in Korea by raising the spirit of reconciliation and cooperation between the two Koreas. It advocates principles and ways of reconciliation on governmental and nongovernmental levels and holds various annual events commemorating inter-Korean or pan-Korean history, jointly with its North Korean counterparts.

People's Solidarity for Participatory Democracy (PSPD), Center for Peace and Disarmament (CPD)
3F Anguk New Bldg.
175-3 Anguk-Dong
Jung-Gu, Seoul, 110-240 Korea
tel: +82 2 723 4250
fax: +82 2 723 5055
e-mail: jjepark@pspd.org
www.pspd.org
The PSPD serves as a watchdog against abuse of political and economic power and advocates alternative policies. The PSPD-CPD promotes peaceful resolution of Korea-related tensions, monitors defense and security policies, and advocates disarmament options.

Women Making Peace (WMP)
4F Women Peace Bldg.
38-84 Jangchung-Dong 1 Ga
Jung-Gu, Seoul, 100-391 Korea
tel: +82 2 2275 4860

fax: +82 2 2275 4861
e-mail: wmp@chollian.net
www.peacewomen.or.kr
The WMP aims to achieve autonomous national unification and peace in the peninsula through public campaigns, education programs, conflict resolution training, and international cooperation. It also works for defense budget cuts and against militarist culture in Korean society.

Francis Daehoon Lee, born in South Korea, is currently a Ph.D. candidate in peace studies, University of Bradford, U.K. deputy secretary of the People's Solidarity for Participatory Democracy, Seoul, and researcher at the Centre for Human Rights and Peace, SongKongHoe University, Seoul.

Notes

1. The armistice agreement was actually signed by the United States on behalf of the United Nations, and therefore the UN is a party in the hostilities.

2. The National Security Act is notorious in that any contact of any sort with North Korea, and even the expression of opinions favorable to North Korea, are punishable by imprisonment.

3. The Perry Process refers to the outcome of close consultations of William Perry, a senior North Korea policy coordinator, and his team with their counterparts in the Republic of Korea and Japan over the renewed threat of the Taepodong-I missile test-fired over Japan on August 31, 1998.

4. The United States wishes to reduce its troop levels on the ground (they are needed elsewhere), and reduce reliance on military bases in the region, both of which are points of friction with local populations. Therefore the strategy is to comply with peace movement pressures for withdrawal, but at the same time increase reliance on sea-based forces and much higher technology to close the gaps created by withdrawal.

9

SOUTHEAST ASIA

9.1

Regional Introduction: Missing the Target? The Human Cost of Small-Arms Proliferation and Misuse in Southeast Asia

David Capie

Southeast Asia is a region afflicted by a large number of civil wars and insurgencies. From Burma's borders with India and Bangladesh in the west, to West Papua in the east, rebel groups, insurgents, and militants have taken up arms to challenge the authority of ruling regimes, to seek profits, or to advance a particular religious or political agenda. In doing so, these armed groups—and their opponents—rely heavily, sometimes exclusively, on small arms and light weapons. This chapter examines the relationship between the proliferation of these weapons and internal conflict and violence in Southeast Asia. It provides an overview of the threats to national and human security presented by small arms, and critically evaluates efforts made to address the problem.

The chapter is divided into three sections. The first section identifies the principal factors that make Southeast Asia susceptible to trafficking in illicit arms. It discusses the key routes through which weapons reach criminals and armed groups in the region, including transnational smuggling and the sourcing of weapons within states. The second section provides a preliminary assessment of the effects of small-arms misuse in the region. It explains some of the direct and indirect impacts and provides introductory data about the human costs of gun violence and armed conflict in the region. The final section assesses the response of civil society groups, national governments, and regional organizations such as the Association of Southeast Asian Nations (ASEAN) to what is increasingly recognized as a small-arms crisis in parts of the region.

Factors Making Southeast Asia Vulnerable

Three factors make Southeast Asia particularly susceptible to the proliferation and misuse of small arms and light weapons: a high demand for arms, a ready supply of surplus weapons, and the fact that the institutional weakness of many of the region's states makes them unable to respond effectively.

Together, these factors combine to create a permissive environment in which arms trafficking can thrive.

The persistence of armed conflict in Southeast Asia creates a high level of demand for weapons and ammunition. While Southeast Asia has not seen a major interstate war for more than two decades, the region continues to be afflicted by civil wars and intercommunal violence. Along Burma's borders with Thailand and Bangladesh, in the southern Philippines, and in Aceh, Maluku, and West Papua in Indonesia, armed groups are fighting either a state or other armed groups, seeking greater political autonomy, independence, or control over resources. In these conflicts, small arms and light weapons are the preferred tools of the trade.[1] They are cheap, easily concealed and transported, highly durable, and simple to maintain. They are also easy to use and well suited to the tactics employed by irregular armed forces, typically ambushes, terrorist attacks, and guerrilla operations. Because it is difficult—though not impossible—for these armed groups to acquire weapons through licit channels, their needs help sustain the illicit trade.

If the prevalence of intrastate conflict creates a demand for small arms, then the ubiquity of weapons in parts of Southeast Asia means there is a ready supply. While seven ASEAN members produce their own small arms, light weapons, or ammunition, and six are known to have exported these in the past, most illicit arms used by insurgents and criminals in the region are not new.[2] Rather, the overwhelming majority of weapons that pass through illicit channels come from existing stockpiles, not new production.

While no reliable baseline figure for Southeast Asia's small-arms holdings exists, millions of small arms and light weapons are known to circulate in states across the region. As is the case globally, by far the majority of these are in private hands. In the Philippines, official records show that 824,328 weapons were registered with the police in early 2003. Estimates as to the number of unregistered guns vary from 270,000 to 600,000.[3] One 2003 press report claimed there were 439,119 firearms "loose" within the country. Another source claims the total number of private weapons may be as high as 5.3 million.[4] The Thai government has reported the country as having 1,080,394 licensed private firearms, but news accounts place the number of licensed weapons at about 3.7 million, and there could be as many as 10 million illicit arms in circulation.[5] Large numbers of military arms are also stockpiled, and many are vulnerable to theft. After the United States withdrew from Indochina in 1975, Vietnam and Cambodia inherited some 2 million firearms and 150,000 metric tons of ammunition. Even after a government crackdown, between 500,000 and 1 million military arms remain in Cambodia alone.[6]

The Pathways of Proliferation

Weapons are diverted from licit holdings to illicit hands through a series of complex channels. The most important are theft from private ownership, leakage from government inventories or stockpiles, and diversions organized through brokers and arms dealers. The scale of these transactions varies enormously, from "straw man" purchases of just a handful of weapons, to boatloads with tons of illicit arms. In addition to these black-market sales, there are so-called gray-market transfers: covert, politically motivated transfers from governments to nonstate actors, typically with the involvement of the military or intelligence agencies.

While it is extremely difficult to gauge the proportion of illicit arms that move through these various routes, there is clear evidence that some of the most important sources are national militaries and police forces. Weapons leak out from state control either by being captured during combat, by being lost or stolen from poorly guarded government armories, or simply by being purchased from disaffected or corrupt members of the security forces. Incidents involving this kind of illegal leakage from national inventories and stockpiles plague Southeast Asia.

Cambodia has historically been the most important source of leaked weapons in the region. After the country's civil war ended in 1991, hundreds of thousands of surplus weapons were collected under various disarmament and demobilization programs. An EU-funded initiative for the collection and destruction of surplus weapons, EU Assistance on Curbing Small Arms and Light Weapons in Cambodia (EU-ASAC), has documented the poor quality of weapons-storage facilities throughout the country. Until the recent introduction of a weapons-security program, tens of thousands of arms taken from former combatants and armed civilians were stored in police stations and poorly guarded depots.[7] Once there, they were an obvious target for poorly paid military personnel seeking to supplement their wages.

Leakage from security forces has also been a serious problem in Indonesia. During intercommunal violence in Maluku in 2000, hundreds of military weapons were stolen from overrun police stations and military armories. In just one incident at Tantui in July 2000, more than 800 military-style rifles were looted, along with thousands of rounds of ammunition.[8] There have also been allegations that weapons and explosives have gone missing directly from the country's national arms producer, PT Pindad.[9]

Militant groups have also tried to acquire weapons from military camps and armories in Malaysia and Thailand. In January 2004, more than thirty members of a separatist group attacked an army depot in the southern Thai town of Narathiwat. They killed four soldiers and made off with more than 100 weapons.[10] Similarly well-planned raids have taken place in Malaysia. In July 2000, fifteen men dressed in army uniforms persuaded sentries to let them into the camp near Grik and seized more than 100 M-16 and Steyr AUG rifles, machine guns, grenade launchers, mortar shells, and thousands of rounds of ammunition.[11] The Malaysian government blamed the raid on an Islamic radical group known as Al-Ma'unah, but an investigation also implicated several soldiers sympathetic to the group.[12] The theft of army weapons from Grik was not without precedent.[13] A criminal gang armed with Malaysian military-issue Steyr rifles was involved in a series of armed robberies during 1999 and 2000 before finally being arrested.[14]

Security Forces Complicity

In addition to leakage through theft and negligence, state security forces are also actively complicit in the transfer of weapons to paramilitaries and rebel groups, either for political purposes or for profit. Indonesia's security forces have been notorious in this respect, most notably when they armed militia groups like Aitarak and Mahidi in the lead-up to the September 1999 independence referendum in East Timor.[15] The Indonesian military forces have also transferred weapons to Islamic militants in Maluku, while the Indonesian police force provided small arms to rival groups. In the rebellious province of Aceh, Indonesean soldiers have sold weapons to the Gerakan Aceh Merdeka (GAM) rebels they are supposed to be fighting.[16] GAM leaders have also claimed that senior Indonesian generals are involved in supplying them with weapons. In Thailand, the country's Fourth Army has been implicated in the sale of its arms to criminal syndicates and Burmese and Acehnese rebels, while in the Philippines, terrorist and insurgent groups openly proclaim that their most important sources of weapons are the armed forces of the Philippines and the Philippines national police.[17] In July 2003 more than 300 members of the armed forces took over a shopping mall in central Manila to protest the involvement of corrupt senior officers in selling their weapons and ammunition to the Moro Islamic Liberation Front (MILF).[18]

Weak States

In addition to an intense demand for weapons and a ready supply, a third factor contributing to small-arms problems in Southeast Asia is the lack of institutional capacity in many ASEAN states. Some countries simply do not have adequate resources for law enforcement. Firearms legislation is often out of date and filled with loopholes.[19] Often, regional militaries have no accurate figures about the size or location of their arms inventories. Audits are rare and poor record keeping makes theft and loss much more likely. The low salaries, poor training, and lack of resources that are available to police and judicial officers further aggravate the situation, encouraging bribery and corruption, and in some cases even allowing the capture of some state institutions.

These institutional weaknesses are compounded by the physical challenges of preventing illicit arms trafficking in Southeast Asia. Poorly demarcated borders create law enforcement problems between Thailand, Laos, and Burma. The Indonesian government faces the nearly impossible task of policing almost 17,000 islands stretching across an expanse equal to one-sixth of the equator. Some of the least-accessible territory anywhere in the world is found along the country's long land border with Papua New Guinea. Maritime boundaries between Eastern Malaysia, the Philippines, and Indonesia are also unclear, and enforcement is complicated by the number of fishermen and refugees who frequently move back and forth across borders. With arms traffickers frequently using small boats and fishing trawlers to move their cargo, already overstretched law enforcement and maritime patrols find themselves looking for needles in haystacks.

Arms-Trafficking Routes

Past analysis of small arms trafficking in Southeast Asia has tended to categorize regional countries as either source, transit, or destination states. While this typology has some explanatory utility, it arguably fails to capture the increasingly complex patterns of proliferation in the region. Weapons flows frequently move both ways across national borders and supply patterns quickly change as levels of demand rise and fall.

Several well-known pipelines are used for the transnational movement of illicit small arms. Typically, these begin in Indochina, the most important source of weapons for the region's many intrastate conflicts. Since the end of its civil war, Cambodia has operated as a kind of weapons supermarket for arms dealers and brokers searching for low-cost military hardware. Surplus arms stolen from weapons storage depots with the connivance of corrupt officials are moved by land across the border into Thailand, where they can be sold to criminal gangs, or transported by sea or over land to markets in Burma, Sri Lanka, and Indonesia. A larger proportion of the weapons—80 percent by one estimate—leaves via southern ports such as Kompong Som (Sihanoukville) and moves along the coastline to Rayong and Pattaya in the Gulf of Thailand.[20]

Well-known buyers of Cambodian arms include the Liberation Tigers of Tamil Eelam (LTTE), Burmese rebels, and armed groups operating in India's northeastern states.[21] Burmese factions like the Shan State Army and Karen National Liberation Army are supplied by land through Thailand, with the porous Thai-Cambodian and Thai-Burmese borders making these transfers relatively easy to accomplish.[22]

According to intelligence sources, the most important sea routes for trafficking out of Thailand are the islands off the coast of Phuket, as well as the southern provinces of Ranong and Satun.[23] Cambodian-sourced weapons destined for the Tamil Tigers are shipped from near Phuket, first on trawlers before later being transferred to speedboats off the coast of Sri Lanka.[24] Totally shutting down the trade is almost impossible, given the thousands of vessels that fish Thai waters and the large number of small islands where weapons can be cached and transshipped.[25] The complicity of the Thai and Burmese militaries in smuggling operations also undermines efforts at law enforcement. At one time an LTTE base on Twante Island south of Rangoon was operated through an understanding with several Burmese generals and the Tatmadaw—the Burmese Army—has also been linked to arms trafficking by the Moyaza pirate group.[26]

But while Thailand is typically portrayed as a transit country, more and more evidence suggests it is also an important source of illicit weapons and ammunition. One important, if only recently recognized, channel involves the domestic retransfer of imported military weapons. In April 2001, Thai airforce officers were implicated in a scam to resell imported duty-free 9 mm Glock pistols onto the local black market.[27] A subsequent investigation revealed that as many as 30,000 weapons had been diverted in this way, with an unknown number sold to armed groups and criminal gangs.[28] In May 2003, agents from the LTTE and GAM were arrested after buying small numbers of weapons from gun shops.[29] The arrests led the Police Crime Suppression Division to conclude that legal gun shops formed the core of the illegal arms trade in Thailand.[30]

A second major arms trafficking pipeline passes from southern Thailand across the Strait of Malacca to Aceh. According to a report by the Indonesian magazine *Forum Keadilan,* GAM is primarily armed with weapons sourced within Indonesia and from Indochina. From Cambodia, arms pass through southern Thailand, often with the help of separatist groups like the Mujahidin Islam of Pattani.[31] The Malaysian city of Penang, with its large Acehnese population, has also been identified as an important transit point. According to officials based in Aceh, weapons are transported across the Straits of Malacca in small boats, often being retransferred again at sea, before landing in Sumatra in places like Lhokseumawe, Padang, Tanjung Balai, and Peureulak.[32] Again, the size of the boats and number of vessels using these waters make interdiction at sea by Malaysian or Indonesian naval and marine forces extremely difficult.

Like Thailand, the Philippines also resists any easy characterization as a source, transit, or destination country. Large numbers of illegal arms are smuggled out of the Philippines to various foreign markets, including Indonesia, Japan, and Taiwan. Another problem is controlling illegal production in the south, particularly in Danao city and Mandaue city in Cebu, where there are more than 3,000 gunsmiths at work.[33] In addition to Danao's two major licensed arms makers, there are many illegal or quasi-legal producers manufacturing *paltik,* or homemade weapons. Many of these are of low quality, often crafted from scrap metal, but there is growing evidence that some producers are now making high-quality, customized military-style small arms as well.[34] Buyers include local crime organizations and rebels, as well as Taiwanese and Japanese crime syndicates.[35] According to a report by the Philippines Centre for Transnational Crime (PCTC), agents collect finished firearms from a variety of small producers and consolidate them for shipment to Japan. Important exit points reportedly include Batangas, Ilocos Sur, and other northern parts of the country.[36] In the southern Philippines, arms trafficking is a serious problem in Agusan, Misamis, Surigao, Sulu, Basilan, Tawi-tawi, and Zamboanga provinces.[37]

But the Philippines is also a destination country and a point of transit for arms shipped to parts of Indonesia, especially the strife-torn regions of Maluku and Sulawesi. Groups in the Middle East were reported to have established links with Islamic armed groups in the southern Philippines from the mid-1970s on. Iran, Lebanon, Pakistan, Sudan, and Libya have all been mentioned as suppliers.[38] Members of the Abu Sayyaf terrorist group and GAM trained in Libya and Tripoli reportedly helped transfer large numbers of Pakistan-made arms to the Moro National Liberation Front.[39] Cold War ideological ties also saw the transfer of abandoned U.S. arms from Vietnam to the left-wing New People's Army in the 1980s.

Philippines Security Personnel at Zamboanga Airport, Mindanao.

More recently, the Al-Qaida and Jemaah Islamiyah terrorist networks have been linked to Filipino armed groups, and there have been reports of arms and ammunition being transferred from Saudi Arabia and Afghanistan.[40] Despite these ties, evidence suggests that Filipino armed groups source most of their weapons locally, and it is these illegal arms that are being passed on to Indonesian groups. The inventory of groups like the MILF and Abu Sayyaf is dominated by Philippines state-issue small arms. According to MILF spokesman Eid Kabalu, local sources are plentiful, while buying arms overseas is a process that is "long, expensive and risky."[41]

Under the Gun: The Impacts of Small Arms Misuse

Clearly there is a permissive environment for the proliferation and misuse of small arms and light weapons in Southeast Asia. What, then, are the impacts of those weapons on peace and security? At the UN Conference on the Illicit Trade in Small Arms and Light Weapons in 2001, states recognized that the excessive accumulation and uncontrolled spread of small arms have a "wide range of humanitarian and socio-economic consequences and pose a serious threat to . . . security, stability and sustainable development at the individual, national, regional and international levels."[42] There is a growing body of evidence establishing clear links between the availability and misuse of small arms and a wide range of negative social indicators. Direct impacts of the misuse of small arms include physical injuries and deaths, psychological trauma, forced displacement, the costs of treating victims, as well as the opportunity costs of long-term disability and lost productivity. Indirect effects can include discouraged investment, impeded economic development, a rise in armed criminality, and weakened social capital. The widespread availability of weapons can also impede the delivery of basic social services and lead international agencies and aid workers to withdraw humanitarian assistance in areas of conflict.

One difficulty with any attempt to assess the impacts of small arms in Southeast Asia—and indeed in many developing states—is a lack of reliable data. Not surprisingly, in war zones information is hard to obtain and rarely accurate. Even away from areas of armed conflict, basic data on firearms-related deaths or injuries are frequently poorly kept or distorted by under-reporting. In some cases, data on firearms-related crime do not exist, or are tightly controlled for spurious "national security" purposes. Methodologically rigorous research on impacts in Southeast Asia is now being undertaken and better data will be available in the future. For the time being, however, the fragmentary figures that are available suggest serious negative impacts from small arms and light weapons that warrant further investigation.

In terms of direct effects, easy access to firearms has been associated with the increased incidence of intrastate conflicts. While small arms by themselves do not cause conflict, their availability can exacerbate conflicts by prolonging violence and increasing its lethality. As a World Health Organization report notes, "The level of weapons technology does not affect the risk of a conflict, but it does determine the scale of any conflict and the amount of destruction that will take place."[43] To take one example from the region, when intercommunal violence originally broke out in Ambon in Indonesia in 1999, swords, spears, and machetes were among the weapons most commonly used. Once firearms were brought into the area (and a large number of homemade weapons were produced) levels of fatalities and violence rapidly increased.[44]

Armed conflict is also a driver of mass displacement, and the presence of small arms has been shown to aggravate forced displacement patterns.[45] As a result of fighting between armed groups and Burma's military junta, more than 125,000 refugees now live in camps along the Thai-Burma border. The militarization and use of these camps for coerced recruitment is also a growing problem.[46] Within Burma itself, there are believed to be between 600,000 and 1 million internally displaced persons (IDPs).[47] Ethnic and religious violence in Indonesia created an estimated 1.3 million IDPs in 2002 and since the government's May 2003 military offensive in Aceh, more than 100,000 people have been displaced.[48]

High levels of violence-induced displacement are also associated with increased risk of illness and disease. While none of the major international datasets on armed conflict measures the indirect death toll caused by war, research by several international relief agencies has found a strong correlation between high rates of armed violence, declining access to social services, and child mortality from nonviolent causes.[49] A 2001 report by the UN Children's Fund assessed Mindanao's child mortality rate at more than 310 per 100,000 per day, a level similar to that seen in Rwandan refugee camps. (A rate of 10 per 100,000 per day is classified as an emergency.)[50] These are indirect victims of gun violence whose deaths are rarely reflected in standard analyses of armed conflict and violence.

Linking the availability of small arms and criminality is more complex and causality less clear-cut. However, high homicide rates in parts of Southeast Asia are associated with ready access to firearms, although the rudimentary nature of the data in some jurisdictions warrants caution. As can be seen in Table 9.1.1, Cambodia, Thailand, and the Philippines—all states known to have very high (if not precisely quantifiable) levels of private firearms ownership—have significantly higher homicide rates than neighboring countries with lower levels of firearms ownership. Research in Mindanao by the British relief agency Oxfam found that 78 percent of all violent deaths and injuries that occurred in crimes reported to the authorities were carried out with military-style weapons.[51] While better data are needed to make an authoritative determination, one judicious analysis of levels of lethal violence in Southeast Asia concludes that the most important explanation for these comparatively high homicide rates is "enduring relatively unfettered [access to] firearms, low enforcement capability and regime influenced policing institutions."[52]

Ready access to firearms by abusive institutions of the state also creates circumstances conducive to serious human rights violations and extrajudicial killings. Thai prime minister Thaksin Shinawatra's recent campaign to crack down on so-called dark influences, has seen a surge in such killings. In a three-month period at the beginning of 2003, more than 2,200 people, including children as young as nine, died at the hands of police adopting a "shoot to kill" approach.[53] In Cambodia, extrajudicial homicides make up over 25 percent of all officially reported deaths and more than 40 percent of deaths covered in the local press. According to Roderic Broadhurst, the high number of extrajudicial killings can be attributed to the "armed nature of most offending, a weak rule of law culture and the poor discipline and training of the police."[54]

Table 9.1.1 Homicide Rates in Southeast Asia

	Gross National Product per Capita (U.S.$)	Gini Coefficient	Homicide Rate (per 100,000)
Cambodia	270	0.40	9.3
Indonesia	998	0.32	0.9
Malaysia	4,287	0.49	2.1
Myanmar	765	n/a	1.4
Philippines	1,203	0.45	16.2
Singapore	31,900	0.39	2.6
Thailand	2,450	0.44	9.6

Sources: Roderic Broadhurst, "Lethal Violence, Crime, and State Formation in Cambodia," *Australian and New Zealand Journal of Criminology* 35, no. 1 (2002): 1–26; *Small Arms Survey 2003: Development Denied* (Oxford: Oxford University Press, 2003); *Asian Development Bank (2002);* World Health Organization, *Global Report on Violence and Health* (Geneva: World Health Organization, 2002).

Note: n/a = not available.

In many countries that have suffered conflict, rates of violence remain high even after the cessation of hostilities. This is in part because violence becomes more socially acceptable, but also because of the ready availability of weapons.[55] According to one report, Phnom Penh has an armed robbery rate four times that of Bangkok (despite its much smaller population) and has the highest number of armed robberies and murders in Southeast Asia. Another estimate is that three Cambodians die a violent death at the hands of military weapons every day.[56] Property crime is also very high. A survey of 783 households in Phnom Penh carried out in 2002 revealed that more than 60 percent had experienced theft in the previous year, mostly carried out by armed gangs.[57] Studies in Cambodia in the 1990s have also linked the ubiquity of small arms to high levels of violence and intimidation against women.[58]

There is also some preliminary evidence about the indirect socioeconomic effects of small arms proliferation and misuse in Southeast Asia. According to one recent survey, these "are more insidious and potentially of greater concern" than direct impacts like death and injury.[59] Research in the southern Philippines demonstrates the deleterious effect that armed conflict has on economic and social development. Violence in Mindanao has not only prevented new development projects from going forward, but also eroded gains from projects already in place.[60] As one analysis has noted, "Poverty and conflict [have] perpetuated a vicious cycle. Poverty fuelled conflict—by magnifying the sense of marginalization and exclusion. Conflict, in turn, aggravate[d] poverty—through its effects on people, institutions and the economy."[61] More specifically, there is evidence of the negative impact of the ready availability of firearms in schools and university campuses in the region.[62] In the Philippines, such violence not only causes direct impacts such as deaths and injuries, but also leads students to avoid school and undermines the quality of the education system, imposing additional social and economic costs.[63]

Finally, small arms proliferation is closely linked to and supports other forms of criminal behavior, including drug trafficking and the illegal extraction of resources such as timber and gems.[64] Links between Thai political, business, and military figures and the Khmer Rouge were well documented through the mid-1990s, with arms and money being exchanged for logging and precious-stone concessions. According to one estimate, logging concessions alone were worth some U.S.$10–20 million a month to the Khmer Rouge, revenue that was used to sustain military operations.[65] The increasing number of guns-for-drugs deals, particularly along the Thai-Burma border, also evidences the nexus between organized crime and arms smuggling. In the past, weapons were frequently exchanged for heroin, such as that produced by Khun Sa's Mong Thai Army. More recently, the bulk of the trade has been in methamphetamine, much of which is produced by ethnic Wa militias operating with impunity in the eastern Shan state after signing cease-fire agreements with Rangoon.[66] An estimated 1 billion speed pills cross into Thailand annually, often in exchange for weapons and ammunition.

Off Target? Local, National, and Regional Responses

The principal focus for international action against the illicit trade in small arms and light weapons has been the United Nations. In July 2001 the UN adopted a program of action designed to combat the illicit trade in small arms and ammunition. It called upon all states to implement adequate legislative and regulatory controls over the production and transfer of firearms, the creation of national coordination agencies to guide policy efforts to combat the illicit trade, better management of military and police stockpiles, destruction of surplus weapons, and improved systems for the marking and tracing of weapons. At the regional level, states were obliged to establish cooperative mechanisms for information sharing among law enforcement, border, and customs control officials. While the program has been criticized by some for not going far enough, it provides a benchmark against which policy responses in Southeast Asia can be assessed.[67]

Civil Society Responses

Internationally, NGOs and civil society groups have been at the forefront of efforts pushing for compliance with the UN program. Organizations like the International Action Network on Small Arms (IANSA) and the "Biting the Bullet" coalition have been vocal critics of governments that have failed to meet the obligations they agreed to in 2001.[68] While NGOs have been less prominent in Southeast Asia—partly because of the illiberal nature of many regimes—a number of civil society actors in several regional states have been active on small arms issues. Perhaps the most successful has been the Cambodian Working Group for Weapons Reduction (WGWR), which has worked closely with both local NGOs and the Cambodian government to address the kingdom's small arms challenge. The WGWR has monitored demobilization activities and engaged in a nationwide education campaign designed to promote awareness about small arms and build a culture of peace. The WGWR has also carried out research on the impact of weapons in communities, including schools, and made recommendations to the Ministry of Interior during the drafting of new firearms legislation.[69]

The Philippines Action Network on Small Arms (PhilANSA) has launched a series of activities to promote public education and awareness about firearms issues.[70] The group began with projects in three regions—Mindanao, the Visayas, and Luzon—each with the aim of helping communities confront the human cost of arms. PhilANSA faces a considerable challenge in its efforts to reduce gun ownership. The Philippines has its own large and well-organized gun lobby, including the "Peaceful, Responsible Owners of Guns" coalition, which has forcefully argued against more restrictive laws on firearms ownership.[71]

Recently, the WGWR and PhilANSA joined forces with the Bangkok-based group Nonviolence International Southeast Asia to create the Regional Action Network to Reduce Arms Violence (RARAV). According to its founders, "RARAV is an open network of NGOs who are concerned with the impact of weapons and armed violence in Southeast Asian society."[72] Its members are committed to undertaking cooperative action to address "militarization, [the] culture of violence, weapons and human trafficking, human rights violations, and the impact of the arms trade." The groups have also taken part in several regional seminars on small arms, at both nongovernmental and governmental levels. In October 2003 they organized activities and demonstrations as part of the international "Control Arms" campaign, founded by Amnesty International, IANSA, and Oxfam.[73]

Uneven Government Action

At the governmental level, action against small arms in Southeast Asia has been extremely uneven. Regimes in Burma, Vietnam, and Laos have paid lip service to the UN's program of action, occasionally citing some elements that suit their interests, but have generally not taken any practical steps to address small arms issues.[74] Elsewhere, there has been some modest progress, but most governments have framed the small arms challenge as a question of transnational crime or terrorism and have focused on adopting supply-side measures. They have been notably unwilling to confront links between the licit and illicit arms trade or address the underlying factors creating a demand for arms.

Some progress has been made in the area of collection and destruction of surplus stocks. In Cambodia, a newly formed National Commission for Weapons Management and Reform has collected some 120,000 weapons, and has destroyed 111,161 through burning and crushing.[75] Cambodia has also introduced a program to secure government weapons stocks. With European and Japanese assistance, arms depots in two of its six military regions have been made secure. In the Philippines, 45,000 weapons had been collected, confiscated, or surrendered to police by December 2002. In addition, 6,500 confiscated weapons were destroyed in July 2001 and a smaller number were destroyed in 2002.[76]

There have also been some efforts to introduce tougher gun control measures in regional states. In 1999 the Thai government launched a pilot project banning the issue of new firearms licenses in the province of Phuket. Bans have also been introduced in other provinces and towns that rely heavily on tourism, including Pattaya and Chiang Rai.[77] This approach was expanded in May 2003, when the Thai Ministry of Interior ordered gun dealers to suspend all sales of rifles to the public and introduced limits on the number of weapons any individual can own.[78] More recently, Prime Minister Thaksin Shinawatra announced his intention to make Thailand a "gun-free society" within six years. However, the policy was greeted with opposition from the public and from the country's gun lobby and it remains to be seen just how effectively it will be implemented.[79]

In February 2003 the Philippines government introduced an executive order banning civilians and off-duty police officers from carrying arms outside their homes. The country also regularly imposes similar bans in the lead-up to elections.[80] Generally, however, changes in regional gun control laws have only been made on an ad hoc basis. Only Cambodia has reviewed and comprehensively overhauled its gun laws. In 2002 it introduced new legislation on small arms that restricts the right to bear arms and imposes higher penalties for violations.

Regional Responses: Rhetoric or Reality?

At the regional level, small-arms and light-weapons problems have been treated primarily as a transnational crime issue. ASEAN's first effort to address small-arms issues came at a conference on transnational crime held in Manila in December 1997. The meeting produced a declaration in which ASEAN members agreed to cooperate on tackling a range of transnational threats, including arms trafficking. The first meeting to focus specifically on small-arms issues came in May 2000, at a regional seminar held in Jakarta. This concluded with a general agreement to focus on strengthening law enforcement and improving coordination and intelligence sharing. In accordance with ASEAN's preference for avoiding formality and legalistic solutions, the agreement was nonbinding.

Efforts to combat weapons trafficking have increased since the September 2001 terrorist attacks in New York and Washington, D.C., and the October 2002 Bali bombing. The United States has pressed Southeast Asian nations to formulate individual and collective responses to terrorism in the region. However, the war on terror has had mixed results for small-arms concerns in Southeast Asia. On the one hand, it has been an important catalyst for improved international cooperation against arms trafficking. A plethora of bilateral and multilateral initiatives have been designed to improve law enforcement, military, customs, and intelligence cooperation between ASEAN states. In May 2002, ASEAN chiefs of police adopted a work program on combating small-arms trafficking. This nonbinding document encourages regional states to exchange information about illicit arms flows, build law enforcement capacity, destroy surplus weapons, and harmonize the marking of their arms and ammunition. Regional militaries have also begun to improve their coordination in patrolling well-known smuggling routes like the Straits of Malacca.[81] With U.S. support, a regional center for counterterrorism in Southeast Asia has been established in Kuala Lumpur, promising to help build capacity in the region to address transnational problems, including arms trafficking.

On the other hand, Washington's apparent preference for military solutions to combat terrorism could actually aggravate aspects of the region's small-arms problem. For example, as part of its campaign against terrorism, the United States gifted the Philippines armed forces more than 30,000 M-16 rifles under its "Excess Defense Articles" program.[82] Given the poor security of many Philippines state armories and evidence that Philippines security forces are complicit in the transfer of arms to terrorists and rebel groups, this seems likely to be counterproductive. The U.S. desire to resurrect military-to-military ties with Indonesia also risks offering legitimacy to an institution that has not yet been fully held accountable for its role in killings in Timor, Aceh, and West Papua. Washington's war on terror also increases the likelihood that Southeast Asian regimes may step up their own misuse of arms, as they begin to see all opposition groups as "terrorists."

Despite the progress that has been made in the last few years, ASEAN as a regional organization has been unwilling to deal with some of the broader consequences of the small-arms challenge. Its model of "sovereignty-enhancing regionalism" and fundamental norm of noninterference means it is unable to effectively address what are deemed to be "internal" issues in member states. Its members have shown no inclination to pool sovereignty, or to give the organization's small, Jakarta-based secretariat the authority and resources needed to play a more active role on security issues, including illicit arms proliferation. As a consequence, there has been impressive rhetoric at the regional level, but only limited practical action. There have been no moves to improve transparency to prevent the diversion of arms transfers in the region or regulate the role of arms brokers, let alone deal with the factors that fuel the demand for weapons. Commitment to the UN process also varies significantly within the region. Only four of ten regional states reported on their implementation of the UN program of action to a follow-up meeting held in New York in July 2003, and just five have appointed a national "point of contact" for small arms issues—one of the least-demanding requirements of the program. The ASEAN experience seems to confirm Aaron Karp's observation that while strong regional institutions force national governments to put their house in order, where regional institutions are weaker, as in Southeast Asia, so too is the pressure for effective action.[83]

Conclusion

This chapter has documented the complex and multidimensional nature of the small arms challenge in Southeast Asia. As long as some governments address small arms issues in a piecemeal and halfhearted fashion, there will continue to be significant negative consequences for both state and human security in the region. Poor regulation, weak law enforcement, and violence in one jurisdiction expose neighboring states to arms flows, crime, and corruption. The serious economic and developmental consequences of inaction are also increasingly apparent and frequently spill over national borders. Failure to address internal issues like societal violence and the factors that create a demand for weapons not only condemns civilians to continued suffering, but also allows the root causes of terrorism to develop and spread. Until Southeast Asian governments recognize the need to forge a broad, multidimensional, and coordinated response to the challenge posed by small arms, the long shadow cast by these weapons will continue to hang over the region.

Website Resources

www.controlarms.org (Control Arms Campaign)
www.hdcentre.org/programmes/small.htm (Centre for Humanitarian Dialogue)
www.iansa.org (International Action Network on Small Arms)
www.smallarmssurvey.org (Small Arms Survey)
www.wgwr.org (Working Group on Weapons Reduction)

David Capie is codirector of the Armed Groups Project at the University of British Columbia, Vancouver, Canada. His most recent book is Under the Gun: The Small

Arms Challenge in the Pacific *(Victoria University of Wellington Press, 2003). He has also published several books on Asia Pacific security issues, including* The Asia-Pacific Security Lexicon *(2001) with Paul M. Evans, and* Small Arms Production and Transfers in Southeast Asia *(2002).*

Notes

I am grateful to Neb Sinthay, Gina Rivas Pattugalan, Andrew Mack, Cate Buchanan, Daniel Eaton, Wendy McAvoy, and Annelies Heijmans for comments and assistance received during the preparation of this chapter. I am also grateful for the research assistance of Bernice Wong.

1. According to one survey, In forty-six of forty-nine major conflicts fought between 1990 and 1998, small arms and light weapons were the only arms used. See Jeffrey Boutwell and Michael Klare, "Small Arms and Light Weapons: Controlling the Real Instruments of War," *Arms Control Today,* August–September 1998.

2. For a detailed discussion of small arms and ammunition production in ASEAN states, see David Capie, *Small Arms Production and Transfers in Southeast Asia,* Canberra Paper no. 146 (Canberra: Strategic and Defence Studies Centre, Australian National University, 2002).

3. According to a Philippines government report to the United Nations, there are 284,100 loose firearms, of this estimate 189,766 were not reregistered, 2,156 were "lost," and 94,313 were in the hands of various armed groups and criminals. How this last figure was calculated is not reported. See *National Report on the Implementation of the Programme of Action (POA) to Prevent, Combat, and Eradicate the Illicit Trade in Small Arms and Light Weapons in All Its Aspects,* Republic of the Philippines, July 3, 2003, available at the Small Arms Survey's database, www.smallarmssurvey.org.

4. *Manila Times,* February 10, 2003. The 5.3 million figure is cited in *Small Arms Survey 2002: Counting the Human Cost* (Oxford: Oxford University Press, 2002), p. 99.

5. Wassayos Ngamkham, "Guns the 'Weapons of Choice' in Murders," *Bangkok Post,* September 15, 2003; "Ban on Sales Won't Work," *Bangkok Post,* September 10, 2003.

6. Michelle Vachon and Ana Nov, "Unreliable Gun Statistics Agree Only That Nation Well-Armed," *Cambodia Daily,* February 20, 2001, p. 8.

7. There has been progress in securing weapons stocks in Cambodia. By the end of 2002, two of the six military regions in Cambodia had had their weapons stocks audited, registered, and stored securely. Eight arms depots in Phnom Penh were also made secure. The country is aiming to implement the program nationwide by 2006.

8. "Calls for Int'l Troops in Maluku Brushed Aside," *Jakarta Post,* August 7, 2000.

9. "Pindad, Police Give Conflicting Account on AG Office Bomb," *Jakarta Post,* July 8, 2000.

10. BBC News, "Armed Raids in Southern Thailand," January 4, 2004.

11. "Military Combs Malaysian Jungle for Missing Weapons," *Straits Times,* July 5, 2000; Thomas Fuller, "Malaysia Armory Thieves Surrounded," *International Herald Tribune,* July 5, 2000.

12. Jestyn Cooper, "Rebel Group Threatens Malaysian Security," *Jane's Intelligence Review,* September 1, 2000; Wan Hamidi Hamid, "Mahathir: Arms Heist Gang out to Topple Government," *Straits Times,* July 11, 2000; "Nine More Soldiers Involved in Arms Heist Questioned," *Straits Times,* July 13, 2000.

13. Four Steyr rifles were stolen from another army camp in Kamaunting, Perak, in July 1999. See Bernama News Agency, "Two Cases of Theft at Army Camps in Last Five Years," November 22, 2000.

14. The group, known as the "Steyr Gang," carried out a number of armed robberies on banks and finance companies, before four members were shot dead by police

and the weapons were recovered. See "Audit Check at Military Camp Armouries After Steyr Thefts," *New Straits Times*, August 8, 1999; and Bernama News Agency, "All Four Stolen Steyr Automatic Rifles Recovered," January 19, 2000. See also Ghazemy Mahmood, "Security Tightened at Military Weapons Stores," Bermana News Agency, January 19, 2000; M. Jeffri Razali, "No Cover-Up of Arms Thefts," *New Straits Times*, February 4, 2000; and Tony Emmanuel, "Steyr Gang 'Mastermind' Nabbed in Police Ambush," *New Straits Times*, August 31, 2000.

15. BBC News, "Indonesia Admits Arming Militias," February 6, 1999.

16. Australian Broadcasting Corporation, "Indonesian Solider Arrested for Aceh Weapons Sales," January 6, 2000.

17. See the comments of Abu Sayyaf, member Abu Solaiman, as recalled by former hostage Gracia Burnham, quoted in Anthony Davis, "Philippine Security Threatened by Small-Arms Proliferation," *Jane's Intelligence Review*, August 2003, p. 34.

18. Friena P. Guerrero, "Mutiny Leaders Blame 'Corruption' in Military," *BusinessWorld Publishing*, August 14, 2003.

19. Some of these loopholes are described in Katherine Kramer, *Legal Controls on Small Arms and Light Weapons in Southeast Asia* (Geneva: Small Arms Survey, 2001).

20. Senior Thai military officer quoted in Craig Skehan, "Thais Run Huge Arms Trade," *Sydney Morning Herald*, August 14, 1999. A British arms dealer interviewed by an NGO working to curb small arms problems claimed to have made purchases from the Cambodian Ministry of Defense, which supplied the arms for shipment in containers at Kompong Som. See *Curbing the Demand for Small Arms: Focus on Southeast Asia* (Geneva: Centre for Humanitarian Dialogue, 2003), p. 22.

21. "Thai Military, Police Officers Arrested for Selling Guns to Sri Lanka Rebels," *The Star*, September 23, 2003; "Arms Seized by Thai Navy Destined for Indian Rebels," *Thailand Times*, March 18, 1997; Anthony Davis, "Thailand Tenders Anti-Trafficking Plan to Others," *Jane's Defence Weekly*, April 21, 1999.

22. Author's interviews, Phnom Penh and Bangkok, November 2000 and February 2001.

23. Davis, "Thailand Tenders Anti-Trafficking Plan."

24. "Chuan Pledges Watch on Tamil Arms Link," *The Nation*, May 29, 1999; Robert Karniol, "Sri Lanka Says Tigers Are Trading Arms in Cambodia," *Jane's Defence Weekly*, October 2, 1996; Bertil Lintner, "LTTE Purchases, a Link with Cambodia," *Jane's Intelligence Review*, December 1, 1996. For a recent analysis on LTTE smuggling operations, see Chris Smith, "In the Shadow of a Ceasefire: The Impacts of Small Arms Availability and Misuse in Sri Lanka," *Small Arms Survey Occasional Paper* no. 11 (October 2003): 10–14.

25. "Thailand, Sri Lanka to Foster Defence Cooperation," *The Nation*, April 9, 1999.

26. "Army Chief Insists Rebels Have Local Base," *The Nation*, March 29, 2000; "Tamil Tigers 'Extend Net in Thailand,'" *The Nation*, August 4, 2000; "Leader of Captured Weapons Linked to Pirates," *Thailand Times*, March 13, 1997; "Navy Seizes Weapons Reportedly Destined for Tamil Tigers," *Thailand Times*, March 12, 1997.

27. "Airforce Firearms Theft: Informants Hand in Twenty-five of the Stolen Glock Pistols, Only Five Still Not Accounted For," *Bangkok Post*, April 16, 2001; "Officer Who Ordered Pistols Claims He Was Duped," *The Nation*, April 19, 2001.

28. "Firearms Imports," *Bangkok Post*, April 28, 2001.

29. Wassayos Ngamkham, "In the Market for a Firearm?" *Bangkok Post*, October 7, 2003.

30. Ibid.

31. "FOKUS: Cara GAM Mengail Dana," *Forum Keadilan* 31, no. 5 (November 2000): 80–86; Muhamad Ayub Pathan, "Arms Trio Linked to Separatists," *Bangkok Post*, July 6, 2003; "Dead Separatist Was a Gun Runner: Thaksin," *The Nation*, August 30, 2003.

32. Aceh-based official cited in interview notes provided to the author during interviews in Jakarta. See also John McBeth, Nate Thayer, and Bertil Lintner, "Worse to Come," *Far Eastern Economic Review,* July 29, 1999.

33. Alexandra A. Seno, "Aiming for legitimacy," *Asiaweek,* January 19, 1996, p. 29.

34. Justin Morozzi, "Rest, Work, and Play by the Gun: Firearms Ownership, Dealership, and Production Are Routine in sleepy Danao," *Financial Times,* April 19, 1997.

35. Author interview with Philippines ambassador to Cambodia H. E. Francisco Atayde, Phnom Penh, February 22, 2001; Disraeli Y. Parreño, "Danao City Big Supplier of Yakuza Guns," *Manila Chronicle,* January 21, 1995, p. 183. On an alleged weapons-for-drugs partnership between Abu Sayyaf and the Hong Kong 14-K crime syndicate, see Donna S. Cueto, "Abu Links to Int'l Drug Ring Probed," *Philippines Daily Inquirer,* July 17, 2000.

36. Rodrigo de Gracia and Camilo Cascolan, "PCTC Paper on Illegal Manufacturing of and Trafficking in Firearms," unpublished paper, The Philippine Center on Transnational Crime, Quezon City (n.d., author's copy), pp. 17–19.

37. Ibid., p. 20.

38. "Abu Sayyaf Weapons Capabilities, Foreign Supporters Listed," *Philippines Daily Inquirer,* July 31, 1994, pp. 1, 12.

39. "Libya-Trained Rebels Blamed for Current Aceh Violence," *Jakarta Post,* July 30, 1999; Cathy Rose A. Garcia and Manolette C. Payumo, "MILF Tells Gov't to Choose: Talk Peace or Resume War," *Business World,* February 22, 2000.

40. "Bin Laden Funds Abu Sayyaf Through Muslim Relief Group," *Philippines Daily Inquirer,* August 9, 2000.

41. Anthony Davis, "Philippine Security Threatened by Small-Arms Proliferation," *Jane's Intelligence Review,* August 2003, p. 33.

42. United Nations, *Report of the United Nations Conference on the Illicit Trade in Small Arms and Light Weapons in All Its Aspects,* A/CONF/.92/15, I, New York, July 9–20, 2001, para 2.

43. World Health Organization, *Global Report on Violence and Health* (Geneva: World Health Organization, 2002), p. 222.

44. These data are drawn from an unpublished 2002 report commissioned by Oxfam.

45. Robert Muggah, "Small Arms and Forced Displacement," *Forced Migration Organization Research Guide* (October 2002), available at www.forcedmigration.org/guides/fmo002.

46. For example, see two reports by Amnesty International, *East Timor: Forced Recruitment and Arrests in Relocation Camps,* ASA 21/139/1999, September 8, 1999, and *Nowhere to Run,* ASA 16/024/2001, December 7, 2001.

47. Global IDP, Myanmar (Burma) database entry, available at www.db.idpproject.org.

48. Department of Foeign Affairs, Republic of Indonesia, "Briefing Paper on Current Development in the Province Nanggroe Aceh Darussalam (NAD), Period 19 May–10 August 2003"; UN Office for the Coordination of Humanitarian Affairs (OCHA), "OCHA Consolidated Situation Report No. 154," November 14, 2003.

49. For example, see the work of the International Rescue Committee cited in *Small Arms Survey 2002: Counting the Human Cost* (Oxford: Oxford University Press, 2002), p. 173.

50. Ibid.

51. *Small Arms Survey 2003: Development Denied* (Oxford: Oxford University Press, 2003), p. 138.

52. Roderic Broadhurst, "Lethal Violence, Crime, and State Formation in Cambodia," *Australian and New Zealand Journal of Criminology* 35, no. 1 (2002):pp. 13–14.

53. Deutsche Presse-Agentur, "Human Rights Group Faults Thailand's Bloody Anti-Drug Campaign," August 21, 2003.

54. Broadhurst, "Lethal Violence," p. 12.

55. World Health Organization, *Global Report on Violence and Health*, p. 15.

56. James East, "Need a Gun? It's Easy to Get One in Cambodia," *Straits Times*, November 26, 2000; Inter Press Service, "Violent Crime Thrives in Wounded Society," August 25, 1998.

57. *Small Arms Survey 2003*, p. 138.

58. A 1994 study, albeit based on a small sample, noted that about 18 percent of women who experienced violence were threatened with a gun. See Cathy Zimmerman, *Plates in a Basket Will Rattle: Domestic Violence in Cambodia* (Phnom Penh: Project Against Domestic Violence, 1994), p. 131.

59. *Small Arms Survey 2003*, p. 156.

60. Ed Quitoriano and Eric Libre, "Reaching for the Gun: The Human Cost of Small Arms in Central Mindanao, Philippines," *Kasarinlan* 16, no. 2 (2001): 13–39.

61. Amina-Bernardo Rasul, "Poverty and Armed Conflict in Mindanao," paper presented to the U.S. Institute for Peace, Washington, D.C., January 10, 2002, p. 18.

62. *Small Arms Survey 2003*, p. 141.

63. Conversely, while levels of violence in Cambodian schools are high, and 30 percent of students report feeling unsafe, studies show that gun violence in schools is minimal. *Cambodian Peace and Disarmament Education Project: Baseline Survey Report* (Phnom Penh: Working Group on Weapons Reduction, June 2003), p. 17.

64. *The Logs of War: The Timber Trade and Armed Conflict* (London: Global Witness, 2003).

65. Pasuk Phongpaichit, Sungsidh Piriyarangsan, and Nualnoi Treerat, *Guns, Girls, Gambling, Ganja: Thailand's Illegal Economy and Public Policy* (Chiang Mai: Silkworm Books, 1998), p. 132.

66. "Speed Tribe," *Time*, December 16, 2002; Anthony Davis, "The Wa Challenge Regional Stability in Southeast Asia," *Jane's Intelligence Review*, January 1, 2003.

67. *Small Arms Survey 2002*, p. 203.

68. For more information on these coalitions, see www.iansa.org and www.international-alert.org/policy/security/biting.htm.

69. *Implementing the Programme of Action 2003: Action by States and Civil Society* (London: IANSA and Biting the Bullet, 2003), p. 124.

70. "Youth for Peace President Back from Exchange Travel," *Minda News*, November 11, 2003.

71. Sol Jose Vanzi, "PROGUN, Solons Question Gun Ban," Philippines Headline News Online, February 1, 2003.

72. Documents provided by the Working Group for Weapons Reduction. I am very grateful to the WGWR's director, Neb Sinthay, for drawing this to my attention.

73. For more information about the various country activities, see the Control Arms website, www.controlarms.org/events/cambodia.htm.

74. For example, the Burmese government frequently makes the argument that transfers to nonstate actors should be illegal. It is, of course, fighting a number of militia groups along the Thai-Burma border.

75. *Working to Build Peace, Security, and Prosperity: Curbing Small Arms and Light Weapons in Cambodia* (Phnom Penh: National Commission for Weapons Management and Reform [NCWMR], July 2003). According to the NCWMR, 36,505 weapons were crushed and 74,656 were burned.

76. *Philippines National Report on the Implementation of the UN Programme of Action*, p. 13.

77. "Take a Break and Park Your Gun," *Phuket Gazette*, November 12, 2003.

78. *National Report of the Kingdom of Thailand on the Implementation of the 2001 United Nations Programme of Action (POA) to Prevent, Combat, and Eradicate the Illicit Trade in Small Arms and Light Weapons in All Its Aspects*, July 2003, p. 5, available at the Small Arms Survey's database, www.smallarmssurvey.org.

79. Nirmal Ghosh, "Thais Shoot Down Proposal to Ban Guns," *Straits Times*, September 17, 2003.

80. "PNP to Start Gun Ban on Dec. 15," *Today* (Manila), November 27, 2003.

81. "Three Straits in Indonesia Prone to Weapons Smuggling—Navy," *Antara*, August 12, 2003. In October 2003 the Japanese government announced it would contribute a coast guard delegation from the police's Sea International Crime Division to help Indonesian law enforcement improve their ability to patrol in national waters. Japan also provided a patrol ship for the operation.

82. The program is managed by the Defense Security Cooperation Agency. For more information, see www.dsca.osd.mil.

83. Aaron Karp, "The Small Arms Challenge: Back to the Future," *Brown Journal of World Affairs* 9, no. 1 (Spring 2002): 183.

9.2

Burma/Myanmar:
Military Rule and Ethnic Conflict

Tom Kramer

Burma has been in a state of civil war since 1948, and has been under military rule since 1962. The military regime has been fighting armed groups representing the various ethnic minorities in the country. It has also been cracking down on the political opposition, led by Nobel Peace Prize winner Aung San Suu Kyi. Although the military government has agreed cease-fires with a large number of the ethnically based armed opposition groups, sporadic fighting and large-scale human rights violations continue to occur. Local and international efforts to overcome the fundamental issues of ethnic conflict and military rule by nonviolent means have yet to materialize. Talks between democratic opposition leader Aung San Suu Kyi and the military that started at the end of 2000 have stalled.

Burma, or Myanmar as it is officially known since 1989,[1] is the largest country of mainland Southeast Asia. It is also one of the most ethnically diverse countries in the world. Since the constitution of 1974, Burma is divided into seven divisions and seven ethnic minority states: Mon, Karen, Kayah, Shan, Kachin, Chin, and Rakhine. These states make up 55 percent of the landmass, but only reflect some of the larger ethnic groups. Reliable statistics on population and ethnic groups are not available, but the military government officially recognizes "135 national races."

The majority Burman population, which is predominantly Buddhist, mainly lives in the central plains and valleys. In contrast, most ethnic minority groups, which make up between 30 and 40 percent of the population, live in the rugged hills and mountains that surround the central lowlands, where they have each developed their own distinctive culture and traditions.

The civil war in Burma started almost immediately after independence in January 1948, with a communist insurgency and army mutinies. After negotiations about the establishment of a separate independent Karen state failed, the Karen National Union (KNU) took up arms in early 1949. Other ethnic minority

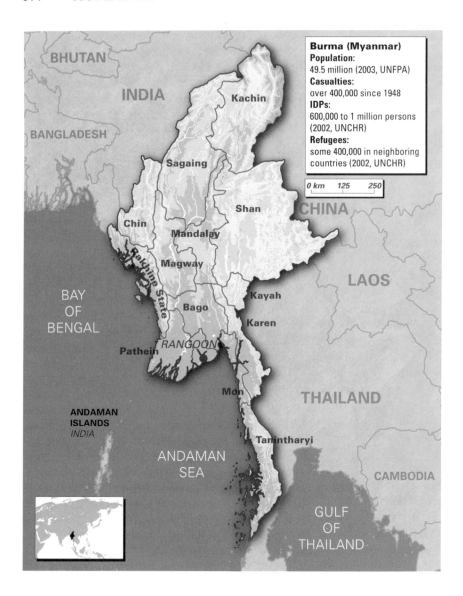

Burma (Myanmar)
Population:
49.5 million (2003, UNFPA)
Casualties:
over 400,000 since 1948
IDPs:
600,000 to 1 million persons
(2002, UNCHR)
Refugees:
some 400,000 in neighboring
countries (2002, UNCHR)

groups in Burma, such as the Mon, Karenni, Pao, and Rakhine and Muslims in Rakhine state followed suit and also began an armed struggle. By the early 1960s the civil war had spread to Shan and Kachin states as well.

In 1962 the army, led by General Ne Win, took power in a military coup. The new regime abrogated the constitution, and turned the country into a one-party state led by the Burmese Socialist Program Party (BSPP). Prime Minister U Nu and several ethnic minority leaders, who had been discussing possibilities to change the constitution to make it more federal, were arrested and put in jail. Ne Win put forward his political ideas in the "Burmese Way to

Socialism," a mixture of Buddhist and socialist ideas. By the early 1970s Burma had been closed off from the outside world, and all large companies, media, and institutes were nationalized. All civil society organizations were banned or placed under strict government control. Members of the political opposition were put behind bars.

By the 1970s the *tatmadaw* (Burmese army) had successfully pushed the ethnic armed groups into the hills of the border regions, using the infamous "Four Cuts" strategy. This campaign, which continues until today, consists of separating armed groups from the civilian population. It has been implemented at a high cost: gross human rights abuses and the relocation of hundreds of thousands of ethnic minority villagers in Karen, Kayah, and Shan states over the past thirty years.

The policies of the governing party, the BSPP, proved to be disastrous. By the 1980s the economy had all but collapsed. Burma, once the world's largest rice exporter, had to apply for least-developed-country status in 1987. In the same year the BSPP took a large amount of the bank notes out of circulation, which overnight wiped out the savings of millions of people.

The economic crisis contributed greatly to the political upheaval of 1988, when, after the unexpected resignation of General Ne Win, student protests in the capital, Rangoon, sparked nationwide mass demonstrations. Protesters called for the introduction of a multiparty system and demanded an end to the military dictatorship. In September 1988 the army crushed the protest movement, killing thousands of demonstrators. In response to the upheaval, the regime reorganized itself, by establishing the State Law and Order Restoration Council, which replaced the former governing BSPP and in practice was a byword for the military regime.

Since the collapse of the Communist Party of Burma in 1989, most ethnic minority armed organizations signed cease-fire agreements with the military regime. These are essentially military accords, which allow groups to control their territory and keep their weapons. The status and activities of the various groups vary. Among the larger cease-fire groups are the United Wa State Army (UWSA), the Shan State Army North (SSA North), the Kachin Independence Organization (KIO), and the New Mon State Party (NMSP).

There are also other smaller groups, including various breakaway groups, some of which have a status more similar to that of a local militia force. While some cease-fire organizations have political agendas, such as the KIO and the NMSP, others seem to be more economically oriented. A number of them, such as the UWSA, are alleged to be heavily involved in the narcotics trade.

After years of self-imposed isolation, Burma's military rulers in 1990 adopted a policy aimed at ending the international isolation, which had been put in place in response to the crackdown on the nationwide protests in 1988 and gross human rights abuses. The army organized elections in May 1990. The opposition party, the National League for Democracy (NLD), led by the charismatic Aung San Suu Kyi, the daughter of independence hero Aung San, won a landslide victory. A number of ethnic minority parties also won seats.

Aung San Suu Kyi, placed under house arrest since 1989, was awarded the Nobel Peace Prize in 1991 for her nonviolent struggle.

However, the army refused to hand over power and instead arrested scores of NLD leaders. The regime declared that a National Convention should first draft a new constitution before a new government could be formed. The regime handpicked the members of this National Convention, which first convened in 1993. In 1995, a few months after Aung San Suu Kyi's release from house arrest, the NLD decided to walk out of the National Convention in protest of political restrictions. In an attempt to break the deadlock, the NLD, in cooperation with a number of ethnic minority politicians, in 1998 set up the Committee Representing the People's Parliament and called upon the regime to convene the parliament. This led to a new wave of arrests.

By 2003 the main ethnic minority armed groups still fighting the military government were the Karen National Union, the Karenni National Progressive Party (KNPP), the Shan State Army South (SSA South), and the Chin National Front (CNF). These groups have been fighting a guerrilla war from small, often mobile bases along the Thai (KNU, KNPP, and SSA South) and Indian (CNF) borders. It is in these conflict areas that the most serious human rights violations are taking place.

There is a host of other smaller armed groups, including the Arakan Liberation Party, the Lahu Democratic Front, and the Wa National Army, all of them based along the Thai border. The Arakan Rohingya National Organization and the National Unity Party of Arakan operate from small bases near the border with Bangladesh. There are also many splinter groups and breakaway factions from larger armed opposition groups, which are active in most conflict areas in the country. Some of them operate with some kind of cease-fire status, such as the Democratic Karen Buddhist Army, which broke away from the KNU in 1995. Others, for instance the Hongsawatoi Restoration Army, broke away from the NMSP cease-fire group, and took up arms again against the military government. In addition, several government-supported militias, such as the various Lahu militias in Shan state, are still active. In January 2004, the SPDC agreed to a temporary verbal truce with the KNU, and both sides agreed to continue talks to reach an official cease-fire agreement.

Conflict Dynamics

The Burmese military regime, which since 1997 has called itself the State Peace and Development Council (SPDC), is more firmly in control than ever before. The Burmese army has expanded significantly, from about 170,000 troops in 1988 to some 400,000 by the year 2000. Armed opposition groups fighting the regime have suffered military setbacks or defeats. Although power is highly centralized, some regional Burma army commanders rule the areas under their control as warlords. The power of the military regime is based on the use of force and intimidation, and its lack of legitimacy became clear in the 1990 election when the military-backed National Unity Party won only ten seats, compared to 492 seats won by the opposition party, the National League for Democracy.

By the year 2004 the intimidation, arrests, forced closure of offices, and forced resignations had severely weakened the NLD's capacity. The NLD has called on the international community to implement economic sanctions against the regime to force it to the negotiation table and adopt substantive political reform. This has led the regime to accuse the NLD of being manipulated and controlled by foreigners (the regime has sometimes called the NLD leadership "axe-handles of external destructive elements").

A wide range of ethnic minority organizations continue to exist, most of them built along ethnic lines, including armed opposition groups, some of which reached cease-fire agreements with the military government, and political parties. They have formed numerous alliances and united fronts, but none have been nationwide and all-inclusive. Ethnic minorities are divided over goals (independence versus federal state) and strategy (armed struggle versus cease-fire). There are also disputes about ideology and economics (including drugs trade), as well as various personal conflicts.

Strong resentment, suspicion, and feelings of mistrust exist among ethnic groups in Burma. Ethnic minority groups feel discriminated against by ethnic Burmans, who have until today dominated the national political arena. The military regime justifies its position by arguing that its rule is necessary to keep the country together and "to save the union." However, ethnic minority leaders say the military regime is building a unitary state based on central Burman identity, and accuses it of "chauvinism" and a policy of "Burmanization." The state promotion of Buddhism, and perceived discrimination of other religions, including Islam and Christianity, is also resented. Since 1988, several anti-Muslim riots have erupted in towns in central Burma. Tensions are particularly strong in Rakhine state, where the Rohingyas, a Muslim minority, face ethnic and religious discrimination. During 1991 and 1992 some 250,000 Rohingyas fled to Bangladesh following a campaign of the Burmese army. Most of them have been repatriated to Rakhine state by the UN High Commissioner for Refugees, but they still suffer from a lack of freedom of movement and are not eligible for Burmese citizenship. Conflicts between ethnic minority groups, for instance between the Rohingya and Rakhine population in Rakhine state, have further blurred the picture.

Humanitarian Crisis

More than fifty years of civil war and decades of military rule have caused great suffering for the peoples of Burma, especially for ethnic minority groups, in whose areas most of the fighting has taken place. As a result, Burma is in the midst of a deep political, economic, and social crisis.

There are no reliable data on the number of conflict-related casualties. Some government officials stated that the death toll "would reach as high as millions." Another source estimates the number of casualties at 10,000 per year in four decades.[2] However, the number of deaths have decreased significantly since the cease-fire agreements of 1989.

The military regime is accused of committing widespread and systematic human rights abuses, including extrajudicial killings and summary executions,

torture, rape, forced relocations, forced labor, confiscation of land and property, extortion, and the use of child soldiers. Harsh laws, which put a lid on the
freedom of expression and association, are used to sentence hundreds of people during trials that fall far short of international standards. Opposition
sources say there are about 1,500 political prisoners in Burma. Most of them
were given long jail sentences without a fair trial. Many of them were also
subjected to ill treatment and torture while in detention. In 2002 the Burmese
army was accused of committing sexual abuses against ethnic minority women
in Shan state.[3] Human rights abuses by armed opposition groups have also
been reported.

The humanitarian crisis further affects both the health and the education
sector. Compared to the defense budget, public spending on health and education remains extremely low. Among the most serious health problems is the
fast-growing HIV/AIDS epidemic. Burma's youth today are seen as a "lost
generation," since high schools and universities have been regularly closed
down since 1988 to counter student protests. Although all have been reopened,
the educational standard remains low.

Economic mismanagement, the ongoing conflict, and continuing uncertainty have created space for people to become involved in various illegal
activities like illicit logging and narcotics production. Burma is, after Afghanistan, the world's largest producer of opium. Most opium is grown in Shan
state, often in areas under the control of cease-fire groups and government-
recognized militias. New reports say that opium production in UWSA-con-
trolled areas has shown a significant decrease, but at the same time the production of methamphetamine has increased dramatically.

Stagnation

In 2003 the political stagnation in Burma continued. After the talks between
Aung San Suu Kyi and the military had started in October 2000, the regime
initially reduced its repression of the NLD to some extent. Its offices in Rangoon were allowed to reopen, and public attacks on the NLD and Aung San
Suu Kyi in the government-controlled press ceased. The regime released some
political prisoners, among them many NLD members. In May 2002 the regime
also lifted the restrictions upon the movement of Aung San Suu Kyi after nineteen months of house arrest. Her release was welcomed inside Burma as well
as abroad, and gave hope that further reform would take place. Aung San Suu
Kyi was allowed to travel through the country, and visited Mandalay and Mon,
Shan, Rakhine, Chin, and Kachin states.

However, the talks between Aung San Suu Kyi and the regime have since
stalled. Some observers contend that they never seriously began, and have yet to
move beyond the stage of confidence building. In early 2003 the regime arrested
several NLD activists and a high-ranking Shan politician, although the latter was
later released. On May 30, 2003, hopes that the talks could be revived and move
on to meaningful political dialogue were shattered when a convoy of Aung San
Suu Kyi and her supporters were attacked by a government-organized mob. In

the incident, an unknown number of NLD members were killed and injured, and Aung San Suu Kyi was arrested and detained at an unspecified place. More NLD members were arrested in the weeks after the attack.[4] This led to strong condemnation by the international community, including from Association of Southeast Asian Nations (ASEAN) member states and Japan, which had previously taken a soft stance with regard to the military regime. In August 2003 the SPDC announced a road map to democracy, including a resumption of the National Convention, without giving any time frame or details on delegates. Since September 2003, Aung San Suu Kyi has again been under house arrest. The SPDC has announced that the National Convention will reconvene in 2004.

Officially, all conflict parties have stated publicly that they aim to work toward a democratic Burma. The regime's vehicle for political reform, the National Convention, has not convened since 1996. The NLD has called for tripartite talks between the military, the democratic opposition, and ethnic groups to find a lasting solution to the current political deadlock. This is supported by most ethnic minority organizations, which now reject separatism and instead call for a federal state and more ethnic nationality rights based on democratic principles.

Ethnic minority groups who are still fighting maintain that they will not enter into a cease-fire with the government without a political settlement, and have formed a new military alliance consisting of the KNU, the KNPP, the SSA South, the CNF and the Arakan Liberation Party. The so-called cease-fire groups, on the other hand, hope that social and economic development in their regions, enabled by the relative stability, will result in progress on the political front and, eventually, more autonomy.

Official Conflict Management
The seventeen cease-fire agreements that have been reached with individual armed groups since 1989 stand out as the most concrete example of conflict management by the Burmese regime. The regime sees the agreements as one of its major accomplishments. The regime leadership maintains that it is not a government, and therefore is not in a position to negotiate political settlements. Instead it has told the groups it has reached cease-fire agreements and waits for a political agreement until the National Convention has finalized the new constitution and a new government has been formed.

Proponents say that the cease-fires at least have put an end to the bloodshed and that the process of resettling displaced persons has begun. The education and health sectors in the cease-fire areas have somewhat improved and people can travel more freely. Opponents point at the increasing numbers of Burmese soldiers being stationed in these areas, and to the lack of political initiatives to follow through on cease-fires. They see the cease-fires as a strategy by the Burmese army to divide the opposition.

Efforts by the international community at conflict management in Burma have been hampered by divisions over goals and strategy. Some countries, such as the United States and some European Union (EU) member states, advocate international political and economic isolation of the regime. Others, including ASEAN member states, Japan, and Australia, feel that change should be stimulated through dialogue and "constructive engagement." ASEAN countries in particular do not want to get involved in what they say are Burma's internal affairs. Meetings to discuss the conflict in Burma organized by the international community in South Korea, the United Kingdom, Japan, and most recently in Bangkok, Thailand, have yet to result in a coordinated and common international policy on Burma.

A key player in conflict resolution efforts is Malaysian diplomat Tan Sri Razali Ismael, the UN Secretary-General's special envoy for Burma. He revealed in early 2001 that the regime and Aung San Suu Kyi had been engaged in a dialogue since October 2000. The talks were secret, and little is known about what was being discussed. The international community supported the talks and expressed "cautious optimism" about their outcome. One major shortcoming of the talks is that representatives of the organizations of the large number of ethnic minorities are not included. Razali has visited the country several times to keep the talks going. He has been credited for the release of Aung San Suu Kyi from house arrest in May 2002. Razali promoted the idea of setting up a joint committee of the regime and the NLD to tackle some of the country's most urgent problems, such as the humanitarian crisis and the HIV/AIDS epidemic. Furthermore, Razali has reportedly put more emphasis on solving the ethnic minority issue.

The situation quickly deteriorated with the government-organized attack on Aung San Suu Kyi and her convoy in May 2003. The talks between the regime and Aung San Suu Kyi came to a halt. In an attempt to secure the release of Aung San Suu Kyi from detention, and to get the reconciliation process back on the track, Razali visited Burma again and continued efforts to get the dialogue back on track.

The International Labour Organization (ILO) in 2000 took the unprecedented step of recommending that its members, as well as UN agencies and multilateral organizations, review their relations with Burma to ensure that they did not contribute to forced labor in Burma. A special ILO commission of inquiry had in 1998 concluded that forced labor was widespread and systematic, and as such constituted a "crime against humanity." In September 2001 an ILO high-level team conducted an extensive visit to the country. After negotiations with the regime, the ILO opened a liaison office in Rangoon in 2002 to monitor the authorities' pledge to end forced labor and provided technical assistance to the regime in eradicating this practice.

The UN Special Rapporteur on the Situation of Human Rights in Myanmar, Paulo Sergio Pinheiro, has visited the country several times since his appointment in 2001. He was the first UN special rapporteur to do so since 1995. Apart from visiting political prisoners, he has also investigated allegations of widespread human rights abuses in ethnic minority areas. He has proposed several options to the regime to conduct a credible investigation of these allegations, and urged the regime to allow the International Committee of the Red Cross (ICRC) access to all conflict areas in the country.

Following the events of 1988 and the new "open door" policy of the regime, most ASEAN nations, specifically Thailand, Singapore, and Malaysia, were keen to invest in Burma, and adopted a policy of "constructive engagement." This policy was seen by critics as a guise to exploit Burma's economic resources. Burma was admitted into ASEAN in 1997, in spite of much criticism from the United States, the EU, and Burmese opposition groups. Burma's relationship with Thailand remains tense, as the Burmese authorities accuse Thailand of supporting armed opposition groups. Thailand in turn blames Burma for failing to control the production and flow of narcotics, especially methamphetamines, into Thailand. This has led to several border conflicts in 2002.

After the May 2003 attack on Aung San Suu Kyi, ASEAN broke its principle of nonintervention in domestic affairs of member states by calling for an easing of tensions in Burma and the early release of Aung San Suu Kyi. The regime failed to accept a proposal by Indonesia to allow ASEAN to help mediate in the political standoff. Thailand proposed to develop a road map for national reconciliation, but has so far not produced any details. In December 2003 Thailand hosted a meeting on Burma attended by selected countries from Asia and Europe, as well as the SPDC. The Thai government has announced it will organize a second meeting in 2004.

Among the regional powers, China is Burma's most important strategic ally. It is a major trading partner for Burma, and has invested hugely in the Burmese economy. China is also a major supplier of military hardware. Japan is Burma's largest aid donor, and has given debt relief and official development assistance to the regime, most recently following Aung San Suu Kyi's release from house arrest in May 2002. The regime's relations with India have improved in recent years. The Indian government is worried about China's growing influence in Burma, and has other concerns, including the presence of several ethnic minority armed groups that are active on both sides of the India-Burma border. At the same time, Indian support for the Burmese democratic opposition is decreasing.

In Europe, the EU has since 1988 adopted several political sanctions against the military government, including an arms embargo and a visa ban for high-ranking regime members and their families. It has also frozen funds held abroad by leaders of the Burmese regime. The EU has over the past few years sent a number of troika missions to Rangoon to try to establish "a meaningful political dialogue" with the regime.

Since 1997 the United States has barred all new U.S. investment in Burma due to the lack of democratic reform, continuing human rights abuses, and the lack of cooperation from the regime to combat the growing drug problem. In 2003, President George W. Bush declared that Burma, together with Haiti and Guatemala, "failed demonstratively to adhere to their obligations under international counter-narcotics agreements and to take the measures set forth in U.S. anti-drug law."[5] The United States banned visitation by high-ranking

Burmese officials, and the Defense Department halted the importation of clothing made in Burma. Following the May 2003 events, the United States increased its sanctions regime in July, banning the import of all goods from Burma and freezing the U.S. assets of the Burmese military government.

Multi-Track Diplomacy

Civil society remains repressed in Burma. After the coup of 1962, independent organizations were either banned or put under strict government control. The military regime has placed strong restrictions on any form of grassroots organizing. Many individuals seeking to establish some form of civil organization have been arrested and given long jail sentences.

The military created its own mass organizations to support government policies, such as the Union Solidarity Development Association. This organization claims to have 16 million of members, but most people are reportedly forced to join, or face difficulties in, or loss of, their career if they do not. Other Government-organized "nongovernmental" organizations include the Myanmar Maternal and Child Welfare Association and the Myanmar Red Cross Society.

Many of the political parties that were established prior to the 1990 elections were subsequently banned; only ten still operate legally, and they remain under strict control. Founding of labor unions or student unions is banned. All media are either state owned or operate under strict government censorship. Internet use is not available for the general public, and e-mail accounts are almost impossible to obtain. All lines of communication, including mail, telephone, fax, and e-mail, are believed to be monitored by the military intelligence service. Armed opposition groups also seem reluctant to allow the establishment of independent organizations in their areas, although this has improved in recent years.

Several religious organizations, notably Christian, but also Buddhist, Hindu, and Muslim, have been able to set up social welfare and development programs, targeting local communities. Some of them, such as the umbrella Myanmar Council of Churches, the Myanmar Baptist Convention, and the Catholic Bishop Conference, have long-standing nationwide networks.

A number of new community-based initiatives have appeared that manage to operate relatively independently. Among these are the Metta Development Foundation and the Shalom Foundation. These organizations work on social and economic development, mainly in ethnic minority areas where cease-fire agreements have created new room to start community-based projects in former war areas. Other initiatives include ethnic minority literacy and cultural associations.

Although most local initiatives focus on development, the Shalom Foundation was set up to promote peace and reconciliation in Burma through conflict management. The organization aims to become involved in practical peace negotiation and mediation, by building up a network of mediators from different ethnic backgrounds. Some church organizations also have set up commissions

Tom Kramer

Burma. Karen refugees.

on "reconciliation and peace." Representatives of these organizations, in their private capacity and not under the mandate of their organization, have played important roles as go-betweens and mediators in various cease-fire negotiations in Kachin, Karenni, and Karen states.

The Karen Development Committee, a social organization working on cultural, educational, and health issues, is also involved in peacebuilding activities. In 2002 it organized a Karen congress attended by Karen delegates representing different geographical areas, religious backgrounds, and organizations. In the same year the three Kachin cease-fire organizations found common ground and jointly supported the newly formed Kachin Nationals Consultative Assembly.

These initiatives are relatively new, and are still in the process of gaining experience and building trust. However, there is a strong feeling among local community workers that they cannot wait for overall political change to come from Rangoon, and must follow through on their own initiatives to improve social and humanitarian conditions in their communities and rebuild the country.

In 2003, about thirty international nongovernmental organizations (NGOs) were operating in Burma. Their overall implementation capacity and the amount of money spent was low. Most international NGOs focus on health (especially HIV/AIDS) and educational programs. An exception to this is the Center for Humanitarian Dialogue, which aims to facilitate dialogue between the regime and opposition groups. The center is working closely with UN Special Envoy Razali, and is meeting regularly with the regime and Aung San Suu Kyi. Razali and the center also try to promote the release of political prisoners, to ease restrictions on political parties, and ensure full cooperation from the SPDC with visits by the ILO and the UN Special Rapporteur on the Human Rights Situation in Burma. The ICRC now has access to the country, and its delegates are allowed to visit people in detention, including political prisoners. It also started a project aimed at protecting and assisting civilians in border areas where the armed conflict continues.

Conflict Resolution

A wide range of Burmese organizations in exile have been trying to promote political change in Burma. These include political groups as well as civil society organizations. Many of them are based in neighboring countries, mainly in Thailand, and to a lesser extent in India and Bangladesh. They put strong emphasis on international advocacy and lobby activities on democratization and human rights. Few have service-providing projects. Most of them advocate international isolation of the Burmese regime in the economic, political, and social fields.

These organizations have developed strong links with lobby and campaign groups in Asia, Europe, and the United States, and have successfully campaigned against foreign investment in Burma, leading to the withdrawal of several international companies, including Carlsberg, Heineken, and more recently, Triumph. These international campaigns have managed to raise media attention, especially by making use of new media such as the Internet, and put Burma firmly on the human rights agenda of the international community.

In 1999, opposition groups in exile set up the National Reconciliation Program (NRP). It aims to be a platform to tackle ethnic, religious, and political conflict, and financially supports initiatives that promote reconciliation, empowerment, and conflict resolution. A practical outcome of the NRP is the Ethnic Nationalities Solidarity and Cooperation Committee (ENSCC), formed in 2001 by ethnic minority armed opposition groups based along the Thai border. The ENSCC formally sees itself as a task force, rather than as a new political organization, and aims to speak on behalf of ethnic minority organizations, including cease-fire groups. It aspires to set up a dialogue process.

Humanitarian Crisis and Political Change

While all sides agree that there is a humanitarian crisis in Burma, the question of how to get aid to those in need has been subject to heated debate. Opponents say that humanitarian aid cannot reach the target population, cannot be adequately monitored, and will only give credibility to the regime. Proponents say that the presence of international NGOs creates greater spaces for others to work in. They also argue that it is not right to punish the population for the wrongdoings of the government, by denying it aid. The HIV/AIDS crisis is used as an example of an issue that cannot wait to be dealt with until a democratic government comes to power. This polarization has greatly hampered communication and cooperation among the NGOs working in Burma, and those working from abroad, mostly from neighboring countries. The NLD and Aung San Suu Kyi maintain that they are not against humanitarian aid, as long as it is given to the right people in the right way. They call for transparency, accountability, and independent monitoring.

Organizations that reached cease-fire agreements have requested international assistance to rebuild their war-torn areas. They have welcomed community development programs of local and international NGOs. However, currently these small-scale initiatives are being carried out in an atmosphere of continued instability, despite the cease-fire agreements. Nevertheless, they are an important shift away from decades of destruction and the huge loss of life.

Ethnic minorities feel marginalized by the predisposition of the international community to focus on the democratic opposition. They sense a lack of interest in and understanding of the changes brought about by the cease-fire process. Similarly, they feel that the international community has shown little interest in ending a civil war that has had such a huge impact on ethnic minority communities.

The debate about conflict in Burma remains highly polarized. Some advocate complete isolation of Burma as the only way to bring the generals to the negotiation table. Others feel that there needs to be more engagement with the regime and military authorities in the social and political fields (in some cases also in the economic field) to try to convince them to begin a process of reforms.

A recent International Crisis Group report on the politics of humanitarian aid to Burma argues that a dual strategy—promoting political change and supporting social development—should be part of an integral approach toward development and conflict resolution in Burma.[6] This line of thinking is supported by some ethnic minority organizations in Burma that, not wanting to wait for change to come from Rangoon, have started their own initiatives to promote peace and development in their regions.

Prospects

Decades of civil war and military rule have had a huge impact on the political, social, and economic climate in Burma. Military rule continues, and there are widespread human rights abuses. There is deep misunderstanding and mistrust among ethnic groups and the immediate future looks grim.

Although the regime is militarily strong, it lacks political legitimacy and remains in power through force. The regime's failure to manage the economy, especially the country's external debt and the current banking crisis, has the potential to lead to new political upheaval. Although the SPDC has officially declared that it wants to transform Burma's political system into a democracy, it has so far taken no political steps toward this goal. The political impasse and stagnation continue. The talks between Aung San Suu Kyi and the regime have not moved beyond the stage of confidence building, and by the end of 2002 had completely stalled. The May 2003 attack on Aung San Suu Kyi and the NLD convoy was a major setback in the process to find a peaceful solution to the political deadlock in Burma. The SPDC has announced a road map to democracy and the reconvening of the National Convention in 2004.

Burmese politics has been characterized by factionalism and personal power struggles, both in the military and in the opposition. There are said to be serious tensions and rivalry between sections of the military, but they have thus far been able to stick together as one group, and little is known of the inside politics.

The NLD has been severely weakened by government repression against the party and the arrests of many of its members. Its main strength lies in the legitimacy stemming from its landslide election victory of 1990 and its non-violent strategy. The NLD's main internal weakness perhaps is also its strength: The party relies heavily on personalities, especially Aung San Suu Kyi, who has considerable personal authority in and outside the country. Critics argue that the NLD has not made enough effort to establish relations with ethnic minority organizations.

Militarily speaking, the armed opposition has either been severely weakened or changed tactics in the last decade and is not posing a real threat to government authority in Rangoon. Ethnic minority organizations, both political parties and armed groups, have sought to create a national platform to discuss the future and prepare for participation in a political dialogue. Some have called for a nationwide cease-fire.

Almost all cease-fire agreements are holding, but there have been no concrete steps to move forward in the political arena. Some of the ethnic organizations are growing impatient with the lack of political reform, but it seems unlikely that they will resume fighting.

Recommendations

After fifty years of civil war and decades of military rule, the peoples of Burma have suffered from huge loss of life and property. It is therefore of utmost importance that all parties take immediate steps to resolve the conflict through dialogue instead of armed conflict. A nationwide cease-fire should be declared as soon as possible.

It is also vital that all parties in the conflict respect fundamental human rights as defined by international law. They should also officially and publicly state their commitment to international humanitarian law. Monitoring of the implementation of international humanitarian standards is necessary. The military government, and also armed opposition groups, should put an end to the use of child soldiers and the laying of land mines.

The military government should end all forms of discrimination against ethnic and religious minorities. Furthermore, it should release all political prisoners and ensure fair trials for everyone. The authorities should stop all forms of torture, as well as extrajudicial executions, rape, forced labor, forced relocations, and extortion. The military government should issue clear orders to all military and security units to stop these practices, and to bring all offenders to justice.

The military government should immediately cease its policy of forced relocations of the civilian population in conflict areas. Neighboring countries, in particular Thailand, Bangladesh, and India, should respect customary international law and allow refuge to all new asylum seekers in their respective countries. They should also refrain from involuntary and forced repatriations, and provide adequate assistance and protection to all refugees.

In order to find a lasting political solution to end the current deadlock, it is essential that all parties involved are included in a platform for discussion on the political future of Burma and the writing of a new constitution. These discussions need to include the military, the NLD, and ethnic minority organizations, representing all ethnic and religious groups. A new constitution should safeguard the rights of all the peoples of Burma.

The international community should commit itself to a more coherent and coordinated strategy to get the dialogue process going again and find common means to promote political change. It should consult with ethnic minority organizations and ensure they are included in this process. The international community should find ways to deliver humanitarian aid directly to the most vulnerable part of the population. It should in particular pay attention to urgent issues such as HIV/AIDS.

Resources

Newsletters

Burma Debate (Open Society Institute; www.burmaproject.org)
Burma Issues (www.burmaissues.org)
BurmaNet News (daily compilation of English-language newspaper articles on Burma; e-mail: burmanet-request@burmanet.org)
The Irrawaddy (www.irrawaddy.org)
Kao Wao (news on Mon state; e-mail: kaowao@shaw.ca)
Mizzima News (news on Burma from India; e-mail: mizzima_editor@hotmail.com)
Narinjara (news on Rakhine state; e-mail: narinjar@aitlbd.net)
S.H.A.N. (news on Shan state; e-mail: shan@cm.ksc.co.th)

Reports

All Burma Students' Democratic Front. *To Stand and Be Counted: The Suppression of Burma's Members of Parliament.* Bangkok, June 1998.
Amnesty International. *Myanmar: Justice on Trial.* July 30, 2003.
———. *Myanmar: Lack of Security in Counter-Insurgency Areas.* London, July 2002.
Ethnic Nationalities Solidarity and Cooperation Committee. *The New Panglong Initiative: Re-building the Union of Burma.* Chiangmai: UNLD Press, 2002.
Human Rights Watch Asia. *Crackdown on Burmese Muslims.* New York, July 2002.
———. *"My Gun Was As Tall As Me": Child Soldiers in Burma.* New York, October 2002.
International Crisis Group. *Myanmar: The Politics of Humanitarian Aid.* Asia Report no. 32. Bangkok, April 2, 2002.
———. *Myanmar: The Role of Civil Society.* Asia Report no. 27. Bangkok, December 6, 2001.
———. *Myanmar Backgrounder: Ethnic Minority Politics.* Asia Report no. 52. Bangkok, May 7, 2003.
Lahu National Development Organization. *Unsettling Moves: The Wa Forced Resettlement Programs in Eastern Shan State.* Chiangmai, April 2002.
Minority Rights Group International. *Burma (Myanmar): The Time for Change.* London, 2002.

Office of Strategic Studies (OSS), Ministry of Defence, Union of Myanmar. *Political Situation of Myanmar and Its Role in the Region.* Lieutenant-Colonel Hla Min, Rangoon, n.d.

Shan Human Rights Foundation and Shan Women's Action Network. *License to Rape: The Burmese Military's Regime's Use of Sexual Violence in the Ongoing War in Shan State.* Chiangmai, May 2002.

Transnational Institute and Burma Center Netherlands, *Strengthening Civil Society in Burma: Possibilities and Dilemmas for International NGOs.* Chiangmai: Silkworm Books, 1999.

Other Publications

Burma: The Challenge of Change in a Divided Society. Ed. Peter Carey. Basingstoke: Macmillan, 1997.

Burma: Insurgency and the Politics of Ethnicity. By Martin Smith. London: Zed Books, 1999.

Burma/Myanmar: Strong Regime, Weak State? Eds. Morten Pedersen, Emily Rudland, and R .J. May. Adelaide: Crawford House, 2000.

Burma in Revolt: Opium and Insurgency Since 1948. By Bertil Lintner. Chiangmai: Silkworm Books, 1999.

Gathering Strength: Women from Burma on Their Rights. By Images Asia/Brenda Belak. Chiangmai: Images Asia, January 2002.

Living Silence: Burma Under Military Rule. By Christina Fink. London: Zed Books, 2001.

Mon Nationalism and Civil War in Burma: The Golden Sheldrake. By Ashley South. London: RoutledgeCouzon, 2003.

Websites

www.amnesty.org (Amnesty International)

www.burmalibrary.org (online Burma library—most of the reports and publications listed above can be found here)

www.burmaproject.org (Open Society Institute)

www.crisisweb.org (International Crisis Group)

www.dvb.no (Democratic Voice of Burma, opposition radio station)

www.myanmar.com (official government site)

www.shanland.org (several Shan organizations)

Resource Contacts

Lian Sakhong, Peace and Conflict Research Department, Uppsala University, e-mail: liansakhong@hotmail.com (also research director, National Reconciliation Program)

Open Society Institute, Burma Project/Southeast Asia Initiative, e-mail: burma@sorosny.org

Robert Templer, Asia Program director, International Crisis Group, e-mail: icgbrussels@crisisweb.org

Chao Tzang Yawnghwe, program director, National Reconciliation Program, e-mail: tzang@attcanada.ca

Harn Yawnghwe, director of the Euro-Burma Office (joint project of the European Commission and the Olof Palme International Center in Stockholm), e-mail: saoharn1@attglobal.net

Organizations

ALTSEAN Burma
c/o Forum-Asia
109 Suthisarnwinichai Road
Samsennok, Huaykwang, Bangkok, Thailand
e-mail: altsean@ksc.th.com

Amnesty International
International Secretariat
1 Easton St.
London WC1X 0DW, UK
www.amnesty.org

Assistance Association for Political Prisoners (AAPP)
P.O. Box 93, Mae Sot 63110
Tak Province, Thailand
e-mail: aappb@cscoms.com

Burma Campaign UK
28 Charles Square
London N1 6HT, UK
e-mail: info@burmacampaign.org.uk
www.burmacampaign.org.uk

Burma Center Netherlands
Paulus Potterstraat 20
1071 DA Amsterdam, Netherlands
e-mail: bcn@xs4all.nl
www.burmacenter.nl

Free Burma Coalition
Washington, D.C., Office
Free Burma Coalition
1101 Pennsylvania Ave., SE #204
Washington, D.C. 20003
e-mail: info@freeburmacoalition.org
www.freeburmacoalition.org

National Coalition Government of the Union of Burma (NCGUB)
NCGUB Information Office
1319 F Street, N.W., Suite 303
Washington, D.C. 20004
tel: +202 639 0639
fax: +202 639 0638
e-mail: ncgub@ncgub.net
www.ncgub.net
NCGUB is constituted by elected members of parliament in exile.

National Council of the Union of Burma (NCUB)
P.O. Box 29, Huamark Post Office
Bangkok, 10243 Thailand
e-mail: ncubfac@loxinfo.co.th
www.ncgub.net
Umbrella organization of prodemocracy Burmese and non-Burmese ethnic
  nationalities.

Women's League of Burma (WLB)
Secretariat: P.O. Box 413, GPO
Chiangmai, 50000 Thailand
e-mail: wlb@chmai2.loxinfo.co.th

---

*Tom Kramer is writer and consultant on Burma. He spent the past decade researching
modern Burmese politics, which included repeated visits to the region. He currently
works freelance and has written policy papers and reports on the country for a wide*

range of institutes and development agencies. He has also published several articles and contributed to other publications.

Notes

1. In 1989 the military government changed the official name of the country from "Burma" to "Myanmar." The opposition has rejected this change, and it has become the subject of a political debate. Although the UN uses "Myanmar," it is not commonly used outside of these official structures. Therefore "Burma" will be used throughout the chapter.

2. Both figures are from Martin Smith, *Burma: Insurgency and the Politics of Ethnicity* (London: Zed Books, 1991), pp. 100–101.

3. See *License to Rape: The Burmese Military Regime's Use of Sexual Violence in the Ongoing War in Shan State* (Chiangmai: Shan Human Rights Foundation and Shan Women's Action Network, May 2002).

4. Amnesty International, *Myanmar: End Crackdown Now,* June 4, 2003, available at www.amnesty.org.

5. White House, Statement by the Press Secretary, Annual Presidential Determinations of Major Illicit Drug-Producing and Drug-Transit Countries, January 31, 2003.

6. International Crisis Group (ICG), *Myanmar: The Politics of Humanitarian Aid,* Asia Report no. 32 (Bangkok: ICG, April 2, 2002).

9.3

Cambodia:
Peacebuilding amid Unresolved Issues

Soth Plai Ngarm

Cambodia is best known for its Angkorian temple complex and for the genocidal regime of the Khmer Rouge. After more than twenty-five years of civil war, today Cambodia can also be recognized for its significant efforts in peacebuilding and postwar reconstruction. As the international community invested billions of U.S. dollars in aid, many rehabilitation programs have been implemented by both internal and external actors. Since the signing of peace agreements in 1991, the programs have constantly shifted, as the society has tried to recover from the scars of both modern and traditional conflicts. Although the international community is generally optimistic about Cambodia's future, many unresolved issues and conflicts must be addressed before Cambodians can experience real peace.

For a long time Cambodia was ruled by the divine right of kings and governed by a deeply embedded traditional class system. However, the decline of this system, in the form of the Khmer empire, began in the twelfth century with accumulated pressures and tensions that led to its final and complete collapse in 1975.

The past conflicts, which have led to widespread destruction, can be conceived of in three significant stages: The first stage was from the fourteenth to the eighteenth century, when the Khmer empire was continuously in conflict with its neighbors Thailand and Vietnam;[1] the second stage was from the nineteenth to the twentieth century, when Cambodia was under the rule of the French protectorate (1863 to 1953);[2] the third stage followed independence from the French (1954) to the 1970s and 1980s, when Cambodia became one of the Cold War battlefields.

Cambodia's modern historical conflicts resulted in a period of chronic war starting in the 1960s—the beginning of the end of social prosperity and development. The Cold War posed an increasing threat to the world, and the communist movement in Southeast Asia (then known as Indochina) was increasing in strength, especially in Vietnam.

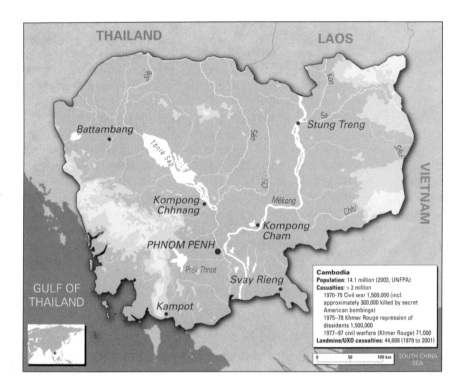

THAILAND   LAOS

Battambang   Stung Treng

Kompong
Chhnang   Mékong

Kompong
Cham
PHNOM PENH

Prêk Thnot
Svay Rieng

GULF OF
THAILAND   Kampot

Cambodia
Population: 14.1 million (2003, UNFPA)
Casualties: > 3 million
1970-75 Civil war 1,500,000 (incl.
approximately 300,000 killed by secret
American bombings)
1975-78 Khmer Rouge repression of
dissidents 1,500,000
1977-97 civil warfare (Khmer Rouge) 71,000
Landmine/UXO casualties: 44,608 (1979 to 2001)

Having just become the leader of the country after gaining its independence from France, King Sihanouk tried desperately to protect his new nation from the effects of the Cold War. His decision to secretly support the North Vietnamese communist forces with supply passages through Cambodia while assuring the United States of his neutrality, led to the 1973 secret U.S. Air Force carpet-bombing of eastern Cambodia. This marked the start of decades of destruction, war, and conflict with the ensuing violence and turmoil.

By 1975 the Cambodian communist movement, the Khmer Rouge had gained momentum, and on April 17 it marched into Phnom Penh, overthrowing the U.S.-backed Lon Nol government. Democratic Kampuchea (DK) was founded. The population was immediately ordered to evacuate all urban centers and form agricultural collectives. Intellectuals and other "enemies of the revolution," including monks, were summarily executed.

In 1977 the DK, with military aid from China, began a series of internal purges of dissidents. A number of DK dissident commanders fled to Vietnam, where they were groomed for a government-in-exile. While almost the entire international community continued to recognize the genocidal DK regime, Vietnam began an offensive in 1978 to "liberate" the Cambodian people from its control. In 1979 Phnom Penh quickly fell to the Vietnamese forces and large numbers of Cambodians fled to the Thai border. The Vietnamese-backed People's Republic of Kampuchea, of socialist orientation, was established.

Almost immediately, resistance forces, comprising the Khmer Rouge, the United Front for an Independent, Neutral, Peaceful, and Cooperative Cambodia (FUNCINPEC), and the Khmer People's National Liberation Force under the leadership of Prince Sihanouk, joined together along the Thailand-Cambodia border to fight the Vietnamese-backed government. The conflict lasted until the signing of the Paris Peace Accords in 1991 and the arrival of the UN Transitional Authority in Cambodia (UNTAC).

The May 1993 election conducted under the auspices of UNTAC marked a turning point for Cambodia. The election helped to establish a new constitutional monarchy under a coalition government with Sihanouk as king. The Khmer Rouge, however, did not participate in the election and returned to insurgency activities in its former strongholds, leaving the newly combined security forces to fight an ongoing civil conflict.

At that time, three factors remained as significant obstacles to Cambodia's national reconciliation and reintegration:

- Those who controlled land and resources questioned whether, after the reintegration, they would have to share or give up what they controlled.
- Those involved in politics were unsure of whether they could work together again after being enemies for so long.
- Most important, everyone feared that one party would be unable to tolerate the others, were one party to take absolute military power.

Cambodia, 1991. A crowd of refugees recently returned from Thailand are held back by a policeman as they wait to greet King Norodom Sihanouk. A helicopter was returning him from exile to become head of state again.

The widespread fear and insecurity at the individual and group level generated by these three factors resulted in a strong aversion to risk, which made imaginative conflict resolution measures difficult to implement. The experience of the Khmer Rouge regime had taught Cambodians that losing power meant a loss of everything, including life. This is critically important for understanding Cambodian conflict and power politics today.

The presence of UNTAC and the election outcome opened up the country to a rapid flow of financial and technical assistance, enabling a large number of actors, including international organizations and nongovernmental organizations, to play constructive roles in rebuilding the country. Despite this newly laid foundation for peace, many issues remained unresolved, especially the ongoing insurgent activities of the Khmer Rouge. In 1997, after months of escalating political tension and violence, the coalition government ended when the two coalition parties—the Cambodian People's Party (CPP) and the royalist FUNCINPEC party—openly competed for the support of armed groups, including Khmer Rouge remnants.[3]

At the time of the second national election in 1998, the Khmer Rouge ended its resistance and joined the government. After the elections the CPP/FUNCINPEC coalition brought five years of relative stability and development to Cambodia, until the third national election in July 2003.

Conflict Dynamics

Today, Cambodia's conflicts are more pragmatic than ideological and thus can be characterized as more development-related than political. Most disputes concern material resources rather than ideas. This is not surprising considering that poverty remains a crucial reality for Cambodians in general. Gross domestic product over the past five years has remained at U.S.$260 per capita.[4] Cambodia's human development index is estimated at 0.517, with only Laos and Bangladesh in Asia having lower scores.[5]

Pertinent conflicts include labor disputes, resource-based conflicts over land, forests, and waterways, corruption, tension as a result of discrimination and racism, border disputes, and election violence and intimidation. These contemporary conflicts have been exacerbated by the widespread availability of small arms, a culture of impunity and violence, contradictions between traditional and modern-day hierarchies, and the rise of private enterprise and the business sector. Unresolved issues about how to reconcile past conflicts (like the ongoing debate on the proposed Khmer Rouge Tribunal) and how to continue the processes of reintegration and demilitarization are also significant. Global issues such as regional and international cooperation to curb terrorism, and other economic and security matters, also impact on the national political agenda.

Any discussion of contemporary conflict in Cambodia must also note the high rate of domestic violence, with NGO statistics putting even the lowest estimates at 25 percent of families[6]—(10 percent is a more common statistic for many developing countries in Asia). This may be attributed to a deeply entrenched culture of violence exacerbated by poverty and unemployment and related to the trauma created by years of war. These issues lead one to question whether Cambodia is really showing signs of positive development or is facing a chronic social crisis.

Communities, local authorities, government departments, national policy-makers, and international corporations have been in almost constant conflict since the 1990s over the management and distribution of forests, fisheries, and land.[7] Traditionally, the most common use of land in Cambodia has been for agriculture. However, there is currently a massive change of land use from traditional to commodity-based, where landownership is legally exchangeable.[8] This is inevitably creating confusion and conflict in a predominantly rural and poor society, where those with education and resources can use the legal system to their own advantage.

Such development-related disputes are paralleled in urban areas, with conflict between garment factory workers and their employers. An International Labour Organization (ILO) report on Cambodia notes, "Factory owners are very powerful and it is very difficult to act against them if they break the law. They have connections at the top level in government."[9]

Corruption is a key element in both resource-based conflicts and labor disputes, as security forces and officials are easily manipulated to support business interests. A large amount of incoming resources, whether aid, taxation, or profit, are "diverted" to support corrupt officials and illegal activities such as drug and human trafficking.[10] In 2001, the Cambodia Human Rights and Development Association (ADHOC), a local human rights organization, reported that for that year 168 women and girls (69 of them were under eighteen years of age) were smuggled into Cambodia and forced to work in the sex industry.[11] Although this is not a confrontational conflict between political parties, the result is the same—violence and death. According to the World Bank, "Even the Government recognizes that a lack of good governance is a serious obstacle, not only to public sector performance, but also to the development of a healthy private sector because it weakens institutions and encourages corruption."[12] The contrast between poor human rights development in Cambodia and its improving economic performance[13] seems to reflect something significant about the new form of conflicts that arise from the process of development.[14] Social reforms to counter these conflicts have yet to be implemented.

In addition to development-related conflict and violence, some political issues remain. On January 29, 2003, an ethnic riot erupted against Thai nationals and businesses in Phnom Penh. Many Thai establishments, including the embassy, were attacked by a mob of young Cambodian extremists. In response to the riot, a Thai group attacked the Cambodian embassy in Bangkok.[15] Bilateral relations with Thailand became strained following the event.[16] The riots were triggered by unfounded rumors that a Thai actress had said that the Angkor Wat temple should be returned to Thailand.[17] This event illustrates complicated, deep-rooted ethnic and historical tensions between Cambodia and its neighbors. Similar tensions also exist between Cambodian and Vietnamese communities, both inside Cambodia and between the two countries. Border conflicts have been traditionally a source of racial tension between Cambodia, Thailand, and Vietnam.

Some people also fear a repetition of past election violence. In September 2002 the Cambodian Human Rights Action Committee, a network of eighteen Cambodian NGOs, documented eighty-two cases of political intimidation and violence since the beginning of the year.[18] Such incidents imply ongoing obstacles to real democratic development where intimidation and violence have become part of the culture. However, observers of Cambodian elections noted an improvement in the implementation of elections during both the 2002 commune elections and the 2003 national elections.

A brief armed incident that took place in Phnom Penh on November 24, 2000, should be noted in any discussion of Cambodian conflict dynamics. A U.S.-based resistance group known as the Cambodia Freedom Fighters attacked a government and military facility. A number of people were killed and injured. The government arrested fifty people allegedly involved in the attack.[19] An incident such as this indicates that Cambodia's past conflicts still need to be addressed in a comprehensive way in order for them to be managed and resolved.

Official Conflict Management

The annual Consultative Group Meeting on Cambodia has been an effective mechanism for pressurizing the government for change. In addition, the International Monetary Fund (IMF), the World Bank, and the Asian Development Bank (ADB) have been using loans to support reform programs, and the UN Development Programme (UNDP) has provided long-term support for community development, capacity building, and good governance.

Substantial financial and technical support has been made in the area of land reform by the German Cooperation Enterprise for Sustainable Development (GTZ), the World Bank, the ADB, and the Japan International Cooperation Agency (JICA), among others. They aim to reform the structures of government by developing a new mechanism to be operated through the Ministry of Land Management, with international supervision and assistance.[20] Activities include development of the land law, a land registration and titling system for the whole country, and conciliation training to provide capacity for the ministry structure, especially cadastral commissions at district and provincial levels. Finland has also been providing technical support on geomapping.

As the application of this new land policy is only just beginning, it is too early to determine the effectiveness of the various projects. Nevertheless, some problems in terms of practicality have occurred, such as the unclear jurisdiction of roles and responsibilities between cadastral committees and local courts over land disputes. For ordinary people seeking to secure their land titles, this confusion is complicated by the various levels and systems. They continue to be disempowered vis-à-vis government, and the new mechanism has not resolved this problem. Until these issues are addressed, land reform policies will not be sufficient alone to resolve Cambodia's land conflicts.

Labor conflicts have intensified in Cambodia over the last five years. The ILO, in addition to its programs to develop employment, construct road-bridges, and conduct vocational skills training,[21] has been attempting to ensure application by the Cambodian government of the ratified ILO conventions.[22] The ILO has also worked to encourage registration of labor unions. Thus far, the ILO has cooperated with the Cambodian Federation of Employers and Business Associations in order to build links with employers. A labor committee has been formed, representing five major worker organizations, the Free Trade Union of Workers of Kingdom of Cambodia, the Workers Union for Economic Development, the Cambodian Union Federation, the Cambodian Federation of Independent Trade Unions, and the National Independent Federation Textile Union of Cambodia. The U.S. government can potentially play an effective role on labor issues, since many of the industrial goods produced in Cambodia, especially garments, are exported to the United States.[23] Such interventions have already improved working conditions, rates of pay, and worker-employer relations.

Corruption is a structural issue that needs strong action. While this may be as simple, for example, as raising basic wages for teachers above U.S.$20 per month, unfortunately there are very few direct measures to address corruption. During the Consultative Group Meeting on Cambodia in 2001, NGOs lobbied governments to consider corruption as one of the key issues in the statement of the NGOs.[24] As a result, the Cambodian government committed itself to implementing key state reforms.[25] Among local NGOs working on corruption, the Centre for Social Development has been the most outspoken and active on the issue.[26]

Despite a number of foreign government agencies working closely with national authorities to combat drug and human trafficking, the identities of such trafficking rings have yet to be fully exposed. The UN agencies, international organizations, and NGOs have also raised concern about this issue. The Cambodian Centre for the Protection of Children's Rights, Gender and Development for Cambodia, and the Ministry of Women's Affairs and Veterans are involved in campaigning against drug and human trafficking. Recently, Gender and Development for Cambodia published a comprehensive report titled *Youth Attitudes Toward Gangs, Violence, Rape, Drugs, and Theft*. The research was supported by the Asia Foundation, the U.S. Agency for International Development, Australia's embassy to Cambodia, and World Vision.

The primary local actor on weapons reduction is the Working Group for Weapons Reduction in Cambodia.[27] In 2001 the government began a program to demobilize the military, with a target of 30,000 soldiers over two years. The World Bank was the major donor, with other agencies such as Japan International Cooperation Agency contributing to the demobilization process.[28] However, only 15,000 were demobilized before the program ran into administrative problems; it has presently been suspended.

At the regional level, the Association of Southeast Asian Nations (ASEAN) has been playing a constructive role in making, keeping, and building peace in

Cambodia. The members of ASEAN address the issues in Cambodia both multi-laterally and bilaterally. Significantly, following the armed conflict between Cambodian People's Party and FUNCINPEC in July 1997, the then ASEAN Troika (the Philippines, Thailand, and Indonesia) and the Friends of Cambodia helped bring the parties back together to settle their conflict through a political process.[29]

Despite deep-rooted prejudice and resentment between people from Thailand and Cambodia, diplomatic, economic, and trade cooperation are the only significant measures being taken to normalize Thai-Cambodian relations following the January 2003 anti-Thai riot. ASEAN, the Japanese government, and the United States were among regional and international diplomatic players to bring Cambodia and Thailand back into cooperation. For their mutual benefit, the two governments have bilaterally decided to put the past behind them and to try and rebuild the relationship. In his opening speech at the ASEAN ministerial meeting, Prime Minister Hun Sen stressed that Thailand and Cambodia have a vision of "shared growth and prosperity, founded on the building of a Cambodia-Thailand Economic Corridor."[30]

Preventive diplomacy is also important to Cambodia's electoral process with an important role for the international community. During the third national election of 2003, the European Union,[31] the Japanese government, UN agencies, and a number of international organizations provided financial support and sent observers to help ensure a free and fair process. U.S. secretary of state Colin Powell introduced two conditions for the normalization of U.S.-Cambodian relations during a visit to Cambodia in June 2003.[32] One was that the Cambodian government guarantee a free and fair election, and the other that the Khmer Rouge Tribunal be implemented.[33]

Tension between the UN and the Cambodian government over the Khmer Rouge trial has been ongoing for several years. Bilateral negotiations between the UN (directly from the office of the Secretary-General) and Cambodia reached a stalemate on at least two occasions. Recently, they made a break-through in agreeing that former Khmer Rouge leaders be put on trial soon. The United States is one of the main international actors to have supported the trial. Locally, the Documentation Centre of Cambodia has collected and preserved evidence of crimes against humanity committed by the Khmer Rouge.[34]

Cambodia's decision to participate in the U.S. war on terror is the result of internal politics. It has encouraged the building of a preventive mechanism as part of regional and international cooperation to address the issue. Two Thai nationals and one Egyptian were arrested in May 2003 for alleged links to terrorists.[35]

The active UN and associated agencies represented in Cambodia are RC System, the Food and Agriculture Organization, the ILO, the United Nations Joint Program on HIV/AIDS, the UN Cambodian Office for the High Commissioner for Human Rights (UNCHOCHR), the UN Development Programme, the UN Educational, Scientific, and Cultural Organization (UNESCO), the UN Population Fund (UNFPA), the UN High Commissioner for Refugees, the UN Children's Fund (UNICEF), the UN Volunteers (UNV), the World Food

Programme, the World Health Organization, and the UN Overseas Development Organization. They have contributed to monitoring and strengthening social structures, and also to practical interventions on a wide range of issues.[36]

While development and governance programs contribute to peacebuilding, it is only UNESCO's "Culture of Peace" program and UNICEF's "Living Values" primary school education curriculum that have directly sought to undertake peace education. A number of foreign governments have been supporting direct peace work in Cambodia, such as Japan, Germany, the Netherlands, the European Union, Sweden, and Canada.

Multi-Track Diplomacy

Actors that have been playing different roles to help maintain peace and security in Cambodia include UN agencies, governmental organizations, international organizations, and local NGOs. They have worked in either bilateral or multilateral ways and as donors or as implementers, focusing on the three societal levels: grassroots, middle, and national.[37] Many have aimed to reinforce the formal systems (e.g., justice, law enforcement, structural reformation), while others focus on strengthening informal systems (e.g., peacebuilding and conflict resolution through practitioners and grassroots communities by revising traditional practices and encouraging application of alternative conflict resolution).

Following the 1993 election, the track-two approach, which involved nongovernmental professional actors, was more active than the track-one approach. International organizations and NGOs could acquire more resources and funding for grassroots and middle-level programs. During those years, program activities seemed to give more attention to a bottom-up approach. Community-based projects were broadly supported, as they were aiming to rebuild social structures using sustainable strategies. The number of local civil society actors rose to about 400 NGOs operating throughout the country.

Key actors in the initial rehabilitation and reconstruction work were international NGOs such as the Mennonite Central Committee, the American Friends Service Committee, Oxfam-Great Britain, Catholic Relief Service, Jesuit Service, Cooperation Internationale pour le Dévelopment et la Solidarité, the Church World Service, and World Vision. They are either facilitators of emergency relief and community development projects, advocacy networks, or financial supporters of local organizations.

At the local level, during the 1990s, a large number of Cambodian NGOs worked on community development projects but only a small number had peace and conflict resolution programs. Among them were the Cambodian Institute for Cooperation and Peace, the Cambodian Development Resource Institute, and the Dharma Yietra Centre for Peace, the latter led by Buddhist patriarch Maha Ghosananda. The center was active until 1997 leading marches for peace into former conflict areas of Cambodia.

After 1997 a significant shift was made by both bilateral and multilateral donors, in preference of supporting programs undertaken through and with government ministries. This shift in fact reinforced actors in the track-one framework, and highlighted the conflict between two contrasting development theories: social transformation through the empowerment of people, and the strengthening of state operational structures for coping with free-market economies.

Despite the shift and subsequent competition for scarce financial resources, a number of civil actors continue to work in the peace and conflict resolution sector. The 2001 *Peace Mapping* report, a study of peacebuilding initiatives in Cambodia, revealed that over thirty NGOs work on various peacebuilding and conflict resolution programs throughout the country.[38]

The Cambodian Centre for Conflict Resolution (CCCR) operates under the auspices of the Cambodian Development Resource Institute and introduced the first conflict resolution training program in 1997. The first core group trained by the CCCR formed themselves into a national networking organization called the Alliance for Conflict Transformation (ACT). ACT's contributions include capacity and skills development, technical support in the area of peacebuilding to other sectors, and advocacy for policy change through workshops, conferences, networking, and research. Significantly, the CCCR, known today as Cambodia Peace and Development, has also provided training courses to commune councils in what are known as the "reconciliation zones," former Khmer Rouge–controlled areas.

The Working Group for Weapons Reduction in Cambodia, the Youth Resource Development Program, Youth for Peace, Khmer Ahimsa, and SILAKA are all implementing peace and conflict resolution programs in Cambodia in the areas of direct action, training, and resource development.

Further efforts to raise awareness on the issue of domestic violence have been significant, with far-reaching educational campaigns. Most notable, however, is the draft legislation on domestic violence, which at the time of writing is before the National Assembly. The movement to address Cambodia's high rate of domestic violence has been strongly led by Cambodian NGOs such as the Project Against Domestic Violence, the Cambodian Women's Crisis Centre, and Gender and Development for Cambodia.[39] The domestic violence law is significant not only because of the seriousness of the issue it seeks to address, but also because of the close cooperation between local organizations and the Ministry of Women's Affairs that has been established through its development.

These concrete initiatives toward peace are enriched by a good understanding of local culture and the conflict context, as well as close connection with local communities. Local initiatives have been enhanced by relationships and funds generated through regional networks and alliances. These institutions include the Southeast Asian Conflict Studies Network and Action Asia, among others.

Generally speaking, however, peacebuilding through commerce (track three) and peacebuilding through personal involvement (track four) have been to date almost nonexistent.

Prospects

> The concepts of human security and peacebuilding are still poorly understood in transitional economies including Cambodia, resulting in ineffective local/ regional development policy responses. Such policies are still aimed at promoting economic growth, as if growth is the only measure of development. Despite the arguments of human security and peacebuilding, there is continuing emphasis on the importance of growth.[40]

Despite massive investment in the postwar reconstruction of Cambodia, support for direct peace work in Cambodia, especially in terms of institutionalization and *local mechanism* development, remains limited.[41] The majority of incoming financial and technical assistance targets economic growth. This may be influenced by a narrow view of root causes of conflict or by the dissemination of international concepts of demographic growth and the trickledown effect of economic development.

Another concrete lesson learned from such imbalance concerns how to address the root causes of conflict in Cambodia, whose capacity to understand the social, economic, and cultural causes of violence, abuse, illiteracy, and poverty is frequently undermined by the necessity of dealing with the results of conflict on a day-to-day basis. This is one of the obstacles to achieving sustainable development and self-reliance. If its level of dependency remains as strong as it is today, Cambodia will not be able to achieve self-management of conflicts and tensions without significant support from outside. Support that only helps Cambodia to address the results of conflict, such as the visible violence and abuses, in fact weakens society's ability to adequately address the root causes of conflict.

The switch in donor strategies toward work undertaken through government structures has been vital. However, it has not been complemented by the appropriate parallel contributions toward civil society actors, particularly in the areas of peacebuilding, attitudinal and behavioral change, and improved social relations. This situation has contributed to competition for donor funding and delayed possible dividends in peace and social reconstruction.

Recommendations

Greater emphasis needs to be placed on ways of dealing with Cambodia's ethnic diversity. Cambodians have been the target of significant campaigns and education strategies pertaining to land mines, small arms, HIV/AIDS, human rights, and health. Very little work has been done in the area of reducing social prejudice and discrimination.

In order to address these issues the following recommendations can be made:

- Increased research and local capacity to translate experiences and theories into practice would help Cambodian society become stronger and more effective in preventing, managing, and dealing with conflicts.

- Greater consideration needs to be given to the root causes of conflict in Cambodian society beyond economic disparity. For sustainable peace, the issues of hierarchical social structures, power imbalances, and discrimination require equal if not more attention than economic growth.
- In order to better link the valuable reforms taking place in the government sector, more work needs to be done in the area of public education to provide access and protection to the civilian population. This might best be pursued through supportive strategic relationships between government and civil society actors.
- Local initiatives and organizations for peacebuilding should be supported and strengthened, and considered as key areas for learning. Cambodia's peace practitioners have a wealth of knowledge and experience, which should be shared in broader contexts for the benefit of others.
- Appropriate mechanisms for reconciliation need to be researched in detail, with the recognition that a national trial of Khmer Rouge leadership will not address individual or community needs in this area.
- Work in the area of domestic violence should be maintained and complemented by new research and programs in the area of community security.
- More efforts need to be made to include the business sector in peacebuilding initiatives. While economic stability might contribute to the peace, unless the mechanisms for achieving this stability are equitable and just, there will be further social crises in Cambodia.

Resources

Newsletters and Periodicals

Cambodia Development Review (Cambodia Development Resource Institute newsletter of the Alliance for Conflict Transformation)

Reports

Dispute Resolution in Cambodia: A Road to Peace and Reconciliation. Eds. Eva Mysliwiec and Catherine Morris. Proceedings of a workshop held November 28–30, 1995, in Phnom Penh, Cambodia. Victoria, B.C.: UVic Institute for Dispute Resolution and Cambodia Development Resource Institute, 1997.

Peace Mapping: A Study of Peace Building Initiatives in Cambodia. By Soth Plai Ngarm. August 2001.

Practical Experiences of Peace Building and Conflict Resolution in Cambodia. Phnom Penh, November 2002.

Other Publications

An Army of Peace: Quest for a Non-Violent Cambodia. Dhammayietra Center for Peace and Non-Violence, 1997. Video.

Between Tiger and Crocodile: Management of Local Conflicts in Cambodia—An Anthropological Approach to Traditional and New Practices. By Fabienne Luco. Phnom Penh: UNESCO, 2002.

"Case Studies in Religion and Peacebuilding: Cambodia." By Catherine Morris. In Harold Coward and Gordon Smith, eds., *Religion and Peacebuilding.* Albany: State University of New York Press, 2003.

"I Live in Fear": *Consequences of Small Arms on Women and Children in Cambodia.* By Sam Oeun Yem and Rebecca F. Catella. June 2001.

An Investigation of Conflict Management in Cambodia Villages: A Review of the Literature with Suggestions for Future Research. By Caroline Hughes. October 2001.

Nature and Causes of Conflict Escalation in the 1998 National Election. By Caroline Hughes and Real Sopheap. January 2000.

Plates in a Basket Will Rattle: Domestic Violence in Cambodia. By Cathy Zimmerman. Phnom Penh, December 1994.

Possibilities to Reduce the Number of Weapons and the Practice of Using Weapons to Solve Problems in Cambodia. By Sinthay Neb and Janet Ashby. July 1998.

Truth, Justice, and Reconciliation in Cambodia: Twenty Years After the Khmer Rouge. By Laura McGrew. 1999.

Victims and Perpetrators: Testimony of Young Khmer Rouge Comrades. By Ea Meng-Try and Sorya Sim. Phnom Penh: Documentation Center of Cambodia, 2001.

Websites

www.act-cambodia.org (Alliance for Conflict Transformation)
www.bigpond.com.kh/users/csd/support.htm (Centre for Social Development)
www.cdri.org.kh (Cambodia Development Resource Institute)
www.cicp.org.kh/public.htm (Cambodia Institute for Cooperation and Peace)
www.dccam.org (Documentation Centre on Cambodia)
www.wgwr.org (Working Group for Weapons Reduction)

Resource Contacts

Youk Chhang, Documentation Centre of Cambodia, e-mail: dccam@online.com.kh
Thida Khus, executive director, Silaka, e-mail: silaka@online.com.kh
Emma Leslie, Secretariat, Action Asia, freelance consultant, e-mail: emma@online.com.kh
Laura McGrew, e-mail: lamcgrew@igc.org
Catherine Morris, director, Peacemaker Trust, Canada, e-mail: cmorris@lampion.bc.ca
Soth Plai Ngarm, executive coordinator, Alliance for Conflict Transformation, e-mail: plaingarm@online.com.kh
Neb Sinthay, executive director, Working Group for Weapons Reduction, e-mail: wgwrdirector@online.com.kh
Ok Serey Sopheak, coordinator, Cambodia Peace and Development, e-mail: sopheak@cdri.forum.org.kh

Organizations

Alliance for Conflict Transformation (ACT)
#34, St. 480, Phsa Deum Thkov, Chamkarmorn
P.O Box 2552, Phnom Penh 3, Cambodia
tel: 023 217 830
e-mail: act@online.com.kh

Cambodia Institute for Cooperation and Peace (CICP)
Government Palace, Sisowath Blvd., Wat Phnom
Phnom Penh, Cambodia
tel: 023 722 759
e-mail: cicp@camnet.com.kh

Cambodia Peace and Development (CPD/CDRI)
#56, St. 315, Beoung Kak 2, Tuol Kork
Phnom Penh, Cambodia
tel: 23 367 115
e-mail: cdri@camnet.com.kh

Centre for Social Development (CSD)
#19, St. 57, Beoung Keng Kang 1, Chamkarmorn
Phnom Penh, Cambodia
tel: 023 364 735/215 685
e-mail: csd@online.com.kh

Documentation Center on Cambodia (DC-CAM)
#70, Sihanouk Blvd.
Phnom Penh, Cambodia
tel: 023 211 875
e-mail: dccam@online.com.kh

Khmer Ahimsa
#30, St. 352, Beoung Keng Kang 1, Chamkarmorn
Phnom Penh, Cambodia
tel: 023 216 400
e-mail: lcn@online.com.kh

Project Against Domestic Violence (PADV)
#15, St. 105/278, Beoung Keng Kang 2, Chamkarmorn
Phnom Penh, Cambodia
tel: 023 721 654
e-mail: padv@online.com.kh

Silaka-Metathor
#10B, St. 57, Beoung Keng Kang 2, Chamkarmorn
Phnom Penh, Cambodia
tel: 023 217 872
e-mail: silaka_ctp@online.com.kh

Youth for Peace (YFP)
#8AB, St. 202, Phsa Deumkor, Tuol Kork
Phnom Penh, Cambodia
tel: 023 881 346
e-mail: youthforpeace@online.com.kh

Youth Resource Development Program (YRDP)
#93, St. 590, Beoung Kak 2, Tuol Kork
Phnom Penh, Cambodia
tel: 023 880 194
e-mail: yrdp@forum.org.kh

Working Group on Weapon Reduction (WGWR)
#55, Sothearos Blvd, Tonle Bassac, Chamkarmorn
Phnom Penh, Cambodia
tel: 023 222 462
e-mail: wgwr@online.com.kh

Soth Plai Ngarm is coordinator of the Alliance for Conflict Transformation, a network of Cambodian NGOs and individual activists working toward social peace and stability. He also serves as the Cambodian representative of the Southeast Asian Conflict Studies Network. For the past nine years, he has been involved in peacebuilding and conflict resolution in Cambodia from the local to the national level, touching on both policy and practical issues. His work involves areas of training, research, issue-based capacity building, networking, and direct interventions.

Notes

1. B. K. Gordon, *The Dimensions of Conflict in Southeast Asia* (Englewood Cliffs, N.J.: Prentice-Hall, 1966), p. 45.

2. Australian government Department of Foreign Affairs and Trade website, www. dfat.gov.au.

3. Ibid.

4. Ibid.

5. UN Development Programme, *Human Development Report 2000: Children and Employment*, website, www.un.org.kh/undp/publications/nhdr/2000.pdf.

6. Asia Human Rights News, "CAMBODIA: Debate Set for Domestic Violence Draft Law 11-11-2002," available at www.ahrchk.net/news/mainfile.php/ahrcnews_200211/2746.

7. Global Witness press releases, available at www.globalwitness.org/press_releases/pressreleases.php?type=cambodia.

8. I was involved in training in land conflict conciliation for cadastral committees from district and provincial levels.

9. "ILO in Cambodia," by Sanjiv Pandita, *Asia Labour Update,* issue 44, July–Sept. 2002 available at www.amrc.org.kh/4406.htm, p. 3.

10. N. Sayres and Th. Lum, *Cambodia: Background and U.S Relation,* CRS Report for Congress, Order Code RS21289, August 21, 2002, p. 6, available at the CRS website, www.us-asean.org/cambodia/crs_report_8_21_02.pdf.

11. ADHOC, *Human Rights Situation 2002* (in Khmer language) (Phnom Penh: ADHOC, 2003), p. 31; e-mail ADHOC at adhoc@forum.org.kh.

12. World Bank website, web.worldbank.org.

13. Despites, critical report about human rights development in Cambodia by local and international human rights organizations, on July 22, 2002, the International Monetary Fund (IMF) claimed satisfactory with Cambodia economic performance and then agreed to immediately release U.S.$11.2 million out of the U.S.$67.3 million of the IMF support program, available at www.inf.org/external/np/sec/pr/2003/pr0319.htm.

14. Human Rights Watch, *World Report 2002,* available at www.hrw.org/wr2k2/asia.html.

15. *The Nation,* Jan. 30, 2003, available at http://203.150.224.53.

16. Australian government Department of Foreign Affairs and Trade website, www.dfat.gov.au.

17. *The Nation,* Jan. 30, 2003.

18. Human Rights Watch, *World Report 2002,* p. 2.

19. Information in relation to human rights and the Cambodia Freedom Fighters is available at the Human Rights Watch website, www.hrw.org/press/2000/12/cambodia1205.htm.

20. For more information on forestry in Cambodia, see www.sustdev.org/explore/forestry/news/02.06.01.shtml.

21. On the ILO in Cambodia, see www.un.org.kh/ilo/index.html.

22. "ILO in Cambodia," by Sanjiv Pandita, available at www.amrc.org.kh/4406.htm, p. 2.

23. Ibid., p. 7.

24. The NGO statement to the 2001 Consultative Group Meeting on Cambodia is available at www.bigpond.com.kh/users/ngoforum/cg2001/government.htm.

25. UN Development Programme, *Reform for What? Reflection on Public Administrative Reform,* June 2002, p. 2, available at www.un.org.kh/undp/publications/cg_par.pdf.

26. The Centre for Social Development is supported by the U.S. Agency for International Development, through the Asia Foundation, by the Swedish International

Development Agency, through DIAKONIA, and by the Danish International Development Agency, through DANCHURCH AID, Website: www.bigpond.com.kh/users/csd/support.htm.

27. Working Group for Weapons Reduction website, www.wgwr.org.

28. JICA, "Peace Building," information kit; see www.jica.go.jp (e-mail: jicagap@jica.go.jp).

29. Australian Department of Foreign Affairs website, www.dfat.gov.au, p. 4.

30. Keynote address to the thirty-sixth ASEAN Ministerial Meeting, available at www.cnv.org.kh/2003_release/160603_asean_amm_36.htm.

31. The European Union Election Observation Mission deployed to Cambodia for the parliamentary election of July 27, 2003. See website: http://europa.eu.int/comm/external_relations/human_rights/ue_election_ass_observ/cambbodia03/ip03_817.htm.

32. U.S. aid to Cambodia had been suspended following the 1997 political violence between coalition parties.

33. V. Sokhen, "U.S. Hints That Aid Could Flow from a Fair Election," *Phnom Penh Post,* June 20–July 3, 2003, p. 4.

34. For information about the documentation center, see www.bigpond.com.kh/users/dccam.genocide/.

35. B. Bainbridge and V. Sokheng, "More 'Terrorist' Arrests to Come," *Phnom Penh Post,* June 19, 2003, p. 1.

36. For more information about the UN in Cambodia see "The United Nations in Cambodia," website: www.un.org/kh.

37. In Cambodia these levels are represented by the government structures—village, commune, district, provincial, and national levels. The grassroots level pertains to village, district, and commune jurisdictions, while activities in the provinces are middle-level interventions.

38. P. L. Soth, *Peace Mapping: A Study of Peace Building Initiatives in Cambodia,* 2001, available from ACT (e-mail: act@online.com.kh).

39. For more information about the Project Against Domestic Violence, e-mail: padv@online.com.kh.

40. S. E. Josefa "Human Security and Peacebuilding: Focus on Local Capacity and Institutional Development," available at www.uncrd.or.jp/res/hsp/resfocus.pdf, p. 1.

41. The local mechanism means resource people, available knowledge, and a functional system at all levels.

9.4

East Timor:
The Role of Civil Society in
Conflict Prevention and Peacebuilding

Helder Da Costa

East Timor, the world's newest nation, is a nation emerging from trauma. Occupying just 15,000 square kilometers on the eastern half of the island of Timor, it is only now experiencing its first years of fragile peace, the beginnings of political, economic, and social recovery, and a start to the process of institution building. Having endured centuries of Portuguese colonialism, Japanese occupation from 1942 to 1945, and twenty-four years of Indonesian occupation, the East Timorese people have affirmed themselves as a determined and resilient nation.

East Timor has only been an independent country since May 20, 2002, when the UN Transitional Administration for East Timor (UNTAET)[1] officially withdrew and handed power to a locally elected parliament.[2] East Timor is a country characterized by a low-base economy, poor internal security, a lack of well-defined property rights, and since the withdrawal of UN interim administration, rising unemployment and increasing poverty. Both President Xanana Gusmão and Prime Minister Mari Alkatiri have taken positive steps to assure the continued support of the international community. Bilateral ties are also being fostered, and in particular, ties with Indonesia are gradually improving. The new government faces the daunting task of lifting the socioeconomic standards of East Timor and building a strong economic base for sustainable growth.[3]

The tremendous hardships suffered by the Timorese people in the recent past can be traced back to the coup d'état in April 1974 by a cartel of left-leaning generals who overthrew the Portuguese dictator Marcelo Caetano.[4] The new regime commenced a decolonization program, presenting the Timorese political elite with three options: full independence, continuing with Portugal under some new and more democratic arrangement, or integration with Indonesia.[5] In Portugal, the revolution had led to economic chaos, demoralizing the overseas administration and undermining its administrative grip on the

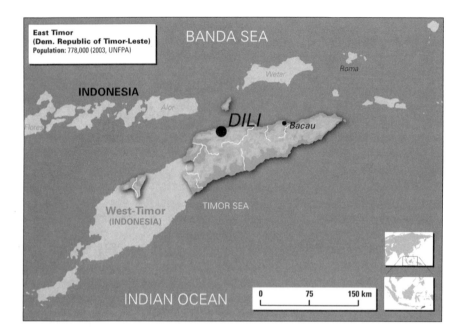

East Timor
(Dem. Republic of Timor-Leste)
Population: 778,000 (2003, UNFPA)

colony, a situation subtly and subversively exploited by the Indonesian gener-als headed by Operasi Komodo.[6] Claiming that intervention was necessary to restore peace and security in East Timor, Indonesia invaded on December 7, 1975. The move was a deliberate project of President Suharto, with conscious support from the United States, Australia, and most Western governments. The remaining Portuguese left the territory, bringing Portuguese rule in East Timor to an end. In July 1976 the Indonesian parliament passed a bill incorporating East Timor into the unitary state of Indonesia as its twenty-seventh province.[7]

During the twenty-four years of occupation, the East Timorese suffered horribly. According to James Dunn, one in four East Timorese died as a con-sequence of the intermittent military offensives staged by the Indonesian mil-itary in East Timor.[8] The Indonesian strategy to control East Timor combined coercion with the incentive of development. Hospitals, roads, and schools were built as Jakarta channeled disproportionate funding to its twenty-seventh province.[9] But these efforts failed to discourage resistance, because develop-ment was accompanied by continued harassment and suspicion rather than genuine political freedom. Perhaps the most notorious example was what has come to be known as the Santa Cruz massacre, which occurred on November 12, 1991, when the Indonesian army opened fire on youthful demonstrators who had gathered at a cemetery to honor the memory of a colleague who had been killed two weeks earlier.

Those opposing Indonesian rule mounted organized resistance, but by the end of 1978, through the application of overwhelming force, the Indonesian military was able to gradually destroy the existing bases of resistance across the country.[10] High-level politicians and military people saved their own lives at the cost of hundreds of arms and hundreds of guerrilla fighters affiliated with the Forcas Armadas da Libertação Nacional de Timor Leste (Falintil),[11] the main armed opposition group, who were assassinated. Educated Timorese, midlevel cadres, and ordinary folk were also massacred.

Under difficult circumstances, the leadership of the proindependence Revolutionary Front for an Independent East Timor (Fretilin) movement decided to continue resistance throughout the territory and to wage guerrilla warfare. Gusmão's strategy in 1983 was to launch a policy of national unity encompassing a pluralist, multiparty system, declare Falintil to be politically unaffiliated, and set up the National Council of Maubere Resistance (CNRM). José Ramos-Horta was appointed as special representative of CNRM abroad. The resistance movement was reinforced during the 1998 Peniche Convention,[12] when the CNRM was subsumed into a new organization, the National Council of Timorese Resistance (CNRT), established as an umbrella organization headed by Xanana Gusmão.[13]

By a combination of internal resistance and international solidarity, the largely nonviolent struggle was sustained over twenty-five years. In 1996 the independence movement gained further international recognition when longtime East Timor national liberation activists José Ramos-Horta and the bishop of Dili, Carlos Ximenes Belo, were awarded the Nobel Peace Prize.[14] In its statement accompanying the award, the committee issued a scathing condemnation of Indonesia's chronic violations of human rights in East Timor.

In 1997 the Indonesian economy was devastated by the collapse of its currency, the rupiah. Mounting pressure at home and abroad forced President Suharto's resignation on May 21, 1998. Vice President B. J. Habibie became president. Racked by an ongoing political and economic crisis, the new administration in Jakarta began indicating that East Timor was a problem it was ready to solve. For East Timor, the windfall was swift. Following Habibie's surprising announcement in January 1999, it appeared that if the people of East Timor rejected the government's autonomy proposal, independence might follow. Independence leaders greeted the unexpected and extraordinary concession with guarded optimism. At an impromptu press conference, Xanana Gusmão simply said, "better late than never" and called for cease-fire negotiations to begin. On May 5, Indonesia and Portugal formally agreed to allow the United Nations to conduct a referendum on Indonesia's autonomy proposal. The agreement included a commitment from Indonesia that, should autonomy be rejected, East Timor would be separated from Indonesia.[15]

Under the UN-sponsored referendum, on August 30, 1999, the East Timorese were asked to either accept or reject integration with Indonesia. Turnout for the historic ballot was 98 percent, with 78.5 percent of the registered electorate voting for a transition to independence. Implementation of the results of the ballot should have been an occasion for celebration. Instead, the Indonesian military and their prointegration militia carried out a scorched earth policy. Countless civilians were victims of murder, rape, and various forms of torture. The military forced people to flee, burning and looting civilian property. About 260,000 people were abducted to West Timor, only a fraction of them militia or proautonomy. During the following two weeks, Indonesian forces and the militias destroyed 75 percent of the buildings and almost all of the infrastructure in East Timor and displaced 75 percent of the population.[16]

By late September 1999, the International Force for East Timor (INTERFET), an Australia-led intervention force authorized by the UN, had taken control and restored order in East Timor.[17] INTERFET's deployment was accompanied by a strong presence of UN agencies, international nongovernmental organizations (NGOs), and other humanitarian actors. Within the country, the CNRT, church groups, local NGOs, and other members of civil society played a key role in assisting the affected population. Once security had been ensured, the humanitarian response was gradually able to extend through the territory over the next two months in order to meet the immediate needs countrywide.[18] Falintil, having protected many of those who sought refuge in the hills, did not engage the Indonesian military during the postballot violence, and on INTERFET's arrival kept largely to its bases in the hills. The East Timorese gradually returned to their villages and towns. In response to the turmoil, during 1999 the last remaining Indonesians finally withdrew from East Timor, paving the way for UNTAET to oversee a transition period that led, ultimately, to independence in May 2002.

Jan Banning/Panos Pictures

East Timor, February 1999.
Around 200 villagers from Turiscai and Same, having fled prointegration militia terror, have found shelter in the Dili suburb of Mota-Uiun.

Conflict Dynamics

East Timor's long history of violence has left scars unhealed to the present day. Divisions in society, reflecting differences in social class, economic and political power, and ideology, are the lasting legacies of the years of foreign rule and significantly contribute to both current conflicts and risks of conflict in the future.

Those divisions manifested themselves throughout the colonial period under Portugal. The cash economy was dominated by a group of Mestizos,[19] Portuguese, and immigrants from China and the Middle East who grew wealthy relative to the remainder of the population. During the Indonesian occupation, from 1975 until 1999, further divisions developed between the various factions engaged in the civil war. The conflict between the pro- and anti-independence movements culminated in the August 1999 referendum and its tragic aftermath.

Even the nationalist groups and East Timorese youth are rife with internal divisions. For example, the youth sector is divided between those who cooperated with, and were paid and protected by, the Indonesian Intelligence, and those who were nationalists. And one consequence of the systematic repression that prevailed during the occupation was that the nationalist groups, though all contributing in their own manner to the struggle, were themselves profoundly divided, with smaller or larger groups and distinctly different characters.[20]

Since the Indonesian withdrawal, a new division has emerged in East Timor between the Timorese diaspora and those who remained in East Timor during the occupation. Many who joined the struggle for independence missed opportunities for education and work experience available in Australia and Portugal. One result is that when the exiles return, they move into the best government and private-sector jobs, causing resentment among those who stayed behind.

Divisions related to educational opportunities and the diaspora are closely linked to divisions around language as well. In colonial times, just 15 percent of the population was literate, and the overwhelming majority spoke the indigenous language, Tetum. But the elite and returned exiles speak Portuguese. The situation is further complicated by the fact that during the Indonesian occupation, Bahasa Indonesian became a working language and was taught in school. English has also become an important working language. The new constitution specifies Portuguese and Tetum as the two official languages.

Finally, the new nation is burdened with ongoing political conflicts rooted in the years of turmoil and occupation. One group, the Popular Council for the Defense of the Democratic Republic of East Timor (CPD-RDTL), rejected the legitimacy of the UN administration and demanded a return to the 1975 constitution. Throughout the territory there have been a series of skirmishes, often politically oriented, involving the CPD-RDTL. In response, President Xanana Gusmão's office organized a national dialogue on January 25, 2003,[21] bringing together representatives of the government and representatives of CPD-RDTL to openly discuss and address their political demands. The dialogue, which was broadcast to the entire nation, did not result in any breakthrough, but provided an opportunity for each side to lay out its own position, and served as an avenue for confidence-building measures.

Official Conflict Management

A variety of different conflict resolution perspectives or positions are applied within a multipolar network.[22] Important players have included UNTAET, agencies such as the UN Children's Fund and the UN High Commissioner for Refugees, other international bodies such as the International Organization for Migration (IOM), the Timorese reconciliation and repatriation organization the Association of Resistance Veterans (ARV),[23] international NGOs, and a range of emerging civil society organizations.

Working with the Timorese leadership, UNTAET created a sound foundation for a modern system of democratic government at the national level. The UN also helped to create the conditions for a lasting political solution between East Timor and Indonesia. The UN peacekeeping force played an important humanitarian role in ensuring the safety and security of the country and its inhabitants. The peacekeepers were pivotal in ending blatant human rights abuses and creating a stable environment for emergency relief and a platform for development.

There were problems worth noting, however. A significant factor undermining the effectiveness of the UN agencies in peacebuilding initiatives in East Timor has been their predisposition to deal with state actors rather than to listen to voices in civil society and address their grievances. Under UNTAET, UN administrators, armed with ready-made prescriptions, failed to adequately invest in building upon the existing strengths and capacities, nor was it inclined to push initiatives suited to the local context. In addition, the UN did not seek to build capacity among already established, robust NGOs in East Timor, instead relying exclusively on international actors.

In terms of political development, UNTAET oversaw positive movement. While the establishment of several political parties reflects a range of political tendencies within East Timorese society, party leaders are generally united on fundamental issues, no significant group feels itself to be marginalized, and no political faction is inclined to revert to violence to achieve its goals. UNTAET has succeeded, in the postconflict period, in achieving the primary objectives of its mission: East Timor has been secured from reprisals by the militias that caused so much havoc, and it has created an environment sufficiently safe that most refugees have returned home.

Multi-Track Diplomacy

Within East Timorese society there are inherent and ongoing tensions related to both residual hostility among former adversaries during the occupation and civil unrest, as well as unresolved conflicts existing among the various elements within the lower levels of Timorese society. During the years of occupation, people at all levels developed their own survival methods and it is not always apparent what actors within East Timor are responsible for what activities, or which outside party can most effectively play a constructive role in reconciliation and reconstruction. Hence, East Timor can clearly benefit from a multiactor, multilevel, and multifaceted approach to address the range of both past conflicts and emerging conflicts now threatening East Timorese society.

At the domestic level, the CNRT has experience in protecting and coordinating the movements and safety of internally displaced persons (IDPs) and refugees since 1999. They have created their own civilian structures—for example, a civil registry and an education program—for those fighting on behalf of the resistance and living in the mountains. The CNRT has assisted the UN in resolving many of the issues inherent in a postconflict society and has been active in preparing East Timor for the transition to an independent state. However, despite the mandate and increased capability of UN civilian police and the newly established Policia Nacional Timor Leste, members of various parallel structures continue to carry out what they perceive to be a "security" function, which often extends to the enforcement of law and order. The country's inadequate police and legal services faced a real test on December 4, 2002, when frustration over economic issues sparked serious rioting, which the state security forces were unable to fully control.[24]

In the postindependence period, the development of civil society groups is vitally important to normal development and a definitive turn away from violence. Local actors are vital in building a culture of prevention and ensuring durable peace.[25] The National Development Plan confirms the legitimacy and importance of civil society in the nation's development framework.[26] Through the NGO Forum, the NGO community has also been engaged as well in driving policy in the early stages.

Two categories of civil society have emerged over the years, namely civil society during the resistance period and civil society during the transition period.[27] East Timor never had the institutions of a sovereign state, but those of a remote colonial outpost of Portugal or the makings of a provincial administration implementing Jakarta's decisions and policies. But civil society in the transition period involves communities and civil society organizations (NGOs, such as the Road to Progress Foundation (ETADEP), HAK Foundation (Foundation for Law, Human Rights and Justice), women's groups, Rede das Mulheres, and the Catholic Church) playing an active role in conflict-related issues designed and executed by local NGOs, often with little involvement of internationals.

Civil society is currently expanding rapidly in numbers and types of activity. The environment in which they operate is broadly supportive.[28] There are now about 230 local NGOs.[29] Through their main umbrella, the NGO Forum, these NGOs have provided an outlet for the younger generation to express their views and to influence national and local policy. Most NGOs in East Timor are engaged in the provision of emergency humanitarian assistance, education, health services, agriculture, development, environmental advocacy, good governance, human rights work, and justice and peace activities.[30] While most of these groups are concentrated in Dili, these organizations are beginning to change the political landscape in all sorts of interesting ways.

Spearheaded by respected Dili-based organizations that emerged between 1996 and 1999, civil society has also been involved in conflict resolution, voter education, and the monitoring of peacebuilding and reconciliation work in East Timor. Most are independent of the United Nations and international agencies, though they do receive funding from outside agencies. Their activities are often in response to internal conflicts in the country. The recent highly successful voter education campaign, resulting in the participation of 86 percent of eligible voters in the presidential election, is an excellent example of civic education promoted by the local organizations.[31]

To spur contributions by civil society in East Timor, NGOs will continue to foster civic education for both citizens and office holders. They have acted as mediators between the United Nations, the emerging government administration, and the population at large. Such interactions help politicians to come to an understanding that they should be accountable to the citizenry, and helps citizens provide feedback and influence their government.

An important development over the past two years has been the emergence of community-based organizations and locally operated radio stations, providing capacity building at the grassroots levels and allowing for balanced and informative programming. The goal is to help communities to articulate their interests, make informed choices, exert influence on government for improved services, and to hold government accountable, consistent with the notion that civic engagement is the demand side of good governance. The facilitation of public interest broadcasting—including at the very local level—is emerging as a critical enabler for accountability and empowerment of poor people.[32]

Particular notice should be paid to developments in civil society in the following areas:

- *Conflict resolution, human rights advocacy and monitoring, and democracy.* Leading civil society groups such as the HAK Foundation, the Sahe Institute for Liberation (SIL), the Kadalak Sulimutuk Institute (KSI), and the East Timor Study Group (ETSG) have played important roles in promoting peacebuilding initiatives throughout East Timor. This has also included the growing role of the labor movement in the villages, initiated by the Labor Advocacy Institute for East Timor. This is a difficult lesson, since the only experience most people have is unaccountable foreign-imposed autocratic government, which they could only resist. Most internationally driven civic education programs have not addressed the issue effectively, although some local ones do a better job.[33] The exemplary conflict management activities of Yayasan Hak, the East Timor Student Solidarity Council (ETSSC), and SIL, which produced leaflets, brochures, and relevant information for distribution at the district and subdistrict levels prior to the elections for the Constituent

Assembly and presidency, were impressive. Combined with the supplemental information provided by media outlets, such as Radio UNTAET, Suara Timor Lorosae, Televisi Timor Lorasea (TVTL), and the Timor Post, they played an important part in stimulating and protecting the country's embryonic democracy—filling an information void that otherwise could have been filled with rumors and misinformation certain to fuel discontent. By expanding their services beyond the Dili, and explaining choices, voting procedures, and the importance of voting, these NGOs are establishing direct links with the population and helping to instill democratic norms in a state that has never experienced democracy, much less self-governance. They are also encouraging the growth of grassroots organization outside of the capital. Local NGOs are indeed fostering the kind of positive civil society that will add qualitatively to conflict prevention and peacebuilding in East Timor.

The Western-based groups active in East Timor (e.g., Oxfam, Caritas, CARE, World Vision, Concern, the International Republican Institute, Catholic Relief Services, the Asia Foundation, and many others) bring many specialized skills to their work in peacebuilding in East Timor. There is a rapidly growing recognition that all of the groups and organizations in this field need each other if they are to make any real contribution to resolving the deep-rooted and intractable conflicts that they are called upon to deal with.

• *Information services.* By providing a channel for communication between the population and elites, civil society organizations are fostering communication and trust in general.[34] Print and electronic media outlets such Suara Timor Lorosae, Timor Post, Talitakum, Lian Maubere, TVTL, Radio Timor Lorosae, and the Catholic outlet Radio Timor Kmanek (RTK) at the national level, as well as community radio stations promoted by the ETSCC in Liquica, can be used for the dissemination of information on conflict management and the promotion of peaceful relations between formerly warring parties. The development of credible media also provides an effective platform for quelling and responding to irresponsible rumors that tend to circulate in the capital. However, there is concern that the press freedom that Timorese media organizations have long dreamed of may not last for long, as the current government is attempting to impose restrictions on the media.

• *Gender balance.* In the past, Timorese women were relegated to a marginal role in East Timorese society. But spurred on by the umbrella organization Rede das Mulheres (REDE), Timorese women have gradually increased their contributions to peacebuilding and political activities. Interventions by the international community and international donors, such as through the World Bank Community Empowerment Programme, have also contributed to promoting the role of women in local governance structures.[35] There is now work under way on the part of the women's support organization the East Timorese Women's Communication Forum

(FOKUPERS), the party-linked women's organization Timorese Women's Organisation (or Organizacao Mulher Timor [OMT]), and the UN to mount a campaign against domestic violence, an issue of importance to vulnerable Timorese women. The public campaign is aided by TVTL, Radio Timor Lorosae, and RTK, which broadcast information to raise public awareness on gender issues. Indeed, East Timorese women were the first to ensure that the UN transition structures incorporated a gender affairs department (as part of UNTAET) and allotted a mix of international and local staff. This department did much to continue to exert the necessary pressure to ensure that gender considerations would be taken seriously, both by the UN transitional authority and by East Timorese political leaders. As a result of direct lobbying to the government, an office for the promotion of equality was established with a view to working on a dual strategy empowering both women in government and the civil service, as well as women in civil society.[36] A sign of increasing women's representation in the national parliament (26 percent) is one obvious consequence. This is an important recognition of the role that East Timorese women have played and continue to play in the area of peacemaking and reconciliation.

• *Education and training.* Universities and independent think tanks are also playing important roles in promoting public awareness on public policy.[37] The ongoing public debate on campus organized by the National University of East Timor, through its National Research Centre (CNIC),[38] in cooperation with the National Democratic Institute for International Affairs (NDI), is an example of an initiative that contributed positively to peacebuilding initiatives. The seminars brought together two potential conflicting parties, the Falintil-FDTL and former Falintil veterans who were not successfully selected into the national defense forces, to openly discuss their views and potential contributions to the country's future development.[39] A more limited but effective focus on issues affecting national interests is being promoted through a Dili-based think tank, the East Timor Study Group,[40] which is a gaining reputation for involving high-level institutions and civil society groups in discussions of public policy issues pertinent to East Timor's current development.

Reconciliation

One concrete step that must be taken to promote national cohesion in East Timor is reconciliation among East Timorese, a point very much supported by the current Timorese leadership.[41] Recognizing that in the postconflict period, communities and political groups in East Timor remain traumatized and unsettled, there has been a need to identify ways in which divisions within and among the communities can be addressed so as to narrow the differences between those who supported independence and those who opposed it, promote reconciliation, strengthen social cohesion, and create a sense of security and closure in society at large.[42] In particular, the issue of justice as it relates to reconciliation is arguably one of the centerpieces of conflict prevention. The Catholic Church has played a pivotal role in promoting reconciliation.

An essential part of the debate on reconciliation and justice focuses on choices confronting East Timor with respect to the appropriate instruments to address its painful past, and in particular the choice between a "retributive" judicial process, with a war crimes tribunal as the principal instrument, or a "restorative" process, with a truth commission as the principal instrument. Much attention has been focused on the legal dimension of the tribunal, its potential impact on sovereignty, and the retributive justice aspects of it. A truth commission is assessed in terms of the ostensible dualism between truth and justice, and the granting of amnesty.[43] The victims of the violence insist on retributive justice, with strong emphasis on the rule of law. But an important consideration—the real impact on society of one or the other procedure—has been largely overlooked in the debate. The question is whether either procedure can really address the root causes of the conflict. If the impact is limited to individuals, then the exercise will not amount to conflict prevention. Unfortunately, little empirical work has been done in this area.

The most notable upshot of these discussions has been the establishment of the Reception, Truth, and Reconciliation Commission (CAVR), which took office in January 2002 pledging "to promote reconciliation, national unity and peace."[44] It has been given a mandate complementary to that of the courts, with the authority to deal with less serious human rights abuses. The commission, which has both national and regional commissioners, is an independent authority whose three functions are to provide a truth-telling forum for victims and perpetrators of human rights violations; to facilitate community reconciliation for lesser crimes; and to make recommendations to the government on further actions on reconciliation and human rights. A "serious crimes" process has been established to run parallel to the CAVR to bring to justice those perpetrators of especially serious crimes who have remained in East Timor.

The CAVR is mandated to establish the truth about past human rights violations that occurred throughout the entire twenty-four years of Indonesian occupation,[45] and report on the underlying causes of these violations. The CAVR seeks to help communities honor those who lost their lives. In understanding the causes of what happened in Timor in this period, it is hoped that the CAVR may also make it a little more difficult for the international community to allow this to ever happen again.[46]

Despite the establishment of the CAVR, a debate continues about the establishment of a international war crimes tribunal in addition to the truth commission. To date, the only actions taken against Indonesians suspected of serious crimes against humanity have taken place in Jakarta, where some—mostly junior—Indonesian military officers were tried at an Indonesian ad hoc human rights trial. Those results have been widely rejected as inadequate by the international community and within East Timor. Many East Timorese demand that the international community take the initiative to prosecute the perpetrators of gross violations of human rights through an international tribunal.

Reconciliation, in this view, is more than a political effort shaped by apologies, handshakes, and embraces. Justice for the perpetrators needs to prevail. However, East Timor's current leadership believes that the national interests of the country are better advanced by avoiding a potential deterioration in the relationship between East Timor and Indonesia, which could ensue if Indonesian suspects faced trial.

Two simplified models of reconciliation are in place in East Timor, namely, one focusing on the political elite and the other on the grassroots.[47] Despite earlier attempts to involve actors at both levels over the years, the end results appear to be mixed.[48] Reconciliation regarding residents of refugee camps is an area that has had, to date, mixed results. Although UN agencies have attempted to implement repatriation programs, weaknesses in these programs have led to the marginalization of armed militias who controlled the refugee camps. This in part is due to attitudinal differences based on ideology, principles of reconciliation, and necessary conditions to achieve a lasting solution. While reconciliation efforts are still under way, a possible explanation for the difficulties can be ascribed to the symbolism of reconciliation, with strong religious undertones and it association with traditional Timorese cultural humanism *(nahe biti)*.

Reconciliation takes time and effective effort. If the process is abandoned before its work is done, the unfortunate consequence may be that long-term reconstruction is hindered rather than helped.

Addressing the Needs of Former Combatants
Many postconflict countries have encountered serious difficulties resulting from a failure to address veterans' issues or the adoption of ill-defined or unsustainable veterans' policies. East Timor is addressing these problems early, which President Gusmão has created two commissions to deal with—one responsible for identifying former combatants of the 1975–1979 period and one charged with identifying Falintil veterans from the 1981–1999 period. However, vital funding to meet the needs of veterans and satisfy their current demands has been inadequate.

The peacebuilding process has also endeavored to identify legitimate former combatants and their families and reintegrate them into civil society. The Falintil Reinsertion Assistance Program (FRAP), undertaken by the IOM under UNTAET, provided initial support in demobilizing members of Falintil by means of U.S.$500 subsidy and various reintegration packages in host communities.[49] Although partially successful as an economic initiative, the program was unable to address wider problems of social integration, which have the potential to create serious and continuing unrest.

Prospects
Rebuilding political, social, economic, and security systems in the aftermath of a prolonged conflict is an extremely daunting task. The key factors are endurance and commitment—the willingness of all actors to engage in long-term rebuilding

and reconciliation efforts—along with sustained investment in the prevention of renewed outbreaks of violence.[50] East Timor faces tremendous challenges on many fronts as it proceeds to develop its political, social, and economic institutions. A fair and effective system of law and order, justice, and good governance must be established to secure democracy and guarantee respect for fundamental human rights.

Progress toward stability will require that a number of issues be addressed. The high levels of frustration among youth and former Falintil combatants, as evidenced by protest and violence, pose one significant challenge in the future. Furthermore, there is a need to apply political pressure to the reconciliation process itself. There is a possibility of increased political and social tension if the process of national reconciliation and peacebuilding falters. Additionally, the weak development of civil society, coupled with the increasing exercise of political control by the ruling party (Fretilin), undermines the development of representative government. Finally, the prospects for peace are threatened by the lack of progress in capacity building at both the national and the local level, and by macroeconomic instability brought on by large budget deficits and weak progress on economic reform. The shortages of human and economic resources could undermine economic performance and perhaps lead to social and political instability.

The peacebuilding process in East Timor depends on a complex of activities and actors: advocacy, conflict management, and education and training by civil society organizations at the national and district levels. It is especially important that women and other marginalized groups begin to participate in decisionmaking at all levels of society. The process will require that connections between citizen and state be strengthened, and that institutions be transformed to create an enabling environment for effective citizen participation, social justice, and the protection of human rights.

Recommendations

There are several strategies available to policymakers and civil society in managing conflict prevention and peacebuilding in East Timor. These include:

Empowerment of Citizens

Communities empowered by a peacemaking agenda often feel a sense of solidarity and confidence that provides momentum for change. The local or grassroots level in East Timor is the most appropriate place to start, where impact is most keenly experienced and where early warning signs of impending conflict will emerge. The grassroots level also provides the most fruitful context for rehabilitation. This is because traditional resources for remedy are present and the conflict is relatively contained. The most effective and lasting way to build peace and avert conflict is to ensure that the people of East Timor, using their own institutional and societal structures, develop the confidence and capabilities to manage their own problems and disputes.

Strengthening Civil Society

Efforts should focus on strengthening East Timor's civil society, and working with nascent government organs (principally at the district and subdistrict levels) to promote more participatory approaches to policy and planning. Citizen participation in public affairs, where debate and discussion of policies and options and deliberation on decisions and choices are encouraged, is essential to democratic governance at all levels. Conflict is mitigated when civil society flourishes and opportunities for democratic participation occur at both the local and the national level. These opportunities are critical in order to inform and educate the people on the roles, functions, and activities of the different organs of the government, donor agencies, NGOs, and other civil society organizations.

Strengthening the Rule of Law

It is essential that all concerned parties, in particular the government and donors, commit over the long-term to the development of an East Timorese society where the rule of law prevails. The administration of justice is central to this goal. A long-term training plan for judges, prosecutors, public defenders, and other court officials should be developed, as well as guidelines for the police, prosecutors, judges, and community leaders that clarify which matters are to be directed to the formal criminal justice process and which matters may be more appropriately dealt with through the traditional justice system. Also, all applicable law in East Timor should be reviewed to identify gaps and ensure consistency with international human rights standards, to enable access to justice, and to provide for necessary assistance or measures to be taken to ensure the functioning of district courts. Finally, an effective and timely dissemination of all applicable laws of the state to the public at large should be set up, through available print and electronic media outlets, and workshops and meetings involving civil society groups at the village level should be organized to enable citizens to familiarize themselves with the laws being promulgated, including their duties and responsibilities as citizens.

Maintaining Peace and Stability Through Reconciliation

Efforts to promote peace and reconciliation among East Timorese at the elite and grassroots levels continue to pose formidable challenges, given the trauma of the war and East Timor's complex history with Indonesia. Care is needed by both countries at the state and civil society levels to put this relationship on a new and positive footing. At both levels, civil society has a vital role to play transforming violent attitudes, behavior, and situations.

Education for Peacebuilding

Peacebuilding activities should be included as part of the new school curriculum to mirror a realistic representation of Timorese history. The need to retain the collective memory of the history of the Timorese struggle for human rights, justice, and peace is a must. The very development of this history could be a helpful process not only in strengthening the national identity but also in effecting collective healing. Church leaders, business groups, NGOs, and academics are urged to be proactive in their contributions.

Encouraging Independent Media Outlets

A critical component for understanding nonviolent conflict resolution is the empowering of local independent media organizations (print and electronic) to bring rapid and drastic changes in conflict management to East Timor. In the capital, newspapers (*STL* and *Timor Post*) and TVTL have constructive roles to play, while at the district and *suco* (village) level, radio appears to be the most effective media outlet. Viable channels also need to be developed to facilitate the flow of information from the people on the ground to policymakers, other government functionaries, and other stakeholders.

Mutual Cooperation Among Various Players in the Country

Civil society should develop a long-term protocol that recognizes the need to work in partnership with UN agencies in East Timor while maintaining a clear and explicit independence. The same holds for the UN and other international agencies, which must take responsibility for proactively reaching out to civil society. Social and political citizenship is integrally related to livelihood, which must be improved through increased fair allocation of resources and reduced threat of civil conflict. In practical terms, civil society and UN agencies, together with government officials, need to find better ways to extend effective citizenship to rural East Timorese men and women, and to supplement their homegrown resourcefulness with earmarked funding, training, and support in peacebuilding activities.

Resources

Reports

Clements, Kevin P., *Civil Society and Conflict Prevention*. Presented at the conference "Facing Ethnic Conflicts: Perspectives from Research and Policy Making, " organized by the Center for Development Research at the University of Bonn, December, 14–16, 2000.

International Peace Academy. *East Timor in Transition: From Conflict Prevention to State-Building*. By Simon Chesterman. 2001. Available at www.ipacademy.org/publications/reports/research/publtimorprint.

———. *Sharing Best Practices on Conflict Prevention: The UN, Regional and Subregional Organizations, National and Local Actors*. Policy report. N.d. Available at www.ipacademy.org

United Nations. *SC Resolution 1272*. UN SCOR (4057th meeting), 2002.

———. *The UN and East Timor: Self-Determination Through Popular Consultation*. New York, 1999.

United Nations Development Programme. Interview: President Xanana Gusmão of Timor-Leste. December 18, 2002. Available at www.reliefweb.int.

———. *Ukun Rasik A'an*. East Timor Human Development Report. Chap. 3, "New Roles for Civil Society." May 2002. Available at www.undp.east-timor.org.

World Bank. *Background Paper for the Donor Meetings on Timor-Leste.* Dili, June 2–3, 2003.

———. *Draft Summary of the Joint Assessment Mission to East Timor.* Darwin, Australia, November, 15, 1999.

———. *Tapping the Power of Grassroots Radio Bank Initiative Incorporating Support for Community Stations.* The Participation and Civic Engagement Group. 2003. Available at www.worldbank.org/participation/events.

Other Publications

"Assessing UNTAET's Role in Building Local Capacities for the Future." By James J. Fox. In Hadi Soesastro and Landry Haryo Subyanto, eds., *Peace Building and State Building in East Timor.* Jakarta: CSIS, 2002, chapter 3, available at http://jsmp.minihub.org/Reports/Fox10nb20nb03.pdf.

"Bilateral Aid to East Timor: An Overview." *La'o Hamutuk Bulletin* (Dili), December 2001. Available at www.etan.org/lb/bulletins/bulletinv2n8.html.

Bridging a Divide: The Creation of a Third Path for Conflict Resolution. By Mikael Weissmann. Department of Peace and Conflict Research, Uppsala University, Sweden, 2002. Available at http://orient4.orient.su.se/easttimor/towardsacivilsociety.pdf.

"Challenges of Operational Conflict Prevention: From Proactive to Reactive Prevention." By Albrecht Schnabel. UNU, presentation for the session "System and Procedures for Conflict Prevention and Resolution." N.d.

"Challenges of Peace and Stability." By Xanana Gusmão. Speech delivered at the University of Melbourne, April 7, 2003. Available at www.etan.org/et2003/april/07/07xg.htm.

East Timor at the Cross Roads. Eds. P. Carey and G. Garter Bentley. Honolulu: University of Hawaii Press, 1995.

East Timor Facing the Future: Reconciliation, Institution Building, and Economic Reconstruction. By J. M. Saldanha and M. Salla. East Timor Study Group. Available at http://rspas.anu.edu.au/etsg/briefs/proc1.rtf.

External Reviewers on Humanitarian Crisis in East Timor, September 1999–May 2000, UN Transitional Administration in East Timor, May 2000. Available at www.reliefweb.int.

"From Resistance to Nation Building: The Challenging Role of Civil Society in East Timor." By Natasha Meden. In *Development Outreach.* Washington, D.C.: World Bank Institute, 2002. Available at http://lnweb18.worldbank.org/eap/eap.nsf/countries/east+timor/d383aa29e775539785256ba0006c2ed2?opendocument.

Indonesia's Forgotten War: The Hidden History of East Timor. By J. G. Taylor. London: Zed Books, 1991.

"Issues in Conflict Resolution." By Dirk Kotzé. *African Journal in Conflict Resolution* no. 1 (2002).

"Nahe Biti: The Philosophy and Process of Grassroots Reconciliation." By Dionisio Babo Soares. Paper presented at the conference "Road to Reconciliation," Bergen, Norway, April 11–12, 2001.

"Nation Building in East Timor." By Jonathan Steele. *World Policy Journal* XIX, no. 2 (Summer 2002), pp. 76–87.

National Development Plan. RDTL Planning Commission, Dili, 2002. Available at www.gov.easttimor.org/web.%20development%20partners/left%20frame.

"NGOs, Civil Society, and Hopes for Democracy in East Timor." By Chris Lundry. Unpublished paper, 2002.

On Amnesty and the Settlement of Crimes Against Humanity: A Pastoral Appeal. By Carlos Filipe Ximenes Belo. Dili, June 29, 2002.

Out of the Ashes: Destruction and Reconstruction of East Timor, by James J. Fox and Dionisio Baba Soares, eds., Adelaide: Crawford House, 1990.

Peace Building and State Building in East Timor. Eds. Hadi Soesastro and Landry Haryo Subyanto. Jakarta: CSIS, 2002.

Peace-Building in East Timor: Good Governance as the Key Ingredient to Success. By Gwi-Yeop Son. Columbia University, New York, 2001. Available at www.barnard. columbia.edu/bcrw.

Peacebuilding in East Timor: The Role and Contribution of the Church. By Carlos Filipe Ximenes Belo. Oslo, December, 2001.

The Political Economy of East Timor Development. By João Mariano Saldanha. Jakarta: Sinar Harapan, 1994.

A Popular Challenge to UNTAET's Achievements. By Lucas Da Costa and Jose Antonio Neves. 2001.

"Reconciliation, Tolerance, Human Rights, and Elections." By Xanana Gusmão. Symposium, National Council, Dili, February 12, 2001. Available at www.etan.org/ et2001a/february/11-17/12pres.htm.

"Reconciliation from Legal Perspective." By Aniceto Guterres Lopes. *La'o Hamutuk Bulletin* (Dili), June 21, 2000.

"The Role of Civil Society Organisations in Sustainable Development in East Timor." By Arsenio Bano. In Russell Anderson and Carolyn Deutsch, eds., *Sustainable Development and the Environment in East Timor,* proceedings of the Conference on Sustainable Development in East Timor, January 25–31, 2001.

The Role of NGOs in Asia: An East Timorese Example. By Jose Ramos-Horta. N.d. Available at www.easttimor.com/lh.html.

"Success, Weakness, and Challenges of Political Transition in East Timor." By Dionisio Babo Soares. In Hadi Soesastro and Landry Haryo Subyanto, eds., *Peace Building and State Building in East Timor.* Jakarta: CSIS, 2002.

"Sustainable Future? How East Timor Manages Its Economy" By Helder Da Costa. *Inside Indonesia* no. 71 (July–September 2002): 8–9.

Suara Timor Lorosae (Dili). January 26, 2003.

Text of the Norwegian Nobel Committee's Citation for the 1996 Peace Prize. Nobel Peace Prize Committee, Oslo, 1996.

Timor: A People Betrayed. By James Dunn. Sydney: Jaracanda Press, 1983.

"Two-Track Transitional Justice Model in Timor-Leste." By Anita Roberts. Presentation at the conference "Activating Human Rights and Diversity," Southern Cross University, Australia. Available at www.scu.edu.au.

United Nations Involvement in Post-Conflict Reconstruction Efforts: New and Continuing Challenges in the Case of East Timor. By Sarah Pritchard. 2001. Available at www.jsmp.minihub.org/reports/pritchardpercent20FF.pdf.

Websites

www.caec-asiaeurope.org (Council for Asia-Europe Cooperation, Publication on East Timor, Kosovo, and Bosnia)

www.easttimor-reconciliation.org (Commission for Reception, Truth, and Reconciliation)

www.etan.org/lh (La'o Hamutuk, East Timor Institute for Reconstruction Monitoring and Analysis)

www.geocities.com/etngoforum/index.html (NGO Forum)

www.jsmp.minihub.org (Judicial System Monitoring Programme)

Resource Contacts

Local Experts

Domingas Alves, East Timorese Women's Communication Forum, e-mail: fokupers@fokupers.minihub.org

Cecilio C. Freitas, executive director of the East Timor NGO Forum, e-mail: etngocentre@hotmail.com

Francisco Da Costa Guterres, Ph.D. candidate, School of International Business and Asian Studies, Griffith University, Nathan, QLD 4111, Australia, e-mail: f.c.guterres@griffith. edu.au (also a Fellow in Law and Politics, East Timor Study Group, Dili)

Julio Martins, NGO Forum team leader of advocacy, e-mail: vique10@yahoo.com

Adriano do Nascimento, La'o Hamutuk, East Timor Institute for Reconstruction Monitoring and Analysis, e-mail: mentoadi@hotmail.com
Aniceto Neves, Perkumpulan HAK, e-mail: yayasanhak@minihub.org
Filomena dos Reis, director, Women's Development and Advocacy, FOKUPERS
Dionisio Babo Soares, deputy country director, Asia Foundation, Jl. Jacinto Candido, Audian, Dili, e-mail: dionisio@tafet.org

International Experts
Rebecca Engel, Center for International Conflict Resolution, Columbia University, e-mail: ree7@columbia.edu
Charlie Scheiner, La'o Hamutuk, East Timor Institute for Reconstruction Monitoring and Analysis, e-mail: laohamutuk@easttimor.minihub.org

---

Helder Da Costa currently serves as tertiary education manager at the Asia 2000 Foundation of New Zealand. He has a master's degree in agricultural economics from Massey University and a Ph.D. in economics from Adelaide University. He was executive director of the National Research Centre, Universidade Nacional Timor Lorosae, Dili, and has lectured in international economics at the same institution. He has been a consultant and reviewer to AusAID, the ADB, the UNDP, ACIAR, and UNOCHA. Among his publications is East Timor Human Development Report 2002: The Way Forward *(coauthor) (Dili: UNDP).*

Notes

I wish to thank Dionisio Babo Soares (RSPAS, Australian National University, Canberra) and Francisco Da Costa Guterres (Griffith University, Brisbane) for their comments on the initial draft of this chapter.

1. UNTAET was established under UN Security Council Resolution 1272 of October 25, 1999. It was empowered to exercise all legislative, executive, and judiciary authority in East Timor. Its main tasks were to provide security and maintain law and order throughout the territory. For a critical assessment of UNTAET in East Timor, see Jonathan Steele, "Nation Building in East Timor," *World Policy Journal* XIX, no. 2 (Summer 2002). See also Hadi Soesastro and Landry Haryo Subyanto, eds., *Peacebuilding and State Building in East Timor* (Jakarta: CSIS, 2002). For a more critical note, see Sarah Pritchard, *United Nations Involvement in Post-Conflict Reconstruction Efforts: New and Continuing Challenges in the Case of East Timor,* 2001, available at www.jsmp.minihub.org/reports/pritchardpercent20FF.pdf.

2. The East Timorese have perceived government as an imposition from the outside not only under Portuguese and Indonesian rule, but also to a certain degree under UNTAET. This has resulted in a general reluctance on the part of East Timorese to engage with government on a constructive basis, and a general reluctance on the leadership's part to take responsibility for a process over which it felt it had little control. Important steps were taken in 2000–2002 that led the East Timorese to take the driver's seat. In the August 2001 elections, sixteen political parties registered and campaigned. While five of these parties were formed in 1974–1975, the other eleven for the most part established themselves in 2000–2001, which had not given them enough time to reflect much beyond campaign slogans and strategies on governance. As shown by the high turnout in both the 1999 referendum and the 2001 Constituent Assembly elections, the East Timorese society is a highly politicized one, but not in a modern way, and politics are still very much driven by personality as opposed to program.

3. See the macroeconomic outlook in the National Development Plan, 2002.

4. See J. G. Taylor, *Indonesia's Forgotten War: The Hidden History of East Timor* (London: Zed Books, 1991).

5. James Dunn, *A People Betrayed* (Sydney: Jaracanda Press, 1983).

6. P. Carey and G. Garter Bentley, eds. *East Timor at the Crossroads* (Honolulu: University of Hawaii Press, 1995).

7. See Dunn, *A People Betrayed,* rev. ed. (Sydney: Jaracanda Press, 1983).

8. Ibid.

9. For details, see Joao Mariano Saldanha, *The Political Economy of East Timor Development* (Jakarta: Sinar Harapan, 1994).

10. See Xanana Gusmão's speech at the symposium "Reconciliation, Tolerance, Human Rights, and Elections," February 12, 2001.

11. Falintil is now restructured as Falintil–Força da Defesa de Timor Leste (Falintil-FDTL), according to the constitution of the Democratic Republic of East Timor.

12. In March 1998 the representatives of a cross-section of East Timorese internal political groups and exiles of all shades attended the convention, held in Peniche, Portugal, to set up a political platform. The decision was to change the name from "CNRM" to "CNRT" under the leadership of Xanana Gusmão.

13. After fulfilling its mission in 1999, and with the advent of multiparty politics in June 2001, the CNRT was dissolved.

14. See Nobel Peace Prize Committee, *Text of the Norwegian Nobel Committee's Citation for the 1996 Peace Prize,* Oslo, 1996.

15. See the "Agreement Text" between Indonesia and Portugal under the UN auspices, May 5, 1999.

16. See the HAK Foundation, and other UN reports.

17. Diplomatic negotiations led to the entry of the International Force in East Timor into Dili on September 19, 1999, under Australian command. Later the Security Council, by Resolution 1272 of October 25, 1999, established UNTAET.

18. See the report External Review of Humanitarian Response to the East Timor Crisis, by the UN Transitional Administration in East Timor, May 24, 2000, available at www.reliefweb.int.

19. *Mestizo* is a Portuguese term for a mixture of Portuguese and Timorese descent.

20. See Mikael Weissmann, *Bridging a Divide: The Creation of a Third Path for Conflict Resolution* (Uppsala, Sweden: Department of Peace and Conflict Research, Uppsala University), pp. 36–38, available at http://orient4.orient.su.se/easttimor/towardsacivilsociety.pdf.

21. See *Suara Timor Lorosae* (Dili), January 26, 2003.

22. For an overview of multi-track diplomacy, see Kevin P. Clements, *Civil Society and Conflict Prevention* (Bonn: Center for Development Research, December, 14–16, 2000).

23. The AVR was created by Xanana Gusmão in 2000 and is now headed by Paulo Assis Belo. Its main activities include reconciliation, humanitarian issues, microcredits, and welfare of former combatants.

24. The background to the riots involved rising frustration with increasing poverty since the withdrawal of the main UN interim administration, lack of economic progress and opportunity, and the country's long history of violence—a history that predates the bloody Indonesian era.

25. See United Nations Development Programme, *Ukun Rasik A' an,* East Timor Human Development Report, chap. 3, "New Roles for Civil Society," May 2002, available at www.undp.east-timor.org.

26. The National Development Plan is the official document published by the New Government of the Democratic Republic of Timor Leste. It outlines the mission, vision for 2020, and development strategies over the next five years.

27. See Natasha Meden, "From Resistance to Nation Building: The Challenging Role of Civil Society in East Timor," in *Development Outreach* (Washington, D.C.: World Bank Institute, 2002).

28. There is no specific legislation governing the structure and responsibilities of NGOs. They can apply for charitable status and thereby benefit from exemptions from

income tax and customs duties for goods imported for the purposes of humanitarian relief, education, and health care.

29. For details, see the NGO Forum website, www.geocities.com/etngoforum/index.html.

30. Personal observation, based on remarks of a few NGO representatives in an informal talk in Dili, February 2003.

31. However, the civic education program, designed by the UN Development Programme and the U.S. Agency for International Development, was fundamentally flawed in that it defined civic participation in government exclusively as voting.

32. See World Bank, *Tapping the Power of Grassroots Radio Bank Initiative Incorporating Support for Community Stations,* The Participation and Civic Engagement Group, available at www.worldbank.org/participation/events.

33. The UN also sponsors programs, as do local and international NGOs.

34. See Chris Lundry, "NGOs, Civil Society, and Hopes for Democracy in East Timor," unpublished paper, 2002.

35. For a brief description of the role of women in East Timor and in postconflict countries see Milena Pires, *Enhancing Women's Participation in the Electoral Process in Postconflict Countries,* January 2004. The experience from East Timor is available at: www.un.org/womenwatch/osagi/meetings/2004/EGMelectoral/EP6-Pires.pdf.

36. Maria Domingas Fernandes was appointed gender adviser to the office the prime minister.

37. There has been a proliferation of private universities in Dili. At least fourteen public universities emerged in Dili in the absence of a proper regulatory framework governing higher-education management in East Timor.

38. See the CNIC website, in Portuguese, www.cnictimor.org.

39. A seminar titled "The Role of Veterans in East Timor's Democracy" was held at CNIC at the National University of East Timor (UNTL) in June 2002, as part of an ongoing series organized by the CNIC in cooperation with the NDI.

40. See the ETSG website, www.rspas.anu.edu.au/etsg.

41. See interview with Xanana Gusmão, December 18, 2002, available at www.reliefweb.int.

42. See Dionisio Babo Soares, "Nahe Biti: The Philosophy and Process of Grassroots Reconciliation," paper presented at the conference "Road to Reconciliation," Bergen, Norway, April 11–12, 2001.

43. Dirk Kotze, "Issues in Conflict Resolution," *African Journal in Conflict Resolution,* no 1, available at www.accord.org.za/web.nsf.

44. See www.easttimor-reconciliation.org.

45. See CAVR Update of June–July 2003.

46. Ibid.

47. See Dionisio Babo Soares, "Nahe Biti: The Philosophy and Process of Grassroots Reconciliation," paper presented at the conference "Road to Reconciliation," Bergen, Norway, April 11–12, 2001, for details.

48. A number of reconciliation meetings have been held involving political elites, representatives of veterans resistance, local leaders, NGOs, and family members, at the international level in Singapore, Darwin, London, Jakarta, Washington, and Canberra, and at the national level in Baucau, Batugade, Suai, and Ainaro.

49. World Bank, *Background Paper for the Donor Meetings on East Timor,* December 9–10, 2002.

50. See Albrecht Schnabel, "Challenges of Operational Conflict Prevention: From Proactive to Reactive Prevention," UNU, presentation for the session "System and Procedures for Conflict Prevention and Resolution," n.d.

9.5

INDONESIA

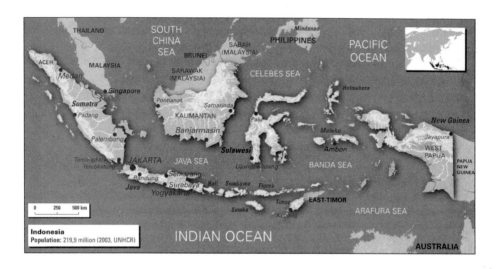

Indonesia
Population: 219,9 million (2003, UNHCR)

9.5.1

Political Transition
and Communal Violence

Harold Crouch

The collapse of President Suharto's military-backed authoritarian regime in May 1998 was greeted with high hopes that it would be followed by a new era of democratization and "good governance." These hopes have been largely disappointed. Although authoritarian restrictions on political freedoms were lifted and the first genuinely free election in forty-four years was held, democracy failed to produce strong and effective governments. Long-simmering social tensions rose to the surface and Indonesia saw the outbreak of violence between ethnic and religious communities as well as renewed fighting between government forces and armed separatist movements.

It is important, however, to place this violence in perspective. Despite the impression often presented outside the country, Indonesia is not a "failed state" in which government authority has virtually ceased to exist. The worst violence since 1998 occurred in a few provinces with relatively small populations—Aceh with about 2 percent of Indonesia's total population, Papua with 1 percent, the two Maluku provinces with 1 percent, West and Central Kalimantan with 2 percent, and Poso (Central Sulawesi) with around 0.2 percent. The inhabitants of the provinces where the state had really "failed" constituted only about 6 percent of the total population and even then parts of these regions remained relatively unaffected. Social conflict also occurred in the provinces inhabited by the other 94 percent, but occasional communal and other clashes in these regions did not result in the high levels of casualties and destruction experienced by the worst-hit provinces. The tragic consequences of social violence for those directly involved should not be ignored, but such violence is not common in most parts of Indonesia.

It should also be noted that much of the violence after 1998 had its roots in the New Order period and earlier. It is not true, as has been suggested in regard to some other countries, that the main source of political violence in Indonesia relates to the elections that are part of the democratization process.[1]

Aceh experienced rebellion in the 1950s,[2] again in the 1970s, and especially after the late 1980s. Armed resistance to Jakarta's rule in Papua commenced almost immediately after its transfer to Indonesia in the early 1960s.[3] Severe ethnic conflict broke out in West Kalimantan in 1997 before the fall of the Suharto regime.[4] While the promise of elections may have triggered some communal clashes after 1998,[5] the roots of conflict in regions such as Kalimantan, Maluku, and Poso lay in rivalries between indigenous communities and migrants who had been encouraged by previous governments to seek opportunities in other parts of Indonesia long before 1998. Many migrants were sponsored under the government's transmigration program, but others moved of their own volition. This factor was also present in the separatist conflicts in Aceh and Papua. All these regions, like others, had also experienced much discontent as a result of the massive exploitation of their resources by interests based in Jakarta whose activities often involved, and were always protected by, the military.

Political conditions since the fall of the authoritarian regime in 1998 have provided the context in which communal and other social violence has taken place. This chapter focuses on:

- The failure of democratic institutions to produce a strong and effective government
- The poor performance of the security forces in dealing with outbreaks of communal conflict
- The absence of an effective judicial system
- The radical decentralization program adopted in 1999
- The reemergence of radical Islamic groups, including one with new international connections

Failure to Establish Strong Democratic Government

After three decades of Suharto's repressive rule, pressures for change were already growing during the 1990s. But it was only after the government proved incapable of dealing with the economic collapse caused by the Asian financial crisis in 1997 that the regime finally fell in the wake of massive rioting in Jakarta in May 1998. Following the constitutional procedure, Suharto was replaced by his vice president, B. J. Habibie. Although Habibie, as Suharto's longest-serving minister, had been at the center of the New Order regime, he quickly appreciated that in the new circumstances Suharto's type of authoritarian rule was no longer viable. Habibie's democratizing reforms were not inspired by the president's sudden conversion to democratic values but by his realization that his tenure in office would be short without them. Habibie released political prisoners, removed restrictions on the free press, permitted the formation of new political parties, and held a free election in June 1999.[6] The reality of the new democratic environment was demonstrated when Habibie himself was removed from office by democratic means in October 1999. His successor, Abdurrahman Wahid, suffered the same fate and was replaced by his vice president, Megawati Sukarnoputri, in July 2001.

The new democratic spirit proved more effective in curbing the authoritarian practices of the Suharto regime than in creating a stable and effective democracy. Instead of the three legal parties of the Suharto era, forty-eight parties were permitted to contest in the 1999 election. In contrast to the old practice whereby the bureaucracy and military ensured overwhelming victories for the government party, Golkar, the 1999 election was free of government interference but failed to produce a clear winner. The nationalist Indonesian Democracy Party of Struggle (PDI-P) led the field with 34 percent of the votes.[7] But victory in the presidential election required an absolute majority in the 700-member People's Consultative Assembly (MPR), which served as an electoral college. During the months of political maneuvering between the general election in June and the presidential election in October, an alliance of Muslim parties blocked the PDI-P's candidate, Megawati, and voted instead for the pluralist-minded Abdurrahman Wahid, whose party had won only 11 percent of the votes in the general election.[8] With such a tiny support base of his own, Abdurrahman had little choice but to form a coalition government whose members were drawn from every significant party, plus the military. After nineteen months, however, Abdurrahman had so alienated his coalition partners that in July 2001 he was dismissed and replaced by Megawati.[9] Like Abdurrahman, Megawati also included representatives of all significant forces in her cabinet, which as a consequence was hardly more coherent than his.[10] Lacking both an inspiring vision and a deep understanding of policy issues, Megawati seemed unable to impose her will on the cabinet and policy was allowed to drift without clear direction.

Indonesia. Villagers look on as their votes are
counted openly in front of a panel of election monitors.

The democratic transition failed to produce strong and effective governments. Apart from their own personal failings, successive presidents were unable to assert their authority because they depended on the support of a fragmented parliament consisting of parties with little interest in cooperating with each other. The result was that the government had difficulty in formulating and implementing clear policies. Loyalty to the government was bought by distributing patronage to supporters. Parties seemed more interested in accumulating funds for the next election than in ensuring that the current government worked effectively.

All three post-Suharto governments were too concerned with self-preservation in Jakarta to devote adequate attention to communal and religious tensions in distant parts of the archipelago. Nevertheless, tentative steps were taken under Megawati toward resolving some of the conflicts. Government-sponsored "peace" agreements were reached between rival groups in Poso (December 2001) and Maluku (February 2002) and the government itself negotiated a "cessation of hostilities" agreement in Aceh (December 2002). The Poso and Maluku agreements have largely held despite sporadic violence, but the Aceh agreement collapsed in May 2003 when a new military offensive was launched after several months of fruitless negotiations.[11]

Poor Performance of the Military and Police

Military action can never deal with the root causes of communal conflict, but once such conflict breaks out, it cannot be stopped without effective military or police intervention. The military provided the backbone of the Suharto regime. It was always represented in the cabinet; several thousand officers were appointed to positions in the civil bureaucracy and parliamentary seats were allocated to military appointees. Social conflict was repressed, often brutally, by the army, which was organized on a "territorial" basis with about two-thirds of its troops dispersed throughout the nation in units that in effect "shadowed" civilian administration.[12] As a key component of the New Order regime, the military after May 1998 shared in the disgrace of the fallen president and was loudly condemned by the newly freed press and political parties for its corruption and brutality while its morale was badly damaged by its inability to save its patron.

After the fall of the Suharto regime, a program of military reform was launched that saw a significant reduction of the military's formal political role. It abandoned the "dual function" ideology that had "justified" its role in government, severed its connection with Suharto's electoral vehicle, Golkar, and adopted a neutral stance in the 1999 general election. Its active officers were withdrawn from the civilian bureaucracy and it agreed to withdraw its appointed representatives in the national and regional parliaments by 2004. No less important were the separation of the police from the military and the transfer of primary responsibility for internal security to the police. In 2002 the reform process culminated in the adoption of a new law on national defense based on the concept of civilian supremacy. The reform process, however, soon lost momentum. As a result, the military continues to exercise informal political influence, particularly through the preservation of its "territorial" structure.[13] This structure also enables the military to continue to play a major role in internal security despite the formal transfer of that responsibility to the police.

A crucial constraint on the development of professional security forces is a severe lack of funds.[14] The Indonesian government's budget provides only about 30 percent of the military's requirements. The remaining 70 percent is left to the military itself to raise. Salaries are extremely low and far from sufficient to maintain even a minimum standard of living, let alone the luxurious lifestyle enjoyed by many senior generals. In practice, individual units and personnel are entrusted with augmenting the military's funds and supplementing their own salaries. It is often believed that the main source of additional income comes from the military's commercial empire, but in reality most of its companies are inefficiently managed and unable to contribute much. Most of the military's extra funds are obtained by means that are best described as "extortion." At the highest level, big kickbacks are obtained when armaments and other equipment are purchased, large contributions are extracted from foreign corporations in resource sectors such as mining and petroleum, and regional governments are forced to pay for the "protection" provided by the military's presence. At the middle level, military officers collect contributions from enterprises in towns and townships and often provide military personnel as "security" guards. Military officers also protect illegal logging, mining, and fishing, as well as smuggling. Unofficial taxes are imposed on goods moving through ports and along highways. At the lowest level, military personnel are involved in protecting prostitution, illegal gambling, petty crime, and narcotics distribution.

The financial position of the police is no less dire and police personnel are engaged in much the same practices as the military, although mainly at the middle and lower levels. As rivals for control of the same resources and sharing responsibility for internal security, army and police units are often involved in "turf" wars that lead to occasional shoot-outs and fatalities.

Military and police forces are underpaid, undertrained, ill-disciplined, and poorly equipped. Factionalism is rife both in the headquarters in Jakarta and in the regions (although, contrary to a common perception, factions are not usually based on religious identity). It is therefore little wonder that their performance in the field leaves much to be desired. In regions facing insurgencies—such as Aceh and Papua—members of the security forces commit human rights abuses with impunity. It seems to be virtually standard practice to burn villages and take other forms of revenge whenever a member of the security forces is killed.[15] In regions affected by religious or ethnic conflict—such as Maluku and Poso—members of the security forces have often taken sides, sometimes joining in the fighting or at least supplying combatants with weapons or bullets. In some cases armaments are supplied by soldiers identified with one side or another for religious or ethnic reasons, but in other cases the motives are purely commercial.[16]

There is much speculation in Indonesia that the military, or at least some elements within it, has actively fostered communal conflict. One possible motive is a desire to destabilize and discredit civilian government (although this argument has been less persuasive under the Megawati government, which has been favorably disposed toward the military). More convincing is the claim that the military in "disturbed regions" has a continuing interest in maintaining at least low-level conflict because turbulent conditions make it easier to extract money by offering "protection" to commercial enterprises in the region. In some cases elements within the military seem to have been involved in efforts to undermine peace negotiations and agreements.

In May 2003 the military launched its largest military campaign since that against East Timor following the breakdown of negotiations with the Independence Movement Group (GAM). Over 40,000 military and police troops embarked on a campaign to eliminate the small GAM force, which military intelligence estimated to number only a few thousand. Although the body count rose sharply in the first months of the military campaign, there is little evidence of success in the battle to win the hearts and minds of the local population.[17]

Rebellion and communal violence are in part consequences of the lamentable condition of the security forces. The behavior of the security forces often creates more problems than it solves. It is inevitable that military and police personnel will continue to alienate local populations as long as they are expected to "live off the land" in order to make up for the huge shortfall in the security budget. The security forces will also continue to fail to win the hearts and minds of populations in disturbed regions as long as effective measures are not taken to ensure that those responsible for human rights violations are made accountable for their behavior. Indonesia badly needs a mobile and professional security force that can nip threats of violence in the bud, but past experience suggests that the presence of military and police "elite" units often exacerbates conflict.

Absence of an Effective Judicial System

The Indonesian courts are riddled with corruption at every stage of the judicial process, from the police to the prosecutors and the judges. As in the security forces, the salaries of legal officials are so low that they have no alternative to seeking supplementary income from other sources. Many obtain the largest part of their incomes from bribes. It is common for judges to collude with prosecutors who prepare weak cases that make it easy for judges to acquit defendants.[18]

In cases of communal violence it is especially difficult to uphold the law. Both sides in communal conflicts are always convinced that they are victims of violence initiated by the other side. When the security forces are incapable of preventing attacks, each side mobilizes in self-defense and then launches counterattacks on the other side. Perpetrators of violence are regarded as heroes fighting to save their community. In such circumstances the police often feel powerless to make arrests for fear of igniting further violence and, even when arrests are made, courts are unwilling to convict. This pattern has been seen in all the regions where mass violence has taken place in Indonesia. Despite thousands of murders in Maluku, no one was ever charged with murder. In Poso, the conviction of several Christians only sparked further violence. In Central Kalimantan, Dayak leaders were arrested but soon released. In face of the failure of the legal system to deal with communal violence, it is sometimes suggested that traditional customary law should be revived. The difficulty with this proposal is that while customary law can sometimes work within cultural communities, it is unlikely to be effective in dealing with conflict between cultural communities that each have their own distinctive customary laws.

The judicial system has also failed to deal effectively with abuses perpetrated by members of the security forces. Under current law, military personnel accused of civil crimes are tried by military tribunals, which are notorious for their light sentences. An exception was made in a law adopted in 2000 to establish special tribunals to hear cases of gross violations of human rights. It was under this law that fifteen members of the security forces and three civilians were charged with responsibility for killings in East Timor before and after the 1999 referendum.[19] All the defendants in the early trials were acquitted, but later, apparently in response to international concern, three army officers, one policeman, and two East Timorese civilians were convicted and sentenced to jail terms ranging from three to ten years. Some, however, have appealed successfully and the others remain free while awaiting the results of their appeals.[20] So far, no member of the security forces has been charged before the special tribunal for offenses committed in Aceh or Papua, and only a few—almost all junior personnel—have been charged before military tribunals, which, as usual, have imposed very light sentences such as the two- to five-year sentences for the seven murderers of Papuan independence leader Theys Eluay. The attitude of the military leadership was revealed when the seven were described as "heroes" by the army chief of staff, General Ryamizard Ryacudu.

The Impact of Regional Autonomy

President Suharto and the military imposed a highly centralized regime on a very diverse population. Despite the façade of elections, provincial governors and district heads—many of whom were Javanese—were in effect appointed by the central authorities, and the structures of regional government made few concessions to local peculiarities. Even the structure of village government was made uniform, based on the Javanese model. Haunted by the memory of the regional rebellions that had broken out during the first decade of independence in the 1950s, Suharto seemed to believe that only uniformity and direct central control—enforced by the military—could hold Indonesia together. Of course, central domination also facilitated the exploitation of the archipelago's natural resources by the Jakarta elite.

Excessive centralization, economic exploitation, and military domination all contributed to growing disaffection in the regions, however, especially in the islands outside Java. In the wake of Suharto's fall from power, the weak Habibie government was confronted by an increase in demands for regional autonomy and in three provinces—East Timor, Aceh, and Papua—it faced armed separatist movements. In the new circumstances, regional autonomy was no longer seen—as it had been by Suharto—as the first step toward national disintegration, but as the most effective means of preserving national unity. In East Timor the government's offer of "special autonomy" was rejected in a popular referendum that in effect opted for independence, but the Habibie government's radical regional autonomy laws were broadly welcomed elsewhere. The laws, which were quickly passed by the national parliament, transferred many central powers not to the 30 provinces but to the 350 districts. The laws also gave the regions access to a vastly increased share of natural resource revenue. The central government calculated that the transfer of authority to districts that were too small to form viable independent states would undermine separatist aspirations.

The implementation of regional autonomy was far from trouble-free.[21] Many of the regulations necessary for a smooth transition had not been issued when implementation began on January 1, 2001. Some central officials fought a rearguard action to retain powers while district heads sometimes assumed that more powers had been transferred than was really the case. Not only was there confusion over which powers had been transferred, but there were also disputes over jurisdiction between districts as well as between districts and provinces. Regional officials sought control of activities that promised high financial returns while they were reluctant to take on services that were expensive to provide. Control over the exploitation of natural resources—forests, mines, land—allowed local officials to make lucrative deals with contractors and often led to the violation of existing laws and regulations. Central officials complained about the spread of corruption in the districts, but given the massive corruption in which central officials were engaged during the Suharto era, their accusations rang rather hollow.

The combination of democratization and decentralization sometimes sharpened ethnic and religious rivalries in districts populated by several communities. In some districts, local governments attempted to promote "native sons" policies, especially in government employment, and even tried to block migration by other ethnic groups. In several cases the competition between ethnic groups for control of resources stimulated attempts to establish new districts or provinces that would ensure the political dominance of particular ethnic communities.[22] In a number of cases ethnic violence seemed linked to local elections when politicians mobilized their own ethnic group against others or even forced members of other ethnic communities to flee from the region.

It is important, however, to keep the impact of democratization and decentralization on ethnic violence in perspective. Democratization and decentralization were nationwide phenomena that affected many multiethnic districts but only occasionally contributed to serious ethnic and religious violence. The genuinely free democratic election in 1999 was remarkably peaceful compared to elections during the New Order period.

Decentralization took a different form in the two provinces (after the secession of East Timor) where armed separatist movements were active. In 2002 special autonomy laws recognized the distinctive character of Aceh and Papua and provided much higher allocations of natural resource income compared to the other provinces. The special autonomy law in Aceh then became the basis for negotiations between the central government and GAM, but the collapse of talks followed by the introduction of martial law in May 2003 in effect restored central government control. In Papua, hope that the passage of the special autonomy law would lessen popular opposition to Jakarta was marred when soldiers murdered the leader of the nonviolent Papuan independence movement and the Megawati government divided the province into three new provinces without even consulting the "autonomous" provincial government.[23]

Islam and Communal Violence

That communal violence has often involved Muslims is hardly surprising given that Muslims make up 87 percent of Indonesia's population. Much violence involving Muslims, however, is not especially motivated by religious concerns. In many cases, what appears to be religious conflict has its roots in ethnic conflict, as for example when migrants who happen to be followers of one religion move to a region that is predominantly of another religion. Tensions are often aggravated when the migrant community acquires a strong position in the local economy or becomes sufficiently numerous to challenge the indigenous community's grip on local politics. These characteristics were prominent in both of Indonesia's "religious wars" since 1998. In the conflict in Poso (Central Sulawesi), the dividing line between Muslims and Christians coincided with that between migrants and indigenous people.[24] In Maluku, conflict between Muslim migrants and indigenous Christians was the trigger that led to a wider conflict that then involved indigenous Muslims.[25] The common perception in the West that these conflicts were the result of Muslim campaigns to eliminate Christians is wrong. In fact Christians were no less involved in killing Muslims than Muslims were in killing Christians.

In some cases of communal violence, Muslims were the main victims, but these conflicts arose from ethnic rather than religious antagonisms. In both West and Central Kalimantan, Muslim migrants from the island of Madura were the targets of campaigns carried out by indigenous people. In West Kalimantan non-Muslim Dayaks and Muslim Malays combined to attack Madurese. In Central Kalimantan, where a substantial proportion of the Dayak population is Muslim, both Muslim and non-Muslim Dayaks were involved in the killing of Madurese.[26] In Papua, Muslim transmigrants from Java were the targets of non-Muslim indigenous violence, while in Aceh Muslim Javanese transmigrants were sometimes attacked by Muslim Acehnese.

Some of the violence, however, was religiously motivated. Attacks by Muslim radicals on churches, temples, and "places of sin" took place occasionally during the New Order period but increased after 1998. Among several new "fundamentalist" organizations were the Defenders of Islam Front (FPI) in Jakarta and the Laskar Jihad. The FPI concentrated on raiding bars, night-clubs, casinos, and brothels while the Java-based Laskar Jihad was formed to support the Muslims in Maluku and Poso against their Christian rivals. In both cases, members of the security forces facilitated the emergence of these groups. In the case of the FPI, members of the Jakarta police welcomed the attacks by the FPI because it enabled them to extract increased protection money from the proprietors of these establishments.[27] In the case of the Laskar Jihad, it seems that some military officers provided assistance to the Laskar Jihad—including arms and military training—with the aim of destabilizing the government of President Abdurrahman after he had taken steps to establish civilian control over the military.[28] In neither case, however, were military and police officers especially sympathetic with the long-term aims of these organizations.

Muslim violence, however, moved to a new level with the emergence of an underground group called Jemaah Islamiyah (JI), which had some contact with Osama bin Laden's Al-Qaida.[29] Unlike the FPI and Laskar Jihad, whose goals were focused on Indonesia itself, the JI's network extended to Malaysia, Singapore, and the Southern Philippines. It was only after a failed plot to blow up the United States and several other embassies in Singapore in December 2001 that the JI's presence became widely known. It was later revealed that the JI had been responsible for a series of church bombings in Indonesia and explosions in Manila in December 2000 as well as the attempted murder of the Philippine ambassador in Jakarta. In October 2002 a JI team was responsible for bomb explosions that killed more than 200 people—most of them Western tourists—on the island of Bali. Following the Bali bombing, the main culprits were soon arrested and the JI network was further exposed. In Jakarta, the "spiritual leader" of the JI, Abu Bakar Ba'asyir, was also arrested—although the charges did not include the Bali bombing. Eventually, in September 2003, he was convicted of treason. This conviction was later quashed on appeal but he served eighteen months in jail for related immigration offenses.

The overwhelming majority of Indonesia's Muslims cannot be labeled as radical or fundamentalist. Nor is there much evidence to support the common perception that political Islam is on the rise. One indication of the size of the fundamentalist community is support obtained in the 1999 election by parties advocating the introduction of *sharia* law. The combined vote for radical Muslim parties amounted to only about 15 percent. These parties continue to participate in the constitutional process in much the same way as the secular parties and are concerned not just with religious issues but also with the material needs of their constituents. Indonesia's current vice president and several cabinet ministers represent "fundamentalist" parties, but their influence on policy has not been decisive.

It is important to recognize that Islamic groups involved in violence and terrorism constitute a tiny minority. Participants in FPI raids and rallies rarely exceeded 1,000, while the Laskar Jihad never mobilized more than 3,000–4,000 fighters in Maluku at any one time. Those actively involved in JI probably number no more than a few thousand. It is significant that the arrests of the leaders of the JI, the FPI, and Laskar Jihad did not lead to widespread public protests. Virtually no public sympathy was expressed—even by members of radical Islamic organizations—for the Bali bombers. This is not to say that Muslim violence, and particularly the JI's link with Al-Qaida, is not a serious threat to stability in Indonesia. But it should be seen in the context of the generally peaceful relations between Muslims and non-Muslims in most parts of the country.

Conclusion

With the overthrow of authoritarian rule in Indonesia, ethnic and religious tensions that had been simmering beneath the surface throughout the New Order period were exposed. The democratization process provided new political freedom but did not produce strong and coherent governments with sufficient authority to tackle the root causes of communal conflict. Moreover, the security forces not only proved to be poor instruments for dealing with communal violence but often themselves contributed to conflict, while a corrupt and incompetent judicial system provided only a weak deterrent to violence. The central government's decentralization program established an infrastructure that could potentially deal more sensitively with local tensions but in the short run sometimes aggravated communal relations. Concurrent with these developments, a new form of Muslim terrorism emerged that threatened to do much harm even though it had no capacity to change the basic structures of the state.

Indonesia has yet to find a formula for resolving the many communal tensions that are inevitable in an extraordinarily diverse society undergoing drastic political change. Nevertheless, outbreaks of severe communal violence have been limited to only a few regions. Whatever other challenges they face, most Indonesians have not directly experienced severe communal violence.

Resources

Reports

International Crisis Group. "Communal Violence in Indonesia: Lessons from Kalimantan." Asia Report no. 19. June 27, 2001.
————. "Indonesia: Ending Repression in Irian Jaya." Asia Report no. 23. September 20, 2001.
————. "Indonesia: The Search for Peace in Maluku." Asia Report no. 31. February 8, 2002.
————. "Aceh: Why the Military Option Still Won't Work." Indonesia Briefing Paper. May 9, 2003. Available at www.crisisweb.org.

Other Publications

"Communal Violence in Poso, Central Sulawesi: Where People Eat Fish and Fish Eat People." By Lorraine V. Aragon. *Indonesia* 72, October 2001.
Local Power and Politics in Indonesia: Decentralisation and Democratization. Eds. Edward Aspinall and Greg Fealy. Indonesia Update Series. Singapore: Institute of Southeast Asian Studies, 2003.
Reformasi: The Struggle for Power in Post-Soeharto Indonesia. By Kevin O'Rourke. Sydney: Allen and Unwin, 2002.

Resource Contacts

Edward Aspinall, School of European, Asian, and Middle Eastern Languages and Studies, University of Sydney, Australia, e-mail: edward.aspinall@asia.usyd.edu.au

Jacques Bertrand, Department of Political Science, Toronto University, Canada, e-mail: bertrand@chass.utoronto.ca

Richard Chauvel, Australia Asia Pacific Institute, Victoria University, Melbourne, Australia, e-mail: richard.chauvel@vu.edu.au

Greg Fealy, Research School of Pacific and Asian Studies, Australian National University, Canberra, Australia, e-mail: greg.fealy@anu.edu.au

Sidney Jones, director, Indonesia Project, International Crisis Group, Jakarta, e-mail: sjones@crisisweb.org

William Liddle, Department of Political Science, Ohio State University, Columbus, e-mail: liddle@polisci.sbs.ohio-state.edu

Kirsten Schulze, Department of International History, London School of Economics, e-mail: k.e.schulze@lse.ac.uk

Rizal Sukma, Center for Strategic and International Studies, Jakarta, Indonesia, e-mail: rsukma@csis.or.id

Harold Crouch is a professor in the Research School of Pacific and Asian Studies at Australian National University. He was director of the Indonesia Project of the International Crisis Group from 2000 until 2002 and taught political science at the University of Indonesia from 1968 until 1971. He is the author of The Army and Politics in Indonesia *(Ithaca, N.Y.: Cornell University Press, 1978).*

Notes

1. Jack Snyder, *From Voting to Violence: Democratization and Nationalist Conflict* (New York: W. W. Norton, 2000).

2. On the rebellion in Aceh in the 1950s, see Nazaruddin Sjamsuddin, *The Republican Revolt: A Study of the Acehnese Rebellion* (Singapore: Institute of Southeast Asian Studies, 1985).

3. Robin Osborne, *Indonesia's Secret War: The Guerrilla Struggle in Irian Jaya* (Sydney: Allen and Unwin, 1985).

4. Human Rights Watch Asia, "Indonesia: Communal Violence in West Kalimantan," vol. 9, no. 10 (c).

5. In the case of Maluku, see Gerry van Klinken, "The Maluku Wars: Bringing Society Back In," *Indonesia* 71 (April 2001), pp. 1–26.

6. David Bourchier, "Habibie's Interregnum: *Reformasi,* Elections, Regionalism, and the Struggle for Power," in Chris Manning and Peter van Diermen, eds., *Indonesia in Transition: Social Aspects of Reformasi and Crisis* (Singapore: Institute of Southeast Asian Studies, 2000), pp. 15–38.

7. Harold Crouch, "Indonesia: Democracy and the Threat of Disintegration," in *Southeast Asian Affairs 2000* (Singapore: Institute of Southeast Asian Studies, 2000).

8. Marcus Mietzner, "The 1999 General Session: Wahid, Megawati, and the Fight for the Presidency," in Manning and van Dierman, *Indonesia in Transition,* Chap. 3.

9. Developments leading to the end of the Abdurrahman Wahid presidency are analyzed in International Crisis Group, "Indonesia's Presidential Crisis," Indonesia Briefing, Jakarta/Brussels, February 21, 2001; and International Crisis Group, "Indonesia's Presidential Crisis: The Second Round," Indonesia Briefing, May 21, 2001.

10. International Crisis Group, "The Megawati Presidency," Indonesia Briefing, September 10, 2001.

11. Edward Aspinall and Harold Crouch, "The Aceh Peace Process: Why It Failed," Policy Paper no. 1 (Washington, D.C.: East West Center, November 2003).

12. Robert Lowry, *The Armed Forces of Indonesia* (St. Leonards: Allen and Unwin, 1996), pp. 91–94.

13. International Crisis Group, "Indonesia: Keeping the Military Under Control," ICG Asia Report no. 9, September 5, 2000.

14. Ibid., pp. 16–17.

15. International Crisis Group, "Aceh: Why Military Force Won't Bring Lasting Peace," ICG Asia Report no. 17, June 12, 2001.

16. International Crisis Group, "Indonesia: The Search for Peace in Maluku," ICG Asia Report no. 31, February 8, 2002.

17. International Crisis Group, "Aceh: How Not to Win Hearts and Minds," Indonesia Briefing, July 23, 2003.

18. Adi Andojo Soetjipto, "Legal Reform and Challenges in Indonesia," in Manning and van Dierman, *Indonesia in Transition,* Chapter 8.

19. International Crisis Group, "Indonesia: Impunity Versus Accountability for Gross Human Rights Violations," ICG Asia Report no. 12, February 2, 2001.

20. International Crisis Group, "Indonesia: The Implications of the Timor Trials," Indonesia Briefing, May 8, 2002.

21. Mark Turner and Owen Podger, *Decentralisation in Indonesia: Redesigning the State* (Canberra: Asia Pacific Press, 2003).

22. For an example, see International Crisis Group, "Indonesia: Overcoming Murder and Chaos in Maluku," ICG Asia Report no. 10, December 19, 2000, p. 6.

23. International Crisis Group, "Dividing Papua: How Not to Do It," Asia Briefing, April 9, 2003.

24. David Rohde, "Indonesia Unravelling," *Foreign Affairs* (July–August 2001), pp. 110–124; Lorraine V. Aragon, "Communal Violence in Poso, Central Sulawesi: Where People Eat Fish and Fish Eat People," *Indonesia* 72 (October 2001), pp. 45–78.

25. Jacques Bertrand, "Legacies of the Authoritarian Past: Religious Violence in Indonesia's Moluccan Islands," *Pacific Affairs* 75, no. 1 (Spring 2002), pp. 57–85.

26. International Crisis Group, "Communal Violence in Indonesia: Lessons from Kalimantan," ICG Asia Report no. 19, June 27, 2001.

27. Based on interviews in Jakarta. See also Kevin O'Rourke, *Reformasi: The Struggle for Power in Post-Soeharto Indonesia* (Crows Nest, NSW: Allen & Unwin, 2002), p. 346, wherein the FPI is seen as linked more to elements in the army than the police.

28. Evidence indicating that Laskar Jihad was supported by some elements in the military is provided in International Crisis Group, "Indonesia: The Search for Peace in Maluku," ICG Asia Report no. 31, February 8, 2002, pp. 5–7. Further circumstantial evidence can be found in O'Rourke, *Reformasi,* pp. 348–349. See also Kirsten E. Schulze, "Laskar Jihad and the Conflict in Ambon," *Brown Journal of World Affairs* 9, no. 1 (Spring 2002), pp. 57–69.

29. The origins and development of Jemaah Islamiyah are discussed in a series of International Crisis Group publications: "Al-Qaeda in Southeast Asia: The Case of the 'Ngruki Network' in Indonesia," Indonesia Briefing, August 8, 2002; "Indonesia Backgrounder: How the Jemaah Islamiyah Terrorist Network Operates," ICG Asia Report no. 43, December 11, 2002; "Jemaah Islamiyah in Southeast Asia: Damaged But Still Dangerous," ICG Asia Report no. 63, August 26, 2003; "Indonesia Backgrounder: Jiham in Central Sulawesi," ICG Asia Report no. 74, February 3, 2004.

9.5.2

Aceh: Civil Society—
The Missing Piece of Peacebuilding

Aguswandi

With the collapse of the peace process and subsequent declaration of martial law in Aceh on May 19, 2003, the Indonesian government again opted for a military approach to managing the decades-long conflict in Aceh. With the imposition of martial law, Aceh is once again under the control of the military, which has almost unlimited authority to shape and implement policy. It is unlikely, however, that the current operation will succeed in solving the crisis, as the conflict is political and as such requires a political solution. Such a solution can be found through involving Acehnese civil society in peacebuilding efforts. A genuine dialogue should be held involving the current conflicting parties—the Independence Movement Group (GAM) and the Indonesian government—along with the significant involvement of civil society.

There is no direct correspondence between the conflict in Aceh and the rise of Acehnese nationalism. For many years the Acehnese have devoted their energy to ending the abuses practiced by different regimes of the Indonesian government and its armed forces. The rise of contemporary nationalism in Aceh is a reaction to the continued experience of oppression.

In 1953, nine years after Indonesia proclaimed its independence, and four years after the Dutch handed full sovereignty of the Dutch East Indies to Sukarno's government, Daud Beureueh led a rebellion in Aceh against the central administration in Jakarta. Interestingly, Beureueh was one of the local leaders who had supported the full integration of Aceh into the new nation-state of Indonesia.[1] During the Indonesian revolution, in the period between 1945 and 1949, Beureueh was involved together with the local population in the struggle against the Dutch, who were trying to reoccupy the country.[2] The Acehnese contributed significantly to the whole struggle, earning Aceh the name *Daerah Modal* (model area), while Beureueh and local leaders became famous as heroes of the republic.

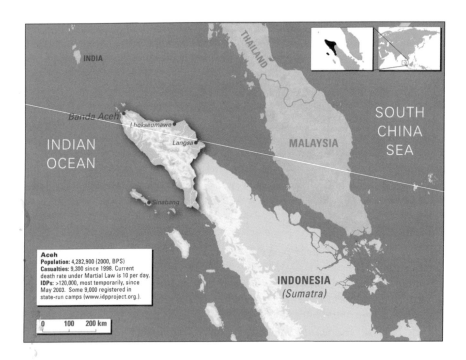

INDIA

THAILAND

Banda Aceh
Lhokseumawe
Langsa
INDIAN
OCEAN

MALAYSIA

SOUTH
CHINA
SEA

Sinabang

Aceh
Population: 4,282,900 (2000, BPS)
Casualties: 9,300 since 1998. Current
death rate under Martial Law is 10 per day.
IDPs: >120,000, most temporarily, since
May 2003. Some 9,000 registered in
state-run camps (www.idpproject.org.).

INDONESIA
(Sumatra)

0   100   200 km

The Beureueh revolt, however, resulted in the Acehnese's first major disappointment with Jakarta's centralist policies in the postcolonial nation-building project. In Aceh, this centralization led to the province of Aceh being incorporated into the territory of North Sumatra.[3] The Beureueh movement, as a revolt against this centralist tendency, did not call for the separation of Aceh from Indonesia. Rather, it questioned the injustice of the policies of a central government, which had not only broken the promise of autonomy, but also abolished the province of Aceh. The Beureueh movement had no specific political demands. It was a movement born out of reaction to the central government's decision to abolish the province of Aceh. Thus, Beureueh effectively criticized the manner in which the Indonesian nation-state was being built in the postcolonial era. Despite this fact, the central government responded by sending thousands of troops and killing many of those involved in the movement. According to one account of the counterinsurgency operation against the rebellion, in March 1954, Indonesian troops executed 148 people from two fishing villages in Jeumpa-Bireuen, North Aceh, in a single incident.[4]

The Beureueh movement was eventually pacified in 1959 through a nonmilitary approach when the central government reestablished Aceh as a province with extensive autonomy in matters of religion, education, and culture. Aceh was named a *Daerah Istimewa* (special region),[5] because of the autonomy it had been granted. However, the large-scale deployment of troops and the brutal operations beforehand generated much bitterness among the local population. This was the seedbed of the antagonism toward the central government in

Jakarta, and was found mostly in rural areas where villagers had been brutalized during the campaign against the Beureueh revolt.

The bitterness grew as the *Daerah Istimewa* status became virtually meaningless and the promises of autonomy went largely unrealized. This was further exacerbated by the rise of the New Order regime, lead by General Suharto, whose nation-building project was based on centralist policies backed by state terror and the massive exploitation of natural resources. Under the New Order, Aceh provided huge quantities of oil; by the 1980s, about 30 percent of exported oil and gas came from Aceh.[6] The boom in income from Aceh's natural resources did not benefit the local people and the problems of unemployment, poverty, and illiteracy remained unaddressed. The extremist tendency of the New Order's nationalization programs destroyed the fabric of Acehnese society and replaced it with an imposed system of government adopted from the Javanese tradition. This in part explains the birth of GAM and Hassan Di Tiro's declaration of Acehnese independence on December 14, 1976. As Robinson observes, it was not by chance that Hasan Di Tiro's declaration coincided with the New Order's policies in Aceh.[7] The reactive character of this declaration can also be seen in the fact that, in 1958, Hasan Di Tiro published a book titled *Democracy for Indonesia,* in which he argued for an ethnofederal system in Indonesia.[8] Thus, GAM, like the Beureueh movement, arose in reaction to the way the Indonesian nation-state was being built, this time as a reaction to the New Order.

In their appeal for support from the Acehnese, Hassan Di Tiro and GAM referred to history to underpin their declaration, arguing that Aceh was an independent state and entity and had never been colonized. However, initially, support for Di Tiro's movement was limited to a few hundred villagers from Pidie, North Aceh, and East Aceh. These villagers and their relatives in the subdistricts as well as some Beureueh followers who were dissatisfied with the previous settlement and had remained in the mountains made up the entire movement.

Nevertheless, as the New Order government and its armed forces began to exploit Aceh's natural resources and to terrorize its people, support for the Di Tiro movement grew stronger. Acehnese discontent with the New Order regime renurtured the antagonistic sentiment against the central government among locals. According to Benedict Anderson, New Order practice caused more and more Acehnese to lose hope and confidence that they had a share in the common Indonesian project.[9] New Order policies served to alienate the Acehnese from this common project.

Conflict Dynamics

Considering the small number of Di Tiro supporters, the New Order decided to declare Aceh a military operation zone (DOM). This decision proved to be the biggest mistake in the central government's handling of the conflict in Aceh. Not only did it fail to deal with GAM, but it also resulted in the escalation of conflict, and even produced a new generation of GAM fighters and supporters.

The failure to address the root causes of the conflict and the mounting brutality toward many ordinary Acehnese by the armed forces resulted in a backlash against the government and its methods of resolving the conflict.

The imposition of the DOM resulted in thousands of locals being killed during the counterinsurgency operation. It is estimated that 7,078 people were victimized during the campaign (see Table 9.5.2.1). Many civilians were killed and went missing and thousands of people were tortured in military camps and prisons. Most of these atrocities were conducted by the armed forces, especially the Kopassus, a special unit of the army that is trained and supported by a number of Western governments. The Kopassus unit committed many atrocities and other kinds of violence, even within the Exxon Mobile compound in North Aceh, which was used by Kopassus as a camp to detain suspected rebels.

Under the DOM, many Acehnese, particularly in Pidie, East Aceh, and North Aceh, lived under constant military surveillance. The situation in Aceh was one of the factors leading to the military's economic and political advance. The imposition of the DOM gave the military a free hand in controlling all entrepreneurial activities in Aceh. Politically, the province became a site for generals to boost their careers, as success in Aceh would open doors to the Cendana inner circle.[10] The economic and political policy of the New Order and its army resulted in the permanent military occupation of Aceh.

The brutality of the DOM only became public after the fall of Suharto. Stories of killing and torture began to attract attention as nongovernmental organizations (NGOs) started investigations and victims of human rights violations started speaking out and demanding justice. The collapse of the New Order regime in 1998 raised Acehnese hopes for a just and democratic society. The dominant discourse in the early post-Suharto period concerned justice and a change in the structural relationship between the political center in Jakarta and the periphery of Aceh.

Unfortunately, this demand for significant change was not acknowledged and President B. J. Habibie failed to fulfill many of his promises, including the promise to deliver justice and change the structural relationship between Aceh and Jakarta. The political problem in Indonesia partly explains the lack of

Table 9.5.2.1 Human Rights Abuses by Conflict Parties in Aceh During the DOM Era (1989–1998)

Type of Violation	Number of Victims
Disappearance	1,958
Killing	1,321
Torture	3,430
Sexual violence	209
Robbery	160
Total	7,078

Source: Institute for Policy Research and Advocacy (Elsham), 1999.

response from the central government, for despite the fact that the political regime had changed, the underlying structural problems of the New Order regime, such as impunity and centralism, continued. The problem for the new regime was that it had to choose between delivering justice for the Acehnese and compromising politically with the military. From Habibie to the present Megawati government, Jakarta has chosen the latter course, which has resulted in continuing problems of impunity. As such, the conflict in Aceh in the post—New Order period is also indirectly a portrait of modern Indonesia and its failed attempt to make the transition to a democratic society.

Total impunity and the post–New Order regime's lack of genuine political will to solve the conflict have led to growing hostility between the Acehnese and Jakarta. GAM's increasing popularity, around 1999, coincided with the launch of new military operations, during which several massacres occurred.[11] For the first time, GAM started to enjoy wide popular support, as many victims of violence began to join the movement. The separatist idea became the hegemonic discourse in Aceh.

In its contemporary form, the armed opposition group GAM can be roughly divided into four groups. The first is the political group, which believes that the transfer of Aceh's sovereignty from the Dutch to Sukarno's government was illegitimate. Geoffrey Robinson has described this group as a collection of intellectuals, local bureaucrats, deserters from the police and military, and local businessmen.[12] These leaders are respected by the local people for their commitment, devotion, and simple ways of life. The commander

North Sumatra, 1999.
Women fighters training at a GAM camp near Lhksemawe, Aceh.

of GAM, Abdullah Syaffie, who was killed in 2002, is the best example of this first group. When he was killed, nobody rejoiced at his death, not even government officials in Aceh.[13] The second group comprises human rights abuse victims. The government's failure to respond to demands for justice has led many to join GAM, not for political reasons but to seek revenge for the impunity of the military. This element comprises the majority of the present members of GAM, most of whom have relatives who were victims during the DOM or under the several military operations in the post–New Order period.[14] A third group within the movement is made up of those who are more interested in exploiting the conflict for economic benefits. Some of these people maintain illicit economic relations with the Indonesian military and police. The fourth group comprises people who have been forced to choose between conflicting parties. Government generalizations have meant that all who are critical of injustices committed by the government and military are being classified as GAM members, and thus face the risk of being arrested or even killed. As a result, many have chosen to join GAM. However, these four elements do not completely describe GAM, as changes occur according to the dynamic of the conflict in Aceh, and are in particular affected by how the Indonesian state responds to the conflict.

Official Conflict Management

The situation in Aceh started to improve when Abdurrahman Wahid (popularly known as Gus Dur) became the fourth president of Indonesia. During his administration, the conflict in Aceh was transformed from a militaristic to a political problem. The most positive step was that Wahid decided to enter into dialogue with the Acehnese.

Even before Wahid became president, he had mentioned on several occasions the possibility of holding a referendum, similar to the one authorized by Habibie in East Timor, as a mechanism for conflict resolution for Aceh.[15] However, the idea was not realized when he became president, and the initiative for the referendum and other kinds of peaceful means of conflict resolution were undermined by many politicians and especially the army. The disunity of Wahid's government was the main obstacle to progress in resolving the Aceh conflict.

However, the move to send Bondan Gunawan, the acting secretary of state in Wahid's cabinet, to meet GAM commander Abdullah Syafii, widened the possibility for dialogue between GAM and the Indonesian government. The initiative for dialogue, supported by pressure from many groups in Aceh and in Jakarta, gained further momentum when the Henry Dunant Center (HDC) offered to act as facilitator for the talks, with the goal of reducing the violence and opening the way for humanitarian assistance in Aceh.[16] Wahid's government decided to accept the HDC offer. After several talks facilitated by the HDC, on May 12, 2000, GAM and the Indonesian government signed an agreement for a "humanitarian pause."

The agreement received widespread support from many Acehnese. The day the agreement was signed, thousands of people in Banda Aceh and in many subdistricts gathered to hold prayers for the success of the pact.[17] The international community also expressed its support, with praise for the agreement coming from the United Nations, the European Union, the United States, and many foreign governments. Many nongovernmental groups launched programs to help villages affected by the conflict.

As a follow-up to the humanitarian pause agreement, several meetings were held in Banda Aceh between representatives of GAM and the Indonesian government to establish mechanisms for its implementation. Besides the establishment of a joint forum as the highest body to resolve any possible deadlock, two other bodies were established: a joint committee on security modalities, to prevent the launch of further military operations, and a joint committee on humanitarian action, to help distribute aid. In addition, a security modalities monitoring team was set up.

However, the agreement did not succeed in demilitarizing conditions on the ground. Representatives of GAM and the Indonesian government were unable to agree on several fundamentals, such as defining the pause or ceasefire, the role of the security forces, and the display of the Indonesian and Acehnese flags. The failure to demilitarize resulted in continuing clashes between Indonesian security forces and GAM fighters. While in the early period of the pause the violence declined significantly, this did not last long. The Indonesian government and GAM continued to disagree on many substantial issues, and soon the violence returned to previous levels.

The situation further deteriorated with the relaunch of military operations in April 2001. The decision to launch the operation was affected by the weakening of Gus Dur's position, giving the military the chance to regain its control in Aceh. Worsening conditions in Aceh and the government's inability to agree with GAM on the demilitarization process opened the opportunity for the renewal of military operations. At the end of his term in office, before being replaced by Megawati Sukarnoputri, Wahid issued Presidential Decree no. 4, in which he authorized a military operation in Aceh and abandoned all previous agreements with GAM.

With Gus Dur's replacement by the popular nationalistic politician, Megawati, the prospects for peace became even gloomier. The constant international pressure, however, forced the Indonesian government to renew talks with GAM, but it was only a matter of time before the talks collapsed, as the military regained control in Indonesian politics. GAM's inflexibility in its demands also contributed to the collapse of the process. However, the current military operation is mainly due to the military's ascendancy in Indonesian politics, especially the "rock" (hard-liner) element within the Indonesian military, which has been pushing for military operations over time as the only conflict resolution tool that can overcome the crisis in Aceh.

Multi-Track Diplomacy

Civil society in Aceh is a potential element in the search for a just and positive peace in the struggle to resolve the conflict in Aceh. Civil groups are interested in transforming the conflict to move beyond the simple discourse of national self-determination, and instead focus more on a broader struggle for people's self-determination for both Acehnese and Indonesian society. Together with many groups outside Aceh, they seek a democratic and peaceful solution to the conflict. In working to create a democratic society in Aceh, they encourage the conflicting parties to pursue their political goals through democratic and nonviolent means.

The story of Acehnese civil society is the story of hope, creativity, and progressive politics. Besides the destruction of life and property, the conflict has also given rise to a new generation of Acehnese who have the vision and determination to create a better society. It is a generation of people who are critical both of state policies in Aceh and of their own society.

Made up of intellectuals, NGOs, students, women's networks, media, and many other sectoral groups, Aceh's emerging civil society has played a significant role in transforming conflict and creating opportunities for building peace (see Table 9.5.2.2). Under the New Order, Acehnese in both rural and urban areas were widely suppressed, but soon after the collapse of the New Order regime, people at all levels of society took initiatives to reclaim space for dialogue and popular engagement with regard to the crisis in Aceh. Their role was so dominant that when a local NGO, Walhi Aceh, carried out a poll on who should represent Acehnese, most of those named were leaders of civil society groups.[18] Acehnese civil society groups have been active locally, nationally, and internationally, and have been working to build further networks across these different levels.

Table 9.5.2.2 Civil Society Initiatives at Local, National, and International Levels

	Social Actors	Demands and Initiatives
Local	Student and youth movement Women's groups NGOs Victims' groups Intellectuals, academics Progressive religious leaders Artists Sectoral organizations such as farmers/fishermen, traders, drivers	Demilitarization: demonstrations, lobbying Peace process: end to military impunity and accountability for human rights abuses, political education to create a critical mass People's empowerment: community support networks, rights education, skills training, capacity-building workshops, debates, forums Justice for victims: human rights documentation, investigation, interviews with victims, legal support
National	Students NGOs Women's groups Intellectuals Solidarity groups Acehnese community in Indonesia	Military and political reform: lobbying, demonstrations, accountability, justice for victims, democratization
International	Solidarity groups Acehnese community abroad International NGOs	Justice and peace Building capacity of civil society International pressure

Because of the severe violence under the DOM, many organizations were formed to investigate and document cases of human rights abuse. Groups like CORDOVA, Koalisi NGO-HAM, and Kontras Aceh worked with national-level human rights groups such as Kontras and Lembaga Bantuan Hukum in compiling chronologies, building databases, and preparing reports on the human rights situation in Aceh. In June 1998 such investigations were followed by persistent advocacy at local, national, and international levels, eventually forcing the Indonesian government to end the DOM.

The Student Movement

Following the end of the DOM, student groups quickly emerged as the most active element within Acehnese civil society. Groups such as Student Solidarity for the People, the Muslim Student Front for Reform in Aceh, and the Aceh Student Coalition for Reform formed during the *reformasi* period, were actively engaged in antimilitary campaigns, advocacy for victims and internally displaced persons, and conducted many protests, hunger strikes, and general strikes. In March 1999 the student movement also campaigned for a boycott of the elections, which resulted in a voter turnout of less than 50 percent, as an act of protest against the central government's decision to maintain the military operation in Aceh.

In terms of political settlement, students were determined to seek a democratic and nonviolent solution and began to campaign around the idea of a referendum as the best solution to the conflict. The idea of a referendum was first voiced at the All-Aceh Student and Youth Congress, held in February 1999 in Banda Aceh. With the participation of more than 200 groups, including many student and youth groups, several mass organizations, and groups of victims of violence, it was decided that an organization should be set up to support the idea of a referendum, leading to the birth of the Aceh Referendum Information Center (SIRA). The congress was organized through the building of a vast network of student and youth movements throughout the province, and soon students became the most prominent civil group in Aceh.

On November 9, 1999, a coalition of many student activists and youth groups in Aceh held the biggest rally in the history of Aceh, with over 1 million people rallying in the capital, Banda Aceh, to demand a referendum in Aceh.[19] It became a landmark for the civil society movement, because not only was the rally a great success, with almost 40 percent of the population turning up, but it was also a very peaceful demonstration. It also put pressure on GAM to support the idea of a referendum for Aceh after seeing the massive support of the population for a referendum as a way of finding the political settlement. By the end of 1999, the word "referendum" appeared throughout Aceh, painted on the walls of public buildings and along streets in towns and villages alike and replacing the purely independence-focused discourse of GAM.

Besides consolidating student groups behind the idea of a referendum, the student congress also established a model for students in strengthening other sectors of civil society. For example, student activists working to build support for victims facilitated a victim congress in 2000, out of which an organization was established called Solidarity for Victims of Human Rights Violations in Aceh. Similar congresses were held by women, ulama, and other groups. The underlying cause of this move was the belief that a truly social movement had to be a people's movement, not just a student movement, with the participation of the majority of the masses.

Mobilizing Rural-Urban Networks

During this time, many students also began to establish posts in the country-side to offer humanitarian assistance, and build support networks between the rural areas and urban centers. One such group was the People's Crisis Center (PCC), established in 1999. It worked to assist and train internally displaced people to rebuild their economic livelihoods, health facilities, and education systems, all of which had been eroded by the armed conflict. With the support of PCC workers, internally displaced villagers learned to be responsible for the management of their camps, handling such tasks as maintaining sanitation, distributing food, providing treatment for the sick, and organizing makeshift classrooms for children whose education had been interrupted by the fighting. The PCC also encouraged processes of collective decisionmaking, which brought about critical changes in social agency within the groups. Women and chil-dren, for example, who had not previously participated in meetings at night, were now actively involved in all discussions where decisions were made. Displaced people were also involved in developing economic cooperatives, cultural-religious activities, and media work, thus enabling them to become active members of the civil movement.

Women's groups also played a prominent organizational role in the rural areas. One organization, Flower Aceh, was founded as early as 1989, and played a major role in supporting victims of rape and gender-based violence under the DOM. Flower Aceh and other women's organizations, including students, estab-lished networks that offered support and training for women in such diverse activities as trauma counseling, rebuilding economic livelihoods, family plan-ning, and community awareness campaigns on gender equality and justice.

The most decisive outcome of popular mobilization was the emergence of a new leadership at many levels of Acehnese society, in both urban and rural areas. Students played the most prominent role in strengthening the various sectors of civil society, and in building networks of urban-rural support. Stu-dents also initiated closer collaboration with Indonesian civil society groups in advocating a peaceful, nonmilitary solution to the conflict, through advocacy, counseling, media campaigns, and cultural exhibitions. Work on the ground was also supported by the presence of foreign groups, such as Oxfam, Save the Children, Peace Brigades International, and the Jesuit Refugee Service.

Organizing at the International Level

Acehnese civil society has also been active at the international level. Many local human rights groups have worked to build networks with other inter-national organizations such as Amnesty International and Human Rights

Watch in their campaign to end the violence in Aceh. The most prominent group advocating human rights in Aceh at the international level is the International Forum for Aceh (IFA), established in 1998 in the United States by Jafar Siddiq Hamzah. In July 1999, the IFA and Forum Asia cosponsored a conference in Bangkok that resulted in one of the first meetings between GAM and the Indonesian government, opening the path for further negotiations between the two sides and the humanitarian pause agreement the following year. In September 2001, exactly a year after Jafar's death, the IFA worked with American University to hold the Acehnese Brotherly Dialogue, during which the Acehnese Civil Society Task Force (ACSTF) was established to coordinate civil society involvement in advancing the peace process, and up until the collapse of the Cessation of Hostilities Agreement (COHA) worked to build dialogue between diverse groups on the ground.

Civil Society and the Peace Process

Even before the humanitarian pause, several groups in Aceh had been demanding an end to violence by both sides. One example was the establishment in January 2000 of Team 21, an umbrella group involving NGOs, student groups, and religious organizations that met with both GAM and Indonesian officials to demand a cease-fire and the establishment of peace zones in Aceh. Several NGOs were even involved in facilitating the meeting between the acting secretary of state of Gus Dur's government, Bondan Gunawan, and the GAM leader in Aceh, Abdullah Syafii, for possibility of a dialogue. It was the first open contact between an Indonesian government official and a GAM leader.

When the HDC went to Aceh, the initiative for a peace process gained momentum and began to dominate the political climate. After several months of closed-door talks, GAM and the Indonesian government agreed to a humanitarian pause in June 2000. However, as negotiations progressed, civil society became increasingly marginalized from the process. The process only recognized the official existence of the armed groups, and the civil society movement soon found itself without a clear formal role, and little safeguard for its activities on the ground. This led to local groups being caught in an ambiguous position between the two armed parties, unable to participate in the peace process as an independent element. Civil society members who were appointed to sit on the joint committees were positioned as representatives either of GAM or of the Indonesian government, leading to the polarization of nonpartisan groups.

These developments coincided with a worsening security situation, during which student activists, humanitarian workers, intellectuals, journalists, and other civil actors became the new targets of the military. Among the increasing incidents of disappearances, arbitrary arrests, torture, killing, and intimidation against civil society were the assassinations of Safwan Idris and Dayan Dawood, the rectors of Aceh's two universities; the kidnapping and murder of IFA chairman Jafar Siddiq Hamzah; and the kidnapping, torture, and execution of humanitarian workers from the organization Rehabilitation of Torture Victims in Aceh. The relaunch of military operations also meant a resumption of violence in the rural areas and increased displacement of the population.

Nevertheless, civil society groups continued to foster the dialogue process while remaining critical of it, with many groups trying to create spaces for peacebuilding activities in villages and towns to socialize the cease-fire ideas, peace education and training, and the building of networks for monitoring. Such efforts, however, were increasingly undermined by the security forces. On May 3, 2002, for instance, a one-day seminar organized by the Acehnese Civil Society Task Force was banned at the eleventh hour by the police. The seminar, titled "Building a New Commitment in Aceh," had intended to seek ways of bringing Acehnese civil society more directly into the peace process.[20] The meeting was to have been addressed by the vice governor of Aceh as well as a representative of GAM, and attended by Acehnese, Indonesian, and international NGO representatives. The ACSTF remained active in building trust and cooperation among diverse groups of Acehnese society throughout the negotiations, including ulama, academics, businessmen, and even members of GAM and the Indonesian security forces, until the breakdown of COHA, and the declaration of martial law on May 19, 2003.

The exclusion of civil society groups from the process of peacebuilding was a denial of the importance of engaging the civilian population as equal partners at all levels of the process. As a result, the far-reaching social change that civil society activism had achieved on the ground was not translated into official engagement in political negotiations. Many Acehnese saw the negotiations not just as a dialogue between two armed groups, but as an opportunity to transform the very social relationships and inequalities that had created the conditions for the conflict. For many ordinary Acehnese, the negotiations were the first step toward changing the unjust system into a society based on democratic participation, as well as political, economic, and social justice.

The potential of civil society remains hindered by other factors. One of these is the weak capacity of civil society groups, which is not only the result of internal capacity, but also due to the long period of suppression during which constant militarization has weakened many critical elements within Acehnese society. Government policies also had the effect of weakening local civil society, disempowering local communities, and creating almost total dependency.

Now under martial law, the constant military presence has resulted in the collapse of the civil space. The civil movement has joined GAM as the prime target of the present war in Aceh. Not only have students, activists, human rights defenders, and community leaders been intimidated, arrested, kidnapped, and killed, but the whole idea of space for dissent is being eliminated, with any opponent of the government being classified as a potential rebel. For example, a few days after martial law was declared, the government named SIRA, Kontras, and Student Solidarity for the People as GAM-sympathizers. Since the declaration of martial law, mass arrest and hunting of activists has been carried out in Aceh. All nonstate groups, in order to carry out their activities, have to get permission from the martial law authority, who is also the commander of military operations. The authority has also closed Aceh to foreign humanitarian workers and foreign journalists. The restriction is also being imposed on any activities by NGOs.

Another major challenge facing this movement in Aceh is to gain support from civil society in the rest of Indonesia. The engagement of both Acehnese and Indonesian civil society could provide alternative support to the whole process of peacebuilding in Aceh. This is even more urgent now that the conflict has become more complex, demanding greater creativity and intelligence for its solution. The present government seems to lack this creativity, resulting in the prioritizing of political processes that do not take into account what is important to ordinary people, and in which they have no means of participation. In addition, the engagement with Indonesian civil society is also important since both Acehnese and the larger Indonesian society are victims of the conflict in Aceh. The Acehnese are the visible victims and the Indonesians are the invisible.

The Acehnese want a positive peace, not a negative one. They do not see conflict as a necessarily bad thing. The Acehnese reject the destructive elements in the conflict, but recognize the positive, constructive, creative potential and opportunities that the conflict presents. The challenge then lies in transforming the destructive tendencies in the conflict into creative tendencies, and in building viable spaces for the flourishing of communities where people are engaged in practicing peace, demanding justice, and engaging in democratic relationships in their everyday lives.

Prospects

There is no easy way of solving the conflict in Aceh. The conflict has been going on for many years and has evolved to a point where a solution is becoming increasingly difficult to find. The complexity of the Aceh problem has been further enhanced by the complex problems of Indonesian politics. It is impossible to fully understand this war in Aceh without understanding the intricate political dynamics in Jakarta that precipitated it. Indonesian politics in the post–New Order period were inevitably messy. Increasing recognition of the New Order's human rights violations and state terrorism, largely carried out by Indonesia's armed forces, meant military reform was a critical element of Indonesia's broad reform agenda *(reformasi)*. Yet it soon became clear that military entrenchment in the civil power structures meant the problem of impunity would not be dealt with; at the same time, endemic corruption and a weak judicial system undermined efforts to make essential structural changes. Many government critics have said that the *reformasi* is dead. Inevitably, the broader political situation in Indonesia has had a direct bearing on efforts to resolve the crisis in Aceh.

Prospects for third-party intervention receded when the New Order fell. Talk of reform was seen as a sufficient indicator that change was inevitable. The reality of the *reformasi* is very different though. The current domestic political situation does not lend itself to conflict resolution. The changes have actually made the Acehnese conflict more complex. However, difficulties in finding a political solution to Aceh's problem should not mean that the only alternative is to let the Indonesian military run the show. This would be the ideal time for the government to incorporate civil society into a search for other solutions. Civil society could provide the initiative, creativity, and willingness to negotiate that are needed in any search for peace. These are certainly not characteristics of the current troubleshooters entrusted with ending the conflict: the military. Over time, they have been the cause of instability, violence, and destruction in both Acehnese and wider Indonesian society. The current repetition of the same tactics and strategy that have failed in every operation in Aceh to date only underlines this.

If the war is to be transformed, third-party intervention or the recognition of civil society is essential. Unfortunately, the official stance that the only parties in the conflict are the government and GAM has closed down the space for civil society to work constructively. The military's absolute control of information about the conflict has almost squeezed that space out of existence as well. As long as they are able to represent only one perspective on the war, not only is pressure to curtail the operation there unlikely to be credible, but they are also free to represent themselves as the only group who can overcome the political crisis in Indonesia. Civil society is not only restricted or discredited with the label "unpatriotic," but actively targeted by the military as well. Intervention with the government will not come from outside the country while there is no verifiable information about the facts within the province. It seems that the two best potential agents for changing Aceh's prospects have been outmaneuvered.

Recommendations

Despite the seemingly insurmountable obstacles to breaking the deadlock, there are still measures that can be taken by various actors, domestically and internationally, to improve Aceh's chances for peace:

- The Indonesian government should immediately end martial law in Aceh and return with GAM to the negotiation table. Other governments, donors, and international supporters of the peace process for Aceh should increase the scope and urgency of current efforts to pressure the Indonesian government to end martial law immediately and actively seek the mediation of an international third party, as well as Acehnese civil society participation in order to find a viable nonmilitary solution to the conflict in Aceh. Association of Southeast Asian Nations member states, besides Japan, the United States, and the European Union, should play a significant role in approaching the Indonesian government.
- The Indonesian government should allow access to international humanitarian organizations and human rights monitors. The UN should continue to pressure the Indonesian government to allow human rights and humanitarian organizations access to Aceh. Various international humanitarian and human rights organizations that have experience working in

Aceh have been trying, repeatedly, to regain access to the province after martial law authorities denied them "Blue Book" renewals in the early stages of the renewed conflict. Few organizations are able to provide their services in the fourteen-day access slots issued by the authorities. The few individual staff who have been permitted brief visits to the province have been forbidden to travel outside the capital to the areas worst affected by the current conflict. Access to the province should not be restricted to a fixed period of time. Agencies should be able to make their own security evaluations outside the capital.

- All levels in the international community must ensure that the peace negotiations at the political level run concurrently with peacebuilding efforts throughout society. UN agencies, governments, donors, and international and local NGOs should support capacity-building programs to prepare the local population for the various stages of the peace process and beyond. Logistical, financial, and political support for domestic civil society groups will assist their work in, for example, the reconstruction of economic, education, and health systems, or political education and empowerment efforts.

- International support for reform and democratization in Indonesia should be a policy priority. The military remains the chief obstacle to finding a political settlement in Aceh and Indonesia. The above recommendations should be coupled with continuing pressure on and assistance to the Indonesian government that will support civil society, and weaken the Indonesian military politically. For example, demilitarization and demobilization, human rights investigations, and restructuring of judicial mechanisms. Until this happens, local and national civil society will struggle to find a solution for the problems. Not until the Indonesian military's political role is diminished will a solution for the crisis in Aceh and in Indonesia at large be found.

- Civil society, on both the Acehnese and Indonesian sides, should work together to find a solution to the crisis in Aceh. This engagement by civil society must run parallel with efforts to facilitate talks between the Indonesian government and GAM. This can be done by developing and maintaining regular contact between, and network building efforts by, NGOs, student groups, intellectuals, and activists from Aceh and the rest of Indonesia. Integrated strategies will assist efforts to define what kind of society they would like to build.

Resources

Newsletters
DTE Bulletin, London
Inside Indonesia, Australia
TAPOL Bulletin, London

Reports

Amnesty International. "Shock Therapy: Restoring Order in Aceh, 1989–1993." London: Amnesty International, 1993.
Human Rights Watch. "Indonesia: Aceh Under Martial Law: Inside the Secret War." December 2003, vol. 15, no. 10 (C).
———. "Indonesia: The War in Aceh." August 2001, vol. 13, no. 4 (C).
International Crisis Group. "Aceh: A Fragile Peace." Jakarta/Brussels, February 27, 2003.
———. "Aceh: Why Military Force won't Bring Lasting Peace." Jakarta/Brussels, June 12, 2001.
Tapol Indonesian Human Rights Campaign. "A Reign of Terror: Human Rights Violation in Aceh, 1998–2000." March 2000.

Other Publications

"Rawan Is As Rawan Does: The Origins of Disorder in New Order Aceh." By Geoffrey Robinson. *Indonesia* no. 66 (October 1998), pp. 127–156.
The Republican Revolt: A Study of the Acehnese Rebellion. By Nazaruddin Sjamsuddin. Singapore: Institute of Southeast Asian Studies, 1985.
The Roots of Acehnese Rebellion, 1989–1992. By Tim Kell. Cornell University Monograph Seris no. 74, Ithaca, N.Y.: Cornell Modern Indonesia Project, Southeast Asia Program, Cornell University, 1995.
The Rope of God. 2d ed. By James T. Siegel. Ann Arbor, Michigan University Press, 2000.
"Whither Aceh." By Priyambudi Sulistiyanto. *Third World Quarterly* 22, no. 3 (2001): 437–452.

Websites

www.acheh-eyes.org
http://tapol.gn.apc.org
http://dte.gn.apc.org

Resource Contacts

Aguswandi, Tapol, e-mail: agus_smur@hotmail.com
Carmel Budiardjo, Tapol Indonesian Human Rights Campaign, London, e-mail: tapol@gn.apc.org
Otto Syamsuddin Ishak, Yappika, Jakarta, e-mail: aroen_jeram@yahoo.com
Sidney Jones, International Crisis Group, Jakarta office, e-mail: sjones@crisisweb.org
Damien Kingsbury, Deakin University, Australia, e-mail: dlk@deakin.edu.au
Liem Sio Liong, Indonesian Kodemo, Amsterdam, e-mail: slliem@xs4all.nl
Lesley McCullogh, SCHRA, Australia, e-mail: lesleymc@deakin.ed.au.
Munir, Imparsial Jakarta, e-mail: munir91@plasa.com
Saeki Natsuko, NINDJA, Japan, e-mail: sekjen@nindja.com

Organizations

Local

Commission for Disappearance and Victims of Violence (KONTRAS)
Jl. Cisadane no. 9
Cikini 10330, Indonesia
tel: +62 21 390 1978
fax: +62 21 319 00627

Imparsial
Jl. Diponegoro no. 9
Jakarta, Indonesia

tel: +62 21 391 3819
fax: +62 21 319 00627

Indonesian Legal Aid Foundation (YLBHI)
Jl. Diponegoro no. 74
Jakarta 10320, Indonesia
tel: +62 21 314 5518
fax: +62 21 330 140

International Crisis Group (ICG), Jakarta Office
Menara Thamrin, 14th Floor, Suite 1402
Jl. M.H. Thamrin Kav. 3
Jakarta 10250, Indonesia
tel: +62 21 398 30303
fax: +62 21 398 30304

International

Support Committee for Human Rights in Aceh (SCHRA)
c/o Network for Indonesian Democracy, Japan (NINDJA)
Chateaux Sawamura A
8 Sugacho Shinjukuku
Tokyo 160-0018, Japan
tel/fax: +81 3 3356 8364

Tapol Indonesian Human Rights Campaign
111 Northwood Road
Thornton Heath, Surrey
CR7 8HW, UK
tel: +44 20 8771 2904
fax: +44 20 8653 0322

Aguswandi is a researcher for the Tapol Indonesian Human Rights Campaign, based in London.

Notes

1. Together with six other prominent ulamas in Aceh, Beureueh advocated the integration of Aceh into the new state of Indonesia under the Sukarno regime through a joint statement.

2. In the period 1945–1949 the Dutch tried to reoccupy Indonesia, which provoked resistance in many places. This period is called a time of revolution in Indonesian history.

3. For a full account of the Beureueh rebellion, see N. Syamsuddin, *The Republican Revolt: A Study of the Acehnese Rebellion* (Singapore: Institute of South Asian Studies, 1985).

4. Support Committee for Human Rights in Aceh (SCHRA), *Aceh: The Untold Story of Aceh—An Introduction to the Human Rights Crisis in Aceh* (Tokyo: SCHRA, 2000).

5. N. Syamsuddin, *The Republican Revolt: A Study of the Acehnese Rebellion* (Singapore: Institute of South Asian Studies, 1985).

6. M. Isa Sulaiman, *Aceh Merdeka: Ideologi, Kepemimpinan dan Gerakan* (Jakarta: Pustaka Al Kautsar, 2000).

7. G. Robinson, "Rawan Is As Rawan Does: The Origins of Disorder in New Order Aceh," *Indonesia* no. 66 (October 1998), pp. 127–156.

8. H. Di Tiro, *Democracy Untuk Indonesia* (Jakarta: Teplok Press, 1999).

9. Benedict Anderson, "Indonesian Nationalism Today and in the Future," *New Left Review* no. 235 (May–June 1999), pp. 3–17.

10. The "Cendana circle" is the term being used to replace "Suharto circle"; Cendana is the place where Suharto's family live. For more information on the military interests in Aceh, see Aguswandi, "Aceh: Tradisi Ketidakadilan," paper presented at a seminar on military interest in Aceh organized by Pusat Pegembangan Studi Kawasan (PSPK), Banda Aceh, May 27, 2000.

11. Priyambudi S, "Whither Aceh?" *Third World Quarterly* 22, no. 3 (2001): 438.

12. Robinson, "Rawan is as Rawan Does."

13. An interview with Otto Syamsuddin Ishak in *Inside Indonesia,* February 2002.

14. In the post–New Order period and before the present imposition of martial law there had been several operations, such as Wibawa (January–April 1999), Sadar Rencon I (May 1999–January 2000), Sadar Rencong II (February–May 2000), Cinta Meunasah I (June–September 2000), Cinta Meunasah II (September 2000–February 2001), OPKH I (February–August 2001), and OPKH II (September 2001–February 2002).

15. *Serambi Indonesia,* September 16, 1999.

16. HDC Mission Statement, available at www.hdcentre.org.

17. *Serambi Indonesia,* May 13, 2000.

18. Walhi Aceh polling, June 1999.

19. The referendum demanded was similar to that held in East Timor, in which independence and autonomy were options people could choose.

20. *Tapol Bulletin,* nos. 166–167 (April–May 2002).

9.5.3

Kalimantan: Unity or Diversity?

John Bamba

Kalimantan has a long history of cultural diversity and ethnic violence, of wealth and exploitation. While tensions among the many Dayaks, Malay, Madurese, and other ethnic groups, including Chinese, have deep roots, under the Suharto dictatorship they were more or less kept under control until the regime fell in 1998. In Kalimantan, the Sanggau Ledo, Sambas, and Sampit conflicts were so devastating that they attracted international attention. Initiatives to transform the conflict have largely failed, and the causes of the conflict remain unresolved. The vast majority of internally displaced persons (IDPs) have been resettled in isolated and undeveloped areas, and ethnic tensions are increasingly reflected in divisions along political and social lines.

Violent ethnic conflicts have had a long, though sporadic, history in Kalimantan. Since 1952,[1] there have been primarily conflicts between Madurese and either Dayaks or Malays,[2] with numerous outbreaks of isolated and small-scale communal fighting, and the loss of many lives on all sides. In recent years, violence has broken out in Sanggau Ledo, West Kalimantan, in 1997, in Sambas, West Kalimantan, in 1999, and in Sampit, Central Kalimantan, in 2001. This chapter focuses primarily on communal violence in the West Kalimantan context involving the Dayak, Madurese, and Malay ethnic groups.

Kalimantan's earliest inhabitants consisted of hundreds of different subethnic and cultural groups, who have come to be collectively known as the Dayaks, despite different languages, social practices, and customs. They were largely forest dwellers, who tended to migrate inland to more isolated parts of the island of Borneo when Arab, Indian, and other Asian traders established ports and trading centers on the coast. The inward migration was also caused by their rejection of Islam, despite efforts by these traders to convert them. Those who did convert were considered "Malay" and gained access to certain social benefits.

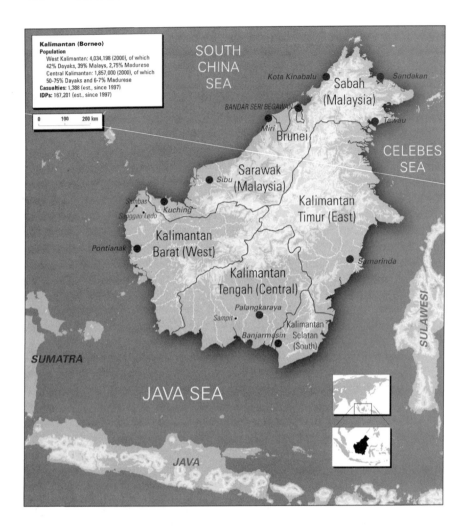

Kalimantan (Borneo)
Population
    West Kalimantan: 4,034,198 (2000), of which
    42% Dayaks, 39% Malays, 2,75% Madurese
    Central Kalimantan: 1,857,000 (2000), of which
    50-75% Dayaks and 6-7% Madurese
Casualties: 1,388 (est., since 1997)
IDPs: 167,201 (est., since 1997)

The Malays are the descendants of both the Muslim traders and the local Dayak converts. They settled predominantly in coastal areas as fishermen, or earned their livelihood, like the Dayaks, as farmers in the interior areas. In modern times, the Malays have tended to have greater political prominence and be better educated as a community than the Dayaks or Madurese.

The history of inequality and the present competition over economic, social, and political positions between the non-Muslim Dayaks and the predominantly Muslim Malays can thus be seen as the primary continuing source of potential conflict between these two ethnic groups—whose different religious affiliations may also have aggravated relations. However, while there are tensions between the Malay and the Dayak, these have never erupted into open violent conflict such as that between the Dayak and the Madurese.

The Madurese migration to West Kalimantan first began in 1904, when they were brought to the region as coolies from the island of Madura, off the northeastern coast of Java, by Malay, Bugis, and Arabic merchants.[3] It was then followed by the Dutch resettlement program *(Kolonisasi)*. Later on, most Madurese migrated voluntarily in search of a better life. These Madurese tended to come from the very poorest part of Madura—a region where resilience, fierce determination, and communal support are important survival skills, and where honor has assumed central importance in the culture. In West Kalimantan, most of them work in the transportation sector in jobs such as pedicab and public bus drivers, and in the informal sector as street vendors or cigarette sellers. Others plant cassava and vegetables on the outskirts of towns and sell these products door to door or in the markets. Few of them are successful businessmen, government officers, and politicians. Although more Madurese are found in towns and cities, some do live in the interior areas as farmers and in coastal areas as fishermen.

The stereotyping typical of ethnic conflict and ethnic relations is widespread in Kalimantan. The Madurese are portrayed as aggressive, quick to use violence, hostile toward other ethnic groups, and criminally inclined. Dayaks are stereotyped as barbaric and backward. Malays are stereotyped as arrogant and cowardly. As with all stereotyping, the portrayals tend to relate to the history of ethnic relations in Kalimantan, and the continuation of stereotypes is supported by current political and economic structures.

Once, Kalimantan had the second-largest tropical rainforest in the world, after the Amazon. However, according to the World Bank, some 746,000 hectares of forest are destroyed annually as a result of logging and mining activities.[4] Deforestation is also caused by burning off forests to clear land for plantations. These lands are mostly owned by private businessmen and financed by foreign investment from Malaysia and Europe.[5]

For Dayaks, whose economic, social, and cultural livelihood depends on the forests, the devastation has led to a sharpened sense of marginalization, and has arguably driven them to use violence to assert themselves. The use of violence has also been linked to a recent identification with a common pan-Dayak sentiment and associated efforts to assert that identity.[6]

Conflict Dynamics

Since the fall of the New Order regime, Dayaks and Malays have sought to use *reformasi* (reforms) to support and build collective identities that they feel have been denied by Jakarta. In the past, violence was often the primary means employed by the Indonesian government to suppress protest; it is now being used by the people to try to redress their grievances. The Dayaks, for example, have been involved in a number of violent ethnic conflicts with the Madurese, and some tend to exploit this violence to project an image of resistance to any future threats.

Geographically, the violence has centered around Pontianak and Sambas in West Kalimantan, and Sampit in Central Kalimantan. Typically, conflicts have been triggered by personal disputes related to disagreements over land, debts, or women. Local accounts of the conflicts tend to identify ethnic and cultural clashes as the primary causes, but injustice, marginalization of the local communities, and divisive and poor government policies are among other root causes of these deadly conflicts. Due to bad governance, poor policing, and accumulated grievances, they easily escalate into communal violence.[7]

Each ethnic group has tended to respond to disputes, including violent disputes, according to its own cultural practices and traditions. This is especially true in the interior areas. A common source of friction is the practice among Madurese men of carrying a sharp knife in public. This is a practice rejected by Dayaks, and viewed in general by non-Madurese as threatening and insulting. Other ethnic groups complain that many Madurese men are quick to use their weapons to resolve disputes, which naturally increases tensions. Malays and Dayaks justify their use of violence against Madurese as a response to their frustration with Madurese violence, including killings of Dayaks and Malays.[8]

The open conflict between the Malay and the Madurese has revealed the seriousness and complexity of ethnic relations in Kalimantan. Many people have been led through press reports to believe that the conflicts between Dayaks and Madurese are linked to a revival of Dayak headhunting traditions,[9] aggravated by the religious divide between the predominantly Christian Dayaks and the Muslim Madurese. But the Sambas case in 1999 involving Malays and Madurese belies this argument, as the Malay had no history of headhunting,[10] and both communities shared the Islamic faith.

In most cases, where the Madurese have been driven out of an area, Malays and Dayaks have appropriated Madurese settlement areas, usually seizing the land but destroying other property such as abandoned houses and vehicles. In appropriating these lands, the Dayak or Malay believe they are reclaiming land previously taken from them. Their actions reflect the underlying nature of the conflict, which, as noted above, is not so much an ethnic or cultural conflict as a conflict rooted in disputes over resource management, economic and political power, and the absence of the rule of law.

Government policy with respect to the indigenous peoples and their customary rights has resulted in their continued oppression and marginalization, and the appropriation of their lands by the state.[11] These indigenous people, then, feel ignored and betrayed. Transmigration programs, which have moved around 8 million people from densely populated islands such as Java and Bali to Kalimantan, Sumatra, and West Papua, are a continuing source of tension, as the local population is faced with competition for access to natural resources, jobs, and political positions.

One feature of the conflicts has been harassment of local leaders and politicians by the government and the police. During the Sanggau Ledo conflict, for example, A. R. Mecer, a prominent former Dayak politician and leader of a Dayak nongovernmental organization (NGO) called Pancur Kasih, was blackmailed with a fake letter that linked him and six other Dayaks to the "Republic of Independent Borneo" (RDM). The letter asserted that the RDM wielded power in West, Central, and South Kalimantan, and in Sabah and Sarawak as well. The letter was sent to the governor (director) of the National Defense Institute, the governor of West Kalimantan, and the commander of the

Sixth Tanjungpura Territorial Military Command. As a result, Mecer was summoned by the police and interrogated for thirty-six hours. On another occasion, Zainudin Isman, a local leader of the Muhammadiyah Group, was arrested and tried for carrying a sharp weapon in his car.[12] He was later found not guilty and released. And Dayak cultural leader Kma Usop, a professor at Palangkaraya University in Central Kalimantan, was also arrested and taken to Jakarta by the police before being eventually released.[13]

When conflicts have occurred, the security apparatus has been very slow to respond, so that personal disputes escalate into wider conflicts and violence. If a conflict spins out of control, then the government has attempted to resolve it through formal peace negotiations, but without adequate representation from the parties involved. The government has also resorted to forced relocations, the use of force to separate the parties, and even force of arms by members of the security forces to try to control the violence. Such actions, however, have had the effect of reinforcing a culture of violence.

At the level of the access to natural resource management, the local populations have been experiencing accelerating pressures from both the voluntarily migrants and transmigrants. The opening up of millions of hectares of areas for foreign investment in palm oil and industrial tree plantation businesses, which have taken advantage of the cheap labor offered by immigrants but provided few job opportunities for the local population, has raised tensions, jealousy, frustrations, and disappointments.[14] The Malays and Dayaks, who had effectively controlled the exploitation of natural resources for centuries, are suddenly confronted with an influx of immigrants who are also participating in the management and ownership of the natural resources.

Charly Flynn/Panos Pictures

Kalimantan. Transmigration in a deforested area.

The conflicts in Sanggau Ledo (Bengkayang district), Sambas (Sambas district), and Sampit (Central Kalimantan) have claimed a total of 1,388 lives, destroyed 9,649 houses and other properties, and forced more than 167,000 Madurese from their homes. By the end of the Sambas conflict in April 1999, most Madurese had left this area; likewise, most had fled Sampit in Central Kalimantan in 2001. By February 2003, more than 45,000 Madurese IDPs were living in East Java and nearly 130,000 were in Madura.[15] Additional IDPs moved to other areas in West Kalimantan, including about 60,000 in IDP camps in Pontianak, the capital of West Kalimantan province. This decreased the likelihood of conflicts recurring, but increased tension in Pontianak. Since the violent conflict ended in Sambas in 1999, virtually no Madurese IDPs have returned to Malay areas, and the Malay communities refuse to discuss reconciliation or consider a return of the Madurese.[16] However, Madurese communities who live in other districts in West Kalimantan, such as in Ketapang, Kapuas Hulu, and Sintang, have not been affected by this forced eviction.[17] According to the UN Office for the Coordination of Humanitarian Affairs (OCHA), since end of 2002 in Central Kalimantan, 107 Madurese families (540 people) have returned from Madura to three areas in Central Kalimantan.[18]

The police and military's responses to some cases in Pontianak city and, later, in Sambas on December 15, 2002,[19] have shown that quick action can prevent situations from escalating. However, in Sanggau Ledo, Sambas, and Sampit, security officers have at other times appeared to abdicate their responsibility to maintain order and have even encouraged the escalation of violence by failing to take appropriate legal action against instigators. Security officers were even reported to be standing around observing the intercommunal violence, claiming that they were prevented from intervening because they lacked sufficient personnel.

Official Conflict Management

To manage the conflict in Kalimantan, the government has applied a strategy consisting of three options: return, empowerment, and resettlement.[20] Under the first option, the government aims to peacefully return the refugees to their normal livelihoods and prior living places. With its empowerment policy, the government aims to provide facilities and job opportunities to the refugees to build new lives in the communities to which they have fled. With its policy of resettlement, the government aims to resettle the refugees in new locations through transmigration programs.

However, in West Kalimantan the local government has given the relocation of IDPs the highest priority. Strong protests by local populations against the attempted return of IDPs has increased the government's reluctance to make serious efforts to find an acceptable solution for the IDPs, and encouraged the use of relocation, no matter how ineffective it is, for addressing the root causes for the conflicts.

In August 2002 a meeting facilitated by the West Kalimantan Regional Commission on Human Rights was attended by Sambas Malay and Madurese representatives. The meeting was preceded by intensive discussions about respective ethnic groups and by a socialization process that resulted in an agreement on reconciliation. It was then followed by another meeting in Singkawang with more participation from local government representatives. The participants in the meeting agreed to discuss and promote the aims of the meeting with their respective community members, and proposed a budget to the local government to fund reconciliation activities between the Malay and Madurese.

The latest meeting of this kind was held on October 25, 2003, in Singkawang and attended by representatives of just two Madurese organizations, one Malay organization, and the police.[21] At this meeting the parties were unable to reach any meaningful agreements to address the situation. Patience is required before any change in attitudes at the grassroots level in the Malay community can be expected. The Sambas Malay community's rejection of the Madurese is aggravated by problems within the Malay community itself: a lack of collaboration and coordination among various groups involved in the reconciliation initiatives, and the limited capacities of these groups. Although millions of dollars in government funds and additional contributions from abroad have been allocated to programs focusing on the relocation of IDPs to new settlement areas, no funds have been specifically earmarked for reconciliation. The root causes of the conflict are not being addressed and conflict resolution efforts have been largely abandoned. Furthermore, some community leaders feel threatened by members of their own community if they agree to the return of the Madurese to Sambas areas.

Based on Presidential Decree no. 3/2001, a national coordinating body, Bakornas PBP, formulated national policies on accelerated handling of IDPs in Indonesia,[22] with a mandate to completely resolve all IDP problems by the end of 2002, and indeed all of the IDP camps in Pontianak have been successfully emptied by the government.

In Central Kalimantan, local government has joined with NGOs to initiate dialogue and training activities at various times. These initiatives have included conflict transformation dialogue and the formulation of work plans, conflict resolution training for the Dayak representatives in Palangkaraya and Madurese IDPs in Madura in April 2002; meetings of the Central Kalimantan team and Madurese team in Yogyakarta, Central Java, in May 2002; meetings of Dayak and Madurese children in their respective areas in July 2002; and the Jamboree of Dayak-Madurese Children, held in Jakarta in August 2002. Despite these achievements, local government still lacks any comprehensive long-term program.

The repeated ethnic conflicts in Kalimantan have also attracted international attention. Most of the activities by UN agencies such as OCHA and the World Health Organization (WHO) have focused on rehabilitation and emergency support, particularly in relation to IDPs. The UN Children's Fund has supported the education of IDP children; OCHA has introduced the guideline principles for internal refugees to the government; and the UN High Commissioner for Refugees and WHO have also supported the Indonesian government in handling IDPs.

Multi-Track Diplomacy

To achieve ethnic reconciliation in Kalimantan, both government institutions and nongovernmental organizations have organized various meetings and workshops, facilitated dialogue, and worked to negotiate peace agreements. Peace talks initiated by the Office of the President, under the name "Deliberation of the Nation's Children" *(Musyawarah Anak Bangsa),* were held in Bogor immediately after the Sampit conflict. However, these initiatives only involved the elite and community leaders, who themselves failed to include their grassroots communities in the process. In many cases, the initiatives began and ended in a seminar, dialogue, or workshop in a hotel in a city.

The NGO community and religious groups have developed and gained substantial space since the *reformasi.* The university students, whose massive demonstrations forced Suharto to step down in May 1998, are an important element within civil society, with the potential power to reshape government policies. Students are grouped in various internal and external organizations. As student pressure through massive demonstrations has proved effective in changing government policies and even in changing the government, students have also become the target of political groups who seek to use them for their political interests.

The role of these civil society groups in peacebuilding efforts is varied. While the students are the most vocal and potent force for change in political life, they are far less active in issues of reconciliation. No student demonstrations have been staged on the issues of ethnic conflict in Kalimantan. In West Kalimantan, student groups have only been involved in emergency initiatives such as providing free goods for IDPs or as participants in various discussions on ethnic relations. A relatively small group of Kalimantan students studying in Java (Yogyakarta) undertook some peacebuilding initiatives by holding interethnic forums, dialogues, and public campaigns.

On the other hand, the leaders of major religions (Islam and Christianity) have distanced themselves from reconciliation efforts, claiming the need to stay "neutral" and refrain from any action that could later result in them being considered "provocateurs" in the conflicts. Such an attitude may have motivated Archbishop Hieronimus Bumbun of Pontianak to declare that the Catholic Church had nothing to do with the ethnic conflict between the Dayak and the Madurese.[23] However, religious organizations have been involved in humanitarian work both during and after a conflict.[24] While most of the religious leaders were involved in interethnic dialogue following the conflicts, they proved to be ineffective in preventing their religious followers from engaging in violence and retaliation. This failure has been especially evident at times of maximum conflict, when active opposition from these leaders might have been expected. One explanation for this passivity is that the religious leaders did not want to be associated with acts of "provocation," as happened to a group of Madurese ulamas linked to an organization known as the Board of Madurese Ulamas Friendship.[25]

Multi-track conflict resolution efforts related to NGO activities and initiatives fall into two main categories: building communication and dialogue between various ethnic communities, especially those in conflict; and providing emergency support. These initiatives have been carried out by local NGOs, by coalitions between local and national NGOs, and by coalitions of local, national, and international NGOs.

The conflict resolution efforts have included organizing forums to discuss reconciliation and peacebuilding initiatives with various local NGOs and among ethnic communities in conflict. Various workshops, training programs, and seminars in conflict resolution have also been carried out at both local and national levels. The issues of peaceful ethnic relations and acceptance of cultural differences have been discussed within various forums and at meetings focusing on human rights, democracy, environmental protection, and regional autonomy, where the central importance of peacebuilding for the success of sustainable development in Kalimantan has been highlighted.

Most NGOs and community groups in Kalimantan that have been involved in responding to the conflict have focused on providing emergency support for IDPs. In each IDP camp in Pontianak there were service posts set up by NGOs to provide support and aid to IDPs, as well as to provide updated information on the daily conditions at the IDP camps. Food, medicine, clothes, and other basic needs were distributed by those NGOs to the IDPs, with financial support provided primarily from international donors. Different types of organizations, including local NGOs, Muslim university student associations, Madurese youth organizations, student and scholar organizations, and Christian organizations, were involved in these activities.

Some international NGOs, including Save the Children, the British Council, and Search for Common Ground–Indonesia, working in cooperation with local NGOs, also carried out activities with a special focus on children, bringing youth of different ethnic backgrounds together to work for conflict resolution and peacebuilding. Other organizations such as the BBC and Kalimantan Review Magazine, along with the British Council once again, worked with local journalists in peace journalism training activities.

Still other NGOs have been working directly with IDPs at relocation sites. World Vision International has been providing seeds and tools and is involved in a land preparation program. Save the Children–UK, Catholic Relief Services, and the International Medical Corps also have programs in relocation areas, and the International Organization of Migration is involved in developing relocation sites.

While activities have focused on emergency relief efforts for the IDPs, little effective work has been done in the area of conflict resolution. Collaboration among NGOs, academics, religious groups, government, and international communities has been poor, resulting in overlapping and inefficient strategies, and communication and coordination among various groups has been limited to sharing information at the initial stages of involvement only. Because of the priority given to handling IDPs, peacebuilding activities have tended to end when the financial means are exhausted or when the IDP camps are emptied.

The work of the Foundation for the Victims of Sambas Social Conflict (YKKSS) reflects this situation. The YKKSS was established by IDP representatives, active NGOs, youth and student volunteers, local legislative and executive representatives, and security officers. The foundation has been working intensively on various negotiations with government institutions, distributing materials and financial support to IDPs, and monitoring the numbers of IDPs in various camps and relocation sites. The foundation is also the member of the Collective Team for the Handling of IDPs in West Kalimantan, with representation from various governmental entities, the police, and the military.

The YKKSS has mainly been involved in the negotiations regarding levels of compensation to be granted as part of arrangements for IDPs to leave the camps and settle in relocation sites. It tends to play the role of a "broker" between the government and the IDPs. Internal conflict within the foundation led it to split into two camps, when a group of IDPs expressed disappointment with the management policies. These internal divisions soon weakened the foundation's legitimacy and ability to function effectively, and management of IDP issues was relegated to local government.

As the discussion above would suggest, most civil society responses to the conflict have focused more on the problems of IDPs than on peacebuilding and conflict transformation. Few initiatives have addressed the root causes of the conflict, and as a result, local people (Malays in Sambas and Dayaks in Sampit) still oppose the return of the Madurese to the homes they fled, and Madurese feelings of discrimination and aggravation continue. An event occurring on December 15, 2002, in Karamungting-Bengkayang district, which nearly escalated into a new outbreak of mass killing, highlights the fragility of the situation, and the urgent need to address the fundamental issues. In view of the fact that reconciliation efforts have so far been focused primarily on the short-term management of IDPs, one organization, Refugees International, has rightly urged international donor agencies to focus their attention on long-term peacebuilding and reconciliation initiatives.[26]

Prospects

While all of the IDP camps in Pontianak have been successfully emptied by the government, no substantial efforts are being made at the government level to address the causes of the conflict, or to work toward real reconciliation between those communities involved in conflict. Although local peoples' access to and management of land and natural resources has always been of crucial importance in the conflicts afflicting Kalimantan,[27] local government has failed to take clear action to address the policies on logging and development of plantations, or transmigration programs, all of which are of crucial importance with respect to access and management concerns.

One of the most difficult challenges for various parties working for conflict resolution in Kalimantan is to end the local peoples' strong resistance to the return of IDPs. The ongoing individual disputes between Madurese and Malay or Dayak are being used to justify claims that these ethnic groups should live separately. Without progress on the issue of return, all reconciliation efforts are doomed to failure.

Still, there are some opportunities to move toward reconciliation. The Malays' willingness to open dialogue with the Madurese, including discussion of the return of IDPs, could be a starting point for meaningful accommodation.[28] Likewise, there have been encouraging signs from the Madurese community. For example, the Madurese community publicly congratulated the Dayaks on their celebration of Naik Dango—the Post-Harvest Festival—and the Association of Madurese Communities took it upon itself to turn in a member of the Madurese community suspected of injuring a Malay during a brawl involving Madurese and Malay youth in Tanjunghulu-Pontianak on October 21, 2003.

It should be noted that in addition to the conflicts between Madurese and Malays, and Madurese and Dayaks, violent conflict between the Dayak and Malay communities remains a possibility. It is difficult to even imagine the impact of such an event, as there is serious risk that the same sort of disaster that befell Maluku could be repeated in West Kalimantan, because such a conflict would be not only ethnic but also religious in nature. The tendency to use violence against members of other communities as an expression of ethnic identity, as the three main communities in Kalimantan compete for political power, remains a source of great concern.

Recommendations

The people of Kalimantan should be given the right to choose and apply their own village government systems, to manage natural resources based on their local cultures and traditions, and to be protected from any development activities, such as the logging, monoculture plantation, mining, and transmigration projects, that may result in the violation of their rights as indigenous peoples.

Serious efforts should be made to develop local cultural and religious values and practices that promote and respect human rights, nonviolence, and tolerance for differences. These efforts should address stereotyping, segregation, and ethnic hatred. Such values and practices should be taught at schools and universities, including those of the military and religious-based educational institutions. Public campaigns should utilize the media and involve religious leaders. The government and various elements of civil society should work hand-in-hand on these initiatives. Considering the potential power of the university students as a force for change, NGOs working on conflict resolution and peacebuilding should aim to involve more students in their work. NGOs should also support and facilitate the use of legitimate customary law by communities as a means to prevent and resolve conflicts.[29]

Broader community consultation and comprehensive participatory analysis of the roots of the violent conflicts are needed. Such consultation and analysis should be undertaken in a way that encourages collaboration between civil society groups and the government. A long-term strategic intervention on conflict resolution, reconciliation, and peacebuilding should be a multidimensional effort involving all stakeholders, at all levels of society, representing a range of experience and expertise.

The police and military should respond responsibly and quickly to any incidents that occur to ensure that they do not escalate. But responsible and quick action does not mean that violence should be the first option, as a violent response to civil unrest is likely to worsen and perpetuate the conflict rather than resolve it. Accordingly, plans to increase the military's presence with additional deployments of personnel, which both the military and the local government in West Kalimantan support, should not be carried out; to date, there has been no evidence that military deployments in Indonesia have been effective in restoring order where intercommunal violence has been a serious problem.

International institutions, especially donor agencies, should focus more on long-term peacebuilding initiatives rather than short-term humanitarian projects such as IDP resettlement.[30] Specifically, they should focus on supporting and building local conflict management capacities, and helping media to provide more accurate and responsible coverage of the conflict. The media's sensationalist style of reporting, using terms such as "headhunters," "cannibalism," "blood drinkers," "savage," "uncivilized,"[31] has promoted false perceptions and misunderstanding among the public, nationally and internationally, about the true nature of the conflict.

There also needs to be greater focus in the education sector on programs that foster peacebuilding and reconciliation, a culture of peace, respect for the nation's diversity, and the protection of human rights. This will necessitate reforms in the educational system and curricula at schools and universities, including those of the military and religious-based educational institutions. As university students have proven to be one of the groups pushing most effectively for reform, it is incumbent upon those working on peacebuilding and reconciliation to involve more students in their activities. Within religious institutions, teachings should aim to encourage tolerance among religious followers. Religious leaders should put reconciliation on their agendas, whether they are engaged in preaching or in discussion in their communities.

In 2002 a program called Deliberation of the Nation's Children was initiated by the minister of internal affairs (Suryadi Sudirja) and attended by the four governors of Kalimantan (West, Central, East, and South) and representatives of East Java, including Madura. It was held in NAM Center, Bogor, West Java. The meeting recommended that similar meetings be held in the respective provinces to formulate regional plans for conflict resolution. These meetings did subsequently take place, under the auspices of the respective provincial governments. However, voicing the oft-repeated rationalization that no funding was available, the principals at these meeting failed to follow up these promising meetings with concrete actions.

The weakness of the various multi-track initiatives taken to date to address Kalimantan's intercommunal violence can be attributed not only to the lack of government support, but also to the limited grassroots participation.

Reconciliation initiatives undertaken so far have been largely prompted and negotiated at the elite level, as the elite groups have tended to be the groups most cooperative and amenable to dialogue. The fact is that leadership within the various communities has been weak due to the long process of marginalization and co-option of local leaders by the previous regime. Where the reconciliation efforts have been targeted at local leaders (both formal and informal) through various peace accords, agreements, and dialogues, the impact at the grassroots level has been minimal. To overcome this problem, two strategies are required: first, develop effective local leadership, and second, build a culture of peace and respect for differences within Kalimantan's diverse society.

These strategies will only be adopted if there are fundamental changes in policies related to people's autonomy and sovereignty with respect to the management of their social, cultural, economic, and political life. However, both the development of local leadership and the construction of a culture of peace are long-term endeavors requiring efforts in the social, cultural, and political domains. Further, they will require cooperation among various parties agreeing to a concerted program and common objectives, and should be initiated through bottom-up, participatory processes.

Resources

Reports
Human Rights Watch Asia. *West Kalimantan: Communal Violence in West Kalimantan* 9, no. 10 (C) (December 1997).
ICG Asia Report no. 18. "Communal Violence in Indonesia: Lessons from Kalimantan." Jakarta/Brussels, June 27, 2001, p. iv.
Refugees International. "Few Options for Madurese IDPs in West Kalimantan." March 29, 2002.
U.S. Agency for International Development. Office of Transition Initiatives (OTI). "OTI Trip Report: West Kalimantan." November 13–19, 2000, p. 11.

Magazines and Magazine Articles
"Dayak Anger Ignored." By Michael Dove. *Inside Indonesia* no. 51 (July–September 1997).
"Ethnic Fascism in Borneo: Old Elites in Central Kalimantan Discover New and Dangerous Strategies." By Gerry van Klinken. *Inside Indonesia* no. 68 (October–December 2001): 30–31.
Kalimantan Review Magazine. No. 45 (May 1999).
———. No. 55 (April 5–May 5, 2000).

Internet Articles
"Analysis: Behind the Borneo Violence." By Jonathan Head. BBC News, Friday, February 23, 2001, 11:26 GMT. Available at http://news.bbc.co.uk/hi/english/world/asia-pacific/default.stm.
"Fight to the Death for Tribal Rights." By Dini Djalal. *Asia Times,* February 20, 1997. Available at www.asiatimes.com/97/02/20/20029704.html.
"Judi Picu Rusuh Karimunting" [Gambling Triggered Karimunting Riot]. AP Post Online, Tuesday, 17 December 2002. Available at www.appost.co.id/berita/utama.php3?id=5646.

"1,200 Go Missing in Ethnic Warfare." By Louise Williams, *Herald* correspondent in Jakarta. Wednesday, March 5, 1997. Available at www.smh.com.au/daily/content/970305/world/world1.html.

Resource Contacts and Organizations

Ikatan Keluarga Besar Madura (IKBM; Association of Madurese Communities)
Jalan Teluk Intan no. 5
Siantan-Pontianak Utara, West Kalimantan
tel: 62 561 881348
contact: Haji Sulaiman

Institut Dayakologi
Kompleks Bumi Indah Khatulistiwa
Jl. Budi Utomo Blok A3, no. 3-4
Pontianak 78241
Kalimantan Barat
tel: 62 561 884567
fax: 62 561 883135
e-mail: dahas@pontianak.wasantara.net.id
www.dayakology.com

Lembaga Adat dan Budaya Melayu (LEMBAYU)
Jalan Tanjung Raya II
Kompleks Delima Mas A/7
Pontianak, West Kalimantan
tel: 62 561 739177
contact: Syarief Toto Taha Alkadrie

Majelis Adat Budaya Melayu (MABM; Council of Malay Adat and Culture)
Jalan Sungai Kawi
Jembatan II no. 123
Pontianak, West Kalimantan
tel: 62 561 732317
contact: Imim Taha

Segerak "Pancur Kasih"
Jalan Budi Utomo, Blok A3
Pontianak 78241, Kalimantan Barat
tel: 0811 569895
e-mail: duwata@pontianak.wasantara.net.id
contact: Stepanus Djuweng

Yayasan Korban Kerusuhan Sosial Sambas (YKKSS; Foundation for the Victims of Sambas Social Conflict)
Jalan Paralel Tol
Gang Melati no. 5
Pontianak Timur, West Kalimantan
tel: 0811 568467
contact: Subro

John Bamba is executive director of Institut Dayakologi, a research and cultural advocacy institution struggling for the revitalization and restitution of Dayak cultural heritage in Kalimantan. Recently, Institut Dayakologi has been involved in various peacebuilding and reconciliation initiatives in collaboration with other NGOs in Indonesia. The institute promotes Dayak culture and peaceful interethnic relations in Kalimantan through its magazine Kalimantan Review. *Bamba has taught Dayakology at Islamic State College and has served on the advisory board of Search for Common Ground–Indonesia.*

Notes

1. Edi Petebang and Eri Sutrisno. *Konflik Etnik di Sambas* (Jakarta: ISAI, 2000), p. 201.

2. One case in the late 1960s involved a Dayak attack on Chinese in West Kalimantan. At the time, the Indonesian army, which was fighting the Sarawak People's Guerrilla Force (PGRS), a communist group backed by Peking and some Chinese communities along the border of Kalimantan and Sarawak-Malaysia, engaged Dayaks to cut off the Chinese support to the PGRS movement (Justus M. van der Kroef, "Sarawak-Indonesia Border Insurgency," *Modern Asia Studies,* vol. 2, part 3, July 1968, p. 245). What began as a limited action evolved into a serious conflict. Around 3,000 Chinese in West Kalimantan were killed and nearly all Chinese living in villages in West Kalimantan were forced to flee to the towns. See Herbert Feith, "Suharto's Search for a Political Format," no. 6 (1968), pp. 88–105; David Jenkins, "Timor's Arithmetic of Despair," *Far Eastern Economic Review,* vol. 29, December, 1978; Robert Peterson, *Storm over Borneo* (London: Overseas Missionary Fellowship, 1968).

3. Hendro Suroyo Sudagung, *Mengurai Pertikaian Etnis: Migrasi Swakarsa Etnis Madura ke Kalimantan Barat* (Jakarta: ISAI, 2000), pp. 76–83.

4. Victor Barber and James Schweithelm, *Trial by Fire: Forest Fires and Forestry Policy in Indonesia's Era of Crisis* (Washington, D.C.: WRO/ World Resources Institute 2000), p. 2.

5. At least sixty-two European institutions and forty-one Malaysian institutions (*New Straits Times* [Malaysia], Thursday, October 2, 1997) are engaged in the cultivation of over 4 million hectares of oil palm plantations. Eighteen European financial institutions have investments in the pulp and paper industry, with a total annual production capacity of 4,841,000 tons of pulp and 4,737,250 tons of paper (Jan Willem van Gelder and Ed Matthew, *Paper Tiger, Hidden Dragons 2: April fools.* February 2002, London: Friends of the Earth, http://www.foe.co.uk/resource/reports/april_fools. pdf). The government plans to expand plantation cultivation from a total of 7.4 million hectares to 30 million, 75 percent of which would be developed by foreign interests, with substantial displacement of indigenous peoples and the destruction of habitat. See "Indonesia: Democratization in the Era of Globalization," Bonn, May 4–6, 1998, available at www.infid.be/bonnconference.html.

6. There is a substantial history of violent conflict among different Dayak subethnic groups, see Nancy Lee Peluso and Emily Harwell, "Territory, Custom, and the Cultural Politics of Ethnic War in West Kalimantan Indonesia." In, *Violent Environments,* Nancy Lee Peluso, Michael Watts, eds. (Ithaca: Cornell University Press, 2001). On the rise of Dayakism, see Gerry van Klinken, "Ethnic Fascism in Borneo: Old Elites in Central Kalimantan Discover New and Dangerous Strategies," *Inside Indonesia* (October-December 2001): 30–31.

7. The Sambas conflict was triggered in January 1999 when a simple dispute involving accusations of theft against a Madurese man and protests of his innocence spun out of control, leading to tit-for-tat violence between Malays and Madurese. When a group of Dayaks were attacked, the Dayak community joined with Malays in what amounted to open war between the Malays and Dayaks on one side and Madurese on the other. The ethnic war lasted almost four months.

8. Violent conflict between the Dayaks and the Madurese erupted fourteen times in West Kalimantan from 1952 to 1997. See Edi Petebang and Eri Sutrisno, *Konflik Etnik di Sambas* (Jakarta: ISAI, 2000).

9. The "headhunting" issue is raised by the press every time violence breaks out in Kalimantan.

10. Nonetheless, some analysts still believe that the headhunting tradition has been a factor in the violence, noting that some Malays are Dayaks who have converted to Islam.

11. Recent reforms since 1998 have addressed issues related to traditional communities, customary land rights, customary law, cultural identity, and the like, using the term *masyarakat hukum adat* (literally meaning "customary-law based communities"), without specifically making reference to "indigenous peoples." Neither the term "traditional communities" nor the term "customary-law based communities" adequately represents the real meaning of "indigenous peoples" as agreed to in international conventions.

12. Zainuddin worked as a journalist for the biggest Indonesian newspaper, *Kompas*, which was owned by a Catholic conglomerate. Zainuddin was a Muslim but identified himself as a Dayak. The police claimed that they had found a provocative pamphlet that implicated Zainuddin. See *TIRAS* no. 5/Thn. III, February 27, 1997.

13. Gerry van Klinken is one of those who strongly believe that Usop had an important role in instigating the ethnic violence in Sampit. See Gerry van Klinken, "Ethnic Fascism in Borneo: Old Elites in Central Kalimantan Discover New and Dangerous Strategies," *Inside Indonesia* (October-December 2001): 30-31.

14. Out of 1,264 cases of crimes and cases related to ethnicity, religion, race, or intergroup relations that occurred at transmigration sites in Indonesia up to the year 2000, about half took place in Kalimantan. For complete data, see the table presented by the Department of Transmigration and Work Force of Indonesia at www.nakertrans. go.id/infotrans/situs/buku%20iii/t3_9.htm.

15. Summary Notes, Mission to Madura Island, East Java, February 17–19, 2003.

16. In early 2002 a Madurese IDP guarded by five army officers returned to Sambas to sell the land he had left, but he was killed by a mob in Sambas market once they found out that he was a Madurese. The Madurese IDPs have also complained that the local government has broken its promise to protect the Madurese property in Sambas and is facilitating Malay occupation or sale of those lands. See Bambang H. S. Purwana, *Intercommunity Ethnic Conflict in Sambas 1999* (Pontiak: Romeo Grafika, 2003), p. 78.

17. In areas other than Sambas district (Bengkayang, Pontianak, Landak, and Sanggau), Dayaks have been more tolerant of the Madurese, who are still able to travel back to their former settlements. However, some areas, such as Salatiga, have been occupied by the Dayaks.

18. Global IDP Database, May 21, 2003, p. 260.

19. On December 15, 2002, a clash between the two ethnic groups almost escalated into wider violence when a Malay was stabbed to death by a Madurese over a gambling dispute. One Malay and one Madurese were killed, sixteen Madurese houses were burned down, and 228 Madurese were evacuated from the areas, but further violence was prevented by quick and firm action by police. Associated Press Post, December 17, 2002.

20. The government has established the National Coordinating Board for Tackling Disasters and Refugees Management, which consists of thirteen departments. The coordinating minister of people's welfare (Menko Kesra) was chosen to chair the board, assisted by a secretary and the director-general of social assistance. The members are the ministers of social affairs, home affairs, defense, public works, communication, and health. Nongovernmental organizations among others are the Red Cross and the Indonesian Scouts. Other agencies, such as the Meteorological and Geophysical Agency and universities involved in scientific and technical work, assist the coordinating body. A working group is responsible for evaluating and preparing a study of recommendations to the chairman. The board formulated "National Policies on Refugee Management in Indonesia," which were discussed and agreed on in a cabinet meeting on September 25, 2001.

21. Associated Press Post, October 26, 2003.

22. See www.who.int/disasters/repo/7420.pdf.

23. In response to the Sampit conflict (Central Kalimantan, 2001), a joint statement was released by all eight bishops in Kalimantan and presented to President Abdurrahman Wahid in Jakarta on March 21, 2001. In their statement, the bishops reiterated that the ethnic conflicts in Kalimantan were not religious conflicts. They argued that the root causes of the conflicts were cultural differences, marginalization of the Dayaks, and the unsatisfactory resolution of past conflicts. See *Kalimantan Review* no. 68/Th/X, April 10–May 10, 2001, pp. 18–19.

24. The parishes in interior areas, such as in Menjalin, Landak district, were used during the 1997 conflict as a camp by Dayak women and children who fled their villages because they feared Madurese attacks. The archdiocese of Pontianak was also reported as getting involved in humanitarian work for the Sambas IDPs in Pontianak city. Women, children, and elderly people also sheltered in mosques and *pesantren* (traditional Islamic educational establishment) during violence, although they were not always exempted from attacks.

25. See *TIRAS*, no. 5/Thn. III, February 27, 1997. For K. H. Abdullah Schal's clarification, see D&R, no. 28/XXVIII, March 1, 1997; and *Forum Keadilan,* no. 24, Tahun V, March 10, 1997.

26. Refugees International, "Few Options for Madurese IDPs in West Kalimantan," March 29, 2002.

27. In all three conflicts (Sanggau Ledo, Sambas, and Sampit) reoccupation of lands abandoned by the Madurese emerged as an issue. See also note 17 above.

28. The most recent example of such dialogue was organized by LPPMKB and IKBMKB of the Madurese, PFKPM (Tebas, Pemangkat, Singkawang, and Sambas) of the Malay, and the police on October 25, 2003, in Singkawang. The Malay participants stated their willingness to accept the return of the Madurese IDPs provided that they were given more time to work within their communities at the grassroots level for acceptance. Associated Press Post, October 26, 2003.

29. There have been complaints by other ethnic groups and government officers regarding what they call the "commercialization" of the Dayak customary law to settle disputes. Heavy monetary fines are imposed—some reach almost 100 million rupiah—accompanied by threats and intimidation. Such practices are not consistent with Dayak customary law, which usually prescribes a settlement involving domestic animals or ceramics, not cash.

30. Refugees International, "Few Options for Madurese IDPs in West Kalimantan," March 29, 2002.

31. John Bamba, "'CNN-Effects' or 'Haatzaai Artikelen'?" Paper presented at the workshop "Covering Conflict for Kalimantan Journalist," held by the BBC and the British Council and Institut Dayakologi in Pontianak, October 22–27, 2001.

9.5.4

Maluku:
The Challenge of Peace

Samsu Rizal Panggabean

Maluku has been the scene of horrific intercommunal violence since early 1999, with thousands of people killed and hundreds of thousands driven from their homes. At the outset, the violence was primarily between an indigenous Christian community on the island of Ambon, and Muslim immigrants, but it evolved into more general violence between the Christian and Muslim communities on Ambon, and subsequently spread to many other islands in the provinces of Maluku and North Maluku. For the most part, order was restored throughout the archipelago by 2000, with the exception of Ambon. Despite leaders of both communities signing the government-sponsored Malino Declaration in February 2002, tensions remain high (as the sudden outbreak of new violence in late April 2004 showed) and few of the provisions included in that declaration have been implemented. A variety of other conflict transformation efforts involving some traditional approaches, as well as interventions from nongovernmental organizations (NGOs) and civil society, could serve as examples of strategies that hold out the promise of reducing tensions.

The eastern Indonesian island group known as Maluku (also called the Moluccas in English) forms the nation's largest archipelago, consisting of approximately 1,000 islands. Divided in 1999 into two provinces, North Maluku and Maluku, the archipelago is largely composed of the forested tops of volcanoes rising out of the sea. The two provinces, with a total population of about 2.1 million inhabitants, have been plagued by serious intercommunal violence since January 1999, particularly severe on the island of Ambon and in Ambon city, the capital of Maluku and the administrative center of the region.

Known to Chinese, Arab, Spanish, Portuguese, and Dutch traders as the "Spice Islands," Maluku was at various times colonized by Spain, Portugal, the Netherlands, and Britain beginning in the sixteenth century, and occupied by the Japanese during World War II. Early contacts with Arab traders led to

416

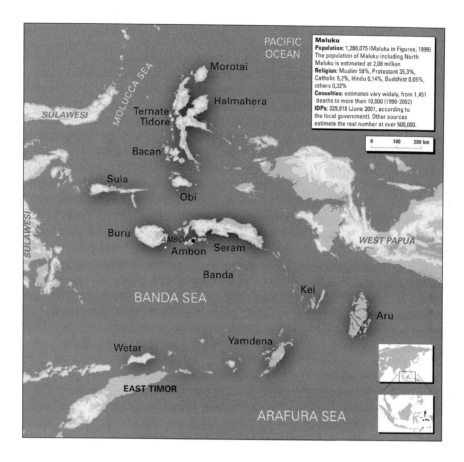

Maluku
Population: 1,286,075 (Maluku in Figures, 1999) The population of Maluku including North Maluku is estimated at 2,08 million
Religion: Muslim 59%, Protestant 35,3%, Catholic 5,2%, Hindu 0,14%, Buddhist 0,05%, others 0,32%
Casualties: estimates vary widely, from 1,451 deaths to more than 10,000 (1999-2002)
IDPs: 329,818 (June 2001, according to the local government). Other sources estimate the real number at over 500,000.

the introduction of Islam in the fifteenth century. The Portuguese brought Roman Catholicism to the islands in the sixteenth century, and the Dutch then introduced Reformed Protestantism in the seventeenth century.

Although much has been made of a long history of peaceful relations between Christians and Muslims in Maluku, the historical record available, writes anthropologist Dieter Bartels, "points to a much more complex picture filled with manipulation, intrigue, and rivalry." The Portuguese, Dutch, and Japanese all tried and "frequently succeeded with manipulation of the elites on [the] basis of religious affiliation, pitting Moslems against Christians." Over the years, and especially during the long Dutch colonial period, the divisions between Christians and Muslims were exploited for political purposes, with the Dutch colonial administration giving Christians preference in filling positions in the bureaucracy and military and, equally important, access to modern education. During the brief Japanese occupation, the situation was reversed. Nonetheless, writes Bartels, except when they were coerced by outside forces, "there seems to be little evidence that [the colonizers] ever instilled deep religious hatred into the general Ambonese population [and] there was never before a situation in the early colonial period when either Ambonese Moslem or Christian villages unified to fight . . . one another."[1]

The manipulative practices begun under colonialism, especially when leadership positions and jobs were at stake, were continued after Indonesian independence. For example, toward the end of President Suharto's long years in office, he used the Indonesian Muslim Intellectuals Association (ICMI), established in 1990, as a means to co-opt middle-class Muslims, and correspondingly, ICMI members used the association as a steppingstone to power. In the 1990s, in order to win support from Muslim groups, Suharto twice appointed Ambonese Muslims to the governorship, rather than giving the jobs to military officers who had previously enjoyed his favor.[2] On both occasions, the other candidate for the job was a Protestant.

While Maluku has traditionally had a very mixed population, the balance between Christians and Muslims has been shifting steadily over the past three decades, primarily due to the "transmigration" policies encouraged under Suharto, which resulted in a steady flow of predominantly Muslim immigrants from more densely populated islands moving to less densely populated regions, including Maluku. The Muslim population in Maluku increased from slightly less than 50 percent of the total in 1971 to nearly 60 percent by 1999. During the same period, the Christian population declined from about 47 percent to roughly 40 percent.[3] The impact of immigration is clearly evident in the increase in nonnative Muslims, from about 5 percent of the total Maluku population in 1971 to more than 14 percent in 1995, with that trend continuing. A substantial proportion of these immigrants came from South Sulawesi, and most of them were ethnically Buton, Bugis, or Makassar.

As part of the transmigration policy, these new arrivals were given land that had usually been taken from the indigenous population. The government also built facilities such as markets, roads, schools, and health centers for the transmigrants. From 1969 to 1999, 25,319 households (almost 100,000 people) were transmigrated to Maluku and North Maluku, with more than half settling in Central Maluku, especially on the islands of Ambon, Seram, and Buru. Additional migration not related to the government policy also took place, though the number of these unofficial migrants is difficult to estimate. Most of these migrants also came from South Sulawesi, with substantial numbers also immigrating from Java. Again, the vast majority of these immigrants were Muslim.

Not surprisingly, the transmigration policy and unchecked migration have been an important source of tensions and discontent in Maluku society. The loss of large tracts of land with little or no compensation, and the economic success and domination of the newcomers, have resulted in long-smoldering resentment among the native population. Most of the affected villages were Christian, whose the inhabitants felt their way of life threatened by the influx of so many Muslim immigrants. In the 1970s, when *transmigrasi* was barely under way, the old villages were sleepy and for the most part only accessible by sea. By the late 1990s, they were all connected by roads along which many new businesses and settlements were located, almost exclusively owned by nonindigenous Muslims.[4] During this same period, Maluku was being rapidly urbanized, a factor that some observers believed added to the sense of insecurity felt among Christians, especially those living in Ambon city.[5]

Another contentious issue in Maluku has concerned the issue of representation. As noted above, under the Dutch colonial administration, Christians had a privileged position with more opportunities for good jobs and education. The result was that when Indonesia became independent, Christians were better prepared than Muslims to participate in many walks of modern life in Maluku, and could more easily move into professional jobs. Denied access to education or positions in the bureaucracy, Muslims came to dominate the marketplace during the colonial period. After independence, when Muslims and Christians had equal access to education and more opportunities for social mobility, the situation began to change, and gradually more and more Muslims were able to compete for positions at all levels of society. The struggle between the two communities for economic and political power was set in motion.

For a long time, Muslims placed a priority on securing representation in government and the bureaucracy. They perceived that they were underrepresented in civil service jobs, especially in Ambon city, and also complained that Muslim students and lecturers suffered from discrimination at the Christian-dominated University of Pattimura. For their part, Christians also felt aggrieved as Muslims, over time, came to occupy more and more government jobs at the provincial level. Christians feared that they were losing the dominant role they had traditionally played.

Another factor that may have contributed to the violence was the breakdown in the traditional structures of governance as a consequence of Indonesian policies on local government. In the 1970s, the central government of Indonesia introduced laws to establish uniform institutions of local government throughout the country. As a consequence, the traditional village leaders (called Raja, Bapa Raja, or Latu Pati) were replaced by village heads and traditional authority was replaced by village government. The traditional role of the Rajas as conflict managers and arbitrators was significantly weakened. In addition, the status of land also changed. In previous times, the land usually belonged to the clan. With the new arrangement, however, land could be registered and bought and sold. As a result, the sale of land was practiced widely, including sale to migrants from South Sulawesi.

The replacement of the clan-based system with a village government system headed by a low-ranking official of the Indonesian bureaucracy was more egalitarian and did make it possible for migrant communities of ethnic Bugis, Butonese, and Makassarese to be represented and to have members of their own communities serve as village head. But these village heads lacked the authority the old Rajas had enjoyed, and when conflict broke out, there were fewer people at the local level with the ability to stop it.[6]

Especially during the "New Order" regime under Suharto, religious education within both the Muslim and the Christian communities tended to emphasize the internal and exclusive dimension of religion at the expense of the external and inclusive dimension. Religious leaders "enjoined their congregations to abandon remnant traditional beliefs."[7] The Christianization process within the Christian community and Islamization process within the Muslim community weakened the *adat,* or customary, institutions and "the ideas of Moslem-Christian brotherhood."[8]

At the same time, this process of religious revitalization increasingly brought religion to center stage in society, with language and religious symbols assuming greater importance with respect to matters such as citizenship, ethnicity, and competition for economic and political power. Within this context, communal and local identity (Ambonese Christians on the one side and Ambonese and non-Ambonese Muslims on the other), national identity (Indonesian Christians and Indonesian Muslims), and international/global identity (Maluku Muslims as part of Islamic universalism and Maluku Christian as part of Christian universalism) took on renewed importance.

The violence in Maluku took place within the context of the Asian economic crisis and the New Order's collapse. With the central government weakened and discredited by economic and political crisis, it was incapable of playing a useful role as conflict manager or of maintaining security, and was unable to intervene, when violence first broke out, to restore order. At the beginning of the riots in 1999, it was primarily the migrant ethnic groups who were the targets of violence perpetrated by Christians. But as the violence continued, and as most of the migrants escaped, it became more and more a conflict between the Christian and Muslim communities. Thus it was the early failure of the police and military to control the situation that transformed the conflict in Ambon from an unfortunate but possibly containable one directed at the migrants into a far more widespread and dangerous "intercommunal" or "interreligious" conflict.

As the violence in Maluku dragged on, the parties to the conflict faced the need to mobilize supporters and resources in support of their struggle. Here again, religion and religious symbols, idioms, and doctrines were used and abused for mobilization purposes. Religious leaders preached defamatory sermons, portraying, for instance, the "enemy" not only as the enemy of God but also as the enemy of the state. Christians were accused of supporting a separatist political movement known as Republik Maluku Selatan (RMS; Republic of South Moluccas). Mosques and churches were drawn into the quagmire and turned into armed fortresses. Holy books and traditions were exploited to persecute members of the opposing community and to point accusing fingers at coreligionists who were not considered "militant" enough; some were labeled as traitors. Hence the violent process of dehumanization intensified within the religious communities in Maluku. Voices advocating peaceful coexistence and tolerance were increasingly viewed with suspicion and suppressed. Just when cooperation and communication between advocates of peace in the different communities was most needed, it was stifled because of the very real risk facing those trying to achieve reconciliation.

Another consequence of the failure to quickly resolve the conflict and restore order was the involvement of forces coming from other parts of Indonesia, and even from outside Indonesia, in what had been a relatively localized conflict. In particular, the arrival in May 2000 of fighters equipped with modern weapons from Laskar Jihad (Holy War Forces) in support of the Muslim community, fundamentally changed the nature of the conflict. Laskar Jihad's arrival reflected, among other things, the inability of the security apparatus to control entry to Maluku and betrayed a pro-Muslim bias among some elements within the military and the government. Similar militias were subsequently organized in the Christian community.

Conflict Dynamics

The violence in Maluku is usually portrayed in sweeping generalizations. The general image produced is of an all-consuming war involving Christian and Muslim communities everywhere in Maluku and North Maluku and continuing unabated from 1999 onward. The true situation has been quite different, with the nature, intensity, and duration of the violence varying significantly from place to place. While continuing violence occurred in the city of Ambon from 1999 to 2002, violence in some districts occurred only during 1999 and order was quickly restored, while in other districts violence only erupted for a relatively short period in 2000. There have been few attempts to differentiate between the nature and extent of violence in different parts of Maluku, to identify which villages and which subdistricts were most severely affected, or to quantify casualties (both deaths and injuries) according to where and when they occurred.[9]

The violence involving members of Christian and Muslim communities in Ambon city was sparked by an argument between a Christian bus driver and a Muslim youth from the Bugis ethnic group on January 19, 1999, coinciding with Idul Fithri, the biggest Muslim holiday in Indonesia, a time when police forces are understaffed because officers take leave for the holiday. This seemingly minor altercation spun out of control and turned into uncontrolled rioting throughout Ambon city, which continued until January 23. Surrounding villages were also drawn into the violence, which included surprise attacks on members of the opposing community, arson, and pitched battles with stones and machetes. Initially, the fighting was mainly between Ambonese Christians and Muslim migrants from South Sulawesi. Later, Ambonese Muslims were also involved in the fighting. In the following months, more incidents took place in the Ambon city and later in other parts of Ambon island.

Just days before the outbreak of violence in Ambon, between January 15 and January 17, Christian and Muslim communities had clashed in Dobo, in the district of Southeast Maluku. The local security apparatus had been unable to manage the violence and requested support from Ambon. The provincial police had responded by sending a mobile brigade on January 19—just hours before the violence broke out in Ambon city.

After the communal riots in Ambon city, violence spread to Central Maluku in February 1999, although the number of incidents was much lower than in the Ambon city. Then, in March, violence spread to the Kei Islands of Southeast Maluku. Here, the most serious incidents, those resulting in deaths,

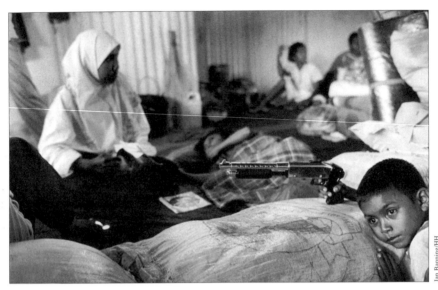

Jan Banning/HH

Ambon 2000. Around six hundred refugees,
Muslims from the island of Saparua, stay in an improvised camp in Tulehu town.

only took place during 1999. Beginning in June 1999, North Maluku was also afflicted by communal violence, but once order was restored in early 2000, the violence ceased altogether. Clearly, the conflict dynamics have been quite different in North Maluku and the Kei Islands as compared to the ongoing violence that has plagued Ambon, including Ambon city, and the nearby Lease Islands. In fact, even in Maluku province, the great majority of serious violent incidents (violence-related deaths, arson, ambushes, shootings, bombings, lynching, violent demonstrations, etc.) occurred in Ambon city, where, in addition, destruction of property was also especially severe.[10]

As violence continued in Ambon city, the conflict became more "weaponized," with more incidents involving handmade guns and bombs. Indeed, incidents involving the use of guns and bombs quadrupled between 1999 and 2001, from nineteen to seventy-six, before a reduction to fifty-two in 2002. Bombings in 1999 numbered eighteen and increased steadily each year to sixty-nine in 2002. But even as this weaponization was occurring, the frequency of violent incidents was decreasing outside Ambon city. Clashes involving Christian and Muslim villagers decreased from sixty-six in 1999, to thirty-two in 2000, to seven in 2001, and to one in 2002. And attacks by one village on another followed a similar pattern, decreasing from twenty-nine in 1999 to just two in 2002.[11]

As the conflict escalated and became increasingly weaponized, the role of security forces took an unfortunate turn, with police—especially local police—and troops drawn into the conflict. In Maluku, these "contaminated" security forces fought alongside their coreligionists; served as patrons, suppliers, and sellers of guns and ammunition; and provided intelligence. They also trained militias and taught them how to make bombs, including, for example, using leftover bombs from World War II found in the coastal waters around Maluku. In addition, as conflict continued, these security forces developed vested interests in the conflict. Members of the security apparatus became involved in economic activities and profited from the conflict, by engaging in trade, providing intervillage and interisland transportation/escort, and selling protection. As reported by the International Crisis Group, "While security forces have no desire to return to the all-out conflict of 1999–2000, their financial interests are served by a high level of public nervousness. Occasional bomb explosions and shootings are sufficient to persuade businesspeople and property-owners to pay for special protection. On several occasions bomb explosions in Ambon have been traced to low-ranking military."[12]

Where the police and the military ended up taking sides in the conflict, as occurred in Maluku, the result was that the violence persisted, and segregation within the security sector was reinforced. Mistrust and suspicion pervaded the police and the military forces, and was prevalent between police and the military, between different police units, between different military units, and between the police and the military on the one hand and the Christian and Muslim militias on the other hand. On several occasions, the Civil Emergency Authority created joint stations where the military and the police were directed to serve together to avoid clashes between security sector units.[13] Such disarray within the security sector served to reinforce the public sense of insecurity and vulnerability.[14]

On the other hand, the military played a far more constructive role in North Maluku and thus contributed to the relatively quick cessation of hostilities there, with no serious incidents after mid-2000. This can be attributed to both the presence of security forces in the area and the efforts of local community leaders and local government. On many occasions after the violence ended, the Indonesian armed forces and the Indonesian police facilitated and supported reconciliation processes, by conveying, for instance, invitations to community leaders in different towns and *kecamatan,* escorting community leaders who sought to initiate the reconciliation process, and providing security at reconciliation meetings.[15]

One of the most serious negative impacts of the conflict was on the health-care system. Health workers including doctors, nurses, and paramedics, who were identified by their religion, had difficulties moving from village to village. Ambulances were similarly denied free access. The violence also caused shortages of drugs, problems of access to health centers and hospitals for individuals and whole communities of the "wrong" religion (many hospitals and health centers only provided service for one religious community), changes in the referral system for medical treatment, and higher prices for medicine and health services. Beyond, that, many hospitals and health centers were damaged or destroyed.

As the conflict escalated, several important developments crucially influenced the course of events. One of these was the arrival of Laskar Jihad in

Maluku, beginning in May 2000. Estimates of its numbers vary from fifteen hundred to several thousand. Laskar Jihad forces were moved into the Muslim neighborhood in Ambon city as well as other villages on the island. Some Laskar Jihad forces also reached Seram and Buru islands and North Maluku. Laskar Jihad believed that the central government was incapable of protecting their fellow Muslims and that the situation for Muslims was worsening as the conflict continued. Through radio broadcasts, publications, and public statements, Laskar Jihad mobilized both humanitarian and armed support for the Muslim cause in Maluku. They also advocated the arrest, trial, and conviction of the Christians they accused of instigating the conflict in January 1999. Although at the beginning few Muslims were enthusiastic about the presence of the Laskar Jihad and most did not identify closely with the militia, many were grateful to it for its role in fending off Christian militias and shifting the balance of power between the two conflicting communities.[16]

Christian leaders saw the presence of the Laskar Jihad, especially the armed elements, as a key obstacle to a longer peace. One response was the establishment of Front Kedaulatan Maluku (FKM; Maluku Sovereignty Front) in June 2000. The Civil Emergency Authority, which had been installed to govern Maluku on June 26, 2000,[17] recognized that Laskar Jihad was impeding efforts to reestablish order and attempted on several occasions to persuade the Jihad forces to scale back their presence in Maluku and to end their incitement to violence. Toward the end of 2000, the Civil Emergency Authority demanded that the central government of Indonesia prevent Laskar Jihad forces from departing from the harbors in Java and South Sulawesi. But the presence of Laskar Jihad continued in Ambon city and in other parts of Maluku until it dissolved itself in October 2002.

Within the Christian community, the FKM engaged in provocative behavior, and the presence of thugs and militias such as Laskar Yesus also exacerbated the conflict in Maluku. Like Laskar Jihad, the FKM concluded that the government of Indonesia was unable to provide security in Maluku and demanded a humanitarian intervention by the international community.

Accounts of the number of conflict-related deaths between 1999 and 2002 vary widely. Official figures put the toll at 1,451 deaths (including 66 troops and 25 police) and 2,140 injured,[18] with about two-thirds of the deaths and injuries in Ambon city.[19] Other estimates of the death toll go as high as 10,000.[20] The local government estimated in June 2001 that the conflict had resulted in 329,818 internally displaced persons (IDPs), while others cite a figure of about 400,000. Approximately 75 percent of the IDPs remained in Maluku, while an estimated 100,000 fled to Southeast Sulawesi. The violence also resulted in the destruction of some 6,488 houses and 243 shops, as well as 66 churches and 36 mosques, and serious damage to the state provincial university and other schools, governmental offices including the governor's office, and as mentioned above, healthcare facilities.[21] Finally, as a result of the conflict, many islands have become strictly segregated along religious lines.

Almost two years of relative peace came to an abrupt end in late April 2004, with a sudden week of violence and a death toll of 38. Hundreds of buildings were torched and thousands of people again fled their homes. The Christian-Muslim clashes in Ambon were sparked by a parade and the raising of their independence flag by the hard-line group of Christian separatists, the RMS, celebrating the anniversary of their movement. Twenty-four hours later, 20 people lay dead. Controversy grew, as the violence was widely blamed on the security forces for not taking preventative measures and appearing unable to stop the fighting. Amidst breakdowns in peace talks and anticipated reprisals, officials attempted to restore order by replacing the Maluku police chief, while deploying hundreds of reinforcements and arresting leaders of the RMS.

Official Conflict Management

The conflict in Maluku started during the presidency of President Habibie, after the thirty-year regime of President Suharto ended in May 1998. Habibie's presidency, however, lasted only until October 1999. Abdurrahman Wahid replaced Habibie but soon delegated the responsibility for dealing with conflict in Maluku and North Maluku to Vice President Megawati Sukarnoputri. President Wahid was skeptical about her chances, however, stating that only the conflicting communities in Maluku could bring the violence to an end.

One of the most significant measures taken by the central government of President Wahid was to declare a civil emergency in Maluku and North Maluku on June 26, 2000. This emergency status provided a wide range of powers to the governors of Maluku and North Maluku, the regional military commander, the regional police chief, and the office of the prosecutor so that they could effectively act to restore order and security. A "Civil Emergency Authority" was given the power to issue decrees, and to limit civil rights and individual freedom.

In Maluku, the local government tried to mitigate the violence through dialogue and reconciliation. In 1999, for instance, the government brought together community leaders from different backgrounds and religions several times. Each time, the participants and the representatives of the local government issued declarations pledging their commitment to restraint and the termination of violence.[22] Several times during the course of conflict, local government also created reconciliation teams with representation from various communities. For instance, in March 1999 the local government created Pusat Rujuk Sosial (PRS; Center for Social Reconciliation) with a mandate to assist the peace and reconciliation efforts of the government in Maluku. The PRS suggested that the root causes of the violence in Maluku need to be examined and that community-based peaceful coexistence efforts should be strengthened, and recommended the establishment of security posts in violence-prone villages.[23]

The Civil Emergency Authority failed to end the violence, contributing to the perception among the Christian and Muslim communities in Maluku that the violence had in fact been engineered from Jakarta. In early 2002 the central government engaged in discussions with both the Christian leaders and Muslim leaders of Maluku, during which leaders from both communities agreed to attend meetings scheduled for February 11–12, 2002, in Malino, South Sulawesi, where they would discuss issues related to ending the conflict and rebuilding the violence-torn society. This was the highest-profile meeting to date, and was attended by thirty-five Muslim and thirty-five Christian participants. The government's mediation team included the coordinating minister of welfare, the coordinating minister for political and security affairs, the national police head, the governor and deputy governor of Maluku, the governor of South Sulawesi, the regional police chief, the regional military commander, the head of the Maluku legislature, and the mayor of Ambon.

At the end of the two-day talks, the participants agreed to the following:

- To end all conflicts and disputes.
- To abide by due process of law enforcement fairly, faithfully, honestly, and impartially, supported by the communities, with an understanding that security officers were also committed to carry out their duties in a professional manner.
- To reject and oppose all kinds of separatist activities that might threaten the unity and sovereignty of the Unitary State of the Republic of Indonesia, including support for the Republic of South Moluccas (RMS).
- That as citizens of the Unitary State of the Republic of Indonesia, the people of Maluku have the right to live and work legally and fairly anywhere in the Republic of Indonesia nationwide, and others have the right to live and work in Maluku, as long as they respect local culture and law, and maintain order.
- To ban and disarm illegal armed organizations, groups, or militias, in accordance with existing law. Outside parties that disturb the peace in the Maluku will be expelled.
- To establish an independent national investigation team to investigate among other things, the tragic incident on January 19, 1999; organizations including the Maluku Sovereign Front, the Republic of South Maluku, the Christian Republic of South Moluccas, Laskar Jihad, and Laskar Kristus; the practice of coercive conversion; and human rights violations.
- To call for the voluntary return of refugees to their homes, and the return of their property.
- To rehabilitate social, economic, and public infrastructures, particularly educational, health, religious, and housing facilities, with support from the Indonesian government.
- That the maintenance of law and order depends on the military and the police coordinating their efforts and pursuing their mission with firmness and resolve; and that the proper functioning of the security services requires reorganization and reequipping of some units and facilities.
- That to ensure good relations and harmony among all communities and religions in Maluku, all evangelical activities must respect the diversity of its peoples and acknowledge local culture.
- That to support the rehabilitation of Pattimura University for the common good, recruitment of staff and students should be transparent, based

on the principle of fairness and a commitment to maintaining quality standards.

Although the Malino Declaration provided a framework for moving forward, implementation was beset by problems. The committees formed in Malino, consisting of representatives of the local government and the communities, failed to implement their mandate because the central government and the Civil Emergency Authority failed to provide them with the support they needed and did not possess the political will to ensure success. The central government failed to fulfill its promises to provide funds for the committee to implement programs such as rehabilitation and reconstruction, and the local governments under the Civil Emergency Authority continued to work independently of the committees. Beyond that, members of the committees did not even manage to meet as intended in the agreement.

Lack of support from the security apparatus was also evident from several crucial incidents that sabotaged the Malino peace process. On April 3, 2002, a bomb exploded in the Christian part of the city of Ambon, killing six people and injuring many others. Several hours later, the office of the governor and provincial government of Maluku was burned. On April 25, a flag-raising incident, with the flags of the Forum Kedaulatan Maluku and the RMS displayed in many parts of heavily guarded Ambon city, also undermined confidence in the Malino Declaration. Three days later, an ambush at the predominantly Christian village of Soya caused twelve deaths. Christian thugs, deeply infiltrated by the security apparatus, were believed to be involved in the ambush.

Besides these official efforts to resolve the conflict at the national and regional levels, the United Nations and the International Committee of the Red Cross, both present in Maluku to address the humanitarian crisis, were also engaged in peripheral ways in conflict resolution activities.[24] Agencies working under the UN umbrella included the Office for the Coordination of Humanitarian Affairs, the UN Children's Fund, the UN Development Programme, the UN High Commissioner for Refugees, the World Food Programme, and the World Health Organization (WHO). Their activities and programs, some of which were implemented in cooperation with NGOs, included projects to bring Muslims and Christians under the same programmatic umbrella, and peacebuilding and conflict resolution programs, such as WHO's Health as a Bridge for Peace program in Maluku in 2000–2001. The activities and programs of the UN in Maluku, however, were hindered by the several violent incidents that resulted in the UN withdrawing its representatives from Maluku and only returning when tensions eased.

Multi-Track Diplomacy

As decentralized responses to the violence, conflict resolution approaches drawing on traditional values and institutions have been widely discussed and debated in Maluku. One of the traditional systems for containing conflict within the pluralistic society characteristic of Maluku is the *pela* system, or an "intervillage alliance system."[25] The *pela* system can be found in most villages on Ambon, Haruku, Saparua, Nusalaut, and Seram islands. Similar alliance systems can also be found on many other islands of Maluku and North Maluku provinces. On the islands of Maluku, most villages are monoreligious in the sense that the entire population of the village is either Muslim or Christian. Therefore, the intervillage alliance can be, in effect, an interreligious alliance.[26] According to Bartels:

> *Pela* alliances are concluded between two or more villages and, in a few rare cases, between clans from different villages. With the exception of the Leitimor mountains on Ambon Island where several neighboring villages are engaged in such pacts, *pela* partners live usually far apart and are often located on different islands. Most alliances are between Christian villages but a considerable number is between Christian and Moslem villages, thus spanning across religious boundaries. Purely Moslem *pela* do not exist.[27]

Historically, the *pela* system has played an important role in containing conflict between Muslim and Christian villages. To quote Bartels again:

> Because of the existence of the *pela* system, any potential antagonism between Ambonese Moslems and Christians was held to a minimum, as opposed to internecine strife so common between the adherents of these religions throughout the world. On the practical level, there was a marked increase of economic exchange and many churches, mosques and schools were being built with the generous help of *pela* partners who supplied labor, work material, money and/or foodstuffs to make those undertakings possible without governmental aid. After a project was finished, the pela partners arrived for its inauguration, and, in case of a church or mosque, both Christians and Moslems entered it together for a common service.[28]

Unfortunately, the *pela* system has no relevance to the villages and neighborhoods of migrants who came from other ethnic groups, notably Makassar, Bugis, and Buton who migrated to Maluku. Nor does the *pela* system apply to the relatively new villages and residential areas that contain families from different religious backgrounds. Moreover, as a mechanism for containing conflict, the *pela* system has been further weakened by two processes: religious education that tends to undermine traditional *adat* (customary beliefs and cultural norms handed down by the ancestors), and the increasing centralization that occurred under the New Order.[29]

In 1999 a new law on local government was introduced that replaced the centralized approach of the New Order with greater autonomy at the village level. While in several provinces of Indonesia this law has facilitated the reemergence of traditional and local forms of governance, violence in Maluku has delayed the implementation of local government reforms. In early 2003, with the support of Baku Bae, a local organization advocating reconciliation, a gathering of Rajas and Latu Patis (traditional leaders) in Ambon ended with the creation of the Latu Pati Forum to discuss governance at village level.[30]

In at least one case, in the village of Waiyame, a less traditional approach was used with considerable success to maintain order. Waiyame (whose name means "water of life") is a village of 5,000 people and Ambon island's largest oil depot. Originally a Christian village, Waiyame now has both Muslim and Christian residents, most of whom are educators, civil servants, and middle-class families. In the older section of the village, there are also residents who are less well-off. The village serves as a commercial hub for surrounding villages and is known for its popular vegetable market. Although it received a significant number of Christian and Muslim IDPs after the riots, Waiyame was the only village on Ambon that was not hit by communal violence. To prevent the conflict from spreading to the village, local Christian and the Muslim leaders created a crisis team, referred to as "Team 20," composed of ten Christians and ten Muslims.[31] According to some, the government's need to protect the oil depot meant that it applied pressure to encourage the community leaders to maintain order. As conflict resolution specialist Christopher W. Moore writes:

> The mission or purpose of Team 20 was to prevent, manage and resolve inter-religious differences in Waiyame, and to stop the spread of violence that had divided the rest of the country from destroying the village. Team 20, as an informal organization, initially based its credibility and strength on the reputation and respect held by members of each community for its individual members, but its leaders believed that they needed formal legitimacy and authority to be more effective.[32]

Team 20 developed a set of behavioral norms for the Waiyame community, including sanctions and penalties for the violators. These norms explicitly embraced freedom of religion and condemned any type of harassment because of religious belief or affiliation, required all rumors about religious conflict to be reported to Team 20 for investigation, and banned all weapons, fighting, defacing of religious buildings, and alcohol consumption in the village. Notably, the norms also specified that a person could not be buried in the village if that person had been killed because of his or her participation in the interreligious conflict. Enforcement reverted to the community; that is, if Muslims broke the rules, they were punished by Muslim leaders, and if Christians violated the norms, their cases were handled in their own community.[33]

Since the outbreak of the conflict in Maluku, NGOs have played an increasingly significant role. In Ambon city, the number of NGOs has increased from about 30 or 40 in 1999 to more than 500 in 2002. Most of the new NGOs are concerned with emergency relief and humanitarian assistance, including the provision of food, water, shelter, and sanitation to IDPs. Many of the local NGOs in Maluku have received substantial support from international NGOs.[34]

During the first year of the violence, there were efforts at the local level and within the NGO network to organize regular meetings between Christian and Muslim leaders and representatives of the NGOs. One of these forums is TIRUS, a humanitarian volunteer team, which was very active at the beginning of the violence. More than sixty NGOs from the Christian and Muslim communities participated in TIRUS activities. The forum has three coordinators, representing the Muslim, Protestant, and Catholic communities respectively. Another intercommunal network is the Caring Women's Movement (GPP), a prominent civil society group formed in September 1999 as a moral movement against violence. More than forty women activists from the Protestant, Muslim, and Catholic communities are involved in the GPP. In addition to organizing rallies against the violence in Maluku, the GPP has also supported women and children victims of violence.

In addition to its work described above on local governance, the Baku Bae movement, formed in March 2000, has been engaged in other ways to bring together local NGOs and community leaders. With the support of civil society organizations in Jakarta, Baku Bae has been an important civil society response to the violence and conflict in Maluku, organizing reconciliation workshops attended by participants from different backgrounds, and promoting intercommunal engagements and economic transactions.

Baku Bae also created several "neutral zones" with the help of the villagers in Maluku. These neutral zones created safe areas on the borders between Christian and Muslim districts for business, education, and the delivery of health services. One zone was established at Nania village, near the Christian town of Passo at the isthmus between the predominantly Muslim Leihitu peninsula in the north of the island and the predominantly Christian Leitimor peninsula in the south.[35] A second zone was at Pohon Pule near the center of Ambon. Sidewalk markets were set up at both Nania and Pohon Pule, where Christians and Muslims participated as vendors and shoppers.

In the Pohon Pule area, Pattimura University was able to establish a temporary campus (to replace the campus destroyed in July 2000) and the army hospital was open to Muslims and Christians seeking medical treatment.[36] Another informal market sprang up in a narrow "neutral" zone at Mardika.[37] Neutral zones, however, have not gone unchallenged. During the latter part of 2001, several bombs exploded near markets, killing some and wounding others.[38]

Baku Bae also facilitated meetings between journalists and lawyers from the two communities, who gathered to discuss ways they might support the peace process. In cooperation with Aliansi Jurnalis Independen (AJI), Baku Bae supported a meeting of Muslim and Christian journalists in March 2001 in Bogor, West Java. This meeting resulted in the establishment of the Maluku Media Center in the neutral zone at Mardika, in Ambon city. This program contributed remarkably to more balanced reporting in Ambon. In January 2002, Baku Bae also held a workshop for Christian and Muslim lawyers in Jakarta. Among other groups for which workshops are planned are intellectuals, teachers, military and police personnel, NGOs, religious leaders, and businesspeople.[39]

Beyond these local efforts, a Jakarta-based NGO, Go-East Institute, also engaged in peacebuilding activities focusing on Maluku, with its sponsorship of the "National Dialogue of the Maluku and North Maluku Community," held near Tual on the Kei Islands in Southeast Maluku. The event was attended by 1,500 Muslims and Christians from all parts of the region. The conference issued a statement promising to continue peace efforts and proposed "the use of local traditions as a meeting point for accommodating the interests of the different groups in the province." It also proposed that "all local traditional leaders, or *Bapa Radja,* once again take the lead . . . but at the same time support state law and guarantee the acceptance of all migrants living in the province."[40] During the meeting, however, some Muslim representatives from Ambon refused to sign the agreement. The head of the Muslim students' association Himpunan Mahasiswa Islam (HMI) in Ambon said that those representatives "could be rejected by our members" if they signed.[41]

In addition to local and national NGOs and civil society groups, international NGOs are also very active in providing aid and other resources to the communities and local NGOs. These include Save the Children (emergency education programs, child protection programs, and peacebuilding among children), CARDI (shelter, water, and sanitation projects as well as education and economic empowerment programs), and the ACF (food distribution, water and sanitation program, and seeds and tools distribution). Among the many international NGOs coming to Maluku, Mercy Corps International (MCI) is noted for its activities in building the capacity of local NGOs in Maluku. It also runs a water and sanitation program and has organized workshops on disaster response. In the field of community development, MCI provided microcredits and organized training on microfinance and financial management for local NGOs. It also supported the establishment of an NGO center in the city of Ambon, to provide a neutral place for broad-based NGOs to operate. In Central Maluku, International Medical Corps helped to reactivate a hospital affected by the violence and to start up an outpatient clinic in August 2001. The presence of the hospital facilitates further reconciliation between the two communities.

As the incidents of violence have decreased and the emergency situation has eased, many NGOs and international NGOs have shifted their activities toward peace advocacy and peacebuilding. More and more NGOs are trying to bring together different ethnic and religious groups under the same program or activity. After the Malino Declaration, many local NGOs became involved in peace and reconciliation promotion. Some served bridging functions between state and civil society.

The experience of NGOs working in Maluku during the past four years raises several issues for consideration. First, with regard to the relationships between NGOs and local government, differences in working styles and organizational culture sometimes create difficulties. NGOs in Maluku sometimes have to play by the rules set by the local bureaucracy, which tries to extort money from their programs in the same way it did when dealing with development projects during peacetime. Second, capacity building is badly needed among the NGOs working in conflict areas such as Maluku. The local NGOs view themselves as important actors in public education and catalysts of peaceful change in Maluku, but to succeed, they require skills and knowledge in conflict management, facilitation, and community organizing. Third, NGOs need to say up front what they can do and what they cannot do in Maluku in order to avoid creating unrealistic expectations. The image of NGOs as charity organizations delivering services to the communities should be avoided.

Prospects

Poor governance, a weakened central government, demoralized, divided, and indecisive security forces, outside intervention, and unresolved social tensions brought about by changing demographics all contributed to the tragic communal violence in Maluku.

Although the Megawati government did finally bring the parties together to produce the Malino Declaration, the basic tenets of this agreement have not been implemented. This failure has several sources: the central government failed to make necessary commitments for implementation of the declaration, the communities were too fragmented to be able to work together to implement the agreement, and both the local government and the representatives of the communities did not work out the details of the relationships between themselves. The deadline to hand in the weapons set by the Penguasa Darurat Sipil Daerah Maluku was initially March 31, 2002. Nevertheless, this could not be accomplished and most weapons still remain in the hands of the society. A sense of extreme insecurity has prevented people, especially youth, from handing in their weapons, and there have not been any meaningful efforts to deal with these problems. The Malino Declaration has also been opposed by several groups. On March 1, 2002, the Forum for Moslem Baguala Women organized strikes to protest the shutting down of the Suara Perjuangan Muslim Maluku radio station. They also denounced TVRI Station Ambon and RRI Ambon as acting provocatively during the conflict and demanded that their activities be halted. Clearly then, despite the relative lack of violence currently, the situation remains extremely volatile.

Another issue facing post-Malino Maluku is the resettlement of internally displaced persons. Many IDPs have returned to their houses only to find that they have been occupied by new settlers who moved into them during the conflict. This has often triggered open confrontation and remains a source of potential violence. There have also been cases where certain groups refuse to allow members of other religious groups to return to their villages. Again, these issues must be addressed if peace and stability are to be restored.

Recommendations

In order to address prospects, taking into account the conflict dynamics, and to increase successful conflict transformation the following recommendations are made:

- The central and local government should push the implementation of the Malino Declaration, especially by specifying its general statements and working out the details of monitoring the implementation. Particular emphasis should be put on the principles of reconciliation, tolerance, mercy, justice, and truth contained in the declaration. The resettlement of IDPs mandated by the declaration should also be implemented by using a comprehensive approach.

• A new, revived *pela* arrangement should be established. Many people still believe in the traditional institution of *pela* as an alliance and cooperation agreement involving villages. It is also important considering its potential as a decentralized mechanism of conflict management. It can be modified and reinvigorated as an alliance system involving villages without regard to the religious and ethnic backgrounds of the populations in those villages. By using territory and place of residence as bases of alliances and not religion or ethnicity, the traditional institution can be adapted to the new situation in Maluku.

• The Waiyame model should be emulated. In contrast to the *pela* system, which focuses on intervillage cooperation, the model is appropriate for conflict management at the village level.

• The city of Ambon, with its two subdistricts of Sirimau and Nusaniwe, should be treated differently. As an urban area where the influence of traditional leaders is weaker, and the traditional norms and customs do not hold sway over much of the population, the city needs other forms of governance based on the participation of civil society, religious leaders, the police, and local government.

• Reforms of the police should be pursued. Police in Maluku suffered from corruption, poor training, low salaries, lack of discipline, and abuse of power. Nevertheless, police are indispensable for maintaining law and order and protecting citizens in Maluku. Significant changes are needed within the police organization. The police need to view their role in society differently—not just as security apparatus and law enforcers but also as "problem solvers." Skills, knowledge, and practice in community policing, especially in postconflict communities, should be introduced to the police forces in Maluku.

• Reforms of military institutions should be intensified. During the conflict, the number of troops deployed to Maluku was much greater than the number of police officers. In mid-2002, there were about four times as many members of the army (more than 4,100) in Ambon as there were police. At the provincial level, one and a half police battalions were deployed, compared to ten army battalions. Many within the military were corrupt and lacking in discipline. There were indications that army special forces personnel were involved in instigating violence prior to, and soon after, the Malino Declaration. The army also upgraded the status of its headquarters in Maluku. As a consequence, the army played a greater role in dealing with security affairs in Maluku, although the formal authority was in the hands of the police. While Indonesia was committed to demilitarization of its society, the reverse occurred in Maluku, so military and political reforms suffered a setback. Therefore, efforts to reduce the military's role in Maluku and to improve the performance of army personnel should be a priority.

Resources

Reports
European Commission Conflict Prevention Assessment Mission. "Indonesia." By Nick Mawdsley, Monica Tanuhandaru, and Kees Holman. March 2002.
Human Rights Watch. "Indonesia: The Violence in Ambon." March 1999.
———. "Mollucan Islands Communal Violence in Indonesia." June 2000.
International Crisis Group. "Indonesia: Overcoming Murder and Violence in Maluku." ICG Asia Report no. 10. Jakarta/Brussels, December 19, 2000.
———. "Indonesia: The Search for Peace in Maluku." ICG Asia Report no. 31. February 8, 2002.
———. "Indonesia's Maluku Crisis: The Issues." ICG Briefing Paper. Jakarta/Brussels, July 19, 2000.
Project Ploughshares. "Indonesia-Molucca Islands (1999 First Combat Deaths)." *Armed Conflict Report 2002.* Last update January 2002. Available at www.ploughshares/content/acr/acr00/acr00-indonesiamoluccaisland.html
United Nations. "Consolidated Inter-Agency Appeal 2001."
United Nations Inter-Agency. "Appeal for the Maluku Crisis." Jakarta, March 2000.

Other Publications
Atlas Maluku. Utrecht: Landelijk Steunpunt Educatie Molukkers, 1998.
Bakubae: Breaking the Violence with Compassion. By Ichsan Malik, et al. Jakarta, 2003.
"Building Peace in Indonesia: Religion Is Both a Help and a Complication As Country Struggles with New Democracy." By Paul Jeffrey. *National Catholic Reporter,* June 6, 2003.
The Community Based Movement for Reconciliation Process in Maluku. By Ichsan Malik. Jakarta: Bakubae Maluku, 2003.
Developing a Village-Level Conflict Management System to Handle and Resolve Religious Conflicts: The Wayame Experience in Ambon, Indonesia. By Christopher W. Moore. 2001.
"Guns, Pamphlets, and Handy Talkies: How the Military Exploited Local Ethno-Religious Tensions in Maluku to Preserve Their Political and Economic Privileges." By George Junus Aditjondro. Revised paper for the proceedings of the conference "Conflicts and Violence in Indonesia," organized by Institute of Southeast Asian Studies, Department of African and Asian Studies, Humbolt University, Berlin, July 3–5, 2000.
"Indonesian Political Developments and Their Implications for the U.S., with Special Reference to the Maluku Crisis." By R. William Liddle. Paper presented to the U.S. Commission on International Religious Freedom, Hearing on the Maluku Islands, Washington, D.C., February 13, 2001. Available at www.geocitie.com/paper/william_liddle.htm.
"Islam and Asian Security." By Robert William Hefner. Strategic Asia 2002–2003: Executive Summary, National Bureau of Asian Research.
"The Maluku War: Bringing Society Back In." By Gerry van Klinken. *Indonesia* 71 (Cornell University, April 2001).
"Pela and the Failure of Reconciliation." By Dieter Bartels. *Maluku World Wide,* July 27, 2000. Available at www.geocities.com/chosye/paper/dieter-Barstels.htm.
"Why Local Conflict Becomes Indonesia's National War." By Dan Murphy. *Christian Science Monitor,* September 20, 2000. Available at www. csmweb2.emcweb.com/durable/2000/09/20/p8s1.htm.
"Your God Is No Longer Mine." By Dieter Bartels. 2000 Unpublished paper.

Websites
www.hawaii.edu/cseas/conf/links.html
www.websitesrcg.com/ambon/index.html

Resource Contacts

M. Adnan Amal, North Maluku, tel: +62 921 24011

M. Najib Azca, e-mail: najibazca2002@yahooo.com.au

Dieter Bartels, www.geocities.com/chosye/paper/dieter-barstels.htm

Konrad Huber, e-mail: konrad_huber@unicef.org

Gerry van Klinken, e-mail: gerryvk@ykt.mega.net.id, editor@insideindonesia.org

Ichsan Malik, Baku Bae Movement, e-mail: bagjanet@indo.net.id

Imam B. Prasodjo, Department of Sociology, Faculty of Social and Political Sciences, University of Indonesia, e-mail: budipras@dnet.net.id

Arifah Rahmawati, e-mail: arifah.rahmawati@csps-ugm.or.id

Daniel Sparingga, Departemen Sosiologi Fisip Universitas Airlangga, Jl. Darmawangsa Dalam Selatan Surabaya, tel: +62 31 503 4015 ext. 262.

Tamrin Amal Tomagola, Jakarta

Lambang Trijono, e-mail: lambang@csps-ugm.or.id

Organizations

Bakubae Maluku Movement
Jl. Mendut no. 3
Jakarta Pusat
tel/fax: +62 021 315 3865
e-mail: bakubaemaluku@hotmail.com

Forum Komunikasi Nusaniwe-Sirimau (Forkonussi)
Ambon
contact: Conny Lelapary
tel: +62 911 351 854

Institut Studi Arus Informasi
Jl. Utan kayu no. 68H
Jakarta 13120
tel: +62 21 857 3388 ext. 125
fax: +62 21 856 7811

Kantor Berita Radio 68H
Jl. Utan Kayu no. 68H
Jakarta 13120
tel: +62 21 857 3388 ext. 132
fax: +62 21 857 3387

Lembaga Pemberdayaan Perempuan dan Anak (LAPPAN)
Ambon
contact: Bai Tualeka
tel: +62 911 314 176
e-mail: bai_lmb@yahoo.com

Mercy Corps
Aman's Building
Jalan Pantai Mutiara no. 53
Ambon
tel: +62 911 315 390
fax: +62 911 315 391

UN Support Facility for Indonesian Recovery (UNSFIR)
Surya Building, 9th Floor
Jl. M.H. Thamrin Kav. 9
Jakarta 10350
tel: +62 21 392 4320
fax +62 21 392 1152

Samsu Rizal Panggabean is a director of the Master's Program in Peace and Conflict Resolution, Gadjah Mada University, Yogyakarta, Indonesia and formerly head of the Centre for Security and Peace Studies at the same university. He teaches conflict analysis and transformation, philosophy of conflict resolution, and international security studies. Currently he is working on a research on "Civil Society and Ethnic Conflict" in six cities of Indonesia, funded by the Ford Foundation, and in collaboration with Professor Ashutosh Varshney (University of Michigan). With Professor Varshney and Muhammad Zulfan Tajuddin, he also is creating a social conflict database for Indonesia, funded by the UN Support for Indonesian Recovery, a project funded by the UNDP. He received educational training from Gadjah Mada University, George Mason University (United States), Uppsala University (Sweden), and the European Peace University (Austria). He has served on the editorial board for the publication Islamika, *as a lecturer at the Islamic University of Indonesia, and as a visiting lecturer at the Magelang Military Academy.*

Notes

1. Dieter Bartels, "Your God Is No Longer Mine," 2000, unpublished paper, p. 6.
2. International Crisis Group, "Indonesia's Maluku Crisis: The Issues," ICG Briefing Paper, Jakarta/Brussels, July 19, 2000, p. 2.
3. These statistics are derived from official census figures of Survei Penduduk Antar Sensus for 1991, 1985, and 1990.
4. Bartels, "Your God," .
5. Lance Castles, "Census Data in Time-Depth Which May Be Relevant to the Conflicts in Maluku," 2000, unpublished paper, pp. 1–2.
6. Human Rights Watch, "Indonesia: The Violence in Ambon," March 1999, p. 9.
7. International Crisis Group, "Indonesia's Maluku Crisis," p. 2.
8. Bartels, "Your God," p. 21.
9. UN Support for Indonesia's Recovery in Jakarta is creating a conflict database for these purposes.
10. See Pemerintah Darurat Sipil Maluku, *Laporan Konflik Maluku* [Maluku Conflict Report], Ambon, November 2002. According to this report, released by the Civil Emergency Authority, 920 out of 1,189 violent incidents (77.4 percent) that took place in Maluku from early 1999 to November 2002 occurred in Ambon city. In addition, 726 out of 1,359 of the violence-related deaths (53.4 percent) occurred in Ambon city. The figures regarding destruction of property also reveal a disproportionate concentration in Ambon city for houses (damaged, burnt, or destroyed; 2,320 out of 6,488, or 35.8 percent), churches (18 out of 66, or 27.3 percent), mosques (15 out of 36, or 57.7 percent), shops and kiosks (213 out of 243, or 87.6 percent), and government buildings (15 out of 22, or 68.2 percent).
11. Pemerintah Darurat Sipil Maluku, *Maluku Conflict Report,* app. tabs. 1.1.a–1.4.a.
12. International Crisis Group, "Indonesia: The Search for Peace in Maluku," ICG Asia Report no. 31, February 8, 2002, p. 21.
13. Pemerintah Darurat Sipil Maluku, *Maluku Conflict Report,* pp. 83–84.
14. Muhammad Najib Azca, "The Role of the Security Forces in Communal Conflict: The Case of Ambon," master's thesis, Faculty of Asian Studies, Australian National University, July 2003.
15. Chris Wilson, "Examining the Successful Reconciliation Process in North Halmahera," 2004, unpublished preliminary research report.
16. On Laskar Jihad, see Kirsten Schulze, "Laskar Jihad and the Conflict in Ambon," *Brown's Journal of World Affairs,* 9, no. 1 (Spring 2002), available at www.watsoninstitute.org/bjwa/archive/9.1/indonesia/schulze.pdf.
17. It stood down in mid-2003.

18. Pemerintah Darurat Sipil Maluku, *Maluku Conflict Report,* app. tabs. 2.1.b.–2.4.b.

19. Ibid.

20. Nick Mawdsley, Monica Tanuhandaru, and Kees Holman, *Report of the EC Conflict Prevention Assessment Mission: Indonesia,* European Commission, March 2002, p. 71. A team of researchers in Maluku and North Maluku is participating in creating the statistics of casualties and damages sponsored by the UN Development Programme and UN Support for Indonesian Recovery.

21. Pemerintah Darurat Sipil Maluku, *Maluku Conflict Report.* app. tab. 8.

22. Ibid., pp. 21, 23.

23. Ibid., pp. 10–11.

24. United Nations, *Consolidated Inter-Agency Appeal for the Maluku Crisis,* 2001.

25. Bartels, "Your God," p. 9.

26. Another traditional institution is *gandong.* If *pela* is a contract-based alliance, *gandong* is based on ancestral or genealogical bonds. Two villages that are bound by *gandong* believe that they share a common ancestor.

27. Bartels, "Your God," p. 10.

28. Ibid., p. 14.

29. International Crisis Group, "Indonesia's Maluku Crisis," p. 2.

30. M. Shaleh Putuhena, "Kerusuhan Maluku: Pengalaman dan Renungan dari Makassar," and R. Z. Leirissa, "'Encounter' Sebagai Mekanisme Gerakan Baku Bae, Maluku," in Ichsan Malik, et al., *Baku Bae: Breaking the Violence with Compassion* (Jakarta: Yappika, 2003).

31. *Tempo,* December 25–31, 2001.

32. Christopher W. Moore, "Developing a Village-Level Conflict Management System to Handle and Resolve Religious Conflicts: The Waiyame Experience in Ambon, Indonesia," 2001, unpublished paper, p. 11.

33. Paul Jeffrey, "Building Peace in Indonesia: Religion Is Both a Help and a Complication As Country Struggles with New Democracy," *National Catholic Reporter,* June 6, 2003.

34. Mawdsley, Tanuhandaru, and Holman, *Report of the EC Conflict Prevention Assessment Mission,* p. 30.

35. *Kompas,* September 8, 2001.

36. *Forum Keadilan* no. 15, July 15, 2001.

37. Ibid.

38. *Koran Tempo,* September 28, 2001.

39. Joint Committee of Baku Bae Maluku, *The Community-Based Reconciliation Process of Baku Bae in Maluku,* Bogor, 2001.

40. "Maluka Dialogue Ends with Peace Commitment,"*Jakarta Post,* March 20, 2001.

41. Ibid.

9.5.5

West Papua: Building Peace Through an Understanding of Conflict

Yohanis G. Bonay with Jane McGrory

There has been conflict in West Papua for forty years. To some extent, it is a conflict in the conventional sense: There are clashes between armed separatists and government forces. But conflict in West Papua also exists in the structures of injustice that affect every aspect and every section of society. The absence of peace today stems from the denial of Papuan aspirations for self-governance with Papua's integration into the Republic of Indonesia in 1963. Real peace can only be secured through resolution of the conflict regarding Papuan sovereignty and governance, accompanied by a process of changing the structures of conflict and establishing the foundations of a peaceful society.

During the former Suharto regime, the province of Papua was known as Irian Jaya. Under Dutch rule, before becoming a part of Indonesia, it was known as Nieuw Guinea. It was not until January 1, 2000, that Abdurrahman Wahid, then president of Indonesia, agreed to adopt "Papua" as the official name of the province.[1] This decision was of no small importance to indigenous communities in Papua. They welcomed the decision as a sign of recognition of the Papuan people and their existence as a nation.

Since the eighteenth century, the South Pacific island of Papua has been an object of imperial ambition, with the British, German, Dutch, and Japanese laying claim to parts of the island at different times. The western half of Papua remained under Dutch control even after other territories of the Dutch East Indies came under Indonesian sovereignty with the declaration of the Republic of Indonesia in 1945. It was not until the 1950s that the Dutch government began a process to relinquish control of this last remaining piece of its former empire in Asia Pacific. The Netherlands promised Papuans independence through a process of decolonization that would lead toward eventual self-rule.

The new government of the Republic of Indonesia regarded the Dutch policy for Papuan independence as a veiled strategy to maintain an outpost of

438

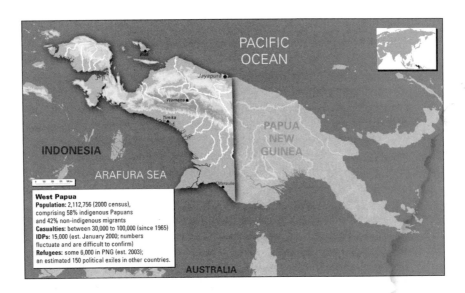

West Papua
Population: 2,112,756 (2000 census), comprising 58% indigenous Papuans and 42% non-indigenous migrants
Casualties: between 30,000 to 100,000 (since 1965)
IDPs: 15,000 (est. January 2000; numbers fluctuate and are difficult to confirm)
Refugees: some 6,000 in PNG (est. 2003); an estimated 150 political exiles in other countries.

Dutch colonial authority in the Pacific. On December 19, 1961, with the aim of ousting the Dutch and establishing its sovereign claim to all territories of the formerly Dutch East Indies, the first president of Indonesia, Sukarno, announced a military plan for the "return" of West Papua (then known by Indonesia as West Irian). Indonesia's military invasion of West Papua attracted international attention amid Cold War anxieties. The United States stepped in to broker a settlement, seeking to win Indonesia's good favor and keep Jakarta out of the Soviet axis. Under this deal—the New York Agreement—West Papua was placed under interim UN administration, known as the UN Temporary Executive Authority in West New Guinea (UNTEA), in October 1962. The territory was subsequently transferred to Indonesian administration in May 1963 with the agreement that a UN-supervised referendum would allow the people of Papua to determine whether they would become part of the unitary state of Indonesia or form their own independent nation in 1969. This referendum was called the Act of Free Choice.

To carry out the Act of Free Choice, Jakarta opted to appoint a consultative council that could represent the West Papuan nation. By carefully assembling a council of 1025 pro-Indonesian "representatives," Indonesia turned the referendum into "act of no choice." Faced with intimidation and coercion, the council returned a unanimous result in favor of integration with Indonesia. Brutality and terror also silenced those protesting the way Papuans were cheated of their right to self-determination.

The majority of Papuans view Indonesia's annexation of Papua as illegitimate. They oppose Indonesian rule and the denial of their desire to govern themselves. In response, the Indonesian government resorted to violence, and so began the conflict that continues today. There are at least four dimensions of violence:

- Open armed conflict between armed separatists—the National Liberation Army (TPN) and the Free Papua Movement (OPM)[2]—and the Indonesian military.
- State violence against ordinary citizens as a consequence of military operations and violent responses by the state apparatus to civilian resistance to Indonesian authority.
- Structural violence through the systems of economic, political, social, and cultural injustice that marginalize ethnic Papuan communities and secure the dominance of Indonesian authority.
- Communal conflict between different religious, ethnic, and subethnic groups.

Each of these dimensions of conflict stems from one root cause: the denial of the Papuan right for recognition and self-governance. In considering the task of peacebuilding in Papua, however, what is important is not only how this root cause of conflict can be "resolved," but also how the consequences and impacts of this root cause can be addressed to bring about just and sustainable peace.

Conflict Dynamics

Open Armed Conflict

Since 1965 there has been open armed conflict between small groups of armed separatists (TPN/OPM) and the Indonesian security forces.[3] The Indonesian military has undertaken successive military operations, ostensibly to crush the "separatist rebellion."[4] For this purpose, 60,000 troops were deployed to West Papua from 1967 to 1972.[5] Current estimates of military and police personnel number 15,000–20,000.[6] TPN/OPM personnel, meanwhile, are estimated at 1,600,[7] which includes a number of units pursuing nonviolent means.[8]

While the TPN/OPM has never been a serious military threat to the superior forces of the Indonesian Armed Forces (ABRI) and Indonesian National Army (TNI), their activities have provided justification for the far-reaching militarization of West Papua. The presence of security forces in West Papua and their modus operandi cannot be separated from their political and economic interests. Politically, the interests of the military are served by the existence of a "threat to national integrity," which bolsters the military's position in national politics. Economically, the military's presence is inextricable from the business interests of the Indonesian armed forces, which includes illegal logging, protection of vital commercial installations, trade in protected wildlife, and so forth. The extrabudgetary income from these activities constitutes an important source of revenue for the underfinanced state security forces.[9]

State Violence

There are two prevalent forms of state violence in West Papua. The first is civilian causalities caused by military operations that are poorly executed or excessive in their brutality. Since 1963, Indonesian military operations against

Rob Huibers/Panos Pictures

Sentani, West Papua, February 2000. Participants in the Mushawara Papua Besar 2000 (Great Papua Deliberation), where the political elite of the Papuas discussed the future of their people after 38 years of Indonesian rule.

the TPN/OPM have often claimed an unjustified toll in civilian causalities and injuries, forced displacement, and the destruction of property.[10] Moreover, military operations create a culture of fear and submission, which is particularly acute in remote inland communities.

The second pattern of state violence is a response to the political movement for West Papuan independence. The state security apparatus has sought to eliminate and silence opponents of Indonesian rule through human rights violations, including forced disappearances, extrajudicial killings, torture, rape, and abduction. Statistics of human rights violations during the New Order regime are difficult to obtain and even more difficult to verify. Some recent reports hint at the current scale of the problem:

- An investigation by Elsham West Papua documented 1,000 cases of gross violations of human rights between 1997 and 2002.
- A recent submission by the World Council of Churches to the UN Commission on Human Rights, in Geneva, referred to an escalation in cases of extrajudicial killings in the period 2000–2002, in addition to 838 cases of arbitrary arrest, interrogation, and abduction.
- Human Rights Watch has documented at least eleven incidents in which excessive military force was used to break up demonstrations of Papuan nationalism during 1999 and 2000, including incidents in Biak, Nabire, and Merauke when the military's use of force to remove the Papuan "Morning Star" flag caused multiple casualties.[11]

One act of state violence particularly injurious to Papuans' sense of justice was the murder of Theys Hiyo Eluay, independence leader and head of the Papuan Presidium Council (PPC), by the Indonesian military on November 11, 2001.

A vicious cycle has developed in which protest movements and public opposition become a justification for extended central government control of Papua; resistance to control meets control of resistance. The prevalence of state violence impacts deeply on the community's confidence in their own security and trust in the public security apparatus.[12]

Structural Violence

The Indonesian government imposes systems of structural violence in Papua that create conditions of economic, political, social, and cultural disadvantage for Papuan communities.[13] This structural violence has created unequal power relations and unequal life opportunities between Papuan and non-Papuan communities.

Despite being one of the richest provinces in terms of natural resources, Papua has one of Indonesia's highest rates of poverty. Papuans have lower access to education, health services, and the media than their counterparts in other areas of Indonesia.[14] In addition, until recent special autonomy measures were implemented, non-Papuans dominated positions in the government bureaucracy, particularly senior positions.[15] There has been very low representation of Papuans in executive and legislative arms of government, as well as in the military and police force. Major businesses are generally owned by investors from outside of Papua. Migrants dominate the local commercial sector.[16] Papuans feel disadvantaged, that they are second-class citizens who can only sit by and watch as outsiders cash in on resources taken from their land.

For almost forty years, until recent autonomy reforms increased Papua's share of income raised in the province, the spoils of economic development were largely channeled straight to Jakarta. Papua got the thin end of the wedge in terms of development's advantages. Papuan's socioeconomic welfare has been undermined by the seizure of traditional lands and the degradation of indigenous culture. Irreversible damage has been inflicted on the environment. A prime example of this is PT Freeport's Grasberg gold and copper mine in Mimika, where there has been massive environmental and social damage in the pursuit of what is said to be one of the world's richest gold reserves.[17]

The Indonesian government has sought to "civilize" Papuans, whom it portrays as primitive people, to make Papuans think, act, and look like "Indonesians." Attempts at "Indonesianization," by banning traditional Papuan apparel, hampering traditional governance, as well as restricting cultural practices and symbols, have undermined the identity and dignity of indigenous Papuans. The breakdown of traditional values and systems has caused various social problems in Papuan communities, including alcoholism, weakened work ethics, and domestic violence.

It should be noted that the degree of structural violence is changing with recent reforms for expanded autonomy, which have opened up opportunities for Papuans in regional and local government agencies. Current efforts toward "Papuanization" of the bureaucracy have enabled Papuans to become more involved in governance and policymaking. A sad fact, however, is that Papuans have shown to be as easily won over by the culture of bureaucratic self-interest and profit-taking as have their predecessors. While regional autonomy goes some way toward addressing structural violence, the structures of injustice and disadvantage have become self-perpetuating. Long processes of education and training will be needed to reverse the economic and social inequality.

Communal Conflict

The demographic makeup of Papua has been altered significantly since Papua's integration into Indonesia, particularly through internal transmigration by people from other parts of Indonesia.[18] As a result of transmigration, both through government programs and spontaneously, large numbers of ethnic Malay, Javanese, and Bugis from western Indonesia came to a community that was almost completely ethnically Melanesian at the time of integration. While many migrants are Muslim, indigenous Papuans are largely Protestant or Catholic. Additionally, migrant communities often have a higher degree of economic wealth than indigenous Papuans. These differences in ethnicity, religion, culture, and socioeconomic status have become fault lines in contemporary Papuan society.

It is also important to note that neither the Papuan nor migrant communities are homogeneous or monolithic. There are significant cultural differences between the more than 250 Papuan subethnic groups, in particular between coastal and inland tribes. Among the migrant community there is also a vast variation, and some "migrants" have lived in West Papua for generations. There is no denying, however, that issues of identity in Papua are complex and contested. Consciousness of ethnic identity and primordial sentiments pervade Papuan society. Stereotyping is prevalent and suspicion between different ethnic and social groups is high. This breeds at least two patterns of communal conflict: social conflict between different ethnic/religious groups, and manipulation of ethnic/religious differences or tensions to serve political interests.

Examples of conflict along communal lines include several recent inter-ethnic clashes at markets in Jayapura during 2000.[19] In these incidents, economic inequality caused feelings of resentment and social jealousy among Papuans toward migrants. In the absence of a mechanism to mediate or express these tensions, the Papuans resorted to violence. Conflict, tension, and polarization between ethnic groups are symptomatic of structural injustices; vertical pressures, such as structures of economic inequality facilitated by government policies, create "cracks" in the community and manifest as violent conflict along communal lines.

Second, it is evident that ethnic sentiment is manipulated and exploited for political purposes. One important study documented the dynamics of a conflict between Papuans and migrants in the highlands town of Wamena in 2000 that led to the deaths of over 30 people (7 Papuans and 24 migrants),[20] the displacement of 10,000, and widespread destruction of property. The study found that, although this conflict has often been explained as an explosion of primordial sentiment, there is reason to believe it was engineered by the military against a background of elite political interests.[21] More recently, concerns have increased about the possibility of interreligious conflict given the arrival of the Islamic militia group Laskar Jihad in West Papua. There are suspicions that support or acquiescence by the security authorities for Laskar Jihad may represent a strategy to instigate religious conflict and manufacture in West Papua the kind of insecurity that serves the military's political interests.[22]

The Situation Today

The situation in West Papua today is characterized by political intolerance for independence aspirations, and this produces actual and potential conflict. Open conflict between separatist groups and the armed forces continues, albeit sporadically. And while state violence has perhaps been curbed by greater media freedom and vocal civil society organizations, the military's audacious murder of independence leader Theys Hiyo Eluay suggests that the brutal ways and means of the armed forces remain unchanged. The structural violence of disadvantaged indigenous communities is largely still intact, despite reforms under special autonomy. The potential for communal conflict remains high.

The current renewal of political intolerance follows a short period of optimism among Papuans about the prospects of actually attaining self-governance. This optimism emerged in 1999 when presidents Habibie and Wahid created space for dialogue on Papuan aspirations. President Wahid also permitted the flying of the Morning Star flag and changed the name of the province to Papua—both significant gestures that fueled Papuan expectations of freedom. The openness of this era was never backed by a real intent within the Indonesian government to seriously consider West Papua's secession from Indonesia. Nevertheless, this period became a significant turning point in the Papuan struggle. The independence movement transformed from a fragmented, armed resistance to a broadly based political movement mainly based on a peaceful approach.

The government of Indonesia is also working to dampen popular aspirations for independence through special autonomy reforms. Special autonomy approaches the "Papuan problem" as a problem of development, with the assumption that it can be resolved by increased revenue and decentralized governance. The reforms have given rise to conflict among Papuans, given divergent views on the merits of special autonomy. Some view special autonomy as the best alternative under the current circumstances and support it on the grounds that expanded autonomy can be a strategic first step toward self-governance and the ultimate goal of independence. Opposition to special autonomy stems from a lack of faith in the Indonesian government, born of experience. Opponents also point out how Papuan objectives for the plan—expanded self-rule—were vastly compromised in negotiation on the final legislation and that the drafting process did not respect for the right of the people to participate in decisionmaking about issues that impact directly on their welfare and security.

The fragility of social stability in Papua was demonstrated in September 2003 when a decision by Jakarta to split Papua into three separate provinces led to violent communal clashes in Timika, the capital of the new Central Irian Jaya province. The proposed division is based on legislation that predates special autonomy and is widely thought to be contradictory to the spirit—if not the letter—of special autonomy legislation,[23] causing polarization between supporters and opponents of the decision. Even prior to the deadly clashes in Timika, the policy had been subject to significant controversy. What is apparent is that special autonomy has not been devised to serve the interests of the Papuan communities or through consultation with the people it affects.

An accumulation of structural and communal tensions is causing a rapid escalation in the potential for violence and horizontal conflict in the community. This undermines the bargaining position of the people, while bolstering the position of political elites who are pushing for a "tough line." Insecurity creates opportunities for the military to extend its control—a situation it exploited during the drafting of special autonomy legislation and recent antiterrorism laws.

Official Conflict Management

Role of the UN

There is widespread disappointment among Papuan activists regarding the role of the United Nations. This disillusion stems from the view that the UN not only has failed to give the situation in West Papua the attention it deserves, but also has not taken responsibility for its complicity in the political deal-making that lead to integration in the first place. The UN, by failing to uphold international practice in the determination of West Papuan sovereignty, is criticized for having neglected its obligations as the referendum's supervisory authority to ensure due process in the 1969 Act of Free Choice.

Skirting the political issue at the source of the conflict, the UN's engagement in West Papua has centered on development assistance. Community development and welfare programs implemented by several UN agencies have helped mitigate some impacts of structural violence.[24] The UN Development Programme also works with the World Bank, the Asian Development Bank, and bilateral donors to improve standards of governance, including the implementation of special autonomy.[25] The most relevant contribution among the work of other international organizations is training in humanitarian law for military and police personnel in Papua conducted by the International Committee for the Red Cross.

Regional Organizations

Regional governments tend to prioritize commercial, security, and political relations with Indonesia, and this overwhelms any humanitarian concerns that might motivate regional organizations to take a political stance on West Papua. Indonesia is a member of the two major regional organizations, the Association of Southeast Asian Nations and the Asia Pacific Economic Cooperation, which generally shy away from the sensitive political problems of member countries.

One regional organization that has made some meaningful attempts to address conflict in Papua is the Pacific Islands Forum. In the past, the forum has been a rare sympathetic voice for the plight of Papuans on the international stage.[26] Member countries Nauru and Vanuatu have been significant driving forces behind regional attention for the West Papuan struggle.[27] In particular, Vanuatu has lobbied for West Papua to be put back on the UN's decolonization list and a review of the legality of the Act of Free Choice by the International Court of Justice.[28] The government in Port Vila has also allowed the PPC and OPM to set up representative offices in Vanuatu.[29]

Outside of the framework of Asia Pacific organizations, regional governments (including the United States and Australia) in the past have expressed concern about the level of violence in West Papua.[30] New Zealand prime minister Phil Goff once offered to serve as a mediator to help resolve conflict in Papua—yet this offer specifically stated an intent to explore options for peace within the framework of Indonesian sovereignty.[31]

Official Domestic Attempts Toward Conflict Resolution

During the New Order rule of West Papua, official attempts toward "conflict resolution" comprised successive military operations to crush separatism and structural violence to quell popular aspiration for independence. With the beginning of the era of Indonesian political reform in 1998, the government's strategies have diversified, but none of these measures have succeeded in moderating the demands for independence or addressing the grievances of Papuan people.

The end of the Suharto regime and its iron-claw grip on West Papua created a short-lived opportunity for high-level political engagement on Papuan aspirations. Forum Rekonsiliasi Rakyat Irian/Papua (FORERI), which comprised various sections of the community, took the lead in the early stages of "national dialogue." The forum sought to streamline perspectives within the struggle against injustice in Papua and to promote dialogue as an alternative to conflict. FORERI also coordinated the meeting by a group of West Papuan representatives, the "Team of 100," with President Habibie on February 26, 1999.

Before long, however, dialogue between the Indonesian government and Papuan leaders became "deadlocked." In an effort to gain new momentum in official negotiations, the broad-based Papuan people's congress held in May–June 2000 agreed to form a new representative body, the Papuan Presidium Council. The PPC, a council of 31 members, has an executive mandate and is accountable to a "panel" of 501 representatives of ten different sectors of Papuan society (indigenous people, women, youth, non-Papuan migrants, professionals, churches, among others). The PPC was mandated by the People's Congress to negotiate with the central authorities on behalf of the Papuan people to bring about independence, and to pursue four policy directions regarding the rectification of history, the development of a political agenda, the stimulation of cooperation and reconciliation among Papuan groups, and the promotion of the rights of indigenous people. However, the PPC was quickly branded by Jakarta as a separatist political group, effectively closing the door to national dialogue and its prospects to fulfill its mandate. Today, PPC members face significant political constraints and intimidation amid renewed intolerance from Jakarta for Papuan freedom.

The role of the PPC in official domestic diplomacy has been hampered not only by the unaccommodating attitude from Jakarta. The PPC itself has faced numerous problems in fulfilling its mandate, and many of these problems underscore the difficulty of forming a truly representative body that reflects a broad cross section of Papuan interests. Although the membership is united in their desire for independence, there are contesting views on how and when this should be achieved and this hampers the PPC's ability to move forward with its agenda. Three years after its formation, some are questioning the role of the PPC and its capacity to represent Papuan aspirations.

The short interlude of national dialogue on the Papuan issue ended in 2001 and political repression returned. The Indonesian government was alarmed by the strength and breadth of the independence movement that grew during the "Papuan spring" and responded by tightening political freedoms. At the same time, the government sought to tackle the problem with a massive welfare program intended to convince reluctant Papuans of the benefits of being part of the Indonesian state,[32] and then by offering of special autonomy in October 2001. Today, as civil and political liberties are tightened, the promises of increased autonomy ring hollow to many ears.

Prospects of dialogue are hampered by a mutual lack of trust and confidence. In the experience of Papuans, concessions from Jakarta have been empty promises that do not translate into substantive changes in their economic, social, or legal standing. For example, Jakarta today permits the Papuan flag and national anthem, but as cultural rather than national symbols. Additionally, while special autonomy increased Papua's share of official revenue from natural resource–related businesses in the province, this has not flowed down to Papuan communities or produced significant improvements in socioeconomic welfare. Jakarta's promises in terms of governance reforms have also fallen short of expectations. Eighteen months after the implementation of special autonomy, only 10 percent of reforms have been implemented.[33] Jakarta has failed to install the Papuan Consultative Assembly (Majelis Rakyat Papua), a local assembly made up of women, religious leaders, and customary (adat) leaders, with an advisory function at the provincial level. The formation of this assembly was an important provision of the 2002 special autonomy laws to democratize local governance. Jakarta's failure to follow through on its formation reflects not only bureaucratic laxity but also its distrust of Papuans; it fears that the Consultative Assembly will become a vehicle for independence aspirations.

Looking back at the processes of official domestic diplomacy over the past four years, it is possible to identify three fundamental flaws to the state of

government in Indonesia that limit the prospects for a consistent or constructive policy on West Papua:

- Indonesia is currently undergoing a transition to democracy. In this
  immature phase of democratic politics, policy is driven by shortsighted
  political motivations.
- Full civil supremacy in governance is yet to be established and the military continue to wield influence in national and local decisionmaking.
- The ongoing economic crisis is used as a rationale or justification for
  claims to, and control of, the abundant natural resources of Papua.

As long as these three factors dictate the central government's policy on West
Papua, the prospects for meaningful engagement and realistic approaches to
conflict management are poor. On a more fundamental level, official diplomacy is constrained by "national interests" that engender intransigence by
Jakarta on the issue of Papuan sovereignty. Jakarta is determined to maintain
the immense security, economic, and political interests concentrated in Papua;
Papua is too valuable to let go.

Multi-Track Diplomacy

At least 140 nongovernmental organizations (NGOs) are operating in Papua,[34]
and there are 72 organizations involved in peacebuilding.[35] Aside from NGOs,
there are numerous community-based organizations, including a growing network of indigenous customary organizations. The Protestant and Catholic
churches have a strong presence in all parts of Papua, in addition to other
denominations. There are often also lay organizations associated with churches,
such as parish councils, youth groups, and women's associations. Islamic organizations, too, have a strong presence, particularly in urban areas. Ethnic community organizations are formed by migrant groups, including organizations for
Minang, Batak, Madurese, and Javanese communities living in Papua.[36] In addition, there are numerous professional associations.

The apparent prevalence of civil society organizations, however, does not
automatically suggest a strong or robust civil society. The nature of these
organizations also has to be taken into consideration. One characteristic immediately relevant in this context is the tendency for civil society to be organized
along ethnic lines, in particular ethnic community councils and indigenous customary organizations. NGOs often have a "Papuan" or "non-Papuan" identity,
generally reflecting the identity of their staff. The ethnic exclusivity of many
civil society organizations and the primordial patterns of organization raise
doubts about the extent to which civil society as a whole functions as an arena
for interaction between people of different ethnic and religious identities.

One important indicator of the strength of civil society is its bargaining
position vis-à-vis the government. There are signs that NGOs are carving out a
role in advocacy on public policy and the drafting of legislation. The most
notable example of this was the contribution of NGOs in the drafting of special

autonomy legislation. At the level of local government, NGOs have also capitalized on opportunities created by decentralization to become involved in drafting local regulations (peraturan daerah) on a range of issues, including social welfare, customary law, and land rights. There are signs that civil society is becoming a counterweight—but also a complementary mechanism—to government authority.

The scope of civil society initiatives for peace has been expanding since the 1990s, prior to which the church was the only real agent of peacebuilding in Papua. In particular, NGO activities in Papua have swelled in the reformasi era. Today, a healthy variety of civil society initiatives can be identified, including initiatives responding to state violence, and those working to change structures of violence; patterns of engagement and confrontation with the government and security apparatus; and initiatives from the heights of international diplomacy to the grassroots of Papuan communities.

There is a fairly clear division of roles among NGOs. International NGOs work mainly at the level of international advocacy to raise awareness of the situation in Papua among foreign governments and publics, or by funding local organizations. The most prominent role of local NGOs is in addressing state violence by investigating and reporting on human rights abuses. In addition to this, there is a community of NGOs and church organizations working in important, albeit less prominent ways, to address the impacts and causes of structural violence through programs for education, community health, and economic empowerment. Additionally, there are a few notable initiatives by religious organizations and NGOs to directly address issues of interethnic and interfaith harmony and tolerance. The dimension of conflict that receives less attention from civil society is open conflict between TPN/OPM and the Indonesian military.

Initiatives by International, Regional, and Local Nonofficial Actors

One of the strengths of peacebuilding initiatives by international and regional organizations is the way they help "put Papua on the agenda" at national and international levels. The international focus they bring to the situation in Papua also helps to place checks on Indonesian actions in Papua and encourage its accountability to international standards. Drawing on data provided by local NGOs and churches, international NGOs—including Amnesty International, TAPOL, Human Rights Watch, the World Council of Churches, the International Crisis Group, and the International Catholic Migration Commission—are prominent campaigners on issues of peace and justice in Papuan on the international level. Additionally, international solidarity movements, in particular in Australia, the UK, and the Netherlands, are active in raising the international profile of the Papuan struggle. The Papuan diaspora in Australia and the Netherlands also works to raise awareness of human rights abuses and issues of self-determination. Backed by the strong presence of the Catholic and Protestant churches in Papua, international church organizations play a role in promoting public awareness, solidarity movements, and lobbying.

International church organizations, such as the World Council of Churches and Franciscans International, have also used their consultative status at the UN Commission on Human Rights to make interventions regarding human rights violations in Papua.[37] On the regional level, the Pacific Concerns Resource Centre is active in raising awareness among governments and publics in the Pacific region of conflict in Papua.

There are also international NGOs working directly in Papua in the area of peacebuilding, including Common Ground Indonesia, InterNews, and World Vision Indonesia. A number of international donor agencies also support the peacebuilding work of local organizations through funding and capacity building.

The international advocacy work of international organizations relies heavily on information from local sources, in particular those working in the field of human rights. Strong players in this field include Elsham Papua, LBH Papua, Kontras Papua, Aliansi Demokrasi Untuk Papua, the church-based Offices of Justice and Peace, and the GKI Division of Law and Human Rights. Activities by these organizations include conflict mapping/surveys, monitoring and investigation, litigation and legal advocacy, campaigning, workshops, and conferences. Additionally, Elsham West Papua supports the training of police in human rights. It has also engaged in dialogue with the TPN/OPM leadership to encourage them to adopt nonviolent strategies. Kontras has been working on a campaign to have a truth and reconciliation commission established. In addition, a women's peace network has been gaining momentum among different elements of civil society in the Papuan capital of Jayapura. The broad participation of women from a variety of ethnic, religious, and professional backgrounds conveys a strong message of inclusiveness and common struggle against violence. The Indonesian Bar Association (Ikadin) is the only professional organization actively working on issues of peace and justice. It provides advocacy (litigation and nonlitigation) for people charged with subversion, including members of the OPM.[38]

There is also a large contingent of NGOs and church organizations working to address conditions of socioeconomic disadvantage. Some programs have a direct link to conflict prevention, such as the work of the Foundation for Entrepreneurship Development–Papua to promote the economic empowerment of Papuan traders in markets, while at the same time creating mechanisms for the peaceful resolution of conflicts that can be used between traders of different ethnic backgrounds. In the development sector, the focus of socioeconomic programs is generally placed on community development and empowerment of disadvantaged Papuan communities. Church organizations have been active in promoting education standards and access to schooling, particularly among students in or from remote Papuan communities. While these programs may not appear to be immediately related to issues of peace or conflict, their contribution in ameliorating the impacts of structural violence and transforming structures of injustice over the long term is significant. By reducing the socioeconomic disparity between Papuan and migrant communities and relieving some of the socioeconomic tensions that complicate intergroup relations, these activities also have an indirect effect in reducing the potential for communal conflict.

Customary organizations (*lembaga masyarakat adat*) are another significant component of civil society. They make a vital contribution to peacebuilding by addressing disputes over natural resources and upholding indigenous rights to land and resources. By reviving custom, or adat, which is integral to Papuan sense of dignity, identity, and community, customary organizations can also play an important role in promoting peace. Adat also offers an indigenous mechanism for conflict resolution and can help mediate community relations.

The reach of churches (all denominations) throughout Papua and their influence on the spiritual and social life of Papuan society also makes them a strong force for building peace. Aside from the human rights and social work of churches, the respect they command as institutions make them powerful proponents of universal principles of nonviolence, peace, and justice.[39] Churches also wield moral authority with government and Papuan elites. Church networks have unrivaled access in almost all areas of Papua, which greatly assists in getting information into remote communities, as well as channeling out information in regard to humanitarian crises and human rights violations.

Across the board, peacebuilding activities tend to focus on addressing state violence or structural conflict. There are very few civil society organizations working explicitly on issues of community conflict or social cohesion. One recent example is a media campaign for interethnic tolerance conducted by the NGO network organization FOKER LSM in 2002. Additionally, the Catholic Church has taken the initiative in promoting interfaith dialogue through the formation of the Interreligious Working Group, which brings religious leaders together for dialogue, issues statements, and organizes events for interfaith understanding, such as a peace march held on September 21, 2002.

In terms of community-based peace initiatives, one noteworthy example is the "zone of peace" concept. The idea originated in June 1999 at meetings organized by students in Yapen Waropen regency. On July 17 that same year, indigenous community leaders and non-Papuan ethnic community leaders came together to draft and sign a peace communiqué. This communiqué declared the region a zone of peace and contained a commitment to work together to maintain peace and prevent external provocateurs from inciting conflict. This initiative took on a Papua-wide dimension when the PPC planned a "peace zone" program for all Papua. It called on all parties, including nonethnic Papuans, government institutions, and the business community, to work together to realize the humanitarian mission of peace.[40] While follow-up from the PPC in concretizing this ideal has been minimal, the "zone of peace" idea has taken on its own momentum, spurning numerous peace initiatives. The concept seems to serve as a "peg" on which to hang different peacebuilding initiatives, and has therefore provided impetus, a guiding framework, and a rallying point for community-based peace initiatives.

Also tied to the "zone of peace" concept were two broadly based initiatives for peacebuilding held in 2002, which reflect an awareness among civil society of the need to build a more consolidated and strategic peace movement. The first was a peace conference jointly hosted by the human rights NGO Elsham, the provincial parliament, and police authorities. One outcome of the conference was the formation of a peace task force intended to serve as a forum for conflict prevention through dialogue. The second was a peacebuilding workshop hosted by the Catholic Church's Office for Justice and Peace. The workshop brought together religious organizations, NGOs, customary organizations, and academics to develop a shared perspective on the causes of conflict, a vision of peacebuilding, and joint or complementary plans to promote a culture of peace in Papua.

Reflection on NGO Initiatives

While it is difficult to imagine the prospects of a just and peaceful future for Papua without an effective NGO sector, the potential of NGOs as agents of peacebuilding should not be romanticized. Many NGOs have weak internal management and this limits their effectiveness. Many organizations—in particular human rights NGOs—are caught up by the urgency of "reacting" to events. While this responsiveness is the strength of their work, it also saps their capacity to work in more strategic and visionary ways to bring about structural change. There are numerous issue-oriented NGOs with narrow interests. These organizations have a real potential to create conflict rather than address it. Legitimate concerns have also been voiced about the viability of project-oriented approaches to the promotion of peace and justice.

Donor practices are part of the problem of project-oriented approaches. Donor organizations fund initiatives that are easily "packaged" as projects; they support peacebuilding activities, such as training and workshops, but do not support more sustained processes to bring about change in the conditions and causes of conflict at all levels. Local peace initiatives have to be molded to fit the donor-defined project structure if they want to be funded. This constrains the creativity, responsiveness, and capacity of local organizations to promote long-term strategies for peace. There is also a kind of self-censorship among donors, which are reluctant to support "radical" activities that carry a risk that their organization could be blacklisted by the Indonesian government. Some international organizations—both donors and advocacy organizations—impose their priorities on local organizations; they are driven by their own interests rather than the interests of the people they claim to be helping. These kinds of problems with international organizations are exacerbated by the fact that many local NGOs are dependent on international funding.

In terms of networking, there are examples of strong and effective coordination between by local NGOs, in particular joint activities by human rights NGOs for dialogue, press conferences, and public campaigning. Effective and sustained networking among NGOs, however, is lacking. The NGO sector tends to be "compartmentalized"; each organization has its activities, focus, and orientation, and goes about its work accordingly. Relations between NGOs are also complicated by competition either for funding, public profile, or "turf."[41]

While individual organizations may be successful in their stated objectives and in implementing their individual programs, they have yet to achieve a kind of "critical mass" and become a significant movement for social change. The two broadly based peacebuilding initiatives referred to above are perhaps a step in this direction. The test of these initiatives lies in their sustainability and the commitment of organizations to continued development of these frameworks.

Politicization is another risk facing NGO initiatives—a risk associated with the intensely political nature of the Papuan problem. FORERI is an example of this. It was intended to act as an open platform for dialogue and management of conflict, but the leadership took a more political direction. The resultant politicization of FORERI undermined the role it could play as an open and inclusive forum.

The issue of identity—Papuan/non-Papuan—is also a sensitive but urgent concern for civil society organizations. While many non-Papuan organizations have unquestionable commitment to promote peace in Papua, the reality is that their role is not entirely accepted by those who conceive Papuan identity in narrow terms. The low levels of pluralism and interethnic tolerance among civil society organizations can be a barrier to developing more cohesiveness. The harsh reality facing civil society is that whatever their achievements in peacebuilding, these efforts can be quickly negated by the actions of errant elements within the government, military, or Papuan society. NGO workers, particularly human rights activists, face obstruction, intimidation, and threats to personal safety.

One of the difficulties in bringing about broad implementation of the "zone of peace" concept is a good example of a core challenge in building peace in Papua. Because of the way it has been co-opted by the security apparatus and government, which took the "zone of peace" concept as a rationale for repression of those they viewed as a threat to peace in terms of stability and national security (and examples of these "threats" included human rights organizations and PPC members), the concept has been endangered. This highlights the most difficult challenge in building a broadly based peace movement in Papua: among NGO workers, independence activists, migrant communities, and Papuan communities—not to mention the security apparatus—there are different concepts and understandings of what "peace" means in the Papuan context. Until there is a common concept that is shared broadly by different sections of civil society, peace initiatives will remain on different roads to different destinations.

Prospects

Thom Beanal, the customary leader of the Amungme people and member of the PPC, has said: "We are asking for independence because we do not want to continue to be killed like this."[42] This comment is representative of the broadly held sentiment among Papuans that regards the question of independence as inextricable from the survival of Papuan people—in both physical and cultural terms. It underscores how resolution of all dimensions of conflict in Papua must address the question of sovereignty. The raw emotion of Thom Beanal's plea also hints at the psychological scars caused by the conflict. The suffering and sense of betrayal among Papuans runs deep, too deep for autonomy or power sharing as an alternative to the broadly held aspiration for "freedom."[43] The political leadership in Papua does not have the capacity or the will to assuage such ardent demands and moderate popular aspirations. The "hardline" proindependence stance of the Papuan community leaves the Papuan elite with only one negotiating position, independence. All the while, Jakarta's insistence on national integrity is unwavering, and the irreconcilable nature of these positions renders the prospects of a negotiated political settlement poor.

In addition, with regional and international powers not willing to challenge the status quo of Indonesian national unity, and given the Indonesian government's allergy to any "foreign intervention," the prospects of international mediation are also slim. Moreover, it has been suggested that the central government is currently moving to limit international access to West Papua in fear of "internationalization" of the Papua problem.[44] As long as armed conflict in West Papua can be written off by the Indonesian government as separatist rebellion, international security intervention or peacekeeping is unimaginable. Perhaps only a humanitarian and human rights disaster the likes of postreferendum East Timor would attract an international response of any significance.

Recommendations

Real peace will only be achieved in West Papua once the following questions are answered:

- How can contesting claims regarding Papuan sovereignty be resolved in a way that respects the right of the Papuan people to self-determination? How can parties engage constructively and openly to address the core question of Papuan sovereignty?
- How can effective and just rule of law be established? How can human rights be upheld and restitution sought for past human rights violations?
- How can the violence (overt and structural) be stopped and community security, social justice, and good governance be established?
- What kind of community does West Papua want to be in the future? What does "peace" mean to the people of West Papua?

Addressing these questions will require concerted action by all stakeholders as they engage in a process to build peace:

- All parties involved should assess critically their role in and responsibility for the conflict in Papua. They should be able to disengage from self-interest and participate in an open process to build a shared understanding of what peace means in the Papuan context and what is needed to achieve it.

- The government of Indonesia should learn the lessons of East Timor and Aceh—that violence is not a viable means for securing national integrity. It should engage in sincere dialogue with the Papuan people based on principles of international law. This is the only way to resolve conflict in Papua that will be accepted by all stakeholders.
- The Indonesian military should reform its system of territorial command, which has created an oppressive military presence and social control at all levels of Papuan society. Responsibility for public security must be handed over to the civilian police force and rule of law upheld.
- Transnational companies and the government of Indonesia should develop community-based approaches to corporate security and reform security policies that rely on the military.
- Transnational companies and other large corporations should uphold the rights of Papuans as subjects of law. There must be an end to exploitation of Papuan communities and the resources or land over which they hold native title.
- The international community should review the legality of the 1969 Act of Free Choice and Papua's integration into Indonesia. In particular, the UN should meet its obligations to recognize the right of the Papuan people for self-determination.
- International organizations (UN agencies, bilateral donors, and NGOs) should ensure that their activities in Papua respect the dignity and capacities of the Papuan people. Priority should be placed on the needs of the Papuan people, rather than their own agendas.
- International organizations and foreign governments should use their influence to force accountability from the Indonesian government regarding the situation in Papua, including protection of human rights workers and legal processes to address past human rights violations.
- The PPC should take a clearer stance on how it will achieve its mandate to bring about independence. This stance must be acceptable to Papuans and the international community, and be able to open the way for dialogue with the government of Indonesia.
- Churches and church organizations should focus more on supporting and promoting peaceful processes of change that are initiated by the community; they should act as a facilitator of community initiatives for peace in a way that respects indigenous capacities for peace.
- NGOs (local and international) should place greater emphasis on empowering the Papuan people as agents of structural change to build a socioeconomic environment that is democratic and just.
- NGOs (local and international) should develop a more "holistic" and strategic approach to peacebuilding that recognizes and capitalizes on the respective roles and strengths of different organizations.

- The Papuan people should take on greater responsibility for their own futures and not depend on political elites to represent their interests. Papuan communities should develop control mechanisms to promote the accountability of their own political institutions and representatives. This will also require that communities themselves reconcile competing interests and become more united. Papuans need to develop capacities and forums that enable them to manage and resolve conflicts that occur within and between their communities.

Resources

Reports

Human Rights Watch. "Indonesia: Violence and Political Impasse in Papua." Human Rights Watch Report, Vol. 13, no. 2 (July 2001). Available at www.hrw.org/press/2001/07/papua0703.htm.

International Crisis Group. "Ending Repression in Irian Jaya." ICG Asia Report no. 23. September 20, 2001. Available at www.crisisweb.org/projects/asia/indonesia/reports/a400414-20092001.pdf.

———. "Indonesia: Resources and Conflict in Papua." ICG Asia Report no. 39. September 13, 2002. Available at www.crisisweb.org/projects/asia/indonesia/reports/a400774_13092002.pdf

International Federation for Election Systems. "Papua Public Opinion Survey Indonesia." Available at www.ifes.org/reg_activities.

Other Publications

"Against Indonesia: West Papuan Strategies of Resistance Against Indonesian political and Cultural Aggression in the 1980s." By B. Giay. In B. Anderson, ed., *Violence and the State in Soeharto's Indonesia*. New York: Cornell Southeast Asia Program, 2001, pp. 129–38.

Indonesia Commission: Peace and Progress in Papua. By D. C. Blair and D. L. Phillips. Report of an independent commission sponsored by the Council on Foreign Relations. Center for Preventive Action, 2003. Available at www.cfr.org/pdf/indonesia_commission.pdf.

The Politics of Power: Freeport in Soeharto's Indonesia. By D. Leith. Honolulu: University of Hawaii Press, 2003.

The Position and Role of Civil Society Organisations in Resolving the Papuan Conflict. By B. Setyanto, B. Sugiono, Y. Reba, and N. Wamafma. Asian House Focus Series no. 12. Schriftenreihe des Asienhauses, 2002. Available at www.asienhaus.de/publikat/focus/focus12/focus12.pdf.

"Trifungsi: The Role of the Indonesian Military in Business." By L. McCulloch. Paper presented at the International Conference on Soldiers in Business: Military as an Economic Actor, Jakarta, October 17–19, 2000. Available at www.bicc.de/budget/events/milbus/confpapers.html.

Websites

www.amnesty.org (Amnesty International)

www.cs.utexas.edu/users/cline/papua/core.html (features the online version of the West Papua Information Kit, produced by the Australian West Papua Association, Sydney www.cs.utexas.edu/users/cline/papua/letter.htm)

www.geocities.com/elshamnewsservice (website of the West Papuan human rights NGO Elsham)

www.gn.apc.org/dte (Down to Earth)

www.gn.apc.org/tapol (Tapol)

www.hrw.org (Human Rights Watch)

www.intl-crisis-group.org (International Crisis Group)

www.irja.org/index2.shtml (online library of resources related to Papua)

www.papuaweb.org (A "clearinghouse" site managed jointly by Papuan and Australian universities to provide official data and academic papers in relation to Papua)

www.rfkmemorial.org/center/pro_act.htm (Robert F. Kennedy Memorial Center for Human Rights)

www.survival.org.uk (Survival International)

Resource Contacts

Kamkei Abepura, Jayapura, Papua, Indonesia

Benny Giay, director, Biro Perdamaian dan Keadilan Gereja KINGMI di Papua

Theo van den Broek OFM, director, Sekretariat Keadilan dan Perdamaian Keuskupan Jayapura (Office for Justice and Peace), Jl. Kesehatan no. 4 Dok II, Kotak Pos 1379, Jayapura, Papua, Indonesia, e-mail: sekkp@jayapura.wasantara.net.id

John Rumbiak, Elsham, United States, e-mail: elsham@usadata.net

Willem F. Rumsarwir, Sekolah Tinggi Teologi, GKI I.S. Kijne, Jl. Sentani 37, Abepura, Papua, Indonesia

Ziegfried Soellner aml., e-mail: szoellner@t.line.de

Organizations

Papua

Aliansi Demokrasi Untuk Papua (Alliance Democracy for Papua)
Jl. Raya Padang Bulan, Depan Asrama Mahasiswa Acemo
Manokwari, Abepura, Jayapura
Papua, Indonesia
tel: +62 0 967 587890
fax: +62 0 967 588365
e-mail: aldepe@jayapura.wasantara.net.id

Biro Perdamaian dan Keadilan Gereja KINGMI di Papua
Kamkei Abepura, Jayapura
Papua, Indonesia
tel: +62 0 961 593349

FOKER LSM Papua
Papua NGO's Forum
Jl. Sentani Raya no. 89, Waena, Jayapura
Papua, Indonesia
tel: +62 0 967 573511
fax: +62 0 967 573512
e-mail: fokerlsm@jayapura.wasantara.net.id

Komisi Untuk Orang Hilang dan Korban Tindak Kekerasan (Kontras; Commission for Disappearance and Victims of Violence)
Jl. Gerilyawan no. 46, Abepura, Jayapura
Papua, Indonesia
tel: +62 0 967 588615
fax: +62 0 967 588615

Lembaga Penelitian, Pengkajian dan Pengembangan Bantuan Hukum (LP3BH)
Jl. Gunung Salju Fanindi, Bengkel Tan no. 18, Manokwari
Papua, Indonesia
tel: +62 0 986 213160
fax: +62 0 986 213160

Lembaga Penguatan Masyarakat Sipil Papua (LPMS; Institute for Civil Strengthening [ICS])
Jl. Arwana II Gang Batu Karang no. 1, Waena, Jayapura
Papua, Indonesia
tel: +62 0 967 573970
fax: +62 0 967 573970/1
e-mail: buset@jayapura.wasantara.net.id

Lembaga Studi dan Advokasi Hak Asasi Manusia (Institute for Human Rights Study and Advocacy)
Jln. Kampus ISTP—Padang Bulan, Jayapura
Papua, Indonesia
tel/fax: +62 0 967 581600/520
e-mail: elshamnewsservice@jayapura.wasantara.net.id

Perkumpulan Terbatas Untuk Pengkajian dan Pemberdayaan Masyarakat Adat Papua (PPMA; Association for Papua Indigenous People's Study and Empowerment)
Jl. Raya ABG Sentani no. 13B, Abepura
Papua, Indonesia
tel: +62 0 967 582681
fax: +62 0 967 587614
e-mail: lppma_irja@jayapura.wasantara.net.id

Sekretariat Keadilan dan Perdamaian Keuskupan Jayapura (Office for Justice and Peace)
Jl. Kesehatan no. 4 Dok II, Kotak Pos 1379, Jayapura
Papua, Indonesia
tel: +62 0 967 534993
fax: +62 0 967 534993
e-mail: sekkp@jayapura.wasantara.net.id

Yayasan Hak Asasi Manusia Anti Kekerasan (YAHAMAK)
Jl. Baru Kompleks Yosepha Alomang, Kelurahan Kisamki Baru, Timika
Papua, Indonesia
tel: +62 0 901 323070
fax: +62 0 901 323070

Yayasan Humi Inane (Suara Perempuan) Jayawijaya
Jl. Yos Sudarso no. 20, Wamena
Papua, Indonesia
tel: +62 0 969 31260
fax: +62 0 969 31278

Yayasan Nanimi Wabili Su (YNWS; Nanimi Wabili Su Foundation)
Jl. F. Kalasuat no. 96, Kelurahan Malangkedi, Sorong
Papua, Indonesia.
tel: +62 0 951 322787
fax: +62 0 951 331102
e-mail: ferdy_rondong@hotmail.com

Yayasan Pengembangan Prakarsa Wirausaha (YPPWI; Foundation for Enterpreneurship Development)
Jl. Raya Sentani no. 92, Padang Bulan, Jayapura
Papua, Indonesia
tel: +62 0 967 581222
fax: +62 0 967 581222
e-mail: yppwi@jayapura.wasantara.net.id
www.yppwi.arecool.net

Jakarta

Aliansi Masyarakat Sipil untuk Demokrasi (YAPPIKA; Civil Society Alliance for Democracy)
Syamsuddin Ishak (Manager Riset)
Jl. Pedati Raya no. 20 RT 007/09
Jakarta Timur, DKI Jakarta, Indonesia
tel: +62 0 21 8191623
fax: +62 0 21 8500670
e-mail: yappika@indosat.net.id
www.yappika.org

International Crisis Group (ICG)
Menara Thamrin, 14th Floor, Suite 1402, Jl. M.H.Thamrin Kav.3
Jakarta 10250, Indonesia
tel: +62 0 21 3983 0303
fax: +62 0 21 3983 0304
e-mail: sjones@crisisweb.org

Lembaga Studi dan Advokasi Masyarakat (Elsam; Institute for Policy Research and Advocacy)
Ifdhal Kasim, SH (Direktur Eksekutif)
Jl. Siaga II no. 31, Pejaten Barat, Pasar Minggu
DKI Jakarta, Indonesia
tel: +62 0 21 7972662/64
fax: +62 0 21 79192519
e-mail: elsam@nusa.or.id, advokasi@indosat.net.id
www.elsam.or.id

Yohanis G. Bonay is a Papuan human rights activist and lawyer. He worked with the Jayapura Branch of Indonesian Legal Aid Institute Foundation from 1986 to May 1998, when he established the Institute for Human Rights Study and Advocacy (Elsham) in Papua. He served as director of Elsham until August 2003, during which time the organization fostered the emergence of a community-based human rights movement and become an internationally respected voice on human rights issues in Papua. Currently, he serves as a member of the Electoral Commission for the Province of Papua. He is frequently called upon to act as an adviser and commentator on human rights by NGOs, the media, and tertiary education.

Jane McGrory works for Cordaid and Catholic Relief Services in support of their peacebuilding programs in Indonesia. In Papua, she has been part of Cordaid's efforts to support the work of local partners in developing broadly based initiatives for peace and justice.

Notes

1. The change to the name of the province was formalized in legislation regarding special autonomy for Papua (Udang-Udang 21/2001).

2. The TPN is the Papua-based military wing of an umbrella group of resistance movements known as the OPM.

3. These are composed of the Indonesian Armed Forces (ABRI), referring to the national security apparatus prior to security reform in 1999, when the armed forces and national police became separate institutions; the Indonesian National Army; and the Police of the Republic of Indonesia.

4. B. Giay, "West Papua: Peace Zone a Possible Dream—The Role of West Papuan Churches and Local Initiatives in the Human Rights Struggle," 2001, unpublished paper, p. 3.

5. J. Mason, "Shadow plays: The Crisis of Refugees and Internally Displaced Persons in Indonesia," Report to the U.S. Committee for Refugees, January 2000, p. 35.

6. C. Richards, "Military Madness," *New Internationalist,* West Papua Special Edition no. 344 (April 2002).

7. *Papua Post,* August 11, 2003.

8. OPM leader Kelly Kwalik has previously declared that he was renouncing violence in 2001. Kwalik said that he and other OPM leaders realized that their guerrilla activities also helped sustain the cycle of conflict in Papua. However, the TPN/OPM is a fragmented organization and its nine units operate autonomously. It is uncertain to what extent units have committed to a strategy of nonviolent means.

9. For more information regarding military businesses see L. McCulloch, "Trifungsi: The Role of the Indonesian Military in Business," paper presented at the International Conference on Soldiers in Business: Military as an Economic Actor, Jakarta, October 17–19, 2000, available at www.bicc.de/budget/events/milbus/confpapers.html.

10. Giay, "West Papua," p. 3.

11. Human Rights Watch, "Indonesia: Violence and Political Impasse in Papua," *Human Rights Watch Report,* vol. 13, no. 2 (July 2001), available at www.hrw.org/press/2001/07/papua0703.htm, p. 23.

12. A recent opinion poll by the International Foundation for Election Systems (IFES) found that the military and police were the least-respected public institutions among Papuans. IFES, "Papua Public Opinion Survey, Indonesia," 2003, available at www.ifes.org/reg_activities/pdf/papua_summary_report_final.pdf, p. 12.

13. The definition of structural violence forwarded by G. Harris and N. Lewis aptly characterizes the nature of structural violence in Papua, identifying it as an systematic program to "maintain the dominance of one group at the center of power over another group . . . [which] at a practical level . . . can mean low wages, landlessness, illiteracy, poor health, limited or non-existent political representation or legal rights, and in general, limited control over much of their lives." G. Harris and N. Lewis, "Structural Violence, Positive Peace, and Peacebuilding," in G. Harris, ed., *Recovery from Armed Conflict in Developing Countries: An Economic and Political Analysis* (London: Routledge, 1999), pp. 29–30.

14. IFES, "Papua Public Opinion Survey, Indonesia," pp. 4–7.

15. International Crisis Group, "Ending Repression in Irian Jaya," ICG Asia Report no. 23, September 20, 2001, available at www.crisisweb.org/projects/asia/indonesia/reports/a400414-20092001.pdf, p. 6.

16. Ibid.

17. The conditions for economic exploitation of Papua were set when PT Freeport began operation in 1967 (notably prior to integration). The giant U.S.-owned mining operation, closely supported by the regime in Jakarta, made Papua a center of Indonesia's economic growth. As a vital national object, the company's contract site attracts a strong police and military presence—a presence that cost PT Freeport a onetime payment of U.S.$35 million and annual payments of U.S.$11 million in security fees. Richards, "Military Madness." This protection money is paid from the massive U.S.$19 billion that Freeport makes in after-tax profits each year.

18. In the 1960s the nonindigenous composed only 2.5 percent of the population, compared to an estimated 30 percent today. International Crisis Group, "Ending Repression in Irian Jaya," pp. 5–6.

19. Elsham, "Insiden di Pasar Abepura," November 11–12, 2000.

20. Statistics regarding fatalities drawn from "Peristiwa Tragedi Kemanusiaan Wamena 6 Oktober 2000 Sebelum dan Sesudahnya: Sebuah Laporan Investigasi," report prepared by the Justice and Peace Center at the Jayapura Diocese (Sekretariat Keadilan dan Perdamaian), KONTRAS Papua, Elsham, and LBH-Jayapura, January 2001.

21. O. Mote and D. Rutherford, "From Irian Jaya to Papua: The Limits of Primordialism in Indonesia's Troubled East," *Indonesia,* vol. 72 (Ithaca: October 2001): 115–140.

22. International Crisis Group, "Indonesia: Resources and Conflict in Papua," ICG Asia Report no. 39, September 13, 2002, available at www.intl-crisis-group.org/projects/showreport.cfm?reportid=774.

23. Legislation for the division of Papua into three provinces was passed on October 4, 1999 (Udang-Udang no. 45) but was not implemented due to public opposition. President Megawati revived plan and issued a Presidential Instruction (no. 1/2003), which ordered the implementation of the 1999 law to divide Papua.

24. D. C. Blair and D. L. Phillips, "Indonesia Commission: Peace and Progress in Papua," report of an independent commission sponsored by the Council on Foreign Relations Center for Preventive Action, available at www.cfr.org/pdf/indonesia_commission.pdf, pp. 34–35.

25. Ibid.

26. Ibid., p. 35.

27. International Crisis Group, "Ending Repression in Irian Jaya," p. 16.

28. "Vauatu Wants West Papua Back on Decolonization List," Port Vila Presse, September 25, 2002.

29. Ibid.

30. International Crisis Group, "Ending Repression in Irian Jaya," p. 16.

31. Ibid., citing "West Papuan to Ignore Warning," *Sydney Morning Herald,* November 24, 2000.

32. International Crisis Group, "Ending Repression in Irian Jaya," p. 18.

33. Laurence Sullivan, a British expert in constitutional law, in an interview with the Australian Broadcasting Corporation, September 11, 2003.

34. Yayasan Pengembangan Prakarsa Wirausaha Papua has compiled a list of active NGOs in Papua, which included over 140 organizations in 2002.

35. The Indonesian Peacebuilding Directory compiled by CRS-Cordaid in 2002 lists seventy-two peacebuilding organizations located in Papua and another fourteen organizations with programs in Papua. Organizations were listed in the directory based on "self-identification" as a "peacebuilding organization" and in accordance with an understanding of peacebuilding as a broad range of actions to promote conditions and relationships that promote peace and justice.

36. B. Setyanto, B. Sugiono, Y. Reba, and N. Wamafma, "The Position and Role of Civil Society Organisations in Resolving the Papuan Conflict," Asian House Focus Series no. 12, Schriftenreihe des Asienhauses, 2002, available at www.asienhaus.de/publikat/focus/focus12/focus12.pdf, p. 32.

37. World Council of Churches (WCC), "Press Release: UN Commission on Human Rights: WCC Addresses Serious Human Rights Situation in Papua, Indonesia, 17 April 2002," available at www2.wcc-coe.org/pressreleasesen.nsf/index/pu-02–11.html; and Franciscan International, "Franciscan International and Dominicans for Justice and Peace Demand an End to Long-Standing and On-Going Human Rights Violations in Papua, Indonesia," statement to the fifty-eighth session of the Commission on Human Rights, Geneva, April 10, 2002.

38. Setyanto et al., "Position and Role of Civil Society Organisations," p. 30.

39. A recent opinion poll found that religious institutions were the most respected type of institution in Papua, according to 50 percent of those surveyed, significantly ahead of the second-most-respected type of institution, regency-level government, according to 5 percent. While the church is obviously not the only religious institution in Papua, it is reasonable to assume that it shares in this high level of respect for religious institutions. IFES, "Papua Public Opinion Survey, Indonesia," p. 12.

40. Giay, "West Papua," pp. 10–14.

41. "Turf" refers to the tendency of organizations to compete to secure and protect the "niche"—in terms of either particular issues, geographic areas, or target communities—that they seek to claim as their exclusive domain and are reluctant to share with other organizations.

42. Thom Beanal, customary leader of the Amungme people and member of the PPC, in dialogue with then president B. J. Habibie in Jakarta, February 26, 1999.

43. The IFES survey found that aspirations for independence were as high as 75 percent among indigenous Papuans. IFES, "Papua Public Opinion Survey, Indonesia," p. 17.

44. Suggested by Franciscan friar and human rights activist Theo van den Broek OFM in "Papua 2003: Situational Report for the Diplomatic Community in Jakarta," April 2003, p. 7.

9.6

THE PHILIPPINES

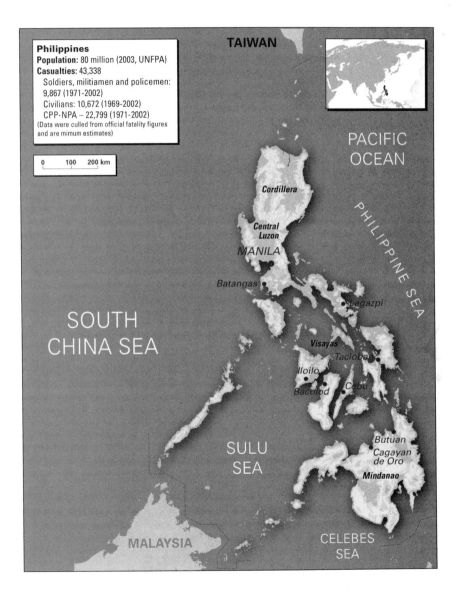

Philippines
Population: 80 million (2003, UNFPA)
Casualties: 43,338
  Soldiers, militiamen and policemen:
  9,867 (1971-2002)
  Civilians: 10,672 (1969-2002)
  CPP-NPA – 22,799 (1971-2002)
(Data were culled from official fatality figures
and are mimum estimates)

0   100   200 km

TAIWAN

PACIFIC
OCEAN

PHILIPPINE SEA

Cordillera

Central
Luzon

MANILA

Batangas

Legazpi

SOUTH
CHINA SEA

Visayas

Tacloban

Iloilo

Cebu

Bacolod

Butuan
Cagayan
de Oro

Mindanao

SULU
SEA

MALAYSIA

CELEBES
SEA

9.6.1

Communist Insurgencies:
Years of Talks, But No Solution Yet

Rey Claro Casambre

The armed conflict between the Philippine government and the National Democratic Front of the Philippines (NDFP) has been raging throughout the country for more than three decades. Under martial rule, from 1972 to 1986, the government pursued a policy of suppression, pacification, and co-option in dealing with this armed challenge. It was only after Ferdinand Marcos was deposed in 1986 that the incoming government initiated peace negotiations with the NDFP. The current peace negotiations began in 1992 under President Fidel Ramos. The talks have produced ten major bilateral agreements, despite long recesses, suspensions and complete breakdowns between a few days or weeks of actual negotiations.[1] After having been recessed and suspended for two-and-a-half years since June 2001, formal talks resumed February 2004 in Oslo, Norway with social and economic reforms now on the agenda.

Armed conflict in the Philippines is rooted in the same iniquitous social, political, and economic structures that plague most Third World countries. Widespread poverty and unemployment, immensely disparate incomes, rampant criminality, graft and corruption, chronic economic depression, and a gargantuan foreign debt—these are the symptoms of centuries-old social malaise afflicting the backward, preindustrial, foreign-dominated Philippine economy and society.

One could plausibly assert that what is now called "globalization" began in 1521 when the Portuguese navigator Ferdinand Magellan "discovered" and claimed for Spain what would be known as the Philippine Islands. He thereby opened up new trade routes for exploiting new sources of cheap raw materials, labor, and most important, gold. These helped stimulate the rise of capitalism until it subsumed feudalism and replaced it as the dominant system in Europe and the world.[2]

The arrival of the Spanish *conquistadores* ushered in three centuries of colonialism. The *encomienda* system of administration was established whereby large tracts of land were awarded by the Spanish king to Spanish officials and religious orders "for meritorious services." Vested with absolute feudal power and privileges, the *encomenderos* imposed exorbitant tributes, land rent, corvée labor, forced servitude, arbitrary evictions, and a host of other abuses on the largely peasant native population. In the eighteenth century, *haciendas* were introduced for large-scale production of agricultural export crops. Thus emerged a local class of merchant capitalists, traders, and a nascent working class. However, the great majority of the native population remained peasants.

The introduction and spread of Christianity by Spanish friars served to perpetuate Spanish rule by inculcating in the natives filial piety, obedience, and sacrifice with the promise of reward in the afterworld. Still, peasant revolts erupted continually. Toward the end of the nineteenth century, Filipino nationalism evolved from a movement for reforms and assimilation into a fight for independence from Spain. The 1896 revolution led by the Katipunan and inspired by the French Revolution eventually dealt deathblows to Spanish colonialism. But the goal of national and social liberation was preempted by the 1898 Treaty of Paris following the end of the Spanish-American War, whereby Spain ceded the Philippines to the ascendant world power, the United States, for U.S. $20 million.

The United States occupied the Philippines after vanquishing the Filipinos in the Philippine-American War of 1899–1902, in which more than 700,000 Filipinos died—roughly one-tenth of the population.[3] They retained the semi-feudal system to keep the Philippines as source of raw materials, a market for surplus products, and a field of investment for surplus capital. A lopsided "free trade" policy and "special relations" between the industrialized United States and the agrarian Philippines stunted the growth of any local industry.[4]

The United States granted the Philippines nominal independence on July 4, 1946. On this same day, incoming president Manuel Roxas signed the U.S.-Philippines Treaty of General Relations, which guaranteed to U.S. citizens and corporations the same property rights enjoyed by Filipinos, granted the United States territorial rights over its military bases in the Philippines, and required Philippine foreign policy to align with U.S. foreign policy. Other treaties followed, effectively surrendering economic sovereignty, territorial integrity, and national patrimony to the Americans. The Philippines was thus transformed from a colony to a "neocolony."

The pattern of unequal colonial trade persisted, resulting in chronic trade, balance-of-payments, and budget deficits as well as a burgeoning foreign debt. Military treaties and agreements allowed the United States to maintain military bases in the Philippines until 1991, and to train, supply, and direct the Armed Forces of the Philippines through a joint military advisory group.

Such overwhelming economic, political, diplomatic, and military advantage was made possible by a Filipino elite nurtured to serve U.S. interests, and a Filipino populace conditioned to look up to the United States as a liberator, benefactor, and friend rather than as invader and colonizer. The United States established an extensive public school system that instilled Western values and

Manila 1990. Civil protest against U.S. military bases.

extolled itself as a "benevolent brother." The upper strata of Philippine society—extremely wealthy and privileged landowners and import-export merchants—became beholden to the United States and served as its local agents. They completely dominated and controlled Philippine society.

The great majority of the Filipino people are peasants (75 percent) and workers (14–15 percent) living in poverty and misery. Government statistics show that in 1991, 5 percent of all landowners owned half the total farmland area. Two-thirds own less than three hectares.[5] Continuous reconcentration through land conversions and landgrabbing by big landlords and multinational corporations has led to the expulsion of many farmers from their plots. Dispossessed and evicted farmers either migrated to the cities in search of employment or resettled on public lands, usually in the mountains. With the industrial sector stagnant, it was the forest frontiers that absorbed the displaced farmers. In the late 1960s these frontiers reached a point of saturation, swelling the ranks of the unemployed and underemployed.

Conflict Dynamics

The 1960s were characterized by severe economic crisis and social unrest with massive demonstrations, strikes, and protest actions by workers, farmers, students, urban poor, church people, indigenous peoples, and various professionals. These were met with violent state repression. More significantly, the crisis was marked by increasingly violent conflict among the various factions of the ruling elite.

On December 26, 1968, a group of cadres of the dormant, Soviet-leaning Partido Komunista ng Pilipinas (PKP) broke away and "reestablished" the

Communist Party of the Philippines (CPP). The CPP established the New People's Army (NPA) as its military arm on March 29, 1969. The NDFP was established in April 1973 as a broad alliance of various organizations under the banner of the national democratic revolution.

The declaration of martial law in 1972 by President Marcos and the incarceration of thousands of activists and critics, including Marcos's business and political rivals, appeared to validate the CPP's reading that the ruling elite had to shift to a more repressive mode of rule in order to remain in power.

From the outset, the CPP/NPA/NDFP launched a "people's democratic revolution" aimed at "overthrowing imperialism, feudalism and bureaucrat-capitalism" and setting up a "people's democratic state." From a few score men and firearms, the NPA grew by 1986 to 10,000 fighters organizing mass bases in the countryside and engaging government troops nationwide. Fourteen years of full-blown dictatorship and unabated counterinsurgency campaigns failed to crush this armed challenge.

The toll of the armed conflict on human life and limb was enormous. A 1984 report based on studies conducted by human rights organizations in the Philippines and abroad showed that under martial law, 160,000 people were killed and thousands tortured all over the Philippines.[6] Hundreds of thousands were illegally detained and humiliated for at least one day, 70,000 of them for more than a month. Up to 6 million people were forced to leave their homes and farms, of whom 2.5 million were permanently displaced farmers. Amnesty International reported 500 "involuntary disappearances" as of 1990.[7]

"People Power"—an unarmed uprising triggered by a military rebellion—overthrew Marcos and ended martial rule in February 1986. In November 1986, the government under the new president, Corazon Aquino, and the NDFP began peace negotiations. A sixty-day cease-fire agreement to build confidence and goodwill for the talks was signed. But before discussion on substantive issues could begin, the negotiations collapsed in January 1987 when government troops fired at unarmed farmers demonstrating near Malacanang Palace, killing nineteen and injuring hundreds. In April 1987, speaking before the Philippine Military Academy graduating class, Aquino declared "total war" against the CPP/NPA/NDFP.

Subsequent efforts to resume peace negotiations during Aquino's term were blocked by preconditions that the NPA lay down its arms or agree to a cease-fire and the government's insistence on the constitution as a framework for negotiations. These were rejected by the NDFP as tantamount to capitulation and anathema to a revolutionary movement seeking to establish a "people's democratic government."

Meanwhile, the government formed regional and provincial Peace and Order Councils (POCs) to infuse socioeconomic and political dimensions to the military campaigns and mobilize local government units and civic organizations into the counterinsurgency effort. The POCs called for peace talks at the local level and oversaw the amnesty and rehabilitation program for surrendering individuals.

The NDFP viewed these moves as schemes to divide the revolutionary forces and foment dissent and demoralization in their ranks.

Local peace talks did not materialize, as local CPP/NPA/NDFP forces abided by the NDFP's policy of negotiating with the government only at the national level. An exception was in the Cordillera region, in northern Luzon, where a breakaway group formed the Cordillera People's Liberation Army (CPLA), which entered into a peace agreement with the government. The CPLA was demobilized and its members integrated into themilitary or military-supervised village militia units.

Official Conflict Management

In 1992, president-elect Fidel V. Ramos called for peace negotiations with the CPP/NPA/NDFP, the Moro National Liberation Front (MNLF),[8] the Moro Islamic Liberation Front (MILF), and military rebels who staged several failed coups against the Aquino government. The military rebels signed a peace agreement with the government in October 1993, while the MNLF signed a "Final Peace Agreement," also with the Ramos government in 1996.

The NDFP responded positively to the offer for peace negotiations for the following reasons:

- To counter any impression that it was the government that genuinely wanted peace while the CPP/NPA/NDFP eschewed it.
- To propagate its program for a people's democratic revolution.
- To achieve immediate gains that benefit the people and the revolutionary movement.

It did so knowing that it risked confusion within its ranks, rendering its forces vulnerable to government offers of amnesty and rehabilitation for those who surrender and return to the mainstream of society.

The NDFP line for the attainment of a just and lasting peace is none other than its general line of the people's democratic revolution, that is, the struggle to overthrow imperialism, feudalism, and bureaucratic capitalism. It states that it has no illusions this can be achieved through peace negotiations alone, and it still considers armed struggle as the principal form of struggle. Even when compared to democratic mass protest actions, the peace negotiations have secondary importance. The NDFP stresses that its strength at the negotiating table derives from its strength on the battlefield and the democratic movement for national and social emancipation. The peace negotiations have the unique advantage of being an arena where the NDFP can assert equality and parity with the government. Thus, the NDFP asserts, peace negotiations do not play the primary role but contribute positively to the quest for lasting peace.[9]

Exploratory talks were held in the Netherlands from August 30 to September 1, 1992, resulting in the signing of the Hague Joint Declaration, which set the objective, substantive agenda, and framework for the government-NDFP peace negotiations.

The National Unification Commission (NUC) was created by Ramos on July 28, 1992, to formulate a general amnesty program and a comprehensive peace process. The NUC submitted its recommendations in July 1993 after a series of provincial, regional, and national consultations. However, in contrast to the openness and wide publicity given to the consultations, these recommendations were not immediately and fully divulged to the public.

Ramos adopted the NUC proposals, and in September 1993 issued an executive order, "Defining the Approach and Administrative Structure for Government's Comprehensive Peace Efforts." The "six paths to peace," which to this day stand at the core of government's peace program, consist of the following:

- The pursuit of social, economic, and political reforms that deal with the root causes of insurgency and social unrest
- Consensus building and empowerment for peace, which seek to make consultations with people a regular part of governance
- Peace talks with the rebel groups aimed at final negotiated settlements
- Reconciliation, reintegration into society, and rehabilitation of rebels, including amnesty and other measures to address the needs of former rebels, demobilized combatants, and civilian victims of the armed conflicts
- The protection of civilians and the deescalation of conflict, which includes such measures as limited suspension of offensive military operations and recognition of peace zones, intensified delivery of basic services to conflict areas, and strict implementation of laws and policy guidelines for the protection of human rights
- Building a positive climate for peace, which includes confidence-building measures between the government and rebel groups, and peace advocacy and education for Philippine society as a whole[10]

Like the NDFP, the Philippines government does not consider the peace negotiations to be the primary means of attaining a just and lasting peace. It asserts that socioeconomic and political reforms are being undertaken with or without peace talks. Nonetheless, peace negotiations have been used to provide some semblance of political stability whenever the government is confronted by crisis situations, especially those that scare away foreign investors.

In his first "State of the Nation address" before Congress in July 1993, President Ramos made the following assessment:

> Our peace initiative has succeeded beyond our expectations. It has brought the military rebels and southern secessionists to the conference table, and *fragmented the insurgent communist party to the core* [italics added].[11]

Ramos was referring to a long-simmering rift within the CPP that broke out in the open soon after the party leadership issued a call in mid-1992 to "reaffirm our basic principles and rectify our errors." A number of leading cadres rejected that call, defied the party leadership and publicly criticized the party center. The CPP/NPA/NDFP appeared deeply divided, with the "rejectionists" having the larger following. However, when the dust had settled, the CPP remained largely intact. The "rejectionists" tried to regroup into a single party, but failed due to political, ideological, and personal differences. They now comprise four distinct groups, with only one waging armed struggle.

The Ramos government initially adopted a wait-and-see attitude, freezing the negotiations with the NDFP after the Hague Joint Declaration was approved. It offered to hold separate talks with the splinter groups, and drew one into peace negotiations, resulting in a cease-fire agreement and a PhP 500 million rehabilitation package.

Exploratory talks between the government and NDFP resumed in 1994, subsequently resulting in agreements on safety and immunity guarantees, ground rules for formal meetings, formation of reciprocal working committees, and other preliminary agreements.

Formal peace talks began on June 26, 1995. In March 1998 both parties signed a Comprehensive Agreement on Respect for Human Rights and International Humanitarian Law (CARHRIHL), the first of four items on the substantive agenda. However, the implementation of the CARHRIHL was shelved after the government objected to a number of provisions implying the NDFP had the political authority to implement CARHRIHL. In May 1999, the government entered into a "Visiting Forces Agreement" with the United States, which the NDFP considered a violation of national sovereignty and thus of the Hague Joint Declaration. This, on top of previous disagreements, resulted in the termination of the peace negotiations in mid-1999.

At issue, in particular, has been the interpretation of "national sovereignty." The government asserts that it is the sole sovereign power and that the republic is indivisible. Thus the NDFP cannot share sovereign power and the authority, for example, to investigate, prosecute, and impose sanctions on violators of human rights and international humanitarian law.[12] Further, all agreements must be interpreted and implemented in accordance with the government constitution and legal processes.

The government is extremely wary that the NDFP would gain a status of belligerency through the negotiations. The NDFP, on the other hand, asserts its status as a revolutionary organization and a belligerent under international law, exercising sovereign power in areas it controls, with an army to defend its constituency and territory. It argues that there is no need to gain belligerency status through the talks, having achieved this on the battlefield and through the establishment of its mass base.

A deeper examination reveals that the NDFP claim to belligerency and political authority is not the crux of the debate. First, the government has been slow to implement provisions of the CARHRIHL that do not involve NDFP political authority, such as review and repeal of repressive government laws, release of political prisoners, and indemnification of human rights victims under martial law. Second, the NDFP cites examples of the government compromising national sovereignty and territorial integrity to the United States, such as the provisions surrendering jurisdiction over U.S. servicemen committing crimes and the terrorist listing of the CPP/NPA and Jose Maria Sison (founding chair of the CCP) by the United States and the European Council.

The more fundamental difference between the government and the NDFP impeding the peace negotiations is a disagreement on the root causes of the armed conflict, and on the nature of a "just and lasting peace." The government considers the following as the roots of the armed conflict: massive and abject poverty, iniquitous distribution of wealth and control over the base of resources needed for livelihood, injustice, and poor governance. These are all acknowledged by the NDFP. But the government is silent on how foreign domination and control has stunted the growth of the Philippine economy and caused suffering and misery. In contrast, the NDFP highlights this as the fundamental problem.

The difference goes beyond semantics. The NDFP points out that rather than address this problem, successive administrations since the Marcos regime have pursued basically the same economic policies that further open up the economy to foreign exploitation and plunder. Thus, measures being pursued by the government, such as Ramos's social reform agenda, fall short when assessed in terms of how economic independence and progress can be achieved to alleviate the people's suffering.

A comparison of the two parties' proposals for social and economic reforms reveals great disparity on how to address the roots of the armed conflict. The government's proposals all lie within the framework of the Philippine constitution and laws, notwithstanding the provision in the "six paths to peace" that reforms "may involve constitutional amendments." In initial negotiations for the Comprehensive Agreement on Social Economic Reform, the government resisted any reference whatsoever to foreign domination and control of the Philippine economy.

From the 1993 NUC list of "reforms which will deal with the root cause of insurgency," to the 2003 government draft "Final Peace Agreement," for example, no constitutional amendment is proposed for land reform or national industrialization, only better and more vigorous implementation of existing laws such as the Comprehensive Agrarian Reform Law.

NDFP proposals, on the other hand, hew closely to the program for a people's democratic revolution. Even as adjustments are made considering the nature of negotiations, these proposals nonetheless aim to dismantle monopolies—foreign and local—from which arise the economic and political power of the ruling elite. The most important of these are in agrarian reform, national industrialization, protection of economic sovereignty and the national patrimony, and upholding the people's basic social and economic rights. Many of these proposals, if agreed upon, would require major constitutional changes.

Without the assistance of a neutral third party, it is unlikely that the peace negotiations would advance this far. From the outset the NDFP has been open to having a foreign neutral third party in the negotiations. But the government argued that the armed conflict was an internal matter that should be resolved without any foreign third-party intervention. The government, wary that having a foreign third party in the negotiations would give the armed conflict an international character, initially insisted on holding the talks in the Philippines, then proposed a "shifting venue." The NDFP objected, pointing to the 1986 experience when CPP/NPA/NDFP personnel who surfaced for the peace talks were subjected to intensive surveillance, identification, and punitive actions.[13] To underscore its point, the NDFP offered to host the peace talks inside its territory, with the NDFP issuing safe-conduct passes to government personnel.

Exploratory and formal talks have been hosted by the Netherlands and Belgium since 1992. The Norwegian government has acted as third-party host since the resumption of formal government-NDFP talks in April 2001. It has taken an even more active role as third-party facilitator since October 2003. Other, less significant activities by outside parties have included an offer from the Swiss government to host talks (rejected by the government),[14] similar offers from the European Parliament, and European Parliament resolutions supporting the negotiations and expressing concern over human rights violations.

In contrast, there is also what might be called foreign third-party conflict "aggravation." For example, the United States, the Netherlands, and the Council of the European Union have jeopardized peace negotiations by listing the CPP/NPA and NDFP chief political consultant Jose Maria Sison as a "foreign terrorist" since August 2002.

The government has itself undermined confidence-building efforts by campaigning for the "terrorist" listing among member states of the European Union in October 2002, welcoming such actions, and then using the "terrorist" listing to pressure the NDFP into agreeing to a "new enhanced process" that would lead to the signing of a "Final Peace Agreement." The NDFP has denounced the listing and the actions of the government as violations of national sovereignty and of the bilateral agreements. It also rejected the government's proposed "new process" and draft "Final Peace Agreement" as "negotiated capitulation."

There is meager involvement by international organizations in advancing the Philippine peace process. Neither the United Nations, nor any official Asian or Southeast Asian regional organization has been directly involved in the government-NDFP peace negotiations. However, the UN Commission on Human Rights (UNCHR) recently issued an official document enumerating positive aspects, subjects of concern, and recommendations in relation to the Philippine government's report on human rights.[15] It commends the government for reforming its legal order, ratifying the Optional Protocol to the Covenant, and facilitating international assistance in relation to education and training on the protection of human rights.

On the other hand, the UNCHR expressed its concern over a whole range of issues including investigations of crimes allegedly committed by state forces against human rights defenders, journalists, and mass leaders; antiterrorist legislation; cases of extrajudicial killings, arbitrary detention, abuse and intimidation of detainees; the persistent and widespread use of torture and inhumane treatment of detainees; trafficking of women and children; warrantless arrests; and continuing reports of displacement of persons and evacuation of populations in areas of counterinsurgency operations. Though not specifically linked to the peace process, such comments contribute to identifying the causes of conflict and the approaches employed by the government to resolve it.

The only international organization directly involved in the government-NDFP peace negotiations, albeit in a low-key mode, is the International Committee of the Red Cross (ICRC). On at least seven occasions, the government and NDFP requested the ICRC to help facilitate the NPA's release of captured police and army officers for humanitarian reasons and as part of the confidence-building measures for peace talks. The ICRC has also been involved in providing information and training to the Armed Forces of the Philippines and the Philippine National Police on international humanitarian law.

Multi-Track Diplomacy

Both the government and the NDFP claim to represent the people's general interest. Accordingly, both consult with organizations and assemblies to inform their efforts at formulating policies and positions reflecting and appealing to a broad cross-section of the population.

There is a strong and vibrant people's movement in the Philippines for sovereignty, freedom, and social justice. It consists of people's organizations (POs), nongovernmental organizations (NGOs), church groups, sectoral organizations (e.g., women, youth, workers, farmers, indigenous peoples, etc.) multisectoral organizations, alliances and coalitions, issue-based organizations, networks, institutions, and even individuals, striving to contribute to the attainment of these ideals.

Reborn and revitalized in the 1960s, this movement was steeled in the crucible of the Filipino people's struggle against the Marcos dictatorship in the 1970s and 1980s. The restoration of formal democratic processes in 1986 after the ouster of Marcos opened up divergent avenues and trajectories for various organizations and individuals. However, they would reconverge under certain conditions and form a core around which the mass of unorganized and hitherto uninvolved could rally. This was vividly displayed in the upsurge that led to the popular uprising "People Power 2" that brought about the ouster of the Estrada government in 2001.

Under normal conditions, these organizations are so diverse and numerous as to defy definition and classification. The Western observer would loosely call them "civil society." But Filipino social scientists advise caution: There is no single term to define this conglomeration of organizations, or a single acceptable definition for "civil society" in the Philippines.[16]

Whatever they are called collectively, these organizations and individuals that comprise the movement for national sovereignty, democracy, and social justice have played a crucial role in peacebuilding efforts in the Philippines. They have been instrumental in calling for peace negotiations and raising issues and advocacies that enhance the peace process. More important, they have amplified and upheld the imperative of addressing the roots of the armed conflict through social, economic and political reforms.

The Coalition for Peace (CfP) played a key role in 1987, in the formation of "peace zones," where the military and NPA combatants were banned or voluntarily withdrew so the people would be spared the ravages of war and work to improve their lives, including organizing themselves for self-empowerment. Unfortunately, the military later insisted on reestablishing their presence. Government co-opted the program by declaring the peace zones "social development areas" and pursued programs and projects without consulting the communities themselves.[17]

The People's Caucus, formed in 1990, consisted of hundreds of organizations and prominent personages, most of whom were at the forefront of the movement against the Marcos dictatorship. It issued on October 14, 1990, a People's Agenda highlighted by a call for the government and NDFP to resume peace negotiations and address the roots of the armed conflict to attain a just and lasting peace.

The multisectoral National Peace Conference (NPC) held in 1990 drafted a "Basic Peace Agenda," which was to be presented to the government and the NDFP. It was reconstituted in 1993 to undertake direct advocacy with government on the basic peace agenda, and provided sectoral participation in the 1993 Social Pact for Empowered Economic Development and the 1994–1995 Social Reform Agenda.[18]

The Multisectoral Peace Advocates (MSPA) actively pushed for the resumption of peace negotiations after they collapsed in 1987. The MSPA consisted of prominent individuals and representatives from the People's Caucus, NPC, Association of Major Religious Superiors, the Philippine Peace Center, the Peace Institute, and others. It advocated negotiations for the attainment of a just and lasting peace by addressing the root causes of the armed conflict.

The Katipunan ng mga Samahan ng Mamamayan (People's Congress), organized to present and advocate a people's agenda and alternatives, held its first session on 25 July 1992 with 120 organizations drawing up ten resolutions adopted as a "People's Agenda for the First 100 Days of the New Government." It pointed out that the armed conflict is rooted in poverty, injustice, foreign domination, and political disempowerment, and called for the holding of peace talks between the government and the NDFP, MILF, and military rebels. It forged, in September 1992, a common statement on the peace process. The second session of the People's Congress, held on August 24, 1993, presented a critique of the NUC report and the Ramos peace program, and reiterated the calls for basic reforms and peace negotiations.

There are currently a number of broad formations engaged in peacebuilding as an element of broader programs. Notable among these are the "Pilgrims for Peace," the "Gathering for Peace," and the "All-Out Peace Group." They have called for the resumption of government-NDFP and government-MILF formal negotiations, protested the Philippine government's all-out support for the U.S. "war against terror," and harshly criticized U.S. interventions in Iraq and elsewhere, including its military involvement in the Philippines.

At the core of these formations are organizations with peace advocacy as a principal or major focus. Among these are the National Council of Churches in the Philippines (NCCP), the National Secretariat for Social Action, Justice and Peace—Catholic Bishops' Conference of the Philippines (NASSA-CBCP), the Gaston Z. Ortigas Peace Institute, the Philippine Peace Center, the Coalition for Peace, the UP Center for Integrative and Development Studies, the Ecumenical Bishops' Forum, and the Bishops-Ulama Forum.

There are many other "cause oriented" formations pursuing particular or broadly-ranging concerns related to the advocacy of national sovereignty, democracy, and social justice. These often link up with the peace advocacy groups and participate in activities sponsored by them.

The largest, most experienced and active among these have expanded their advocacy by linking their particular concerns to national issues. Many organizations of workers, peasants, women, youth, professionals, and indigenous peoples, consider the interests of their constituencies inextricably linked to the overall pursuit of freedom, democracy, and social justice. It then becomes necessary for them to participate more actively in peacebuilding activities.

Understandably, the church sector in the Philippines is the most active and experienced, and has the most sustained activity in peacebuilding, including wide-ranging forms of support to the government-NDFP and government-MILF peace negotiations. Whatever the church, peacemaking is an integral and essential component of its ministry. The NCCP and NASSA-CBCP, for example have had long-running, comprehensive peace programs that include faith-based peace education, research, training, information dissemination, networking, and the like. The spirit and practice of ecumenism have also significantly facilitated the expansion and advance of peacebuilding by the various churches.

Similarly, human rights advocates are the natural allies and coworkers of the peace advocates. Most of the current crop of human rights leaders had their baptism by fire as activists during the martial law years. The lesson is not lost on them: defending, upholding, and promoting human rights cannot be done merely on a case-by-case basis, and involves more than the advocacy of civil and political rights. The pursuit of the full range of social, economic, cultural, and political rights is itself the pursuit of a just peace. Among the human rights organizations that actively link their human rights advocacy to peacebuilding are the Alliance for the Advancement of People's Rights, the Organization of Ex-Detainees Against Detention and Amnesty, the Philippine Alliance of Human Rights Advocates, the Task Force Detainees of the Philippines, and the Ecumenical Movement for Justice and Peace.

Special mention should be made of government officials who have played crucial roles in the peace process. These include the incumbent vice-president Teofisto Guingona, senator Loren Legarda, former senator Wigberto Tanada, and other national and local officials who have, at critical junctures, defied protocol and risked sanctions in opposing official policy and measures that impeded peace negotiations.

Three prominent multisectoral leaders elected into Congress under the Bayan Muna (People First) Party in 2001 have articulated in their privilege speeches and resolutions the various positions of peace advocates in pushing for negotiations and striving for a just and lasting peace. However, they warn their constituency against any illusion of legislation being passed that would address the roots of the armed conflict, in an institution heavily dominated by big landlords and *compradors*.

International church organizations such as the World Council of Churches, the National Christian Council of USA and the Church World Service, the United Council of Churches in Canada, the Christian Conference of Asia, Norwegian Church Aid, and other member or allied national churches and church councils quietly and indirectly support peacebuilding efforts through their local churches, church councils, and NGO partners.

The Mennonite Central Committee, a relief, service, community development, and peace agency of the North American Mennonite and Brethren in Christ churches, is a long-standing partner and supporter of the conflict-resolution and prevention efforts in the Philippines, both in the Moro areas and outside.

Amnesty International has investigated and documented human rights violations in the Philippines since the martial law years. It is perhaps the first international organization to document human rights violations under the Marcos regime and succeeding governments, and to draw international attention to them.

International Alert supports conflict resolution programs and projects in the Philippines through local partners. International Alert's founder, and former Amnesty International secretary-general, Martin Ennals, helped arrange a meeting between Aquino emissary Edilberto de Jesus and NDFP representative Luis Jalandoni in San Remo, Italy, in June 1990.

In sum, all these efforts taken collectively have created a significant positive impact on conflict-resolution and peace-building in the Philippines. They have shown that intervention by the people, especially those who suffer the most from the present dispensation, are needed to push the peace process forward.

Prospects

The resumption of the government-NDFP formal peace talks on February 10, 2004, reopened the door to negotiations on the substantive agenda and further confidence-building measures. The two Oslo Joint Statements issued by both panels in February and April 2004 announced agreements on addressing the issue of the "terrorist" listing of the CPP, NPA, and Jose Maria Sison, operationalizing the Joint Monitoring Committee, the release of political prisoners by the government, indemnifying human rights victims under the Marcos regime, and accelerating the talks on social and economic reforms.

Encouraged by these positive developments, which it has evidently and considerably helped realize, the people's movement for genuine peace is likewise gaining momentum.

The Filipino people above all stand to benefit concretely from the resumption and advance of the peace talks through the implementation of the

CARHRIHL, addressing pressing concerns as part of goodwill and confidence building measures, and the articulation of basic problems and their corresponding possible solutions. Further, the enhanced prospects for a genuine peace, though still distant, instill in the people faith and confidence in themselves and hope in their future.

The peace negotiations are bound to gain more international support. The third party facilitator, the government of Norway, has successfully hosted and facilitated the series of informal and formal talks that have put the negotiations back in track. The participation of international NGOs in the peace process is also bound to increase as the talks advance.

Recommendations

The Philippine experience in conflict resolution validates the criteria for an efficacious approach prescribed by Hugh Miall, Oliver Ramsbotham, and Tom Woodhouse in "calling for a broad approach to conflict resolution."[19] The government-NDFP negotiations and the agreements reached show that progress is possible so long as (1) the parties enter into the negotiations without preconditions or any imposition from either side or outside parties, (2) the agreements are crafted in precise language that strikes a balance between commitment and flexibility, (3) there is mutuality and reciprocity in the provisions, and (4) they deal with the core issues and bring about basic changes in society, "in accordance with mutually acceptable principles, including national sovereignty, democracy and social justice."[20]

The most difficult but essential aspect of successful peacebuilding is to ensure that the peace process deals with the core issues—that it is aimed at addressing the root causes of the armed conflict, especially the social and economic ones. With respect to bilateral peace negotiations, conflict resolution and prevention means ensuring that agreements identify and address the root causes of conflict, prevent their perpetuation and aggravation, and thereby avert the recurrence of violent conflict.

Second, addressing the root causes of armed conflict is invariably a long drawn-out and complicated process. Thus the peace process must be so designed as to generate immediate tangible gains that benefit the people in general, mitigate the adverse effects of the armed conflict, and serve to build confidence and goodwill as the negotiations advance towards the goal of a lasting peace.

This is the advantage of having the agreement on the respect for human rights and international humanitarian law as the first item of the substantive agenda. Its implementation could at once, in the absence of a settlement, mitigate the human cost of the armed conflict. The returns in terms of imbuing both combatants and noncombatants with greater respect for human rights are invaluable, if intangible. The forging of the CARHRIHL likewise helped build confidence in the capabilities of the two parties to move forward to the more contentious item on the agenda, the socioeconomic reforms.

Third, the peace process needs all the help it can get. Third-party official intervention can be either positive (offers of good offices, hosting, facilitation) or negative (like the "terrorist" listings). Intervention by other international organizations can be positive if they contribute to the identification, elaboration, and resolution of the causes of armed conflict, and if they help the parties build on their bilateral agreements rather than try to impose their own ideas. Neutrality should mean not taking the side of either party. In the Philippine context, the kind of neutrality that is good, possible, and necessary makes the interests of the greater majority of the Filipino people the paramount consideration in determining what position to adopt vis-à-vis the twists and turns in the negotiations.

The government-NDFP armed conflict has never been purely an internal affair, with the United States playing a dominant role in Philippine politics, economy and social-cultural life. September 11, 2001, has injected renewed U.S. military activity in the country under the guise of "counterterrorism," The inclusion of the CPP, NPA, and Jose Maria Sison on foreign "terrorist" lists underscores the negative impact of international geopolitics on the government-NDFP conflict and conflict-resolution.

Fourth, the government and NDFP must uphold and comply with bilateral agreements that have proven to be effective in advancing the talks and achieving further substantial agreements. Foremost is the Hague Joint Declaration which serves as the framework and foundation of the negotiations.

And fifth, there is a vast potential for building a strong peace constituency in the people's movement clamoring for socioeconomic and political reforms. To a larger extent, such potential lies in both the organized and the still-unorganized grassroots masses in the countryside, who are most directly affected by the armed conflict, and who stand to benefit most by its just resolution.

The NGOs, POs, and other organizations and individuals involved in this people's movement have presented sharp critiques of the present system, policies, and related factors, and clamor for basic reforms. But they still have to link their advocacy to the peace process, particularly the peace negotiations, and affirm their roles as true stakeholders.

There is a pressing need for further peace education and information work among the populace, the POs, NGOs, and other sectoral and grassroots organizations, and for involving them into activities that directly support and enhance the peace process.

In the end it is the people's conscious and sustained participation in the peace process that will push it forward in the direction of addressing the roots of the armed conflict. The Filipino people are the final arbiters on what will bring about genuine peace.

Realistically speaking, a just and lasting peace in the Philippines is still far beyond the horizon. The peace process has stretched out over many years. The ultimate resolution of the conflict will only come with much more painstaking work not only inside the negotiating room, but more decisively, outside its walls.

Resources

Publications

Philippines: "Disappearances" in the Context of Counter-Insurgency. By Amnesty International. London, February 1991, p. 7.

Overview, Status and Prospects of the Peace Negotiations Between the Government and the NDFP. By Silvestre Bello III, Quezon City, April 24, 2003. (Handout)

The Ramos Peace Program: Towards a Genuine and Lasting Peace or a Mere Pacification Campaign? By UN judge Romeo T. Capulong. Philippine Peace Center Policy Paper no.1. Makati, 1994.

Ten Years, Ten Agreements. Ed. Rey Casambre. NCCP and Philippine Peace Center, Quezon City, 2002.

The Philippines, 1986–1998: Narrative. By Maria Serena Diokno.
www.usc.edu/dept/las/ir/cis/cews/database/philippines/philippines.pdf.

Peace Matters: A Philippine Peace Compendium. By Miriam Coronel Ferrer. Quezon City: University of the Philippines Press and the UP Center for Integrative and Development Studies, 1996.

Pilgrim Voices: Citizens as Peacemakers. Ed. Ed Garcia. International Alert. Quezon City: Gaston Z. Ortigas Peace Institute and Ateneo Center for Social Policy and Public Affairs, 1994.

Participative Approaches to Peacemaking in the Philippines. By Ed Garcia. Tokyo: United Nations University, 1993.

Waging Peace in the Philippines: Looking Back, Moving Forward. Eds. Ed Garcia, Ed Legaspi, and Karen Tanada. Quezon City: Gaston Z. Ortigas Peace Institute, 2003.

Manila Covenant on Peace for Life: Another World Is Possible! By International Ecumenical Conference on Terrorism in a Globalized World. Conference Declaration and Workshop Reports. Manila, September 2002.

Documents of the Second Regular Session. By Katipunan ng mga Samahan ng Mamamayan (People's Congress). August 24, 1993.

Toward an Agreement on Human Rights and International Humanitarian Law. By Philippine Peace Center. Philippine Peace Center Policy Paper no. 4, Makati, 1998.

The People's Struggle for a Just Peace. By Jose Maria Sison. Utrecht: International Network of Philippine Studies, June 1991.

Philippine Economy and Politics. By Jose Maria Sison. Quezon City: Aklat ng Bayan, 1998.

"Concluding Observations of the Human Rights Committee: Philippines," in *Consideration of Reports Submitted by State Parties Under Article 40 of the Covenant.* November 6, 2003. ("Covenant" refers to the 1966 International Covenant of Civil and Political Rights)

Websites

www.opapp.gov.ph/peaceagreements.htm (Office of the Presidential Adviser on the Peace Process, Office of the President, Republic of the Philippines)

www.philippinerevolution.org (Philippine Revolution Web Central—CPP, NPA, NDFP, CPP-Public Information Office, *Ang Bayan*)

www.inps-sison.freewebspace.com (International Network for Philippine Studies) (Philippine Peace Center)

www.codewan.com.ph/caucus/about/a_2000_1211_08.htm (Gaston Z. Ortigas Peace Institute)

www.iisd.org/50comm/commdb/list/c01.htm (National Peace Conference)

www.justpeace.net.ph/process/body.htm (information on the status of peace negotiations of the government of the Philippines with the various rebel groups)

Resource Contacts

Fidel V. Agcaoili, spokesperson and member, NDFP Negotiating Panel; co-chair, Joint Monitoring Committee, e-mail: misha@wish.net

Silvestre Bello III, chair, government Negotiating Panel for the CPP/NPA/NDFP (2001–present), e-mail: mcm_villarta@mail.com

Romeo T. Capulong, senior legal adviser, NDFP Negotiating Panel, e-mail: jcapulong@tri-isys.com

Teresita Deles, presidential adviser on the peace process, e-mail: stqd@opapp.gov.ph

Luis Jalandoni, chair NDFP Negotiating Panel, e-mail: ndf@wanadoo.nl

Maria Lorenzo Palm-Dalupan, former executive director, OPAPP, e-mail: dalupan@cistron.nl

Tomas Millamena, independent observer, Joint Monitoring Committee, chair, NCCP; Obispo Maximo, Iglesia Filipina Independiente, e-mail: ifiphil@hotmail.com

Karen Tañada, executive director Gaston Z. Ortigas Peace Institute; member, government Reciprocal Working Committee for Social and Economic Reforms, e-mail: peace@codewan.com.ph

Jose Maria Sison, NDFP chief political consultant, e-mail: joma-inps@wanadoo.nl

Jose Yap, special emissary of president Ramos to the NDFP (1992); advisor, government Negotiating Panel for the CPP/NPA/NDFP (2001–present), e-mail: capitol@mozcom.com

Organizations

All-Out Peace
c/o Gaston Z. Ortigas Peace Institute
2/F Hoffner Bldg., SDC, Ateneo de Manila University
Loyola Heights, Quezon City, Philippines
tel: +63 2 426 6122
fax: +63 2 426 6064
e-mail: peace@codewan.com.ph, gzopeace@admu.edu.ph

Coalition for Peace
c/o Gaston Z. Ortigas Peace Institute
2/F Hoffner Bldg., SDC, Ateneo de Manila University
Loyola Heights, Quezon City, Philippines
tel: +63 2 426 6122
fax: +63 2 426 6064
e-mail: peace@codewan.com.ph, gzopeace@admu.edu.ph

Philippine Peace Center
4/F KAIJA Bldg, 7836 Makati Ave. cor Valdez St.
Makati City, Metro Manila, Philippines
tel.: +63 2 899 3403
fax: +63 2 899 3416
e-mail: ppc@pinas.net

Pilgrims for Peace
879 EDSA
Quezon City, Metro Manila, Philippines 1101
tel: +63 2 410 7623
fax: +63 2 925 1786
e-mail: justpeacenow@hotmail.com

Rey Claro Casambre is the executive director, cofounder, and a board member of the Philippine Peace Center, which was established in 1992 and has been assisting in the

government-NDFP peace negotiations since then. He is a key initiator and convenor of Pilgrims for Peace, a broad formation of peace advocates actively supporting and intervening in the peace negotiations. He has authored analytical articles and edited publications on the armed conflict and conflict resolution and prevention in the Philippines.

Notes

1. Philippine Peace Center, "Timeline of the government-NDFP Peace Negotiations," Makati, 2002

2. Karl Marx, *Capital,* vol. I (Moscow: Progress, 1978), p. 703.

3. Luzviminda Francisco, "The First Vietnam: The U.S.-Philippine War of 1899," app. 5 of *Conspiracy for Empire: Big Business, Corruption and the Politics of Imperialism in America, 1876–1907.* By Luzviminda Bartolome Francisco and Jonathan Shepard Fast. *Bulletin of Concerned Asian Scholars,* vol. 4, no. 4 (December, 1973): pp 324–325.

4. The U.S. Payne Aldrich Act of 1909 decreed tariff-free importation of finished products from the United States in exchange for raw materials from the Philippines.

5. Bureau of Agricultural Statistics (of the Department of Agriculture of the Philippines), *1991 Statistical Handbook on Agrarian Reform,* Manila, 1991.

6. Ecumenical Movement for Justice and Peace and Task Force Detainees, "The Human Rights Situation and Militarization in the Philippines: Trends and Analysis." 1984.

7. Amnesty International, *Philippines: "Disappearances" in the Context of Counter-Insurgency.* (London, February 1991), p. 7.

8. The Bangsa Moro (Moro Nation) consists mainly of Muslim people in Mindanao, in the Southern Philippines. The MNLF led an armed secessionist movement in 1972 and signed the 1976 Tripoli Agreement and the 1996 Final Peace Accord with the government. The MILF was formed from a faction of the MNLF led by Hashim Salamat that rejected the Tripoli Agreement.

9. Jose Maria Sison, "History and Circumstances Relevant to the Question of Peace," in *The People's Struggle for a Just Peace* (Utrecht: International Network of Philippine Studies, June 1991), p. 3.

10. The "six paths to peace" are reiterated in the Arroyo administration's Executive Order no. 3, "Defining Policy and Administrative Structure for Government's Peace Efforts" (February 28, 2001).

11. Cited by Rome T. Capulong in *The Ramos Peace Program: Towards a Genuine and Lasting Peace or a Mere Pacification Campaign?* (Makati: Philippine Peace Center, 1994), p. 3.

12. Silvestre Bello III, "Overview, Status and Prospects of the Peace Negotiations Between the Government and the NDFP," handout at the Media Roundtable discussion "Prospects on the Resumption of Peace Talks Under the Arroyo Administration." Quezon City, April 24, 2003, p. 2.

13. Government intelligence officials reported that their intelligence stock on the CPP/NPA/NDFP increased by 60 percent after the 1986–1987 cease-fire and peace talks.

14. "Switzerland Offers Good Offices for Peace Talks Between NDFP and Aquino Government in Geneva: Aquino Government Rejects Offer," *Neue Zuricher Zeitung,* May 17, 1991.

15. "Concluding Observations of the Human Rights Committee: Philippines," in *Consideration of Reports Submitted by State Parties Under Article 40 of the Covenant.* November 6, 2003, pp. 1–4. ("Covenant" refers to the 1966 International Covenant of Civil and Political Rights.)

16. Ledivina V. Carino and the PNSP Project Staff, *Volunteering in Cross-National Perspective: Evidence from Twenty-four Countries. Working Papers of the Johns Hopkins Comparative Nonprofit Sector Project,* no. 39 (Baltimore: Johns Hopkins Center for Civil Society Studies, 2001).

17. Ging Quintos Deles, "Unarmed Forces in the Philippines," in Ed Garcia, ed. *Pilgrim Voices: Citizens as Peacemakers* (Quezon City: Gaston Z. Ortigas Peace Institute and Ateneo Center for Social Policy and Public Affairs, 1994), pp. 55–59.

18. See http://iisd.org/50comm/commdb/desc/dOl.htm.

19. Hugh Miall, Oliver Ramsbotham, and Tom Woodhouse, "Calling for a Broad Approach to Conflict Resolution," in Monique Mekenkamp, Paul van Tongeren and Hans van de Veen, eds., *Searching for Peace in Central and South Asia.* (Boulder: Lynne Rienner, 2002), p. 34.

20. Luis Jalandoni and Jose Yap, "The Hague Joint Declaration," signed and issued by Cong. Jose Yap, representing President Ramos, and Luis Jalandoni, representing the NDFP, The Hague, September 1, 1992.

9.6.2

Mindanao:
Conflicting Agendas, Stumbling Blocks, and
Prospects Toward Sustainable Peace

Rufa Cagoco-Guiam

No area in the Philippines has seen as much bloodshed and violence as the central and western regions of the southern island of Mindanao—the country's second-largest island—where a predominantly Muslim population continues its struggle for a Muslim homeland.[1] Despite a peace agreement signed in 1996, resulting in the Autonomous Region of Muslim Mindanao (ARMM), peace continues to elude Mindanao's population of 18 million. However, civil society groups continue to work toward building a growing constituency for peace, hoping to exert pressure on both government and rebel panels.

Before colonial rule, Mindanao Muslims (also referred to as Bangsamoro or Moro peoples) were already socially, politically, and economically organized into the two sultanates of Maguindanao and Sulu. These sultanates evolved as quasi-nation segmentary states whose territories and areas of influence increased and decreased depending on the overall leadership abilities of their sultans. Lineage and kinship combined with more elaborate structures to manage production and defense in the sultanates. Their wealth was based on their flourishing long-distance bulk trade with China and Arabic countries in the Middle East, including Yemen. The long-distance trade brought in not only traders but also Arab Islamic missionaries to Mindanao, Sulu, and Tawi-tawi. This paved the way for the Islamization of many areas in Mindanao starting as early as 1380, roughly the date attributed to the oldest material evidence of Islamic presence, that of a grave marker in Simunul, Tawitawi. The sultanates played an important role in providing the foundation for Mindanao Muslims upon which to base their distinctive identity as a people separate from those of Luzon and the Visayas who were Christianized under Spanish colonial rule.

The Spanish colonial period began with the establishment of a government in Manila, in the northern part of the islands it called the Philippines, starting in the late 1500s. For more than three centuries, the Spanish colonial government Christianized the indigenous populations in Luzon and the Visayas. These

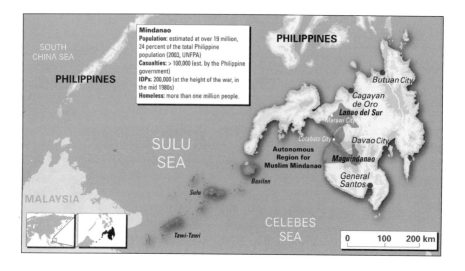

Christianized indigenous populations of the north were used by Spain to fight against the Mindanao Moros in its pacification campaigns. Despite some Spanish footholds in northern, eastern, and southwestern Mindanao, the Spaniards failed to colonize Muslim-dominated areas. The Moros fiercely resisted Spanish colonial rule. Although Spain failed to establish full political control over the Moros and the territories of the Sultanates, it engaged them in relentless armed campaigns and undermined the sultanates' economic base through trade blockades.

The United States defeated Spain in a series of armed confrontations that culminated in the decisive Battle of Manila Bay in 1898, effectively ending Spanish rule in the Philippines. The two parties signed the Treaty of Paris in December 1898, ending the war and giving the United States full possession of the Philippine archipelago, including Mindanao.

U.S. colonial rule in the Philippines lasted for over four decades, from the turn of the century until July 4, 1946, when the United States granted independence. Like Spain, the U.S. colonial government established its central government in Manila. Unlike Spain, however, the U.S. colonial government emphasized education rather than proselytization in the name of Christianity. U.S. officials used education as "a tool of conquest."[2] Thus they were quite successful in convincing Moro leaders to send their sons and daughters to U.S.-established schools. Consequently, many Moro leaders were convinced they were better off under a U.S. administration, with their province (Sulu) as a "permanent territory" of the United States, rather than be assimilated into an independent Philippine state.[3]

Both Spanish and U.S. colonial rule started a process that irreversibly altered the demographic composition in Mindanao. Where once they were dominant in number and political influence, the Muslim Moros soon became a minority in Mindanao. Through central government–sponsored migration, land-seeking Christianized Filipinos from Luzon and the Visayas came to Mindanao in droves. Settlers populated Mindanao's most productive agricultural lands and were successful in growing staple crops like rice, corn, and coconuts. Transnational corporations were granted huge landholdings for pineapple, banana, and rubber plantations. Wealthy loggers from both Luzon and the Visayas grabbed giant forest concessions.[4]

These developments, resulting from colonially imposed land laws (like the Land Registration Act of 1902, the Philippine Commission Act no. 718, and the Public Land Act of 1903) that did not recognize *adat* (Moro customary law) on land stewardship, slowly stoked feelings of resentment among the Muslims against the central government administration in Manila. Moreover, heightened tensions and animosities between settler populations and the impoverished and minoritized Muslim/Moros groups gradually evolved into Muslim rebellion in the 1960s and early 1970s. Initially, the rebellion was a series of isolated uprisings that rapidly spread in scope and size. But one group, the Moro National Liberation Front (MNLF), chaired by Nur Misuari, then an instructor at the University of the Philippines, managed to bring most partisan Moro forces into the loosely unified MNLF framework. In 1972 the MNLF declared in its manifesto the goal of establishing of the Bangsamoro Republic, and declared armed struggle as means for achieving the Moro people's complete freedom and independence from the perceived oppression of Filipino colonialism.

A series of incidents convinced many Muslim intellectuals, and even politicians, that armed struggle was the only way to redress their grievances and to attain their inherent right to self-determination. Foremost among these incidents was the Jabidah Massacre in March 1968, in which more than twenty Sama youth from Sulu were allegedly killed by soldiers of the Philippine army under instructions from their chief of staff, who was himself under the command of President Ferdinand Marcos. Allegedly, upon President Marcos's instructions, the Philippine military recruited Sama youth to be trained in preparation for an invasion to Sabah. The Philippine government under Marcos was taking steps toward staking its territorial claim over Sabah, which historically had been part of the Sulu sultanate. The youth were to become a guerrilla-type group to be deployed in Sabah, but they were not told about the intentions of President Marcos at the time of their recruitment. After their training, when they were told what their mission was, the Muslim Sama youth staged a mutiny in protest. Many of the youths had distant relatives living in Sabah, and could not accept being used as an instrument for waging war against their fellow Muslims there. The young mutineers were reportedly massacred on Corregidor Island. One of them, Jibin Arula, survived and sought the help of some politicians, notably the late senator Benigno Aquino. Aquino initiated a series of congressional investigations of the incident. However, these investigations failed to establish the truth behind it and several versions of the event exist. Many Muslims believe that the government under Marcos was solely responsible for the carnage, and this incident was enough to jump-start the so-called Moro insurgency in Mindanao.[5]

Mindanao. Combatants of the Muslim MNLF guerrilla army.

Conflict Dynamics

A number of writers cite deep animosities and prejudices between a Christian-dominated central government and the minoritized Muslim groups as one of the triggers of the war in Mindanao.[6] Some three-and-a-half centuries of colonial rule have spawned such feelings among the highly diverse communities in Mindanao.

Spanish colonial administrators perpetuated negative images of the Moros, or Muslims, in Mindanao. Such attitudes may have originated in their own violent colonial history under the Muslim Moors of Morocco and other parts of North Africa, who subjugated the natives of the Iberian Peninsula for almost 800 years. The Spanish colonial administration's failure to win converts among the fierce Moro groups reinforced their prejudices against a group who embraced the culture and beliefs also embraced by their archenemies. The colonial administration also used the Christianized Indios from Luzon and the Visayas in their pacification campaigns against the Moros.[7]

The U.S. colonial government dealt in similar negative images of Muslims, while befriending some of the more compliant local leaders.[8] One U.S. governor-general during colonial times was tellingly quoted as saying, "A good Moro is a dead Moro."[9]

The assertion of a distinct identity separate from the majority Christianized Filipinos is also one of the most important motivations for the continuing struggle of the Bangsamoro people for self-determination, which they view as their God-given right. They therefore believe they are waging a just war.

The conflict in Mindanao reached its peak in the early 1970s, with massive air, land, and sea attacks against MNLF positions, causing tremendous loss of life and destruction of property. According to government estimates, from 1970 to 1976 alone, an average of eighteen people were killed every day. From 1970 to 1996, the Philippine government spent a total of PhP 73 billion pesos, or about U.S.$138 million at the current exchange rate of 53 Philippine pesos per U.S. dollar.[10] The late president Ferdinand Marcos disclosed once that more than 11,000 Philippine army soldiers were killed in the first eight years of the war (1972–1980).[11]

Calls for a cease-fire started in 1973, when the dictatorial Marcos regime learned of an impending oil embargo to be imposed by oil-producing countries. The Organization of Arab Petroleum-Exporting Countries decided to impose an oil embargo on all countries that supported Israel. The Philippines was one of those countries, and at that time had "only three months supply of crude oil and it was getting 93.3% of its total energy demands from two Arab states . . . Saudi Arabia and Kuwait, both of which were enemies of Israel."[12]

In 1976, through the mediation and participation of the Organization of Islamic Conference (OIC), more specifically the Quadripartite Ministerial Commission, chaired by Libya, the Philippine government and the MNLF leadership signed the Tripoli Agreement. The agreement provided for an autonomous arrangement for thirteen provinces in Mindanao, Sulu, and the Palawan Islands claimed by the MNLF as part of their areas of influence. But this agreement was doomed from the start.[13] It left out significant issues and many of its provisions were not implemented because of questions in interpretation.

With the collapse of the Tripoli Agreement, the MNLF resumed its armed struggle against Philippine military forces. Unfortunately, it was also at this time that the MNLF was facing deep divisions within its central leadership. This led to the creation of two separate factions: the Moro Islamic Liberation Front (MILF), led by a Maguindanaon religious teacher, or *ustadz,* Salamat Hashim, and the MNLF-Reformist group, led by a Maranaw, Dimas Pundatu.

After the downfall of former president Marcos following the "People Power" movement in 1986, a new national government administration was put in place, with Cory Aquino as president. Aquino immediately arranged for a meeting with Nur Misuari and the MNLF in Sulu. While this move drew the ire of the rival MILF leadership,[14] it paved the way for the series of negotiations carried out during the Aquino administration. Unfortunately, it took another ten years to forge an agreement. On September 2, 1996, under the presidency of Fidel V. Ramos, the "Final Peace Agreement" (FPA) was signed.

However, eight years after the signing of the FPA, Mindanao is nowhere near achieving lasting peace. While peace with the MNLF continues to hold, government forces have faced a new challenge from the MILF, against which, in March 2000, then president Joseph Estrada declared an all-out war. Estrada's war has spawned a renewed cycle of hostilities in the mountainous areas of central and western Mindanao, where the MILF has major camps. From January to June 2002, some 196 individuals were reported to have died from the conflict, 97 MILF fighters, 25 members of the Philippine army, and 74 civilians.[15] Violent clashes resumed early in 2003 between MILF and government forces. The number of casualties continues to rise, as does the number of refugees. *Time* magazine reports that fighting in February 2003 caused the deaths of at least 160 MILF rebels and 8 Philippine soldiers, and the displacement of more than 40,000 residents in one town alone.[16]

Presently, war has become the daily reality for many residents of central Mindanao, owing largely to the Philippine government's hard-line stance against "local terrorists." The MILF have been tagged as such, and is accused of having close links with Osama bin Laden's Al-Qaida network of international terrorists. Bombings in several key Mindanao cities have been blamed on the "terrorist" activities of the MILF.[17]

Official Conflict Management

For more than two decades, the Philippine government has resorted primarily to the use of military might to manage the conflict in Mindanao. At the height of the "Moro insurgency" in the mid-1970s, about 80 percent of the entire Philippine military force was deployed in Muslim-dominated areas in Mindanao.[18] This has continued up to the present, as the alleged mountain lairs of the MILF rebels in central Mindanao continue to be the targets of the Philippine military's mortars and howitzers.

Notwithstanding the military strategies for "containing" the conflict, the Philippine government has also tried to pursue the "carrot" approach, albeit with not as much emphasis as the "stick," or military, approach. Interestingly, the government has tended to adopt the carrot approach when external actors exert pressure on it to do so.

In 1975 the martial law regime of President Ferdinand Marcos relented and started calling for a cease-fire in preparation for peace talks with the MNLF leadership. This was because of the above-mentioned oil embargo against countries, including the Philippines, that supported Israel, and the low levels of Philippine oil reserves. As a result of this more conciliatory approach, the Philippine government and the MNLF signed the first Tripoli Agreement in December 1976 in Libya. President Muammar Qaddafi of Libya brokered and facilitated the signing of this historic but ultimately ineffective document. The Tripoli Agreement collapsed and the hostilities between the Philippine military and the MNLF forces resumed early the following year.

Several years and two Philippine presidents later, the "Final Peace Agreement" was signed. It is noteworthy to cite the key role of the member countries of the Organization of Islamic Conference in making this historic event possible. The OIC convinced both Nur Misuari and President Ramos to come to terms on a "final resolution" of the war in Mindanao. Pundits view president Ramos's willingness to agree to "forge a comprehensive and enduring settlement" as the result of a calculated move on his part to elicit the financial support of OIC countries for a postwar reconstruction program in Mindanao.[19] The signing on September 2, 1996, of the FPA was accompanied by elaborate ceremonies in Manila.

The OIC has used various means of so-called Islamic diplomacy in drawing on the principle of *ummah* (community of believers in Islam), in addition to conventional mediation and the use of "good offices" in responding to the conflict in Mindanao.[20] Lawyer Soliman Santos Jr. notes that OIC aid was "constant throughout the process . . . the OIC could not wait for the outcome of the negotiations before acting to ameliorate the plight of Muslims in the Philippines."[21]

The UN administration in the Philippines was among the first international donors to respond to the call of the government for development assistance. This and the aid coming from other international donors are perceived to be part of government's official commitment to manage the conflict to prevent a resurgence of violence in the areas that have suffered so heavily in terms of both lost lives and property damage.

During the short-lived term of President Joseph Estrada (June 1998–January 2001), official conflict management shifted, with a renewed emphasis on the stick approach. In April 2000, Estrada launched an "all-out war" after government troops engaged the MILF in pocket skirmishes in central Mindanao. This war spawned even more rigidly hard-line positions among the MILF leadership and led to the recruitment of more followers and sympathizers to the rebel cause.[22] No substantial talks took place during Estrada's brief administration.

The 1987 Philippine constitution provides for the supremacy of the civilian-led police force in ensuring peace and order. However, this provision has been observed more in the breach than in practice. The military has played, and continues to play, a crucial role in influencing major decisions in the Mindanao conflict. Opinion makers even believe the military is the de facto "determinant" of official government policy in Mindanao. An extreme view looks at the military as the "power" behind Filipino presidents, with the "all-out war" of Estrada, for example, reflecting the preponderant military influence on a sitting president.

Currently, the Arroyo administration's policies on the conflict in Mindanao are embodied in an executive order that the president signed on February 28, 2001, just a few days after assuming office following the ouster of Estrada. Executive Order no. 3 provides "the framework for the implementation, coordination, monitoring and integration of all government initiatives and the participation of civil society in the pursuit of a just and lasting peace." Under this order, the Office of the Presidential Adviser on the Peace Process (OPAPP) is mandated to pursue a peace agenda encompassing three principles for a "comprehensive peace process," as well as the "six paths to peace." Both the principles and the paths to peace are derived from the work of the National Unification Commission, created during the Ramos administration.[23]

In theory, official conflict management of the Arroyo administration is based on waging an "all-out peace," in contrast to the policy of President Estrada. Immediately after assuming office, she sent emissaries to the MILF to resume talks. Subsequently, she also named Mindanawons to her newly formed cabinet and even appointed an all-Mindanawon peace panel to negotiate with the MILF. This panel was quite different from the past panels, as it was headed by a civilian, Jesus Dureza, who had previously been Arroyo's presidential assistant for Mindanao. President Arroyo also named two women, one a former Mindanao State University president and a Maranaw Muslim, and the other a prominent Christian woman leader based in Davao, as part of the five-person peace panel.

To manifest her all-out concern for peace in Mindanao, President Arroyo also convened all government line agencies to form a presidential task force to lead rehabilitation of the areas in Mindanao devastated by her predecessor's all-out war in 2000.[24] Arroyo also saw to it that peace talks got back on track in 2001. In that year, the Malaysian prime minister helped the Arroyo government convince the MILF to resume talks, leading to the signing of an agreement to resume official talks on March 24.

In March, MILF representatives met with some MNLF leaders in Malaysia. The MNLF leaders would later call themselves the members of the "Executive Council" or the "Council of 15." Some pundits claim this was the initial phase of an MNLF "coup" against Misuari. This coup was insinuated to have been initiated by the people in the Malacanang Presidential Palace, and by president Arroyo herself.

Consequently, Misuari was ousted as chairman of the MNLF, and the Executive Council assumed collective leadership of the group. The council "retired" Misuari, naming him "MNLF chairman emeritus." Misuari rejected such a post and accused the council members of betraying him and the MNLF.

In the same year, the Philippine Congress passed RA 9054, or the "Expanded ARMM" law. Congress also set the date for a plebiscite in Mindanao to ask voters in the ARMM whether they were in favor of expanding it. Those in the non-ARMM provinces were asked if they favored being included in an expanded ARMM. But despite president Arroyo's campaign for a yes vote, the voters delivered a resounding no. Only one additional province (Basilan, excluding its city of Isabela) and one city (Marawi, in Lanao del Sur) opted to be included in the expanded ARMM. Aside from the popular no vote, there was also very low turnout in many polling places in southern and western Mindanao.[25]

In June 2001 the government and MILF panels held talks in Tripoli, Libya, that resulted in the signing of the Tripoli Peace Agreement of 2001. This agreement called for discussions on security, rehabilitation and development of conflict-affected areas, and ancestral domain. From then on, more talks took place, mostly in Malaysia.

On November 24, 2001, MNLF leader Misuari was arrested in Malaysia on charges of rebellion after a group of his loyal supporters attacked security posts in Jolo, Sulu. Meanwhile, one of the leaders of the coup against Misuari, Parouk Hussin, was elected governor of the ARMM during the regional elections that same day. The elections were widely perceived as Malacanang-influenced. Several accusations were hurled by Hussin's rival candidates, who claim that the election results were rigged at Malacanang's behest.

The events in 2002 revived the cycle of violence of the previous year. Skirmishes resumed in various places in Mindanao in February and led to president Arroyo's decision to suspend formal peace talks with the MILF in

March. In May, however, the talks resumed and led to the signing on May 6, 2002, in Kuala Lumpur, Malaysia, of a joint communiqué on the isolation and interdiction of all criminal syndicates and kidnap-for-ransom groups operating in Mindanao. The following day, another document was signed jointly by the responsible persons for both parties in Putrajaya. From June to November, a series of talks and meetings were held, and several local monitoring teams in various parts of central and western Mindanao were trained. By December, the members of the government panel announced that a peace agreement was expected to be forged within the first quarter of 2003.

On February 10, 2003, the government peace panel presented its draft final peace agreement with the MILF to some leaders of the Philippine Congress. But the following day, Philippine military forces stormed the Buliok complex, believed to be the residential compound of MILF leader Hashim Salamat. That day was also a Muslim holiday, the Feast of Sacrifice (Eid'l Adha). At this point, the peace process stalled. MILF leaders refused to meet with government negotiators unless the Philippine military troops moved out of Pikit, central Mindanao.

In March, April, and May 2003, several bombing incidents shook Davao city and the town of Siocon, Zamboanga del Sur. All bombing incidents were attributed to, and denied by, the MILF. Thirty-eight people died in the two Davao city bombings, while twenty-two people lost their lives in the Siocon bombing. These incidents undermined the gains that had been achieved early on in the Arroyo administration. The unfortunate events have also hardened the positions as well as highlighted the contrasting agendas of the two parties. This has inevitably had an impact on the relations between many Bangsamoro, Christian, and Lumad communities.

These events, coupled with the Arroyo administration's avowed all-out support for the worldwide campaign against "terrorism," have led to the failure of the administration to achieve the "comprehensive, just, and lasting peace" it envisioned for Mindanao. At least for the near future, peace remains an elusive dream for residents of both central and western Mindanao.

Multi-Track Diplomacy

The Philippines probably provides Southeast Asia with its most dynamic and vibrant citizen activism. This is manifested through the proliferation of private, nonprofit organizations and groups formed outside of government for social development and advocacy. Such groups are referred to as nongovernmental organizations (NGOs) or, more recently, as civil society organizations (CSOs). There is a lot of confusion and debate on the use of such terms; for this chapter, the acronyms *NGO* and *CSO* are used interchangeably to mean nonprofit, nongovernmental formations that are committed to a wide range of social development work.

The forerunners of these groups were the cooperatives established during pre–martial law days. During martial law, several "cause oriented" groups like Bayan and other left-leaning organizations had already established inroads in the "parliament of the streets." These included various forms of mass action and mobilizations of grassroots communities in rallies and picketing actions against the martial law regime. After the end of martial law, many of these organizations became full-fledged, legally registered organizations with the country's Securities and Exchange Commission. The post–martial law period opened democratic space in Philippine politics, thus paving the way for organizing a wide variety of people's movements, grassroots organizations, and other groups aimed primarily at conducting a wide range of social development work, including peace advocacy.

For the past two or three decades, these organizations have worked to challenge the established government and to present alternative strategies to benefit the poor, deprived, and marginalized sectors of society. Many of these organizations have attained a status of respectability and credibility especially in terms of their various services to the poor and marginalized. Because of their efforts to provide services and resources that are more traditionally the responsibility of the state, they are able to claim a certain level of influence, especially among their beneficiaries and partners. This is the main source of their strength.

The groups that have established nationwide presence and affiliates or networks are those that are relatively stable and more active in raising issues and concerns of marginalized sectors within the public arena. These include so-called cause-oriented groups among the basic sectors, like farmers, transport workers, and urban and rural poor. Their leadership and members are in the forefront of mass and protest actions against controversial government policies and strategies.

In terms of conflict resolution, conflict transformation, conflict prevention, and overall peacebuilding, civil society groups in Mindanao still have a long way to go, especially in mounting concerted efforts to push for peace. While there are a substantial number of civil society groups addressing the need for sustainable peace in Mindanao, their efforts still lack the synergy needed to have a substantial impact on the comprehensive peace process that is unfolding in the region. For one thing, the groups addressing peace concerns come from various political or ideological orientations. Those that have different or even opposing ideologies tend to have strained relationships, thus leading to conflicts and tensions within civil society itself.[26]

There is further the perennial problem of inadequate funds to run programs and projects that support the efforts of NGOs to forge lasting peace in Mindanao. A consequence is that these nongovernmental groups or organizations compete with each other for scarce development funding and resources. This is another source of potential conflict among civil society leaders. Many of the groups, especially the small and recently organized ones, still need to establish credibility or a track record in order to access funds from foreign development partners.

Another vulnerability is the lack of professional preparation or technical skills specific to conflict transformation work among many peace advocates or peace animators. Many of the peace workers in Mindanao get involved as a consequence of their socioeconomic development work, and many civil society groups in Mindanao started out as social development NGOs before evolving into peace advocacy groups. Nevertheless, a professional, skilled, and committed sector of peace workers has arisen in Mindanao.

Civil Society Peace Initiatives in Mindanao

A wide range of peace initiatives are under way in Mindanao, including seminars on the history of the armed conflict, peace journalism, dialogues on life and cultures, and advocacy and lobbying activities to bring about the inclusion of civil society representatives in the official peace process conducted through the facilities of the Philippine government. Still another type of initiative has focused on training peace workers or animators for various conflict management, resolution, and peacebuilding and peace education activities.

In 1996, Catholic and Protestant bishops met with Muslim religious leaders through the initiatives of the OPAPP. This meeting led to the formation of the Bishops-Ulama Forum (BUF), a group largely responsible for the institutionalization of the "Mindanao Week of Peace." This celebration originally started as the annual activity of the Peace Advocates of Zamboanga (PAZ). The BUF has played a very active role in peacemaking through local mediation and localized confidence-building initiatives (e.g., the "Priests, Imams, and Pastors" group in Kidapawan city, Cotabato). Despite its efforts, it has been quite severely criticized by various civil society groups for opting to remain silent at critical moments in the peace negotiation process, even at times when violent clashes occurred between armed groups.

In December 2001 a group of Mindanao women leaders, calling itself the Mindanao Commission on Women, met in Davao city. Led by a member of the government peace panel, the group has on various occasions called for the active role of women in peacemaking efforts, aside from publishing a yearly report on the situation of women in Mindanao.

More recently, with the outbreak of the latest hostilities, initiatives were focused on assisting the displaced civilian population for their multifarious needs (from physical to psychosocial) in the evacuation centers. Relief and rehabilitation programs as well as the provision of psychosocial services, such as trauma healing for the children caught in the conflict, have been provided by the Balik-Kalipay (Return to Happiness) Foundation, the Tabang Mindanaw Foundation, and the Ecumenical Commission for Displaced Families and Communities. These organizations are based mainly in Cotabato city and Maguindanao and Cotabato provinces.

Civil society groups have also criticized the media for exacerbating age-old animosities among the diverse peoples in Mindanao. Some Mindanao-based media practitioners have realized that if they are "part of the problem, they must also be part of the solution." As Carol Arguillas, director of Mindanao News and Information Cooperative Center (MindaNews), noted at a forum in General Santos city on September 18, 2003, "Media reports can either help resolve or exacerbate conflicts. . . . We blame the government, . . . the rebels, politicians, but we in media forget we are to blame too."[27] On May 18, 2002, Arguillas and more than fifty Mindanao-based journalists, radio broadcasters, publishers, and radio and television managers signed a covenant, "This Is Our Mindanao," after the holding of the First Mindanao Media Summit in Davao city. During this summit, media practitioners addressed the various factors that result in journalists, through their news coverage and commentaries, aggravating the already strained relations among the diverse groups of people in Mindanao. Some public officials and civil society leaders also attended the summit as observers. The summit ended with a commitment from the media practitioners to forge partnerships with the academe and other sectors in peacebuilding efforts. Such efforts will focus on the need for media practitioners themselves to understand fully the roots of the conflict in Mindanao.

A factor that tends to perpetuate conflict between the Bangsamoro, Lumad, and Christian communities is the marginalization of both Bangsamoro and Lumad compared to most Christian communities. As such, socioeconomic development programs, while not directly working for peace, are also important and appropriate. These are implemented by nongovernmental resource or service centers that provide microcredit facilities for livelihood and enterprise development among their partners or beneficiaries. Many of their activities are geared mainly toward economic empowerment, but will eventually be geared toward political empowerment or the widening of popular participation in local governance as well.

Both small and large civil society formations have addressed the need for mutual understanding of the two major ways of life—Islam and Christian—in Mindanao. Working for such understanding has been recognized as an initial step in the pursuit of sustainable dialogue. Educational forums and seminar workshops on the historical background of the conflict in Mindanao, given by Mindanao-based historians and resource persons, are useful in helping participants to learn about the historical roots of the conflict. Through workshops, participants formulate steps toward lessening the levels of animosity between groups that have been at war in Mindanao or the southern Philippines.[28] Such initiatives have been conducted by groups like the Silsilah Movement in Zamboanga city, the Mindanao Coalition of Development NGOs, and smaller groups like the Maguindanao Development Foundation (southern Cotabato), the Kadtuntaya Foundation (Cotabato city and Maguindanao), the Kalimudan Foundation (Marawi city and Lanao del Sur), and PAZ.

International, regional, and local NGOs have also provided funds and technical assistance to deliver much-needed relief and rehabilitation to areas seriously affected by the conflict in Mindanao. Among these are Oxfam-GB, the VSO-Toscadar Programme, Accion, the Community and Family Services International, and Catholic Relief Services (CRS).

In addition, CRS, has conducted an annual workshop through the Mindanao Peacebuilding Institute in each of the past four years. The institute provides thematic training on the culture of peace, conflict management, conflict transformation, and peace education. Participants come not only from Mindanao but also from other parts of the country, as well as from other Asia Pacific countries (including Pakistan, India, Indonesia, and Vietnam).

Localized peacebuilding efforts, such as the establishment of "peace zones," have become centerpieces of "pragmatic peace" in communities that have seen bitter conflict. In these areas, members of a diverse community (Muslims, Christians, and indigenous peoples) agree to come together and work to forge long-lasting peace. Such efforts have taken place in Maladeg, Zamboanga del Sur, and in Sapad, Lanao del Norte—places that witnessed bloody fighting between Muslim rebels and members of the Philippine army at the height of the war in the mid-1970s.[29]

Other examples of grassroots initiatives toward peacebuilding have recognized people-initiated and community-based principles of conflict resolution in small communities that have seen the worst consequences of the hostilities from 2000 to 2003. These include the efforts of both Muslim and Christian residents in several villages in Cotabato who declared their areas "spaces for peace." Such initiatives took place in at least five different barangays in the town of Pikit. One of the initiators of the "spaces for peace" efforts is a Catholic parish priest, Bert Layson, of the Oblates of Mary Immaculate (OMI). Layson is cochair of the Mindanao People's Caucus (MPC). The two other cochairs are a Moro and a Lumad (indigenous people). The composition of the cochairship reflects the tripartite character of the MPC.

In Kauswagan, Lanao del Norte, a group was organized in the wake of President Estrada's declaration of all-out war in 2000. Kauswagan hosts a portion of a major MILF camp. The group, called "Pakigdait," a Cebuano-Visayan term meaning "mutual understanding," organized a series of forums and symposia that promoted mutual understanding between Muslim and Christian residents in the area. The seminars they have conducted since 2000 have aimed to "heal the ruined relationships between Muslims and Christians" that were spawned by Estrada's all-out war. Its conveners include both Christian and Muslim (Maranaw) civil society leaders in the central Mindanao area.

For their part, various academic institutions in Mindanao have contributed to the popularization of the peace agenda in the academe. For instance, Notre Dame University in Cotabato city has become the trendsetter among Mindanao institutions that offer a graduate-degree course in peace and development (at both the master's and the doctoral level). Ateneo de Davao University has even gone the extra mile in recognizing the efforts of nongovernmental or civil society individuals in promoting peace and development. It has recently offered an equivalency program at both the undergraduate and the graduate level for those who have had long years of experience in actual peacebuilding or peacemaking efforts as well as in other fields of specialization. The Extended Tertiary Educational Accreditation Program was started in 2001 and has since graduated two students from the master's program in peace and development.

Several organizations have addressed the peace process in statements about the government-MNLF peace agreement. For example, the Bangsamoro Women

Conference on the Peace Process, held on September 7, 2002, in Cotabato city produced a strongly worded declaration, urging, among other things, the unconditional release of Nur Misuari from prison and the implementation of all provisions of the 1996 peace agreement.[30] Some have played advocacy roles on issues directly related to the peace process.

In 2001 a Mindanao People's Caucus was organized in Davao city to promote mutual understanding among the three peoples of Mindanao. Taking the lead in the mobilization of this tripeople caucus is the Initiatives for International Dialogue, also based in Davao city. The caucus has been quite active in mobilizing mass action, urging unity among the diverse peoples in Mindanao, and in calling for sobriety during times of crisis, like the bombing incidents in Davao city in March 2003.

Reflection on NGOs

In general, there has been a substantial improvement in the relations among civil society groups in Mindanao, especially where forging coalitions for peace is concerned. While there are still divisions, civil society groups are now more than willing to collaborate, especially in efforts to put pressure on both government and rebel groups to stop the war. This is indicated by the presence of "consortiums" like the Consortium of Bangsamoro Civil Society Organizations. Members come from various political orientations, and are of various sympathies (some are pro-MNLF and others are pro-MILF).

Moreover, there is now a vibrant collaboration effort between the academic sector (both governmental and private) and purely NGO groups in developing a "Mindanao Studies Project" that aims at establishing a database for peace and development resources in Mindanao. The Mindanao Studies Consortium is composed of ten universities (five of which are government-owned or state universities; the other five are private, sectarian [Catholic] universities) and one NGO resource center based in Davao city (the Alternate Forum for Research in Mindanao).

NGOs and civil society groups working for peace are relatively free to conduct their activities and pursue their respective goals. On the part of the government, it is to its advantage that civil society groups are active in helping to forge peace. The government does not have the resources needed (personnel, material, and financial) to attain the "comprehensive, just, and lasting peace" envisioned in President Arroyo's Executive Order no. 3. It needs all the help it can get from both groups and individuals in the communities affected by the armed conflict. By getting the support of NGOs for the government's peace agenda, the government is already winning half the battle for the hearts and minds of constituents, be they Muslims, Christians, or indigenous peoples.

In the same vein, the MILF also needs wide support, not necessarily in waging what it perceives as a just struggle against the Philippine government, but more importantly in helping people understand the root causes of the conflict. Thus it welcomes NGOs that promote mutual understanding among Muslims and Christians in Mindanao. Although its methods are often "unpeaceful," as the MILF has pronounced repeatedly through its spokesperson, peace is as much its goal as it is government's.

Civil society groups occupy a unique niche in society. This stems from their immense potential in promoting empowerment of citizens and in forging wide participation in an envisioned "comprehensive peace process." While NGOs and civil society groups exist outside of government bureaucracy, they have conducted activities and have performed roles and duties that are otherwise the concern of government. In the context of the overall peace process, these activities range from conducting seminars and workshops for mutual understanding and dialogue, to distributing relief and rehabilitation assistance, including the provision of basic and psychosocial services for the displaced populations.

In terms of influencing government decisions on the peace process, the collective efforts of civil society groups in Mindanao appear to have influenced the presidential decision to appoint an "all Mindanao" peace panel to face the MILF peace negotiators. This is quite a breakthrough given the composition of the peace panel in the previous negotiations. Moreover, for the first time in the history of peace negotiations, two Mindanao women leaders have been appointed members of the peace panel.

Intensive lobbying by groups like the Mindanao People's Caucus has resulted in the inclusion of a Lumad representative in the government peace panel's technical committee. Datu Al Saliling of Carmen, Cotabato province, has been appointed by the presidential assistant for Mindanao, Jesus Dureza, to the technical working group on ancestral domain. This implies a recognition of the fact that the indigenous Lumad populations need to be considered in the course of the peace negotiations with the MILF. In past peace negotiations and agreements, the Lumad populations in Mindanao have not been given a voice, much less a seat at the negotiation table. Datu Al's appointment is quite a feat, given the past administration's "sins of omission" in not including the Lumad in the peace negotiations. But it still falls short of recognizing the indigenous peoples' crucial role in charting a common course for Mindanao's future. Their inputs are invaluable in widening and elevating the levels of social discourse for Mindanao and its diverse peoples.

It remains to be seen whether the panel of Mindanao-based peace advocates and professionals can substantially influence the course of the talks and the efforts to eventually produce a mutually acceptable agreement in the coming months. Earlier, there had been reports of the panel members' disappointment in having been sidelined in "back channeling" efforts that have led since 2003 to the signing of interim agreements.[31]

Prospects

As noted earlier, prospects for ending the war in Mindanao remain bleak at this point. Father Roberto Layson, OMI, cochair of the Mindanao People's Caucus and coordinator of the Interreligious Dialogue of the Missionary Oblates of Mary Immaculate, laments in a book of his memoirs of the war: "In war, the real enemy is war itself. War makes people cruel."[32]

On February 8, 2003, the Philippine military bombarded the Buliok complex in Pikit. The complex is believed to be the residence of the Salamat Hashim, MILF chairman; many civilians had to seek refuge. This incident shattered the hopes of the priest for a final resolution of the conflict. While Layson also denounces what he considers "insincerity" on the part of the MILF in not respecting a previous cease-fire agreement, he holds the government more accountable for all the suffering of the evacuees in his town. "As a state, [the Philippine government] is supposed to have the moral high ground to exhaust all peaceful means to prevent war."[33]

Another Mindanao conflict expert, lawyer Soliman Santos Jr., has also expressed pessimism and disappointment at the turn of recent events in central Mindanao. Santos assessed March 2003 that "nothing much will happen in the next months of the Arroyo presidency in terms of coming up with an acceptable agreement. . . . This administration will just be made to pass, and wait for a newly elected president in 2004."[34]

Santos, however, sees some cause for optimism and hope in the "softening" of the MILF's stance. He believes that the MILF has "bent over backwards" to accommodate the popular call for a resumption of the talks with the government to keep the peace negotiations on track. He also says that the dynamism of civil society efforts could be another source of hope that something positive will come out of recent events, no matter how tragic they have been for Mindanao.

Recommendations

Various civil society formations have proposed two options to end the war and find a long-lasting solution to the conflict in Mindanao: the implementation of a federal system of government for the entire Philippines, and the holding of a UN-supervised referendum.

In May 2001 a group of experts convened in Davao City to prepare the broad outlines of a draft constitution for an envisaged "Federal Philippine Republic." This gathering was made possible through the conveners of the Kusog Mindanaw (Strength of Mindanao), a broad coalition of civil society groups and individuals who work toward a more peaceful and progressive Mindanao.

On December 17–20, 2002, the Mindanao Peoples' Summit was held at Southern Christian College in Midsayap, northern Cotabato. The summit produced the Midsayap 2002 Declaration, which called on the Philippine government "to hold a United Nations–supervised Referendum in the Bangsamoro Areas of Mindanao."

The Mindanao Peoples' Peace Movement pledges to support and promote this proposal through a multi-track strategy, including, but not limited to, legislative pressure, people's initiatives, peace constituency building, and national and international lobbying. The group believes that only through a referendum will the Bangsamoro be given the opportunity to determine for themselves their fate and political future. At least 500 representatives of people's organizations and other civil society groups in Mindanao attended the summit.

On February 22, 2003, the Mindanao Summit of Muslim Leaders was held in Davao city. The gathering of Muslim leaders from different provinces in Mindanao passed a thirteen-point declaration on peace and development addressed to the national government. The declaration was summarized in four major calls, namely:

- "No to all-out war in Mindanao."
- "No to *Balikatan* [literally, shoulder to shoulder, referring to the joint military exercise between Philippine and U.S. army troops] in Sulu."
- "Yes to federalism."
- "Yes to US development, but not *military* assistance" [italics added].[35]

While diverse in political orientations and loyalties, the participants in the summit were united in their calls for the national government to "address the endemic poverty" in Mindanao. They also urged the national government to "take the path of peace and campaign against using war and aggression as an instrument of national and international policy."[36]

There are other efforts that could be undertaken to put the Mindanao peace process back on track for its final resolution:

- A rethinking of military strategies in Mindanao, including the possibility of a gradual or eventual pullout of military installations and forces, especially those in areas that are now slowly stabilizing in terms of peace and order. Both governmental and nongovernmental organizations could lobby for the implementation of the constitutional provisions on the supremacy of the civilian-led Philippine National Police to protect the country's citizens. However, this could be a formidable stumbling block, as the military has always played a crucial role in influencing policy on Mindanao affairs.
- Sustained social discourse on the issue of a "multination" state, to accommodate excluded identities in a definition of the Philippine national identity. Moreover, there is a need to have wide discussions on a whole range of alternatives and possibilities for the future of Mindanao's diverse peoples.
- Peace constituency building on all fronts, and at all educational levels, with a corresponding and sustained capacity-building program for peace workers. This could include modules to train various sectors, even the military, to help them understand the roots of the conflict in Mindanao.
- A much bigger and more extensive role in the current phase of the government-MILF peace process for external players like the OIC, starting with the leadership of Malaysia. Such a role should include not only the brokering and facilitation of a "Final Peace Agreement," but also monitoring and

overall peacekeeping as well as the provision of financial assistance for nongovernmental initiatives to forge long-lasting peace in Mindanao.

Handled properly, Mindanao could be the key that unlocks the potential for a vigorous regional economy and, ultimately, a dynamic national economy built on self-reliance, fairness, justice, and empowerment of its citizens. Mindanao has a vibrant civil society network composed of divergent groups and formations that are committed to social development for its diverse peoples. It is rich in natural resources and cultural diversity. Its wellsprings of indigenous knowledge systems, especially in conflict resolution and transformation, remain a largely untapped resource. All these could be harnessed to form a vigorously developing society.

Resources

International Reports

"Child Soldiers in Central and Western Mindanao: A Rapid Assessment." By Rufa Cagoco-Guiam. Geneva: International Labour Organization, 2002.

"A Critical Collaboration: Civil Society Participation in the Peace Process." By Rufa Cagoco-Guiam. In *An International Review of Peace Initiatives.* Accord Series. London: Conciliation Resources, 1999.

"The MNLF-GRP Peace Process: Mindanao in Transition." *Accord* (London) 3, nos. 1–2 (January–June 1999).

Other Publications

"The Compliant and the Defiant." By Jeremy Beckett. In Alfred W. McCoy and Ed C. de Jesus, eds., *Philippine Social History: Global Trade and Local Transformations.* Quezon City: Ateneo de Manila University Press, 1998.

In War, the Real Enemy Is War Itself. By Roberto Layson, OMI. Davao City: Initiatives for International Dialogue, 2003.

Organizations in Two Provinces in the Autonomous Region in Muslim Mindanao. By Rufa Cagoco-Guiam. General Santos City: Center for Peace and Development Studies, Mindanao State University, 2002. Unpublished.

Rebels, Warlords, and Ulama: A Reader on Muslim Separatism and the War in Southern Mindanao. Eds. K. Gaerlan and M. Stankovitch. Quezon City: Institute for Popular Democracy, 2000.

Revolt in Mindanao: The Rise of the Islam in Philippine Politics. By T. J. S. George. Kuala Lumpur: Oxford University Press, 1980.

"Separatism, Autonomy, and Democratization in the Southern Philippines: Issues and Challenges." By Rufa Cagoco-Guiam. Paper commissioned for the Separatism, Autonomy, and Democratization Project, funded by the United States Institute for Peace, 2002. Unpublished.

The SPCPD: A Response to the Controversy. Ed. Miriam Coronel-Ferrer. Quezon City: UP Center for Integrative and Development Studies, 1997.

Under the Crescent Moon: Rebellion in Mindanao. By M. Dañguilan Vitug and G. M. Gloria. Quezon City: Ateneo Center for Social Policy and Public Affairs and Institute for Popular Democracy, 2000.

Understanding Mindanao Conflict. By Patricia P. Diaz. MindaNews Publications, 2003.

Websites

http://mnlf.net (MNLF website)

just_peace@yahoogroups.com (e-mail for reports and updates on the activities of national civil society groups engaged in peace advocacy, like the Gaston Z. Ortigas Peace Institute)

www.c-r.org (maintained by Conciliation Resources, a small NGO that publishes *Accord: An International Review of Peace Initiatives;* the June 1999 issue focused on the Mindanao peace process between the MNLF and the government of the Philippines; an update of the MILF-GRP peace process is currently being prepared)

www.mindanews.com (Mindanao stories, news, and other incisive comments on the conflict and endemic poverty in Mindanao; site is maintained by the Mindanao News and Information Cooperative Center, headed by Carolyn O. Arguillas)

www.respond.org (maintained by the Responding to Conflict organization; mailing address is 1046 Bristol Road, Selly Oak, Birmingham B29 6LJ, UK; the organization put out a training manual, *Working with Conflict: Skills and Strategies for Action,* by Simon Fisher et al., in 2001)

Resource Contacts

Carolyn O. Arguillas, e-mail: carol@mindanews.com

Jamail Kamlian, vice chancellor for research and extension, Mindanao State University, Iligan Institute of Technology, Iligan City, Mindanao

Eliseo R. Mercado Jr., OMI, e-mail: junmeromi@yahoo.com, ermomi@hotmail.com

Macapado A. Muslim, chancellor, Mindanao State University, General Santos City.

Grace Rebollos, director, People's Center for Peace and Development Initiatives

Irene Santiago, convener, Mindanao Commission on Women, e-mail: irenesantiago@yahoo.com

Soliman M. Santos Jr., e-mail: gavroche@info.com.ph

Western Mindanao State University, Zamboanga City, e-mail: rebollos@wmsu.edu.ph

Organizations

Bangsamoro Women Foundation for Peace and Development, Inc.
Door 1, Salic Apt. Rabago St.
Corner Espino Ext., Cotabato City, Philippines
tel: +63 064 421 6154
e-mail: bmwf@microweb.com.ph

Initiative for International Dialogue
27 Galaxy St. GSIS Heights
Matina, Davao City
tel: +63 82 299 2574 75
fax: +63 82 299 2052
e-mail: iid@iidnet.org

Mindanao Center for Peace and Development
Gomez Compound, Yniquez St.
Ma-a, Davao City
tel: +063 082 244 0648
e-mail: infos@skyinet.net

Mindanao Commission on Women
121 University Avenue, Juna Subdivision
Matina, Davao City
tel +63 082 298 4031
e-mail: mc_women@hotmail.com

Peace Advocates Zamboanga Foundation, Inc.
c/o Angel Calvo, CMF
Claret School, San Jose, Zamboanga City
tel +63 062 991 1168
e-mail: acalvo@mozcom.com

Rufa Cagoco-Guiam is director of the Centre for Peace and Development Studies at Mindanao State University in General Santos city. She is an anthropologist and free-lance media practitioner involved in advocacy for peace, women's issues, and consultations with various nongovernmental organizations. She is also associate professor and coordinator of Mindanao State University's graduate program in public administration. She has written several articles on the peace process and on gender situational analysis of Bangsamoro women in Mindanao. In February 2002, her book Child Soldiers in Central and Western Mindanao *was published in Geneva by the International Labour Organization.*

Notes

1. This chapter focuses on the conflict between the Philippine Republic's armed forces, and the Bangsa Moro (Moro National Liberation Front–Moro Islamic Liberation Front).

2. B. R. Rodil, *The Minoritization of the Indigenous Communities of Mindanao and the Sulu Archipelago* (Davao City: Alternate Forum for Research in Mindanao, 1994), p. 51.

3. Ibid., p. 54.

4. Macapado A. Muslim and Rufa Cagoco-Guiam, "Mindanao: Land of Promise," *Accord* no. 6 (1999): 11–13. See also Rufa Cagoco-Guiam, *Child Soldiers in Central and Western Mindanao: A Rapid Assessment* (Geneva: International Labour Office, 2002).

5. Rufa Cagoco-Guiam, "Separatism, Autonomy, and Democratization in Southern Philippines: Issues and Challenges," paper presented at a forum of writers for the Separatism, Autonomy, and Democratization in Asia project, Hotel Gran Mahakam, Jakarta, January 22–25, 2002, pp. 3–4.

6. See, for example, the works of B. R. Rodil, Samuel K. Tan, and Macapado A. Muslim cited in the Resources section of this chapter.

7. *Indios* was a term the Spanish colonizers used to refer to the natives in Luzon and the Visayas whom they had converted to Christianity.

8. See Jeremy Beckett, "The Compliant and the Defiant: Maguindanao Datus Under Colonial Rule," in Alfred W. McCoy and Ed C. de Jesus, eds., *Philippine Social History, Global Trade, and Local Transformations* (Quezon City: Ateneo de Manila University Press, 1998), pp. 391–414.

9. Rufa Cagoco-Guiam, "Telling the Truth of the Other: Images of Islam and Muslims in Southern Philippines," in Melinda Quintos de Jesus, ed., *The Media and Peace Reporting: Perspectives on Media and Peace Reportage* (Pasig City: Office of the Presidential Adviser on the Peace Process, 2000), pp. 62–80.

10. See Carolyn O. Arguillas, "The Cost of War," *MindaNews,* March 12, 2003, available at www.mindanews.com.

11. Macapado A. Muslim and Rufa Cagoco-Guiam, "Mindanao: Land of Promise," *Accord* no. 6 (1999): 16.

12. B. R. Rodil, *Kalinaw Mindanaw: The Story of the MNLF Peace Process, 1975–1996* (Davao City: Alternate Forum for Research in Mindanao, 2000), pp. 3–4.

13. One reason that the agreement was doomed from the start was that it should have been implemented in accordance with the Philippine constitution and legal processes. For example, the implementation of autonomy would have to pass through

the process of enactment of law and then plebiscite to determine which provinces would be part of the autonomous region. It sought to circumvent, rather than resolve, the issue of self-determination.

14. I witnessed one huge anti-MNLF and anti-Cory rally in 1987 in Cotabato city, where MILF speakers took turns in condemning the meeting as "divisive," and saying that it would "co-opt some of the Moro leaders like Misuari to give concessions to the Philippine government."

15. Computed from the tally sheet of conflict-related casualties, annex to the Midyear Briefing of IBON Databank, specifically from the article "Stabilization and Recovery?" by Antonio A. Tujan Jr. (Manila: IBON Databank, 2002).

16. See Zoher Abdoolcarim, "Terrorist Refuge," *Time,* February 24, 2003. Davao-based *MindaNews* claims the number of MILF casualties is bloated in the *Time* report. MILF deaths are estimated to be only sixty. From an informal interview with Carolyn Arguillas, editor-in-chief of *MindaNews,* March 4, 2003. See www.mindanews.com.

17. As of this writing, Davao city, the premier city in Mindanao and the center of commerce and trade in the region, has been wracked by several bombings: one at the Davao International Airport on March 4, 2003, that killed seventeen people and wounded scores of others; and the latest bombing incident, at Davao's Sasa Wharf Passenger Terminal on April 2, 2003, that killed sixteen and injured more than thirty.

18. Muslim and Cagoco-Guiam, "Mindanao," p. 16.

19. See ibid., p. 19.

20. See Soliman Santos Jr., "Islamic Diplomacy, Consultation, and Consensus," *Accord* no. 6 (1999): 20–23.

21. Ibid., p. 23.

22. See Cagoco-Guiam, "Separatism, Autonomy, and Democratization," p. 31.

23. See *Semi-Annual Accomplishment Report, First Semester, 2002* (Manila: Office of the Presidential Adviser on the Peace Process, 2002), p. 1.

24. Rufa Cagoco-Guiam, "Negotiations and Detours: The Rocky Road to Peace in Mindanao," in *Accord: The Mindanao Peace Process,* supplement to *Compromising on Autonomy* (London: Conciliation Resources, August 2003), p. 6.

25. Ibid.

26. These are among the issues and challenges confronting civil society relations in the Philippines listed by Karina Constantino-David in her paper "From the Present Looking Back: A History of Philippine NGOs," in Sidney Silliman and Lela Garner Noble, eds., *Organizing for Democracy: NGOs, Civil Society, and the Philippine State* (Quezon City: Ateneo de Manila University Press, 1998).

27. Carol Arguillas, "Media and Peace Building in Mindanao," presentation at the Seminar-Workshop on Learning from Public Participation in Peace Processes, Vancouver Hall, Sydney Hotel, General Santos City, September 18, 2003, jointly sponsored by the Conciliation Resources, London, and Catholic Relief Services–Mindanao Regional Office, and conducted by the Center for Peace and Development Studies, Mindanao State University, General Santos City.

28. See Rufa Cagoco-Guiam, "An Exploratory Study of Civil Society Organizations Among Muslim Communities in Two Provinces in the Autonomous Region in Muslim Mindanao," unpublished report to the Konrad Adenauer Foundation, December 2002.

29. For details on how these peace zones came into being, see Karl M. Gaspar et al., *Mapagpakalinawon: A Reader for Mindanao Peace Advocates* (Davao City: Alternate Forum for Research in Mindanao and Catholic Relief Services, Mindanao Regional Office, 2002).

30. Representatives of sixteen Bangsamoro civil society organizations attended the conference. These organizations are based in different regions in Mindanao and included the following: the Bangsamoro Women Solidarity Forum, the Bangsamoro Women Foundation for Peace and Development, the Federation of United Mindanawan

Bangsamoro Women, the Bangsamoro Women Professionals and Employees Organization, the Consortium of Bangsamoro Civil Society Organizations and Its Affiliates, the Asian Muslim Action Network in the Philippines, the Maranao People's Development Center, the Salam Women Organization, Ompongan O Mga Bae sa Ranao, the Peace and Development Advocates League of Maguindanao, Lumah Ma Relaut, HAGS, the MaálJamaáh Development Foundation, the Kadtuntaya Foundation, and the Bangsamoro Youth Assembly. More than 200 participants, mostly women, were in attendance. I was invited to speak on increasing public mechanisms for participation in the peace process.

31. This was disclosed in an informal conversation between myself and a woman member of the government peace panel in early March 2003 in Davao city.

32. See the postscript in Roberto Layson, OMI, *h 9.7* (Davao City: Initiatives for International Dialogue, 2003), p. 67–68.

33. Ibid.

34. From a phone interview with Soliman M. Santos Jr., March 31, 2003.

35. Carolyn O. Arguillas, "Mindanao's Muslim Leaders: Heed Our Calls," February 22, 2003, available at www.mindanews.com.

36. Ibid.

9.7

South China Sea:
Managing Territorial and Resource Disputes

Aileen Baviera

Sometimes called the "mother of all territorial disputes" due to the number of claimants and stakeholders, the complexity of the claims, and the wide range of interests involved, the South China Sea disputes have the potential to trigger armed conflict in East Asia. The claimants have entered into the early stages of a conflict prevention process, characterized by confidence-building measures and agreement on fundamental principles of conduct. Various Track Two initiatives and proposals point the way forward on how to calm these troubled waters, but the first prerequisite—political will on the part of the claimant governments—is not yet in place.

The South China Sea (SCS) disputes refer to competing territorial and jurisdictional claims over four groups of islands, reefs, and atolls, along with their surrounding waters, lying strategically between China and Southeast Asia. These disputes, which focus specifically on Pratas Reef, Macclesfield Bank, the Paracels, and the Spratlys,[1] existed prior to World War II, when claims were made by China and the two colonial powers, Japan and France. After the war, France withdrew from the region and Japan renounced its claims in the San Francisco Peace Treaty, without specifying to which country or countries they were being relinquished, therefore triggering subsequent competition among littoral states, with rival claims pursued by mainland China, Taiwan, and four Southeast Asian states.[2]

The area is strategically important for various reasons, but most of all because critical sea-lanes traverse the waters, linking Northeast Asia and the Western Pacific to the Indian Ocean and the Middle East. More than half the world's shipping tonnage reportedly sails through the South China Sea each year, including more than 80 percent of the oil destined for Japan, South Korea, and Taiwan.[3]

China and Taiwan share the same historical basis for their claims, citing Ming dynasty chronicles as well as a 1947 map published by the Republic of

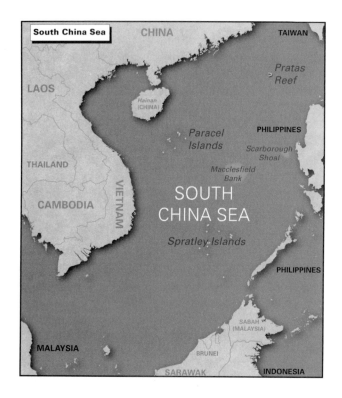

China enclosing virtually the entire sea in nine dotted lines. The two do not appear to compete directly with each other and have even explored cooperation in the past to advance common claims.[4] However, there are recent indications that Taiwan wants to distinguish its claim from that of the People's Republic of China (PRC).[5]

Of the four island groups, Pratas and Macclesfield Bank are claimed by both China and Taiwan, with Taiwan occupying Pratas. Macclesfield Bank is completely submerged and therefore unoccupied. The Paracels are the subject of disputes between China/Taiwan and Vietnam, which led in 1974 to brief PRC–South Vietnam armed confrontations, ending with Vietnam's expulsion from the islands and their occupation by PRC. The entire Spratly group— some 100 islets and outcroppings spread over 410,000 square kilometers of the South China Sea with a total land area of less than 5 square kilometers—is also claimed by China/Taiwan and Vietnam, while only certain parts are claimed by the Philippines, Malaysia, and Brunei. Vietnam and China also clashed in this area in 1988, resulting in the sinking of three Vietnamese vessels and the loss of seventy soldiers. It is believed that Vietnam now occupies around twenty-two features in the Spratlys, China fourteen, the Philippines eleven, Malaysia ten, Taiwan one (the largest feature—Itu Aba), and Brunei none.[6] Except for a few islands that have been converted into civilian facilities by Taiwan and Malaysia, the Spratlys are occupied by military troops. A fifth area, not previously treated as part of the disputes but considered by China to be part of its claim, is an uninhabited rocky outcrop known as Scarborough Shoal, which has recently become a bone of contention between China and the Philippines. (For the basis of the claims, see Table 9.7.1.)

Collectively, these disputes are perceived to be a regional flashpoint, with the possibility of armed confrontation persisting, although to a considerably lesser degree than in other conflict areas in the region such as the Taiwan Strait or the Korean Peninsula. At stake in the disputes are issues of sovereignty and territorial integrity, competition for access to the ocean's living resources (fisheries and other marine flora and fauna) and nonliving resources (oil, gas, and other mineral deposits)[7], freedom of passage and navigation in vital trade and communication sea-lanes, and control for the purposes of security against external threats.

Vietnam and China have long been at loggerheads over the Paracels and Spratlys, symptomatic of larger historical, cultural, and ideological animosities.[8] Until 1992, when China's passage of its Law on Territorial Sea and Contiguous Zone reiterated extensive claims over the entire South China Sea, the other Association of Southeast Asian Nations (ASEAN) claimants generally viewed the China-Vietnam dispute with concern from the sidelines. That year, following fresh tensions between Beijing and Hanoi, ASEAN issued its first collective official statement—commonly referred to as the Manila Declaration on the South China Sea—calling on the parties concerned to exercise self-restraint and to commit to peaceful conflict resolution.

Larger events in the region during the post–Cold War period contributed to the increasing importance of the South China Sea, raising the stakes for those involved. In 1994 the UN Convention on the Law of the Sea (UNCLOS)

Table 9.7.1 South China Sea: Claimants, Basis, and Extent of Claims

China (People's Republic of China)	Historical grounds, including naval expeditions by Han dynasty (A.D. 110) and Ming dynasty (A.D. 1403–1433).
	A 1947 map published by the Republic of China shows that its claim includes all islands within nine dotted lines; no specific claims to adjacent waters are mentioned but are presumed by many.
Taiwan (Republic of China)	Same as People's Republic of China.
Vietnam	Historical grounds dating to French colonial period.
	Claims Paracels, and whole of Spratlys and its continental shelf.
Philippines	Proximity principle; exploration and "discovery" of territory that was unoccupied at the time.
	Claims only some islands in eastern part of Spratlys.
Malaysia	Based on continental-shelf principle.
	Claims only some islands in southern part of Spratlys.
Brunei	Based on continental-shelf principle.
	Claims only a small corridor and one island overlapping with Malaysian claim.

took effect, hastening competition for extended jurisdictions over ocean areas, at a time when the pressures of population growth and rapid industrialization appeared to increase global demand for ocean-based food and energy sources. The rise of China as a regional power, fueled by over a decade of high economic growth, led to a worrisome combination of renewed nationalism among its people, greater assertiveness in its foreign policy, and a more ambitious military modernization program focused on maritime power projection. These developments occurred concurrent with a reduction in the U.S. military presence, following the closure of U.S. bases in the Philippines and a shift to the so-called places, not bases approach, thus adding an element of uncertainty to the regional security environment. Meanwhile, Vietnam had joined ASEAN (after relations had improved following the end of Hanoi's occupation of Cambodia), with the perhaps unintended result that the South China Sea disputes became reframed as a China-ASEAN problem, since Taiwan's role remained unclear and all the four other claimants were now ASEAN members.

There are other parties that are directly or indirectly concerned with the outcome of the disputes. Many countries have a stake in continued freedom of navigation, safety, and security, and some have an unstated interest as well in the presumed energy reserves in the ocean floor. At the subnational level, stakeholders include fisherfolk, fishing enterprises, shipping companies, and coastal communities in the littoral states, whose existence and livelihood depend on access to rich fishing grounds and navigation routes. Supranationally, the scientific community and environmental conservationists also take an interest in these waters because of what study of them may reveal about how their resources could be better managed. Clearly, though, the rival sovereignty claims and the contest for expanded maritime jurisdictions, backed by armed capabilities, constitute the fundamental source of conflict. (See Table 9.7.2 for a brief chronology on the disputes.)

Conflict Dynamics

Thus far, the use of force has been limited to just a few parties and cases and has resulted in relatively small-scale clashes. Apart from the hostilities between China and Vietnam already cited, there have also been occasional standoffs between opposing navies of the various claimants, warning shots fired by military troops, harassment and arrest of fisherfolk on grounds of illegal entry or poaching, the sinking or seizure of civilian vessels and properties, and in a few cases, verbal tussles among political leaders.[9] But despite signs of continuing military buildup in the area, there have been no serious battles fought between the armed forces of any of the claimant nations since the Sino-Vietnamese clashes in 1988.

Recent attention has focused on tensions between the Philippines and China over Beijing's 1995 occupation of the Mischief Reef, claimed by the Philippines, and Chinese fishing in both disputed areas and Philippine territorial waters. Yet although the animosity generated by the Mischief Reef issue is a serious concern, the two governments have not allowed the disputes to disrupt

Table 9.7.2 South China Sea: Selected Chronology of Incidents

1974	Chinese seize the Paracel Islands from South Vietnam.
1988	Chinese and Vietnamese navies clash at Johnson Reef in the Spratlys. Several Vietnamese boats are sunk and over seventy sailors killed.
1992	Vietnam accuses China of landing troops on Da Luc Reef. China seizes almost twenty Vietnamese cargo ships transporting goods from Hong Kong between June and September.
	China passes Law on Territorial Sea and Contiguous Zone, laying claim to Paracels and Spratlys, among others.
1993	China's South Sea Fleet conducts major maneuvers in South China Sea.
1994	China builds a new airstrip on the Paracels.
	China and Vietnam have naval confrontations within Vietnam's internationally recognized territorial waters over Vietnam's Tu Chinh oil exploration blocks 133, 134, and 135. Chinese claim the area as part of their Wan' An Bei–21 (WAB-21) block.
1995	China occupies Mischief Reef near the Philippines.
	Taiwanese artillery is fired at a Vietnamese supply ship.
1996	China ratifies UNCLOS but declares baselines around the Paracels.
	Chinese vessels engage in a gun battle with a Philippine navy gunboat near Capones Island.
1997	China sets up an oil rig on Vietnam's continental shelf.
	The Philippine navy orders a Chinese speedboat and two fishing boats to leave Scarborough Shoal; later removes Chinese markers and raises Philippine flag.
	China sends three warships to survey Philippine-occupied Panata and Kota Islands.
1998	China upgrades structures on Mischief Reef.
	Philippines brings U.S. representative Dana Rohrabacher on overflight of Mischief Reef; U.S. State Department reportedly tries to prevent him from taking the trip.
	Vietnamese soldiers fire on a Philippine fishing boat near Tennent (Pigeon) Reef.
1999	A Chinese fishing boat is sunk in a collision with a Philippine navy vessel on two separate occasions near Scarborough Shoal.
	Philippine defense sources report that two Malaysian fighter planes and two Philippine air force surveillance planes nearly engaged over a Malaysia-occupied reef in the Spratly Islands; Malaysian Ministry of Defense denies there was a standoff.
	Vietnam expands structures on three reefs; the Philippines and Taiwan protest.
	Philippines protests Vietnamese troops firing at its air force reconnaissance plane.
	Philippine navy ship runs aground on Scarborough Shoal, sparking China to send navy patrol.
2000	Philippines files diplomatic protest against Beijing after its navy spots six Chinese vessels loaded with coral anchored off Scarborough Shoal. A navy patrol boat tries to ward off the vessels but later retreats.
2001	Two Chinese navy vessels and a survey and research ship are sighted in Scarborough Shoal.
	U.S.-Philippines joint exercises are held near the Spratly area; China protests.

Sources: Energy Information Administration, www.eia.doe.gov; Aileen S. P. Baviera, "Ocean of Opportunity or Sea of Strife: Transforming the South China Sea Conflict," paper presented at the seminar "Conflict Prevention and Peacebuilding in Southeast Asia: Regional Mechanisms, Best Practices, and ASEAN-UN Cooperation in the Twenty-First Century," Manila, February 21, 2002.

the normal course of relations. A similar reluctance to make the disputes a central issue in their bilateral diplomacy can be observed among all other claimants. China-ASEAN relations have not, in fact, revolved around this single issue, nor have the disputes hindered the development of comprehensive bilateral relations between China on the one hand and individual ASEAN states on the other hand. Neither have they prevented China and ASEAN from pursuing policy coordination in ongoing multilateral arenas such as the ASEAN Regional Forum, the ASEAN-China dialogue partnership, or the more recent ASEAN Plus Three (China, Japan, and Korea) framework. In this context, governments in the region tend to look at the South China Sea problem as a potential conflict—perhaps an accident waiting to happen—rather than as an active one requiring their urgent attention.

China's role in the development of the conflict is seen as crucial because it is the most powerful claimant, holds the most extensive claims, and has been known to use military force in pursuit of its other territorial claims. China has also appeared the most unyielding in its position, continuing to assert its "indisputable sovereignty" and insisting on handling the sovereignty disputes only bilaterally with each of the other claimants. In early 1996, Beijing unilaterally declared baselines around the Paracels and announced that it would do the same for other territories at a later date. The following year, Hanoi protested China's construction of an oil rig on part of its continental shelf. In late 1998, China expanded its Mischief Reef presence into what Philippine defense authorities described as an "emerging military facility" equipped with helipads, gun platforms, and radars.

China is not, however, the only party guilty of apparent unilateral assertions of sovereignty or provocative acts. In 1999, shortly after holding a consultation with China intended to help build mutual confidence, the Philippine navy in separate incidents in May and June intercepted Chinese fishing boats near Scarborough Shoal, and "accidentally sank" two vessels.[10] Malaysia soon afterward set up markers and sent "scientific and research personnel" to areas just outside the Philippine-claimed area.[11] It was also reported to have begun building a base on Philippine-claimed Investigator Shoal. In October 1999, Vietnam expanded structures on three of its occupied reefs, triggering protests from the Philippine and Taiwan governments.

The costs of the escalating tensions can be measured in terms both of consequences and of opportunities lost. They have contributed to arms buildups in the region to secure maritime interests. During the 1980s, Indonesia, Malaysia, the Philippines, Singapore, and Thailand—joined later on by Vietnam—each began gradually to shift its security focus from internal to external concerns, including the control of its territorial waters, assertion of a 200-mile exclusive economic zone, and the securing of trade-related sea-lanes. China also began to develop the ability to mount better-integrated military operations in the South China Sea, fueling suspicion about its intentions not only among the claimants but also among other members of the international community, including major powers such as the United States and Japan.[12] One may even argue that China's maritime ambitions in the South China Sea have given credence to a "China threat" theory and have helped to justify the pursuit of a balance-of-power strategy by countries in the region.

South China Sea. Filipino Navy patrolling.

Meanwhile, the harassment of fishermen of different nationalities has led to the obstruction of economic activities, and an increase in diplomatic tensions. The disputes have also impeded more rational development of the ocean's resources, as claimants have failed to establish cooperative regimes that could otherwise help promote both better development and more sound environmental practices.

Official Conflict Management

Various official initiatives to address the potential conflict have been undertaken since the 1990s, including proposals raised unilaterally by the claimants themselves, bilateral agreements among them, multilateral consultations, and even actions by countries that are not parties to the disputes.

The first government to put forward a strategy for resolution was China, which in the late 1980s broached the idea of shelving the sovereignty disputes and pursuing joint development of the oceans instead. Unfortunately, no detailed proposal followed, while its continued assertions of "indisputable sovereignty" belied its words of compromise. In 1995 the Philippines proposed demilitarization of the islands and a freezing of the status quo—meaning that no further militarization should take place. Such unilateral declarations were largely dismissed as rhetoric, since neither the political will nor the mechanisms for the claimants to reach agreement existed at the time.

Bilateral consultations have focused on reducing the risk of violence by placing the maritime and territorial disputes on the agenda of normal diplomatic processes. Examples include the China-Vietnam delimitation of the

Tonkin Gulf in 2000, and the Philippines-China and Philippines-Vietnam "codes of conduct" of 1995 and 1996 respectively. The codes of conduct called for peaceful settlement of the disputes in accordance with recognized principles of international law, urged the parties to undertake confidence-building measures while refraining from use or threat of force, and expressed the need to cooperate for the protection and conservation of maritime resources. But however helpful it has been in encouraging dialogue among the parties, bilateral diplomacy has not prevented claimants from taking potentially provocative actions against each other, nor is it likely to lead to a comprehensive resolution of disputes that are, after all, multilateral in nature.

Multilateral ASEAN-China efforts to defuse tensions have also made slow progress in recent years. China apparently started to take ASEAN seriously when, in the aftermath of its occupation of Mischief Reef in early 1995, the association closed ranks and severely criticized China's actions. Consultations that were held in Hangzhou in 1995 marked the first time China agreed to discuss the Spratlys dispute multilaterally with the ASEAN claimants. The disputes have since then become part of the agenda of annual China-ASEAN meetings, involving all of ASEAN and not just the claimants.

In 1997 the top leaders of China and ASEAN held their first summit and issued a joint statement on ASEAN-China cooperation for the twenty-first century. On the subject of the disputes, the statement said that the two sides shall "continue to exercise restraint and handle relevant differences in a cool and constructive manner."[13] In 1998 the ASEAN governments resolved to work for a regional code of conduct to prevent the further escalation of conflict. Following much internal negotiation among ASEAN members and then between ASEAN and China, a regional Declaration of Conduct on the South China Sea was finally agreed upon in November 2002. While the declaration is not legally binding and still falls short of specific measures for conflict prevention, it binds the parties to common principles (such as those embodied in the UN Charter, the UN Convention on the Law of the Sea, the Southeast Asian Treaty of Amity and Cooperation, and the "Five Principles of Peaceful Coexistence") as well as to consultative and peaceful processes of dispute settlement. Other provisions of the declaration include calls for the exercise of self-restraint; mutual notification of military exercises; and the extension of humanitarian treatment to all persons in situations of danger or distress in the area. The declaration also includes provisions promoting exploration or cooperation in marine environmental protection, scientific research, safety of navigation, search and rescue, and efforts aimed at combating transnational crime.[14] However, the agreement may be viewed with some degree of skepticism since claimant Taiwan is not a party, it provides for no verification measures, and it fails to spell out any agenda for future action.

The ASEAN Regional Forum (ARF), an Asia Pacific–wide security dialogue mechanism initiated by ASEAN in 1993, has also taken a keen interest in the subject of the disputes. Because of China's objection to the involvement of other parties, the South China Sea issue has not been included on the ARF agenda. Nevertheless, other countries such as the United States and Australia have used the meetings to express their concerns about the apparent escalation of the disputes.

The disputes were also discussed during the 1999 UN General Assembly, after the Philippines had earlier called for UN assistance for their resolution. During the meeting, China, with the support of Malaysia, stressed that it advocated settlement through peaceful means but opposed intervention from nations outside the region. Vietnam and the Philippines, meanwhile, called for restraint and peaceful settlement but asserted before the General Assembly their rights as coastal states.[15] Disagreement among the four major claimants at the 1999 General Assembly is indicative of the difficulties the United Nations faces should it attempt to define a role for itself with respect to the conflict. Interestingly, parties to the disputes have not considered the question of whether the Hamburg-based International Tribunal on Law of the Sea (ITLOS), an institution created by UNCLOS, might also eventually play a role.[16] Nonetheless, their common adherence to UNCLOS already binds the claimants to some form of cooperation with the United Nations on this issue.

As far as the official track is concerned, only the bilateral consultations and the China-ASEAN dialogue can claim to have made any real progress— however modest—perhaps reflecting the claimants' preferences for a solution that will be crafted by the parties directly concerned.

Multi-Track Diplomacy

Unofficial or Track Two diplomacy has also played a role in the conflict management efforts. Foremost among such initiatives is the Indonesia-initiated and Canada-supported Workshop on Managing Potential Conflicts in the South China Sea (MPCSCS), which at first involved only ASEAN countries but eventually expanded to include Taiwan, China, and the new ASEAN members. Most participants in the meeting are officials acting in their personal capacities and technical experts working at the behest of their governments. It is considered Track Two because it has no official standing, and any conclusions or recommendations arising from the discussions are nonbinding to the governments represented.

The workshops, which have been held regularly since 1990, have focused on such areas as resource assessment; marine scientific issues; safety of navigation, shipping, and communication; and legal matters, under the principle of addressing the less sensitive issues first and saving the most difficult ones until after the parties have attained higher comfort levels in dealing with each other. The goal of the MPCSCS is not to resolve the sovereignty or the jurisdictional disputes, but rather "to address areas of co-operative marine management and thereby promote a political environment more amenable to the resolution of jurisdictional conflicts."[17] Confidence-building measures and proposals for practical cooperation are thus also discussed.

Many cooperative projects have been proposed but their implementation has been snagged by the reluctance of governments to compromise on the issue of sovereignty.[18] On the other hand, as an indirect result of the talks, certain parties have been inspired to explore functional cooperation with each other, such as the Philippines and Vietnam, which have held joint oceanographic and marine scientific research expeditions in the disputed areas. Unfortunately, the Canadian government ended its funding for the Indonesian workshops in 2002 after more than a decade, placing the future of the process in question.

Another Track Two initiative is that of the Council for Security Cooperation in Asia Pacific (CSCAP), a regional network of security scholars and practitioners. CSCAP has been active in submitting policy recommendations to governments in the region, particularly in the promotion of confidence building. Its Maritime Cooperation Working Group is currently involved in drafting a maritime security cooperation agreement for the Asia Pacific. The working group has produced a number of publications and two reports that were submitted to the ARF-CSCAP Memorandum no. 4, titled "Guidelines for Regional Maritime Cooperation," and CSCAP Memorandum no. 5, titled "Cooperation for Law and Order at Sea."[19] While the recommendations are nonspecific to the South China Sea, they have particular significance because of their comprehensive coverage and the involvement in the process of participants from all the South China Sea claimant countries.

The ASEAN Institutes of Strategic and International Studies (ASEAN-ISIS) is a network of think tanks in Southeast Asia that also takes an interest in conflict resolution processes. Established in 1984 and now composed of ten member institutes representing each of the ASEAN countries, it has submitted several memoranda to ASEAN, including a 1995 memo titled "The South China Sea Disputes: Renewal of a Commitment to Peace," which directly addresses the issues.

By placing the South China Sea conflict on its agenda of international conferences involving security specialists from the Asia Pacific region, ASEAN-ISIS has also encouraged the exchange of information and explored ways of mitigating the security threat perceptions surrounding the maritime disputes. It has convened three meetings of an ASEAN Experts Group on the Law of the Sea. Its separate dialogues with counterpart research institutes in China and Taiwan periodically touch upon the disputes, but are not limited to the subject. The main handicap of ASEAN-ISIS is that most of its members are organizations that either fall under or are very close to their respective governments, and therefore cannot stray too far from official positions. It has also been difficult to sustain cooperation between Track Two and ASEAN's official track on maritime issues, because, relative to new troubles such as the effects of the 1997 Asian financial crisis, terrorism, and political instability in some member countries, maritime concerns in general and the South China Sea disputes in particular are viewed with less urgency.

A new regional initiative, created in 1999, with some prospects for contributing to the development of new approaches to conflict resolution is the Southeast Asia Conflict Studies Network (SEACSN), which comprises individuals and institutions involved in peace and conflict resolution research and practice. It promotes research on various conflict situations through fellowships or exchanges, and organizes workshops and seminars to compare and discuss experiences in conflict analyses and resolution.[20] Though it is more academically rather than policy oriented, as compared to the ASEAN-ISIS, SEACSN may also be well positioned to engage in peace advocacy, as its networks extend not only to peace researchers and strategic studies experts, but to the nongovernmental sector as well. The network held its first workshop on interstate conflicts in Penang in 2002, including a session on the South China Sea. Its programs are currently supported by the Swedish International Development Agency.

Engagement on the South China Sea issues is not restricted to personnel in the diplomatic and defense establishments, scholars, or Law of the Sea experts; fisheries experts, oil and energy specialists, marine scientists, and environmentalists have become involved as well. The MPCSCS or Indonesia workshops may be seen as a model for how technical experts can work in tandem with officials. Over time, the process has underlined what has become a symbiotic relationship between the former, whose knowledge base helps guide the decisionmakers through a better understanding of the costs of conflict and the benefits of cooperation, and the latter, whose decisions will ultimately affect the advocacy for sustainable ocean development.

The United Nations also provides environmental experts opportunities to indirectly contribute to peace in the South China Sea at the Track Two level. The UN Environmental Program has an East Asian Seas group that is working on a strategic action program for the South China Sea. Similarly, the UN Development Programme is supporting a major regional initiative known as "Partnerships in Environmental Management for the Seas of East Asia," whereby twelve countries in the region (Brunei, Cambodia, China, Indonesia, Japan, Malaysia, North Korea, the Philippines, South Korea, Singapore, Thailand, and Vietnam) are working together to protect the life-support systems of the East Asia seas and to enable the sustainable use of their renewable resources through intergovernmental, interagency and intersectoral partnerships.[21] The Global Environmental Facility (GEF) has provided funds for the program to address marine pollution problems and to engage in partnership-building activities. But the participants' avoidance of activities that will require cooperation in the disputed areas precludes GEF from playing a more useful role in addressing the disputes; the projects have instead been limited to coastal locales.

Perhaps due to the complex nature of these conflicts, and the urgent need to address internal social and political problems, it has been difficult for other nongovernmental organizations (NGOs) or civil society groups to establish a clear stake for themselves vis-à-vis the South China Sea disputes, not to mention delineating a role that they might fill. The nature of civil society itself varies widely among the claimant countries, with autonomous organizations quite active in the Philippines, Taiwan, and Malaysia but largely still irrelevant in the social and political contexts of China, Vietnam, and Brunei. Even in the first three countries, where civil society might have an impact on peace advocacy, the inclination of certain groups has instead been to promote nationalist objectives and support state sovereignty rather than encourage compromise with their neighbors. Public opinion in the claimant states is also more likely to favor strong state action to defend national interests, rather than to view the disputes as international conflicts requiring resolution. In the Philippines, local environmentalist NGOs in its SCS-frontline province of Palawan have pressured Manila to punish fully the Chinese fishermen who are often apprehended in both the country's internal waters and nearby disputed areas.

Instead of coming from civil society, the nonstate conflict prevention initiatives have arisen from the emergence of epistemic communities of security specialists, Law of the Sea experts, marine scientists, and environmentalists in the region and beyond, who through their pooled knowledge, shared beliefs, and common norms have themselves become engaged in the confidence-building and dialogue processes.[22] Such epistemic communities may not always be able to influence policy outcomes, but in the case of the South China Sea disputes they have certainly helped enlarge the constituency for the peaceful and cooperative resolution.

Many proposals for management of the disputes have emerged from these epistemic communities, the most prominent of which are very briefly discussed here. Ambassador Hasjim Djalal, prime mover of the MPCSCS workshops, has in an unofficial capacity proposed a formula for defining the areas of jurisdiction of the claimant states. His formula suggests that each state claim a 200-nautical-mile exclusive economic zone from its baselines, then delimit overlaps with neighboring countries by negotiating median lines. His proposal has become known as the "donut formula" because of the hole it leaves in the middle of the disputed maritime region, marking the high seas area for common use. Mark Valencia of the Honolulu-based East-West Center has suggested establishing a cooperative regime to be managed by a multilateral "Spratlys Development Authority," under which China and Taiwan would lay down their historical claims in exchange for a 51 percent stake in the proceeds from the resources that are developed.[23] Stein Tonnesson of Norway suggests a six-stage strategy for China that will lead to shelving its sovereignty claim over Scarborough Shoal and the Spratlys in exchange for others recognizing its sovereignty over the Paracels. All claimants will then transfer the Spratlys to a regional or international authority, which will manage it as a marine park.[24] Marine scientists such as John McManus have also proposed transforming the seas into a marine park.[25]

Some proposals emphasize the need for parties to negotiate the delimitation of their boundaries, where possible, and to pursue confidence-building and conflict prevention measures in the interim. In areas where the multilateral claims and the military occupations so greatly overlap, thereby making delimitation difficult, the proposed formula is for parties to establish joint development zones (JDZs).[26] Such JDZs are motivated by practical rather than political considerations, and would therefore take the form of provisional arrangements. They may be implemented with or without the final settlement of a maritime boundary. The JDZ approach is attractive because, by its flexible and provisional nature, it is able, in principle, to reconcile the needs of parties to simultaneously preserve sovereignty and territorial integrity, promote peace and security with their neighbors, and advance profitable economic uses of the ocean.[27]

The main value of these proposals from the scholars and scientists is that they compel policymakers to open their minds to the realm of the possible, as well as the necessary and desirable, rather than to be constrained by what might, in a bureaucrat's view, seem only impolitic or insurmountably difficult. Their main shortcoming is the lack of influence over, or even support from, the official track. Nonetheless, even if the political will to implement the proposals is sorely lacking at this point, it is important to continue to refine them and bring them to the attention of governments, highlighting not only their technical sophistication, but more important, their peacebuilding potential.

Prospects

The international community's interest in the maritime disputes has waxed and waned in the past decade or so, mirroring the pattern of tensions among the claimants. Since 1999, there has in fact been an overall improvement in China-ASEAN relations, bilaterally (particularly China's relations with Vietnam, the Philippines, Malaysia, and Indonesia) and multilaterally, as seen in ASEAN-China Free Trade Area initiatives and the ASEAN Plus Three cooperation. Following the 1997 Asian crisis, China gave much-needed financial support to Thailand and Indonesia, and has emphasized building economic links with Southeast Asia. Moreover, since the September 11, 2001, terrorist attacks on the United States, concern in the world and the region has shifted from the so-called China threat to the dangers of terrorism and weapons of mass destruction.

Given the improved relations among the parties to the disputes, the challenge is for governments to avoid becoming complacent or ignoring the continuing potential for conflict escalation. Instead, the November 2002 China-ASEAN Declaration of Conduct on the South China Sea should mark the beginning of new efforts to further institutionalize cooperative and consultative mechanisms for dealing with the disputes. There is a need for the parties to translate the agreed principles of self-restraint and constructive approaches into measures that will further deescalate tensions, including conversion of military presence into civilian presence, negotiation of boundaries and overlapping zones, and development of a modus vivendi on fishing and oil exploration in disputed areas.

Notably, it will only be possible to begin considering the economic potential of the area and promoting its sustainable use when the perceptions of threats to security have been minimized. Apart from state security, human security—including the protection and promotion of the welfare of peoples of the littoral states—must be a priority concern.[28] Indeed, there are stakeholders who remain underrepresented in the process. Among these are coastal communities, fisherfolk, maritime traders, and other seafarers whose survival may depend on the oceans (as the ocean's survival depends on them) far more than their nations' politicians realize. Thus far, their voices have barely been heard.[29]

Recommendations

While the disputes over ownership of territory remain intractable, a number of constructive proposals have been raised in relation to the settlement of the maritime jurisdiction issues. One is that the parties should learn from the already successful experiences of maritime delimitation and joint development in the region. They should focus on building resource management regimes, perhaps low-level and informal initially but ultimately geared to formal cooperation. The process should be multi-track and involve diplomatic, military, management, scientific, and technical personnel, among others.[30]

In the process, the parties should refrain from unilateral provocative acts, including passing new legislation and making major military moves. Instead, they should try to build mutual trust as well as encourage domestic public opinion away from hard-line nationalist sentiments and toward a desire for principled compromise and cooperation.

Given the power asymmetry among the parties and the history of the use of force among them, some experts deem it helpful to consider convening a nonpartisan international body to either help organize the agenda and the process of conflict prevention and conflict resolution, or engage in actual mediation or arbitration. Canada and the Scandinavian countries appear to have built track records in promoting research and dialogue on this issue, and their physical distance, middle-power status, and noncontroversial relations with the littoral states enhance their credibility to act as honest brokers. There are also existing formal mechanisms for dispute settlement that may be tapped, such as the International Court of Justice, the International Tribunal on the Law of the Sea, and ASEAN's very own High Council.[31]

In view of the sensitivity of some parties to direct external intervention, other countries such as the United States, Japan, or Australia should focus their contributions to peace in the South China Sea on encouraging a positive atmosphere for claimants to enter into negotiations, while discouraging any one country from unilaterally seeking a solution by use of force.[32]

Ultimately, however, building peace in the South China Sea requires a transformation of the understanding of security from one that is state-centered and guaranteed only by the ability to assert sovereignty backed up by military means, into one that reconciles the needs of each human being, each community, and each state with the needs of both neighboring peoples and our ocean environment.

Resources

Publications

Calming the Waters: Initiatives for Asia Pacific Maritime Cooperation. Eds. Sam Bateman and Stephen Bates. Canberra Papers on Strategy and Defence no. 114. Canberra: Strategic and Defence Studies Centre, Australian National University, 1996.

"China and the South China Sea: A Peace Proposal." By Stein Tønnesson. *Security Dialogue* 31, no. 3 (September 2000): 307–326.

China and the South China Sea Disputes. By Mark J. Valencia. Adelphi Paper no. 298. Oxford: Oxford University Press for the IISS, 1995.

China's Ocean Frontier: International Law, Military Force, and National Development. By Greg Austin. St. Leonards: Allen and Unwin, 1998.

Conflict Situations and Conflict Management in the South China Sea. By Ramses Amer. UPSK Occasional Paper no. 5/00. Universiti Kebangsaan Malaysia Strategic and Security Studies Unit, 2000.

"Creeping Assertiveness: China, the Philippines, and the South China Sea Dispute." By Ian James Storey. *Contemporary Southeast Asia* 21, no. 1 (1999): 95–118.

The Kalayaan Islands (Spratlys) in Philippine Foreign Policy. By Aileen S. P. Baviera. Panorama vol. 2. Manila: Konrad Adenauer Stiftung, 1999.

"Managing Potential Conflicts in the South China Sea: Informal Diplomacy for Conflict Prevention." By Hasjim Djalal and Ian Townsend-Gault. In Chester A. Crocker et al., eds., *Herding Cats: Multiparty Mediation in a Complex World.* Washington, D.C.: U.S. Institute of Peace Press, 2000.

Maritime Cooperation in the Asia-Pacific Region: Current Situation and Prospects. Ed. Sam Bateman. Canberra Papers on Strategy and Defence no. 132. Canberra: Strategic and Defence Studies Centre, Australian National University, 1999.

The Sino-Vietnamese Approach to Managing Boundary Disputes. By Ramses Amer. Maritime Briefing vol. 3, no. 5. Durham: International Boundaries Research Unit, 1997.

The South China Sea Dispute: Prospects for Preventive Diplomacy. By Scott Snyder. Special Report. Washington, D.C.: U.S. Institute of Peace Press, August 1996.

The Spratly Islands: A Study on the Limitations of International Law. By R. Haller-Trost. Occasional Paper no. 14. University of Kent at Canterbury, 1990.

The Spratly Islands Dispute: Who's on First. By Daniel Dzurek. Maritime Briefing vol. 2, no. 1. Durham: International Boundaries Research Unit, 1996.

"The Spratlys: A Test Case for China's Defense and Foreign Policy." By Ji You. Paper presented at the Workshop on the Spratly Islands: A Potential Regional Conflict, Institute of Southeast Asian Studies, Singapore, December 8–9, 1993.

"Taiwan's South China Sea Policy." By Cheng-yi Lin. *Asian Survey* 37, no. 4 (April 1997): 323–339.

Websites

http://faculty.law. ubc.ca/centres/scsweb/ (University of British Columbia Faculty of Law, South China Sea Working Group)

www-ibru.dur.ac.uk/index.html (International Boundaries Research Unit, University of Durham)

www.asean.or.id (ASEAN Secretariat)

www.cscap.org/maritime.htm (CSCAP Maritime Cooperation Working Group)

www.csis.org/html/pacnet/html (Pacific Forum–CSIS Online Journal Comparative Connections/China-ASEAN Relations)

www.taiwansecurity.org (Taiwan Security Research)

Organizations

Academia Sinica, Taiwan
Yann-huei Song
e-mail: yhsong@eanovell.ea.sinica.edu.tw

Archipelagic and Ocean Studies Network,
University of the Philippines
Gil Jacinto
www.geocities.com/arcoast

ASEAN Institutes for Strategic and International Studies
Clara Joewono, Head of Secretariat
www.aseanisis.org

Center for Strategic and International Studies
Jakarta
Jusuf Wanandi
www.csis.or.id

China Institute for Marine Affairs
State Oceanic Administration
Gao Zhiguo
e-mail: zgao@public.bta.net.cn
Jawhar Hassan
www.jaring.my/isis

*Council for Security Cooperation in the Asia Pacific/Maritime Cooperation Working
    Group*
Commodore Sam Bateman (ret.), cochair
Admiral Sunardi, cochair
www.cscap.org/maritime.htm

Faculty of Law, National University of Hanoi
Nguyen Hong Thao
e-mail: thaonh@vista.gov.hanoi

Hainan Research Institute for the South China Sea
Wu Shicun
www.hriscs.com.cn/index_en.asp

Institute of International Relations
Ministry of Foreign Affairs, Vietnam
Nguyen Nam Duong
e-mail: nguyennamduong2001@yahoo.com

Philippine Center for Marine Affairs
Jay Batongbacal
e-mail: philmar@pworld.net.ph

Southeast Asia Conflict Studies Network (SEACSN)
Kamarulzaman Askandar
www.seacsn.net

Southeast Asia Program on Ocean Law and Policy (SEAPOL)
Phiphat or Frances Lai
www.seapol.org

UNDP Partnerships in Environmental Management for the Seas of East Asia (PEMSEA)
Chua Thia Eng
www.pemsea.org

---

*Aileen Baviera is an associate professor and dean at the Asian Center, University of the
Philippines. She holds a Ph.D. in political science. Her main research interests are
contemporary China studies, Asia Pacific security, and regionalism in East and Southeast Asia.*

Notes

1. The claimants have their own place names for the islands in their respective
languages. Since the simple use of names already reflects assertions of sovereignty on

the part of the claimants, this chapter shall use only the names most commonly used in international sources.

2. Kimie Hara, *Cold War Wedges of China? The San Francisco System and the Cold War Frontiers in the Asia-Pacific—China's Territorial Problems as a Case Study,* East-West Center Politics and Security Working Paper no. 2 (Honolulu: East-West Center, September 2000).

3. Brad Glosserman, "Cooling South China Sea Competition," *PACNET Newsletter* (Pacific Forum–Center for Strategic and International Studies) no. 22A (June 1, 2001).

4. Mark Valencia, *China and the South China Sea Disputes,* Adelphi Paper no. 298 (Oxford: Oxford University Press, 1995), pp. 39–41. There were discussions between China's CNOOC, Taiwan's China Petroleum Corporation, and U.S.-based Chevron for an exploration joint venture in the East China and South China Seas. In 1994 a joint academic conference on the SCS was held. Taiwan at some point even proposed the formulation of a joint legal position. Djalal and Townsend-Gault also note that Taiwan and China shared similar positions in the Indonesia-sponsored Workshops on Managing Potential Conflicts in the South China Sea, Hasjim Djalal and Ian Townsend-Gault, "Preventive Diplomacy: Managing Potential Conflicts in the South China Sea," in Chester A. Crocker, ed., *Herding Cats: Multiparty Mediation in a Complex World* (Washington, D.C.: U.S. Institute of Peace Press, 2000), pp. 107–133.

5. Valencia, *China and the South China Sea Disputes,* p. 23. Such indications include the conversion of the Pratas and Itu Aba military garrisons into civilian facilities, participation by Taiwan representatives in unofficial meetings concerning the disputes involving ASEAN but not China, and recent writing by Taiwan scholars. Taiwan had earlier been reported to be considering changing its claim to only those islands already occupied by itself and China. For details of Taiwan's position, see Lin Cheng-yi, "Taiwan's South China Sea Policy," *Asian Survey* 37, no. 4 (April 1997), available at www.catsic.ucsc.edu.

6. Djalal and Townsend-Gault, "Preventive Diplomacy," pp. 107–133.

7. The South China Sea is estimated to produce 10 percent of the world's annual fisheries catch—over 5 million tons a year, according to the UN Environmental Program, as cited in Environment News Service, "Asian Nations Put Quarrels Aside to Save South China Sea," 2000, available at www.hartcons.com. On the other hand, estimates of oil and natural gas reserves differ from one source to another, with most not too hopeful and the most optimistic estimates coming from China. Chinese media sources have referred to the sea as the "second Persian Gulf," and some experts assert that it could contain as much as 130 billion barrels of oil and natural gas, although the costs of exploring and exploiting would be immense.

8. These include 1,000 years of Chinese domination of Vietnam, land border issues, and Vietnam's close ties with the former Soviet Union, among others.

9. Aileen S. P. Baviera, "Ocean of Opportunity or Sea of Strife: Transforming the South China Sea Conflict," paper presented at the Seminar on Conflict Prevention and Peacebuilding in Southeast Asia: Regional Mechanisms, Best Practices, and ASEAN-UN Cooperation in the Twenty-First Century, Manila, February 21, 2002.

10. "China Still Wants to Get Paid for Fishing Boat That Sank in the Spratlys," *Today,* June 5, 1999, p. 12.

11. "Malaysia Lays Reef Markers," *Today,* June 20, 1999, p. 1; and "Malaysia Admits Sending Scientists to Spratlys," *Today,* June 21, 1999, p. 12.

12. Shawn Crispin, "Arms: On Their Marks," *Far Eastern Economic Review,* October 5, 2000.

13. Joint Statement of the Meeting of Heads of State/Government of the Member States of ASEAN and the President of the People's Republic of China, Kuala Lumpur, December 16, 1997.

14. Declaration on the Conduct of Parties in the South China Sea, November 4, 2002.

15. Thalif Deen, "China Insists Spratly Islands Dispute Is Regional," *IPS Report,* December 7, 1999.

16. Since its establishment in October 1996, the International Tribunal on the Law of the Sea has passed judgment on cases involving questions of commercial activities in exclusive economic zones, the right of hot pursuit, conservation of highly migratory fish stocks, and freedom of navigation.

17. See the website of the South China Sea Working Group, University of British Columbia, http://faculty.law.ubc.ca/centres/scsweb.

18. For a detailed report of the workshop process and outcome until 1998, see Djalal and Townsend-Gault, "Preventive Diplomacy." For analysis, see Liselotte Odgaard, "Conflict Control and Crisis Management Between China and Southeast Asia: An Analysis of the Workshops on Managing Potential Conflict in the South China Sea," available at www.stanford.edu/~fravel/chinafp/scs.htm, also printed in Dieter Mahncke et al., eds., *ASEAN and the EU in the International Environment* (Baden-Baden: Nomos Verlagsgesellschaft, 1999).

19. See the website of CSCAP Maritime Cooperation Working Group, www.cscap.org/maritime.htm.

20. See the website of the Southeast Asia Conflict Studies Network, www.seacsn.net.

21. See the website of UNDP–Partnerships for Environmental Management of the Seas of East Asia, www.pemsea.org.

22. Tom Naess, "Epistemic Communities and Environmental Cooperation in the South China Sea," Centre for Development and Environment, University of Oslo, available at www.sum.uio.no/southchinasea/publications/pdf-format/naess.pdf. See also Peter M. Haas, ed., "Knowledge, Power, and International Coordination," *International Organisation* (Special Issue) 46, no. 1 (Winter 1992). Haas defines epistemic communities as channels through which new ideas circulate from societies to government as well as from country to country, through "a network of professionals with recognized expertise and competence in a particular domain and an authoritative claim to policy-relevant knowledge within that domain or issue-area."

23. Valencia, *China and the South China Sea Disputes,* pp. 50–67.

24. Stein Tonnesson, "Here's How to Settle Rocky Disputes in the South China Sea," *International Herald Tribune,* September 6, 2000. For details, see Tonnesson's article "China and the South China Sea: A Peace Proposal," *Security Dialogue* 31, no. 3 (September 2000): 307–326.

25. John W. McManus, "The Spratly Islands: A Marine Park?" *Ambio* 23, no. 3 (May 1994): 181–186.

26. "Joint development" refers to an agreement to develop together or through some form of cooperation the resources of a designated zone that is the subject of conflicting claims. Townsend-Gault defines joint development as "the pooling of sovereignty or sovereign rights exercised by two or more States over the [mineral] resources of an area." Jagota offers a more general definition within the context of the Law of the Sea Convention, that joint development zones are provisional arrangements covering the whole or part of the overlapping claimed areas, with or without the settlement of a maritime boundary. S. P. Jagota, "Maritime Boundary and Joint Development Zones: Emerging Trends," in *Ocean Yearbook,* vol. 10 (Chicago: University of Chicago Press, 1993), p. 112.

27. Aileen S. P. Baviera and Jay Batongbacal, "When Will Conditions Be Ripe? Prospects for Joint Development in the South China Sea," in Mely C. Anthony and Mohamed Jawhar Hassan, eds., *Beyond the Crisis: Challenges and Opportunities,* vol. 3 (Kuala Lumpur: ISIS Malaysia, 2000).

28. Interest in human security concerns in the South China Sea has focused largely on environmental degradation. Only a third of the region's mangrove forests remain. Rising levels of sedimentation and nutrients, and destructive fishing practices, have

devastated sea-grass communities—like mangroves, another key breeding ground for fish. Two-thirds of the waters' major fish species are being overexploited, with the over 5 million tons of fish that are harvested from the sea each year. Since the South China Sea provides 25 percent of the protein needs for 500 million people—80 percent of the protein in the Philippine diet alone—and a livelihood for some 270 million, one scholar commented that "this is a human security concern of enormous significance." Glosserman, "Cooling SCS Competition," citing the Fourth South China Sea Workshop, a Track Two meeting conducted by the Institute of Strategic and Development Studies (Manila) and the Pacific Forum CSIS (Honolulu), and hosted by the Institute of International Relations, National Chengchi University, Taipei, April 2001.

29. A rare study of the impact of the disputes on local fishing communities in China's Hainan province can be read in Zha Daojiong, "Localizing the South China Sea Disputes: The Case of China and Hainan," *Pacific Review* 14, no. 4 (December 2000): 575–598. A similar study on how fisheries disputes in the South China Sea have affected Palawan in the Philippines is being undertaken as of early 2003 by Baviera and Batongbacal of the University of the Philippines.

30. David Ong and B. A. Hamzah, "Disputed Maritime Boundaries and Claims to Offshore Territories in the Asia Pacific Region," in Sam Bateman and Stephen Bates, eds., *Calming the Waters: Initiatives for Asia Pacific Maritime Cooperation,* Canberra Papers on Strategy and Defence no. 114 (Canberra: Australian National University, Strategic and Defence Studies Centre, 1996), p. 41.

31. Djalal and Townsend-Gault, "Preventive Diplomacy," pp. 125–133.

32. Scott Snyder, *The South China Sea Dispute: Prospects for Preventive Diplomacy,* U.S. Institute of Peace Special Report (Washington, D.C.: U.S. Institute of Peace, August 1996), pp. 15–16.

10

PACIFIC ISLANDS

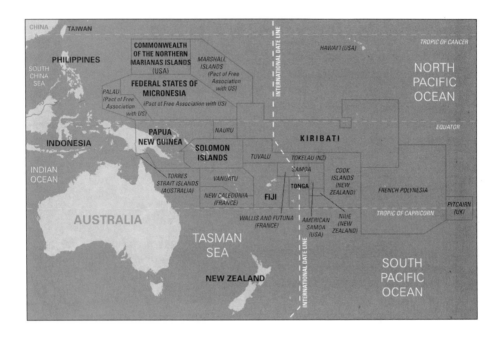

10.1

Regional Introduction: Creating Peace in the Pacific— Conflict Resolution, Reconciliation, and Restorative Justice

Nic Maclellan

Overseas governments have a record of sending police and military forces to the Pacific Islands to assist in peacemaking and peacekeeping operations. The latest intervention in the Solomon Islands comes after a series of violent conflicts in recent decades—small by global standards but significant for small island developing states. But armed conflicts like those in Bougainville, West Papua, and the Solomon Islands are not the norm in the region. This chapter looks at the sources of conflict in the Pacific region, and highlights efforts by Pacific church, women's, and community groups to promote peacemaking, reconciliation, self-determination, and restorative justice.

From the Operation Kumul intervention of troops from Papua New Guinea in Vanuatu in 1980, to Operation Helpem Fren—the Regional Assistance Mission to the Solomon Islands (RAMSI)—in 2003, overseas governments have a record of sending police and military forces to the Pacific Islands to assist in peacemaking and peacekeeping operations. The latest intervention in the Solomon Islands, involving police and soldiers from nine Pacific countries, comes after a series of violent conflicts in recent decades—small by global standards but significant for small island developing states. These included:

- Conflicts over democratic rights, land, and indigenous paramountcy in Fiji with coups d'état in May 1987, September 1987, and May 2000.[1]
- A war in Bougainville between 1989 and 1998, in which more than 12,000 people died during a blockade of rebel areas and armed clashes between the Bougainville Revolutionary Army (BRA), the Papua New Guinea Defense Force (PNGDF), and pro–PNG Resistance militias.[2]
- An armed conflict that erupted in the Solomon Islands in 1998, between rival militias—the Isatabu Freedom Movement of Guadalcanal and the Malaita Eagles Force—and the overthrow of the government in June

2000, resulting in more than 200 deaths and an estimated 15,000–20,000 internally displaced people.[3]

- Violent clashes in 1984–1988 in New Caledonia between the French state, local European settlers, and the Kanak independence movement, FLNKS.[4]
- Indonesia's ongoing occupation of West Papua since the 1969 Act of Free Choice, which has sent thousands of refugees across the border into Papua New Guinea.[5]

Talk of "the Pacific" can often encourage an underlying assumption that all island societies are the same—but there is in fact a vast diversity of social, political, and economic circumstances across the twenty-eight countries and territories in the islands region, with populations ranging from over 5 million people to just 50.[6] Most Pacific Island nations achieved political independence later than developing nations in Africa and Asia, and the legacies of colonialism are a vital influence on conflicts in the region. The issue of colonialism has dropped off the international agenda, but there are still many colonized peoples in the Pacific asserting their right of self-determination in line with UN principles and practice on decolonization.[7]

In some cases, political parties or indigenous sovereignty movements are calling for greater autonomy within the nation-state—while in several others, the demand is for full political independence. This issue affects many territories in the Pacific, under different political and constitutional arrangements: New Caledonia, French Polynesia, and Wallis and Futuna (France); Guam, American Samoa, the Commonwealth of the Northern Marianas Islands, and Hawaii (United States); Tokelau (New Zealand); Pitcairn (United Kingdom); Easter Island (Chile); West Papua (Indonesia); Torres Strait Islands (Australia); and Bougainville (Papua New Guinea).[8]

Sources of Conflict

Media commentators often present conflicts in the Pacific as "ethnic" clashes—between Fijians and Indians, Kanaks and French settlers, Guadalcanal islanders and Malaitans—suggesting that conflicts arise from the failure of island communities to adapt to Western models of democracy, governance, and economic development. But debates over identity and ethnicity take place in a broader context of economic and political change, affected by the failure of a development model promoted by former colonial powers and overseas aid donors. The major source of crisis in the islands is not "ethnic violence" but the militarization of political and social disputes, arising from the interaction of local struggles for power and resources—particularly land, paid employment, and services—and global economic trends that disadvantage small island developing states.[9]

The Australian and New Zealand governments' response to conflict in Pacific states has been influenced by the perception that they are following the path of "failed states" in Africa.[10] Recent military deployments in the Melanesian islands have highlighted concern over the so-called arc of instability to the north and east of Australia and the potential "Balkanization" of Indonesia and Papua New Guinea.[11]

But armed conflicts like those in Bougainville, West Papua, and the Solomon Islands are not the norm in the region. It is important to look at the unique and complex circumstances of each society. Most Polynesian and Micronesian nations—which have a strong chiefly tradition, a monolingual society, and the safety valve of emigration—don't face the so-called ethnic conflict of multilingual Melanesian societies.

To investigate the sources of conflict in Pacific societies, it is vital to look at the political ecology of the region. For example, the Asian Development Bank (ADB) estimated that in 1997–1998, the Solomon Islands saw a 15–20 percent drop in gross domestic product in just one year, partly due to withdrawal of capital after the financial crash in Asia and exacerbated by the El Niño drought in 1998. Further analysis is needed to understand the interplay of all these factors as sources for the violence that erupted in 1999—and responses to conflict must address the interplay of social, cultural, and economic factors with global trends in the movement of capital, labor, and trade.[12]

Land and Resource Conflicts

For indigenous peoples in the Pacific, land is at the center of life: as a source of livelihood through subsistence activities; a source of power, authority, and status through ownership; and above all as a source of security and identity. Around the region, there are significant variations in land tenure systems, but issues of landownership, land usage, or land degradation are at the heart of many conflicts in the Pacific.[13] There are fundamental conflicts between land and resource owners, governments, and transnational corporations over who controls the vast wealth of the Pacific. There are extensive reserves of timber and strategic metals such as copper, gold, nickel, and cobalt throughout Melanesia. The island nations' 200-mile Exclusive Economic Zones (EEZ) give sovereignty and control over fisheries and marine resources around every islet, reef, and archipelago. The ocean seabed also harbors wealth such as polymetallic nodules and oil and gas reserves.

The ways in which natural resources are extracted can devastate ecosystems and destroy indigenous cultures and livelihoods, as was shown with major projects such as Ok Tedi (PNG), Panguna (Bougainville), and Freeport (West Papua). Clear-cut logging and the disposal of mining tailings have caused serious environmental damage and local landowners have fought back against this despoliation. In turn, governments have relied on police and military forces to control these enclave resource developments, sparking a cycle of repression, conflict, and further militarization.

Lack of Substantive Democracy and Economic Restructuring

Many independent Pacific nations are still seeking to overcome the administrative, legal, and constitutional legacies of colonization: national boundaries

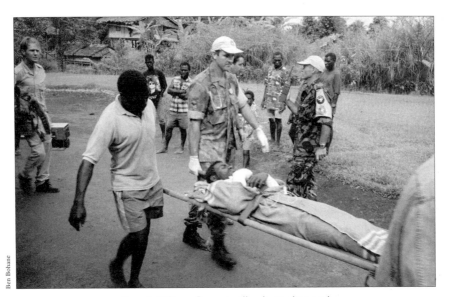

Ben Bohane

So-vele Village, Bougainville. Australian and
New Zealand peacekeepers carrying a wounded guerrilla for medevac.

that arbitrarily divide linguistic and cultural groups; education programs that cannot guarantee jobs in the wage sector for the young; and systems of law, administration, and economic development that have created unequal access to power and resources (particularly between kinship groups on different islands).

Countries that only achieved self-government and independence in the 1970s and 1980s are trying to meld customary systems of governance and law with Western parliamentary traditions and judicial structures.[14] Moves to transform institutions of government inherited from colonial administrations have been tentative and underresourced, and the alienation of many grassroots people from the institutions of *gavman* (government) underlie the violent conflicts of the past decade.

Since the early 1990s, academic and policy debate about conflict in the Pacific has been influenced by the "good governance" agenda being promoted by the World Bank, the ADB, and other donors.[15] Donor programs on good governance have emphasized the role of civil society and "nonstate actors." But these programs have often failed to define the place of customary authorities and indigenous structures that are so important in the region.

As part of a broader global trend, trade policy is a new arena of debate between the Organization for Economic Cooperation and Development countries and island nations in the Pacific, being driven by multilateral institutions. The action plan developed by the Forum Economic Ministers' Meetings and adopted by the Pacific Islands Forum sets out a neoliberal agenda for regional economic restructuring, including liberalization of trade and removal of tariffs; reduction of staffing in the public sector; flexible labor markets; corporatization and privatization of government agencies in transport, communications, energy, water, and other sectors; introduction of value-added taxes; and removal of some controls on the finance sector.[16]

There has been growing concern about the social and cultural impacts arising from the neoliberal orthodoxy that underlies these structural adjustment programs. Public-sector employees, farmers' groups, and university students have resisted government cutbacks, and churches and nongovernmental organizations (NGOs) have established a Pacific Action Network on Globalization.[17] A regional gender and trade network is analyzing the impact of World Trade Organization policies on Pacific women and young people, and feminist scholars and activists have been documenting the particular impacts of debt, trade, and reform policies on women and poverty.[18]

Protests over structural adjustment have been sharpest in Papua New Guinea and Fiji. Four people were shot dead by the police during the June 2001 protests in Port Moresby against corruption in government, privatization policies, and the way that government cost-cutting under World Bank programs hit the poor hardest.

Militarization of Conflict

Although internal repression has not reached the level seen in many other Asian states, a worrying feature of some Pacific island nations is the militarization of their police forces and engagement of military forces in political life. With no credible external military threats, security doctrines have now turned inward to deal with threats to the security of the state from resource and landowners, indigenous groups, and movements for democratic rights.

In a worrisome development, a number of states have seen the intervention of military forces in the civil affairs of the society: two coups d'état in Fiji in 1987 and a civilian putsch and military takeover in 2000; the 1996 kidnapping of Vanuatu's president by Mobile Force members; and the PNGDF intervention in Bougainville. The Bougainville crisis contributed to increased conflict in the neighboring Solomon Islands, as the Solomon's police increased their military capacity to cope with cross-border raids by PNGDF troops in hot pursuit of BRA militants and civilian refugees.

The blurring of roles and responsibilities between military and unarmed constabulary is a major concern. In Papua New Guinea, PNGDF military troops have also been used in the policing of industrial disputes; clashes with land and resource owners over mineral and timber projects; and crackdowns on *raskol* (criminal gangs) and unemployed youths.[19]

Foreign governments have contributed to this process of militarization. Australia, the United States, France, and New Zealand are all suppliers of military equipment and training programs to the Pacific Islands, although island nations are diversifying their military aid links beyond their former colonial powers (e.g., China and Israel, seeking diplomatic support from the Pacific Islands Forum bloc, have supplied military aid to island states).[20]

There are regular joint exercises, such as Australia's training of the PNGDF and Kopassus troops from Indonesia, France, and the United States holding joint war games with the Tonga Defense Services, even though there is no credible military threat to Tonga. Australia has pursued a policy of offering military-oriented support to local police forces.[21] In late 2003, Australia announced that it would send 200 police to Papua New Guinea, to participate directly in policing operations.

As well as the direct effects of military operations, the culture of militarism can affect the ethos of a society. The role of troops in internal operations has indirect spillover to other sectors of society (e.g., incidences of domestic violence against Papua New Guinea women by soldiers returning from Bougainville; the use of stolen military weapons in robberies in postcoup Fiji; the gun culture that has flourished in the Solomon Islands among marginalized youth). In the highlands of Papua New Guinea, long-standing tribal warfare has become more vicious, with increasing use of high-powered rifles and heavy weapons.

Pacific Responses to Conflict

An analysis of conflict resolution and peacebuilding in Pacific countries reveals a number of common strands. As detailed in the following chapters, it is the complex interplay of all these elements that can make or break a peace process:

- The importance of operating at a range of levels: from community to national, from regional to international
- The importance of time—allowing people to meet, consult, and decide at their own pace
- The often undervalued Pacific traditions of consensus; talking together; the power of the spoken word, shame, and personal pledges and commitment
- The need to engage a range of players—not just government officials, soldiers, and leaders of armed militias, but the full range of civil society, church, and customary leaders
- The key role of women's groups, church leaders, and customary authorities in catalyzing grassroots consultation, disarmament, and reconciliation initiatives
- The catalyzing effect of outside groups—whether through lobbying and advocacy by solidarity and human rights groups, or the provision of resources and meeting spaces by outside governments and neutral brokers

Government Policy Through the Pacific Islands Forum

Over the last decade, the Pacific Islands Forum has increasingly addressed security and conflict issues in the region. The forum has issued a series of statements on security at its annual meetings, such as the 1992 Honiara Declaration on Law Enforcement Cooperation, the 1997 Aitutaki Declaration on Regional Security Cooperation, and the 2000 Biketawa Declaration.

The forum has made increased efforts to coordinate law enforcement and security agencies around the region—police, customs, intelligence, and judicial—and to develop a common approach to weapons control and gun smuggling.

However, there have been expressions of concern over the slow implementation of these regional policy frameworks and the lack of capacity in some forum countries to meet the provisions of these declarations. NGOs have been critical of the forum for being slow to address crises within the boundaries of postcolonial states (such as Bougainville and West Papua).[22]

Island nations are increasing their contact with international networks such as the Alliance of Small Island States, the UN Secretariat, and the Commonwealth Secretariat, and developing a new policy on engagement with "nonstate actors." This has led to engagement in postconflict and decolonization monitoring (e.g., Commonwealth missions to the Solomon Islands and Fiji; UN representation in postconflict Bougainville; UN Decolonization Committee special missions to Tokelau; Pacific Islands Forum special missions to New Caledonia and French Polynesia). Fiji has a long-standing involvement in international peacekeeping operations,[23] and soldiers and police from other island states have played important roles in Bougainville and Solomon Islands peacekeeping.

Governance and Constitutional Reform

One major focus for conflict resolution has been constitutional review and the use of legal processes to address violations of human rights. NGOs such as the Citizens' Constitutional Forum in Fiji and the Tonga Human Rights and Democracy Movement have used the courts to promote and defend civil and political rights. Fiji provides a striking example of the successes and limits of legal strategies to reform the constitution after the 1987 coups, as discussed in Chapter 10.2.

Other groups, such as Transparency International and the Ombudsman Commissions in Papua New Guinea, Samoa, and Vanuatu, use legal processes to monitor arbitrary or corrupt government actions and support judicial review or repeal of unjust legislation.

Apart from Australia and Aotearoa/New Zealand, the Fiji Human Rights Commission is the only governmental human rights commission in the Pacific Islands—a body entrenched in Fiji's 1997 constitution together with a bill of rights and extensive antidiscrimination provisions. The Asia Pacific Forum for Human Rights Institutions has been working to establish other such government commissions in the Pacific (especially in Papua New Guinea), and an important seminar was held on standards for Pacific human rights commissions at the University of the South Pacific, Suva, Fiji, in 1999. However, efforts to establish a regional human rights structure have thus far been unsuccessful.[24]

Legal reviews are also part of self-determination processes. Nationalist movements in New Caledonia, French Polynesia, Tokelau, and Bougainville are debating constitutional frameworks that address issues of indigenous rights, citizenship, and decentralization of powers.[25] The constitutions of Fiji and the Federated States of Micronesia (FSM) include entrenched provisions for regular review, and the FSM has held two constitutional conventions to discuss proposed amendments. In New Caledonia, the signing of the 1998 Nouméa Accord opened the way to the devolution of powers, a multiparty government, and a vote on self-determination after a period of increasing autonomy for fifteen to twenty years.[26] The people of Bougainville have also established a consultative process to develop a new constitution that could be put to the population for ratification in a vote on self-determination.

Human Rights Education and Advocacy from a Pacific Perspective

A primary focus on constitutional change and civil and political rights down-plays the larger question of addressing the underlying causes of conflict, often relating to land, cultural identity, leadership, and social and economic rights.

Pacific NGOs have initiated a wide range of programs on human rights and peacemaking, drawing on custom and Christian values that meet with the values and experience of island communities. They are working to present the language of international human rights instruments in accessible and popular formats and in local languages.[27]

Human rights initiatives occur at both the regional and the national level. Pacific NGO delegations attended the Vienna Conference on Human Rights and other global summits throughout the 1990s, and have organized key regional seminars on human rights issues (including legal literacy training, economic social and cultural rights, women's rights, intellectual property rights and traditional knowledge, decolonization and demilitarization, etc.).[28]

While a key focus has been to develop a Pacific perspective on human rights, national and regional NGOs have cooperated with overseas training, advocacy, and solidarity programs. Regional NGO bodies such as the Pacific Regional Human Rights Education Resource Team and the Pacific Concerns Resource Centre have extensive networks in Europe, Asia, and the Americas to coordinate education and training programs for church and NGO activists on international human rights instruments.

There is vibrant civil society debate on human rights in the region, and grassroots activists are drawing on a synergistic mixture of Christian and Melanesian values to promote "restorative justice."[29] There are also many debates taking place over the content of "human rights." Some activists question whether the Western emphasis on individual rights is helpful, given the Pacific's communal and collective culture. In contrast, some women's groups argue that an uncritical acceptance of "community" and "the Pacific way" can ignore the particular oppression of women and young people in Pacific custom.[30]

Women and Churches at the Forefront

Pacific women's groups and churches have expressed concern that peace negotiations and cease-fires can center on the armed state and armed militias, without acknowledging the concerns of wider civil society and the need for restorative justice.[31] As described in the following chapters, a notable feature of efforts for peacebuilding, reconciliation, and reconstruction after recent conflicts has been initiatives by women, which have challenged the "boys with guns" culture:

- The Bougainville Inter-Church Women's Forum was central to kickstarting peace negotiations in the mid-1990s after years of violence, while NGOs such as the Bougainville Community-Based Integrated Humanitarian Program and the Leitana Neihan Women's Development Agency have worked to address the impact of the crisis on women and other noncombatants.[32]
- In June 1999, women in the Solomon Islands initiated a Reconciliation and Peace Committee, with work continuing today through the Women's Peace Initiative and involving members of the Federation of Women, the Family Support Centre, and Women for Peace.[33] The Solomon Islands Christian Association (SICA) and the SICA Peace Office have been central focal points for reconciliation and reconstruction efforts.
- In Fiji, the Women's Peace Vigil was initiated by the National Council of Women two days after the May 2000 coup. They met daily in the Anglican Cathedral in Suva to provide a secure venue for dialogue and prayer, and support for the hostages held in parliament.[34]

Grassroots women have personally challenged armed soldiers and militia gunmen to halt their attacks on noncombatants, often highlighting their role as mothers, sisters, and wives. The use of "shame" and loss of face—a central part of most Pacific cultures—has had a powerful disarmament effect in reaching young men who have abandoned their responsibility to community values of peace and order.[35]

In national elections, many church and women's organizations have run awareness campaigns to counter vote rigging, fraud, and "pork barreling"—challenging "big man" politicians who have used private militias to back their campaigns (a striking example was the 2002 elections in the Southern Highlands of Papua New Guinea, which were postponed after extensive violence).

The issue of violence against women, sex tourism, and sexual abuse of women and children is of growing concern around the region. The plague of sexual violence is being challenged by support and advocacy centers linked through networks such as the Pacific Women's Network Against Violence Against Women.[36] Such advocacy centers have combined with local women's groups to address the specific impacts of violence against women during and after situations of armed conflict.[37]

Many organizations have also drawn on traditions of spiritual peacemaking, given the central role played by Christian churches throughout the region.[38] In Fiji's multiconfessional society, interfaith dialogue between the Christian, Hindu, and Muslim communities plays an important part in postcoup reconciliation, while in New Caledonia, Christian theologians have contributed to the Kanak liberation struggle.[39] Church organizations have an increasing focus on postconflict reconciliation, peacemaking, and interfaith dialogue.[40]

In the wake of violent clashes in the Solomon Islands and Bougainville, the formal peace treaty did not mean demilitarization: Hundreds of high-powered guns remain in the hands of former militants, and criminal behavior by unemployed former fighters is an ongoing concern for local communities. NGOs have been active in promoting "zones of peace," to remove weapons from warring communities and promote conflict resolution and mediation. NGOs have commenced links with the International Action Network on Small Arms (IANSA), and in 2003 the Small Arms Survey project issued a major study on the impact of small arms on Pacific Island communities.[41]

In Pacific cultures, the public expression of peace and reconciliation is a central element of conflict resolution. The importance of custom and ceremony in peacebuilding is a crucial part of island society. In Bougainville, armed militants of the Bougainville Revolutionary Army and pro–Papua New Guinea Resistance forces have joined together for peace ceremonies with the exchange of pigs and shells and the symbolic breaking of bows and arrows. Such public ceremonies are a first step that allows former combatants to make their private peace with the families of those they've killed, opening the way for emotional healing and reintegration into their communities. Bougainville's reconciliation efforts emphasize traditional peacemaking processes, to promote the reconstruction of social harmony and transcend the "payback" mentality.[42]

A dispute between the Vanuatu police and paramilitary Vanuatu Mobile Force (VMF) was calmed by a "Kastom Peace Reconciliation" on August 31, 2002, initiated by the Malvatumauri (Vanuatu National Council of Chiefs). The public ceremony, attended by the prime minister, high chiefs, police, and VMF leaders, involved the exchange of pigs and mats as compensation for their actions in disturbing the public peace.[43] In postcoup Fiji, there were a series of roundtable discussions called Talanoa, supported by the Pacific Islands Development Program in Hawaii. The Talanoa talks attempted to bring together politicians and community leaders for informal talks to end the polarization of postcoup politics.

But in a small island community, where nearly everyone knows everybody else, there are particular problems in addressing issues of payback, revenge and reconciliation, memory and forgiving. Melanesian custom can be distorted, as detailed in Chapter 10.4: Traditional ways can be discredited when the government pays out significant sums to former combatants (a process viewed by many as extortion rather than customary symbolic recompense). The length of time needed for customary processes can clash with Western deadlines.[44]

There is ongoing debate about how to meld customary peacemaking with formal legal processes. Should tribunals be created for war crimes, or will this harm reconciliation efforts? Should amnesty be extended for crimes committed during civil conflicts? While statesmen preach reconciliation with former enemies, others have advocated the establishment of truth and reconciliation commissions to address human rights abuses or crimes against humanity.[45]

Some NGOs in Fiji and the Solomon Islands maintain that general amnesties and the demand for reconciliation allows coup supporters to avoid any acknowledgment of—let alone punishment for—their role.

Military Forces, Training, and Human Rights

In spite of the importance of indigenous customary authority, foreign governments can play a catalyzing role, creating neutral space for dialogue and supplying police and peacekeeping forces to separate or disarm combatants. The New Zealand government played an important role as a facilitator for peace talks in the Bougainville conflict—supplying financial resources and neutral meeting places to bring together a range of political leaders for inter-Bougainville dialogue in a series of meetings between 1990 and 1998.[46] These talks were vital in creating agreement on the central issues (cease-fire, truce, peace monitoring). The military stalemate in Bougainville and the 1997 Sandline crisis were also significant turning points in Papua New Guinea, affecting Australian policy and government attitudes toward the role of military forces in the region.[47]

In recent years, there has been a new focus on peacekeeping operations involving Australia, New Zealand, and Pacific Island forces, including the South Pacific Peacekeeping Force in Bougainville (1994), the Truce Monitoring Group and Peace Monitoring Group in Bougainville (from 1997), the International Force for East Timor and the UN Transitional Administration for East Timor in East Timor (from 1999), and the International Peace Monitoring Team (from 2000) and Regional Assistance Mission for the Solomon Islands (from 2003).

There is a growing body of literature that analyzes these peacekeeping and peacebuilding operations, which have provided significant contrasts in operational styles.[48] In all cases, Australia has contributed greater resources than Pacific counterparts, but has also been regarded as less of a neutral player than New Zealand, Fiji, Vanuatu, or Tonga. The armed military intervention in East Timor has been contrasted to the unarmed peace monitors in Bougainville, and many commentators have noticed the important cultural role played by islanders from Vanuatu, Fiji, and Tonga. The Bougainville operation involved multinational civilian as well as military peace monitors. In spite of the pride of the Australian Defence Force contingent in the fact that it went to Bougainville unarmed, female and indigenous peace monitors have bemoaned the lack of resources provided by macho military men to work with women's organizations.[49]

The Red Cross, the Fiji Women's Crisis Centre, and other Pacific human rights NGOs have begun programs to train police, judiciary, and military forces in international humanitarian law (IHL), with information on sexual violence, rape, HIV/AIDS, and human rights law. The Asia Pacific Military Law training course at the University of Melbourne involves military forces from Papua New Guinea, Tonga, and Fiji, and has established a regional IHL resource center and library. NGOs are also lobbying governments to ratify IHL conventions (such as Protocol 2 of the Geneva Conventions, on civil disturbances).

But there are limits to retraining military forces and disarming militias. Extensive "engagement" between the Australian Defence Force and Indonesia's elite Kopassus special forces has not ended human rights abuses.[50] Demobilizing poorly paid troops leaves them without hope or jobs: in 2001, PNGDF soldiers rebelled and seized arms in their Port Moresby barracks, when a Commonwealth review team recommended significant cuts to the size and operations of the army after the Bougainville war.[51] Former militia members employed as Solomon Islands "special constables" after the 2000 Townsville Peace Agreement demanded compensation at gunpoint when the government tried to dismiss them.

Conclusion

Government-sponsored peace agreements and the deployment of peacekeeping operations have had some initial successes in addressing conflict in the Pacific. But there are a range of underlying causes that must be addressed if long-term peace is to be restored. Conflict resolution must actively engage with a spectrum of players—not just government officials, soldiers, and armed militias, but the full range of civil society, church, and customary leaders involved in peacemaking, reconciliation, self-determination, and restorative justice.

The focus on ending armed conflict needs commensurate and ongoing efforts to address the sources of conflict, which often arise from the policies of overseas governments: clashes between landowners, government, and transnational corporations over the impact of resource projects on culture and environment; militarized responses from the state to the demands of landowners, indigenous groups, and movements for democratic rights and self-determination; and opposition to the effects of structural adjustment programs.

There is enormous potential for strengthening women's groups, church organizations, and customary authorities involved in disarmament, development, and reconciliation. The following chapters outline such initiatives in Fiji, Bougainville, and the Solomon Islands.

Nic Maclellan has worked as a journalist, researcher, and community development worker in the Pacific Islands. Between 1997 and 2000, he lived in Fiji, working with the Pacific Concerns Resource Centre in Suva. He is coauthor of three books on Pacific issues, including La France dans le Pacifique: De Bougainville à Moruroa *(Paris: Editions La Découverte, 1992);* After Moruroa: France in the South Pacific *(Melbourne: Ocean Press, 1998); and* Kirisimasi *(Suva: Pacific Concerns Resource Centre, 1999).*

Notes

1. From the vast literature on Fiji's coups, see Paul Reeves, Tomasi Vakatora, and Brij Lal, *The Fiji Islands: Towards a United Future,* Parliamentary Paper no. 34 (Suva: Parliament of Fiji, 1996). Two volumes of research papers of the Fiji Constitution Review Commission have been published as Tomasi Vakatora and Brij Lal, eds., *Fiji in Transition* (vol. 1) and *Fiji in the World* (vol. 2) (Suva: University of the South Pacific, 1997). See also 'Atu Bain and Tupeni Baba, eds., *Bavadra: Prime Minister, Statesman, Man of the people* (Nadi: Sunrise, 1990); and Brij Lal, ed., *Fiji Before the Storm: Elections and the Politics of Development* (Canberra: Australian National University, Asia Pacific Press, 2000).

2. Donald Denoon, *Getting Under the Skin* (Melbourne: Melbourne University Press, Melbourne, 2000); Yauka Aluambo Liria, *Bougainville Campaign Diary* (Eltham: Indra, 1993).

3. Amnesty International, *Solomon Islands: A Forgotten Conflict*, ASA 43/005/2000, September 7, 2000. See also Tarcisius Tara Kabutaulaka, "Beyond Ethnicity: Understanding the Crisis in the Solomon Islands," *Pacific News Bulletin*, May 2000; and Oxfam Community Aid Abroad (CAA), *Australian Intervention in the Solomons: Beyond Operation Helpem Fren* (Melbourne: Oxfam CAA, 2003).

4. Nic Maclellan and Jean Chesneaux, *After Moruroa: France in the South Pacific* (Melbourne: Ocean, 1998).

5. Rex Rumakiek, "Human Rights Violations in West Papua," in Pacific Concerns Resource Centre (PCRC), *No Te Parau Tia, No Te Parau Mau, No Te Tiamaraa* (Suva: PCRC, 2000), p. 40.

6. The largest Pacific state Papua New Guinea has 5.1 million people; the British territory of Pitcairn, listed with the UN Decolonisation Committee as a non-self-governing territory, has less than fifty people, the descendants of the Bounty mutineers. For country information, see Brij Lal and Kate Fortune, eds., *The Pacific Islands: An Encyclopedia* (Honolulu: University of Hawaii Press, 2001).

7. A detailed study of the role of the UN Decolonisation Committee can be found in Carlyle Corbin, "What Future for the United Nations' Decolonisation Process?" *IWGIA Indigenous Affairs* no. 1 (January–March 2000), pp. 4–13.

8. For a history of Pacific colonization, see K. R. Howe, R. C. Kiste, and Brij Lal, *Tides of History: The Pacific Islands in the Twentieth Century* (St. Leonards: Allen and Unwin, 1994).

9. Greg Fry, "Political Legitimacy and the Post-Colonial State in the Pacific: Reflections on Some Common Threads in the Fiji and Solomon Islands Coups," *Pacifica Review* 12, no. 3 (October 2000): 295–304. Thanks to Cathy Emery for references.

10. Ben Reilly, "The Africanisation of the South Pacific," *Australian Journal of International Affairs* (Canberra), November 2000; Donald Denoon, "Black Mischief: The Problem with African Analogies," *Journal of Pacific History* 34, no. 3 (1999): 281–289.

11. See, for example, Greg Sheridan, "Breaking Up Brings no Benefit: We Are Witnessing the Balkanisation of the Region," *The Australian,* June 9, 2000; and Greg Sheridan, "Danger on the Doorstep," *Weekend Australian,* March 24–25, 2001. For an insightful reply to the crisis-mongers, see Greg Fry, "Conflict and Conflict Resolution in the South Pacific: Regional Dimensions," in *Dialogue,* November 2000.

12. Office of Pacific Operations, Asian Development Bank (ADB), *Impact of the Asian Financial Crisis on PMDC Economies* (Manila: ADB, 1998). For the concept of political ecology and the link between El Niño, free trade, and conflict in the Pacific, see Mike Davis, *Late Victorian Holocausts: El Niño Famines and the Making of the Third World* (London: Verso, 2001), pp. 97–98, 108.

13. "Land, Labour, and Independent Development," chap. 5 in *The Cambridge History of the Pacific Islanders* (Cambridge: Cambridge University Press, 1995).

14. Tess Newton Cain, "Convergence or Clash? The Recognition of Customary Law and Practice in Sentencing Decisions of the Courts of the Pacific Islands Region," *Melbourne Journal of International Law* 2 no. 1 (June 2001): 48–68; Paul de Dekker and Jean-Yves Faberon, *Custom and the Law* (Canberra: Asia Pacific Press, 2001).

15. Peter Lamour, *Governance and Good Government: Policy and Implementation in the South Pacific* (Canberra: National Centre for Development Studies, Australian National University in Canberra, 1995); Peter Lamour, ed., *Governance and Reform in the South Pacific,* Pacific Policy Paper no. 23 (Canberra: National Centre for Development Studies, Australian National University in Canberra, 1998); Cluny McPherson and La'avasa McPherson, "Where Theory Meets Practice: The Limits of the Good Governance Program," in Elise Huffer and Asofou So'o, eds., *Governance in Samoa: Pulega i Samoa* (Canberra: Asia Pacific Press, 2001).

16. The Pacific Islands Forum represents heads of government of all the independent and self-governing Pacific Island countries, Australia, and New Zealand. Since 1971 it has provided member nations with the opportunity to express their joint political views and to cooperate in areas of political and economic concern. The sixteen-member Pacific Islands Forum links Australia, New Zealand, and the independent island states of Papua New Guinea, the Solomon Islands, Vanuatu, Fiji, Kiribati, Tuvalu, the Cook Islands, Tonga, Samoa, the Marshall Islands, the Federated States of Micronesia, Palau, Niue, and Nauru. With the exception of New Caledonia, which has observer status with the forum, the French and U.S. colonies in the region are not forum members, though they are members of other regional intergovernmental organizations.

17. Ecumenical Centre for Research, Education, and Advocacy, "Regional Consultation on Globalisation, Trade, Investment, and Debt," Nadave, Fiji, April 30–May 4, 2001.

18. See, for example, Clare Slatter, "Banking on the Growth Model? The World Bank and Market Policies in the Pacific," in 'Atu Emberson-Bain, ed., *Sustainable Development or Malignant Growth? Perspectives of Pacific Island Women* (Suva: Marama, 1994), pp. 17–36; and Clare Slatter, "Economic Agendas, Internal Impacts, and Growing Dissent: Economic Restructuring in the Pacific," and Vaine Wichman, "A General Discussion on the Social Impacts of the Economic Reform Programme in the Cook Islands," both in "Making a Difference: Women and Globalisation," *Tok Blong Pasifik* 53, no. 2, 2001.

19. Sinclair Dinnen, *Law and Order in a Weak State: Crime and Politics in Papua New Guinea* (Adelaide: Crawford House, 2001); Glenn Banks, "Razor Wire and Riots: Violence and the Mining Industry in Papua New Guinea," in Sinclair Dinnen and Allison Ley, eds., *Reflections on Violence in Melanesia* (Leichhardt: Federation Press, 2000), Chapter 18.

20. For example, after Australia and New Zealand cut military aid programs to Fiji after the 1987 military coups because of human rights concerns, France joined Singapore and Malaysia to fill the gap. Israel has provided Uzi submachine guns to the Tonga Defense Services, and China's defense minister, General Chi Haotian, announced a grant of U.S.$500,000 to the Fiji military forces during a February 1998 visit to Suva. "China Donates to Fiji Soldiers," *Fiji Daily Post,* February 12, 1998.

21. Nic Maclellan, "Policing the Economy in Papua New Guinea," *Arena* no. 86 (Autumn 1989).

22. For example, Pacific Concerns Resource Centre, "Pacific Islands Forum Should Do More on West Papua," *Pacific News Bulletin,* July 2001, p. 3.

23. Fiji has sent police or Fiji military force personnel to peacekeeping and monitoring roles in Zimbabwe, Namibia, Lebanon, Sinai, Cyprus, Bosnia, East Timor, Bougainville, and the Solomon Islands. Indeed, peacekeeping operations are a major source of income and employment for young Fijian men. There are also negative spin-offs—for example, a former Fiji military force soldier used an M-16 rifle in a supermarket robbery; the M-16 was reportedly smuggled from Lebanon, where the soldier had been part of Fiji's military contingent in the UNIFIL peacekeeping force; others have faced allegations of smuggling tons of ammunition from Israel into Lebanon, and then to Fiji in 1996. See "Ex-Soldier Admits Using M-16 in Foodtown Heist," *Fiji Daily Post,* November 7, 1997; and "Army Faces Arms Smuggling," *Fiji Daily Post,* March 23, 1998.

24. Citizens Constitution Forum (CCF) and Institute of Justice and Applied Legal Studies (IJALS), *The Importance of National Human Rights Institutions* (Suva: CCF, 1998); Caren Wickliffe, *Human Rights Education in the Pacific,* Journal of South Pacific Law Working Paper no. 1 (Port Vila: USP, 1999).

25. Aliki Faipule Kolouei O'Brien, "The Modern House of Tokelau," *Pacific News Bulletin,* June 2000; Yash Ghai and Tony Regan, "Constitutional Accommodation and Conflict Prevention," in Andy Carl and Lorraine Garasu, eds., "Weaving Consensus: The Papua New Guinea–Bougainville Peace Process," *Accord* no. 12 (2002); Nic

Maclellan, "New Caledonia–Nouméa Accord," *Australian Indigenous Law Reporter* 7, no. 1 (2002): 88.

26. Nic Maclellan, "The Nouméa Accord and Decolonisation in New Caledonia," *Journal of Pacific History* 34, no. 3 (1999): 245–252.

27. Examples include the translation of the Convention for the Elimination of All Forms of Discrimination Against Women (CEDAW) into Bislama (the pidgin language of Vanuatu) by the late Grace Mera Molisa, or a Tahitian artist's drawing of the Universal Declaration of Human Rights in reo Maohi language, produced by the human rights group Ligue des Droits de l'Homme de Polynésie–Teturaetara.

28. See, for example, Pacific Concerns Resource Centre (PCRC), *Report of the Inaugural Indigenous Peoples of the Pacific Workshop on the UN Draft Declaration of the Rights of Indigenous Peoples,* Suva, Fiji, 1996 (Suva: Government of the Republic of Fiji and PCRC, 1997); and PCRC, *Proceedings of the Indigenous People's Knowledge and Intellectual Property Rights Consultation* (Suva: PCRC, 1997).

29. Pat Howley, *Breaking Spears and Mending Hearts: Peacemakers and Restorative Justice in Bougainville* (Leichhardt: Federation Press, 2002).

30. Margaret Wilson and Paul Hunt, eds., *Culture, Rights, and Cultural Rights: Perspectives from the South Pacific* (Wellington: Huai, 2000).

31. Civil society perspectives on peacemaking were outlined at an important seminar in October 2000. See Pamela Thomas, ed., "Conflict and Peacemaking in the Pacific: Social and Gender Perspectives," *Development Bulletin* no. 53 (October 2000).

32. Lorraine Garasu, "The Role of Women in Promoting Peace and Reconciliation," in Carl and Garasu, "Weaving Consensus." Helen Hakena, "War Leads to Human Rights Abuses," *Pacific Women Against Violence Newsletter* 4, no. 4 (April 1999).

33. Alice Pollard, "Resolving Conflict in Solomon Islands: The Women for Peace Approach," and Daley Tovosia Paina, "Peacemaking in the Solomon Islands: The Experience of the Guadalcanal Women for Peace movement," both in Thomas, "Conflict and Peacemaking in the Pacific," pp. 44–46, 47–48.

34. Sharon Baghwan Rolls, "Gender and the Role of the Media in Conflict and Peacemaking: The Fiji Experience," in Thomas, "Conflict and Peacemaking in the Pacific": 62–64.

35. For discussion of "shame" as an element in Pacific peacemaking, see Howley, *Breaking Spears and Mending Hearts,* pp. 30–31, 129–132.

36. Information on the Pacific Women's Network can be found in the quarterly newsletter *Pacific Women Against Violence* or at www.fijiwomen.com. See also "Non-Government Organisations and Domestic Violence," sec. 3 in Sinclair Dinnen and Allison Ley, eds. *Reflections on Violence in Melanesia* (Leichhardt: Federation Press, 2000).

37. On Bougainville, see Ruby Mirinka, "Our Mothers and Children Are Dying: Military Offensives Against the Island of Bougainville," in Emberson-Bain, *Sustainable Development or Malignant Growth?* p. 230; and Michelle Tonissen, "The Relationship Between Development and Violence Against Women in Post-Conflict Bougainville," in Thomas, ed., "Conflict and Peacemaking in the Pacific," p. 26. On Timor, see *Violence by the State Against Women in East Timor* (Melbourne: East Timor Human Rights Centre, 1998); and Melinda Sissons, *From One Day to Another: Violations of Women's Reproductive and Sexual Rights in East Timor* (Melbourne: East Timor Human Rights Centre, 1998).

38. Christine Weir, "The Churches in Solomon Islands and Fiji: Responses to the Crises of 2000," in Thomas, "Conflict and Peacemaking in the Pacific," p. 49. For historical comparison, see Christine Weir, "'The Gospel came . . . fighting is ceasing among us': Methodist Representations of Violence in Fiji and New Britain, 1830–1930," in Dinnen and Ley, *Reflections on Violence in Melanesia* (Leichhardt: Federation Press, 2000), Chapter 3.

39. Pothin Wete, *Agir ou meurs: L'Eglise Evangélique de Calédonie vers Kanaky* (Suva: Pacific Theological College, 1988); Erich Weingartner: *New Caledonia: Halfway to independence?* (Geneva: World Council of Churches, 1996).

40. The Fiji-based Ecumenical Centre for Research, Education, and Advocacy (ECREA) has developed a manual for teaching conflict resolution adapted for Pacific audiences: Arlene Griffen, ed., *Creating a Culture of Peace: A Training Manual for Pacific Peace Builders* (Suva: ECREA, 2002).

41. I attended the 1998 founding meeting of IANSA in Brussels as a representative of the Suva-based Pacific Concerns Resource Centre. The Small Arms Survey project has issued an important research study on the region: Conor Twyford and Phil Alpers, S*mall Arms in the Pacific,* Occasional Paper no. 8 (Geneva: Small Arms Survey, March 2003).

42. For detailed examples, see Howley, *Breaking Spears and Mending Hearts.* See also Liz Thompson's award-winning video *Breaking Bows and Arrows* (Paddington: Firelight and Tiger Eye, 2001).

43. "PCRC Welcomes Vanuatu Peace and Reconciliation," *Pacific News Bulletin,* August 2002, p. 1.

44. For example, in New Caledonia, attempts to use "the Pacific way" to reconcile long-running conflict between Kanaks and Wallisians in the village of Saint Louis have been hampered by looming congressional elections in 2004, rivalry between chiefs aligned with the pro- and anti-independence parties, and heavy-handed intervention by the French police.

45. For a valuable comparative analysis of truth and reconciliation commissions in Europe, Africa, and Latin America, see Elizabeth Stanley, "What next? The Aftermath of Organised Truth Telling," in Bill Rolston, ed., "Truth?" special edition of *Race and Class* 44, no. 1 (July–September 2002).

46. The Endeavour Agreement (1990), Burnham 1 (July 1997), Burnham 2 (October 1997), Cairns (November 1997), and Lincoln (January 1998). See Moses Havini, "The History of Bougainville/PNG Peace Accords," in Pacific Concerns Resource Centre (PCRC), *Proceedings of the Third NGO Parallel Forum, Rarotonga, Cook Islands, September 1997* (Suva: PCRC, 1998); and Robert Tapi, "From Burnham to Buin," in Carl and Garasu, "Weaving Consensus."

47. On Bougainville and Sandline, see Sean Dorney, *The Sandline Affair* (Sydney: ABC, 1998); Mary-Louise O'Callaghan, *Enemies Within* (Sydney: Doubleday, 1999); and Sinclair Dinnen, Anthony Regan, and Ron May, eds., *Challenging the State: The Sandline Affair in PNG,* NCDS Pacific Policy Paper no. 30 (Canberra: Australian National University, 1998).

48. Bob Breen, *Mission Accomplished: East Timor ADF Participation in INTERFET* (St. Leonards: Allen and Unwin, 2000); Bob Breen, *Giving Peace a Chance: Operation Lagoon, Bougainville 1994—A Case Study of Military Action and Diplomacy,* Canberra Papers on Strategy and Defence no. 142 (Canberra: Strategic and Defense Studies Centre, Australian National University, 2001); Monica Wehner and Donald Denoon, eds., *Without a Gun: Australians' Experiences Monitoring Peace in Bougainville, 1997–2001* (Canberra: Pandanus Books, 2001); Bob Breen, *A Good Thing Worth Doing: Peace Monitoring in Bougainville, 1997–1998* (forthcoming); "International Peace-Building Initiatives," in Carl and Garasu, "Weaving Consensus." Rebecca Adams, ed., *Peace on Bougainville: Truce Monitoring Group—Gudpela Nius Bilong Peace* (Wellington: Centre for Strategic Studies New Zealand/Victoria University Press, 2002).

49. Melissa Bray, "A Woman in Buin," and Tracey Haines, "An indigenous Monitor," both in Wehner and Denoon, *Without a Gun,* pp. 131–133.

50. Former Australian foreign minister Gareth Evans has acknowledged the weakness of efforts to improve the professional standards of the Indonesian armed forces:

"Many of our earlier training efforts helped only to produce more professional human rights abusers." "Indonesia's Military Culture Has to be Reformed," *International Herald Tribune*, Opinions, July 24, 2001.

51. Nic Maclellan, "Defence Force Mutiny in Papua New Guinea," *Pacific News Bulletin*, April 2001, pp. 7, 12–13.

10.2

Fiji:
Enabling Civic Capacities for
Conflict Prevention and Peacebuilding

Satendra Prasad and Darryn Snell

Fiji remains a deeply divided nation. The Fiji Islands have witnessed a cycle of coups, armed insurrection, political unrest, and ethnic conflict since the military coups of 1987. While the country has not erupted into full-blown civil or ethnic war, the instability has caused considerable social and economic setbacks. Since 1987 a variety of civil society organizations have promoted efforts to rebuild the democratic processes and interethnic relations, with varying degrees of success. However, their more recent efforts have been hampered by the inability of the principal political parties to establish a broad-based multiparty government that reflects the ethnic diversity of society and that is consistent with the power-sharing provisions of the constitution. As a result, Fiji is still locked into a dangerous cycle of ethnic hostility and competition. This continues to extract a high price from its developmental efforts.

Prior to the military coups of 1987, Fiji was the envy of the South Pacific. Politically it had remained stable since independence in 1970 and had made considerable advances in education, health, and other sectors. The military coups of 1987 and the failed coup and subsequent political crises of May 2000 reversed many of these advances as the country became internationally isolated, foreign investment declined, and the domestic environment for commerce deteriorated sharply. Dwindling tourist numbers, large-scale emigration of skilled and professional workers, and increased international competition in the sugar and garment industries also increased Fiji's economic difficulties, leading to a continuing decline in its fortunes. Between 1986 and 2003, Fiji experienced a deterioration in all indicators of human development—with its position on the UN Development Programme's human development index falling from 44 in 1986 to 81 in 2003.[1]

Growing poverty, particularly in urban areas, has become a serious problem. The UN Development Programme estimates that one in three families

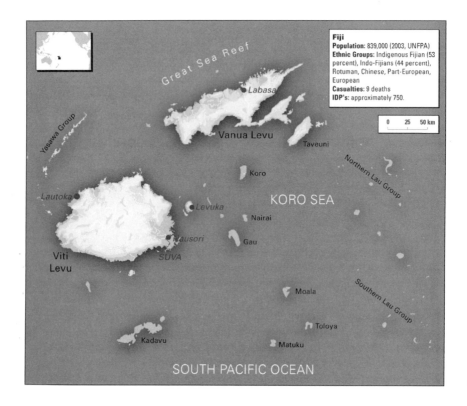

Fiji
Population: 839,000 (2003, UNFPA)
Ethnic Groups: Indigenous Fijian (53 percent), Indo-Fijians (44 percent), Rotuman, Chinese, Part-European, European
Casualties: 9 deaths
IDP's: approximately 750.

live in poverty.[2] In the capital, Suva, youth unemployment runs at 60 percent. The majority of these youth are indigenous Fijians. Job creation in the formal sector, outside of the garment and textiles industries, has remained dismal. Fiji's rural agriculture sector has also been in a state of decline resulting from uncertainties in the sugar industry and anxieties about land leases among the mainly Indo-Fijian tenant community.[3]

Fiji's political uncertainty contributed to a radical reorientation of the economy. Following the coups of 1987 and the subsequent economic downturn, the country adopted a harsh structural adjustment program. This committed Fiji to restructuring its economy through policy measures that included corporatization and privatization of state enterprises, deregulation of the labor market, promotion of trade liberalization, devaluation of the Fiji dollar, and reforms in the public sector.[4] Between 1989 and 1999, these policies were vigorously pursued by successive governments. However, following the general elections in 1999, a new coalition government led by the Fiji Labor Party (FLP) rolled back aspects of the structural adjustment reforms. This ended with its removal from office in 2000. The Soqosoqo Duavata ni Lewenivanua (SDL) government, which took office after the elections of 2001, reaffirmed the basic parameters of economic policy that had been introduced in 1989.

During both the 1987 and 2000 upheavals, the Indo-Fijian population experienced significant levels of violence and human rights abuse. There were many cases of looting and burning of Indo-Fijian shops, enterprises, and farms, and desecration of their places of worship. In May 2000, these events escalated to such an extent in some regional areas that whole Indo-Fijian villages had to be evacuated by humanitarian agencies after a series of beatings, thefts, and continued threats by indigenous youth with the apparent complicity of elements within the police and military forces.[5]

The numbers of deaths attributed to political and ethnic violence in Fiji have been marginal. No deaths were reported during the "bloodless" 1987 coups, due largely to the fact that the military was mostly united behind the coup. In May 2000, however, the coup was largely civilian-led but received some support from factions within the military. Throughout the crisis the military struggled to regain control of its divided forces. While the military succeeded in restoring order and arresting the coup leaders by mid-July without major altercations, the divisions within the military continued to present problems for some time. In November 2000, soldiers in the elite Counter Revolutionary Warfare Unit (CRWU) attempted to take control of the military's headquarters in Suva. This event coincided with the interim government's decision to charge the coup leaders with treason. The mutiny involved the takeover of the armory by the CRWU and an attempt to capture the army's chief commander, Frank Bainimarama, who successfully evaded capture. A counteroffensive ensued that involved a gun battle in which eight soldiers were killed and twenty-four were injured before the insurrection was put down. This incident shocked the nation,[6] and demolished the myth that Fiji had a highly professional and internally disciplined military. Factions within the military had clearly fallen prey to the provincial and tribal machinations that erupted during the grab for political power following the capture of the government in 2000.

The Colonial Legacy

Fiji's postcolonial history was never going to be easy. The country had become deeply racialized by nearly 100 years of British colonial policies. The British maintained a system that sought to exploit the riches of Fiji while "protecting" the indigenous population. Between 1889 and 1916, over 50,000 indentured laborers were recruited from colonial India to help develop export industries, sugar in particular. The majority of these laborers remained in Fiji at the end of the indenture period in 1920 and the colonial administration maintained a series of policies to keep the two major groups separated. These policies included laws protecting indigenous land rights; the establishment of separate administrative arrangements for indigenous, Indo-Fijian, and other communities; labor-market policies that restricted the recruitment of indigenous Fijians and regulated workers from other communities in commercial employment; and the establishment of a separate system of governance for indigenous Fijians that included the Bose Levu Vakaturaga (Great Council of Chiefs) and provincial- and district-level councils. The Great Council of Chiefs, consisting of high chiefs, served as a mechanism to resolve leadership challenges and customary rights (especially land rights)—issues that often divided the indigenous population. It also served as the medium through which colonial development policies were communicated to the indigenous Fijian population.

By the time of independence, Fiji was a divided and inequitable society. While indigenous Fijians owned over 80 percent of Fiji's land, they were disadvantaged in education and commerce, sectors in which Indo-Fijian and European/part-European communities performed much better. The colonial administration's labor-market policies meant that indigenous Fijians were also disadvantaged in most formal employment categories at the time of independence.[7] There were notable exceptions, however. The military and the police force were dominated by indigenous Fijians, as were most senior government positions. The rise of segmented labor markets was to become a source of open hostility in the postcolonial period.

The constitutional framework that was adopted at the time of independence reinforced ethnic separateness. The 1970 constitution provided for fifty-two seats in the House of Representatives. These seats were partitioned according to the ethnic categories; twenty-seven seats were "communal" (twelve each reserved for indigenous Fijians and Indo-Fijians, and three for "general electors"—a category that at the time of independence was dominated by Europeans and part-Europeans). Under these arrangements, political parties continued to be ethnically based. Indo-Fijians founded and strongly supported the National Federation Party, while indigenous Fijians rallied behind the Alliance Party.[8]

The Alliance Party controlled the government from 1970 to 1987. In the 1987 general elections, the Alliance Party was defeated by the FLP Coalition. The FLP, established in 1985, represented the country's first multiethnic political party. Timoci Bavadra, appointed prime minister of the FLP Coalition soon after the election, became the first "commoner" indigenous Fijian prime minister. The FLP Coalition was elected on a populist platform that sought to address the needs of the country's workers, farmers, and disadvantaged. Among the proposals were plans to strengthen the country's trade union movement, introduce progressive taxation, and nationalize strategic industries.

In May 1987, a month after the general election, third-ranking Lieutenant Colonel Sitiveni Rabuka staged a military coup. This action, he proclaimed, was necessary to preserve indigenous rights. He abrogated the 1970 constitution and formed a government consisting of a large number of Alliance Party members who had been defeated in the 1987 elections.[9]

In 1990 a new constitution was established through presidential decree. The 1990 constitution aimed to ensure indigenous Fijian dominance of government. Under the 1990 constitution, indigenous Fijians received a disproportionate number of "communal" seats, and the offices of president, prime minister, chief justice, and heads of the military, police, and senior public service were reserved for indigenous Fijians. Ideally, Rabuka hoped the 1990 constitution would help the country overcome the international isolation it had endured since 1987. The 1990 constitution, however, was seen as so overtly racist that local and international condemnation and pressure continued.

Throughout this period, nonindigenous Fijians, particularly Indo-Fijians, were increasingly isolated. Ethnonationalists in government justified this on the grounds that they were *vulagis* (visitors) rather than citizens. Efforts to declare Fiji a Christian state only deepened Indo-Fijians' feelings of marginalization.

The Rabuka-led Soqosoqo ni Vakavulewa ni Taukei (SVT) Party, unsurprisingly, was elected and reelected in the 1992 and 1994 general elections. The SVT government bowed to domestic and international pressure and agreed to review the 1990 constitution. A commission was established to review the 1990 constitution and by 1997 the principal political parties and ethnic group leaders had agreed to a multiracial and democratic constitution.[10]

The 1997 constitution removed the blatantly racist elements of the 1990 constitution. At the same time, however, the 1997 constitution sought to preserve indigenous group rights. It ensured that indigenous Fijians, who were a majority in the population, received a majority of seats in parliament. Indigenous group rights were also firmly protected through veto powers of the nominated representatives of the Great Council of Chiefs in an unelected upper house.[11]

More important, the 1997 constitution introduced changes that sought to encourage the different ethnically based political parties to cooperate with one another. Largely through pressure by civic agencies, constitutional dialogue and discussion were made open to the public from early on. Extensive public discussions fed into the formal constitution-making process. New opportunities for cross-ethnic group dialogue on divisive political questions were created, contributing to improvements in interethnic group relations and leading eventually to the almost unanimous acceptance of the constitution by parliament and by the Great Council of Chiefs.

Elections under the 1997 constitution led to the formation of an FLP-led multiparty government in 1999.[12] Mahendra Chaudhry was sworn in as Fiji's first nonindigenous prime minister. Like in 1987, this government was forcibly removed from power in May 2000 by ethnic Fijian nationalists supported by some military officers. Following extensive international condemnation, fresh general elections were held in May 2001. This election brought to power the nationalist Fijian SDL Party under Prime Minister Qarase. The FLP, however, performed well, winning the second-greatest number of seats. In spite of constitutional provisions for multiparty government, the SDL-led government initially excluded the FLP; following directives from the courts in October 2003, it offered a token participation to the FLP. Politics in Fiji remain divided by this issue.

Conflict Dynamics

The takeover of parliament on May 19, 2000, was preceded by months of agitation by various groups dissatisfied with the FLP Coalition's policies. The Chaudhry-led government had worked quickly to deliver on its campaign promises. The government reversed plans to privatize the civil aviation and electricity industries, sought to resolve difficult issues surrounding land tenure

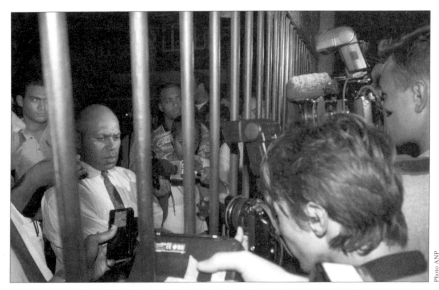

Photo ANP

Suva, May 21, 2000. Coup leader George Speight (in tie)
holds a press conference through the iron gates outside the
Parliament Buildings. Speight's attempt to overthrow the
Fijian government did not work because he lacked military backing,
Prime Minister Adi Kuini Speed said the next day.

and the sugar industry, took on government corruption and corporate tax
evaders, and worked to introduce a minimum wage and improved labor legislation. These policy changes upset a wide range of people and entrenched
interests. Business owners were unhappy with the government's pro-worker
stance and the fact that several government ministers were trade union leaders.
Landowners were uneasy about government plans to alter the land tenure system. Former politicians, many of whom had been in control of government
since 1987, were finding it difficult to be in opposition or outside politics. The
Chaudhry government's inquiries into past government corruption increased
their unease.[13]

Indigenous Fijian nationalists were the most vocal about their dislike for
the Chaudhry government. Ethnonationalists, soon after the Chaudhry government took office, expressed their dissatisfaction with having an Indo-Fijian as
prime minister. Initially, few people took much notice of their activities or
statements. They did not have the support of the Great Council of Chiefs, president, or the military, and thus could do little to alter the situation. Over time,
however, the nationalists began to gain support from a growing number of
indigenous Fijian church leaders, chiefs, and disenchanted unemployed youth.

To confront this "*vulagi* led" government, a narrow base of disenchanted
politicians were able to whip up simmering resource-based grievances. They
sought the support of elements in fundamentalist church groups to pursue the

goal of declaring Fiji a Christian state. They gathered support among disenchanted urban Fijian youths—the unemployed and the underemployed underclass who had little stake in the formal sector of employment and felt excluded from it. They exploited the real sense of economic exclusion felt by indigenous Fijians in the central provinces on Viti Levu. These provinces had provided the land upon which the hydroelectricity dam that powered the coastal cities was built, and they felt that they had been grossly undercompensated for this. Furthermore, they saw that employment opportunities in the capital and urban areas were taken not only by Indo-Fijians, but also by Fijians from outer islands.

A number of ethnonationalist protest marches were organized throughout the country. The largest march took place on the day of the attempted coup. As some 10,000 people marched through the streets of Suva, a group of armed men stormed parliament and took the government hostage. George Speight, chairman of the Fiji Hardwood Corporation until dismissed by the Chaudhry government,[14] led the armed group. Speight and his supporters held nearly all the elected members of the Chaudhry government hostage for fifty-six days. They demanded that the 1997 constitution be abrogated and a new exclusively indigenous Fijian government be installed.

For the first two weeks of the crisis the country suffered from widespread lawlessness. The nationalists' march in downtown Suva turned into a riot with widespread looting and burning. Similar but smaller-scale events spread to other towns and villages. The military struggled to gain control of the situation and for a period of time it was unclear whom it supported. The military eventually succeeded in bringing the situation under control by imposing a state of emergency and direct military rule that involved isolating Speight and his supporters. The military negotiated the release of the hostages, but the Chaudhry government was not to be allowed to return to power. The military appointed an interim government headed by Laisenia Qarase.

Qarase's SDL Party narrowly won the general elections in September 2001. While the FLP performed quite well, the Qarase government refused to form a multiparty government. He formed a government that included only one Indo-Fijian. Much to the dismay of many civil society organizations, Qarase included a number of nationalists in the government who had backed Speight and the takeover. The Qarase government maintained a largely nationalist agenda. A "blueprint" for the advancement of indigenous Fijians was developed and changes to the constitution that would ensure indigenous supremacy in government were once again proposed.[15]

The 1997 constitution, through its provisions for multiparty government, sought to moderate this sort of extremist politics. Qarase, however, simply ignored these provisions bringing about a legal challenge by the FLP. After nearly two years in lower and appeal courts, the Supreme Court ruled on the case. It upheld the constitution's power-sharing arrangements and ordered the "Prime Minister to select persons from the FLP for appointment to Cabinet, to advise the President to appoint those persons as ministers and to appoint them to cabinet."[16] Qarase publicly declared he would abide by the decision of the Supreme Court. However, as of this writing, he has yet to negotiate in good faith with the FLP about its inclusion in government, and has offered to the FLP little more than token representation in the cabinet.

The Qarase government's nationalist position has prevented any meaningful reconciliation between indigenous Fijians and Indo-Fijians. The view of the government-established Ministry for Reconciliation is that reconciliation must occur between indigenous Fijians first and be based on Christian teachings.[17] It is highly unlikely under the current government that the ministry will expand its work to include reconciliation between ethnic communities despite calls to do so from the leader of the opposition, Mick Beddoes, and many civil society organizations.

The government is also unhappy with ongoing court trials and court-martials for individuals accused of being involved in the attempted coup. Members of the Qarase government are seeking to have those charged released and those found guilty pardoned and provided traditional ceremonies of apology. The fact that some of Qarase's ministers stand accused of involvement in the coup attempt plays no small role in the government's stance.

Relations between the government and the military appear to have become strained over this issue. Commander Frank Bainimarama has made it clear that he wants those involved in the attempted coup held accountable and disciplined for their actions. Whether such a position will help strengthen or further divide the military is uncertain. What is clear is that the government has decided not to renew Bainimarama's position as commander. This may be part of the government's attempt to assert its control over the military. If this is the case, the nationalist elements within the government may be able to gain the upper hand of the military.[18]

The government's efforts to appease the extremist ethnonationalist elements within itself have worked to calm tensions temporarily. These tensions are likely to erupt again in the longer term if the underlying currents that contribute to the ethnonationalist sentiments, such as poverty and economic exclusion, are not addressed. Serious commitment to tackling such critical issues has not been demonstrated thus far. The government's affirmative action programs are oriented toward expanding the number of indigenous Fijians in business rather than reducing the number of unemployed and impoverished youth who fall victim to political manipulation during political upheavals.

The net result is that Fiji remains locked in a low-investment and low-growth trap, adding to heightened interethnic group tensions. A volatile situation could once again arise if the military becomes divided and/or military-government relations deteriorate. It is clear that Fiji will continue to face broad developmental challenges that are exacerbated by simmering ethnic tensions and continued bad governance.

Official Conflict Management

Fiji receives significant overseas development assistance. In 2001, it received U.S.$26 million, roughly U.S.$31.6 per capita.[19] The European Union (EU),

Japan, Australia, and New Zealand are its key donors. The EU has displayed its strong commitment to linking continued developmental assistance to good governance conditionalities that arise from the Lomé and the Cotonou development cooperation agreements between the African, Caribbean, and Pacific countries and the EU.

While the developmental scope of the Commonwealth Secretariat is extremely limited, it wields considerable influence in Fijian society. Building on the lessons from the era of coups in Africa, the Commonwealth now has a Millbrook Plan of Action to define its response to countries wherein governments are unlawfully removed. This action plan allows for the establishment of a ministerial-level contact group to speedily engage with authorities in troubled countries and to negotiate a road map for return to legality. The Commonwealth Secretariat, through its contact group, applied considerable pressure upon the Qarase-led interim government to adopt a road map that would lead to fresh, internationally supervised elections under the 1997 constitution and the prosecution of those involved in the coup attempts. Fiji's suspension from Commonwealth councils reinforced this message.

In June 2000 the EU suspended most of its nonhumanitarian assistance to Fiji and sought and received commitments for a road map to constitutionality from the Qarase-led interim government. This road map resembled the one negotiated by the Commonwealth Secretariat. It included a commitment from Fiji that those responsible for holding hostage the elected government would be brought to justice and be excluded from government, that the regime would respect the 1997 constitution, that internationally supervised elections would be held within twelve months, and that the constitution would be fully complied with in the formation and operation of the government. The sanctions that applied would be progressively lifted as Fiji took steps forward.

The United Nations also applied pressure on the interim government and Fiji's military forces to uphold the 1997 constitution during the 2000 political crisis. The UN Secretary General sent his special envoy, the late Sergio De Mello, to Fiji early in the 2000 crisis when the government was still being held hostage. The UN maintains significant leverage over Fiji's military, which plays a key role in UN's global peacekeeping operations. This is an important source of income for the military. The participation of elements within the military in the takeover of the parliamentary complex threatened the further participation of Fiji's security forces in UN peacekeeping operations. Many UN and multilateral agencies, including the Asian Development Bank, cut off contact with the new Qarase-led government and only restored these links when progress on reestablishing the democratic process was demonstrated. These direct and subtle pressures helped the Commonwealth Secretariat and EU to extract a firm commitment to the road map.

These multilateral efforts were further complemented by actions of key bilateral actors. Australia, New Zealand, and the United States used their aid and more direct political leverage to pressure a speedy return to constitutionality. They engaged with Fijian authorities and the South Pacific Forum Secretariat—a grouping of leaders from the South Pacific region. As a result, the forum agreed to its own Millbrook Plan of Action, referred to as the Biketawa Declaration. This changed the region as well. For the first time, South Pacific regional heads of governments agreed to intervene in the affairs of member states when they faced serious political crisis. The forum set up contact groups to maintain dialogue with the new regime and encourage it to return to constitutionality.

These official engagements did not take place in a vacuum. The international community represented by the Commonwealth Secretariat, the EU, and UN agencies engaged with Fiji in such a coherent way largely as a result of well-organized representations from Fiji's civil society and their international counterparts. They harnessed the available international instruments and helped international agencies to think through a feasible road map for constraining ethnic violence and promoting peacebuilding.

Domestically, Fiji's higher courts played an active role in reversing the abrogation of the 1997 constitution. The High Court and the Supreme Court nullified the abrogation of the constitution by the military. Unlike the 1987 coups, when the courts buckled under pressure and legitimized the Rabuka regime, after the 2000 upheavals, citizens' groups, individuals, and political parties aggressively used the courts to rein in antidemocratic developments quite successfully. The Fiji Human Rights Commission—a creation of the 1997 constitution—has also played an extremely active role in using the courts to seek redress for human rights violations. Both developments suggest that the institutional environment has the capacity to sustain the democratic and human rights gains from the 1997 constitution.

Multi-Track Diplomacy

Fiji has a well-developed and active civil society that includes various nongovernmental organizations (NGOs), trade unions, and church groups, which have played an active role in constraining state excesses and promoting interethnic group dialogue. Civil society initiatives were quite varied as events transpired following the immediate crisis on May 19, 2000. One of the most difficult challenges for Fiji's civil society was the complex nature of the Fijian crisis, in which ethnic relations was only one component. Even greater tensions and divisions were exposed within the indigenous Fijian community, arising from perceptions about inequality and political marginalization between different provinces and regions. Such tensions required sets of interventions and targeted responses on the part of civil society different from those that primarily revolved around the tensions between ethnic groups. The role and response of civic agencies to the past and ongoing problems associated with the attempted coup are considered below.

The May 19, 2000, takeover of parliament, while unexpected, was not unprecedented, and Fiji's civil society had learned a lot following the 1987 coups about combining domestic campaigning with international pressure to help restore democracy. During the period of military rule under the Rabuka regime, there was a tendency for Fiji's civil society organizations to operate independently. Trade unions, for example, worked through their international trade union networks to introduce trade bans in order to exert pressure on the military regime. The bans proved effective in delaying shipments and flights to Fiji and frustrating the military government, but these unilateral moves were not popular with other civil society organizations that perceived them as ineffective and harmful to Fiji's citizens and workers. Furthermore, when the trade unions undertook such large campaigns alone, they were easily isolated and targeted. These lessons were to prove useful in shaping the direction of civil society–led democracy campaigns in May 2000.

Prior to 1987, Fiji's civil society had little or no experience in working on cross-community issues, or on issues specifically related to the promotion of democratic governance. It was assumed that a Westminster-type system of government, dominated by the two large political parties, would take care of such problems. Fiji's elections prior to 1987 were largely free and fair, and interethnic relations were generally congenial, though strong undercurrents that could lead to open conflict were always present. But as civil society came to grips with new challenges such as promoting dialogue on constitutional accommodation and the protection of indigenous, group, minority, and human rights, many organizations came into more open conflict with successive governments. Often after 1987, governments worked to divide civil society organizations along ethnic lines. By appealing to ethnic group solidarity, the post-1987 governments portrayed indigenous Fijians who were active in trade unions and nongovernmental organizations as disloyal to indigenous Fijians.

By May 2000, Fiji's civil society organizations had matured considerably, as had their working relationships with one another. Several new organizations, including the Citizens' Constitutional Forum (CCF), the country's foremost civic NGO, had also arrived on the scene and had developed specific work programs in response to the increasingly strained interethnic environment following the 1987 coup. The 1999 general elections, the first held under the 1997 constitution, were in many ways a high point for Fiji's civil society and signaled the beginning of a new era. Years of dedicated work by NGOs, church, community, and political leaders had gone into the development and implementation of the 1997 constitution.[20] As a result, Fiji's civil society organizations had built up solid working arrangements with one another. By opening community discussion on constitutional issues, civil society had reached out to significant cross sections of the communities, often undercutting the monopoly of access that political elites and traditional leaders had enjoyed. Many church and community leaders continued to work with NGOs on conflict prevention, voter education, and constitution awareness campaigns prior to and during the election. They also exerted informal pressure on ethnically based political parties to promote reconciliation, social justice, and the interests of all communities during the electoral campaign.

When events unfolded on May 19, 2000, Fiji's civil society organizations had the hindsight of 1987, newly strengthened partnerships, and a capacity to effectively network domestically and internationally, enabling them to respond quickly and decisively to the crisis. From early in the 2000, crisis joint campaigns were formed between NGOs including the CCF, the Fiji Women's Crisis Centre, the Fiji Women's Rights Movement (FWRM), the Fiji Trade Union Congress (FTUC), churches, and religious organizations. The largest of these initiatives came to be known as the "Fiji Blue Campaign" and sought to put pressure on the military to resolve the hostage crisis and return the country to constitutional rule. The FTUC, as a member of the campaign, called for punitive trade disruptions and secured the support of members of the civil society coalition at the outset. The coalition secured the backing of the Fiji Employers' Federation and many of Fiji's commerce chambers. This initiative went far in drawing international attention to the severity of the situation and ensuring that the military remained committed to defeating the coup attempt.

Operating independently, civil society organizations sought to bring about stability and reduce ethnic tensions within their spheres of influence. Women's groups collaborated to hold peace vigils throughout the fifty-six days when the government was being held hostage. The FTUC and its affiliated unions worked with employers negatively affected by the political crisis to find alternative solutions to layoffs and mass redundancies. With exception of the Methodist Church, the leaders of other mainstream churches condemned the violence and worked to counter the nationalist rhetoric and misinformation that was occurring in the outer villages. Working with local chiefs, they sought to prevent community members from joining the coup supporters in parliament grounds and to recall those who had joined the ranks of Speight and his group. They undercut efforts that sought to use public media to promote the cause of those who were holding the government hostage.

Media became the means for control of hearts and minds, especially of rural Fijian communities who had rallied behind Speight and his group. The supporters of the coup trashed the national television station and threatened to burn down newspaper companies. They had used simplistic nationalist rhetoric revolving around the dilution of indigenous rights to whip up popular support. Elements within different church groups had also rallied behind the Speight group and couched their own contributions in terms of presumed threats to Christianity by Hindus and other non-Christian groups. They used the press and the pulpit to rally supporters to parliament to effectively work as human shields. Except for some internal elements, all national media strongly condemned the coups and slowly regained editorial control over the elements that were promoting the nationalist/fundamentalist push for political power.

Most government agencies continued to function throughout the crisis, although the loyalty of many within them oscillated. Some of these agencies and departments provided invaluable support to Fiji's civil society organizations. One of the most significant government bodies to become actively involved in the campaign to bring the situation under control was the Fiji Human Rights Commission, a statutory organization established in 1999 as a requirement of the 1997 constitution. Its responsibilities included investigating and resolving complaints of human rights abuses, providing legal advice on human rights issues, and acting as a source of human rights information. During the civil unrest the commission continued with this mandate by monitoring the security situation and informing the international community about ongoing affairs. The commission investigated allegations of human rights violations and breaches of the bill of rights by the police, military, and prison authorities during the state of emergency.[21] International human rights organizations, such as Amnesty International, came to rely upon the commission and Fiji's civil society organizations to conduct their own campaigns in the international arena.

The joint civil society initiatives, combined with these various efforts, went a long way toward ensuring that Fiji's military would bring the situation under control. However, the manner in which the military resolved the crisis and appointed an interim administration was far from satisfactory. Soon after the tensions had eased and the military had regained control, Fiji's civil society attempted to restore the country to democratic rule. They relied predominately upon the court system to make this happen and maintained dialogue with the military leadership.

A citizen named Chandrika Prasad mounted the first legal challenge. Prasad, with the support of a number of NGOs and the assistance of the Fiji Human Rights Commission, filed a case in the Supreme Court that challenged the legal basis of the state of emergency declared by the president on May 19 and the abrogation of the 1997 constitution. On November 15, 2000, Justice Anthony Gates ruled that the attempted coup of May 19 was unsuccessful, that the 1997 constitution remained the supreme law of Fiji, and that the interim government was illegally holding office. The interim government appealed the ruling, but on March 1, 2001, it was upheld.

The Supreme Court decision paved the way for a return to constitutionality. The interim administration, however, proved unwilling to uphold the ruling. Local NGOs and civil society organizations used their international networks to lobby European governments, Australia and New Zealand, as well as the UN and its Committee on the Elimination of Racial Discrimination for support. They drew up a blacklist of individuals thought to be associated with the coup attempt, some of whom were included in the interim administration, and called upon the international community to forbid them access to other countries. They also called upon the international community to withdraw nonhumanitarian development assistance until democracy and the rule of law returned. International support wavered, however, following the release of the hostages and the arrest of the coup leaders. London-based Conciliation Resources, one of the international NGOs that provided assistance to Fiji's NGOs in their negotiations with foreign governments, described the outcome as "a cold reminder of government's inclination to prioritize stability over liberty and justice."[22]

Soon after the appeals court ruling, the CCF launched another court case. The CCF asked the High Court to direct the president to reinstate the Chaudhry government rather than order new elections. The High Court controversially rejected this challenge and instead supported a fresh election. Without international support for the reinstatement of the Chaudhry government, this decision preserved the interim administration's control of government until the 2001 general elections.

Since the 2001 general elections, Fiji's civil society organizations have turned much of their attention toward promoting peacebuilding, reconciliation, and compliance with the constitution. The Ecumenical Centre for Research, Education, and Advocacy (ECREA), for example, has organized educational materials for young students on human rights and racial discrimination. ECREA has also worked in remote communities that were badly affected by the political unrest. It has held workshops with local communities and community leaders, asking them to consider the root causes for the May 2000 violence and to reflect upon their actions. ECREA hopes these types of workshops will help local communities come to terms with the May 2000 civil unrest and reconcile themselves with other communities.

The Fiji Human Rights Commission has taken a significant step toward developing a strategic race-relations strategy, something no other organization has sought to do. One of the commission's primary objectives is the development of a proactive race-relations strategy that endeavors to "lower the race relations temperature" in Fiji.[23] However, the commission has been hampered by budget and staffing constraints that prevent it from extending its work beyond the main urban centers. As a result, many of the remote islands and regional areas, where Speight received significant support, remain beyond the reach of the commission and other civic agencies.

The political crisis of May 2000 overturned many of the earlier gains toward democracy and an improved investment climate. It also challenged much of the work undertaken by civil society organizations both locally and abroad. One of the major challenges facing Fiji's civil society is weariness from the continuing uphill struggle. Long-standing members of civil society are making the difficult decision to join the mass migration from Fiji.

One of the ways that organizations are seeking to overcome financial constraints and "burnout" while strengthening their united voice is through coalition building—a lesson learned from the Fiji Blue Campaign. The NGO Coalition of Human Rights is one example. Presently chaired by the CCF, it includes representatives from the FWRM, the Women's Crisis Centre, ECREA, and the FTUC. Like the Fiji Human Rights Commission, it is involved in education and advocacy issues surrounding human rights. Its nongovernmental status, however, enables it to challenge the government's human rights record in ways the commission finds difficult.

The current environment is mixed. On the one hand, the situation has stabilized sufficiently for civil society organizations to return to their missions prior to May 19, 2000. On the other hand, civil society organizations are operating in a climate of heightened ethnic tension and polarization. NGOs that are seen as sympathetic to a particular political agenda or ethnic group concern are often accused by political and community leaders of being aligned with a particular party or group. In an atmosphere of suspicion and hatred, these smear campaigns can be quite damaging. As a result, NGOs are forced to spend valuable time and resources in defending their organizations.

The CCF has been one of the organizations most affected by these changes. It played a very vocal role in responding to the 2000 coup attempt. It worked with its international partners to put pressure on the military to uphold the rule of law and the restoration of democracy. The organization paid a price for its stand. The Qarase government withdrew the CCF's charitable status, and its executive director, Reverend Akuila Yabaki, was suspended from the Methodist Church. The withdrawal of the charitable status has placed the CCF in a financially vulnerable position. So far, however, it has managed to secure financial support from various international bodies, including the EU, the International Centre for Human Rights and Democratic Development (Canada), the Methodist Church (UK), the Church Development Service (Germany), and the Australian, U.S., and New Zealand governments to continue its work.

Divisive politics have also plagued the country's trade union movement. While Fiji's trade union movement proved effective in promoting workplace interethnic dialogue and reconciliation and maintained pressure upon the government, it has since suffered from internal divisions. In 2002 a breakaway group of trade unions formed another trade union center, named the Fiji Island Council of Trade Unions (FICTU). The council has received favorable support from the Qarase government, and it has adopted a policy of only including FICTU members in its consultative committees, forcing it into an antagonistic position with government.

Prospects

Ever since 1987 coups, the primary agents for dialogue between ethnic leaders and groupings have come from Fiji's civil society. Civic agencies have skillfully used international agencies to create opportunities for dialogue in a hostile interethnic-relations climate. Following the 2000 crisis, this modality has proved useful in turning Fiji away from a potential degeneration into more extreme and widespread ethnic violence. In the current climate, however, organizations that are committed to promoting interethnic dialogue remain vulnerable.

Fiji's NGOs are vulnerable to threats from the government, extremist groups, and security agencies. Their vulnerability is amplified during periods of heightened conflict. In response, organizations like the CCF, the FWRM, and the FTUC have developed strong international connections, which became channels for communication during the 2000 crisis and allowed many international agencies to make informed decisions in response to the crisis. Such relationships need to be sustained.

At the official level, an initiative taken by the director of the East West Centre at the University of Hawaii soon after the overthrow of the FLP-led government in 2000 resulted in the opening of an informal diplomacy track referred to as *Talanoa* (casual talks). While these talks assisted the key parties in reaching some accommodation on land lease questions, they failed to help the parties resolve the multiparty government deadlock. *Talanoa* has kept open a line of communication between SDL and FLP leaders. In the lead-up to the 2001 elections, this process helped to reduce communal temperatures. Clearly, external mediators can help to keep leaders engaged informally even when interethnic group relations are extremely strained.

But domestic civic agencies also have a central role to play in the conflict transformation process. State institutions in Fiji are closely identified with the indigenous Fijian group and thus have limited scope for promoting conflict resolution. Multiethnic NGOs have a huge potential to overcome the limits of state action.

In trying to promote peacebuilding and conflict resolution, many international agencies and governments have exclusively engaged with Fiji's political leadership. At the same time, however, they have identified such leaders as the primary problem in Fiji. The clearest lesson is the need for international agencies to broaden their engagement in Fiji so as to include governmental and nongovernmental agencies and engage with a broader community leadership base. The dividends for sustainable peacebuilding and conflict transformation, especially during periods when ethnic conflict and tension are inflamed, are likely to be greater.

Recommendations

To mitigate the adverse impacts of ethnically divided political institutions, Fiji needs to broaden the space of intercommunity, civil society, and state dialogue. Broad-based dialogue will open more opportunities for engaging political and ethnic group leaders. This can be achieved by making parliamentary committees and governmental institutions more open to public consultation, by requiring that major policy matters be subjected to public consultations, and by enabling civic groups to make submissions on major policy issues to the parliamentary committees.

More formal opportunities, such as the *Talanoa* process, need to be vigorously supported. While this process primarily involves party political actors, the interaction between party political leaders and civil society can be enhanced on its sidelines to complement this process.

Civil society capabilities need to be strengthened to better inform national decisionmaking. In Fiji, because political parties are almost exclusively ethnically based, policies are debated and constructed through ethnic lenses. Improved conflict sensitivity of public policies is likely to have favorable consequences on interethnic group relations.

Accountability institutions such as the Fiji Human Rights Commission, the Office of the Auditor General, and the Office of the Ombudsman can be weak in the face of strong governments. Civic agencies can support hesitant accountability institutions in confronting antidemocratic tendencies of governments. Opportunities for dialogue between accountability institutions and civil society thus need to be broadened. For this effort to be successful, the international community and donor agencies must take the necessary steps to support NGOs and to engage with such institutions more meaningfully and in a sustained manner.

The domestic base for supporting the civic sector is narrow. Donors need to recognize that NGOs have been the primary drivers for democratic change in Fiji. Donor funding that is channeled through government departments places NGOs in a vulnerable position, particularly for those that are critical of government directives. Donors need to be able to support a greater cross section of NGOs directly, rather than through the government. Civic capacities to evaluate conflict and interethnic-relations consequences of donor and domestically supported developmental projects also need to be strengthened.

Civic agencies need to improve their skills in engaging with rural communities, security institutions, and provincial councils on issues such as managing resource conflicts, undertaking conflict prevention, and improving interethnic group dialogue. Working with the security forces and the government on efforts to review and reduce the size of the armed forces is a priority area. Civic agencies need to continue to promote broader understanding about human, group, and minority rights and encourage communities to use legal, constitutional, and parliamentary means more effectively in order to redress long-held grievances. This requires capacity building, resources, and the development of responsive institutional infrastructure.

In the longer term, conflict resolution and peacebuilding will only be sustainable if Fiji's governments move away from short-term and populist affirmative action measures and adopt a vigorous developmental framework. Domestic political stability, a sustained policy environment, and selective development of sectors that fully utilize Fiji's human resource and the best combination of local and international private-sector skills are necessary to create meaningful jobs in the urban sector and linked opportunities for those in the rural sector. It is in the developmental arena that the longer-term solutions to conflict prevention lie.

Resources

Reports

Collaborative for Development Action. "Constraints and Contributors to Violent Conflict in Fiji." By K. Doughty, D. Snell, and S. Prasad. 2003. Available at www.cdainc.com.

Fiji Human Rights Commission. "The Fiji Human Rights Commission Strategic Plan 2001–2003." Suva, 2001.

UN Development Programme. *Fiji Poverty Report: 1994.* 1994. Available at www.undp.org.

U.S. Department of State. Bureau of Democracy, Human Rights, and Labour. *Fiji Country Report on Human Rights Practices.* 2002. Available at www.state.gov.

Other Publications

Christianity, Poverty, and Wealth at the Start of the Twenty-First Century. By C. Khan and K. Barr. Suva: ECREA, 2003.

Confronting Fiji Futures. Ed. A. Haroon Akram-Lodhi. Canberra: Asia Pacific Press, 2000.

Constitution of the Republic of Fiji Islands. Government of Fiji, Suva: Government Printer, 1997. Available at www.ccf.org.fj.

Coup: Reflections on the Political Crisis in Fiji. Eds. Brij V. Lal and Michael Pretes. Melbourne: Pandanus Books, 2001.

Economic Development, Democracy, and Ethnic Conflict in the Fiji Islands: Minority Rights and Development Macro Study. By S. Prasad, J. Dakuvula, and D. Snell. London: Minority Rights Group and Citizens Constitutional Forum, 2001.

Fiji in Transition. By B. Lal and T. Vakatora. Suva: School of Social and Economic Development, University of the South Pacific, 1997.

Fiji and the World. By B. Lal and T. Vakatora. Suva: School of Social and Economic Development, University of the South Pacific, 1997.

"Forging a Formula for Peaceful Co-Existence." In P. Woodrow, *Fiji: A Case Study on the Citizen's Constitutional Forum.* 2000. Available at www.cdainc.com (Collaborative for Development Action).

Government by the Gun: The Unfinished Business of Fiji's 2000 Coup. By R. Robertson and W. Sutherland. New York: Zed Books, 2001.

Limits and Possibilities for Civil Society–Led Re-Democratisation: The Fijian Constitutional Debates and Dilemma. By S. Prasad. 1996. Available at www.c-r.org (Conciliation Resources).

Protecting Indigenous Rights and Interests in Fiji. By Citizens' Constitutional Forum (CCF). Suva: CCF, 1996.

Stocktake of Civic Education Initiatives in Fiji. By A. Griffen. 2003. Unpublished report.

Your Constitution, Your Rights. By Citizens' Constitutional Forum (CCF). Suva: CCF, 2002.

Websites

www.ccf.org.fj (Citizens' Constitutional Forum)
www.ecrea.org.fj (Ecumenical Centre for Research, Education, and Advocacy)
www.fiji.gov.fj (Fiji government)
www.fijilive.com (Fijilive online news)
www.fijiwomen.com (Fiji Women's Crisis Centre)

Resource Contacts and Organizations

Citizens' Constitutional Forum
tel: +679 3309 011, +679 9921 037
fax: +679 3308 380
contact: Akuila Yabaki, e-mail: yabaki@ccf.org.fj

Conciliation Resources
tel: +44 207 359 7728
fax: +44 207 359 4081
contact: Andrew Carl or Kushma Ram, e-mail: conres@c-r.org and kushma@c-r.org

Ecumenical Centre for Research, Education, and Advocacy
tel: +679 3307 588
fax: +679 3311 248
contact: Aisake Casimira, e-mail: admin@ecrea.org.fj

Fem'Link Pacific
tel: +679 3307 207, +679 9244 871
fax: +679 3301 925
contact: Sharon Bhagwan Rolls, e-mail: femlinkpac@connect.com.fj

Fiji Disabled People's Association
tel: +679 3311 203
fax: +679 3301 161
contact: Angeline Khan, e-mail: ubp@connect.com.fj

Fiji Human Rights Commission
tel: +679 3308 577
fax: +679 3308 661
contact: Shaista Shameem, e-mail: sshameem@humanrights.org.fj

Fiji Human Rights Group
tel: +679 3311 700, +679 9923 477
fax: +679 3303 469
contact: Roy Krishna, e-mail: roy_k@fsm.ac.fj

Fiji I Care
tel: +679 3301 753
fax: +679 3301 753
contact: Suresh Khatri or Ratu Meli Vesikula, e-mail: slkhatri@connect.com.fj

Fiji Media Watch
tel: +679 3308 605
fax: +679 3305 775
contact: Larry Hannan, e-mail: lhannan@relpac.com.fj

Fiji Trade Union Congress
tel: +679 3315 377
fax: +679 3300 306
contact: Felix Anthony, e-mail: ftuc1@connect.com.fj

Fiji Women's Crisis Centre
tel: +679 3313 300, +679 9992 875
fax: +679 3313 650
contact: Edwina Kotoisuva, e-mail: fwcc@connect.com.fj

Fiji Women's Rights Movement
tel: +679 3313 156
fax: +679 3313 466
contact: Asenaca Colowaimailto, e-mail: wrm@connect.com.fj

Fiji Young Lawyers' Association
tel: +679 3314 400
contact: Faiyaz Khaiyum

Greenpeace Pacific
tel: +679 3312 861
fax: +679 3312 784
contact: Angie Heffernan, e-mail: aheffern@dialb.greenpeace.org

National Council of Women Fiji
tel: +679 3315 429
fax: +679 3315 429
contact: Abua Salato, e-mail: ncwf@connect.com.fj

Women's Action for Change
tel: +679 3314 363
fax: +679 3305 033
contact: Peni Moore, e-mail: wac@connect.com.fj

Satendra Prasad is former head of the Department of Sociology at the University of the South Pacific, Fiji. He is a founding member of the Citizens' Constitutional Forum, through which he was closely involved in discussions that led to the promulgation of the 1997 constitution. He works closely on issues related to governance, development, and peacebuilding, and is currently working as a governance and institutional development specialist in Afghanistan.

Darryn Snell lectures in sociology and social justice at Monash University, Australia, and was a visiting lecturer at the University of the South Pacific, Fiji, in 1998–1999. He has worked extensively on development questions in Fiji. He has an ongoing association with the Citizens' Constitutional Forum, the Fiji Trade Union Congress, and several other nongovernmental organizations in Fiji.

Notes

1. UN Development Programme (UNDP), *Human Development Report 2003*, available at www.undp.org.

2. UNDP, *Fiji Poverty Report 1994*, available ay www.undp.org.

3. B. Prasad and S. Kumar, "Institutional Rigidities and Economic Performance in Fiji," in A. Haroon Akram-Lodhi, ed., *Confronting Fiji Futures* (Canberra: Asia Pacific Press, 2000), pp. 11–132.

4. K. Ram, "Militarism and Market Mania in Fiji," in A. Emberson-Bain, ed., *Sustainable Development or Malignant Growth? Perspectives of Pacific Island Women* (Suva: Marama, 1994), pp. 237–249; Satendra Prasad and Darryn Snell, "Globalisation, Economic Crisis, and the Changing Face of Labour Relations in Fiji Islands," unpublished report prepared for the Fiji Trades Union Congress, 2002.

5. K. Doughty, D. Snell, and S. Prasad, "Constraints and Contributors to Violent Conflict in Fiji" (Cambridge: Collaborative for Development Action, 2003), available at www.cdainc.com.

6. R. Robertson and W. Sutherland, *Government by the Gun: The Unfinished Business of Fiji's 2000 Coup* (New York: Zed Books, 2001).

7. S. Prasad, D. Snell, and K. Hince, *Employment and Industrial Relations in the South Pacific* (Sydney: McGraw Hill, 2003).

8. S. Prasad, J. Dakuvula, and D. Snell, *Economic Development, Democracy, and Ethnic Conflict in the Fiji Islands: Minority Rights and Development Macro Study* (London: Minority Rights Group and Citizens' Constitutional Forum, 2001).

9. B. Lal, *Coups in Paradise: Race, Politics, and Military Intervention* (London: Zed Books, 1989).

10. See B. Lal and T. Vakotora, *Fiji in Transition* (Suva: School of Social and Economic Development, University of the South Pacific, 1997).

11. *Constitution of the Republic of Fiji Islands* (Suva: Government Printer, 1997).

12. The coalition government was made up of the FLP, two indigenous Fijian breakaway parties from the SVT, and a party consisting of "general" electors.

13. D. Snell and S. Prasad, "Behind the Fiji Crisis: Politics of Labour in an Ethnically Divided Society," *Arena Journal* no. 15 (2000): 39–56.

14. Fiji Hardwoods Corporation is a government agency that oversees the development of commercial harvesting opportunities of large-scale hardwood timber.

15. L. Qarase, "Blueprint for the Protection of Fijian and Rotuman Rights and Interests and the Advancement of Their Development," July 13, 2000, available at www.fijivillage.com.

16. *Fijilive,* July 18, 2003, available at www.fijilive.com.

17. A. Casimira, "The Need to Review Reconciliation" (Suva: Ecumenicial Centre for Research, Education, and Advocacy, 2002), available at www.ecrea.org.fj.

18. Doughty, Snell, and Prasad, "Constraints and Contributors to Violent Conflict in Fiji."

19. UNDP, *Human Development Report 2003.*

20. B. Lal and T. Vakotora, *Fiji and the World* (Suva: School of Social and Economic Development, University of the South Pacific, 1997).

21. S. Shameem, "The Fiji Human Rights Commission" (Suva: Fiji Human Rights Commission, 2003), available at www.humanrights.org.fj.

22. Conciliation Resources, *Annual Report, 1999* (London: Conciliation Resources, 2000).

23. Fiji Human Rights Commission, "The Fiji Human Rights Commission Strategic Plan 2001–2003" (Suva: Fiji Human Rights Commission, 2001).

10.3

Papua New Guinea: A Success Story of Postconflict Peacebuilding in Bougainville

Volker Böge and Lorraine Garasu

In 1998, after almost a decade of war, postconflict peacebuilding began on the island of Bougainville. So far, despite setbacks, the peace process has been a success story with all parties observing a cease-fire agreement. Substantial progress has been made on reconstruction, rehabilitation, and reconciliation. However, while a solution to the political problems underlying the conflict has been agreed upon, obstacles remain that need to be overcome on the way to sustainable peace. Weapons disposal is not yet complete and maintaining law and order is a serious challenge. The psychological and spiritual wounds of protracted fighting have not yet been healed, while important steps in the implementation of the political solution to the conflict still have to be taken, and economic and social conditions need substantial improvement. However the success to date has been made possible by the leadership and participation of the community in the peace process. In traditional ceremonies and processes, former militants, women, churches, and nongovernmental organizations (NGOs) have joined together to make a peace otherwise unobtainable through official channels. This chapter does not discuss the historical, political, or economic causes of the conflict but portrays an ongoing community-based indigenous peace process.

The island of Bougainville is situated just within the eastern boundary of Papua New Guinea (PNG), but ethnically and geographically it is closer to the Solomon Islands in the South Pacific, with which it maintains social and cultural ties. Its 8,800 square kilometers make it the largest island of this archipelago. Constitutionally, however, it belongs to the state of Papua New Guinea, which became independent in 1975. Together with the neighboring island of Buka to the north and several small atolls, it formed one of the nineteen provinces of PNG. From 1988 to 1998, the 180,000 inhabitants of Bougainville suffered under fierce jungle warfare, said to be the longest and

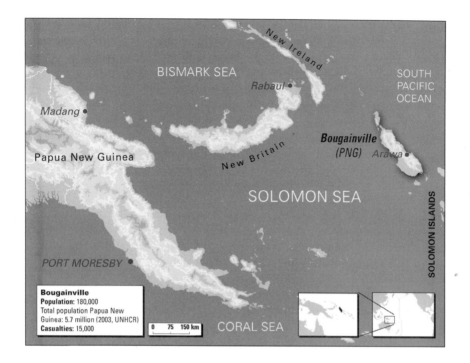

Bougainville
Population: 180,000
Total population Papua New
Guinea: 5.7 million (2003, UNHCR)
Casualties: 15,000

most bloody conflict in the South Pacific since the end of World War II. Armed violence started at the end of the 1980s. At its core were problems related to the social and environmental effects of a large, open-pit copper mine. The Panguna mine in central Bougainville had been opened in 1972 and was at that time the largest open-pit mine in the world. It was run by the mining company Bougainville Copper Limited (BCL), a subsidiary of the British-Australian mining giant Rio Tinto Zinc (RTZ)/Conzinc Riotinto of Australia (CRA), with a minority shareholding in the name of the Papua New Guinea government. The RTZ and CRA have since merged into Rio Tinto.

In the 1970s and 1980s the Panguna mine was the backbone of PNG's national economy, and the largest provider of foreign exchange. At the same time, large-scale mining posed a serious threat to the traditional Bougainvillean way of life, which was closely connected to the land. Given the presence of workers from other provinces of Papua New Guinea and large cash inflows, the traditional fabric of social relations among clan communities was disrupted.

Both the BCL and the PNG central government disregarded the negative environmental and social side effects of the mining operations. The people affected by the mining felt economically exploited and socially marginalized, and so demanded compensation for environmental damage and loss of land, and a larger share of the revenues generated. The mining company and the central government rejected the demands of the landowning clans for compensation and for environmental protections to be imposed on the mine—

which had always operated without any environmental restraints. Local young people brought the mine to a standstill in late 1988 by acts of sabotage.

As the police riot squads were unable to cope with the activities of the protesters, the central government sent troops to the island in March 1989. Members of the clans in the mine area then founded the Bougainville Revolutionary Army (BRA) and began fighting the government forces. In this way the conflict surrounding the mine escalated into a war that started in central Bougainville and soon spread across the whole island. The BRA soon adopted a secessionist stance and called for self-determination and political independence for Bougainville, pointing to ethnic differences between the Bougainvilleans and the rest of the Papua New Guineans and stressing historical and cultural ties with the neighboring Solomon Islands, thus repeating calls for secession that had already been made in the 1960s and 1970s. As it had done previously, the PNG central government rejected the BRA's demands for independence and insisted on the sovereignty and territorial integrity of the state of PNG. It felt authorized to fight the "criminal elements" of the BRA with all means available.

The central government's stance was supported by former colonial power Australia. Australia feared that PNG, whose population consists of more than 700 ethnolinguistic groups, might disintegrate as a state should the Bougainville secessionists succeed, thus setting a precedent for others. Therefore, and in the interest of the Australian mining company, the Australian government assisted the PNG government in its fight against the secessionist movement.

The secessionists, on the other hand, received virtually no outside assistance. There was some sympathy for their cause in the neighboring Solomon Islands—the BRA was able to make use of the islands closest to Bougainville as an area for retreat and supplies, and in the course of the war thousands of Bougainvilleans fled to the Solomon Islands, especially in search of medical care. However, the world at large almost totally ignored the demands of the secessionists, and internationally few took notice of the jungle war that was raging on a remote South Pacific island.

Conflict Dynamics

The BRA managed to overrun and shut down the Panguna mine at a very early stage in the fighting, and the mine has remained closed ever since; even today it is in the hands of a faction of the secessionists. In the first phase of the war—due to the brutality of the government forces toward the civilian population—the BRA managed to win the support of many of the islanders and to recruit more and more young men—some 2,000 in total—to its cause. Waging guerrilla warfare, the BRA made successful military strikes against the riot squads of the PNG police and the Papua New Guinea Defense Force (PNGDF), which was far better equipped both materially and in terms of personnel, as it enjoyed substantial Australian military support (training, weaponry, and at times even "military advisers").

In March 1990 the government forces were compelled to withdraw entirely from the island. The central government then ordered a total blockade of

Bougainville, which led to the death of thousands of islanders in the following years, mainly as a result of the collapse of the medical care system. In May 1990, as a reaction to the blockade, the BRA proclaimed the independence of the "Republic of Bougainville" and established an interim government of its own, with Francis Ona, the person originally at the forefront of the antimine protests, as its president. However, not one country in the international community recognized the new state.

After 1992 the PNGDF managed to recapture parts of the island with the support of local Bougainvillean auxiliary units, the so-called resistance forces, which developed out of village protection groups formed during the time of unrestrained BRA rule, when the BRA proved incapable of maintaining law and order. Some BRA units or splinter groups lacked discipline, and attacked civilians and perpetrated human rights abuses. The resistance also contained disaffected former BRA combatants who had defected for various reasons.

The resistance, enlisting probably 1,500 fighters, fought the BRA along-side the PNGDF. It was equipped and supported by the PNGDF and during the last years of the war and actually bore the brunt of the fighting on the government side, but was at no time formally amalgamated into the government forces. Commanding and controlling the resistance forces therefore posed a lasting problem to the military and political leadership of the PNG side. However, their formation partly changed the character of the conflict. From being a war of Bougainvilleans against "foreign" government troops, it became a war among Bougainvilleans themselves. From then on, traditional conflicts between different groups and clans, who supported either the BRA or the resistance, were also fought under the umbrella of the "great" war of secession.

At times, resistance units would wage their own "private" wars against BRA units over merely local issues, especially land disputes. Moreover, it was not unusual for individual resistance or BRA units to change sides. Neither were all resistance units reliable allies for the government side, nor was the BRA a unitary force with clear chains of command and control.

For years neither side was able to achieve a decisive military break-through. The BRA were able to retain most of its heartland in central Bougainville around the Panguna mine and in the south, while the PNGDF and the resistance forces mainly controlled the north, the eastern coastal strip, and the neighboring island of Buka, where the effects of mining had hardly been felt and where separatist support was generally weaker. In 1996 the last massive offensive of the PNGDF and resistance forces collapsed after a few weeks.

In March 1997 an attempt by Prime Minister Julius Chan's PNG government to regain control of the Panguna mine and to destroy the BRA by secretly enlisting British South African mercenary troops from the firms of Sandline International and Executive Outcomes ended in disaster. Leading PNGDF officials detained the imported Sandline staff and troops. Huge demonstrations against the mercenaries in the capital city of Port Moresby forced Chan to resign and the mercenaries to leave the country. After that, the war dragged on at a level of low intensity.

Following PNG elections in June 1997 a new government under Prime Minister Bill Skate came to power. Skate declared that his government was willing to negotiate with the secessionists. A decisive factor in this development was no doubt the change in the position of the Australians, whose massive military support had enabled the central government and its PNGDF to continue with the war up to that point, but who finally recognized that a military solution to the conflict was impossible. The Australian government had already begun to change its attitude before the Sandline crisis of March 1997. However, that crisis was the event that finally gave the Australian side the opportunity to put its changed approach into practice.

Moreover, after almost ten years of bloodshed and privation, the Bougainville population was exhausted and war-weary. There was a widespread desire for peace and a return to normalcy that neither the BRA nor the resistance could ignore. Civilians suffered most in the jungle war. About 15,000 men, women, and children are said to have died in the conflict; only a minority of them were fighters who died in combat. The majority of the war-related deaths were due to the effects of the blockade, which banned all imports, even medicines. At times, more than half of the island's population were forced to flee their homes and find refuge in the jungle in either bush-camps in BRA-controlled areas or in so-called care centers (camps under the control of the government troops). Several thousand found refuge in the neighboring Solomon Islands.

Infrastructure, public administration, and in particular health and education services broke down entirely. Roads and bridges were destroyed, economic activities came to a standstill, copra and cocoa, the island's main cash crops, could no longer be marketed and exported, hospitals, health posts, and schools were forced to close, and a whole generation of young Bougainvilleans missed out on formal education. In towns and larger population centers the majority of the buildings were destroyed, while whole villages were razed. The war was accompanied by massive violations of human rights; arbitrary arrests and killings, torture, murder, and "disappearances" were commonplace, as were evictions, massacres, rapes, sexual harassment, and other attacks on women and children.[1] Consequently, by the time a substantial peace process was set in motion in June 1997, Bougainville society was deeply wounded, physically, mentally, socially, and spiritually.

Official Conflict Management

In 1997 the New Zealand government facilitated several meetings and rounds of negotiations. On the one side were the BRA and the interim government, on the other the central government, the resistance forces, and the transitional government (the latter was the provincial government established in 1995, which cooperated with the central government and was based on PNGDF-controlled Buka, an island with the administrative headquarters adjacent to Bougainville).

In addition, representatives of other social groups on the island also attended those meetings, forming a third-party group and reflecting the interests of the "grassroots." This third party consisted of representatives of modern civil society—NGOs, especially church groups and women's groups—and of representatives of traditional authorities—village elders, chiefs, and clan leaders.

Talks and negotiations resulted in the so-called Burnham Declaration (July 1997), in which the parties committed themselves to a peaceful solution of the conflict, and the Burnham Truce (October 1997, named after the New Zealand military base where it was negotiated). The latter provided for a truce of ninety days that was to be monitored by a neutral international observer group. The Burnham Truce was signed not only by the top political and military leaders of the conflicting parties but also by representatives of civil society and traditional authorities and by the local commanders of the BRA and the resistance. This made it more binding socially and easier to implement. Agreements made between the "top brass" are of doubtful value if the formal political and military leaders have only limited control over their respective forces.

By taking part in negotiations and signing the agreement, field commanders also had a larger stake in the truce and felt a greater obligation to observe it. Likewise, the representatives of civil society and traditional clans thereby took on a shared responsibility for keeping the truce and stabilizing the situation. This inclusive approach was followed throughout the ensuing peace process and decisively contributed to its success. Local commanders and representatives of civil society, chiefs, and elders were involved in every stage of the process and organized local peace committees as their own responsibility and contribution, thus linking the peace process at the top with manifold peace processes at the bottom of society.

Torsten Blackwood/EPA Photo AFP

Arawa, Papua New Guinea, April 30, 1998.
Resistance fighters and guerrillas from the Bougainville Revolutionary Army arrive at the signing of the Bougainville cease-fire agreement.

In January 1998 the parties negotiated and signed the "Lincoln Agreement on Peace, Security, and Development on Bougainville" at Lincoln University in Christchurch, New Zealand. It laid down the principles for the envisaged peace process and paved the way for a peaceful resolution to the conflict. All sides agreed in principle to demilitarize the conflict and agreed upon a procedure for its further political treatment. As agreed at Lincoln University, the truce became an official cease-fire on April 30, 1998. It was declared "permanent and irrevocable." The cease-fire was to be overseen by a peace monitoring group, which was an unarmed unit of initially some 300 men and women, both military and civilian from Australia, New Zealand, Fiji, and Vanuatu. In addition to the monitoring group, a UN observer mission was invited to Bougainville; in August 1998, following a UN Security Council resolution, this small mission, the UN Observer Mission on Bougainville, began its work.

During the cease-fire ceremony on April 30, 1998, Sam Kauona, military leader of the BRA at the time, declared the war to be over. And in fact, the cease-fire has held to the time of this writing (May 2004). Therefore, one can justifiably speak of April 30, 1998, as the end of the war on the island. Nevertheless, subsequent developments have once again demonstrated that the end of a war does not necessarily mean peace. Even today, Bougainville is still in the process of postconflict peacebuilding, which must be understood as a complex and lengthy process of transition from war to peace.

In the field of official conflict management there have been many steps forward since 1998 (and occasional stalemates and setbacks), which cannot be outlined here in full. Central to these efforts has been the attempt to elaborate a common position among the various parties on the Bougainville side (as mentioned above, the Bougainvilleans were far from united), then present the central government with a unified position and find a compromise acceptable to both it and the Bougainvilleans.

Three main issues had to be tackled: a referendum about the future political status of Bougainville, the question of autonomy or complete independence, and weapons disposal. It was only after numerous rounds of talks and negotiations that the differences regarding these questions could be sorted out. Finally, on August 30, 2001, the Bougainville Peace Agreement (BPA) was signed. The BPA can be said to present a comprehensive political settlement, as it provides for

- Far-reaching political autonomy for Bougainville within the constitutional framework of PNG
- A referendum on the future political status of Bougainville in ten to fifteen years' time, including the option of complete independence
- Weapons disposal in a three-stage process

For a transitional period, Bougainville has been granted a special form of autonomy. It will have its own constitution and its own autonomous government with competencies in almost all political fields, including taxation, mining, public service, police, judiciary, and even—to a certain extent—foreign affairs. No more than fifteen years and no less than ten years after the establishment of the autonomous government, a referendum on the future political status of Bougainville is to be held among Bougainvilleans. The choices offered at the referendum must include independence for Bougainville—this means that the option of complete independence, although deferred, remains open. This is what the BRA had been fighting for and the central government had consistently rejected. It was only after a breakthrough on the key issue of referendum was achieved that the other issues could also be tackled.

Elections for, and establishment of, the autonomous government can only take place after the completion of a comprehensive weapons disposal process, which is to have three stages: first, weapons are to be locked away locally in containers under the control of local commanders; second, the collected weapons are to be collected in more central containers under a double-key regime (one key held by a local commander, one key held by a UN representative); third, "the final state of the weapons" is to be decided (practically, this means destruction). In addition to weapons disposal, the presence of the PNGDF on the island was to be substantially reduced—this has been accomplished.

The process of weapons disposal started in December 2001 and has progressed well so far, although it is still not completed. In most areas, the second stage is under way, and in some districts the process has gone even further, with weapons having been destroyed. In 2001–2002, a constitution for an autonomous Bougainville was drafted. The draft was presented to the public in early 2003 and is being discussed broadly at the grassroots level all over Bougainville. The constitution will be inaugurated by a constituent assembly, and on the basis of that, constitution elections for the Bougainville autonomous government will take place, probably in 2004, depending on further progress in weapons disposal. Relations between Bougainville and the central government are managed by a so-called joint supervisory body established in February 2003, which has the task of supervising the implementation of the BPA and sorting out any problems that might arise in Bougainville-PNG relations.

Multi-Track Diplomacy

In the context of a largely traditional rural society as it still exists in Bougainville today, the concepts of "multi-track diplomacy" and "civil society" naturally differ from modern, Western-style perceptions. In Bougainville, the range of political parties, unions, employer associations, media, NGOs, and the like, that constitute "civil society" in the Western sense of the term, is not present.

Rather, for Bougainville, civil society is closely linked to the traditional societal fabric of village life. Even associations that can be called "NGOs" are embedded in traditional structures, or to be more precise: Only if they are embedded in those traditional structures can they be of importance for peacebuilding and multi-track diplomacy. In fact, the strength of the Bougainville peace process, which decisively contributed to its success, was the combination of traditional Melanesian ways of "diplomacy" based on custom on the one hand, and modern "civil society" ways on the other. This also means that actors such as chiefs and village elders, men and women with spiritual authority, are part of what constitutes "civil society" in the Bougainville context.

Peacebuilding in Bougainville was thus "multi track" in the sense that, foremost, customary conflict resolution and peacebuilding resources and mechanisms were added to and combined with official conflict management at the political level. Only a few of the participants were officials of any recognized government. In order to build peace at the grassroots, customary rules and rituals were used in many places all over Bougainville during the transition process from war to peace.

At the core of customary peacebuilding is reconciliation and the restoration of community. This is basically achieved via compensation, which breaks the cycles of payback and blood feuding. This kind of peacemaking involves a long and often complicated process of negotiation, in which the chiefs or elders on both sides act as the middlemen. They lay down the conditions for the peace agreement and the form and amount of compensation—for example, pigs, traditional foods, strings of shell money. Once both sides have agreed upon the outcome of negotiations, there is a ceremony of restoration in which the whole community is included. The ceremony is a sign for the community that the conflict has ended and harmony has been restored. Included in such a ceremony are rituals and symbolic actions and objects, the dividing up and sharing of food, the breaking of spears and arrows, the chewing of betelnut, exchanges of gifts, and singing, dancing, and feasting. These symbolic activities are expressions of commitment and trust and are more important and more powerful than mere spoken or written words. Since the end of the war in Bougainville, many such peace processes and peace ceremonies have taken place between villages and clans all over the island, involving all members of the affected communities. Hence this community-based approach is all-inclusive, and although it is very different from a modern, Western, individualistic approach (which one usually associates with the notion of civil society), it is genuinely civil society–centered, if the term "civil society" is understood to also embrace the local village structures.

In fact, it is not an exaggeration to say that only "diplomacy" on this "track" made peace possible. It substantially contributed to the stabilization of the whole peace process. Official conflict management on Track One would not have been successful without this customary "diplomacy" at the grassroots level—not to mention that customary ways and means and traditional authorities were also included in Track One conflict management at the official political level.

"Civil society" played a role in peacebuilding by assisting the customary conflict resolution and adding certain "modern" aspects to it that enhanced its efficiency. However, it was only by accepting custom as the starting point of any peacebuilding activities that modern NGOs could make a major contribution to the peace process. Most prominent in this respect were the churches and women's groups. Most Bougainvilleans are devout believers, and the churches are the most significant institutions of civil society, as they virtually reach out to every village. Churches are interwoven with indigenous Melanesian culture so that they combine custom and Christianity, which makes them effective peacebuilders at the grassroots level. In many cases, local and regional peace processes were set in motion by church people.

During the war the churches, through their own networks, organized relief supplies in terms of medicines, clothes, and household items. Furthermore, the three mainstream churches on the island (Roman Catholic, United Church, Seventh-Day Adventist) hosted renewal programs to bring about healing and reconciliation. In the Catholic Church, a program called "Healing of Memories Retreats" started as early as 1992, initially facilitated by Sister Veronica Kihono of the Congregation of the Sisters of Nazareth, with the help of lay workers. The retreats aimed at mutual forgiveness and reconciliation. These retreats were well attended by the people from all the churches and the combatants from both the BRA and the resistance. Several former combatants became lay workers for the retreat team.

The women from the churches have been especially active in building peace. Given the high societal status of women in the mostly matrilineal societies in Bougainville, they were in a position to negotiate peace in their communities and to use their influence as go-betweens with the warring factions to initiate and maintain dialogue. Mothers went into the bush to attempt to bring their sons home. Moreover, women's groups and individual women leaders also became important players in the political arena. They organized peace marches, peace vigils, peace petitions, and prayer meetings for peace, thus putting pressure on the male leaders of the warring parties. In July 1995 the Bougainville Inter-Church Women's Forum (BICWF) was established, uniting women from all denominations who were willing to work for peace. The BICWF organized a Women's Peace Forum, which was held in Arawa in August 1996. It was attended by about 700 women from across the island who spoke freely of their fears about the conflict and their desire for peace, and who formed working groups to put in place concrete plans toward achieving a lasting resolution to the conflict. That conference was an important step on the road to the peace process, which started a year later in Burnham, New Zealand.

Despite having important roles and responsibilities in Bougainville's culture, women have struggled to participate directly in the formal political peace process, which has been dominated by men. However, women's different forms of support for a political solution to the conflict, often expressed from the sidelines at official meetings or through discreet lobbying of the different parties, have maintained vital pressure on the men to continue the search for peace. Although women took part in all the decisive rounds of negotiations at the official political level, they were clearly underrepresented. This is also the case regarding the official political bodies, for example the Bougainville People's Congress and the interim provincial government. The question of women's participation in structures of the new autonomous government also remains open. Women leaders in Bougainville demand that women be given the opportunity to participate fully in political life.

Women still bear the brunt of work in several NGOs that are seeking to achieve reconstruction and reconciliation in today's postconflict situation. For example, the Bougainville Community Integrated Development Agency (BOCIDA) was the lead agency in delivering humanitarian assistance during the war. It is now focusing its work on literacy, reproductive health, and education. The Leitana Nehan Women's Development Agency offers a range of services for women and youth, such as counseling and a program to combat violence against women. The BICWF has shifted the focus of its work to literacy, small business training, and capacity building for women and local women's organizations.

These and other women's NGOs (e.g., Bougainville Women for Peace and Freedom, the District Women's Council, the Provincial Women's Council, and the Church Women's Organization) are closely linked to the grassroots and thus in a position to work for the stabilization of the situation on the ground. They can do this because they were present with the people during the war already and—similar to the churches—won the trust of the people because they stayed by them even in the hardest of times. Their members eat the same food, and respect the customs and understand the way of Melanesian village life—because they are part of it. This holds true for only a handful of other NGOs, for example the Paruparu Education Development Center.

Special mention should also be made of the Peace Foundation Melanesia, whose members worked for peace in Bougainville even in times of the fiercest warfare. At the core of the foundation's activities are workshops to train grassroots people as mediators in conflicts at the local level. Peace Foundation Melanesia managed to train a total of 160 trainers between 1994 and 2000. They in turn helped to conduct 250 mediation courses for a total of more than 6,400 participants. As with the healing-of-memories seminars of the Catholic Church, these courses of Peace Foundation Melanesia did not introduce fixed, external, modern, Western-style concepts of conflict resolution into the Bougainvillean environment, but built upon the customary indigenous experiences.

A key element in the approach of Peace Foundation Melanesia is the concept of restorative justice—the idea that people can overcome conflict, guilt, and grievance through processes of mediation aimed at achieving a win-win outcome of mutual forgiveness, reconciliation, and restoration of harmony in the community—rather than revenge and punishment. This approach is remarkably similar to customary ways of resolving conflicts in Bougainville and in Melanesia in general. Hence the success of Peace Foundation Melanesia's courses, which have contributed greatly to spreading the idea of peaceful conflict resolution at the grassroots level even during times of war. The importance of the fact that hundreds and thousands of ordinary Bougainvilleans have participated in these courses and in the healing-of-memories seminars and similar endeavors of other groups cannot be overestimated.

Furthermore, leaders of the warring parties were also trained in conflict resolution. For example, Ruby Miringka (then director of BOCIDA) ran a course in 1996 for members of the political wing of the BRA, following her attendance at a University of New South Wales, Sydney, diplomacy training program. Australian lawyer Leo White ran a course on negotiation skills for leaders of the conflict parties in 1997 that obviously contributed to the success of the Burnham talks. Whereas these are positive examples of external civil society assistance to the Bougainville peace process, one cannot gloss over the fact that external interference can also have detrimental effects.

After the cease-fire and the stabilization of the security situation on the ground, a considerable number of foreign development agencies, international NGOs, and UN programs and institutions became active in Bougainville, trying to assist in reconstruction and peace building. AusAID, the Australian government's development agency, became the largest donor, spending considerable amounts of money on large projects such as building hospitals and schools, but also delivered small grants for community projects. The New Zealand Official Development Assistance supports the reintegration of former combatants through vocational training and related activities. The European Union assists in rebuilding infrastructure and cash crop rehabilitation. The UN Development Programme has been funding a program for rehabilitation, reconstruction, and development, assisted by the United States and Canada.

A considerable number of Australian and other foreign NGOs run programs on the island. One almost gets the impression that there is "too much" help: too much money, too much outside interference, too many foreign ideas. There is the imminent danger of suppressing local indigenous initiatives and of proffering paternalistic attitudes. In an artificial "civil society" with no links to the grassroots village level, NGOs completely dependent on donor money and with no basis in the Bougainvillean society might be the negative outcome—probably with serious repercussions for peacebuilding.

Already, some international NGOs have been targeted by disgruntled youths. Those NGOs set up their own offices and infrastructure at considerable expense and in visible contrast to the lack of resources available to local groups. The display of their comparative wealth has caused resentment, apparent in their targeting by youths who have stolen vehicles and supplies. External NGOs are not always prudent in choosing local partners, and outside assistance is spread unequally, for example preferring coastal areas with easier access to the mountainous interior or former government-controlled areas to former BRA-controlled regions. This might trigger new conflicts.

Local groups often feel sidelined by the richer and more powerful international NGOs and criticize them for establishing programs without prior consultation and for bypassing existing local initiatives. The imminent danger exists that external assistance creates dependency and that external models of "development" again contribute to conditions that were causes of the war in the first place.

All outside agencies must always be aware that they are guests on the island and that through the war and especially the postwar period of reconstruction and reconciliation the people of Bougainville have developed self-confidence, have learned to trust their own strength, and are both willing and capable of taking care of their own affairs and remaining in control of their own destiny. This self-assurance and cooperative spirit will develop an indigenous "civil society" that is intimately interwoven with the traditional society and its customs. Only if this is achieved will peace be sustainable, and will conflicts be solved nonviolently.

The ground for such a civil society was laid during and after the war; then civil society proved strong enough to force the political and military leadership to negotiate peace and continued to assist in the peace process both at the grassroots as well as at the official level. No leader today dare ignore civil society. The success story of peacebuilding in Bougainville is also a success story of civil society intervention.

Prospects

Thus far, Bougainville is a success story of postconflict peacebuilding. This can be attributed to a number of key factors. One of them is the linking of the peace process from above with manifold peace processes from below. Peacebuilding was not confined to negotiations in the political field between the top representatives of conflicting parties. Rather, the grassroots, former militants, and civil society took over ownership of the process to a large extent. All stakeholders at all levels of society were included and participated in the process. Of special importance was the involvement of women, who on account of the matrilineal organization of most of the traditional communities on the island have a strong social position and who spoke out strongly for peace. Representatives of civil society and traditional authorities were present and active in negotiations, and they took the task of peacebuilding at the grassroots level into their own hands. In doing so, they combined modern civil society styles and methods of conflict resolution and traditional, customary means of peacebuilding. At the core of the latter is accepting responsibility, leading to reconciliation, restoration of justice, and thus social harmony (via compensation for damage done and wrongs committed). Only in that way could the mind-set of payback be changed and sustainable peace achieved.

Customary reconciliation was crucial in resolving bitter divisions at the local level. Customary processes and ceremonies were combined with Christian elements, and church people were particularly active in initiating and stabilizing grassroots peace processes, providing an adequate role for reconciliation in the peacebuilding process. It was acknowledged that peacebuilding is a complicated and painful psychological and spiritual process.

It must also be acknowledged that peacebuilding is not a quick fix. Conflict parties in the Bougainville case took their time to come to sustainable solutions. After almost ten years of war, Bougainville has now witnessed six years of peacebuilding, with more than twenty rounds of negotiations, and the BPA envisages a transitional period of another ten to fifteen years. A solid foundation for this period has been laid, and thus prospects for peace on the island look good, if all parties keep to the inclusive, patient, and consensual approach they followed in recent years.

However, it can be foreseen that frictions and problems lie on the road ahead. Not all factions are actively involved in the peace process (Francis Ona and his Me'ekamui Defense Force [which split from the BRA], who are in control of the Panguna mine, remain outside, although they tacitly accept the process). The law and order situation on the ground is strained and violence is common. Many young former combatants lack personal and professional prospects in civil life. Weapons disposal has not yet been fully accomplished, and questions of justice, amnesty, and pardon need further consideration. Elections for an autonomous government might cause new strife as well as more confidence among Bougainvilleans. The fiscal base for autonomy is far from consolidated and revenues for the autonomous government will be constrained for some time to come. Administrative capacity is weak, economic recovery is still limited, and infrastructure development slow. The future of the Panguna mine has not been addressed at all. Furthermore, the peace monitoring group withdrew in mid-2003, and the UN also seems to be preparing to say goodbye to Bougainville. It has to be hoped that the external support for the peace process, which has had important positive stabilizing effects, will not be withdrawn too early.

Recommendations

The following recommendations are important to contribute to the ongoing peacebuilding and reconciliation processes in Bougainville:

- Patience is highly recommended. All stakeholders have shown impressive patience during the last years, and it would be very foolish to become impatient and nervous in the present stage of the process. Unfortunately, there are signs of the latter: the withdrawal of the peace monitoring group, the ever more pressing attitude of the central government regarding weapons disposal, and the frustration of many Bougainvilleans with the slow pace of economic recovery and social betterment.
- The strength of Bougainvillean peacebuilding so far has been its process orientation in the context of long-term thinking, both at the top political level and at the grassroots level. Parties should adhere to that attitude. Reconciliation processes on the ground, at the village-to-village and clan-to-clan level, should continue and be extended.
- The autonomy arrangements should be fully implemented step by step. External assistance should be given in a long-term perspective, including help in funding the autonomous government.
- Weapons disposal should continue without putting participants under undue pressure by setting deadlines (which, as experience from other places amply shows, will not be met). Rather, people still holding weapons should be patiently put under moral pressure and made to feel ashamed.

- The draft constitution should be subject to wide public consultation with enough time.
- Elections for and establishment of an autonomous government should go ahead as soon as possible (and even if the last weapon has not been handed in), but be well prepared, even if this means some delay. Crucial to the future of the peace process will be that the people of Bougainville have an autonomous government that will be accepted by the great majority and thus be legitimate and trusted (even if its funds and administrative capacity will probably be severely limited for quite some time). Such a government will be in a position to lead the island on the road to reconstruction, rehabilitation, reconciliation, and self-determination, so that finally the people of Bougainville will be capable of deciding their future by means of a referendum on a solid societal basis and under peaceful conditions.

Resources

Reports
Amnesty International. *Bougainville: The Forgotten Human Rights Tragedy.* ASA 34/ 01/97. London, 1997.
Parliament of Australia. Joint Standing Committee on Foreign Affairs, Defence, and Trade. *Bougainville: The Peace Process and Beyond.* Canberra, September 27, 1999.
UN Inter-Agency Mission. *The Rehabilitation and Reconstruction of Bougainville, Papua New Guinea: A Needs Assessment and Programme Proposal.* Draft Report. Ed. John R. Rogge. Port Moresby, 1995.
UN Development Programme. *Bougainville Rehabilitation, Reconstruction, and Development Project: Achieving Sustainable Human Development Through Strengthening Social Capital in Bougainville.* By Colleen Peacock-Taylor (team leader), Naihuwo Ahai, Elizabeth Momis, and Enaha Kwa. PNG/98/002/07/UNOPS. November 1999.
World Council of Churches Programme Unit IV. *Stories of Bougainville.* Report of Women's Team Visit (Brenda Fitzpatrick). Geneva, 1993

Publications
Bergbau—Umweltzerstörung—Gewalt: Der Krieg auf Bougainville im Kontext der Geschichte ökologisch induzierter Modernisierungskonflikte. By Volker Böge. Hamburg, 1998.
Bougainville: Perspectives on a Crisis. Ed. Peter Polomka. Canberra, 1990.
Bougainville: Rebuilding Trust and Rebuilding People. By Naihuwo Ahai. Discussion Paper no. 9. Armidale: Centre for Peace Studies, University of New England, 1996.
The Bougainville Crisis. Eds. Ron J. May and Matthew Spriggs. Bathurst, 1990.
The Bougainville Crisis: 1991 Update. Eds. Donald Denoon and Matthew Spriggs. Canberra, 1992.
"The Bougainville Political Settlement and the Prospects for Sustainable Peace." By Anthony J. Regan. *Pacific Economic Bulletin* 17, no. 1 (2002): 114–129.
Breaking Spears and Mending Hearts: Peacemakers and Restorative Justice in Bougainville. By Pat Howley. London: Leichhardt, 2002.
Building Peace in Bougainville. By Geoff Harris, Naihuwo, Ahai and Rebecca Spence. Waigani, Armidale, 1999.
Conflict Potential and Violent Conflicts in the South Pacific: Options for a Civil Peace Service. By Volker Böge. Working Paper no. 1/2001. Hamburg: Research Unit of Wars, Armament, and Development, 2001.

Getting Under Their Skins: Australia and the Making of the First Bougainville Agreement. By Donald Denoon. Melbourne, 2000.
Weaving Consensus: The Papua New Guinea–Bougainville Peace Process. Eds. Andy Carl and Lorraine Garasu. Conciliation Resources Accord no. 12. London, 2002.
Without a Gun: Australians' Experiences Monitoring Peace in Bougainville, 1997–2001. Eds. Moinica Wehner and Donald Denoon. Canberra, 2001.

Websites
http://rspas.anu.edu.au/melanesia/bougainville.htm (Bougainville Resource Page, Research School of Pacific and Asian Studies, Australian National University)
www.dfat.gov.au/geo/png/bougainville (Australian Department of Foreign Affairs and Trade, Bougainville Peace Process)
www.dod.gov.au/belisi (Australian Defence Force, Operation Bel Isi, Peace Monitoring Group, Bougainville)
www.eco-action.org/bougainville (Bougainville Freedom Movement)
www.pcrc.org.fj (Pacific Concerns Resource Centre)
www.unpo.org/member/bougain/bougain.html (Bougainville Page, Unrepresented Nations and Peoples Organisation)

Resource Contacts
Volker Böge, Bonn International Center for Conversion, e-mail: boege@bicc.de
Donald Denoon, Research School of Pacific and Asian Studies, Australian National University, Canberra ACT 0200, Australia
Lorraine Garasu, CSN, Bougainville Inter-Church Women's Forum (BICWF), e-mail: bicwf@dg.com.pg
Vikki John, Bougainville Freedom Movement, e-mail: vikki@law.uts.edu.au
Martin R. Miriori, secretary, Bougainville Interim Government, e-mail: miriori@bart.nl
Anthony Regan, State, Society, and Governance in Melanesia Project, Research School of Pacific and Asian Studies, Australian National University, Canberra, e-mail: anthony.regan@anu.edu.au
Heinz Schürmann-Zeggel, Amnesty International, Pacific Desk, e-mail: hschurma@amnesty.org

Organizations

Conciliation Resources
173 Upper Street
London N1 1RG, UK
tel: +44 (0) 20 7359 7728
fax: +44 (0) 20 7359 4081
e-mail: accord@c-r.org
www.c-r.org

European Centre on Pacific Issues (ECSIEP)
P.O. Box 151
3700 AD, Zeist, Netherlands
tel: +31 30 692 7827
fax: +31 30 692 5614
e-mail: ecsiep@antenna.nl
www.antenna.nl/ecsiep

Pacific Concerns Resource Centre
83 Amy Street, Private Mail Bag
Suva, Fiji
tel: +679 304 649

fax: +679 304 755
e-mail: pcrc@is.com.fj

World Council of Churches
Pacific Desk
150 Route de Ferney
P.O. Box 2100
CH-1211 Geneva 2, Switzerland
tel: +41 22 791 6218/6219
fax: +41 22 788 0067
e-mail: tevi@wcc-coe.org
www.wcc-coe.org

Volker Böge works at the International Center for Conversion in Bonn, Germany. The conflict in Bougainville has been the subject of his dissertation, as well as various books, articles, and papers. His present work includes a project on postconflict peacebuilding and traditional instruments and mechanisms of conflict resolution.

Lorraine Garasu is a member of the Congregation of the Sisters of Nazareth and program coordinator for the Bougainville Inter-Church Women's Forum, Integrated Literacy Program. She is a community development worker and a skilled trainer in conflict management and women's issues.

Note

1. Those who were "disappeared" suffered beatings, questioning under torture, and sometimes death.

10.4

The Solomon Islands:
Conflict and Peacebuilding

Bob Pollard and Matthew Wale

Violent conflict in Solomon Islands began in 1998 and continued mid-2003. Over the course of this five-year period, more than 20,000 civilians were displaced, hundreds were killed, the state was incapacitated, and the economy was crippled. Although active hostilities ceased in 2000, following the signing of a peace agreement in Australia, an atmosphere of lawlessness persisted until 2003. In July 2003 a regional assistance mission was deployed to help restore law and order. It involved over 2,000 military and police personnel from Australia, New Zealand, and five Pacific Island nations. The mission has made significant progress in disarmament of militants, the restoration of law and order, and the return of government functions. However, serious concerns remain about fundamental issues of nationhood, peace, justice, and development. The consolidation of current advances and the potential for sustained improvements rely on the engagement of ordinary people and civil society, particularly the churches, in issues of reform.

The Solomon Islands is a developing country located in the southwest Pacific Ocean. It comprises over 900 islands spread over 1.6 million square kilometers of ocean territory. The bulk of the population is located on six main islands: Guadalcanal, Malaita, Choiseul, Santa Isabel, Makira, and New Georgia.[1] There are numerous indigenous cultural groups, each with distinct languages and territories.[2] Only 16 percent of the population is urbanized, with the remaining 84 percent living in several thousand villages. Tribes and kin groups hold the great majority of land, under customary arrangements, and it is on these tracts that most villages are located. Subsistence livelihoods including gardening, fishing, and hunting sustain the rural majority. There is limited participation of villagers in the cash economy, mainly in the form of cash cropping (coconuts, cacao) or fishing and garden production for the local market.

Lack of services and very limited opportunities for cash generation in the villages have driven a rapid urbanization process,[3] particularly of youth from densely populated areas. A national development emphasis focused on the capital, Honiara, and its surroundings has meant that most infrastructure investment is concentrated there, as well as most economic opportunities. This has made Honiara and its environs of northern Guadalcanal a magnet for migrants from throughout the country, but especially the neighboring island of Malaita.

The earliest contact between European explorers and the indigenous peoples of the Solomons occurred in the sixteenth century, when a Spanish explorer from Peru reached the islands. But the contact was brief, and because of a mapping error, they were "lost" to Western sailors for 200 years, until a British sailor located them. Still, no effort was made to colonize the islands. Beginning in the 1870s, however, slave traders began engaging in the practice of "blackbirding"—forcibly seizing Solomon Islanders to work as indentured laborers on the plantations of Queensland, Fiji, Samoa, and New Caledonia. Local resentment led to the killings of missionaries and shipwrecked sailors. Partly in response to the appeals of the missionaries, the British declared a protectorate over the Solomons in 1893. Except for the Japanese occupation during World War II, the British retained control until 1976, when autonomy was granted. The Solomon Islands achieved full independence in 1978.

The issues that ignited the conflict on Guadalcanal arose from an intersection of land relations, people, culture, and notions of development. The strength of ties between kin group and their land throughout the Solomons means that habitation and economic activities on customary land have very complex social and cultural implications. Following the establishment of Honiara as the national capital after World War II, there was a steady influx of settlers from other provinces into the area, in response to the economic and educational opportunities available there.

Several factors caused Malaita to be overrepresented in the migrant flow to Guadalcanal. The large population and density in parts of Malaita is a key factor. With approximately a third of the country's population but only a sixth of the landmass, population pressures there are more marked than elsewhere. Another driving force for Malaitan emigration is the island's long exposure to migrant labor as a lifestyle and economic option; Malaitans made up a majority of a total of some 30,000 indentured laborers during the "blackbirding" period. Under less oppressive circumstances, the Malaitans continued to leave their own homes to work as laborers when Solomon Island plantations were established as the mainstay of the colonial economy. Until the middle of the twentieth century, almost three-quarters of plantation labor within the Solomons was composed of Malaitans. Resource scarcity relative to population has continued to make migrant labor an attractive proposition for Malaitans.

By the late 1990s, there were many sizable Malaitan settlements on northern Guadalcanal. One issue that arose concerned the improper and unwelcome settlement and use of land by settlers. Although many settlers originally obtained permissions for land and resource use from landowners, their communities often overstepped agreed boundaries or extended beyond the original agreed basis for settlement, turning them into squatters with a significant socioeconomic footprint.

A second issue arose around the relations between settler and local host peoples. Settler and indigenous Guadalcanal values often clashed,[4] and with a growing non-Guadalcanal presence, Guadalcanal peoples felt they were being culturally marginalized in their own land. These issues were highlighted by a number of murders of Guadalcanal villagers in the Mount Austen area of Honiara, and became the basis of a 1988 petition by Guadalcanal leaders to the government, calling for a cessation of such killings and the adoption of a federal government system.[5]

A third issue was the apparent lack of economic benefit to the Guadalcanal people and province from the many significant investments on the island, most notably Honiara town and the large palm oil plantations of northeastern Guadalcanal.[6] This perception of relative deprivation was fueled by the degree to which Malaitans and other non-Guadalcanal people were successfully exploiting economic opportunities—for instance jobs and the provision of services—made available by those same large investments.

These issues, and Guadalcanal resentment around them, grew over the decades,[7] and were exacerbated by instances of violence between Malaitans and local people, including a number of murders of Guadalcanal persons throughout the 1970s, 1980s, and 1990s. These grievances came to a violent head in 1998.

Conflict Dynamics

Late in 1998, a small gang of Guadalcanal youth initiated a series of attacks on migrant settlements on northern Guadalcanal. In a shootout with police,[8] one of the gang was killed and the remainder were arrested. Two of the leaders, Harold Keke and his brother, Joseph Sangu, were released on bail and escaped from Honiara. Soon after, in 1999, they formed the militant group, the Guadalcanal Revolutionary Army (GRA), and began a widening pattern of attacks on migrant communities throughout Guadalcanal. During the first part of 1999, these attacks, including the razing of settlements, killings, and other human rights abuses, caused widespread panic among the predominantly Malaitan settler community. Over the space of the year, an estimated 20,000–30,000 people were displaced from rural Guadalcanal—often with complete loss of home and possessions—into Honiara and its environs, often continuing on to Malaita.

By 2000, rural Guadalcanal had been essentially cleared of all migrants, but the cost had been the closure of all industries, the closure of almost every school, and deprivation of access to medical facilities for most Guadalcanal people. Thousands of Malaitans had lost their livelihood and all they owned. Many were forced to return to a "home" they had never known. This has in turn led to many internal problems and tensions in Malaita.

During this period, the frequency and severity of clashes between the GRA and national paramilitary forces escalated,[9] particularly around the national resource projects at Solomon Islands Plantations Limited (SIPL) and Gold Ridge. This escalation was paralleled by a weakening confidence in the impartiality of the police force, with doubts about the vigor of Guadalcanal officers' execution of their duties against Guadalcanal militant elements.

These doubts, together with considerable loss of life, property, and pride on the part of evicted Malaitan settlers, found expression in late 1999 through the formation of an opposing militia, the Malaita Eagle Force (MEF). The MEF, which had strong links to a number of senior police officers, carried out a raid on the Auki police armory in late 1999, securing a number of modern military-style weapons. Thus equipped, the MEF began active operations against the GRA, Guadalcanal militants, and even civilian populations outside Honiara. Because of the high proportion of police officers of Malaitan extraction, the correspondence between MEF and police forces developed rapidly, with the police force becoming increasingly Malaitan-dominated due to the departure of Guadalcanal and other officers. An internal split also emerged between leadership of different factions within the Guadalcanal militancy, leading to the formation of a new militia, the Isatabu Freedom Movement (IFM), separate from the GRA.[10]

The fighting between police and MEF forces, and the Guadalcanal militias, moved inward from the Guadalcanal hinterland to a rough perimeter around Honiara, with particularly clear lines at the eastern and western ends of the town. In 2000, instances of atrocities by both sides, particularly against civilians, reached a high and, together with the apparent encroachment of the capital by GRA forces, led to widespread rumors of a planned assault on Honiara itself.

During the first part of 2000, with wide-scale destruction and the displacement of thousands of citizens, the Ulufa'alu government had entered into quiet negotiations with the European Union (EU) to secure a SI$300 million financial assistance package to enable reconstruction and provide aid to displaced persons. A high-level delegation from the EU visited Honiara in early June 2000, and the agreement for the aid package was to be signed on the morning of June 5, 2000. But on that very day, at least in part as a preemptive response to the rumors of an assault on Honiara, the MEF took over the national police armory and staged a coup, placing the elected prime minister, Bartholomew Ulufa'alu, under house arrest and forcing him to resign.

The EU delegation was trapped in Honiara for a number of days. Australia and New Zealand evacuated their citizens, along with other foreign nationals, in the days following the coup. They sent their foreign affairs ministers to visit Honiara immediately after the forced resignation of Prime Minister Ulufa'alu. Their message was, again, to "find a local solution." The Australian foreign affairs minister, Alexander Downer, offered his phone number, saying, "Give me a call when you have found a solution, and we will come in and help." Downer even offered to assist "compensation payments" and a gun buyback scheme if peace could be restored—comments later refuted by his own government. Nonetheless, the promise had an effect: parliament moved to elect a new government, with Manasseh Sogovare as prime minister. The Sogovare

Ben Bohane

Guadalcanal, Solomon Islands.
IMF guerrillas in a Moro Movement Village.

government was obviously banking on Downer's pledge and made commitments on that basis. The Australian and New Zealand governments quickly recognized the election of Sogovare as prime minister by parliament in July 2000, despite the fact that parliament had been under serious duress and six members of the fifty-seat house had been unable to attend because of threats by the militants.

In successfully executing the coup, the MEF effectively gained control of the bulk of military weaponry in the country, and established control over the entire capital. With the benefit of this position, open assaults were launched on Guadalcanal militants at both eastern and western ends of Honiara, driving them back from the town. Following the coup, MEF leadership rapidly lost control of their own forces holding the capital, with disastrous effect on law and order. By carrying out the coup in coordination with elements of the police, the MEF had effectively co-opted law enforcement, which was subsequently unable to reassert itself. The months following the coup were characterized by general lawlessness and thuggery throughout Guadalcanal and parts of Malaita, a situation that paralyzed government, the economy, and even traditional relations in certain regions.

Then, in October 2000, an Australia-brokered peace plan was consummated with the signing of a peace agreement in Townsville, Australia, between the two militant forces and the national government. This Townsville Peace Agreement (TPA) was in essence a capitulation to the demands of both militant groups.[11] The TPA reflected the militants' desire to avoid liability for individual and corporate criminal actions, their wish for compensation for property and human loss during the hostilities, and their interest in progress in key areas identified as significant or "root" causes of the conflict.

While successful in halting open armed hostilities, and officially disbanding militia groups, the TPA failed to provide a basis for the reinstitution of civil order, nor did it address deep issues underlying the origins of the conflict. Accordingly, while open warfare ceased and individual militants reconciled, thuggery, intimidation, and community violence continued to destabilize Guadalcanal, Honiara, national governance institutions, and through them, the country as a whole. Because tensions remained high within Guadalcanal militant groups, the MEF has been unwilling to disarm.

The underlying feelings of injustice that fueled the conflict—ones that almost every Guadalcanal person felt strongly, and that most Malaitans could easily identify with as well—have not been successfully addressed, and the economic circumstances continue to perpetuate injustice. Existing avenues for resolving the injustice have been ineffective. The political forums have seemed incapable of addressing the fundamental concerns, and the unstable and unprincipled nature of politics in the Solomon Islands subsequent to independence has offered very little hope for change. The evolving political culture has been one of different factions consumed by their desires to gain and/or retain power, creating an unstable political climate that has made it impossible to develop or implement any policies geared for the long term.

Efforts at serious reform have inevitably been compromised by the actions of politicians seeking immediate personal benefits. Sadly, there has been a clear lack of proactive leadership with integrity, and as a result the Solomon Islands has been labeled in the international community as a "failed state."

Unfortunately, alternatives for addressing injustice within traditional society have not, in general, been effectively exploited. The formal governance structures of the Solomon Islands do not make any provision for a role in society for traditional leadership structures. Existing apart from the formal structures, these various traditional structures within the language groups have themselves been under severe strain and have been quite marginalized. Other institutions, such as the churches, gave very little serious attention, prior to the conflict, to the justice issues, presuming them to be the domain of the government or the courts.

In December 2001, general elections were held, but the installation of a new government failed to change this fundamentally unstable environment. The newly elected prime minister, Sir Allan Kemakeza, openly identified and sympathized with militants, and his administration operated under constant threat of former militant elements and their associates.

However, with ever-increasing pressures accruing from the charged atmosphere and ongoing instability, the Kemakeza administration asked for outside assistance, including significant military and police forces, to restore order and bring stability. In July 2003 the Australian-led Regional Assistance Mission to the Solomon Islands (RAMSI) deployed over 2,000 Australian, New Zealand, and Pacific Island troops, police, and officials to reestablish the rule of law and public order, which it was able to do without further violence. The intervention was, in general, welcomed by ordinary citizens, who viewed it as an effective action for further reducing the influence of the already weakened militias. RAMSI's seizure and destruction of thousands of firearms and arrest of dozens of key militant figures throughout the last half of 2003 represents the first milestone on the path to a truly postconflict situation in the Solomon Islands.

Official Conflict Management

Early Efforts
During 1999 and into early 2000 the Solomon Islands government continued to be indecisive about the escalating violence.[12] The increasing militancy of both Guadalcanal and Malaitan armed groups in early 2000 led the prime minister to request Australian and New Zealand military assistance to help the Solomon Island government control the conflict. However, the Australian and New Zealand governments refused to intervene directly in the manner requested.

In 1999 the Solomon Islands government appealed to the Commonwealth Secretariat for assistance in dealing with the escalating conflict. Former Fijian military coup maker and prime minister Sitiveni Rabuka was sent to the Solomon Islands as an envoy assisted by Ade Adefue, an officer of the Commonwealth

Secretariat. Rabuka's first comments on arrival were to compare the Solomon Island conflict with that of Fiji, where, supposedly, indigenous Fijians were fighting for their rights against the Indian settlers. The direct corollary was that the Guadalcanal militants were fighting for their rights against (predominantly) Malaitan settlers. In light of the abuses and losses they had suffered at that stage of conflict, most Malaitans found this statement highly inflammatory and lost any hopes that their justified concerns would be seriously considered by Rabuka. Rabuka spent the bulk of his time negotiating a series of peace accords between the Guadalcanal militants and the government. None of the accords lasted, however, or slowed the militant activities. This period was characterized by indecisive leadership from the government and ambiguous signals to the Guadalcanal militants as to whether they were viewed as criminals or genuine justice fighters.

The Townsville Agreement

The Townsville Peace Agreement, described above, required both militant groups to surrender all arms and stolen property within thirty days in exchange for amnesty for all crimes except human rights abuses—a provision that was clearly to the advantage of both sides. The agreement also included an assurance from the government of donor assistance to help rehabilitate and rebuild the economy. Furthermore, the government was committed to finding money to pay compensation to all victims of the conflict. It is important to note that at the negotiations in Townsville, the government was extremely weak—at best totally bereft of any moral authority, at worst a puppet of the MEF. Relative to the Isatabu Freedom Movement (IFM) and the government, the MEF was clearly in the strongest negotiating position. The TPA embodied an approach to peacemaking that relied more on financial incentives than either humanitarian concerns, negotiated compromises, or any efforts to address the roots cause of the conflict or grievances of the parties. The delegates to the talks were paid generous allowances as enticement to attend and sign. In the agreement, the government promised to pay "compensation" for lost lives, property, and earnings. It was clear to the government even then that there was no way it would be able to live up to those commitments. This extravagance was fueled by promises of aid by Australia—or so the government and militia groups believed. But the monetizing of the peace process at Townsville had a severely negative impact on Solomon Islands economy and society, and served to undermine traditional cultural values and conflict resolution principles. It also laid the basis for corruption in the government's payment of compensation.

Since early on in the conflict, victims have demanded reparations. Reparation claims have taken two factors into account: the need of victims for restoration from loss suffered, and compensation for the injustice done. Compensation draws on traditional custom, whereby a perpetrator restores his or her relationship with a victim by offering compensation. The process involves the acknowledgment of wrongdoing by the perpetrator and a sense of punishment, as well as the acknowledgment of the perpetrator to the extent of loss incurred by the victim. In an attempt to defuse the cycle of violence, the Sogo-vare government, just weeks into its time in office, started paying out SI\$100,000 "compensation" to families of people killed in the conflict, regard-less of the circumstances.[13] This set a precedent on the value of a life at SI\$100,000. When the cease-fire agreement was signed, it was accompanied by the payment of SI\$12 million "compensation" by the Sogovare government to the two provincial governments and to the militants. But these payments by the government bore no resemblance to traditional customary reconciliation processes, wherein the symbolic rather than the material aspect is of tanta-mount importance. In fact, the Guadalcanal militia and provincial government had refused to recognize the Sogovare government, which they felt had been installed by the MEF while parliament was under duress. After the lump-sum payments, however, both the Guadalcanal provincial government and militia quickly recognized the Sogovare government. The deputy prime minister at the time, Allan Kemakeza, who was also in charge of the peace process, believed the government had to spend money to achieve peace. In practice this meant the government had to pay relatively large amounts to key militia lead-ers to entice them to come to the negotiating table. It was a turning point in the Solomon Island peace process, though the payments also had grave implica-tions for the process of governance and for society more generally.

The government procured a U.S.\$25 million commercial loan from Tai-wan in 2001 to pay compensation to the victims of the conflict.[14] The com-pensation payments fueled a culture of corruption, with senior politicians and public servants implicated in schemes whereby they received substantial amounts of money from the compensation fund, to which they had no legiti-mate claim.

Although, the Townsville Peace Agreement extended amnesty to fighters on both sides, conditioned on full disarmament by both parties, neither party fully disarmed. The deadline for disarmament was extended three times. The final deadline, May 31, 2002, produced a significant surrender of arms, but MEF leaders publicly refused to disarm, claiming they were acting on the advice of the prime minister. The surrender of arms was given a boost when the police conducted their own surrender of arms exercise. But disarmament remains incomplete. The surrender of arms was further complicated by the occasional issue of arms by the police to special constables (mostly former militants) for operations to apprehend criminals. As a result, it was unclear how many weapons were still out in the community.

The Townsville Peace Agreement provided for the establishment of an independent national Peace Monitoring Council (PMC),to officially monitor the implementation of the agreement. The PMC was keen to be seen to be as "neutral" by the parties to the agreement, including the government. Particu-larly in the early days, it did not want to be seen as a leader in the peace process but as a monitor of developments, whose responsibility was to report back to the parties. The need to report back to bodies that were supposed to have disbanded proved to be a major flaw of the TPA.

International Engagement

After declining to take an active role in conflict resolution following the June 2000 coup, Australia ultimately did engage in peacemaking by hosting the Townsville talks that led to the TPA in October 2000. Australia's unusual approach was to fly the leaders of the militant groups and the government to Townsville and give them three days to produce a peace agreement (the process ended up taking six days).

Following the signing of the TPA, Australia and New Zealand provided and funded the unarmed International Peace Monitoring Team (IPMT) to help monitor its implementation. The international peace monitors, in collaboration with local counterparts, actually did much more than monitoring. They were able to provide human faces to the international concern felt for ordinary Solomon Islanders who were victims of this conflict. They were able to facilitate simple confidence-building measures and provide limited humanitarian assistance. The IPMT was withdrawn at the end of May 2002, in the belief that at this point the issue had become one of restoring law and order and no longer required peace monitoring.

Given the absence of leadership by the Solomon Islands government, the Peace Monitoring Council became, by default, the official lead body in the peace process. After the conclusion of the Townsville Peace Agreement, a National Peace Council was established to supersede and to continue the work of the PMC. The National Peace Council kept on many people from the PMC as staff.

The United Nations was not officially requested by the Solomon Island government to engage in the situation until mid-2002. It had been involved in the Solomon Islands prior to the conflict by way of the UN Development Programme (UNDP) and a UN representative remained in country during 2000–2001. The UNDP did, in 2002, take a lead role in attempting to demobilize the special constables and former militants and facilitate constitutional reform required by the TPA. The demobilization of special constables is still in progress (in late 2003) and involves the UNDP soliciting the agreement of individual special constables to disarm and terminate from the constabulary for a lump-sum payment. Most special constables have participated in this program and have terminated from the constabulary, a division of the police. These special constables were recruited from the two militia groups and were a source of further compromise within the police. Worse, a number of these special constables have violently coerced payments from the national treasury. Increasingly, the government has been unable to make any payments to health and education services because of the sustained pressure from special constables for payments from the treasury.

In late 2001 a representative office of the UN High Commissioner for Human Rights was established in Honiara. This office was very effective in raising awareness about human rights issues and assisting government and civil society groups in considering alternative responses to the situations. For the groups and individuals concerned about human rights abuses and violations in the Solomon Islands, the presence of the office was an important indication that people outside the country were concerned about these events.

Multi-Track Diplomacy

The term "civil society" came to prominence in the Solomon Islands during the period of the conflict. The network of local civil society organizations has played a constructive role for peacebuilding and justice. However, there has been considerable resentment by some of the militant leaders that civil society groups would dare to challenge their power, claimed through the barrel of the gun. Similarly, the government has at times been upset that civil society groups, as unelected bodies, would challenge their decisions and even intimidate elected leaders by shows of public strength.

Active civil society in the Solomon Islands comprises churches, women's groups, some nongovernmental organizations NGOs, the business community, union groups, and others. Individuals and community leaders, too, are able to exercise influence. The concept of civil society has a unique nature in a village-based, largely rural society like the Solomon Islands. Unlike in developed societies, consciousness has grown of one being part of civil society regardless of whether or not one is a member of an organization. Further, with this new consciousness has come the almost sudden resolve to "take on" government and militia on issues of justice and accountability. This consciousness has allowed for the development of a tangible forum for the airing of views on issues of concern. The forum links the urban civil society organizations with the rural "civil society" groups, which are in fact mostly concerned individuals from the villages. Whereas, before, the villagers never expressed their voice on issues of national importance, the forum has given them the opportunity to give voice, outside the mechanisms of parliament, to their concerns. Apart from the structures of traditional society, the churches are the most significant institution, with broad networks that reach to the grassroots. NGOs are a growing force, while the business and union sectors are essentially restricted to the urban centers.

Traditional Melanesian society is based on the strength of blood relationships. It is a tie that both binds people to each other and to the land. The family/clan is the base institution in society. The concept of a provincial or national government is at best distant and at worst a foreign and imposed concept in Solomon Islands society.[15] The concept of nationhood is extrinsic to ordinary life in Solomon Islands society. Allegiances are first and foremost to one's kinfolk, second to the language group, and third and more weakly to one's island. The communities of the Solomon Islands have at no time in their history made a deliberate choice to be a nation-state. The traditional leadership structures of the different communities have until recent times provided the organizational leadership for their own communities.

Christianity came to the Solomon Islands in the late 1800s. Five denominations hold the allegiance of more than 90 percent of the population. These churches form the Solomon Islands Christian Association (SICA). Every village is identified as associated to one or a number of the churches. Women's groups, which are active in almost every village, are a central part of the churches.

A number of local NGOs have been formed in recent decades. Only a small number have been sustainable, the most notable being the Solomon Islands Development Trust, an NGO that focuses on village development. An umbrella body for the NGO community, the Development Services Exchange, was formed in the 1980s but has struggled.[16]

The National Council of Women is an umbrella body for women's organizations in the country, focusing on national policy issues. Its prime constituents are Honiara-based women's groups. A Honiara-based interdenominational and interprovincial group of women was formed in 2000, calling themselves the "Women for Peace."

The government is the major employer in the Solomon Islands. Businesses, which are almost entirely urban-based, are a small but powerful sector of Solomon Islands society. The Chinese community dominates the business sector.

While the business sector is powerful, the Council of Trade Unions is also an important sector. The Council of Trade Unions is a somewhat disorganized sector in society. The public-sector unions are the largest union bodies.

A few international NGOs have representation in the country, but on the whole they have kept a low profile. The Red Cross has been active as a humanitarian agency.[17]

Roles in Conflict

During the early stages of the conflict most parts of society looked to the police or government, including the provincial governments, to address the problems. By early 2000 it was becoming clear that the conflict was escalating, that the government and police on their own could not resolve it, and that a national crisis was unfolding. Now that a semblance of order has been restored, the police have serious work to do to regain their status. Much suspicion remains about their allegiances and, because they were marginalized by the more aggressive militias, their ability to reassert authority. There is some fear that their marginalization may be perpetuated by the presence of Australian police who have taken up duty since the arrival of RAMSI.

While militant factions had lost confidence in the government, they still retained respect for the churches, and church leaders had access to warring parties, who began looking to the churches to possibly take on a mediating role. The Solomon Islands Christian Association was the obvious body to lead the churches' engagement, but was ill prepared to do so. SICA established a peace office in August 2000. As the militants lost confidence in the government and the Commonwealth envoy efforts faltered, SICA was turned to by default. In addition to the mediating role, SICA became conscious of the prophetic role that it had to play. With the continuing conflict and human rights abuses and violations, SICA believed that it had a moral responsibility to speak out and condemn these acts. However by doing so, SICA inhibited the mediating role it could play. In the small Solomon Islands society, the militant leaders became personally offended by their public condemnation by church leaders. SICA's delay in getting organized left it open to criticism from the Malaitan Eagle Force for not speaking out earlier against the human rights abuses by Guadalcanal militants.

An instrumental group in conflict prevention has been the Church of Melanesia Brotherhood Order, called the Tasius. This group of dedicated young men was often in the midst of the two militant groups, preventing them from shooting at each other. They were in constant demand by individuals or groups in fear or needing security. The Tasius were able to go to places that the police could not or would not go, and thus played an important mediating role. The Tasius have importantly assisted in the disarmament process, approaching former militants and persuading some to hand over their guns.

As the conflict intensified, the Women for Peace group took on an active role of visiting the militants and their leaders. The place of women in conflict resolution is traditionally significant within much of Melanesian society.[18] The women came as "mothers," appealing to the men and boys to refrain from violence. The "mothers" also took on active roles of facilitating humanitarian assistance to families suffering because of the conflict and engaged in civil society initiatives toward peace. The need for trauma counseling has been great. Various groups have received assistance with trauma counseling training. A lead agency was the SICA Federation of Women's Groups, which provided a large amount of counseling training, as well as actual counseling.

In August 2000 the SICA Peace Office organized a national peace conference on board the New Zealand frigate *Te Kaha,* attended by about 120 participants.[19] The participants were invited from all the provinces, and included church and community leaders, women, and a few youth as well. Provincial legislators also participated, but national parliamentarians did not. The reason for the national peace conference was the observation that the government formed after the coup had a very unhealthy relationship with the militant groups, particularly the MEF. There was widespread acknowledgment that the government was not acting in the interests of the whole nation, but rather for the benefit of a very small minority—those in the MEF leadership and close associates. The most powerful power broker in the Sogovare government was the chairman of its caucus. He was the real power behind the prime minister, and it showed in the benefits accrued to himself, close associates, and family. He had relatives in the MEF and used them effectively as a power base. He was responsible for the recruitment of the special constables, even against the wishes of the commissioner of police. He was also deciding which payments were priority out of the national treasury. The remissions of customs duty to close associates have also been credited to him and the minister of finance. It was recognized that if a sustainable solution to the conflict was to be achieved, it would require a government that could act impartially and with consideration for the whole society. One of the resolutions of the conference was a call for a commission to establish the truth about the beginnings of the conflict and subsequent events.

The national peace conference was initially scheduled to take place after the cease-fire talks. The minister for national unity, peace, and reconciliation was persuaded to allow the conference to happen prior to the cease-fire talks so that the government could be armed with the views of wider society when it engaged the militant factions. The resolutions of the national peace conference resulted in violent attacks on some of the organizers and participants. The conference was in many ways the birth of a genuinely collaborative civil society force in the Solomon Islands. Despite the strong resolutions passed by the national peace conference, or more likely because of the strong positions taken, no civil society representatives were invited to participate in the cease-fire or peace talks.[20] This again reflected the weak position of government, which was under the influence of the militants.

In early 2001 as the economy continued to deteriorate, the Solomon Islands Chamber of Commerce took the initiative to call together the churches, the business community, women's groups, and NGO representatives to discuss what could be done to address the serious circumstances that the economy faced. This coalition of civil society bodies, which came to incorporate the unions, youth representatives, and a variety of other organizations and individuals, called itself the Honiara Civil Society Network (CSN). The CSN met regularly to discuss events and issues as well as to decide on actions that could be taken, either corporately or individually. The CSN was a network of groups and individuals, and it was deliberately decided that is would not be another formal organization, but remain a loose coalition.[21]

The Solomon Islands Christian Association Peace Office (SICAPO) took on the secretariat role of the network. Some of the activities engaged in by the CSN included taking public stands against acts of violence and human rights abuse, publicizing and disseminating information about issues including government corruption, organizing meetings of the network, and arranging delegations to meet leaders and international representatives.

The media organizations in the country were under duress during the conflict. The local newspaper deliberately decided to avoid news items that might provoke the MEF, which controlled the Honiara area. The national radio broadcaster took a more active role, also engaging in the civil society network. However, it must be said that serious limitations existed, and still exist, with respect to capacity of the media to engage in investigative journalism.

During 2001 the PMC announced that it planned a review of the Townsville Peace Agreement (TPA). The CSN saw this as a prime opportunity to raise the concerns of wider society about the direction and nature of the peace process. A nationwide consultation process ensued, organized by SICAPO and involving some respected senior citizens. This was particularly important because the other six provinces had felt largely marginalized during the conflict. Not only had the conflict ruined the national economy, but now the two provinces of Guadalcanal and Malaita were monopolizing the minimal resources that remained. The consultation process was largely successful. All provinces were visited and public meetings held. For many the consultations presented the first opportunity for them to see the TPA and to have its contents explained. During each public meeting, attendees were given the opportunity to prepare resolutions to be submitted to the TPA review.

The resolutions of the provincial consultations were combined and, along with the submission by the PMC itself, composed the major submission to the review. Two or three provincial governments did not make submissions at all but stated that their concerns were included in the civil society submission. Tension again surfaced about the appropriate role and place of civil society groups at the actual review meeting. The MEF and government were the main objectors to civil society representation.[22]

By the time of the review, the Isatabu Freedom Movement and the Guadalcanal Revolutionary Army had fractured and reverted to a loose coalition of Guadalcanal militants, many of whom had tried, with limited success, to return to civilian life. Although the Isatabu Freedom Movement was difficult to reconstitute, the Malaitan Eagle Force had retained greater cohesion; however, over time, and through efforts of peacebuilders, there had been some disbanding of the MEF as well. Unfortunately, the review prompted regrouping by militant groups, particularly the MEF.

The concerns at the review revolved around issues of disarmament, continued criminal activity, the relationship between the militants and the police, the need to demobilize special constables appointed after the TPA, and the continued pillaging of the public purse. The need for a truth commission as a way of establishing the actual story and providing an opportunity for reconciliation was again raised in the submission by civil society. The CSN had drafted a framework for a truth and reconciliation process, which it had circulated among communities, that called for community tribunals to handle minor crimes (more serious crimes would be handled by courts), with provisions for perpetrators to perform community service instead of doing jail time, as a way to break the cycle of impunity.

During the review meeting one of the leaders of the CSN, a SICAPO officer, was assaulted by a senior police officer, in full uniform, who was also a prominent MEF leader. The minister of police and other senior government officers witnessed the assault. No disciplinary action was taken against the police officer concerned. The review was suspended the following day because the IFM and Guadalcanal delegations withdrew after an IFM leader was brutally murdered in Honiara. The review was never reconvened.

In 2001 the government decided that because of the conflict it would be inappropriate to hold the general elections due late that year. The CSN took an active role in opposing the idea of postponing the general elections. The government attempted to make a constitutional change that would allow it to hold on to power for a further year or more. The government twice withdrew the motion from parliament when it recognized that it did not have the parliamentary numbers or public support.

Women and youth placarded the entrance to parliament in peaceful opposition. This was a real shock to many politicians. The Civil Society Network began to be perceived by the government as the pseudo opposition. The churches were roundly criticized by the government for moving outside their "spiritual" sphere and taking a public stand on governance issues. There was broad public consensus that the postcoup government was illegitimate and that a general election was a necessary step in the peace process. With the aid of donors a general election was successfully held in early December 2001.[23]

Reflections on Multi-Track Approaches

The participation of civil society in the formal peace process has been essentially prohibited by the militant groups and a weak government. The militants saw themselves as the legitimate parties to determine the destiny of the country, given the fact that they had "risked their lives" for the nation. The government readily acquiesced to this position, and more seriously, it questioned the right of unelected persons to speak with any authority about the concerns of the nation. Within this matrix the civil society bodies have been marginalized. With the arrival of RAMSI, there was some hope that the situation might change, but RAMSI has tended not to consult with civil society representatives. Without more input from civil society, there is reason to wonder if the stability that now exists will be sustainable projecting out over five or ten years or more.

Despite its exclusion in the past and continuing in the present, it has been the civil society groups—the women, the churches, the community leaders, and the Peace Monitoring Council—that have played significant roles in directing the conflict toward peace. Unfortunately, most politicians have failed to rise above political opportunism, even during the times of serious turmoil. The recent political history of the Solomon Islands has been characterized by "quick fix" solutions. What's more, RAMSI—admittedly in a sensitive and delicate position—has tended to "protect" corrupt government officials, parliamentarians, and militia leaders. While this may help RAMSI to effectively assert authority in the short term, it may have more serious long-term implications.

Civil society groups, too, have been too quick to assume that the conflict can be easily resolved and that the Solomon Islands can quickly return to "normal," in the sense of going back to how things were before the conflict started. Looking toward the future, the role of civil society groups, including the civil society network, must be strengthened to work for good governance, national unity, and a Solomon Islands that takes responsibility for its own future. Prospects for long-term stability will not improve greatly until these fundamental justice issues are confronted.

The conflict has required Solomon Islands leaders to take stock and rebuild the foundations of the nation. This requires proper and thorough understanding of the causes and dynamics of the conflict. An appropriate truth commission is essential if society is to learn from the experience and find healing. This is not a quick-fix solution. It is also essential to build appropriate democratic institutions—that is, institutions that are not carbon copies of Western systems but that reflect the cultural traditions and realities of Solomon Islands society.

Prospects

An obvious lesson that should be learned from the Solomon Islands conflict is the need to ensure that fundamental justice issues are addressed before they lead to violence. The existence of injustice has been clear for the past couple of decades, and it was wrong for civil society groups to leave these issues to the state, and wrong of the government to think that people would ultimately accept their bureaucratic bungling as dealing with the issues.

No one predicted that the Solomon Islands conflict would erupt. At the time, it was uncertain what exact factors triggered the violence, whether they were social, political, or simply criminal, but when criminal activities first emerged, they should have been dealt with decisively. Indecisive action by political leaders, and the choice of an ostensible "Melanesian way," simply exacerbated the situation. The "Melanesian way" has provided a cop-out for those (in government) who did not want to deal substantively with justice issues. In most situations, they have dealt with these issues in ways that were inconsistent with local customs and culture, and yet they still say they have followed the "Melanesian way." No one has been able to say exactly what this way is, as there is no such thing. Understanding precisely what led to the tragedy in the Solomon Islands is a prerequisite for acquiring the capacity to avoid future tragedies. Therefore, an authoritative mapping of the conflict is needed.

The police force had been neglected for many years and thus as a result was caught ill-prepared for the conflict. The lack of an effective police force gave the militants a major advantage in waging war on the population of Malaita and Guadalcanal. Given the involvement of the police force in the conflict, it is not certain that reform will be even possible with existing personnel. External assistance to strengthen the police force in the early days of the conflict might have saved many lives and could have released the pressure on the Malaitan community to form their own militant group. Unless the quality of the police force is substantially improved, the risks of a repeat of the past remain significant.

The peace process, and especially the TPA, was characterized by a lack of ownership. This was largely due to the fact that people felt there was little or no consultation with the community and therefore the process and agreement were prejudiced against the interests of the communities. Communities were only called on to implement an agreement others constructed to serve narrow interests. There was also a lack of ownership of the issues. When the "demands" were first publicly stated by the premier of Guadalcanal, the response from the national government was that these were Guadalcanal issues, notwithstanding the fact that the issues were common to all provinces. Because of this lack of ownership of the issues, Guadalcanal felt it had to turn to militancy to force resolution, and there was no effort made by the national government to engage all the provinces in a dialogue over the issues and seek longer-term outcomes that were not reactionary. Genuine reconciliation of the thorny issues that ignited the Solomons will not occur unless there is a sense of "ownership" among and within the communities of the processes and the outcomes of processes to end the conflicts.

The weak security sector was matched by very poor governance. For example, the Guadalcanal provincial government was a key body that could have helped resolve the conflict in the early stages, but the leadership lacked integrity and became instead an obstacle to peace. Prior to the coup, the Ulufa'alu government failed to provide decisive leadership. The postcoup governments have shown themselves to be complicit with the corruption that fuels conflict. Until Solomon Islands voters choose enough leaders who have integrity and give priority to national rather than personal interests, the prospects for improvement do not look good.

External assistance needs to be directed at enabling Solomon Islanders to address their issues themselves. Assistance with a truth commission will be critical. Assistance with rebuilding the police force will be essential. If civil society can continue to play an active role and grow in strength and influence, it may ultimately mean that Solomon Islands society will be able to take responsibility for its own destiny.

Recommendations

Aid donors must be very careful not to reward corrupt governments and strengthen their hands. Instead, it would be advisable not only to withhold funds from those who are likely to squander them, but also to invest in capacity building so as to make assistance more effective and less likely to disappear into the bank accounts of corrupt officials.

The high level of illiteracy had a huge bearing on the conflict. Geographic areas providing a majority of the militants were also those with the highest illiteracy rates in the country. Illiteracy leaves communities vulnerable to opportunistic individuals. Literacy is also important to ensure that the electorate is better informed and can return better leaders to positions of responsibility in parliament and the provincial assemblies. Basic literacy taught in vernacular must become a core element of the primary education system.

The truth and reconciliation commission provides the most significant opportunity for Solomon Islands society to deal constructively with the past. This is essential to enable the story of the conflict to be told so that society can learn from the experience. National unity, which is fundamental to a secure future, has been torn. Deliberate attention must be given to the question of nationhood, and in what form. However, constitutional changes should not be attempted until the conflict has been satisfactorily dealt with by a truth commission.

Major economic reform is a prerequisite for national survival. Major political reform is also overdue. There is a need to create a more direct accountability relationship between the electorate and the executive government and parliament. Weak government has been a hallmark of this fragile democracy since independence. Without a responsible and relevant parliament, the Solomon Islands will continue to descend into failure and corruption.

Australia has, in the past, provided training to government officials to try to improve governance in the Solomon Islands, but this has generally been training for high-ranking officials. It may be more advisable to provide training to officials at regional or even local levels, since a centralized governmental system is essentially inappropriate in the Solomon Islands context and irrelevant at the village level. It would be more effective to focus on building capacity at the middle level of government and to link those organs to the existing traditional system prevalent in Melanesian society.

The engagement of civil society groups, especially the churches, provides the best opportunity for reform and an educated electorate. The 2006 general elections will be the next opportunity for major change that may put the country on a better footing for the future.

Resources

Published Documents

Central Bank of Solomon Islands. *Central of Solomon Islands Annual Report 2001.* Honiara: Central Bank of Solomon Islands, 2002.

Dinnen, S. "Political Chronicles: Winners and Losers—Politics and Disorder in the Solomon Islands, 2000–2002." *Journal of Pacific History* 37, no. 3 (2002).

Liloqula, Ruth, and Alice Arhe'eta Pollard. "Understanding Conflict in Solomon Islands as a Practical Means to Peacemaking: Men, Women, and the Church—The Women for Peace Analysis and Approach." Presented at the Symposium on Conflict and Peacemaking in the Pacific: Social and Gender Issues, Canberra, October 2001.

Short, F. Letter to the Editor. *Pacific Islands Report,* July 30, 2002.

Solomon Islands Government. *Solomon Islands Human Development Report.* Windsor, Queensland 4030. Mark Otter, 2002.

———. *Report on 1999 Population and Housing Census.* Honiara: Statistics Office, 2000.

World Bank Country Profile. Solomon Islands Data Profile. World Development Indicators Database. April 2002.

Contacts

Chairman, National Peace Monitoring Council, Honiara

Sinclair Dinnen, Governance in Melanesia Project, Australian National University, Canberra

Johnson Honimae, General Manager, Solomon Islands Broadcasting Association, Honiara

Ruth Liloqula, Alice Arhe'eta Pollard, Women for Peace, Honiara

John Roughan, Solomon Islands Development Trust, Honiara

Matthew Waletofea, Judith Fangalasu'u, Joseph Foukona, Solomon Islands Christian Association Peace Office, Honiara

Ashley Wickham, Solomon Islands Office of the UN High Commissioner for Human Rights, Honiara

---

Bob Pollard is a Solomon Islander/New Zealander. He attended secondary school and university in Canterbury, New Zealand, and studied theology for three years in Melbourne, Australia. Apart from his studies, he has lived his entire life in the Solomon Islands. His career has focused on education, including teaching, management, and consultancies. During the conflict period in the Solomon Islands, he was actively engaged with the churches and the burgeoning civil society movement.

Matthew Wale is a Solomon Islander and strong advocate for civil rights. During the conflict he worked with the Solomon Islands Christian Association, advocating on human rights issues, mediating between the warring militias, and engaging with the

government and the police on issues of good governance. He has been engaged in the proposal to establish a truth and reconciliation commission for the Solomon Islands, as well as an independent human rights commission.

Notes

1. All six main islands are greater than 1,000 square kilometers in area. Figures taken from www.db.idpproject.org (Global IDP Project).

2. There are currently sixty-eight living indigenous language groups in the country, some with additional dialects. The consequence of this diversity is that languages are spoken by very small groups of people, often inhabiting very limited areas. Language and place of origin remain very important factors in Solomon society—the normal first question asked about a given person is their island origin, or if known, the language group/geographical locale within that island.

3. Much of this migration has been from central and northern Malaita to Honiara and its environs, especially to the coastal areas to the east and west of the capital. This has resulted over the years in the growth of considerable peri-urban settlements, largely on customary land of the northern coast of Guadalcanal.

4. For instance, land in Guadalcanal is matrilineally inherited, while in Malaita it is inherited through the male (patrilineal). Intermarriage between Malaitan men and Guadalcanal women sometimes resulted in frictions due to the extent of the man's dominance in his wife's land affairs.

5. Federal government has long been seen as a remedy for many issues related to the problems of national unity in the Solomons. Federalism has been seen to ensure greater autonomy and governmental recognition of traditional authority, as well as providing a basis for greater capture by local communities of economic benefits from resource extraction.

6. Solomon Islands Plantations Limited (SIPL) was a joint venture between the Solomons government and Commonwealth Development Corporation. It involved an estate of 6,000 hectares of oil palms planted on north Guadalcanal land leased from customary owners. At its height, SIPL was the country's largest employer, with up to 2,000 direct employees.

7. As early as the 1950s, Guadalcanal community leaders were expressing concerns about the adverse impacts on their people of the influx of migrants to Honiara and environs.

8. The shootout ensued from the gang's raid of a police post at Yandina in the Russell Islands group of the Solomons. The officers there were overpowered and the post's firearms seized. Police forces pursued the gang and a firefight occurred on Bungana Island, some thirty kilometers north of Guadalcanal.

9. The Police Field Force division was the paramilitary wing of the Royal Solomon Islands Police. It was formed during the Bougainville conflict, as a response to concerns about transborder violence by PNG military forces in particular.

10. The GRA continued to be led by Harold Keke, while the leadership of the IFM consisted of a different set of individuals, George Grey, Andrew Te'e, and Selwyn Saki amongst them.

11. Harold Keke and his GRA group were not signatories to the TPA. His continued apparent belligerence and possession of arms was used as justification for non-disarmament by Guadalcanal and Malaitan militias alike.

12. The Ulufa'alu government did not appoint any one person in the cabinet to be responsible for attending to the violence. The police arrested key Guadalcanal militants in early 1999 but the courts gave them bail. They absconded and did not keep the bail conditions.

13. Over public radio on the payment of the first SI$100,000, Sam Alasia, special adviser to Prime Minister Sogovare, stated that this was done consistent with Melanesian custom.

14. Taiwan has insisted that this is a commercial loan; however, the initial conditions of the loan have not been met and still the loan was drawn down. The fact that it was a loan that would bind future generations of Solomon Islanders from all provinces has been a contentious issue further undermining national unity.

15. Attempts at governance structures beyond the clan include the Vaukolu of Gela in the late 1880s, assisted by John Plant of the Melanesian Mission, and the Ma'asina Ruru movement instigated on Malaita in the 1950s.

16. For a list of key national NGOs see the website http://makcell.logic11.com.

17. For a list of key international NGOs see the website http://makcell.logic11.com.

18. Ruth Liloqula and Alice Aruheeta Pollard, "Understanding Conflict in Solomon Islands as a Practical Means to Peacemaking: Men, Women, and the Church—The Women for Peace Analysis and Approach," presentation at the Symposium on Conflict and Peacemaking in the Pacific: Social and Gender Issues, Canberra, October 2001, p. 16.

19. The conference was generously funded by the New Zealand government.

20. A small number of civil society representatives did attend as observers only.

21. A draft charter was drawn up to help people understand what the new group calling itself the CSN was.

22. See the civil society submission to the TPA review.

23. The general elections resulted in two-thirds of sitting members losing their seats.

PART 3

Directory

Introduction to the Directory

The directory that follows contains profiles and contact information for about 350 organizations working in the fields of conflict prevention and peacebuilding across Asia Pacific. The prime focus is on key organizations—mainly nongovernmental—that are based and active in these regions. It also includes a selection of organizations from North America and Europe that are involved in relevant activities in Asia Pacific. Finally, relevant regional and intergovernmental organizations like the ASEAN and UN are included.

Because organizations working in the field of development cooperation, humanitarian aid, or human rights have increasingly incorporated the goals of conflict prevention and peacebuilding into their prime mandate, we have also opted to include organizations that, at first sight, might not be seen as conflict prevention organizations.

The organizations are listed by country of location. For larger international NGO networks, we included the profile of the headquarter's office, including the contact details of regional offices. However, there are a few exceptions to this selection criterion. We included a small number of local offices in certain countries where the concerned NGO has very specific programs that differ from those of the headquarters.

The shaded box that appears at the upper right of each profile presents the organization's main activities in conflict prevention and peacebuilding.

The countries/regions in which the organization's activities are focused are presented above the organization's name.

As far as possible, the given number of staff and budget relates to the organization's specific activities in the field of conflict prevention and peacebuilding.

Additional information on some organizations may be found in the survey chapters in Part 2 of this book. Some of this information has been omitted here due to space limitations.

East Timor, Indonesia, South Pacific

Action in Solidarity
with Asia and the Pacific

EDUCATION
ACTION
ADVOCACY

Action in Solidarity with Asia and the Pacific (ASAP) is a network of activists in Australia building solidarity with and support for movements for social justice, genuine democratization, and self-determination around the Asia Pacific region. ASIET was founded in 1991 as Action in Solidarity with Indonesia and East Timor (ASIET) to reverse Australia's neo-liberal and military interventionist foreign policy in the Asia-Pacific region. Work is particularly focused on areas directly targeted by such policy, including Indonesia, East Timor, and the South Pacific. Their goal is to achieve this by promoting and actively building people-to-people solidarity in Australia and to overcome the struggles for democracy by promoting self-determination and economic justice in Asia Pacific.

c/o 23 Abercrombie St.
Chippendale NSW
PO Box 458 Broadway
NSW 2007
Australia

Tel: +61 (2) 9690 1240
Fax: + 61 (2) 9690 1381
asap@asia-pacific-action.org
www.asia-pacific-action.org

Contact: Max Lane, Chairperson
Budget: < $25,000
Number of staff: 4
Publications: Aceh: Indonesia's Dirty War (July 2003)

Asia Pacific

Australian Agency
for International Development

ACTION
ADVOCACY

The Australian Agency for International Development (AusAID) has become one of the leading donors in the Asia Pacific region. Its program strongly focuses toward assisting countries particularly in the areas of governance, service delivery, peacebuilding, and in the promotion of regional stability. In June 2002, AusAID's Peace, Conflict and Development Policy was formulated with the aim to improve the aid program's ability to respond to threats to peace and stability. There will be greater emphasis on conflict prevention and peacebuilding, along side its more traditional missions of humanitarian relief and reconstruction.

AusAID has also taken a lead role in post-conflict recovery programs in the region (e.g., Bourgainville, Solomon Islands). Australia supports peace and reconciliation processes; the demobilization and reintegration of ex-combatants; demining; and reconstruction and the revival of the economy.

62 Northbourne Avenue
GPO Box 887
Canberra ACT 2601
Australia

Tel: +61 (2) 6206 4000
Fax: +61 (2) 6206 4880
infoausaid@ausaid.gov.au
www.ausaid.gov.au

Contact: Bruce Davis, Director General
Publications: contact books@ausaid.gov.au for copies of publications

Asia-Pacific

Australian Centre
for Peace and Conflict Studies

RESEARCH
EDUCATION

The Australian Centre for Peace and Conflict Studies (ACPACS) is established as a research centre located within the Faculty of Social and Behavioural Sciences at the University of Queensland. ACPACS is a key Australian centre with a nationally and internationally recognized focus on research and professional practice in peacekeeping, peacebuilding, and economic, social, and political development.

The functions of the Australian Centre for Peace and Conflict Studies are:

1. To conduct research into the causes of international conflict, international security, modes of conflict resolution, and emerging peacebuilding approaches, with special reference to the Asia-Pacific region. Research includes peacebuilding in East Timor, the transition from confrontation to cooperation on the Korean peninsul, and Ethics and Foreign Policy;

2. To coordinate world class undergraduate and postgraduate programs to equip students with the knowledge and practical skills in mediation, conflict resolution, and peacekeeping and peacebuilding in the contemporary global context;

3. To provide advanced level short courses and training for government and non-governmental organizations engaged in peacekeeping, peacebuilding, development activities, humanitarian intervention, and work in conflict contexts; and

To provide expert advice to public and private sector organizations on issues concerned with conflict and its resolution drawing on interdisciplinary expertise in the social, political, economic, legal, ethnic, and cultural context of conflict in national and international arenas.

School of Political Science
  and International Studies
General Purpose North III
  Building (39A)
University of Queensland
Brisbane, QLD 4072
Australia

Contact: Professor Kevin Clements

Publications: Newsletter; *The Politics of Nuclear Non-Proliferation,* 2002; *Conceptualizing the West in International Relations,* 2002

Tel: +61 (7) 3365 3043
Fax: +61 (7) 3365 1388
k.clements@uq.edu.au
www.polsis.uq.edu.au/acpacs/

Global

Caritas Australia

EDUCATION
ACTION
ADVOCACY

Caritas Australia is a Catholic aid agency that works through partnerships with local organizations to bring relief and aid to people in emergency situations caused by natural disasters or conflict. In addition, the organization raises funds for its aid projects and provides educational resources about developmental issues. Many of the projects in the Asia-Pacific region that are supported by Caritas Australia are related to peacebuilding. In Bougainville, Caritas Australia initiated the Bougainville Rehabilitation Program, which aims to help the Bougainville community overcome the trauma of ten years of conflict, focusing on education, health, women, young men, peace and reconciliation, and trauma counselling.

19 MacKenzie Street
North Sydney
NSW 2060
Australia

Tel: +61 (2) 9956 5799
Fax: +61 (2) 9956 5782
annak@caritas.org.au
www.caritas.org.au

Contact: Anna Kiousis

Publications: Ozspirit, weekly online magazine; *Reconciliation: Stories of the Heart, Sounds of the Rock CD,* a joint initiative of Caritas Australia, Catholic Mission and ANTaR; and several videos and workbooks

Global

Centre for Peace and Conflict Studies

RESEARCH
EDUCATION

Established within the University of Sydney in 1988, Centre for Peace and Conflict Studies (CPACS) promotes interdisciplinary research and teaching on the causes of conflict and the conditions that affect conflict resolution and peace. The centre aims to facilitate dialogue among individuals, groups, or communities who are concerned with conditions of positive peace, whether in interpersonal relationships, community relations, within organizations, or internationally. CPACS also runs a conflict resolution desk, which provides customized workshop and consultancy and mediation services.

Mackie Building K01
University of Sydney
NSW 2006
Australia

Tel: +61 (2) 9351 7686
Fax: +61 (2) 9660 0862
cpacs@social.usyd.edu.au
www.arts.usyd.edu.au/cpacs

Contact: Emeritus Professor Stuart Rees, Director

Budget: $25,000–$100,000

Number of staff: 5

Publications: PeaceWrites, biannual newsletter; *Passion for Peace,* 2003; *Peace-building: The Challenge for East Timor,* 2000

Global

Centre for Peace Studies

RESEARCH
EDUCATION

The Centre for Peace Studies is one of the few research centres in the world where students can obtain a Ph.D. in Peace and Community Development Studies. The centre also offers undergraduate and postgraduate units in Peace and Community Development Studies. The centre is involved in ongoing research projects on issues pertaining to recovery from armed conflict in East Timor and Bougainville.

University of New England
Armidale
NSW 2351
Australia

Tel: +61 (2) 6773 5095
Fax: +61 (2) 6773 3350
rspence1@metz.une.edu.au
www.une.edu.au/arts

Contact: Dr Rebecca Spence

Budget: $25,000–$100,000

Number of staff: 4

Publications: Building Peace through Volunteering: Experiences of Working in Post-conflict Situations, 2003; *Building Safer Sustainable Communities: The Challenge of Working in Post-conflict Recovery Situations,* 2003; *Building the Road as We Walk It: Peacebuilding as Nonviolent Revolutionary Praxis,* 2002; *Post-conflict Peacebuilding: Who Determines the Peace?* 2001; *Building Peace in Bougainville,* 1999.

Asia-Pacific

Conflict Management Research Group

RESEARCH
EDUCATION

CMRG was established in 1993 with the objective of promoting the study and management of conflict, in particular for the benefit of the diverse cultural groups in contemporary Australia. Research and consultancy projects of the group have focused on the education and training of mediators in a wide range of court-based and community settings and on researching a wide range of issues including domestic violence; conflict and bullying in schools; children's rights and legal processes; and restorative justice. The CMRG is a partner in the project "Culture of Peace News Network" together with UNESCO and the International Conflict Resolution Centre at Melbourne University. The CMRG is also the founder and administrative center of the Asia-Pacific Mediation Forum (www.unisa.edu.au/cmrg/apmf) that is sponsored by the World Mediation Forum (www.mediate.com/world).

University of South Australia
St Bernards Road
Magill
South Australia 5072
Australia

Tel: +61 (8) 8302 4375/8
Fax: +61 (8) 8302 4377
dale.bagshaw@unisa.edu.au
www.unisa.edu.au/cmrg/

Contact: Dale Bagshaw, Director

Number of staff: 15

Asia-Pacific

Conflict Resolution Network

RESEARCH
EDUCATION
ACTION
ADVOCACY

The Conflict Resolution Network is a non-profit NGO founded in 1973 as the Peace and Conflict Resolution Program of the United Nations Association of Australia. The Conflict Resolution Network aims at being a resource and information center to all who wish to advocate, research, learn, teach, and implement the theory and practice of Conflict Resolution. It does this through a national and international network and concerns itself with the resolution of all conflicts, from the global and international to the personal. In addition, its website contains much training material which can be downloaded and disseminated.

PO Box 1016.
Chatswood
Sydney
NSW 2057
Australia

Tel: +61 (2) 9419 9500
Fax: +61 (2) 9413 1148
crn@crnhq.org
www.crnhq.org

Contact: Dr Stella Cornelius, Director
Number of staff: 4
Budget: $25,000 to $100,000
Publications: Everyone Can Win; The Gentle Revolution; Conflict Resolution Trainers' Manual, 12 Skills

China and Taiwan

Contemporary China Centre

The Contemporary China Centre was established in 1970 as a research facility concerned with scholarly social-science analysis of post-1949 China and Taiwan. The Centre is part of the Division of Society and Environment of the Research School of Pacific and Asian Studies. The Centre's main research relates to the modern political and legal arenas and to the social–anthropological ramifications of political and economic change in the People's Republic of China, Taiwan, and Hong Kong. As part of its program, the Centre publishes *The China Journal,* a periodical issued twice a year.

Research School of Pacific
and Asian Studies
Australian National University
Canberra ACT 0200
Australia

Tel: +61 (2) 6125 4150
Fax: +61 (2) 6257 3642
ccc@coombs.anu.edu.au
http://rspas.anu.edu.au/ccc/

Contact: Mrs. Heli Brecht, Centre Administrator

Number of staff: 20

Publications: The China Journal. The centre also produces a commemorative series of lecture papers, the *George Ernest Morrison Lectures in Ethnology,* as well as a number of monographs jointly with M. E. Sharpe, New York, as part of its *Contemporary China Papers* book series.

Asia-Pacific

International Conflict Resolution Center

RESEARCH
EDUCATION

The International Conflict Resolution Center (ICRC) aims to research, teach, and disseminate information about the theory and practice of non-violent conflict resolution. Its interdisciplinary research focuses on the psychology of reconciliation and cultural aspects of conflict resolution strategies. The Center also provides short courses and distant education courses in mediation, research supervision for Masters and Doctoral students, and mediation consultancy services in dispute resolution. The ICRC is the Research Development and Training Site for UNESCO's Culture of Peace Media and News Network.

Psychology Department
University of Melbourne
Victoria 3010
Australia

Tel: +61 (3) 8344 7035
Fax: +61 (3) 9347 6618
icrc@psych.unimelb.edu.au
www.psych.unimelb.edu.au/icrc

Contact: Dr Di Bretherton, Director

Number of staff: 12

Budget: $1,00,000–$500,000

Publications: ICRC Newsletter (online); *The Qualities of Peacemakers,* 2001; *Conflict, Culture and Language,* 2001; and several others

Asia

Monash Asia Institute

RESEARCH
EDUCATION

The Monash Asia Institute (MAI) was established by the Monash University, a research center on Asia. Its role is to serve as an umbrella organization for six research centers on Asia within the university, including the National Centre of South Asian Studies. The institute organizes conferences, dialogues, and policy-oriented research on Asian subjects dealing with a wide range of critical regional issues such as the nuclear confrontation in South Asia and relations between North and South Korea. The teaching program is providing postgraduate courses in Asian Studies and Development Studies. An Asian Studies research library is available for students and other researchers.

Building II
Monash University
Victoria 3800
Australia

Tel: +61 (3) 9905 2124
Fax: +61 (3) 9905 5370
monash.asia.institute@adm.monash.edu.au
www.arts.monash.edu.au/mai

Contact: Marika Vicziany, Director

Publications: The MAI is one of the largest specialist publishers on Asia in Australia: see the MAI website for an on-line catalogue and information about the most recent publications.

Global

Oxfam Community Aid Abroad

Oxfam Community Aid Abroad works across 31 countries in Asia Pacific, Africa, Central America, and Indigenous Australia, and does this in partnership with local communities to overcome poverty and injustice. Oxfam Community Aid Abroad's work includes long-term development projects, responding to emergencies, and campaigning for a more just world. Themes that are addressed are: human rights, the environment, sustainable agriculture, gender and development, HIV/AIDS, community education, and indigenous peoples. For instance in East Timor, Oxfam Community Aid Abroad supported national NGOs to restart their activities after the referendum, and provided support of advocacy initiatives on human rights (in particular gender and active participation of the East Timorese in the reconstruction process).

156 George Street
Fitzroy, Melbourne
Victoria
Australia 3065

Contact: Andrew Hewett

Tel: +61 (3) 9289 9444
Fax: +61 (3) 9419 5318
enquire@caa.org.au
www.oxfam.org.au

Asia-Pacific

Research School of Pacific and Asian Studies

The Research School of Asia-Pacific Studies (RSPAS) is a large research center at the Australian National University in Canberra. RSPAS is home to a number of departments, programs, and projects such as the Contemporary China Center; the Center for the Contemporary Pacific, and the State Society and Governance in Melanesia Project. In 2001 the Center for Conflict and Post-Conflict Studies, Asia-Pacific (CCPCSAP) was established. The Center builds on existing research interests within RSPAS on Indonesia (particularly in Aceh and Papua), East Timor, the Philippines (particularly Muslim Mindanao), Burma/Myanmar, Papua New Guinea (especially Bougainville), Fiji, and the Solomon Islands.

Australian National University
Canberra
ACT 0200
Australia

Tel: +61 (2) 6125 2183
Fax: +61 (2) 6157 1893
director.rspas@anu.edu.au
http://rspas.anu.edu au/
www.ccpcsap.org/

Contact: Professor James J. Fox, Director or Ron May, Head of Conflict and Post Conflict Studies Asia Pacific

Number of staff: 120 academic staff

Publications: RSPAS Print News Announcements, a monthly overview of new publications by the RSPAS; *Political Crises in North East Asia: An Anatomy of the Taiwan and Korean Crises,* 2001; *The Day the World Changed? Terrorism and World Order,* 2001

Pacific

State, Society and
Governance in Melanesia Project

RESEARCH
EDUCATION

State, Society and Governance in Melanesia Project (SSGMP) started in 1996 to encourage scholarship on governance and state-society relations and to generate dialogue throughout Melanesia and the Pacific Islands on these issues. The Project's key objective is to increase awareness and understanding of the problems of governance and the relationships between society and state in Melanesian countries. The primary mechanisms for achieving this objective are research, publication, conferences, workshops; collaboration with institutions and scholars within the region; practical engagement as advisers and consultants in conflict management and other programs, and increased interface between the academic and policy communities.

Research School of Pacific
  and Asian Studies
Australian National University
Canberra ACT 0200
Australia

Tel: +61 (2) 6125 8394
Fax: +61 (2) 6125 5525
ssgm@anu.edu.au
http://rspas.anu.edu.au/melanesia

Contact: Jeanette Regan, SSGM Project Administrator

Number of staff: 8

Publications: Disorderly Democracy: Political Turbulence and Institutional Reform in Papua New Guinea, 2003; *Perspectives on Conflict and Post Conflict,* 2003; and many others

Global

International Cooperation
for Development and Solidarity

ACTION
ADVOCACY

The Vatican II Council in 1964 set up this co-ordination body for Catholic aid agencies; the current name was recognized in 1981. The International Cooperation for Development and Solidarity (CIDSE) network now has 14 members from developed countries worldwide. The CIDSE Peace and Conflict Coalition (PCC) seeks to engage in effective Northern advocacy on peace-related issues by linking activities with partners. Currently its main focus is on natural resources fuelling conflict throughout the world. The Coalition studies each case individually which links Northern lobbying with concrete actions to support Southern advocacy. In parallel the PCC is part of an international coalition of more than 75 NGOs calling on oil, gas, and mining companies to publish payments that they make to national governments.

Rue Stévin 16
B-1000
Brussels
Belgium

Tel: +32 (2) 230 7722
Fax: +32 (2) 230 7082
postmaster@cidse.org
www.cidse.org

Contact: Christiane Overkamp, Secretary General

Number of staff: 11 secretariat staff

Publications: A number of papers available online

Balkans, Africa, Asia

International Crisis Group

RESEARCH
ADVOCACY

The work of the International Crisis Group (ICG) is grounded in field re-search. Teams of political analysts, based on the ground in countries at risk of conflict, gather information from a wide range of sources, assess local condi-tions, and produce regular analytical reports containing practical recommenda-tions targeted at key international decision-takers. ICG's reports are distributed widely to officials in foreign ministries and international organizations and made generally available at the same time via the organization's website. ICG works closely with governments and those who influence them, including the media, to highlight its crisis analysis and to generate support for its policy pre-scriptions. In Asia, ICG is present in Burma, Cambodia, Indonesia, and in Cen-tral Asia.

149 Avenue Louise, level 24
1050 Brussels
Belgium

Tel: +32 (2) 502 9038
Fax: +32 (2) 502 5038
icgbrussels@crisisweb.org
www.crisisweb.org

Contact: Gareth Evans, President and Chief Executive
Number of staff: 58
Budget: > $1,000,000
Publications: Indonesia: Ending Repression in Irian Jaya, 2001; *Burma/Myanmar: How Strong is the Military Regime?* 2000; *Cambodia: The Elusive Peace Dividend,* 2000

Global

Médecins Sans Frontières

EDUCATION
ACTION
ADVOCACY

Médecins Sans Frontières (MSF) is an international humanitarian aid organiza-tion that provides emergency medical assistance to populations in danger in more than 80 countries. In carrying out humanitarian assistance, MSF is also mandated to raise awareness of crisis situations. MSF acts as a witness and will speak out, either in private or in public, about the plight of populations in dan-ger for whom it works. MSF has headquarters for field operations in France, Switzerland, Luxembourg, Spain, the Netherlands, and Belgium. A further 14 sections, from Sweden to Australia, support operations in the form of represen-tation, recruitment of field volunteers, fundraising, and information etc.

39, Rue de la Tourelle
1040 Brussels
Belgium

Tel: +32 (2) 280 1881
Fax: +32 (2) 280 0173
office-intnl@brussels.msf.org
www.msf.org

Publications: MSF International Activity Report; MSF Reference books

South and Southeast Asia

Action Asia

**EDUCATION
ACTION
ADVOCACY**

Action Asia was established in 2000 as a network of individuals and organizations working toward conflict transformation in the Asian region. It is linked to Action International, a network based in South Africa. Through the sharing of experiences at the grassroots level of conflict transformation, the network hopes to create a pool of skills and knowledge. One of its current programs, the Southeast Asia Conflict Transformation training program, organizes visits of Burmese peacebuilders to Cambodia for peacebuilding training. The Action Asia network comprises core members from Afghanistan, Bangladesh, Sri Lanka, Burma, Cambodia, and the Philippines.

PO Box 2552
Phnom Penh
Cambodia

Tel: +855 (12) 764 097
Fax: +855 (23) 885 414
ActionAsia@online.com.kh

Contact: Emma Leslie, Secretariat
Number of staff: Volunteers only
Budget: < $60,000
Publications: Action Asia, newsletter;
contributor to *Transforming Conflict,* Action
International

Cambodia

Alliance for Conflict Transformation

**RESEARCH
EDUCATION
ADVOCACY**

The Alliance for Conflict Transformation (ACT) was formed in 1998 and formalized in 2002 by a group of long-time peacebuilding practitioners. It aims to develop and strengthen social mechanisms for peace in Cambodia. ACT conducts conflict resolution and peacebuilding trainings for civil society and government organizations. Other activities are research, consultation, and network building. Parts of ACT's activities have developed from the Cambodia Peace Building Study Group of the Working Group for Weapons Reduction.

#34, St. 480, Phsa Deum Thkov
Chamkarmon, PO Box 2552
Box CCC 402, Phnom Penh
Cambodia

Tel/fax: +855 (23) 217 830
ACT@online.com.kh
www.act-cambodia.org

Contact: Soth Plai Ngarm, Executive
Coordinator
Budget: $25,000–$100,000
Number of staff: 10
Publications: Newsletter

Cambodia

Cambodian Defenders Project

EDUCATION
ADVOCACY

Since its establishment in 1995, the main aim of the Cambodian Defenders Project (CDP) has been to provide free legal defense for the poor and vulnerable. The organization has also become involved in awareness raising and advocacy. CDP's Legal Awareness Program organizes frequent seminars on law, criminal investigation techniques, trial techniques, and specific issues such as domestic violence. In 1997, it established the Women's Resource Center to meet the specific needs of victims of domestic violence and to raise awareness about the issue of trafficking women.

12, Street 282
Sankat Boeng Keng Kang 1
Phnom Penh
Cambodia

Contact: Mr. Vuth Heng, Administrator
Number of staff: 57

Tel: +855 (23) 720 032/901 199
Fax: +855 (23) 720 031
cdp@cdpcambodia.org
www.cdpcambodia.org

Cambodia

Cambodia Human Rights and Development Association

RESEARCH
EDUCATION
ACTION
ADVOCACY

The Cambodian Human Rights and Development Association (ADHOC) is the largest human rights organization in Cambodia. It was founded in 1992 by a group of former political prisoners. With 18 regional offices spread throughout Cambodia, the organization is active in training, advocacy, and monitoring of human rights. ADHOC holds human rights workshops in rural communities and educates government officials and university students. It places special emphasis on women's rights. ADHOC actively participates in various national, regional, and international human rights seminars and forums. It is a part of the Cambodian Human Rights Action Committee, a coalition of human rights organizations that lobbies with the Cambodian government and bilateral and multilateral donors.

1, Street 158
Oukghna Troeung
PO Box 1024
Beng Raing, Daun Penh
Phnom Penh, Cambodia

Tel: +855 (23) 218 653
Fax: +855 (23) 217 229
adhoc@bigpond.com.kh
www.bigpond.com.kh/users/adhoc

Contact: Thun Saray, President
Number of staff: 78
Budget: $500,000–$1,000,000 (2000)
Publications: Neak Chea Bulletin, fortnightly magazine in Khmer; *Human Rights Situation in Cambodia,* 2001; *Rule of Law and Human Rights,* paper for the NGO statement for the 2000 Consultative Group meeting in Paris, 2000; *Three Freedoms,* an update on the freedom of expression, association and assembly, 1999.

Cambodia

Cambodian Institute
for Cooperation and Peace

RESEARCH
EDUCATION
ADVOCACY

The Cambodian Institute for Cooperation and Peace (CICP) is an independent research institute founded in 1994. The institute promotes human rights, the advancement of democracy within civil society, and peace and cooperation within Cambodia as well as between Cambodia and other regional and international institutions. To this end, the CICP conducts research and organizes meetings and training programs.

Room 1G, Government Palace
Sisowath Quay, Wat Phnom
PO Box 1007
Phnom Penh 12202
Cambodia

Tel: +855 (23) 722 759
Fax: +855 (23) 362 520, 722 759
cipc@camnet.com.kh
www.cipc.org.kh

Contact: Kao Kim Hourn, Executive Director

Number of staff: 14

Budget: $100,000–$500,000 (1998)

Publications: Civil Society, newsletter; The Cambodian Journal of International Affairs, journal; *ASEAN A-Z: A Lexicon of ASEAN-Related Terminology,* 2001; *The Role of Think Tanks in Cambodia: Achievements, Challenges and Prospects,* 2001

Cambodia

Cambodian Institute of Human Rights

RESEARCH
EDUCATION
ADVOCACY

The Cambodian Institute of Human Rights (CIHR) is involved in the education, training, documentation, and research of human rights. The CIHR believes that basic human rights and democratic values must form the basis of a successful peace process in Cambodia. The Institute teaches human rights education to primary school teachers and good governance practices to public servants. The CIHR was also a founding member of the Coalition for Free and Fair Elections (COFFEL), an umbrella organization of over 100 NGOs that was formed in 1996 to promote free and fair elections. It has published and distributed many documents about human rights, the Cambodian constitution, and other issues.

30 Street 57
PO Box 550
Sangk at Boeung Keng Kang 1
Khan Chamcar Morn
Phnom Penh, Cambodia

Tel: +855 (23) 210 596
Fax: +855 (23) 362 739
CIHR@camnet.com.kh
www.ned.org/grantees/cihr/sands.html

Contact: Mr. Kassie Neou, Executive Director

Number of staff: 74

Budget: $50,000–$100,000 (1998)

Cambodia

Cambodian League for the Promotion and Defense of Human Rights

ACTION
ADVOCACY

The aim of the Cambodian League for the Promotion and Defense of Human Rights (LICADHO) is to strengthen Cambodian civil society through the promotion and protection of human rights and the rule of law. The organization aims to influence and educate the government and institutions in Cambodia to respect human rights and the rule of law. LICADHO's programs include the promotion and protection of women's rights, children's rights, and the rights of other vulnerable groups within Cambodian society. The League monitors human rights by collecting and publishing information on human rights violations and works together with regional and international organizations such as Forum Asia and Amnesty International.

103 Street 97
PO Box 499
Phnom Penh
Cambodia

Contact: Kek Galabru, Director
Number of staff: 128
Budget: $500,000–$1,000,000

Tel: +855 (23) 360 965
Fax: +855 (23) 360 965/217 626
licadho@camnet.com.kh
licadho@everyday.or.kh

Cambodia

ACTION
ADVOCACY

Cambodian Women's Crisis Center

The Cambodian Women's Crisis Center (CWCC), a non-profit organization, was established in March 1997. It was created by a group of women who perceived that levels of violence against women and children were severe and that assistance services were lacking. CWCC's vision is to eliminate violence against women, such as trafficking, rape, and domestic violence, in order to achieve peace, development, and happiness for all. CWCC has three regional offices and shelters. The central office is based in Phnom Penh and there are regional offices in Banteay Meanchey and Siem Reap provinces. CWCC encourages women who have been victims of gender-based abuse and their children to help themselves through providing crisis intervention services. CWCC also aims to reduce violence against women through training, media campaigns, community organizing, and legal advocacy.

#42F, Street 288
Sangkat Psar Deum Thkaov
Khan Chamkarmon
PO Box 2421
Phnom Penh, Cambodia

Tel/Fax: +855 (23) 982 158

Banteay Mean Chey Office:
Palelay, O Chrov, Banteay Mean Cheay

Tel/Fax: +855 (63) 963 276
cwccct@forum.org.kh

Cambodia

Cambodian Women's Development Association

ADVOCACY

The Cambodian Women's Development Association (CDWA) is committed to the advancement of women's social and economic rights. The NGO aims to empower women in both their productive and reproductive capacities by providing education and access to resources. CDWA is involved in advocacy and lobbying for women to participate in commune council elections and to be represented in commune administration. In these ways, CDWA seeks to address the socioeconomic and psychological problems resulting from Cambodia's two decades of civil war while enhancing the contributions of women to the process of national development.

18 Street 242
Sangkat Beung Prolit
Khan 7 Makara
PO Box 2334
Phnom Penh 3, Cambodia

Tel: +855 (23) 210 449
Fax: +855 (15) 917 679
cwda@bigpond.com.kh
www.bigpond.com.kh/users/cwda/

Contact: Ms. Kien Serey Phal, Director
Number of staff: 29
Budget: $100,000–$500,000 (1998)

Cambodia

| RESEARCH |
| EDUCATION |
| ACTION |

Centre for Peace and Development

The Centre for Peace and Development (CPD—formerly the Cambodian Centre for Conflict Resolution) was established by the Cambodia Development Resource Institute (CDRI) in 1996 to support the management, transformation, and resolution of conflict by peaceful means.

The CDP's activities have been in four areas.

Public policy dialogue: In preparation for the commune elections in February 2002, the CPD organized monthly conflict prevention roundtable meetings, bringing together representatives from political parties, NGOs, media, and government. In 1999, CPR undertook a fact-finding mission to the former Khmer Rouge areas in the Northwest of Cambodia to assess reintegration and reconciliation. The Centre has also been involved in discussions concerning the Khmer Rouge Tribunal, and has helped formulate a Land Policy Framework to assist the peaceful resolution of conflicts related to land and food security.

Research: The CPD conducts research into the causes of conflict in Cambodia. One of the Centre's research projects focused on the nature and causes of conflict during the 1998 election.

Training: Training is the Centre's main priority. The organization has developed a manual for conflict management trainers and has focused on training NGO staff and government officials to work together.

Networking: The Centre's fourth focus is on developing and maintaining links and networks of support within Cambodia as well as on a regional level. CPD staff has been involved in a number of conferences and seminars on conflict resolution.

c/o Cambodia Development
    Resource Institute
56 Street 315
Tuol Kork
PO Box 622
Phnom Penh, Cambodia

Tel: +855 (23) 880 734/883
    603/368 053/367 115
Fax: +855 (23) 366 094
cdri@camnet.com.kh or
    pubs@cdri.forum.org.kh
www.cdri.org.kh

Contact: Ok Serei Sopheak, Coordinator

Number of staff: 5

Publications: Cambodia Development Review, quarterly newsletter of the CRDI; Monthly Flash Report on Cambodian Economy; *The Buddha as Peacemakers,* 2000; *Mindful Mediation: Handbook for Buddhist Peace Makers,* 1998 (in Khmer); *An Investigation of Conflict Management in Cambodian Villages; Nature and Causes of Conflict Escalation in the 1998 National Election; Technical Assistance and Capacity Development in an Aid-dependent Economy; The Experience of Cambodia*

Cambodia

Center for Social Development

RESEARCH
EDUCATION

The Center for Social Development (CSD) was founded as a local NGO in 1995. The organization strives to further develop transparency and good governance in Cambodian society. To this end, the Center organizes forums on various issues of national and social concern. In 1998 CSD conducted Cambodia's first survey on *Public Attitudes Towards Corruption,* presently a second, more detailed, survey on the same subject is carried out. CSD also publishes independent reports in the monthly bulletin on the activities of the National Assembly and the Senate, and provides advice on the drafting of new laws under its Parliamentary Watch and Legal Unit projects. Under the Coalition for Transparency Cambodia (CTC) Project, CSD and its working group has been a major stakeholder in the drafting and passing of the long-awaited Anti-Corruption Law, and putting forward the issue of anti-corruption to increase public awareness. The organization is also involved with Cambodian elections.

House 19, Street 57
Sangkat Boeung Keng Kang 1
Khan Chamkar Mon
PO Box 1346
Phnom Penh, Cambodia

Tel: +855 (23) 364 735
Fax: +855 (23) 364 735
csd@online.com.kh
www.online.com.kh/users/csd/

Contact: Ms. Chea Vannath, President and Mr. Heav Veasna, Managing Director

Number of staff: 25

Budget: $250,000–$500,000

Publications: Monthly Research Bulletin (ongoing); *Cambodia: Building a Coalition for Transparency*, 2002

Cambodia

Gender and Development for Cambodia

EDUCATION
ADVOCACY

Gender and Development for Cambodia (GAD/C) is a local non-government organization that aims to promote gender equity in social, economic, and political processes in Cambodia through sustained efforts to advocate for policy and legislative reform in relation to women's rights. GAD/C carries out this mission in partnership with other Cambodian NGOs, international and multilateral organizations, state institutions, and other organizations of civil society. GAD/C implements three mutually reinforcing programs: Training and Internship; Advocacy and Networking; and Information, Education, and Communication (IEC).

House 4, Street 294
Sangkat Tonle Bassac
PO Box 2684 Phnom Penh 3
or CCC Box 128
Khan Chamcarmon, Phnom Penh
Cambodia

Tel/Fax: +855 (23) 215 137
gad@bigpond.com.kh
www.bigpond.com/kh/users/gad

Contact: Ms. Ros Sopheap, Executive Director

Publications: Gender in TVET, a study of the situation of young women studying Non Traditional skills in Cambodia, 2002; *Women in Poverty in Phnom Penh* and the *Series of Gender Handbooks: Gender Awareness, Gender policy, Gender Mainstreaming and Gender Indicator.*

Cambodia

Khmer Institute of Democracy

EDUCATION
ACTION
ADVOCACY

The Khmer Institute of Democracy (KID) was established in 1992 to promote democratic values in Cambodian society, including human rights and the rule of law. To this end, KID organizes workshops and field training for grassroots government officials and citizens on democracy and the rule of law. Other activities of the Institute include radio programs, conferences of parliamentarians, and a proto-ombudsman system for which KID trains voluntary citizens advisors.

#5 Street 57
Sangkat Boeung keng kang
Khan Chamcar Mon
PO Box 117
Phnom Penh
Cambodia

Tel: +855 (23) 214 928
Fax: +855 (23) 216 208
director.kid@bigpond.com.kh
www.bigpond.com/kh/users/kid

Contact: Lao Mong Hay, Executive Director

Number of staff: 21

Budget: $100,000–$500,000 (2000)

Cambodia

Konrad-Adenauer Foundation – Cambodia

EDUCATION
ACTION
ADVOCACY

The activities of the Konrad-Adenauer-Stiftung (KAF) in Cambodia focus on assisting democracy building, the establishment of rule of law, the development of media and media professions, and the development of rural areas. In cooperation with the Khmer Institute for Democracy, KAF organizes orientation and training courses on procedures and mechanisms of democracy, rule of law, and good governance. Together with the Buddhism for Development Movement, KAF provides assistance to small businesses, farmers, and communities in rural areas and to former Khmer Rouge fighters to be integrated again in rural society. KAF cooperates with the Club of Cambodian Journalists and the Department of Media and Communication at the Royal University of Phnom Penh in order to develop quality standards, independence, and influence of media professions and media enterprises.

4 Street 462
Chamkar Mon
PO Box 944
Phnom Penh
Cambodia

Tel: +855 (23) 213 363
Fax: +855 (23) 213 364
konrad@bigpond.com.kh

Contact: Peter Koeppinger, Country Representative
Number of staff: 19
Budget: $1,200,000–1,300,000

Cambodia

Legal Aid of Cambodia

EDUCATION
ACTION

Legal Aid of Cambodia is an association of Cambodian lawyers dedicated to the establishment of a legal system based on human rights and the rule of law. The organization's main aim is to make legal aid accessible for the most vulnerable parts of society. Its lawyers offer legal service at no financial charge, and the organization focuses on making legal services accessible for rural communities. The organization was set up in 1995 by some of the first new legal defenders in Cambodia after the civil war.

43 Street 306
Boeung Kengkang I
Camkarnorm
PO Box 1197
Phnom Penh, Cambodia

Tel: +855 (23) 215 274/214 824
Fax: +855 (23) 212 206
lac@bigpond.com.kh
www.lac.org.kh

Contact: Choeung Sokha, Director
Number of staff: 70
Publications: Legal Aid of Cambodia Quarterly, newsletter

Cambodia

Local Capacities for Non-violence Khmer Ahimsa Organization

EDUCATION
ACTION

Local Capacities for Non-violence (LCN) started as a project of the American Friends Service Committee. Funded by UNICEF, the project completed a two-year research project to help identify indigenous strategies to cope with violence in Cambodian communities. The goal of the LCN–Khmer Ahimsa is to empower people to use their non-violent capacities by supporting and encouraging community-level initiatives to build peace and reduce violence and injustice in Cambodia. LCN–Khmer Ahimsa helps to rebuild some of the customs that can support peacebuilding within communities, such as re-establishing traditional meeting houses and strengthening the community of Buddhist monks. Combining Buddhist believes and traditional customs, LCN–Khmer Ahimsa organizes workshops at the community level to promote non-violent conflict resolution and aims to bring several organizations together to form an Active Non-violence Working Group in order to expand the outreach of non-violence and conflict resolution in Cambodia.

Khmer Ahimsa
30 Street 352
Beoung Keng Kang 1
Chamkarmorn
Phnom Penh, Cambodia

Tel: +855 (23) 216 400
Fax: +855 (23) 364 232
lcn@online.com.kh

Contact: Judy Saumweber, LCN project

Budget: $25,000–$100,000 (2000)

Number of staff: 4

Cambodia

Mennonite Central Committee – Cambodia

EDUCATION
ACTION

The Mennonite Central Committee (MCC)—Cambodia is a part of the international NGO Mennonite Central Committee based in Canada and the United States. Since 1979, peace and reconciliation has been a part of MCC's mandate in Cambodia, alongside other activities in relief, education, and small enterprise development. MCC seconds expatriate volunteers to a number of organizations and projects in Cambodia, such as the Working Group for Weapons Reduction and Youth For Peace, which provide introductory peace education concepts to students in Phnom Penh high schools and conducts workshops on peace education, human rights, and conflict resolution at its student center.

Street 404/475 house #20
Tumnup Tuk
Phnom Penh
Cambodia

Tel/Fax: +855 (23) 215 994
mcc@online.com.kh

Contact: Chris Landes, facilitator Partnership Program; Sherry and Larry Groff, co-country representatives

Number of staff: 1 national/7 expat

Budget: $100,000

Cambodia

NGO Forum on Cambodia

The NGO Forum on Cambodia is an umbrella organization of over 70 local and international NGOs. The NGO Forum coordinates and supports advocacy activities of these NGOs within Cambodia as well as on an international level. Together with the Cooperation Committee for Cambodia and MEDiCAM, the NGO Forum coordinates the NGO Statement to the annual international Consultative Group Meeting. In 2002, it coordinated a review of NGO observations on the first year of implementation of the Government Action Plan. These reports are published on the Forum's website. The NGO Forum brings NGOs together in working groups to organize seminars, discussions, and campaigns on different issues. The current working groups are on Development Issues, Environment, Gender, Resettlement, Pesticides, Sesan River Protection, and Forest Livelihoods. Starting in 2004, NGO Forum intends to focus increasingly on land issues.

PO Box 2295
Phnom Penh 3
Cambodia

Tel: +855 (23) 986 269
Fax: +855 (23) 214 429
ngoforum@ngoforum.org.kh
www.ngoforum.org.kh

Contact: Russell Peterson, Representative

Number of staff: 10

Budget: $400,000

Publications and Joint Statements: NGO Recommendations to Enhance the Success of the Royal Government of Cambodia's Governance Action Plan, 2002; NGO Statement to the Consultative Group Meeting on Cambodia, 1999–2002; Cambodia's National Poverty Reduction Strategy Paper—Suggestions for NGO Follow-up, Monitoring and Advocacy, June 2003; *A Rapid Comparison of the NGO Statement to the 2002 CG Meeting* and the *Final Draft of Cambodia's National Poverty Reduction Strategy,* June 2003.

Cambodia

ADVOCACY

Project Against Domestic Violence

The Project Against Domestic Violence (PADV) is a local non-profit NGO established in August 1997. PADV envisions a society where women and men enjoy equal rights to a life free from violence and cruel, inhumane, or degrading treatment. PADV aims to prevent, reduce, and eventually eliminate domestic violence in Cambodia, so that families can live in peace and happiness. For this it aims to collaborate with the Ministry of Women's and Veteran's Affairs, and local and international NGOs in lobbying for support of domestic violence law.

#15, St. 105/278
Beoung Keng Kang 2
Chakarmorn
Phnom Penh, Cambodia

Contact: Sath Salim, Program Manager

Number of staff: 22

Publications: Newsletter

Tel: +855 (23) 721 654
Fax: +855 (23) 721 654
padv@online.com.kh

Cambodia

EDUCATION
ADVOCACY

Silaka – Metathor

Silaka is a NGO that was founded in 1993 with the purpose of contributing to the development of social infrastructure in order to assist in the rehabilitation and reconstruction of Cambodian society. Silaka aims to build capacity of public service institutions by direct transfer of skills and knowledge to Cambodian NGOs, and government staff. Metathor—Conflict Transformation Program is a new project in Silaka that aims to contribute to peacebuilding in Cambodia. Metathor provides training, network support, technical advice, and capacity building to participants of the program. They are invited to learn about the role of conflict, how conflict may affect society, and how conflict can be transformed into opportunities for growth and development.

#10B, St. 57
Boeung Keng Kang 2
Chamkarmon
Phnom Penh, Cambodia

Contact: Ms. Thida C. Khus, Executive Director or Ms. Dor Soma, Program Coordinator

Number of staff: 20

Tel: +855 (23) 217 872
Fax: +855 (23) 213 108
silaka@online.com.kh

Cambodia

STAR Kampuchea

EDUCATION
ACTION

Since 1997, STAR Kampuchea has been active in promoting and supporting civil society in Cambodia, with the ultimate goal of building a true democracy. Its objectives are to mobilize Cambodian civil society organizations to advocate for good legislation, judiciary, and governance by reinforcing respect for laws and, secondly, to strengthen Cambodian civil society organizations to be dynamic and skillful advocates. In cooperation with 37 non-governmental organizations and 7 major trade unions, STAR Kampuchea organizes NGO fairs and workshops and conducts numerous training courses. In addition, STAR Kampuchea established 4 provincial advocacy networks to help villagers to advocate for themselves, and also launched a Legislative Development Program.

16, Street 398
Sangkat Boeung Kengkang I
Khan Chamcarmorn
Phnom Penh, Cambodia
PO Box 177
Phnom Penh, Cambodia

Tel: +855 (23) 211 612
Fax: +855 (23) 211 812
star@forum.org.kh; sarin@forum.org.kh
www.forum.org.kh/~star-ldp/back_to_welcome.htm

Contact: Mr. Nhek Sarin, Executive Director; Ms. Chet Charya, Deputy-Executive Director

Number of staff: 19

Budget: $200,000

Publications: STAR Kampuchea, Bi-monthly Newsletter and Legislative Development Newsletter

---

Cambodia

Working Group for Weapons Reduction in Cambodia

RESEARCH
EDUCATION
ACTION
ADVOCACY

The Working Group for Weapons Reduction (WGWR) was a coalition of local and international NGOs cooperating to address issues related to the proliferation and misuse of small arms and light weapons, and to peacebuilding in Cambodia. In June 2002, WGWR restructured and became an independent organization that is now governed by a board of directors. Currently, WGWR has four projects including public education, monitoring and research, information and advocacy, and NGO partnership. In 2002, WGWR was involved in a review of the government demobilization strategy.

55 Sothearos Blvd
PO Box 630
Phnom Penh, Cambodia

Tel: +855 (23) 222 462
Fax: (c/o AFSC) +855 (23) 213 447
wgwr@online.com.kh
www.wgwr.org

Contact: Mr. Neb Sinthay, Executive Director

Number of staff: 18

Budget: Approx. $200,000 to $300,000 annually

Publications: Several reports and various small-arms education materials

Cambodia

Youth for Peace

Youth for Peace (YFP) is a local non-profit NGO founded in January 2000 by four individuals who were committed to the development of young people and building peace in Cambodia. YFP is a member of the Asian Youth Network for Human Development, and co-operates with the Department of Youth of the Ministry of Education. YFP offers four main programs: Education for young people about living in a society with a culture of peace; empowering, encouraging, and supporting youth initiatives to act for peace, development, and social justice; Youth for Peace created Cambodian National Network for Peace and Democratization. The organization also has an action of immediate response to violence by peaceful action like peace walk or advocacy.

#8AB, St. 202
Phademkor
Tuol Kok
Phnom Penh, Cambodia

Contact: Mr. Outh Renne, Representative
Number of staff: 7

Tel: +855 (23) 881 346/(11) 717 442
Fax: +855 (23) 881 346
youthforpeace@online.com.kh

Cambodia

Youth Resource Development Program

The main goal of the Youth Resource Development Program (YRDP) is to raise awareness, promote and enable critical thinking and analytical skills, and foster a sense of responsibility in Cambodian youth. YRDP aims to create learning conditions for young people and to empower them. It also wants the Cambodian youth to acquire empowerment skills to undertake useful activities for the development of their communities and country and build peace through developing critical thinking and deep dialogue and apply alternatives to violence. YRDP is providing non-formal education on peacebuilding through developing critical thinking and analytical skills on personal and societal development. Its Social Development Courses offers education on, primarily, Conflict Resolution, Love and Marriage, and Active Non-Violence.

93 Street 590
Boeung Kak 2
Tuol Kok
Phnom Penh, Cambodia

Contact: Mr. CHEANG Sokha, Executive Director
Number of staff: 10
Budget: $25,000–$100,000

Tel: +855 (23) 880 194
Fax: +855 (23) 880 059
yrdp@forum.org.kh

East Asia, Pacific

Pacific Campaign for Disarmament and Security

RESEARCH
ADVOCACY

Established in 1985 the Pacific Campaign for Disarmament and Security (PCDS) is committed to peace and disarmament in this region through providing research, information, and support within its worldwide network. The PCDS focuses on non-military solutions to regional and national conflicts, which includes the development of demilitarization, political and human rights, enhancement of the role of NGOs, and the promotion of disarmament initiatives. It also works on exposing military alliances, removing foreign military, and reallocating military expenditure to basic human needs. Currently the PCDS is working on projects aiming to build support for a Northeast Asia Nuclear Weapon Free Zone through regional and U.S. assurances. The second project is focused on establishing non-governmental consultation with the ASEAN Regional Forum in order to promote peoples' participation.

PCDS Resource Office
3780 Lake Road
Denman Island
British Columbia
Canada VOR 1TO

Tel/Fax: +1 (250) 335 0351
pcdsres@island.net
www.island.net/~pcdsres/

Publications: North Korea's Nuclear Bombshell and a Non-Governmental Response, 2003; The War on Terrorism in the Asia-Pacific, 2002; Japan Erodes Pacifist Constitution in the War on Terrorism, 2002; ASEAN Regional Forum: North Korea Takes Center Stage, 2001

Pacific

Pacific People's Partnership

RESEARCH
EDUCATION
ADVOCACY

Pacific People's Partnership (PPP) was founded in 1975 and has developed into Canada's leading social justice and development education organization working with Pacific island peoples to create lasting solutions to militarism, poverty, and environmental degradation. PPP is devoted to international research, education, and advocacy on issues of concern for the South Pacific region, such as peace and militarism, sovereignty and de-colonization, human rights and indigenous people's rights, environmental issues, and women's role in preserving traditional knowledge. While research, education, and advocacy remain PPP's top priority, they also directly support the work of community-based groups in the Pacific, as well as projects that facilitate links between indigenous peoples in the Pacific and First Nations peoples in Canada.

Suite 407-620 View Street
Victoria, BC V8W1J6
Canada

Tel: +1 (250) 381 4131
Fax: +1 (250) 388 5258
general@pacificpeoplespartnership.org
www.pacificpeoplespartnership.org

Contact: Rita Parikh, Executive Director

Budget: $250,000

Number of staff: 1–2

Publications: Tok Blong Pasifik and various videos available to buy.

Indonesia

Peace Brigades International Indonesia Project

ACTION

Peace Brigades International Indonesia Project (PBI-IP) was founded in 1999 and focuses on protective accompaniment for human rights and humanitarian aid workers in conflict areas. PBI actually seeks to secure and expand the space in which civil society operates through the use of a protective presence of their international volunteers. PBI also aims to promote international under-standing of the situation in Indonesia and the work of Indonesian organiza-tions, and to empower civil society through the above mentioned activities. In Indonesia, PBI-IP works closely to protect human rights and humanitarian workers in Aceh such as Koalisi NGO HAM, RPUK, SPKP HAM.

Box 9, 33 Boundary Trail
Clearwater, R0K 0M0 Manitoba
Canada

Tel: +1 (204) 873 2563
Fax: +1 (775) 242 5240
pbiip@mb.sympatico.ca
www.peacebrigades.org

Contact: Celia Guilford, Project Coordinator

Number of staff: 4 staff; 20 volunteers in Indonesia; 20 volunteers outside Indonesia

Budget: $500,000–$1,000,000

Publications: Pa Khabar, newsletter

Taiwan Strait

Association for Relations Across the Taiwan Straits

ACTION
ADVOCACY

The Association for Relations Across the Taiwan Strait (ARATS) was founded in 1991 in Beijing, China. The Association takes charge of contacting and negotiating with the Straits Exchange Foundation in the position of a non-government organization. Nevertheless it is supervised and directed by the Chinese government to handle technical and business matters in cross-strait affairs. The foundation aims to promote development of cross-straits relations resulting in the peaceful reunification of China and Taiwan. It focuses on areas such as progressively building cooperation among NGOs in Taiwan; negotiating with the Taiwan Strait Exchange Foundation to address issues like smuggling and hijacking in the Taiwan Straits; negotiating with concerned authorities or persons in Taiwan to settle fishery disputes and trespassers into the opposite area. The foundation further provides policy guidance and services regarding trade and investments in China.

No. 6-1, Guanganmen Nanjie
Xuanu District
Beijing
China

Contact: Wang Daohan, Director

Tel: +86 (10) 8353 6622
Fax: +86 (10) 63571505/ 8353 6622/ 8353 2364
english@cn5c.com

China

China Association for NGO Cooperation

EDUCATION
ACTION

The China Association for NGO Cooperation (CANGO) is a network of 91 Chinese NGOs that address poverty alleviation, environmental protection, and social development in China's poor, remote, and minority-inhabited regions. CANGO acts as an intermediary agency between international and Chinese NGOs to strengthen fundraising, provide technical support, and build capacity of grassroots social organizations in China. It organizes seminars and conferences, such as the Business and Civil Society Forum and a workshop on Protected Area Management. In November 2002, CANGO opened its training center at the Tranjin University for Technical Education. This countrywide initiative aims to provide free training to NGOs from all sectors on issues such as leadership, project and program management, fundraising and resource mobilization, and strategic planning.

18 Bei San Huan Zhong Lu
Beijing 100011
People's Republic of China

Contact: Haoming Huang, Executive Director

Number of staff: 10

Tel: +86 (10) 6201 1832
Fax: +86 (10) 6201 1328
info@cango.org
www.cango.org

Asia-Pacific, Japan, Russia

RESEARCH

China Centre for International Studies

Formerly know as the Centre for International Studies of the State Council, the China Centre for International Studies took its name in 1988. This research and consulting center engages mainly in the field of major political, economic, and security issues. Based on the results of these findings, advisory opinions are also provided to the government. The CCIS also hosts international conferences, symposiums, and seminars on topics of world concern. Other activities include bilateral dialogue on world and regional situations held annually between CCIS and other institutions. The center is comprised of the research departments on International Politics; Development of International Economy, Science and Technology; International Security and Strategy; and the Asia Pacific Region.

PO Box 1744
22 Xi'anmen Da Jie
Beijing 100007
China

Number of staff: 22

Tel: +86 (10) 6309 7083
Fax: +86 (10) 6309 5802

China

Chinese People's Association for Peace and Disarmament

RESEARCH
EDUCATION

CPAPD is an NGO working for peace and disarmament in China. The organization's aims are to promote mutual understanding and cooperation between Chinese peoples and those in other parts of the world in order to strive for disarmament, world peace, and the elimination of nuclear weapons and other weapons of mass destruction. To this end, CPAPD researches on peace, security, arms control, and development. Together with other international research and advocacy organizations, it sponsors seminars on regional and international security and development issues. In China CPAPD, together with the China Association for Science and Technology and some 40 other organizations, sponsors the activities of the yearly International Week of Science and Peace. These include peace education and the promotion of scientific progress for the benefit of peaceful development.

PO Box 188
15 Wanshou Road
Beijing 100036
People's Republic of China

Contact: Madame He Lui, President

Number of staff: 20

Publications: Peace, quarterly bulletin in English

Tel: +86 (10) 6827 1736
Fax: +86 (10) 6827 3675
Chinapeace@cmmail.com

Asia-Pacific
Institute of Asia-Pacific Studies

Established in 1988, the Institute of Asia-Pacific Studies (IAPS) is one of the research institutes in the Chinese Academy of Social Sciences (CASS). It focuses mainly on contemporary politics, economic development, foreign relations, social and cultural issues, as well as regional integration and cooperation in the Asia-Pacific region. This research institute is funded by the central government and its research programs are both academic and policy oriented. The IAPS has four research departments: Economic Studies; Security and Foreign Relations; Political and Social Studies; and Culture Studies, and also has several centers and associations under the exclusive or joint management of the institute.

Chinese Academy of Social Sciences
3 Zhang Zizhong Rd. Beijing
100007 China

Tel: +86 (10) 640 63922
Fax: +86 (10) 640 63041
admin@iapscass.cn or twukong@yahoo.com
www.iapscass.cn

Contact: Tang Shiping, Head of the Department of Security and Foreign Relations

Number of staff: 40

Publications: East Asian Cooperation and Integration: Where to Go, 2002; *Changing Sino-U.S. Japanese Relations,* 2000; *Good Governance: The Lessons of the Asian Crisis,* 1999; *Institution-building under "10+3" Tackling the Practical Issues,* 2003; *The Rise of China as a Security Linchpin,* 2003; *What China Should Do About North Korea,* 2003.

East Timor

East Timor Institute for Reconstruction Monitoring and Analysis, La'o Hamutuk

RESEARCH
EDUCATION
ADVOCACY

East Timor Institute for Reconstruction Monitoring and Analysis or La'o Hamutuk (Walking Together) is an East Timorese organization, founded in 2000, that seeks to monitor and report on the activities of the principal international institutions present in Timor Loro Sa'e as they relate to the physical and social reconstruction of the country. The institute operates under the assumption that the people of East Timor must be the ultimate arbiters of the reconstruction process and, thus, that the process should be as democratic and transparent as possible. In addition to providing information on and analysis of the reconstruction and development processes, La'o Hamutuk works to improve communication between international institutions and organizations and the various sectors of East Timorese society. Finally, La'o Hamutuk serves as a resource center.

Institutu Timor Lorosa'e ba Analiza
no Monitor Rekonstrusaun
PO Box 340, Dili
East Timor

Tel: +670 (390) 325 013
laohamutuk@easttimor.minihub.org
www.etan.org/lh

Number of staff: 9

Budget: $100,000–$500,000

Publications: The La'o Hamutuk Bulletin (a periodic publication with in-depth analytical articles and editorials), *Disorder in East Timor: The International Community Must Accept Responsibility,* 2002

East Timor

East Timor NGO Forum

EDUCATION
ADVOCACY

The East Timor NGO Forum's vision is to contribute to the building of a pluralist, democratic, just, and sustainable development in East Timor, based on environmental principles. This is to be achieved through the development of a strong, independent, and responsible civil society committed to upholding and making real in all sections of society, the full range of human rights that all East Timorese, particularly the vulnerable, can enjoy. This also includes the liberation from domination while encouraging the free pursuit of development in East Timor. To realize the vision of the NGO Forum it is necessary to promote a culture of learning, cooperation, and partnership with the community; to promote respect for human rights and good practice among East Timorese NGOs, local NGOs, and other development actors, both domestic and international, and to serve as a collective, independent, non-partisan voice for the rights and needs of the community.

Ngo forum Nasional Timor Lorosae
KaiKoli St. Dili
East Timor, 322773

Tel: +670 (390) 322772
etngocentre@hotmail.com
www.geocities.com/etngoforum/

Contact: Cecilio Caminha Freitas,
Executive Director

Number of staff: 23

East-Timor

East Timorese Women's Communication Forum

The East Timorese Women's Communication Forum (Fokupers) was founded in 1997. It focuses on political victims and gives counseling and other forms of assistance to female victims of violations, including ex-political prisoners, war widows, and wives of political prisoners. Its mandate also includes promoting women's human rights among the local population, especially the East Timorese women. Its activities revolve around: conducting workshops discussing ways to enhance or develop further women's participation in Timorese society; focusing on receiving trauma counseling training for their staff in order to provide counsel to women victims; supporting women survivors of violence; and to end violence against women through advocacy and education; supporting community-based local groups in different areas of the country; and publishing relevant materials.

Rua Governador Celestino da Silva
Farol, Dili, Timor Lorosa'e
East Timor

Tel: +670 (390) 321 534
fokupers@fokupers.minihub.org

Contact: Manuela Leong Pereira, Director and Maria Domingas Alves
Number of staff: 5 and many volunteers

East-Timor

HAK Foundation

HAK Foundation (Foundation for Law, Human Rights and Justice) was established in 1997. It was founded by a number of East Timorese young intellectuals and NGO activists because of their interest for human rights. HAK Foundation aims to accomplish a critical, independent, and open society for the people of East Timor—all of which are based on the principles of democracy. To attain social justice, HAK Foundation provides advocacies for human rights violations in conjunction with people empowerment involving transfer of knowledge, quality improvement, and social control. Ever since its establishment, HAK Foundation has been handling several cases on human rights violations, which involves civil and political rights, as well as economic, social, and cultural rights. These cases are supported in litigation as well as non-litigation (mediation, campaigns, and lobbying).

Jln. Gov. Serpa Rosa T-091
PO Box 274
Farol, Dili
Timor Lorosae

Tel: +670 (390) 313 323
Fax: +670 (390) 313 324
direito@yayasanhak.minihub.org or yayasanhak@minihub.org
www.yayasanhak.minihub.org/

Contact: Jose Luis De Oliveira, Program Manager
Number of staff: 12

East Timor

International Federation
for East Timor

Founded in 1991, the International Federation for East Timor (IFET) is a federation of NGOs, with an interest in the decolonization process of East Timor as well as various aspects of peoples lives in and from the territory, as they too are effected by the process of decolonization. The IFET also wishes to assure that human rights are properly maintained in East Timor according to international standards. The objectives of the IFET are: to provide support from the international civil society for the people of East Timor in freely exercising their rights to political, economi,c and social self-determination; to endeavor to guarantee internationally recognized human rights and justice for all involved in East Timor's evolution to full and genuine independence; to assist the United Nations in helping East Timor reach these goals by providing information to UN officials and organs; mobilizing international public opinion; and advocating with UN officials and governments of member states. IFET also facilitates information exchange and coordinated international campaigns among NGOs and international institutions.

PO Box 88
Dili
East Timor

Tel: +670 723 4335
Fax: +670 331 7294
ifet@etan.org
www.etan.org/ifet

Tel: +1 (718) 596 7668
Fax: +1 (718) 222 4097
john@etan.org

Contact: Charles Scheiner, Secretary or John M. Miller, UN Representative

Number of staff: IFET is a network, with no permanent office or staff. All work is done be volunteers from the member organizations of the federation.

Budget: < $25,000

Publications: open letters to UN and other officials, released for media and public information. See examples at: www.etan.org

East Timor

Judicial System Monitoring Program

EDUCATION
ADVOCACY

Judicial System Monitoring Program (JSMP) is a human rights project set up by the East Timorese Jurist's Association and the Timorese/International organization La'o Hamutuk. JSMP aims to assist the UN Transitional Administration in East Timor, the East Timorese public, and the international community by making recommendations for ongoing reform of the fledgling judicial system of East Timor.

The main objective of the program is to improve the quality of justice provided by the newly established judicial system and to promote human rights and the rule of law in a meaningful and transparent manner for the people of East Timor through: sending legal observers to monitor the serious crimes trials; providing legal analysis and thematic reports; and dissemination of information on the developments of the justice system as a whole. The program's courtroom observation work focuses on the cases related to the violence in 1999, which include crimes against humanity, genocide, and torture.

PO Box 275
Rua Setubal, Kolmere
Dili, East Timor

Tel/Fax: +670 (390) 323 882
info@jsmp.minihub.org
www.jsmp.minihub.org

Contact: Christian Ranheim,
christian@jsmp.minihub.org

Publications: JSMP's regular news service

East Timor

Kadalak Sulimutuk Institute

RESEARCH
EDUCATION

Kadalak Sulimutuk Institute (KSI) is an East Timorese non-governmental organization founded by Nobel Peace Laureate Bishop Belo as a center for peace and development in the newly independent East Timor or Timor Lorasa'e. It is involved in education and conflict resolution of West Timorese refugees. KSI conducts research in the field of ethnic relations, reintegration of refugees, land and property disputes, and impact of public policy. KSI further conducts training and organizes workshops to support peace and development in East Timor

Jl. Bebonok Dili Cornoro
PO Box 420
Dili, East Timor

Tel: +670 (390) 325 188

Contact: Antero Bendito Da Silva

East-Timor

Sahe Institute for Liberation

The Sahe Institute for Liberation (SIL) aims to support the active participation of the East Timorese community in the process of developing a nation state through the dissemination of information and discussions or seminars. SIL is the transformation of a study group called Sa'he Study Club (SSC) formed by East Timorese student activists and Indonesian prodemocracy activists in 1998 in Jakarta, Indonesia. SSC held weekly seminars since forming, first in Jakarta and then in Dili, until being forced to leave in early September. After the referendum, SSC was reformed and became an institute known as Sahe Institute for Liberation (SIL). Since then, they have published a pamphlet critiquing the World Bank and have coordinated youth projects in community education.

Sahe Institute for Liberation
c/o. Hak Foundation, Dili
East Timor

Sahe_Lib@yahoo.com

Contact: Aderito de Jesus Soares, Coordinator

Publications: SSC has published books about Amilcar Cabral, Samora Machel, the East Timorese political party Fretilin, and the East Timorese poet Francisco Borja da Costa. Prior to the ballot, SSC published a critical analysis of Indonesia's autonomy offer and distributed it as a pamphlet throughout East Timor.

East-Timor

Timor Institute of Development Studies

The Timor Institute of Development Studies, called East Timor Study Group before, is an independent and nonpartisan think tank on public policy issues. Its aim is to provide high quality public policy research on East Timor and its relations with neighboring countries. Therefore, in January 2002, they restructured ETSG to only three centers (compared to the previous four). These are: Center for Democracy and Social Studies (CDSS) that focuses on good governance; Center for Economic Studies (CES) that focuses on economic growth and poverty reduction; and Center for Applied Science and Technology Studies (CASTS) that focuses on technology, energy, and the environment. The centers are supported by the Administration and Finance Unit, Library Unit, and Conference Center.

Rua Maucocomate
Becora-Dili, Timor Lorosae
PO Box 181, Dili
East Timor

Tel/Fax: +670 (390) 323 889

Contact: João M. Saldanha, Executive Director

Number of staff: 10

East Timor

United Nations Mission
of Support in East Timor

ACTION

The United Nations Mission of Support in East Timor (UNMISET) was established by Security Council Resolution 1410 on 17 May 2002. The mission was established to: provide assistance to core administrative structures critical to the viability and political stability of East Timor; to provide for an interim law enforcement and public security and assist in the development of a new law enforcement agency in East Timor; and to contribute to the maintenance of the external and internal security of East Timor.

On 20 May 2002 East Timor became an independent nation. Although the road to independence started decades ago, the first UN mission was established in 1999. When in October 1999 the Indonesian People's Consultative Assembly formally recognized the result of the popular consultation, which started the process of transition toward independence, the United Nations Transitional Administration in East Timor (UNTAET) replaced the United Nations Mission in East Timor (UNAMET), which was established to carry out the consultation. UNTAET was established as a multidimensional peacekeeping operation fully responsible for the administration of East Timor during its transition to independence.

As a successor mission, UNMISET, adopted a milestone-based approach toward gradual withdrawal from the territory and supports the East Timorese authorities in the areas of stability, democracy and justice, internal security and law enforcement, and external security and border control.

UNMISET Headquarters
Dili
East Timor

Budget: $190,000,000
Number of staff: 4,200

www.un/org/depts/dpko/missions/unmiset/index.html

Fiji

Citizens' Constitutional Forum

The Citizens' Constitutional Forum (CCF) began as a series of national consultations on constitutional matters in 1993 and was formally registered in 1996. After the promulgation of the 1997 Constitution, the forum began to educate Fijians about its provisions. It published a popular version of the constitution in English, Hindi, and Fijian and began work on promoting multiculturalism, human rights, and a fairer electoral system. Since the coup in 2000, the work of the CCF has focused on the restoration of parliamentary democracy, respect for human rights, and the rule of law. The CCF lobbies foreign governments for support to return Fiji to a parliamentary democracy, and is taking legal action against the current president and interim administration.

7A Thurston Street
PO Box 12584
Suva, Fiji

Tel: +679 (3) 08 379
Fax: +679 (3) 08 380
ccf@ccf.org.fj
www.ccf.org.fj

Contact: Rev. Akuila Yabaki, Executive Director

Number of staff: 4

Budget: $100,000–$500,000 (2000)

Publications: Your Constitution, Your Rights, 1998;
*Economic Development, Democracy and Ethnic
Conflict in the Fiji Islands* (together with Minority
Rights Group International), 2001

Fiji

Pacific Concerns Resource Centre – Demilitarization Desk

The Demilitarization Desk of the Pacific Concerns Resource Centre (PCRC) serves as the secretariat for the Nuclear Free and Independent Pacific (NFIP) Movement. The Desk acts for over 100 affiliated NGOs and CBOs from around the Pacific. It collects and disseminates information, advocates and lobbies, promotes discussion and understanding, and mobilizes resources within and outside the region on five campaign areas: demilitarization, decolonization, environment, human rights and good governance, and sustainable human development. The Demilitarization Desk is undertaking a comprehensive study on the state of militarism in the Pacific.

83 Amy St Toorak
Private Mail Bag
Suva, Fiji

Tel: +679 (3) 30 4649
Fax: +679 (3) 30 4755
pcrc@connect.com.fj
www.pcrc.org.fj/pcrc_demilitarisation.htm

Contact: Mrs. Lorine Chan Tevi, Secretary

Number of staff: 13

Budget: $500,000

Publications: Pacific News Bulletin

Fiji

Ecumenical Centre for
Research Education and Advocacy

The Ecumenical Centre for Research Education and Advocacy (ECREA) was formerly known as the Fiji Council of Churches Research Group. ECREA researches social, economic, religious, and political issues, and organizes workshops and seminars to raise awareness on such issues. It also trains local Christian leaders in social analysis and lobbies the government on matters of concern. ECREA's four programs focus on economic and social justice, regional economic justice, social empowerment and education, and gender and communication. In 2001, ECREA organized the national workshop "Towards a Culture of Peace," which brought together a number of organizations and individuals involved in peacebuilding in Fiji. In January 2003, ECREA published the book *Intercultural Exercises,* written by Father Frank Hoare. The exercises are intended to help students explore cultural differences in a positive way. The Ministry of Education in Fiji has accepted the book as an official resource for schools.

PO Box 2300
Government Buildings
Suva, Fiji

Tel: +679 (3) 07 588
Fax: +679 (3) 11 248
fccrgroup@is.com.fj

Contact: Aisake Casimira, Director
Number of staff: 8
Budget: $25,000–$100,000 (1998)

Fiji

Fem'Link Pacific

Fem'Link Pacific is a Suva-based women's NGO committed to "Linking Women with the Media." The organization wants to bring the stories of Suva women and their communities to the forefront and to share these stories with the rest of Fiji, with the hope that through this community-centered initiative it will not only increase awareness of critical social, political, and economic issues, but also serve as a means to promote reconciliation and peace in Fiji.

Fem'Link Pacific's Media Initiatives for Women in 2001 completed distribution of their pilot community video *fem'TALK* to over 50 women's groups, their civil society partners, and political parties. The community video *Not Just Sweet Talk* features more than 20 women and young women addressing all kind of social topics.

Government Building SUVA
PO Box 2439
Fuji

Tel: +679 (3) 313 211
Fax: +679 (3) 301 925
femlinkpac@connect.com.fj

Contact: Caines Jannif, Coordinator

Fiji

**EDUCATION
ACTION
ADVOCACY**

Fiji Council of Social Services

The Fiji Council of Social Services (FCOSS) is an umbrella organization of 300 member organizations working on social welfare, community development, and environment awareness. The Council was established in 1957 to provide a focal point for civil society organizations in Fiji, and works to support and strengthen these local organizations. FCOSS serves as Fiji's national member to a number of international forums and prepares submissions to governmental and international bodies on a variety of issues. It also provides training to strengthen management capacity of organizations. The Council runs programs and campaigns on child development, disaster response coordination, the elderly, and the prevention of drug and substance abuse.

256 Waimanu Road
PO Box 13476
Suva, Fiji

Tel: +679 (3) 312 649
Fax: +679 (3) 302 936
fcoss@connect.com.fj

Contact: Mohammed Hassan Khan, Executive Director

Number of staff: 10

Budget: $25,000–$100,000

Publications: Voluntary Action Network, quarterly newsletter; *Family Network,* quarterly newsletter; *Drugnet,* quarterly newsletter; Basic Counselling Skills, Conflict Resolution, Crime, Deviance and Delinquency, Violent Encounters

Fiji

**RESEARCH
EDUCATION
ACTION**

Fiji Human Rights Commission

When the Constitutional Review Committee was drafting Fiji's 1997 Constitution, it recognized the need for the country to have a Human Rights Commission. The Commission comprises three members. At its inception in 1999, the Commission initially concentrated on its education function—publishing pamphlets and conducting workshops and training for trainers and human rights activists as well as the police and prison authorities. In the aftermath of the events of May 2000, the Commission concentrated on its function of investigating allegations of human rights violations and breaches of the Bill of Rights by the police, military, and prison authorities during the State of Emergency. With the same focus, the Commission is continuing its promotion and educational function.

Level 2, Civic Towers
Victoria Parade
Suva, Fiji

Tel: +679 (3) 308 577
Fax: +679 (3) 308 661
info@humanrights.org.fj
www.humanrights.org.fj

Contact: Dr. Shameem Shaista, Director of the Commission

Number of staff: 14

Fiji

Fiji Women's Crisis Centre

RESEARCH
EDUCATION
ACTION
ADVOCACY

The Fiji Women's Crisis Centre (FWCC) provides crisis counseling and other support to women and children who are victims of violence committed against them by men. The center is also involved in community education and research on gender violence. The FWCC is also involved in public advocacy and community education on gender violence. Together with a number of women's organizations in the Pacific region, the FWCC forms the Pacific Women's Network Against Violence Against Women and organizes regular regional meetings in which the role of women in peacebuilding has been one of the themes discussed. Together with other women's organizations in Fiji, the Fiji Women's Crisis Centre was involved in protests and public vigils at the time of the coup in 2000.

88 Gordon Street
PO Box 12882
Suva, Fiji

Tel: +679 (3) 313 300
Fax: +679 (3) 313 650
fwcc@connect.com.fj
www.fijiwomen.com

Number of staff: 17

Publications: FWCC Local and Regional Newsletters; *Breaking the Silence;* Brochures on Child Sexual Abuse, Sexual Harassment, Domestic Violence and Rape; Community Education Program—Trainers Manual; Counselors Training Program—Trainers Manual; *Beneath Paradise* Poetry Booklet

South Pacific

Institute of Justice and Applied Legal Studies

EDUCATION
ADVOCACY

The Institute of Justice and Applied Legal Studies (IJALS) was established at the University of the South Pacific in 1996. The Institute works together with national and regional organizations in the areas of law and social justice. IJALS also provides technical assistance and specialist training in legal drafting, law reform, civil litigation, and criminal advocacy.

Lower Campus
University of the South Pacific
PO Box 1168
Suva, Fiji

Tel: +679 (3) 212 801
Fax: +679 (3) 314 273
pulea_m@usp.ac.fj
www.usp.ac.fj/ijals

Contact: Ms Mere Pulea

Fiji

Interfaith Search Fiji

Interfaith Search Fiji started as a series of regular prayer meetings after the 1987 coup. Today, it is made up of 16 different religious member organizations, roughly one third each Christian, Hindu, and Muslim. The organization aims to build respect and understanding between people of different religious organizations in Fiji, mainly through the organization of interreligious dialogues. Interfaith Search Fiji also speaks out on issues related to religious freedom through newsletters and letters to editors.

Interfaith Search Fiji
5 Bau St Flgstf
Suva, Fiji

Tel: +679 (3) 308 346

Fiji

National Council of Women Fiji

The National Council of Women Fiji (NCWF) was established in 1968 as a national coordinating body for the different women's groups that were being established to address social, economic, political, and spiritual issues that were emerging. After the coup of May 19, 2000 the NCWF, together with other women's organizations such as the Fiji Women's Crisis Centre and the Fiji Women's Rights Movement, organized a number of peaceful protest actions such as a daily peace vigil and the "women in black" campaign. In May 2000 the NCWF founded a special organization to co-ordinate these actions, the Women's Action for Democracy and Peace (WADaP). WADaP continues to address the long-term consequences of the coup and strives to maintain a gender perspective in reconciliation and reconstruction efforts. WADaP has four teams: Human Rights and Peace, Multiculturalism, Good Governance, and Economic Empowerment.

PO Box 840
Suva, Fiji

Tel: +679 (3) 315 429/311 880
Fax: +679 (3) 315 429
ncwf@connect.com.fj

Contact: Miriama Leweniqila, President
Number of staff: 3
Budget: $25,000–$100,000

Fiji

EDUCATION
ADVOCACY

NGO Coalition on Human Rights

A meeting organized by the Fiji Women's Crisis Centre in December 1998 led to the formation of the NGO Coalition on Human Rights which consists of 15 local and regional NGOs committed to the promotion of human rights. The Coalition is a coordinating network for non-governmental organizations engaged in different aspects of human rights education, advocacy, or project work. Its aim is to raise awareness in the community of human rights and the various human rights instruments, and to explain human rights in a way that is relevant to people's daily lives. Members of the Coalition are working together by providing support for each other's activities as well as sharing skills, networks, and resources. By joining forces the members of the Coalition have been able to gain larger audiences as well as a higher public and media profile for both the participating organizations and human rights issues.

PO Box 12584
Suva, Fiji

Contact: Rev. Akuila Yabaki

Tel: +679 (3) 08 379
Fax: +679 (3) 08 380
ccf@is.com.fj

South Pacific

EDUCATION

Pacific Foundation for the Advancement of Women

The Pacific Foundation for the Advancement of Women (PACFAW) works in different aspects of gender advocacy in seven Pacific countries: Fiji, Cook Islands, Kiribati, Papua New Guinea, Solomon Islands, Tonga, and Tuvalu. PACFAW's programs focus on trade and economic reform and its consequences for women, human rights/good governance, and strategic leadership/management. The Foundation trains women in political skills in order to increase the number of female parliamentarians.

PO Box 3940
Samabula
6 MacGregor Road
Suva, Fiji

Tel: +679 (3) 304 961
pacfaw@connect.com.fj
www.pacfaw.org.fj

Contact: Ms Salamo Fulivai, Executive Director
Number of staff: 9
Publications: PACFAW Gender Advocacy Newsletter; PACFAW Brochure; PACFAW Training Manual; Analysis of Regional Strategy Paper and Regional Indicative Programme for the Period 2002–2007 Pacific ACP/European Community; PACFAW Beijing Plan of Action Report for Cook Islands; PACFAW Beijing Plan of Action Report for Tonga; Status of Women Report for Cook Islands; Status of Women Report for Tonga

Pacific

Pacific Islands Association of NGOs

EDUCATION
ADVOCACY

The Pacific Islands Association of Non-Governmental Organizations (PIANGO), formally established in 1991, is a regional network of NGO focal points or coordinating bodies known as National Liaison Units (NLUs) based in 22 Pacific Island countries and territories. PIANGO exists to enable the Pacific extended family of NGOs to more effectively promote and advance the interest and well-being of their people. More specifically, PIANGO is a network of Pacific NGOs, existing to facilitate communication, provide a common voice at regional and international forums, and assist NGOs to strengthen and develop Pacific identities, unity, cultures, and forms of social action, as well as to improve the well-being of the communities they serve. PIANGO activities are clustered around three main themes; Organizational Development; Providing a Common Voice for Pacific NGOs; and Collection and Dissemination of Information.

Level 3 Lords Building
19-23 Cummings St
Suva, Fiji
PO Box 17780
Suva, Fiji

Contact: Felicity Bollen, Director
Number of staff: 4

Tel: +679 (3) 302 963
Fax: +679 (3) 317 046
piango@connect.com.fj
www.piango.net

Pacific

Pacific Islands Forum

ACTION

The Pacific Islands Forum is the main regional intergovernmental organization in the Pacific region. It represents the heads of government of all the independent and self-governing Pacific countries, Australia, and New Zealand, and it convenes annually. The Forum Secretariat, located in Fiji, undertakes activities under guidelines decided by the Forum leaders. Its work is divided in four divisions: Trade and Investment, Development and Economic Policy, Corporate Services, and Political and International Affairs. The Forum has developed activities related to regional security, weapons control, and regional responses in times of crisis, including support for good governance, human rights, and democracy.

Forum Secretariat
Private Mail Bag
Ratu Kukuna Road
Suva, Fiji

Contact: Noel Levi, Secretary General
Number of staff: Approx. 70

Tel: +679 3312 600
Fax: +679 3301 366/3302 214
info@forumsec.org.fj
www.forumsec.org.fj

South Pacific

Pacific Network on Globalisation

The Pacific Network on Globalisation (PANG) is an NGO, founded in 2001, with the mission to research, disseminate information, and raise awareness of globalization and economic injustice issues. It also organizes campaigns and does advocacy and lobbying work on fair trade issues. Its activities are focused around monitoring the impact of free trade agreements, economic reform, and TNCs. PANG organizes anti-war events targeted at civil society and grassroots movements, and the PANG Coordinator is the spokesperson of the Fiji Anti-War Movement (FAWM).

PO Box 15473
5 Ban Street
Suva, Fiji

Tel: +679 (3) 316 722
Fax: +679 (3) 311 248
pang@connect.com.fj

Contact: Stanley Simpson, Coordinator
Number of staff: 2
Publications: Tracking Trade Liberalisation: A Case Study of Samoa; A Critical Analysis of PICTA; A Rice Case Study of Fiji.

Fiji

Women's Action for Change

Women's Action for Change (WAC) was founded in 1993 to empower and assist women. In recent years, the organization has expanded its mandate to include awareness raising on issues of human rights and social justice. The WAC Theatre is a drama company that aims to promote human rights and social justice messages through the performance of plays. One of its plays, "Bats and Birds," focuses on Fiji's history and conflicts. Women's Action for Change also runs rehabilitation projects for ex-prisoners, and a childcare center for children of low-income garment workers. Finally, the WAC supports gay, lesbian, bisexual, and transgender people through workshops, lobby networks, and support groups.

PO Box 12398
333 Waimanu Road
Suva, Fiji

Tel: +679 (3) 314 363
Fax: +679 (3) 305 033
wac@connect.com.fj

Contact: Penni Moore, Director, Carlos Perera, Sexual Minorities Project Director
Number of staff: 7 in theatre group and 4 in Sexual Minorities groups

Global

TRANSCEND

TRANSCEND was founded in 1993 as a conflict mediation organization. It is a network of scholars and practitioners concerned with peace and development. Its view is that conflicts are not to be prevented, but transformed in nonviolent and creative ways. TRANSCEND's activities are based on four pillars: action, education/training, dissemination, and research. The most important is action and that the activity focuses on peaceful conflict transformation.

The TRANSCEND Peace University (TPU) is the organization's peace education/training arm, delivering on-site and on-line courses. It was established in 2001 with the purpose of preparing participants with the knowledge and skills required for professional peace work, with an emphasis on professional experience. Current mediation attempts include Hawaii-Pacific, China, Korea, Japan–Okinawa, and Japan/Korea–China–U.S.A.

51 Bois Chatton
F-01210 Versonnex
France

Tel: + 1 (914) 773 3440 (USA)
Fax: + 1 (609) 799 2581 (USA)
transcend@transcend.org
www.transcend.org

Contact: Johan Galtung, Director

Publications: What Kind of Peace is Being Built? Critical Assessments from the South; Transcending the State: From States of War to Communities of Peace—New Discourses, New Visions, New Realities; If Gandhi were Alive Today, Using the Methods of Contemporary NGOs; Cultural Peace: Some Characteristics; From Polyglot to Polycultural: A Next Step in Raising Children

French Polynesia

Association Moruroa e Tatou

| RESEARCH |
| EDUCATION |
| ACTION |
| ADVOCACY |

Created on the 4th July 2001 in Tahiti, the Association Moruroa e Tatou (AMT) is an organization that promotes the right to information on the health consequences of participation in nuclear testing programs, the right to access radiological and medical files, and the right to indemnify oneself. In order to obtain these objectives, the organization aims to gather available information and to inform their members on their legal rights. The AMT also works alongside l'association des Vétérans, which is specialized in the effects of nuclear testing and participated in the creation of the International Network on Nuclear Testing in Paris, 2001. During 2003 the AMT conducted activities like meeting the Minister of Health in Papeete, visiting Hiroshima and Nagasaki, meeting with the Secretary of State of Papeete and the President of Tahiti, participating in the "Europe Pacifique Solidarité" conference in Strasbourg, and attending the "Nuclear Free and Independent Pacific" conference in Tonga.

Contact: Roland Oldham, President

403 Boulevard Pomare
Papeete, Tahiti
French Polynesia

Number of staff: 8

Tel: +68 (9) 430 905
moruroaetatou@mail.pf

French Polynesia

Evangelical Church of French Polynesia

| RESEARCH |
| ADVOCACY |

Established in 1963 by the former French Society of Evangelical Missions, the Evangelical Church officially covers areas such as security and environmental issues and the maintenance of the Maohi cultural identity. The ECFP is made up of several academics and professionals with a focus on theological education. This region has been the site for nuclear testing and the ECFP works on identifying the consequences. In addition, networking with other organizations is undertaken in order to demand that military archives on this subject be opened by independent researchers. This organization supports the freedom that comes from the establishment of human rights and for an investigation to be undertaken on the French Polynesian justice system.

B.P. 113
Papeete, Tahiti
French Polynesia

Tel: + 68 (9) 460 600
Fax: + 68 (9) 419 357
eepf@mail.pf
wwwcevaa.org/international/pacifique/polynesie1.htm

Global

Bonn International Center for Conversion

RESEARCH
EDUCATION

Established in 1994, this independent non-profit organization is dedicated to promoting and facilitating the processes whereby people, skills, technology, equipment, and financial and economic resources can be shifted away from the defense sector and applied to alternative civilian uses. Through research and analysis, technical assistance and advice, retraining programs, publications, and conferences, BICC supports governmental and non-governmental initiatives as well as public and private sector organizations by finding ways to reduce costs and enhance effectiveness in the draw down of military-related activities. As a result, BICC contributes to disarmament, demilitarization, peacebuilding, post-conflict rehabilitation, and human development. It aims to solve the problems associated with disarmament through conducting research, supporting public and private organizations, and mediating the conversion process.

An der Elisabethkirche 25
53113 Bonn
Germany

Tel: +49 (228) 911 960
Fax: +49 (228) 241 215
bicc@bicc.de
www.bicc.de

Contact: Peter J. Croll, Director

Number of staff: 32

Publications: Annual conversion survey, the BICC disarmament and conversion studies and other books. *Restructuring of Korea's Defence Aerospace Industry,* 2003

Asia

Asian Centre
for the Progress of Peoples

ACTION
ADVOCACY

Founded in 1979, the Asian Centre for the Progress of Peoples (ACPP) is an independent, though Catholic-inspired, service center for the promotion of peace and justice in Hong Kong and Asia. ACPP's main program is the Hotline Asia project, which appeals for solidarity on peace and justice issues in Asia to a wide network of organizations and individuals.

1/F. 52 Princess Margaret Road
Kowloon, Hong Kong

Tel: +852 (2) 712 3989/714 5123
Fax: +852 (2) 712 0152
hotline@acpp.org
www.acpp.org

Contact: Mr. James Tan, Chairperson

Publications: Justice and Peace Workers Bulletin, quarterly e-bulletin, *Social Concern Notes,* Urgent Appeals

Asia

Asian Human Rights Commission

EDUCATION
ADVOCACY

The Asian Human Rights Commission (AHRC) was founded as an independent NGO in 1986. The Commission's goals are to promote greater awareness and realization of human rights in the Asian region, as well as to mobilize Asian and international public opinion to address human rights violations. To this end, the AHRC investigates alleged human rights violations and cooperates with other human rights organizations to raise awareness, provide human rights training, and to organize workshops and seminars. In its projects, the AHRC has focused on a wide variety of issues and countries, such as China, Sri Lanka, Cambodia, the Philippines, the promotion of the Asian Human Rights Charter, indigenous people's groups, and the promotion of national institutions on human rights.

Unit D, 7th Floor
Mongkok Commercial Centre
16-16B Argyle Street
Kowloon, Hong Kong

Tel: +852 (2) 698 6339
Fax: +852 (2) 698 6367
info@ahrchk.net
www.ahrchk.net

Contact: Basil Fernando, Executive Director

Number of staff: 11

Publications: Human Rights Solidarity, Newsletter; *Torture: A Crime Against Humanity,* 2001; *Monitoring the Right for an Effective Remedy for Human Rights Violations,* 2001; *Buddhism, Human Rights and Social Renewal,* 2000; *Rule of Law, Human Rights and Legal Aid in Southeast Asia and China,* 1999 (with the International Human Rights Law Group); *Demoralization and Hope,* 2000; *Hong Kong after 1997: The First 1000 Days,* 2000 (with the Hong Kong Christian Institute); *Problems Facing the Cambodian Legal System,* 1998

Asia

Asia Monitor Resource Centre

RESEARCH
EDUCATION

The Asia Monitor Resource Centre (AMRC) aims to support democratic and independent labor movements in Asia. To this end, the AMRC monitors and researches information on aspects of labor in Asia, including women in Asian Export Processing Zones, the impact of transnational corporations' subcontracting on workers, and the monitoring of workers' conditions in the sport shoe, garment, and toy industries. The AMRC also organizes campaigns, seminars, and meetings on these and linked issues.

8b, 444 Nathan Road
Kowloon, Hong Kong

Tel: +852 (2) 332 1346
Fax: +852 (2) 385 5319
admin@amrc.org.hk
www.amrc.org.hk

Contact: Apo Laung, Executive Director
Budget: $25,000–$100,000
Number of staff: 10
Publications: Asian Labour Update,
quarterly newsletter

Asia

Asian Peace Alliance

ADVOCACY

In October 2001, representatives of several civil society organizations, coalitions and peace groups in Asia gathered in Hong Kong for a public forum jointly organized by ARENA (Hong Kong) and Focus on the Global South (Bangkok) to discuss the regional impact and implications of the September 11 tragedy and the U.S. military campaign against Afghanistan. APA was formally launched through an assembly held in August 2002 in Quezon City, Philippines, attended by more than 100 participants from all over Asia. This consultation considered ways by which civil society organizations could effectively address and respond to these and other emerging peace and security issues. APA exists to strengthen peace movements in Asia, muster a regional people's response to address threats to peace in the region, and promote alternative constructs and practices of peace and people's security.

Flat 6, 13th Floor, Block A
Fuk Keung Industrial Building 66-68
Tong Mi Road
Kowloon, Hong Kong SAR

Tel: +852 (2) 805 6193/6270
Fax: +852 (2) 504 2986
arena@asianexchange.org
www.arenaonline.org

Contact: Aida Jean Nacpil Manipon,
Coordinator Secretariat

Asia

Asian Regional Exchange for New Alternatives

The Asian Regional Exchange for New Alternatives (ARENA) is a regional network of Asian scholars that aims to contribute to processes of people-oriented change. ARENA members come from a wide range of Asian countries to advocate alternative paradigms and development strategies. ARENA undertakes research, facilitates networking, and organizes workshops and dialogues that focus on issues such as: economic globalization and its impact on human security; the agenda of sustainable development; democratization and governance; gender issues; and people's empowerment.

Flat 6, 13th Floor, Block A
Fuk Keung Industrial Building 66-68
Tong Mi Road
Kowloon, Hong Kong SAR

Tel: +852 (2) 805 6193/6270
Fax: +852 (2) 504 2986
arena@asianexchange.org
jeannie@asianexchange.org
www.arenaonline.org
www.asianexchange.org

Contact: Aida Jean Nacpil Manipon, Coordinator Secretariat
Number of staff: 5
Publications: Asian Exchange, bi-annual journal; *Communiqué,* occasional newsletter

Asia

Documentation for Action Groups in Asia

The Documentation for Action Groups in Asia (DAGA) is a research and information center for action groups in Asia. Its main aim is to collect, analyze, and make available information for action. The organization publishes a newsletter and dossiers on human rights issues in the Asian region in addition to organizing workshops and training programs in the areas of peace and conflict transformation, focusing on non-violence and indigenous/traditional methods of conflict resolution. On its website, DAGA publishes articles on various conflicts, including a section on just peace and positive stories of peacebuilding, contributed by various practitioners and scholars in the region.

96 Pak Tin Village Area 2
Mei Tin Road
Shatin, Hong Kong

Tel: +852 (2) 697 1917
Fax: +852 (2) 697 1912
dagainfo@daga.org.hk
www.daga.org

Publications: DAGAInfo, Newsletter; *The War on Terror: Reordering the World,* 2002; *Taming Global Financial Flows,* 2000; *The Koreas: Chronological review of DPRK-ROK Dialogue and Efforts for Unification: 1945–1997,* 1997; *Dossiers on Mindanao, Burma, China and the WTO, India, Kashmir and East Timor*

China

Human Rights in China

RESEARCH
EDUCATION
ADVOCACY

Founded by Chinese scientists and scholars in 1989, Human Rights in China (HRIC) is an international NGO that is committed to promoting human rights and advancing the institutional protection of these rights in China. Furthermore, HRIC encourages victims of human rights abuses to seek redress under domestic law or, if necessary, assists in seeking international intervention. In addition, if Chinese domestic law contravenes international human rights standards, HRIC advocates its amendment or repeal. HRIC uses five interrelated strategies to foster human rights values: to act as a human rights resource center; to facilitate and empower Chinese human rights activism; to educate and inform; to research and publish information; and to advocate and monitor Chinese government compliance with ratified instruments.

Hong Kong GPO
PO Box 1778
Hong Kong

Tel: +852 (2) 710 8021
Fax: +852 (2) 710 8027
hrichina@prochina.org.hk
http://iso.hrichina.org

Publications: China Rights Forum, a quarterly English or Chinese-language journal about the human rights situation in China; *Empty Promises: Human Rights Protections and China's Procedure Law*, 2001

Asia

Oxfam Hong Kong

RESEARCH
EDUCATION
ACTION
ADVOCACY

Oxfam Hong Kong is an independent development and relief agency based in Hong Kong since 1976 and member of Oxfam international. Oxfam Hong Kong supports poor people regardless of race, sex, religion, or politics in their struggle against poverty, distress, and suffering. Its vision is a world where people are equally assured of their rights with dignity and respect, including access to food, shelter, employment, and health care, in a sustainable manner. Oxfam Hong Kong supports the Asia-Pacific campaigns to ban land mines, conducts job training for victims, and disseminates public awareness mailings to community groups, schools, and NGOs, and advertises in major newspapers for public support.

17/F., China United Centre
28 Marble Road
North Point, Hong Kong

Tel: +852 (2) 520 2525
Fax: +852 (2) 527 6307
info@oxfam.org.hk
www.oxfam.org.hk

Contact: Chong Chan-yau, Director

Publications: Curse of the Bombes: A Case Study of Saravan Province, Laos, 1998; *Land Mines and Underdevelopment: A Case Study of Quang Tri Province, Central Vietnam*, 1995

Tibet

Tibetan Center for
Human Rights and Democracy

RESEARCH
EDUCATION
ACTION
ADVOCACY

Tibetan Center for Human Rights and Democracy (TCHRD) was founded in 1996. The NGO has had a branch office in Kathmandu, Nepal, since 1998. TCHRD is independent of the Tibetan Government-in-Exile, and is based in Dharamsala, India. It is funded by donations from individual supporters and foundations around the world. To achieve its objectives TCHRD undertakes activities such as monitoring and researching the human rights situation in Tibet; producing documents and reports relating to specific human rights issues in Tibet and disseminating these internationally; lobbying international bodies to highlight and support the human rights of Tibetan people; and educating the Tibetan community-in-exile in the principles of human rights and democracy.

Top Floor, Narthang Building
Gangchen Kyishong
Dharamsala 176 215 (HP)
India

Tel: +91 (1892) 23 363
Fax: +91 (1892) 24 957
dsala@tchrd.org
www.tchrd.org

Publications: Human Rights Update, monthly newsletter; *Annual Report 2002: Human Rights Situation in Tibet,* 2002; *Dispossessed: Land and Housing Rights in Tibet,* 2002

Tibet

EDUCATION
ACTION
ADVOCACY

Tibetan Women's Association

The Tibetan Women's Association (TWA) was officially founded in Tibet in 1959 as a force against the illegal imprisonment and torture of thousands of Tibetan women in Lhasa. TWA was reinstated in India in 1984 and now works through 12 branches in India and 44 branches worldwide. The TWA has over 11,000 members and is committed to raising public awareness about the abuses faced by Tibetan women in Tibet. The TWA further addresses religious and cultural issues, educational needs, social welfare, the environment, and the political participation and social empowerment of women. In addition, the TWA has developed many community projects aimed at raising awareness and empowering Tibetan women.

Central Executive Committee
Bhagsunath Road
PO Box Mcleod Ganj
Dharamsala-176219
Kangra (H.P.)
India

Tel: +91 (1892) 221 527/198
Fax: +91 (1892) 221 528
twa@del2.vsnl.net.in
www.tibetanwomen.org

Contact: B. Tsering Yeshi, President

Number of staff: 7 Executives

Publications: Dolma: The Voice of Tibetan Women, TWA magazine published every 18 months; *Our Will Against Their Might: Female Prisoners of Conscience in Occupied Tibet,* 2002; *Undying Spirit: 40 Years of Tibetan Women in Exile* (video); *Voices in Exile: Tibetan Women's Journeys* (video).

Aceh

Aceh Human Rights NGO Network

ACTION
ADVOCACY

In 1998, fifteen NGOs concerned with human rights abuses in Aceh founded the Koalisi NGO HAM Aceh. Their goal was to build a regional and international network for human rights advocacy in Aceh. The Network envisages a society in which the values of humanity, social justice, gender, and democracy are respected. The Koalisi campaigns to raise awareness of the human rights situation in Aceh, locally as well as internationally. It investigates and records human rights violations; provides assistance for victims through litigation and non-litigation approaches; and lobbies the local and central governments to address human rights violations and the rehabilitation of victims. On the grassroots level, the Koalisi has established Centers of Human Rights Legal Assistance in six different conflict areas within Aceh. These centers consist of human rights lawyers and litigators, and facilitate human rights assistance on the village level.

Jalan Sudirman No. 11A
Banda Aceh 23239
Indonesia

Tel: +62 (651) 41 998/47 898
Fax: +62 (651) 47 839
koalisi@asia.com
www.koalisi-ham.org

Contact: Maimul Fidar,
Director PB-HAM, Risman A.
Rachman, Director

Number of staff: 12

Aceh

Aceh Legal Aid Foundation – LBH Banda Aceh

RESEARCH
EDUCATION

As a result of Military Operation Region in Aceh there were lots of human rights violations to the civil community. Realizing this condition, the Legal Aid Foundation in Jakarta considered it important to set up an institution working in legal aid in Banda Aceh in order to defend the interest of civil community whose rights are being neglected. Founded on November 30, 1996, this foundation is intended to defend the legal rights of the oppressed civil society.

The main activities of this foundation are gender, law, environment, human rights, democracy, informal sector, and labor issue. All those activities are carried out in the form of community development and assistance as well as advocacy. This foundation has organized various discussions and provided advocacy for several cases, especially the human rights violations in Aceh. It participates in Regional Forum of NGOs of Aceh and WALHI Aceh. At the national level it is a member of the Indonesian Legal Aid Foundation.

Jalan Teungku Chik Pantee Kulu Lt. II, No. 12
Banda Aceh 23242, Daerah Istimewa Aceh

Tel: +62 (651) 23 321
Fax: +62 (651) 31 116
lbh-banda@wasantara.net.id

Contact: Abdul Rahman Yakob,
SH, Director

Number of staff: 6

West Kalimantan

EDUCATION
ACTION

Akar Pama Foundation – YAPAMA

Yayasan Akar Pama started as a study group in 1998 by student activists in West Kalimantan and became a foundation in 2001. YAPAMA focuses on the development of multi-ethnic communities in West Kalimantan, that are empowered, independent, and able to think critically about issues of faith, human rights, gender equity, justice, and peace. YAPAMA's mission is to empower multi-ethnic communities through community organization and to defend victims of human rights abuses while building their own organizational capacity.

Jl. Paris II
Komplek Alex Griya Permai
  I Blok D-15
Pontianak, Kalimantan Barat 78241
Indonesia

Tel: +62 (561) 712 146
Fax: +62 (561) 881 849
akar_guns@yahoo.com

Contact: Charles, Director
Number of staff: 4; 6 volunteers

West Papua

RESEARCH
EDUCATION
ADVOCACY

Alliance for Democracy in Papua – AIDP

The Alliance for Democracy in Papua (AIDP, Aliansi Demokrasi Untuk Papua) is an independent NGO, established in 2000, that fights for and gives a voice to community aspirations for democracy and justice in Papua through advocacy, political education, publications, research, promoting community access, and by developing networks. Its main task are: policy advocacy in lawmaking and the lawmaking obligations of legislative institutions; promotion of accuracy and completeness of information regarding all kinds of developments in Papua; strategic studies of trends with regard to politics, organizations, bureaucracy, and military actors, in particular focusing on the authority inherent in each of these structures and the effects of this in the community; research, studies, assistance, training, and support for the process of building, strengthening, and developing the position and sovereignty of the people; and effectiveness of internal and external networks that promote AIDP's vision.

Jl. Raya Padang Bulan
Depan Asrama Mahasiswa Acemo
Manokwari, Abepura, Jayapura
Papua

Tel. +62 (967) 587 890
aldepe@jayapura.wasantara.net.id

Contact: Latifah Anum Siregar
Number of staff: 9

Southeast Asia

Association for
Southeast Asian Nations

ACTION

Since 1967 the Association for Southeast Asian Nations (ASEAN) has stimulated social, economic, and cultural cooperation in Southeast Asia. In 1976 its
members signed an important treaty to promote regional peace and stability
through political and security dialogue. This treaty also provides a code of
conduct for the peaceful settlement of disputes. Abiding respect for justice and
the rule of law in the relationship among countries in the region and adherence
to the principles of the United Nations Charter are part of this declaration. A
historical highlight for ASEAN was the settlement of the Cambodian conflict
through mediation and diplomacy in the early 1990s. A further step toward
conflict prevention was the creation of the ASEAN Regional Forum. Since the
admission of Cambodia in 1999, ASEAN represents all Southeast Asian states.
There are connections with dialogue partners, including India.

70A, Jl. Sisingamangaraja
Jakarta 12110
Indonesia

Tel: +62 (21) 726 2991, 724 3372
Fax: +62 (21) 739 8234, 724 3504
public@aseansec.org
www.aseansec.org

Contact: H.E. Ong Keng Yong, Secretary-
General

Publications: ASEAN Annual reports (1980
till 2003), ASEAN Public Information
Series, ASEAN Briefing Papers, Hand-
book on Selected ASEAN Political
Documents, ASEAN Regional Forum
Documents Series 1994–2002

Asia Pacific

Association for Southeast
Asian Nations – Regional Forum

ACTION

The Association for Southeast Asian Nations—Regional Forum (ARF) was
established by ASEAN in 1994 with the purpose of promoting political and
security dialogue and cooperation in the Asia-Pacific region. At this moment
participants are the ten ASEAN members and 11 ASEAN dialogue and consultative partners from Asia and beyond. The forum emphasizes the importance of
confidence building measures to the overall ARF process and that these efforts
need to be intensified. The ARF process provides an annual ministerial meeting
and several supporting bodies, such as Inter-Sessional Meetings (on CBM) and
related Track-Two meetings. Recently an extended discussion on the concept of
preventive diplomacy has emerged among the member states.

The ASEAN Secretariat
70A, Jl. Sisingamangaraja
Jakarta 12110
Indonesia

Tel. +62 (21) 726 2991
Fax. +62 (21) 739 8234
public@aseansec.org
www.aseansec.org/arf.htm

Contact: M. C. Abad, Jr., Head of Public
Affairs Office

Number of staff in the Secretariat: 150

Publications: Annual Security Outlook

Maluku

Bina Swadaya

RESEARCH
EDUCATION
ADVOCACY

Bina Swadaya is a non-profit NGO (founded in 1967) dedicated to empowering the poor on institutional and business issues. Its mission is to strive for pro-poor development policies and to bridge the socioeconomic gap in order to create a fair and just social structure. This organization works on capacity building foremost, while also establishing a solid network and outreach program through education, publishing, and researching. Bina Swadaya has a Humanitarian Aid department that focuses exclusively on conflict prevention/resolution programs, including a Peace-Based Reconciliation program focusing on the (North) Maluku region.

Gunung Sahari 111/7
10610
Indonesia

Tel: +62 (21) 420 4402
Fax: +62 (21) 420 8412
binaswadaya@binaswadaya.org
www.binaswadaya.org

Contact: Bambang Ismawan, Director
Number of staff: 6 for conflict
prevention/resolution (750 total)

Budget: $25,000 to $100,000

Publications: Newsletter; *Pluralism, Humanity and Anti-Discrimination; Peace vs. War*

Aceh

Care for Human Rights Foundation – YPHAM

RESEARCH
EDUCATION
ADVOCACY

Established in July 1998, Care for Human Rights Foundation (YPHAM, Yayasan Peduli Hak Asasi Manusia) was called Forum Peduli HAM (Human Rights Care Forum), but since 2001 it changed to YPHAM. The organization strives to promote and improve human rights conditions in Aceh through a human rights awareness program. It mainly carries out human rights training that ranges from human rights education to forensic training; dissemination of human rights information through its newsletter and seminars, advocacy, and campaign work; and investigation and documentation. Its documentation collection is mostly used for sources of research on Aceh. Along with its mission, YPHAM is also doing programs regarding conflict resolution, peacebuilding, and good governance.

Jalan T. Hasan Dek No. 160
Beurawe, Banda Aceh
Nanggroe Aceh Darusallam
Indonesia

Tel: +62 (651) 24726
Fax: +62 (651) 32242
ypham_aceh@yahoo.com or fpham@aceh.wasantara.net.id

Contact: Saifuddin Bantasyam, Executive Director
Number of staff: 10; some volunteers

Indonesia

CARE International Indonesia

ACTION

CARE International Indonesia works in a counterpart relationship with the Ministry of Home Affairs. CARE International Indonesia has been active in Indonesia since 1967. Beginning with food distribution in Java, the organization has since expanded into a wide range of programming from Emergency to Emergency Recovery (Transitional) to Development. Development programs at CARE International Indonesia have prioritized water and sanitation, health, agriculture, environment, small economic activities development, good governance, and civil society. CARE International Indonesia is carrying out extensive programming in East and West Java, East Kalimantan, Central, South and Southeast Sulawesi, Nusa Tenggara Barat (NTB), and the West Timor and Flores regions of Nusa Tenggara Timur (NTT).

Jl. Pattimura, No. 33
Kebayoran Baru, Jakarta
12110 DKI Jakarta
Indonesia

Contact: Steve Gilbert, Assistant Country Director, Programming
Number of staff: 300

Tel: +62 (21) 7279 6661
Fax. +62 (21) 7222 552
sgilbert@cbn.net.id
www.careinternational.org.uk/cares_work/where/indonesia/

Indonesia

ACTION
ADVOCACY

Catholic Relief Service Indonesia

Catholic Relief Service (CRS) Indonesia is part of the international NGO Catholic Relief Service. In Indonesia CRS has been involved in relief and development work since the early 1950s and its vision is to work for a just and peaceful society. Its mission is to improve equality for those in greatest need while strengthening solidarity among Indonesia's diverse ethnic and religious communities. CRS works in areas of health, agriculture, emergency response, micro-finance, and peacebuilding, and offers services to communities regardless of a community's faith. CRS implements its programs through local partners.

In its Peacebuilding Program, CRS aims to increase the capacity and effectiveness of peacebuilding practitioners through capacity building of partners, providing resources for networking, documenting and disseminating good practices, and research into indigenous conflict resolution approaches. More broadly, civil society is strengthened through training, promoting gender awareness in peacebuilding, building strong community media, and promotion of good governance through education of civil society groups, religious, and other informal leaders. Peacebuilding is also integrated with relief and development programs to enhance the overall institutional focus and strategic direction toward peace and justice. In Southeast Asia CRS has offices and programs in countries such as Vietnam, East Timor, Philippines, Cambodia, Burma, and Thailand.

Jl. Wijaya I, 35
Kebayoran Baru
Jakarta, 12170
Indonesia

Tel: +62 (21) 725 339
Fax: +62 (21) 725 1566
crsindo@crs.or.id
www.catholicrelief.org

Contact: Mike Frank, Executive Director of CRS Indonesia

Number of staff: 10 persons in Peacebuilding Program

Peacebuilding budget: $300,000 (at country level)

Publications: *The Peacebuilding Toolkit; The Indonesian Peacebuilding Directory* (in collaboration with Cordaid); *Peace by Peace: Good Practice in Peacebuilding in Central Java, Indonesia; Conflict is the Beginning of Peace: Stories and Good Practice from Field Workers Serving East Timor Refugees in West Timor; Not Eno: Documentation of Information Dissemination Program on East Timor Commission on Truth, Acceptance and Reconciliation by West Timor NGO Coalition.*

Indonesia

Center for Research on Intergroup Relations and Conflict Resolution

RESEARCH
EDUCATION

The Center for Research on Intergroup Relations and Conflict Resolution (CERIC, Pusat Studi Hubungan Antar Kelompok dan Resolusi Konflik) is a research organization that studies the dynamics of inter-community group relationships as potential sources of conflict, through transparent and focused research methods. CERIC conducts training about conflict prevention and group mediation for the general public and works to develop approaches to education that are based on the understanding of the relationship between groups, and conflict resolution, through curriculum and syllabus development. Research activities are conducted through various programs, such as workshops, training, seminars, studies, and publications. CERIC also works to build networks with universities and NGOs, both within Indonesia and internationally.

Gedung C Lantai Kampus Fisip Ul
Depok, DKI Jakarta 16424
Indonesia

Tel: +62 (21) 787 3838
Fax: +62 (21) 787 3777
ceric@cbn.net.id

Contact: Imam B. Prasodjo, Director
Number of staff: 8; 19 volunteers

Indonesia

Center for Security and Peace Studies, Gadjah Mada University

RESEARCH
EDUCATION
ADVOCACY

The Center for Security and Peace Studies, Gadjah Mada University (CSPS-UGM) is a non-profit academic institution that was founded in October 1996. Its mission is to reshape conceptions of security and peace, with the goal of raising public awareness about international, regional, and national security and peace issues. Its main objectives are to produce a high quality of research, training, and advocacy in conflict and peace issues areas. CSPS-UGM focuses on Security Sector Reform, Conflict Resolution, Conflict Prevention and Post-conflict Reconstruction, and Media and Networking. These issues are translated into various activities such as research, training, facilitation, and policy advocacy, in several regions in Indonesia. In addition to its role as a national coordinator of the Southeast Asian Conflict Studies Network (SEA-CSN) in Indonesia, CSPS maintains good cooperation and networking with many national and international partners.

Sekip K-9
Yogyakarta 55281
Indonesia

Tel/Fax: +62 (274) 520 733
Csps-ugm@jmn.net.id
www.csps-ugm.or.id

Contact: Lambang Trijono, Director
Number of staff: 16
Budget: $25,000-$100,000
Publications: Newsletter; *Building Sustainable Peace and Fostering Development in Papua* (a final report of the e-conference), 2002

Indonesia and East Asia

Center for Strategic and International Studies

The Center for Strategic and International Studies (CSIS) is a private non-profit organization that was founded in 1971. CSIS undertakes policy-oriented studies on domestic and international affairs as an independent voice in the government and private sector, and as a contributor to public debates. The Center's main activities are research, policy advice, networking, data collecting, and publishing books and journals that are distributed regionally. CSIS has an on-going program of conflict resolution in Aceh and Papua that aims to develop modalities for conflict resolution through conflict analysis and dialogue projects with government, local leaders, and civil society organizations. CSIS also plays a significant role in the Council for Security Cooperation in Asia Pacific and has constructed an international network with many institutions, including the Henry Dunant Center (Switzerland).

Jl. Tanah Abang III No. 27
Jakarta 10160
Indonesia

Tel: +62 (21) 386 5532/386 5535
Fax: +62 (21) 380 9641/384 7517
csis@csis.or.id
www.csis.or.id

Contact: Rizal Sukma
Budget: $25,000–$100,000
Publications: Peace Building and State Building in East Timor, 2002.

Indonesia

Center for the Study and Promotion of Peace

The mission of the Center for the Study and Promotion of Peace (Pusat Studi dan Pengembangan Perdamaian) is to empower individuals and communities for peacebuilding in families, religious communities, working places, and within society based on love, truth, justice, and peace. It does this through the research and promotion of peace, education and training, consultation and conflict intervention, trauma healing, and the provision of information. Some of the projects are: Trauma Healing and Conflict Resolution; Police Training in Cooperative Conflict Resolution; Peer Mediation; Empowering Area Facilitators; Independent Team for Reconciliation in Ambon; and Promoting Reconciliation and Human Rights in the Process of Democratization in Papua.

Pusat Studi dan Pengembangan Perdamaian
Universitas Kristen Duta Wacana
Jl. Dr. Wahidin 5-19
Yogyakarta 55224
Indonesia

Tel: +62 (274) 563 929 ext.108
Fax: +62 (274) 513 235
pspp@ukdw.ac.id
www.ukdw.ac.id/pspp/indexeng.html

Contact: Rev. Paulus S. Widjaya, Ph.D and Rev. Jozef M. N. Hehanussa, M.Th.
Number of staff: 5

Indonesia

Civil Society Alliance for Democracy – Yappika

RESEARCH
ADVOCACY

Aliansi Masyarakat Sipil untuk Demokrasi was established in 1991 to promote the development of a civil society that is democratic, independent, and respects pluralism. Yappika has three strategic programs in development: it supports social initiatives to promote social reconciliation, aims to strengthen the capacity and governance of civil society, and focuses on developing the social economy of the community. Yappika has, in the past, carried out research in both Aceh and Papua and, at this time, conducts a study into the peace agreement regarding the Maluku conflict.

Jl. Pedati Raya No. 20 RT 007/09   *Contact:* Otto Syamsuddin Ishak, Manager
Jakarta Timur   *Number of staff:* 22
DKI Jakarta 13350
Indonesia

Tel: +62 (21) 819 1623
Fax: +62 (21) 850 0670
yappika@indosat.net.id
www.yappika.or.id

Indonesia

Commission for Involuntary Disappearances and Victims of Violence – KONTRAS

EDUCATION
ACTION

The Commission for Involuntary Disappearances and Victims of Violence (KONTRAS) was formed in March 1998 by the coalition of 12 pro-democracy NGOs and activists in response to the Indonesian government's silence regarding disappearances of some activists. KONTRAS carries out programs mainly on integrated legal aid that includes legal consultancy for the victim and his/her family, legal advocacy to plead for state responsibility, post-trauma healing and rehabilitation for the victim and family, and investigations. Other programs are documenting human rights violation cases, monitoring of human rights situations, and also forming public opinion for human rights education and awareness purposes. In 2001, KONTRAS built Voice of Human Rights, a radio for human rights education. It works together with national NGO networks as well as international networks.

Jl.Cisadane No. 9   *Contact:* Ori Rahman, Presidium
Menteng   Coordinator
Jakarta Pusat
Indonesia

Tel: +62 (21) 390 1978
Fax: +62 (21) 314 1484
kontras@clon.net.id
www.desaparecidos.org/kontras/links.html

Kalimantan

Commission for Socioeconomic Justice and Peace Development – PSE and KKP

RESEARCH
ACTION
ADVOCACY

The Commission for Socioeconomic Justice and Peace Development (PSE and KKP, Komisi Pengembangan Sosial Ekonomi, Keadilan dan Perdamaian) is a church-affiliated organization committed to underprivileged, oppressed, poor, and marginalized people. PSE and KKP works to fight together with these people through campaigning, promoting awareness, and socioeconomic development (income generation). They also focus on empowering grassroots communities and promoting awareness of moral crisis within the community, increasing awareness of rights and responsibilities through courses in farming, and forming inter-ethnic self-reliance groups among target communities.

Jl. WR. Supratman 100
PO Box 1270
Pontianak
Kalimantan Barat 78011
Indonesia

Contact: P. Yeremias
Number of staff: 4; 6 volunteers

Tel: +62 (561) 748 116
Fax: +62 (561) 748 116
pse_kap@pontianak.wasantara.net.id

Indonesia

Common Ground Indonesia

RESEARCH
EDUCATION
ACTION
ADVOCACY

Common Ground Indonesia is a program designed by the Search for Common Ground based in the United States. The program's maxim is to create a shared peaceful and just life by transforming ways of dealing with conflict, using methods that generate solidarity, participation and pluralism. The Indonesian projects focus on working with communities and civil-society organizations in conflict vulnerable areas in Central and Western Kalimantan, Madura, and Papua. The program enables these groups to develop the skills needed to prevent and resolve conflict, through training and capacity building. Indonesia now has its first ever radio drama about conflict and conflict transformation, called Menteng Pangkalan, aired on over 160 radio stations across Indonesia. In addition, there is a comic book program established as an educational tool for conflict transformation, as well as a film festival.

Griya Upakara Bld. Jl Cikini
IV No. 10, Unit 10. 3rd Floor
Jakarta 10330
Indonesia

Contact: Vanessa Johanson, Country Director
Publications: Women Transforming Conflict: Assessment Report, January 2003

Tel: +62 (21) 392 3738
Fax: +62 (21) 392 5216
commonground@indocg.org
www.sfcg.org

Indonesia

Community Recovery Program

ACTION

The Community Recovery Program (CRP, Program Pemulihan Keberdayaan Masyarakat) was founded in Jakarta. Its original founders include Emil Salim, Erna Witoelar, Ismid Hadad, Bambang Ismawan, and a number of other community leaders. CRP is a mechanism for channeling assistance through NGOs and community self-reliance groups to vulnerable communities in Indonesia that have suffered the greatest impact of the economic crisis. Communities receiving assistance devise activities that promote the empowerment of individuals and groups with the assistance of NGOs. Community empowerment and institution strengthening contribute to promoting to the future strength and viability of civil society. In addition to providing assistance to victims of the economic crisis, CRP also helps victims of violence in places such as Maluku, Aceh, and Central Kalimantan. The approach of the organization is participatory with CRP only acting as a facilitator.

Jl. Tebet Barat Dalam IV No. 10
Jakarta Selatan
12810 DKI Jakarta
Indonesia

Tel: +62 (21) 828 0050
Fax: +62 (21) 8370 4405
indocrp@indocrp.or.id
www.indocrp.or.id

Contact: Amrullah, Program manager
Number of staff: 22
Budget: US$1,000,000

Indonesia

Consortium for Assisting the Refugees and Displaced in Indonesia

EDUCATION
ACTION
ADVOCACY

Consortium for Assisting the Refugees and Displaced in Indonesia (CARDI) is a non-profit, humanitarian consortium established by the Danish Refugee Council, the Norwegian Refugee Council, the International Rescue Committee, and Dutch Refugee Foundation that are sharing the same mandate of providing assistance and solutions to refugees and displaced persons in Indonesia. They have pooled their resources in order to reduce the suffering of conflict-affected communities and mitigate the effects of internal displacement in Indonesia, while building a stronger civil society.

In collaboration with local and international NGOs, Indonesian authorities and UN Agencies, CARDI strives to meet the needs of communities affected by conflict. Its main activities concentrate around emergency relief, capacity building for community-based organizations and local NGOs, education, community development, peace education or conflict management activities in areas with high numbers of IDPs/refugees, economic empowerment (e.g. income generation, vocational training etc.), support for return and resettlement, water and sanitation, and other activities aimed at reinforcing the capacity of communities to address the consequences of conflict or forced displacement and to resume a peaceful and sustainable coexistence.

For 2002–2003, CARDI's programs were:

- Youth Civic Participation Initiative, conducted together with UNICEF's support to strengthen the foundation of social recovery in North Maluku postconflict communities by mobilizing youth from all religious backgrounds to address conflict in nonviolent ways, through a combination of peer-to-peer education and radio programming.
- Emergency Education and Psychosocial Support in Ambon Island, to mitigate the effect of violence and displacement on Malukan displaced young people through a network of youth centers, offering structuring activities, life skills and peace education.
- Information Centers in North Sulawesi and North Maluku, to allow displaced persons to make informed decisions about their future and to facilitate a peaceful reunion with their former neighbors.

CARDI
Jl. Cibulan 16 A
Jakarta 12170
Indonesia

Tel: +62 (21) 726 2452
Fax: +62 (21) 726 2452 ext.105
cardi@cbn.net.id

Contact: Hervé de Bailleux
Number of staff: 20
Budget: $100,000 to $500,000

Sulawesi

Consortium of Local NGOs of South Sulawesi—KL2SS

ACTION

Established in 1998, the Consortium of Local NGOs of South Sulawesi is an alliance of 24 local NGOs. Each organization represents one regency/town in South Sulawesi. They are concerned about the welfare of marginalized communities who are poor, weak and have been left behind in the development process. The NGOs pool their resources and work together to overcome the socioeconomic problems faced by society. This ideal and spirit of struggle is embodied in KL2SS's motto "Together Against Poverty." To achieve its goal, KL2SS carries out some strategic activities such as increasing family income by developing economic enterprises, promoting environmental conservation, improving family health, advocating the rights of civil society, developing human resource, information dissemination, and providing consultation.

Jl. Tengko Situru No. 5
Malangngo, Rantepao
Tana Toraja
Sulawesi Selatan

Contact: May Januar, Coordinator
Budget: $25,000–$50,000

Tel: +62 (423) 23 985/21 365
Fax: +62 (423) 21 855

Maluku

Crisis Centre Diocese of Amboina

RESEARCH
ACTION

The Crisis Centre Diocese of Amboina (CCDA) was founded in July 1999 by Bishop P.C. Mandagi Msc. During the conflict in the area, which started in January 1999, the CCDA worked in the fields of intervention and reconciliation efforts, evacuation and emergency aid for refugees, funding, humanitarian assistance, human rights promotion, mediation, and development/rehabilitation. CCDA also built networks with international agencies as well as with local government authorities and national or local communities, and with individual Muslim leaders. In June 2000 it started to disseminate information on the conflict to the international community. As in October 2002 the conflict was considered to have come to an end, the Crisis Centre since then has restricted itself to a general stand-by and backing up, but has been continuing their regular newsletter publication.

Puspaskup
Jl. Pattimura 32
Ambon 97124
Indonesia

Tel: +62 (911) 342 195
Fax: +62 (911) 355 337
crisiscentre01@hotmail.com
www.malra.org/posko

Contact: C.J. Böhm and Felix Wee
Budget: < $25,000
Number of staff: 2
Publication: Newsletter *The Situation in Ambon/Moluccas* consists of reports on the conflict in Maluku and reconciliation efforts

Kalimantan

Dialogue Forum of South Kalimantan – Forlog Kalsel

RESEARCH
EDUCATION
ACTION
ADVOCACY

Forum Dialog Antar Kita Kalimantan Selatan was initiated by local organizations as a follow up of Dian Interfidei's seminar on pluralism, dialogue, and conflict. Awareness of the importance of disseminating pluralism ideas to prevent or resolve conflict makes LPKOP, STT GKE, MASIKA, GMKI, PMII, Yowana, Peradah, LK3, and Gemabidhi work together to do public campaigning through discussion and the media, as well as training. They conduct training in postconflict areas, e.g., Central and South Kalimantan, on conflict management and also some research and publishing to promote peace journalism. They also work cooperatively on facilitating dialogue, trauma counseling, and postconflict rehabilitation.

Jl. Simpang Gatot Subroto VII/
Rama Rt. 29 No. 61
Banjarmasin 70235
Kalimantan Selatan
Indonesia

Contact: Gazalirrahman, Secretary
Number of staff: 3; 8 volunteers
Budget: < $25,000

Tel/Fax: +62 (511) 271 689
lk3@indo.net.id

Indonesia

Forum for Community Participation

RESEARCH
ACTION

Forum for Community Participation (FPPM) is a non-profit, non-partisan forum founded on local ability and diversity. Its vision is the development of civil society at the grass-roots level—a kind of civil society that is able to analyze, access, and manage the issues that have an impact on its environment and promote broad interaction as a working example of "self-governance." It wants to achieve this by building networks and communication between interested parties and practitioners of community development; facilitating innovative participatory approaches which make it possible for members of the community to interact actively; to support the community's ability to access and to have control over available resources and develop contacts with the outside world; facilitating activities for human resource development through exchange of information and experience within a framework of learning together; and carrying out studies and advocacy concerning policy at central and regional levels.

Taman Duren Sawit Blok AI No. 09
Jl. Rawa Domba, Jakarta Timur
13440 DKI Jakarta
Indonesia

Contact: Tri Bangun Asih, Secretariat
Number of staff: 23

Tel/Fax: +62 (21) 860 4606
forumppm@indo.net.id
www.fppm.org

Indonesia

Human Rights Commission – Komnas HAM

EDUCATION ACTION

Human Rights Commission (Komnas HAM, Komisi Nasional Hak Asasi Manusia) is a governmental institution that was founded originally by a presidential decree in 1993, which was reinforced by UU No. 39/1999 on Human Rights and the role of Komnas HAM. Its mission is to resolve human rights violation cases and to engage in human rights education. Even though it is mandated by the state, Komnas HAM is impartial and independent. Its members are prominent figures that are well known as human rights defenders and elected through a test by parliament.

To achieve its mission, Komnas HAM functions as a body to receive complaints on human rights violations, investigate cases, especially prominent human rights cases, and make recommendations on how to follow up the case to government and judicial body.

Current priorities are the Maluku and Tanjung Priok case. Complementing this role, Komnas HAM carries out research into bill/policy regarding human rights issues, on international human rights instruments, advocates the bill to complement with human rights values as well as to public interest, and/or to recommends the instruments to ratify. Komnas HAM also provides human rights education for people, especially NGOs, religious leaders, military, police, judicial officials, and so forth. To disseminate the idea of human rights, Komnas HAM publishes a monthly newsletter, executes a human rights campaign, and conducts seminar. To accomplish its goal, Komnas HAM also builds international networks.

Jl. Latuharhary No. 4B
Menteng, 10310, Jakarta Pusat
Indonesia

Tel: +62 (21) 392 5230
Fax: +62 (21) 392 5227
info@komnas.go.id
www.komnas.go.id

Indonesia

Indigenous Peoples Alliance
of the Archipelago – AMAN

The Indigenous Peoples Alliance of the Archipelago (AMAN, Aliansi Masyarakat Adat Nusantara) is an independent social organization with a membership that is drawn from indigenous communities from all corners of the Indonesian archipelago. AMAN is an umbrella organization that works with indigenous communities to maintain their traditional rights, existence, and sovereignty. This can be achieved when communities can organize themselves in just ways and manage their natural resources sustainability.

AMAN's program consists of developing their network and protecting the rights of indigenous communities through advocacy. In addition, they focus on strengthening the economy, education and women of indigenous communities.

Jalan B No. 4
Rawa Bambu Satu
Pasar Minggu
Jakarta Selatan 12520
Indonesia

Tel/Fax: +62 (21) 780 2771
rumahaman@cbn.net.id

Contact: Emilianus Ola Kleden, Director
Budget: $25,000–$100,000
Number of staff: 6

Indonesia

Indonesia Anti-Discrimination
Movement – GANDI

Indonesian Anti-Discrimination Movement (GANDI, Gerakan Perjungan Anti-Diskriminasi) was established as a coordinating body to work for the eradication of discrimination in Indonesia. Following the events of 1998, there emerged a collective awareness among various community stakeholders, such as Indonesian businesspeople of Tionghoa ethnic group and Islamic Kiai from NU (such as Gus Dur) that there was something wrong with the nation and that this situation had to be fixed through collective action. With a vision of bringing about respect for equality, tolerance, and diversity, GANDI was established. Currently, GANDI tends to focus more on strengthening efforts to bring about justice, equality, and diversity. It is currently working on the national law regarding citizenship and vital statistics.

Jl. Raya Kebayoran Lama No. 72
Jakarta Barat
DKI Jakarta 11540
Indonesia

Tel: +62 (812) 949 4284
Fax: +62 (21) 5367 8143
wisantara@yahoo.com

Contact: Wahua Effendy
Number of staff: 6; 5 volunteers

Indonesia

Indonesia Center for Environmental Law – ICEL

RESEARCH
EDUCATION
ADVOCACY

Indonesia Center for Environmental Law (ICEL, Lembaga Pengembangan Hukum Lingkungan) is an independent NGO that works in the field of environmental law. It is active in advocacy and empowerment to promote the fulfillment of rights and management of the environment and natural resources in ways that are just and sustainable. Activities include providing training in environmental law and enforcement; training and workshops; compiling guidelines to promote protection of the environment; and providing legal assistance on environmental law cases. ICEL has worked with various stakeholders, including central government, regional government, academic, and NGOs to promote policy advocacy issues related to the environment and development.

Jl. Dempo II No. 21
Kebayoran Baru
Jakarta Selatan
DKI Jakarta 12120
Indonesia

Contact: Indriany Augustine
Number of staff: 22

Tel: +62 (21) 726 2740/723 3390
Fax: +62 (21) 726 9331
s_indri@lycos.com
icel@indosat.net.id

Indonesia

Indonesia Forum for the Environment – WALHI

EDUCATION
ADVOCACY

The Indonesia Forum for the Environment (WALHI, Wahana Lingkungan Hidup Indonesia) is a non-governmental organization and community group concerned with environmental issues. WALHI was formed in response to concern about environmental issues and injustice in the mismanagement of natural resources as a consequence of development. Activities include strengthening the community, civil society, and indigenous organizations through training in analysis of laws and policies pertaining to the environment and management of natural resources, training in organizational management, and the development of human resources through training and education.

Jl. Tegal Parang Utara 14
Jakarta 12790
Indonesia

Tel: +62 (21) 794 1672
Fax: +62 (21) 794 1673
info@walhi.or.id
www.walhi.or.id

Indonesia

Indonesian Alliance of Independent Journalists – AJI

EDUCATION
ADVOCACY

The Indonesian Alliance of Independent Journalists (AJI, Aliansi Jurnalis Independen Indonesia) was formed as a non-profit journalists' union. The organization was founded in 1992 in response to restrictions placed on freedom of expression in Indonesia and the centralization of information into the hands of the state media. Its mission is to protect, and act as an advocate for, press freedom and democracy in Indonesia. AJI places great emphasis on democracy development, and capacity building for journalists through training, and networking. In addition to these activities, AJI also engages in negotiation and mediation, advocacy, and development/rehabilitation.

The Maluku Media Centre project, run by AJI, attempts to educate and persuade journalists to report less subjectively on the conflict in Maluku, the aim of which ultimately is to promote peace in the region. AJI seeks to build international and national networks.

Jalan LAN I no. 123 A
Pejompongan
Jakarta, 10210
Indonesia

Tel: +62 (21) 571 1044/56
Fax: +62 (21) 571 1063
ajioffice@aji-indonesia.or.id
www.ajinews.or.id

Contact: Ati Nurbaiti, Executive Director
Number of staff: 10
Budget: $25,000–$100,000

EDUCATION

Indonesian Pluralism Institute

Institut Pluralisme Indonesia (IPI) was founded in Jakarta in 2000 with the aim of developing pluralism as the basis for dialogue and cooperation in Indonesian society. IPI's vision is to create understanding, solidarity, and cooperation among individuals and social groups in Indonesia, without discrimination on the basis of ethnic background, religion/belief, gender, political persuasion, socioeconomic status, or regional origin. Activities include the development of a blood donor system, research into pluralist education, the development of training materials for pluralism, conflict transformation and leadership, and the facilitation of youth dialogue circles.

Jl. Percetakan Negra C-553 Lantai 4
DKI Jakarta 10570
Indonesia

Tel/Fax: +62 (21) 422 6449
ipi@cbn.net.id
    or ilmasy@yahoo.com

Contact: William Kwan HL
Number of staff: 3,600 volunteers

Kalimantan

Institut Dayakologi

ACTION

Since 1991, Institut Dayakologi (ID), a community-based NGO, has been actively working for the revitalization and restitution of Dayak cultural heritage in Kalimantan through research, strategic studies, collaboration, publication, and documentation. ID strives to empower the Dayak peoples by the purpose of advocacy at local, national, and international level. In order to fulfill the objective, ID undertakes activities that revitalizes the peoples' customary religion, customary institutions, law, and local knowledge, and encourages local initiative. In collaboration with local, national, and international NGOs, as well as the media, ID is actively involved in peacebuilding efforts through workshops, public discussion, trauma counseling, reconciliation, civic education, and early-warning system activities.

Kompleks Bumi Indah Khatulistiwa
Jl. Budi Utomo Blok A3, No. 3-4
Pontianak 78241
Kalimantan Barat
Indonesia

Contact: John Bamba, Director
Number of staff: 30; 9 volunteers

Tel: +62 (561) 884 567
Fax: +62 (561) 883 135
i.dayakologi@ptk.centrin.net.id
www.dayakology.com

West Papua

Institute for Human Rights Studies and Advocacy – West Papua

**EDUCATION
ADVOCACY**

The Institute for Human Rights Studies and Advocacy-West Papua (ELSHAM) is an independent, Papua-based human rights organization with a mission and vision of demilitarization, justice, peacebuilding, self-determination, and empowerment. A group of lawyers, NGO activist,s and church leaders established ELSHAM in 1998 determined to rectify the long history of human rights violations and structural violence in West Papua. Through its four programs: education, legal aid, research, and gender issues, ELSHAM works to empower communities by building awareness and understanding of universal human rights. Since its establishment, ELSHAM has also been a vocal and high profile advocate on human rights developments in West Papua, frequently investigating and reporting on cases of human rights violations.

Jln Kampus ISTP-Padang Bulan
Jayapura
West Papua
Indonesia

Contact: Aloysius Renwarin,
Acting Director

Tel: +62 (967) 581 600
Fax: +62 (967) 581 520
elshamnewsservice@jayapura.wasantara.net.id
www.geocities.com/elshamnewsservice

Indonesia

Institute for Interfaith Dialogue in Indonesia – Interfidei

Since 1991, Institut Dialog Antar-Iman di Indonesia has been conducting work related issues of humanitarian concern in Indonesia. Interfidei is intended as a forum where religious concepts can be discussed together. It values the legacy of religious thought and respects all religions in their diversity. Its main activities are promoting tolerance and pluralism through public discussion, providing training, research, and conducting religious studies courses. In tandem with this, Interfidei also publishes books and bulletins, in addition to capacity building of personnel and organizations. The importance of networking for the organization is reflected in Interfidei's work with local and international NGOs and governments. At the local level, Interfidei encourages dialogue through a capacity building program. Forum Dialog "Antar Kita" in West Kalimantan and South Sulawesi are the result of Interfidei's efforts.

Jl. Banteng Utama 59
Kaliurang Km. 8
Yogyakarta 55581
Indonesia

Tel/Fax: +62 (274) 880 149
profide@yogya.wasantara.net.id

Contact: Elga Sarapung, Director
Number of staff: 12
Budget: $50,000–$100,000

Kalimantan

Institute for Community Legal Resource Empowerment – LBBT

Lembaga Bela Banua Talino (LBBT) is a non-governmental organization that facilitates the development of the resources of customary law to build a community that is independent in terms of the law and advocacy; that respects for human rights; shows concern for the environment and is based on gender equity and democracy. Activities include organizing community events, policy study, and critical legal education.

Jl. Budi Utomo Blok A3 No. 5
Pontianak
Kalimantan Barat 78241
Indonesia

Tel: +62 (561) 885 623
Fax: +62 (561) 884 566
banua@pontianak.wasantara.net.id

Contact: C. Kanyan, Director
Number of staff: 12; 1 volunteer

Indonesia

Institute for Policy Research and Advocacy – ELSAM

Lembaga Studi dan Advokasi Masyarakat (ELSAM) is an NGO working on policy advocacy, which was established in 1993. It aims to establish a society that respects human rights, justice, and democracy. To achieve this goal, ELSAM conducts some programs on policy/legal research, legal drafting, policy advocacy that relates to human right issues, human rights education/training, and disseminating information on human rights. ELSAM has succeeded in its advocacy that the Indonesian government ratifies the Civil and Political Rights Covenant, and has also actively participated in drafting the legal basis and framework for the Truth and Reconciliation Commission in Indonesia, now under discussion in parliament. ELSAM also publishes books on human rights, the *Judicial Monitoring Review*, analyzing the judicial process in accordance with human rights parameters, and the bulletin *ASASI*, summarizing human rights abuses. The publications are aimed at the public, decision-makers, and law enforcement officials.

Jl. Siaga II No 31, Pasar Minggu
Jakarta 12510
Indonesia

Contact: Ifdhal Kasim,
Executive Director

Number of staff: 20 persons

Tel: +62 (21) 797 2662 / 7919 2564
Fax: +62 (21) 7919 2519
elsam@nusa.or.id or advokasi@indosat.net.id
www.elsam.or.id

Indonesia

Institute for Social Transformation – INSIST

INSIST Foundation is an NGO based in Yogyakarta. The organization works nationally. It was founded in 1997 with the vision of "civil society" as a social movement that organically, with the people, engages in "counter-hegemonic work" against the dominant ideas of neo-liberalism and the state becoming the guardian of global capital. INSIST aims to realize these goals with a range of efforts and ways to find a new path through: young volunteers for social movements who gather in Indonesia; volunteer for Social Movement program (Involvement); and the Indonesian Research and Advanced Co-education Fellowship Program for Community Empowerment (Fellowship) program.

Blimbingsari CT IV No. 38
  (Sekip Blok T/7)
Sleman
Yogyakarta
Indonesia 55281

Tel: +62 (274) 561 847
Fax: +62 (274) 583 314
donmarut@insist.or.id
insist@insist.or.id
www.insist.or.id

Contact: Mr. Donatus K. Marut, Executive Director
Publications: Facilitation Manual for Revitalisation of People's Rights, 2000

Maluku

Institute for Women and Child Empowerment – LAPPAN

Lembaga Pemberdayaan Perempuan dan Anak was founded in 2002. LAPPAN is an NGO which fights for women and children's rights, and empowers women and children through reducing economic inequality and peacebuilding. Its main activities are peace education on community level through seminars, discussions, and trauma counseling for women and children from different parties in the conflict. LAPPAN conducts management conflict training for journalists and coordinators of refugee camps. It also conducts peace education for high school teachers in order to enable them to critically and actively change life skills of the students through curriculum reform and to promote peace and pluralism.

Jl. Pintu Air Kompleks THR
Kelurahan Waihaong
Ambon 97112
Maluku
Indonesia

Tel: +62 (911) 314 176 / 312 022
Fax: + 62 (911) 312 007
lappan_thr@yahoo.com

Contact: Baihajar Tualeka, Executive Director
Number of staff: 7

Aceh

Institute of Civil Society Empowerment – Yayasan Cordova

RESEARCH
EDUCATION

Cordova is an NGO which has been active since 1990 in Kutaradja, Aceh. Cordova aims to support the empowerment of civil society, so that it has a commitment to uphold human rights and principles of life in a democratic political system. Cordova's activities include documentation, investigation, and publication, as well as education, and are characterized by democratic and humanitarian values. Cordova has carried out various forms of investigation and studies regarding issues of human rights and democratization problems and has published several titles about human rights cases. Cordova has experience in holding different forms of workshops, seminars, and training.

Jl. As Sumantrani No. 3
Darussalam
Banda Aceh 23111
Indonesia

Contact: Risman A.Rachman, Director and
T.M. Zulfikar Arifin, Program Manager
Number of staff: 6; 3 volunteers

Tel: +62 (651) 51 157
Fax: +62 (651) 54 186
cordova@aceh.wasantara.net.id

Indonesia

Institute of Islam and Social Studies – LKIS

RESEARCH
EDUCATION
ADVOCACY

Javanese Muslim activists founded LKIS (Lembaga Kajian Islam dan Sosial) with the objective of transformative-pluralist society, where members are sharing and communicating peacefully. Besides getting funding from donors, LKIS established a publishing company to subsidize day-to-day activities and the programs. LKIS conducts some main programs on audio-visual media to disseminate the idea of pluralism; it does research to provide alternative thought on Islam and pluralism and has monthly discussion groups on pluralism, civil society, and Islam tolerance. LKIS provides alternative education on religion critics, politics of Islam, religion and feminism, and religious dialogue. Its goals are civic education, advocacy, publication, and building networks. Some of its activities have already been successful, such as civic education in "pesantren" (Muslim school) in Tasikmalaya to educate the "santri" to be tolerant and work for their community to promote pluralism.

Jl. Pura I/1 Sorowajan
Yogyakarta
Indonesia

Contact: Jadul Maula, Executive Director

Tel/Fax: +62 (274) 524 901
lkis@indosat.net.id
www.lkis.or.id

Indonesia

International NGO Forum
on Indonesian Development

The International NGO Forum on Indonesian Development (INFID) was established in June 1985 under the name of INGI (Inter-NGO Conference on Inter-Governmental Group on Indonesia—IGGI matters) based on the initiative of several Indonesian NGOs and their partners in the Netherlands. INFID is an open and pluralistic network of NGOs from Indonesia and various member countries of the Consultative Group for Indonesia (CGI) as well as of international organizations with an interest in and commitment to Indonesia.

INFID's aim is to give voice to the perspective and common concerns of the people represented by NGOs involved in Indonesia vis-à-vis governments, multilateral development agencies, and the private sector involved in Indonesia. INFID aims at facilitating communication between NGOs inside and outside Indonesia in order to promote policies to alleviate structural poverty and to increase the capacity to improve conditions of the poor and disadvantaged in Indonesia.

Jl. Mampang Prapatan XI/23
Jakarta 12790
Indonesia

Tel: +62 (21) 7919 6721/2
Fax: +62 (21) 794 1577
infid@infid.org
www.infid.org

Contact: Ms. Binny Buchori, Executive Secretary at the INFID Secretariat

European Liaison Office
Vlasfabriekstraat 11
1060 Brussels
Belgium

Tel: +32 (2) 5361 950/1
Fax: +32 (2) 5361 906
infid@infid.be

Contact: Dr. Klaus H. Schreiner, Liaison Officer at the European Liaison Office

Indonesia

Kalyanamitra

EDUCATION

Kalyanamitra, meaning "Good Friends," is a women's NGO, founded in 1985. Its mission is to build democracy and gender equity through trauma recovery and assisting women victims of violence. Its principle activities are education through training, data collecting and fact-finding, human rights promotion, as well as democracy development. A key objective is to build networks nationally and internationally such as with CARE-Netherlands and Brot fur die Welt, Germany. Kalyanamitra does not have a specific division for conflict resolution, but it supports these activities through education. For example, it has co-organized a psychosocial training for Baileo Maluku volunteers and their community networks in Central and Southeast Maluku in 2002.

Jl. Kaca Jendela II No. 9
Rawajati, Kalibata
Jakarta 12750
Indonesia

Tel: +62 (21) 790 2102
Fax: +62 (21) 790 2112
ykm@indo.net.id

Contact: Ruth Indiah Rahayu
Number of staff: 20
Budget: < $25,000

Maluku

Lepa-Lepa Maluku Foundation – LEMA

ADVOCACY

Lepa-Lepa Maluku Foundation (LEMA) works to build a stronger society that is peaceful and able to manage natural resources in a self-reliant way. Their mission is to address poverty and improve the quality of life, to build communities that are just and peaceful, and to work toward building peace and establishing peace as a part of community life. Activities include negotiation and mediation in Maluku through indigenous practices, hereditary lines, and empowerment of the fishing sector. In addition, LEMA is involved in economic empowerment issues in conflict areas, including reconciliation, negotiation, mediation, and trauma counseling.

Jl. Pelita Ohoibun Atas
Tual, Maluku Tenggara
Maluku 97611
Indonesia

Tel/Fax: +62 (91) 622 163

Contact: Theo Fanumby, Executive Director
Number of staff: 6; 4 volunteers

Maluku

EDUCATION
ACTION

Mercy Corps

Mercy Corps has been working in Maluku province in eastern Indonesia for over two years. Mercy Corps funds emergency (shelter, water and sanitation, NFI distributions, etc.) and economic empowerment (microcredit, fisheries, and agricultural activities, etc.) projects, as well as capacity building and peacebuilding activities through local organizations. Recognizing that many people have been affected by the conflict, Mercy Corps funds projects that support those who are vulnerable and most in need, including host communities, not just internally displaced persons (IDPs).

Mercy Corps have set an example by being the first international organization to have a mixed team of Muslims and Christians working out of one office in a neutral area of Ambon (the provincial capital). Mercy Corps' approach to peacebuilding in Maluku is also practical rather than theoretical, for instance, creating space for interaction and facilitating dialogue between people from different communities to share common concerns and ideas. Mercy Corps opened an NGO Community Centre in Ambon where local NGOs can hold workshops and meetings, and have access to computers and other resources.

In selecting which projects to fund, Mercy Corps looks at how the activities will bring people together, the numbers of people represented from the different communities, as well as how these activities will promote peaceful change in the long run.

Jl. Mutiara 53A, Ambon
97123 Maluku

Tel: +62 (911) 315 390
Fax: +62 (911) 315 391
b_dayna@yahoo.com
info@mercycorps.org (US office)
www.mercycorps.or.id

Contact: Dayna Brown, NGO
Development Officer

Number of staff: 100

Sumatra

RESEARCH
ADVOCACY

Mitra Bentala

Founded in 1995 Mitra Bentala is an NGO that is dedicated to raising community awareness in the seacoast, the small islands and in the management of sustainable resources of Sumatra. Mitra Bentala focuses on three main activities: empowering the community, advocacy, and policy researching. Although there is not a specific department for conflict prevention and resolution the staff is involved in advocacy issues during periods of conflict. Parties involved in conflict resolution include academics, NGOs, the media, and groups of fishermen. Mitra Bentala is active in a network formed in the Lampung province and includes regional and local organizations involved in issues concerning the environment, human rights, and related activities.

Jalan Flamboyan No. 18
Enggal Bandar Lampung
Provinsi Lampung 35118
Indonesia

Tel/Fax: +62 (721) 241 383
yamitra@indo.net.id

Contact: Mr. Guswarman, Director
Number of staff: 7; 2 volunteers
Budget: less than $25,000

Indonesia

EDUCATION
ADVOCACY

National Commission on Violence against Women

National Commission on Violence Against Women (Komisi Nasional Anti Kekerasan terhadap Perempuan) is an independent organization but was founded by presidential decree in response to people's, especially women's, demand for state responsibility in May 1998 riots that discriminated against and made Chinese women victim of rape. Its mission is to increase the awareness of people on violence against women, to advocate law and policy toward improvement of protection for women, and to strengthen capacity of preventing violence and assisting the recovery of abused women. Its programs cover evaluation of governmental actions to protect women from any violence, giving recommendation to government for policy drafting to protect women's rights, strengthen capacity of its networks for improvement of victim support system, and also education for awareness.

Jl. Latuharhari 4B
Jakarta 10310
Indonesia

Tel: +62 (21) 390 3963
Fax: +62 (21) 390 3922
andy@komnasperempuan.or.id
www.komnasperempuan.or.id

Contact: Kamala Chandrakirana, Secretary General
Number of staff: 6

Sumatra

Network of Independent Organizations for People's Empowerment – JOIPaRa

EDUCATION
ADVOCACY

Jaringan Organisasi Independen untuk Penguatan Rakyat began as a small group of NGOs in North Sumatra, which then combined their capacity and mission into the Working Group for Capacity Building in 1992. In 2000, the working group changed its name to JOIPaRa. Their main focus is the grassroots people in the villages and urban society in Sumatra, especially in North Sumatra, Lampung, and Jambi. Meanwhile they also build national and international networks for the benefit of their work. They support the establishment of community organizations through their community organizers, and assist grassroots people by providing civic-political education, policy advocacy, institutional capacity building training, and network development.

Jl. Medan Tanjung Morawa
Km. 20.5 Psr. VII No. 112
Tanjung Morawa, Deli Serdang 20362
Sumatra Utara
Indonesia

Tel: +62 (61) 794 3929
Fax: +62 (61) 799 0436
joipara@yahoo.com

Contact: Syamsul Bahri, General Secretary

Number of staff: 4

West Papua

Office for Justice and Peace – SKP Jayapura

EDUCATION
ACTION
ADVOCACY

Office for Justice and Peace (SKP Jayapura, Sekretariat Keadilan dan Perdamaian Keuskupan Jayapura) is an institution under the Jayapura Catholic Diocese, which focuses on four areas. It firstly aims to provide advocacy in cases of human rights violations by reporting and working with the victim, religious communities, and the NGO community. Secondly, the institution wants to comprehensively raise awareness and understanding of problems faced in Papua through contribution to seminars and a series of publications, "memoria passionis," and "political notes." Thirdly, SKP Jayapura works to find peaceful solutions through the strengthening of civil society, reconciliation, mediation, or negotiation. And finally, the institution works together in cooperation with a range of partners and people of different religions, cultures, and political ideologies, which share the same concern, programs, methodology, and focus, at the local (Papua), national, or international levels.

Jl. Kesehatan No. 4 Dok II
Kotak Pos 1379, Jayapura
Papua 99013

Tel/Fax: +62 (967) 534 993
sekkp@jayapura.wasantara.net.id

Contact: Theo van den Broek, Director

Number of staff: 5; 55 volunteers

Budget: $60,000

Global, Indonesia

Oxfam Great Britain, Indonesia

RESEARCH
ACTION
ADVOCACY

Oxfam Great Britain started to work in Indonesia in 1972. Based on its mission to work with others to find appropriate solutions to reduce poverty and suffering, Oxfam specializes its capacity in some major areas such as development/rehabilitation, human rights promotion, humanitarian assistance as well as conflict reduction, fact-finding and data collecting, and advocacy works that may consist of lobbying, policy advise, research, etc. Other areas that also fall under Oxfam's concern are capacity building, education, and media. For some small projects, Oxfam may provide funds and work closely with their partners.

Specifically in conflict reduction in Indonesia, Oxfam has worked with local NGOs developing community-based conflict resolution program.

1. With Baku Bae movement in Ambon Central Maluku during 2001–2002. This program is targeting the grassroots community to facilitate peace-building efforts involving ex-combatants, informal leaders, and other key component of communities.
2. Another initiative is also in Maluku—Southeast Maluku on conflict resolution using the livelihood approach as part of the Integrated Social and Economic Development program for Maluku. The main partner is Baileo Network (coalition of 9 NGOs in Central and Southeast Maluku) and will be finished by April 2004.
3. In Central Sulawesi—Poso, with LPSHAM in establishing and supporting inter-community dialogue and early warning system in early 2003. The program involves 17 villages where communities could share their concern and interest within and/or with other communities as well as local government and security forces. Oxfam is planning to continue the support in the coming years in the area.

Puri Gejayan Indah Blok B
   No. 20A
Gejayan
Yogyakarta 55281
Indonesia

Tel/Fax: +62 (274) 584 722
oxfam-ids@oxfam.or.id
www.oxfamgb.org/eastasia

Contact: Leopold Sudaryono,
Conflict Reduction Officer
Number of staff: 40
Budget: $25,000 to $100,000

West Papua

Papua Legal Aid Foundation – LBH Papua

EDUCATION
ADVOCACY

Lembaga Bantuan Hukum Papua was founded in 1985, through the initiative of a number of churches in Papua and constitutes the 14th branch of the Indonesian Legal Aid Foundation (YLBHI). LBH Papua is a community-based civil society organization, which believes state mechanisms must protect the people and guarantee economic, social, cultural rights, and basic freedoms. Programs include education for increasing awareness, community legal aid, policy advocacy through workshops, courses, training, dialogue on legal awareness, policy advocacy, and legal defense of victims of human rights violations. These activities are undertaken to promote the capacity of the community to voice their aspirations and know their rights and responsibilities.

Jl. Gerilyawan No. 46
Abepura, Jayapura
PO Box 224 Abepura
Papua

Tel: +62 (967) 581 710
Fax: +62 (967) 582 559
jprlbh@jayapura.wasantara.net.id

Contact: Demianus Wakman, Director
Number of staff: 21; 3 volunteers
Budget: < $25,000

West Papua

Papua NGO's Forum – FOKER LSM Papua

EDUCATION
ADVOCACY

FOKER is a networking forum for NGOs in Papua that was established in 1991. As a networking forum, FOKER works to build more just and diverse structures, to promote the interests of the economically disadvantaged and indigenous communities in Papua (both men and women) to enable them to gain access and take control of the economic, political, social, and cultural resources at their disposal, and to allow them to take charge of their own futures. Its activities include: consultation and dialogue between NGOs that are concerned about poor people; facilitating and utilizing research; supporting NGOs created with the aim to respond to issues relevant to the Papuan context through focused dialogue and consultation; and training for capacity building of organizations and organizational management to improve the quality of advocacy and community assistance activities.

Jl. Sentani Raya No. 89
Waena, Jayapura
99358 Papua

Tel: +62 (967) 573 511
Fax: +62 (967) 573 512
fokerlsm@jayapura.wasantara.net.id

Contact: Golda Aronggear, S.H., Secretary
Number of staff: 6; 6 volunteers

Maluku

Peace Building Institute – Institut Titian Perdamaian

EDUCATION
ACTION

The Peace Building Institute–Institut Titian Perdamaian, formally "The Baku Bae Movement," is the community-based reconciliation process mediated by civil society components as an alternative to conflict resolution and reconciliation in current Indonesian political context. The Institut Titian Perdamaian is an indigenous idiom that reflects the spirit of peace, commonly used in children games to restore friendship after a quarrel. This movement is utilized to halt ethnic and religious "war" in Maluku Island.

The Institut Titian Perdamaian movement was initiated by civil society elements (scholars, NGO activist, lawyer, journalist, religious, and informal leaders) with the five stages of intervention. First, representation and informal leaders of conflicting parties were facilitated by initiators of Institut Titian Perdamaian movement to gather outside the Molucan island, exchange experiences, reflecting on each other's experiences, and having intensive dialogue to understand the nature of the conflict. In the second step, dialogue was intensified in several workshops among the representatives of the Molucan people. The third step was asking conflicting communities their view regarding the nature of conflict, their reactions, how to halt the conflict, and their hopes and aspirations. The result was disseminated to the communities, in the hope that it would raise the communities' awareness about the nature of the conflict, while at the same time transforming their conflict ethos to a peaceful ethos. The fourth step involved locating a neutral zone where the two communities were secured in undertaking intergroup activities. The last stage was the public announcement of the Institut Titian Perdamaian, where a public discourse was encouraged. In the long term, the truth in terms of law enforcement was implemented after the communities were healed and reconciled.

The success of the Institut Titian Perdamaian movement suggests the benefit of a bottom-up approach and the role of civil society in strengthening and empowering survivors to build their own reconciliation processes.

Jl. Mendut no. 3
Jakarta Pusat
Indonesia

Contact: Ichsan Malik

Tel: +62 (213) 153 865
bagjanet@indo.net.id or titian-damai@plasa.com

Sulawesi

Poso Media Center

RESEARCH
ADVOCACY

Pusat Media/Informasi Poso (PMC) is a non-governmental organization formed by NGO activists, journalists, academics, practitioners of law, and religious leaders as a mechanism for facilitating discourse among all interest groups, especially those in Poso.

PMC is intended to serve as an information center providing information on conflict/peace analysis and studies to any interested party. PMC seeks to clarify biased information from the mass media. One program is monitoring the media (media watch), producing alternative media (peace journalism), and undertaking legal and human rights advocacy.

JL. K. S. Tubun No. 28
Pulu, Sulawesi Tengah 94112
Indonesia

Tel: +62 (451) 422 229
pmc@telkom.net

Contact: Amran Amier
Number of staff: 12; 5
volunteers

Aceh

Sahara Foundation

RESEARCH
ACTION
ADVOCACY

Sahara was formed to meet community's aspirations and promote community participation. It focuses on active participation of society in determining, implementing, and monitoring development and freedom of access to all areas for self-development.

Its mission is to build the capacity of community groups to determine their rights and equality in all decisionmaking and active self-development to strengthen civil society. Activities include research, investigation, campaigning and lobbying, legal drafting, education and workshops, strengthening the rights of indigenous communities, and developing a strong network.

Jl. Kol. H. Habib Muhammad Syarief No. 1
Kelurahan Simpang Empat
Lhokseumawe
Aceh Utara
NAD 24314 Indonesia

Tel/Fax: +62 (64) 546 484
sahara@lhokseumawe.wasantara.net.id

Contact: Saifuddin Irhas,
Executive Secretary
Number of staff: 12; 30
volunteers

Sulawesi

South Sulawesi Forum
for Dialogue Among Us – FORLOG

EDUCATION
ADVOCACY

Driven by concern of the increasingly prevalent conflicts in parts of Indonesia, activists from a wide range of backgrounds agreed to establish Forum Dialog Antar Kita Sulawesi Selatan in 1999 in a seminar facilitated by Dian Interfidei. It consists of about 50 members and has demonstrated its commitment in promoting pluralism and tolerance to prevent conflict by conducting many activities and being actively involved in the mediation process in conflict in Poso. Pluralism and tolerance is promoted through public campaigns such as radio broadcasts, organizing public seminars and discussions etc. FORLOG also actively works for democratization, trauma counseling, and peace journalism. The focus is on the medium and grassroots level where "intellectual dialog" is complemented by creating room for shared inter-religious and inter-cultural experience and peace/humanitarian activities.

Jalan Bonto Ramba No. 8
Makassar 90221
Indonesia

Tel: +62 (411) 854 703
forlog@gmx.net
www.geocities.com/forlog

Contact: Alimuddin, Programme Coordinator

Number of staff: about 50 persons
(all volunteers)

Budget: < $10,000

Publications: Lintas, journal

Sulawesi

Tengko Situru' Foundation – YTS

The Tengko Situru' Foundation was established in 1974 in South Sulawesi. YTS works to empower society by assisting self-help groups in South Sulawesi. These groups comprise four units and focus on activities to promote community empowerment. These activities include peacebuilding initiatives such as strengthening civil society, gender issues, democratization, advocacy/lobbying, and civic education.

Jl. Tengko Situru' No. 5
  Malangngo' Rantepao
Tana Toraja
Sulawesi Selatan 91831
Indonesia

Tel: +62 (423) 23 985/21 365
Fax: +62 (423) 21 855
tengkos@indosat.net.id

Contact: May Januar, Director

Number of staff: 32; 4 volunteers

Maluku

Tita Mae Foundation – YTM

The Tita Mae Foundation is a non-governmental organization that engages in humanitarian work in Maluku. It was established in 1989 through reform of Yayasan Rela, which was founded in 1990. Hence, YTM has been active since 1999, and was named YTM, based on legal registration in 1999. Activities include economic projects and physical/mental rehabilitation for displaced people, advocacy on community rights, trauma counseling for children, and training in management and human resource management. YTM is also involved in reconciliation work in cooperation with other NGOs in Maluku.

Jl. Dr. Kayadoe Sk 26/1
Ambon, Maluku
Indonesia

Tel/Fax: +62 (911) 352 443
titamae@ambon.wasantara.net.id

Contact: John Lefmanut, Director

Number of staff: 4; 4 volunteers

Indonesia

United Nations Support Facility for Indonesian Recovery

RESEARCH
EDUCATION

The United Nations Support Facility for Indonesian Recovery (UNSFIR) is a project established by the government of Indonesia and the UNDP to stimulate examination of policy options for the country at an important point in the country's development. The work aims to engender wide public discussion of the issues involved in order to build a new social and political consensus for effective and lasting policy implementation. To facilitate this process of public discussion of policy alternatives, UNSFIR with various national partners created the Indonesian Public Policy Network or popularly known as JAKAKI. JAJAKI is intended to be a network of national institutions that aims to provide a platform to support informed public discussion of fresh and innovative approaches on some of the most pressing issues facing Indonesia.

Surya Building, 9th Floor
Jl. MH Thamrin Kav. 9
Jakarta 10350
Indonesia

Tel: +62 (21) 392 4320
Fax: +62 (21) 392 1152
niken.laksmita@undp.org
www.unsfir.or.id

Contact: Satish C. Mishra, Head/ Chief Advisor

Publications: The Right to the Development, 2003; *Formulating A Strategic Approach to Poverty Reduction: From A Global Framework to An Indonesian Agenda,* 2002; *Anatomy of Social Violence in the Context of Transition: The Case of Indonesia 1990–2001,* 2002; *Regional Disparity and Center-Regional Conflicts in Indonesia,* 2001

Indonesia

Voice of Human Rights in Indonesia – SHMI

EDUCATION
ADVOCACY

Suara Hak Asasi Manusia di Indonesia is a progression of POKASTIM (The Working Group for Welfare and Education of East Timorese), which suspended its activities with the independence of East Timor. SHMI addresses issues of human rights and democratization in East Timor and undertakes investigations of acts of violence in the community when presented with cases of human rights violations. It also holds dialogue and provides education for victims of the New Order, and facilitates dialogue between communities/ humanitarian organizations and the government in cases of human rights violations, acts of violence and so forth. SHMI is involved in advocacy, publications and arranging seminars and workshops on human rights. It is also active in networking with other organizations within Indonesia and internationally.

Jl. Kayu Manis Barat No. 7
DKI Jakarta 13130
Indonesia

Tel: +62 (21) 858 0405
Fax: +62 (21) 858 2405
shmi@cbn.net.id

Contact: Ade Rostina Sitompul, Program Coordinator

Number of staff: 7; 50 volunteers

Aceh

Women Activities for Rural Progress – Yayasan Flower Aceh

ACTION
ADVOCACY

Yayasan Flower Aceh, founded in 1989 in Aceh, is an NGO fighting for the rights of marginalized women and to realize a supportive environment that attaches importance to women's rights and gender justice. The vision comes from the experience of Acehnese women who have been abused and marginalized in conflict situations as well as in the society. Even though Flower does not have a specific department that deals with conflict, they work closely with conflict victims. In the past 15 years, Flower has actively promoted human rights and mainly conducts women empowerment programs through training, research, humanitarian assistance, and publications. In response to the current situation, Flower has joined with local and international NGOs in order to conduct conflict resolution training for women and public campaigns for public awareness.

Jl. T. Mohd Taeb Peurelak/Gabus No. 15
Lampriet, Banda Aceh
Nanggroe Aceh Darussalam 23126
Indonesia

Tel: +62 (651) 32 229
Fax: +62 (651) 26 848
flower@aceh.wasantara.net.id

Contact: Elvida, Coordinator for Public Campaign and Research
Budget: $25,000–$100,000
Number of staff: 3

Kalimantan

Women Institution for Study and Advocacy – eLPeKA

ADVOCACY

Lembaga Perempuan Kajian dan Advokasi is a women's NGO, which envisions gender equality in social, political life, and before the law. eLPeKA is concerned with sex worker (women) trafficking and the condition of women in an ethnic-separated society in West Kalimantan. West Kalimantan has faced ethnic conflict between the Dayak and the Madurese peoples. eLPeKA campaigns against women trafficking in the Municipality of Sambas, Pontianak and Sanggau, conducts training on human rights for NGO and promotes public dialogue about women's rights, and advocacy on relevant cases.

Jl. A. Yani Parit H. Husin II
Komplek Alex Griya 1A Blok D No. 15
Pontianak Selatan
Kalimantan Barat 78124
Indonesia

Tel: +62 (561) 712 146
Fax: +62 (561) 886 373
elpeka-ptk@yahoo.com or asmaniar@yahoo.com

Contact: Asmaniar, Executive Director
Number of staff: 5

Kalimantan

EDUCATION
ACTION

Yayasan Madanika

Yayasan Madanika is a non-profit organization founded in 1998 with a mission to stimulate civil society in Indonesia, especially in West Kalimantan. For its goal, Madanika put its program mainly in democracy development, education, media, and mediation. Working with CESDA USAID, Madanika conducted workshops and dialogues to reduce conflict by targeting high school educators and students. Its strategy is to approach conflict prevention through civic education. It raises social awareness about the values of a civil society through critical study and a process of media development, encouraging the formation of a middle class as a pillar for the development of civil society, while also developing a climate for dialogue by supporting reconciliatory efforts with a social approach.

Jl. Dr. Wahidin Sudirohusodo
Kompleks Sepakat Damai Blok I No. 6
Pontianak 78116
Kalimantan Barat
Indonesia

Contact: Pahrian Ganawira Siregar,
Executive Director

Budget: < $25,000

Number of staff: 2

Tel/Fax: +62 (561) 573 276
madanika@pontianak.wasantara.net.id

Sulawesi

EDUCATION
ACTION
ADVOCACY

Yayasan Pelita Kasih Abadi

Yayasan Pelita Kasih Abadi (PEKA) is a local NGO dedicated to empowering civil society in the struggle for justice, equality, social welfare, and health care. Founded in 1996, PEKA has established an Advocacy for Peace program that aims to promote peacebuilding in North Sulawesi and to prevent conflict through good governance and the promotion of peaceful conflict resolution techniques. The program also covers helping IDP's children from North Maluku in Bitung and Manado. High on their agenda are peace (journalism) training and advocacy for justice and peace among the young and the Minahasa province. PEKA works alongside civil society and grassroots organizations, IDP's and government officials. Internationally they work with OTI/ USAID, CRS, CSSP/USAID, all based in Jakarta, and the British Council.

Jl. Mogandi No. 36
Malalayang Satu
Manado
North Sulawesi
Indonesia

Contact: Th. Yuswandani Adiloekito
SH, Director and person in charge of
the Advocacy for Peace program.

Number of staff: 14; 6 staff for
conflict prevention

Tel: +62 (431) 828 046
Fax: +62 (431) 882 8045
ypekamdo@indosat.net.id

Budget: $25,000–$100,000

Publications: DODOKU, newsletter

Global

Concern

RESEARCH
EDUCATION
ACTION
ADVOCACY

Founded in 1968 Concern works with international and local partners, engages in long-term development work and emergency situations while undertaking development education and advocacy. Concerns ethos is to empower poor people to become the central actors in the development of their communities. It has a strict ethic of balancing enthusiasm for responding in difficult situations with a prudent approach to risk-taking. Concern recently celebrated 10 years in Laos PDR and assists four thousand isolated ethnic minority villagers in 12 villages. Primary schools were repaired and rebuilt and subsequently attendance has risen. Other support has included the management of rice mills, improvement of infrastructure, development of community disaster management, and the establishment of a savings and credit scheme. Concern has also established similar programs in East Timor, Cambodia, and the DPR of Korea.

52-55 Lower Camden Street
Dublin 2
Republic of Ireland

Tel: +35 (31) 475 4162
Fax: +35 (31) 475 7362
info@concern.ie
www.concern.ie

Indonesia

West Papua Action

EDUCATION
ADVOCACY

West Papua Action (WPA) was founded in 1996 at a conference opened by then Irish President Mary Robinson. It works at all levels in Irish society to raise awareness of the ongoing denial of human rights in West Papua, including the denial of the right to self-determination. It works with the general public, students, politicians, the media, and NGOs. Internationally, it cooperates with other organizations that are working in solidarity with the people of West Papua.

134 Philsborough Road
Dublin 7
Republic of Ireland

Tel: +35 (31) 860 3431
Fax: +35 (31) 882 7576
wpaction@iol.ie
www.westpapuaaction.buz.org

Contact: Mark Doris, coordinator

Publications: West Papua News, newsletter; *West Papua in the Global Community,* booklet

Global

Foundation for Advanced Studies on International Development

RESEARCH
EDUCATION

FASID was established as an NGO in 1990. Its main aim is the education and training of Japanese development officials and research on international development. The Foundation's research programs study trends in development assistance, with attention for links between development aid and conflict resolution and peacekeeping efforts.

Chiyoda Kaikan Building, 5th Floor
1-6-17 Kudan-Minami
Chiyoda-ku
Tokyo 102-0074
Japan

Tel: +81 (3) 5226 0301
Fax: +81 (3) 5226 0023
pub@fasid.or.jp
www.fasid.or.jp

Contact: Mr. Kenichi Yanagi, President; Mr. Masaki Saito, Executive Director

Budget: conflict prevention: $25,000–$100,000

Number of staff: 50

Publications: Agenda for International Development: Coping with Marginalization, 2002; *Report on the Forum Evolving Concept of Peacebuilding: Natural Resource Management and Conflict Prevention,* 2001

Global

Goi Peace Foundation

EDUCATION
ACTION

The mission of the Goi Peace Foundation is to build an international peace network and to stimulate the global trend toward a culture of peace. The foundation sponsors festivals and organizes symposia and lectures that promote a culture of peace. The foundation presents an annual peace award to honor individuals and organizations in various fields that have contributed to the advancement of world peace. It also develops educational programs, such as the international essay contest for young people.

Heiwa Daiicho Building 1-4-5
Hirakawa-cho Ciyoda-ku
Tokyo 102-0093
Japan

Tel: +81 (3) 3256 2071
Fax: +81 (3) 3239 0919
info@goipeace.or.jp
www.goipeace.or.jp

Contact: Patrick Petit, European Representative

Number of staff: 14

Publications: Creating Peace, quarterly magazine

The Goi Peace Foundation
European Office
Johann-Fichte Street 11, 7th Floor
D-80805 Munich, Germany

Tel: +49 (89) 3600 4312
Fax: +49 (89) 3600 4313
E-mail: GoiPeace@web.de

Japan

Hiroshima Institute
for Peace Education

RESEARCH
EDUCATION

The Hiroshima Institute for Peace Education was established in 1972 with the aim to develop peace education for elementary and junior high school children, based on the nuclear atomic bombing of Hiroshima in 1945. The Institute aims to pass on the experience of Hiroshima to coming generations. To this end, it researches and edits peace education materials, organizes visits of war monuments, holds lectures about the bombing of Hiroshima, and conducts research into peace education. It also organizes an annual peace education symposium for teachers.

2-8-32 Hikari-machi
Higashi-ku
Hiroshima-city 732-0052
Japan

Tel: +81 (8) 2264 1751
Fax: +81 (8) 2264 1757
hipe@mac.potato.ne.jp
www1.ocn.ne.jp/~hipe

Contact: Setsuko Tammitsu, Chairperson
Budget: $25,000–$100,000
Number of staff: 2
Publications: Peace Education Research, annual publication; Teaching materials: *Hiroshima and the 15 Years War; Hiroshima—Living in this Nuclear Age;* and *A Standard Curriculum for Peace Education*

Asia-Pacific

Hiroshima Peace Institute

RESEARCH
EDUCATION

The Hiroshima Peace Institute (HPI) was established as a research institute at Hiroshima City University in 1998. The HPI conducts research related to peace, inspired by the city's historical experience. The Institute is dedicated to the ultimate goals of complete disarmament and the elimination of nuclear weapons. The HPI conducts research into topics such as the theory of peace, the methodology of peace research, the nuclear holocausts in Hiroshima and Nagasaki, the proliferation and abolition of both conventional and nuclear weapons, peace, conflict resolution, and culture movements in the Asia-Pacific region. Besides research, the Institute also organizes workshops and conferences.

Hiroshima Mitsui Building,
    12th Floor
2-7-10 Otemachi
Nakaku Hiroshima 730-0051
Japan

Tel: +81 (82) 544 7570
Fax: +81 (82) 544 7573
office-peace@peace.hiroshima-cu.ac.jp
http://serv.peace.hiroshima-cu.ac.jp

Contact: Haruhiro Fukui, President
Budget conflict prevention: $100,000–$500,000
Number of staff: 19
Publications: Hiroshima Research News, newsletter (three times yearly)

Global

RESEARCH

Institute for Peace Science

The Institute for Peace Science at Hiroshima University (IPSHU) was established in 1975 as a university-wide facility for the collection of data and research into peace science. The institute collects, analyzes, and disseminates data related to peace science and promotes cooperation between peace researchers and research institutions. IPSHU organizes annual symposia on a variety of topics related to peace and conflict studies, as well as research seminars throughout the year.

Higashisenda-machi 1-1-89
Naka-ku
Hiroshima 730-0053
Japan

Tel: +81 (82) 542 6975
Fax: +81 (82) 542 0585
heiwa@hiroshima-u.ac.jp
http://home.hiroshima-u.ac.jp/heiwa/

Contact: Shuichi Nakayama, Director
Budget: $25,000–$100,000
Number of staff: 6
Publications: Hiroshima Peace Science, annual journal

Global

ACTION

Interband

Interband is a NGO dedicated to peacebuilding and democratization. The organization focuses on three activities: election monitoring, reintegration of demobilized soldiers, and the elimination of small arms in post-conflict situations. Together with local NGOs and the Asian Network for Free Elections, Interband has monitored elections and promoted democratization in the Asian region in Sri Lanka, Bangladesh, Pakistan, Cambodia, East Timor. In Cambodia, Interband also works with local NGOs to support the reintegration of demobilized soldiers and the elimination of small arms.

2816-22 Shinohara-cho
Kohoku-ku
Yokohama-shi
Kanagawa 222-0026
Japan

Tel: +81 (45) 439 4003
Fax: +81 (45) 439 4004
info@interband.org
www.interband.org

Contact: Nobuhiko Suto
Budget: $25,000–$100,000
Number of staff: 5
Publications: Peacebuilding, bi-annual bulletin

Global

Japan Center for Conflict Prevention

The Japan Center for Conflict Prevention (JCCP) aims to strengthen the contribution of the Japanese non-governmental sector to conflict prevention in the world. In addition to the head office in Tokyo, JCCP has representative offices in Sri Lanka, Cambodia, and Afghanistan, where, together with local NGOs, it organizes conflict prevention workshops, "small arms and weapons for development" programs, vocational training for ex-combatant youth, and other conflict prevention activities. JCCP also starts a humanitarian de-mining operation in Sri Lanka in 2004.

JCCP runs an annual post-graduate program for conflict prevention, consisting of a three-week seminar and a two-month overseas training course. JCCP produces the Directory of Organizations for Conflict Prevention in Asia and the Pacific, listing more than 400 NGOs, research institutes, and intergovernmental agencies active in conflict prevention in Asia and the Pacific. The online version of the Directory can be found at CP-Net, JCCP's web-based Conflict Prevention Network (www.conflict-prevention.org), where there is also a specialist database, a conflict prevention events calendar, and databases of conflict prevention activities and online resources. JCCP also runs the Dialogue Web page for Conflicts Worldwide (www.dwcw.org), providing a venue for ongoing open dialogue on many of the conflicts in the world. The e-Symposium on Conflict Prevention series is held on DWCW on an annual basis, bringing people from all over the world together to discuss timely conflict prevention topics online.

2-17-12-803 Akasaka
Minato-ku
Tokyo 107-0052
Japan

Tel: +81 (3) 3584 7457
Fax: +81 (3) 3584 7528
tokyo@jccp.gr.jp
www.jccp.gr.jp

Contact: Mr. Ito Kenichi, President or
Mr. Asomura Kuniaki, Executive Director
Budget: $1,000,000
Number of staff: 17
Publications: Japan Center for Conflict Prevention Bulletin, quarterly bulletin; *Directory of Organizations for Conflict Prevention in Asia and the Pacific,* 2003; *On Modern Preventive Diplomacy,* 2000; *An Introduction to Preventive Diplomacy,* 1999

Global

Japan Center for Preventive Diplomacy

EDUCATION
ACTION
ADVOCAC

The Japanese Center for Preventive Diplomacy (JCPD) was established in 1999 to promote the role of Japanese civil society in the field of preventive diplomacy. The Center runs programs in Southwest and Southeast Asia and in the Middle East, with activities ranging from peace education and preventive diplomacy workshops to fact-finding missions. It also established a postgraduate program for preventive diplomacy. Together with the Japan Institute of International Affairs, the Center has published a directory of organizations working for conflict prevention in Asia and the Pacific. It also maintains a dialogue website for conflicts worldwide.

2-17-12-803 Akasaka
Minato-ku
Tokyo, 107 0052
Japan

Tel: +81 (3) 3584 7457
Fax: +81 (3) 3589 5120
jcpd@jfir.or.jp
www.jcpd.gr.jp

Contact: Ito Kenichi, President or Asomura Kuniaki, Executive Director

Number of staff: 13

Budget: > $1,000,000

Publications: JCPD Newsletter, quarterly newsletter; *Directory of Organizations for Conflict Prevention in Asia and the Pacific,* 2000; *On Modern Preventive Diplomacy,* 2000; *An Introduction to Preventive Diplomacy,* 1999

Global

Japan International Cooperation Agency

ACTION

Japan's official development cooperation (ODA) is based on the concepts of "humanitarian and moral considerations" and "the recognition of interdependence among nations." ODA takes into account the following four principles: (1) Environmental conservation and development should be pursued in tandem. (2) Any use of ODA for military purposes or for aggravation of international conflicts should be avoided. (3) Full attention should be paid to trends in the recipient countries' military expenditures, their development and production of weapons of mass destruction and missiles, their export and import of arms, and so on, in order to maintain and strengthen international peace and stability. (4) Full attention should be paid to efforts toward democratization and the introduction of a market-oriented economy, the situation regarding the securing of basic human rights, and the level of freedom in the recipient country.

Based on JICA's experience in Cambodia and Afghanistan, it will be increasingly active in carrying out post-conflict reconstruction and development assistance.

6-13F, Shinjuku Maynds Tower
1-1, Yoyogi 2-chome
Shibuya-ku
Tokyo 151-8558
Japan

Publications: Annual reports, newsletters and study reports

Tel: +81 (3) 5352 5311
www.jica.go.jp

Global

Japan Institute of International Affairs

The Japan Institute of International Affairs (JIIA) was established in 1958 and consists of five separate research centers: Russian Studies, Asia-Pacific Studies, American Studies, Global Issues, and a Center for the Promotion of Disarmament and Non-Proliferation. The institute researches topics that are relevant to the foreign policy of Japan and organizes seminars, conferences, and symposiums, in collaboration with a number of research institutes throughout the world. It serves as the Japanese representing organization in both the Pacific Economic Cooperation Council (PECC) and the Council for Security Cooperation in the Asia-Pacific (CSCAP). The JIIA has co-organized international symposia on UNTAET: Debriefing and Lessons and on Conflict Prevention in Asia.

11F Kasumigaseki Building
3-2-5 Kasumigaseki
Chiyoda-ku
Tokyo 100-6011
Japan

Tel: +81 (3) 3503 7263
Fax: +81 (3) 3503 7286
info@jiia.or.jp
www.jiia.or.jp

Contact: Yukio Satoh, President

Budget: > $1,000,000

Number of staff: 50

Publications: Kokusai Mondai (Japanese), monthly journal; *Roshia Kenkyu* (Japanese), bi-annual journal; *Japan Review of International Affairs,* quarterly journal; *JIIA Newsletter,* monthly; *Directory of Organizations for Conflict Prevention in Asia and the Pacific,* 2002

Global

National Institute for Research Advancement

The National Institute for Research Advancement (NIRA) is a research institute with several programs focusing on conflict prevention and peace. The NIRA has researched topics such as "Internal Conflicts in Sub-Sahara Africa and Preventive Diplomacy," "Human Security: Examining the Role of Civil Society," and "Regional Policies Contributing to International Peace—Modeled on Hiroshima as a Representative of Peace in the Twentieth Century." NIRA provides research information, exchanges research with other organizations in Japan and abroad, and organizes conferences. It publishes a worldwide directory of think-tanks.

Yebishu Garden Place Tower, 34th Floor
4-20-3 Ebisu
PO Box 5004
Yebishu Garden Place Post Office
Shibuya-ku
Tokyo 150-6034
Japan

Tel: +81 (3) 5448 1735
Fax: +81 (3) 5448 1745
www@nira.go.jp
www.nira.go.jp

Contact: Yotaro Kobayashi, Chairperson or Takafusa Shioya, President

Budget: > $1,000,000

Number of staff: 47

Publications: NIRA Newsletter; NIRA Policy Research, monthly journal; *NIRA Review,* quarterly journal; *NIRA's World Directory of Think Tanks,* updated every three years

Indonesia

Network for Indonesian Democracy Japan

RESEARCH
ADVOCACY

The Network for Indonesian Democracy Japan (NINDJA) is an NGO, which was founded in 1998. NINDJA's mission is to contribute to the progress of democratization in Indonesia and to support the people's struggle for the improvement of their human rights. The organization collects information from grassroots in Indonesia, and if serious human rights violations are identified they convey this information to the Japanese Ministry of Foreign Affairs, to parliament members, and to its Japanese and international NGO network. NINDJA has semi-regular meetings with the Ministry of Foreign Affairs regarding the Aceh conflict. NINDJA is further the secretariat of the Supporting Committee for Human Rights in Aceh (SCHRA).

Chateaux Sawamura A
8 Ssuga-cho, Shinjuku-ku
Tokyo160-0018
Japan

Tel/Fax: +81 (3) 356 8364
office@nindja.com
www.nindja.com

Number of staff: 12 volunteers

Publications: Indonesia Failed in Democratization/Reformation, 2003; *Ache in Dark: Human Rights Violations by the Military,* 2001; *Bleeding Maluku: Conspiracy of Indonesian Military and Politics,* 2001

Global

Niwano Peace Foundation

RESEARCH
EDUCATION

The Niwano Peace Foundation was established in 1978 to contribute to the realization of world peace and the enhancement of culture by promoting research and other activities based on religious spirit. The Foundation commissioned research and carries out its own research, each year on a different topic of social significance. The Niwano Peace Foundation Peace Research Institute conducts research into peace-related issues from a religious viewpoint. The Foundation organizes lectures and symposia, and sponsors various international exchange activities for religious young people.

Shamvilla Catherina 5F
1-16-9 Shinjuku
Shinjuku-ku
Tokyo 160-0022
Japan

Tel: +81 (3) 3226 4371
info@npf.or.jp
www.npf.or.jp

Contact: Nichiko Niwano, President

Number of staff: 5

Publications: Niwano Peace Foundation Report, bi-annual in Japanese; *Echoes of Peace,* bi-annual in English; *Peace and Religion,* annual in Japanese

Global
Peace and Governance Program
at the United Nations University

RESEARCH
EDUCATION

The mission of the United Nations University (UNU) is to contribute, through research and capacity building, to efforts to resolve the pressing global problems that are the concern of the United Nations, its peoples and member states. The UNU fosters an environment for the acquisition, advancement, and dissemination of policy-relevant knowledge in a spirit of scholarly and critical inquiry for the purpose of enhancing the security, welfare, and quality of human life. The method of the UNU—research and capacity building through a global network of scholars and institutions—distinguishes it both from other UN organizations and from other universities. The mission of the Peace and Governance Program is to contribute to the promotion of sustainable peace and good governance. The Program organizes and supports research that produces policy-oriented recommendations for current problems, and also that which identifies longer-term trends and patterns in international politics that hold implications for peace, security, and governance. The Program is also committed to the training and capacity building needs that arise from this research activity.

The work of the Peace and Governance Program, which are mostly collaborative research projects on global issues related to peace and governance, is carried out by academic staff in Tokyo, at the UNU regional centers/programs, and project collaborators around the world. The Program selects and formulates projects in consultation with partners in the academic community and international organizations.

Peace and Governance Program
United Nations University
53-70 Jingumae 5-chome,
  Shibuya-ku
Tokyo 150-8925, Japan

Tel: +81 (3) 3499 2811
Fax: +81 (3) 3406 7347
sawada@hq.unu.edu
www.unu.edu/p&g

Contact: Professor Ramesh Thakur, Senior Vice Rector for Peace and Governance and Ms. Yoshie Sawada, Programme Administrative Assistant

Number of staff: 8

Publications: Refugees and Forced Displacement: International Security, Human Vulnerability, and the State, 2003; From Civil Strife to Civil Society: Civil and Military Responsibilities in Disrupted States, 2003; Conflict Prevention: Path to Peace or Grand Illusion? 2003.

Global

Peace Boat

EDUCATION
ACTION
ADVOCACY

Peace Boat is a Japan-based international NGO that organizes educational peace voyages on a large passenger ship four times a year to promote peace, human rights, sustainable and democratic development, and respect for the environment. Peace Boat seeks to create awareness through a global educational program, which takes place in a neutral space on the ship, as well as in the countries the Peace Boat visits. Peace Boat together with NGO partners and local communities in up to 50 countries around the world develops cooperative projects and collaborative advocacy campaigns to strengthen grassroots level activism. In 2003, Peace Boat's key regional campaigns included; advocating for a Nuclear Weapons Free Zone in North East Asia; promoting the constitutional renunciation of war world-wide; publishing an equitable account of twentieth century history in textbook form for Asian school students; working to clear landmines in Cambodia and Afghanistan; and mobilizing participants for the World Social Forum in India January 2004.

2F, 3-14-3, Takadanobaba
Shinjuku-ku
Tokyo 169-0075
Japan

Tel: +81 (3) 3363 7561
Fax: +81 (3) 3363 7562
pbglobal@peaceboat.gr.jp
www.peaceboat.org

Number of staff: 50
Contact: Yoshioka Tatsuya, Director

Global

Peace Depot

RESEARCH
EDUCATION

Peace Depot is a non-governmental research organization engaged in peace related research, education, and information dissemination. Peace Depot aims to be a think-tank on peace related issues and promotes the cooperation between grassroots movements and the disclosure of information on defense and diplomacy matters. The organization's main programs lie in the area of nuclear disarmament, regional security in the Asia-Pacific, and the training of NGO activists and peace researchers through international cooperation and exchange.

3-3-1-102 Minowa-cho
Kohoku-ku, Yokohama
Kanagawa 223-0051
Japan

Tel: +81 (45) 563 5101
Fax: +81 (45) 563 9907
office@peacedepot.org
www.peacedepot.org

Contact: Hiro Umebayashi, President
Number of staff: 3
Publications: Peace Depot Newsletter,
bi-annual newsletter

Global

Peace Studies Association of Japan

RESEARCH
EDUCATION

Peace Studies Association of Japan (PSAJ) is a large national peace research organization. The purpose of PSAJ is to focus on conflicts between nations, to carry out scientific research on the causes of any resultant strife and conditions for peace, and to contribute to academic progress in related fields of study. PSAJ was founded in 1973 and organizes study meetings and lectures, two major conferences every year, and smaller ad hoc meetings. PSAJ also coordinates national and foreign academic associations and other related institutions, as well as the promotion of intellectual exchange among researchers. The research activities are based on study commissions of PSAJ. PSAJ is a member of the International Peace Research Association.

c/o Prof. KAWAHARA Akira
Faculty of Law, Chuo University
742-1 Higashinakano, Hachioji
Tokyo 192-0393, Japan

Tel: +81 (426) 74 3220/3195/3953
Fax.: +81 (426) 74 3133
psaj@tamacc.chuo-u.ac.jp
wwwsoc.nii.ac.jp/psaj/about-e.html

Contact: Kawahara Akira, Secretary General

Publications: Peace Studies Newsletter

Global

Peace Winds Japan

ACTION

Peace Winds Japan (PWJ) is an NGO that provides humanitarian assistance to victims of conflict throughout the world. It aims to help resolve and prevent conflict and strive for change in the social structures that create the need for assistance. The activities of PWJ include conflict prevention, emergency assistance, post-conflict rehabilitation, and development assistance. Peace Winds has branches in Northern Iraq, East Timor, Mongolia, Indonesia, and Sierra Leone.

2-11-5 Sakurashinmachi
Setagaya-ku
Tokyo 154-0015
Japan

Tel: +81 (3) 5451 5400
Fax: +81 (3) 5451 5401
meet@peace-winds.org
http://peace-winds.org

Contact: Seiko Indo, PR Officer
Budget: $6,500,000

Global

Sasakawa Peace Foundation

ACTION

Sasakawa Peace Foundation's mission is to contribute to the welfare of humankind and the sound development of the international community, and thus to world peace. Sasakawa Peace Foundation conducts activities, which foster international understanding, exchange, and cooperation. The foundation undertakes surveys and research, develops human resources, invites and dispatches personnel, and organizes international conferences and other forums in order to accomplish the organization's mission.

The Nippon Foundation
  Building, 4th Floor
1-2-2 Akasaka
Minato-ku
Tokyo 107-8523
Japan

Tel: +81 (3) 6229 5400
Fax: +81 (3) 6229 5470
spfpr@spf.or.jp
www.spf.org

Contact: Mr. Setsuya Tabuchi, Chairman
Number of staff: 34
Publications: Newsletter, quarterly publication

Global

Toda Institute for
Global Peace and Policy Research

RESEARCH
EDUCATION

The Toda Institute for Global Peace and Policy Research is an NGO dedicated to the pursuit of peace through peaceful means and a complete abolition of war. The Institute focuses on an international dialogue on four major themes: Human Security and Global Governance, Human Rights and Global Ethics, Social Justice and Global Economy, and Cultural Identity and Global Citizenship. The Institute organizes conferences and seminars, conducts research, and brings out publications on these and related issues. Currently, the Toda Institute, together with international partners, runs two research programs: "Globalization, Regionalization and Democratization: A Multi-Civilization and Dialogic Research Project" and "Human Security and Global Governance."

15-3 Samon-cho
Shinjuku-ku
Tokyo 160-0017
Japan

Tel: +81 (3) 3356 5481
Fax: +81 (3) 3356 5482
todainst@mb.infoweb.or.jp
www.toda.org

Contact: Majid Tehranian, Director
Budget: > $1,000,000
Number of staff: 8
Publications: Peace and Policy, bi-annual
journal; *Peace Worlds on the Move: Globalization, Migration and Cultural Security,* 2004;
Managing the Global: Globalization, Employment and Quality of Life, 2004; *Dialogue of Civilizations: A New Peace Agenda for a New Millenium,* 2001.

Korean Peninsula

Civil Network for a Peaceful Korea

ADVOCACY

Civil Network for a Peaceful Korea (CNPK) seeks to monitor media reports concerning the Korean peninsula to check if there are false, exaggerated, or distorted ones, because the media takes a critical role in forming the international agenda regarding North Korea and reunification. CNPK publishes the results of regular media monitoring on its website. It also intends to expand the current narrow scope of North Korean issues by actively publicizing an agenda needed for peace and reunification of the two Koreas. CNPK hopes to encourage an active exchange of opinions among people as well as the formation of peace-oriented public consensus and to contribute to the dismantling of the Cold War mentality of people. CNPK activities consist of: constant monitoring of foreign and domestic media reports on the Korean peninsula; active efforts to list arms reduction issues; regular conferences on peace on the Korean peninsula; and translation of local and foreign media reports.

#184-3, Pulun-dong
Jongro Gu
Seoul, Korea

Tel/Fax: +82 (2) 393 3509
network@peacekorea.org
www.peacekorea.org

Contact: Mr. Chung Wook-sik,
Representative
Number of staff: 3; 21 volunteers

Asia-Pacific

Forum of Democratic Leaders in the Asia-Pacific

ACTION
ADVOCACY

The Forum of Democratic Leaders in the Asia-Pacific is a forum of solidarity for democratic leaders in the Asia Pacific region. It supports activities for democratic change by individuals and organizations working in the region. The forum also works to protect fundamental human rights, which it sees as essential for a peaceful transition from an authoritarian to a democratic government. Furthermore, the forum promotes the idea of global democracy, by sponsoring and supporting international cooperation between NGOs, governments, and academia. The forum sponsors and participates in international conferences and workshops on these matters, and establishes special committees and working groups to focus on particular issues. One of the forum's advisors is Nobel Peace laureate Daw Aung San Suu kyi.

Suite 501 Aryung Building
506-20 Changchun-dong
Seadaemun-ku
Seoul, Korea

Tel: +82 (2) 322 4491
Fax: +82 (2) 322 4494
fdlap@chollian.dacom.co.kr
www.nancho.net/fdlap/

Contact: Han Song Joo, Co-President
Budget: $100,000–$500,000
Publications: FDL-AP Quarterly,
annual journal

Global

Global Cooperation Society Movement

ACTION

The Global Cooperation Society Movement (GCS) is a social movement committed to the creation of "a spiritually beautiful, materially affluent and humanly rewarding" society. The GCS Movement began in Korea in the 1950s and was launched as an international initiative in 1975. During the 1980s national chapters were established in countries throughout the world. The movement played a substantial role in the establishment of the UN International Day of Peace. In 1999, GCS hosted a first major NGO gathering in Seoul, dedicated to improving NGO organization and empowerment. It has also published a World Encyclopedia of Peace.

Kyung Hee University
1 Hoigi-dong
Dongdaemun-gu
Seoul 130-701, Korea

Tel: +82 (2) 961 216/163
Fax: +82 (2) 961 225
gcs@nms.kyunghee.ac.kr
www.gcs-ngo.org

Contact: Dr. Young Seek Choue, President

Number of staff: 15

Publications: Oughtopia, annual journal; *Compatriot and Mankind,* 2000; *Will World Peace Be Achievable in the 21st Century?* 2000; *World Encyclopedia of Peace,* 1999; *Global Vision Toward the Next Millennium: Modern Civilization and Beyond,* 1999

Global, Korean Peninsula

Good Friends

RESEARCH

Good Friends is an international non-profit and non-sectarian organization committed to active implementation of peace and human rights, including the well being of refugees and displaced people in Asia and beyond. The major activities of Good Friends are to provide humanitarian assistance to refugees from all over the world, to achieve peaceful resolution in conflict areas, and to take actions to improve and protect human rights. Good Friends focused in the past on information dissemination to North Korean refugees and provided the refugees with humanitarian aid. Currently, Good Friends' main activities are focused on promoting reconciliation between North and South Korea. It also aims to improve human rights for the North Korean people.

Good Friends
1585-16, Seocho-3-dong
Seocho-gu
Seoul, Korea 137-875

Tel: +82 (2) 587 0662
Fax: +82 (2) 587 8998
goodfriends@jungto.org
www.jungto.org/gf

Contact: Erica Kang, Project Coordinator

Korean Peninsula

Korean Council for
Reconciliation and Cooperation

ACTION
ADVOCACY

The Korean Council for Reconciliation and Cooperation (KCRC) promotes national reconciliation and peaceful reunification in Korea by raising the spirit of reconciliation and cooperation between the two Koreas. It advocates principles and ways of reconciliation on governmental and non-governmental levels and holds various annual events commemorating inter-Korean or pan-Korean history, jointly with its North Korean counterparts.

4F Donggu International Bldg.
Youido-Dong
Youngdeungpo Gu
Seoul 150-010, Korea

Tel: +82 (2) 761 1212
Fax: +82 (2) 761 6590
kcrc@kcrc.or.kr
www.kcrc.or.kr

Korean Peninsula

Korean Institute
for National Reunification

ACTION

The Korean Institute for National Reunification was established by the South Korean government in 1991 to conduct research on the peaceful settlement of the Korean conflict and the reunification of the two Koreas. The institute provides analyses and policy recommendations on reunification, the (human rights) situation in North Korea, international relations between North Korea, South Korea, and their four neighbor countries. The Centre for North Korean Society and Human Rights was established as a special research focus within the institute in 1996. It publishes an annual white paper on the human rights situation in North Korea. The centre is also involved in settlement support and protection of North Korean escapees and the organization of reunions of families divided by the North-South political border.

553-353, Suyu6-dong
Kangbuk-ku
Seoul, Korea 142-887
SL Tobong

Tel: +82 (2) 901 2529/900 4300
Fax: +82 (2) 901 2547
webmaster@kinu.or.kr
www.kinu.or.kr

Contact: Young-Kyu Park, President

Number of staff: 60

Publications: White Papers on Human Rights in North Korea; Analysis on Transition of Policy Changes of Sectors in Kim Jong Il Regime: Research Based on Editorials, Axioms and Discourses from Nodong Shinmum, 2001; Analysis on Selected Works of Kim Jong Il, Characteristics and Prospect for Changes in North Korea's Foreign Policy, 2001; Fact-finding Survey on the Acceptance of North Korean Culture, 2001

Korean Peninsula, Russia and US

Korean Institute
of International Studies

Founded in 1965, the Korean Institute of International Studies (KIIS) is an independent NGO with a number of research programs that focus on peace and security in Asia, in particular East Asia. The KIIS sponsors many annual conferences with institutes in the United States, China, Japan, and Russia, while holding bilateral roundtable conferences with China and Russia. Aside from providing research into peace and security issues in the region, the KIIS emphasizes the importance of timely and workable policy recommendations.

5th Floor Daeyu Building
Banpo-dong
Swocho-Gu
Seoul, Korea

Tel: +82 (2) 543 6075/6076
Fax: +82 (2) 543 1073/1074
kiiss1965@yahoo.com

Contact: Chong-ki Choi, President
Budget: $25,000–$100,000
Number of staff: 30
Publications: The Korean Journal of International Studies, Policy Studies (Korean)

Korean Peninsula

Network for North Korean
Democracy and Human Rights

The mission of the Network for North Korean Democracy and Human Rights (NKnet) is to contribute to the realization of human rights and democracy in North Korea. To this end, NKnet supports and networks with other local civil groups, international organizations, and human rights groups. The network launches aid projects to North Korean people and refugees, and disseminates information on North Korea via online newsletters. NKnet is also involved in research and the establishment of a Committee for the Truth about North Korea.

110-045# 2nd Floor Hongsung Bldg.
18-5 Chebu-dong
Chongno-go
Seoul, Korea

Tel: +82 (2) 723 6711/2
Fax: +82 (2) 723 6715
solidarity@nknet.org
www.nknet.org

Publications: Keys, quarterly journal; online newsletters through e-mail

South Korea

People's Solidarity for Participatory Democracy

ACTION
ADVOCACY

The People's Solidarity for Participatory Democracy (PSPD) was founded in 1994, one year after South Korea's first democratically elected government was established. The PSPD is a civil organization dedicated to the promotion of justice and human rights in Korean society through participation of the people. It acts as a watchdog against the abuse of power, and raises awareness, campaigns, and questions on social and political activities. To this end, the PSPD has set up a number of different bodies: the Judiciary Watch; the National Assembly Watch; the Centre for Democracy in Science and Technology; the Transparent Society Campaign; Freedom of Information and Tax Reform; Restoration of Citizens' Rights Campaign; the Public Interest Law Centre; the Participatory Economy Committee; the Social Welfare Committee; and the Committee for International Solidarity.

3F, New Anguk Bldg.
175-3 Anguk-Dong
Chongno-Gu
Seoul 110-240, Korea

Tel: +82 (2) 723 4250
Fax: +82 (2) 723 5055
pspdint@pspd.org
www.pspd.org

Contact: Youngmi Yang, International Coordinator

Publications: PSPD Review; Judiciary Watch, quarterly magazine; *National Assembly Watch,* quarterly magazine; *Asia Solidarity Quarterly,* quarterly magazine

South Korea

ACTION
ADVOCACY

Sarangbang Group for Human Rights

The Sarangbang Group for Human Rights aims to promote and popularize human rights advocacy and build a progressive human rights movement in South Korea. Since its inception in 1993, the Sarangbang Group has been publishing the first daily newspaper specializing in human rights issues. The group monitors and campaigns on human rights issues such as the National Security Law, prison conditions, and the situation of irregular workers. It organizes the annual Seoul Human Rights Film Festival and various other human rights education projects such as workshops for college students, school teachers, and NGO activists and summer human rights camps for youth and children.

4th Floor, 8-29,
   Myunglyun dong 2ga
Jongno-gu
Seoul 110-522, Korea

Tel: +82 (2) 741 5363
Fax: +82 (2) 741 5364
rights@chollian.net
www.sarangbang.or.kr

Contact: Joon-shik Suh, Director

Budget: $25,000–$100,000

Number of staff: 11

Publications: The National Security Law Report, 1997, 1998, 2000 and 2001; Get Up, Stand Up for Your Rights, 2000; Pathfinder for Human Rights Education, 1999

Northeast Asia

RESEARCH

Sejong Institute

The Sejong Institute's security studies program provides analysis of and offers policy proposals on Korea's security environment. Apart from a focus on the reunification of Korea, the institute also tries to expand its scope of inquiry from a more traditional concept of security to a comprehensive one, by including issues related to environment, energy, science and technology, and the relation between information and security.

PO Box 45
Pundang
Sungnam 463-660
Korea

Tel: +82 (2) 31 750 7500
Fax: +82 (2) 2233 8832
jcbaek@sejong.org
www.sejong.org

Contact: Dr Baek Jong-Chun, President

Budget: > $1,000,000
Number of staff: 75

Korean Peninsula

RESEARCH
EDUCATION

Women Making Peace

The aim of Women Making Peace (WMP) is to realize reunification and peace on the Korean peninsula and to promote peace in the wider Asian region and throughout the world. Since 1991, a group of women organized conferences on "Peace in Asia and the Role of Women." These conferences brought together women from South Korea and North Korea for the first time since the division of Korea. In 1997, the Korean organizing committee of these conferences created Women Making Peace. WMP conducts research on the conditions necessary for reunification and presents policies from a feminist perspective toward this goal. It tries to facilitate women's participation in activities concerning reunification, international affairs, and defense. The organization provides training for peacemakers and leadership training for women. WMP also supports conflict resolution activities by other peace groups in international conflict areas.

4th Floor, the Women's House of Peace
38-84 Jangchoong-Dongha
Joong-ku
Seoul 100-391, Korea

Tel: +82 (2) 275 4860
Fax: +82 (2) 275 4861
wmp@peacewomen.or.kr
www.peacewomen.or.kr

Contact: Lee Hyunsook
Publications: Women Making Peace, quarterly newsletter; *Women and Peace,* Research Reports

Indonesia

Borneo Resource Institute

RESEARCH
EDUCATION
ACTION

The Borneo Resource Institute (BRIMAS) is an indigenous NGO that works at grassroots level with the indigenous Dayak people of Borneo. The institute aims to educate indigenous communities about their rights, to assist, and to empower them. BRIMAS addresses the people's self-reliance and promotes community-based sustainable resource management. BRIMAS organizes capacity building training in local communities and co-ordinates lawsuits on customary land and human rights related cases. The institute is also assisting communities in the development of sustainable livelihood projects and has a special program focusing on the roles and rights of indigenous women in Borneo.

Lot 1046, 2nd Floor
Shang Garden
Jalan Bulan Sabit
98000 Miri, Sarawak
Malaysia

Publications: Papit Bulletin

snanet@tm.net.my
brimas.www1.50megs.com

Asia Pacific

Council for Security Cooperation in the Asia Pacific

ACTION

The Council for Security Cooperation in the Asia Pacific (CSCAP) is a Track Two security forum. It provides an informal place for scholars, officials, and others in their private capacities to discuss political and security issues. The staff organizes working groups in order to create space for specific themes and to provide policy recommendations to intergovernmental bodies. In a recent CSCAP workshop, a working definition and statement of principles on Preventive Diplomacy was formulated. This was immediately presented at a large Asian forum. CSCAP has member committees in twenty countries in the region. It is also associated with the Department of Public Information of the United Nations.

Institute of Strategic and
  International Studies Malaysia
1 Persiaran Sultan Salahuddin
PO Box 12424
50778 Kuala Lumpur
Malaysia

Tel: +60 (3) 293 9366
Fax: +60 (3) 293 9430
jawhar@isis.po.my
www.cscap.org

Contact: Mohamed Jawhar Hassan, Director General

Publications: CSCAP Newsletter; AUS-CSCAP Newsletter; The Relationship between Terrorism and Order at the Sea, 2003; The Practice of the Law of the Sea in the Asia Pacific, 2002; Regional Maritime Management and Security, 1998

Malaysia

Institute of Islamic Understanding Malaysia – IKIM

RESEARCH

Institut Kefahaman Islam Malaysia was initiated by then Malaysian Prime Minister Dr. Mahathir bin Mohamed in 1992. The institute functions as a think tank on national and international issues related to Islam and the relationship between Islam and the dynamics of the contemporary Malaysian society in particular and Muslim society in general. The institute aims to educate on Islam and to create awareness of international issues that have an impact on Muslims. IKIM also provides a platform for discussions between Muslim and non-Muslim scholars.

2, LanggakTunku
Off Jalan Duta
50480 Kuala Lumpur
Malaysia

Tel: +60 (3) 6204 6200
Fax: +60 (3) 6201 4189
monir@ikim.gov.my
www.ikim.gov.my

Contact: Dr. Abdul Monir bin Yaacob, Director General

Budget: > $1,000,000

Number of staff: 47

Malaysia

Institute of Strategic and International Studies

RESEARCH

As an independent research organization, the Institute of Strategic and International Studies (ISIS) focuses on independent policy research and the fostering of dialogue between the public sector, the private sector, and academia. The institute's main research areas include defense, security, and foreign affairs. It organizes the annual Asia-Pacific Roundtable conference, a Track -Two security dialogue that focuses on confidence building and conflict reduction.

1 Persiaran Sultan Salabuddin
PO Box 12424
50778 Kuala Lumpur
Malaysia

Tel: +60 (3) 2693 9366
Fax: +60 (3) 2693 9430/9475/8485
webmaster@isis.po.my
www.jaring.my/isis/index.htm

Contact: Dr. Noordin Sopiee, Chairman

Publications: Social Security in Malaysia and Singapore, Practices, Issues and Reform Directions, 1994; *Confidence Building and Conflict Reduction in the Pacific,* 1993; *Southeast Asia and Regional Peace,* 1992; *The Spratlys Disputes and Prospects for Settlement,* 1992

Global

International Movement for a Just World

RESEARCH
ADVOCACY

The International Movement for a Just World is an international NGO that aims to respond to the challenges posed by the injustice created by globalization. The movement wants to develop international awareness of this injustice throughout the world. To this end, articles, commentaries, and publications related to globalization, international justice, and the role of Islam written by authors linked to the movement are placed on its website. The organization also organizes conferences on these topics.

PO Box 288
Jalan Sultan
46730 Petaling Jaya
Selangor, Malaysia

Tel: +60 (3) 7727 6386
Fax: +60 (3) 7727 7389
muza@po.jaring.my
www.just-international.org

Contact: Chandra Muzzafar, President

Budget: $50,000–$100,000

Number of staff: 3

Publications: Muslims, Dialogue, Terror, 2003; *Alternative Politics for Asia: A Buddhist-Muslim Dialogue,* 2003; *Human Wrongs,* 2003

Southeast Asia

National Consciousness Movement

RESEARCH
ADVOCACY

National Consciousness Movement—Aliran Kesedaran Negara (ALIRAN) is a Malaysian reform movement that focuses on raising awareness and is dedicated to justice, freedom, and solidarity. In its publications and on its website, ALIRAN provides space for criticism and independent analyses of political events in Malaysia and Southeast Asia. Issues included are for example human rights, multi-ethnic religious dialogue, and the abolition of the internal Security Act in Malaysia. ALIRAN also acts as the secretariat for Charter 2000, a citizen's initiative to promote media freedom.

103 Medan Penaga
11600 Jelutong
Penang, Malaysia

Tel: +60 (4) 658 5251
Fax: +60 (4) 658 5197
alirankn@hotmail.com
www.malaysia.net/aliran

Contact: P. Ramakrishnan, President

Budget: < $25,000

Number of staff: 4

Publications: Lidah Aliran, Newsletter; *Aliran Monthly,* Monthly News Bulletin

Malaysia

RESEARCH
ADVOCACY

National Human Rights Society

The National Human Rights Society—Persatuan Kebangsaan Hak Asasi Manusia (HAKAM) promotes, preserves, and defends human rights in Malaysia. The society campaigns for the abolishment of laws that are inconsistent with human rights, addresses complaints about human rights violations, and lobbies the government to ratify international and regional human rights instruments. An important focus of HAKAM is the campaign to abolish the Internal Security Act and to free political prisoners in Malaysia.

5th Floor, Wisma Harwant
Jalan Tuanku Adbul Rahman
50100 Kuala Lumpur
Malaysia

Contact: Elizabeth Wong, Secretary-General

Number of staff: 11

Tel: +60 (3) 2693 8828
Fax: +60 (3) 2693 2868
hakam@hakam.org
www.hakam.org

Southeast Asia

RESEARCH
EDUCATION
ACTION

Research and Education for Peace

The Research and Education for Peace at the University Sains Malaysia (REP-USM) was formed in 1995. Through its research, education, and training programs, REP-USM aims to contribute to peaceful living. REP-UGM is the secretariat for the Southeast Asian Conflict Studies Network (see separate entry).

REP-UGM has a number of projects concerned with conflict resolution. The Taiping Peace Initiative, which is organized jointly with the Taiping Tourist Association, USM, and the United Nations, aims to promote a culture of peace in three dimensions: inner peace, peace with other people, and peace with the environment. The Southeast Asian Public Policy Conflict Management project looks at the management of public policy related conflicts in Southeast Asia.

Finally, REP-UGM also offers a variety of courses, seminars, workshops, counseling and customized training through its Mediation and Reconciliation Services (MARS) project. In this manner, the project aims to promote awareness of the need for early conflict prevention and peaceful conflict resolution.

School of Social Sciences
Universiti Sains Malaysia
11800 Pulau Pinang
Malaysia

Contact: Dr. Kamarulzaman Askandar, Coordinator

Budget: $25,000–$100,000

Number of staff: 6

Tel: +60 (4) 657 888 ext. 2123
Fax: +60 (4) 657 7070
rep@usm.my
zam@usm.my
www.soc.usm.my/research/repusm/index.htm

Southeast Asia

Southeast Asian Conflict Studies Network

The Southeast Asian Conflict Studies Network (SEASCN) is a network of individuals and institutions engaged in peace and conflict research and practice. It aims to act as a channel for discussion and cooperation between researchers working in conflict analysis and conflict resolution in the region. In each of its eight member countries, national coordinators are compiling information for a directory of individuals and organizations working in peace and conflict research in Southeast Asia. The network also organizes regular regional workshops on issues such as the role of women in conflict management and the impact of political and socioeconomic changes in Southeast Asia.

Research and Education for Peace Unit
School of Social Sciences
Universiti Sains Malaysia
11800 Penang, Malaysia

Tel: +60 (4) 657 7888 ext. 2568/2123
Fax: +60 (4) 657 7070/0918
zam@seacsn.net
www.seacsn.net

Contact: Dr Kamarulzaman Askander, Regional Coordinator

Publications: Malaysia's Role in the Peace Negotiations Between The Philippine Government and The Moro Islamic Liberation Front, 2003; *The SEACSN Bulletin,* 2003; *Management and Resolution of Inter-State Conflicts in Southeast Asia,* 2003

Global

Third World Network

The Third World Network (TWN) is an independent non-profit international network of organizations and individuals involved in issues relating to development, the Third World, and North-South issues. Its objectives are to conduct research on economic, social, and environmental issues pertaining to the South; to publish books and magazines; to organize and participate in seminars; and to provide a platform representing broadly Southern interests and perspectives at international forums such as UN conferences and processes. The TWN's international secretariat is based in Penang, Malaysia. It has offices in Delhi, India; Montevideo, Uruguay (for South America); Geneva, Switzerland; and Accra, Ghana. TWN has affiliated organizations in several Third World countries, including India, the Philippines, Thailand, Brazil, Bangladesh, Malaysia, Peru, Ethiopia, Uruguay, Mexico, Ghana, South Africa, and Senegal. It also cooperates with several organizations in the North.

Third World Network
121-S, Jalan Utama, 10450
Penang, Malaysia

Tel: +60 4 2266 728/159
Fax: +60 4 2264 505
twnet@po.jaring.my
www.twnside.org.sg

Publications: Third World Resurgence, a monthly magazine

Malaysia

Voice of the Malaysian People

EDUCATION
ACTION
ADVOCACY

The Voice of the Malaysian People—Suara Rakyat Malaysia (SUARAM) was formed in 1989 by a number of activists to campaign for the abolition of the Internal Security Act (ISA) in Malaysia. Over the years, this campaign evolved into a movement for human rights and democracy. SUARAM's vision is to empower people and build a mass movement to work for a peaceful, free, equal, and just society. SUARAM monitors and documents human rights violations, assists victims of human rights violations, and networks with other social interest groups. The movement campaigns for specific issues such as the abolition of the International Security Act, an independent and effective National Human Rights Commission, and several environmental issues.

383, 1st Floor, Jalan 5/59
Petaling Gardens
46000 Petaling Jaya
Selangor, Malaysia

Tel: +60 (3) 7784 3525
Fax: +60 (3) 7784 3526
suaram@suaram.org
www.suaram.org

Publications: Human Rights Status Report, Annual Publication

Mongolia

Liberty Center

EDUCATION
ADVOCACY

The Liberty Center was established in 2000 to promote human rights and justice through public outreach, education, and advocacy for legislative reform. The center provides consultancy to protect people's rights and liberties, and has supported a TV series on human rights issues in Mongolia. It publishes alerts on specific human rights violation cases and lobbies to rectify these. The Liberty Center also collects announcements of foreign study opportunities, seminars, meetings, and calls for papers, and disseminates these in daily newspapers and on its website.

Mongoliin Zaluuchuudiin
Holboonii bair, no. 301
Ulaanbatar 48
Ulaanbaatar
Mongolia

Tel: +976 (11) 321 297
Fax: +976 (11) 320 753
liberty_c@mongolnet.mn
libertycent@yahoo.com
www.libertycenter.org.mn

Contact: Ts. Oyungerel, Executive Director

Number of staff: 3

Mongolia
Political Education Academy

The Political Education Academy strives to support and develop democracy, rule of law, and individual human rights and liberties in Mongolia. The academy provides training and seminars in Ulaanbaatar and in its regional centers in Darkhan-Uul, Dornod, Dundgobi, Uvurkhangai, Khuvsgul, and Khov-daimags. Topics include School of Democracy; Radio and TV—"Democracy and Development" programs; Citizen's Political and Economic Information; The Principles of Human Rights; The Concept and Development of the Constitution; and Freedom of the Press and Democracy. In 2002, the Political Education Academy organized over 700 seminars that reaches more than ten thousand people. In addition to these training activities, the Political Education Academy also researches several topics on democracy and civil society, and publishes research outcomes and training materials.

PO Box 337
Ulaanbaatar 210 620
Mongolia

Tel: +976 (11) 350 550/547
Fax: +976 (11) 350 926
peacademy@mobinet.mn
www.owc.org.mn/pea

Contact: Mr Damba Ganbat, Executive Director
Number of staff: 28
Publications: Shine Toli, quarterly magazine;
The Grand Failure: The Birth and Death of Communism in the Twentieth Century; International Relation in Twentieth Century; World Policy and International Relation.

Mongolia
Women for Social Progress Movement

The Women for Social Progress Movement (WSPM), founded in 1992, strives to educate people on democratic governance and provides support to improve the economic situation of women. In 1997, the WSPM established the Voter Education Centre. Its activities include radio and television programs to educate people on democratic governance and the training of rural activists. It publishes newsletters that compare the voting records of members of parliament with their campaign platforms and a *Citizen's Guide on the Government,* which includes the salaries and phone numbers of members of parliament.

National History Museum
Room 1 and 2
PO Box 20a
Ulaanbaatar 11
Mongolia

Tel/Fax: +976 (1) 322 340
wsp@magicnet.mn
www.mol.mn/wsp

Contact: R. Burmaa, Chairperson
Budget: $100,000–$500,000
Number of staff: 6
Publications: Voter Education Center newsletter; Citizen's Guide to the Government

Global

Action by Churches Together
Netherlands

RESEARCH
EDUCATION
ACTION
ADVOCACY

Action by Churches Together (ACT) is part of a global ecumenical network of the World Council of Churches and supports hundreds of sister organizations all over the world. ACT is primarily concerned with the struggle against injustice. ACT Netherlands collaborates with local churches, women groups, labor unions, and human rights organizations. Its activities include fundraising for projects and informing the public. A new campaign is launched each year.

Landelijk Dienstencentrum
    van de Samen op
    Weg-kerken
PO Box 456
3500 AL Utrecht
The Netherlands

Contact: Bea Stolte-van Empelen,
Program Officer

Tel: +31 (30) 880 1456
Fax: +31 (30) 880 1457
info@kerkeninaktie.nl
www.kerkinactie.nl

Burma

Burma Center Netherlands

EDUCATION
ADVOCACY

The Burma Center Netherlands (BCN) is an information and lobby-center, which aims to raise awareness in the Netherlands for the situation in Burma and strives toward support within the European Union for democratization processes in Burma. In this context the BCN actively approaches national and EU policymakers and the media. This independent foundation works closely together with other European Burma Groups and has, over the last years, acted as a clearinghouse of all the groups' activities aimed at the European Union. In its information work the BCN gives special attention to issues as human rights, the rights of the indigenous peoples, democratization, tourism, and foreign investments in Burma. The BCN intermediates for Burmese NGOs in terms of funding and information gathering upon request.

Burma Centrum Nederland
Paulus Potterstraat 20
1071 DA Amsterdam
The Netherlands

Publications: Burma Behind the Mask,
1997; *Strengthening Civil Society in
Burma*

Tel: +31 (20) 671 6952
Fax: +31 (20) 671 3513
bcn@xs4all.nl
www.burmacenter.nl

Global

Cordaid

Cordaid (Catholic Organization for Relief and Development) was established in 1999 following the merger of Bilance, Caritas Netherlands, and Memisa, three Catholic development organizations based in the Netherlands. Cordaid now works together with more than a thousand local organizations. Cordaid is engaged in all aspects of development cooperation including emergency aid, structural poverty alleviation, and health care. Cordaid views conflict prevention and reconciliation as integral themes within a more comprehensive development program. For example, in its programs to enhance disaster preparedness, it sees preparedness against "complex political emergencies"—and thus conflict prevention—as an integral component. Within East Asia, Cordaid carries or carried out activities in Indonesia, The Philippines, and Papua New Guinea.

Cordaid
PO Box 16440
2500 BK The Hague
The Netherlands

Tel: +31 (70) 313 6300
Fax: +31 (70) 313 6301
cordaid@cordaid.nl
www.cordaid.nl

Contact: Jan Nielen, head of Asia department

Number of staff: 285

Publications: Fighting against Poverty and Injustice, general information about Cordaid; *Partnerbulletin,* information for local counterparts.

Global

European Center
for Conflict Prevention

RESEARCH
ADVOCACY

The European Center for Conflict Prevention (ECCP) is an independent NGO based in the Netherlands that promotes effective conflict prevention and peace-building strategies, and actively supports and connects people working for peace world-wide. The ECCP serves as an information point, a network organization, and an advocate for the field of conflict prevention and peacebuilding in general. ECCP's activities revolve around:

1. Documenting and disseminating comprehensive information on conflicts and various approaches to conflict prevention and peacebuilding by civil society worldwide.
2. To increase cooperation and networking among different actors (civil society, IGOs, governments, policymakers, academics, media) working on conflict prevention and peacebuilding worldwide.
3. To advocate inclusive and multi-track approaches for conflict prevention and peacebuilding, including support for local capacities for peace, to governments, the donor community, civil society, and a broad public.

Among ECCP's programs, two are implemented globally: The Searching for Peace Program and Global Partnership for the Prevention of Armed Conflict.

The Searching for Peace project aims to provide actual information on violent conflicts and conflict prevention in the region, an inventory on who is doing what by producing a directory of organizations as well as strengthening networking and coordination among local and regional networks and promote multi-track diplomacy. Lastly, it aims to describe, discuss and promote effective approaches, lessons learned and recommendations on conflict prevention and peacebuilding.

The Global Partnership for the Prevention of Armed Conflict is an integrated global program of research, discussion, and network building, leading to an international conference at the UN headquarters, New York, in mid 2005. NGOs and civil society organizations from 15 regions worldwide will finally formulate a Global Action Agenda, containing concrete proposals to support and enhance the role of civil society and NGOs, and to facilitate future cooperation between the civil society and NGOs and the UN, Regional Organizations, and governments. ECCP further acts as the secretariat of the European Platform for Conflict Prevention and Transformation—an open network of about 150 organizations—and initiates, co-ordinates and implements the activities of the platform.

PO Box 14069
3508 SC Utrecht
The Netherlands

Tel: +31 (30) 242 7777
Fax: +31 (30) 236 9268
info@conflict-prevention.net
www.conflict-prevention.net

Contact: Paul van Tongeren, Executive Director
Number of staff: 15

Publications: Conflict Prevention Newsletter, quarterly newsletter; *The Power of the Media: A Handbook for Peacebuilders,* 2003; *Searching for Peace in Europe and Eurasia: An Overview of Conflict Prevention and Peace-building Activities,* 2002; *Searching for Peace in Central and South Asia: An Overview of Conflict Prevention and Peace-building Activities,* 2002; *Towards Better Peacebuilding Practice,* 2002; *People Building Peace: 35 Inspiring Stories from Around the World,* 1999; and *Prevention and Management of Violent Conflicts: An International Directory,* 1998

Pacific

European Center on Pacific Issues –
Europe Pacific Solidarity

RESEARCH
ACTION
ADVOCACY

The European Center on Pacific Issues (ECSIEP) is the secretariat of the Europe Pacific Solidarity Network. ECSIEP serves as an information center on developments in the Pacific and acts as an interface between Pacific civil society and European organizations and institutions. European NGOs and church organizations working on peace, environmental, and development issues in the Pacific established the Europe Pacific Solidarity (EPS) network. Since 1989, the Europe Pacific Solidarity network organizes annual seminars at which activists of the network meet and discuss the current developments in the Pacific and their involvement. ECSIEP brings together all initiatives from organizations working in this field in Europe, keeps in contact with the European Commission, and assists Pacific civil society representatives to meet the right people, organizations, and institutions when traveling to Europe.

ECSIEP maintains regular contact with churches and NGOs in the Pacific and supports their campaigns and activities. Projects and campaigns over the past years addressed issues like French nuclear testing, climate change, sustainable forestry, the ACP-EU partnership agreements, and the involvement of civil society in this process, mining, sustainable development, and conflicts. Through its website, list servers, and meetings, ECSIEP maintains a high quality of knowledge about developments related to tensions, conflict, and potential conflict situations in the Pacific region.

PO Box 151
3700 AD Zeist
The Netherlands

Tel: +31 (30) 692 7827
Fax: +31 (30) 692 5614
ecsiep@antenna.nl
www.antenna.nl/ecsiep

Contact: Peter van der Vlies, Coordinator
Publications: EPS Bulletins

Global

European Network Against Arms Trade

RESEARCH
ADVOCACY

Established in 1984 during an international conference on arms production and military exports, the European Network Against Arms Trade (ENAAT) now has participants from 13 countries. ENAAT is opposed to the export of arms to countries that are involved, or about to be involved, in armed conflict. Each participant is dedicated to working together to solve the arms trade problem, yet each works independently. Some participants are campaigning organizations, others lobbyists. Research organizations, journalists, and grass-root organizations are also actively involved. ENAAT publishes the EU Annual reports on Arms Trade on its website.

Anna Spenglerstraat 71
1054 NH Amsterdam
The Netherlands

Tel: + 31 (20) 616 4684
Fax: +31 (20) 692 5614
amokmar@antenna.nl
www.enaat.org

Publications: Indonesia: Arms Trade to a Military Regime, 1997

Global

Interchurch Organization for Development Cooperation

EDUCATION
ADVOCACY

Founded in 1964, the Interchurch Organization for Development Cooperation (ICCO) is rooted in the Dutch Protestant-Christian tradition and is partner in various national and international ecumenical networks. In 2000 ICCO merged with SOH (Dutch Interchurch Aid – DIA) and Service Abroad (DOG). It has developed its own program for development cooperation in order to close the gap between North and South. ICCO focuses on promoting processes that lead to a fairer distribution of power and prosperity worldwide while also making a relevant contribution to structural poverty alleviation in developing countries. Attention in Asia and the Pacific over the coming years will be focused on sustainable and equitable economic development, democratization, and peacebuilding.

PO Box 151
3700 AD Zeist
The Netherlands

Tel: +31 (30) 692 7811
Fax: +31 (30) 692 5614
info@icco.nl
Fili-desh@icco.nl
Indo-Indo@icco.nl
www.icco.nl

Contact: Jack van Harn, General Director

Number of staff: 214

Publications: On the Road to Justice, ICCO Policy Plan 2001–2005.

Global

International Fellowship of Reconciliation

EDUCATION

Founded in 1919 to oppose all war and to search for alternatives to violent conflicts, IFOR's current aims are to work toward nuclear disarmament. IFOR covers nonviolence; education, and training; women peacemakers and children's rights; disarmament and peace teams; and inter-religious cooperation. Its training projects help grassroots organizations and local actors to develop educational and training programs in nonviolent conflict resolution. IFOR publishes newsletters, brochures, and leaflets on peace and reconciliation.

Spoorstraat 38
1815 BK Alkmaar
The Netherlands

Tel: +31 (72) 512 3014
Fax: +31 (72) 515 1102
office@ifor.org
www.ifor.org

Contact: David Mumford, International Coordinator

Publications: IFOR In Action, a quarterly e-mail newsletter; *Cross the Lines newsletter*

Global

Netherlands Institute for Multiparty Democracy

RESEARCH
EDUCATION
ACTION
ADVOCACY

The Netherlands Institute for Multiparty Democracy (IMD) was set up as a foundation in 2000 by Dutch political parties, in response to the international requests for support by political parties and groups abroad. Its main objective is to support the process of democratization in young democracies in order to help create a well-functioning, sustainable, pluralistic system of party politics. IMD set up a program in Indonesia and has participated in many debates over the future of Indonesia as a unified state, along with exchanging views about democratization. IMD identified the need for training and support in many areas, among MPs and established politicians, regional administrators, and emerging political figures alike. IMD is hoping to provide a foundation through an "Academy for Democracy" and would target the young, women, and people who are active in politics in the provinces. Its main focus would be the democratic skills needed to function in political for and on representative bodies, and the development or reinforcement of citizens' democratic skills.

Korte Vijverberg 2
2513 AB The Hague
The Netherlands

Tel: +31 (70) 311 5464
Fax: +31 (70) 311 5465
info@nimd.org or jantuit@nimd.org
www.nimd.org

Contact: Jan Tuit, senior policy officer

Publications: IMD monthly newsletter; The Democratic Deficit, 2002; *Network Democracy: Enhancing the Role of Parties,* 2001

Global

Netherlands Institute of
International Relations Clingendael

The overall objective of the Clingendael Institute is to promote a better understanding of international affairs among politicians, academicians, civil servants and diplomats, the media, and the public at large. The Clingendael "Conflict Research Unit" (CRU) is part of Clingendael's research department and focuses on the study of intrastate conflict and conflict management, especially in the developing world. The CRU focuses in particular on the current "gap" between academic research and policy at a time when efforts to prevent and resolve violent conflicts are demanding new conceptual and analytical frameworks. The goal of CRU research is to develop innovative perspectives and policy approaches to intrastate conflict.

PO Box 93080
2509 AB The Hague
The Netherlands

Tel: +31 (70) 324 5384
Fax: +31 (70) 328 2002
gfrerks@clingendael.nl
www.clingendael.nl/cru

Contact: Professor Georg E. Frerks, Head of Conflict Research Unit

Budget: > $1,000,000

Publications: Women's Roles in Conflict Prevention, Conflict Resolution and Post-Conflict Reconstruction: Literature, 2002.

Global

Novib/Oxfam Netherlands

Novib (Netherlands Organization for International Development Cooperation) works for sustainable development by supporting the efforts of poor people in developing countries and by serving as their advocate in the North. The three broad goals are to alleviate structural poverty, to educate the Dutch population on development issues, and to advance the interest of the poor in policymaking. Novib promotes dialogue in areas of conflict, lobbies in the international arena, undertakes fact-finding activities, and organizes conferences. It works closely with the 11 sister organizations of Oxfam International, with more than 3,000 local counterparts and supports international groups such as International Alert and Synergies Africa. Current campaigns are Make Trade Fair, Control Arms, and Education Now.

PO Box 30919
2500 GX The Hague
The Netherlands

Tel: +31 (70) 3421 777
Fax: +31 (70) 3614 461
info@novib.nl
www.novib.nl

Contact: Jan Ruyssenaars, Policy Advisor Human Rights and Conflicts

Africa, the Balkans, Indonesia,
Latin America, the Middle East, Chechnya

ACTION

Pax Christi Netherlands

Pax Christi is an international movement for peace and reconciliation, non-violence, and human rights. The organization invites opponents in conflicts to meet and encourages gestures of reconciliation. Pax Christi members visit those involved in or affected by armed conflict: victims and peace groups, socially committed religious movements, authors and other opinion leaders, and the warring parties, their politicians, and warlords. It expresses solidarity through organizing capacity training for young people, women, and NGOs, and supports local civil peace initiatives in the region and lobbies international organizations.

Godebaldkwartier 74
3511 DZ Utrecht
The Netherlands

Tel: +31 (30) 233 3346
Fax: +31 (30) 236 8199
reactie@paxchristi.nl
www.paxchristi.nl

Contact: Jan Gruiters, Director
Number of staff: 25

Global

RESEARCH
ADVOCACY

Transnational Institute

The Transnational Institute (TNI) was founded in 1974 as a worldwide fellowship of committed scholar-activists. The TNI program Asia Europe Relations "The People's Agenda" has been developed in close cooperation with partner organizations in the Asian region and is currently focusing on Globalization and Militarization; Democratic Transitions and People's Power in Asia; Europe's Asia policy—Trade, Investment and ODA flows; Impact of WTO (GATS), World Bank and IMF policies and social movements and alternatives for the 21st century. Democratization and human rights in Asia are important parts of TNIs Asia program, which participates in solidarity campaigns, facilitates consultations and advocacy initiatives between Asian activists and European counterparts, development NGOs, politicians and policy-makers. TNI is currently involved in studying the impact of European water corporations' investments in the drinking water utilities in major cities in Asia, like Manila and Jakarta. TNI has also been monitoring the struggle for labor rights in South Korea and has assisted in publicizing the international campaign against the repression of Korean Congress of Trade Unions (KCTU) leadership.

Paulus Potterstraat 20
1071 DA Amsterdam
The Netherlands

Tel: +31 (20) 662 6608
Fax: +31 (20) 675 7176
asia@tni.org
www.tni.org/asia

Contact: Brid Brennan
Number of staff: 3
Publications: ASEM Watch (regular TNI bulletin);
Drugs and Conflict in Burma, Dilemmas for Policy Responses, 2003

Global

Unrepresented Nations and Peoples Organisation

EDUCATION
ACTION
ADVOCACY

One of the aims of the Unrepresented Nations and Peoples Organisation (UNPO) is to assist its 51 member nations, peoples, and minorities in preventing violent conflicts, or in resolving them through negotiations and political means. Through its Conflict Prevention Program, UNPO provides training in diplomacy and conflict resolution, professional services, and advice relevant to these purposes. UNPO also encourages and facilitates dialogue between potential adversaries and carries out behind-the-scenes diplomacy. UNPO is dedicated to the five principles enshrined in its Charter: Non-violence, Human Rights, Self-determination and Democracy, Environmental Protection, and Tolerance.

PO Box 85878
2508 CN The Hague
The Netherlands

Tel: +31 (70) 364 6504
Fax: +31 (70) 364 6608
unpo@unpo.org
www.unpo.org

Contact: Cathy Shin, Conflict Prevention Program Coordinator

Budget: $100,000–$500,000

Publications: UNPO News, quarterly newsletter; *Nonviolence and Conflict: Conditions for Effective Peaceful Change,* 1998; *UNPO Monitor of the United Nations Working Group on Indigenous Populations,* 1997

Pacific

Council for International Development

EDUCATION
ADVOCACY

The Council for International Development (CID) works to strengthen the capacity of international aid programs by the New Zealand government and community organizations. CID serves as an umbrella agency for 61 member organizations that are directly involved in development and aid issues, of which some are related to peace and reconciliation issues. CID provides a forum for discussion on international development issues; supports national and international networking; raises developmental issues to political parties; and raises awareness on international aid and development needs. One of its responsibilities is training and capacity building for its members. In some of CID's courses facets of peace and reconciliation issues are included. One of CIDs roles is to service and facilitate the NGO Disaster Relief Forum (NDRF), which is an informal grouping of those agencies that are involved with disaster relief and emergency management work.

5th Floor, PSA House
11 Aurora Terrace
PO Box 12-470
Wellington
New Zealand

Tel: +64 (4) 472 6375
Fax: +64 (4) 473 6274
cid@clear.net.nz
www.cid.org.nz

Contact: Rae Julian, Executive Director

Budget: $100,000–$500,000

Number of staff: 5

Publications: Newsletter, 3 times a year

Global

Disarmament and Security Center

RESEARCH
EDUCATION

The Disarmament and Security Center was established in 1998 as a specialist branch of the New Zealand Peace Foundation (see separate entry). The center's broad objective is to provide a resource center for alternative thinking on disarmament and security issues, both within New Zealand and internationally. Current activities focus on supporting nuclear disarmament initiatives; rebutting nuclear deterrence doctrine and offering safer alternatives; promoting non-provocative, non-nuclear security policies and conflict resolution in the Asia-Pacific region; and ways to implement the UN Study on Disarmament and Non-Proliferation Education. It highlights the key role of women in nurturing peace; and its youth work includes providing lecturers for the Peace Studies course at the University of Canterbury, helping Christchurch develop as a Peace City, and helping to build a national youth peace network.

PO Box 8390
35 Rata Street
Riccarton
Christchurch
New Zealand

Tel: +64 (3) 348 1353/1350
Fax: +64 (3) 348 1353
kate@chch.planet.org.nz
www.disarmsecure.org

Contact: Dr Kate Dewes, ONZM and Commander Robert Green, Royal Navy (Ret), Coordinators

Budget: $25,000-100,000

Number of staff: 5

Publications: The Naked Nuclear Emperor— Debunking Nuclear Deterrence, 2003; *Re-Thinking Nuclear Deterrence,* 2001

New Zealand

Foundation for Peace Studies New Zealand

EDUCATION

Since its establishment in 1975, the Foundation for Peace Studies New Zealand ("The Peace Foundation") has initiated peace education for schools, homes, and wider communities. The organization's Cool Schools program teaches primary and secondary teachers and students how to peacefully resolve conflicts and handle anger. It also offers conflict resolution and mediation services and runs a family health program to help parents prevent family violence against children. The Peace Foundation established the Media Peace Awards to recognize those who are actively contributing towards reducing violence. The organization is also involved in the organization of various other events.

PO Box 4110
29 Princes Street
Auckland 1
New Zealand

Tel: +64 (9) 373 2379
Fax: +64 (9) 379 2668
peace@fps.pl.net
www.peace.net.nz

Contact: Wendy John, General Manager

Budget: $100,000–$500,000

Number of staff: 7

Publications: Peaceworks, quarterly newsletter; *Volcanoes: Handling Anger CD Rom,* 2003; *Little Volcanoes,* 2003

Asia Pacific, Southern and East Africa, Latin America

New Zealand Agency
for International Development

EDUCATION
ADVOCACY

New Zealand Agency for International Development (NZAID) is a semi-autonomous agency of the Ministry of Foreign Affairs and Trade. New Zealand's aid program is designed to contribute to peace, security and development within the Pacific Island states and the poorer East and Southeast Asian countries. The key policy principles include partner responsibility, human rights, capacity building, and good governance. There are a number of bilateral programs established in the Pacific. In the Solomon islands NZAID focuses particularly on education and on law and justice sectors as well as support to civil society and sustainable livelihoods. In Papua New Guinea the agency assists with the upgrading of educational levels through study awards in New Zealand and capacity building of NGOs. In Bougainville, NZAID's program continues to be focused on re-integration of former combatants, re-establishment of civil authority, and on rebuilding the islands' infrastructure.

Private Bag 18-901
Wellington
New Zealand

Contact: Peter Adams, Executive Director

Tel: +64 (4) 439 8200
Fax: +64 (4) 439 8515
enquiries@nzaid.govt.nz
www.nzaid.govt.nz

Global

New Zealand Center
for Conflict Resolution

RESEARCH
EDUCATION

The New Zealand Center for Conflict Resolution (NZCCR) was established in 1996 as a research center in the School of Law at Victoria University in Wellington. The center promotes the study of conflict and conflict resolution in domestic as well as international contexts. The center researches conflict and the resolution of disputes and develops dispute resolution courses. It also organizes lectures and seminars by a variety of speakers.

Victoria University of
   Wellington Law School
Government Buildings
15 Lambton Quay
PO Box 600
Wellington
New Zealand

Contact: Ian MacDuff, Director
Number of staff: 2

Tel: +64 (4) 463 6327
Fax: +64 (4) 463 6365
law-centres@vuw.ac.nz
www.vuw.ac.nz/nzccr

Global

Operation Peace Through Unity

Operation Peace Through Unity (OPTU) is an accredited NGO in association with the UN Department of Public Information. It has been involved in a variety of peace related issues since its foundation in 1975. Some examples include the UK World Disarmament Campaign in the 1980s and the Peace Child Musical. OPTU has initiated and sponsored a Culture of Peace project, which involves the building of a peace artwork to signify a future culture of peace and non-violence.

Te Rangi
4 Allison Street
Wanganui 5001
New Zealand

Tel/Fax: +64 (6) 345 5714
optubrookiana@xtra.co.nz
www.isleofavalon.co.uk/manytomany.html

Contact: Anthony and Gita Brooke, Co-founders

Publications: Many-to-Many, quarterly newsletter

Global

Oxfam New Zealand

Oxfam New Zealand works with communities in developing countries to overcome poverty and injustice by addressing the causes of inequality and powerlessness, and building the capacity of its partners to advocate for change. In New Zealand Oxfam NZ campaigns against injustice to influence governments and international institutions. In Asia Pacific Oxfam NZ provides support for community development, protection of women's rights, health care, and emergency response in Afghanistan, Cambodia, East Timor, Fiji, India, Indonesia, Papua New Guinea, Solomon Islands, Somoa, and Vanuatu.

Level 1, 62 Aitken Terrace
Kingsland
PO Box 68357
Auckland, 1032
New Zealand

Tel: +64 (9) 355 6500
Fax: +64 (9) 355 6505
oxfam@oxfam.org.nz
www.oxfam.org.nz

Contact: Barry Coates, Director

New Zealand, Pacific

ACTION
ADVOCACY

Peace Movement Aotearoa

Peace Movement Aotearoa (PMA) is the national networking organization in New Zealand for those concerned with peace and related issues. PMA provides news and views on armed conflict, weapons production and sales, militarization and human rights abuses; suggestions for alternative ways of thinking and peaceful resolution of conflict; information on peace initiatives, peaceful protest, and preventing war. Its primary focus is on New Zealand and the Pacific. PMA is committed to social change through non-violent means; they are working for a world with real security, lasting peace, and justice for everyone. PMA's networking and information services include: frequent e-mail updates and alerts on a wide range of peace issues; national "what's on where" listings sent by e-mail every week; a comprehensive up-to-date website; free web pages for groups working for peace; and the Internet Peace Gateway. PMA is funded by donations from supporters.

PO Box 9314
Wellington
New Zealand

Budget: < $25,000
Number of staff: 1, 5 volunteers

Tel: +64 (4) 382 8129
Fax: +64 (4) 382 8173
pma@apc.org.nz
www.converge.org.nz/pma/

Global
Women's International League for Peace and Freedom

EDUCATION
ACTION

Women's International League for Peace and Freedom (WILPF) New Zealand is part of the international women's peace organization established in 1915 to *"bring together women of different political beliefs and philosophies who are united in their determination to study, make known and help abolish the causes and the legitimization of war."*

WILPF International has consultative status at the UN, and they use this to ensure women's voices for peace are heard at that level. In New Zealand, it is committed to honoring the Treaty of Waitangi, as it perceives this as a positive way to prevent conflict and to remedy past and present injustice.

There are WILPF groups in 42 countries, all working toward the same goals: an end to war, violence, and coercion; peaceful negotiated solutions to conflicts; universal disarmament and the diversion of resources away from armed forces and weapons to meeting human needs; the elimination of all forms of inequality, oppression, discrimination, and exploitation; the establishment of an international economic order based on meeting the needs of people, not on privilege and profit; environmentally and socially sustainable development; and reform and strengthening of the United Nations to assist with achieving the above goals.

WILPF New Zealand's current work, among others, includes: active opposition, campaigning, and lobbying the government, other governments, and international bodies, on issues concerning West Papua and Aceh and the Indonesian government's continuing oppression of these communities; working with the women in West Papua; working for demilitarization and disarmament in the Pacific; supporting indigenous struggles especially in New Zealand where the government is intent on passing new legislation to deprive Maori of rights guaranteed in the Treat of Waitangi of the control of the foreshore and seabed; working with other organizations to oppose the wars in Afghanistan and Iraq and any New Zealand involvement in these wars.

WILPF Aotearoa
PO Box 47-189, Ponsonby
Auckland
New Zealand

Contact: Joan MacDonald

Fax: +64 (9) 360 8005
Joanmac@pl.net
www.converge.org.nz/pma/wilpf/

Balkans, Asia, Middle East, South America, Sub-Saharan Africa

RESEARCH

Chr. Michelsen Institute

The Chr. Michelsen Institute (CMI) is a private social science foundation working on issues of development and human rights, primarily in sub-Saharan Africa, Asia, the Balkans, South America, and the Middle East. It carries out both basic and applied research. In its "Human Rights and Democratization" program, CMI focuses on peace, reconciliation, and democratization; the adequacy of conflict prevention mechanisms and peacebuilding; good governance and the rule of law; judicial reform; and human rights protection.

Fantoftvegen 38
PO Box 6033 Postterminalen
5892 Bergen
Norway
_____
Tel: +47 (55) 574 000
Fax: +47 (55) 574 166
cmi@cmi.no or
    gunnar.sorbo@cmi.no
www.cmi.no

Contact: Gunnar M. Sørbø, Director

Number of staff: 60

Publications: Frustrations with a Paternalistic Humanitarian Industry, 2003; *Growth and Ethnic Inequality, Malaysia's New Economic Policy,* 2003; *Malaysia's New Economic Policy: An Overview,* 2003; and several others

Global

RESEARCH
EDUCATION

International Peace Research Institute

International Peace Research Institute (PRIO) was founded in 1959 and was one of the first centers of peace research in the world. The institute is independent. PRIO studies the driving forces behind violent conflict and ways that peace can be built, maintained, and spread. This is at the core of all institute activities. PRIO also conducts policy-oriented activities and hosts the editorial office of two international journals published by Sage in London. There are three research programs: Foreign and Security Policies; Ethics, Norms and Identities; and Conflict Resolution and Peacebuilding. The operational projects under the latter program are Assistance to Mine-Affected Communities (AMAC) and Norwegian Initiative on Small Arms Transfers (NISAT). In 2002 PRIO established the Center for the Study of Civil War. Of special relevance is the "Security and Maritime Conflict in East Asia" project.

Fuglehauggata 11
N-0260 Oslo
Norway
_____
Tel: +47 (22) 547 700
Fax: +47 (22) 547 701
info@prio.no or stein@prio.no
www.prio.no

Contact: Dr. Stein Tonnesson, Director

Number of staff: 50

Publications: Journal of Peace Research; Security Dialogue journal; "Class" in Tibet: Creating Social Order Before and During the Mao Era, 2003; and several other reports

Bougainville

Bougainville Inter-Church Women's Forum

The Bougainville Inter-Church Women's Forum (BICWF), a community based organization, was founded to promote Christian unity and the development of reconciliation and peace in Bougainville. It grew out of the strong tradition among women in Bougainville to organize within their churches. By drawing in "non-politicized women" and as a pan-Bougainvillean and ecumenical organization, the BICWF complemented the work of the Provincial Council of Women and their district structures. Dialogue work was done in northern Bougainville with the Bougainville Resistance Army, the Bougainville Revolutionary Army, the Papua New Guinea Government, and the Papua New Guinea Defense Force on various abuses of the rights of the civilian population. The present work revolves around programs such as Learning from the Bougainville Peace Process, which is aimed at reducing conflict and to help workshop participants understand their own conflict resulting from the Bougainville Crisis. The BICWF was part of an Accord project and developed an education pack of materials about the conflict and peace process for use in critical literacy training workshops across Bougainville.

Sevillehaus
Kokopau
PO Box 209
Buka
Bougainville
Papua New Guinea

Tel: +675 (973) 9983
Fax: +675 (973) 9157
bicwf@dg.com.pg

Contact: Sister Lorraine Garasu, CSN Director

Budget: < $25,000

Number of staff: 8 office staff (of which 2 active in conflict prevention/resolution activities) and 70 field workers

Publications: Multitrack Diplomacy, 2003; *Weaving Consensus: The PNG-Bougainville Peace Process,* 2002; *Learning from the Bougainville Peace Process,* 2002; *Healing Divisions after Conflict in Bougainville,* 2001

Papua New Guinea

Foundation for
People and Community Development

EDUCATION
ADVOCACY

The activities of the Foundation for People and Community Development (FPCD) focus on advocating and fostering human dignity and respect, sustainable development and the development of self-reliance. The FPCD has several programs including an Awareness Community Theater that promotes awareness of environmental, social, and developmental issues through theater. The foundation also has a Conflict Management Program that aims to reduce conflict over natural resource management and development issues through workshops and roundtable discussions.

PO Box 1119
Boroko
NCD
Papua New Guinea

Contact: Yati A. Bun, Executive Director
Budget: $25,000–$100,000
Number of staff: 27

Tel: +675 (325) 8470
Fax: +675 (325) 2670

Papua New Guinea

Individual and
Community Rights Advocacy Forum

EDUCATION
ADVOCACY

The Individual and Community Rights Advocacy Forum (ICRAF) has been promoting, monitoring, and advocating human rights, women's rights, and land rights, as well as environmental protection in Papua New Guinea since 1992. The ICRAF has a Human Rights Litigation program that is involved with human rights violations, in particular police brutality and state violence. The forum also runs a special women's desk that acts as a women's crisis center and looks into the rights of children. The ICRAF organizes training and workshops on Land and Environmental laws, women's rights, and human rights, and also has conducted protest marches on women's and forestry issues to raise awareness.

Section 240, Lot 38
Agolo/Ala Street
Gerehu stage 2
PO Box 155
University PO
NCD
Papua New Guinea

Contact: Hilan Los, Acting Director
Budget: $100,000–$500,000

Tel: +675 (326) 2469/2385
Fax: +675 (326) 2703

Bougainville

Leitana Nehan
Women's Development Agency

The Leitana Women's Development Agency (LNWDA) was established in 1995 with the goal to create a worl that is safe for women and children. The agency organizes workshops to educate on violence against women and provides crisis-counseling services for families and female victims of violence. LNWDA runs a program "Strengthening Communities for Peace," which involves teams of volunteers visiting communities and schools throughout Bougainville to raise awareness on violence, human rights, and peace.

c/o PO Box 86
Buka
Bougainville
Papua New Guinea

Contact: Helen Hakena

Tel/Fax: +675 (973) 9962

Papua New Guinea, Solomon Islands

Peace Foundation Melanesia Inc.

The Peace Foundation Melanesia was established in 1989 as the Foundation for Law, Order and Justice, with an advocacy role in improving and promoting the use of traditional methods of mediation within the introduced Western legal system. In 1994 in response to the Bougainville crisis the emphasis of the foundation changed to that of providing training to the grassroots in People Skills, Conflict Resolution, and Restorative Justice.

In 2002 there was another important shift in policy, which resulted in the establishment of a Peace and Good Order Committee made up of village leaders, leaders of the local churches, women's groups, and youth groups. This committee appoints mediators to resolve all conflicts within their village or community, including all matters that are referred to the formal sector legal system through the village courts and police.

The Peace Foundation Melanesia currently conducts training throughout Papua New Guinea and have also provided training to the Papua New Guinea and Solomon Islands Police Forces and Corrective Services.

PO Box 1272
Port Moresby NCD
Papua New Guinea

Tel: +675 (321) 3144
Fax: +675 (321) 3645
peacefound@global.net.pg
www.restorativejustice.org/default.htm

Contact: Dr. Pat Harley, Executive Director
Budget: 100,000–$500,000
Number of staff: 12 including more than 70 trainers
Publications: Breaking Spears and Mending Hearts and Training Manuals, 2000

Philippines

Alliance for the Advancement of People's Rights

RESEARCH
EDUCATION
ACTION
ADVOCACY

Alliance for the Advancement of People's Rights (KARAPATAN) is an umbrella organization set-up in 1995 by individuals, groups, and organizations working for the promotion and protection of human rights in the Philippines. Its founders and member have been in the forefront of the human rights struggle in the Philippines since the time of Marcos' martial law regime.

Currently KARAPATAN is involved in activities like education and training to raise people's awareness of their rights via education modules and seminars; campaign, and advocacy to develop a strong public opinion and to generate support for human rights issues and concerns; and services for the welfare and legal needs of political prisoners, torture victims, relatives of disappeared and victim killings, displacement, and others. It further gathers information on particular cases of human rights violations and on the general human rights situation in the country in its Documentation and Research Program. These analyses are sometimes sent out as urgent action alerts.

#43 Masikap St.
Central District
Quezon City 1101
Philippines

Number of staff: 7

Tel: +63 (2) 435 4146
Fax: +63 (2) 928 6078
Krptn@philonline.com and karapatan@edsamail.com.ph
www.karapatan.org

Asia-Pacific

Asia-Pacific
Peace Research Association

The Asia-Pacific Peace Research Association (APPRA) is an international NGO of peace researchers, peace advocates, and peace educators. It functions as an independent regional branch of the International Peace Research Association (IPRA). Its goal is to promote interdisciplinary research on peace and conflict through international collaboration. APPRA organizes regional conferences, supports scientific journals, and assists in the collaboration of different peace research institutes and associations throughout the region.

41 Raja Matanda
Project 4, Quezon City
Phillippines 1109

Tel: +63 (2) 913 9255/439 9119
Fax: +63 (2) 913 6435/913 9255
info@appra.org
www.appra.org

Contact: Mary-Soledad Perpiñan,
Secretary General

Publications: APPRA Waves, newsletter

Philippines, Mindanao

Bishops-Ulama Forum

The Bishops-Ulama Forum is a dialogue forum between Catholic bishops, Muslim religious leaders, and Protestant Bishops in Mindanao. The forum convenes four times per year to discuss areas of common concern to promote a culture of peace. In addition, it initiates regional forums to address local issues of peace and solidarity together with religious leaders of indigenous people. Through these efforts, the Bishops-Ulama Forum aims to strengthen the spiritual and cultural bases for peace, and to provide an important addition to political and socio-economic peacebuilding efforts in Mindanao.

D5 Kimberley Building
Bonifacio Avenue
9200 Iligan City
Philippines

Tel: +63 492 0096
Fax: +63 223 8120
kalinaw@mindanao.com
www.mindanao.com/kalinaw/buf/buf.htm

Philippines

Center for Peace Education

EDUCATION
ADVOCACY

The Center for Peace Education was established in 1997 to institutionalize and strengthen peace education in Miriam College. To this end, the center trains the faculty in peace education, develops a curriculum, and organizes conflict resolution education sessions for students and the faculty. The center also conducts workshops on peace education, non-violent conflict resolution, and mediation for teachers, social development workers, and grassroots leaders. It is also involved in advocacy, and has convened a Peace Education Network to join together the schools and organizations that are doing schools-based and community-based peace education. The center is also linked with other peace-oriented groups and centers in the country and is associated with the Hague Appeal for Peace Global Campaign for Peace Education and with the Peace Education Centers Network coordinated by the Peace Education Center of Teachers College, Columbia University.

Miriam College
U.P PO Box 110
Diliman, Quezon City
Philippines

Contact: Loreta N. Castro, Director
Number of staff: 3

Tel: +63 (2) 435 9231/580 5400
Fax: +63 (2) 924 9769
lcastro@mc.edu.ph
www.mc.edu.ph/center_for_peace.htm

Philippines, Mindanao

Community Organizers Multiversity

RESEARCH
EDUCATION

Community Organizers Multiversity, or CO Multiversity, is a capability building institution that has a broader perspective on the empowerment process. The organization aims to respond to the difficult challenges faced by the marginalized communities to address the impact of poverty due to the globalization process. The learning processes of the training modules are based on the lessons of the past and guided by the new issues of the present which confronts many people's organizations and development NGOs especially on the questions of strategies and tactics of empowerment, the use of power, empowering dispute resolution management processes, and peace and development questions in Mindanao. CO Multiversity organizes trainings and researches issues affecting grassroots organizations.

23-B Matulungin Street
Brgy. Central
Quezon City 1100
PO Box 2631
QCCPO 1166 Quezon City
Philippines

Contact: Ma. Fides Bagasao,
Executive Director
Number of staff: 24
*Publications: Promotion of a Common
Rural Community Organizing
Standard in the Philippines,* 1998;
*Rural Community Organizing in the
Philippines,* 1996

Tel/Fax: +63 (2) 922 2026
sanayan@comultiversity.org.ph
www.comultiversity.org.ph

Philippines

Consortium of Bangsamoro NGOs and POs in Mindanao

RESEARCH
EDUCATION
ACTION
ADVOCACY

The Consortium of Bangsamoro NGOs and POs in Mindanao is a network of 31 NGOs and People's Organizations (POs) covering thirteen provinces all over Mindanao. The consortium aims to improve the quality of life of the Bangsamoro people, and to uphold their rights to live in a just, progressive, and peaceful society. It does this through (1) policy research and advocacy on issues and concerns that persist to affect the Bangsamoro people; (2) establishing and maintaining a wide network of contacts among international organizations, support groups, parallel organizations, and concerned individuals who sympathize with the cause of the Bangsamoro; (3) campaigns to help the Bangsamoro people to deepen their understanding of their social, cultural, economic, and political situation; (4) capacity building of the necessary expertise and degree of professionalism of its member organizations in implementing their respective programs so they can better serve the people.

2-3/F Demonteverde Building
Dona Pilar St.
Purok Maharlika, Poblacion IV
Cotabato City, Mindanao
Philippines

Contact: Guiamel Alim

Tel: +63 (64) 421 4222
Fax: +63 (64) 421 2072
guimel@microweb.com.ph or kadtun@hotmail.com

Philippines

Ecumenical Movement for Justice and Peace

ACTION
ADVOCACY

The Ecumenical Movement for Justice and Peace (EMJP) was formed on 28 July 1979 by members of various religious orders and congregations who opted to live out their mission by taking the stand of the marginalized and exploited sectors in Philippine society. The EMJP is one of the pioneering human rights organizations in the Philippines during the height of martial law in the late 1970s. Its membership is composed of church people, professionals, youth, and students. EMJP works closely with its regional and provincial chapters throughout the Philippines, to serve the victims of conflicts through campaigns, training and the establishment of local human rights committees.

#43 Masikap St.
Central District
Quezon City 1101
Philippines

Contact: Rev. Alfredo Faurillo (Board member)

Tel: +63 (2) 435 4146
Fax: +63 (2) 928 6078
emjp2004@yahoo.com

Philippines

Gaston Z. Ortigas Peace Institute – National Peace Conference

ACTION
ADVOCACY

The first National Peace Conference (NPC) in 1990 brought together representatives from many different sectors of Philippine society in order to forge a national vision and agenda for peace. Today, it is a non-partisan, multi-sectored citizens assembly of a wide diversity of sectors, including farmers, urban poor, indigenous peoples, women, and youth. The goal of the NPC is to pursue its Basic Peace Agenda through lobbying the government, focusing on social justice, the peace process, human rights, good governance, environmental concerns, and sociocultural transformation. The conference supports peace talks between the government and armed opposition groups and advocates active citizens' participation in the peace process.

Gaston Z. Ortiga Peace Institute
Social Development Complex
Ateneo de Manila University
Loyola Heights, Quezon City
Philippines

Contact: Karen Tañada, Executive Director

Tel: +63 (2) 426 6122/ 6001
Fax: +63 (2) 426 6064
peace@codewan.com.ph

Burma, East Timor, Philippines, Mindanao

Initiatives for International Dialogue

The Initiatives for International Dialogue (IID) is a NGO that strives to strengthen South-South solidarity. To this end IID, together with other national and regional groups, campaigns and lobbies on various issues in Burma, East Timor, and Mindanao. For example, IID advocates the engagement of a people's constituency in the peace process in Mindanao, tri-partite dialogue in Burma and international sanctions against perpetrators of human rights violations in East Timor. In addition to its lobbying and advocacy activities, IID is also involved in curriculum development, training, and the organization of solidarity discussions and forums. IID functions as the secretariat of the Mindanao Peoples Caucus (MPC).

27-G Galaxy Street
GSIS Heights, Matina
Davao City
Philippines

Tel: +63 (82) 299 2574/5
Fax: +63 (82) 299 2052
info@iidnet.org or
    davao@iidnet.org
www.iidnet.org

Manila Liaison Office:
Door 15 Casal Building,
    15 Anonas Road, Project 3
Quezon City, Philippines

Tel: +63 (2) 911 0205
Fax: +63 (2) 435 2900
manila@iidnet.org

Contact: Augusto Miclat Jr., Executive Director
Number of staff: 21
Publications: Peaceweaving: Cotabato local peace dialogues, 2002; *Peacebuilder Kit for Mindanao,* 2002

Philippines

Institute for Popular Democracy

The Institute for Popular Democracy (IPD), founded in 1986, is a political research and advocacy institute serving social movement groups, NGOs in development work, and progressive local government officials. At the core of IPD's identity is its commitment to democratization and social development. IPD focuses on local and national issues affecting areas that continue to be economically backward and that are subject to various forms of local authoritarianism. IPD locates itself at the interstices of civil society, the economy, and the state. IPD's immediate constituency is the NGO grassroots community and progressive political formations. IPD reaches out as well to the broader community of groups and individuals who seek national reform: media, academe, and reform-minded policy-makers in government and in the business community. IPD conducts training on "Democratizing Local Governance," on "Electoral Campaign Management," "Voters' Education: New Politics and Active Citizenship," and "Political Education: Basic Understanding On Democratization."

45 Matimtiman Street
Teachers Village
Quezon City
Metro Manila
Philippines

Tel: +63 (2) 434 6674
Fax: +63 (2) 921 8049
ocd@ipd.org.ph
www.ipd.ph

Contact: Joel Rocamora, Director

Publications: Political Brief, monthly e-letter; *Work in Progress,* occasional.

South China Sea

Institute for Strategic and International Studies

RESEARCH
ACTION

The Institute for Strategic and International Studies (ISIS) has organized a series of dialogues on the South China Sea since 1995. This series of workshops aims to clarify the security implications for neighboring states, should conflict arise in the South China Sea. The workshops bring together representatives of governments, NGOs and academia and attempt to arrive at a better understanding of and generate appropriate policy responses to the security issues surrounding the South China Sea problem. So far, workshops have been held in 1995, 1997, and 2000.

Room 311, P.S.S. Center
Commonwealth Avenue, Diliman
Quezon City 1001
Philippines

Tel: +63 (2) 929 0889
Fax: + 63 (2) 922 9621
isdsphil@cnl.net

Contact: Professor Malaya Ronas or Ms. Rowena Layador

Budget: $50,000–$100,000

Number of staff: 7

Philippines

Legal Rights and
Natural Resources Centre

RESEARCH
EDUCATION
ACTION
ADVOCACY

The goal of the Legal Rights and Natural Resources Centre (LRC) is to empower marginalized peoples that are dependent on natural resources, so that these resources can come to be managed and conserved in equitable and ecologically sustainable ways. LRC provides critical analyses of the policies and laws concerned with indigenous peoples and natural resources, organizes paralegal trainings with partner communities, and files court cases. The center also lobbies through the media, and networks with local, national, and international organizations to find support for its campaigns. The LRC is in close contact with grassroots communities through its regional branches. LRC is also the official Philippine affiliate of Friends of the Earth International.

#7 Marunong Street
Central District Diliman
Quezon City 1100
Philippines

Tel: +63 (2) 926 4409
Fax: +63 (2) 920 7172
lrcksk@info.com.ph
www.lrcksk.org

Contact: Ms. Milagros Ballesteros

Publications: Mapping the Earth, Mapping Life,
2001

Mindanao

Mindanao Coalition
of Development NGOs

ADVOCACY

Mindanao Coalition of Development NGOs (MINCODE) is a coalition of nine networks of NGOs and people's organizations based in Mindanao. These networks represent various sectors: the church, cooperatives, social development agencies, intermediary organizations, and sectoral groups. It serves as an advocacy body that raises the needs and aspirations of marginalized sectors for sustainable, gender-fair, and participatory development. From 1993 to 1996, its member networks spearheaded region-wide consultations among development NGOs, with the goal of building consensus on an integrated and comprehensive development agenda for Mindanao. Validated in 1996 as the "People's Development Program in Mindanao" (PDPM), this groundbreaking document marks the first time for the Mindanao NGO community to articulate a common development vision for the region. The PDPM currently serves as the basis for MINCODE's various endeavors.

110 Maa Road
DBP Village
Davao City
Philippines

Telefax: +63 (82) 299-0625
secretariat@mincode.org
www.mincode.org

Contact: Aileen A. Fermalino

Asia

EDUCATION

Mindanao Peacebuilding Institute

Organized by Catholic Relief Services (CRS), the Mennonite Central Committee (MCC) and the Catholic Agency for Overseas Development (CAFOD), the Mindanao Peacebuilding Institute (MPI) is an annual intensive training event that seeks to promote peaceful and just communities in the Asia Pacific region through training. Since 2000 to date, it has brought together more than 450 peacebuilders and practitioners from twenty-one countries.

The MPI, as envisioned, provided a unique experience in that it brought together a wide range of people with vast experience, knowledge, and skills in peace-related work. The intensive training in areas such as religious peacebuilding, conflict transformation, community-based peacebuilding, and other themes increased people's skills, drawing on the shared knowledge of both the participants and the facilitators.

Mennonite Central Committee
   Asia Peace Resource
Davao City
Philippines

Contact: Jon Rudy

Tel: +63 (82) 297 8203
mccapr@myrealbox.com
www.mcc.org/areaserv/asia/philippines

Mindanao

Mindanao Peoples Caucus

ACTION
ADVOCACY

Formerly the Mindanao Tri-People's Caucus, the Mindanao Peoples Caucus (MPC) was established during the Tri-Peoples Grassroots Dialogue organized by the Initiatives for International Dialogue (IID) in April 2001 in response to the challenge of peace-building work among the tri-peoples (indigenous peoples, Bangsamoro and Christian settlers). MPC is composed of more than fifty grassroots leaders coming mainly from the conflict areas where the major camps of the Moro Islamic Liberation Front (MILF) are located. Additionally, there are also non-government organizations that are officially affiliated with MPC. MPC's mandate is to give community leaders, whether Moro, settler, or indigenous, greater representation within the official peace process between the MILF and the government of the Philippines, and to ensure that grassroots' concerns are headed by both sides. So far, MPC has been successful in positioning itself as a key player in the talks, having been officially recognized as an observer in the GRP-MILF peace talks, which is unprecedented in the series of talks conducted since 1976. Initiatives for International Dialogue functions as MPC's secretariat.

27-G Galaxy Street
GSIS Heights, Matina
Davao City
Philippines

Contact: Augusto Miclat Jr.

Tel: +63 (82) 299 2574/5
Fax: +63 (82) 299 2052
iid@skyinet.net
www.iidnet.org

Philippines

National Council of Churches in the Philippines

ACTION
ADVOCACY

The National Council of Churches in the Philippines, founded in 1963, is a fellowship of ten mainline Protestant and non-Roman Catholic churches and nine service-oriented institutions with an estimated 13 million members. The NCCP's engagement in the peace process, involving the government of the Philippines and the National Democratic Front of the Philippines (NDFP), began in 1987. Since then, the council has articulated its commitment to peace building as an integral part of the church's ministry. A Joint Peace Consultation between the NCCP and the Catholic Bishops' Conference of the Philippines was held in 1994 to identify collaborative efforts for peace. From the consultation was born the Joint NCCP-CBCP Peace Committee that has intermittently released statements in support of principled peace negotiations. In 1997, it was deemed that NCCP's ecumenical overseas partners be brought into the peace program more intentionally by creating the International Peace Advisory Committee to advise the NCCP on the appropriate role it might play in the negotiations. Also in 1997 and in 2001, the NCCP lent its office as the third party depository of GRP-NDFP peace talks documents.

879 Epifanio delos Santos Avenue
West Triangle, Quezon City
1100 Philippines

Tel: +63 (2) 929 3745/ 925 1797
Fax: +63 (2) 926 7076
nccp-ga@philonline.com

Contact: Ms. Sharon Rose Joy Ruiz-Duremdes, General Secretary
Number of staff: 26

Philippines

National Secretariat of Social Action, Justice and Peace

ACTION
ADVOCACY

The National Secretariat of Social Action, Justice and Peace (NASSA) is an Episcopal Commission of the Catholic Bishops Conference of the Philippines and functions as the country representative of Caritas International. The organization strives toward a socially just and equitable society, and aims to strengthen the voice of the poor in developmental processes. To this end, NASSA supports and promotes political education, environmental protection, human rights, and child protection.

National Secretariat for Social Action
CBCP Building
470 General Luna Street
Intramuros
1002 Manila
Philippines

Tel: +63 (2) 527 4163/527 4148
Fax: +32 (2) 527 4144
staff@nassa.org.ph
www.nassa.org.ph

Contact: Most Rev. Dinualdo Gutierrez (Bishop of Marbel), Chairperson
Publications: NASSA News, bi-monthly newsletter; *Managing Advocacy through Social Transformation,* 2003

Philippines

Philippine Peace Center

The Philippine Peace Center (PPC) is a non-profit, NGO that is committed to the attainment of a just and lasting peace in the Philippines. Since its establishment in 1992, the PPC has directly and actively assisted in the peace negotiations between the government of the Republic of the Philippines (GRP) and the National Democratic Front of the Philippines (NDFP). The PPC has provided direct technical and consultative assistance to the negotiations through research, documentation, and facilitation of communications between the two parties. It has also contributed specific services, playing key roles in the implementation of confidence and goodwill measures such as the releases of prisoners held by both parties, and the holding of a national solidarity conference that preceded the resumption of formal negotiations in April 2001. PPC is one of the key conveners of the Pilgrims for Peace, a broad multi-sectoral alliance of peace advocates, and the drafter of a statement calling for the resumption of peace negotiations.

4/f Kaija Bldg.
7836 Makati Ave.
　Cor Valdez Makati City
Metro Manila
Philippines

Tel: +63 (2) 899 3403/899 3439
Fax: +63 (2) 899 3416
crcc@accessway.ph

Contact: Rey Claro C. Casambre, Director

Publications: Toward an Agreement on Human Rights and International Humanitarian Law, 1998; *Which Way to a Just and Lasting Peace?* 1996

Mindanao

Sumpay Mindanao Inc.

Sumpay Mindanao works toward the building of sustainable communities in Mindanao, by realizing alternative models of development that arise from peoples own initiatives. One of Sumpays programs is the Organizational Development and Peace Constituency Building program. This program aims to strengthen the organizational structures of peoples organizations at the community level. Sumpay also works on peace education and advocacy among the three peoples of Mindanao, by organizing seminars on conflict transformation, youth peace camps and facilitating peace dialogues. Sumpay works together with a large number of local community development partners in Mindanao.

Door 1 Kurut Apartment
Doña Josefa Celdran Avenue
3rd East St., Rosario Heights
Brgy. Tubod
Iligan City 9200
Mindanao, Philippines

Tel/Fax: +63 (63) 223 2508
sumpay@mozcom.com

Contact: Ma. Gittel J. Saquilabon, Executive Director and Eva Olaer-Ferraren, Executive Director
Stichting Sumpay Mindanao International
Sint Jacobsstraat 16, Amsterdam 1012 NC
Netherlands

Number of staff: 7
Budget: < $25,000

Global

Third World Studies Center

RESEARCH
EDUCATION

As an internationally oriented academic agency the Third World Studies Center (TWSC) accumulates and exchanges knowledge and know-how on human aspects of processes of political, economic, social, and cultural change. The center has five research areas of which the study of human security in conflict situations is one. The research for the human security in conflict situations focuses on the relationship between conflict and insecurity, with the aim to identify economic, political, social, and cultural policies, which promote stable, secure, and peaceful societies. Conflict prevention and conflict resolution are key areas of analysis. The TWSC has also co-sponsored international conferences and workshops such as the Asian Peace Assembly (APA), Asia-Pacific Peace Research Association (APPRA), and Waging Peace in the Philippines. TWSC acts as Secretariat of the Philippine Campaign to Ban Landmines, and is a member of the Steering Committee of the Philippine Action Network on Small Arms.

Basement, Palma Hall
PO Box 210
University of the Philippines
Diliman, Quezon City 1101
Philippines

Tel: +63 (2) 920 5428
Fax: +63 (2) 920 5301
twsc@kssp.upd.edu.ph
www.upd.edu.ph/~twsc/

Contact: Teresa S. Encarnacion Tadem, Director

Publications: Kasarinlan, bi-annual journal; *People's Initiatives: Engaging the State in Local Communities in the Philippines and Thailand,* 2003

Asia Pacific

Institute of Defense and Strategic Studies

RESEARCH
EDUCATION

The Institute of Defense and Strategic Studies (IDSS) was established at Nanyang Technological University in 1996. It conducts research and provides education on security and strategic issues, with a focus on Asia Pacific and security implications for Singapore and other countries in the region. In the past, research topics included "Non-Traditional Security Issues in Southeast Asia," "Comparative Regionalism," and "Evolving Approaches to Security Cooperation in the Asia-Pacific." The institute provides educational opportunities through the Master of Science in Strategic Studies and Master of Science in International Relations programs.

Institute of Defense and
    Strategic Studies
Nanyang Technological University
South Spine S4, Level B4
Nanyang Avenue
Singapore 639798

Tel: +65 (67) 906 982
Fax: +65 (67) 932 991
wwwidss@ntu.edu.sg
www.idss.edu.sg

Contact: Barry Desker, Director

Budget: $1,000,000

Number of staff: 50

Publications: The OSCE and Co-operative Security in Europe: Lessons for Asia, 2003; *The South China Sea Dispute in Philippine Foreign Policy,* 2003; *The War on Terror and the Future of Indonesian Democracy,* 2003; and several other reports and books

Southeast Asia

Institute of Policy Studies

RESEARCH

The Institute of Policy Studies is engaged in policy-oriented research on topics including management of ethnic relations, United Nations peacekeeping and conflict resolution, and ASEAN-EU relations. The institute's objective is to promote interest in these and other issues relevant to Singapore, and to act as a bridge between the government, business, scholars, journalists, and others in Singapore. To this end the institute also organizes conferences, lectures, and briefings.

29 Heng Mui Keng Terrace
Singapore 119620
Kent Ridge PO Box 1088
911103 Singapore

Tel: +65 (6) 215 1010
Fax: +65 (6) 777 0700
ips@ips.org.sg
www.ips.org.sg

Contact: Professor Tommy Koh, Director

Number of staff: 10

Publications: The Study of Ethnicity, National Identity and Sense of Rootedness in Singapore, 2002; Remaking Singapore: Recommendations from IPS, 2002; The Reform Process of United Nations Peace Operations, 2001

Asia-Pacific

Institute of Southeast Asian Studies

RESEARCH

The Institute of Southeast Asian Studies (ISEAS) is a regional center dedicated to the study of sociopolitical, security, and economic trends and developments in Southeast Asia and its wider geostrategic and economic environment. The institute's aim is to develop a community of scholars interested in the region and to engage in related research and to participate in the exchange of ideas. The intention is to enhance public awareness and to facilitate the search for viable solutions to the problems confronting the region.

ISEAS offers three programs: Regional Economic Studies; Regional Strategic and Political Studies; Regional Social and Cultural Studies. The Regional Strategic and Political Studies (RSPS) program seeks to address the strategic issues affecting the Southeast Asian and Asia-Pacific region and to understand the dynamics of political change with the regional states.

30 Heng Mui Keng Terrace
Pasir Panjang
Singapore 119614

Tel: +65 (67) 780 955
Fax: +65 (67) 781 735
admin@iseas.edu.sg
www.iseas.edu.sg

Contact: Mr. Kesavpany, Director

Publications: INAUGURAL, ISEAS Newsletter; *Regional Outlook: Southeast Asia 2004–2005, 2003; Islam and the State in Indonesia, 2003; Security and Southeast Asia: Domestic, Regional and Global Issues, 2003*

Global

Singapore Institute
of International Affairs

RESEARCH
EDUCATION

The Singapore Institute of International Affairs (SIIA) is Singapore's oldest think-tank, founded in 1961. As a representative of the ASEAN-ISIS dialogue process, the SIIA organizes a number of regional dialogues and conferences, such as the Asia-Pacific Roundtable and the ASEAN-ISIS Human Rights Colloquium. The SIIA researches issues such as East Asian regionalism, Asia-EU relations, environment, and human rights, and civil society. The institute organizes public lectures and seminars, and has established exchange and training programs with developing Asian countries, focusing on ASEAN policy and research, governance, and trade and investment regimes.

6 Nassim Road
258373 Singapore

Tel: +65 (67) 349 600
Fax: +65 (67) 336 217
siia@pacific.net.sg
www.siiaonline.org

Contact: Simon SC Tay, Chairman

Budget: $100,000–$150,000

Number of staff: 8

Publications: China, ASEAN and East Asia: Partnership with a Rising Power, 2002; *Comparing Apples with Mangoes and Durian: Human Rights Systems in Europe and Southeast Asia,* 2002; *Preventive Diplomacy in the ASEAN Region—Possibilities for Good Offices and Special Envoys,* 2000

Solomon Islands, the Pacific

Development Services Exchange

RESEARCH
EDUCATION

Development Services Exchange (DSE) is a non-profit NGO and was founded in 1988 as the umbrella body of the NGO community in the Solomon Islands. It strives to strengthen the NGO Community and encourages people-oriented sustainable development within Solomon Islands.

PO Box 556
Honiara
Solomon Islands

Tel: +677 (2) 3670
Fax: +677 (2) 7414
dse@solomon.com.sb

Contact: Edgar S Pakoa, General Secretary
Budget: < $25,000
Number of staff: 2

Solomon Islands, the Pacific

Lauru Land Conference of Tribal Community

EDUCATION

The Lauru Land Conference of Tribal Community (LLCTC) was founded in 1981. LLCTC is an ecumenical NGO seeking to empower grass-roots communities to continue to live peacefully and harmoniously with one another in their traditional environment. LLCTC works with cultural, judicial and Christian norms and values, to promote conflict resolution, and to ensure people are working together ecumenically. In 2002, the Lauru Christian Association (LCA) was formed to carry out conflict prevention and reconciliation programs. The Social Integration Program is one of the conflict prevention/ reconciliation programs addressing land reform issues, integration of various groups, inter-racial education, and human resources development.

PO Box 131
Munda Post Office
Western Province
Solomon Islands

Tel: +677 61071
Fax: +677 61150
llctc@solomon.com.sb

Contact: Esau Tza, Director
Budget: $25,000–$100,000
Number of staff: 15

Solomon Islands

Melanesian Brotherhood

ACTION

The Melanesian Brotherhood was founded by Ini Kopuira, a Solomon Islander on the Island of Guadalcanal in 1925. These days more than 400 brothers are working in the Solomon Islands, Papua New Guinea, Vanuatu, the Philippines, and the U.K. The ethos of the community is to live a religious life but in a Melanesian, indigenous way. Their way of life reflects many of the strengths of Melanesian tradition and they respect traditions and customs of working together and sharing all they believe God provides. In 1999 the Melanesian Brotherhood decided that they had to become more directly involved in trying to de-escalate the ethnic conflict in the Solomon Islands in order to prevent further hostilities. In May 2000 the group chose and commissioned a team of brothers to directly work for peace and they became the go-betweens, with the aim to stop the killing and hatred. They are considered impartial and trustworthy and are seen as representing a restored community.

The Motherhouse of the
  Melanesian Brotherhood
Tabalia
PO Box 1479
Honiara
Solomon Islands

Tel: +677 (2) 6355
Fax: +677 (2) 3079
brotherhood@deedes.demon.co.uk
www.orders.anglican.org/mbh/

Contact: Brother Henry Gerenui

Solomon Islands

OHCHR Field Office in Solomon Islands

EDUCATION
ADVOCACY

The Office of the High Commissioner for Human Rights maintains a field office in Honiara to implement activities designed to promote and protect human rights. While the OHCHR does not have an investigative role, the field office works with and supports the initiatives of NGOs and civil society organizations. Currently it targets problem areas to provide information on human rights issues and support animators and facilitators who continue the work in rural communities.

Other activities are assisting in the truth and reconciliation process, helping to plan the setting up of a National Human Rights Commission, training prison personnel and police in human rights awareness, and assisting the government to work toward legislative changes that will enforce human rights treaties and conventions.

OHCHR Field Office
PO Box 1375
Honiara
Solomon Islands

Tel: +677 (2) 8749
Fax: +677 (2) 8751
humanrights@solomon.com.sb

Contact: Human Rights Advisor
Budget: $100,000–$500,000
Number of staff: 4

Solomon Islands

Solomon Islands Civil Society Network

EDUCATION

Solomon Islands Civil Society Network (CSN) was set up to create a support-network of civil society organizations, to establish new partnerships, to develop and raise awareness on civil society issues, and to be able to reach out to all communities in the country. The CSN aims to develop an action program for civil society organizations on areas such as good governance; human rights; environmental issues; peace and justice issues; and social security. This will result in establishing a formally constituted Solomon Islands civil society network organization, with the CSN becoming the formal secretariat. To this end a small office has been opened in Honiara, which supervises the administration.

PO Box 1004
Honiara
Solomon Islands

Tel: +667 (2) 1058
Fax: +667 (2) 1058
civils@solomon.com.sb

Contact: Philip Jionisi
Budget: < $25,000
Number of staff: 1

Solomon Islands

Women for Peace

EDUCATION
ACTION
ADVOCACY

Formed in 2000 the Women for Peace (WFP) group is independent of any political, religious, or ethnic movement and utilizes non-violent and peaceful methods. It engages with the Malaita Eagle Force (MEF), Istanbu Freedom Movement (IFM), churches, NGOs, chiefs, community leaders, government, and the international community. Their objective is to actively and effectively support and encourage women's initiatives for peace. The group consists of women of all ages, religions, walks of life, and provinces who reside in Honiara and includes the sisters of the Catholic Church and Church of Melanesia. Since forming, the WFP group has encouraged various sectors within the government and the communities to work together and settle differences at the negotiation table. The WFP focuses on building trust and confidence with the two militant groups and encourages them to lay down their arms. In addition, the group has briefed a number of government officials on the group's objectives and planned activities and made suggestions on matters of concern.

c/o R. Liloqula   *Contact:* Ruth Liloqula
PO Box 1807
Honiara
Solomon Islands

Tel/Fax: +677 (3) 8757
temale@welkam.solomon.com.sb

Global

Department of Peace and Conflict Research – Uppsala University

RESEARCH
EDUCATION
ADVOCACY

The Department of Peace and Conflict Research at Uppsala University was established in 1971 to conduct research and offer courses in peace and conflict studies. Besides its educational activities, the department runs interdisciplinary projects dealing with the origins and dynamics of conflicts, conflict resolution, and international security issues in a number of regions including West, Central and Southeast Asia. The department also runs a Conflict Data Project, which continuously collects data on armed conflicts and has published statistics on major armed conflicts in the SIPRI Yearbook since 1988. The Department publishes annual reports of all armed conflicts.

Uppsala University
Box 514
751 20 Uppsala
Sweden

Tel: +46 (18) 471 000
Fax: +46 (18) 695 102
info@pcr.uu.se
www.pcr.uu.se

Contact: Amer Ramses, Associate Professor for the Southeast Asia program

Number of staff: 33

Budget: > $1,000,000

Publications: States in Armed Conflict, 2001; *A Century of Economic Sanctions: A Field Revisited,* 2000; *Gendering UN Peacekeeping: Mainstreaming a Gender Perspective in Multidimensional Peacekeeping Operations,* 1999

Global

International Institute for Democracy and Electoral Assistance

Created in 1995, the International Institute for Democracy and Electoral Assistance (IDEA) is an inter-governmental organization that promotes and advances sustainable democracy and improves and consolidates electoral processes world-wide. Where other organizations stop after the first democratic election has been held, IDEA aims to help the country after the election to build a true, long-term, democratic state.

In the region the institute is helping the democratic process in Indonesia, South Asia, and Burma/Myanmar. The formulation and promotion of acceptable standards and guidelines on electoral and democratic principles is an important activity of the institute. It has produced "codes of conduct" for election managers and observers, and a similar code for political parties for campaigning during elections is on the way. IDEA has a special Conflict Management Program Team. It has published a handbook for would-be democracy builders in countries emerging from deep-rooted conflict and outlines options that negotiators can draw upon when trying to build democracy.

Stromsborg
103 34 Stockholm
Sweden

Tel: +46 (8) 698 3700
Fax: +46 (8) 202 422
info@idea.int
www.idea.int

Publications: Country-specific reports; *Democratization in Indonesia: An Assessment,* 2000; *Consolidation Democracy in Nepal,* 1997; Forum and Conference Reports; International IDEA Information.

Asia, Africa, the Caribbean and Latin America

Swedish NGO Foundation for Human Rights

The Swedish NGO foundation for Human Rights is a non-profit foundation, which was set up in 1991. A board of directors governs the foundation. The foundation's activities are based on supplementing its partner organizations in the field of human rights and democracy. The foundation emphasizes that economic, civil, cultural, political, and social rights are universal, indivisible, independent, and interrelated, while aspiring to gender balance.

The foundation assists the struggle for human rights in Burma. Financial support is given to a documentation center in Thailand run by Burmese refugees and to an organization educating activists in human rights.

Drottninggaten 101
S-113 60 Stockholm
Sweden

Tel: +46 (8) 5454 9970
Fax: +46 (8) 3030 31
info@humanrights.se
www.humanrights.se

Contact: Anita Klum, Secretary-General
Number of staff: 11
Publications: Human Rights, newsletter

Global
Center for Humanitarian Dialogue

The Center for Humanitarian Dialogue (CHD), formally known as the Henry Dunant Centre for Humanitarian Dialogue, is an international organization working for the promotion of humanitarian dialogue. It facilitates dialogue among the principal humanitarian actors, stakeholders, and aid recipients to enhance understanding of acute and future humanitarian problems. Central to its mission are four guiding principles: partnership, transformation, common understanding, and dialogue.

CHD believes that more attention has to be paid to the prevention of conflicts. To this end, its prime activity is to foster dialogue between parties in order to help reconcile their differences.

Through dialogue in conflict, the center's projects aim to bring parties together to reach agreements that contribute to the resolution of conflict, e.g. in Aceh, Indonesia, and Burma. Its outreach work with humanitarian organizations and diplomats have improved awareness of the center's approach and reputation. The result has been in suggestions for new projects and the center now regularly briefs diplomats in Geneva about its work.

114, Rue de Lausanne
CH-1202 Geneva
Switzerland

Tel: +41 (22) 908 1130
Fax: +41 (22) 908 1140
info@hdcentre.org
www.hdcentre.org

Contact: Martin Griffiths, Director

Number of staff: 5

Publications: Politics and Humanitarianism Coherence in Crisis? 2003; *The Role of Non-state Actors in Building Human Security, the Case of Armed Groups in Intra-state Wars,* 2000

Global

International Catholic Migration Commission

EDUCATION
ACTION
ADVOCACY

The International Catholic Migration Commission (ICMC) works with refugees, internally displaced people, forced migrants, and trafficked persons. ICMC responds to immediate needs whilst also working for durable solutions. ICMC programs focus on counter-trafficking, survivors of torture, trauma recovery and education, tolerance building, micro-grants, community services, small business development, return/reintegration assistance, refugee identification and processing, cultural orientation training, and the provision of protection for refugees, returnees, and the internally displaced.

In Indonesia there are a number of established programs. Since 2000, ICMC has supported organizations working on human rights in conflict areas, sustainable community recovery in Maluku, combating the trafficking of women and children, support and protection for female-headed households in Aceh, and addressing the needs of IDPs in North Sumatra. In addition, there is a program focusing on training local NGOs on torture awareness and the necessary counseling skills, while developing a survivor of torture network.

37-39 rue de Vermont
Case Postale 96,
1211 Geneva 20,
Switzerland

Tel: + 41 (22) 919 10 20
Fax: + 41 (22) 919 10 48
canny@icmc.net,
secretariat.ch@icmc.net
www.icmc.net

Jalan Terusan Hang Lekir I/5
Kebayoran Lama
Jakarta 12220
Indonesia

davy@icmc.net

Contact: William Canny, Secretary General, or Charles Davy, Regional Director—Indonesia and East Timor

Number of staff: 75

Budget: $2,500,000

Publications: ICMC Report on the World Conference Against Racism, Racial Discrimination, Xenophobia and Related Intolerance, 2001; *Trafficking of Women and Children in Indonesia,* 2003

Global

International Committee of the Red Cross

RESEARCH
EDUCATION
ACTION
ADVOCACY

The International Committee of the Red Cross (ICRC) is an impartial, neutral, and independent organization whose exclusively humanitarian mission is to protect the lives and dignity of victims of war and internal violence and to provide them with assistance. Considering its direct humanitarian involvement in conflict situations, the ICRC has indeed a great interest in all efforts that may be deployed to prevent conflict, promote a culture of peace, and prevent human suffering. Although its direct role in conflict prevention as such can only be limited, due to its primary concern to be present beside the victims and accepted by all the parties engaged in the conflict, the ICRC remains available to offer its services to the parties to facilitate possible meetings between them for example.

19 Avenue de la Paix
1202 Geneva
Switzerland

Tel: +41 (22) 734 6001
Fax: +41 (22) 733 2057
webmaster.gva@icrc.org
www.icrc.org

Contact: Paul Grossrieder, Director General
Number of staff: 825 (HQ), 9,000 (field, for all activities)
Budget: > $1,000,000 (for all activities)
Publications: The International Review of the Red Cross, quarterly magazine; *Strengthening Protection in War: A Search for Professional Standards*, 2001; *The ICRC and Civil-Military Relations in Armed Conflict*, 2001

Global

International Federation of Red Cross and Red Crescent Societies

EDUCATION
ACTION

Founded in 1919 in the aftermath of World War I with five founding member Societies, the International Federation of Red Cross and Red Crescent Societies is now the world's largest humanitarian organization. The mission is to improve the lives of vulnerable people by mobilizing the power of humanity. Conflict prevention is a priority implicit in the activities of the International Federation of Red Cross and Red Crescent Societies rather than a program area. Based on the Seven Fundamental Principles of the Red Cross and Red Crescent Movement and on explicit policy decisions by the governing bodies, the organization pursues the goal of preventing conflicts through the dissemination of knowledge, development of attitudes, providing forums for contacts, endeavoring to foster development, and providing assistance to direct and indirect victims of conflict. With 169 National Societies, the federation is well placed to fulfill this mission.

PO Box 372
CH-1211 Geneva 19
Switzerland

Tel: +41 (22) 730 4222
Tel: +41 (22) 733 0395
secretariat@ifrc.org
www.ifrc.org

Contact: Markku Niskala, Acting Secretary-General
Publications: Red Cross, Red Crescent, quarterly magazine; *Beyond Conflict: the International Federation of Red Cross and Red Crescent Societies, 1919–1994,* 1997

Global

International Organization for Migration

RESEARCH
EDUCATION
ACTION
ADVOCACY

Established in 1951, the intergovernmental International Organization for Migration (IOM) is the leading international organization for migration and is committed to the principle that humane and orderly migration benefits migrants and society. The department of the IOM responsible for conflict prevention is called the Emergency and Post-conflict Division. It has special expertise in the stabilization and development of communities and communal governance following the return of displaces persons in East Timor, but similar projects are also being executed elsewhere. In emergency and post-crisis situations IOM plays an active role in Afghanistan, East Timor, and Kosovo.

17 route des Morillons
PO Box 71
1218 Geneva 19
Switzerland

Tel: +41 (22) 717 9111
Fax: +41 (22) 798 6150
info@iom.int
www.iom.int

Contact: Hans Petter, Chief of Emergency and Post-conflict Division

Number of staff: 250

Budget: > $1,000,000

Publications: IOM News, quarterly newsletter; *Migration and Development: A Perspective from Asia,* 2003; *Labour Migration in Asia: Trends, Challenges and Policy Responses in Countries of Origin,* 2003

ACTION

International Peace Bureau

Founded in 1982, the International Peace Bureau (IPB) claims to be the world's largest comprehensive international peace federation. It is not strictly an organization for pacifists but also includes women's, youth, workers, religious, political, and professional bodies. The IPB's role is to support peace and disarmament initiatives with the main programs focusing on disarmament and human security. Other areas of focus include nuclear weapons abolition, conflict prevention and resolution, human rights, international humanitarian law, women, and peace and peace education.

With 235 member organizations, the IPB also acts as publishing house and conference organizer, and gives logistic assistance to visiting NGOs in Geneva. The IPB's resource center acts as a directory and an educational resource with historical accounts and links to related resources.

International Peace Bureau
41 Rue de Zurich
CH-1201 Geneva
Switzerland

Tel: +41 (22) 734 6429
Fax: +41 (22) 738 9419
mailbox@ipb.org
www.ipb.org

Contact: Colin Archer, Secretary-General

Global

Office for the Coordination of Humanitarian Affairs

EDUCATION
ACTION
ADVOCACY

The UN Office for the Coordination of Humanitarian Affairs (OCHA) is mandated to coordinate UN assistance. It is committed to conflict prevention through advocacy efforts and humanitarian policy development. OCHA discharges its coordination function primarily through the IASC, with the participation of humanitarian partners such as the Red Cross Movement and NGOs. At present, OCHA maintains 32 field offices in Africa, Asia and Europe including the Integrated Regional Information Network (IRIN). Instrumental in implementing its conflict-prevention goal is its leading role in the UN Framework for Coordination Team, an inter-agency body that identifies countries at risk and promotes appropriate preventive and preparedness measures.

Office for the Coordination
of Humanitarian Affairs
United Nations
Palais des Nations
1211 Geneva 10
Switzerland

Tel: +41 (22) 917 1234
Fax: +41 (22) 917 0023
ochagva@un.org
www.reliefweb.int/ocha_ol/

Contact: Ramesh Rahjasingham, Humanitarian
Affairs Officer

Publications: OCHA News; Memorandum of
Understanding between the United Nations
and the Government of Hellenic Republic
and the Government of Turkey on Cooperation
in the Field of Humanitarian Emergency
Response, 2002; OCHA and the East Timor
Crisis, 1999

Global

RESEARCH

Small Arms Survey

Established in 1999 the Small Arms Survey is an independent research project located at the Graduate Institute of International Studies, Geneva. It is an international source of public information on all aspects of small arms and a resource center for governments, policymakers, researchers, and activists. International staff works closely with a worldwide network of researchers and partners.

Ground Floor
Avenue Blanc 47
1202 Geneva
Switzerland

Tel: +41 (22) 909 5777
Fax: +41 (22) 909 2738
smallarms@hei.unige.ch
www.smallarmssurvey.org

Contact: The Information Department

Publications: Small Arms Survey Yearbook
2001–3; Small Arms in the Pacific, 2003; Legal
Controls on Small Arms from Society: A Review
of Weapons Collection and Destruction
Programs, 2001; Humanitarianism Under
Threat: The Humanitarian Impact of Small
Arms and Light Weapons, 2001

Global

Swiss Platform for Conflict Prevention and Transformation

RESEARCH
EDUCATION

The Swiss Platform for Conflict Prevention and Transformation is an open and informal network of more than 20 organizations that are based in Switzerland and involved in conflict prevention and resolution in the international arena. The Swiss Platform was launched in 1997 by the Center for Applied Studies in International Negotiations (CASIN) and is affiliated with the European Platform for Conflict Prevention and Transformation. The primary objective of the Swiss Platform is to facilitate the exchange of information and experiences among interested organizations, and to stimulate cooperation and synergy among them.

c/o CASIN
7 bis Avenue de la Paix
PO Box 1340
1211 Geneva 1
Switzerland

Tel: +41 (22) 730 8660
Fax: +41 (22) 730 8690
jff@casin.ch
www.casin.ch

Contact: Jean F. Freymond, Director

Budget: $100,000–$500,000

Publications: Collapse in Cancun: NGO and Civil Society Perspectives on the 5th WTO Ministerial, 2003; *The Anti-War Movement Waging Peace on the Brink of War,* 2003; *Administration and Governance in Kosovo: Lessons Learned and Lessons to Be Learned,* 2003

Global

RESEARCH
ADVOCACY

World Council of Churches

The World Council of Churches (WCC) brings together more than 340 churches, denominations, and church fellowships in over 100 countries and territories throughout the world, representing some 400 million Christians.

The purpose of the International Affairs, Peace and Human Security team is to help "formulate the Christian mind" and "bring that mind effectively to bear" upon these issues. It does this by informing and addressing public issues that have a claim on the Christian conscience. Furthermore it monitors, analyzes, and provides information on international political trends—for example on critical situations like East Timor and Sri Lanka. It provides a platform for information-sharing and joint advocacy on critical situations of human rights violations and conflicts, and on opportunities to support peacemaking initiatives.

The WCC Peacebuilding and Disarmament Program seeks to assist individuals, families, churches, societies and the international community to manage and resolve conflicts, and become more skilled in transforming them through non-violent action. It promotes creative approaches to conflict management, and transformation through developing and/or highlighting innovative community approaches to overcome violence.

Special emphasis is placed on situation of armed conflicts and violence, as well as advocacy for the effective control and reduction of conventional weapons, the elimination of nuclear weapons, and non-military approaches to peace and security.

150 route de Ferney
PO Box 2100
1211 Geneva 2, Switzerland

Tel: +41 (22) 791 6111
Fax: +41 (22) 791 0361
infowcc@wcc-coe.org
www.wcc-coe.org/wcc/

Contact: Mr. Peter Weiderud, Program Executive/Team Coordinator—International Affairs, Peace and Human Security

Budget: > $1,000,000

Global

Chung-Hua Institution for Economic Research

RESEARCH

The Chung-Hua Institution for Economic Research (CIER) was formally established in 1981 as a non-profit and autonomous research organization. The institution undertakes advanced research both on the national and international economics, and on selected areas of concern. It also stimulates academic exchange and facilitates closer contact between scholars, both at home and abroad, by conducting symposiums, seminars, and other activities of scientific interest. The CIER plays an important role in strengthening economic ties between the Republic of China and the rest of the world, through the sponsorship of international conferences, and by forging links with individual scholars and research organizations in other countries

75 Chang-Hsing St.
Taipei City
Taiwan, 106
R.O.C.

Tel: +886 (2) 2735 6006
Fax: +886 (2) 2735 6035
info@mail.cier.edu.tw
www.cier.edu.tw

Asia-Pacific, Taiwan Strait, Americas and Europe

Foundation on International and Cross-strait Studies

RESEARCH
ADVOCACY

Founded in 1994, the Foundation on International and Cross-strait Studies (formerly Chinese Eurasian Foundation) is a private, non-profit, non-partisan research institution dedicated to public policy analysis and impact. Initiated by a group of former government officials, business executives, and senior scholars, the Foundation is committed to be a leading think-tank in Taiwan. It convenes meetings involving government officials and experts from academia and political parties to discuss major policy issues.

The foundation's primary missions are: to raise public awareness of national security interests, to provide policy options for government and private sectors, to enhance studies in the areas of Europe, Americas, and Asia-Pacific, to promote understandings across the Taiwan Strait, and to sponsor international exchanges and collaborations.

It conducts studies with strategic implications to international and regional security. Issues such as U.S. security policy in Asia, PRC military modernization, Sino-Russian strategic partnership, and Beijing's policy toward Taiwan are key research projects of the foundation.

88 Chung-Hsiao East Rd.
Section 2, Suite 1402
Taipei
Taiwan, 10046
R.O.C.

Tel: +886 (2) 2396 8760
Fax: +886 (2) 2391 7350
webmaster@fics.org.tw
www.fics.org.tw

Taiwan Strait

Friends of Hong Kong and Macau Association

RESEARCH

Founded in 1992, the association is a non-profit organization that aims to improve friendships with Hong Kong and Macau citizens and to help maintaining freedom, democracy, and prosperity of these areas. The missions of this organization include; improving the cultural, economic and trade exchange between Taiwan, Hong Kong, and Macau; to strengthen research and reports on issues about Hong Kong and Macau; and to analyze and evaluate the changing situation in the Taiwan Strait; and to provide these analyses as reference recourse for government's policymaking.

9F., No. 5-3, Sec. 1
Sinyi Rd., Jhongjheng District
Taipei City 100
Taiwan
R.O.C.

Tel: +886 (2) 2395 6541/7184
Fax: +886 (2) 2395 6474

Taiwan Strait

Future China Research, Cross-Strait Interflow Prospect Foundation

RESEARCH

Founded in 1997, the foundation is a nonprofit and autonomous research organization dedicated to the cross-strait relation and international issues. Its research focuses on the key areas including the cross-strait relation promoting, diplomatic policy, international security, international relations, international strategy, and international economy. The foundation strives to promote academic exchange and cooperation by strengthening contacts with Mainland China and with international academic organizations, and secondly by exchange visits with think-tanks from Mainland China and all over the world.

No. 1, Lane 60, Sec. 3
Tingjhou Rd.
Taipei City
Taiwan, 106
R.O.C.

Tel: +886 (2) 2365 4366
Fax: +886 (2) 2367 6511/2367 9193
info@future-china.org.tw
www.future-china.org

Global

Institute of International Relations – National Chengchi University

RESEARCH

The Institute of International Relations (IIR) is Taiwan's largest research institution dedicated to the understanding of the cross-strait affairs and international issues. The institute is divided into four main divisions. The first division conducts research on the international political and economic relations of America, Europe, and Africa. The second division covers similar topics in Asia, Oceania, and the Pacific Rim. The third and fourth divisions focus on mainland China affairs: the former researches such areas as ideology, politics, law, foreign relations, and military affairs in the PRC, while the latter analyzes China's social, economic, cultural, and minority affairs. IIR has an impressive array of resources and has produced over 150 books, monographs, and other volumes. IIR also produces a wide range of journals.

National Chengchi University
No. 64 Wan Shou Road
Taipei
Taiwan
R.O.C.

Publications: Issues and Studies, quarterly journal

Tel: +886 (2) 8237 7277
Fax: +886 (2) 2937 8609
iir@nccu.edu.tw
http://iir.nccu.edu.tw

Taiwan Strait

Mainland Affairs Council

RESEARCH
ACTION
ADVOCACY

In an attempt to strengthen mainland policymaking, the government established the Mainland Affairs Council (MAC) in 1991 whose main function is—as the central competent authority at cabinet level—to coordinate policy matters concerning Mainland China. MAC's aim is to promote peace between Taiwan and the mainland by following the principles of reconciliation and cooperation with a long-term view of positive cross-strait relations.

Many public opinion surveys are carried out in order to determine cross-strait relations, the results of which are freely available online. Research projects are undertaken by the Information and Research Center, an off-shot established in 1994, which compiles developments related to Mainland China. The MAC works closely with academics and non-government agencies to establish solid cross-strait relations. Every three months the "Report and Evaluation of Developments in mainland China" is published and distributed to agencies and individuals, covering various areas as foreign affairs and policies towards Hong Kong, Macau, and Taiwan.

15 Floor, No 2-2, Sec. 1
Jinan Road
Taipei
Taiwan
R.O.C.

Tel: +886 (2) 2397 5589
macst@mac.gov.tw
www.mac.gov.tw

Taiwan

National Policy Foundation

This foundation was reorganized in 2000 to form a non-profit institution whose purpose is to improve public policy and decisionmaking through extensive research. Its main expertise is research into national policy within areas like Foreign and Security Policy; Constitution and Law; Economy and Technology; Monetary and Public Finance Policies, and Social Security. The NPF holds regular conferences on these topics in an attempt to bridge the gap between the government and opposing groups, while actively promoting cross-strait relations through international exchanges.

National Policy Foundation
16 Hang Chow South Road
Sec 1
Taipei 100
Taiwan
R.O.C.

Tel: +88 (6) 22 343 3399
Fax: +88 (6) 22 343 3357
npf@npf.org.tw
www.npf.org.tw

Contact: Mr. Hsung Hsiung Tsai, President
Number of staff: 483
Publications: U.S. Arms Sales and Cross-Strait Conflict, 2003; *Status Quo and Prospect of Cross-Strait Relations,* 2000

Taiwan Strait

Strait Cultural and Economic Association

The association is a non-government organization serving to increase the cultural, academic, and trade exchanges in Taiwan Strait. It aims to improve the reciprocal exchange and to promote peace in Taiwan Strait. The association facilitates exchange visits of scholars, experts, and students from Taiwan and Mainland China; promotes cultural exchanges; and promotes exchange visits of trade groups from Taiwan and Mainland China.

3F., No. 226, Jhongyang Rd.
Sindian City
Taipei County 231
Taiwan
R.O.C.

Tel: +886 (2) 2218 7588
Fax: +886 (2) 2218 9341
Wjh.tang@msa.hinet.net
http://203.75.105.158

Taiwan Strait

Strait Peaceful
Re-Unification Association

EDUCATION
ADVOCACY

The Strait Peaceful Re-Unification Association is a non-governmental organization dedicated to promote cross-strait reciprocal exchange and peaceful co-existence. It aims at the peaceful re-unification in Taiwan Strait. It organizes cross-strait activities to improve mutual understanding like symposium to discuss political, diplomatic, trade, economical, and cultural issues. These discussions aim to improve the opposing relationship, to generate opinions from civil groups as reference resources for government's policymaking; and to visit Mainland China to express Taiwan's opinion toward Mainland China's Taiwan policy.

Room 2405, 24F
No. 333, Sec. 1
Jilong Rd., Sinyi District
Taipei City 110
Taiwan
R.O.C.

Tel: +886 (2) 8789 0538
Fax: +886 (2) 2757 7271
spra@tpts8.seed.net.tw
www.spra.org.tw

Taiwan Strait

Taiwan Businessmen in China

RESEARCH
ADVOCACY

Founded in 2001, the institute is a non-government organization dedicated to facilitate affairs related to the cross-strait business exchange and to develop Taiwan business in China. The institute's concrete activities include lobbying for the establishment of a "trade fund" for Taiwan businessmen in China, the promotion of a clear position for Taiwan businessmen in China through public opinion and discussion, and to lobby the government for subsidy, guidance and assistance to Taiwan businessmen in China.

11F.-2, No. 10
Lin-sen South Rd.
Jhong-jheng District
Taipei City
Taiwan
R.O.C.

Tel: +886 (2) 2358 2353
Fax: +886 (2) 2358 2301

Taiwan Strait, Japan, PRC, US and Asia-Pacific

Taiwan Strait, Japan, PRC, US and Asia-Pacific

Taiwan Security Research

Taiwan Security Research (TSR) is an academic and non-governmental website designed to disseminate current event information on Taiwan's security and regional security issues. TSR now acts as a timely and objective information service to the academic community as regards peace and security issues across the Taiwan Straits and the Asia-Pacific region. This website encompasses many news articles relating to regional topics, dating from 1998.

Taiwan Security Research
21, Hsu Chow Rd
Taipei
Taiwan 100
R.O.C.

Tel: +886 (2) 2351 9641
Fax: +886 (2) 2357 0487
pyang@ccms.ntu.edu.tw
www.taiwansecurity.org

Contact: Dr. Philip Yang, Director

Budget: $100,000–$500,000

Number of staff: 2

Publications: Rein in at the Brink of Precipice: American Policy Toward Taiwan and U.S.-PRC Relations, 2003; PRC Security Relations with the United States: Why Things Are Going So Well, 2003; Taiwan Strait I: What's Left of "One China"? 2003; Taiwan Strait III: The Chance of Peace, 2003; Taiwan's Threat Perceptions: The Enemy Within, 2003

Taiwan Strait

Taiwan Strait Exchange Foundation

Founded in 1991, the Straits Exchange Foundation (SEF) is the only private organization empowered by the government to handle relations with the Chinese mainland. The SEF deals with technical and business matters that involve the ROC government's public authority but would be inappropriate for the ROC government to handle directly under its current policy of no official contacts with mainland authorities. The foundation's primary aims to promote the interflow between Taiwan and the Mainland China; to help people in Taiwan resolve problems caused by the cross-strait interflow; and to negotiate with the Association for Relations Across the Taiwan Straits in the position of a non-government organization.

The foundation's concrete activities are organizing the cross-strait activities to increase contact, formulating policies and regulations about how to achieve that, producing relevant laws and regulations to facilitate cross-strait exchange, collecting advices from civil groups as reference recourse for government's policymaking; and negotiating with the Association for Relations Across the Taiwan Straits.

17 F., No. 156, Sec. 3
Min-Sheng E. Rd.
Taipei City
Taiwan, 106
R.O.C.

Tel: +886 (2) 2718 7373
Fax: +886 (2) 2514 9962
service@sefweb.sef.org.tw
www.sef.org.tw

Burma

All Burma Students' Democratic Front

The All Burma Students' Democratic Front (ABSDF) is the largest multi-ethnic student and youth organization on Burma's borders. It was founded in 1988 and is fighting for democracy and human rights in Burma alongside other democratic forces. The aims of the ABSDF are to liberate the peoples of Burma from the oppression of military dictatorship, to achieve democracy and human rights, to attain internal peace, and to bring about the emergence of a federal union in Burma. To achieve these, the ABSDF is organizing people throughout Burma to be politically motivated forces by implementing networks, solidifying the opposition's unity and activities, and mobilizing the international community to exert effective pressure on the military regime.

PO Box 31
Mae Sariang
Mae Hong Son 58110
Thailand

Tel/Fax: +66 (53) 621 186
absdfhq@cscoms.com
www.geocities.com/absdf_au

Contact: Kyaw Thura, Secretary of Foreign Affairs

Publications: The Notifications of CRPP, 2000; *Significant Events in Burma's Politics,* 2003; *Letters to a Dictator—Part II,* 1999; *Burma and the Role of Women: Chronological Events,* monthly publication; *Military Echelon, Cries From Insein,* yearly publication; *Dawn Oway,* quarterly publication.

Southeast Asia, Burma

Alternative ASEAN Network on Burma

The Alternative ASEAN Network on Burma (ALTSEAN-BURMA) is a network of activists, NGOs, academics, and politicians who support human rights, democracy, and peace in Burma. All the members are from Southeast Asia. They maintain a contact list of people from outside the region who have an interest on the relationship between the ASEAN and Burma's military junta, the State Law and Order Restoration Council (SLORC).

ALTSEAN-Burma initiates and implements a range of activities to support human rights, democracy, and peace in Burma, and ultimately, in the rest of Southeast Asia. Its activities are mainly oriented to campaign work, advocacy, networking, and resource production. ALTSEAN-Burma is not a funding agency.

PO Box 296
Ladprao Post Office
Bangkok 10310
Thailand

Tel: +66 (2) 850 9008
Fax: +66 (2) 693 4939
altsean@altsean.org
www.altsean.org

Asia

Asian Cultural Forum
on Development

RESEARCH
EDUCATION
ACTION
ADVOCACY

Established in 1975, the Asian Cultural Forum on Development (ACFOD) has members in some 30 countries in the Asia Pacific region. The forum advocates for development and aims to promote peace, harmony, and human rights. ACFOD names human resource development as its main concern and also mobilizes action campaigns on issues of concern. The forum has initiated talks with the LTTE guerillas in Sri Lanka and the separatist movements in Nepal, as well as in Bangladesh and Burma. In the future ACFOD plans to be involved in training on conflict resolution, non-violence, and mediation.

494 Lardprao 101 Road, Soi 11
Klong Chan, Bangkapi
PO Box 26
Bungthonglang
Bangkok 10240
Thailand

Tel: +66 (2) 377 9357/370 2701
Fax: +66 (2) 374 0464
acfodbkk@ksc15.th.com
http://ksc11.th.com/acfodbkk/

Contact: Professor Banton Ondam, Coordinator
Number of staff: 5
Budget: $25,000–$100,000

Asia

Asian Resource Foundation

EDUCATION
ADVOCACY

The Asian Resource Foundation (ARF) was established in 1996. The organization aims to develop awareness about the root causes of conflict, facilitate dialogue, and train young people about tolerance and peace. Together with local and national partners, the ARF is also involved in lobbying and the development of networks among peace activists and organizations. In 2002, the ARF co-organized the Interfaith Peace Forum in Bangkok, which addressed the impact of the war on terrorism.

1562/113 Soi 1/1
Mooban Pibul
Pracharaj Road, Bang Sue
Bangkok 10800
Thailand

Tel: +66 (2) 913 0196
Fax: +66 (2) 913 0197
arf@arf-asia.org
www.arf-asia.org

Contact: M. Abdus Sabur, Secretary General
Budget: $50,000–$100,000
Number of staff: 3
Publications: Crisis of Violence in Asia, Interfaith Peace Forum Report, 2002; *International Workshop on Multi-Ethnic Asia, Report,* 2002

Asia-Pacific

Asia Pacific Forum on Women, Law and Development

EDUCATION
ADVOCACY

The Asia Pacific Forum on Women, Law and Development (APWLD) was established as a network in 1986 after a series of dialogues between Asia Pacific women lawyers, social scientists, and activists. The main objective of the network is to enable women in the region to use law as an instrument of social change for equality, justice, and development. The APWLD engages in advocacy, education, training, and other activities to address issues affecting marginalized women in the region, such as human rights, participation in political processes, labor, and migration. The forum has developed partnerships with other NGO's in the region in order to strengthen and expand networks that are working on women, law, and development.

Santitham YMCA Building
3rd floor, Room 305-308
11 Sermsuk Road, Soi Mengrairasmi
Chiangmai 50300
Thailand

Tel: +66 (53) 404 613/4
Fax: +66 (53) 404 615
apwld@apwld.org
www.apwld.org

Contact: Mary Jane N. Real, Regional Coordinator

Number of staff: 7

Budget: $500,000–$1,000,000

Publications: Forum News, tri-annual newsletter; *Identity and Gender Based Politics,* 2002; *Guidelines on Strategies and Responses to the Needs of Burmese Migrant Women in Thailand,* 2000

Asia and the Pacific

Asia Pacific Network for International Education and Values Education

EDUCATION

The Asia-Pacific Network for International Education and Values Education (APNIEVE) was established in 1995. The major objectives of APNIEVE are to promote and develop international education and values, education for peace, human rights, democracy, and sustainable development through inter-country co-operation among individuals and institutions working in these fields. APNIEVE is composed of individual members and institutional members from both government and non-government sectors. The individual members are specialists, educators, teachers, and students engaged in international education and values education for peace, human rights, democracy, and sustainable development in Asia Pacific, and others who are genuinely committed to promote these areas of education.

c/o UNESCO—Bangkok
920 Sukhumvit Rd., Prakananong
Bangkok 10110
Thailand

Tel: +66 (2) 3910879
Fax: +66 (2) 3910866 Attn. APNIEVE
n.zhou@unescobkk.org
www.unescobkk.org/education/aceid/apnieve.htm

Contact: Mr. Zhou Nan-zhao, Coordinator of APEID

Asia-Pacific

Asia-Pacific Regional Resource Center for Human Rights Education

The Asian Pacific Regional Resource Center for Human Rights Education (ARRC) was established in 1992, and aims to serve as an institute and a network facilitator for human rights education in Asia Pacific. The center organizes human rights education training workshops, develops training materials, and organizes forum, conferences, and human rights education campaigns. It has also completed a recent Peace Education manual titled, *Human Rights Education Pack, New Edition*. In 2001, ARRC organized the Southeast Asia Training of Trainers for Peace Building to promote human rights education as a tool for conflict prevention and peacebuilding in the region.

2738 Ladprao 128/3
Klongchan, Bangkapi
Bangkok 10240
Thailand

Tel: +66 (2) 731 0829/377 5641
Fax: +66 (2) 731 0829
arrc@ksc.th.com
www.arrc-hre.com

Contact: Theresa J. Limpin, Regional Coordinator
Number of staff: 6
Publications: Making a Difference, Newsletter; *Report on Southeast Asia Training of Trainers for Peace Building*, 2001; *Asian Human Rights Education Trainer's Colloquium*, 2000

Burma

Assistance Association for Political Prisoners

In order to give effective and efficient assistance to their fellow political prisoners, and to honor student leader Min Ko Naing who has been held under detention by the military regime since 1989, former political prisoners established the Assistance Association for Political Prisoners (AAPP) in 2000 on the 11th anniversary of Min Ko Naing's arrest. AAPP's objectives are to report on the military regime's oppression of political prisoners presently detained; to encourage the support of international governments and organizations; to secure fundamental human rights for political prisoners; to aid in the reconstruction of the ex-political prisoners' life; and to protect the political prisoners upon their release from prison from harassment and intimidation by the military regime. AAPP activities include assisting families of political prisoners to visit the prisoners and supporting prisoners by providing necessities such as food and medicine and monitoring conditions in prisons. AAPP also publicizes arrests, conditions, and life stories of imprisoned political activists and artists, and assists former political prisoners with their mental and physical rehabilitation from torture and isolation.

PO Box 93
Mae Sot
Tak Province, 63110S
Thailand

Tel: +66 (1) 324 8935
aappb@cscoms.com
www.aappb.net

Contact: Bo Kyi, Joint Secretary
Publications: Spirit for Survival; Letter From Burma and Ten Years On

Global

Focus on the Global South

RESEARCH
ADVOCACY

Focus on the Global South is an NGO that researches and advocates for various issues of concern to the developing world. One of the organization's thematic areas is peace and security. In its research and publications, Focus on the Global South attempts to address the roots of conflict and advocates for disarmament and conflict resolution through diplomacy. The organization has organized various conferences on security issues and actively participates in alternative security projects, such as an international peace mission to Basilan in the Philippines in 2002. Focus on the Global South is also researching an Alternative Multilateral Security System for the Asia-Pacific, which aims to strengthen cooperation between peace activists throughout the region.

c/o CURSI
Wisit Prachuabmoh Building
Chulangkorn University
Phayathai Road
Bangkok 10330
Thailand

Tel: +66 (2) 218 7363/5
Fax: +66 (2) 255 9976
admin@focusweb.org or
    jim@focusweb.org
www.focusweb.org

Contact: Dr. Walden Bello, Executive Director

Budget: $100,000–$500,000

Number of staff: 18

Publications: Basilan: The Next Afghanistan?
Report of the International Peace Mission to
Basilan, Philippines, 2002; *Prospects for Good
Global Governance: The View from the South,*
2002; *Declaration and Papers from the Conference on Korean Reconciliation and Reunification for Global Peace,* 2001

Asia

Forum-Asia

RESEARCH
EDUCATION
ACTION
ADVOCACY

Forum-Asia was launched in December 1991, to facilitate collaboration among human rights organizations in Asia so as to develop a regional response for the promotion of human rights and democracy in the region. Collaboration between members of Forum-Asia is based on the understanding that human rights and fundamental freedoms are indivisible and interdependent. They include not only civil, political, economic, social, and cultural rights but also the rights of peoples to pursue freely their economic, social, and cultural development.

Forum-Asia strives towards the promotion and protection of human rights in the Asian region through collaboration and cooperation among human rights organizations in the region.

111 Suthisarnwinichai Rd
Samsennok Huay Kwang
Bangkok, 10320
Thailand

Tel: +66 (2) 276 9846/7
Fax: +66 (2) 693 4939
info@forumasia.org
www.forumasia.org

Contact: Rashid Kang

Greater Mekong region

Foundation for International Human Resource Development

RESEARCH
EDUCATION
ACTION

The Foundation for International Human Resource Development (FIHRD) aims to improve the standard of human resources in the Greater Mekong region. To this end, the foundation researches current social and economic conditions and their impact on human resource development in the region and proposes solutions for shortcomings, for example through trainings. The foundation organizes an annual Leadership Forum. In 2002, the theme of this international conference was "Rethinking of Globalization: Networking and Partnership."

7th Floor, S.P. Building B
338 Phaholyothin Road
Samsennai, Phythai
Bangkok 10400
Thailand

Tel: +66 (2) 619 0512/0513/273 0180
Fax: +66 (2) 273 0181
fihrd@bkk3.loxinfo.co.th
www.fihrd.or.th

Contact: Chira Hongladarom, Secretary-General

Budget: $50,000–$100,000

Number of staff: 7

Southeast Asia

Images Asia

RESEARCH
EDUCATION

Images Asia is an alternative media organization involved in the documentation, multimedia production, and dissemination of information on human rights issues in Southeast Asia. The organization's activities include human rights documentation and media intervention training. It focuses on issues such as Burma, drug trafficking, ethnic affairs, the environment, women, landmines, and children. Images Asia maintains a library with slides, videos, and photographs from throughout the region that span the last ten years.

Images Asia (IA) and
    Borderline Video
PO Box 2, Prasingha Post Office
Chiang Mai 50200
Thailand

Tel: +66 (1) 884 4034
images@cm.ksc.co.th

Contact: Sam Kalayanee

Publications: A Question of Security: A Retrospective on Cross-border Attacks on Thailand's Refugee and Civilian Communities along the Burmese Border Since 1995, 1998; *All Quiet on the Western Front? The Situation in Chin State and Sagaing Division,* 1998

Thailand, Southeast Asia

Institute for Dispute Resolution

RESEARCH
EDUCATION

The Institute for Dispute Resolution is an academic institute that was founded in September 1995. Its goals are to firstly perform and facilitate research, case studies, and conflict management training especially in the dispute cases related to the natural resources, environment, and public policy. Secondly, it wants to establish an information center especially for the data related to major conflicts occurring in Thailand and in some international events. Lastly, its goal is to provide academic and professional services in term of training, lecturing, consultation, and mediation to other agencies.

One of the programs of the institute is the Southeast Asian Conflict Management Capacity Building Training Program, which aims at increasing the conflict management capacity of participants by Training Workshop, Field Trips, and Case Study Implementation. The institute is part of the Southeast Asian Conflict Studies Network

Institute for Dispute Resolution
Khon Kaen University
Amphur Muang
Khon Kaen, 40002
Thailand

Tel: +66 (4) 320 2425/320 2222
Fax: +66 (4) 320 2788
idr@kku.ac.th
http://idr.kku.ac.th

Contact: Dr Suwit Laohasiriwong, Director *or* Ms. Ang Ming Chee, Project Coordinator

Number of staff: 4

Publications: Social Transformation and Conflicts in Southeast Asia: Proceedings of the sixth Southeast Asian Conflict Studies Network Regional Workshop, 2003

Thailand

King Prajadhipok's Institute – Center for Peace Promotion

RESEARCH
EDUCATION

King Prajadhipok's Institute (KPI) is a national academic institution committed to the development of democracy. The Center for Peace Promotion researches and promotes non-violent conflict resolution methods. The main activities of the center are research into the prevention and resolution of conflicts and the promotion of networking, capacity building, and the practical application of theoretical knowledge concerning peaceful conflict resolution. The center organizes seminars, awards prizes in conflict resolution research and its application, and has established local, national, and international networks.

47/101 Moo 4, Tiwanond Road
Talad Kwan Subdistrict, Muang District
Nonthaburi 11000
Thailand

Tel: +66 (2) 527 7830/9
Fax: +66 (2) 527 7826/8
anocha@kpi.ac.th
www.kpi.ac.th

Contact: Prof. Dr. Vanchai Vatanasapt

Publications: Developing Democracy Under a New Constitution in Thailand: A Pluralist Solution, 2001

Southeast Asia

Nonviolence International
Southeast Asia

Nonviolence International Southeast Asia (NISEA) was established in Bangkok in 1992, as an independent branch of the international NGO Nonviolence International. It provides assistance to individuals, organizations and governments seeking nonviolent means to bring about social and political change. Its vision is to strengthen people's ability to use the power of nonviolence as a means to bring about changes that reflect the truth, justice and the desire for human development on the personal, social, economic and political levels. Nonviolence International believes that every cultural and religious tradition in the world contains the seeds of truth through nonviolence, and they encourage activists of different traditions to seek nonviolent solutions that respect their cultural identities. To this end, NISEA provides training, organizes seminars and publishes research on nonviolent struggles in Southeast Asia. It is a founding member of the Working Group for Weapons Reduction in Cambodia and part of the International Action Network for Small Arms and the International Campaign to Ban Landmines. At the moment their Cease-fire and Peace Accord Program is aimed at encouraging a negotiated settlement to the civil war in Burma by targeting the leadership of armed ethnic organizations, military junta, democratic opposition, regional governments, UN Agencies and INGOs. To this end they encourage the formulation of options by stakeholders in the conflict to move beyond current positions.

104/20 Latprao Soi 124
Wangtonglang
Bangkok 10310
Thailand

Tel: +66 (2) 934 3289
Fax: +66 (2) 934 3289
seasia@nonviolenceinternational.net
www.nonviolenceinternational.net/seasia

Contact: Yeshua Moser-Puangsuwan, Regional Coordinator
Budget: $25,000–$100,000
Number of staff: 4
Publications: Whose Security Counts? 2003; *From War to Peace,* 2002; *Truth is Our Only Weapon,* 2000; *One Million Kilometers for Peace,* 1999

Asia

Santi Pracha Dhamma Institute

ACTION
ADVOCACY

Since its establishment in 1986, the Santi Pracha Dhamma Institute (SPDI) has been active in campaigns for democracy and human rights. One of its main projects is called Alternative Politics for Asia. This project aims to create an alternative political movement in Asia based on traditional spiritual values to address structural, political and grassroots issues. To this end, the SPDI has held a series of dialogues, including a Buddhist-Muslim dialogue and a European-Asian dialogue. The institute is part of the Sanithirakoses-Nagapateepa Foundation, a Buddhist-inspired umbrella organization for five cooperating sister organizations in Thailand.

666 Charoen Nakhorn Road
Klongsan
Bangkok 10600
Thailand

Contact: Pracha Hutanuwatr

Tel: +66 (2) 438 9331/2
Fax: +66 (2) 860 1277
spd@ksc.th.com
www.sulak-sivaraksa.org/network25.php

Southeast Asia

South East Asian Committee for Advocacy

RESEARCH
ADVOCACY

All activities of the South East Asian Committee for Advocacy's (SEACA) focus on advocacy capacity building. Its three strategic projects include Research Capacity Development, Media and Communications Skills Development and Advocacy Strategy and Techniques Development. Research Capacity Development aims to promote skills in policy research and analysis, participatory policy research and alternative policy development. Media and Communications Skills Development promotes the usage of popular media and communication tools appropriate for grassroots communities. Advocacy Strategy and Techniques Development is being implemented in the form of internship for advocates from Southeast Asia. All these strategic projects have follow-up activities at country level through national and local trainings, workshops, consultation meetings, to ensure that more numbers of people from civil society organizations have appropriate skills for advocacy work.

2556 (51/498) Soi 128/2 Ladprao Road
Klongchan Bangkapi
Bangkok 10240
Thailand

Tel: +66 (2) 377 2939
Fax: +66 (2) 731 0583
seaca@ksc.th.com or info@seaca.net
www.seaca.net

Thailand

Spirit in Education Movement

The Spirit in Education Movement (SEM) provides training and workshops on topics such as community building, meditation, social action, NGO management and conflict resolution, rooted in Buddhism philosophy. Under its Grassroots Leadership Training Program, SEM aims to empower grassroots leaders of marginalized communities in Thailand and the wider Southeast Asian region. In the future, SEM hopes to extend this program to the establishment of an Alternative College to run two-year courses teaching empowerment for sustainable communities.

666 Charoen Nakhorn Road
Klongsan
Bangkok 10600
Thailand
_____

Tel: +66 (2) 314 7385/16
Fax: +66 (2) 314 7385
sem@semsikkha.org
www.sulak-sivaraksa.org/network23.php

Contact: Ms. Wallapa Kuntiranon
Budget: < $25,000
Number of staff: 8
Publications: Seeds of Peace, journal of the Sanithirakoses-Nagapateepa Foundation; *Alternative Development from a Buddhist Perspective:* SEM course report

Burma

Women's League of Burma

Founded on December 9, 1999 the Women's League of Burma (WLB) is an umbrella organization comprising eleven already-existing women's organizations of different Burmese ethnic backgrounds. Its mission is to work for the advancement of the status of women and to increase their decision-making participation in all areas of society. This includes participation in the democracy movement and in the peace and national reconciliation processes through capacity building, advocacy, research and documentation.

The second Forum of Women's Organizations of Burma was held in Chiang Mai in Dec 7-9, 1999. Women had the opportunity to share their views on the ways and means to find a common platform and how to work together to promote the role and participation of women at all levels.

PO Box 413
Chiang Mai 50000
Thailand
_____

wlb@womenofburma.org
www.womenofburma.org

Publications: Overcoming Shadows, 2004

Tonga

Human Rights and Democracy Movement in Tonga

The Human Rights and Democracy Movement in Tonga was formed in the late 1970's by a small group of Tongans who believed that change was needed to bring about more democratic governance in Tonga. It was formally established and recognized as the Pro-Democracy Movement in 1992 and in September 2002 it further changed into its current form. The Movement primarily strives to serve the people of Tonga. Its working philosophy is based on the text of the Universal Declaration of Human Rights and Christian principles. The Movement's annual work programme is focused primarily on public education and advocacy.

1st Floor, Siasi 'o Tonga Building
Fatafehi Road, (Kilikali)
PO Box 843
Nuku'alofa, Tonga

Tel: +676 (2) 5501
Fax: +676 (2) 6330
demo@kalianet.to
www.planet-tonga.com/HRDMT

Contact: Lopeti Senituli, Director of HRDMT Office

Number of staff: 3

Publications: Basic Proposals for an Alternative Structure of Government for Tonga, 2003; *Convention on Constitution and Democracy in Tonga,* 2003; *Taimi 'o Tonga and the Future of the Rule of Law in Tonga,* 2003

Global

Amnesty International

With national sections in over fifty countries, Amnesty International (AI) is one of the world's leading human rights organizations. Apart from focusing on individual cases of human rights abuse, it also reports on systematic violations, offers recommendations on how to prevent these and put pressure on governments through public and lobby campaigns to heed them. For sudden escalations of human rights violations, the organization has a special crisis response team. AI's human rights education work also contributes to the prevention of violent conflict.

99-119 Rosebery Avenue
London EC1R 4RE
United Kingdom

Tel: +44 (20) 7814 6200
Fax: +44 (20) 7833 1510
info@amnesty.org.uk
www.amnesty.org.uk

Contact: Campaigning and Crisis Response Program

Number of staff: 120 at AIUK

Budget: > $1,000,000

Publications: Annually over 200 books, reports and circulars in over a dozen languages

Global

Bradford University –
Department of Peace Studies

RESEARCH
EDUCATION

The Department of Peace Studies at Bradford University was established a quarter of a century ago and has grown to be the largest university center for peace studies in the world. Together with 20 lecturers and research fellows, the department works primarily in the following areas: international politics and security studies, development and peace, regions in conflict, conflict resolution, politics and society, international politics and the environment. The Department also has a large publishing program, including publication of its regular Newsletter three times a year and the Bradford Arms Register Studies (BARS) Project.

Further applied work in conflict resolution is conducted within the Department's Center for Conflict Resolution. This Center, an applied research unit within the Department, combines theoretical studies in peacekeeping, mediation and conflict resolution with a range of practical programs, many of them concerned with training mediators and peacemakers in areas in conflict.

Richmond Road
Bradford BD7 1DP
U.K.

Tel: +44 (1274) 23 5235
Fax: +44 (1274) 23 5240
n.lewer@bradford.ac.uk
www.brad.ac.uk/acad/peace

Contact: Dr. N. Lewer, Head of Center for Conflict Resolution
Number of staff: 20

Publications: Newsletter; Women, Gender and Peacebuilding, 2000; *International NGOs and Peacebuilding: Perspectives from Peace Studies and Conflict Resolution,* 1999

Burma

Burma Campaign UK

RESEARCH
EDUCATION
ADVOCACY

The Burma Campaign UK (BCUK) campaigns for human rights and democracy in Burma. BCUK works for the freedom of all the peoples of Burma regardless of race, ethnicity, gender or age. BCUK aims to achieve the restoration of human rights and democracy in Burma through: the discouragement of trade, investment and tourism (including pressure for sanctions); the raising of public awareness of issues relating to Burma and increasing international pressure on the UK government, on the European Union (EU), the Association of Southeast Asian Nations (ASEAN) and the United Nations (UN). It achieves this through direct lobbying of the UK government and EU; campaigning (e.g. "Cut The Lifeline" Campaign); education of the public; lobbying businesses and research. Since 1991 it has achieved results such as forcing Premier Oil to withdraw from Burma as well as various tour operators.

The Burma Campaign UK
28 Charles Street
London N1 6HT
United Kingdom

Tel: +44 (2) 7324 4710
Fax: +44 (2) 7324 4717
info@burmacampaign.org.uk
www.burmacampaign.org.uk

Contact: Mark Farmaner
Budget: $100,000–$500,000
Number of staff: 4
Publications: METTA which is published twice a year

Global

Catholic Institute for International Relations

ACTION
ADVOCACY

This international charity is working for sustainable development and the eradication of poverty. Founded in 1940, CIIR's roots are in gospel values and a progressive Catholic tradition and works with civil society organizations and governments in 11 countries worldwide. It is a membership organization, with over 1500 members worldwide. Through direct support and by international policy advocacy the CIIR seeks to help the poor and excluded and to advocate for change.

CIIR is active in Latin America, the Caribbean, Africa, the Middle East and Southeast Asia. In Southeast Asia CIIR focuses on Justice on Gender and Ethnicity, Sustainable Environment, Building Just Societies, Just Economies, HIV/AIDS and Peace and Conflict.

In 2000 the Advocacy Capacity Building in Asia project was set up in collaboration with Southeast Asian civil organizations from Thailand, Philippines, Cambodia, Malaysia, Indonesia, Vietnam, Burma and East Timor. The objects of the program are to encourage the successful implementation of pro-poor policies in this region.

Unit 3 Canonbury Yard
190a New North Road
London N1 7BJ
United Kingdom

Tel: +44 (20) 7354 0883
Fax: +44 (20) 7359 0017
rolando@ciir.org
www.ciir.org

Contact: Rolando Modina, Asia Regional Manager

Budget: > 1,000,000

Number of staff: 49

Publications: *Democratizing Development: Civil Society Advocacy in Southeast Asia,* 2000; *Time to Change the Prescription: A Policy Response to the Asian Financial Crisis,* 1999; *South Korea: Model and Warning,* 1995

Tajikistan, Fiji, Sri Lanka, Cambodia,
Philippines, Caucasus, Angola, West Africa, Uganda

RESEARCH
EDUCATION
ACTION
ADVOCACY

Conciliation Resources

Founded in 1994, Conciliation Resources (CR) is a non-governmental international service for conflict prevention and resolution seeking to provide sustained assistance to partner organizations and their initiatives at community and national levels. In Asia Pacific, the Accord program has had projects on the peace processes in Tajikistan, Sri Lanka, Cambodia, Mindanao and Fiji. An "education pack" of training and discussion materials is produced to accompany the Accord publications. Other project activities in these countries have included policy seminars, briefing meetings, and other initiatives to encourage the development of strategies that will consolidate the peace processes in the respective countries.

173 Upper Street
London N1 1RG
United Kingdom

Tel: +44 (20) 7359 7728
Fax: +44 (20) 7359 4081
conres@c-r.org
www.c-r.org

Contact: Andy Carl
Number of staff: 14 (UK)
Budget: > $1,000,000
Publications: Accord: An International Review of Peace Initiatives

Global

RESEARCH
EDUCATION
ACTION
ADVOCACY

Forum on Early Warning and Early Response

The Forum on Early Warning and Early Response (FEWER) is an independent global network of organizations committed to preventing conflict by providing early warning and informing peacebuilding efforts. FEWER's activities are led by its members. The network is composed of NGOs, UN agencies and academic institutions who work together to exchange knowledge and experience in the field of early warning, conflict prevention and conflict resolution. FEWER's motivation is strictly humanitarian. The services provided by FEWER are oriented towards the promotion of human rights, sustainable development and peace. FEWER provides local perspectives on the causes and dynamics of violent conflict and peace building to different policy-making communities.

FEWER actively works in Southeast Asia, particularly in the Philippines, Cambodia and Indonesia.

Old Truman Brewery
91-95 Brick Lane
London E1 6QN
United Kingdom

Tel: +44 (20) 7247 7022
Fax: +44 (20) 7247 5290
secretariat@fewer.org
www.fewer.org

Contact: David Nyheim, Director
Budget: $500,000–$1,000,000
Number of staff: 8
Publications: Development in Conflict: A Seven Step Tool for Planner (joint initiative), 2001; *Conflict Analysis and Response Definition: Abridged Methodology* (joint initiative), 2001

Tibet

Free Tibet Campaign

EDUCATION
ADVOCACY

Established in 1988 as an independent membership organization, the Free Tibet Campaign stands for the Tibetans' right to determine their own future. It campaigns for an end to the Chinese occupation of Tibet and for the Tibetans' fundamental human rights to be respected.

A number of campaigns are detailed on the website. Approximately 35 local groups work on behalf of the Free Tibet Campaign in local communities across the U.K. These groups are the vital link to the grassroots support for Tibet that enables awareness to be spread within local communities.

28 Charles Square
London N1 6HT
United Kingdom
—————
Tel: +44 (20) 7324 4605
Fax: +44 (20) 7324 4606
mail@freetibet.org
www.freetibet.org/

Contact: Alison Reynolds, Director
Number of staff: 7
Publications: Quarterly membership newsletter

South East Asia, Middle East, Northern Ireland,
Basque Country, West Africa, South Africa

Initiative on Conflict Resolution and Ethnicity

RESEARCH
EDUCATION
ADVOCACY

A joint program of the United Nations University and the University of Ulster, the Initiative on Conflict Resolution and Ethnicity (INCORE) aims to integrate research, training, practice, policy and theory, and to provide an international focus on ethnic violence. INCORE's Policy and Evaluation Unit was established in 1998 to examine, research, and analyze the ways in which conflict management research and practical lessons from past practice are currently utilized by policymakers. INCORE's Conflict Data Service, available on its website, provides current and historical information on all major on-going conflicts, theme sites on a variety of issues relevant to conflict, and information on conflict resolution institutions throughout the world.

Aberfoyle House
Northland Road
Derry/Londonderry BT48 7JA
Northern Ireland
United Kingdom
—————
Tel: +44 (28) 7137 5500
Fax: +44 (28) 7137 5510
incore@incore.ulst.ac.uk
www.incore.ulst.ac.uk

Contact: Professor Mari Fitzduff, Director
Number of staff: 13
Budget: $100,000–$500,000
Publications: Ethnic Conflict Research Digest, journal; Ethnic Studies Network Bulletin; *From Protagonist to Pragmatist: Political Leadership in Societies in Transition,* 2001; *Assessment of UN Research Needs,* 1999

Global

International Action Network on Small Arms

ADVOCACY

The International Action Network on Small Arms is the global network of civil society organizations working to end the proliferation misuse of small arms and light weapons by bringing together the voices of NGOs and individuals across the world. It was founded in 1998 and has grown to more than 500 participating groups, which include policy development organizations, national gun control groups, research institutes, aid agencies and human rights organizations.

IANSA aims to reduce small arms violence through a number of means. It is raising awareness among policymakers, the public and the media whilst promoting the prevention work of NGOs and providing them with a forum to share experiences. It establishes regional networks and promotes the voices of victims in regional and global policy discussions.

PO Box 422
8-17 Tottenham Court Road
London W1T 1JY
United Kingdom

Tel: +44 (20) 7953 7664
contact@iansa.org
www.iansa.org

Contact: Rebecca Peters, Director

Publications: IANSA Report, Implementing the Program of Action, 2003

Global

International Alert

RESEARCH
EDUCATION
ACTION
ADVOCACY

International Alert is a non-governmental organization based in the UK. The organization was set up in 1985 as an action-based, non-governmental organization to contribute to the prevention and resolution of violent internal conflict. Together with different organizations and individuals, IA has worked to peacefully resolve many of the world's most intractable disputes. IA seeks to strengthen the ability of people in conflict situations to make peace by facilitating dialogue at different levels of society in conflict and helping develop and enhance local capacities through funding or training. The creation of the organization was a response to the rise in violent conflict within countries and the subsequent abuse of individual and collective human rights in conflict situations. Today there is an ever more pressing need for conflict resolution and peacebuilding efforts.

346 Clapham Road
London
SW9 9AP
United Kingdom

Tel: +44 (0) 20 7627 6800
Fax: +44 (0) 20 7627 6900
general@international-alert.org
www.international-alert.org

Contact: Dan Smith OBE, Secretary General

Number of staff: 63

Publications: Biting the Bullet Briefing Paper 16 on the Regulation of Civilian Possession of Small Arms and Light Weapons, 2003; *Cost of the War: Economic, Socio-political and Human Costs of the War in Sri Lanka,* 2001

Global

International Institute for Strategic Studies

Founded in 1958 the International Institute for Strategic Studies (IISS) is devoted to the study of the problems of conflict, however caused, that have, or potentially have, an important military content. To this end, the Institute's research program has been concerned not just with the military aspects of security but also with the social and economic sources of conflict, as well as the political and moral implications of the use and existence of armed force.

The IISS continues to stimulate debate through its conference program and its publications, notably the Adelphi Paper series. Research activities undertaken concern the strategic implications of the "new terrorism," Defense Policy, Conflict Resolution, Peace Operations and Humanitarian Intervention, and Regional Security Studies.

There is an established program covering a wide range of Asia-Pacific security issues covering the Taiwan Strait, the Korean Peninsula, maritime Southeast Asia, and South Asian nuclear weapons. Content includes studying the core regional disputes, exploring broader influences on regional security rooted in economic, environmental and energy-based factors while also focusing on China's evolving role in the international systems.

Arundel House
13-15 Arundel Street
Temple Place
London WC2R 3DX
United Kingdom

Tel: +44 (20) 7379 7676
Fax: +44 (20) 7836 3108
huxley@iiss.org
www.iiss.org

Contact: Dr. Tim Huxley, Senior Fellow Asia-Pacific Security or Adam Ward, Senior Fellow East Asian Security.

Publications: Adelphi Paper series

Global

Minority Rights Group International

RESEARCH
ACTION
ADVOCACY

Minority Rights Group International (MRG) is a non-governmental organization working to secure rights for ethnic, religious, and linguistic minorities worldwide, and to promote cooperation and understanding between communities. MRG has over 30 years of experience promoting the rights of marginalized, non-dominant groups within society. MRG has four main activities: researching and publishing; advocacy to secure the rights of minorities; educating children and teachers on minority issues; and cooperative efforts with other organizations and activists who share its aims to build alliances, discuss ideas, develop skills and further minority rights worldwide.

Floors 2-4, 54 Commercial Street
London E1 6LT
United Kingdom

Tel: +44 (20) 7422 4200
Fax: +44 (20) 7422 4201
minority.rights@mrgmail.org
www.minorityrights.org

Contact: Alan Phillips, Director
Number of staff: 26
Budget: > $1,000,000
Publications: Outsider, newsletter;
World Directory of Minorities, 2001;
Muslim Women in India, 1999; *Forests and Indigenous Peoples of Asia,* 1999

Global

Oxfam

EDUCATION
ADVOCACY

Founded in 1942 as the Oxfam Committee, whose main aim was to ensure the Greeks obtained relief during occupation, Oxfam now works actively with others to overcome poverty and suffering throughout the world. Oxfam's donors, supporters, staff, project partners and participants are working together to implement project activities. The staff covers a vast range of activities including donating, fundraising, campaigning, volunteering or working "on the ground."

Oxfam-GB has offices in six East Asian countries and supports partners in three more. The core programs are in sustainable livelihoods, education and complex emergencies. Oxfam GB currently supports people affected by conflict in Indonesia and southern Philippines.

Oxfam Supporter Services Department
Oxfam House
274 Banbury Road
Oxfam OX2 7DZ
United Kingdom

Tel: +44 (870) 333 2700
Fax: +44 (1865) 312 600
oxfam@oxfam.org.uk
www.oxfam.org.uk

Budget: > 1,000,000

Colombia, Guatemala, Indonesia and Mexico

EDUCATION
ACTION
ADVOCACY

Peace Brigades International

Peace Brigades International (PBI) works to open a space for peace in which conflicts can be dealt with non-violently. PBI use a strategy of international presence and concern that supports local initiatives and contributes to developing a culture of peace and justice. It acts on request of local non-violent groups working for human rights and social change in regions where there is oppression and conflict.

The aim of PBI's international presence—defined as one or more of the following: physical presence, physical accompaniment, public relations, networking, observing, reporting, and building international support networks—is to accompany both political and social processes through a joint strategy of deterring violence and promoting active non-violence. Its international teams of volunteers use methods such as protective accompaniment, peace education, independent observation and analysis of the conflict situation.

International Office
Unit 5, 89-93 Fonthill Rd
London N4 3HT
United Kingdom

Tel: +44 (20) 7561 9141
Fax: +44 (20) 7281 3181
info@peacebrigades.org
www.peacebrigades.org

Budget: > 1,000,000

Number of staff: Indonesia Team – 18 volunteers

EDUCATION

Responding to Conflict

Responding to Conflict (RTC) is an international, non-profit agency which focuses on building action-oriented capacity for conflict transformation and peace-building in countries where it is most needed. RTC provides advice, cross-cultural training and longer-term support to people working in the areas of peace, development, rights and humanitarian assistance in societies that are affected or threatened by violent conflict. RTC works with a range of partners from community-based organisations to government bodies and international agencies; and in a variety of fields: from rights, development, environmental protection and relief to reconciliation and conflict resolution. RTC's approach to learning aims to be practical, participative and experience-based. The ten-week Working with Conflict course brings together people working in areas of instability and violence. The one-week Strengthening Policy and Practice workshop is concerned primarily with policy formation and implementation in conflict-affected areas.

1046 Bristol Road
Birmingham B29 6LJ
United Kingdom

Tel: +44 (121) 415 5641
Fax: +44 (121) 415 4119
enquiries@respond.org
www.respond.org

Contact: Simon Fisher, Director

Number of staff: 11

Publications: Working with Conflict Skills and Strategies for Action

Aceh

Support Committee
on Human Rights in Aceh

EDUCATION
ACTION
ADVOCACY

The Support Committee on Human Rights in Aceh (SCHRA) is a platform of human rights and peace groups around the world. SCHRA networks and coordinates activities on the human rights situation in Aceh. The steering committee of SCHRA consists of organizations based in Indonesia, Malaysia, the Philippines, Japan, Australia, New Zealand, the United States of America, the United Kingdom and the Netherlands. A 24-point program of action was developed in a meeting in December 2003 in Kuala Lumpur consisting of burning issues like campaigning for the ending of martial law in Aceh and protesting against the trials of hundreds of Acehnese citizens allegedly involved in the rebellion against the government in Jakarta.

c/o Tapol, the Indonesian Human Rights Campaign
111 Northwood Road,
Thornton Heath,
Surrey CR7 8HW,
United Kingdom

Tel: +44 (20) 8771 2904
Fax: +44 (20) 8653 0322
tapol@gn.apc.org
www.gn.apc.org/tapol

Global

EDUCATION

American Friends Service Committee

Founded by the Quakers in 1917, the American Friends Service Committee carries out service, development, social justice and peace programs throughout the world. AFSC's work is based on the Quaker's belief in the worth of every person and faith in the power of love to overcome violence and injustice.

AFSC created the East Asia Quaker International Affairs Program to promote dialogue on peace and justice issues and to overcome political division in East Asia, especially in North Korea and the improvement of U.S.–DPRK relations. AFSC supports efforts of East Asian people to reduce tension, in particular within the Korean peninsula, and to encourage demilitarization in the region. Since 1994 it has sponsored conferences on alternative security and tolerance building, organized discussions on peace education in Beijing and has made exchanges possible for leaders from South Korea, China and Vietnam in order to observe the impact of globalization.

The Southeast Asia Quaker International Affairs Program established in 1968 offered young leaders from the newly emerging nations a chance to meet their counterparts from other countries to discuss common issues. Currently the AFSC in Southeast Asia is seeking ways in which the program might lesson tensions, promote communications or encourage the prospects for the peaceful resolution of conflicts.

AFSC National Office
1501 Cherry Street
Philadelphia PA 19102
United States

Tel: +1 (215) 241 7000
Fax: +1 (215) 241 7275
afscinfo@afsc.org
www.afsc.org

Asia

RESEARCH
EDUCATION

Asia Foundation

The Asia Foundation consists of a widespread network, which stretches throughout Asia Pacific and the United States. The foundation has focused on issues ranging from effective law, governance and citizenship to the equal participation of women, and peace and stability in the region. The government and law program includes programs on conflict resolution, election and non-governmental organization support. In this connection, the foundation has supported a study of how the structures and procedures of alternative dispute resolution may be institutionalized in Indonesia. The Foundation also offers an inter-faith and inter-ethnic conflict resolution program.

465 California Street 14th Floor
San Francisco, CA 94104
United States

Tel: +1 (415) 982 4640
Fax: +1 (415) 392 8863
info@asiafound.org
www.asiafoundation.org

Contact: William P. Fuller, President

Publications: Democratic Transitions and the Role of Islam in Asia, 2000; *Approaches to Human Rights in Southeast Asia,* 2000; *Focus on Pakistan,* 2000; *Funding Civil Society in Asia: Philanthropy and Public-Private Partnerships,* 1997

Asia Pacific

Asia Pacific Center
for Justice and Peace

RESEARCH
EDUCATION
ADVOCACY

The Asia Pacific Center for Justice and Peace (APCJP) works with organizations in the Asia and Pacific region to strive for political, social and economic justice. The Peace, Human Rights and Democracy program focuses on key areas of ethnic and political conflict that are under-reported or misreported in the U.S. Its mission is to provide a link between grassroots organizations in the Asia Pacific and policy makers in Washington.

110, Maryland Avenue, NE
Suite 504
Washington, DC 20002
United States

Tel: +1 (202) 543 1094
Fax: +1 (202) 546 5103
apcjp@igc.org
www.apcjp.org

Contact: Miriam Young,
Executive Director
Number of staff: 6

Burma

ACTION
ADVOCACY

Burma Project

The Burma Project, established by the Open Society Institute in 1994, is dedicated to increasing international awareness of conditions in Burma and to helping the country make the transition from a closed to an open society. To this end, the Burma Project initiates, supports, and administers a range of programs and activities around the globe. Examples include efforts by and for multiethnic, grassroots organizations dedicated to the restoration and preservation of fundamental freedoms; education programs for Burmese students, a professional and vocational training for young Burmese abroad who plan eventually to return to live and work in a democratic Burma.

Some examples of Burma Project activities are: support for publications in Burmese and other indigenous languages; publication of a bimonthly magazine, Burma Debate, which serves as a forum for discussion of central issues concerning Burma; supplementary educational grants and an internship program for Burmese students

Burma Project/Southeast Asia Initiative
Open Society Institute
400 W. 59th St.
New York, NY 10019
United States

Tel: +1 (212) 548 0632
Fax: +1 (212) 548 4655
burma@sorosny.org
www.burmaproject.org

Contact: Maureen Aung-Thwin,
Director
Publications: Burma News Update

Global

Carnegie Commission on Preventing Deadly Conflict

RESEARCH
ADVOCACY

In May 1994 the Carnegie Corporation of New York established the Carnegie Commission on Preventing Deadly Conflict to address the looming threats of intergroup violence to world peace and to advance new ideas for the prevention and resolution of deadly conflict. In December 1997 the Commission published its final report. In it, it "seeks to demonstrate the need for a new commitment—by governments, international organizations, opinion leaders, the private sector, and an informed public—to prevent deadly conflict and to marshal the considerable potential that already exists for doing so." Though originally envisaged as a three-year project, the Commission has decided to continue its activities. The Commission's conceptual approach hinges on three questions: What is the problem posed by "deadly conflict" within or between states? How should (outside) help be structured? And who should do this work? It serves both as a strategic framework for thinking about preventing mass violence and as an analytic structure to guide its work.

Since it's founding the Commission has worked to deepen understanding of human conflict and conflict prevention. Through sponsored research carried out by many organizations and individuals, the Commission has encouraged fresh thinking about these problems that are so crucial to the future of humanity. The Commission also sponsors conferences around the world and convenes seminars. It conducted case studies of possible 'missed opportunities' in former Yugoslavia, Rwanda, Nagorno-Karabakh, Chechnya and Somalia. The Commission also plans to study successful prevention efforts and identify the political, diplomatic, economic, military and social tools available to help prevent deadly conflict.

The Commission, which meets quarterly, is composed of sixteen eminent international leaders and scholars who have long-standing experience in conflict prevention and resolution.

2400 N. Street
N.W., Sixth Floor Washington
DC 20037-1153
United States

Tel: +1 (202) 429 7979
Fax: +1 (202) 429 9291
pdc@carnegie.org
www.ccpdc.org

Contact: Jane E. Holl, Executive Director

Budget: > $1,000,000

Number of staff: 10

Publications: Preventing Contemporary Intergroup, Violence Education for Conflict Resolution, 1999; The Warning-Response Problem and Missed Opportunities in Preventive Diplomacy, 1997

Global

Carter Center

The Carter Center works to advance peace and health worldwide. Founded in 1982 by former US President Jimmy Carter and Rosalynn Carter, the Atlanta-based Center focuses in its conflict resolution program on peaceful prevention and resolution of conflicts, primarily civil wars. An array of associated programs reinforces the Center's conflict resolution work. These include activities to improve nations' capacities for sustainable development, promote and protect human rights and strengthen democracy.

Through its Conflict Resolution Program (CRP), the Carter Center marshals the expertise of peacemakers worldwide to prevent and resolve armed conflicts around the globe. It is the base for the International Council for Conflict Resolution, a small body of internationally recognized experts and world leaders. They are engaged on an individual basis in ongoing CRP projects. The CRP regularly monitors many of the world's armed conflicts in an attempt to better understand their histories, the primary actors involved, disputed issues, and efforts being made to resolve them. When a situation arises where President Carter has a unique role to play and specific conditions have been met, the CRP directly supports his intervention.

In order to make mediation more effective the Center fosters collaboration among individuals, NGOs, official agencies and corporations. It tries to identify creative ways to address problems, seeks partners to implement solutions and aims to build the internal capacity of countries to ensure continued growth and progress. The Center works in China, Indonesia, North Korea and East Timor.

One Copenhill
453 Freedom Parkway
Atlanta GA 30307
United States

Tel: +1 (404) 331 3900
Fax: +1 (404) 402 5145
carterweb@emory.edu
www.cartercenter.org

Contact: Ben Hoffman, Director of the Conflict Resolution Program

Budget: > $1,000,000

Publications: Carter Center News Biannual; The Kashmiri Conflict: Historical and Prospective Intervention Analyses, 2002; 1995–1996 State of World Conflict Report, 1997

Global

Catholic Relief Services

EDUCATION
ACTION
ADVOCACY

Founded in 1943 by the Catholic Bishops of the United States the Catholic Relief Services provides direct aid to the poor and involves people in their own development. Motivated by religion the policies and programs reflect and express the teaching of the Catholic Church. The CRS helps victims of natural and man-made disasters, provides assistance to the poor, supports self-help programs and actively collaborates with groups of goodwill and non-sectarian persons.

In South Asia CFS focus on promoting a culture of peace, equity and women's empowerment. They work towards strengthening civil society, improve community livelihoods and promote education in areas where child labor is an acute problem. In East Timor the CRS' goal is to facilitate a non-violent and just society by strengthening the capacity of communities and institutions to build a peaceful and democratic nation. The program in North Korea focuses on providing support for rehabilitation and reconciliation.

Catholic Relief Services
209 West Fayette Street
Baltimore, MD 21201-3443
United States

Tel: +1 (410) 625 2200
WebMaster@CatholicRelief.org
www.catholicrelief.org

China

Center for China-US Cooperation

EDUCATION
ADVOCACY

The Center for China-US Cooperation is joint venture between Chinese and US intellectuals, investors, officials, academics, entrepreneurs and others committed to the search for mutual understanding between China and the United States and the positive resolution of disputes. Founded in 1998 by the University of Denver's Graduate School of International Studies (GSIS), the CCUSC will continue to serve as a bridge between the two societies in a search for mutual understanding, prudent policies and the positive resolution of disputes.

Center for China-US Cooperation
Graduate School of International Studies
The University of Denver
2201 South Gaylord
Denver CO 80208
United States

Tel: +1 (303) 871 2401
Fax: +1 (303) 871 2456
szhao@du.edu
www.du.edu

Contact: Suisheng Zhao, Executive Director

Budget: > $1,000,000

Number of staff: 6

Global

Collaborative for Development Action

ADVOCACY

Incorporated in 1985, the Collaborative for Development Action (CDA) consulting agency has worked in over seventy-five countries to support local economic and social development. Current projects include the Local Capacities for Peace Project (LCPP) and the Reflecting on Peace Practice Project (RPP). The LCPP seeks to identify ways in which assistance given in conflict settings may be provided so that it contributes to peace building. In the RPP, all kinds of agencies collaborate in gathering experiences from their recent conflict-focused programs and identify what works and what does not work. Both projects are based on field-based case studies of work in different areas of the world.

Collaborative for Development Action
130 Prospect Street
Suite 202
Cambridge MA 021 39
United States

Tel: +1 (617) 661 6310
Fax: +1 (617) 661 3805
cda@cdainc.com
www.cdainc.com

Contact: Dr. Wolfgang Heinrich,
Project Co-ordinator Local
Capacities for Peace Project
Number of staff: 6
*Publications: Do No Harm: How Aid
Can Support Peace—Or War,* 1999;
*Rising from the Ashes: Development
Strategies in Times of Disaster,* 1998

Global

Conflict Prevention and Peace Forum

RESEARCH
EDUCATION

The Conflict Prevention and Peace Forum (CPPF) was established in 2000 to strengthen the knowledge base and analytical capacity of UN system and local Indonesian organizations and academics. CPPF works to help the UN system have a better understanding of the areas of conflict in Indonesia, covering conflict prevention and management, peacemaking and peacebuilding. CPPF follows scholarly and other expert analysis on issues of concern to the UN; recommends experts on or from countries threatened by or experiencing conflict; hosts off-the-record consultations between outside experts and UN officials; conducts technical evaluations related to conflict prevention and peace-building; provides research materials for UN training needs; and otherwise supports peace efforts.

810 Seventh Avenue
31st Floor
New York, NY 10019
United States

Tel: +1 (212) 377 2700
Fax: +1 (212) 377 2727
cppf@ssrc.org
http://cppf.ssrc.org/

Contact: Elizabeth Cousens, Director
Number of staff: 4

China

Dui Hua Foundation

RESEARCH
ADVOCACY

Incorporated in 1999, the Dui Hua Foundation (meaning "dialogue" in Chinese) is a non-profit organization dedicated to improving human rights by means of dialogue between the United States and China. The founder was an early advocate of corporate responsibility and has intervened on behalf of many Chinese political detainees. The organization's researchers conduct extensive searches of Chinese publications to uncover information about cases of Chinese citizens allegedly detained for the non-violent expression of their political and religious rights. More than 1,400 cases have been uncovered in this way, the majority of which are unknown to the rest of the world. In addition, material on statistics, regulations and legal discussions on counterrevolution and related offenses have been discovered.

Based in San Francisco, Dui Hua maintains a political database with information on more than 7,000 individuals. It uses this information to develop prisoner lists used by governmental and non-governmental bodies in their human rights dialogues with China. Dui Hua is the only non-governmental human rights organization to which the Chinese government provides information on its political and religious detainees. At the invitation of the Chinese government, Dui Hua has visited several prisoners in the country.

A key part of Dui Hua's mission is outreach. The Executive Director speaks to a number of academic and educational institutions in the United States and abroad and gives testimony to committees and commissions of Congress.

The Dui Hua Foundation
450 Sutter Street, Suite 900
San Francisco, CA 94108
United States

Tel: +1 (415) 986 0536
Fax: +1 (415) 986 0579
duihua@duihua.org
www.duihua.org

Contact: John T. Kamm, Chairman and Executive Director

Number of staff: 7

Publications: Dialogue, quarterly newsletter; *Individuals Detained During the Spring 1989 Disturbances in Beijing,* 1999

East Timor

East-Timor Action Network

RESEARCH
ADVOCACY

The East-Timor Action Network (ETAN) was founded in 1991 after the Santa Cruz massacre to support human rights and self-determination in East Timor. This grass-roots human rights organization grew from individual pressure on the US government to change the US policy and to promote East Timor's genuine self-determination. The movement encompasses contacts in many cities. Once the US cut all military ties with Indonesia, ETAN's aim adapted to change US foreign policy and to raise public awareness surrounding the core issues. ETAN works closely with the people of East Timor to focus their support and to support those still receiving brutality from the Indonesian military.

ETAN/US National Office
PO Box 15774
Washington, DC 20003-0774
United States

Tel: +1 (202) 544 6911
Fax: +1 (202) 544 6118
karen@etan.org
www.etan.org

Contact: Karen Orenstein, Washington Representative

Publications: Indonesian Court's Final East Timor Sentence "A Joke," 2003; *Powell Urged to Raise Aceh War at ASEAN Meeting,* 2003; *People of Faith Call for International Tribunal for East Timor, Regardless of Indonesian Court Verdicts,* 2003

Burma

Free Burma Coalition

EDUCATION
ACTION
ADVOCACY

Founded by a group of Burmese and American graduate students at the University of Wisconsin at Madison in 1995, the Free Burma Coalition (FBC) is an Internet-based organization with grassroots member groups and affiliates in 28 countries. Through public education, policy advocacy, consumer boycotts, and divestment campaigns, FBC works to raise awareness about human rights violations in Burma.

Since its inception, FBC has grown to become one of the largest human rights campaigns via both Internet and traditional activism, as well as the world's largest network of Burmese freedom fighters in exile. It is internationally recognized as a pioneer in the effective use of the Internet for promoting awareness about political repression. It is a key network and an important forum for exchanging ideas and perspectives. It actively mobilizes global citizens and Burmese freedom fighters and aims to secure financial and intellectual resources.

Free Burma Coalition
1101 Pennsylvania Ave, SE #204
Washington, DC 20003
United States

Tel: +1 (202) 547 5985
Fax: +1 (202) 544 6118
info@freeburmacoalition.org
www.freeburmacoalition.org

Global

Harvard Program on Humanitarian Policy and Conflict Research

RESEARCH
EDUCATION

Harvard Program on Humanitarian Policy and Conflict Research was founded in August 2000. The Program is dedicated to a people-centered approach to the concept of security. Through policy research and development, training, and advisory services, the Program works to enhance the protection of civilians in conflict areas, to improve the strategic planning of international responses to armed conflicts and complex humanitarian emergencies, to encourage a multi-disciplinary dialogue on the sources of insecurity, and to formulate concrete, practical options to address those sources.

There have been five portals developed for intergovernmental organizations, CSO and grassroots people in Indonesia, Nepal, Central Asia, Economics and Conflict, and International Humanitarian Law. The Program focuses its works in several main areas in Asia—including Indonesia, Nepal, Central Asia, Sri Lanka and some work in the Middle East and Africa (DRC). The Program works together with UN (including EOSG, DPA, UNDP, OCHA), other international NGOs (e.g. Conflict Prevention and Peace Forum in New York and Amnesty International) and also with local NGOs (e.g. Center for Peace and Security Studies (CSPS) at Gadjah Mada University in Indonesia, and CPAU (Center for Peace and Unity) in Peshawar Pakistan).

Program on Humanitarian Policy
and Conflict Research
Harvard University
1033 Massachusetts Ave, 4th Floor
Cambridge, MA 02138
United States

Tel: +1 (617) 384 7407
Fax: +1 (617) 384 5908
hpcr@hsph.harvard.edu or
    cpihpcr@hsph.harvard.edu
www.hsph.harvard.edu/hpcr

Contact: Mr. Claude Bruderlein, Program Director

Budget: $100,000 to $500,000

Number of staff: 7 persons

Publications: Afghan Legal Reform: Challenges and Opportunities, 2003; *Report on the Feasibility of Creating an Annual Human Security Report,* 2002. *People's Security as a New Measure of Global Stability, International Review of the Red Cross,* June 2001; *The Role of Non-State Actors in Building Human Security: The Case of Armed Groups in Intra-State Wars,* 2000

Global
Human Rights Watch

RESEARCH
ACTION
ADVOCACY

Human Rights Watch (HRW) is the largest human rights organization based in the United States. Its researchers conduct fact-finding investigations into human rights abuses in all regions of the world. In Asia, HRW monitors closely the countries suffering from major conflict such as East Timor. HWR publishes dozens of books and reports every year, all of which can be found on its website and provides up-to-date reports of ongoing conflicts. Other recent actions in regard to Asia are the Landmine Monitor Report 2000 (covers also the Asia Pacific region), policy recommendations to governments, and current campaigns such as The Campaign to Ban Landmines and Stop the Use of Child Soldiers.

350 Fifth Avenue, 34th floor
New York, NY 10118 3299
United States

Tel: +1 (212) 290 4700
Fax: +1 (212) 736 1300
hrwnyc@hrw.org
www.hrw.org

Contact: Kenneth Roth, Executive Director

Number of staff: more than 150

Publications: Malaysia: End Intimidation of News Website, 2003; *Human Rights Watch World Report,* 2001; *Crisis of Impunity: The Role of Pakistan, Russia and Iran in Fueling the Civil War in Afghanistan,* 2001; *Indonesia: Violence and Political Impasse in Papua,* 2001; *Behind the Kashmir Conflict: Abuses by Indian Security Forces and Militant Groups Continue,* 1999

Tibet
International Campaign for Tibet

RESEARCH
EDUCATION
ACTION
ADVOCACY

A non-profit membership organization established in 1998, the International Campaign for Tibet's (ICT) mission it to promote human rights and self-determination for Tibetans and to protect their culture and environment. The ICT conducts fact-finding missions to Tibet, India and Nepal and networks with exiled Chinese democracy and overseas Chinese organizations while conducting research on Chinese rule of Tibet.

International Campaign for Tibet
1825 K Street NW, Suite 520
Washington, DC 20006
United States

Tel: +1 (202) 785 1515
Fax: +1 (202) 785 4343
info@savetibet.org
www.savetibet.org

Contact: John Ackerly, President

Publications: Tibet Press Watch, journal; *Tibetan Environmental and Development News,* newsletter; *Jampa: The Story of Racism in Tibet,* August 28, 2001; *The Right to Self-Determination—The Legal Cornerstone to Tibet's Future,* 2002.

Global

International Campaign to Ban Landmines

EDUCATION
ADVOCACY

The International Campaign to Ban Landmines (ICBL) is an advocacy coalition composed of more than 1300 member organizations working in over 80 countries to achieve full universalization and implementation of the 1997 Mine Ban Treaty. Its members include human rights, humanitarian, children's, peace, disability, mine action, development, arms control, religious, environmental and women's groups who work locally, nationally and internationally to end the global landmine crisis.

Launched in 1992, the ICBL and its then-coordinator Jody Williams were awarded the Nobel Peace Prize in 1997. This civil society effort helped to spur the global movement against landmines, which resulted in the 1997 Mine Ban Treaty. As of January 2004, 150 countries have signed and 141 had ratified the Treaty. Campaigners continue to work to ensure that all countries join the treaty and to ensure that all States Parties fully implement their treaty obligations, as well as supporting sustained and appropriate victim assistance and mine clearance programming.

110 Maryland Avenue NE
Suite 509, Box 6
Washington, DC 20002
United States

Tel: +1 (202) 547 2667
Fax: +1 (202) 547 2687
icbl@icbl.org
www.icbl.org

Publications: Landmine Monitor
Number of staff: 6

Aceh

International Forum for Aceh

EDUCATION
ADVOCACY

The International Forum for Aceh (IFA) is a non-governmental organization actively campaigning for peace and human rights in Aceh. The IFA has worked to inform the international community about human rights violations in Aceh, and helped to organize several seminars on Aceh involving NGOs and others. The organization has also been active in raising the issue of human rights violations at the UN Human Rights Commission in Geneva.

50-02 47th Street, 2nd Floor
Woodside
New York, NY 11377
United States

Tel: +1 (718) 937 0510
Fax: +1 (718) 786 2935
acehforum@aol.com
www.aceh.org/ifa/index.htm

Contact: Robert Jereski, Executive Director

Global

EDUCATION

International Medical Corps

Established in 1984 by volunteer doctors and nurses, International Medical Corps (IMC) is a private, voluntary non-profit organization dedicated to saving lives and relieve suffering through health care training and relief and development programs.

IMC places emphasis on training local medical personnel in order that they can rebuild their own health care systems. This is achieved through extensive hands-on training in the full range of health and managerial skills needed to restore self-reliance. Those that train with IMC go on to teach others in their communities.

1919 Santa
Monica Blvd., Suite 300
Santa Monica
CA 90404-1950
United States

Tel: +1 (310) 826 7800
Fax: +1 (310) 442 6622
imc@imcworldwide.org
www.imc-la.com

Contact: Burkhard Gnarig, Chief Executive Officer, International Save the Children Alliance

Global

EDUCATION
ADVOCACY

Mennonite Central Committee

MCC is a service, peace and service agency whose mission identifies those most in need. This organization maintains operations in 13 countries within East/Central/Southern Asia. To name a few examples, MCC has been working in Cambodia since the major emergency crisis of 1979; in North Korea since 1995 by supplying agricultural and emergency assistance; in Vietnam since 1954, when it responded by offering refugee services at the time of the north-south migration.

Although the projects may not directly involve conflict resolution, MCC holds true to the biblical teaching of non-violence and the integration of the principles of peacemaking in all its missions.

Mennonite Central Committee
International Peace Office
21 South 12th Street
PO Box 500
Akron PA 17501-0500
United States

Tel: +1 (717) 859-1151
Fax: +1 (717) 859-2171
mailbox@mcc.org
www.mcc.org

Contact: Larry Guengerich, Media contact
Number of staff: Volunteers only
Budget: < $25,000

Asia

Nautilus Institute for Security and Sustainable Development

EDUCATION

Launched in 1993, the Nautilus Institute is a transnational, nongovernmental network of non-proliferation specialists, regional security experts and non-governmental organizations from Northeast Asia and North America. An international group of eminent persons from China, Europe, Japan, North Korea, South Korea and the U.S. advise the network. The Institute also provides daily news summaries of peace and security issues in the region to its e-mail participants, commissions papers from scholars around the world and distributes the papers electronically.

The Nautilus Institute
746 Ensenada Avenue
Berkeley CA 94707
United States

Contact: Brandon Yu, Program Officer

Tel: +1 (510) 526 9296
Fax: +1 (510) 526 9297
npr@igc.apc.org
www.nautilus.org/napsnet/index.html

Asia, Central and Eastern Europe, Balkans, CIS countries

ACTION

Open Society Institute

The Open Society Institute (OSI) is a private operating and grant-making foundation that promotes the development and maintenance of open societies around the world. OSI does this by supporting an array of activities dealing with building free and open societies through educational, social, legal and health-care reform and by encouraging alternative approaches to complex and controversial issues. The Constitutional and Legal Policy Institute program supports legal reform, basic rights and democratic institutions in Central Asia, Mongolia and Central and Eastern Europe. The Burma Project/Southeast Asia Initiative focuses on open society throughout the region, but works mainly with Burma and Indonesia. Organizations based within other Southeast Asian countries have received grants to aid their projects.

400 West 59th Street
New York, NY 10019
United States

Contact: Ms. Maureen Aung-Thwin,
Director of the Burma Project/Southeast
Asia Initiative

Tel: +1 (212) 584 0632
Fax: +1 (212) 548 4655
maungthwin@sorosny.org
www.soros.org/osi

Publications: A Prayer for Burma: A Burmese Expatriate Reflects on His Homeland, 2003; *From the Land of Green Ghosts: A Burmese Odyssey,* 2002

Asia Pacific

School of Hawaiian, Asian and Pacific Studies

The School of Hawaiian, Asian and Pacific Studies (SHAPS) represents the ongoing commitment of the University of Hawai'i to enhance international awareness and intercultural understanding throughout the educational experience. In fulfilling this commitment, SHAPS has become a large resource facility for Asian and Pacific studies.

Established in 1987, SHAPS offers academic programs in Asian Studies, Hawaiian Studies, and Pacific Islands Studies. SHAPS also has centres for Chinese Studies, Hawaiian Studies, Japanese Studies, Korean Studies, Pacific Islands Studies, Philippines Studies, South Asian Studies, and Southeast Asian Studies. Through these centres and programs, SHAPS helps to coordinate the efforts of some 300-faculty specialists throughout the university who offer more than 600 courses related to Hawai'i, Asia, and the Pacific.

School of Hawaiian, Asian
    and Pacific Studies
University of Hawaii at Manoa
Moore Hall 315
1890 East-West Road
Honolulu, HI 96822
United States

Tel: + (808) 956 8922
Fax: + (808) 956 6345
edgara@hawaii.edu
www.hawaii.edu/shaps/

Contact: Edgar A. Porter, Interim Dean

Global

Search for Common Ground

Search for Common Ground, in partnership with the European Center for Common Ground, is an international non-profit peace and conflict resolution organization. Its goal is to transform conflict into cooperative action. Search for Common Ground believes in long-term commitment in conflict areas in which they work. Search for Common Ground is convinced that traditional adversarial approaches are increasingly irrelevant in dealing with today's conflicts. The organization encourages a new level of thinking based on a non-adversarial framework.

Over the years, the organization has developed a toolbox that includes twenty-four different tools for conflict resolution and prevention. These include such traditional methods and approaches as training, capacity building and convening adversaries for dialogue, as well as less standard methods such as TV and radio productions, investigative reporting, sports, culture and music.

1601 Connecticut Ave. N.W.
Suite 200
Washington, DC 20009
United States
_____
Tel: +1 (202) 265 4300
Fax: +1 (202) 232 6718
search@sfcg.org
www.sfcg.org

Contact: Susan Collin Marks, Executive Vice-President

Number of staff: 360

Publications: Common Ground Newsletter

Global

Southeast Asia
Quaker International Affairs

Established in1968 by the American Friends Service Committee to enable the leaders of the emerging nations to meet and discuss issues of common concern with their counterparts from other countries. Later the representatives from this program were able to bring together grass-root groups with planners and administrators. Currently this program is exploring the tensions in Southeast Asia and seeking ways to promote peaceful resolutions of conflicts, internally and externally, particularly in Indonesia.

AFSC National Office
1501 Cherry Street
Philadelphia, PA 19102
United States
_____
Tel: +1 (215) 241 7000
Fax: +1 (215) 241 7275
afscinfo@afsc.org
www.afsc.org

Contact: Paul Lacey, Presiding Clerk

Budget: > $1,000,000

Publications: Getting a Word in Edgewise: Conscientious Objectors Gain Momentum in South Korea, 2003; *Scenes of Healing and Reconstruction: Afghanistan Summer Progress Report,* 2003

Global

United Nations Development Programme

EDUCATION
ACTION
ADVOCACY

Over the past several years the United Nations Development Program (UNDP) has come to place greater emphasis on conflict prevention. The Emergency Response Division sees poor governance as a major factor in the development of man-made crises, so it works on capacity building for good governance nationally and internationally by means of preventive development and training. Among other things, the Program provides electoral assistance, support for judiciaries, and public-sector management.

UNDP's core goal of supporting sustainable human development is in itself a strong foundation for the prevention of conflict in the long term. UNDP's mission in the Asia and Pacific is to empower people and organizations to achieve Sustainable Human Development in the region. In Indonesia UNDP has a Crisis Prevention and Recovery Program; in the Philippines a Peace and Development Program; in Cambodia UNDP focuses on judicial and legal reform, public finance reform, administrative reform, and anti-corruption within the Cambodian Government. In East Timor UNDP supports, among others, the reconciliation process and the strengthening of a parliamentary democracy.

Regional Bureau for Asia and the Pacific
304 E. 45th Street
New York, NY 10017
U.S.A.

Tel: +1 (212) 906 5324
Fax: +1 (212) 906 5364
aboutundp@undp.org
www.undp.org

Contact: Robert Piper, Deputy Director Emergency Response Division

Publications: Transition 1999: Regional Human Development Report for Central and Eastern Europe and the CIS, 1999; Central Asia 2010: Prospects for Human Development, 1999; The New Yalta: Commemorating the 50th Anniversary of the Declaration of Human Rights in the RBEC Region, 1999; Poverty in Transition? 1998.

Global

United Nations
Development Fund for Women

| RESEARCH |
| EDUCATION |
| ACTION |
| ADVOCACY |

UNIFEM works for women's empowerment and gender equality. UNIFEM has an established program in Asia, which focuses on implementing the Beijing Platform for Action and other UN global commitments through political and economic empowerment of women and through the full realization of women's human rights. Women remain under-represented in parliaments, corporate boardrooms, peace negotiations and the many other venues in which decisions are made. UNIFEM programs promote women's leadership in all sectors. UNIFEM's Peace and Security Program aims to strengthen the gender focus in prevention and early warning mechanisms, improving protection and assistance for women affected by conflict; by making women's and gender perspectives central to peace processes and supporting gender justice in post-conflict peacebuilding. In 1997, UNIFEM Pacific became the newest Regional Office.

304 E. 45th Street
15th Floor
New York, NY 10017
U.S.A.

Tel: +1 (212) 906 6400
Fax: +1 (212) 906 6705

Pacific Regional Office
c/o UNDP
Private Mail Bag
Suva, Fiji

Tel: +679 (3) 301 178
Fax: +679 (3) 301 654
amelia@unifempacific.com
www.unifem.org
www.unifem-eseasia.org

East and Southeast Asia Regional Office
UN Building 5th Floor
Rajdamnern Avenue
Bangkok 10200, Thailand

Tel: +662 (2) 882 093
Fax: +622 (2) 806 030
unifem-bkk@mozart.inet.co.th

Contact: Amelia Kinahoi Siamomua,
Regional Program Director (Pacific)
Lucita S. Lazo, Regional Program
Director (SE Asia)

Global

United States Institute of Peace

RESEARCH
EDUCATION
ACTION

The United States Institute of Peace (USIP) is a federal institution created and funded by the Congress to strengthen the nation's capacity to promote the peaceful resolution of international conflict. Established in 1984, the Institute meets its congressional mandate through an array of programs, including grants, conferences and educational activities. USIP seeks to support policy makers by providing independent and creative assessments of how to deal with international conflict situations by political means. In Asia, the Research and Studies Program conducts frequent working group meetings directed towards building confidence on the Korean Peninsula.

USIP's activities are based on six interconnected methods of curbing international conflict: Expanding society's knowledge; support for policy-makers; dispute resolution; training professionals; strengthening education; and increasing public understanding. The Institute works with leading thinkers from government, academia and NGOs to carry out independent research and policy assessments available to all.

1200 17th Street NW
Suite 200
Washington, DC 20036-3011
United States

Tel: +1 (202) 429 3828
Fax: +1 (202) 429 6063
usip_requests@usip.org
www.usip.org

Number of staff: 16

Publications: Peace Watch Newsletter; Guide to IGO's, NGO's and the Military in Peace and Relief Operations, 2001; US Leadership of the Cambodia Settlement and Normalization with Vietnam, 2000

Pacific

Foundation of the Peoples
of the South Pacific International

EDUCATION
ACTION

The Foundation of the Peoples of the South Pacific International (FSPI) is a network of eleven NGOs of different Pacific countries. The members of the FSPI include FSP Fiji, Foundation for People and Community Development in Papua New Guinea, FSP Kiribati, O le Siosiomaga Society in Samoa, the Solomon Islands Development Trust, Tonga Trust, Tuvalu Association of Non-Government Organizations and FSP Vanuatu.

The Foundation's Conflict Management for Community Based Resource Development Program targets conflicts of interest that may hamper the achievement of sustainable rural livelihoods and the reduction of poverty. These conflicts range from local disputes between community groups over the access to natural resources to negotiation between local producers, distributors and government regulators. FSPI has been working with communities in Papua New Guinea and Fiji to strengthen its capacity to resolve conflicts over resources or mitigate potential conflict through improved project planning and customary approaches.

FSPI Regional Office
PO Box 951
Port Vila
Vanuatu

Tel: +678 (2) 2915
Fax: +678 (2) 4510
ici@fsp.org.vu
www.fsp.org.vu

Contact: Rex Horoi, Executive Director
Budget: $25,000–$100,000
Number of staff: 14

Vietnam

RESEARCH
EDUCATION

The Institute for International Relations

The Institute for International Relations (IIR) was established in 1959 as an affiliation and think-tank of the Ministry of Foreign Affairs of Vietnam. It has research, training and networking functions, which are aimed at assisting Vietnamese foreign policy makers and practitioners to develop comprehensive approaches to strategic thinking in foreign affairs, in order to cater for diplomats and others with an interest in international relations.

IIR is the centre for strategic studies in Vietnam and an active participant in global and regional networks linking scholars, analysts and institutions in the field, including the network of ASEAN Institutes of International and Strategic Studies (ASEAN-ISIS) and the Council for Security Cooperation in the Asia-Pacific Region (CSCAP). It also has close connections with strategic and international studies institutions in many countries in Asia, Asia-Pacific, Europe, and America as well as foundations interested in the field such as the Asia Foundation, the Ford Foundation, the UNDP, the Japan Foundation, SIDA, and CIDA.

The faculty and research staff of IIR are actively involved in the study of issues related to security and stability in the world and the Asia-Pacific and their implications for Vietnam, of which peace and conflict study is a major area. They have participated in many international and exchange programmes and authored a great number of publications in peace and conflict studies. IIR is also active in organizing national, regional and international conferences and workshops on peace and development. It is currently the national coordinator of the Southeast Asian Conflict Studies Network in Vietnam.

MOFA Vietnam
69 Chua Lang
Dong Da, Hanoi
Vietnam

Contact: Mr. Pham Cao Phong,
Coordinator International Peace
and Security Studies

Tel: +84 (4) 834 3542
Fax: +84 (4) 834 3543
E-mail: iirmofa@hn.vnn.vn or seacsn-vn@hn.vnn.vn

Selected Bibliography

Abuza, Zachary, *Militant Islam in Southeast Asia: Crucible of Terror*, Boulder, CO: Lynne Rienner Publishers, 2003.

Adams, Rebecca (ed.), *Peace on Bougainville—Truce Monitoring Group—Gudpela Nius Bilong Peace*, Wellington: Center for Strategic Studies New Zealand/Victoria University Press, 2002.

Ahai, Naihuwo, *Bougainville: Rebuilding Trust and Rebuilding People*, Discussion Paper No. 9, Armidale, Australia: Center for Peace Studies, University of New England, 1996.

Akram-Lodhi, A Haroon (ed.), *Confronting Fiji Futures*, Canberra: Asia Pacific Press, 2000.

Alagappa, Muthiah, *Asian Security Order: Instrumental and Normative Features*, Stanford CA: Stanford University Press, 2003.

Amer, Ramses, *Conflict Situations and Conflict Management in the South China Sea*, UPSK Occasional Paper No. 5/00, Malaysia: Universiti Kebangsaan Malaysia Strategic and Security Studies Unit, 2000.

Amnesty International, *Shock Therapy: Restoring Order in Aceh 1989–1993*, London: Amnesty International, 1993.

———, *Papua New Guinea, Bougainville: The Forgotten Human Rights Tragedy*, London: Amnesty International, 1997.

———, *People's Republic of China: Gross Violations of Human Rights in the Xinjiang Uighur Autonomous Region*, London: Amnesty International, 1999.

———, *East Timor: Forced Recruitment and Arrests in Relocation Camps*, London: Amnesty International, 1999.

———, *Myanma: Justice on Trial*, London: Amnesty International, 2003.

———, *Philippines: Torture Persists—Appearance and Reality Within the Criminal Justice System*, London: Amnesty International, 2003.

Anderson, Benedict, *Imagined Communities: Reflections on the Origin and Spread of Nationalism*, London: Verso, 1983.

Anderson, B. (ed.), *Violence and the State in Soeharto's Indonesia*, New York: Cornell Southeast Asia Program Publications, 2001.

Anthony, Mely C., and Mohamed Jawhar Hassan (eds.), *Beyond the Crisis: Challenges and Opportunities Vol. II.*, Kuala Lumpur: ISIS Malaysia, 2000

Asia Foundation, *Governance Reform and Lessons from the Economic Crisis in Asia*, San Fransisco: Asia Foundation, 1999.

Aspinall, Edward, and Greg Fealy (eds.), *Local Power and Politics in Indonesia: Decentralization and Democratization*, Indonesia Update Series, Singapore: Institute of Southeast Asian Studies, 2003.

Austin, Greg, *China's Ocean Frontier: International Law, Military Force and National Development,* St. Leonards: Allen & Unwin, 1998.

Babbage, Ross, *Recovering from Terror Attacks: A Proposal for Regional Cooperation,* ASPI Occasional Paper 01, Canberra: Australian Strategic Policy Institute, 2002.

Bacevich, Andrew, *American Empire,* Cambridge, MA: Harvard University Press, 2002.

Ball, Desmond, *Building Blocks for Regional Security: An Australian Perspective on Confidence and Security Building Measures (CSBMs) in the Asia/Pacific Region,* Canberra Papers on Strategy and Defense No. 83, Canberra: Strategic and Defense Studies Center, Australian National University, 1991.

——— (ed.), *The Transformation of Security in the Asia/Pacific Region,* London: Frank Cass, 1996.

———, *Implications of the East Asian Economic Recession for Regional Security Cooperation,* Working Paper No. 331, Canberra: Strategic and Defense Studies Center, Australian National University, January 1999.

———, *The Council for Security Cooperation in the Asia Pacific (CSCAP): Its Record and its Prospects,* Canberra Papers on Strategy and Defense No. 139, Canberra: Strategic and Defense Studies Center, Australian National University, October 2000.

Ball, Desmond, and Amitav Acharya (eds.), *The Next Stage: Preventive Diplomacy and Security Cooperation in the Asia-Pacific Region,* Canberra Papers on Strategy and Defense No.131, Canberra: Strategic and Defense Studies Center, Australian National University, 1999.

Ball, Desmond, and Barry Desker, CSCAP Co-chairs, *The ARF Into the 21st Century,* Kuala Lumpur: CSCAP, May 2002.

Ball, Desmond, and Pauline Kerr, *Presumptive Engagement: Australia's Asia-Pacific Security Policy in the 1990s,* Sydney: Allen & Unwin, 1996.

Banister, Judith, *China's Changing Population,* Stanford, CA: Stanford University Press, 1987.

Barnett, Robert, and Shirin Akiner (eds.), *Resistance and Reform in Tibet,* Bloomington, IN: Hursts/University of Indiana, 1994.

Bateman, Sam (ed.), *Maritime Cooperation in the Asia-Pacific Region: Current Situation and Prospects,* Canberra Papers on Strategy and Defense No.132, Canberra: Strategic and Defense Studies Center, Australian National University, 1999.

Bateman, Sam, and Stephen Bates (eds.), *Calming the Waters: Initiatives for Asia Pacific Maritime Cooperation,* Canberra Papers on Strategy and Defence No.114, Canberra: Strategic and Defense Studies Center, Australian National University, 1996.

BCN and TNI, *Strengthening Civil Society in Burma: Possibilities and Dilemmas for International NGOs,* Chiangmai: Silkworm Books, 1999.

Bello, Walden, *Deglobalization,* London, Zed Books, 2002.

Bello, Walden, and Stephanie Rosenfeld, *Dragons in Distress: Asia's Miracle Economies in Crisis,* San Francisco: Food First, 1990.

Benson, Linda, *The Ili Rebellion: The Moslem Challenge to Chinese Authority in Xinjiang, 1944–1949,* New York: M.E. Sharpe, 1990.

Berghof Research Center for Constructive Conflict Management, *Berghof Handbook for Conflict Transformation,* Berlin: Berghof Research Center for Constructive Conflict Management, 2001.

Bernstein, Richard, and Ross H. Munro, *The Coming Conflict with China,* New York: Alfred A. Knopf, 1997.

Bhattarai, Teeka (et al.), *Forests and Indigenous Peoples of Asia,* London: Minority Rights Group International, 1999.

Böge, Volker, *Conflict Potential and Violent Conflicts in the South Pacific: Options for a Civil Peace Service,* Armament and Development Working Paper No 1, Hamburg: Research Unit of Wars, 2001.

Booth, Ken, and Tim Dunne (eds), *Worlds in Collision: Terror and the Future of Global Order,* London: Palgrave Macmillan, 2002.

Boutros-Ghali, Boutros, *An Agenda for Democratization,* New York: United Nations, December 1996.

Breen, Col. Bob, *Mission Accomplished—East Timor ADF Participation in INTERFET,* St. Leonards: Allen & Unwin, 2000.

———, *Giving Peace a Chance—Operation Lagoon, Bougainville 1994: A Case Study of Military Action and Diplomacy,* Canberra Papers on Strategy and Defence No. 142, Canberra: SDCS, 2001.

Brenner, Robert, *The Boom and the Bubble,* New York: Verso, 2002.

Brown C., (ed.), *Lost Liberties: Ashcroft and the Assault on Personal Freedom,* New York: The New Press, 2003.

Brown Journal of World Affairs, Brown University, Providence, RI.

Brown, Michael (ed.), *Ethnic Conflict and International Security,* Princeton, NJ: Princeton University Press, 1993.

Buckley, Mary, and Rick Fawn (eds.), *Global Responses to Terrorism: 9/11, Afghanistan and Beyond,* London: Routledge, 2003.

Cagoco-Guiam, Ruva, *Child Soldiers in Central and Western Mindanao: A Rapid Assessment,* Geneva: International Labour Office, 2002.

Cambodia Development Review, Cambodia Development Resource Institute, Cambodia.

Cambridge History of the Pacific Islanders, Cambridge: Cambridge University Press, 1995.

Capie, David, *Small Arms Production and Transfers in Southeast Asia,* Canberra Paper No. 146, Canberra: Strategic and Defense Studies Center, Australian National University, 2002.

Capie, David, and Paul Evans, *The Asia-Pacific Security Lexicon,* Singapore: Institute of Southeast Asian Studies, 2002.

Carey, Peter (ed.), *Burma: the Challenge of Change in a Divided Society,* Basingstoke, UK: Macmillan, 1997.

Carey, Peter, and G. Carter Bentley (eds.), *East Timor at the Crossroads: The Forging of a Nation,* Honolulu: University of Hawaii Press, 1995.

Carl, Andy, and Sister Lorraine Garasu (eds.), "Weaving Consensus: The Papua New Guinea—Bougainville Peace Process," *Accord,* Issue 12, London: Conciliation Resources, 2002.

Carnegie Endowment for International Peace, "Korean Security: The Highest Hurdle," *Proliferation Brief,* Vol.3, No. 30, October 20, 2000.

Casambre, Rey (ed.), *Ten Years, Ten Agreements,* Quezon City: NCCP/Phillipine Peace Center, 2002.

Central Asian Survey, Carfax Publishing, Taylor and Francis Group, London.

Center for Humanitarian Dialogue, *Curbing the Demand for Small Arms: Focus on Southeast Asia,* Geneva: Center for Humanitarian Dialogue, 2003.

Chan, Anita, *China's Workers under Assault—the Exploitation of Labor in a Globalizing Economy,* Armonk, NY: M. E. Sharpe, 2001.

Chang, Gordon G., *The Coming Collapse of China,* London: Century, 2001.

Chen, Jack, *The Sinkiang Story,* New York: Macmillan, 1977.

Chi, Su and Cheng An-kuo (ed.), *A Historical Account of the Consensus of 1992,* Taipei: National Policy Foundation, 2002.

China Quarterly, Cambridge University Press, School of Oriental and African Studies, United Kingdom.

Christensen, Thomas J., "PRC Security Relations with the United States: Why Things are Going so Well," *China Leadership Monitor,* No. 8, August 2003.

Chomthongdi, Jacques-chai, "The IMF's Asian Legacy," in *Prague 2000: Why We Need to Decommission the IMF and the World Bank,* Bangkok: Focus on the Global South, 2000.

Clements, Kevin, *Civil Society and Conflict Prevention*, Bonn: Center for Development Research, 2000.

Collier, Paul, and Anke Hoeffler, "On the Economic Causes of Civil Wars" *Oxford Economic Papers*, Vol. 50, No. 4, 1998.

Contemporary Southeast Asia, Institute of Southeast Asian Studies, Singapore.

Coronel-Ferrer, Miriam (ed.), *The SPCPD: A Response to the Controversy*, Quezon City: UP Center for Integrative and Development Studies, 1997.

Coward, Harold, and Gordon Smith, *Religion and Peacebuilding*, Albany, NY: SUNY Press, 2003.

Crocker, Chester A. (ed.), *Herding Cats: Multiparty Mediation In a Complex World*, Washington DC: United States Institute of Peace Press, 2000.

Dañguilan Vitug, M., and G. M. Gloria, *Under the Crescent Moon: Rebellion in Mindanao*, Quezon City: Ateneo Center for Social Policy and Public Affairs and Institute for Popular Democracy, 2000.

Deal, David, *National Minority Policy in Southwest China, 1911–1965*, Ph.D. dissertation, University of Washington, 1971.

De Dekker, Paul, and Jean-Yves Faberon: *Custom and the Law*, Canberra: Asia Pacific Press, 2001.

Denoon, Donald, *Getting under the Skin*, Melbourne: Melbourne University Press, 2000.

Dent, Christopher M., (ed.), *Economic and Security Cooperation in the Asia-Pacific Region*, Basingstoke, UK: Palgrave Macmillan, 2004.

Diaz, Patricia P., *Understanding Mindanao Conflict*, Philippines: MindaNews Publications, 2003.

DiFilippo, Anthony, *The Challenges of the U.S.-Japan Military Arrangement: Competing Security Transitions in a Changing International Environment*, New York: M.E. Sharpe, 2002.

Dickens, David (ed.), *The Human Face of Security: Asia-Pacific Perspectives*, Canberra Papers on Strategy and Defense No. 144, Canberra: Strategic and Defense Studies Center, Australian National University, 2002.

Dinnen, Sinclair, Anthony Regan, and Ron May (eds.), *Challenging the State—the Sandline Affair in PNG*, NCDS Pacific Policy Paper No. 30, Canberra: Australian National University, 1998.

Dinnen, Sinclair, *Law and Order in a Weak State—Crime and Politics in Papua New Guinea*, Adelaide: Crawford House, 2001.

Dinnen, Sinclair, and Allison Ley (eds.): *Reflections on Violence in Melanesia*, Leichhardt, NSW: Federation Press, 2000.

Dosch, Jorn, and Manfred Mols (eds.), *International Relations in the Asia-Pacific: New Patterns of Power, Interest, and Cooperation*, New York: St. Martin's Press, 2000.

Doughty, K., D. Snell, and S. Prasad, *Constraints and Contributors to Violent Conflict in Fiji*, Cambridge: The Collaborative for Development Action, 2003.

Drifte, Reinhard, *Japan's Security Relations with China since 1989: From Balancing to Bandwagoning?* London: Routledge/Curzon, 2003.

Dunn, James, *Timor a People Betrayed*, Milton, Queensland: Jaracanda Press, 1983.

Dupont, Alan, *East Asia Imperilled: Transnational Challenges to Security*, Cambridge: Cambridge University Press, 2001.

Edström, Bert, (ed), *Interdependence in the Asia Pacific*, Stockholm: Swedish Institute for International Affairs and Center for Pacific Asia Studies, 2001.

Eichengreen, Barry, and Donald Mathieson, *Hedge Fund and Financial Markets*, Occasional Paper 166, Washington, DC: International Monetary Fund, 1998.

Eide, A., et al., *The Universal Declaration of Human Rights: A Commentary*, Oslo: Scandinavian University Press, 1992.

Emberson-Bain, A., (ed.), *Sustainable Development or Malignant Growth? Perspectives of Pacific Island Women*, Suva: Marama Publications, 1994.

Esposito, J. L., *Islam: The Straight Path*, New York: Oxford University Press, 1998.

Esposito J.L., and J.O. Voll , *Islam and Democracy,* New York: Oxford University Press, 1996.

Far Eastern Economic Review, Hong Kong: Dow Jones & Company.

Fiji Human Rights Commission, *The Fiji Human Rights Commission Strategic Plan 2001–2003,* Suva: Fiji Human Rights Commission, 2001.

Fink, Christina, *Living Silence: Burma Under Military Rule,* London: Zed Books, 2001.

Fitzgerald, Frances, *Fire in the Lake,* New York: Random House, 1973.

Forbes, Andrew, *Warlords and Muslims in Chinese Central Asia,* Cambridge: Cambridge University Press, 1986.

Foreign Affairs, Council of Foreign Relations, New York.

Foreign Policy, Carnegie Endowment for International Peace, Washington, DC.

Fox, James J., and Dionisio Babo Soares (eds), *Out of the Ashes: Destruction and Reconstruction of East Timor,* Adelaide: Crawford House, 1990.

Franke, Herbert, and Denis Twitchett, *Cambridge History of China: Volume 6: Alien Regimes and Border States (907–1368),* Cambridge: Cambridge University Press, 1994.

Funabashi, Yoichi, Michel Oksenberg, and Heinrich Weiss, *An Emerging China in a World of Interdependence,* New York: The Trilateral Commission, 1994.

Gaerlan K., and M. Stankovitch (eds.), *Rebels, Warlords and Ulama: A reader on Muslim Separatism and the War in Southern Mindanao,* Quezon City: Institute for Popular Democracy, 2000.

Garcia, Ed, *Participative Approaches to Peacemaking in the Philippines,* Tokyo: United Nations University, 1993.

———, (ed.), *Pilgrim Voices: Citizens as Peacemakers,* Quezon City: International Alert/Gaston Z. Ortigas Peace Institute and Ateneo Center for Social Policy and Public Affairs, 1994.

George, T.J.S., *Revolt in Mindanao: The Rise of the Islam in Philippine Politics,* Oxford: Oxford University Press, 1980.

Gladney, Dru C., (ed.), *Muslim Chinese: Ethnic Nationalism in the People's Republic of China,* Cambridge, MA: Harvard University Press, 1996.

———, *Ethnic Identity in China,* Fort Worth, TX: Harcourt Brace, 1998.

———, *Making Majorities: Constituting the Nation in Japan, Korea, China, Malaysia, Fiji, Turkey, and the United States,* Stanford, CA: Stanford University Press, 1998.

Global Witness, *The Logs of War: The Timber Trade and Armed Conflict,* London: Global Witness, 2003.

Goodman, David S.G., and Gerald Segal (eds.), *China Rising: Nationalism and Interdependence,* London: Routledge, 1997.

Gordon, B.K., *The Dimensions of Conflict in Southeast Asia,* Englewood Cliffs, NJ: Prentice-Hall, Inc., 1966.

Green, Stephen, *Reforming China's Economy: A Rough Guide,* London: Royal Institute of International Affairs, 2003.

Griffen, Arlene, (ed), *Creating a Culture of Peace: A Training Manual for Pacific Peace Builders,* Suva: ECREA, 2002.

Haller-Trost, R., *The Spratly Islands: A Study on the Limitations of International Law,* Occasional paper No. 14, Canterbury: University of Kent, 1990.

Hara, Kimi, "Cold War Wedges of China?: The San Francisco System and the Cold War Frontiers in the Asia-Pacific—China's Territorial Problems as a Case Study," *East-West Center Politics and Security Working Paper Series No. 2.* Honolulu: East-West Center, September 2000.

Harding, Harry, (ed.), *China's Foreign Relations in the 1980s,* New Haven, CT: Yale University Press, 1982.

Harris, Geoff, Naihuwo Ahai and Rebecca Spence, *Building Peace in Bougainville,* Armidale: Waigani, 1999.

Harris, G., (ed.), *Recovery from Armed Conflict in Developing Countries: An Economic and Political Analysis,* London: Routledge, 1999.

Harris, Peter, and Ben Reilly (eds), *Democracy and Deep-Rooted Conflict: Options for Negotiators,* Stockholm: International Institute for Democracy and Electoral Assistance, 1998.

Harris, Stuart, and Andrew Mack (eds.), *Asia-Pacific Security: The Economics-Politics Nexus,* Sydney: Allen & Unwin, 1997.

Harrison, Selig S., *Korean Endgame: A Strategy for Reunification and US Disengagement,* Princeton, NJ: Princeton University Press, 2002.

Harvard Asia Pacific Review, Cambridge, MA.

Heberer, Thomas, *China and Its National Minorities: Autonomy or Assimilation?* Armonk, NY: M. E. Sharpe, 1989.

Heijmans, A., N. Simmonds, and L. Trijono, *Lessons Learned from Peacebuilding Efforts in Southeast Asia and the Pacific,* workshop proceedings, European Center for Conflict Prevention (ECCP), and the Center for Security and Peace Studies, Yogyakarta, 2003.

Henderson, Callum, *China on the Brink,* New York: McGraw-Hill, 1999.

Hermes, Niels, *New Explanations of the Economic Success of East Asia: Lessons for Developing and Eastern European Countries,* Groningen: University of Groningen, Center for Development Studies, 1997.

Hirschman, Albert O., *Exit Voice and Loyalty: Responses to Decline in Firms, Organizations, and States,* Cambridge MA: Harvard University Press, 1972.

History and Anthropology, London: University of Durham/Routledge.

Hocking, J., *Terror Laws: ASIO, Counter-Terrorism and the Threat to Democracy,* Sydney: University of New South Wales Press, 2003.

Howley, Pat, *Breaking Spears and Mending Hearts—Peacemakers and Restorative Justice in Bougainville,* Leichhardt, NSW: Federation Press, 2002.

Huffer, Elise, and Asofou So'o (eds): *Governance in Samoa: Pulega i Samoa,* Canberra: Asia Pacific Press, 2001.

Human Rights Watch, *Western Hypocrisy and Chinese Diplomacy,* New York: Human Rights Watch, 1999.

———, "Indonesia: The War in Aceh," Vol. 13, No. 4 (C), August 2001.

———, *Crackdown on Burmese Muslims,* New York, July 2002.

———, "Indonesia: Aceh Under Martial Law: Inside the Secret War," December 2003, Vol. 15, No. 10 (C).

Huntington, Samuel P., *The Clash of Civilizations and the Remaking of World Order,* New York: Simon and Schuster, 1996.

Huxley, Tim, *Defending the Lion City: The Armed Forces of Singapore,* London: Allen & Unwin, 2001.

International Affairs, Columbia University, New York.

International Commission on Intervention and State Sovereignty, *The Responsibility to Protect,* Ottawa: International Development Research Centre, 2001.

International Crisis Group (ICG), "Indonesia: Keeping the Military Under Control," *ICG Asia Report No. 9,* Jakarta/Brussels, 5 September 2000.

———, "Indonesia: Overcoming Murder and Chaos in Maluku," *ICG Asia Report No. 10,* Jakarta/Brussels, 19 December 2000.

———, "Indonesia: Impunity versus Accountability for Gross Human Rights Violations," *ICG Asia Report No. 12,* Jakarta/Brussels, 2 February 2001

———, "Aceh: Why Military Force Won't Bring Lasting Peace," *ICG Asia Report No. 17,* Jakarta/Brussels, 12 June 2001.

———, "Communal Violence in Indonesia: Lessons from Kalimantan," *ICG Asia Report No. 19,* Jakarta/Brussels, 27 June 2001.

———, "Myanmar: The Role of Civil Society," *ICG Asia Report No. 27,* Bangkok/Brussels, 6 December 2001.

_____, "Indonesia: The Search for Peace in Maluku," *ICG Asia Report No. 31,* Jakarta/Brussels, 8 February 2002.

_____, "Myanmar: The Politics of Humanitarian Aid," *ICG Asia Report No. 32,* Bangkok/Brussels, 2 April 2002.

_____, "Indonesia Backgrounder: How the Jemaah Islamiyah Terrorist Network Operates," *ICG Asia Report No. 43,* 11 December 2002.

_____, "Myanmar Backgrounder: Ethnic Minority Politics," *ICG Asia Report No. 52,,* Bangkok/Brussels, 7 May 2003.

_____, "Jemaah Islamiyah in Southeast Asia: Damaged But Still Dangerous," *ICG Asia Report No. 63,* 26 August 2003.

International Security, MIT Press, Cambridge, MA.

Jane's Intelligence Review, Coulsdon, UK, Jane's Information Group,

Japan Center for Conflict Prevention (JCCP), The Japan Institute of International Affairs (JIIA), *Directory of Organizations for Conflict Prevention in Asia and the Pacific 2003,* Tokyo: JCCP/JIIA, 2003.

Japanese Journal of Political Science, Cambridge University Press, New York.

Japan Forum on International Relations (JFIR) Policy Council, *Economic Globalization and Options for Asia: The 19th Policy Recommendations of the Policy Council,* Tokyo: JFIR, 2000.

Johnston, Alistair Iain, and Robert S. Ross, eds, *Engaging China: The Management of an Emerging Power,* London: Routledge, 1999.

Journal of Contemporary China, Carfax Publishing, University of Denver, Denver, CO.

Journal of Pacific History, Carfax Publishing, Australian National University, Canberra, Australia.

Journal of Peace Research, Peace Research Institute, Oslo, Norway.

Journal of Strategic Studies, Frank Cass Publishers, London, United Kingdom.

Kartha, Tara, Siddiqua Agha, Ayesha, *Curbing the Weapons of Civilian Destruction in South Asia,* Mumbai: International Centre for Peace Initiatives, 1999

Kasarinlan: Philippine Journal of Third World Studies, Third World Studies Center, University of the Philippines, Quezon City, Philippines

Kepel, G., *Jihad: The Trial of Political Islam,* London: I.B. Taurus 2002

Khan, Azizur Rahman, and Carl Riskin, *Inequality and Poverty in China in the Age of Globalization,* New York: Oxford University Press, 2001

Khan, C., and K. Barr, *Christianity, Poverty and Wealth at the Start of the Twenty-First Century,* Suva: ECREA, 2003

Kihl, Young Whan, and Peter Hayes (eds), *Peace and Security in Northeast Asia: The Nuclear Issue and the Korean Peninsula,* New York: M. E. Sharpe, 1997.

Kim, Samuel S. (ed.), *China and the World: Chinese Foreign Relations in the Post-Cold War Era,* Boulder, CO: Westview Press, 1994.

Kim, Sunhyuk, *The Politics of Democratization in Korea: The Role of Civil Society,* Pittsburgh: University of Pittsburgh Press, 2000.

Klintworth, Gary, (ed.), *Asia-Pacific Security: Less Uncertainty, New Opportunities?* Melbourne: Longman, 1996.

Kolko G., *Another Century of War?* New York: The New Press, 2002.

Kongdan, Katy, (ed.) *Korea Briefing 1997–1999: Challenges and Change at the Turn of the Century,* New York, M.E.Sharpe, 2000.

Korean Journal of Defense Analysis, Korean Institute of Defense Analyses, Seoul, South Korea.

Kramer, Katherine, *Legal Controls on Small Arms and Light Weapons in Southeast Asia,* Geneva: Small Arms Survey, 2001.

Lampton, David, (ed.), *The Making of Chinese Foreign and Security in the Era of Reform,* Stanford, CA: Stanford University Press, 2001.

Lardy, Nicholas, *China in the World Economy,* Washington, DC: Institute for International Economics, 1994.

Lattimore, Owen, *Pivot of Asia: Sinkiang and the Inner Asian Frontiers of China and Russia*, Boston: Little, Brown, 1950.

Lal, B., *Coups in Paradise: Race, Politics and Military Intervention*, London: Zed Books, 1989.

Lal, B., and T. Vakatora, *Fiji in Transition*, Suva: School of Social and Economic Development, University of the South Pacific, 1997.

Lal, B., and T. Vakatora, *Fiji and the World*, Suva: School of Social and Economic Development, University of the South Pacific, 1997.

Lal, Brij (ed.), *Fiji Before the Storm—Elections and the Politics of Development*, Canberra: Asia-Pacific Press, Australia National University, 2000.

Lal, Brij V., and Michael Pretes (eds), *Coup: Reflections on the Political Crisis in Fiji*, Melbourne: Pandanus Books, 2001.

Lamour, Peter, *Governance and Good Government—Policy and Implementation in the South Pacific*, Canberra: NCDS, 1995.

———, (ed.), *Governance and Reform in the South Pacific*, Pacific Policy Paper No. 23 Canberra: NCDS, 1998

Layson, Fr. Roberto, *In War, the Real Enemy Is War Itself*, Davao City: Initiatives for International Dialogue, 2003.

Lee, Bernice, "The Security Implications of the New Taiwan," *Adelphi Papers #331*, New York: Oxford University Press, 1999.

Lee, Chyungly, *Cooperative Monitoring Center Occasional Paper No. 26*, Albuquerque, NM: Sandia National Laboratories, March 2003.

Lefort, Claude, and Roger B. Thompson (eds.), *The Political Forms of Modern Society: Bureaucracy, Democracy, and Totalitarianism*, Cambridge, MA: Polity Press, 1986.

Leifer, Michael, "The Asean Regional Forum," *Adephi Paper* No. 302, 1996 IISS Oxford University Press.

Leith, D., *The Politics of Power: Freeport in Soeharto's Indonesia*, Honolulu: University of Hawaii Press, 2003.

Lintner, Bertil, *Burma in Revolt: Opium and Insurgency Since 1948*, Chiangmai: Silkworm Books, 1999.

Liria, Yauka Aluambo, *Bougainville Campaign Diary*, Indra: Eltham, 1993.

Lowry, Robert, *The Armed Forces of Indonesia*, St. Leonards: Allen & Unwin, 1996.

Luijun, Sheng, *China's Dilemma: The Taiwan Issue*, London: I.B. Tauris/Institute of Southeast Asian Studies, 2001.

———, *China and Taiwan: Cross-Strait Relations under Chen Shui-Bian*, London: ZED Books/Institute of Southeast Asian Studies, 2002.

Mack, Andrew, and John Ravenhill (eds.), *Pacific Cooperation: Building Economic and Security Regimes in the Asia-Pacific Region*, Sydney: Allen & Unwin, 1994.

Mackerras, Colin, *China's Minorities: Integration and Modernization in the Twentieth Century*, Hong Kong: Oxford University Press, 1994.

Mahncke, Dieter, et al. (eds.), *ASEAN and the EU in the International Environment*, Baden-Baden: Nomos Verlagsgesellschaft, 1999.

Mair, Victor, (ed.). *The Bronze Age and Early Iron Age People of Eastern Central Asia: Volume II*, Washington DC: Institute for the Study of Man, 1998.

Mann, Michael, *The Sources of Social Power*, Vol. 1, Cambridge: Cambridge University Press, 1986.

Manning, Chris, and Peter van Diermen, (eds.), *Indonesia in Transition: Social Aspects of Reformasi and Crisis*, Singapore: Institute of Southeast Asian Studies, 2000.

Mawdsley, Nick, Monica Tanuhandaru, and Kees Holman, *Report of the EC Conflict Prevention Assessment Mission, Indonesia*, The European Commission, March 2002.

May, Ron J., and Matthew Spriggs (eds.), *The Bougainville Crisis*, Bathurst, NSW: Crawford House Press, 1990.

McCoy, Alfred W., and Ed C. de Jesus (eds.), *Philippine Social History, Global Trade and Local Transformations*, Quezon City: Ateneo de Manila University Press, 1998.

Mekenkamp, Monique, Paul van Tongeren, and Hans van de Veen (eds.), *Searching for Peace in Central and South Asia*, Boulder, CO: Lynne Rienner Publishers, Inc., 2002

Miall, Hugh, Oliver Ramsbotham, and Tom Woodhouse, *Contemporary Conflict Resolution*, Cambridge, MA: Polity Press, 1999.

Minority Rights Group International, *Burma (Myanmar): The Time for Change*, London: Minority Rights Group International, 2002.

Modern China, Thousand Oaks, CA: Sage Publications, nd.

Mosely, George, *The Party and the National Question in China*, Cambridge MA: MIT Press, 1966.

Mulvenon, James, "Missile Defenses and the Taiwan Scenario," *Report No. 44*, Washington, DC: Henry L. Stimson Center, 2002.

Nagel, Stuart, (ed.), *Handbook of Global Legal Policy*, New York: Marcel Dekker, 1999.

National Commission for Weapons Management and Reform, *Working to Build Peace, Security and Prosperity: Curbing Small Arms and Light Weapons in Cambodia*, Phnom Penh: National Commission for Weapons Management and Reform, July 2003.

National Report of the Kingdom of Thailand on the Implementation of the 2001 United Nations Programme of Action (POA) to Prevent, Combat and Eradicate the Illicit Trade in Small Arms and Light Weapons in All its Aspects, July 2003, http://www.smallarmssurvey.org.

Niksch, Larry, *Regional Security Consultative Organizations in East Asia and their Implications for the United States*, CRS Report for Congress, Washington, DC: Congressional Research Service, January 1994.

Nordlinger, Eric A., *Conflict Regulation in Divided Societies*, Center for International Affairs, Cambridge, MA: Harvard University Press, 1972.

Nye, J.S. *The Paradox of American Power: Why the World's Only Superpower Can't Go It Alone*, Oxford: Oxford University Press, 2002.

Oberdorfer, Don, *The Two Koreas: A Contemporary History*, London: Little, Brown and Company, 1998.

O'Callaghan, Marie-Louise, *Enemies Within*, Sydney: Doubleday, 1999.

Organski, A.F.K., *World Politics*, New York: Knopf, 1958.

Organski, A.F.K., and Jacek Kugler, *The War Ledger*, Chicago: University of Chicago Press, 1980.

O'Rourke, Kevin, *Reformasi: The Struggle for Power in Post-Soeharto Indonesia*, St Leonards, NSW: Allen and Urwin, 2002.

Osborne, Robin, *Indonesia's Secret War: the Guerilla Struggle in Irian Jaya*. Sydney: Allen & Unwin, 1985.

Pacific Affairs, University of British Columbia, Vancouver, Canada.

Pacific Concerns Resource Centre, *Proceedings of the Indigenous People's Knowledge and Intellectual Property Rights Consultation*, Suva: ECRC, 1997.

Pacifica Review, School of Sociology, Politics and Anthropology, La Trobe University, Victoria, Australia.

Pedersen, Morten, Emily Rudland, and R.J. May (eds.), *Burma/Myanmar: Strong Regime, Weak State?* Adelaide, NSW: Crawford House Publishing, 2000.

Perry, E., and M. Selden, (eds.), *Chinese Society: Change, Conflict and Resistance*, London: Routledge, 2000.

Perry, Charles M., and Toshi Yoshihara, *The U.S.-Japan Alliance Preparing for Korean Reconciliation & Beyond*, Cambridge, MA: Institute for Foreign Policy Analysis, 2003.

Phongpaichit, Pasuk, Sungsidh Piriyarangsan, and Nualnoi Treerat, *Guns, Girls, Gambling, Ganja: Thailand's Illegal Economy and Public Policy,* Chiang Mai: Silkworm Books, 1998.

Pillsbury, Michael, *China Debates the Future Security Environment,* Washington, DC: National Defense University Press, 2000.

Prasad, S., J. Dakuvula, and D. Snell, *Economic Development, Democracy, and Ethnic Conflict in the Fiji Islands: Minority Rights and Development Macro Study,* London: Minority Rights Group and Citizens Constitutional Forum, 2001.

Prasad, S., D. Snell, and K. Hince, *Employment and Industrial Relations in the South Pacific,* Sydney: McGraw Hill, 2003.

Polomka, Peter, (ed.), *Bougainville: Perspectives on a Crisis,* Canberra: Strategic and Defence Studies Centre, Research School of Pacific Studies, Australia National University, 1990.

Postiglione, Gerard A., (ed.) *China's National Minority Education: Culture, State Schooling and Development.* New York: Garland Press, 1999.

Quintos de Jesus, Melinda, (ed.), *The Media and Peace Reporting: Perspectives on Media and Peace Reportage,* Pasig City: Office of the Presidential Adviser on the Peace Process (OPAPP), 2000.

Ramos-Horta, Jose, *The Role of NGOs in Asia, An East Timorese Example,* nd, www.easttimor.com/lh.html.

Robertson, R., and W. Sutherland, *Government by the Gun: The Unfinished Business of Fiji's 2000 Coup,* New York: Zed Books, 2001.

Robinson, Thomas W., and David Shambaugh, *Chinese Foreign Policy: Theory and Practice,* Oxford: Claredon Press, 1995

Rodil, B.R., *The Minoritization of the Indigenous Communities of Mindanao and the Sulu Archipelago.* Davao City: Alternate Forum for Research in Mindanao, 1994.

———, *Kalinaw Mindanaw: The Story of the MNLF Peace Process, 1975–1996,* Davao City: Alternate Forum for Research in Mindanao, 2000.

Ross, Robert S., (ed.), *East Asia in Transition: Toward a New Regional Order,* New York: M. E. Sharpe, 1995.

Rudelson, Justin Jon, *Oasis Identities: Uyghur Nationalism along China's Silk Road,* New York: Columbia University Press, 1998.

Russett, Bruce, *Grasping the Democratic Peace,* Princeton NJ: Princeton University Press, 1993.

Saldanha, Joao Mariano de Sousa, *The Political Economy of East Timor Development,* Jakarta: Sinar Harapan, 1994.

Scobell, Andrew, (ed.), *The Costs of Conflict: the Impact on China of a Future War,* Carlisle, PA: Strategic Studies Institute, 2001.

Security Dialogue, International Peace Research Institute, Sage Publications, Oslo, Norway.

Segal, Gerald, "China Changes Shape: Regionalism and Foreign Policy," *Adelphi Paper 287,* London: Brassey's for IISS, 1994.

Shambaugh, David, (ed.), *Contemporary Taiwan,* London: Oxford Press, 1998.

———, (ed.), *Is China Unstable,* Armonk, NY: M. E. Sharpe, 2000.

———, *Modernizing China's Military: Progress, Problems and Prospects,* Berkeley, CA: University of California Press, 2002.

Shinn, James, (ed.), *Weaving the Net: Conditional Engagement with China,* New York: Council on Foreign Relations Press, 1996.

Siegel, James T., *The Rope of God,* Ann Arbor: Michigan University Press, 2000.

Silliman, Sidney, and Lela Garner Noble (eds.), *Organizing for Democracy: NGOs, Civil Society and the Philippine State,* Quezon City: Ateneo de Manila University Press, 1998.

Simon, Sheldon, *Evaluating Track II Approaches to Security Diplomacy in the Asia Pacific: The CSCAP Experience,* Seattle: National Bureau of Asian Research, Special Report, September 2001.

SIPRI Yearbook 1999: Armaments, Disarmament and International Security, Oxford: Oxford University Press, 1999.

Sison, Jose Maria, *Philippine Economy and Politics*, Philippines: Aklat ng Bayan, Inc.,1998.

Sissons, Melinda, *From One Day to Another—Violations of Women's Reproductive and Sexual Rights in East Timor*, Melbourne: East Timor Human Rights Center, 1998.

Sjamsuddin, Ndazaruddin, *The Republican Revolt: A Study of the Acehnese Rebellion*, Singapore: Institute of Southeast Asian Studies, 1985.

Small Arms Survey 2002: Counting the Human Cost, Oxford: Oxford University Press, 2002.

Small Arms Survey 2003: Development Denied, Oxford: Oxford University Press, 2003.

Smith, Martin, *Burma: Insurgency and the Politics of Ethnicity*, London: Zed Books, 1999.

Smith, Warren W., Jr., *Tibetan Nation: A History of Tibetan Nationalism and Sino-Tibetan Relations*, Boulder, CO: Westview Press, 1996.

Snyder, Jack, *From Voting to Violence: Democratization and Nationalist Conflict*, New York: W. W. Norton, 2000.

Snyder, Scott, *The South China Sea Dispute: Prospects for Preventive Diplomacy*, Special Report, Washington DC: United States Institute for Peace, August 1996

Soesastro, Hadi, and R. Subyanto, (eds), *Peace Building and State Building in East Timor*, Jakarta: CSIS, 2002.

Son, Gwi-Yeop, *Peace-Building in East Timor: Good Governance as the Key Ingredient to Success*, New York: Columbia University, 2001.

Soros, George, *On Globalization*, New York: Public Affairs, 2002.

South, Ashley, *Mon Nationalism and Civil War in Burma: The Golden Sheldrake*, London: Routledge/Couzon, 2003.

Southeast Asian Affairs, Institute of Southeast Asian Studies, Singapore

Spence, Jonathan D., and John E. Wills Jr. (eds.), *From Ming to Ch'ing*. New Haven, CT: Yale University Press, 1979

Sukma, Rizal, and Edy Prasetyono, *Working Paper 9: Security Sector Reform in Indonesia: The Military and the Police*, Netherlands: Netherlands Institute of International Relations, Clingendael, Conflict Research Unit, February, 2003

Survival, Oxford University Press, United Kingdom

Sutter, Robert, (ed.), *Taiwan in World Affairs*, Boulder, CO, Westview Press, 1994

Swanström, Niklas, *Foreign Devils, Dictatorship, or Institutional Control: China's Foreign Policy Toward Southeast Asia*, Uppsala, Sweden: Uppsala Universitet, Department of Peace and Conflict Research, 2001.

Syamsuddin, N., *The Republican Revolt: A Study of the Acehnese Rebellion*, Singapore: Institute of South Asian Studies, 1985.

Taylor, John G., *Indonesia's Forgotten War: The Hidden History of East Timor*, London: Zed Books, 1991.

Taylor, Trevor, and Seizaburo Sato, (eds.), *Future Sources of Global Conflict*, London: Royal Institute of International Affairs, 1995.

Tehranian, Majid, (ed.), *Asian Peace: Security and Governance in the Asia-Pacific Region*, London: I.B. Tauris, 1999.

Thiparat, Pranee, (ed.), *The Quest for Human Security: The Next Phase of ASEAN?* Bangkok: Institute of Security and International Studies, Chulalongkhorn University, 2001.

Tilly, Charles, *The Politics of Collective Violence*, Cambridge: Cambridge University Press 2003.

Tsering Shakya, *The Dragon in the Land of Snows: A History of Modern Tibet since 1947*, London: Random House, 1999.

Turner, Mark, and Owen Podger, *Decentralisation in Indonesia: Redesigning the State* Canberra: Asia Pacific Press, 2003.

Twyford, Conor, and Phil Alpers: *Small Arms in the Pacific*, Occasional Paper No. 8, Geneva: Small Arms Survey, March 2003.

Ullman, Harlan K., and James P. Wade, *Shock and Awe: Achieving Rapid Dominance*, Washington , DC: National Defense University Press, 1996.

United Nations, *Report of the United Nations Conference on the Illicit Trade in Small Arms and Light Weapons in All its Aspects*, New York, 9–20 July 2001, (A/CONF/.92/15).

United Nations Development Programme (UNDP), *Fiji Poverty Report: 1994*, New York, United Nations, 1994.

———, Mission Report, Bougainville Rehabilitation, Reconstruction and Development Project. Achieving Sustainable Human Development through strengthening social capital in Bougainville. Peacock-Taylor, Colleen (Team Leader)/Ahai, Naihuwo/ Momis, Elizabeth/Kwa, Enaha. November 1999 (PNG/98/002/07/UNOPS).

UNDP, *Human Development Report 2003*.

U.S. Dept of Defense, *United States Security Strategy for the East Asia Pacific Region*, Washington, DC: Office of International Security Affairs, February 1995.

Valencia, Mark, "China and the South China Sea Disputes," *Adelphi Paper 298*, Oxford: Oxford University Press, 1995.

Valencia, Mark J., Hon M. Van Dyke, and Noel A. Ludwig, *Sharing the Resources of the South China Sea*, Honolulu: University of Hawaii Press, 1997.

Vaughn, Bruce, (ed), *The Unraveling of Island Asia? Governmental, Communal, and Regional Instability*, Westport, CT: Praeger, 2002.

Verhoeven, Juliette, and Jim Wake (eds.), *Conflict Prevention in Central Asia: The Role of the OSCE: A Report on a Conference*, The Hague, March 7th and 8th, 2002, Den Haag: Ministerie van Buitenlandse Zaken, Utrecht: European Centre for Conflict Prevention (ECCP), 2002.

Washington Quarterly, Center for Strategic and International Studies, Washington DC.

Waslekar, Sundeep, (ed.), *Political Leaders and Track Two Diplomacy in South Asia*, New Delhi: International Centre for Peace Initiatives, 1995.

———, *A Handbook for Conflict Resolution in South Asia*, New Delhi: Konark Publishers, 1996.

Weber, Maria, *Reforming Economic Systems in Asia: A Comparative Analysis of China, Japan, South Korea, Malaysia and Thailand*, Cheltenham: Edward Elgar and Instituto per gli Studi di Politica Internazionale, 2001.

Wehner, Monica, and Donald Denoon (eds.): *Without a Gun—Australians Experiences Monitoring Peace in Bougainville 1997–2001*, Canberra: Pandanus Books, 2001.

Weingartner, Erich, *New Caledonia—Halfway to Independence?* Geneva: World Council of Churches, 1996.

Weissmann, Mikael, *Bridging a Divide—The Creation of a Tribal Path for Conflict Resolution*, Uppsala, Sweden: Department of Peace and Conflict Research, Uppsala University, 2002.

Wilson, Margaret, and Paul Hunt (eds.): *Culture, Rights and Cultural Rights—Perspectives from the South Pacific*, Wellington: Huai, 2000.

Worcester, K., S. Avery Bermhanzohn, and M. Ungar, (eds.) *Violence and Politics: Globalization's Paradox*, New York: Routledge 2001.

World Bank, *The East Asian Miracle—Economic Growth and Public Policy*, Oxford: Oxford University Press, 1993.

World Health Organization, *Global Report on Violence and Health*, Geneva: World Health Organization, 2002.

Yee, Herbert, and Ian Storey (eds.), *The China Threat: Perceptions, Myths and Reality*, London: Routledge/Curzon, 2002.

Zhao, Suisheng, (ed.), *Across the Taiwan Strait: Mainland China, Taiwan, and the 1995–1996 Crisis*, New York: Routledge, 1999.

———, (ed.), *Chinese Foreign Policy: Pragmatism and Strategic Behavior*, New York: M. E. Sharpe, 2004.

Subject Index

Index of Organizations

Page numbers presented in bold type indicate an entry in the Directory.

About the
Searching for Peace Program

The Searching for Peace Program of the European Centre for Conflict Prevention (ECCP) consists of several regional projects. The ultimate aim of these projects is to contribute to a peaceful transformation of violent conflicts around the world by filling the gaps in information, communication, and coordination that exist in the fields of conflict prevention and peacebuilding. The Searching for Peace publication series is the result of an ongoing process involving research and regional seminars, as well as collaboration with local partners, practitioners, and prominent international scholars.

Searching for Peace in Asia Pacific is the fourth book in the series, following *Searching for Peace in Central and South Asia, Searching for Peace in Europe and Eurasia,* and *Searching for Peace in Africa.* Subsequent volumes will cover the Middle East and North Africa, and Latin America and the Caribbean.

About the Book

Fourth in an acclaimed series, *Searching for Peace in Asia Pacific* offers critical background information, up-to-date surveys of the conflicts in Northeast Asia, Southeast Asia, and the Pacific, and a directory of some 400 organizations working in the field of conflict prevention and peacebuilding in the Asia Pacific region. The authors provide detailed, objective descriptions of ongoing activities, as well as assessments of the prospects for conflict resolution.

Annelies Heijmans is coordinator and **Nicola Simmonds** is project officer of the Asia Pacific Program of the European Centre for Conflict Prevention (ECCP). **Hans van de Veen** is senior journalist and coordinator of an independent network of journalists, Environment and Development Productions, based in Amsterdam.

European Centre for Conflict Prevention
PO Box 14069
3508 SC Utrecht
The Netherlands

Tel: +31 30 242 7777
Fax: +31 30 236 9268
info@conflict-prevention.net
www.conflict-prevention.net